Law of Guarantees

AUSTRALIA
LBC Information Services
Sydney

CANADA and USA
Carswell
Toronto—Ontario

NEW ZEALAND
Brooker's
Auckland

SINGAPORE AND MALAYSIA
Sweet & Maxwell Asia
Singapore and Kuala Lumpur

Law of Guarantees

FOURTH EDITION

Geraldine Mary Andrews, Q.C.
*LLB, LLM (King's College London) of
Gray's Inn and Lincoln's Inn, Barrister*

Richard Millet, Q.C.
*BA (Trinity Hall, Cambridge) of
Lincoln's Innn, Barrister*

LONDON
SWEET & MAXWELL
2005

Published in 2005 by
Sweet & Maxwell Limited of
100 Avenue Road, London NW3 3PF
(http://www.sweetandmaxwell.co.uk)

Typeset by LBJ Typesetting of Kingsclere
Printed in England by MPG Books Ltd, Bodmin, Cornwall

A CIP catalogue record for this book
is available from the British Library

ISBN 0 421 88540 8

First edition 1992
Second edition 1995
Third edition 2001
Fourth edition 2005

No natural forests were destroyed to make this product,
only farmed timber was used and replanted.

ISBN 0-421-88540-8

9 780421 885400

Foreword

By The Rt. Hon. Lord Justice Jacob

In classical Newtonian mechanics, the two-body problem was completely soluble. But once a third body was introduced, the equations of motion simply could not be solved completely, and the best that could be done was a series of approximations. In law, I suppose, an analogy of the two-body problem is the set of rules which govern the relations between the parties ("principal" and "creditor") to a bi-partite contract. But, unlike mechanics, no one would say that the rules are completely soluble—law is more unpredictable than Newtonian mechanics. Nonetheless, we do have some fairly well established ground rules which solve most problems. If one presses the imperfect analogy with mechanics a little further, it is fair to say that the legal three-body problem ("surety", "principal" and "creditor"), just as in mechanics, becomes much more complex than the two-body case. To reduce the rules to some sort of order, one has to graft onto, or adapt, the two-body rules.

What Geraldine Andrews and Richard Millett have done is to set about reducing the three-body problem to a state of intelligibility—to bring order out of potential chaos. And they have done so magnificently. If one dips into the text, almost anywhere you find a clear discussion of the rules. Where they are uncertain the authors say so (and generally give their preferred answer). Where they are clear, you can understand them readily.

Bringing a work such as this up to date is the sort of job which can be done in a fairly slapdash way—you just footnote new cases and fiddle with the text a bit. On the other hand, it can be done carefully—re-writing whole sections or chapters where events have made this necessary. This book shows the authors have taken the latter approach—there are entirely newly written parts for those areas of law which have undergone most change. A revised insolvency chapter and major re-writes of the parts dealing with the decision in *Etridge* and the new cases on performance guarantees are but examples which show that these authors have set about this edition with vim. Quite how they managed to do this, whilst conducting busy practices, will remain a mystery. We should be grateful they have done it.

The Rt. Hon. Lord Justice Jacob
November 2004

Preface

The old joke among Wall Street lawyers, that the definition of a surety is "a shmuck with a pen", holds perhaps as true today among their English counterparts as it did when this work was first published in 1992. It is a particular feature of the guarantee as an instrument that anybody who signs, it is taking a very serious financial risk. There are many cases in the recent law reports which illustrate all too clearly how often the surety who is giving a guarantee fails to understand the extent of the risk he or she is running.

The law governing the obligations assumed by sureties is complex, ancient and, in many areas, arcane and inconsistent. It has developed into what we know today from a large body of cases decided in the 19th Century or earlier. Standing back from the detail, one can trace, in the evolution of a coherent body of the law of guarantees, the history of social and economic change in England. The principles of contract and equity in the 19th Century combined to provide rules which strove to balance risk fairly as between creditor and surety—equity in particular providing its own protection to the surety in the form of the remedy of subrogation. In the first part of the 20th Century, at the zenith of the doctrine of the freedom of contract as a cornerstone of commerce, banks became the primary form of creditor and established their own standard forms of guarantee, containing conditions which removed much of the protection that the law and equity provided to the surety. Later, in the second half of the 20th Century, and with the rise of the consumer society, Parliament intervened to protect the rights of the individual and to impose fair dealing where the vulnerable could not achieve it for themselves. At the turn of the new century, in an era of individual enterprise, the House of Lords, for the second time in a decade, has had to spell out the rules relating to undue influence and the duties of banks and solicitors in the common situation where a wife has provided a guarantee or charge to the bank for her husband's business debts.

The last four years since the third edition of this work have been a busy period for guarantee lawyers. In *Royal Bank of Scotland v Etridge (No.2)* [2002] 2 A.C. 773, the House of Lords eventually laid to rest many of the ghosts that continued to haunt the portals of the law of undue influence in the context of guarantees following its decision in *Barclays Bank plc v O'Brien* [1994] 1 A.C. 180. It examined the extent of the application of the doctrine of constructive notice in all cases where the surety is non-commercial, and gave useful guidance, not only to the lenders who may be affected by the doctrine, but to the lawyers who undertake the task of advising the surety in this context. In *Yorkshire Bank plc v Tinsley* [2004] 3 All E.R. 463, the Court of Appeal have solved the "subsequent transaction" problem, by extending the taint of undue influence, beyond the transaction to which it gave rise, to later transactions by the same lender in substitution for the earlier. The scope and nature of any duty of disclosure in the context of guarantees have also came under scrutiny in cases such as *Far Eastern Shipping Co Public Ltd v Scales Trading Ltd* [2001] 1 All E.R. (Comm) 691, and most recently in the *Etridge Case*, where the House of Lords affirmed the obligation to disclose "unusual features", and brought into sharper focus the boundaries of the duty.

In *Actionstrength Ltd v International Glass Engineering spa* [2003] 2 A.C. 541, the House of Lords has considered the application of the Statute of Frauds 1677 and whether its effect can be avoided by resort to the doctrine of estoppel. In the area of insolvency, in *Re West End Networks* [2004] 2 All E.R. 1042, the House finally overruled *In Re a Debtor (No.66 of 1955)* [1956] 2 W.L.R. 94, thereby bringing certainty to the question of whether contingent claims by the surety against the debtor at the moment of insolvency are provable in the latter's insolvency. The question of the juridical nature of a claim on a guarantee, whether for debt or damages, has been revisited at first instance in *Hampton v Minns* [2002] 1 W.L.R. 1. The law of subrogation in the context of guarantees has also moved on, not least with the assistance of a valuable judgment of the Court of Appeal in *Liberty Mutual Insurance Co (UK) Ltd v HSBC Bank plc* [2002] EWCA Civ 691.

In the Commonwealth too, there have been developments. For example, in Australia, in *Gattellaro v Westpac Banking Corpn* [2004] 204 A.L.R. 258 the High Court considered the enforceability of a guarantee conditional on co-execution by a third party, and in New Zealand in *Stotter v Equiticorp Australia Ltd (in liquidation)* [2002] 2 N.Z.L.R. 686, Fisher J. has produced a scholarly and incisive exegesis on the extent to which a creditor must give credit, in the insolvency of the debtor, for sums received from the debtor or the surety prior to the liquidation.

As with all earlier editions, we have attempted to move away from the traditional use of the phrases "debtor" and "guarantor" because they are too narrow and all too often inappropriate. Not all commercial contexts in which the law of suretyship applies necessarily involve debts or guarantors. Accordingly, where possible, we have used the words "surety" and "principal" to denote these persons. The creditor remains "creditor" (or "bank").

The sheer increase in the number of cases in this area, both in England and in the Commonwealth, the proliferation of many new series of law reports, and the advent of on-line law reporting have together meant that we have not been able to run to earth every case worthy of commentary. As in the past, we have done our best to ensure that we have identified the decisions of importance which practitioners will be able to use as the starting point (and we hope end point) for their researches.

We have aimed to provide a guide to the law in this area and its operation in various commercial contexts as comprehensive and comprehensible as possible, and to set out the underlying principles which govern. We have also tried to identify and explore practical legal problems that confront the practitioner on a daily basis. Where there are questions not solved by the cases, we have attempted to provide what we regard as definitive answers; but sometimes that itself has proved impossible. The responsibility for the suggested solutions is of course ours, as it is for all errors of commission and omission. The law is stated as at August 1, 2004, although we have included, where possible, some later cases.

Once again we have, in producing this edition, been greatly assisted by a host of friends, colleagues and members of the judiciary, who have alerted us to cases and issues, and provided us with transcripts, suggestions and inspiration. They are too many to thank by name. We would single out Jonathan Drakeford for his valuable trawls of the Australasian reports and legal websites. We also gratefully acknowledge the assistance and support of our publishers, particularly Sarah Watt, and our editor, Silvia Segatori, whose patience and amenability has been often saintly, and we also extend our thanks to David Grief, our senior clerk, and his team for sympathetically organising our diaries and keeping us cheerful.

Finally, we give, as ever, our special thanks to Lord Saville and Lord Millett, without whose ideas and encouragement the first edition in 1992 would probably not have been written, and who have continued to provide us with support and inspiration since its first publication. To them this book is dedicated.

Geraldine Andrews Q.C.
Richard Millett Q.C.

Essex Court Chambers,
24 Lincoln's Inn Fields,
London WC2A 3EG.

December 1, 2004

Contents

Chapter 7: Enforcement of Contracts of Suretyship

Chapter 8: Revocation of Contracts of Suretyship

Chapter 9: Discharge of the Surety

Chapter 10: Rights of the Surety Against the Principal

Table of Cases

Table of Statutes

Table of Statutory Instruments

Table of EC/EU Legislation & Conventions

Chapter 1

Definitions and Characteristics

Suretyship

Suretyship is the generic term given to contracts by which one person (the **1–001** surety) agrees to answer for some existing or future liability of another (the principal) to a third person (the creditor), and by which the surety's liability is in addition to, and not in substitution for, that of the principal. In most cases, the contract will involve the assumption by the surety of personal liability to the creditor. However, it may also consist of the provision by the surety of a pledge or security in support of the performance of the principal's obligation, for example, a charge on property.[1]

Rights of a surety

The obligations of a surety are usually created expressly by contract, but it **1–002** is unnecessary for a person to contract as guarantor in order to acquire the rights of a surety. A person who, on the face of a contract, appears to be under a primary obligation to the creditor, may nevertheless acquire the rights of a surety by giving him notice. For example:

> D and S enter into a contract with C under which they undertake to be jointly liable for the repayment of money advanced by C to D. Subsequently D and S agree that as between themselves, D is to assume the primary responsibility for repayment of C, and S is to be secondarily liable. Once notice of this arrangement has been given to C, he is bound to respect S's position as a surety, even if he does not assent to the modification of the original arrangement, and even if by this time the debt has fallen due for repayment. This will not prevent C from suing S (rather than D) for the debt but he must respect S's rights as surety, for example, by preserving his rights to other securities.[2]

In certain cases, where there is a primary and secondary liability of two persons for the same debt, they will stand in the relationship to each other

---

1 *Smith v Wood* [1929] 1 Ch. 14; *Re Conley* [1938] 2 All E.R. 127, *Deutsche Bank v Ibrahim* [1992] 1 Bank. L.R. 267.
2 *Rouse v Bradford Banking Co* [1894] A.C. 586. This case finally decided that the assent of the creditor to a modification of the original position was unnecessary and that, in accordance with the approach taken by the courts of equity, notice was sufficient.

of principal and surety even though there is no express contract of suretyship between them.[3] Thus the acceptor of an accommodation bill of exchange is a surety for the payment by the drawer, and the maker of an accommodation note is in the position of a surety, with all the surety's rights.[4] However, the relationship of principal and surety will not always arise in such circumstances. For instance, if property which was subject to a mortgage has been sold, and the mortgagor remains under a liability to the mortgagee, he does not become a surety for the purchaser: *Re Errington* [1894] 1 Q.B. 11. Similarly, if a person assigns a lease and the assignee covenants to indemnify him against liability for breaches of covenants in the lease, the assignee thereby undertakes a primary liability as between himself and the assignor, but the assignor does not become a surety for the assignee.[5] A transferor of shares does not become the guarantor of the transferee, though he may be liable by statute to pay calls if the transferee does not.[6]

Contracts of suretyship

1–003   Contracts of suretyship fall into two main categories; contracts of guarantee and contracts of indemnity. Guarantees and indemnities have many similar characteristics, and similar rights and duties arise between the parties. Consequently, it is not unusual to find the term "guarantee" used loosely to describe a contract which is in reality an indemnity (and vice versa). However, despite the similarities, it is often important to ascertain into which of these two categories a particular agreement falls. This can have a significant bearing on the enforceability of the contract against the surety, and the extent and nature of his liability, in two particular respects.

First, contracts of guarantee, but not contracts of indemnity, are prima facie unenforceable by the creditor if they do not comply with the requirements of s.4 of the Statute of Frauds 1677.[7] Secondly, the liability of a guarantor is normally co-extensive with the liability of the principal. Therefore, if the obligation of the principal to the creditor is unenforceable, or has been discharged, the liability of the surety may depend on whether the contract is a guarantee or an indemnity.[8]

In addition to guarantees and indemnities, there are various types of commercial contract, such as performance bonds (sometimes called perfor-

---

3 See *Duncan, Fox & Co v North and South Wales Bank* (1880) 6 App. Cas. 1 at 11, discussed below at para.1–006.

4 See, *e.g. Re Acraman Ex p. Webster* (1847) De G. 414; *Bailey v Edwards* (1864) 4 B. & S. 761; *Ex p. Yonge* (1814) 3 Ves. & B. 31 at 40, *per* Lord Eldon L.C.

5 *Baynton v Morgan* (1888) 22 Q.B.D. 74; see also *Allied London Investments v Hambro Life Assurance Ltd* (1984) 269 E.G. 41; *Selous Street Properties Ltd v Oronel Fabrics Ltd* (1984) 270 E.G. 743.

6 See Gore-Browne, *Companies* (Jordans, 44th ed., 1986), Ch. 16; *Roberts v Crowe* (1872) L.R. 7 C.P. 629; *Re Contract Corporation, Hudson's Case* (1871) L.R. 12 E.Q. 1; *Helbert v Banner, Re Barned's Bank* (1871) L.R. 5 H.L. 28.

7 See Ch.3.

8 See Chs 6 and 9.

mance guarantees), export credit guarantees, and carnets, which may be described as contracts of suretyship, or which are very closely related to them, and yet have special distinct characteristics which it is more appropriate to consider independently. These will therefore be dealt with in detail in Chapters 14 to 17 of this book. Chapter 18 will deal with the special considerations which may apply to contracts of guarantee in the context of the relationships between landlord and tenant and their respective assignees.

Contracts of guarantee

Definition

A contract of guarantee, in the true sense, is a contract whereby the surety (or guarantor) promises the creditor to be responsible, in addition to the principal, for the due performance by the principal of his existing or future obligations to the creditor, if the principal fails to perform those obligations. In *Wardens and Commonalty of the Mystery of Mercers of the City of London v New Hampshire Insurance Company* (1991) 3 J.I.B.F.L. 144, Phillips J. cited with approval the following definition of a guarantee which is given in *Halsburys Laws of England* (4th ed. 2004 reissue) at para.101: **1–004**

> "A guarantee is an accessory contract by which the promisor undertakes to be answerable to the promisee for the debt, default or miscarriage of another person,[9] whose primary liability to the promisee must exist or be contemplated."[10]

Although the expressions "creditor" and "debtor" are often used to denote the underlying obligee and obligor, the liability which is guaranteed may consist of performance of some obligation other than the payment of a debt, and does not have to be a contractual liability, although it usually is.

The liability of the guarantor has been defined as a liability not only to perform himself if the principal fails to do so, but to procure that the principal performs his obligations.[11] However, given that in practice the guarantor is rarely in a position to compel the principal to perform his obligations, it is probably more accurate to describe the guarantor's promise as a promise that the obligation will be performed, in the sense that the guarantor will be personally liable for the debt, default or miscarriage of the principal. This analysis has been preferred in Australia:

---

9 The words "debt, default or miscarriage" are taken from the Statute of Frauds (1677) s.4, see Ch.3.

10 For a list of other definitions of guarantee that have been given in textbooks and treatises from time to time, see *Re Conley* [1938] 2 All E.R. 127, at 130–131.

11 *Moschi v Lep Air Services Ltd* [1973] A.C. 331 especially *per* Lord Diplock at 348–349. *Cf. General Produce Co v United Bank* [1979] 2 Lloyd's Rep. 255, where Lloyd L.J. at 258 refers to two classes of guarantee, a promise which becomes effective if the debtor fails to perform his obligations, and a promise that the debtor will perform his obligations.

in *Sunbird Plaza Pty Ltd v Maloney* (1988) 166 C.L.R. 245 Mason C.J. went so far as to describe Lord Diplock's definition of the nature of the guarantor's obligation as "fictitious and quite unrealistic". Therefore, even if the guarantor has not in terms guaranteed the payment of damages to the creditor, he will normally be liable in damages to the same extent as the principal for breach of the latter's obligations.[12]

The description of the guarantor's obligation as a promise to answer for the principal's default may well be apposite for the majority of guarantees, but it does not prevent a contract of guarantee from providing on its true construction that the guarantor will pay a sum of money to the creditor upon default by the principal, in which case his liability will sound in debt rather than in damages. For example, in *Hampton v Minns* [2002] 1 W.L.R. 1, a contract which not only contained a guarantee of "the payment or discharge . . . of all monies and liabilities which shall be for the time being be due owing or incurred by the Principal to you" but also an express undertaking that the undersigned would on demand discharge those moneys and liabilities, was construed as giving rise to an obligation in debt.

Essential characteristics

Secondary liability

1–005 The essential distinguishing feature of a contract of guarantee is that the liability of the guarantor is always ancillary, or secondary, to that of the principal, who remains primarily liable to the creditor.[13] There is no liability on the guarantor unless and until the principal has failed to perform his obligations.[14] In *Lakeman v Mountstephen* (1874) L.R. 7 H.L. 17, Lord Selborne put the matter succinctly at 24:

> "There can be no suretyship unless there be a principal debtor, who of course may be constituted in the course of the transaction by matters *ex post facto* and need not be so at the time, but until there is a principal debtor there can be no suretyship. Nor can a man guarantee anybody else's debt unless there is a debt of some other person to be guaranteed."[15]

---

12 *Moschi v Lep Air Services*, above, and see further para.7–018.
13 A surety's obligation is secondary where the agreement leaves another person primarily liable for the performance of that obligation: see, *e.g. Mallett v Bateman* (1865) L.R. 1 C.P. 163 (Ex Ch), *Harburg India Rubber Comb Co v Martin* [1902] 1 K.B. 778 at 784; *Fahey v MSD Spiers Ltd* [1973] 2 N.Z.L.R. 655. *Clipper Maritime Ltd v Shirlstar Container Transport Ltd* ("*The Anemone*") [1987] 1 Lloyd's Rep. 546 at 555. In *Clement v Clement* (unreported) CAT No.1336 of 1995, October 20 (discussed in para.1–013 below) Peter Gibson L.J. said (at p.7 of the transcript): "The crucial question is whether by the actual words used, the obligation undertaken is dependent on the continued existence of the liability of [the principal]. . .". For a good example of the distinction between a primary obligation and a secondary obligation, see *Birkmeyr v Darnell* (1704) 1 Salk 27, 91 E.R. 27.
14 Thus, a contract of guarantee has been described as a contract to indemnify the creditor on the occurrence of a contingency, namely the default of the principal debtor: see *Sampson v Burton* (1820) 4 Moore C.P. 515, 129 E.R. 891.
15 See also the observations of Donaldson J. in *General Surety & Guarantee Co Ltd v Francis Parker Ltd* (1977) 6 B.L.R. 16 at 21.

It follows from the secondary nature of the obligation, that the guarantor is generally only liable to the same extent that the principal is liable to the creditor, and that there is usually no liability on the part of the guarantor if the underlying obligation is void or unenforceable, or if that obligation ceases to exist. This is known as the principle of co-extensiveness. There are, however, a number of established exceptions to the principle of co-extensiveness under which the guarantor may find himself liable to the creditor, notwithstanding the unenforceability of the principal obligation.[16]

A contract under which the liability of the principal debtor is extinguished or replaced by the liability of some other person cannot be a contract of guarantee. In *Re International Life Assurance Society and Hercules Insurance Co Ex p. Blood* (1870) L.R. 9 Eq. 316, the holder of a policy of life assurance was informed that the insurer had been dissolved, and had transferred its business and assets to the H Company. He was offered either a new policy or an indorsement of the old policy by the H Company "guaranteeing its due fulfilment". He opted for the latter. It was held by the Vice-Chancellor that the indorsement constitued a novation and not a contract of guarantee, as it was obvious from the context of the transaction that there was no intention that the original insurer should remain liable on the policy.

Creditor must be a party

It is essential that the creditor should be a party to a contract of guarantee, **1–006** because he is the person to whom the guarantor makes the promise to be answerable for the debt, default or miscarriage of the principal. Any contract of suretyship to which the creditor is not a party must be a contract of indemnity.

Thus, in *Duncan, Fox & Co v North & South Wales Bank* (1880) 6 App. Cas. 1 at 11, Lord Selborne identified three specific types of contract of suretyship:

(a) those in which there is an agreement to constitute, for a particular purpose, the relation of principal and surety, to which agreement the creditor thereby secured is a party;

(b) those in which there is a similar agreement between the principal and surety only, to which the creditor is a stranger; and

(c) those in which, without any such contract of suretyship, there is a primary and secondary liability of two persons for one and the same debt, the debt being, as between the two, that of one of those persons only, and not equally of both, so that the other, if he should be compelled to pay it, would be entitled to reimbursement from the person by whom (as between the two) it ought to have been paid.

---

16 See further Ch.6.

Of these types, only the first category would embrace a true contract of guarantee—the others are illustrations of contracts of indemnity between surety and principal alone. In such cases, the creditor is entitled to treat the surety as a principal. However, as already stated, once the creditor has been given notice of the agreement, he is bound to give effect to the rights of the surety against him and against any co-sureties.[17]

So, for example, if A and B are jointly indebted to C, and A and B agree between themselves that B shall act as surety only, C will retain the right to recover the debt from B as a principal debtor, because he is not a party to the agreement, even if he has notice of it.[18] However, once C has notice of the agreement between A and B, he will be bound to do nothing to prejudice the rights of the surety, B, in his dealings with other securities, or by agreeing to a material variation in C's contract with A (such as giving A more time to pay, without B's assent).[19]

This rule, which is of equitable origin, applies equally whether the agreement between A and B is made before or after they become indebted to C.

Writing and signature

1–007 A third distinguishing characteristic of a contract of guarantee is that, unlike a contract of indemnity, the essential elements of the agreement are required by s.4 of the Statute of Frauds 1677 to be made or recorded in writing and signed by the guarantor or by someone with his authority. This is because the statute applies to contracts under which the surety assumes a secondary rather than a primary liability.

However, not all guarantees fall within the ambit of the Statute of Frauds 1677. Further, the absence of a written agreement or memorandum is not necessarily fatal to the enforcement of a guarantee, and does not affect the underlying validity of the contract.[20] Therefore, although the need for writing is often described as an essential characteristic of a guarantee, it is more accurate to describe it as a normal prerequisite to enforcement.

Guarantees and insurance

1–008 Contracts of insurance and contracts of guarantee are both examples of contracts which protect the creditor from loss. However, the scope of a contract of guarantee is narrower than the potential scope of a contract of insurance, which may protect the insured against contingencies other than

---

17 *Duncan, Fox & Co v North & South Wales Bank*, above at 12; *Rouse v Bradford Banking Co* [1894] A.C. 586; *Oriental Finance Corporation v Overend, Gurney & Co* (1871) 7 Ch. App. 142, *affd* L.R. 7 H.L. 348 at 361.

18 *Duncan, Fox & Co v North & South Wales Bank* (1880) 6 App. Cas. 1 at 11–12, *per* Lord Selborne; *Nicholas v Ridley* [1904] 1 Ch. 192. See also *Esso Petroleum Co Ltd v Alstonbridge Properties Ltd* [1975] 1 W.L.R. 1474.

19 *Overend Financial Corporation v Overend, Gurney & Co* [1871] 7 Ch. App. 142, *affd* L.R. 7 H.L. 348; *Rouse v Bradford Banking Co* (1894) A.C. 586 *per* Lord Watson at 598; *Goldfarb v Bartlett and Kremer* [1920] 1 K.B. 639 at 647–648.

20 See further Ch.3.

the non-performance by another person of obligations or duties owed to the insured. A contract of insurance is a contract whereby the insurer agrees, in consideration of the payment to him of a premium, to pay a specified sum to the insured on the occurrence of a specified event.[21] His liability does not depend on the existence of a principal, or even on default; for example, the contract may provide for payment simply in the event that the principal does not pay (albeit that he may be justified in withholding payment). An underwriter is not a surety. He is under a primary obligation to make payment, not a collateral liability to answer for the obligations of the principal. He will normally have no influence at all over the principal's performance of those obligations. Consequently an event which might discharge a surety will not discharge the insurer from his liability.[22]

One context in which this distinction may prove to be of some importance is where an insurance company provides a mortgage protection policy to the creditor by way of additional security for a loan secured by a mortgage. The premium for such a policy is often paid by the mortgagor. The answer to the question whether the contract with the insurance company is a contract of guarantee or a contract of insurance could, in certain circumstances, have a significant effect on the rights and obligations of the issuer of the policy, the creditor, and the mortgagor or other sureties. The following two cases illustrate the type of difficulties which can arise.

In *Re Denton's Estate* [1904] Ch. 178, the late Mr Denton was a party to a joint and several covenant with the mortgagor in which he agreed to pay on demand the principal and the interest subject to a limit of £1,000. The deed expressly provided that although as between Mr Denton and the mortgagor he was to be regarded as a surety only, as between Mr Denton and the bank, he was to be considered a principal debtor for the whole mortgage debt. The bank had effected a "mortgage insurance policy" with the plaintiff. In due course the mortgagor defaulted, the plaintiff paid under the policy and sued Mr Denton's estate. It was argued that the "policy" was not one of insurance, but of guarantee, and that the plaintiffs stood in the position of co-sureties with Mr Denton and therefore had to contribute to the loss. The Court of Appeal held (Vaughan Williams L.J. expressing considerable hesitation) that despite the form of the "policy" being that of a policy of insurance, in substance it was a guarantee. However, since the guarantee extended to covering Mr Denton's own obligations to the bank as well as those of the mortgagor, there was no right of contribution.[23]

In *Woolwich Building Society v Brown* [1996] C.L.C. 625, the mortgagor claimed that the creditor, a building society, was obliged to give credit, in computing its claim against him, for money received by it under what was described as an "indemnity guarantee" issued by an insurance company (the premiums for which were paid by the mortgagor). Under the terms of

---

21 See *Prudential Insurance v IRC* [1904] 2 K.B. 658 at 663, *per* Channell J.
22 See, *e.g. Dane v Mortgage Insurance Corporation* [1894] 1 Q.B. 54; *Finlay v The Mexican Investment Corporation* [1897] 1 Q.B. 517.
23 Applying *Craythorne v Swinburne* (1807) 4 Ves. 160, and see generally Chs 11 and 12.

the contract, the insurers were liable to pay a sum which was calculated not by reference to what the mortgagor owed, but by reference to a formula, on the occurrence of three specific events:

(1)   the building society exercising its right of sale of the mortgaged house;

(2)   the mortgagor failing to make any payment;

(3)   the proceeds of sale being less than the outstanding debt.

In the light of these factors, Waller J. held that the contract was a contract of insurance, and that accordingly the insurers were entitled to pursue their subrogated claim in the name of the building society for the full indebtedness, without giving credit for the sum which they had paid. He also expressed the view that even if the contract had been a guarantee, the same result would have been reached.

Sometimes it will be just as easy for the creditor to insure against the default of the principal as it will be for him to obtain a guarantee, and the premium may be a comparatively small price to pay for the relative security of insurance provided by a large commercial institution. On the other hand, the creditor may prefer to dictate the precise terms of the contract which protects him against the anticipated loss, and he may be in such a strong bargaining position with the principal that he can require and obtain the protection of a guarantee without having to make any payment.

The fact that the doctrine of utmost good faith applies to all contracts of insurance may be another matter which the creditor will take into consideration. Contracts of guarantee are not generally subject to this doctrine, although there is a limited duty of disclosure.[24] However, a contract of guarantee may be expressed in the form of a contract of insurance.[25] It has been said that many contracts may be described by either term, and that the question whether a contract is one of the utmost good faith depends on its true character: *Seaton v Heath* [1899] 1 Q.B. 782 at 792, *per* Romer L.J.[26] Accordingly, the question whether the doctrine of the utmost good faith applies may turn on the true construction of the contract, and there is no reason why the duty of disclosure of material facts should not be expressly incorporated into a contract of guarantee. Certain types of export credit guarantee have this feature.[27]

Types of guarantee

1–009   There is a considerable variety in the types of guarantee into which parties may enter. They may be very specific, relating to a particular defined obligation of the principal and to no other obligation, or very widely drawn,

---

24 *London General Omnibus Co Ltd v Holloway* [1912] 2 K.B. 72 at 81, *per* Farwell L.J. and at 85, 86 *per* Kennedy L.J., and see further Ch.5, paras 5–015–5–027.
25 See, *e.g. Re Denton's Estate* [1904] 2 Ch. 178, above.
26 *Revsd* without affecting this point [1900] A.C. 135.
27 See Ch.15.

covering any present and future obligations of the principal to the creditor, whatsoever and howsoever arising. Similarly, the guarantee may be for a limited period or completely open-ended. Some of the different types of guarantee are identified below.

Bipartite and tripartite guarantees

The simplest form of guarantee is the one in which the creditor, principal and surety are all parties to the contract and all three agree that the principal is to be primarily liable and that the guarantor's liability is secondary. However, although the creditor is an essential party to a contract of guarantee, it is by no means unusual for the contract to be made between the guarantor and the creditor alone.

For example, the surety may be induced to give the guarantee by some person other than the principal (for example, the principal's spouse), and may not enter into any contractual relationship with the principal.[28] The contract may also be entered into at the express or implied request of the surety, as when a person who purchases goods manufactured by the principal persuades the creditor to supply the principal with raw materials on advantageous credit terms, by offering him a guarantee of the indebtedness which arises on the underlying trading account. In such a situation, the principal need not even know of the arrangements made between the creditor and the guarantor, though he usually would be aware of them.

Continuing and limited guarantees

Although it is common for a guarantee to be limited in duration, a **1–010** guarantee may also be entered into for an indefinite period. A continuing guarantee is one which extends to a series of transactions, whether or not over a limited period. Guarantees of overdraft facilities afforded by a bank to a trading company are often both continuing and of unlimited duration, though it is common in such contracts to include a provision enabling the guarantor to give a specific period of notice to the creditor to determine his future liability. If there is no express period of notice, the question whether the guarantor can terminate his liability (in the absence of a repudiation by the creditor, or frustrating event) will depend on the construction of the particular contract and on the nature of the principal debtor's underlying obligation.[29]

A guarantee may in terms refer only to the obligations arising under an identified contract or even to a specific obligation, for example, the obligation to pay the purchase price under a particular contract of sale. At the other extreme, the guarantee may cover "liability in respect of any loss, damage, claims, costs charges and expenses (including interest) and any other liability whatsoever and howsoever arising" which the principal may incur to the creditor.

---

28 See, for example, *Brown Shipley & Co Ltd v Amalgamated Investment (Europe) BV* [1979] 1 Lloyd's Rep. 488 (guarantee of a loan to a subsidiary at the request of the parent company).
29 See Ch.8.

Guarantees payable on demand

1–011 A guarantee may contain an express stipulation that the surety is to be liable to make payment to the creditor "on demand".[30] In such event, the obligation of the guarantor to pay does not arise until the demand has been made on him, though his underlying liability arises at the date of the principal's default. The demand will usually be construed as a procedural requirement included for the guarantor's protection, which he may waive, rather than as a condition precedent to liability, which he may not. The demand marks the time from which the surety's liability can be enforced: *Stimpson v Smith* [1999] 1 W.L.R. 1292 at 1304, *per* Tuckey L.J., The fact that the obligation of the principal is to pay on demand will not automatically mean that the creditor is obliged to make a demand on the surety as well. The guarantee may contain an express provision requiring such a demand to be made on the principal before a demand is made on the surety: it may also contain a provision requiring the creditor to give the surety notice of default by the principal before he takes proceedings against the surety.[31] It is more common, however, for a modern guarantee to contain a provision expressly negating any obligation on the part of the creditor to make a demand on the principal, to notify the surety of his default, or to take any other step before enforcing the guarantee. Whilst a demand will often be made an express prerequisite to bringing a claim under a normal guarantee, the expression "demand guarantee" is apt to cause confusion, because in certain contexts it is synonymous with a performance bond (see para.1–015 and Chapter 16). For example, that is the meaning which the expression bears under the ICC Uniform Rules for Demand Guarantees (ICC publication No.458), discussed in Chapter 16.

Contracts of indemnity

Definition

1–012 An indemnity, in its widest sense, comprises an obligation imposed by operation of law or by contract on one person to make good a loss suffered by another. Thus most contracts of insurance and all contracts of guarantee fall within the broad definition. However, the expression "contract of indemnity" is more often used to denote a contract where the person giving the indemnity does so by way of security for the performance of an obligation by another. It is this type of contract with which this book is concerned.

Essential characteristics

1–013 In a contract of indemnity, unlike a contract of guarantee, a primary liability falls upon the surety, and that liability is wholly independent of any liability which may arise as between the principal and the creditor (unless

---

30 See, *e.g. Romain v Scuba TV Ltd* [1997] Q.B. 887; *Sicklemore v Thistleton* (1817) 6 M. & S. 9; *Bradford Old Bank v Sutcliffe* [1918] 2 K.B. 833; *Re Brown's Estate* [1893] 2 Ch. 300; *General Financial Corporation of Canada v Le Jeune* [1918] 1 W.W.R. 372 (Can).

31 *Bache & Co (London) Ltd v Banque Vernes et Commerciale de Paris* [1973] 2 Lloyd's Rep. 437; *Phillips v Fordyce* (1779) 2 Chit. 676; see also *Bonthrone v Paterson* (1898) 35 Sc. L.R. 344; *Britannia Steamship Insurance Association Ltd v Duff* [1909] S.C. 1261 (Scot).

the indemnifier undertakes a joint liability with the principal). Of course, it is usually implicit in such an arrangement that as between the principal and the surety, the principal is to be primarily liable, so that if the surety has to pay first, he has a right of recourse against the principal.

The fact that the obligation to indemnify is primary and independent has the effect that the principle of co-extensiveness and the requirements of s.4 of the Statute of Frauds 1677 do not apply to contracts of indemnity. Thus an indemnity not only effectively shifts the burden of the principal's insolvency onto the surety, but also potentially safeguards the creditor against the possibility that his underlying transaction with the principal is void or otherwise unenforceable.[32] Further, the discharge of the principal or any variation or compromise of the creditor's claims against him will not necessarily affect the liability of the surety under a contract of indemnity.[33] Otherwise, the rights and duties of the parties to a contract of indemnity are generally the same as those of the parties to a contract of guarantee.

The question whether a particular contract happens to be a guarantee or an indemnity, and whether the normal incidents of a contract of that class have been modified, is a matter of construction in each case, and is often very difficult to resolve. A contract of suretyship which contains a provision preserving liability in circumstances in which a guarantor would otherwise be discharged (such as the granting of time to the principal or a material variation of the underlying contract without the surety's consent) will usually be construed as a guarantee, because such a provision would be unnecessary if the contract was an indemnity.

The contract may also contain a provision to the effect that the surety is to be liable in circumstances in which the principal debtor has ceased to be liable, *e.g.* on the release of the principal debtor by the creditor. Although it may be argued, by parity of reasoning, that this tends to indicate that the contract is a guarantee, such a provision may point towards the opposite conclusion because it may show that it was intended that the liability of the obligor should continue regardless of what might happen to the principal debtor. A good illustration of this is to be found in the unreported Court of Appeal case of *Clement v Clement* (CAT No.1336 of 1995, October 20).

A dispute between a husband, his wife and their son about the running of a family-owned company was settled on terms that the parents sold their shares and retired from the company. In return the company agreed that it would pay the father a pension during his lifetime and, if he died before his wife, the company would pay her a reduced pension from the date of his death for the rest of her life. Both pensions were index-linked. The son sent his parents a letter in the following terms:

> "By an agreement of even date ('the Agreement') between First Fashions Ltd ('the Company') and yourselves the Company cove-

---

32 See, *e.g. Yeoman Credit v Latter* [1961] 1 W.L.R. 828; *Goulston Discount Co Ltd v Clark* [1967] 2 Q.B. 493. *Cf. Bentworth Finance v Lubert* [1968] 1 Q.B. 680.
33 See Ch.6.

nanted to pay certain retirement benefits. Now I undertake that if the Company . . . fail(s) to pay the sums covenanted to be paid by it I or my personal representatives will pay such sums or so much of them as shall not be paid. This guarantee shall continue in force until the death of the survivor of you . . ."

The Company subsequently went into voluntary liquidation and the liquidator disclaimed the pension contract. On the law as it then stood, it was believed that the disclaimer determined both the liability of the Company and the liability of any guarantor.[34] The son therefore sought to argue that the letter was a guarantee. Warner J. and the Court of Appeal held that despite the fact that the letter described itself as a "guarantee" it was an indemnity. On the true construction of the conract, the obligation to pay the pension until the death of the surviving parent arose regardless of what might happen in the meantime to the Company or to its liabilities. It did not depend on the continued existence of the liability of the Company.

If the contract provides that the surety is to be liable in circumstances in which the principal debtor was never liable (*e.g.* because the principal debtor lacked the capacity to contract), it may indicate that the contract is an indemnity.[35] A contract which provides for the surety to be liable in circumstances in which the principal debtor has rescinded or avoided the underlying contract may prove exceptionally difficult to classify. Indeed, it is possible that a clause which purports to preserve the guarantor's liability in the event that the underlying transaction is void or avoided will be ineffective, because the guarantee as a whole never comes into effect: this could occur, for example, if the consideration for the guarantee is expressed to be the entry into the principal contract.

"Principal debtor" clauses

1–014   It is common for standard form bank guarantees and similar documents to contain a provision that the surety is to be liable "as principal debtor" or that the creditor may treat him as a principal debtor or "primary obligor" in certain circumstances. A provision of this kind is typically found at the end of a clause which expressly preserves the guarantor's liability in circumstances in which he would otherwise be released. An example is the clause in *National Westminster Bank v Riley* [1986] B.C.L.C. 268 which provided that "this guarantee shall not be discharged nor shall the Guarantor's liability under it be affected by anything which would not have discharged or affected the Guarantor's liability if the Guarantor had been a principal debtor to the Bank instead of a Guarantor". The Court of Appeal held that this precluded the guarantor from raising an argument by way of

---

34 Following *Stacey v Hill* [1901] 1 K.B. 660, which was subsequently overruled by the House of Lords in *Hindcastle Ltd v Barbara Attenborough Associates Ltd* [1997] A.C. 70, see Ch.18.
35 See, *e.g. Alliance Acceptance Co v Hinton* [1964] 1 D.C.R. (NSW) 5.

defence that he had been discharged from liability by virtue of a fundamental breach of the contract with the borrower by the Bank. However even as a self-standing provision it may be construed as having that effect: see, *e.g. Heald v O'Connor* [1971] 1 W.L.R. 497.[36] The prevailing view appears to be that the incorporation of a "principal debtor" clause will not usually suffice in itself to determine the nature of the contract: it will not automatically convert a guarantee into an indemnity.[37]

Similarly, the contract may include a separate provision by which the surety contracts in terms to indemify the creditor against loss or damage suffered by him arising out of or consequential upon his having entered into the agreement with the principal. The question whether this provision will affect the nature of the contract as a whole, or whether it will give rise to independent obligations, is one of construction. If the obligation to indemnify is couched in terms which make it plain that it is predicated upon there being an underlying liability of the principal, the contract will remain a guarantee. This may explain the decision of the Court of Appeal in *Stadium Finance Co Ltd v Helm* (1965) 109 S.J. 471 to the effect that a contract was a guarantee, notwithstanding that it was headed "indemnity form" and containing the following term:

"I will indemnify and keep indemnified you, your successors and assigns from all loss and damage suffered and all claims costs and expenses made against or incurred by you in any way arising out of or consequent upon your having entered into such agreement, whether arising out of a breach by the customer of any of the terms and conditions thereof or otherwise including any such loss or damage etc. aforesaid as may arise from the said agreement being (for whatever reason) unenforceable against the customer."

A more common approach, if the language of the contract permits it, is to treat the contract as giving rise to separate enforceable obligations of indemnity and guarantee: see, *e.g.* the Australian case of *Citicorp Australia Ltd v Hendry* [1985] 4 N.S.W.L.R. 1 where the contract was treated as a guarantee which contained an additional liability under the indemnity clause. However, the language of the indemnity clause is all-important; in that particular case the indemnity provision did not preserve the liability of the guarantor when the sums payable under the principal contract were irrecoverable by the creditor because they were in the nature of a penalty.

---

36 See also *Fletcher Organisation Pty Ltd v Crocus Investments Pty Ltd* [1988] Qd. R. 517; *Orme v DeBoyette* [1981] 1 N.Z.L.R. 576, but *cf. Dunlop New Zealand Ltd v Dumbleton* [1968] N.Z.L.R. 1092 and *Payton v SG Brookes & Sons Pty Ltd* [1977] W.A.R. 91.
37 See *Heald v O'Connor* [1971] 1 W.L.R. 497, *per* Fisher J. at 503; *General Produce Co v United Bank* [1979] 2 Lloyd's Rep. 255 *per* Lloyd J. at 259; *Brown Brothers Motor Lease Canada Ltd v Ganapahi* (1982) 139 D.L.R. (3d) 227; *Credit Suisse v Borough Council of Allerdale* [1995] 1 Lloyd's Rep. 315 *per* Colman J. at 366–367.

Performance bonds

1–015 Bonds are simple covenants by one person to pay another, either conditionally or unconditionally. A performance bond, also commonly called a performance guarantee, or (confusingly) a demand guarantee, is a binding contractual undertaking given by a person, usually a bank, to pay a specified amount of money to a named beneficiary on the occurrence of a certain event, which is usually the non-fulfilment of a contractual obligation undertaken by the principal to the beneficiary.

Performance bonds are not guarantees in the true sense, but are a particularly stringent form of contract of indemnity. They are often drafted in such a way that the liability to pay will arise on a mere demand by the beneficiary, even if there is reason to doubt that the primary obligation has been broken. The rights and duties of the parties to a performance bond will depend on the terms of the contract which has been agreed between them, and are not subject to the usual equities which apply to ordinary contracts of guarantee or indemnity.

It is often a difficult task for the court to determine whether, on its true construction, a particular contract which provides for payment on demand is a performance bond (under which the obligation to make payment is autonomous and is triggered by a demand or a demand plus the provision of certain specified documents) or whether it is a guarantee in the true sense (sometimes referred to in this context as a "see to it" guarantee) where the obligation to pay is conditioned on proof by the creditor of default. Performance bonds are discussed in detail in Chapter 16. See also Precedent 5.

Chapter 2

Contractual Requirements

Introduction

A contract of guarantee or indemnity governed by English law must be   **2–001**
formed, like any other contract, by offer and acceptance, with the intention
of creating legal relations, and must be supported by consideration if it is
not given under seal. Its terms must also be sufficiently certain and
complete to enable the court to give effect to them.[1]

Offer and acceptance

The resolution of the question whether there has been an offer to   **2–002**
guarantee or indemnify, or an acceptance of that offer, depends on the facts
of each particular case, and may be a matter of the proper construction of
relevant documents passing between the creditor and the alleged surety.[2]
Thus, in *M' Iver v Richardson* (1813) 1 M. & S. 557, the defendant gave a
letter to the debtors, A & Co, which said:

> "I understand A & Co have given you an order . . . I can assure you,
> from what I know of A's honour and probity, you will be perfectly safe
> in crediting them to that amount; indeed, I have no objection to
> guarantee you against any loss from giving them this credit."

The letter was handed over by A & Co to the plaintiffs, who subsequently
attempted to sue the defendant upon it as a guarantee. It was held:

(a)   that the wording of the letter did not evince a clear consent by the
      defendant that it should be treated as a guarantee, rather than as a
      mere indication that he would be willing to give a guarantee if
      application were made to him in the future; and

---

1 For examples of cases in which a guarantee was held to be too vague to be enforceable, see
  Westhead v Sproson (1861) 6 H. & N. 728; *Morrell v Cowan* (1877) 6 Ch. D. 166.
2 Thus it is a question of construction whether the words used amount to a guarantee or an
  offer to give one: see *Jones v Williams* (1841) 7 M. & W. 493; *Bank of Montreal v Munster
  Bank* (1876) I.R. 11 C.L. 47. The question whether a particular offer has been accepted is a
  question of fact, the answer to which may be inferred from all the circumstances of the
  transaction. See, *e.g. Marsden & Son v Capital & County Newspaper Company Ltd* (1901) 46
  S.J. 11, CA.

(b) that there was no notice given to the defendant by the plaintiffs that they were treating the letter as a guarantee.

Accordingly, there was neither an offer nor a communicated acceptance, and the plaintiffs' claim failed.[3]

If the creditor acts on the surety's promise to his detriment to the knowledge of the surety, this may be sufficient communication to the surety of the creditor's acceptance of the surety's offer: see, *e.g. Jays v Sala* (1898) 14 T.L.R. 461, where the supply of goods by the creditor to the principal in the presence of the surety was held sufficient to constitute acceptance of a written offer to guarantee payment for the principal's personal orders "should you require it".[4] Such reliance on the surety's promise might also give rise to the operation of the doctrine of promissory estoppel where appropriate. However, a proposal which is expressly made "subject to contract" cannot contain an offer which is capable of acceptance—whether by conduct or otherwise. A binding contract cannot be made unless and until the "subject to contract" condition has been removed. As Langley J. said in *Carlton Communications Plc v The Football League* [2002] EWHC 1650 (Comm) August 1, 2002 at para.52: ". . . a subject to contract proposal is the antithesis of or at the least incompatible with a unilateral offer. The former is not open to acceptance: it is the essence of the latter that it is". Thus in that case, a statement in an initial bid for broadcasting rights that "ONdigital and its shareholders will guarantee all funding to the FL outlined in this document" was held not to have been a unilateral offer to guarantee the obligations of ONdigital to the Football League under the contract eventually made between them, because that initial bid was expressly made "subject to contract".

If the offer contemplates an express notification of acceptance or a particular mode of acceptance, failure to comply with its terms will normally mean that there is no binding guarantee.[5] However, the contract must make it clear that the prescribed means of acceptance is the only means available to the offeree. If it does not, then acceptance communicated to the offeror by any other means which is no less advantageous to him will suffice to bind him.[6] In the absence of an express stipulation as to the means of acceptance, conduct consistent with acceptance may suffice to bind the parties. Thus, if the surety couples his undertaking to pay with a request to the creditor to adopt a particular pattern of behaviour, such as

---

3 See also *Symmons v Want* (1818) 2 Stark 371; *Mozley v Tinkler* (1835) 1 C. M. & R. 692; *Nash v Spencer* (1896) 13 T.L.R. 78; *Newport v Spivey* (1862) 1 New. Rep. 30.
4 See also, *e.g. Sorby v Gordon* (1874) 30 L.T. 528, *A.A. Davison Proprietary Ltd v Seabrook* [1931] A.L.R. 156.
5 See, *e.g. Gaunt v Hill* (1815) 1 Stark. 10, *Newport v Spivey* (1862) 7 L.T. 328; *Chitty on Contracts* (Sweet & Maxwell, 29th ed., 2004), Vol. 1, paras 2–063–2–067.
6 See, *e.g. Yates Building Company v RJ Pulleyn & Sons Ltd* (1975) 237 E.G. 183, CA, in which an option had to be exercised by a notice in writing sent by registered post. It was held that the requirement of using registered post was inserted purely for the benefit of the offeree, and that a notice given by ordinary post within the prescribed time was sufficient to amount to a valid exercise of the option.

extending credit to the principal, supplying goods, or employing someone, his offer may be accepted by the creditor doing what was asked.[7]

In appropriate circumstances, acceptance may even be inferred from silence and inactivity on the part of the creditor. In *Pope v Andrews* (1840) 9 C. & P. 564, the guarantors asked the creditors' agent to make a proposal to the creditors that they should accept a guarantee of the payment of the price of goods delivered to the debtor, by instalments. The agent agreed, and forwarded the signed guarantee to the creditors, who kept it for three weeks before returning it. It was held that the creditors had accepted the guarantor's offer and were bound by the guarantee. Coleridge J. gave the following instruction to the jury:

> "If a person offers a guarantee, and more still, if he signs a guarantee by which he makes himself liable, and that be sent to the other party, such other party, if he means not to accept the guarantee, is bound expressly to dissent within a reasonable time, and if he keeps the guarantee an unreasonable time, he is bound to accept it just the same as if he had assented to it by words; and if he has ever accepted it either by word or by act he cannot afterwards retract."[8]

However, the conduct said to constitute acceptance must be consistent with the offer which was made. Thus in *Glyn v Hertel* (1818) 8 Taunt. 208, 2 Moore C. P. 134, S offered to guarantee a loan of £5,000 to be made by C to D, who was already indebted to C for a considerable sum, for which C held a promissory note and other security. C subsequently cancelled the promissory note and delivered up the security to D, who then delivered the same security back again with a fresh promissory note. It was held that this transaction did not constitute a future loan within the terms of the offer to guarantee and S was not bound.

If acceptance is intimated by someone other than the proposed guarantor (such as the principal), that person must have the guarantor's authority to bind him. The dangers of a creditor committing himself to the contract with the principal in the expectation (however justified) that a guarantee will be produced, are illustrated by *The "Anangel Express"* [1996] 2 Lloyd's Rep. 299. The defendant company, Newco, proposed to charter vessels from a German shipping company named KSH, to carry various shipments of pig iron which they had sold to a steel mill in Korea. KSH usually chartered in vessels from other shipowning companies to fulfil its own commitments. In the course of negotitations for the charter of the vessel "Anangel Express" from the plaintiff shipowners to KSH, the owners indicated that they wanted a performance guarantee from Newco in respect of KSH's obligations under the charterparty. This requirement was not made known to

---

7 See, *e.g. Jays Ltd v Sala* (1898) 14 T.L.R. 461; *Oldershaw v King* (1857) 2 H. & N. 517; *Kennaway v Treleavan* (1839) 5 M. & W. 498, *Brett v Tarr* (CAT No.1234 of 1997, July 9).
8 *Cf. Mozley v Tinkler* (1835) 1 Cr. M. & R. 692, where on its true construction, the guarantee contemplated communication of acceptance by the creditor.

Newco until some three days after the fixture recap had been sent, in which it was stated "charterers agree to performance guarantee to be as per Owners wording on Newco letter headed paper and signed by Newco". When KSH defaulted in payments under the Charterparty, the owners sought to claim against Newco. Waller J. dismissed the claim, on the basis that there was no agreement for a guarantee made between Newco and the plaintiff, and even if (which was doubtful) there was any binding agreement as between KSH and Newco that the latter would give a guarantee if requested, so such guarantee was ever actually asked for or produced. KSH's agreement, set out in the fixture recap, was not binding upon Newco.

A decision on virtually identical facts which went the other way was *Clipper Maritime Ltd v Shirlstar Container Transport Ltd ("The Anemone")* [1987] 1 Lloyd's Rep. 546. In that case, the company secretary of the alleged guarantor had no authority in his own right to commit the company to a guarantee without the approval of the man who controlled the company. Staughton J. held on the evidence that the controller expressly or implicitly authorised the secretary to commit the company into promising to give a guarantee of performance of the charterparties, but even if there was no such authority, the secretary's acts were ratified by the controller in subsequent conversations with the shipowner's solicitors.

If no time limit for acceptance is stipulated in the offer, the acceptance must be given within a reasonable time: *Payne v Ives* (1823) 3 Dow. & Ry. K.B. 664 at 668, *per* Holroyd J. It must also be absolute, unqualified and sufficiently certain. In *Morten v Marshall* (1863) 2 H. & C. 305, the creditor's agreement to accept the guarantee was expressly conditional upon the provision of references by the surety. It was held that the creditor could waive that condition, since it was imposed by him for his own benefit, but the guarantee would not become valid and enforceable until he gave notice to the surety that he no longer required the references.

The offer to contract usually comes from the surety. However, if the true position is that the creditor has offered to contract by requesting the guarantee, and the guarantee is provided in compliance with that request, there is no further requirement that the creditor should notify the surety that he has accepted the guarantee.[9]

Revocation by the surety

2–002/1 It is not uncommon for a surety to change his mind and wish to cancel his suretyship. The position of the surety who wishes to revoke his offer at or before the inception of the contract is considered below. The position of the surety who wishes to cancel or revoke after the contract has become binding on him is discussed in Chapter 8.

---

9 *Fraser v Douglas* (1906) 5 W.L.R. 52 (Can).

Revocation before acceptance

As a general contractual principle, a promise which is not made under seal **2–003**
may be revoked at any stage before it is accepted (or acted upon so as to
create a promissory estoppel).[10] Consequently, the question whether the
surety is entitled to revoke a guarantee prior to the partial or full
performance of the consideration given for it essentially depends upon
whether his offer has been accepted or acted upon. This in turn may
depend on the true construction of the contract of guarantee or indemnity.

Unilateral and bilateral offers

It is often more difficult to determine whether and when an offer to act as **2–004**
surety has been accepted than is usually the case in respect of other forms
of contract. The issue of acceptance may be very closely connected with
other issues such as whether consideration has been given and whether
conditions precedent have been fulfilled. It may be hard to say in a given
case whether as a matter of contractual intention and interpretation the
surety's offer is unilateral, *i.e.* not binding until it is acted upon by the
creditor, or whether, on the contrary, there is a binding promise given by
the creditor in return for the promise to guarantee, and the contract is
operative and bilateral even if the creditor's promise has not yet been acted
upon.[11]

If, as a matter of construction, the offer takes the form of a unilateral
undertaking that if the creditor does something in the future, (*e.g.* supplies
goods to the principal), the surety will guarantee payment, the creditor does
not accept the offer (or give consideration) until he complies with its terms.
In such a case, the surety is entitled to revoke his offer until the terms are
fulfilled at least in part, because "this promise [of the surety] itself creates
no obligation. It is, in effect, conditioned to be binding if the [creditor] acts
on it, either to the benefit of [the surety] or to the detriment of himself":
Offord v Davis (1862) 12 C.B.N.S. 748, *per* Erle C.J. at 757.[12]

In that case the surety, in consideration of the creditor discounting bills
of exchange for the principal at the surety's request, had undertaken to
guarantee payment of all such bills of exchange to the extent of £600 for 12
months. Before any bills had been discounted, the surety requested the
creditor not to discount any such bills. Despite this, the creditor went
ahead, and when the principal dishonoured the bills, he sued the surety on
the guarantee. It was held that the surety was not liable.

The following example illustrates the effect of the rule: C, the creditor, is
a manufacturer of chemicals who intends to make up a special order for D,
the principal. S, the surety, agrees to guarantee payment of the price of the
chemicals. S changes his mind and purports to revoke the agreement:

---

10 *Dickinson v Dodds* [1876] 2 Ch. D. 463; *Daulia Ltd v Four Millbank Nominees Ltd* [1978] 1
    Ch. 231 at 239, *per* Robert Goff L.J.
11 See generally *Chitty on Contracts (op. cit.)*, Vol. 1, paras 2–076–2–079.
12 See also *Daulia Ltd v Four Millbank Nominees Ltd* [1978] 1 Ch. 231 at 239.

(a) before C has started to make up the order or has acted in any way upon S's promise;

(b) after C has actually started to manufacture the chemicals for D's order, but before he has entered into a binding contract with D;

(c) after C has entered into a binding contract with D to supply the chemicals ordered by D.

In situation (a), S is entitled to revoke the guarantee, but not in situation (b) or (c). In situation (b), C has acted to his detriment in reliance on the promise made by S. In situation (c), C has not only acted to his detriment, but by undertaking a binding contractual liability to D, he has at least partly performed his part of the contractual bargain with S.

If the surety dies before his offer has been accepted, this operates as a revocation: *Dickinson v Dodds* [1876] 2 Ch. D. 463 at 475, *per* Mellish L.J.

When the offer becomes irrevocable

2–005   On the other hand, if the offer by the surety is given in consideration of an express promise by the creditor to enter into a transaction with the principal, so that there is a binding and enforceable bilateral agreement at that stage, the surety will be unable to revoke his offer even before the creditor has acted upon it. That is also the case if the surety's promise is in a deed.

Thus, in the example given above, if C were to enter into an agreement with S, under which C promised S that he would supply D with chemicals manufactured by C, in return for S undertaking to guarantee payment by D for those chemicals, the fact that C has not yet begun to manufacture the chemicals, and the absence of a binding contract between C and D for their supply, would probably not justify any revocation by S.[13]

Given that fine distinctions have been drawn between cases in which the contract was held to be binding immediately, and cases in which it was not binding until acted upon by the creditor, a creditor who wishes to protect himself against the possibility of revocation of the surety's offer is probably best advised either to ensure that the guarantee is embodied in a deed, or to furnish a nominal consideration to the surety at the time when the guarantee is given. It is unlikely that he would be able to avoid the consequences of the rule in *Offord v Davies* by inserting a clause in the contract which provides that the guarantee shall be terminable only on the happening of a certain event, *e.g.* the giving of notice by the surety. Although there appears to be no reported decision on this point, it is unlikely that such a clause would be construed as applying to any situation

---

13 For an illustration of the difficulty of distinguishing between a case in which the consideration is an agreement to supply goods and a case in which the consideration is the supply of goods themselves, see *Greenham Ready Mixed Concrete v CAS (Industrial Developments) Ltd* (1965) 109 S.J. 209, discussed at para.2–010 below.

occurring before the guarantee becomes a binding contract. Further, if the surety can revoke the whole offer, there is no logical reason why he should not be entitled to revoke one of its terms.

Prospective consumer credit agreements

If a person provides or agrees to provide security in respect of a *prospective* **2–006** agreement or transaction regulated by the Consumer Credit Act 1974, then by virtue of s.113(6) of that Act the security is only enforceable after the time when the regulated agreement or transaction is made, and until that time, the surety has the right to give notice to the creditor requiring that s.106 of the Act shall apply to the security. Once that notice takes effect, s.106 treats the security as never having effect and obliges the creditor to return any property or money which he has received in respect of the contract of suretyship, and to remove or to cancel any entry pertaining to the security which he may have made in any register (for example, the Companies Register).

The surety therefore has an unfettered right to revoke his contract of guarantee or indemnity at any time until the creditor has entered into the envisaged regulated agreement with the principal. This is in keeping with the general policy enshrined in s.113, of preventing the creditor from evading the provisions of the Act or its consequences by taking security from some person who is not directly protected by it, with the result that the surety would be constrained to pursue lesser remedies against the consumer principal. These provisions are considered in greater detail in Chapter 17.

Privity of contract

The general rule in English law is that a contract can only be enforced by **2–007** those who are parties to it, or by those who acquire contractual rights by assignment, novation or operation of law, or by the beneficiary of a trust of a contractual promise. The Contracts (Rights of Third Parties) Act 1999, which applies to contracts made on or after May 11, 2000 (six months after the Act came into force) and, by express agreement, to contracts made between November 11, 1999 and May 10, 2000, has made substantial inroads into the doctrine of privity of contract. As a result, a contract of guarantee may now expressly or by implication confer contractual rights upon a third party, such as a creditor of the original creditor, provided that (1) a term of the contract purports to confer a benefit upon the third party, and (2) the third party is expressly identified either by name, or as a member of a class or as answering a particular description: for example, "the creditor's nominee" or "the unsecured creditors of X Ltd". If those conditions are fulfilled, then the Act will confer rights on the third party unless on a proper construction of the contract it appears that the parties did not intend the contract to be enforceable by him.[14] This means that he will have the same remedies available to him for the purpose of enforcement as the direct contracting parties.

The Act could prove useful if the guarantee is liable to be affected by changes in the identity of the creditor (for example, where a guarantee is given to the current members of a partnership), but there is a danger that the normal rules on insolvency could be circumvented by virtue of creating a directly enforceable right on the part of one of the creditors of the original creditor (such as a parent company) to claim the fruits of the guarantee, thus taking it out of the assets made available to the general body of creditors. However, its impact can be avoided with ease by inserting an express provision into the contract excluding its application, and such a provision is to be found in most standard forms of guarantee.

Consideration

2–008   On general contractual principles, the contract of guarantee must be supported by consideration if it is not embodied in a deed.

The consideration must move from the creditor rather than from the debtor, though in certain circumstances consideration provided by the creditor's agent may suffice.[15] The consideration need not directly benefit the surety, though it may often do so.[16] It is also possible for the consideration to move to a third party, though there do not appear to be many reported cases dealing with that situation. An example of such a situation is where the creditor agrees to release a guarantee given to him by someone other than the surety (often a relative, or spouse of the surety) in return for the provision of a fresh guarantee by the surety.

In most cases, however, the consideration will consist entirely of some advantage given to or conferred on the principal by the creditor at the request of the surety, such as forebearance from suing him or the compromise of existing legal proceedings against him,[17] loaning him

---

14 See, *e.g. Malyon v New Zealand Methodist Trust Association* [1993] 1 NZLR 137 in which the NZ Court of Appeal held that s.4 of the New Zealand Contracts (Privity) Act 1982, which is in similar terms, did not allow a landlord to enforce a guarantee contained in a deed of assignment of the lease because on its true construction the guarantee given for the assignee's obligations was intended only to benefit the tenant (assignor) and not the head landlord. *Cf. Re A & K Holdings Pty Ltd* [1964] V.R. 257.
15 *White v Cuyler* (1795) 6 Term Rep. 176 at 177; *Dutchman v Tooth* (1839) 5 Bing N.C. 577; *Fleming v Bank of New Zealand* [1900] A.C. 577, PC.
16 *Morley v Boothby* (1825) 10 Moore C.P. 395, 3 Bing. 107; *Ex p. Minet* (1807) 14 Ves. 189 at 190, *per* Lord Eldon L.C.; *Seaton v Heath* [1899] 1 Q.B. 782 at 793, CA (reversed on a different point *sub nom. Seaton v Burnand* [1900] A.C. 135). For an example of a case where the surety did benefit directly see *Re Willis Ex p. Brook* (1850) 6 De G. M. & G. 771.
17 See, *e.g. Crears v Hunter* (1887) 19 Q.B.D. 341, *Oldershaw v King* (1857) 2 H. & N. 517, *Miles v New Zealand Alford Estate Co* (1886) 32 Ch. D. 266, and the cases referred to at paras 2–013–2–014.

money,[18] supplying him with goods on credit,[19] or, in the case of a fidelity guarantee, taking him into the creditor's service or employment.[20]

If there is no consideration, or if the consideration totally fails, the guarantee will be unenforceable and the surety is entitled to have his guarantee delivered up to be cancelled. If the consideration is expressly identified in the guarantee, and the relevant act or omission has not occurred, the guarantee will fail for want of consideration even if the creditor has provided something which is just as good, or which might have constituted consideration had the guarantee been silent.[21] The mere existence of an antecedent debt is not valuable consideration, nor is the mere existence of a "default or miscarriage of another" for which the guarantor agrees to answer.[22]

A good illustration of this is the case of *Brett v Tarr* (unreported) CAT No.1234 of 1997, July 9. Two companies controlled by T had been granted successive licences by B of certain business premises which he owned. Each company went into liquidation owing arrears of licence fees. Despite this history, B granted a fresh licence of the same premises, terminable upon one month's notice, to a third company controlled by T. Two months later, B decided to change the locks and deny T access to the premises. When T attempted to get in, B told him that he would not be allowed access unless he agreed to take "personal responsibility" for the arrears and for future payments of the licence fees. T raised no objection, but he did not say that he agreed. However, he did say that if he was not given access to the premises he would be unable to earn any money with which to pay B. B let him in, and the company licensee continued to pay the licence fees as they fell due until the licence was terminated. B subsequently sent T two self-serving letters which purported to confirm that T had agreed to assume personal liability for all outstanding arrears. T failed to respond. After selling the premises, B sued T for the arrears.

At first instance, the judge held that T's conduct in entering the premises on the understanding that he would only gain continuing access if he accepted personal responsibility for payment of the arrears amounted to an

---

18 See, *e.g. Hartland v Jukes* (1863) 1 H. & C. 667; *Grahame v Grahame* (1887) 19 L.R. Ir. 249; *Edwards v Jeavons* (1848) 8 C.B. 436; *Broom v Batchelor* (1856) 1 H. & N. 255.
19 See, *e.g. Mockett v Ames* (1871) 23 L.T. 729; *Morrell v Cowan* (1877) 7 Ch. D. 151; *Wood v Benson* (1831) 2 Cr. & J. 94; *Johnston v Nicholls* (1845) 1 C.B. 251.
20 See, *e.g. Leathley v Spyer* (1870) L.R. 5 CP 595; *Kennaway v Treleavan* (1839) 5 M. & W. 498; *Newbury v Armstrong* (1829) 6 Bing. 201.
21 This can give rise to fine distinctions. Compare the decision in *Gobblers Inc Pty Ltd v Stevens* (1994) A.N.Z. Conv. R. 110 with the very similar case of *Chan v Cresdon Pty Ltd* (1989) 168 CLR 242. In the first case the stated consideration was "granting this lease to the lessee" and no lease was granted. Even though a statutory tenancy arose by virtue of the landlord allowing the lessee into possession, it was held that there was no consideration. In the second case, the consideration was stated to be "entering into this lease" and it was held that the execution of an instrument equivalent to an equitable lease would have been sufficient to satisfy that term, though the claim failed on other grounds.
22 *Wigan v English and Scottish Law Life Assurance Association* [1909] 1 Ch. 291; *Forth v Stanton* (1669) 1 Sand. 210 at 211(a), 211(b), note f; *Crofts v Beale* (1851) 11 C.B. 172; *French v French* (1841) 2 Man. & G. 644.

acceptance of B's offer.[23] However, the resulting contract was a contract of guarantee and since there was no written note or memorandum to satisfy the requirements of s.4 of the Statute of Frauds (see Chapter 3), the agreement was unenforceable. B appealed, alleging that the contract was an indemnity. The Court of Appeal held that there was no binding oral agreement because there was no consideration. The pleaded consideration had been B's refraining from enforcing his rights to determine the licence, but the Court of Appeal held that he had no such rights at the time, as licence payments by the company were up to date and no notice to terminate the licence had been served, let alone expired. B's refusal of access to T had therefore been unlawful. The judge had stated that the consideration was forbearance by B to sue, but there was no evidence to justify that finding and there was nothing which B could have sued T for. In the circumstances, the Statute of Frauds point did not arise and the Court refused to examine what was described in the judgments as the "elusive" terms of the alleged contract, to determine whether or not it was a guarantee.

Guarantee in the form of a promissory note

2–009   Where the guarantee is given in the form of a promissory note or bill of exchange for the payment of a debt, it has been suggested by some commentators that the creditor need not prove that fresh consideration for the note was given, because s.27 of the Bills of Exchange Act 1882 provides that an antecedent debt or liability is sufficient consideration for a promissory note or bill of exchange.[24] However, this argument was dismissed by the Court of Appeal in *Oliver v Davis* [1949] 2 K.B. 727, in which it was held that if the "antecedent debt or liability" was that of a third party, there must be some relationship between the giving of the bill and the antecedent debt or liability. Accordingly, the creditor would have to show consideration for the giving of the bill or note, *e.g.* forbearance to sue the principal on the antecedent debt or liability.[25]

Guarantees of pre-existing liabilities

2–010   In many cases, the guarantee will be taken either simultaneously with the transaction guaranteed or before the creditor enters into the transaction with the principal. When this happens, there will normally be no difficulty in establishing consideration: the consideration is usually the creditor's agreement to enter into the other transaction.

However, if the guarantee is intended to relate to a pre-existing liability of the principal, it is important for the creditor to take care to ensure that it

---

23 Although the Court of Appeal did not find it necessary to decide the case on this point, it appears from the tenor of the judgments that this was a finding which they found difficult to support.
24 McGuinness, *The Law of Guarantee* (Carswell/Sweet & Maxwell, 1986) at para.4.77.
25 *Cf. Meredith v Chute* (1702) 2 Ld. Raym. 759.

is not unenforceable. A guarantee given for purely past consideration is unenforceable if it is not given under seal. Thus, if the creditor has already provided the consideration, *e.g.* by performing services, supplying goods or giving credit to the principal so that the principal is already liable to the creditor before the guarantee is taken, then in the absence of some fresh consideration the guarantee will be unenforceable.[26]

A possible exception is illustrated by the case of *Simmons v Keating* (1818) 2 Stark. 426. In that case the creditor had agreed to supply goods to the principal before the guarantee was made, but did not actually supply them until afterwards. The guarantee was held to be enforceable. At first sight this result would appear to be contrary to two established rules, namely, the rule that past consideration is no consideration and the rule that performance of an existing liability to a third person is usually not good consideration either.

One possible explanation for this is that the creditor, being an unpaid seller, forbore or agreed to forbear to exercise either a lien over the goods or his right of stoppage in transit, and that this was sufficient consideration despite the existence of his pre-existing obligation to supply. However, this theory, which would confine the "exception" to cases involving the sale of goods, may be unduly artificial. An alternative, wider view is that on its facts, the case is merely an illustration of the rule in *Pao On v Lau Yiu Long* [1980] A.C. 614, namely that an act done before the giving of a promise can be good consideration if it was done at the promisor's request, the parties had understood that the act was to be remunerated either by payment or the conferment of a benefit (*i.e.* the provision of a guarantee) and the payment or conferment of a benefit would have been enforceable had it been promised in advance.[27] This rule is likely to prove useful if, as frequently happens, there is a lapse of time between the advance of moneys to the principal by the creditor, and the execution of the written guarantee on the promise of which the advance was made.

In determining whether the consideration given for a contract is past, the exact order in which the relevant events occur will not be decisive. The court is entitled to look at the substance of the matter, and it may determine in an appropriate case that the underlying transaction for which the guarantee is given, and the guarantee itself, are really part of a single transaction or a series of inter-related and mutually supportive linked transactions. This approach was followed in *Leeds Health Authority, General Utilities Plc v Phoenix Imaging Systems Ltd* [1998] EWHC Tech 325, April 28, 1998 (H.H. Judge Thornton Q.C.). L, an area health authority, entered into negotiations with P for the supply to two hospitals of a specialist

---

26 See, *e.g. French v French* (1841) 2 M. & G. 644; *Astley Industrial Trust Ltd v Grimston Electric Tools Ltd* (1965) 109 S.J. 149; *Power v Ahern* [1935] Q.W.N. 22 (Aus). See also the discussion in the English edition of O'Donovan and Phillips *The Modern Contract of Guarantee* (Thomson Sweet & Maxwell, 2003) at paras 2–52–2–53.
27 See also *In Re Casey's Patents* [1982] 1 Ch. 104 *per* Bowen L.J. at 115–116; *Bradford v Roulston* (1858) 8 I.C.L.R. 468.

diagnostic x-ray system, and for the subsequent maintenance of the system. P had an exclusive distributorship agreement with F, the manufacturer of the equipment. L required the supply and maintenance contract to be guaranteed by an English company. P's principal shareholder, CGEM, obtained the agreement of its English parent, GU, to provide such a guarantee, on condition that CGEM provided it with a counter-guarantee and that F, in turn, would provide CGEM with a back-up guarantee. On December 17, 1991, F sent a fax to CGEM, copied to P, in which it stated that it was prepared to provide a backup guarantee for the orders from the two hospitals. On December 20, 1991, GU and CGEM gave their guarantees, and L contracted with P for the supply and maintenance of the system. However, F's guarantee (contained in a tripartite "guarantee and indemnity" agreement between F, GU and CGEM) was not given until April 1992. The agreement provided that "in consideration of CGEM and GU respectively entering into the guarantees specified in Schedule 1 hereto, F hereby undertakes and agrees to indemnify each of CGEM and GU against all losses, claims, proceedings, expenses and liabilities which may be made or taken against either of them by reason of or pursuant to the said guarantees or either of them." However, the guarantees specified in Schedule 1 were those which had been executed in December 1991.

When P became insolvent and demands were made under the chain of guarantees, F defended the claim on the basis that the tripartite agreement was void for lack of consideration. It argued that the consideration referred to in the text of the agreement had occurred four months earlier, and therefore was past consideration. The court held that the tripartite contract was part of a group of contracts which were mutually dependent upon each other, and therefore the entry into the December guarantees and the supply agreement was good consideration for F's promise. Moreover, both of the December 1991 guarantees had been provided on the strength of a contractual undertaking given by F to provide a backup guarantee, and the April guarantee was entered into in fulfilment of that contractual undertaking. Further consideration for the April guarantee was provided by GU in two ways, by providing the original guarantee to L in the knowledge that F was going to support CGEM's counter-guarantee with its own back-up guarantee, and by joining in the tripartite agreement, under which, by necessary implication, GU gave up its guarantee from CGEM in return for a direct guarantee by F.

Apart from insisting that the contract of guarantee be made under seal, there are three ways in which the creditor may overcome the potential difficulty of past consideration:

(a) by furnishing a purely nominal consideration;

(b) by agreeing to supply further goods, credit or services to the principal, or actually making such supplies; and

(c) by agreeing to accept a compromise, reschedule a debt or withdraw legal proceedings against the principal.

Nominal consideration

It has been said that the consideration given for the guarantee has to be **2–011** real rather than illusory.[28] Nevertheless, Wilmot J.'s observation in *Pillans and Rose v Van Mierop and Hopkins* (1765) 3 Burr. 1664 at 1666 that "the least spark of a consideration will be sufficient" is especially apposite in the modern commercial climate, for courts are extremely reluctant to conclude that a commercial transaction which the parties plainly intended should be binding and enforceable should fail for want of consideration. Similarly, if there is ambiguity as to the nature of the consideration given, the courts will normally favour a construction which will support the obligation.[29]

The court will not inquire into the value of the consideration given; it need not be of commensurate value with the promise. Thus the payment of even a small sum of money may suffice. For example in *Dutchman v Tooth* (1839) 5 Bing. N.C. 577, the consideration advanced by the creditor to the guarantor was 2s 6d; and in *Johnston v Nicholls* (1845) 1 C.B. 251 it consisted of small credit advances made to the principal after the guarantee was entered into. It is possible for example, for good consideration to consist of the surrender to the surety of a piece of paper which may or may not amount to an enforceable written guarantee: *Haigh v Brooks* (1839) 10 Ad. & El. 309, *affirmed* 10 Ad. & El. 323.[30]

Supplies of goods, credits or services

As a matter of principle, no distinction should be drawn between a case in **2–012** which, relying on a guarantee, the creditor enters into a binding agreement to supply future goods, credit or services to the principal and a case in which he actually makes the supplies. In each of these situations the principal has obtained a benefit, either by the actual supply, or by the accrual of a cause of action against the creditor if he fails to keep his promise. Nevertheless, there are some authorities which appear to support the proposition that an agreement to supply in the future is insufficient consideration unless the creditor goes on to perform the agreement.

> In *Greenham Ready Mixed Concrete v CAS (Industrial Developments) Ltd* (1965) 109 S.J. 209, D had incurred an unacceptable level of indebtedness to C for past supplies of building materials. C refused to continue supplying D unless a guarantee was obtained. S agreed to provide such a guarantee which was stated to be "in consideration of C recommencing to supply goods to D". Although C was willing to recommence the supplies, D never ordered any more goods from C

---

28 *White v Woodward* (1848) 5 C.B. 810. This merely means that the consideration has to be sufficient in law to support a contract, and not, for example, "a mere moral commitment": *per* Lord Denman C.J. in *Eastwood v Kenyon* (1840) 11 Ad. & El. 438 at 450–451.
29 *Broom v Batchelor* (1856) 1 H. & N. 255. Extrinsic evidence may be admissible to prove the consideration: see *Pao On v Lau Yiu Long* [1980] A.C. 614 *per* Lord Scarman at 631–632.
30 See also *Westlake v Adams* (1858) 5 C.B.N.S. 248.

and none were supplied. C's action on the guarantee failed on the grounds that no true consideration had been given for it: the promise was illusory since C was not obliged to supply more goods to D unless C wanted to, and therefore the consideration had to be the actual supply of goods.

It appears that the true explanation for the decision in this case and in older authorities which produced similar results (*Morrell v Cowan* (1877) 6 Ch. D. 166, *Westhead v Sproson* (1861) 6 H. & N. 728) lies in the construction of the agreement in question as one which stipulated that the consideration had to be the actual supply of the goods by the creditor rather than the creditor's agreement to do so. Furthermore, in *Morrell v Cowan* and in *Westhead v Sproson* the agreements were held to be too vague to be enforceable. It should be possible to avoid such a problem by using a different form of words, *e.g.* by expressing the guarantee to be given "in consideration of the creditor agreeing to supply the principal with goods if and when the principal so requires".

Other means

Forbearance to sue

2–013   The creditor's forbearance from suing the principal may amount to good consideration to support a guarantee. In *Miles v New Zealand Alford Estate Co* [1866] 32 Ch. D. 266 Bowen L.J. set out (at 289) the two alternative circumstances in which forbearance to sue can constitute consideration:

(a) where the creditor promises to forbear, in consideration for the guarantee; and

(b) actual forbearance by the creditor given at the request of the guarantor and in return for something.

In the case of actual forbearance, the request of the guarantor may be express or implied: see *Crears v Hunter* (1877) 19 Q.B.D. 341 *per* Lopes J. at 346. Although mere voluntary inaction by the creditor will not suffice, a court will readily infer that the inaction is attributable to an express or implicit request by the surety. Thus, if there is a pre-existing debt, the existence of which cannot in itself amount to consideration, the inference will often be drawn that the guarantee was given on the understanding that the creditor would forbear from taking action with respect to that debt: see, *e.g. Glegg v Bromley* [1912] 3 K.B. 474 *per* Parker J. at 491; *Fullerton v Provincial Bank of Ireland* [1903] A.C. 309 at 313–316.

For example, in *Wynne v Hughes* (1873) 21 W.R. 628, C had a claim against D's estate for a debt, but before he took any proceedings C's agent wrote to D's brother, S, and asked him to "be good enough to arrange something by tomorrow". S replied: "I undertake to pay £500 on the account between my late brother . . . and your client on or before this day three weeks". C refrained from suing D's estate for three weeks and it was held that he could recover the £500 from S.

Although the forbearance usually takes the form of the creditor refraining from instituting legal proceedings or proving in a bankruptcy or winding-up, it may consist of the creditor refraining from asserting any legal right, (for example, the right to terminate a line of credit), or the rescheduling of the agreed timetable for payment of the debtor's existing indebtedness under his contract with the creditor. However, the creditor must forbear from the assertion of an actual right. If there is nobody he can sue for payment of the debt, a promise to forbear from suing is no consideration.[31]

Moreover if a guarantee is given as a security for an existing loan facility, care has to be taken to ensure that the lender does something more by way of providing consideration that simply maintaining the status quo. This is illustrated by the recent Australian case of *McKay v National Australia Bank Ltd* [1998] 1 V.R. 173. The bank obtained a fresh guarantee from the sureties, which was expressed to be in consideration of the bank "providing banking accommodation" to the principal "and/or forbearing to enforce immediate payment" of moneys owing by the principal to the bank. However, no new financial accommodation was provided when the guarantee was given, and the bank had never made any demand for repayment of the existing facility. The Supreme Court of Victoria reversed the decision of the trial judge that by permitting the guarantors to maintain the principal's account in debit, and thereby giving them time to organise their financial affairs, the bank had provided "banking accommodation" which constituted good consideration. Ormiston J.A. said, at 186:

> "Though 'providing banking accommodation' is an expression of wide connotation, it cannot be taken to cover the mere acquiescence in the maintenance or continuation of an existing facility or arrangements by way of banking accommodation. The expression connotes that some additional or new accommodation be made available to a borrower, even though that may in certain circumstances be satisfied by an agreed rearrangement of an existing facility or accommodation or even by specific agreement as to confirmation of existing arrangements. What it cannot connote, however, is mere acquiescence in an existing state of affairs between the relevant parties."

If no express time for forbearance is stipulated by the surety, a reasonable time may be implied, and if so implied would be sufficient consideration: *Oldershaw v King* (1857) 2 H. & N. 517.[32] It may be possible

---

31 *Jones v Ashburnham* (1804) 4 East. 455; *White v Bluett* (1853) 23 L.J. Ex. 36. See also *Brett v Tarr* (unreported) CAT No.1234 of 1997, 9 July, discussed in para.2–008 above.
32 See also *Crears v Hunter* (1887) 19 Q.B.D. 341; *Wynne v Hughes* (1873) 21 W.R. 628; *Alliance Bank v Broom* (1864) 2 Dr. & S. 289. *Cf. Semple v Pink* (1847) 1 Exch. 74, also reported under the name of *Temple v Pink* 16 L.J. Exch. 237. As to the computation of a reasonable time for the purposes of a Statute of Limitations, see *Henton v Paddison* (1893) 68 L.T. 405, 9 T.L.R. 333.

to construe the agreement so as to imply a particular period of forbearance: see, *e.g. Payne v Wilson* (1827) 7 B. & C. 423.

A useful illustration of the principles discussed above is the case of *Provincial Bank of Ireland v Donnell* [1934] N.I. 33. The defendant's husband's bank account was secured by two policies of life insurance, and was overdrawn. The defendant undertook to pay the premiums of the policies "in consideration of advances heretofore made or that may hereafter be made". The plaintiff bank admitted that it had no intention of making any further advances. The bank's forbearance to sue for the overdraft had not resulted from any implied or express request from the wife, and the mere mention of future advances did not amount to consideration. The bank was not obliged to make any future advances and did not do so. In the circumstances, it was held that there was no consideration for the undertaking.

If the creditor breaks his promise and commences proceedings, the guarantee will be unenforceable: *Cooper v Joel* (1859) 1 De G. F. & J. 240; *Rolt v Cozens* (1856) 18 C.B. 673.

Compromise or withdrawal of proceedings

2–014   An agreement to withdraw civil proceedings is good consideration for a guarantee: *Harris v Venables* (1872) L.R. 7 Exch. 235. So is an agreement to compromise existing litigation: *Miles v New Zealand Alford Estate Co* (1886) 32 Ch. D. 266 and an agreement to suspend execution of a judgment: *Pullin v Stokes* (1794) 2 Hy. Bl. 312. If the compromised or withdrawn claim was "a serious claim honestly made", it does not matter whether it would have succeeded or not: *Miles v New Zealand Alford Estate Co.*, applying *Callisher v Bischoffscheim* (1870) L.R. 5 Q.B. 449. Consequently, the surety who seeks to defend a claim on a guarantee on the ground of lack of consideration, where the consideration is a compromise of a dispute, faces the onerous task of establishing that the creditor's claim was frivolous or vexatious, and possibly also that the creditor knew that his claim was frivolous or dishonest, so that there was no bona fide compromise.[33]

Thus, for example, if the surety agrees to give the creditor a fresh guarantee in return for the cancellation of a previous guarantee given either by himself or by a third party, or the settlement of an action brought on the earlier guarantee, it is unlikely to be any answer to a claim on the fresh guarantee to say that the earlier guarantee was invalid (*e.g.* because there was no consideration for the promise) or unenforceable (*e.g.* because it did not comply with the requirements of s.4 of the Statute of Frauds).

The creditor, however, must ensure that the compromise entered into with the principal corresponds with the terms undertaken to be entered into in the contract of guarantee, for if it does not, the guarantor will not be liable: see, *e.g. Clarke v Green* (1849) 3 Exch. 619.

---

33 See the observations of Cotton L.J. in *Miles v New Zealand Alford Estate Co* (1886) 32 Ch. D. 266 at 283–284.

The withdrawal of proceedings at the request of the surety is good consideration whether or not there is a promise that new proceedings will not be started.[34] Consequently, if the consideration for the guarantee is to be the withdrawal of existing legal proceedings, rather than their compromise, the surety should take care to ensure that the guarantee is phrased in such a way as to prevent the creditor from discontinuing the existing proceedings and immediately starting fresh proceedings: see *Harris v Venables* (1872) L.R. 7 Exch. 235. Service of a statutory demand under what is now s.268 of the Insolvency Act 1986 does not constitute the commencement of "proceedings" for this purpose.[35]

Unlawful consideration

If the consideration to be given in support of a guarantee is unlawful, the guarantee will be void and unenforceable. The guarantee is also unenforceable if the underlying debt or obligation is illegal, though this is not necessarily the case with a contract of indemnity.[36] The illegality need not be criminal or quasi-criminal in nature.   **2–015**

Unlawful detention

It may be good consideration to refrain from enforcing an irregular court order which has resulted in the unlawful detention of a party in custody, particularly if no objection has been taken to the order at the time when the guarantee is given. This is illustrated by the case of *Decouvreur v Jordan*, *The Times*, May 25, 1987, CA (CAT No.525 of 1987). In that case the plaintiff's former husband had been committed to prison for contempt of court for his failure to obey a court order to discharge a mortgage over the matrimonial home. Two sureties had subsequently agreed to guarantee the fulfilment by the husband of his obligations under the order, and as a result the plaintiff withdrew her opposition to the husband's application to be released from the order for his committal. The husband defaulted, and the guarantors sought to argue that the consideration was illegal because the court had no power to commit the husband and his detention was therefore unlawful. The Court of Appeal held that even upon the assumption that the court was not empowered to commit the husband, the order for his committal was valid and enforceable, however irregular, unless and until it was discharged. Since at the time when the guarantees were given, no   **2–015/1**

---

34 *Crears v Hunter* (1887) 19 Q.B.D. 341; *Oldershaw v King* (1857) 2 H. & N. 517; see also *Clarke & Walker Property Ltd v Thew* (1967) 116 C.L.R. 465.

35 *Clarke & Walker Property Ltd v Thew* (1967) 116 C.L.R. 465, a decision relating to a demand under s.223 of the Companies Act 1948.

36 See Ch.6 below, at para.6–019. For examples of cases in which the underlying illegality tainted the indemnity see *Haseldine v Hosken* [1933] 1 K.B. 822, a case of an unsuccessful claim to an indemnity arising out of a champertous agreement; and *Smith v White* (1866) L.R. 1 Eq. 626, where covenants in the assignment of a lease to indemnify the lessee of premises known to be used as a brothel, from the various covenants in the lease, including a covenant to keep the premises in good repair, were held to be unenforceable against the assignee's estate.

objection had been taken to the regularity of the court order, the wife had something of value which she could enforce, and the withdrawal of her opposition to the application to be released from the order was good consideration for the promises made by the sureties.

Wrongful preference

2–016   A guarantee which amounts to a wrongful preference is void as a matter of public policy, even if the guarantor is a party to the preference and it might therefore be said that he was relying on his own wrong in resisting the claim on the guarantee. Thus for example in *Wood v Barker* (1865) L.R. 1 Eq. 139, a bankrupt entered into a composition with his creditors. He made a secret arrangement with one of his creditors to pay him in full, in consideration of that creditor becoming a surety for the payment of the composition. The court set aside the guarantee.[37]

Avoiding prosecution

2–017   A guarantee will not be enforced if it has been given in order to stifle a criminal prosecution, whether or not the promise to refrain from prosecution is made expressly or implicitly.[38] However, the fact that the parties have agreed that criminal charges will not be pressed is not necessarily fatal; it has been held in Ireland that this is only the case if there were reasonable grounds for believing at the time when the guarantee was given that an offence had been committed or if the parties to the guarantee made that assumption when they entered into the agreement.[39]

There is little case law on this matter, which could prove to be a pitfall for the unwary in cases involving the abstraction of funds into a foreign jurisdiction. It is often the case that a plaintiff who claims that the defendant has stolen moneys from him seeks to trace the moneys or their proceeds into bank accounts or other assets situated abroad. Frequently the plaintiff will need to invoke criminal or quasi-criminal proceedings in the jurisdiction in which the assets or accounts are held in order to preserve them from dissipation while he pursues his civil remedies against the defendant in that jurisdiction or elsewhere. He may also need to be joined as a *partie civile* to the criminal action in order to make good his claim to the stolen funds, so that criminal and civil proceedings run in tandem in the foreign court.

When an application for a freezing order has been made successfully in England or elsewhere, it is fairly common practice for the defendant to procure that a bank guarantee be given in order to release his frozen assets; the guarantee may be given by an English bank and subject to English law

---

37 See also *Jackman v Mitchell* (1807) 13 Ves. 581; *Coleman v Waller* (1829) 3 Y. & J. 212; *McKewan v Sanderson* (1875) LR 20 Eq 65; *Coles v Strick* (1850) 15 QB 2, *Nerot v Wallace* (1789) 3 Term Rep. 17.
38 *Jones v Merionethshire Permanent Benefit Building Society* [1891] 2 Ch. 587, *affd* [1892] 1 Ch. 173; *Cannon v Rands* (1870) 23 L.T. 817; *Seear v Cohen* (1881) 45 L.T. 589.
39 *Rourke v Mealy* (1878) 4 L.R. Ir. 166.

and will probably be backed by a counter-guarantee or some other form of security provided by the defendant to the bank. However, if the consideration for the bank guarantee (and any counter-guarantee) is wholly or partially the discontinuance of a criminal or quasi-criminal action abroad, would such guarantees be enforceable if they were subject to English law?

This problem has not yet been considered by the English courts. It is probable that the public policy behind the rule would be interpreted in such a way as to prevent an iniquitous result which would deprive the plaintiff of his security. The rule might perhaps be expressly confined to criminal proceedings within the jurisdiction, or to criminal proceedings for a substantive offence rather than to proceedings primarily designed to preserve assets, which happen to have the characteristics of a criminal prosecution in the relevant jurisdiction. Nevertheless, while the position remains uncertain, any bank approached to give a guarantee in such circumstances, and any creditor considering accepting a guarantee in return for the release of funds frozen in the course of criminal or quasi-criminal proceedings abroad, should take care to protect their position as far as possible. This could possibly be achieved by ensuring that some other, genuine, consideration is given and referred to expressly in the body of the guarantee, or by ensuring that any relevant guarantee is embodied in a deed.

Evidence of consideration

By virtue of s.3 of the Mercantile Law Amendment Act 1856 the **2–018** consideration is not required to be set out in the document containing or evidencing the guarantee. However, if the consideration is set out in that document, the strict rule of evidence is that oral evidence is inadmissible to prove that the consideration was other than that expressed in the contract: *Oldershaw v King* (1857) 2 H. & N. 517. Consequently there is always still a risk that a lack of care in drafting the terms of the guarantee could lead to difficulties in its enforcement.

There are a number of reported cases in which the wording of the written guarantee suggested that the consideration was past consideration, when in fact it was future, or the wording made it unclear whether the consideration was past or future. In cases such as these, extrinsic evidence is admissible to resolve the ambiguity: and sometimes the courts have held that words which on their face appear quite unambiguous were capable of ambiguous interpretation, in order to mitigate the harshness of the rule.[40]

Evidence may also be adduced to show that an oral agreement of guarantee was entered into before the consideration was given, and that it was subsequently reduced to writing: see *Mumford v Gething* (1859) 7 C.B.N.S. 305. It is unfortunately still fairly common practice for a bank to agree to make a single advance to a company on the basis of a prior or

---

40 See, *e.g. Broom v Batchelor* (1856) 1 H. & N. 255; *Butcher v Steuart* (1843) 11 M. & W. 857; *Goldshede v Swan* (1847) 1 Exch. 154. See further Ch.4 at paras 4–005–4–006.

contemporaneous agreement by its directors to give personal guarantees, and then to wait and send on the relevant documents for signature days, or even weeks, after making payment to the company. While the exception to the parol evidence rule illustrated by *Mumford v Gething* may assist the bank in such circumstances, it is not always easy to establish an oral contract and the timing of events may enable the guarantor at least to resist summary judgment. Accordingly, it is always advisable for a creditor to take care to ensure that he does not expose himself to the argument that the consideration for the guarantee appears on its face to be past.

Contracts under seal

2–019 It is fairly common for a contract of suretyship to be embodied in a deed. The requirement for a deed executed by an individual to be sealed was abolished by the Law of Property (Miscellaneous Provisions) Act 1989, s.1(1)(b), which came into force on July 31, 1990. On the same date, the requirement for a company in England and Wales to have a common seal was abolished. A document signed by a director and the secretary of a company, or by two directors of a company, and expressed in whatever form of words to be executed by the company, has the same effect as if executed under the common seal of the company—Companies Act 1985, s.36A. If the document makes it clear on its face that it is intended by the person or persons making it to be a deed, then it will have effect, upon delivery, as a deed, and it is presumed to have been delivered upon its being executed unless a contrary intention is proved. Nevertheless, it is still common to refer to deeds as "documents given under seal".

A deed has other advantages besides the fact that valuable consideration need not be proved. The limitation period for actions brought on a specialty is normally twelve years from the date of accrual of the cause of action (Limitation Act 1980, s.8), though there are exceptions.[41] Moreover, a person who, by virtue of a deed, takes the benefit of a condition or agreement in respect of land or other property, has the right under s.56 of the Law of Property Act 1925 to bring proceedings in his own name to enforce the benefit, even if he is not a party to the deed.[42]

In *OTV Birwelco Ltd v Technical & General Guarantee Co Ltd* [2002] 4 All E.R. 668, an interesting argument arose about the effect on a contract of suretyship executed under seal, of non-compliance with the technical requirements of the Companies Act 1985. A company, W, was subject to a management buy-out through a new company called WME. After the takeover, WME carried on exactly the same business, adopting the trading

---

41 See Ch.7 paras 7–015 and 7–016.
42 Similar rights are conferred on an intended beneficiary under a contract by the Contracts (Rights of Third Parties) Act 1999, though this only applies where the third party is expressly identified in the contract by name or as a member of a class or as answering a particular description: s.1(3). See further para.2–008 above. However the parties may (and frequently do) contract out of these provisions.

name of W. WME was engaged as a subcontractor to carry out some building works by the main contractor, O, who knew about the takeover. WME applied, in the name of W, to a professional surety, T, for a performance bond obliging the surety to discharge damages sustained by O as a result of any default by the sub-contractor in performance of the sub-contract. In consideration of a substantial premium, T executed and properly affixed its common seal to a bond. The other party to the bond was described in the body of the deed as "W", and the company seal used to seal the deed bore the name, "W" instead of the registered name of WME. Some time later, WME ceased trading and defaulted on the sub-contract. O brought a claim on the bond. Since O was not a party to the bond, the proceedings could only succeed if the bond had been validly executed as a deed. T argued that the sub-contractor was WME but the other party to the bond was a different company, namely, W, and therefore it was not answerable for WME's default. Even if this was incorrect, the bond was a nullity, as it had been executed in the name of W, and the requirements of the Companies Act 1985 had not been complied with in various respects.

Judge Thornton Q.C. held that extrinsic evidence was admissible to prove the identity of the other contracting party to the deed, and that the bond was entered into by WME trading as W, so that the sub-contractor and the other party to the deed were one and the same. There was nothing in s.36A of the Companies Act 1985 which required a company to use its registered name, rather than its trading name, in the body of deeds or bonds. This meant that unless the bond was sealed in a way which rendered it a nullity or unenforceable against the surety, O was entitled to enforce it. However, there had been an infringement of s.350(1) of the Companies Act 1985. That section provides that a company which has a common seal shall have its name engraved in legible characters on the seal, and if it fails to comply with this requirement, it shall be liable to a fine. In this case, the provisions of s.350 had not been complied with, because the common seal used by WME was engraved with its trading name instead of its registered name. However, the judge decided that the consequences of non-compliance were not such as to render the bond a nullity or unenforceable. He observed that the 1985 Act does not give any express indication of what the consequence should be if the statutory formalities as to the seal are not observed, other than that the company and any person authorising the breach are liable to a fine. He decided that there would be no propor-tionality between the loss that might ensue if all deeds and bonds entered into with one of the contracting parties using the right type of seal and the other using the wrong type of seal were automatically nullified and rendered unenforceable by either party to the deed. On the particular facts of the case, the effect of acceding to the surety's argument would be that it would be unjustly enriched by the receipt of the substantial premium paid for the bond, whereas the entirely innocent O, the person intended to benefit from its creation, would be deprived of the rights it was intended to enjoy. Although this part of the judge's reasoning would not apply to a case in which the sealing formalities had not been observed by the normal type of company guarantor, who does not receive payment for standing surety, the first ground on which he rejected the defendant's argument would hold equally good in that context. The judge also held that even if he was wrong on this point, and the seal could not be relied upon, the signature of the bond by two directors, one of whom was also the company secretary of WME, would have been sufficient in the alternative to demonstrate compliance with the formal requirements of s.36A of the 1985 Act.

Chapter 3

Formal Requirements

The Statute of Frauds 1677

The Statute of Frauds 1677, s.4 provides that: **3–001**

> "no action shall be brought . . . whereby to charge the defendant upon any special promise to answer for the debt default or miscarriages of another person . . . unless the agreement upon which such action shall be brought or some memorandum or note thereof shall be in writing and signed by the party to be charged therewith or some other person thereunto by him lawfully authorised."

Introduction

The Statute of Frauds was enacted in order to meet a danger perceived by   **3–002**
the legislature that certain types of contract could be established by false evidence or "by evidence of loose talk, when it never was really meant to make such a contract": *per* Lord Blackburn in *Steele v M'Kinlay* (1880) 5 App. Cas. 754 at 768. It appears that over three centuries later, this danger is still perceived as being sufficiently prevalent in the modern commercial climate to justify retaining the rule. Section 4 of the Statute of Frauds originally applied to five classes of contract, but it was replaced by other legislation in the case of contracts for the sale or other disposition of land.[1] In 1937, the Law Revision Committee[2] recommended the repeal of s.4, but a minority headed by Goddard J. dissented in relation to guarantees, and no action was taken by Parliament at that juncture. In 1953, the Law Reform Committee,[3] whilst endorsing the recommendation of its predecessor that s.4 should be largely repealed, unanimously recommended that it should continue to apply to guarantees. The repeal in respect of the remaining three classes of contract was effected by the Law Reform (Enforcement of Contracts) Act 1954.

The main reason given by the dissenting minority in 1937 for retaining the requirement of writing for contracts of guarantee (which was endorsed by the subsequent Law Reform Committee) was that there was a real

---

1 Section 40 of the Law of Property Act 1925, since superceded by s.2 of the Law of Property (Miscellaneous Provisions) Act 1989.
2 Sixth Interim Report, Statute of Frauds and the Doctrine of Consideration, Cmd. 5449.
3 First Report, Statue of Frauds and s.4 of the Sale of Goods Act 1893, Cmd. 8809.

danger of inexperienced people being led into undertaking obligations which they did not fully understand, and that opportunities would be given to the unscrupulous to assert that credit was given on the faith of a guarantee which the alleged surety had no intention of giving. A guarantee was said to be a special class of contract, being generally one-sided and disinterested as far as the surety was concerned (in the vast majority of cases, the surety was getting nothing out of the bargain) and the requirement of writing would ensure that the terms of the guarantee were settled and recorded. The view was also expressed that the requirement of writing would give the proposed surety an opportunity for thought.

Despite its laudable aim, the Statute of Frauds has proved in practice to be used more often as a weapon for the unscrupulous, than as a protection for the innocent. As a result, there have been hostile judicial observations about the statute almost from the time of its enactment. Despite this, many years after the latest decision was made by Parliament in 1953 to retain the requirement of writing for guarantees, the policy behind the requirement continues to receive occasional judicial commendation. For example, in *Autocar Equipment Ltd v Motemtronic Ltd and Searle* (unreported) CAT No.656 of 1996, June 20, Henry L.J. said (at pages 24–25 of the transcript):

> "I have made it clear that in my judgment the mischief aimed at by Section 4 of the Statute of Frauds 1677 remains as valid as ever it did . . . This matter seems to me to be one of practical importance. Where there is an oral promise to answer eventually for the legal default of another the precise wording of that oral promise will often be difficult to ascertain, and often an uncertainty will lie over it even after the Court has found what the words used were. The result may often be commercially improbable and the requirement of a written note or memorandum should operate to make sense of the agreement."

More recently, in *Technology Partnership Plc v Afro-Asian Satellite Communications (UK) Ltd* (unreported) CAT No.1588 of 1998, there was a divergence of views on the question whether s.4 was still an appropriate form of safeguard. The issue in the appeal was whether two letters written on company notepaper by C, described as the "moving spirit" behind a group of companies, constituted sufficient memoranda of an oral guarantee given by C in respect of the indebtedness of one of the companies to the plaintiff. The Court of Appeal held that they did not. Peter Gibson L.J. said that it was a decision which he reached with some regret, and that it was unfortunate that by reason of s.4 of the Statute of Frauds, C escaped the possibility of being held personally liable for his word:

> "I would for my part question whether today it is still necessary to give such special protection to those who give guarantees . . . It may well be that some protection is required for guarantors such as the possibility of being able to escape the guarantee within a limited period. But it does seem to me to be arguable that the sanction contained in s.4 is

out of all proportion to the mischief which it was originally intended to combat."

Pill L.J., however, disagreed. He said:

"For my part, I see a practical purpose in the existence of safeguards for those alleged to be guarantors . . . I am not persuaded by anything in this case that it would in modern conditions be safe or appropriate to permit a contract of guarantee to be established merely by oral evidence."

When the House of Lords considered the policy behind s.4 in the recent case of *Actionstrength Ltd v International Glass Engineering SpA* [2003] 2 A.C. 541,[4] the majority appeared to agree with Peter Gibson L.J.'s view. Regret was expressed that a party, making and acting on what was thought to be a binding oral agreement, would find his commercial expectations defeated when the time for enforcement came and the other party successfully relied upon the lack of a written memorandum or note of the agreement. Lord Bingham (with whom Lord Woolf and Lord Walker agreed) said at para.7:

"It may be questionable whether, in relation to contracts of guarantee, the mischief at which section 4 was originally aimed is not now outweighed, at least in some classes of case, by the mischief to which it can give rise in a case such as the present, however unusual such cases must be. But that is not a question for the House in its judicial capacity."

In that case, the defendant, SG, had entered into a contract with I as main contractor for the construction of a factory in Yorkshire for the manufacture of float glass. The claimant, A, was a recruitment agency engaged by I as a sub-contractor to provide labour for the project. I fell seriously into arrears in the payment of A's invoices, and A threatened to withdraw all labour from the site unless the arrears were paid. A held various meetings with representatives of SG, to try to find a solution. A alleged that in the course of those meetings it was agreed by SG that if A did not withdraw its workforce from the site, if I then failed to pay A any sums which were or became owing to it, SG would redirect sums which were due to I from SG to settle A's invoices. A acted on that assurance. However, after about another month of work on the site, the indebtedness of I to A had increased significantly. A terminated the contract with I and withdrew the workforce. It then sued both I and SG, but I went into liquidation.

SG sought summary judgment against A on the basis that, even if there had been an agreement in the terms alleged by A, that agreement was a

---

4 Discussed further in paras 3–006 and 3–031 below.

guarantee, and because it was made orally and there was no written record of it, it was unenforceable by virtue of s.4 of the Statute of Frauds. The judge (Mitting J.) refused the application on the basis that the alleged agreement was an indemnity, but the Court of Appeal (Simon Brown, Peter Gibson and Tuckey L.JJ.) [2002] 1 W.L.R. 566 reversed him on that point, whilst acknowledging that it was an interesting and not entirely easy issue.[5] They also held that s.4 of the Statute of Frauds was a complete answer to A's claim because the facts did not give rise to an arguable estoppel. The case went to the House of Lords on the estoppel point, and the decision of the Court of Appeal was upheld, notwithstanding the apparent injustice to A if A's version of events was correct.

As Lord Bingham pointed out in para.5, the reasons given by the dissenting minority of the Law Revision Committee for retaining the rule in relation to conventional consumer guarantees had little bearing on a case such as this. This was not a bargain struck between inexperienced people, liable to misunderstand what they were doing: "these were not small men in need of paternalist protection". SG had a clear incentive to enter into the agreement and, on the assumed facts, had time to think again before committing itself. Moreover, SG had something to gain from the bargain. The termination of A's contract with I would have been seriously prejudicial to SG, whose interest was to take expeditious possession of a completed factory. SG received the benefit of the work done by the labour which A supplied over the weeks that followed the alleged agreement, and the indebtedness of I to A increased five-fold over that period. Moreover, it was doubtful whether those who made the assumed agreement appreciated that it was in law a guarantee. In those circumstances, it is hardly surprising that little enthusiasm was expressed for the outcome of the appeal by three members of their Lordships' House.

By contrast, Lord Clyde and Lord Hoffmann forebore to express any view about whether the policy behind the statute was justifiable in modern times. Lord Hoffmann acknowledged that if a judge found A's version of events to be correct, to hold the promise unenforceable would certainly appear unfair: morally, there would be no excuse for SG not keeping its promise. However, although there was a natural inclination to try and find some way in which the putative injustice could be avoided, it was important to bear in mind that the purpose of the statute was precisely to avoid the need to decide which side was telling the truth about whether or not an oral promise had been made, and exactly what had been promised. Parliament decided that there had been too many cases in which the wrong side had been believed, and a strong Law Reform Committee had recommended the retention of the rule in 1953. He said (at para.20):

"The terms of the statute .. show that Parliament, although obviously conscious that it would allow some people to break their promises,

---

5 See the discussion in para.3–006 below.

thought that this injustice was outweighed by the need to protect people from being held liable on the basis of oral utterances which were ill-considered, ambiguous or completely fictitious. This means that while normally one would approach the construction of a statute on the basis that Parliament was unlikely to have intended to cause injustice by allowing people to break promises which have been relied upon, no such assumption can be made about the statute . . . it must not be construed in a way which would undermine its purpose."

It remains to be seen whether a future Law Reform Committee will adhere to the views of its illustrious predecessors, or whether it will recommend either the complete abolition of the rule, or a modification to restrict the statutory protection to those (such as consumers) who may be perceived to be still in need of it.

The recognition that the statute can operate unfairly to deprive a creditor of his legitimate commercial expectations also gave rise to ingenious attempts by litigants to circumvent it. In the early years after its enactment, one method particularly favoured was to treat the surety's oral promise to be answerable for another as a false representation as to credit for which he was liable in tort: see, *e.g. Pasley v Freeman* (1789) 3 Term Rep. 51. However, this was stopped by the passing of the Statute of Frauds Amendment Act 1828 (Lord Tenterden's Act), s.6, which prevented representations of this kind from being actionable unless made in writing.[6]

Although attempts to circumvent the operation of the Statute of Frauds have been frowned on subsequently,[7] the courts will be vigilant to prevent it from being misused. As Lord Birkenhead observed in *United States of America v Motor Trucks Ltd* [1924] A.C. 196 at 200: "the Statute of Frauds is not allowed by any court administering the doctrines of equity to become an instrument for enabling sharp practice to be committed". In *Steadman v Steadman* [1976] A.C. 536 at 558 this observation was echoed by Lord Simon in the context of a discussion of the doctrine of part-performance, when he said that "Equity would not, as it was put, allow the Statute of Frauds 'to be used as an engine of fraud'." The extent to which principles of equity may be used in guarantee cases to meet a defence of non-compliance with s.4 is discussed in paras 3–030–3–032 below.

In practice, most contracts of suretyship which are entered into in a commercial context are either made in writing or made orally and confirmed in writing, and thus the number of cases in which a defence based on s.4 of the Statute of Frauds has been raised successfully has decreased in recent years. Nevertheless the statute can still prove to be a pitfall for the unwary creditor. A further modern illustration is the case of *Deutsche Bank v Ibrahim* [1992] 1 Bank. L.R. 267. The principal was

---

6 See generally *Halsbury's Laws* (Butterworth's, 4th ed., 2004 reissue), Vol. 20 at paras 142–143.
7 See, *e.g.* the observations of Pollock C.B. in *Mallett v Bateman* (1865) L.R. 1 C.P. 163 at 170–171.

required by the plaintiff bank to provide security for an overdraft facility. He therefore deposited with the bank the title deeds to some flats which he had purchased but which were registered in the names of his daughters. The bank sought a declaration that there was a valid equitable mortgage; the daughters successfully counterclaimed delivery up of the title deeds. The court held that the deposit was made by way of guarantee of the repayment of the loan to the father, and that therefore, as there was no memorandum signed by the daughters complying with the requirements of s.4 of the Statute of Frauds, the bank's claim was unenforceable.[8]

Contracts to which s.4 applies

"Special promise"

3–003   A "special promise" means an express promise, and does not include implied promises which arise by operation of law: *Gray v Hill* (1826) Ry. & M. 420. It is not confined to promises made in contracts under seal or of record: *Holmes v Mitchell* (1859) 7 C.B.N.S. 361 at 368–369. Indeed, such a restriction would render the statute meaningless.

"Debt default or miscarriage"

3–004   Each of these words has a distinct legal meaning; together they would appear to cover any form of legal liability. A "debt" is a past contractual liability: *Castling v Aubert* (1802) 2 East. 325 at 330–331, *per* Lord Ellenborough C.J. A "default", however, is probably wide enough to encompass a future liability including a non-contractual liability: see *Kirkham v Marter* (1819) 2 B. & Ald. 613. Even if "default" is not that wide, the word "miscarriage" would appear to encompass any other form of civil liability (*Kirkham v Marter, per* Abbott C.J. at 616). Accordingly an agreement between S and C that if D does not pay compensation to C for a tort committed by D, S will make payment of that compensation, prima facie falls within the terms of the statute. On the other hand, an agreement by a "surety" to answer for the non-performance by the principal of his obligations to another will not be a guarantee if on its true construction, his liability arises even if the non-performance is not a breach of contract. See, *e.g. Northwood Development Co Ltd v Aegon Insurance Co (UK) Ltd* [1994] 10 Const. L.J. 157, where the underlying contract terminated automatically upon the principal (a contractor) going into liquidation, and his continuing non-performance which triggered the obligation to pay was therefore not a breach.

"Another person"

3–005   Although the words "debt default or miscarriages of another person" are wide enough to cover all types of contract of suretyship (indemnities also involve one person becoming responsible for the debts of another) it was

---

8 A mortgage can no longer be created in this way, by virtue of the provisions of s.2 of the Law of Property (Miscellaneous Provisions) Act 1989: see, *e.g. United Bank of Kuwait Plc v Sahib* [1997] 1 Ch. 107, CA.

established from a very early date that the section only applies where there is some person other than the surety who is primarily liable to the creditor, *i.e.* where it is a guarantee in the true sense.[9] It does not apply to a contract where the surety assumes a primary liability, or to a contract where the promise is made to anyone other than "the person to whom another is already or is to become answerable".[10] It will apply both to a guarantee and to a binding agreement to give a guarantee.[11]

The statute does not apply to a contract under which, on true analysis, the "surety" is promising to pay his own debt and not the debt of another.[12] Examples of such contracts include an agreement to pay a sum by way of compromise of a claim made against the promisor and third parties (even though the promisor may have had a good defence to the claim against him);[13] a promise to be answerable for payments due from the promisor's own agent (for whose default he would be vicariously liable);[14] a promise to pay money owed by the promisor to the promisee in satisfaction of the promisee's indebtedness to a third party;[15] a promise to be answerable for a debt only to the extent of the promisor's own indebtedness to the creditor;[16] and a promise by a judgment debtor to allow the judgment creditor to hold the judgment as security for the indebtedness to the creditor of a third party.[17]

The statute is therefore the origin of the distinction between contracts of guarantee and contracts of indemnity, the latter falling outside s.4, the former often, but not necessarily, falling within it.

Contract distinctions

The distinction between a contract of guarantee and a contract of indemnity has often led to a fine line being drawn by the court.[18] A comparison of two cases illustrates the difficulty which may be caused by the subtlety of the distinction. In *Guild & Co v Conrad* [1894] 2 Q.B. 885, S orally   3–006

---

9 *Birkmyr v Darnell* (1805) 1 Salk. 27, 91 ER 27; *Lakeman v Mountstephen* (1874) L.R. 7 H.L. 17; *Harburg India Rubber Comb Co v Martin* [1902] 1 K.B. 778, CA. See also the cases cited in *Halsbury's Laws*, Vol. 20, para.151, n.2.

10 *Per* Vaughan Williams L.J. in *Harburg India Rubber Comb Co v Martin* [1902] 1 K.B. 778 at 784, and see below.

11 *Mallett v Bateman* [1865] L.R. 1 C.P. 163; *Compagnie Générale d'Industrie v Solori SA* (1984) 134 N.L.J. 788, *Clipper Maritime Ltd v Shirlstar Container Transport Ltd (The "Anemone")* [1987] 1 Lloyd's Rep. 546.

12 *Hodgson v Anderson* (1825) 3 B. & C. 842; *Ardern v Rowney* (1805) 5 Esp. 254. See also *Marginson v Potter & Co* (1976) 11 A.L.R. 64 (Aus).

13 *Orrell v Coppock* (1856) 2 Jur. N.S. 1244; *Stephens v Squire* (1696) 5 Mod. Rep. 205.

14 *Masters v Marriot* (1693) 3 Lev. 363.

15 *Andrews v Smith* (1835) 2 Cr. M. & R. 627; *Hodgson v Anderson* (1825) 5 Dow. & Ry. K.B. 735.

16 *Ardern v Rowney* (1805) 5 Esp. 254.

17 *Macrory v Scott* (1850) 5 Exch. 907.

18 In *Yeoman Credit Ltd v Latter* [1961] 1 W.L.R. 828 at 835, after analysing the foundation for the distinction, Holroyd Pearce L.J. said that it "has raised many hair-splitting distinctions of exactly that kind which brings the law into hatred, ridicule and contempt by the public".

promised C that if C would accept certain bills of exchange from a firm in which S's son was a partner, he, S, would provide C with funds to meet the bills. It was held that the contract was an indemnity and enforceable, because the contract was not a contract to pay if the son's business did not pay, but a contract to pay in any event.

On the other hand, in *Harburg India Rubber Comb Co v Martin* [1902] 1 K.B. 778, S was a director of a company who made an oral promise at a meeting of its creditors that he would endorse bills to the creditors for the amount of the company's debt. The court held that this was a promise to pay a debt for which the company remained primarily liable, and therefore unenforceable.

A simple test to see whether the surety's liability is original or contingent is to ask whether he would be liable irrespective of whether the principal is liable or has made default. If the answer to that question is yes, then the liability is original and the contract falls outside the Statute of Frauds.

It is a question of fact in each case whether the arrangement is one under which the surety's liability is original or collateral, and this means that the court will consider each case on its particular circumstances, and the language which was used by the parties at the time, though indicative of the nature of the bargain, will not necessarily be conclusive: *Simpson v Penton* (1834) 2 Cr. & M. 430. For this reason, the numerous decisions in past cases are of limited usefulness in determining on which side of the line a particular agreement will fall.[19] However, certain features which emerge from the cases may assist. For example, one useful exercise is to ascertain whether the goods have been debited to the principal or to the surety in the creditor's books of account. If they have been debited to the debtor, that is strong prima facie evidence that the surety's obligation was collateral rather than original.[20] On the other hand, if the surety has a direct interest in the underlying transaction this will often be an indication that his liability is intended to be original.

The principles stated above may be illustrated by considering the situation in which one person, S, agrees with a supplier of goods, C, to pay for goods which C supplies to another person, D. If the arrangement is that S will pay in any event, then the contract falls outside the statute: see *Edge v Frost* (1824) 4 D. & R. 243, *Lakeman v Mountstephen* (1874) L.R. 7 H.L. 17 and *Simpson v Penton* (1834) 2 Cr. & M. 430. If both D and S undertake liability for payment, so that they are jointly liable for the debt, again the case falls outside the statute, because S is under a direct and not a contingent liability to C: see *Scholes v Hampson and Merriot* (1806) *Fell on Mercantile Guarantees* (2nd ed.) at 27, 28. On the other hand, if S agrees that he will only make payment if D does not, the matter is within the scope of s.4: *Anderson v Hayman* (1789) 1 Hy. Bl. 120.

In determining whether the surety's liability is original or contingent, the court will be concerned with the substance of the transaction and not just

---

19 For examples of promises which have been held to be original and not collateral see the list in *Halsbury's Laws* (*op. cit.*), Vol. 20 at para.147.
20 *Austen v Baker* (1698) 12 Mod. Rep. 250; *Storr v Scott* (1833) 6 C. & P. 241.

with its form: see *Harburg India Rubber Comb Co v Martin* (above) at 784–785. In *Actionstrength Ltd v International Glass Engineering SpA* [2002] 1 W.L.R. 566 the Court of Appeal[21] had to consider whether a promise made to a creditor to pay an amount owed to him by a debtor out of funds which the promisor himself owed to the debtor, fell within the Statute of Frauds. The alleged agreement was a promise by an employer to redirect moneys due to a contractor and use them to pay a sub-contractor to whom the contractor owed money. Although the original contractor plainly remained liable to the sub-contractor, the alleged surety raised the interesting argument that there is no guarantee within the Statute of Frauds when the promisor does not undertake to be liable generally, but only in respect of specific funds or sources within his control. Reliance was placed upon *Andrews v Smith* (1835) 2 C.M. & R. 627, *Steggall & Co. v Lymburner* (1912) 14 W.A.L.R. 201, and a passage at p.68 of the Australian edition of O'Donovan & Phillips, *the Modern Contract of Guarantee* (3rd ed.).[22]

In *Andrews v Smith* the defendant was a surveyor who was retained by the owner of a building to receive and pay over to a contractor named Hill such moneys as were due to him. The plaintiff agreed with the defendant that he would supply materials to Hill on the defendant's promise to pay for them out of the moneys which he received to pay Hill. Although Hill agreed with this arrangement, he was never a party to any contract and therefore there could be no primary debt for which the defendant had a secondary liability. However, it was held that even if Hill had been liable, if the defendant contracted merely to apply Hill's funds for the purpose of paying the debt, the agreement would not fall within the Statute of Frauds. In *Steggall v Lymburner* the defendant deducted from the wages of an employee, at his request or with his consent, the amount of a debt due by the employee to the plaintiffs, and promised the plaintiffs to pay the amount due to them. McMillan J. (with whom Burnside J. agreed) held that the Statue of Frauds had nothing to do with the case because the promise was a promise to pay the defendant's own debt, although it operated in discharge of the debt of his creditor.

In *Actionstrength* the Court of Appeal distinguished both these cases on the basis that the consent of the original debtor (Hill and the employee, respectively) to the arrangements was central to the reasoning of the court. The debtor's instructions, or at any rate the defendant's promise given with the debtor's consent, created a primary liability to pay. The arrangement operated in a similar way to a novation or an assignment, in that the payment by the defendant to the plaintiff would have extinguished his liability to the original debtor. However, an arrangement of this nature to which the original debtor did not consent, would not have that effect. Simon Brown L.J. readily accepted that there is no guarantee within the

---

21 The case went to the House of Lords on a different point: see the commentary in paras 3–002 above and 3–031 below.
22 See now the commentary in the English edition of O'Donovan and Phillips (Thomson Sweet & Maxwell 2003) at paras 3–008 and 3–009.

Statute of Frauds unless the promisor's own funds are put at risk, but that was not the case in either *Andrews v Smith* or *Steggall v Lymburner*. He said, in para.35:

> "If payment to the creditor (of an assumed contingent liability) is to be made only from funds which the promisor would otherwise have to pay the debtor, that is one thing and understandably outside the Statute. The payment claimed here seems to me quite another thing. It is, indeed, on analysis quite inaccurate to describe it as a payment out of funds otherwise due to the first defendant. Rather it would be a payment out of the second defendant's own funds, since the first defendant would still remain entitled to be paid."

Peter Gibson L.J., delivering a concurring judgment, also pointed out that whilst there may be a distinction between a promise by a promisor to pay out of his own funds, and a promise by a fiduciary to pay out of another's funds entrusted to him for that purpose, neither of the cases relied upon was concerned with a distinction between a promise by a promisor to pay out of his own general assets and a promise to pay out of a specific fund or asset (belonging to him). The suggestion by the editors of O'Donovan & Phillips in the passage cited from the 3rd edition that the Statute does not apply "if the liability merely attaches to a particular asset belonging to the promisor, rather than to the promisor's assets generally" was rejected by the Court of Appeal. The judgment of Higgins J. in the case of *Harvey v Edwards Dunlop & Co Ltd* (1927) 39 C.L.R. 302 (a decision of the Australian High Court) cited in support of that proposition, was said to be too slender to sustain it—none of the other judges concurred in his reasoning and, as Peter Gibson L.J. pointed out in para.50, that reasoning was not in truth supported by the judgment of Dixon A.J. in the court below, though Higgins J. mistakenly believed that it was. In any event, the suggestion was incompatible with *Morley v Boothby* (1825) 3 Bing 107, a case in which Best C.J. held that a promise fell within s.4 notwithstanding that the source of the moneys to answer for the promisor's promise was designated. As the Court of Appeal pointed out, it is commonplace nowadays for guarantees to be limited in amount; there would appear to be no justification in principle for drawing a distinction between a promise to answer for the debt of another up to £100,000 out of the promisor's general assets, and a promise to satisfy that debt by selling an asset worth £100,000 or paying £100,000 out of a designated account. Peter Gibson L.J. said that the law relating to s.4 of the Statute of Frauds was already overburdened with fine distinctions, and he thought it would be regrettable to add another one.

Contracts outside the scope of s.4

3–007 There are a number of established categories of case in which the liability of the surety is original and the Statute does not apply.

Promises to the principal or co-principal

In order to fall within s.4 of the Statute of Frauds, the agreement must be **3–008** made "to answer for the debt default or miscarriage of another" and therefore the promise has to be made to the creditor: *Eastwood v Kenyon* (1840) 11 Ad. & El. 438. Accordingly, if the promise is made to the principal himself, the agreement falls outside the terms of the Statute, because the promise is to answer for the promisee's own debt and not the debt of "another".[23]

Similarly a promise made by one co-debtor to another is excluded from the terms of s.4:[24]

> A, a reputable and influential businessman who is acquainted with the directors of a company, D, which is seeking the advance of a substantial loan from a bank, is asked by B, one of the directors of D, to join B and his fellow directors as personal guarantors of the loan because this would have a very favourable effect on the bank's decision to advance the money. A is persuaded to agree, on the basis of a verbal promise made to him by B, that if the bank calls on the guarantee, B will pay any sum for which A is liable to the bank. B's oral promise is outside the scope of the Statute of Frauds and is enforceable by A.

Guarantee of debts due to a partnership

In *Re Hoyle, Hoyle v Hoyle* [1893] 1 Ch. 84, a majority of the Court of **3–009** Appeal expressed the view that an oral promise made by a partner in a firm to his co-partners to guarantee them against loss in respect of an existing debt due to the firm from his son, was not within s.4 of the Statute of Frauds, on the basis that it was a promise to indemnify the other partners and not a promise to pay a debt due to those partners if the son did not. The reason given by Bowen L.J. (at 99) was that the promise could not have been made to the creditor, *i.e.* to the firm as a whole, because a man cannot make a promise to himself and others, and the case is therefore often cited as an example falling within this exception. However, the reasoning of Bowen L.J. is at least questionable, and it may be that a court faced with the same issue nowadays would find a different route to reach the conclusion that the agreement was an indemnity.

Promises made to third parties

A promise made to someone who is not a party to the contract between the **3–010** principal and the creditor, that the principal will perform the contract, is not within s.4: *Hargreaves v Parsons* (1844) 13 M. & W. 561. So, for example, an oral promise made by a charterer to the shipowner's agent at

---

23 *Eastwood v Kenyon* (1840) 11 Ad. & El. 438; *Castling v Aubert* (1802) 2 East. 325; *Gregory & Parker v Williams* (1817) 3 Mer. 582; *Adams v Dansey* (1830) 6 Bing. 506; *Wildes v Dudlow* (1874) L.R. 19 Eq. 198; *Re Bolton* (1892) 8 T.L.R. 668; *Guild v Conrad* [1894] 2 Q.B. 885.
24 See, *e.g. Thomas v Cook* (1828) 8 B. & C. 728; *Rae v Rae* (1857) 6 I. Ch. R. 490.

the port of discharge that if the shipowner does not pay the agent's fees, the charterer will, is an indemnity and not a guarantee. Similarly a promise made by S to a bailiff executing judgment that S will pay the amount of the judgment debt owed by D, in consideration of the bailiff forbearing to proceed with execution, is outside the Statute of Frauds.[25]

Novation

3–011 An agreement under which the creditor agrees to release the principal from liability in substitution for a new agreement under which either the principal and the surety are both liable (jointly or severally) or under which the surety alone is liable, is not within s.4 of the Statute of Frauds. In such circumstances the surety is not agreeing to be liable for the debt of another because that debt has been released; instead he is undertaking a fresh, independent liability of his own.[26]

The release of the principal may be, and often is, effected by his discharge from execution of a judgment debt.[27] However the release or discharge must be absolute, unconditional and effective. If the creditor simply agrees to forbear to sue the principal, or makes an agreement to release the principal with the surety alone, it is possible that the principal's underlying liability has not been replaced by the arrangements with the surety and the promise by the surety might then amount to a promise to pay the debts of another.[28]

Joint liabilities

3–012 If the surety agrees with the creditor to become jointly liable with the principal (whether or not there is a release of the original debt) then he is undertaking a personal liability rather than a liability to answer for the debt of another and his promise falls outside the scope of s.4.[29] That position is unaffected by whatever private arrangements the principal and surety may have entered into, *e.g.* if they agree that as between themselves the principal is to be primarily liable. An example illustrates this:

> A is a small manufacturer of garments made from natural fibres coloured with organic dyes. A enters into a joint venture arrangement with B, a large retail company which will use its chain of shops to sell the garments. In order to promote the products A and B approach C, an advertising agency. A cannot afford to finance suitably glossy advertisements. A and B enter into an oral contract with C whereby

25 *Reader v Kingham* (1862) 13 C.B.N.S. 344; see also *Love's* case (1706) 1 Salk. 28 and *Cripps v Hartnoll* (1863) 4 B. & S. 414.
26 See, *e.g. Browning v Stallard* (1814) 5 Taunt. 450; *Goodman v Chase* (1818) 1 B. & Ald. 297; *Re Lendon and Lendon Ex p. Lane* (1846) De G. 300; *Commercial Bank of Tasmania v Jones* [1893] A.C. 313.
27 *Goodman v Chase* (1818) 1 B. & Ald. 297; *Bird v Gammon* (1837) 3 Bing. N.C. 883; *Lane v Burghart* (1841) 1 Q.B. 933; *Butcher v Steuart* (1843) 11 M. & W. 857.
28 See, *e.g. King v Wilson* (1875) 2 Stra. 873; *Fish v Hutchinson* (1759) 2 Wils. 94.
29 See, *e.g. Thomas v Cook* (1828) 8 B. & C. 728; *Wildes v Dudlow* (1874) L.R. 19 Eq. 198.

they agree jointly to pay C for the advertisements. However, they agree between themselves that B will pay C, and A will reimburse B out of the profits of the joint venture. The agreement between A, B and C is one under which A and B are each under an original liability to C and the Statute of Frauds need not be complied with.

Lack of co-extensiveness

If the liability of the surety is greater than that of the principal, the contract **3–013** is an indemnity and falls outside s.4. So, for example, an agreement in which S agrees to indemnify C against "any loss you might suffer by reason of the fact that D for any reason does not repay the loan . . ." is not a guarantee because S's liability is not necessarily the same as D's. Thus, recourse agreements taken by hire purchase companies from a car dealer providing for payment by the car dealer in the event of the default of the hirer would normally be outside the Statute of Frauds even if they were made orally. The finance company may not be able to recover the full hire-purchase price from the defaulting hirer, but the dealer would normally be liable under the recourse agreement to pay for all losses, and his liability would therefore be different and independent from the hirer's.[30]

Similarly, if the surety agrees to pay regardless of whether the principal is liable, or in circumstances in which there is considerable doubt as to the principal's liability, he is not undertaking to pay in respect of the "debt default or miscarriage of another". Accordingly, if it is clear from the nature of the contract that it was entered into specifically to safeguard against the possibility that the principal would not be liable to the creditor, the contract does not fall within the statute: *Lakeman v Mountstephen* (1874) L.R. 7 H.L. 17.

Incidental guarantees

Even if the promise by the surety is plainly a promise to answer for the debt **3–014** default or miscarriage of another, the contract will not fall within s.4 of the Statute of Frauds unless the main or immediate object of the contract is to secure the payment of the debt or the fulfilment of a duty by another person: *Harburg India Rubber Comb Co Ltd v Martin* [1902] 1 K.B. 778. The rule was summarised by Vaughan Williams L.J. in that case at 786:

"If the subject-matter of the contract was the purchase of property— the relief of property from a liability, the getting rid of incumbrances, the securing greater diligence in the performance of the duty of a factor, or the introduction of business into a stockbroker's office—in all those cases there was a larger matter which was the object of the contract. That being the object of the contract, the mere fact that as an incident to it—not as the immediate object but indirectly—the debt of

---

30 See, *e.g. Goulston Discount Co v Clark* [1967] 2 Q.B. 493; *Yeoman Credit Ltd v Latter* [1961] 1 W.L.R. 828. See also Consumer Credit Act 1974, s.113(7) as amended by the Minors Contracts Act 1987, s.4(1).

another to a third person will be paid, does not bring the case within the section."

Cases within this exception usually (but not invariably) have the feature that the surety derives some tangible benefit from agreeing to pay the debt of another. These cases usually fall into two distinct categories, namely those in which the surety is earning money (usually a commission) from the transaction, and those concerning the release of property which is subject to a lien or other encumbrance in which the surety has an interest. However, these categories are not exhaustive.

It is sometimes said that if the surety has an ulterior motive for giving the guarantee, the contract will fall outside s.4 (the ulterior motive usually being the benefit to himself). That approach, which is derived from some fairly wide propositions in the case of *Sutton v Grey* [1894] 1 Q.B. 285, is probably too simplistic and should be treated with caution.[31] The mere fact that the surety may have an ulterior motive for entering into the transaction, or may gain some benefit from it, will not necessarily mean that the payment of the debt is not the main object of the transaction, though it may be an indication. It could not be said, for example, that the fact that the surety was motivated by pity or by affection for the principal would alter the nature of a contract from a guarantee into an indemnity. Thus, if the director of a company guarantees to pay its debts, the fact that he was induced to enter into that agreement because he had a legal or equitable charge over the company's assets would not alter the nature of the agreement, nor would the fact that he thought it would be advantageous to him if the company were allowed to continue trading.[32]

Where the surety earns money from the transaction

3–015 In *Sutton v Grey* [1894] 1 Q.B. 285 the surety made an oral contract with a firm of stockbrokers to introduce clients to them in consideration of the payment of commission of half the profits gained on transactions entered into by the stockbrokers for clients introduced by him. The contract included a promise that he would indemnify the stockbrokers in respect of half the losses they made on any such transactions. It was held that the surety had an independent interest in the transaction (namely the earning of his commission) when the main object of the contract was to regulate the terms of his employment with the stockbrokers. Therefore, s.4 was inapplicable and the indemnity was enforceable.

Thus, if a person contracts to buy goods as agent for a principal on terms that he is to be liable to pay the price if his principal fails to pay, the contract will fall outside the statute even though the agent is agreeing to be liable for the debts of his principal. The main object of the arrangement is

---

31 "It is not a question of motive—it is a question of object"—*per* Vaughan Williams L.J. in *Harburg India Rubber Comb Co v Martin* [1902] 1 K.B. 778 at 786.
32 See also *Harburg India Rubber Comb Co v Martin* [1902] 1 K.B. 778; *Davys v Buswell* [1913] 2 K.B. 47.

to effect a sale of goods. Similarly, if a *del credere* agent, in return for a higher commission, guarantees the solvency of purchasers to whom he is selling goods on behalf of his principal, the main object of the transaction is to secure the exercise of greater care by the agent in selecting solvent purchasers. It will be noted that in all these examples, it could be said that the real motive for the agent entering into such an agreement is to earn his commission.[33] However, it is probably unlikely that a creditor could procure the enforceability of an oral guarantee by providing for a payment to be made to the surety as consideration for his promise, and then alleging that the case fell outside the Statute of Frauds simply because the surety was motiviated by that payment to enter into the contract. In such a case, it is unlikely that the real object of the transaction would be to pay the surety or to regulate his conduct, whatever his motivation might be.

Securing the release of property

If a person agrees to pay the creditor in order to secure the release of an **3–016** encumbrance or a lien over property in which he has an interest, the mere fact that he is effectively agreeing to pay someone else's debt will not bring the case within s.4. The main object of the transaction is to secure the release of the property, and that will also be the surety's motive in making the payment.[34] For example, if a cargo receiver agrees to pay freight to a shipowner in order to receive delivery of his goods, the agreement is probably not within the Statute of Frauds.[35] Similarly, if a sub-purchaser agrees to pay the unpaid seller directly, the statute will not apply.[36]

In order to fall within this exception, the surety's interest in the property must be a species of interest known to the law.[37] The lien or encumbrance must be exercised by reference to the debt which the surety agrees to pay.[38] It also seems that if this exception is to apply, the lien or encumbrance should be in place at the time when the surety agrees to pay, although there appears to be no good reason to draw a distinction between a promise made in order to avert an encumbrance, and a promise made in order to release the property once the encumbrance has been placed on it.[39] Furthermore, the property probably has to be surrendered to the surety, or

---

33 *Couturier v Hastie* (1852) 8 Exch. 40; reversed on other grounds (1856) 5 H.L.C. 673; *Morris v Cleasby* (1816) 4 M. & S. 566.

34 *Castling v Aubert* (1802) 2 East. 325; *Williams v Leper* (1766) 3 Burr. 1886; *Walker v Taylor* (1834) 6 C. & P. 752; *Edwards v Kelly* (1817) 6 M. & S. 204; *Bampton v Paulin* (1827) 4 Bing. 264.

35 However, *cf. Gull v Lindsay* (1849) 4 Exch. 45.

36 *Fitzgerald v Dressler* (1859) 7 C.B.N.S. 374; *Marginson v Potter & Co* (1976) 11 A.L.R. 64 (Aus).

37 *Harburg India Rubber Comb Co v Martin* [1902] 1 K.B. 778; *Davys v Buswell* [1913] 2 K.B. 47.

38 *Thomas v Williams* (1830) 10 B. & C. 664. If the promise is severable, it may be good as regards the secured debt even if it is unenforceable as against the unsecured debt: *Wood v Benson* (1831) 2 Cr. & J. 94.

39 This appears to have been the effect of *Gull v Lindsay* (1849) 4 Exch. 45. See further *Bank of Scotland v Wright* [1991] B.C.L.C. 244, *per* Brooke J. at 264.

at least to his order, rather than to the principal or some third party.[40] However, cases in which the surety promises to pay a debt in return for the release of a lien or other encumbrance over property in which he has no interest may still fall outside s.4 of the Statute of Frauds because they are within some other exception, for example because the promise was made to the principal or a third party, or there was a novation, or the surety was undertaking a personal liability for the debt.

Variations must comply with s.4

3–017 If the parties to a contract of guarantee which complies with the requirements of s.4 subsequently reach an agreement to vary its terms, the new terms must also be evidenced by a document complying with s.4 if the agreement, as varied, is to be enforceable.[41] It is well established that if the variation is purely oral and the requirements of s.4 are not complied with, the original agreement is still enforceable as if it had not been varied: see *Morris v Baron & Co* [1918] A.C. 1 at 16 and the cases there cited. This produces the anomalous result that the contract which is susceptible of enforcement is not in fact the true agreement between the parties.[42] However, in practice this is unlikely to produce a result unfair to defendants, because s.4 does not prevent the guarantor from raising the variation as a defence to any claim made against him on the unamended version.[43] The rule does not apply, however, to a subsequent agreement terminating or avoiding the contract of guarantee: *Morris v Baron & Co* (above). Nor does it apply to variations of the underlying contract between the principal and the creditor, even though it might be said that by consenting to such variations the surety is agreeing to vary the terms or scope of the original guarantee. In *Credit Suisse v Borough Council of Allerdale* [1995] 1 Lloyd's Rep. 315[44] one of the issues which arose was whether the principal and the creditor had agreed to material variations of the principal contract and thereby discharged the surety, a local authority. The creditor bank argued that the council was precluded by estoppel or waiver from asserting that the variations had discharged the guarantee; the council in turn contended that even if the bank would otherwise have been entitled to rely upon an

---

40 *Clancy v Piggott* (1835) 2 Ad. & El. 473; *Rounce v Woodyard* (1846) 8 L.T.O.S. 186; *Bull v Collier* (1842) 4 I.L.R. 107, *Fennell v Mulcahy* (1845) 8 I.L.R. 434. *Cf. Houlditch v Milne* (1800) 3 Esp. 86.

41 See further, the discussion in McGuinness, *The Law of Guarantee* (*op. cit.*) at Ch.5.7 and the Canadian cases cited there. *Cf. Re A Debtor (No.517 of 1991) The Times*, November 25, 1991 in which a debtor was held to be entitled to raise a cross-claim based on an alleged oral variation of the guarantee in respect of which the creditor had served a statutory demand.

42 Though the oral variation may be set up as a defence if the original agreement is sued on, and therefore the anomaly should have no practical effect: see *Re A Debtor (No.517 of 1991) The Times*, November 25, 1991 (Ferris J.).

43 Nor does the parol evidence rule, which has no application to variation or discharge by subsequent agreement: see *Gross v Lord Nugent* (1833) 5 B. & Ad. 58, at 64.

44 Upheld [1997] Q.B. 306. The Statute of Frauds and estoppel points were not pursued in the Court of Appeal.

estoppel, it could not do so because of s.4 of the Statute of Frauds. Colman J. held that on the evidence, the council had consented to the variations but that if it had not consented, the bank's case on waiver or estoppel would have failed. Nevertheless he went on to consider, *obiter*, at 370–372, the effect of s.4 of the Statute of Frauds on the hypothesis that both those findings were incorrect. He held that if a surety gave his consent to a material variation of the principal contract, and thereby lost his right to be discharged from liability, there was no creation of a new guarantee. The creditor would still be suing on the original guarantee and if that satisfied the requirements of s.4, the Statute of Frauds would have no further application. The surety's consent to the variation did not have to be made or evidenced in writing. If that analysis is correct, it follows that the position is no different if the creditor alleges that it would be unconscionable for the surety to rely on the material variation because of his conduct or representations. Again, the creditor is still trying to sue on the original guarantee. There is no basis on which it could be said that the policy behind the Statute of Frauds was being evaded.

However, even if this analysis proved to be incorrect and the bank was suing on a different or varied guarantee, Colman J. would have concluded that the Statute of Frauds did not preclude the bank from reliance on the estoppel. Applying dicta of Viscount Radcliffe in *Kok Hoong v Leong Cheong Kweng* [1964] A.C. 993 at 1015, the Statute of Frauds ought to be treated as regulating procedure, not striking at essential validity. Thus it does not supersede the ability of the court to treat as unconscionable, and therefore to disallow, reliance on discharge of an original guarantee where there has been an extension of time to pay or a material variation of the underlying contract to which the guarantor has not assented.

Collateral contracts

It seems most unlikely that a court would ever allow s.4 to be circumvented **3–018** by proof of an oral collateral contract which contradicts, or is otherwise inconsistent with, the terms of a written guarantee. In some cases, chiefly those in which a party has been induced to sign a written agreement by a promise by the other contracting party that he will not enforce a particular term of it, or an assurance on a particular matter, the court has held that there was a collateral contract and that the parol evidence rule does not apply.[45] However, in *Hawrish v Bank of Montreal* [1969] S.C.R. 515, the Supreme Court of Canada held that evidence of a collateral agreement which contradicted the terms of a written guarantee was inadmissible. In that case, the terms of the standard form bank guarantee signed by the guarantor expressly provided that no representations had been made by the bank to the guarantor and that it contained the whole agreement between

---

45 See the discussion of collateral contracts and the parol evidence rule in *Chitty on Contracts*, (29th ed., Sweet & Maxwell 2004) para.12–096 and following, and in McGuinness, *The Law of Guarantee (op. cit.)* paras 5.28 and following.

them. The guarantor admitted that he had not read the guarantee, but sought to allege that the bank manager had orally assured him that the guarantee was limited to the existing indebtedness of the principal company, and that he would be released from the guarantee as soon as the bank obtained alternative security.[46] These terms were completely inconsistent with the terms of the written guarantee.

The defence based on the alleged collateral contract succeeded at trial, but the guarantor lost on appeal to the Court of Appeal and the Supreme Court, where Judson J. stated:[47]

> "The appellant further submitted that the parol evidence was admissible on the ground that it established an oral agreement which was independent of and collateral to the main contract . . . but a collateral agreement cannot be established where it is inconsistent with or contradicts the written agreement."

On the other hand, in such a situation parol evidence could be admissible for the purposes of raising a defence of misrepresentation, and possibly equitable defences such as estoppel—see, *e.g.* the unreported case of *Bank of Baroda v Shah (Dilip)*, July 30, 1999, in which the Court of Appeal upheld a defence based on alleged oral assurances given by the bank to the guarantor that it would release him from his guarantee when he ceased to be a director of the principal company. The assurances were proved at trial and it was held that the bank was estopped from reneging on them and seeking to enforce the guarantee after the director resigned.

If the guarantee itself takes the form of a collateral agreement, it is probable that the Statute of Frauds will apply to it. In *Autocar v Motemtronic Ltd and Searle* (unreported) CAT No.656 of 1996, June 20, the issue before the Court of Appeal was whether an oral assurance given by S that, in the event that his company became liable to return a payment to Autocar, he would ensure that it had sufficient funds to meet that obligation, was a binding collateral warranty. It was held by the majority (Henry and Aldous L.JJ., Staughton L.J. dissenting) that the promise made by S was merely a "statement of comfort" and not a guarantee. However the majority went on to express the view that if the promise had been binding, it would have fallen within s.4 of the Statute of Frauds.

Contracts which fall partly within the Statute of Frauds

3–019   If a contract which does not satisfy the evidential requirements of s.4 of the Statute of Frauds contains several obligations on the part of the guarantor, only one of which is an obligation to act as guarantor, the question whether any part of the contract beside the guarantee is enforceable will depend on

---

46 He did not raise a defence of misrepresentation.
47 *ibid.*, at 520.

whether, as a matter of construction, the guarantee obligation is severable from the rest.[48]

Achieving enforceability under s.4

Where the contract is one which falls within the ambit of s.4 of the Statute **3–020**
of Frauds, the section prescribes two alternative means of achieving enforceability, namely:

(a) the agreement upon which the action is to be brought must be in writing and signed by "the party to be charged therewith or some other person thereunto by him lawfully authorised"; or

(b) a memorandum or note of the agreement must be similarly signed. In this event, the agreement itself may be oral.

These requirements have been considered in many authorities concerning the sale of land, since s.4 used to apply to contracts for the sale of land before it was replaced (and in effect re-enacted) by s.40 of the Law of Property Act 1925.[49] It is possible, therefore, to apply the principles in those cases to cases involving contracts of guarantee. For a detailed consideration of the requirements of the section in the context of sales of land, see Megarry & Wade, *The Law of Real Property* (Sweet & Maxwell, 5th ed., 1984), pp.575–587.[50]

The distinction between the two ways of achieving enforceability was the subject of consideration by the House of Lords in the leading modern authority on s.4 of the Statute of Frauds, *Elpis Maritime Co Ltd v Marti Chartering Co Inc (The "Maria D")* [1991] 2 Lloyd's Rep. 311. In that case M, who were brokers and agents acting for Turkish charterers, had orally guaranteed the payment of outstanding freight and demurrage to the plaintiff shipowners. A charterparty consisting of a front page, a second page with printed clauses on it, and six pages of typed clauses, was drawn up and signed by the owners and M. The front page was stamped and signed by M "for and on behalf of charterers as brokers only". Each succeeding page was stamped and signed by M without qualification. One of the typed clauses stated that "M guarantees . . . outstanding demurrage, if any, and for balance freight". M contended that they had signed the charterparty as brokers only and that the guarantee was unenforceable.

---

48 See *Chater v Beckett* (1797) 7 Term Rep. 201; *Lord Lexington v Clarke* (1689) 2 Vent. 223; *Thomas v Williams* (1830) 10 B. & C. 664; *Wood v Benson* (1831) 2 Cr. & J. 94.
49 This provision has in turn been repealed and replaced by s.2 of the Law of Property (Miscellaneous Provisions) Act 1989.
50 N.B. the editors of Megarry & Wade have not reproduced this historical commentary in the current (6th) ed. 2000. See also *Halsbury's Laws* (*op. cit.*), Vol. 42, paras 31–36, 39, 40–43. Other relevant authorities include those concerning the sale of goods or chattels: the need for a memorandum of those contracts was set out in s.17 of the Statute of Frauds and s.4 of the Sale of Goods Act 1893, now abolished, which were in similar terms to s.4 of the Statute of Frauds.

The House of Lords held that M had no arguable defence to the claim on the guarantee, despite the fact that there was an arguable issue as to whether M had signed all the pages as agents for the charterers or for themselves as a contracting party. This issue meant that the position of M had to be considered on two separate assumptions. The first was that M signed the page containing the guarantee as a contracting party. If that was so, the prior oral contract of guarantee was subsumed in the written agreement and the latter was signed by M, the party to be charged therewith, as principals. Consequently, the agreement had satisfied the first means of enforceability prescribed by s.4. The alternative assumption was that M signed the charterparty solely as agents for the charterers. The charterparty contained a sufficient note or memorandum of the prior oral agreement, and it was signed by M, the party to be charged. Since the note or memorandum did not have to be the agreement itself, the capacity in which M signed it was irrelevant and the second means of enforceability prescribed by s.4 had been fulfilled.

It follows that the capacity in which the alleged guarantor has signed the document on which the creditor seeks to rely is only relevant if there was no oral agreement and the only question which arises is whether there is a written agreement of guarantee between the creditor and guarantor, signed by the latter.[51]

Memorandum and agreement

3–021   If the agreement was not made in writing, the note or memorandum of it need not be made contemporaneously with it, as the contract exists independently of the memorandum.[52] This usually means that the memorandum is made after the agreement—indeed in *Barkworth v Young* (1856) 4 Drew. 1, the written memorandum was made some 14 years after the contract itself.

There was at one time some doubt as to whether a document which was brought into existence before the contract was made (*e.g.* a written offer signed by the guarantor) would ever suffice to constitute a memorandum for the purposes of s.4, even if it could be shown that the parties subsequently made an oral agreement on exactly the same terms. The language of the statute appears to presuppose that there is an agreement already in existence, because there must be a memorandum of that agreement. In *Munday v Asprey* (1878) 13 Ch. D. 855, Fry J. said at 857 that the statute requires that the plaintiff should prove that a concluded agreement should exist at the time when the memorandum was signed. However, that dictum was in direct contradiction to several earlier authorities in which it had been held that an offer signed by the party to be

---

51 See, *e.g. Young v Schuler* (1883) 11 Q.B.D. 651, as explained by Lord Brandon in *The "Maria D"* [1991] 2 Lloyd's Rep. 311 at 314–316. It is doubtful whether the guarantor in *Minories Finance v Attam,* (unreported) CAT No.1094 of 1989, November 13, would have obtained leave to defend on this point if that case had been decided after *The "Maria D".*

52 *Longfellow v Williams* (1804) Peake, Add. Cas. 225; *Re Hoyle* [1893] 1 Ch. 84.

charged could amount to a sufficient memorandum if the evidence showed that it was unconditionally accepted.[53]

This doubt was resolved by Devlin J. in *Parker v Clark* [1960] 1 W.L.R. 286 at 295–296, in which Fry J.'s dictum was held to be incorrect and contrary to authority (at least so far as written offers to contract are concerned). This result does not violate the underlying policy of the statute, since in those circumstances there is no question of the guarantor being held liable on an offer which he never made, by virtue of perjured evidence. However, if the offer is alleged to have been accepted orally, the court may regard the onus of proof on the offeree as a fairly heavy one.[54] In *New Eberhart Co Ex p. Menzies* (1889) 43 Ch. D. 118 at 129, Bowen L.J. said that the written offer cases "pushed the literal construction of the Statute of Frauds to a limit beyond which it would perhaps be not easy to go". However, it would appear that this line of authority is confined strictly to situations in which the document preceding the contract contained the offer which was subsequently accepted.[55]

In *Carlton Communications Plc v Football League* [2002] EWHC 1650 (Comm), unreported, August 1, 2002, Langley J. rejected a claim by the Football League that Carlton and Granada, the major shareholders in ONdigital were jointly and severally liable to it as guarantors of ONdigital's obligations under a contract made in June 2000. The central issues were whether there was a binding contract of guarantee and if so, whether the requirements of s.4 of the Statute of Frauds had been complied with. The Football League placed heavy reliance on a statement made in an Initial Bid document submitted by ONdigital that "ONdigital and its shareholders will guarantee all funding to the FL outlined in this document". It submitted that this was a unilateral offer capable of acceptance by conduct, and that the Football League had accepted the offer by entering into the contract with ONdigital. The Initial Bid was expressed to be "subject to contract". The judge held that there was no offer to guarantee which was capable of acceptance because "a subject to contract proposal is the antethesis of or at the least incompatible with a unilateral offer". However even if the offer had been capable of acceptance by conduct as the Football League contended, there was no compliance with s.4 of the Statute of Frauds. The judge followed the decision of the Court of Appeal in *Tiverton Estates Ltd v Wearwell Ltd* [1975] 1 Ch. 146 in which it was held that a document marked "subject to contract" could not satisfy the Statute of Frauds because it could not acknowledge or recognise the existence of a contract. Moreover, the document relied on by the Football League did not contain a statement of all the material terms of the contract, since the Initial Bid referred only to the funding in the Initial Bid itself, which was

---

53 See, *e.g. Powers v Fowler* (1855) 4 E. & B. 511; *Reuss v Picksley* (1866) L.R. 1 Exch. 342; *Smith v Neale* (1857) 2 C.B.N.S. 67.
54 See the observations of Maugham J. in *Watson v Davies* [1931] 1 Ch. 455 at 468.
55 See *Tiverton Estates Ltd v Wearwell Ltd* [1975] Ch. 146 disapproving *Law v Jones* [1974] Ch. 112.

£240 million, and not the sums for which ONdigital were eventually liable under the June contract, which were substantially greater, £315 million. Finally, the Initial Bid was not signed by Carlton or Granada or by an agent lawfully authorised by them to do so. The judge found that Carlton and Granada were unaware that a guarantee was being proposed or offered, and that ONdigital had no authority, whether actual or ostensible, to bind them to any such contract.

It is an essential requirement that the memorandum is in existence prior to the commencement of the action in which the creditor seeks to enforce the guarantee.[56] However, it is not essential that it should remain in existence until the creditor sues the guarantor. If the original written agreement, memorandum or note has been lost or destroyed, oral evidence may be adduced to prove that it existed and that the requirements of the statute were fulfilled: *Barrass v Reed, The Times*, March 28, 1898; *Crays Gas Co v Bromley Gas Consumers Co, The Times*, March 23, 1901, CA.[57]

Form of memorandum

3–022 The agreement or memorandum must be in writing (which includes typing, printing, lithography, photography and other modes of representing or reproducing words in a visible form).[58] The written evidence of the agreement need not be in any special form, provided that all the essential terms of the agreement (except the consideration) are adequately set out in writing. The memorandum must state the terms of the contract and contain an express or implied recognition that a contract was entered into.[59] However it need not be a lengthy or complex document. For example, in *Birmingham Joinery Ltd v Phillips* [1999] EWCA Civ 866 (unreported) February 26, 1999, P, the main shareholder and marketing manager of a joinery company which had received a statutory demand from one of its creditors, went to a meeting with the creditors at which it was agreed he would give a personal guarantee to secure the company's indebtedness. He then wrote a letter to them expressing pleasure that they were able to reach an agreement to pay the accounts for September, October and November and setting out the total sum agreed including interest and costs. The letter continued "I have pleasure in enclosing our post dated cheque and my own personal guarantee which you were happy about in respect of security". No guarantee was in fact enclosed. When the creditors sent their own form of

---

56 *Lucas v Dixon* (1889) 22 Q.B.D. 357; *Sievewright v Archibald* (1851) 17 Q.B. 103; *Re Hoyle* [1893] 1 Ch. 84; see also the rather unusual circumstances of *Farr, Smith & Co v Messers Ltd* [1928] 1 K.B. 397, in which the memorandum consisted of a pleading drafted in an earlier action.

57 See the recent case of *Gattellaro v Westpac Banking Corporation* [2004] 204 A.L.R. 258 for the problems which the loss of the original document can create for either party. See also *Barber v Rowe* [1948] 2 All E.R. 1050; *Last v Hucklesby* (1914) 58 S.J. 431; *Giasoumi v Hutton* [1977] V.R. 294.

58 Interpretation Act 1978, s.5 and Sch.1.

59 *Welford v Beazely* (1747) 1 Ves. Sen. 6; *Jones v Williams* (1841) 7 M. & W. 493; *Tiverton Estates Ltd v Wearwell* [1975] Ch. 146, applied in *Clipper Maritime Ltd v Shirlstar Container Transport Ltd ("The Anemone")* [1987] 1 Lloyd's Rep. 546 *per* Staughton L.J. at 555–556.

guarantee to P, he declined to sign it. The Court of Appeal rejected P's argument that the letter was an insufficient memorandum because it was to be construed as referring to a further separate document, the terms of which were unknown. Since the oral guarantee relied on by the creditor was a simple unconditional agreement by P at the meeting to guarantee the debts of the company to the creditor, to the extent quantified at the meeting, together with interest and costs, the letter was a sufficient memorandum of that agreement. The extent of that liability was accurately set out in the letter.

It is not essential to refer to the contract as a guarantee, because what matters is the substance of the contract and not the name given to it by the parties.[60] The documentation need not be addressed to the creditor, or indeed addressed to anyone at all.[61] Indeed the creditor may not have seen it.[62] It may not have been brought into existence specifically to record the agreement. A wide variety of documents ranging from letters to a recital in a will have been held to be sufficient. Indeed in *Re Hoyle* [1893] 1 Ch. 84, A.L. Smith L.J. observed at 100: "I should say that an entry in a man's diary, if it were signed by him and the contents were sufficient, would do".[63] A document acknowledging the existence of a contract, but repudiating liability under it may amount to a sufficient memorandum.[64] However, it will not include any document which denies the existence of a contract, such as a written offer "subject to contract".[65] Nor will it normally include a former guarantee which has been released or discharged. In *Silverburn Finance (UK) Ltd v Salt* [2001] 2 All E.R. (Comm) 438, the directors of a company had given written personal guarantees in respect of the company's liabilities under a contract which had terminated. The guarantees had come to an end at the same time as the main contract. About a month later, the company entered into a fresh contract with the same creditor on the same terms as before. The question arose as to whether fresh guarantees, on the same terms as before, were brought into existence by necessary implication, but the Court of Appeal held that the requirements of s.4 of the Statute of Frauds were an insuperable obstacle to that argument. The previous guarantees were "only written evidence of guarantees that have since ceased to exist" and there had been no express agreement to treat them as evidence of any fresh agreement to guarantee the new contract.

It is possible for the requirements of the statute to be satisfied by reading more than one document together. If the terms of the contract are

---

60 *Seaton v Heath* [1899] 1 Q.B. 782 *per* Romer L.J. at 792; *Re Denton's Estate* [1904] 2 Ch. 178.

61 *Gibson v Holland* (1865) L.R. 1 C.P. 1; *Bateman v Phillips* (1812) 15 East. 272; *Jones v Williams* (1841) 7 M. & W. 493.

62 See, *e.g. Macrory v Scott* (1850) 5 Exch. 907.

63 For further examples see *Halsbury's Laws* (*op. cit.*), Vol. 48, at para.32.

64 *Dewar v Mintoft* [1912] 2 K.B. 373; see also *Bailey v Sweeting* (1861) 9 C.B.N.S. 843; *Wilkinson v Evans* (1866) L.R. 1 C.P. 407; *Buxton v Rust* (1872) L.R. 7 Exch. 279; *Thirkell v Cambi* [1919] 2 K.B. 590 (cases on sale of goods).

65 *Carlton Communications v The Football League* [2002] EWHC 1650 (Comm) discussed at para.3–021 above, *Thirkell v Cambi* [1919] 2 K.B. 590; *Tiverton Estates v Wearwell* [1975] Ch. 146; *Daulia Ltd v Four Millbank Nominees Ltd* [1978] Ch. 231.

contained in a series of documents all bearing the signature of the guarantor, and it is clear on their face that they refer to the same transaction, the documents may be read together.[66] However, if the document containing the guarantor's signature does not contain all the terms of the agreement it must contain some reference, express or implied, to any other document which it is sought to read with it, and if the identity of that other document is unclear, oral evidence may be adduced in order to identify it: *Timmins v Moreland Street Property Ltd* [1958] Ch. 110.[67] Oral evidence cannot be adduced in order to connect documents which cannot be connected by express reference or by reasonable inference from the circumstances of the case.[68]

The application of these principles is usefully illustrated by three modern cases. First in time is the Court of Appeal decision in *Jay v Gainsford* (unreported) CAT No.362b of 1977, October 4. The plaintiffs were seeking to rely on a series of letters written to them by a company. Two of the letters plainly sufficed to meet the requirements of the Statute of Frauds for the purpose of evidencing earlier oral agreements by two individuals to guarantee loans made by the plaintiffs to the company. Those loans had been repaid. A third letter written on the company's headed notepaper some years after the second letter, referred to a new loan being made "on the same terms and conditions as our existing deposit" but did not identify the "existing deposit" or refer back to the earlier letters. On an appeal against an order for summary judgment, the Court of Appeal held that the defendants had at the very least a good arguable case that the documents could not be read together so as to satisfy the requirements of s.4, and indicated that without further documentary evidence to provide the necessary link, the defence was likely to succeed.

Similarly, in *Barclays Bank v Caldwell* (unreported) July 25, 1986, (Harman J.) the bank entered into a collateral agreement in a side letter, signed only by the bank's representative, that the guarantee would apply only to the "top slice" of the indebtedness of the principal. The guarantee itself made no mention of the side letter and it was held that the documents could not be read together for the purposes of satisfying s.4 of the Statute of Frauds. On the other hand, in *Clipper Maritime Ltd v Shirlstar Container Transport Ltd ("The Anemone")* [1987] 1 Lloyd's Rep. 546, Staughton J. held that certain telexes, together possibly with the addition of a charterparty which was signed by the guarantor company, could be read together so as to form a sufficient memorandum.

---

66 *Sheers v Thimbleby & Son* (1897) 76 L.T. 709.
67 See also *Oliver v Hunting* (1890) 44 Ch. D. 205; *Coe v Duffield* (1822) 7 Moore C.P. 252; *Sheers v Thimbleby & Son* (1897) 76 L.T. 709; *Ridgway v Wharton* (1857) 6 H.L. Cas 238; *Macrory v Scott* (1850) 5 Exch. 907; *Brettel v Williams* (1849) 4 Exch. 623; *Stead v Liddiard* (1823) 1 Bing. 196; *McEwan v Dynon* (1877) 3 V.L.R. 271 (Aus).
68 *Timmins v Moreland Street Property Co Ltd* [1958] Ch. 110 at 130 *per* Jenkins L.J.; *Boydell v Drummond* (1809) 11 East. 142; *Smith v Dixon* (1839) 3 Jur. 770; *Peirce v Corf* (1874) L.R. 9 Q.B. 210; *Long v Millar* (1879) 4 C.P.D. 450.

Contents of the memorandum

The memorandum must contain evidence of all the material terms of the **3–023**
contract, except the consideration. Oral evidence may be adduced to show
that the documentation on which the plaintiff is seeking to sue does not
contain all the material terms of the contract: *Beckett v Nurse* [1948] 1 K.B.
535. Oral evidence may also be adduced to explain the meaning of
expressions used in the documents or to identify a particular document
referred to in another document so as to connect them. Thus in *Perrylease
Ltd v Imecar AG* [1988] 1 W.L.R. 463, Scott J. held that s.4 of the Statute of
Frauds did not preclude the admissibility of extrinsic evidence firstly to
identify the true name of a company which was misdescribed in the
guarantee, and secondly to identify the liability being guaranteed regardless
of whether it was a present or future liability.[69] However, oral evidence
cannot be used to supplement an incomplete memorandum, or to provide a
link between a series of documents when there is no sufficient apparent
connection between them.[70]

Oral evidence of the circumstances in which the contract came to be
executed is also inadmissible for the purpose of determining the capacity in
which the alleged surety signed the document of guarantee. Thus in
Cheshire Building Society v Shrigley Developments Ltd (unreported) CAT
No.932 of 1996, July 8 the Court of Appeal determined by looking at the
document alone whether the defendants had signed as witnesses or
guarantors, and refused to consider affidavit evidence from a solicitor who
sought to explain the circumstances in which they signed it.

The problems which can arise as a result of the requirement that all
material terms should be evidenced in the document signed by the
guarantor are illustrated by the case of *Minories Finance v Attam* (unreported) CAT No.1094 of 1989, November 13. The defendant alleged that
the printed guarantee form which he signed had left a blank space for the
rate of interest payable on the underlying debt, which someone on the
creditor's side had subsequently filled in with the figure of 3 per cent. The
Court of Appeal upheld an order which granted him unconditional leave to
defend, observing that the plaintiffs ran the potential risk of losing the case
either because the contract was insufficiently certain (if no agreement had
been reached as to the rate of interest, a material term) or, if 3 per cent had
been agreed, because the agreement which was signed did not include that
material term when the guarantor signed it. The secondary part of this
rationale may be open to doubt in the light of the reasoning of the Court of
Appeal in *Raffeiren Zentralbank v Crosseas Shipping* [2000] 1 W.L.R. 1135.
Even if the rate of interest might be regarded as material, if it had already

---

69 The statement in Rowlatt, *Principal and Surety* (Sweet & Maxwell, 4th ed., 1982) that
"where the liability to be guaranteed is a future liability it must appear in the writing what
the liability is to be which the guarantee is to cover" was disapproved by Scott J. at 472.
70 *Fitzmaurice v Bayley* (1860) 9 H.L. Cas 78; *Holmes v Mitchell* (1859) 7 C.B.N.S. 361;
Imperial Bank of Canada v Nixon [1926] 4 D.L.R. 1052; *State Bank of India v Kaur* [1996] 5
Bank. L.R. 158; and see the cases cited at footnotes 60 and 61 above.

been agreed with the surety, its insertion on the document after he had signed it would merely correct a mistake and it is likely that the creditor would be entitled to seek an order for rectification and enforcement—see para.3–032 below. As in *Jay v Gainsford*, the plaintiffs in the *Attam* case had problems in establishing the necessary link between the guarantee document and an earlier document referring to the 3 per cent rate which would enable them to be read together as a sufficient memorandum. This case can be contrasted with *MP Services Ltd v Lawyer* (1996) 72 P. & C.R. D49 in which the surety unsuccessfully argued before the Court of Appeal that a letter of guarantee did not meet the requirements of the Statue of Frauds because it did not spell out the interest rate of the loan. It was held that the promise to guarantee repayment of the debt "together with interest thereon" was a sufficient reference to the rate of interest prescribed by the terms of the underlying loan agreement.

The necessity for expressing the consideration in writing was abolished by the Mercantile Law Amendment Act 1856, s.3. Cases decided prior to the enactment of that statute should therefore be treated with some caution, because often the only reason why a particular memorandum was held to be insufficient was that the consideration was not stated in it. However, the 1856 Act does not make a promise good which was not good before.[71] If the document does refer to a particular consideration, then it appears that the parties are bound by it: so that if the expressed consideration is clearly bad, and there is no ambiguity, the contract will be unenforceable.[72]

The memorandum must make it plain who the parties to the contract are. Thus it has been held that failure to name the person to whom the guarantee is given is fatal.[73] However, if the written documentation contains sufficient references to enable the person giving the guarantee or benefiting from it to be readily identified, it will suffice.[74] It is also highly unlikely that a mistake as to the name of one of the parties would be fatal.[75] It is permissible to look at extrinsic evidence to resolve any uncertainties or ambiguities within a contract as to the identity of the contracting parties: see the speech of Lord Hobhouse in *Shogun Finance Ltd v Hudson* [2003] 3 W.L.R. 1371, especially at para.49, and *OTV Birwelco v Technical and General Guarantee Co Ltd* [2002] 4 All E.R. 668. In *Dumford Trading AG v*

---

71 *Holmes v Mitchell* (1859) 7 C.B.N.S. 361 at 367, *per* Byles J. See also *Sheers v Thimbleby & Son* (1897) 76 L.T. 709.
72 See *Wood v Priestner* (1866) 'L.R. 2 Exch. 66 *per* Bramwell B. at 70; *Oldershaw v King* (1857) 2 H. & N. 517.
73 *Williams v Lake* (1859) 2 E. & E. 349; *A Macdonald & Co v Fletcher* (1915) 22 B.C.R. 298 *AGS Electric Ltd v Sherman* (1997) 108 D.L.R. (3d) 229 (Can).
74 *Dutchman v Tooth* (1839) 5 Bing. N.C. 577; *Sims v Robertson* (1921) 21 S.W.N.S.W. 246 (Aus); *A Macdonald & Co v Fletcher* (above). See also *Freeman v Freeman* (1891) 7 T.L.R. 431 and *Pearce v Gardner* [1897] 1 Q.B. 688, in which the envelope containing the letter signed by the party to be charged was read with its contents in order to supply the missing name and address of the party benefiting from the contract.
75 *Perrylease Ltd v Imecar AG* [1988] 1 W.L.R. 463, *per* Scott J. at 469; see also the Canadian cases of *Brock & Co v Young* (1910) 8 E.L.R. 244 and *Tower Paint & Laboratories Ltd v 126019 Enterprises Ltd (Stainco Edmonton)* (1983) 27 Alta. L.R. (2d) 154.

OAO Atlantrybflot [2004] EWHC 1099, the contracts of loan and guarantee named as guarantor a company (Z) with an address in Kaliningrad, Russia. That address was the registered office of O, Z's parent company. Z's office was elsewhere. The claimant sued O, who argued that Z was the guarantor and that the guarantee failed to comply with s.4 of the Statute of Frauds because it had not been signed by anyone acting on behalf of Z. It was held by Judge Chambers Q.C. that the address was as much a part of the identification of the guarantor as the name, and that since the address given was not Z's but O's, it was permissible to resort to extrinsic evidence to resolve the uncertainty as to which of the two companies was in truth the guarantor. That evidence pointed unequivocally to O, and once it was clear that the person who signed the guarantee did so under a power of attorney from O, the finding that s.4 of the Statute of Frauds had been complied with was inevitable.

It would not suffice if the document merely makes an incidental reference to the names of the parties, without making it clear that they are the parties to the contract.[76] If the guarantee is given to a class of persons, *e.g.* the creditors of a company, it is sufficient for the class to be described in the documents, rather than each and every member of it.[77] The memorandum must also sufficiently identify the principal whose obligations to the creditor are the subject-matter of the guarantee. Failure to do so will have serious consequences, not only because of s.4 of the Statute of Frauds, but also because the omission may result in the guarantee being void for uncertainty. One of the fundamental ingredients of a guarantee is the existence of a primary liability of some other person for which the guarantor has undertaken secondary liability to the creditor. If the principal is not identified, that liability may also be unidentified and uncertain, and the parol evidence rule may preclude evidence being adduced to cure the deficiency. The Canadian case of *Imperial Bank of Canada v Nixon* [1926] 4 D.L.R. 1052 concerned a standard form bank guarantee in which a blank space was left for the insertion of the name of the principal, followed by the words "hereinafter called the customer". By an oversight, the name of the principal debtor was not filled in. At first instance, the court allowed an endorsement on the back of the guarantee form to be admitted in evidence for the purpose of identifying who "the customer" was. The appellate division of the Ontario Supreme Court reversed this decision.

There was no evidence that the endorsement was made when the guarantee was signed, and in any event there was insufficient linkage between the contents of the endorsement and the body of the guarantee to enable the court to read the two together in order to determine who the principal debtor was. Parol evidence to connect the endorsement with the guarantee was disallowed. Orde J.A. said, at 1058: "I think I am safe in saying that in no case where oral evidence has been admitted to illuminate

---

76 *Vandenbergh v Spooner* (1866) L.R. 1 Exch. 316; *Newell v Radford* (1867) L.R. 3 C.P. 52.
77 *Jones v Williams* (1841) 7 M. & W. 493; *Marsden v Capital & County Newspaper Co* (1901) 46 S.J. 11.

the memorandum or note in writing of a contract within the purview of the Statute of Frauds [it] has gone the length of supplying a missing term of the contract itself." Dismissing the argument that the addition of the words "herein called the customer" sufficiently identified the person to whom the advances are made to allow parol evidence, the judge pointed out that the word "customer" was simply a symbol to avoid the continual repetition of the customer's name, and that it might just as easily have been "X" or "debtor". The point was that the contract was wholly incomplete because it failed to mention or to indicate in any way who the principal debtor was; the name of any customer of the bank or indeed anyone else could have been inserted in the blank space consistently with the language of the rest of the contract. The court held that to admit evidence to supply an omission of this character would be in effect to repeal the Statute of Frauds. That case was followed more recently in Canada in *AGS Electric Ltd v Sherman* (1979) 108 D.L.R. (3d) 229, a case in which the names of both the creditor and the principal were omitted from the document.

The identical point arose before the Court of Appeal in *State Bank of India v Kaur*, reported *sub nom. State Bank of India v Gurmit* [1996] 5 Bank. L.R. 158; and was decided in the same way. The defendant executed a document entitled "guarantee of advance" in favour of a bank which assigned it to the plantiff. The guarantee was neither dated nor witnessed. The name of the principal debtor was omitted. The space for the maximum amount of the guarantee was left blank; the original bank's solicitor swore an affidavit showing that it was intended to be for about half the amount demanded from the defendant. The main point taken by the defendant was that the guarantee did not comply with s.4 of the Statute of Frauds because it did not identify the principal debtor. The Court of Appeal agreed that this was fatal, as was the lack of a date and the failure to include the agreed limit. Extrinsic evidence was inadmissible to fill in the blanks. The plantiff sought to rely upon a "principal debtor" clause in the guarantee which, it was argued, meant that the contract was really a contract of indemnity, but the Court of Appeal held that this clause did not save the contract.

It is doubtful whether in a case of that kind, the existence of a separate indemnity clause in the contract would suffice to protect the creditor. If, as a matter of construction, the indemnity clause is regarded as an additional obligation in a contract which is nevertheless to be regarded as a contract of guarantee, and which does not conform with the requirements of s.4 of the Statute of Frauds, it is likely that it would be as unenforceable as any other term in that contract. The indemnity clause would only work in this context if it were possible to infer from its language that it was a self-standing and independent contract whose survival was in no way predicated upon the existence of the rest of the contract of guarantee or upon the existence of any underlying obligations on the principal debtor. If not, the failure to identify the principal debtor, even in a contract of indemnity, could mean that the terms of the agreement were insufficiently certain to make it enforceable.

The question whether an obvious omission of this type could be "cured" by bringing proceedings for rectification, and enforcement of the rectified guarantee, has now been addressed by an English court, albeit only at the stage of an interim hearing, in the unreported case of *GMAC Commercial Credit Development Ltd v Kalvinder Singh Sandu* [2004] EWHC 716 (Comm). The judge, Mr Richard Siberry Q.C., ruled that it is possible to obtain rectification if, as a result of a common mistake, the terms of a guarantee do not reflect the true intentions of the contracting parties, and that there is nothing in principle which distinguishes guarantees from the land cases in which it has long been established that rectification is available. This point is discussed further in para.3–032 below.

Signature

The agreement, note or memorandum must be signed "by the party to be charged" or by his authorised agent. There is no requirement that it should be signed by the other contracting party.[78] The capacity in which the guarantor signs it is only relevant if the written document is said to be the agreement itself (as opposed to a memorandum or note evidencing the agreement). In that case, it may be relevant to the question whether or not he agreed to be bound by the contract personally.[79] Similarly, his intention in signing the document is probably irrelevant if the issue is whether there is a sufficient memorandum or note: as Bowen L.J. said in *Re Hoyle* [1893] 1 Ch. 84 at 99 "the court is not in quest of the intention of parties, but only of evidence under the hand of one of the parties to the contract that he has entered into it".[80]

3–024

The "signature" need not be in any particular place, so long as it has the effect of authenticating the relevant parts of the document.[81] Thus in *Bluck v Gompertz* (1852) 7 Exch. 862, an indorsement by the guarantor correcting a mistake on the face of a written guarantee already signed by him was held to be sufficiently authenticated by his earlier signature of the document.[82] Similarly the signature need not be a "signature" in the popular sense: it suffices if it is printed or written or typewritten by the guarantor or by his agent, and it can appear at the head of the document.[83] A signature by initials, or by means of a stamp or mark is sufficient.[84] However the

---

78 *Laythorp v Bryant* (1836) 2 Bing. N.C. 735, *Liverpool Borough Bank v Eccles* (1859) 4 H. & N. 139. Of course, the parties are free to make signature by the creditor a term of the contract, and it may also be evidence of the acceptance by the creditor of the terms of the guarantor's offer.

79 See *Elpis Maritime Co Ltd v Marti Chartering Co Inc. (The "Maria D")* [1991] 2 Lloyd's Rep. 311.

80 See also *Gibson v Holland* (1865) L.R. 1 C.P. 1; *Wilkinson v Evans* (1865) L.R. 1 C.P. 407. *Cf. Morton v Copeland* (1855) 16 C.B.N.S. 517 and *Hall v Merrick* (1877) 40 U.C.R. 566 (Can).

81 *Caton v Caton* (1867) L.R. 2 H.L. 127; *Durrell v Evans* (1862) 1 H. & C. 174; see also *Hill v Hill* [1947] Ch. 231 *per* Morton L.J. at 240.

82 However, the original signature may not authenticate a subsequent substantive alteration of the terms of the contract: see *New Hart Builders v Brindley* [1975] Ch. 342.

83 *Leeman v Stocks* [1951] Ch. 941; *Evans v Hoare* [1892] 1 Q.B. 593; *Bilsland v Terry* [1972] N.Z.L.R. 43.

84 *Chichester v Cobb* (1866) 14 L.T. 433; *Caton v Caton* (1867) L.R. 2 H.L. 127 at 143. For a more recent example of the application of the rule to a guarantee see *Decouvreur v Jordan* CAT No.523 of 1987, 18 May (*The Times*, May 25, 1987).

signature should give some indication of a name: a memorandum signed "your affectionate mother" has been held to be insufficient.[85]

The guiding principle as to what will constitute a signature is whether the "signature" authenticates the note or memorandum as evidencing a binding agreement. The purpose for which the person signed it is irrelevant.[86] Accordingly, it has been held that a letterhead with the guarantor's name on it may suffice, if the guarantor drew up the document or authorised his agent to send it to the other contracting party.[87] However, where a person signs a blank form and it is subsequently filled in by another in terms of a guarantee, the signature would not authenticate that document as a binding agreement so as to satisfy the requirements of s.4.[88] Similarly, if the guarantor simply fills in his name, or allows someone else to fill in his name, along with other details on a standard guarantee form, this may not necessarily constitute a "signature" because it does not in itself signify assent but merely contemplation of assent.[89] However in *Decouvreur v Jordan* a person who had orally agreed to guarantee the obligations of a party under a court order, who printed and partly wrote his name on a written draft minute of guarantee drawn up by counsel but failed to add his usual signature, was held liable. The Court of Appeal held that on the facts of the case, the guarantor had identified himself and could clearly only have done so with the objective intention of adopting the guarantee.[90]

The signature of a contracting party as a witness, or in some other expressed capacity may be sufficient to bind him if there is evidence that there was an oral agreement to guarantee.[91] The signature by one surety of a document expressed to be a joint guarantee by that person with another is binding on the party who signs it, unless it is an agreed condition precedent to his liability that all the sureties shall sign.[92]

Signature by an agent

3–025 The Statute of Frauds expressly permits the guarantee document to be signed by an agent. The agent must be duly authorised to sign, and such authority may be given either orally or in writing.[93] In addition, the

---

85 *Selby v Selby* (1817) 3 Mer. 2.
86 Thus, *e.g.* in *Jones v Victoria Graving Dock Co* (1877) 2 Q.B.D. 314, the contract was sufficiently evidenced by an entry in a company minute book signed by the chairman of the company.
87 *Evans v Hoare* [1892] 1 Q.B. 593 at 596; *Schneider v Norris* (1814) 2 M. & S. 286; *Tourret v Cripps* (1879) 48 LJ Ch. 567; *Casey v Irish Intercontinental Bank* [1979] I.R. 364 (Ire).
88 *Hall v Merrick* (1877) 40 U.C.R. 566 (Can).
89 See *Morton v Copeland* (1855) 16 C.B. 517, but *cf. VSH Ltd v BKS Air Transport Ltd* [1964] 1 Lloyd's Rep. 460.
90 See CAT No.525 of 1987, May 18 (*The Times*, May 25, 1987).
91 *The "Maria D"* [1991] 2 Lloyd's Rep. 311; *Young v Schuler* (1883) 11 Q.B.D. 651; *VSH Ltd v BKS Air Transport Ltd* [1964] 1 Lloyd's Rep. 460; *Wallace v Roe* [1903] 1 I.R. 32.
92 *Norton v Powell* (1842) 4 Man. & G. 42: compare *Fitzgerald v M'Cowan* [1898] 2 I.R. 1. See also *James Graham & Co v Southgate-Sands* [1986] Q.B. 80 and *Ford & Carter Ltd v Midland Bank Ltd* (1979) 129 N.L.J. 543, HL, discussed in detail at paras 4–022 and 6–012.
93 *Emmerson v Heelis* (1809) 2 Taunt. 38; *Coles v Trecothick* (1804) 9 Ves. 234. As to apparent or ostensible authority see *Irving Oil Ltd v S & S Realty Ltd* (1983) 48 N.B.R. (2d) (Can).

signature by an unauthorised agent may be ratified subsequently by the principal.[94] It is unnecessary for the agent to be *sui juris*.[95] If he does not sign expressly as an agent, oral evidence is admissible to prove the capacity in which he signed it, so as to make an undisclosed principal liable.[96] If the agent has authority to bind his principal to the guarantee, it will not matter if his signature is put on the document as a witness, any more than it would matter if his principal had signed the note or memorandum personally as a witness.[97]

The burden of proving that the agent was authorised rests on the party seeking to uphold the guarantee.[98] It must be shown that the agent was authorised to sign the note or memorandum as a record of the agreement: accordingly, if a party instructs his solicitor to draw up a draft contract, the solicitor will not have implied authority to sign it as a memorandum on his behalf: see *Smith v Webster* (1876) 3 Ch. 49. The authority of the agent is a question of fact to be determined in each particular case: in the *Carlton Communications* case, discussed in para.3–021 above, the judge decided that ONdigital had no authority to bind Carlton and Granada to any gurantee, whereas in *Marubeni Hong Kong and South China Ltd v The Mongolian Government* [2004] 2 Lloyd's Rep. 198, Cresswell J. held that the guarantee had been issued with the express actual authority of the defendant government. In that case the judge held that although the question whether actual authority had been conferred on an agent was a matter to be determined by the law of Mongolia (that being the legal system governing the contractual relationship between the principal and the alleged agent), any issues of usual, apparent or ostensible authority, or of ratification, fell to be determined in accordance with the putative proper law of the alleged contract, which in that case was English law. In so doing, he applied Dicey and Morris, rule 198, as approved by Roch L.J. in *Presentaciones Musicales SA v Secunda* [1994] Ch. 271 at 283, holding that it applied as much to governmental entities and public bodies as it did to private entities.

Any issue as to express, implied or ostensible authority will be settled in accordance with usual agency principles. Certain agents have implied authority to sign a guarantee.[99] There are some old authorities which

---

94 See, *e.g. Maclean v Dunn* (1828) 4 Bing. 722; *Marsh v Joseph* [1897] 1 Ch. 213.
95 *Watkins v Vince* (1818) 2 Stark. 368 (signature by a minor on behalf of his father held to be binding on the father).
96 See, *e.g. Young v Schuler* (1883) 11 Q.B.D. 651. Of course the signatory may still be personally liable in accordance with normal agency principles: see, *e.g. Higgins v Senior* (1841) 8 M. & W. 834; *Basma v Weekes* [1950] A.C. 441.
97 *Welford v Beazely* (1747) 1 Ves. Sen. 6; *Wallace v Roe* [1903] 1 Ir. 32. Compare *Gosbell v Archer* (1835) 2 Ad. & El. 500, probably explicable on the grounds that the agent had no authority to bind his principal to the sale contract.
98 *Banbury v Bank of Montreal* [1918] A.C. 626; *John Griffiths Cycle Corpn Ltd v Humber & Co Ltd* [1899] 2 Q.B. 414 (reversed on a different point *sub nom. Humber v Griffiths* (1901) 85 L.T. 141).
99 See Fell's *Law of Mercantile Guarantees* (2nd ed.), pp.89, 94; de Colyar's *Law of Guarantees* (3rd ed.), p.178 and following.

suggest that this class of agents does not include solicitors: it is a question of fact in each case whether the solicitor was authorised.[1] However in *United Bank of Kuwait Ltd v Hammoud* [1988] 1 W.L.R. 1051 at 1063 Staughton L.J. (with whom Lord Donaldson M.R. agreed) sounded a note of caution about "the elderly cases . . . . showing what types of transactions are not within the ordinary authority of a solicitor". He pointed out that the work that solicitors do can be expected to have changed since 1888, it has changed in recent times and is still changing, and said that he preferred to have regard to the expert evidence of today when deciding what transactions are or are not within the ordinary authority of a solicitor.

A memorandum may be signed by one person as agent for both contracting parties, but (outside the special case of a partnership, discussed below) one contracting party cannot sign as agent for the other.[2] If the agent acts within the scope of his authority, the mere fact that the agent may be acting in his own interests when he signs the agreement for his principal is insufficient to entitle the principal to repudiate liability: *Hambro v Burnand* [1904] 2 K.B. 10.

Partnerships and companies

3–026 The partners who sign a guarantee on behalf of a partnership will be personally liable on the guarantee: *Re Smith, Fleming & Co Ex p. Harding* (1879) 12 Ch. D. 557. If they have express authority to sign, or the remaining partners ratify the guarantee, then of course the partnership will be bound. The difficulties arise when only one or some of the partners sign the guarantee and the issue is whether they had implied or ostensible authority to bind the firm. In those circumstances, the starting-point must be s.5 of the Partnership Act 1890, which provides as follows:

> "Every partner is an agent of the firm and his other partners for the purpose of the business of the partnership; and the acts of every partner who does any act for carrying on in the usual way business of the kind carried on by the firm of which he is a member bind the firm and his partners, unless the partner so acting has in fact no authority to act for the firm in the particular matter and the person with whom he is dealing either knows that he has no authority, or does not know or believe him to be a partner."

The application of this section to a guarantee purportedly given on behalf of a firm by some of its partners was considered by the Court of Appeal in *Bank of Scotland v Henry Butcher & Co* [2003] 2 All E.R. (Comm) 557. The defendant firm of surveyors had thirteen partners. The partnership deed

---

1 See, *e.g. Hasleham v Young* (1844) 5 Q.B. 833; *Forster v Rowland* (1861) 7 H. & N. 103; *Matthews v Baxter* (1873) L.R. 8 Exch. 132; *Earl of Glengal v Barnard* (1836) 1 Keen 769 at 787, on Appeal (1848) 2 H.L. Cas. 131, and the cases cited in *Halsbury's Laws* (*op. cit.*), Vol. 42, para.42.

2 *Sharman v Brandt* (1871) L.R. 6 Q.B. 720; *Wright v Dannah* (1809) 2 Camp. 203.

expressly provided that a partner could not give a guarantee on behalf of the partnership without the consent of the other partners. The firm entered into a consultancy agreement with H, which was in the nature of a joint venture under which the firm was to obtain a share of the profits on the business deals carried out with H, in return for providing H's bankers with a guarantee of his overdraft up to a limit of £200,000. A deed of guarantee of the overdraft was signed by four of the partners "as partners and individuals". When H defaulted and the bank sought to enforce the guarantee, the firm raised the defence that the guarantee was not binding on those partners who had not signed it because the four signatories had no authority, actual, implied or ostensible, to bind the partnership.

At first instance, [2001] 2 All E.R. (Comm) 691, Mr Michel Kallipetis Q.C., sitting as a deputy High Court judge, found on the evidence that all the partners had given their consent to the guarantee by consenting to the joint venture transaction, of which it clearly formed an integral part. He also found that the guarantee was given in the course of partnership business and the firm was bound by virtue of s.5 of the Partnership Act 1890 with or without the consent of the remaining partners. His judgment and reasoning were upheld by the Court of Appeal. As Chadwick L.J. pointed out in paras 88–89 of his judgment there are two distinct limbs to s.5 of the Partnership Act 1890. The inquiry under the first limb is whether the act of one partner, A, is done for the purpose of the business of the partnership. If it is, then, in doing that act, A is the agent of the firm acting with implied authority, and the other partners are bound by what he has done. If it is not an act done for the purpose of the business of the partnership, then the second limb of s.5 comes into play and the inquiry then becomes whether A's act is an "act for carrying on in the usual way business of the kind carried on by the firm". If it is, the person with whom A is dealing is entitled to treat the act as done for the purpose of the business of the partnership unless he knows that A has in fact no authority, or does not know or believe A to be a partner. In effect, A has ostensible authority to bind the firm in relation to acts which appear to be for the purpose of the business of the partnership because they are acts which could be done in the carrying on in the usual way of business of the kind carried on by the firm.

The firm had submitted that a partner in a professional partnership does not have implied or ostensible authority to give a guarantee on behalf of the partnership, relying upon a number of 19th century authorities.[3] In the Court of Appeal, Munby J. said that he entirely agreed with the views expressed by Staughton L.J. in *United Bank of Kuwait Ltd v Hammoud*

---

3 *Duncan v Lowndes* (1813) 3 Camp. 478; *Sandilands v Marsh* (1819) 2 B & Ald 673; *Hasleham v Young* (1844) 5 Q.B. 833; and *Brettel v Williams* (1849) 4 Exch. 623. In *Ex p. Gardom* (1808) 15 Ves. Jun. 286, an argument that one partner had no implied authority to bind the partnership to a guarantee was abandoned and Lord Eldon expressed the opinion that it had been rightly given up; however if that observation was intended to be of general application it was disapproved in *Brettel v Williams* and is contrary to the *ratio* in *Duncan v Lowndes*.

[1988] 1 W.L.R. 1051 at 1063 that elderly authorities as to what transactions were or were not within the ordinary authority of a professional should be approached with caution. However, as the judge had rightly decided, the present case was on all fours with *Sandilands v Marsh* (1819) 2 B. & Ald. 673. That case was still good law, proceeding as it did on the basis of the underlying rule, later enacted as the first limb of s.5 of the Partnership Act 1890, that a firm is bound by acts done by a partner for the purpose of partnership business. The guarantee given by Henry Butcher & Co was an integral part of the transaction with H. As the judge had said, "if the guarantee entered into by one partner is an integral part of a contract which the partnership has entered into, then that is sufficient to render it partnership business even if the full details of the guarantee were not known to every partner". Once a partnership has treated a particular transaction as part of its business then, whether or not that transaction is part of the regular business of the partnership, the partnership is bound not just by the transaction itself but by any other liabilities which are an integral part of it.

The Court of Appeal confirmed the general principle that one partner cannot bind the others in a matter which is unconnected with or outside the business of the partnership. It also said nothing to criticize the decision in *Brettel v Williams* (1849) 4 Exch. 623 in which a guarantee was held to have been outside a partner's authority to bind the firm. The case was distinguishable from *Sandilands v Marsh* because the guarantee, though given in relation to a transaction which the firm approved, was not an integral part of that transaction and was not necessarily contemplated by the transaction itself. In such a case today, the party seeking to enforce the guarantee would probably have to seek to rely upon the second limb of s.5 of the Partnership Act 1890. The decision in *Bank of Scotland v Butcher* gives welcome guidance in an area of the law in which there had been no previous modern authority. Nevertheless, a person seeking a guarantee from a partnership would still be well-advised to take the precaution of insisting that all the partners sign the memorandum.

Section 36 of the Companies Act 1985 provides that any contract which if made between private persons would by law be required to be in writing, signed by the parties to be charged therewith, made on behalf of the company must also be in writing and be signed by any person acting under its authority, express or implied. It may be varied or discharged in the same manner. So far as deeds are concerned, following the abolition (on July 31, 1990) of the requirement for a company in England or Wales to have a common seal, a document signed by a director and the secretary or by two directors and expressed (in whatever words) to be executed by the company will have the same effect as if executed under the common seal of the company.[4] If, despite this simpler alternative route, the deed is still

---

4 Section 36A of the Companies Act 1985 as brought into effect by s.130 of the Companies Act 1989. See also s.1(2) of the Law of Property (Miscellaneous Provisions) Act 1989.

executed under the common seal of the company, there are a number of formal requirements which have to be complied with under s.36A and s.350 of the Companies Act 1985. The seal must have the company's registered name engraved or embossed upon it in legible characters, and any requirements in the Articles of Association (for example, a requirement that the sealed document be signed by a director and the company secretary or by two directors) must also be followed. In *OTV Birwelco Ltd v Technical and General Guarantee Co Ltd* [2002] 4 All E.R. 668, (discussed in more detail in Chapter 2, at para.2–021 above) it was held that the failure by the *counterparty* to comply with these formal requirements did not render a surety bond a nullity or unenforceable. The reasoning in that case would seem to apply equally to a failure by the surety itself to comply with those requirements. Since it is likely that the deed to which a defective seal has been attached would also have been signed by two directors or one director and the company secretary anyway, the chances of such technical arguments having any practical effect on the enforcement of a guarantee under seal would appear to be remote.

In the normal course of events, the persons signing a contract of guarantee on behalf of a company will be one or more of its directors. Subject to the provisions of ss.108, 109 and 111 of the Companies Act 1989, a company will not be bound by a guarantee which is *ultra vires*.[5] In that event, the directors who signed the guarantee may be held personally liable for breach of warranty of authority.[6] The question of whether the directors of the company were entitled to bind the company by a guarantee given by them will depend on the facts of the particular case, and on the scope of their authority. A general power of management may suffice to give the directors implied authority, if the giving of a guarantee is fairly within the scope of the company's business.[7]

The signature of a document on behalf of a company by a director may result in his being held personally liable as a surety, either because the document is a sufficient memorandum of an oral agreement with him, or because as a matter of construction of the written agreement he has undertaken personal liability instead of, or as well as, the company.[8] Thus in *VSH Ltd v BKS Air Transport* [1964] 1 Lloyd's Rep. 460, a director who signed a contract on behalf of a company who alleged that he signed purely in his capacity as agent for the company, was held liable as a guarantor because the document which he signed was a sufficient memorandum of a

---

5 *Colman v Eastern Counties Railway Co* (1846) 10 Beav. 1; *Small v Smith* (1884) 10 App. Cas. 119; *Re Era Life Assurance Society* [1866] W.N. 309, and see generally Gore-Browne, *Companies* (Jordans, 44th ed., 1986), Ch.3 and see also Ch.6, p.48.

6 *Chapleo v Brunswick Building Society* [1881] 6 Q.B.D. 696.

7 Compare, *e.g. Re West of England Bank Ex p. Booker* (1880) 14 Ch. D. 317, and *Re Cunningham & Co Ltd, Simpson's Claim* (1887) 36 Ch. D. 532.

8 See, *e.g. Sun Alliance Pensions Life & Investments Services Ltd v RJL and Anthony Webster* [1991] 2 Lloyd's Rep. 410.

prior oral contract of guarantee which he had made, and the capacity in which he signed it was irrelevant.[9]

Consequently, a person who is asked to sign a guarantee or similar document on behalf of a company should take care to ensure that the wording precludes the possibility of his being held personally liable to the creditor.[10] The usual forms of signature indicating that the document is signed by a director or other person purely in the capacity of an officer of the company are as follows:

The X Company Ltd or	For and on behalf of the X Co Ltd
By: *John Jones*	*John Jones*
Managing Director	Managing Director

Of course, if the document which has been signed "for and on behalf of" a named company is in the form of a guarantee of the indebtedness of that very same company, the probabilities are that the person who signed it did intend to undertake a personal liability as guarantor. Otherwise the "guarantee" would be meaningless.[11]

Effect of non-compliance

3–027 Where the contract is one to which s.4 applies, and the requirements of the statute are not complied with, the contract will be unenforceable, but not void: *Maddison v Alderson* (1883) 8 App. Cas. 467. This is because the statute is merely an enactment as to evidence. As a result, an oral contract of guarantee which is valid by its proper law, being the law of another country, and prima facie enforceable in that other country, may nevertheless be unenforceable by action in England, because the Statute of Frauds is part of English procedural law.[12]

Money paid by the surety under a contract which is unenforceable by reason of s.4 cannot be recovered from the creditor: *Shaw v Woodcock* (1827) 7 B. & C. 73. A purely oral guarantee may also be raised by way of set-off as a defence to a related claim, but probably not as an independent counterclaim, since that would involve bringing an action on the guarantee: see *Lavery v Turley* (1860) 6 H. & N. 239; *Re A Debtor (No.517 of 1991) The Times*, November 25, 1991.

---

9 For an example of a situation in which two letters written by or on behalf of the company constituted sufficient memoranda of prior oral guarantees by two of its auditors see *Jay v Gainsford* (unreported) CAT No.362b of 1977, October 4.

10 See, *e.g. W & T Avery Ltd v Charlesworth* (1914) 31 T.L.R. 52; *Chapman v Smethurst* [1909] 1 K.B. 927; *Re Dover & Deal Railway Etc. Co, Lord Londesborough's Case* (1854) De G. M. & G. 411; *Dutton v Marsh* (1871) L.R. 6 Q.B. 361; *Alexander v Sizer* (1869) L.R. 4 Exch. 102.

11 See *Minories Finance Ltd v Attam* (unreported) CAT No.1094 of 1989, November 13, in which the guarantor was perhaps fortunate to obtain leave to defend on this point.

12 *Leroux v Brown* (1852) 12 C.B. 801, and see also *Compagnie Générale d'Industrie v Solori SA* (1984) 134 N.L.J. 788, in which Hirst J. held that a s.4 defence to a French guarantee was not made out.

If a surety wishes to take a point on the Statute of Frauds it must be raised expressly. Since non-compliance with s.4 does not extinguish a claim, an action may be commenced on an oral guarantee, and if the point is not taken by way of defence, the contract will be enforced. It is therefore permissible for the creditor to initiate bankruptcy proceedings by service of a statutory demand on the guarantor. A statement of claim which pleads an oral contract of guarantee is not susceptible to being struck out as disclosing no reasonable cause of action.[13] However, the defendant may succeed in an application under Rules 3 or 24 of the CPR if he makes it plain that he is going to plead s.4 of the Statute of Frauds and if it is clear that there is no scope for reasonable argument about the existence of a sufficient note or memorandum.

If the defendant admits or avers in his statement of case (or in an affidavit) that there was a contract, he will probably be taken to have admitted its enforceability unless he raises the defence of the Statute of Frauds simultaneously.[14] Indeed, the suggestion was made in *Spurrier v Fitzgerald* (1801) 6 Ves. Jun. 548, that the defence must be raised at exactly the same time as the contract is admitted in the pleading (that was a case in which the defendant sought to raise the point in trial). If this is correct, it leaves open the question whether a defendant is ever entitled to amend to take the point, having admitted the existence of the oral contract in his original defence. The tenor of the cases appears to be that he should not be allowed to do so. In *Steven's Textiles v Jackson* (unreported, December 31, 1980) there was a dispute as to whether the defendant had orally agreed to the name of a second company being added as a principal debtor to the plaintiff's standard form after he had signed it as guarantor. The dispute was resolved at trial in favour of the plaintiff, and the Court of Appeal refused the defendant leave to amend the defence to plead s.4 of the Statute of Frauds. If the defendant acts consistently with his admission of liability, by pleading tender and paying the money into court, clearly the Statute of Frauds will not preclude the plaintiff from recovery: *Middleton v Brewer* (1790) 1 Peake 20.

The potential impact of EU law

In a case concerning an oral contract of guarantee, in which the surety is   **3–028** domiciled in England and is prima facie required to be sued here by virtue of the provisions of the Brussels Convention on Jurisdiction and the Enforcement of Judgments (as enacted by the Civil Jurisdiction and Judgments Act 1982 and extended to the EFTA States by the Lugano Convention of September 1988, ratified by the UK on May 1 1992), a number of important questions arise. First, if England is one of a number

---

13 *Fraser v Pape* [1904] 91 T.L.R. 340; *Linkmel Construction Ltd v New Spiral Housing Association Ltd* (unreported) CAT No.205 of 1988, March 8.
14 *Lucas v Dixon* (1889) 22 Q.B.D. 357, *per* Bowen L.J. at 361, and the cases cited at 358. See also *Humphries v Humphries* [1910] 2 K.B. 531.

of potential fora under the Act and Conventions, and the creditor begins proceedings here without considering the effect of the Statute of Frauds and subsequently finds that the guarantee is prima facie unenforceable because of s.4, can he commence fresh proceedings in one of the other available fora instead? If so, in what circumstances (*e.g.* what happens if a relevant limitation period has expired in the only other available forum)?

Secondly, if England is the only available forum under the relevant Convention, would the provisions of EU law override s.4 to avoid the unjust result that a domestic procedural rule as to evidence in the only forum in which the creditor can bring suit would operate to deprive him of all remedy? Detailed consideration of these questions and others in similar vein is outside the scope of this work. However, it is extremely unlikely that the court would be prepared to apply the Statute of Frauds so as to achieve a result which is contrary to the basic objectives of the Judgments Convention or the underlying principles of EU law. Nevertheless, it may be that until these questions are resolved, it would be a safer course for any creditor under such a guarantee made with an English surety to bring his proceedings in another jurisdiction (if he can do so under the Conventions, when applicable) and then enforce his judgment in England.

Possible ways to circumvent s.4

Solicitors' undertakings

3–029   The court has the power to enforce a verbal undertaking given by a solicitor (by virtue of its summary jurisdiction over officers of the court): *Re Greaves* (1827) 1 Cr. & J. 374n. The same rule has been held to apply to a verbal guarantee given by a solicitor which would otherwise be unenforceable by virtue of s.4 of the Statute of Frauds: *Evans v Duncombe* (1831) 1 Cr. & J. 372; see also *Re A Solicitor* (1900) 45 S.J. 104. However it is questionable whether this power would be exercisable in respect of undertakings given by the solicitor other than in his professional capacity. There would appear to be no good reason why a guarantee or undertaking given by a solicitor in his private capacity should be treated differently from a guarantee or undertaking given by anyone else.

The doctrine of part-performance

3–030   A contract which is unenforceable because it lacks some requisite formality (*e.g.* a signature) may be enforced in equity if it has been partly carried into effect by one of the parties. Although the doctrine of part-performance may be used to assist those who rely on other types of contract falling within the Statute of Frauds or similar statutory provisions, such as contracts for the sale of land, it probably does not enable a creditor to enforce an oral guarantee. In *Maddison v Alderson* (1883) 8 App. Cas. 467 at 490, Lord Blackburn said that to hold otherwise would be to render the statute a nullity.[15] *Maddison v Alderson* was apparently not cited to Staughton J. in

---

15 This approach has been followed in Canada: see *Rink v March* [1921] 1 W.W.R. 919, but *cf. Huron County v Kerr* (1868) 15 Gr. 265.

Clipper Maritime Ltd v Shirlstar Container Transport Ltd ("The Anemone")
[1987] 1 Lloyd's Rep. 546, with the result that there was an inconclusive
discussion in the judgment (at 557). However the judge concluded, without
expressing an opinion on the difficult questions of law which he identified
as arising, that the facts of that case would not have sufficed to found an
argument based on part-performance. The principal difficulty is that the
creditor would have to prove that he did something which was unequivocally referable to the guarantee (as opposed to the underlying contract
with the principal) and that in consequence it would be inequitable for the
guarantor to rely on the statute.

Estoppel

In *Decouvreur v Jordan*,[16] the judge at first instance had held that the   **3–031**
purported guarantor was estopped from denying that he had signed the
relevant memorandum. This point did not arise for consideration on
appeal, but Nourse L.J. said "there is grave doubt whether an agreement
which cannot be enforced directly for lack of a sufficient note or memorandum can be indirectly enforced through the medium of an estoppel".[17] In
the same way as with part-performance, it is difficult to envisage a case of a
guarantee in which the facts would give rise to an estoppel arising out of
the behaviour of the guarantor, or representations made by him, without
subverting s.4 of the Statute of Frauds. The person who would claim to
have acted to his detriment would usually be the creditor, but he would
probably have done nothing more than advance money or supply goods or
services to the debtor as envisaged by the guarantee. That was the critical
problem facing the claimant in *Actionstrength Ltd v International Glass
Engineering Ltd* [2003] 2 A.C. 541, the facts of which are summarised in
para.3–002 above. A appealed to the House of Lords on the basis that it
had kept its labour force on site and continued to work on the project on
the faith of an assumption that it had a binding contract with the
"guarantor", SG, though there was no evidence that SG had done anything
to encourage that belief. The estoppel argument had been described by
Simon Brown L.J. in the Court of Appeal as "quite hopeless". Perhaps
unsurprisingly, the appeal was dismissed. Lord Bingham and Lord
Hoffmann both pointed out that it would be tantamount to repealing s.4 if
they were to allow the creditor to rely on credit advanced on the strength of
nothing more than an assumption that he had a valid guarantee, when the
"guarantor" had done nothing to foster that assumption.

However, despite these acknowledged difficulties, there are a number of
reported cases in which an estoppel has operated so as to relieve the
creditor from the consequences of s.4. For example, in *Humphries v
Humphries* [1910] 2 K.B. 531, a tenant had been sued by his landlord for
the arrears of rent due under a lease which did not comply with the

---

16 (Unreported) May 24, 1985, upheld on appeal on different grounds, CAT No.525 of May
   18, 1987 (*The Times*, May 25, 1987).
17 *ibid.*, at p.18 of the transcript.

requirements of s.4 of the Statute of Frauds. The tenant failed to raise any defence based on s.4, but chose instead to allege that there was no binding agreement. He lost that point, and judgment was given for the landlord. In a subsequent action brought to recover fresh arrears under the same lease, the Court of Appeal held that the tenant was estopped from raising the defence. The existence of a binding agreement had been proved in the earlier proceedings to the satisfaction of the court, and it would be unconscionable for the tenant to be allowed to rely on a statute concerned with evidence in order to defeat a legitimate claim under that proved contract. It is possible to regard this as a simple example of the operation of an issue estoppel, but the reasoning of the court suggests that they were applying the wider principle of estoppel in pais by virtue of the tenant's behaviour.

In *Kok Hoong v Leong Cheong Kweng* [1964] A.C. 993 at 1015, Viscount Radcliffe described the Statute of Frauds as belonging to a category which "though declaring transactions to be unenforceable or void, are nevertheless not essentially prohibitory and so do not preclude estoppels", citing *Humphries v Humphries* as an illustration. In the light of this analysis, there is probably no reason why, as a matter of principle, the doctrine of estoppel should not operate as an answer to a defence based on s.4, if the circumstances would otherwise warrant it, provided that it is not applied in such a way as to deprive s.4 of all effect. Accordingly, if the guarantor made numerous representations to the creditor that he would not rely on the statute and the creditor could prove that he acted on those representations to his detriment, the guarantor may be estopped from going back on his word. This was accepted by Lord Walker in the *Actionstrength* case. Lords Bingham, Woolf, Clyde and Walker also expressed the view that a representation by the surety that he had validly executed a guarantee when he knew that he had not (*e.g.* if he was aware that his signature had been forged) could give rise to an estoppel, provided that the representation was relied upon by the creditor to his detriment.

The relationship between the doctrine of estoppel by conduct and the Statute of Frauds and similar statutory provisions was considered by the High Court of Australia in the case of *Waltons Stores v Maher* (1987) 164 C.L.R. 387, which concerned an agreement for a six-year lease of land which had not been sufficiently evidenced in writing to satisfy the relevant statute. Although on the facts the doctrine of part-performance did not apply, the High Court held that the lessors were estopped in equity from denying that there was a valid and enforceable agreement. However, the members of the court did not adopt a unanimous approach in their explanation of why the doctrine of equitable estoppel enabled a party to circumvent a statutory provision couched in the same terms as s.4 of the Statute of Frauds. Three different reasons were given for the result:

(1) There was no action brought on any contract to which the statute applied. Thus Brennan J. said at 433: "the action to enforce an equity created by estoppel is not 'brought upon any contract', for the equity

arises out of the circumstances. This is not to say that there is an equity which precludes the application of the statute. It is to say the statute has no application to the equity."

(2) The estoppel precluded the lessors from denying a valid and enforceable contract, and therefore it also precluded them from taking a point based on non-compliance with the statute, because that went to the question of enforceability.

(3) The lessors were estopped from denying that the transaction had been completed by the exchange of contracts and this narrower estoppel involved the assumption that the agreement had been duly executed.

Although that decision could be of some assistance to a party who seeks to persuade a court that the doctrine of equitable estoppel may be an answer to a defence based on s.4 of the Statute of Frauds, it must be approached with some caution. The doctrine of estoppel has achieved a wider application in certain Commonwealth jurisdictions, including Australia, than it has in England to date. Thus Brennan J.'s reasoning is not easy to reconcile with the traditional English approach of treating estoppel as a shield rather than as a sword. It must also be noted that it was a case involving real estate, and a slightly more flexible approach to the enforcement of such contracts has always been adopted: for example, as stated earlier, the doctrine of part-performance may apply to contracts for the sale of land, but will not apply to guarantees. As the House of Lords has now confirmed in the *Actionstrength* case, the mere fact that the parties acted on the assumption that the guarantee was operative would not in itself give rise to any relevant estoppel, because this could probably be said in all such cases.

The related problem of whether the doctrine of estoppel by convention as expounded in *Amalgamated Investment and Property Co v Texas Commerce International Bank* [1982] Q.B. 84 and subsequent cases, can ever apply to a guarantee, and if so how this can be reconciled with s.4 of the Statute of Frauds, has been considered both in England and Australia. In *Coghlan v SH Lock* (1985) 4 N.S.W.L.R. 158 (reversed on different grounds (1987) 8 N.S.W.L.R. 88), it was held that as a matter of construction a guarantee did not cover a particular liability, but that the sureties and the creditors had always assumed that it did and had acted on that assumption. A majority of the New South Wales Court of Appeal held that the sureties had actively contributed to the creditor's mistaken assumption about the legal effects of the guarantee, and that an estoppel by convention therefore precluded them from relying on the Statute of Frauds. The estoppel point did not arise for consideration by the Privy Council because they reversed the decision of the lower courts on the construction point.

The identical point arose for determination in *Bank of Scotland v Wright* [1991] B.C.L.C. 244. The facts were very similar to those in *Coghlan v Lock*. A director of a holding company had guaranteed the indebtedness of that company to the plaintiff bank. The main issue between the parties (which was resolved in favour of the bank) was whether as a matter of construction the guarantee covered liabilities of the company as surety for the indebtedness to the bank of one of its subsidiaries. However, the bank argued in the alternative that both parties had treated the guarantee as extending to the liabilities of the subsidiary, even if as a matter of construction it did not, and that the guarantor was therefore estopped from relying on s.4 of the Statute of Frauds to the extent that the terms of the guarantee were not fully evidenced in writing.

After summarising the requirements for the doctrine of estoppel by convention to apply, Brooke J. held that on the facts of the particular case the behaviour of the guarantor could not be said to be unconscionable save to the extent that it might be said to be unconscionable in principle for any guarantor to seek the protection of the Statute of Frauds—a point which has not yet been decided, but which might be difficult to run in the face of the decision in *Actionstrength*. Although he expressed doubts as to whether a situation would ever arise in which the facts could give rise to an estoppel by convention without rendering s.4 of the Statute of Frauds nugatory, the judge expressly left the matter open, indicating that the point might be arguable in different circumstances, in the light of Viscount Radcliffe's observations in *Kok Hoong v Leong Cheong Kweng*.[18] In *Actionstrength*, Lord Bingham was the only member of the House of Lords to express any view on this point. He accepted that estoppel by convention could apply.

It would appear, therefore, that if the creditor is able to satisfy the fairly stringent requirements needed to raise an estoppel by convention on the facts of a particular case, the court might well be persuaded that the guarantor is precluded from raising a defence that the terms of the contract which the parties mutually assumed to be binding upon them were not evidenced in writing in accordance with s.4 of the Statute of Frauds. Indeed, it would be anomalous if a principal would be estopped in certain circumstances from denying that a contract had a particular construction, but a guarantor guilty of identical behaviour would not be estopped.

Rectification and enforcement

3–032 It has long been established in cases involving contracts other than guarantees which failed to comply with the requirements of s.4 of the Statute of Frauds, (or a re-enactment of that section), because of the mistaken omission of a material term about which there was no dispute, that an action for rectification of the contract can be brought, and that this may be coupled with a claim for enforcement of the rectified contract without offending the Statute. In *United States of America v Motor Trucks Ltd* [1924] A.C. 196, certain land which was part of the property to be transferred under a contract of sale was mistakenly omitted from the schedule to the contract. The Privy Council upheld a decision by the judge to rectify the agreement. Lord Birkenhead said, at 200–201:

---

18 See also *Credit Suisse v Borough Council of Allerdale* [1995] 1 Lloyd's Rep. 315 at 371–372, affirmed without comment on this point [1997] Q.B. 306.

". . . the plaintiff must show first that there was an actually concluded agreement antecedent to the instrument which is sought to be rectified; and secondly, that such agreement has been inaccurately represented in the instrument. When this is proved either party may claim, in spite of the Statute of Frauds, that the instrument on which the other insists does not represent the real agreement. The statute, in fact, only provides that no agreement not in writing and not duly signed shall be sued on; but when that written instrument is rectified there is a writing which satisfies the statute, the jurisdiction of the Court to rectify being outside the prohibition of the statute . . .

. . . There seems no reason in principle why a Court of equity should not at one and the same time reform and enforce a contract . . . since the Judicature Act the Court can entertain an action in which combined relief will be given simultaneously for the reformation of a contract, and for the specific performance of the reformed contract."[19]

In the recent case of *GMAC Commercial Credit Development Ltd v Kalvinder Singh Sandhu* [2004] EWHC 716 (Comm) Mr Richard Siberry Q.C., sitting as a deputy High Court judge, followed that reasoning and rejected an argument by the defendants that, as a matter of principle, to permit rectification to create a valid and effective guarantee where none otherwise existed would breach the requirements of s.4 of the Statute of Frauds. On that occasion, however, the court only had to decide whether there was a sufficiently arguable case for rectification. It remains to be seen, therefore, in what circumstances an English court would accede to an application to rectify and enforce a written contract of guarantee which omits a material term, in the face of a pleaded defence relying on s.4 of the Statute of Frauds. It has already been seen that Lord Blackburn in *Maddison v Alderson* (1883) 8 App. Cas. 467 expressed the view at 490 that the doctrine of part-performance, used in land cases to ameliorate the effect of the Statute of Frauds where there has been a change in the possession of the land, is not applicable in this context. Therefore one cannot be too complacent about drawing analogies with remedies used in sale of land cases. Yet in the very same passage in *Maddison v Alderson* Lord Blackburn appears to recognise that it would be strange to apply an equitable principle to one of the cases in the same section of the statute and not to all of the others. This approach found favour with the judge in the *GMAC* case, who expressed the view that there was no reason in principle for distinguishing, in this context, between contracts for the sale of land and contracts of guarantee.

In *Imperial Bank of Canada v Nixon* [1926] 4 D.L.R. 1052, referred to in para.3–023 above, the Ontario Supreme Court (Appellate Division) specifically left open the question of what would have happened if a claim for

---

19 Affirming and approving the decision of the Court of Appeal in *Craddock Brothers v Hunt* [1923] 2 Ch. 136. See also *Samson v Butt* [1927] N.Z.L.R. 119.

rectification had been brought, but did so in terms which suggested that such a claim might have succeeded.[20] In a later Canadian case, *Shaffer v O'Neill* (1943) 2 W.W.R. 641, the District Court of Saskatchewan allowed rectification of a guarantee so as to supply a missing name. However, in *Barclays Bank v Caldwell* (unreported, July 25, 1986),[21] Harman J. refused the bank's application for leave to amend to seek rectification for the guarantee by introducing the terms of the side letter into it, though an important factor in his decision was the timing of the application—it was made after judgment had been delivered.

In *Eason v Brownrigg* (unreported, Ch. D., H.H. Judge Weeks Q.C. April 3, 1998) the court granted rectification of a lease to include a covenant by the directors of the tenant company to give personal guarantees, which had been deleted from the landlord's standard form by mistake. The evidence in support of the claim for rectification was strong—the directors had agreed in principle to give guarantees, and there had been discussion between the parties about the possibility of reducing the number of guarantors to two, which the landlord had refused to do. The judge held (distinguishing *Racal Group Services Ltd v Ashmore* [1995] S.T.C. 1151) that if a draft had been submitted with the covenant in it, it would have been signed. It does not appear, however, that any point was raised on the Statute of Frauds. If the principle of rectification can be used to create a written guarantee, where none existed before, as part of a wider contract (such as a lease or a mortgage) it must follow that rectification is available to cure a mistake in the text of the guarantee itself.

Although there may be no reason in principle why the doctrine of rectification should not be used to make good omissions in a written guarantee in the same way as in any other type of contract, it may be that in practice the prerequisites for the remedy are difficult to establish in this particular context, where particular care is likely to be taken to avoid depriving a defendant of a legitimate statutory defence.[22] It is rarely the case that the written guarantee is merely a reflection of a pre-existing agreement which has been concluded orally; on the contrary, it is generally the intention of the parties that there should be no binding agreement until the guarantee is signed.

In such cases, is there any means of achieving rectification? How, for example, does one establish evidence of common mistake? One ingenious solution was devised (with success) in New Zealand in the case of *Whiting v Diver Plumbing & Heating Ltd* [1992] 1 N.Z.L.R. 560. That was a case in which, once again, the name of the principal debtor had been omitted from the signed guarantee. The creditor initially brought proceedings for sum-

---

20 Riddell J.A. said, at 1054: "this is not a case in which the plaintiff sets up a mistake in reducing the contract to writing or appeals to the equitable doctrine that equity looks to that as done which ought to have been done. Had this been the case, it is possible other considerations would arise. . . ".

21 Referred to in para.3–022 above.

22 Rectification would have been no answer in *State Bank of India v Kaur* [1996] 5 Bank. L.R. 158, since there was dispute as to the identity of the proposed principal.

mary judgment, but the guarantor's defence affidavit sought to rely upon the provisions of the Contracts Enforcement Act 1956 (the New Zealand re-enactment of s.4 of the Statute of Frauds). The plaintiff thereupon abandoned its summary judgment application and amended its statement of claim to include a claim for rectification. The plaintiff then sought leave to serve interrogatories on the guarantor, including the following question:

"At the time you executed the form of guarantee, did you intend and believe it to be an effective guarantee of payment to the Plaintiff [Diver Plumbing] for work undertaken by the Plaintiff for Construction Development Ltd in the six month period [following] execution of the guarantee?"

The guarantor objected to the interrogatory, on the grounds that answering it would create the very memorandum which was lacking, and thus deprive him of a legitimate defence to the claim. He relied on *Imperial Bank of Canada v Nixon* and on two other cases, *Simon v Gardiner* [1942] G.L.R. 338, a decision of the High Court of New Zealand, and *Lovell v Lovell* [1970] 3 All E.R. 721, a decision of the English Court of Appeal. In *Simon v Gardiner* Fair J. disallowed an interrogatory in the context of an action for specific performance of a purely oral contract for the sale of land, on the grounds that it would deprive the defendant of his pleaded defence based on the Statute of Frauds. In *Lovell v Lovell* an interrogatory was disallowed because the answer would have created a written acknowledgment of indebtedness so as to start time running afresh for limitation purposes and to defeat a plea of time bar. However, in that case Salmon L.J. drew a distinction between getting an answer which would be evidence of a prior acknowledgment, and one which would itself constitute such an acknowledgment. That distinction commended itself to Tipping J. in *Whiting v Diver Plumbing and Heating*. He held that there was a difference between administering an interrogatory which would create a memorandum where there was no writing at all, and administering one was designed to assist a party to rectify an agreement where, by mistake, only part of that agreement had been reduced to writing. He said (at 568) that in his judgment interrogatories of this kind should be allowed in aid of a bona fide rectification suit and went on to explain what he meant by this:

"For there to be a bona fide claim to rectification in the present context it seems to me that there must at least be an instrument which has been signed or otherwise authenticated by or on behalf of the defendant ... an interrogatory should not be allowed in aid of a rectification suit if its effect would be to require the defendant to create against himself some writing where no such writing existed before. In any such case it is unlikely that there would be an instrument capable of rectification in any event."

Since in that case the guarantor had signed a guarantee, and the interrogatory was designed to elicit relevant evidence from him as to whose name was intended to be inserted in the blank as the name of the debtor, the interrogatory was permissible. Tipping J. went on to say that this was not a case of driving a horse and cart through the provisions of the Statute, but rather an example of equity relieving against the rigours of the Statute in an appropriate case. It is clear from his judgment, however, that he was of the view that it would be no bad thing if a horse and cart *were* to be driven through the Statute: judicial opinion in this country is not, as yet, so markedly robust.

Indorsers of bills of exchange

3–033   In *Grunzweig und Hartmann Montage v Irvani* [1988] 1 W.L.R. 1285, affirmed [1990] 1 W.L.R. 667, the claim was made against the defendant on the basis that he had become surety for the obligations of the drawees of certain bills of exchange by signing his name on the drafts and authorising the addition of the words *"bon pour aval pour les tirés"* to his signature. One of the defences raised was that the obligations of the defendant could only be categorised as those of a guarantor of the bills of exchange and that s.4 of the Statute of Frauds was not satisfied. Saville J. and the Court of Appeal held that if the statute applied, its requirements were satisfied, but that under the present state of the authorities the Statute of Frauds had no application to liabilities arising under bills of exchange.

First, it was held that under the applicable proper law of the contract, the obligations of the defendant arose out of his being a party to the bill of exchange rather than under a separate contract of guarantee. Although the agreement could be described in one sense as a contract of guarantee, the Statute of Frauds is no answer to a claim under a bill. The decision of Goddard J. in *McCall Brothers v Hargreaves* [1932] 2 K.B. 423 was followed and approved.[23] Secondly, Saville J. held that, on the evidence, the obligations of the defendant were not co-extensive with those of the principal debtor and therefore as a matter of construction his promise was not a promise "to answer for the debt default or miscarriage of another person". This particular point was not considered by the Court of Appeal.

Other statutory requirements

Consumer protection legislation

3–034   Where the contract is one which is regulated by the Consumer Credit Act, certain formalities have to be observed by the creditor, and if he fails to do so, he may be precluded from enforcing the contract against the surety. A detailed consideration of the Consumer Credit Act in the context of guarantees and indemnities is to be found in Chapter 17.

A similar piece of consumer protection legislation is E.C. Council Directive 85/577 which applies to certain contracts negotiated away from

---

23 See further Lord Blackburn in *Steele v McKinlay* (1880) 5 App. Cas. 754, at 769–770, *Macdonald v Nash* [1924] A.C. 625 and *Wilkinson v Unwin* (1881) 7 Q.B.D. 636.

business premises, under which a trader supplies goods or services to a consumer. The mischief against which the legislation is aimed is "doorstep selling", which may pressurise the consumer into making a contract which he later regrets. Like the Consumer Credit Act, it provides for a "cooling off" period during which the consumer may cancel the contract on notice to the trader, who is required to inform the consumer of his rights under the Directive.

In *Bayerische Hypothetiken-und-Wechselsbank AG v Dietzinger* (Case 45/96) [1998] 1 W.L.R. 1035, the European Court of Justice considered the extent to which the Directive applied to guarantees. The defendant entered into a guarantee of his father's overdraft with a bank. The father ran a building firm. The guarantee was signed at his father's home, during a visit there by an employee of the bank. The defendant argued that he had not been told of his right under Directive 85/577 to cancel the contract of guarantee, and that therefore it was unenforceable against him. The Court held that the contract of guarantee fell outside the terms of the Directive, but *not* on the basis that the goods or services were being supplied to a third party under a different contract, rather than to the "consumer" himself. Instead, it held that the Directive did not apply to a contract concluded by a natural person not acting in the course of a trade or profession which guaranteed the repayment of a debt contracted by a third party who *was* acting in the course of a trade or profession. This left open the prospect that a guarantee of an underlying obligation which is not entered into by the principal in the course of a trade or profession (such as a domestic loan) might be held to fall within the terms of the Directive in the future. However, the chances of this happening now seem slender, in the light of a more recent ruling by the European Court of Justice on Council Directive 87/102, the European Consumer Credit Directive, which is aimed at the harmonisation of consumer protection legislation within the European Community. The case, *Berliner Kindl Brauerei v Siepert* (Case 208/98) [2000] 3 E.C.R. 1741 concerned a guarantee provided by S to a German brewery as security for a loan made by the brewery to D to enable D to open a restaurant. S was not told that he had any period of "cooling off", but within the year allowed by German domestic legislation for consumers to change their minds, he told the brewery that he no longer wished to guarantee the loan to D, and purported to withdraw his consent. The brewery called in the loan and sued S under the guarantee. The German court sought a ruling from the European Court on whether Directive 87/102 applied to a guarantee by a "consumer", (that is, someone not acting in the course of a trade or profession) to secure the repayment of credit granted to a third party, also not acting in the course of a trade or profession, by a commercial establishment. The European Court ruled that the Directive did not apply, indeed, that on its true construction guarantees had been deliberately excluded from its ambit. The Directive was almost entirely concerned with information to be given to the principal debtor, and with the protection to be afforded to him. As the Advocate General pointed out in his opinion, the risks of a guarantor are mainly of a different nature to those which affect the principal who undertakes the primary liability, (for example, the risk that the principal will default or become insolvent) and the extension of the Directive contended for would not protect guarantors against those risks.

The Unfair Contract Terms Act 1977

3–035 Guarantees and indemnities frequently contain terms which purport to exclude the creditor from liability for negligent acts, omissions or misrepresentations on his part, and perhaps less often may contain terms excluding the creditor from liability for breaches of the contract. Provided that the creditor's rights and obligations arise in the course of a business, which is normally the case, and the contract is governed by English law, then the provisions of s.2(2) of the Unfair Contract Terms Act will prevent him from restricting or excluding his liability for negligence unless the term satisfies the requirement of reasonableness set out in s.11.

Similarly, if the surety deals as a consumer, or on the creditor's written standard terms of business, s.3 will apply the reasonableness test to terms which purport to exclude the creditor from liability for breach of contract. Since the surety will be dealing as a consumer in all cases in which he makes the contract other than in the course of a business, and the creditor makes the contract in the course of a business, these provisions could prove to be important in some cases. However, the safeguards contained in the Act should not be regarded as a reason for any potential surety not to read all the small print of a standard form bank guarantee or any other such document and to avail himself of the opportunity of seeking legal advice before he agrees to sign it.

The Unfair Terms in Consumer Contracts Regulations 1999

3–036 These regulations, (SI 1999/2083), which came into force on October 1, 1999 replace the 1994 regulations, (SI 1994/3159), implementing the EU Council Directive 93/13 of April 5, 1993.[24] The regulations supplement and to a certain extent supersede the protection in the 1977 Act, but unlike that statute, they do not extend to any contracts in which the party other than the seller or supplier is not a consumer, nor do they relate to non-contractual notices. Nevertheless the effect of the regulations on those contracts to which they apply is much wider than the protection afforded by the Act. Unlike the 1977 Act, the regulations will apply to any relevant contract which contains a choice of law clause which applies or purports to apply the law of a non-Member State, if the contract has a close connection with the territory of the Member States.[25] Accordingly the supplier or seller

---

24 The Directive should have been implemented by all Member States by December 31, 1994. The failure by the UK government to implement it by that date may give rise to an action in damages by consumers against the government if they are unable to invoke its provisions against a supplier or seller which is a private company or individual in respect of contracts made between December 31, 1994 and July 1, 1995.

25 Reg.7.

cannot evade the application of the regulations by inserting in a contract which otherwise has close connections with England, a choice of law clause in favour of Australia or one of the Channel Islands (and that is so even if the choice of law clause might be objectively justifiable on the grounds of equally strong connections with the chosen country).

Subject to the exceptions contained in Sch.1, the regulations apply to any term in a contract concluded between a seller or supplier (in either case acting for purposes relating to his trade, business or profession when he makes the contract) and a consumer, where the term has not been individually negotiated.[26] It is a moot point to what extent the regulations will be held to apply to banks at all. Third-party guarantees are not themselves contracts of sale, or for the supply of services, and the Directive was intended to harmonise the laws of Member States relating to the terms of such contracts as between the seller of goods or supplier of services on the one hand, and the consumer of them, on the other. However, at least in theory the bank is supplying banking services to the principal debtor at the request of the guarantor. It remains to be seen whether the regulations will be interpreted widely so as to cover ancillary contracts directly relating to the performance of contracts for the supply of banking services.

The jurisdiction is still in its infancy, but even before the 1999 regulations were adopted the signs were that a fairly wide construction was likely to be adopted domestically. For example, in *Camden LBC v McBride* (unreported, November 11, 1998, H.H. Judge Tibber) a local authority acting as landlord was trying to obtain a possession order against a secured tenant. It sought to rely on a term in the lease which provided that the landlord was entitled to possession if, in the landlord's opinion, the behaviour of the tenant constituted a nuisance or annoyance to other people. The Judge held that the landlord was a "supplier" within the meaning of the 1994 Regulations, and the term enabling it to be the sole judge of whether the circumstances amounted to a nuisance was struck down as unfair.

If the regulations are applied to bank guarantees, it will be seen that there is considerable scope for an interventionist judiciary to redress the balance between creditor and surety significantly.

The burden of proving that the term has been individually negotiated rests on the supplier or seller. A term will always be regarded as not having been individually negotiated where it has been drafted in advance and the consumer has not been able to influence its substance. Even if a term, or particular aspects of it, has been individually negotiated, the contract may still be subject to the regulations if an overall assessment of it indicates that it is a pre-formulated standard contract—reg.5(3).

Whereas the 1977 Act is concerned with clauses which exempt or exclude liability of the party who is not a consumer, the Directive and regulations

---

26 A consumer is defined as a natural person, who in making the relevant contract is acting for purposes outside his business. The regulations therefore do not apply to corporate sureties or to professional sureties. Likewise, a personal guarantee given by a company director for the supply of goods to the company would fall outside the scope of the regulations.

seek to invalidate terms of any kind which are too one-sided in favour of the seller or supplier. If a term in a relevant contract is "unfair" within the test in reg.5, it will not be binding upon the consumer, although the contract will continue to bind both parties if it is possible for it to exist without that term. Regulation 7 imposes a requirement on the seller or supplier to ensure that any written term of a contract is expressed in plain intelligible language. If there is any doubt about its meaning, the interpretation most favourable to the consumer will prevail.

The test of unfairness

3-037   Regulation 5 provides that an "unfair term" means any term which, contrary to the requirement of good faith, causes a significant imbalance in the parties' rights and obligations under the contract to the detriment of the consumer. The assessment of fairness or unfairness must take into account the nature of the goods or services and all other circumstances attending the conclusion of the contract, and all the other terms of that contract or of any other contract upon which it depends: reg.6(1). In the context of suretyship, this means that the terms of the principal contract may be scrutinised as well as the terms of the guarantee, and the circumstances in which the guarantor came to sign the guarantee will also be of material significance. However if the terms concerned are in plain intelligible language the assessment shall not relate to the definition of the main subject matter of the contract or the adequacy of the price or remuneration as against the goods or services supplied. Thus a clause which identifies the contract as an indemnity rather than a guarantee is unlikely to infringe the regulations if it is written in plain English.

Although it is difficult to predict with any certainty all the types of clause in a contract of suretyship which might be regarded as causing a "significant imbalance" in the rights and obligations of the parties, some assistance may be gained from the list in Sch.2 of the types of terms which may be regarded as "unfair". These include a term which has the object or effect of inappropriately excluding or limiting the legal rights of the consumer against the seller or supplier or any third party in the event of total or partial non-performance or inadequate performance of any of the contractual obligations, including the option of offsetting a debt owed to the seller or supplier against any claim which the consumer may have against him. It is common for a guarantee to contain a term which provides that the guarantor will pay the money on demand "without set-off or counterclaim". Whilst such clauses have been enforced, see, *e.g. The "Fedora"* [1986] 2 Lloyd's Rep. 441, a clause of this type has been struck down as prima facie unreasonable under the 1977 Act: *Stewart Gill Ltd v Horatio Myer & Co Ltd* [1992] Q.B. 600, and there are clear indications in the regulations that such a clause in a guarantee given by a consumer would not be regarded as fair.[27]

---

27 Other express examples appearing in the list are penalty clauses and terms which irrevocably bind the consumer to terms with which he had no real opportunity of becoming acquainted before the conclusion of the contract.

On the other hand, before the Regulations, a provision in a refinancing agreement for interest to be paid at the rate of 42 per cent per annum was held to be neither unfair nor an extortionate credit bargain under the Consumer Credit Act: *Petrou v Woodstead Finance* [1986] F.L.R. 158. The reason appears to have been that the refinancing was in circumstances of last resort, when an order for possession had already been made over the defendant's property, and thus it was only to be expected that any fresh loan would be subject to terms of this kind. Other provisions which are obviously vulnerable include provisions which purport to exclude the rights of the guarantor to share in any security held by the creditor until all of the debtor's obligations have been discharged in full, or which prevent the guarantor from competing with the creditor or enforcing any rights which he may have against the debtor once he has paid all or part of the sums due under the guarantee. However, there are other terms which are less obviously "unfair" which may nevertheless be susceptible to attack, for example, the commonplace clause which denies the surety the right to claim discharge when the creditor grants time to the principal debtor or varies the principal contract without the guarantor's consent. Recently an exclusive jurisdiction clause has been held by the European Court to fall foul of Directive 93/113: *Oceano Grupo Editorial SA v Quintero*, Cases 240/98 to 244/98, June 27, 2000. The Court held that national courts should exercise a power of their own motion to decline jurisdiction conferred upon them by such a clause when it was imposed unfairly on a consumer.[28]

Consequently, the introduction of these regulations is likely to have a radical impact not only upon the terms of standard forms of guarantee or indemnity but also upon the behaviour of the parties before the contract is made. In particular, creditors may consider that it is a wise precaution to ensure that the guarantee is provided to the consumer surety well in advance of the proposed date of signature, together with the underlying contract, and that they should insist, so far as is possible, that he takes legal advice before he signs it. It remains to be seen how far the approach of the courts in the application of the regulations will go to redress the balance of bargaining power in this context.

The Stamp Acts

Section 14(4) of the Stamp Act 1891 provided that an instrument of guarantee executed in the United Kingdom or relating to any property or matter situate or done or to be done there is not, save in criminal proceedings, available for any purpose whatever, and cannot be given in evidence unless stamped according to the law in force at the time of its execution.[29] However, this provision is highly unlikely to have any material **3–038**

---

28 The list in Sch.3 includes a term "enabling the seller or supplier to alter the terms of the contract unilaterally without a valid reason which is specified in the contract".
29 This provision was similar in effect to s.4 of the Statute of Frauds and probably reversed the effect of the earlier decision in *Haigh v Brooks* (1839) 10 Ad. & El. 309, on appeal (1840) 10 Ad. & El. 323, that an unstamped guarantee could be produced in evidence.

bearing on a modern action to enforce a guarantee, since the requirements for stamp duty to be paid have now all been abolished. The requirement that stamp duty should be paid on the memorandum of a guarantee neither under seal nor given for periodical payments was repealed in 1970.[30] *Ad valorem* duty was abolished by the Finance Act 1971, s.64, and the only surviving fixed duty of 50p on all documents executed under seal (including guarantees) was abolished by the Finance Act 1985, s.85(1) and Schs 24 and 27.

---

30 Finance Act 1970, s.32(a), Sch.7, para.1(2)(a).

Chapter 4

Construction

Introduction

There are many different varieties of guarantee or indemnity, some of **4–001** which have already been referred to in Chapter 1. It is therefore important that anyone advising a creditor seeking this form of security, or advising a potential surety, should be aware of these varieties so that the type which is most suited to the needs of the particular case, or which affords his client the best protection, can be selected. Likewise, a lawyer who is asked to give advice on the rights and obligations of the parties to a contract of suretyship which has already been executed, will be concerned with determining the proper construction to be placed on its terms. This chapter considers the general principles of construction applicable to all types of guarantee or indemnity, and then examines various different forms of contract and their effect.

It is appropriate to begin with a word of caution. Previous case law may give a very helpful indication of the approach which the court may take to a particular form of contract or the interpretation which may be given to certain words or phrases, but one must never lose sight of the fact that ultimately what has to be determined is the intention of the parties to the contract in question. Thus factors such as the context in which a phrase occurs, the wording of other parts of the contract and the factual matrix, may result in identical or similar wordings being given completely different interpretations in two different guarantees. This is particularly apparent when one looks at the reported decisions on specific or continuing guarantees. Accordingly, anyone engaged in the task of construing such a contract should take care to treat the case law as a useful source of guidance rather than as providing a conclusive determination of the meaning of that particular agreement.

Principles of construction

General approach

Contracts of guarantee
There is a substantial body of authority which indicates that contracts **4–002** of suretyship are to be construed in the same way as any other

contract.[1] However, there are also numerous cases at the highest level which support a rule that contracts of this kind must be strictly construed so that no liability is imposed on the surety which is not clearly and distinctly covered by the terms of the agreement. Thus in *Blest v Brown* (1862) 4 De G. F. & J. 367 at 376, Lord Campbell stated:

> "It must always be recollected in what manner a surety is bound. You bind him to the letter of his engagement. Beyond the proper inter-pretation of that engagement you have no hold upon him. He receives no benefit and no consideration. He is bound, therefore, according to the proper meaning and effect of the written agreement he has entered into."[2]

Indeed, there are many judicial dicta which go so far as to suggest that guarantees are to be construed in favour of the surety: see for example, the observations of Bayley B. in *Nicholson v Paget* (1832) 1 C. & M. 48 at 52, Donaldson J. in *General Surety & Guarantee Co v Francis Parker Ltd* (1977) 6 B.L.R. 16, at 21, and Lord Oliver in *Coghlan v SH Lock (Australia) Ltd* (1987) 8 N.S.W.L.R. 88. However this is probably not an independent rule of construction, but merely a reflection of the effect usually produced by the strict construction approach coupled with the application of the *contra proferentem* rule in cases of ambiguity. The usual result of the application of that rule is that the construction which is more favourable to the surety will be adopted, because in most cases, the terms of the contract will have been drafted by the creditor.[3] However, the *contra proferentem* rule will not be used to impose an interpretation on a contract which was clearly not intended: *Tam Wing Chuen v Bank of Credit and Commerce Hong Kong Ltd* [1996] 2 B.C.L.C. 69; *Egan v Static Control Components (Europe) Ltd* [2004] 2 Lloyd's Rep. 429, discussed below. It remains to be seen whether, in a case of ambiguity, the court would still construe the contract in a manner more favourable to the surety if he, rather than the creditor, was respon-sible for drawing up the terms of the contract, or whether the *contra*

---

1 *Wood v Priestner* (1866) L.R. 2 Exch. 66; *Mayer v Isaac* (1840) 6 M. & W. 605; *Eshelby v Federated European Bank* [1932] 1 K.B. 254 at 266 affirmed [1932] 1 K.B. 423). See also *Reid Murray Holdings Ltd (in liq.) v David Murray Holdings Pty Ltd* (1972) 5 S.A.S.R. 386 at 406 and the other Australian cases referred to by O'Donovan & Phillips, *The Modern Contract of Guarantee* (Law Book Company (Australia), 3rd ed. 1996), p.217, n.5.

2 See also *Straton v Rastall* (1788) 2 Term Rep. 366; *Wheatley v Bastow* (1855) 7 De G. M. & G. 261 at 279; *Bacon v Chesney* (1816) 1 Stark. 192; *Stamford, Spalding & Boston Banking Co v Ball* (1862) 4 De G. F. & J. 310, *Eshelby v Federated European Bank Ltd* [1932] 1 K.B. 254, affirmed [1932] 1 K.B. 423; *Eastern Counties Building Society v Russell* [1947] 1 All E.R. 500 at 503; *Jones v Mason* (1892) 13 N.S.W.L.R. 157 (Aus).

3 See, *e.g. Eastern Counties Building Society v Russell* [1947] 2 All E.R. 734 at 736 and 739; *Barclays Bank v Thienel* (1980) 247 E.G. 385; *National Bank of New Zealand v West* [1977] 1 N.Z.L.R. 29 at 34 (reversed on the facts [1978] 2 N.Z.L.R. 451); *Coghlan v SH Lock (Australia) Ltd* (1987) 8 N.S.W.L.R. 88 *per* Lord Oliver at 92, *Ankhar Pty Ltd v National Westminster Finance (Aust) Ltd* (1987) 162 C.L.R. 549; *Re a Debtor (No.1594, of 1992), The Times*, December 8, 1992 Knox J. If the surety is a consumer, see the Unfair Terms in Consumer Contracts Regulations 1999, discussed in Ch.3, above.

proferentem rule would operate in such a case for the benefit of the creditor.[4]

As with any other contract, the court will always try to construe the language of the guarantee so as to give a fair effect to the intention of the parties, to the extent that the language used enables it to do so. Thus in *Coghlan v Lock* (above), Lord Oliver, having referred to the principles that guarantees were to be construed strictly, to be read *contra proferentem* and in case of ambiguity to be construed in favour of the surety, as if they were well-established and independent principles of construction of guarantees, continued:

> "these principles do not, of course, mean that where parties to such a document have deliberately chosen to adopt wording of the widest possible import, that wording is to be ignored. Nor do they oust the principle that where wording is susceptible of more than one meaning regard may be had to the circumstances surrounding the execution of the document as an aid to construction."

Accordingly, the court is entitled to look at the surrounding circumstances in order to identify the scope and object of the contract of suretyship, to the same extent that it would be entitled to look at the factual matrix as an aid to the construction of any other commercial agreement.[5] This point was emphasised by the Court of Appeal in the recent case of *Egan v Static Control Components (Europe) Ltd* [2004] EWCA Civ 392, an example of a situation in which a strict or literal construction of the guarantee plainly would have produced a result which was the opposite of what the contracting parties really intended.

E had signed a guarantee of payment to the claimants, S, of certain of the trade debts of a company, T, of which he was a director. The guarantee was in identical terms to a standard precedent for a continuing guarantee of future debts found in the *Encyclopedia of Forms and Precedents*, Vol. 17(2), and provided, so far as is material, that

> "In consideration of your having agreed at my request to supply TBS.. ("the Trader") with goods for his business, supply of component parts ("Trade Goods")
> Now I, Paul Egan . . . agree that

---

4 This approach was favoured by Parker L.J. in *Mercers of City of London v New Hampshire Insurance Co* [1992] 2 Lloyd's Rep. 365 at 368 col. 2, and see the comments of Kirby P. in *Tricontinental Corp Ltd v HDFI Ltd* (1990) 21 NSWLR 689 at 694–695.
5 See, *e.g. Heffield v Meadows* (1869) L.R. 4 C.P. 595 *per* Willes J. at 599; *Hoad v Grace* (1861) 7 H. & N. 494; *Leathley v Spyer* (1870) L.R. 5 C.P. 595; *Nottingham, etc. Hide Co Ltd v Bottrill* (1873) L.R. 8 C.P. 694; *Hyundai Shipbuilding & Heavy Industries Co Ltd v Pournaras* [1978] 2 Lloyd's Rep. 502 at 506; *The "Kalma"* [1999] 2 Lloyd's Rep. 374 at 378 col 1. See also *Bridgestone Australia Ltd v GAH Engineering Pty Ltd* (1997) 2 Qd.R. 145 at 158, the other Australian and New Zealand authorities referred to by O'Donovan & Phillips (*op. cit.*) at p.217, n.2, and the discussion below at para.4.006.

1. I shall be responsible to you for the price of all trade goods that you may supply to the trader but so that my liability to you shall be in respect of the whole debt but shall in no event exceed the sum of £150,000

2. This guarantee is a continuing guarantee and security. . . ."

The guarantee contained no time limit, but provided that E had the right to revoke it at any time by notice, as to all dealing after the date of such notice. E had previously signed an identical guarantee with a lower limit of £75,000, but this was released when the relevant guarantee was signed. At that time, T was indebted to the claimants in a sum in excess of £140,000 for goods already supplied to it by S. S was concerned as to the company's ability to make payment of that indebtedness. There was a meeting between S's representatives and T's audit manager, Mr Jones, at which it was made clear to the latter that S required an increase in E's personal guarantee from £75,000 to £150,000. It was agreed at that meeting that further stock would be supplied by S to T, but subject to a limit of £12,000 per week; that the period of credit afforded to T would be reduced; and that there would be a schedule of payments so as to reduce the overall level of credit and debt. On the same day, E signed the relevant guarantee. Some months later, T was put into administrative receivership owing S about £111,000. The greater part of that debt related to goods supplied prior to the execution of the £150,000 guarantee. E contended that on its true construction, that guarantee only bound him in respect of future supplies to T, and that his liability was therefore only about £14,000.

The Court of Appeal upheld the decision of the Recorder that on its proper construction, the guarantee covered both past and future debts. They made it clear that the principles enunciated by Lord Hoffmann in *Investors Compensation Scheme v West Bromwich Building Society* [1998] 1 W.L.R. 896 at 912H–913F applied as much to the construction of a guarantee as to any other contract. Although the words "all trade goods that you may supply to the trader" taken in isolation might well have been construed as referring only to future supplies, the words "my liability to you shall be in respect of the whole debt" were capable of referring to the existing debt, as well as to any future debt. Since the factual background showed that there was no commercial sense in S agreeing to forego the protection of the existing guarantee and substituting a guarantee which related only to future sales, any reasonable person would conclude that para.1 of the guarantee was intended to extend and did extend both to the present and future indebtedness—in effect providing an increase in the limit of the existing security. Whilst there can be little doubt of the correctness of the Court of Appeal's decision on the facts, it had the slightly perturbing result that a standard precedent for a continuing guarantee of future indebtedness was construed in a way that the draftsman of that precedent (and most of those who use it) are unlikely to have anticipated. Thus those who use standard form precedents as the basis of their agreements can no longer be certain that they will be construed in a uniform manner. Holman J. added this, in para.19 of the judgment:

"[Counsel] submitted that to adopt the construction that I have would be 'creative' or involve 'rewriting' the guarantee and would fail to respect the approach of construing a guarantee strictly. I cannot accept the submission. There has been no creativity and no rewriting, but simply ascertainment of the meaning of the document by the objective approach described by the House of Lords. That being the task, it may be that the concept that a guarantee should be 'strictly construed' now adds nothing."

A guarantee must be given a reasonable interpretation within the context in which it has been given.[6] In dealing with the contract of suretyship as a commercial agreement, the court does not adopt an unduly technical approach, no doubt in recognition of the fact that very often these types of agreement are negotiated and drawn up between creditors and sureties personally, without involving their lawyers. Accordingly, the court will seek to construe the document in such a way as to reflect what may fairly be inferred to have been the objective intention and understanding of the parties.[7] A surety will not be relieved from liability because the language that has been used exposes him to a wider liability than he subjectively intended, even if the court may be of the opinion that had he appreciated the full consequences resulting from the guarantee, he would not have entered into it.[8]

A good illustration of the modern commercial approach to the construction of guarantees, applying the principles stated above, is to be found in a series of recent cases concerned with one of the most difficult questions of construction that can arise; namely, whether the liability of the principal debtor covered by the guarantee includes a contingent liability incurred by the named debtor as a surety for someone else.[9] In all these cases this question was ultimately decided in favour of the creditor, though the traditional "strict construction" approach might have produced a different result (and in two of the cases did produce that result until the matter reached the Privy Council).

---

6 *Lloyd's v Harper* (1880) 16 Ch. D. 290 at 303, *per* Fry J., *Johnston v Nicholls* (1845) 1 C.B. 251 at 269, *per* Maule J.
7 See, *e.g. Bank of Montreal v Munster Bank* (1876) I.R. 11 C.L. 47 at 55 *per* Fitzgerald J; *York City & Country Banking Co v Bainbridge* (1880) 43 L.T. 732; *Barber v Mackrell* (1892) 68 L.T. 29; *Other v Iveson* (1855) 3 Drew. 177 at 182, *per* Kindersley V.-C.; *Credit Suisse v Borough Council of Allerdale* [1995] 1 Lloyd's Rep. 315 at 358–359.
8 *Stewart and McDonald v Young* (1894) 38 S. J. 385; *Bank of BNA v Cuvillier* (1861) 14 Moo. P.C. 187, *per* Lord Cranworth; *London Assurance Co v Bold* (1844) 6 Q.B. 514.
9 *National Bank of New Zealand v West* (1978) 2 N.Z.L.R. 451, PC (reversing (1977) 1 N.Z.L.R. 29); *Coghlan v SH Lock (Australia) Ltd* (1987) 8 N.S.W.L.R. 88, PC (reversing (1985) 4 N.S.W.L.R. 158); *Bank of Scotland v Wright* [1991] B.C.L.C. 244. See also *Cambridge Credit Corpn Ltd v Lombard Australia Ltd* (1977) 14 A.L.R. 420, *Catley Farms Ltd v ANZ Banking Group (NZ) Ltd* [1982] 1 N.Z.L.R. 430, *Estoril Investments Pty Ltd v Westpac Banking Corp* (1993) 6 B.P.R. 13, 146.

Contracts of indemnity

4–003 Although the distinction between a guarantee and an indemnity may be a very fine one, there is clear authority that contracts of indemnity are to be construed strictly in favour of the indemnifier.[10] Thus in the absence of a clear and express provision, an indemnity will not usually be construed in such a way as to protect the person in whose favour it is given from the consequences of his own wrongful act, or negligence.[11] However, there is no real justification for adopting a different approach to the construction of a contract of indemnity from the appropriate approach to construction of a contract of guarantee or any other commercial contract. In each case, the ultimate objective is to ascertain the plain and obvious intention of the contracting parties, and it is desirable that in future both types of contract should be approached in the same manner. However, it remains to be seen whether the slightly more liberal approach evolving in the construction of guarantees will be adopted in the case of indemnities.

Contracts of indemnity are not restricted to those in which the loss against which the promisor has agreed to indemnify the promisee arises as a result of the acts or defaults of a third person. Thus it is even more difficult to lay down any general rules of construction for an indemnity than it is for a guarantee. The extent of a person's liability under an indemnity depends on the nature and terms of the contract, and each case must be governed by its own facts and circumstances.[12]

Construction in accordance with proper law

4–004 A guarantee or indemnity given in one country to secure the performance of an obligation arising in another country may involve the application of the principles of private international law to resolve the following questions:

(1) By what law is the contract of suretyship to be construed?

(2) By what law is it to be determined whether or not the principal has fulfilled his obligations?

The first question is to be approached in the same way as for any other type of contract. If the parties have made an express choice of law in the contract, effect will be given to that choice. If they have not, and the

---

10 See, *e.g. Smith v South Wales Switchgear Ltd* [1978] 1 All E.R. 18; *General Surety and Guarantee Co v Francis Parker Ltd* (1977) 6 B.L.R. 16 at 21; *Greenwell v Matthew Hall Pty Ltd (No.2)* (1982) 31 S.A.S.R. 548. Compare the trend towards a more liberal approach to contracts of guarantee, considered above.

11 *Smith v South Wales Switchgear Ltd* (above); *Canada Steamship Lines v R* [1952] A.C. 192; *North of England Hydro Electric Board v Taylor* (1955) S.L.T. 373; *Gertsen v Municipality of Metropolitan Toronto et al. (No.2)* (1973) 43 D.L.R. (3d) 504 (Can).

12 *Gillespie Bros & Co Ltd v Roy Bowles Transport Ltd* [1973] 1 Q.B. 400. For a list of examples of decisions on particular wordings, see *Halsbury's Laws (op. cit.)*, Vol. 20, para.354, n.1.

contract was made on or after April 1, 1991, then by virtue of the Contracts (Applicable Laws) Act 1990 the provisions of the Rome Convention 1980 will apply.[13] A detailed analysis of these provisions is outside the scope of this work, but particular reference should be made to Art.4, Art.5, Art.13 and Art.1(2)(c). In general terms, the Convention merely affirms the principle which was previously applicable, and which will still apply to contracts entered into prior to April 1, 1991, namely that the law which will be applied ("the proper law") will be the system with which the contract is most closely connected.[14] The Convention creates a presumption that this will be the law of the country in which the surety is resident or incorporated or has his principal place of business, rather than the country in which he has to effect payment to the creditor. This presumption appears to reinforce the approach of the court in earlier cases.[15]

If, as is usually the case, the obligations which are guaranteed arise out of a contract between the principal debtor, D, and the creditor, C, the same approach will be used to ascertain the proper law of the underlying contract, which will be the law used to determine whether or not there has been any relevant breach. It may be that if the transactions are properly viewed as part of an indivisible commercial package, the presumption in favour of the surety's place of residence or business will be displaced by the proper law of the underlying contract. Thus for example in *The Broken Hill Proprietary Co Ltd v Xenakis* [1982] 2 Lloyd's Rep. 304, a guarantee in respect of any sums which were awarded in an arbitration pursuant to the terms of a charterparty was held by Bingham J. to be governed by the same proper law as the underlying charterparty. However, the court must be careful not to give undue weight to a choice of law clause in the underlying contract when deciding which system of law is most closely connected to the guarantee. The Court of Appeal gave that warning in *Samcrete Egypt Engineers & Contractors SAE v Land Rover Exports Ltd* [2002] C.L.C. 533. An Egyptian company had given a guarantee to L in respect of the obligations of L's Egyptian distributor, T. The contract between L and T contained a choice of law clause which provided that English law was to apply to that contract, but there was no similar clause in the guarantee. The judge had decided that the choice of law clause was the determinative factor rebutting the presumption under Art.4(2) of the Convention in favour of Egypt: the Court of Appeal upheld the decision, but on different grounds, namely that payment under the guarantee was to be made in England, and therefore any default was enforceable there.

Different rules apply to performance bonds. The prima facie rule is that a performance bond given by or on behalf of a party to the underlying contract will be governed by the law of the place where payment is to be made under it, and not necessarily the law of the underlying contract:

---

13 See generally, Plender, *The European Contracts Convention* (Sweet & Maxwell, 1991).
14 See generally Dicey & Morris, *The Conflict of Laws* (Sweet & Maxwell, 12th ed. 1993, and supp. 1997), Chs 32 and 33.
15 See, *e.g. Ex p. Littlejohn* (1843) 2 M.D. & De G. 182.

Attock Cement Co Ltd v Romanian Bank For Foreign Trade [1989] 1 W.L.R. 1147. In the absence of express stipulation, the place of payment of a performance bond will be the place at which demand is made and not the place where the payee is located: *Britten-Norman Ltd v State Ownership Fund of Romania* [2000] Lloyd's Rep. (Bank.) 315. However if a counter-guarantee is given by one bank to another which has issued a performance bond, it is likely that the proper law of the performance bond will be held to be the proper law of the counter-guarantee, on the basis that the natural expectation of the parties was that both contracts should be governed by the same law so as to avoid the risk of payment without reimbursement: see *Turkiye Is Bankasi AS v Bank of China* [1993] 1 Lloyd's Rep. 132 and *Wahda Bank v Arab Bank Plc* [1996] 1 Lloyd's Rep. 470 at 473, CA. If the underlying obligation of D, for which S stands as surety to C, is said to arise in tort, matters may be more complex. It may be simply a question of construction of the contract of suretyship whether, on the facts, the act or omission of D was an obligation for which S had promised to indemnify or compensate C. On the other hand, the question may arise whether D is under any liability to C. If the wrong was committed in England and would be actionable in England as a tort, no problem should arise. If it was committed in another country, the question may be determined by simply ascertaining whether what D did was an actionable wrong by the law of the place where the act was committed (the *lex loci delicti*) or possibly by the law which has the most significant relationship with the occurrence and the parties (the "proper law of the tort").[16]

Special rules apply to the determination of the law governing the various rights and obligations of parties to bills of exchange, and these were considered in detail by Saville J. and the Court of Appeal in *Grunzweig und Hartmann Montage v Irvani* [1988] 1 W.L.R. 1285, affirmed [1990] 1 W.L.R. 667.[17] In particular, the *lex loci contractus* determines whether the signature of a party on the bill, together with the words *"bon pour aval pour les tirés"* which were added with his consent, imposes on that party the obligations of a guarantor or those of an indorser.[18]

Construction *ut res magis valeat quam pereat*

4–005 As a general principle, the court will interpret the contract so that the protection which it affords to a creditor is real rather than illusory. This is merely an application of the general rule of interpretation that a contract will be construed in such a way as to give effect to its terms wherever possible.[19] A good illustration is provided by the case of *Nelson Gardner Ltd*

---

16 See Dicey & Morris (*op. cit.*), Rule 203(2), and generally Ch.35.

17 These rules have been preserved by the Rome Convention, Art.1(2)(c).

18 See also *Banco Atlantico SA v The British Bank of the Middle East* [1990] 2 Lloyd's Rep. 504.

19 See, *e.g. Stewart and McDonald v Young* (1894) 38 S. J. 385; *Broom v Batchelor* (1856) 1 H. & N. 255; *Jones v Mason* (1892) 13 N.S.W.L.R. 157, *International Leasing Corp (Vic) Ltd v Aiken* [1967] 2 N.S.W.L.R. 427 at 454, *Re Interwest Hotels Pty Ltd (in liq.)* (1993) 12 A.C.S.R. 78, *Simclar International Circuits Ltd v Rodime Plc* (1992) G.W.D. 9–466 (Scotland).

v Cowburn (unreported) CAT No.219 of 1989, March 7. The document relied on by the creditor company, a letter written by a director of that company to the surety, began by setting out a schedule for the repayment of moneys then outstanding on the debtor's account with the company. In a subsequent clause it stated as follows:

"With immediate effect personally and/or from your other companies guarantee that amount outstanding at any time over normal trading terms ie current month and previous month."

The defendant contended that the agreement was uncertain because it was not clear whether he or one of his other companies was to be the guarantor, and the companies had never executed any form of guarantee. The Court of Appeal held that the clause meant that the defendant was to be personally liable as guarantor, but that if he wished, he could arrange for one of his other companies to pay. Another point taken by the defendant, that any obligations which he undertook as guarantor were to be construed as limited in time to the period scheduled earlier in the agreement for the repayment of sums due to the creditor, was also rejected, on the grounds that the construction for which he contended was uncommercial because the period of the guarantee would then be so short that it would not afford any substantial protection to the creditor. In *Re Interwest Hotels Pty Ltd (in liq.)* (1993) 12 A.C.S.R. 78, the guarantee was given by a company which had no assets in its own right, but which was the trustee of a substantial unit trust. The deed of guarantee made no mention of the trust and the issue was whether it had entered into the guarantee in its own right or as trustee. Eames J., sitting in the Supreme Court of Victoria, held that where a company known to have only acted in the past in a trustee capacity, claims to have given a worthless guarantee by acting in a personal capacity, "that company faces an evidential burden if it is to establish that a contract which defies commercial logic in such a manner is one which has been accepted on that basis by the other party to the contract". However, on the evidence before him, the judge reached the conclusion that the parties had agreed to make such a contract, and that the guarantee was worthless unless the company acquired assets thereafter.

Another example of the application of the principle, which is common in the context of contracts of suretyship, occurs when the consideration referred to in the contract is susceptible to being interpreted as either past consideration or future consideration. In such a case the court will normally adopt the construction which makes the contract valid and enforceable. Thus in *Broom v Batchelor* (1856) 1 H. & N. 255, the guarantee was given in the following terms:

"In consideration of the credit given by B to E, I hereby agree to guarantee the payment of all bills of exchange drawn by the said B and accepted by E. Also I hereby agree to guarantee the payment of any balance that may be due from the said E to the said B. This guarantee

to include all bills of exchange now running as well as the balance of
account at this day."

Evidence was admitted to show that at the time the guarantee was given,
there were bills running and an account due from E to B, and that future
dealings between those parties were contemplated. It was held that the
guarantee extended to future as well as past transactions and was therefore
valid and enforceable.[20]

In general terms, if the consideration is expressed in the past tense, such
as "in consideration of your having resigned from your employment", "in
consideration of your having supplied goods to D" or "in consideration of
your having entered into a settlement agreement with D", the court will
strive wherever possible to interpret this as meaning that a contemporaneous or future act of resignation, supply or settlement occurring or
contemplated after the agreement was made, was the agreed consideration
for it.[21]

Admissibility of oral and extrinsic evidence

4-006   If the meaning of the contract is clearly apparent from the face of the
document, then the court will not permit extrinsic evidence to be adduced,
including evidence of the circumstances in which the guarantee was given:
London Assurance Co v Bold (1844) 6 Q.B. 514 at 525, *per* Coleridge J.
Similarly, oral evidence is normally inadmissible if it would alter, vary or
contradict the written terms of the agreement.[22] In the light of the very
broad modern approach to the admissibility of evidence of the "factual
matrix" of a commercial contract for the purposes of construction, reflected
in the principles set out by Lord Hoffmann in *Investors Compensation
Scheme Ltd v West Bromwich Building Society* [1998] 1 W.L.R. 896 at 912H–
913F, the parol evidence rule is probably of less practical importance
nowadays. An important exception to the rule is that extrinsic evidence is
admissible in order to prove that the surety was induced by fraud or
misrepresentation to enter into the agreement, or to prove duress or undue
influence or similar vitiating conduct.[23] Thus for example in *Hutchison v
Hooker* (1883) 2 N.Z.L.R. (S.C.) 134, the guarantor of a judgment debt was
entitled to adduce evidence to prove that the creditor had no real cause of
action and that he had colluded with the debtor in order to enter a

---

20 See also *Wood v Priestner* (1866) L.R. 2 Exch. 66, in which an agreement to give a
   guarantee "for coal supplied" by C to D was held to be a continuing guarantee for such
   coal as might be supplied from time to time.
21 See, *e.g. Morrell v Cowan* (1877) 6 Ch. D. 166; *Steele v Hoe* (1849) 14 Q.B. 431; *Goldshede v
   Swan* (1847) 1 Exch. 154; *King v Cole* (1848) 2 Exch. 628; *Tanner v Moore* (1846) 9 Q.B. 1;
   Butcher v Steuart (1843) 11 M. & W. 857; *Payne v Wilson* (1827) 7 B. & C. 423; *cf. Chalmers
   v Victors* (1868) 18 L.T. 481.
22 See *Goss v Lord Nugent* (1833) 5 B. & Ad. 58 at 64–65, *per* Denman C.J.; *Jacobs v Batavia
   & General Plantations Trust Ltd* [1924] 1 Ch. 287 at 295, *per* Lawrence J.; *Holmes v Mitchell*
   (1859) 7 C.B.N.S. 361.
23 See, *e.g. Toronto Dominion Bank v Paconiel Investments Inc.* (1992) 6 O.R. (3d) 547.

fraudulent judgment. Oral evidence will also be admissible in a claim for rectification of a written contract, to establish that the document does not accurately reflect the bargain which the parties made.[24]

On the other hand, if the contract is ambiguous, extrinsic evidence, including oral evidence, may be adduced in order to construe it.[25] Thus oral evidence may be used to show whether the guarantee is a continuing guarantee or a specific guarantee,[26] whether the expressed consideration is past, present or future,[27] what the consideration was,[28] what liability the guarantor has undertaken,[29] which of several named companies was the correct offeree,[30] whether the written agreement or memorandum was signed as principal or agent,[31] and to identify documents or other matters referred to.[32] It is often difficult to establish what extrinsic evidence will be admissible and what will be excluded. Evidence of the detailed negotiations between the parties before the contract is concluded is generally inadmissible for the purposes of interpreting the contract, because it usually affords little or no assistance in determining which of the various changing positions adopted by the parties in the course of the negotiations was finally adopted (see *Prenn v Simmonds* [1971] 1 W.L.R. 1381 at 1384–1385, and the third of Lord Hoffmann's principles in *Investors Compensation Scheme Ltd v West Bromwich Building Society* (above)). Occasionally, however, evidence of what was said during the pre-contractual negotiations may be the only satisfactory means of resolving ambiguity. In the unreported case of *BP Australia Ltd v Wales*, Supreme Court of New South Wales, February 12, 1983,[33] the court admitted evidence of pre-contractual negotiations in order to determine whether a guarantee for the due payment for "all goods from time to time supplied by the company to the customer" related only to fuel supplies or to supplies of goods of any kind.

The name and form of the document

The name given to a particular contract in its title or in the body of the documentation, such as "guarantee", "indemnity" or "insurance", or the form which it takes, are not conclusive as to its nature, because that is **4–007**

---

24 For a full discussion of the parol evidence rule, see *Chitty on Contracts* (*op. cit.*), Vol. 1 at paras 12–081 *et seq.*
25 *Goldshede v Swan* (1847) 1 Exch. 154; *Bank of New Zealand v Simpson* [1900] A.C. 182.
26 *e.g. Nottingham Hide, etc. Co v Bottrill* (1873) L.R. 8 C.P. 694.
27 *e.g. Goldshede v Swan* (1847) 1 Exch. 154; *Colbourn v Dawson* (1851) 10 C.B. 765; *Butcher v Steuart* (1843) 11 M. & W. 857.
28 *Shortrede v Cheek* (1834) 1 Ad. & El. 57; *Bainbridge v Wade* (1850) 16 Q.B. 89; *Colbourn v Dawson* (1851) 10 C.B. 765; *Lilley v Midland Brick Co Pty Ltd* (1992) 9 W.A.R. 339.
29 *e.g. Broom v Batchelor* (1856) 1 H. & N. 255; *Hoad v Grace* (1861) 7 H. & N. 494. See also *Perrylease v Imecar* [1988] 1 W.L.R. 463; *State Bank of India v Kaur* [1996] 5 Bank. L.R. 158; *Re Interwest Hotels Pty Ltd (in liq.)* (1993) 12 A.C.S.R. 78; *Maddestra v Penfolds Wines Pty Ltd* (1993) 44 F.C.R. 303; and the cases cited in Ch.3.
30 *Boral Resources (Q) Pty Ltd v Donnelly* [1988] 1 Qd R. 506.
31 *Young v Schuler* (1883) 11 Q.B.D. 651.
32 *Shortrede v Cheek* (1834) 1 Ad. & El. 57; *Bateman v Phillips* (1812) 15 East. 272; *Holmes v Mitchell* (1859) 7 C.B.N.S. 361 at 368; *Brown v Fletcher* (1876) 35 L.T. 165.
33 Referred to by O'Donovan & Phillips, *The Modern Contract of Guarantee* (*op. cit.*) at p.236, n.155.

determined by the substance of the agreement.[34] However, the name given to the contract may be some evidence of the intention of the parties (see *Dane v Mortgage Insurance Corporation* [1894] 1 Q.B. 54).

Recitals and side notes

Contracts of guarantee

4–008   Although the recital is part of the guarantee, and may therefore be looked at in construing the document as a whole, as a general rule the recitals in a guarantee will not govern the effect of the operative words in the body of the contract.[35] Thus in *Bank of British North America v Cuvillier* (1861) 14 Moo. P.C. 187, the issue was whether the surety, S, was liable for all liabilities of D to C, or only those which were referable to a firm of which D had been a member. The recital stated that D, being a member of a firm, was required to borrow money to meet the obligations of the firm. However the body of the guarantee stated that S agreed to be surety to C for "all debts contracted or that might be contracted to and in favour of C". It was held that S was liable for any debts incurred by D to C; the recital merely set out the context in which the borrowing was required, and did not control the generality of the subsequent operative words.

However, if the recital is so inconsistent with the operative words of the guarantee that the latter must be qualified in order to give effect to the plain and obvious intention of the parties, the recital may qualify the more general words in the body of the contract. Thus in *Pearsall v Summersett* (1812) 4 Taunt. 593, the operative wording stated that S was to be liable for all moneys that C had already or might thereafter advance to D, but the recital expressly stated that the guarantee was given to secure the pre-existing liabilities of D to C. It was held that S was liable for those debts only.[36]

One particular type of contract of surety, the fidelity bond, by which a bond is given to guarantee the due and proper performance of his duties by an agent or employee, is frequently explained or restricted by its recitals. Thus in *Lord Arlington v Merricke* (1672) 2 Saund. 403, a bond which recited that D was to be employed for six months was interpreted as meaning that S was only liable for defaults by D during that period. Similarly in *Napier v Bruce* (1842) 6 Cl. & Fin. 470, a bond was given for the due fulfilment of the duties of an agent under an agency agreement, the

---

34 *Seaton v Heath* [1899] 1 Q.B. 782 at 792, *per* Romer L.J. (reversed without affecting this point [1900] A.C. 135); *Re Denton's Estate* [1904] 2 Ch. 178 at 188, *per* Vaughan Williams L.J. See also the observations of Lord Diplock in *Moschi v Lep Air Services Ltd* [1973] A.C. 331 at 349.

35 At least when the meaning of the operative part of the guarantee is clear and unambiguous: *Australian Joint Stock Bank v Bailey* [1899] A.C. 396; *Sansom v Bell* (1809) 2 Camp. 39.

36 See also *Australian Joint Stock Bank v Bailey* [1899] A.C. 396; *Re Medewe's Trust* (1859) 26 Beav. 588; *Sansom v Bell* (1809) 2 Camp. 39; *Plaster Decoration and Papier Mâché Co Ltd v Massey-Mainwaring* (1895) 11 T.L.R. 205; *cf. Bank of India v Transcontinental Commodity Merchants Ltd and Patel* [1982] 1 Lloyd's Rep. 506; [1983] 2 Lloyd's Rep. 298.

terms of which were specifically set out in the recital. The general wording of the bond stipulated that:

> ". . . during the whole time . . . the agent . . . shall continue to act as agent foresaid, in consequence of the above recited agreement, he shall well and truly account for and pay to us, the employers all sums of money received by him on our account."

It was held that the surety was not liable for the agent's failure to account to his employers for sums of money received by him on their account other than pursuant to the agency referred to in the recital.[37]

In certain circumstances, a statement of certain facts in the recital to a guarantee may operate as an estoppel against a party (usually the surety) who subsequently seeks to deny those facts. However, it will be a matter of construction of the contract whether the recital was intended to be a statement which all the parties to the agreement mutually admitted to be true, in which case it will operate as an estoppel against all of them, or whether it was merely a statement of one party only, in which case it will only operate as an estoppel against him: *Greer v Kettle* [1938] A.C. 156.[38]

Guarantees, particularly guarantees given to a bank, are often made on a standard printed form supplied by the creditor. This may contain footnotes and side notes which are intended to provide guidance to the person filling in the form. The notes may be used as an aid to construction in case of ambiguity, but will not be allowed to produce a result which would plainly contradict the obvious meaning of the contract. Thus in *Bank of Baroda v ANY Enterprises Ltd* (unreported) CAT No.1088 of 1986, December 4, the standard guarantee form signed by the defendants contained a proviso which allowed for a maximum monetary limit to be inserted. The space left for the insertion of a maximum sum had been left blank, and initialled in the margin by the defendants. However, the printed side note in the text said that if the guarantee was to be unlimited the proviso should be deleted. The defendants sought to argue that the guarantee was limited, but the Court of Appeal held that as a matter of obvious construction, the guarantee was unlimited despite the fact that the proviso had been left in the text.[39] This case may be contrasted with the more recent decision of the Court of Appeal in *State Bank of India v Kaur* [1996] 5 Bank. L.R. 158, where the guarantee was intended to be limited, but the limit was not inserted in the guarantee.[40]

---

37 See also *Hassell v Long* (1814) 2 M. & S. 363; *Augero v Keen* (1836) 1 M. & W. 390; *Liverpool Waterworks Co v Anderson* (1805) 6 East. 507; *Kitson v Julian* (1855) 4 E. & B. 854; *Keith v Fenelon Falls, Union School Section* (1882) 3 O.R. 194 (Can). *Cf. Birmingham Corporation v Wright* (1851) 16 Q.B. 623; *Oswald v Berwick-upon-Tweed Corporation* (1856) 5 H.L. Cas. 856.

38 See also *Anglo-Californian Bank Ltd v London and Provincial Marine and General Insurance Co Ltd* (1904) 20 T.L.R. 665; *Stroughill v Buck* (1850) 14 Q.B. 781 at 787, *per* Patterson J.

39 See further, *Bank of Baroda v Patel* [1996] 1 Lloyd's Rep. 391.

40 See also *Relwood Pty Ltd v Manning Homes Pty Ltd* [1990] 1 Qd.R. 481, a case in which there was an intention to limit the surety's liability, but no agreement was reached on what the limit should be.

Contracts of indemnity

4-009 It has been said that a contract of indemnity is not to be restricted by its recitals: *Re Baker, Collins and Rhodes* (1881) 20 Ch. D. 230. If this means nothing more than that if the wording in the body of the contract is plain, the recitals will not qualify it, then there would appear to be no distinction in this regard between contracts of indemnity and contracts of guarantee.[41] On the other hand, there would appear to be no justification for an artificial rule which precludes the court from considering the effect of a recital to an indemnity, in circumstances in which an identical recital would qualify the meaning and extent of a guarantee, and it is highly unlikely that a modern court would adopt such an approach.

The consideration clause as an aid to interpretation

4-010 The consideration for a guarantee need not be stated in the contract.[42] However, if the guarantee does refer to a specific consideration, this will be taken into account in construing the document as a whole, and may be a useful aid to determining the nature and extent of the surety's liability.[43] Thus in *Martin v Wright* (1845) 6 Q.B. 917, a guarantee expressed to be "in consideration of your agreeing to supply goods to K at two months' credit" was held to be a continuing guarantee rather than a specific one. If the only consideration referred to is plainly bad, *e.g.* if it is clearly past consideration, the contract will be unenforceable.[44]

On the other hand, it is unlikely that the consideration clause would override any clear and unambiguous meaning in the body of the guarantee, even if the expressed consideration is inconsistent with that meaning. In *Bank of India v Transcontinental Commodity Merchants Ltd and Patel* [1982] 1 Lloyd's Rep. 506, affirmed [1983] 2 Lloyd's Rep. 298, the contract provided that "in consideration of the Bank of India . . . affording banking facilities" the guarantor promised to pay on demand "all and every sum and sums of money which are now or shall at any time be owing to the bank anywhere on any account whatsoever". Bingham J. and the Court of Appeal held that the reference to "banking facilities" did not narrow the scope of the very wide language used in the body of the guarantee so as to limit the liability of the guarantor to the payment of sums advanced under "banking" transactions only.[45]

---

41 See the discussion at para.4–008 above.

42 Mercantile Law Amendment Act 1856, s.3. See Ch.3, above.

43 *National Bank of New Zealand v West* [1978] 2 N.Z.L.R. 451 at 458; *National Bank of Nigeria Ltd v Awolsi* [1964] 1 W.L.R. 1311; *Bank of India v Transcontinental Commodity Merchants and Patel* [1982] 1 Lloyd's Rep. 506 at 512; *Geelong Building Society (In Liquidation) v Encel* [1996] 1 V.R. 594.

44 *Wood v Priestner* (1866) L.R. 2 Exch. 66, *per* Bramwell B. at 70; *Oldershaw v King* (1857) 2 H. & N. 517. See also *Bailey v Manos* [1992] A.C.L. Rep. 220 FCI.

45 The opposite approach was adopted by Sheppard J. in the unreported Australian case of *Scholefield Goodman and Sons Ltd v Gange* (December 4, 1979), see the discussion in O'Donovan & Phillips (*op. cit.*) at p.221. However this case must be approached with some caution, not least because of the somewhat unorthodox approach to construction in favour of the guarantor adopted by the learned judge.

Joint and several liability

It will frequently be the case that the creditor requires more than one **4–011** surety, for example when two directors of a company are required to guarantee the due fulfilment of its obligations to pay rent to the landlord of its office premises. When this occurs, the sureties may be jointly liable, severally liable or jointly and severally liable. Similarly, in contracts of indemnity, the surety may enter into a joint or joint and several liability with the principal or with another surety. In determining the type of liability undertaken by the parties to a particular contract, the rules of construction which are applied are the same for contracts of suretyship as for contracts generally. No special formula is needed to create a joint or several liability. If two persons covenant for themselves, without any words of severance, that they or one of them shall do something, a joint obligation is created; therefore, if it is intended to make the surety's obligation entirely independent from that of his co-obligors, clear and specific words of severance are required: see *White v Tyndall* (1888) 13 App. Cas. 263 at 269.[46] However, by s.81 of the Law of Property Act 1925, a covenant or obligation under seal made with two or more persons jointly is construed, in the absence of the expression of a contrary intention, as also being made with each of them.

Difficult questions of construction may arise when a court has to determine whether two or more sureties are each liable in respect of the same obligation or have distinct liabilities and separate obligations. These difficulties most often occur when the question is whether the sureties are liable for the full amount of the indebtedness, or whether they are each liable for part of that amount.[47] If they are jointly liable for the entire debt, then the creditor should join them all as defendants in any action to recover that debt: *Kendall v Hamilton* (1879) 4 App. Cas. 504.[48] If each surety is severally liable for a particular share of the overall indebtedness, the creditor may sue each one individually to recover the part of the debt to which his liability relates.[49] This type of agreement also has disadvantages. For example, appropriately skilful drafting may create the possibility of a surety being discharged from his several liability before the creditor is fully paid. This may occur if S is liable only for the first £100 of a debt and T is liable for the balance; once the principal has repaid more than £100, S will be released from liability.

Thus the most advantageous contract from the creditor's point of view is one which makes the sureties jointly and severally liable. This enables him

---

46 For examples of words construed as giving rise to several liabilities, see *Collins v Prosser* (1823) 1 B. & C. 682; *Fell v Goslin* (1852) 7 Exch. 185. See also *Armstrong v Cahill* (1880) 6 L.R. Ir. 440. For an example of a contract of indemnity which was construed as joint, rather than joint and several, see *Sumner v Powell* (1816) 2 Mer. 30, affirmed (1823) Turn. & R. 423.
47 Compare, *e.g. Armstrong v Cahill* (1880) 6 L.R. Ir. 440, and *Collins v Prosser* (1823) 1 B. & C. 682 with *Wallace v Roe* [1903] 1 Ir. 32.
48 *Other v Iveson* (1855) 3 Drew. 177; *Berwick-upon-Tweed Corporation v Murray* (1857) 7 De G. M. & G. 497. See also the Civil Liability (Contribution) Act 1978, s.3.
49 *Collins v Prosser* (1823) 1 B. & C. 682.

to bring an action against any one or more of them in respect of the whole debt, leaving that person to seek contribution from the co-sureties and to run the risk that the co-sureties may become insolvent.[50] However, the creditor must ensure that all the sureties sign such a guarantee,[51] unless there is an express provision in the guarantee to the effect that the signatories are bound even if the other intended sureties do not sign, see for example the clause in *Bank of Scotland v Henry Butcher & Co* [2001] 2 All E.R. (Comm) 691. Moreover he would be well advised to include adequate safeguards to protect him against releasing all the sureties by releasing or compromising his claims against some of them.[52]

Limitation to liability of the parties named

4–012   A guarantee given to secure the liability of a named person will not usually be interpreted as extending to cover the liability of another person, or the liability of the named person jointly with another person, unless the contrary intention clearly appears.[53] Thus a guarantee will not extend as a matter of course to any liability undertaken by the named principal's executors.[54] Prima facie, a surety, S, who engages to be answerable for the debts of D to C will not be taken as guaranteeing the debts of D and D's partners to C.[55] Even if the surety knows that the principal has a partner, this will not necessarily mean that he intends to cover the liabilities of the partnership; indeed, naming the principal alone may evince quite the opposite intention.[56] However, if it is clear from the surrounding circumstances that the surety intended to guarantee the liabilities of the firm, the mere fact that the guarantee only names one of the partners will not preclude the surety from being held liable for the firm's indebtedness.[57] On the other hand, if one person executes a guarantee in a form designed to be executed by joint sureties, it will be enforceable against him if there is evidence that in fact he knew and intended that he would be the only surety: *Walter & Morris Ltd v Lymberis* [1965] S.A.S.R. 204.

A guarantee given in respect of a group of persons will not usually be interpreted as covering the liability of only some of them, or some of them with others, unless it clearly provides for this. Similarly, a contract of

---

50 See generally *Ellis v Emmanuel* (1876) 1 Exch. D. 157 especially at 162 *per* Blackburn J.

51 See the discussion of conditional guarantees later in this Chapter at para.4–022.

52 See *Ward v National Bank of New Zealand* (1883) L.R. 8 App. Cas. 755 *Bank of Montreal v Dobbin* [1996] 5 Bank. L.R. 190, *Gattellaro v Westpac Banking Corporation* [2004] 204 A.L.R. 258 and Ch.12.

53 It may, however, indirectly cover another person's liability by covering the named debtor's contingent liabilities: see, *e.g. National Bank of New Zealand v West* (1978) 2 N.Z.L.R. 451; *Coghlan v SH Lock (Australia) Ltd* (1987) 8 N.S.W.L.R. 88; *Bank of Scotland v Wright* [1991] B.C.L.C. 244.

54 *Barker v Parker* (1786) 1 T.R. 287.

55 *Montefiore v Lloyd* (1863) 15 C.B.N.S. 203.

56 *Mills v Alderbury Union* (1849) 3 Exch. 590; *London Assurance v Bold* (1844) 6 Q.B. 514.

57 *Leathley v Spyer* (1870) L.R. 5 C.P. 595, and see generally *Bank of Scotland v Henry Butcher & Co* [2001] 2 All E.R. (Comm) 691 and [2003] 2 All E.R. (Comm) 557, discussed in Ch.3, para.3–026.

suretyship given for the benefit of a named person or group of persons will not usually be enforceable by anyone other than those persons.[58] In the case of a partnership, this principle was given statutory effect by s.18 of the Partnership Act 1890, which provides that a continuing guarantee given either to a firm, or to a third person in respect of the transactions of a firm, is, in the absence of agreement to the contrary, revoked as to future transactions by any change in the constitution of the firm in question.

There is no particular difficulty in achieving continuity in a security despite changes in the persons intended to be secured, by use of an appropriate form of wording. An example is the case of *Metcalf v Bruin* (1810) 12 East. 400, in which a bond was given to indemnify "the company and the directors and all the members thereof" in respect of the due performance of his duties by a clerk to an unincorporated association. The bond was held to remain in full force during the clerk's period of service, despite changes during that period in the individual members of whom the association was composed.

However, care must be taken to use sufficiently precise language. If the guarantee is intended to survive the death or retirement of any of the partners or the joinder of new partners, it should say so clearly.[59] A mere reference to the firm by name will probably not suffice to demonstrate an intention that the guarantee should continue after changes in the existing partnership.[60] The draftsman must also be mindful that he should always ensure that the document containing or evidencing the agreement identifies with sufficient clarity and certainty the person or persons to whom the guarantee is given. Therefore, if a guarantee is given to a partnership, and it is intended to survive any changes in that partnership, it is probably more sensible to insert a separate clause in the body of the agreement dealing with the matter expressly, than to try to cater for changes by defining "the partnership" or "the firm" in the widest possible terms.

If the named beneficiary of the guarantee is a company, and that company subsequently merges with another, it is likely that the new amalgamated company will be entitled to sue on the guarantee as assignee, because the new company will usually take over all the prior rights (and often also the obligations) of the companies which constitute it.[61] This has been held to be the position on the amalgamation of companies by statute which expressly provided for the new company to take over and enforce the rights of action given to the old company.[62] However, if the surety is a

---

58 However it may be enforced by the undisclosed principal of an agent: see *Bateman v Phillips* (1812) 15 East. 272. It may also be enforced by a trustee, or by an assignee, provided that the benefit of the contract is assignable, see Ch.7.

59 For an example of a guarantee which covered defaults of surviving partners after the death of one of them, but not defaults after the retirement of one of them, see *University of Cambridge v Baldwin* (1839) 5 M. & W. 580.

60 *Backhouse v Hall* (1865) 6 B. & S. 507.

61 If the company changes its name and shareholders but remains the same legal entity, the guarantor will not be released: *Gill & Duffus SA v Rionda Futures Ltd* [1994] 2 Lloyd's Rep. 67.

62 *LB & SC Railway v Goodwin* (1849) 3 Exch. 320; *Eastern Union Railway v Cochrane* (1853) 9 Exch. 197. See also *National Bank of Greece and Athens v Metliss* [1958] A.C. 509 (change in the identity of the surety company).

company which merges with another company, the prudent creditor should obtain a fresh guarantee from the amalgamated company in order to fully protect his position.

Liability for assigned debts

4–013   A further issue which sometimes arises is whether the guarantee is to be construed as extending to moneys initially owed by the principal to a third party, when the debt has been assigned by the third party to the creditor. In *Kova Establishment v Sasco Investments Ltd* [1998] 2 B.C.L.C. 83, the issue was whether an "all moneys" guarantee and legal charge were to be construed as extending to the liability of one of the principal debtors under a prior (unsecured) loan made by a third party, which had been assigned by the third party to the creditor after the guarantee and legal charge had been executed. At first sight, the wording of the guarantee and charge appeared to be wide enough to cover the liability, but the judge (Mr John Martin Q.C., sitting as a deputy judge of the Chancery Division) held that it did not, because the provision relating to interest under the earlier loan was different from the rate of interest under the guarantee and charge. He held that the interpretation contended for by the creditor would have been to give carte blanche to a variation of the terms of any debt the creditor might care to acquire, and thus possibly to alter the amount which the guarantor, but not necessarily the principal, was obliged to pay. This, of course, would offend against the principal of co-extensiveness, see para.4–014 below. The judge was not prepared to infer that this was the intention of the contracting parties. In reaching his conclusion, the judge applied dicta of Needham J. in the unreported Australian case of *Skylink International Courier Pty v Grellman* (Supreme Court of New South Wales, September 21, 1987).[63]

The principle of co-extensiveness

4–014   If the contract of suretyship is a guarantee in the true sense, namely one which contains a promise to answer for the "debt default or miscarriage" of another, then there is a strong prima facie rule of construction that the surety's obligations are to be interpreted as co-extensive with those of the principal debtor. Accordingly, it has been held that the obligations of a guarantor of "the due fulfilment of any obligation" of a party to a charterparty which contained an arbitration clause, covered the debtor's liability to pay interest and costs as well as the principal sum awarded by the arbitrators.[64]

When a surety guarantees the performance of a contractual liability on the part of the principal to make certain payments to the creditor by

---

63 See also *Re Clark's Refrigeration Transport Pty Ltd (in liq.)* [1982] V.R. 989 and *Katsikalis v Deutsche Bank (Asia) AG* [1988] 2 Qd.R. 641.
64 *Compania Sudamericana de Fletes SA v African Continental Bank Ltd* [1973] 1 Lloyd's Rep. 21. However *cf. Re Kitchin* (1881) 17 Ch. D. 668; *Bruns v Colocotronis ("the Vasso")* [1979] 2 Lloyd's Rep. 412.

instalments, there may now be difficulties in construing the contract of guarantee in accordance with the principle of co-extensiveness. The starting point of those difficulties is *Moschi v Lep Air* [1973] A.C. 331. In that case, the debtor defaulted under a contract for payment by instalments for services already provided by the creditor. The creditor treated the contract as repudiated. The question which arose was whether the creditor could sue the surety for the balance of moneys due under the contract at the time of the repudiation, notwithstanding that when he accepted the repudiation the debtor's primary obligation to pay specific instalments of money became translated into a secondary obligation to pay damages. The House of Lords held that the surety was liable: he was under an obligation to see to it that the debtor performed his contractual obligations, so that when the debtor defaulted, the surety became liable to "pay the creditor a sum of money for the loss he thereby sustained".[65]

However, it was quite clearly envisaged in that case that the liability of the debtor and the guarantor would remain co-extensive and that no rule of construction would be used to breach this fundamental principle. Thus Lord Diplock said at 349:

"... whenever the debtor has failed voluntarily to perform an obligation which is the subject of the guarantee the creditor can recover from the guarantor as breach of his contract of guarantee whatever sum the creditor could have recovered from the debtor himself as a consequence of that failure. The debtor's liability to the creditor is also the measure of the guarantor's."

Despite this clear affirmation of principle, the Court of Appeal and House of Lords subsequently construed two similar guarantees in a way which, at least prima facie, appears to derogate from the principle of co-extensiveness. In two cases concerning guarantees of instalments due from purchasers of ships under shipbuilding contracts, the surety was held liable for the payment of certain accrued instalments rather than the damages which the debtor was liable to pay for breach of his obligation to pay those instalments.[66]

The courts purportedly relied on what was said in the *Lep Air* case in order to reach this result. It may be that the cases turned on their special facts and that when construed against the factual matrix the "guarantees" were in truth indemnities, though the reasoning is hard to reconcile with that explanation. It also appears that the principle of co-extensiveness may not have played a very substantial part in the argument. Until the matter is resolved, however, particular care will have to be used when drafting or advising on the construction of such contracts of guarantee.[67]

---

65 See the speech of Lord Diplock at 351.
66 *Hyundai Shipbuilding & Heavy Industries Co Ltd v Pournaras* [1978] 2 Lloyd's Rep. 502 and *Hyundai Heavy Industries Co Ltd v Papadopoulos* [1980] 1 W.L.R. 1129; see further *Stocznia Gdanska SA v Latvian Shipping Co* [1998] 1 W.L.R. 574; *BOC Group Plc v Centeon LLC* [1999] 1 All E.R. Comm. 53.
67 The principle of co-extensiveness and the *Hyundai* cases are considered in more detail in Ch.6 at paras 6–002 and 6–030 respectively.

Different forms of contract

4–015   The prospective parties to a contract of suretyship should consider carefully:

(a) what liabilities of the principal they intend to cover; and

(b) the precise extent of the liability of the surety under it.

An example illustrates some of the different possibilities which may occur:

> C is a manufacturer of textiles. D is a manufacturer of fashion garments who is regularly supplied by C with cloth. D's trade is seasonal by nature, and his garments have to be made well in advance of each coming fashion season. D's profitability depends on how well a particular line of fashion garments sells or is likely to sell in the shops. C knows that cashflow can be a problem for D and says that he must insist on cash on delivery terms unless D can find a guarantor. S, a retailer who is impressed by the general quality of D's garments, agrees to provide the guarantee if D will supply S's shops exclusively with his fashion collection for the next season.
>
> C, D and S must first decide which liabilities S is to guarantee, whether the extent of his liability is to be limited in any way, and when that liability is to accrue. There are a number of possibilities. S could guarantee the payment of:

(a) debts arising out of certain specific orders for textiles supplied by C to D (a specific guarantee);

(b) any balance that may be outstanding from time to time on D's account with C (a continuing unlimited guarantee);

(c) all debts that have already been incurred by D for supplies already made to him by C (a retrospective guarantee);

(d) all debts which may arise in the future between D and C (a prospective guarantee);

(e) all existing debts and any debts which may arise in the future in respect of cloth supplied by C to D (a retrospective and prospective guarantee);

(f) any balance that may be outstanding from time to time on D's account with C for more than 30 days (a continuing guarantee limited by time);

(g) any balance that may be outstanding on the account between C and D from time to time but with a maximum liability of £50,000 (a continuing guarantee for an unfixed sum but limited in amount);

(h) the price of the next £50,000 of cloth which is delivered from C to D (a guarantee for a limited sum);

(i) any balance that may be outstanding on account from time to time provided that D continues to supply S exclusively with his products (a conditional continuing guarantee);

(j) the price of all goods supplied by C to D between March 1 and July 30 that year (a guarantee limited in time).

It would also be possible to use combinations of the types of guarantee illustrated above to achieve the particular kind of agreement which C, D and S consider to be the most appropriate to suit their needs.

Retrospective and prospective guarantees

A prospective guarantee is one which relates to liabilities which may arise **4–016** in the future between the creditor and the principal. A retrospective guarantee is one which covers a pre-existing liability between the principal and the creditor. Most modern guarantees will clearly indicate that the guarantee applies to obligations already incurred by the principal towards the creditor as well as those which may fall due in the future, and are therefore both prospective and retrospective. A common form of wording in the guarantee is that the surety will pay "all monies which are now or may from time to time hereafter be owing or remain unpaid". Provided that future obligations are clearly covered, a guarantee will be prospective regardless of the fact that the consideration for it was a forebearance to sue for past indebtedness,[68] or the fact that the recital refers to past indebtedness.[69]

It is perfectly possible for the guarantee only to cover future liabilities of the principal to the creditor. In *Fahey v MSD Spiers* [1973] 2 N.Z.L.R. 665, NZ CA, the surety undertook to be liable for "any materials which are purchased from" the creditor, and it was held that the guarantee related to future indebtedness only.[70] Equally, it is perfectly possible for a guarantee to cover past indebtedness only, although there may be problems as to the consideration for the guarantee.[71] Thus, if such a guarantee is required, the creditor must take care to ensure either that some fresh consideration is given, or, preferably, that the guarantee is embodied in a deed.

An illustration of the difficulties which may occur when a guarantee is construed as being purely retrospective is the case of *Bell v Welch* (1850) 9 C.B. 154. The principal, R, was indebted to the creditor bank. The guarantee recited that he owed the creditor £800, and it was expressed to be "to the extent of £1,000 advanced or to be advanced to R, but the said indemnity to cease when the said R shall have paid the sum of £1,000 to the

---

68 *Coles v Pack* (1869) L.R. 5 C.P. 65.
69 *Sansom v Bell* (1809) 2 Camp. 39; *cf. Pearsall v Summersett* (1812) 4 Taunt. 593, where the recital as to past liabilities was held to override the substantive part of the guarantee which referred to future liabilities; see further para–4.008.
70 See also *Re A Debtor (No.1594 of 1992), The Times*, December 8, 1992, Knox J.
71 As to the effect of past consideration, see *Chitty on Contracts (op. cit.)*, Vol. 1, paras 3–026–3–027, and Ch.2.

credit of his account". In fact, the principal owed the creditor the sum of
£1,400 at the time the guarantee was given. It was held that the guarantee,
construed against the factual matrix when it was given, did not disclose a
good consideration; even though the words "advanced or to be advanced"
might be taken to include future as well as past advances, the sureties could
not be taken to have guaranteed future advances of £1,000.[72]

The main problems of construction arise when the substantive provisions
of the guarantee are ambiguous as to whether the liability is to be
retrospective or prospective. In *Morrell v Cowan* (1877) 7 Ch. D. 151 the
guarantee provided that "in consideration of you . . . having at my request
agreed to supply and furnish goods to C, I hereby guarantee to you . . . the
sum of £500". The guarantee was to last for six years after it was given. The
Court of Appeal held that the guarantee related only to the price of goods
supplied to the principal after the guarantee had been executed. There was
no consideration at the time the promise was given by the surety, since the
creditor was under no obligation to supply goods to the principal, but
consideration arose once the creditor had complied with the principal's
request for a supply of goods.[73]

Where there is an ambiguity, as in *Morrell v Cowan*, the courts have
tended to avoid the difficulties caused by past consideration by interpreting
the guarantee as covering future obligations.[74] However, circumstances may
indicate that it was intended to cover both past and future liabilities. Thus
in *Chalmers v Victors* (1868) 18 L.T. 481, S gave a guarantee stating that he
"engaged to be responsible for liabilities incurred by D to the extent of £50
to C". D was already indebted to C in the sum of £41. It was held that S's
guarantee covered the £41 debt already in existence and up to £9 of any
further indebtedness.

Where the consideration is future advances by the creditor, and past
transactions are intended to be covered, the courts have in the past
demanded the clearest terms,[75] although the modern approach is to regard
the guarantee as both prospective and retrospective.[76]

Other circumstances which have been taken to indicate that the guarantee is intended to have prospective effect are that the guarantee has been
given for more than the amount of the existing indebtedness,[77] that the
creditor refused to perform his own side of the bargain until the guarantee
had been executed,[78] and (though this should be treated with caution) that

---

72 See also *Bank of Montreal v Sperling Hotel Co Ltd* [1973] 4 W.W.R. 417 (Can).
73 *Per* James L.J. at 154.
74 See *Johnston v Nicholls* (1845) 1 C.B. 251; *Chapman v Sutton* (1846) 2 C.B. 643; *Chalmers v
    Victors* (1868) 18 L.T. 481; *Broom v Batchelor* (1856) 1 H. & N. 255; *Goldshede v Swan*
    (1847) 1 Exch. 154, and the discussion of the principle *ut res magis valeat quam pereat* at
    para.4-005 above.
75 *Morrell v Cowan* (1877) 7 Ch. D. 151, *per* James L.J. at 154.
76 See; *e.g. Egan v Static Control Components (Europe) Ltd* [2004] 2 Lloyd's Rep. 429,
    discussed in para.4-002 above; *Fahey v MSD Spiers Ltd* [1975] 1 N.Z.L.R. 240 at 244.
77 *Chalmers v Victors* (1868) 18 L.T. 481.
78 *Smith v Passmore* (1883) 4 L.R. (NSW) 274.

transactions subsequent to the execution of the guarantee took place between the principal and the creditor.[79]

Further, the recitals to the instrument of guarantee may assist in showing that it is only to be retrospective in effect. In *Re Medewe's Trust* (1859) 26 Beav. 588, the recital referred to the balance owing by the principal on three accounts. The guarantee was limited to £3,000 for whatever balance "shall or may be found due on the balance of the said several accounts". It was held that the guarantee covered only existing indebtedness, the word "shall" conveying only the uncertainty as to the exact amount then due, to be settled by agreement between them.

Where the guarantee is prospective, and is intended to cover a transaction to be performed in the future but which has been contracted for at the time of the execution of the guarantee, the guarantee will extend to it.[80]

An additional matter which could adversely affect the effectiveness of a retrospective guarantee from the creditor's point of view is the operation of the rule in *Devaynes v Noble, Clayton's* case (1816) 1 Mer. 572.[81] The problem arises whenever there will be further dealings between the principal and the creditor after the retrospective guarantee is given:

> D owes C £2,500 in respect of cloth which has already been supplied to him. S provides C with a guarantee under seal which states that "S agrees to guarantee payment to C of the sum of £2,500 owed to C by D in respect of cloth already supplied to D at the date hereof". Content in the knowledge that the indebtedness to date has been secured, C then supplies D with further cloth worth £2,000, and D subsequently pays him that sum. C then calls on S to pay him the £2,500 due for the earlier supplies.

If the rule in *Clayton's* case applies, the £2,000 paid by D to C would fall to be appropriated to the earliest debts which arose between D and C; and therefore S's liability would be reduced to £500 (£2,500 less £2,000). C would be unable to recover any part of the £2,000 for the further supplies from S because his guarantee was expressly limited to past supplies.[82] On the other hand, if the circumstances were exactly as stated in the example, save that S's guarantee stated "S agrees to guarantee payment to C of all sums which may become due and owing from D to C in respect of cloth which C may supply hereafter to D", the rule in *Clayton's* case could operate to C's advantage, because the £2,000 paid by D would be applied to

---

79 *Wood v Priestner* (1866) L.R. 2 Exch. 66; but it is doubtful if evidence of subsequent conduct would be admissible to interpret the guarantee: see *James Miller and Partners Ltd v Whitworth Street Estates* [1970] A.C. 583.
80 *Simmons v Keating* (1818) 2 Stark. 426.
81 Discussed at length in Ch.9 below, at para.9–007. It should be remembered that this is a general presumption as to the appropriation of payments into a current account where the debtor has not expressly appropriated them to a particular debt and no contrary intention is evident from the circumstances.
82 *Re Medewe's Trust* (1859) 26 Beav. 588.

reduce the pre-existing liabilities of D and not to reduce the indebtedness for the fresh supplies of cloth which S had guaranteed.[83]

In order to avoid the unfortunate result which the rule in *Clayton*'s case may cause him if he does not take care to expressly appropriate particular payments to particular invoices as and when they are made, a creditor who deals with the debtor on a regular basis should take pains to ensure that the guarantee is continuing and not retrospective. If the surety is reluctant to give an open-ended continuing guarantee, it could be limited in amount to the value of any existing liability, or limited in some other way.

Specific and continuing guarantees

4–017   A specific guarantee is one which covers a particular liability, or a particular transaction or series of transactions, for example, the sums due under an identified series of invoices. Common examples are guarantees given in conjunction with hire-purchase or credit sales agreements, or guarantees of repayment of instalments due under a mortgage of a housc or ship. A continuing guarantee is one which covers liabilities or transactions which continue to occur between the principal and creditor, such as the debts which fall due from time to time on a running account between a supplier of goods and a regular purchaser, or between a banker and its customer.

If the contract is a specific guarantee, payment for the goods sold, or repayment of the loan, ends the surety's liability; if it is continuing, he remains liable if further goods are supplied or moneys advanced up to any relevant limit.

It is not always easy to ascertain precisely into which category a particular guarantee belongs, and if the surety intends only to guarantee a particular transaction, he should ensure that this is clear.[84] There is no hard and fast rule which is used to determine whether a guarantee is specific or continuing, and the construction of one does not necessarily assist in the construction of another given in different circumstances.[85] Further, the cases are somewhat difficult to reconcile.[86]

For example, an agreement that "you may let D have cloth to £500 for which I will be answerable at any time" could be interpreted either as a specific guarantee, which covers only D's liability on any one delivery of cloth to D worth £500, or as a continuing guarantee which covers any outstanding balance on account of up to £500. Each case depends on the particular language used, and often the factual matrix will be determinative. In the example given, a different result might be reached if D had made a special order of cloth worth £500 which C had refused to supply unless he had a guarantee, because D's existing credit limit had been exhausted, from

---

83 See *Kirby v Duke of Marlborough* (1813) 2 M. & S. 18; *Williams v Rawlinson* (1825) 3 Bing. 71, *National Bank of New Zealand Ltd v Macintosh* (1881) 3 N.Z.L.R. 217.
84 *Merle v Wells* (1810) 2 Camp. 413, at 414 *per* Lord Ellenborough.
85 *Coles v Pack* (1869) L.R. 5 C.P. 65, at 70 *per* Bovill C.J.
86 *Chalmers v Victors* (1868) 18 L.T. 481, at 489 *per* Bovill C.J.; *Nicholson v Paget* (1832) 1 Cr. & M. 48; *Mayer v Isaac* (1840) 6 M. & W. 605, *per* Alderson B.

the result which might be reached if £500 were the regular credit limit for all supplies made by C to D from time to time. Consequently, the construction of one such document affords very little or no assistance to the construction of another, as the case of *Coles v Pack* (1869) L.R. 5 C.P. 65 illustrates.[87]

Generally, where there is an ambiguity, the court will lean in favour of construing the guarantee as a specific rather than a continuing one, in operation of the *contra proferentem* canon of construction.[88] However, the court may look at the surrounding circumstances in which the guarantee was given,[89] and the subject-matter of the transaction.[90] For example, in the Irish case of *Governor of the Bank of Ireland v McCabe* (1995) 4 J.I.B.L. 9–71, Egan J. held that a guarantee in respect of a loan which was stated to be "binding as a continuing security" was nevertheless a specific guarantee discharged when that loan was repaid to the bank. If the guarantee contains indications that it is to apply to a general course of dealing between the principal and the creditor rather than a specific transaction or advance, it may be construed as continuing. The intention to give a continuing guarantee may be inferred simply from the reference to "any debt" or "any sums of money" supplied to the principal.[91] It may also be inferred from the fact that the principal's business is such that it requires periodic supplies,[92] or from the past dealings between the principal and the creditor,[93] or from the fact that all the parties knew that the debtor and creditor had a running account.[94] It has even been inferred from subsequent dealings,[95] although the modern view is that evidence of subsequent dealings is not generally admissible as an aid to construction.[96]

In *Mayer v Isaac* (1832) 1 C. & M. 48 the guarantee provided that "in consideration of your supplying my nephew Vogel with china and earthenware, I hereby guarantee the payment of any bills you may draw on him on account thereof, to the amount of £200". Alderson B held that the guarantee was a continuing guarantee, contemplating "the continuance of a supply on one side, and on the other a liability for any default during that supply; and then it defines the extent to which the defendant will be bound upon this continuing or running guarantee, viz, £200". He distinguished the

---

[87] See also the cases referred to in Rowlatt, *Principal and Surety* (Sweet & Maxwell, 5th ed., 1999), pp.53–5.

[88] As to which see para.4–002, and see *Nicholson v Paget* (1832) 1 Cr. & M. 48, at 54 *per* Bayley B.; *cf. Mayer v Isaac* (1840) 6 M. & W. 605.

[89] *Heffield v Meadows* (1869) L.R. 4 C.P. 595; *Walker v Hardman* (1837) 4 Cl. & Fin. 258; *Chalmers v Victors* (1868) 18 L.T. 481.

[90] *Johnston v Nicholls* (1845) 1 C.B. 251.

[91] *Bastow v Bennett* (1812) 3 Camp. 220; *Mason v Pritchard* (1812) 2 Camp. 436; *Nottingham Hide, Skin & Fat Market Co v Bottrill* (1873) L.R. 8 C.P. 694.

[92] *See v Farey* (1889) 10 N.S.W.L.R. 72.

[93] *Johnston v Nicholls* (1845) 1 C.B. 251.

[94] *Heffield v Meadows* (1869) L.R. 4 C.P. 595.

[95] *Burgess v Eve* (1872) 26 L.T. 450.

[96] *James Miller and Partners Ltd v Whitworth Street Estates (Manchester) Ltd* [1970] A.C. 583; *Amalgamated Investment and Property Co Ltd v Texas Commerce International Bank* [1982] Q.B. 84.

guarantee from the one in *Nicholson v Paget* (1840) 6 M. & W. 48, which referred to a liability for the price of a specific consignment of gin.[97]

Where the guarantee is limited in amount, this is not necessarily an indication that the surety's liability is to be limited to a specific transaction.[98] Indeed it is common to find such limitations in continuing guarantees. For example, an agreement to guarantee payment of all sums not exceeding £2,000 in total which might from time to time be advanced by a bank to its customer on account, would be a continuing guarantee.[99] A limit will usually be interpreted as restricting the surety's liability rather than making that liability conditional upon the creditor only advancing a sum up to that amount to the principal debtor.[1] However, if the contract indicates that a particular debt or transaction is contemplated, it is likely to be construed as a specific guarantee. Thus if the amount of the guarantee precisely equates with a particular debt the court may infer from the facts that it was intended to relate to that debt only. For example, in *Plaster Decoration & Papier Mâché Co Ltd v Massey-Mainwaring* (1895) 11 T.L.R. 205, D had contracted with C for building works costing £1,500 and had paid £200 when S gave a guarantee of £1,300 for the price of building works carried out by C for D. The court held that the guarantee related only to the specific balance which was then outstanding in respect of the work already carried out, and that the guarantee did not cover additional work subsequently contracted for by D.

There is a special rule of construction governing guarantees embodied in a promissory note, given for a fixed sum on a fixed day. In *Re Boys, Eeds v Boys* (1870) L.R. 10 Eq. 467, it was held that where a promissory note is given by a surety for a specified sum, payable on a fixed day, there is a presumption that it has been given in consideration of an advance made at the date of the note, and that if the payee asserts that the note was intended to secure payment of the balance of a running account, the burden of proving that assertion rests on him.[2] The presumption may be rebutted by evidence to the contrary showing that it is for future advances.[3] Further, the fact that the promissory note is payable on demand rather than on a fixed day may mean that it is interpreted as a continuing security.[4]

---

97 See also the guarantees held to be continuing in *Allen v Kenning* (1833) 9 Bing. 618 ("an inducement to you to continue your dealings with" the creditor); *Martin v Wright* (1845) 6 Q.B. 917 ("in consideration of your agreeing to supply goods to K at two months' credit"); *Hargreave v Smee* (1829) 6 Bing. 244 ("according to the custom of their trading with you").

98 *Laurie v Scholefield* (1869) L.R. 4 C.P. 622, and see the authorities referred to in O'Donovan & Phillips (*op. cit.*), p.228 esp. n.98.

99 See, *e.g. Batson v Spearman* (1838) 9 Ad. & El. 298; *Laurie v Scholefield* (1869) L.R. 4 C.P. 622.

1 See, *e.g. Total Oil Products (Aust) Pty Ltd v Robinson* [1970] 1 N.S.W.R. 701; *Matthews Thompson & Co Ltd v Everson* (1934) 34 S.R. (NSW) 114.

2 *Cf. Pease v Hirst* (1829) 10 B. & C. 122 where the promissory note was clearly intended to be a continuing security. See also *Walker v Hardman* (1837) 4 Cl. & Fin. 258.

3 For example by an attached memorandum: *Hartland v Jukes* (1863) 1 H. & C. 667; *Henniker v Wigg* (1843) 4 Q.B. 792.

4 *Pease v Hirst* (1829) 10 B. & C. 122.

Limited guarantees

Guarantees may be limited in time or in amount, or both. A guarantee may **4–018** also be limited by reference to the nature of the underlying principal obligation or contract which is being guaranteed. These different types of limitation are considered in turn below.

Guarantees limited in time

A creditor who takes a guarantee limited in time to supplies made between **4–019** certain dates may again have to take care to avoid the consequences of the rule in *Clayton's* case. This is illustrated by the following example based on the facts set out above at para.4–015:

> D's leanest trading period each year is the one immediately before the new autumn fashion season has begun in September, when he has made his garments, but sales have not yet generated substantial profits. S therefore agrees to guarantee payment of all liabilities arising on D's trading account with C during the three months from June to August, and does so in the terms that "this guarantee is to be a continuing guarantee of all liabilities of D to C incurred between 1 June and 31 August 2000". On August 31 D's indebtedness is in excess of £30,000, but in September he begins to obtain payments for the garments and pays £35,000 to C. Despite this, fresh supplies of cloth made to him by C from September onwards result in a substantial debit balance on the running account which eventually causes C to terminate the account.

Notwithstanding the use of the word "continuing" in the guarantee, S's liability is confined to any debts which were incurred during the specific period. Accordingly if the £35,000 paid to C is appropriated to the earliest debts arising under the running account, in accordance with the rule in *Clayton's* case, the value of S's guarantee will disappear once a sufficient payment has been made to cover the indebtedness arising on invoices for cloth supplied to D during the limited period. This problem could be avoided by the use of appropriate language in the guarantee, for example by inserting a clause to the effect that "S shall remain liable to C on the amount outstanding on D's account on August 31 notwithstanding any subsequent payments into or out of the account by D".

A limitation in time may be implied by reference to the duration of the underlying contract between the creditor and principal. As a general rule, a guarantee for the performance by a person of obligations arising under a contract of service, a contract for services, or a tenancy agreement, will normally be interpreted as limited to the duration of the underlying contract, even if this is not expressly stated in the guarantee. Thus if a surety guarantees the due performance by the principal of his duties as an office holder, and the appointment of the principal to that office is for a limited period, the surety's liability may be confined to the performance of the principal's duties during that period, even if he is reappointed for a further period with the knowledge of the surety.[5] On the other hand, if the guarantee expressly covers the possibility of an extension of the principal's term of office, it is likely to be interpreted as applying to any extended term.[6] Where the recital stipulates a period of employment, there are cases which suggest that the guarantee will be confined to that period, notwithstanding clear wording in the main body of the guarantee instrument to the effect that it is to extend to all times during which the principal continues in that employment or office.[7] The modern approach to construction, however, is to give precedence to what is in the body of the instrument.

If the office, employment or tenancy is for an indefinite period, or continues from year to year until determined, the liability of the guarantor will usually continue until the underlying contract is determined or materially varied, whether or not a fresh agreement arises on its determination.[8] A guarantee of the obligations of a tenant under a lease for a fixed period will not usually extend beyond the duration of that tenancy.[9] Thus a guarantee will not extend to obligations under a statutory continuation of the tenancy when the original period expires, unless the wording clearly contemplates this.[10]

If a guarantee given to cover contingent liabilities of the principal is expressly limited in time, a question of interpretation which frequently arises is whether the guarantee covers only liabilities which accrue during the limited period, or whether it extends to liabilities which arise after that period has expired, as a result of transactions entered into during that period. Again this is a matter which will depend on the wording of the particular contract of suretyship and the nature of the underlying transaction. In *Hollond v Teed* (1848) 7 Hare 50, a guarantee was given to a banking house, consisting of several partners, for the repayment of such bills drawn upon them by one of their customers, as the bank might honour, and any advances they might make to the same customer, within a specified time. One of the partners died before the specified period had expired, and the guarantee ceased upon his death. It was held that bills accepted before the date of actual termination and payable afterwards were covered by the guarantee. No decision was made on the question whether bills accepted on the day before the termination date stated in the contract, and payable subsequently, would also have been covered. However, it is likely that the result would have been the same had this point been in issue; the banking house was bound to honour the bills on their due dates, and the act of

---

5 *Kitson v Julian* (1854) 4 E. & B. 854; *Wardens of St Saviour's, Southwark v Bostock* (1806) 2 B. & P.N.R. 175; *Bamford v Iles* (1849) 3 Exch. 380.
6 *Augero v Keen* (1836) 1 M. & W. 390.
7 *Liverpool Waterworks Co v Atkinson* (1805) 6 East. 507; *Peppin v Cooper* (1819) 2 B. & Ald. 431; *Kitson v Julian* (1885) 4 E. & B. 854.
8 *Birmingham Corporation v Wright* (1851) 16 Q.B. 623; *Frank v Edwards* (1852) 8 Exch. 214.
9 *Holme v Brunskill* (1878) 3 Q.B.D. 495; *Giddens v Dodd* (1856) 3 Drew. 485; *Tayleur v Wildin* (1868) L.R. 3 Ex. 303; *Freeman v Evans* [1922] 1 Ch. 36.
10 Compare *Junction Estates Ltd v Cope* (1974) 27 P. & C.R. 482, and *Plesser v Davis* (1983) 267 E.G. 1039, with *Associated Dairies v Pierce* (1982) 265 E.G. 127.

acceptance gave rise to the liability which the guarantee was plainly intended to cover.

In *Rank Enterprises Ltd v Gerard* (unreported, Commercial Court, July 14, 1997) Toulson J. determined a number of questions of construction of a guarantee given in connection with an agreement for the purchase of three ships. The guarantee was in respect of "any claims incurred prior to the time of delivery" made against the vessels, and was to remain in force for one year. Two actions had been commenced in Malta, impugning the authority of the selling companies to sell the vessels and seeking declarations that the supposed sales were nullities. The buyers started proceedings under the guarantee. It was held that "claims incurred prior to delivery" meant "claims in respect of any liabilities incurred prior to delivery" and not "claims that liabilities had been incurred prior to delivery". A "claim" did not require the formal institution of proceedings, but there had to be a demand which carried with it a real and present threat of seizure or arrest of the vessel. The one year time-limit merely required the making of a claim against the vessel within that period, rather than the sustaining of any loss, damage or expense arising out of such a claim.

Guarantees limited in amount

Guarantees limited in amount pose special problems. The limitation may 4–020 take effect in one of two different ways. The guarantee may be in respect of the whole of the liability of D to C, but with a limitation placed on the amount for which the surety is to be liable. Alternatively, it may cover only part of the total liability of D to C, co-extensive with the amount of the guarantee. The difference is between a promise by the guarantor that he will be liable for £100 of any amount which D shall owe C (a partial liability), and a promise to guarantee the payment for all goods supplied by C to D, subject to the limitation that he is not to be called on to pay more than £100 (a liability for the whole, subject to a monetary limit). The distinction may be vitally important, particularly on the bankruptcy of D. This is a matter which is discussed in detail in Chapter 13.

It is a question of construction in each case which form the guarantee takes: *Re Rees Ex p. National Provincial Bank of England* (1881) 17 Ch. D. 98. Certain principles of construction have been laid down to assist in the determination of which type of guarantee is involved in a particular case. If the guarantee is a continuing guarantee, limited in amount, to secure a floating balance which may be due from time to time from the principal to the creditor, then prima facie it is to be construed as applying to only part of the debt, co-extensive with the amount of the guarantee.[11] The reason for this prima facie rule is that the creditor can increase the total debt without reference to the surety, and if the contract were to be construed as covering the entire indebtedness, this could gravely prejudice the surety in the event

---

11 *Ellis v Emmanuel* (1876) 1 Ex. D. 157; *Huggard v Representative Church Body* [1916] 1 I.R. 1; *Re D (A Lunatic Patient) (No.2)* [1926] V.L.R. 467 at 486.

of the debtor's bankruptcy.[12] However, the language of a limited guarantee given to secure a floating balance may clearly indicate an intention that it is to apply to the entire debt.[13] The wording of standard form bank guarantees usually makes it clear that the surety is to be liable for the whole debt, but with a limit on his liability.[14] However, a standard form guarantee which provides a space for the limit to be inserted will be construed as an unlimited guarantee if the space is left blank.[15]

On the other hand, a guarantee limited in amount given for a debt already ascertained which exceeds that limit, is not prima facie to be construed as a guarantee for part of the debt only.[16] It has been suggested by some commentators that such guarantees are prima facie to be construed as guarantees for the whole debt subject to the limit specified,[17] but the cases do not appear to go this far; the better view is that there is no prima facie rule and that each contract has to be considered on its own wording.

If the guarantee is a continuing guarantee covering future transactions, and there is no express stipulation for a limit on liability, then it will usually be construed as being unlimited in amount: *Coles v Pack* (1869) L.R. 5 C.P. 65.

Guarantees limited by reference to the principal transaction

4–021   It is possible for the guarantee to be limited by reference to the type of principal transaction guaranteed.[18] In *United Dominions Trust Ltd v Beech* [1972] 1 Lloyd's Rep. 546 the guarantee provided that:

> "in consideration of your providing banking facilities to [the principal] we hereby jointly and severally guarantee the prompt payment of all or any sums of money for which [the principal] may become liable to you and we hereby jointly and severally guarantee to hold you harmless of any loss or damage which you may sustain by reason of your having extended the above-mentioned banking facilities."

---

12 See, *e.g.* the observations of Lord Hatherley in *Hobson v Bass* (1871) 6 Ch. App. 792 at 795. See also *Bardwell v Lydall* (1831) 7 Bing. 489.

13 *Re Sass*, below; *Re Rees*, above; *Ellis v Emmanuel*, above; *Midland Banking Co v Chambers* (1869) 4 Ch. App. 398.

14 See, *e.g. Re Sass Ex p. National Provincial Bank of England* [1896] 2 Q.B. 12 ("this guarantee is to be security for the whole amount now due or owing") and Precedent 1.

15 *Caltex Oil (Australia) Pty Ltd v Alderton* (1964) 81 W.N. (NSW) (Pt 1) 297; see also *New Zealand Loan and Mercantile Agency Co Ltd v Paterson* (1882) N.Z.L.R. 1 CA 325; *Bank of Baroda v ANY Enterprises Ltd* (unreported) CAT No.1088 of 1986, December 4; *Bank of Baroda v Patel* [1996] 1 Lloyd's Rep. 391. *Cf. State Bank of India v Kaur* [1996] 5 Bank. L.R. 158.

16 Compare *Thornton v M'Kewan*, (1862) 32 L.J. Ch. 69; *Ex p. Rushforth* (1805) 10 Ves. 409; *Re Garner, Ex p. Holmes* (1839) Mont. & Ch. 301; *Hobson v Bass* (1871) 6 Ch. App. 792 with *Gee v Pack* (1863) 33 L.J.Q.B. 49; *Paley v Field* (1806) 12 Ves. 435; *Gray v Seckham* (1872) 7 Ch. App. 680; and see the discussion in Ch.12.

17 See *Chitty on Contracts* (*op. cit.*), Vol. 2 at para.44–064.

18 This is also a very common form of limitation to be found in contracts of indemnity.

It was held that the guarantee was limited to liabilities of the principal incurred in respect of banking facilities afforded it by the creditor, and not in respect of goods and debts discounted through the creditor bank, which was not a banking activity.[19]

This case may be contrasted with *Bank of India v Transcontinental Commodity Merchants and Patel* [1982] 1 Lloyd's Rep. 506, where the recital to the guarantee expressed it to have been given in consideration of the creditor "affording banking facilities" to the principal, but the main body of the guarantee covered all sums which should be owing to the creditor "on any account whatsoever". Bingham J. took the view that the expression of consideration should not be taken to limit the guarantee to debts arising from banking facilities.[20]

In *Banner Lane Realisations Ltd (in liq.) v Berisford Plc* [1997] 1 B.C.L.C. 380, a settlement agreement had been entered into between a parent company, B, and its former subsidiary, W, which was the subject of a management buy-out. In consideration of B continuing to guarantee W's overdraft with its bank, W granted it a debenture as security for all monies outstanding, up to a limit of £1 million, in respect of W's "present or future indebtedness [to B] under the settlement agreement". Subsequently administrative receivers were appointed under the debenture. The bank called on B to pay under the guarantee, which it did, and B claimed repayment from W. By that time, however, B's primary liabilities under the settlement agreement had all been discharged. B argued that it was not liable because there was no "indebtedness" under the settlement agreement. The Court of Appeal, however, held that a debt, in this context, was not confined to a present obligation to pay a sum certain, and that the expression "future indebtedness" encompassed a present obligation to pay an as yet unquantified sum in the future or on a contingency.

Conditional guarantees

A guarantee may be made expressly conditional on the existence or occurrence of some event, or such a condition may be implied in order to give the bargain business efficacy.[21] Although these conditions may appear to be mainly favourable to the surety, they can also benefit the creditor by postponing the accrual of his cause of action against the surety.   **4–022**

Conditions precedent to the liability of the surety

If a guarantee is conditional, the condition will normally take the form of a condition precedent to the surety's liability. Thus if the agreement clearly contemplates that another person is going to execute the guarantee as co-surety, the guarantee may be read as subject to the condition precedent that the guarantee is executed by that co-surety: *Evans v Bremridge* (1856) 25   **4–023**

---

19 *United Dominions Trust Ltd v Beech* [1972] 1 Lloyd's Rep. 546 at 551.
20 At 512 (affirmed [1983] 2 Lloyd's Rep. 298).
21 See, *e.g. Guy-Pell v Foster* [1930] 2 Ch. 169.

L.J. Ch. 102 at 334.[22] This will usually be the case if the guarantee is stated to be joint and several. In *James Graham & Co (Timber) Ltd v Southgate-Sands* [1986] Q.B. 80, the evidence was that the parties mutually contemplated a joint and several guarantee being given by all three of the directors of the borrowing company; one of the signatures was forged, and the Court of Appeal held that the other guarantors who signed were not liable because the condition precedent had not been fulfilled. In a similar case in Australia, *Keith Murphy Pty Ltd v Custom Credit Corporation Ltd* (1992) 6 W.A.R. 332, it was held that a provision in the contract pertaining to the release of one of the joint and several obligors did not negate the general rule that all the contemplated guarantors must sign a joint and several guarantee before the guarantee is to become operative. Again, the forgery of the signatures of some of the guarantors proved fatal.[23] It is possible, however, that a guarantee expressed to be in joint form will be enforceable against only one signatory, if it can be shown that the guarantor intended to be bound as sole guarantor: *Walter & Morris Ltd v Lymberis* [1965] S.A.S.R. 204.[24] or if there is a specific provision in the contract protecting the creditor, such as the clause in the guarantee given by the partners in *Bank of Scotland v Henry Butcher & Co* [2001] 2 All E.R. (Comm) 691. The obligation to ensure that the agreement is executed by all the contemplated parties lies on the creditor, and the known insolvency of one of the named co-sureties will not in itself dispense with the requirement of obtaining that person's signature: *Fitzgerald v M'Cowan* [1898] 2 I.R. 1.

Similarly, if the parties agree to the provision by the principal of additional security for the liability to be guaranteed, the guarantee may be read as only becoming operative if the additional security is provided. This condition may be express, as in the Australian case of *Malone v Wright, Heaton & Co* (1895) 6 Q.L.J. 270, or implied, as in *Greer v Kettle* [1938] A.C. 156. An example is the Irish case of *Hong Kong and Shanghai Banking Corporation v Icarom Plc (Meadows Indemnity Co Ltd, Third Party)* (1993) Irish Law Times, 142. A Greek businessman, operating through a Swiss company, Amaxa, wanted to finance the purchase of an interest in a hotel in Corfu, but Amaxa was unable to raise a loan from various banks because of inadequate security. Amaxa approached the defendant, an insurance company, for a "credit guarantee insurance agreement" which would be security for the loan. The plaintiff bank made the loan to Amaxa, secured by the credit guarantee insurance ("CGI") agreement, which both Blayney

---

22 *Cf. Norton v Powell* (1842) 4 Man. & G. 42.
23 See also *Marston v Charles K Griffith & Co Pty Ltd* (1982) 3 N.S.W.L.R. 294, (but *cf. Taubmans Pty Ltd v Loakes* [1991] 2 Qd. R. 109); *Hong Leong Finance Ltd v Goy Khim Teik* [1994] 1 S.L.R. 366 (Singapore).
24 See also *McNamara v Commonwealth Trading Bank of Australia* (1984) 37 S.A.S.R. 232, and *BP Australia Ltd v Anderson* (unreported) Supreme Court, South Australia, November 24, 1994, where one of the two joint guarantors refused to sign the guarantee, but the other guarantor was held to have dispensed with the condition of execution by the co-guarantor by allowing the document which he had signed to be forwarded by fax to the plaintiff. See also *Gattellaro v Westpac Banking Corporation* [2004] 204 A.L.R. 258.

J. and the Supreme Court subsequently categorised as a contract of guarantee. The defendant obtained an agreement from Meadows that they would "reinsure" the defendant's liability provided that the loan to Amaxa was properly secured. The defendant took security for the loan from Amaxa in the form of shares in the Greek hotel. It subsequently transpired that the transfer contravened Greek law, but despite this, the defendant was held liable under the CGI agreement. The Supreme Court upheld the judge's decision that whether the contract between the defendant and Meadows was one of insurance or one of guarantee, it was an agreement which arose if and only if the loan to Amaxa was secured in the manner intended by the parties. Since the security was unenforceable, the defendant was not entitled to an indemnity in respect of the money paid to the plaintiff under the CGI agreement.

However, a mere stipulation in the contract for the provision of additional security will not in itself suffice to establish a condition precedent. There must be some evidence to show that the parties to the contract of suretyship regarded it as an essential term. The creditor may require the provision of additional security simply for his own protection, and if there is no evidence to show that the surety, at least, insisted that his liability should depend on the provision of the additional security there will probably be no basis for the implication of a condition precedent.[25]

If the contract of suretyship, as a matter of construction, does not require the security to be in place before that contract is entered into, it may suffice if the additional security is provided at any time before the surety is called upon to meet his liability: see *Australia & New Zealand Banking Group Ltd v Beneficial Finance Corp Ltd* (1983) 44 A.L.R. 241, PC in which a floating charge was not executed for some eight months after the guarantee.

In the absence of an express provision, a guarantee would not normally be read as subject to a condition precedent that the principal or a co-surety should provide additional security or execute a guarantee for an entirely different liability, because that would not affect the surety's rights; similar reasoning may preclude the introduction of implied conditions precedent of this type into a contract of indemnity.[26]

It might also be held in an appropriate case that a contract of suretyship is conditional upon the creditor entering into a valid and enforceable contract with the principal.[27] Thus in *Walton v Cook* (1889) 40 Ch. D. 325, a surety for the payment of sums under a composition made by a bankrupt with his creditors was discharged from liability when the composition was annulled by the court; and in *Bentworth Finance Ltd v Lubert* [1968] 1 Q.B. 680, a person who gave an indemnity to a finance company in respect of a

---

25 *Byblos Bank SAL v Al-Khudhairy* [1987] B.C.L.C. 232; *J G L Investments Pty Ltd v Maracorp Financial Services Ltd* [1991] 2 V.R. 168; *Capital Bank Cashflow Finance v Southall* [2004] EWCA (Civ) 817, discussed at 12–001 below.

26 *Coope v Twynham* (1823) 1 T. & R. 426.

27 See, *e.g. Associated Japanese Bank (International) Ltd v Credit du Nord SA* [1989] 1 W.L.R. 255, where the guarantee related to a "leaseback" agreement in respect of machines which it transpired did not exist.

hire-purchase agreement was not liable because the finance company had failed to perform a condition precedent to the hire-purchase contract, namely to provide the hirer with a log book for the car which was the subject of the transaction. If the contract of suretyship is a guarantee, the principle of co-extensiveness would normally operate to protect the surety in this type of case: if the underlying contract is invalid or unenforceable against the principal, the guarantor would not be liable. An interesting aspect of the two cases referred to is that the contracts of suretyship were indemnities, so that the principle of co-extensiveness did not apply: the result was reached purely as a matter of construction.

Other conditions precedent to the surety's liability may include entry by the creditor into a settlement agreement with the principal, or the release of some other security, for example an earlier guarantee which the new contract is to replace. The safest and simplest way to perform the latter type of condition is to execute a deed of release. If physical delivery up to the surety or some other person of any document is required, the creditor should take care to ensure that the performance of the condition is adequately evidenced, to avoid later dispute. The document should preferably be handed over in person, the delivery witnessed, and the recipient should be required to sign a document then and there, acknowledging delivery of the document. If this means of proceeding is impossible, then the creditor should at least use registered post to despatch the document and keep as many records as possible of its despatch to the right address. The creditor should also try to obtain acknowledgement of its receipt by the surety.

By far the most common type of condition precedent to the liability of the surety is an express provision which requires that the creditor should take some specified step, such as giving him notice of default,[28] making a demand on the surety or on the principal,[29] or suing the principal,[30] before he starts proceedings against the surety. In the absence of an express provision the creditor may proceed against the surety without prior notice to him or demand against him and without taking any proceedings against the principal.[31]

Express conditions precedent are likely to be strictly construed, in accordance with the general approach to construction of contracts of suretyship. Thus in *Hill v Nuttall* (1864) 17 C.B.N.S. 262, the surety requested the creditor to deliver a quantity of 500,000 best bricks to D, a government contractor, in order to enable D to carry out a particular

---

28 *Eshelby v Federated European Bank* [1932] 1 K.B. 423; *The "Queen Frederica"* [1978] 2 Lloyd's Rep. 164 *Oval (717) Ltd v Aegon Insurance Co (UK) Ltd* (1997) 54 Con.L.R. 74. See also *Bache & Co v Banque Vernes et Commerciales de Paris* [1973] 2 Lloyd's Rep. 437, in which the notice was also conclusive evidence of default by the debtor.

29 *Re Brown's Estate* [1893] 2 Ch. 300; *Bradford Old Bank Ltd v Sutcliffe* [1918] 2 K.B. 833; *Tate v Crewdson* [1938] Ch. 869 at 874, *per* Morton J. See also *Dow Banking Cpn v Mahnakh Spinning and Weaving Cpn* [1983] 2 Lloyd's Rep. 561, and *Stimpson v Smith* [1999] 2 W.L.R. 1292, where it was held that one of a number of co-sureties may waive the requirement of a demand on the surety.

30 *Holl v Hadley* (1835) 2 Ad. & El. 758; *Lawrence v Walmsley* (1862) 12 C.B.N.S. 799.

31 *Moschi v Lep Air* [1973] A.C. 331 at 348, and see the discussion in Chs 7 and 11.

building contract. The surety guaranteed payment of the price "when the amount of the contract is paid". D was paid a certain amount in advance by the government, but was subsequently dismissed and the work was completed by someone else. It was held that the condition precedent was not fulfilled, and the surety was not liable, because the full amount of the contract had not been paid to D (albeit that he had been paid something and had been dismissed because of his own default).[32] See also *Frans Maas (UK) Ltd v Habib Bank AG Zurich* [2001] 1 Lloyd's Rep. Bank 14 (Sir Christopher Bellamy Q.C.), where a demand which failed to assert in terms that the principal had failed to pay was held to be a bad demand under a performance guarantee.

Conditions limiting the extent or duration of the liability of the surety
A condition may also limit the extent or duration of the liability of the **4–024** surety under the contract of suretyship. For example, a guarantee of a company's overdraft could be given by a director for so long as he remains a director of the company; a retailer of goods supplied by the principal might agree to guarantee the principal's account with his own suppliers provided that the principal continued to supply the retailer. Similarly, as already illustrated above, a guarantee of a running account could be made subject to the express proviso that the indebtedness will not exceed a particular sum, or that if it does exceed a particular sum, notice should be given to the surety.[33]

In such cases, the court is unlikely to interpret the contract in such a way as to deprive the creditor of his rights against the surety as soon as the condition ceases to be fulfilled. Thus, when the company director resigns or is removed, his liability for the debts of the company may cease as to the future, but he would probably remain liable for debts which accrued during his directorship. Similarly, if the amount imposed on the running account by the surety is exceeded, the guarantee would normally be interpreted as limiting his liability to the sum stipulated, unless the language used makes it plain that he is to be discharged from liability altogether if more than that sum is allowed to fall due.

Another possible restriction which a surety may impose is that any claim against him must be met out of a specific fund[34] or that payment will be made out of any moneys which he, the surety, may owe the principal on another transaction.[35]

---

32 See also *BLM Holdings Pty Ltd v Bank of New Zealand* [1994] 11 J.I.B.L. 227, NSW CA and *Halsbury's Laws* (*op. cit.*), Vol. 20 at para.197.
33 See, *e.g. Gordon v Rae* (1858) 8 E. & B. 1065, in which, however, failure to give the surety notice of the increased indebtedness did not discharge him from liability.
34 See, *e.g. Brown v Fletcher* (1876) 35 L.T. 165; *Wilson v Craven* (1841) 8 M. & W. 584; *Stephens v Pell* (1834) 2 Cr. & M. 710.
35 *Parkins v Moravia* (1824) 1 C. & P. 276; *Dixon v Hatfield* (1825) 2 Bing. 439; *Steggal v Lymburner* (1912) 14 W.A.L.R. 210 (Aus).

Chapter 5

Vitiating Elements in the Contract

Introduction

5–001 A contract of suretyship, like any other contract, may be void or voidable by reason of undue influence, duress, mistake (including *non est factum*), misrepresentation, or fraud. In fairly rare cases, the contract may be susceptible to avoidance on the grounds that it was *ultra vires* the surety or illegal.[1] In addition, the special nature of the contract and the relationship between the parties may give rise to a defence of non-disclosure. A detailed general discussion of these defences is beyond the scope of this book; however, this chapter considers their particular application in the context of contracts of suretyship, and certain of the practical implications for the parties. A related matter, which is discussed in Chapter 6, is the effect of the unenforceability of the underlying contract between the creditor and the principal, on the contract between the creditor and the surety.

Mistake

5–002 As with any other contract, a fundamental mistake by all, or sometimes by one, of the parties to it may make a contract of suretyship null and void, or voidable.[2] If the contract is fundamentally different from what the parties believed it to be, it will be void at common law.[3] In *Great Peace Shipping Ltd v Tsavliris Salvage Ltd* [2003] Q.B. 679, the Court of Appeal held that if a contract were to be avoided for common mistake, there had to be a common assumption as to the existence of a state of affairs, and no warranty by either party that that state of affairs existed. Further, the non-existence of the state of affairs must not be attributable to the fault of either party. If it was possible to perform the letter of the contract, but it was alleged that there was a common mistake in relation to a fundamental assumption which rendered performance of the essence of the obligation impossible, it was necessary to construe the contract in the light of all the

---

1 The effect of illegal consideration has already been considered in Ch.2 (see para.2–015).
2 See generally the discussion in *Chitty on Contracts* (Sweet & Maxwell, 29th ed., 2004), Ch.5.
3 *Bell v Lever Brothers* [1932] A.C. 161.

material circumstances in order to determine whether or not the contract could be avoided. However, there was no equitable jurisdiction to rescind the contract for common mistake in circumstances falling short of those in which the contract would be regarded as void at common law. This means that the contract cannot be set aside on terms, though in appropriate cases restitutionary remedies may be available.[4]

Since the decision of the House of Lords in *Kleinwort Benson v Lincoln City Council* [1998] 3 W.L.R. 1095, it does not matter whether the mistake is one of law or of fact. It is generally more difficult to procure a remedy for a unilateral mistake than for a mistake which is mutual, particularly if the contract is in writing, as most contracts of suretyship will be. A guarantor cannot avoid liability simply on the basis that he misunderstood the contract, even if the court forms the view that he would not have signed it had he appreciated what its provisions actually meant, for example, if he signed an "all monies" guarantee believing it to be limited in amount or limited to specific transactions. However, if he can prove that he was under a fundamental mistake as to the nature or effect of the guarantee or its subject-matter at the time when he entered into it,[5] and that the creditor knew this and failed to correct his mistake, the guarantee will be voidable, or alternatively it may be rectified to accord with the surety's understanding of its terms.[6] In general there is no room for the doctrine of constructive knowledge, and mere suspicion by the creditor that the surety is labouring under a misapprehension will not suffice. Nevertheless, the law in this area is still developing and recent authorities indicate that where there is unconscionable conduct, rules of equity will be applied in such a way as to relieve the innocent party from the consequences of his mistake: see, *e.g. Commission for The New Towns v Cooper* [1995] Ch. 259 in which the Court of Appeal rectified a contract pertaining to the sale of land because one party, suspecting the other to be mistaken in its understanding of the terms of the contract, did what it could to prevent the error from being discovered. See also *Taylor v Johnson* (1983) 151 C.L.R. 422.

The surety will be unable to obtain relief in respect of the consequences of a mistake if the contract expressly or by implication visits the consequences of such a mistake upon him.[7] Nor will he be able to obtain relief

---

4 Disapproving and refusing to follow. Solle v Butcher [1950] 1 K.B. 671 on the grounds that it is incompatible with *Bell v Lever Brothers* (above). For a full discussion of the case and its implications see Chitty, *op. cit.*, at paras 5–043–5–049.

5 See, *e.g. Small v Currie* (1854) 1 Drew 102 at 114; *Royal Bank of Canada v Hale* (1961) 30 DLR (2d) 138; *Royal Bank of Canada v Oram* (1978) 1 W.W.R. 564. A mistake as to the commercial consequences of the contract will not suffice: *Clarion Ltd v National Provident Institution* [2000] 1 W.L.R. 1888.

6 See, *e.g. Agip SpA v Navigazione Alta Italia SpA (The "Nai Genova" and "Nai Superba")* [1984] 1 Lloyd's Rep. 353; *Royal Bank of Scotland v Purvis* (1990) S.L.T. 262; *Royal Bank of Canada v Oram* (above); *General Credits Ltd v Ebsworth* [1986] 2 Qd R 162.

7 *Associated Japanese Bank (International) Ltd v Credit du Nord SA* [1989] 1 W.L.R. 255 *per* Steyn J. at 268; *William Sindall Plc v Cambridgeshire County Council* [1994] 1 W.L.R. 1016 *per* Hoffmann L.J. at 1035.

from the consequences of his mistaken belief, if that belief was unreasonable.[8]

Forms of mistake

5–003   A good modern illustration of the operation of the relevant common law and equitable principles in connection with a contract of suretyship is the case of *Associated Japanese Bank (International) Ltd v Credit du Nord SA* [1989] 1 W.L.R. 255. The defendants had agreed to guarantee the obligations of B under an agreement which he had made for the sale to the plaintiffs, and leaseback from them, of four industrial machines. At all material times, B had represented that the machines existed and the plaintiffs and the defendants reasonably believed him. It transpired that B had been fraudulent and that there were no such machines. The defendants' primary contention, that the existence of the machines was a condition precedent to the contract of suretyship, succeeded.

However, Steyn J. also found for the defendants on the ground of mutual mistake. After a detailed and careful examination of the law of mistake, he held that the subject-matter of the guarantee was essentially different from what it was reasonably believed to be in that the prime security to which the guarantors would be looking, namely the four machines, did not exist. He also stated that even if he had not decided in favour of the defendants on construction and common law mistake (which meant that the contract was void), he would have held that the guarantee should be set aside on equitable principles.

Associated Japanese Bank v Credit du Nord was a case of mistake as to the subject-matter of the underlying contract and the security available to the guarantor. Mistake as to the parties to the underlying contract may also relieve the surety from liability. Thus in *Provident Accident & White Cross Insurance Co v Dahne and White* [1937] 2 All E.R. 255, the surety had agreed to indemnify the givers of a bond which was intended to be given in favour of the rural district council. The bond was given to the county council instead; the surety was not liable. Similarly in *De Brettes v Goodman* (1855) 9 Moo. P.C.C. 466, the seller and the surety both believed that a sale of certain property was being made to several co-purchasers. In fact, the agent who purported to act on behalf of all the "purchasers" only had authority to bind one of them. The surety, who had guaranteed payment of one of the instalments of the purchase price, was discharged from liability by reason of his mistaken belief as to the identity of the persons whose liability he was undertaking to guarantee.

However, there are limits to the powers of the court to intervene in cases where one or both of the parties are labouring under a misapprehension. In

---

8 See *McRae v Commonwealth Disposals Commission* (1951) 81 C.L.R. 377 and *Associated Japanese Bank (International) Ltd v Credit du Nord SA* [1989] 1 W.L.R. 255 at 268, cited with approval by the NZ Court of Appeal in *Great Peace Shipping* at paras 77–80 and 90–91.

Capital Bank Cashflow Finance Ltd v Ian Southall [2004] EWCA Civ 817, June 29, 2004, the Court of Appeal held that equity could intervene when one surety's signature was expressly or impliedly conditional on another's, but there was no room for any wider equitable relief in a case where there was only an unexpressed common expectation that guarantees would be given in identical terms. A bank had entered into a finance agreement with a company, relating to its trade debts, which contained various warranties by the company including a warranty in Clause 9(d) that each of the company's customers would pay the full amount of each debt by the late payment date. As security for the agreement, two of the company's directors gave personal undertakings to indemnify the bank against any loss suffered in consequence of any breach of the warranties given by the company. For some reason, which was never explained, the undertaking signed by one director, S, referred to the warranty in Clause 9(d), but the undertaking signed by the other director, M. did not. The Court of Appeal held that the bank was entitled to take two indemnities in different terms, whether it did so deliberately or by inadvertence or mistake. Absent any condition which obliged the bank to procure that M executed an identical indemnity, then even though all parties had expected the undertakings to be in identical terms, it was not open to S to argue that the bank's failure to obtain identical undertakings from his fellow surety afforded him any right to equitable relief.

Non est factum

The principle of *non est factum* is a special category of the law of mistake, and is extremely narrow in scope. It is a defence which may be available to someone who has been misled into executing a deed or signing a document which is fundamentally different from that which he intended to execute or sign. His mistake must have been as to the essential nature of the transaction, rather than as to its terms; a mistake as to the legal effect of those terms by the signatory or by his legal adviser will not suffice. In most cases in which the defence is raised, the mistake will have been induced by fraud, though this is not an essential or decisive factor.[9]

    5–004

Non est factum is one of the most difficult defences to establish, and in view of the criteria which the person seeking to raise such a defence must satisfy, it will rarely be available to a surety. Those criteria were set out in the leading case of *Saunders v Anglia Building Society* (sometimes also referred to as *Gallie v Lee*) [1971] A.C. 1004. The person seeking to raise the defence must prove:

(a)   that there was a radical (or fundamental) difference between what he signed and what he thought he was signing;

(b)   that the mistake was as to the general character of the document, as opposed to its legal effect; and

---

9 *Foster v Mackinnon* (1869) L.R. 4 C.P. 704 *per* Byles J. at 711; see also *Prudential Trust Co v Cugnet* [1956] S.C.R. 914.

(c) lack of negligence, *i.e.* that he took all reasonable precautions in the circumstances to find out what the document was.[10]

The facts of *Saunders v Anglia Building Society* illustrate how difficult it can be in practice to establish those criteria:

> An old lady who had a leasehold interest in a house, gave the deeds to her trusted nephew, P, intending to make a gift to him with immediate effect. She knew that P wanted to raise money on the house, and that a friend of his, L, was to collaborate with him in this regard. Subsequently, L asked her to sign a document. She had broken her spectacles and was unable to read it, so she asked L what it was. He told her it was a deed of gift to P, who was present and did not dissent, and she executed it in that belief. In fact it was an assignment by her of the property to L, for £3,000, which L never paid nor intended to pay. L had arranged with P that L would mortgage the property and pay a sum thus raised to P. L mortgaged the property to a building society but paid no money to P. When he defaulted, the building society sought repossession of the property.

The defence of *non est factum* failed. The aunt was temporarily unable to read the document, but she did try to find out what it was, and the House of Lords held that in those circumstances she had not been negligent. However, the character of the transaction was not "wholly different" from what she believed it to be. It was a transfer of the property, albeit to L rather than to P. The aunt had intended to gift the property to P in order that he could raise money on security of the property in conjunction with L; the assignment to L would have achieved the same purpose if L had carried through his arrangement with P.

If the person who signs the document does so with a particular objective in mind which could be achieved by signing a document of that kind, the defence of *non est factum* will fail: see *Mercantile Credit v Hamblin* [1965] 2 Q.B. 242, cited with approval by Lord Pearson in *Saunders v Anglia Building Society* [1971] A.C. at 1031. Likewise, if the signatory would have signed the document even if he had been told the truth about its character and the nature of the transaction, the defence will not succeed.

It is only in the rarest of cases that someone who can read, but who fails to read a document before signing it, would be able to establish the lack of negligence necessary to make good a defence of *non est factum*, even if he acts in reliance on a person whom he trusts. Lord Pearson gave the

---

10 The Australian High Court subsequently held in *Petelin v Cullen* (1975) 132 C.L.R. 355, that negligence of the signatory is irrelevant if no innocent third party is involved, *i.e.* if the other party to the action is the one whose behaviour caused the signatory to believe that he was signing a different document. No such exception was envisaged in *Saunders v Anglia Building Society*, but the development has much to recommend it, because otherwise the wrongdoer might benefit from his wrongdoing.

example of a busy company director who, for reasons of expedience, signs a pile of documents left on his desk by his secretary with only the spaces for his signature exposed. Such a person may not be negligent in the ordinary sense of the word, but he may be taken to have intended to sign those documents whatever they might be, and therefore to have assumed the risk of a fraudulent substitution or insertion in the pile. Thus in *Norwich Building Society v Steed* [1993] Ch. 116 the defence of *non est factum* was not available when the evidence established that a lady who had signed a power of attorney placed before her by her daughter, on the basis that she did not know what she was signing but trusted her daughter, would have signed anything the daughter put before her. In that case it was impossible to prove that the signatory was labouring under any misapprehension as to the nature of the document she was signing, because she did not care what it was. A person who places trust in his legal adviser to explain the documents to him will be unable to rely on the defence: *Bradley West Solicitors Nominee Co v Keeman* [1994] 2 N.Z.L.R. 111. The case contains a useful analysis of the authorities by Tipping J. at 118–123.

In the light of the observations made in *Saunders v Anglia Building Society*, the case of *Muskham Finance v Howard* [1963] 1 Q.B. 904 would probably be differently decided today. In that case, the defence of *non est factum* was successfully raised by a surety who had signed a document described by a dealer as a "release form". The document was in fact an indemnity, which was partially covered by other papers when he signed it, but which the signatory could have read had he liked.

It is difficult to envisage any circumstances in which a person of full capacity would be able to rely upon the defence, because if someone has taken reasonable care to ascertain what he is signing, it would be most unusual if he does not realise what the document actually is. However, it is possible that the defence may still succeed, albeit in rare cases. The type of case in which it is most likely to succeed is one of misplaced trust, where the nature and contents of the document would not be readily apparent to the person reading it. For example, if the guarantee is written in a foreign language which the signatory does not understand, and the signatory requests a translation before he signs it, but someone gives him a fraudulent translation which relates to a document of a radically different nature, the defence might be available to him.[11] However, mere illiteracy or inability by the surety to read a document in English would not be enough in itself to afford him a defence, for example on the basis that the lender owed him a duty to explain the document properly: *Barclays Bank v Schwartz, The Times*, August 2, 1995.

---

11 See *Lloyds Bank Plc v Waterhouse, The Independent*, February 27, 1990, [1991] Fam. Law 23, CA in which the defence, raised by an illiterate farmer, succeeded. He had signed an "all moneys" guarantee in the mistaken belief that it was limited to the money required for a particular purpose. See also *Lewis v Clay* (1897) L.J. Q.B. 224, where the defendant was induced to sign bills of exchange by a friend who pretended that he was merely witnessing the friend's signature on highly confidential documents, the material parts of which were covered up; *Hambros Bank Ltd v British Historic Buildings Trust* [1995] N.P.C. 179.

Although the surety may be unable to make out a case of *non est factum*, in appropriate cases the circumstances in which he came to sign the document may give rise to other defences such as fraud or undue influence. For example, if in *Norwich Building Society v Steed* the document signed by the mother had been a guarantee or a legal charge, and possibly even if her daughter had signed a guarantee or legal charge pursuant to a power of attorney obtained in those circumstances, the mother might have been able to rely on the defence of undue influence (see para.5–030 below).[12]

Fraud or misrepresentation

5–005   The surety may be able to resist a claim on a contract of suretyship if he was induced to enter into it by fraud or misrepresentation, though if the fraud or misrepresentation was made by someone who was not a party to it or the agent of such a party, the normal rule is that the contract is enforceable.[13] If the contract of suretyship is set aside for fraud or misrepresentation, the parties are usually entitled to be put back in the position in which they would have been if the contract had not been made. This sometimes raises the interesting question of whether a previous guarantee replaced by the one which has been set aside is to be treated as though it were still in force. It has been held in New Zealand that if a guarantor who has already guaranteed the indebtedness to a bank of one of its customers is induced by the misrepresentation of an agent of the bank as to the solvency of that customer to enter into a fresh guarantee of the customer's liabilities, he must put the bank into the position in which it would have been under the original guarantee if the second guarantee is set aside: *Ward v National Bank of New Zealand* (1886) 4 N.Z.L.R. 35. It is highly questionable, however, whether the creditor would be entitled to insist on the restoration of the status quo in this way if he had any complicity in, or actual or constructive notice of, a misrepresentation which led the guarantor to replace his original guarantee.

There is now clear authority as to what will happen in the reverse situation, *i.e.* where it is the *first* transaction which is capable of being set aside. In *Yorkshire Bank Plc v Tinsley* [2004] EWCA Civ 816, [2004] 3 All E.R. 463, discussed in para.5–046 below, the Court of Appeal decided that if the earlier transaction is tainted and the creditor has or is deemed to have notice of the vitiating factor (in that case, undue influence) then the replacement transaction is unenforceable even if that transaction was free of any further wrongdoing. This principle will only apply, however, if the creditor is the same in both transactions—there is no reason why a subsequent lender should be adversely affected by flaws in a transaction that he is refinancing, at least in the absence of knowledge that the earlier transaction was voidable. It was suggested by some members of the Court

---

12 See, *e.g. Avon Finance Co Ltd v Bridger* [1985] 2 All E.R. 281. See also *Lloyds Bank v Waterhouse* (above).
13 See *Chitty on Contracts* (*op. cit.*), para.6–020.

of Appeal in *Yorkshire Bank v Tinsley* that the creditor may be able to prevent the second transaction from being set aside by taking steps to procure that the surety takes independent legal advice at the time of that transaction (even though, *ex hypothesi*, the purpose of procuring such independent legal advice would **not** be to ensure that the surety was properly informed about the second transaction). The jurisprudential basis for that suggestion is somewhat unclear.

Fraud or misrepresentation by the creditor

If the relevant fraud has been committed by the creditor himself, or by his agent, then the contract of suretyship is voidable by the surety.[14] In such circumstances it is no answer for the creditor to say that the surety might have found out the truth by making proper enquiry.[15] Of course, if the creditor has induced the contract by misrepresentation, the surety need not prove that the misrepresentation was fraudulent in order to obtain the remedy of rescission.

5–006

The misrepresentation may consist of the assertion of something which is false, or it may consist of the suppression or concealment of the truth so as to mislead the surety. For example, in *Willis v Willis* (1850) 17 Sim. 218, certain property was conveyed by A to B "free from incumbrances", save for certain incumbrances listed in a schedule, in consideration of B and C, his surety, doing certain things. One incumbrance which A knew about, but had forgotten, was omitted. It was held that C was discharged from his liability as surety. Similarly, in *Blest v Brown* (1862) 4 De G. F. & J. 367, a surety had asked the agent of the creditors whether there were any trade debts then owing from the principal to them, and the agent had said no. It transpired that there was a trade debt outstanding, but the usual credit period allowed to the principal had not yet expired. The surety was relieved from his bond on the ground of misrepresentation.[16]

A more recent example is the Australian case of *O'Brien v Australia & New Zealand Bank* (1971) 5 S.A.S.R. 347. Two brothers, who were farmers, had agreed to sell their farm to a company. The purchase price was payable by instalments over a period of some years. When the company ran into financial difficulties, the bank manager at the branch where it had a substantial overdraft suggested that the brothers should buy shares in the company utilising a loan of Aus $5,000 from the bank, using their farm as security. They were induced to sign a mortgage and a guarantee, which they were led to believe was only for the company's future indebtedness, but in fact covered the previous overdraft. When they queried why the bank required security over property worth $50,000 for such a relatively small

---

14 See, *e.g. Spencer v Handley* (1842) 4 Man. & G. 414, a case of alleged fraudulent concealment.
15 *Central Railway Co of Venezuela v Kisch* [1867] L.R. 2 H.L. 99.
16 See also *Stone v Compton* (1858) 5 Bing. N.C. 142; *Cooper v Joel* (1859) 1 De G. F. & J. 240; *Dominion of Canada Guarantee & Accident Co v Housing Commission of City of Halifax* [1927] 4 D.L.R. 161.

loan, the bank manager made an untruthful excuse. The court set aside the contracts of suretyship on the grounds of misrepresentation and non-disclosure, indicating that if it had been necessary to decide whether or not to set the contract aside for unilateral mistake known to the other party, that point would also have been resolved in favour of the sureties.

The misrepresentation does not have to be fraudulent, or even negligent, to give rise to a right to rescind. The fact that the statement is untrue will be enough, though a statement will be treated as true if it is substantially correct and the difference between the statement and the truth would not have induced a reasonable person to enter into the contract: *Avon Insurance v Swire* [2000] 1 All E.R. (Comm) 573. An example of a case in which innocent misrepresentation enabled the surety to avoid the guarantee is *MacKenzie v Royal Bank of Canada* [1934] A.C. 468:

> S charged her shares to secure debts owed by her husband's company to a bank. The company ran into financial difficulties and was eventually reconstructed so that all of its debts were discharged in return for a transfer of all its assets to the bank. The guarantee was discharged by this release of the principal debt to the bank. However, a new company was then formed to buy back the assets from the bank with funds provided by a fresh loan. S was told by the bank manager that her shares in the company were "gone" and that her only hope of saving them was to give a fresh guarantee. It was held that S could rescind the second guarantee on the grounds of that innocent misrepresentation.

There are dicta which suggest that because of the nature of the contract of suretyship, it may only take a relatively minor misrepresentation to enable the surety to avoid the contract. In *Davies v London and Provincial Marine Insurance Co* (1878) 8 Ch. D. 469 at 475, Fry J. expressed the view that "very little said which ought not to have been said, and very little not said which ought to have been said, would be sufficient to prevent the contract being valid".[17] However, it is clear that in the case of misrepresentation by concealment, or non-disclosure, only misrepresentation or concealment of matters which were material to the risk of the surety and which ought to have been disclosed will make the contract avoidable.[18] It is likely that the same standard of materiality would be applied to positive misrepresenta-tions: if the misrepresentation is not material to the risk, the probabilities are that the court would find that the surety was not induced by it to enter into the contract of suretyship.

As with any other type of contract, the misrepresentation must be one of fact and not of law or opinion[19] though an expression of opinion by one

---

17 This dictum was approved in *Bank of New South Wales v Rogers* (1941) 65 C.L.R. 42 at 59–60.

18 *Seaton v Heath* [1899] 1 Q.B. 782, reversed on the facts [1900] A.C. 135. See below, paras 5–014–5–016.

19 See, *e.g. National Bank of New Zealand v Macintosh* (1881) 3 N.Z.L.R. 217, but *cf. Ward v National Bank of New Zealand* (1886) 4 N.Z.L.R. 35.

party may encompass a representation that he has a sufficient factual basis for expressing that opinion. In this context, the distinction between representations of fact and law may be particularly difficult to draw. A (mistaken) statement by the creditor about the effect of a clause in the contract of suretyship might be held to be a statement of law, rather than fact, but if both parties act on the mistaken assumption that the clause means one thing when in fact it means another, there may be room for the operation of the doctrine of estoppel by convention: see, *e.g. National Westminster Finance NZ v National Bank of New Zealand* [1996] 1 N.Z.L.R. 548.

Likewise, a representation as to future conduct by the creditor may not give rise to a claim to rescind, but it may afford the surety a defence on other grounds, such as an equitable (promissory) estoppel or collateral contract.

Complaints made by sureties about misrepresentations by the creditor usually fall into one or more of the following categories:

(1) Statements made by the creditor or its agents about the nature and extent of the surety's liability under the guarantee (*e.g.* a statement that the guarantee is limited to a certain sum when it is an "all moneys" guarantee, or that it covers future indebtedness when in fact it covers past indebtedness[20]);

(2) statements about the nature and extent of the principal's liability or his ability to meet his obligations;

(3) statements about the creditor's policy or likelihood of enforcement.

It is fairly common for the surety to complain that he was reassured by the creditor that the guarantee would be a "mere formality", or that it was highly unlikely that he would ever be called upon to pay under it; but it has been held in Australia that the expression of an opinion that the creditor would be unlikely to place reliance upon the guarantee is not a promise that it will never be enforced: *Morris v Wardley Australia Property Management Ltd* (1994) A.S.C. 56–268. However, a binding promise or an assurance that the creditor will release the surety in certain circumstances or a promise not to enforce the guarantee may give rise to a defence. The difficulty for the surety generally lies in proving that the promise was made by the creditor in the first place, since the surrounding documentation will usually contradict it. However, such a defence was successfully established in the case of *Bank of Baroda v Shah (Dilip)*, (July 30, 1999), CA. The bank required personal guarantees to be given by all the directors of a company to which it intended to grant financial assistance. One of the directors was given a verbal assurance by the bank's representative that he would be released from his guarantee on his resignation as a director. On the

---

20 As in *O'Brien v Australia & New Zealand Bank Ltd* [1971] 5 S.A.S.R. 347.

strength of that assurance, he entered into a share purchase agreement with his fellow-directors, and gave the guarantee. After he had resigned, the Bank reneged on its assurance and tried to enforce the guarantee against him. A strong Court of Appeal (Evans, Lindsay and Schiemann L.JJ.) upheld the decision of the trial judge that the Bank was estopped from enforcing the guarantee.

Clauses protecting the creditor from allegations of misrepresentation

5–007   It is fairly common for standard form guarantees to contain a clause by which the guarantor acknowledges that no representations or promises have been made to him by the creditor or his agents, and that in entering into the contract, he has not relied on anything said or done by the creditor beforehand. This type of provision is generally encompassed within or accompanies an "entire agreement" clause. Although such a provision will not protect the creditor if he has been fraudulent, it may give rise to an estoppel precluding the guarantor from raising other types of misrepresentation by way of defence, provided that the necessary degree of reliance and detriment can be shown by the creditor. Such a clause would probably also have to satisfy the requirement of reasonableness under the Unfair Contract Terms Act 1977 and s.3 of the Misrepresentation Act 1967 and possibly also the Unfair Terms in Consumer Contracts Regulations 1999 (see Chapter 3 above).

A less common alternative is a clause which states that no agent has any authority to make any binding representations on behalf of the creditor. Again, such a clause will generally be upheld: see, *e.g. Bank of Nova Scotia v Zackham* (1983) 3 D.L.R. (4th) 460.

Fraud or misrepresentation by the surety

5–008   Contracts of suretyship entered into as a result of misrepresentation by either contracting party are liable to be rescinded, or damages may be awarded in lieu of rescission under s.2(2) of the Misrepresentation Act 1967. Whilst it is rare to find a lender seeking the rescission of the original contract of suretyship, he may well seek the rescission of a compromise or variation entered into with the surety. An example is *UCB Corporate Services Ltd v Thomason* [2004] EWHC 1164 (Ch) May 19, 2004. A husband and wife had entered into two personal guarantees to secure the borrowings of a company, which subsequently went into liquidation. The bank then entered into a "waiver agreement" with them releasing them from their liability under the guarantees, on the basis that they had made a full disclosure of their assets. The agreement provided that in the event that further material assets were discovered in which they had a proven beneficial interest as at the date of the waiver agreement, the bank would be entitled to treat the agreement as at an end and proceed for the full sum due under the guarantees. Five years later the bank sought to enforce the guarantees, claiming that there had been non-disclosure or material misrepresentation by the sureties at the time of the waiver agreement regarding, among other matters, the ownership of two properties. Pumfrey J. held that as the waiver agreement specifically set out the grounds on which it could be set aside for non-disclosure, it was not open to the bank to seek to set it aside on the basis of non-disclosure of other information. The bank was entitled in principle to rescission because certain representations made to it by the sureties had been untrue. The delay did not make it unconscionable for the bank to seek rescission, but no allegation of fraud was pursued, and the court had a discretion as to whether or not to order the relief sought. After considering the loss caused by the misrepresentation and comparing it with the loss which would be caused to the sureties by granting rescission, the discretion was exercised in favour of refusing rescission. The bank's claim for damages in lieu of rescission also failed. If the bank would not have entered into the agreement had it known the true facts, its only alternative recourse was to issue bankruptcy proceedings against the sureties, but there was no evidence that it would have made a better recovery by taking that course than it actually recovered.

Fraud or misrepresentation by the principal

If the misrepresentation, whether fraudulent or otherwise, was made by the principal, the question whether the creditor is entitled to enforce the contract of suretyship becomes more difficult to answer. The general rule, stated in a number of cases, is that the surety must establish that the creditor or his agent was a party to the fraud or misrepresentation, or that the creditor had knowledge of it at the time when the surety entered into the contract.[21] **5–009**

Knowledge by the creditor

If the creditor knows, before the contract is made, that it has been procured by fraud or misrepresentation on the part of the principal, he will be precluded from enforcing it. This is merely an example of the wider equitable principle enunciated by Kindersley V.-C. in *Small v Currie* (1854) 2 Drew. 102, which also embraces undue influence and mistake: **5–010**

> "If the person taking the indemnity does either by the frame of the instrument or by any representations made to the surety or in any other manner mislead the surety as to the effect of it or occasion his misapprehending it . . . or if he knows or has reason to believe that the surety misapprehends the nature or effect of the instrument and allows him to execute it without removing such apprehension in any such cases a court of equity would interfere to prevent any advantage being taken."

In effect, the failure of the creditor to correct the misapprehension of the surety operates in the same way as an equitable estoppel, to prevent him from taking advantage of the error of which he was aware.

---

21 *Greenfield v Edwards* (1865) 2 De G. J. & Sm. 582; *Spencer v Handley* (1842) 4 Man. & G. 414, *Matthews v Bloxsome* (1864) 4 New Rep. 139.

For these purposes, in any case where the surety is a professional or commercial surety, the knowledge of the surety which must be established is probably actual knowledge or recklessness: *Spencer v Handley* (1842) 4 Man. & G. 414.[22] An example of a case where actual knowledge by the bank manager of the falsity of statements made to the guarantors led to the bank being held liable is *Goad v Canadian Imperial Bank of Commerce* (1968) 67 D.L.R. (2d) 189. Apart from the special circumstances in which constructive notice will affect the creditor, addressed in the leading case of *Royal Bank of Scotland v Etridge (No.2)* [2002] 2 A.C. 773,[23] there appears to be no English authority directly in point which addresses the position where the circumstances would put a reasonable man in the creditor's position on enquiry and he ought to have discovered that the surety had been misled, but did not.[24] It is important to note, however, that since the decision in *Etridge* the principle of constructive notice will come into play in **any case** where the surety is not a commercial surety. In all other cases, the probabilities are that because the defence of the surety is strongly akin to that of unilateral mistake,[25] the court would adopt a similar approach to the approach taken in the mistake cases and hold that negligent failure by the creditor to discover the surety's misapprehension (at least in cases not involving fraud) is insufficient to relieve the surety. In such cases, the surety is expected to look after himself.[26]

Where the principal acts as agent for the creditor

5–011   If, on the facts of the particular case, the surety is able to establish that the principal acted as the creditor's agent when he made the fraudulent assurance or other misrepresentation to him, the contract may be set aside. The surety has to establish that the principal acted as the agent of the creditor for the purpose of making representations to him or for the purpose of procuring the contract. This is unlikely to be proved in the majority of cases.

Some of the early decisions on this topic established that the mere fact that the principal was asked or even told by the creditor to procure a guarantee would normally be insufficient to establish agency. In the

---

22 In certain situations, however, constructive notice of the wrongdoing will be imputed to the creditor: see the discussion of *Barclays Bank Plc v O'Brien* [1994] 1 A.C. 180 and *Royal Bank of Scotland Plc v Etridge (No.2)* [2002] 2 A.C. 773 at paras 5–030 and following.

23 See paras 5–030 *et seq.*

24 See, however, *Owen and Gutch v Homan* (1853) 4 H.L. Cas. 997, in which it was said that if a reasonable person in the creditor's position would suspect fraud, he has a duty to ensure that the surety is not misled. This may, however, be a reference to wilfully closing one's eyes to the obvious. "Nelsonian knowledge" has always been treated as a species of actual knowledge. See also *Woodchester Equipment Leasing Co v Capital Belts Ltd* (CAT No.335 of 1995, April 12) discussed at para.5–035 below.

25 However, the defence is not identical: the misrepresentation or fraud may not have related to the contract of suretyship but may, for example, have related to such diverse matters as the underlying contract or the existence of other securities.

26 This approach appears to accord with the observations of Lord Scott in *Royal Bank of Scotland v Etridge (No.2)* [2002] 2 A.C. 773 at paras 185–189, and with the general rules relating to non-disclosure.

Canadian case of *JR Watkins Co v Hannah* [1926] 4 D.L.R. 93 the creditor had refused to supply the debtor with more goods unless he procured satisfactory guarantees of his existing and future indebtedness. It was held by the judge at first instance that there was insufficient evidence of agency to make the creditor liable for any fraudulent misrepresentation of the debtor, even though the creditor had left the debtor in charge of procuring the requisite guarantees.[27]

Similarly, in an analogous case where a bank required security for further advances to a trade customer, and the customer procured an insurance policy for the benefit of the bank by making a false statement to the insurers about his financial position, Bray J. and the Court of Appeal held that the customer was not the agent of the bank for the purpose of making representations to the insurers.[28] Bray J. gave the example of a proposed lender asking the intending borrower to procure a guarantee or other security and the intending borrower saying that he will try and get one, and thereafter bringing either the surety himself or a document signed by the surety: "Is the debtor or intending borrower the agent of the lender to make representations? Surely not."[29]

These observations have been fully endorsed by the approach of the Court of Appeal and the House of Lords in *Barclays Bank v O'Brien* [1993] Q.B. 109; [1994] 1 A.C. 180.

Scott L.J. said that the principal is not in general the agent of the creditor, whether or not the creditor leaves it to the principal to procure third party security, and this is so *a fortiori* where the surety is a professional surety who charges a fee for so acting.[30] This was approved by the House of Lords [1994] 1 A.C. at 194.[31]

Earlier cases which seemed to import notions of agency into the creditor-principal relationship by reason of the fact that the creditor entrusted the principal with the task of finding a surety, or procuring the signature of the surety on the contract of suretyship or ancillary security documents,[32] were

---

27 That particular finding was apparently undisturbed on appeal, although a retrial was ordered on the grounds that *non est factum* was an available defence.
28 *Comptoire Nationale v Law Car and General* (unreported), Bray J., October 21, 1908, CA, June 10, 1909, the facts of which are set out in detail in McGillivray and Parkington on *Insurance Law* (Sweet & Maxwell, 8th ed., 1988), para.844. (Later editions of the textbook do not reproduce the facts.)
29 See also *JR Watkins Medical Co v Lee* (1920) 52 D.L.R. 543.
30 [1993] Q.B. 109 at 126.
31 This also appears to be the law in New Zealand, see, *e.g. Contractors Bonding Ltd v Snee* [1992] 2 N.Z.L.R. 157 and in Australia, see, *e.g. Begbie v State Bank of New South Wales Ltd* (1994) A.T.P.R. 41–288, in which any concept of "equitable agency" was rejected; *Burke v State Bank of New South Wales Ltd* (1994) 37 N.S.W.L.R. 53; *HG & R Nominees Pty Ltd v Fava* [1997] 2 V.R. 368; *Lisciandro v Official Trustee in Bankruptcy* [1996] 139 A.L.R. 689.
32 In particular, *Chaplin & Co v Brammall* [1908] 1 K.B. 233; *King's North Trust v Bell* [1986] 1 Q.B. 119; *Shephard v Midland Bank Plc* [1987] 2 F.L.R. 175, *Avon Finance Co Ltd v Bridger* [1985] 2 All E.R. 281 and *BCCI v Aboody* [1990] 1 Q.B. 923 especially *per* Slade L.J. at 972–973. See also in Australia, *Challenge Bank v Pandya* (1993) 60 S.A.S.R. 330 at 343 which was the subject of considerable judicial disapproval and which the Federal Court of Australia refused to follow in *Lisciandro v Official Trustee* [1996] 139 A.L.R. 689.

using the wrong language to implement what the House of Lords in *O'Brien* eventually defined as a principle based on the doctrine of constructive notice.

Fraud and the commercial surety

5–012 Despite the extension by the House of Lords in *Royal Bank of Scotland v Etridge (No.2)* [2004] 2 A.C. 773 of the classes of case in which the principle of constructive notice first laid down in *Barclays Bank v O'Brien* may arise, there is still a substantial body of cases in which the surety will not have that special protection. Yet, as in the case of other commercial contracts, despite taking reasonable precautions to protect his position, he may still be the victim of a fraud or misrepresentation by the principal. The question of whether there are any exceptions to the rule that the fraud or misrepresentation of the principal will not affect the enforceability of the contract of suretyship in the absence of notice or complicity by the creditor or proof of agency, is one on which there is little authority. Some possible exceptions are considered below.

Tripartite contracts

5–013 If the contract which the surety seeks to set aside is a tripartite contract between himself, the creditor and the principal, he probably has fairly strong grounds for setting it aside if he has been induced to enter into that contract by fraud or some other misrepresentation on the part of the principal, even if the creditor knows nothing about the fraud or misrepresentation. Since the person who made the misrepresentation, the principal, is a contracting party, the surety would have a prima facie right to have it set aside as against him, and therefore it probably could not survive as regards any other contracting party. To hold otherwise would be to produce the most unsatisfactory position that the contract was enforceable for some purposes and not for others. Consequently, a surety may well improve his prospects of protection against fraud or misrepresentation by the principal if he insists, where possible, on a tripartite agreement. However, there appears to be no direct authority on this point.

Where the fraud gives rise to a defence of mutual mistake or non est factum

5–014 If the fraud of the principal operated on the minds of the creditor and the surety, then it is possible that the defence of mutual mistake would arise, as it did in the case of *Associated Japanese Bank (International) Ltd v Credit du Nord SA* [1989] 1 W.L.R. 255 (see para.5–003 above).

If the fraud operated on the mind of the surety alone, then it is unlikely that he would be able to set aside the guarantee in the absence of actual or constructive notice. However in certain circumstances the fraudulent misrepresentation of the principal may concern the nature of the document which is to be signed by the surety, in which case the defence of fraud may overlap with the defence of *non est factum*. Thus in *Foster v Mackinnon* (1869) L.R. 4 C.P. 704, the defendant was fraudulently induced to indorse the back of a bill of exchange by a representation that he was signing a guarantee similar to one which he had signed on a previous occasion, and the defences of fraud and *non est factum* both succeeded.[33]

The relationship between the two defences in the context of a contract of suretyship is illustrated by the Canadian case of *JR Watkins Co v Hannah* [1926] 4 D.L.R. 93. The creditor, C, had refused to supply D with more goods unless D procured satisfactory guarantees of his existing and future indebtedness. The surety, S, was illiterate, and said that he had been duped by D into signing the guarantee in the belief that he was signing a reference on D's application for a pedlar's licence. The judge had dismissed the defence (without deciding the truth of the allegation of fraud) on the grounds that there was insufficient evidence that D had acted as the agent of C for the purposes of procuring the guarantee. On appeal, a retrial was ordered on the grounds that *non est factum* could have been raised as a defence notwithstanding the lack of evidence of agency, applying *Foster v Mackinnon*.[34]

It is clear that if a defence of *non est factum* can be established, it will relieve the surety from liability even to a wholly innocent creditor who loaned money to the fraudulent principal on the strength of the guarantee. The fact that the fraud was not committed by the principal while acting as the creditor's agent is irrelevant. The reason for this appears to be that a fraud of this nature prevents any *consensus ad idem*, so that the contract is not merely voidable, but void *ab initio*. It is extremely doubtful, however, whether the cases go so far as to put fraudulent representations as to the fundamental nature of the contract into a special category so as to obviate the necessity of proving knowledge, complicity or agency if *non est factum* is *not* established. There is nothing in the cases referred to which directly support the existence of such an exception, or indeed justify it.

A more difficult question is what effect, if any, the negligence of the surety has on his ability to raise fraud, as opposed to *non est factum*, as a defence in circumstances of this kind. Although it is clear that the negligence of the surety will preclude him from setting up the defence of *non est factum*, nevertheless, as a general rule, the negligence of the surety is no answer to a claim that the contract is voidable for the fraud of the creditor or his agent. Furthermore, the negligence of a signatory is no bar to a successful plea of undue influence, in circumstances in which a plea of *non est factum* would fail.[35]

Since the decision in *Saunders v Anglia Building Society* [1971] A.C. 1004, there is some doubt as to whether, in cases where the fraudulent misrepresentation by the principal relates to the nature of the document which is signed, the negligence of the surety would prevent him from avoiding

---

33 See also *National Provincial Bank v Jackson* (1886) 33 Ch. D. 1; *Lewis v Clay* (1897) 67 L.J. Q.B. 224.
34 Despite the fact that part of the decision, relating to the effect of negligence of the surety, would now be regarded as wrong, it is submitted that the decision is otherwise sound.
35 *Avon Finance Co Ltd v Bridger* [1985] 2 All E.R. 281.

liability on the alternative ground of fraud. In *Carlisle & Cumberland Banking Co v Bragg* [1911] 1 K.B. 489, the defendant signed a guarantee without reading it. He was induced to do so by a rogue, who told him that it was a copy of a document which he had signed the previous day, which the rogue said had been ruined by the rain. Although the defendant was found to have been negligent, his defence of *non est factum* and fraud succeeded, because the Court of Appeal said that his negligence was irrelevant. The reasoning behind this decision was plainly flawed, because it was founded on the proposition that the surety owed no duty of care to the creditor.

The case was followed in Canada in *JR Watkins Co v Hannah* [1926] 4 D.L.R. 93. However, it was overruled, at least so far as *non est factum* is concerned, in *Saunders v Anglia Building Society*, where the House of Lords explained that the fact that a person may be precluded by his own negligence from establishing a defence of *non est factum* (which is essentially a species of mistake) is based not on concepts of duty of care, but on the principle that no man may take advantage of his own wrong.[36] Although Lord Hodson confined his criticism of *Carlisle & Cumberland Banking Co v Bragg* to this narrow point, Lord Pearson's criticism is wider and appears to indicate that where fraud and *non est factum* overlap, the negligence of the surety might prevent him from obtaining relief.[37] That suggestion is both heretical and unattractive. The negligence of the innocent party has never been a good defence to a claim based on actionable misrepresentation, whether fraudulent or otherwise. There is no justification for creating an exception in those cases in which the surety happens to be running a defence based on *non est factum* as well.

In any event, nothing was said to indicate that negligence of the surety would prevent relief from being obtained against a creditor who was directly or vicariously responsible for the fraud, or who had actual or constructive knowledge of it, and it is highly unlikely that the case would be regarded as supporting that proposition. Indeed, the House of Lords was considering a case in which the building society had no knowledge of, or complicity in, the fraud of L, and there was no question of agency. Thus the aunt could not have used fraudulent misrepresentation as an alternative to her defence of *non est factum*, regardless of any question of negligence on her part.

It would appear that, in a case which does not involve a surety who is known to the creditor to be susceptible to undue influence, the following conclusions can be drawn from the authorities referred to above:

(1) If the facts give rise to a defence of *non est factum*, the question of whether the principal was the agent of the creditor or whether the creditor knew of the fraud is strictly irrelevant. If the relevant criteria, including absence of negligence, are satisfied, the contract of surety-

---

36 See *Saunders v Anglia Building Society* (above) at 1019, 1038.
37 Compare Lord Hodson at 1019 with Lord Pearson at 1037–1038.

ship will be unenforceable. However the chances of a commercial surety proving the requirements of this defence must be regarded as almost impossible, and a non-commercial surety may have a better prospect of setting aside the contract on other grounds.

(2) If the fraudulent misrepresentation as to the nature of the contract has been made by the creditor or by the principal acting as his agent, the fraud may be an independent defence available to the surety even if he cannot prove *non est factum*, and his negligence will not be an answer to the fraudulent misrepresentation, though it may defeat *non est factum*. The mere fact that the creditor has left it to the principal to find a surety, or to obtain the signature of the surety, will not make the principal the agent of the creditor for this purpose.

(3) If the fraudulent misrepresentation as to the nature of the contract was made by the principal without the knowledge (actual or constructive) or complicity of the creditor, and the principal was not the creditor's agent, then if negligence by the surety precludes him from raising the defence of *non est factum*, he cannot rely on the fraudulent misrepresentation as an alternative ground for avoidance, any more than he could rely on a negligent or innocent misrepresentation in those circumstances. However, this is not a result of his negligence, but an application of the general rule that a misrepresentation by a third party will not affect the creditor's right to enforce the contract.

Concealment and non-disclosure

The creditor is generally under no duty to disclose material facts to the surety. This is because a contract of guarantee, unlike a contract of insurance, is not to be treated as a contract *uberrimae fidei*—of the utmost good faith.[38] Thus in *Seaton v Heath* [1899] 1 Q.B. 782, Romer L.J. stated at 792:

> "ordinary contracts of guarantee are not amongst those requiring '*uberrima fides*' on the part of the creditor towards the surety; and mere non-communication to the surety by the creditor of facts known to him affecting the risk to be undertaken by the surety will not vitiate the contract, unless there be fraud or misrepresentation . . . whether the contract be one requiring '*uberrima fides*' or not must depend upon its substantial character and how it came to be effected."[39]

As a general rule, therefore, the creditor is not obliged to disclose anything he knows which affects the principal's credit, or of any circumstances unconnected with the transaction in which he is about to engage, which

5–015

---

38 *North British Insurance Co v Lloyd* (1854) 10 Exch. 523; *Railton v Matthews* (1844) 10 Cl. & F. 934; *London General Omnibus Co v Holloway* [1912] 2 K.B. 72.
39 The case was reversed on the facts without affecting this point [1900] A.C. 135.

render his position more hazardous, unless the surety makes specific inquiry.[40] The surety bears the primary obligation to inquire into, and determine, all the relevant facts.

The policy underlying this general rule, which is that a surety is expected to look after himself, was encapsulated in this further passage from the judgment of Romer L.J. in *Seaton v Heath* [1899] 1 Q.B. 782 at 793:

> "In general, the creditor does not himself go to the surety, or represent, or explain to the surety, the risk to be run. The surety often takes the position from motives of friendship to the debtor, and generally not as the result of any direct bargaining between him and the creditor, or in consideration of any remuneration passing to him from the creditor. The risk undertaken is generally known to the surety, and the circumstances generally point to the view that as between the creditor and surety it was contemplated and intended that the surety should take upon himself to ascertain exactly what risk he was taking upon himself."[41]

Thus the creditor is generally entitled to assume that the prospective surety will acquaint himself with the extent of the principal's indebtedness, his current financial position and his past track record, so that he can fairly assess the risk that he is undertaking. If he could be expected to find out the material facts by exercising due diligence then as a general rule he will not be able to complain that the creditor did not tell them what they were: *Wason v Wareing* (1852) 15 Beav. 151. Useful summaries of matters which the Courts have previously decided are not disclosable to a prospective surety are to be found in *Halsbury's Laws* (4th ed., 2004 reissue) Vol. 20(1) at para.125 and in O'Donovan and Phillips, *The Modern Contract of Guarantee* (English ed., 2003) at paras 4–20 to 4–21.[42] For specific examples of matters which the surety would normally be expected to discover for himself, see the discussion in paras 5–019 and 5–020 below.

However, if the surety puts a question to the creditor, he must answer it fairly and not mislead: *Westminster Bank Ltd v Cond* (1940) 46 Com. Cas. 60.[43] The creditor is not obliged to make inquiries before answering, but only to answer the question truthfully from the information which he already has: *Parsons v Barclay & Co and Goddard* (1910) 103 L.T. 196. Likewise, if he has represented a particular state of affairs to the surety and

---

40 *Wythes v Labouchere* (1859) 3 De G. & J. 593 at 609, *per* Lord Chelmsford L.C. See *e.g. Roper v Cox* (1882) L.R. I.R. 200 (non-disclosure of previous irregularities, delays by a tenant in paying rent and substantial arrears, did not relieve a surety who gave a guarantee for the rent payments).
41 See also, *e.g. Behan v Obelon Pty Ltd* (1985) 157 C.L.R. 326; *Pooraka Holdings Pty Ltd v Participation Nominees Pty Ltd* (1991) 58 S.A.S.R. 184; *AD & JA Wright Pty Ltd v Custom Corp Ltd* (1992) 108 F.L.R. 45.
42 Alternatively see the Australian 3rd ed. at pp.128–130.
43 See also; *O'Brien v Australia & New Zealand Bank Ltd* (1971) 5 S.A.S.R. 347; *CIBC v Larsen* [1983] 5 W.W.R. 179.

it comes to his knowledge, before the contract is entered into, that there has been a material change of circumstances, he will be obliged to tell the surety about it. He must also correct any mistake or misapprehension by the surety of which he has actual knowledge before the contract is made.[44] The law in this area is still developing. In the light of the approach of the Court of Appeal in *Commission For The New Towns v Cooper* [1995] Ch. 259, the prudent creditor would now be well advised to take steps to correct any mistake which he reasonably suspects that the surety has made, at least if that mistake is one of interpretation of the terms of the contract.

Despite the principle that there is no general duty of disclosure, it is has also been established that a limited principle of non-disclosure of material facts known to the creditor does operate in the context of contracts of suretyship, though its precise nature and extent has been a matter of considerable debate, and may not yet be settled. The most recent restatements of the principle are to be found in two of the speeches in *Royal Bank of Scotland v Etridge (No.2)* [2002] 2 A.C. 773, though even these formulations differ in a potentially material respect. Lord Nicholls said in para.81:

> "It is a well-established principle that, stated shortly, a creditor is obliged to disclose to a guarantor any unusual feature of the contract between the creditor and the debtor which makes it materially different in a potentially disadvantageous respect from what the guarantor might naturally expect. The precise ambit of this disclosure obligation remains unclear".

Thus the emphasis in Lord Nicholls' formulation is on features of the underlying contract between principal and creditor. Lord Scott considered the matter at greater length in paras 185–188, in which, after consideration of the main authorities, he expressed the view that the obligation should, at least, extend to

> "unusual features of the contractual relationship between the creditor and the principal debtor, or between the creditor and other creditors of the principal debtor, that would or might affect the rights of the surety".

It is submitted that this wider formulation of the established minimum extent of the principle is to be preferred. It would cover an informal arrangement between the principal and the surety, such as the practice adopted by the bank in *Commercial Bank of Australia v Amadio* (1983) 151 C.L.R. 447 of selectively dishonouring cheques drawn on the borrower's

---

44 *Royal Bank of Scotland v Greenshields* (1914) S.C. 259; *Davies v London & Provincial Marine Insurance Co* (1878) 8 Ch. D. 469 at 475–476; *Small v Currie* (1854) 2 Drew. 102; *Royal Bank of Canada v Hale* (1961) 30 D.L.R. (2d) 138; *Royal Bank of Canada v Oram* [1978] 1 W.W.R. 564; *Taylor v Johnson* (1983) 151 C.L.R. 422.

account so as to create the impression that its business was more successful than it was, the secret arrangement between the bank and its customer in *Pendelbury v Walker* (1841) 4 Y. & C. Ex. 424, and the conspiracy to defraud the Russian exchange control authorities in *Far Eastern Shipping Co Public Ltd v Scales Trading Ltd* [2001] 1 All E.R. (Comm) 319 discussed below. All those arrangements had as much potential to injure the surety as a formal contractual obligation. So would an arrangement (contractual or otherwise) between the creditor and other creditors of the principal debtor to postpone the creditor's secured claims against the principal behind the claims of the other creditors, thus potentially impairing the value of the surety's future rights of subrogation and increasing the chances of the guarantee being called on: that was what happened in *Bank of Scotland v Bennett*, one of the appeals decided in *Royal Bank of Scotland v Etridge (No.2)* [2002] 2 A.C. 773 at 871–878. See in particular paras 346–351 of the speech of Lord Scott, to the effect that the obligation to disclose this "ranking agreement" to the surety fell within the ambit of the general duty of disclosure, regardless of whether or not the surety happened to be the spouse of the principal debtor or of the person who owned the principal debtor company. Lord Nicholls, Lord Hobhouse and Lord Bingham all agreed with the reasons given by Lord Scott for allowing that appeal.

The jurisprudential basis for the duty of disclosure is somewhat unclear. In some cases the duty has been said to arise from the presumed basis of the guarantee: see *e.g. Westpac Securities v Dickie* [1991] 1 N.Z.L.R. 657 at 662–663. However the rationale which appears to be most favoured is that the failure to make disclosure amounts to an implied representation that the undisclosed facts do not exist. Indeed the origins of the principle can be traced back to dicta in certain 19th century cases to the effect that asking the surety to enter into the contract involves a representation that there is no unusual feature about the transaction affecting the risks which he is being asked to undertake: see, *e.g. Lee v Jones* (1864) 17 C.B.N.S. 482 at 503.[45] In *Bank of India v Patel* [1982] 1 Lloyd's Rep. 506 at 515 col. 1, Bingham J. said that the surety would be discharged, *inter alia*, "if the creditor is guilty of concealment amounting to misrepresentation". This passage was approved by Robert Goff L.J. when the case went to the Court of Appeal: [1983] 2 Lloyd's Rep. 298 at 301–302. Despite this rationale, the principle does not appear to be confined to circumstances where the non-disclosure can be characterised, without undue artificiality, as tacit mis-representation. If this were so, then contracts of suretyship would be no different from any other ordinary contract. In *Credit Lyonnais v ECGD* [1996] 1 Lloyd's Rep. 200 Longmore J. expressed the view that the concept of "implied representation" could not apply to banking cases so easily as perhaps it could to a guarantee of an employee's fidelity. As the House of Lords has now acknowledged in *Royal Bank of Scotland v Etridge, (No.2)*

---

45 See also *London General Omnibus Co Ltd v Holloway* [1912] 2 K.B. 72 at 78, *Geest v Fyffes* [1999] 1 All E.R. (Comm) 672 at 682–683.

the principle is an independent one, though its precise boundaries have yet to be defined.

Unusual features

The recent restatements of the principle in the House of Lords have both **5–016** emphasised that, so far as the underlying contractual relationship between principal and creditor is concerned, the duty relates only to "unusual features", which is no doubt intended to reflect the general rule that the surety is expected to find out for himself anything material to the risk which might be expected to arise in the ordinary course of events. If the matter is something which the creditor would normally expect the surety to find out for himself, the defence will not run—see *e.g. Bank of Scotland v Henry Butcher & Co* [2001] 2 All E.R. (Comm) 691.[46] Of course there is no duty to disclose something that is already known to the prospective surety. Tipping J. said in the New Zealand case of *Shivas v Bank of New Zealand* [1990] 2 N.Z.L.R. 327 at 364 that "the bank's duty of disclosure must be assessed against what the bank might reasonably have expected the intending guarantors to know already or to be able to ascertain without difficulty should they have been minded to do so." On the other hand, if the creditor makes an incorrect assumption that the prospective surety is aware of something which falls within the ambit of the duty, this will not suffice to meet the defence, even if that assumption is reasonable. It has never been an answer to a misrepresentation claim that the party who made the misrepresentation genuinely and reasonably believed that the other contracting party knew the truth.

In *Hamilton v Watson* (1845) 12 Cl. & Fin. 109, Lord Campbell put the matter on the basis that there should be voluntary disclosure of "anything that might not naturally be expected to take place between the parties who are concerned in the transaction". It is clear that the principle catches any secret arrangements made between the principal and creditor which will have a potentially adverse effect on the surety. The surety is entitled to expect that the creditor and principal have not entered into some private arrangement between themselves which might have the effect of varying the degree of the surety's responsibility beyond that which he would ordinarily expect. Thus in *Pidcock v Bishop* (1825) 3 B. & C. 605, it was agreed between the vendors and purchaser of goods that the purchaser should pay 10 shillings per ton beyond the market price, and that the money was to be applied to repay an old debt due to one of the vendors. It was held that this bargain should have been disclosed to the surety who guaranteed payment of the price, because the vendor was obliged to appropriate to payment of another debt, part of the moneys which the surety might reasonably have supposed would go towards defraying the debt for the payment of which he had made himself collaterally responsible.[47] Similarly, if the principal and

---

46 Discussed at 5–017 below. See also *Wason v Wareing* (1852) 15 Beav. 151; *Bank of Australasia v Reynell* (1891) 10 N.Z.L.R. 257.
47 Compare *Mackreth v Walmesley* (1884) 51 L.T. 19, in which the fact that the principal had agreed to pay part of the guaranteed loan to a previous surety was not revealed to the surety, but the contract was upheld. See also *Stone v Compton* (1838) 5 Bing. N.C. 142.

creditor have entered into an arrangement which would give the creditor a wrongful preference over other creditors, both the agreement and any guarantee of it will be unenforceable: *Pendlebury v Walker* (1841) 4 Y. & C. Ex. 424.[48] In *Lewis v Jones* (1825) 4 B. & C. 506, it was held that any private bargain, the effect of which is to give the creditor an advantage over other creditors, will vitiate a guarantee thereby obtained.

A more recent example of a secret arrangement adverse to the surety is the bargain made between the creditor and principal in *Levett v Barclay's Bank Plc* [1995] 1 W.L.R. 1260. The sureties had agreed to deposit certain stocks which they owned as security for loans made to the borrowers, who were in severe financial difficulties. The sureties expected the stocks to be returned to them on maturity. Unbeknown to them, the borrowers had arranged with the bank that the proceeds of the stocks on maturity would be used to repay the loan. Michael Burton Q.C., sitting in the High Court, held that the arrangement between the borrowers and the bank by which the assets belonging to the surety were bound to be used to repay the loan, should have been disclosed. This arrangement turned the risk of realisation into a certainty, which the sureties would not expect, and the sureties were entitled to recover the sum paid to the bank on maturity of the stocks.

Another example is to be found in the extraordinary facts of *Far Eastern Shipping Co Public Ltd v Scales Trading Ltd* [1999] 3 N.Z.L.R. 26. A guarantee was given by F, a Russian shipping corporation, to S, a New Zealand company, as security for trading debts owed to S by A, an associated trading company of F.A imported goods, particularly apples, into Russia. S failed to disclose to F that it had an agreement with A that, as and when requested to do so by A, it would add a margin to the true price (which became known as the "RFK margin") and submit an invoice for the inflated amount. A would pay the inflated amount to S which would then remit the margin to a third party outside Russia at A's direction. This device was used to defraud Russian exchange control authorities. At trial F's representative gave unchallenged evidence that F knew nothing of these dishonest arrangements and the judge held that the guarantee was unenforceable. S appealed to the New Zealand Court of Appeal, where it succeeded in persuading the court that it had a discretion either under two New Zealand statutes (of which there is no English equivalent) or at common law or in equity to hold the innocent party to the bargain he would have made but for the non-disclosure or misrepresentation. One of the arguments raised by S was that the trial judge had applied too rigorous a test of the duty to disclose, which he had formulated thus: "a creditor who has obtained a guarantee without disclosing to the guarantor unusual aspects of the underlying relationship with a debtor may later be disqualified from enforcing the guarantee". The Court of Appeal rejected that argument, stating (at 34):"There is little if any difference between the

---

48 See also *Re Mason Ex p. Sharp* (1844) 3 Mont. D. & De G. 490; *Clarke v Ritchey* (1865) 11 Gr. 499 (Can); *Bank of Australia v Wilson* (1885) 3 N.Z.L.R. 130.

"unusual", the "different from natural expectation" and the "presumed basis of the contract". What is or is not "unusual" is always a question of fact, tempered by common sense. It will depend to a major extent upon context. It is unusual to find a camel in Lambton Quay. It is not unusual to find a camel in Wellington Zoo. The Judge did not err in the simple formulation adopted. It was not too rigorous".

The case went to the Privy Council [2001] 1 All E.R. (Comm) 319 on the issue of principle whether the court had a discretion to allow the creditor to enforce a guarantee which had been tainted by non-disclosure. The Privy Council decided that it was unnecessary for it to express any final view on whether the court had any power at common law (or under the statutes,) to impose any terms on the innocent party who was entitled to rescission for non-disclosure. It decided that the decision of the Court of Appeal to impose such terms was unjustified on the facts and on the evidence, because it rendered F's right to cancel the guarantee nugatory. Although F might be said to have gained the benefit of freights earned on the carriage of apples on its vessels in consequence of the continuation of the apple trade between F and S, which would have stopped had the guarantee not been given, the non-disclosure by S deprived F of the ability to decide for itself whether it wanted those benefits and advantages sufficiently strongly to be willing to become involved in a trade which included the dishonest RFK arrangements. That was enough to make it wholly inequitable to hold F to any part of the bargain.

The formulation of the principle by Lord Campbell in *Hamilton v Watson* left open the question whether it was only unusual features of the transaction between principal and creditor which had to be disclosed, or whether the limited requirement of disclosure extended to other trans-actions, or indeed to all material facts which the surety would not expect to exist, *e.g.* facts relating to dealings between the principal and third parties, such as co-sureties. In *London General Omnibus Co v Holloway* [1912] 2 K.B. 72, a case concerning a fidelity guarantee, Vaughan Williams L.J. inclined to the latter view, citing Lord Campbell's observations in *Hamilton v Watson* as a mere example of the more general proposition that "a creditor must reveal to a surety every fact which under the circumstances the surety would expect not to exist, for the omission to mention that such a fact does exist is an implied representation that it does not". He described this principle as one of "undue concealment". This approach was followed in the New Zealand case of *National Mortgage & Agency Co of New Zealand Ltd v Stalker* [1933] N.Z.L.R. 1182, in which it was said that it depended on the nature of the transaction in each case whether the material fact not disclosed was impliedly represented not to exist.

However, when the matter was considered more recently by the High Court of Australia in *Commercial Bank of Australia v Amadio* (1983) 151 C.L.R. 447, which concerned a guarantee given to a bank by a father in respect of his son's overdraft, the principle of "undue concealment" was given short shrift. The transaction was set aside by the majority of the High

Court as an unconscionable bargain,[49] but as various alleged non-disclosures were also raised by the father in his defence, Gibbs C.J. considered (at 455–456) the ambit of the law of disclosure in respect of guarantees. He preferred the narrower view that disclosure was only required "where there is a special arrangement between the bank and the customer of a kind which the surety would not expect", and doubted the correctness of Vaughan Williams L.J.'s analysis. He pointed out that if a bank was required to disclose to a surety the details of all unusual transactions which, to the knowledge of the bank, had taken place between the customer and third parties, it might prove to be both vexatious and misleading, as well as a breach of confidence. He concluded that "the obligation is to reveal anything in the transaction between the banker and the customer which has the effect that the position of the customer is different from that which the surety would naturally expect, particularly if it affects the nature or degree of the surety's responsibility". The more restrictive approach in *Amadio* was subsequently followed by the New South Wales Court of Appeal in the case of *Westpac Banking Corporation v Robinson* (1993) 30 N.S.W.L.R. 668 at 688–689[50] and by Longmore J. in *Credit Lyonnais v ECGD* [1996] 1 Lloyd's Rep. 200, who cited *Amadio* with approval.[51]

Nevertheless, in *Royal Bank of Scotland v Etridge (No.2)* [2002] 2 A.C. 773 at para.187 Lord Scott cited Vaughan Williams L.J.'s general proposition without criticism. Indeed, he applied it to the facts of *Bank of Scotland v Bennett*. It is now clear from para.188 of his speech (and from the actual decision of the House of Lords to allow the appeal in *Bennett*) that the principle of disclosure extends to unusual features of the relationship between the creditor and other creditors that would or might affect the rights of the surety. This is nothing new: in certain circumstances it may be incumbent on the creditor to disclose to the surety the existence and nature of an agreement between himself and someone other than the principal: see, *e.g. Stiff v Eastbourne Local Board* (1868) 19 L.T. 408, on appeal (1869) 20 L.T. 339. In that case it was held that there was an obligation on the creditor (the employer on a building project) to inform a surety for a contractor that he had entered into a separate arrangement with another party to complete the same project. It remains to be seen whether, for example, "unusual" arrangements made between the creditor and co-sureties would be disclosable. In principle there would appear to be no reason to distinguish such arrangements from arrangements between the creditor and other creditors. They could have a direct bearing on the risk

---

49 See para.5–043 below.
50 See also *Goodwin v National Bank of Australasia* (1968) 117 C.L.R. 173 and *Union Bank of Australasia v Piddy* [1949] V.L.R. 242.
51 Longmore J. said (at 227) that he was comforted by the fact that the same test appeared to have been applied by Michael Burton Q.C. in *Levett v Barclays Bank* [1995] 1 W.L.R. 1260 at 1275, but *Levett* was a case which directly concerned the dealings between the principal and the creditor.The Court of Appeal and House of Lords did not consider this aspect of the case.

which the guarantor is being asked to undertake. For example, the guarantor might believe that he is one of a number of sureties and that he would therefore have a potentially valuable right of contribution if called upon. If, prior to the relevant contract of suretyship, the creditor made a special (and concealed) arrangement with one of the other intended sureties which would have the effect of releasing him from his obligations in certain circumstances, it could raise very interesting questions, particularly if the contract of guarantee was one which allowed the creditor to release or abstain from perfecting other securities.

Fraud or dishonesty of the principal

Credit Lyonnais v ECGD raises a further issue about the scope of the duty of disclosure, namely, whether and in what circumstances the creditor is under a duty to disclose a fraud by the principal. The case involved a longstanding fraud perpetrated upon the plaintiff bank by a Mr Chong, who pretended that he had sold goods for export to Nigeria and obtained substantial sums of money from the bank by selling it false bills of exchange which had been indorsed by imaginary buyers. The purchases were made against a series of ECGD guarantees[52] that the buyers would pay for the goods in due course. When the bank sued on the guarantees, one of the issues which arose was whether the bank was obliged to disclose to ECGD certain knowledge or suspicions which it had about Mr Chong and his dealings. These included the fact that various Mareva injunctions (freezing orders) had been obtained against Mr Chong's companies, and the suspicion which, it was argued, the bank must have had about the existence of any genuine goods or purchasers for such goods at the time when it applied for certain of the later ECGD guarantees. Longmore J. held that it was not so obliged, partly because he applied the narrower formulation of the principle of disclosure favoured in *Amadio*. However, he also made it clear that the principle of non-disclosure would not extend to requiring the creditor to divulge mere suspicions, as opposed to matters of which he had actual knowledge. This approach was entirely consistent with earlier English authority: see, *e.g. National Provincial Bank of England Ltd v Glanusk* [1913] 3 K.B. 335.[53] In Australia, in *Wesptac v Robinson* (1990) A.S.C. 56–002 Brownie J. held that the lender was under a duty to disclose a fraud in respect of the principal debtor's internal operations which was a "virtual certainty"—though the decision was reversed on appeal on the facts (1993) 30 N.S.W.L.R. 668.

In *Bank of Scotland v Henry Butcher* [2001] 2 All E.R. (Comm) 691, the trial judge, Michel Kallipetis Q.C. considered the authorities at paras 74–81 and accepted that matters amounting to "equitable impropriety" should be disclosed. The guarantors alleged that it was evident to the bank that the

5–017

---

52 See Ch.15.
53 See also *Royal Bank of Scotland v Greenshields* [1914] S.C. 259; *Bank of Scotland v Morrison* [1911] S.C. 593. *Bank of Scotland v Gow or Porteous* (unreported) July 30, 1956.

principal, H, was using the account for "high living" rather than for the purposes of his business, and that this should have been disclosed to them, but the judge found on the evidence that there was nothing exceptional about the expenditure which would have suggested to the bank that H was using the account for anything other than business purposes. Indeed, the bank was under no better position than the guarantors to assess the honesty of H at any material time, and it was not until H misappropriated certain funds belonging to the sureties and put them into his own account that either party was aware that he was in fact behaving dishonestly. This point was not appealed.

The preponderance of authority appears to support the proposition that it is incumbent on the creditor to disclose a material fraud by the principal of which he is aware (no doubt this would also encompass "Nelsonian knowledge"). If Vaughan Williams L.J.'s formulation of the principle is the correct one, there is no difficulty in fitting the obligation to disclose such matters within it—the surety would not expect the principal to have behaved dishonestly, so the dishonesty can be described without artifice as an "unusual feature" of the transaction. On the other hand, if the narrower formulation is preferred, it would have to be justified as a self-standing principle. It is submitted that there is no justification for a rule that obliges the lender to confess to his own dishonest dealings with the principal, but keep quiet about relevant dishonesty of the principal of which he is aware, and of which the surety is unaware, when the dishonesty in either case is equally likely to damage the surety. For example, if the lender under a debt-factoring agreement discovered on taking an audit that many of the "debts" he had factored were fictitious, he would be the victim of the fraud, but nevertheless a failure to reveal the fraud to a prospective surety of the borrower's obligations under the agreement would be hard to justify. In such circumstances, the risk undertaken by the surety that the borrower's customers would not pay the debts when they fell due would be a certainty in the case of the non-existent debts, and the contract of suretyship would be radically different from what the surety would expect it to be.

Other unusual facts

5–018   There are few reported cases in which the creditor was obliged to reveal "unusual" facts to the surety which fall outside the categories of dealings between the creditor and the principal, the creditor and third parties and dishonest conduct by the principal. One such is *Burke v Rogerson* (1866) 14 L.T. 780. A guarantee was given by the directors of a company for the payment by the company of the purchase price for two ships. The vendor, to whom the guarantee had been given, failed to disclose that one of the ships was laden with munitions of war destined for Trebizond, a belligerent port. It was held that the dangerous nature of the cargo, which exposed the vessel to extraordinary risk, was concealed both from the company and the sureties and that both the underlying contract and the guarantee were unenforceable. It is questionable, however, whether that case would be decided the same way now, given the approach of Longmore J. in *Credit*

Lyonnais v ECGD. By way of contrast, the facts of *Seaton v Heath* indicate that if the complaint relates to a feature of the transaction which the surety would expect to exist, it will be very difficult for him to make out a case of non-disclosure, even if that feature has extraordinary or unusual characteristics. Underwriters at Lloyds had guaranteed the solvency of S, who was a surety to C for a loan given to D. C did not tell the underwriters about the extremely high rate of interest which was charged on the loan (over 30 per cent). The Court of Appeal held that the fact ought to have been disclosed, but this decision was reversed by the House of Lords on the ground that the rate of interest was not material [54]

In *Geest Plc v Fyffes Plc* [1999] 1 All E.R. (Comm) 672 the court had to consider the duties of disclosure by an existing guarantor to someone whom he wishes to take over his obligations as surety. The plaintiff company guaranteed the performance of its subsidiary under a charterparty, and also gave confirmation to the owners of the vessel that the company would remain its subsidiary. Notwithstanding that confirmation, it then sold the subsidiary to a joint venture company owned by the defendant and another company. The defendant agreed to use all reasonable endeavours to obtain the consent of the owners' bank (which was financing the chartering operation) to its substitution as guarantor, and meanwhile to indemnify the plaintiff and provide security. When the bank refused its consent and the subsidiary defaulted, the plaintiff sought an order for specific performance. The defendant resisted the order on the grounds of alleged fraud and non-disclosure, relying in particular on the fact that the plaintiff had not told it about the confirmation which it had given to the owners that it would remain the parent company of the charterer. Colman J. held that the omission to disclose the confirmation was not material; there was no general duty of disclosure, but rather a duty not to make implied misrepresentations.

Disclosure obligations and specific types of contract

Bank guarantees

It seems that in the normal case of a surety who gives a guarantee to a bank for the overdraft of a customer, it would require extremely unusual circumstances (such as those in the cases of *Levett* and *Amadio*) to impose a duty of disclosure on the bank. In *London General Omnibus Co v Holloway* [1912] 2 K.B. 72, Farwell L.J. distinguished such cases from fidelity bonds on the grounds that "guarantees for overdrafts are required for the purpose and not on the chance of being used . . . the surety may well complain, 'I did not know your servant was a thief', but he cannot be heard to complain, 'I did not know that your customer had been overdrawing his account'".

5–019

There is no presumption that a customer's account stands clear at the time that the guarantee is given.[55] Thus the fact that there is already a

---

54 [1899] 1 Q.B. 782; [1900] A.C. 135.
55 *Kirby v Duke of Marlborough* (1813) 2 M. & S. 18, *per* Lord Ellenborough L.C. at 22. Compare the facts of *Lee v Jones* (1864) 17 C.B.N.S. 482, where the non-disclosure amounted to a misrepresentation.

substantial indebtedness to the bank is something which it is generally incumbent on the surety to find out for himself. It has been held that a bank was under no duty to tell the proposed guarantor of a wife's bank account that her husband, who had power to draw on the account, was an undischarged bankrupt.[56] Other examples of facts which were not required to be disclosed include the fact that the principal was in serious financial difficulties[57]; that the bank had suspicions that the principal was defrauding the guarantor, or was otherwise dishonest[58]; that the contingency against which the guarantee was given had probably already occurred[59]; that the advance was to be used merely to pay off an existing debt to the bank[60] or to a previous surety[61]; that the principal was merely a guarantor to a third party[62]; or that a co-surety, who had induced the surety to enter into the guarantee and had signed it on her behalf, had no assets.[63] In *Bank of Scotland v Henry Butcher & Co* [2001] 2 All E.R. (Comm) 691, the trial judge rejected the argument by the sureties, who had guaranteed an overdraft facility afforded by the bank to H, that the bank was under a duty to disclose to them the fact that it had withheld payment on certain cheques which H was intending to re-present once the guarantee was given. This point was not appealed.

Fidelity bonds

5–020   The principles to be derived from the banking cases should extend to virtually all other types of contract of suretyship. Thus in the majority of cases the creditor is safe if he says nothing, which can be very hard on the surety. There is, however, one class of case in which the principle of non-disclosure is applied more favourably to the surety, and that is where the surety has been asked to guarantee the due performance of his duties by an employee or official under a fidelity bond or similar contract. In such cases, the employer (or obligee) not only has a duty to disclose to the surety any previous dishonesty of the employee of which he is aware,[64] but a duty to divulge facts which give him reason to believe that there has been misconduct. [65] If he does not do so, the contract may be avoided by the

---

56 *Cooper v National Provincial Bank Ltd* [1946] K.B. 1.
57 *Lloyd's Bank v Harrison* (1925) 4 L.D.B. 12; 58 *National Provincial Bank of England Ltd v Glanusk* [1913] 3 K.B. 335; *Royal Bank of Scotland v Greenshields* [1914] S.C. 259; *Bank of Scotland v Morrison* [1911] S.C. 593.
58 *Bank of Scotland v Gow or Porteous* (unreported) July 30, 1956.
59 *Welton v Somes* (1889) 5 T.L.R. 184.
60 *Hamilton v Watson* (1845) 12 Cl. & Fin. 109; *National Mortgage & Agency Co of New Zealand Ltd v Stalker* [1933] N.Z.L.R. 1182.
61 *Mackreth v Walmesley* (1884) 51 L.T. 19.
62 *Goodwin v National Bank of Australasia* (1968) 117 C.L.R. 173; *Wythes v Labouchere* (1859) 3 De G. & J. 593.
63 *Behan v Obelon Proprietary Ltd* (1985) 157 C.L.R. 326.
64 *Smith v Bank of Scotland* (1813) 1 Dow. 272, *London General Omnibus Co Ltd v Holloway* [1912] 2 K.B. 72 explaining *Railton v Mathews* (1844) 10 Cl. & Fin. 934; *Thomas v Watkins Products Inc* (1965) 54 D.L.R. (2d) 252.
65 *London General Omnibus Co Ltd v Holloway* [1912] 2 K.B. 72 at 80. For examples of mere irregularities not amounting to misconduct see *Caxton & Arrington Union v Dew* (1899) 68 L.J.Q.B. 380 and *Durham Corporation v Fowler* (1889) 22 Q.B.D. 394.

surety, notwithstanding that the non-disclosure was neither wilful nor intentional.[66] However, if the surety knows of the dishonesty of the employee from another source, he will not be discharged from liability, at least if the concealment by the employer was not deliberate.[67] If the fidelity guarantee is a continuing guarantee, this special duty of disclosure will continue to operate throughout the duration of the contract of suretyship, so that if the employer discovers that the agent has been dishonest and nevertheless continues to employ him, without telling the surety, the surety will not be liable for any subsequent dishonesty by the employee.[68] On the other hand, if the person to whom the bond is given is unable to dismiss the employee or office holder from his office, this rule may not apply.[69] It has also been held in Ireland that the defence of even deliberate non-disclosure of the misconduct of an office holder, whose honesty was guaranteed by the bond, is not available to the surety against a public officer who is entitled to enforce the bond. In those circumstances there is no privity between the public officer and the surety, as there would be between a private person to whom the bond was given and the surety.[70]

Knowledge of the creditor

It is probable that the limited principle of disclosure only extends as far as unusual facts of which the creditor is actually aware. It has already been shown that (outside the special rules applying to fidelity guarantees) suspicion is insufficient. It is unlikely, therefore, that an English court would adopt the dictum by King C.J. in the Australian case of *Pooraka Holdings Pty v Participation Nominees Pty Ltd* ((1991) 58 S.A.S.R. 184 at 193 that the obligation related to (*inter alia*) unusual features "of which the creditor *ought* to be aware . . .". In *Royal Bank of Scotland v Etridge* [2002] A.C. 773 at para.188, Lord Scott said that this statement of the extent of the disclosure obligation may be too wide. Certainly it would appear to be wider than any formula accepted in England and Wales to date and contradicts the established law that (absent an *Etridge* situation) the creditor is only under a duty to correct positive misrepresentations of which he is actually aware.

5–021

On the other hand, the degree of knowledge by the creditor of the surety's *lack* of knowledge of the salient fact is unlikely to be confined to actual knowledge, but would probably extend to cover a case where the creditor would not expect the unusual feature to be known to the surety. If it transpires that the surety *was* aware of the feature, there would be no actionable non-disclosure, as his decision to enter into the contract would have been unaffected by the creditor's failure to reveal it to him.

---

66 *Railton v Mathews* (1844) 10 Cl. & F. 934; *London General Omnibus Co v Holloway* [1912] 2 K.B. 72.
67 *Peel v Tatlock* (1799) 1 Bos. & P. 419; *Goring v Edmonds* (1829) 3 Moo. & O. 259; see also *Caxton & Arrington Union v Dew* (1899) 68 L.J.Q.B. 380.
68 *Phillips v Foxall* (1872) L.R. 7 Q.B. 666; *Sanderson v Aston* (1873) L.R. 8 Ex. 73.
69 *Caxton & Arrington Union v Dew* (1899) 68 L.J.Q.B. 380.
70 *Lawder v Lawder* [1873] 7 I.C.L.R. 57.

Effect of non-disclosure

5–022   Whether the creditor is obliged to make disclosure, or whether he has made an implied misrepresentation by his conduct, silence, or by concealing material facts from the surety, will depend on the facts of each particular case.[71]

The requirement that disclosure be made is often referred to as a "duty" or "obligation", although in the strict legal sense it is not, because failure to disclose material facts does not found an independent cause of action or give rise to a claim for damages. However, the consequence of such failure is that, by the application of equitable principles, the creditor will be precluded from enforcing the contract, or the surety will be entitled to have it set aside. In *Westpac v Dickie* [1991] 1 N.Z.L.R. 657, it was held that if the material fact which is not disclosed to the surety is inconsistent with the presumed basis of the contract of guarantee, the failure to disclose in effect amounts to a misrepresentation and therefore will vitiate the contract (or give rise to a right to rescind). The question whether there is a power at common law to impose terms on the innocent party who is entitled to rescind for non-disclosure remains open, the Privy Council having declined to decide the point in *Far Eastern Shipping Co v Scales Trading* [2001] 1 All E.R. (Comm) 319 (discussed above at para.5–016) See also the discussion in para.5–047 of the question whether it is open to the Court to grant partial rescission in the context of *Barclays Bank v O'Brien* relief.

Is the obligation a continuing one?

5–023   There is no English authority which goes so far as to suggest that the creditor must disclose unusual facts *after* the contract of guarantee has been executed (save in the special case of fidelity guarantees, discussed above). The duty not to misrepresent material facts ends when the contract is made and if the basis of the limited principle of disclosure is an implied representation that the unusual fact does not exist, then the duty of disclosure should do likewise. In New Zealand it has been held that there is no continuing duty of disclosure, since the relationship between the parties is not one of the utmost good faith: see *Clark v Westpac Banking Corporation* (HC New Plymouth) (1996) C.P. 21/96, November 7, 1996, and *Westpac Banking Corporation v Hansen* (HC Wellington) (1997) C.P. 43/97, July 7, 1997 (referred to in N.Z.C.L.D. 5th Series part 15 at 1594). However, in Canada it was held in *Toronto Dominion Bank v Rooke* (1983) 3 D.L.R. (4th) 715 that the limited duty of disclosure also applied at the time when the surety's consent to a variation of the contract was sought. If the requirement that certain unusual facts be disclosed is merely an illustration of equity intervening to prevent one party to a transaction from

---

71 *Hamilton v Watson* (1845) 12 Cl. & F. 109; *Davies v London and Provincial Marine Insurance Co* (1878) 8 Ch. D. 469, *per* Fry J. at 474–475; *Lloyds Bank v Harrison* (1925) 4 L.D.B. 12, *per* Pollock M.R. at 14; *Workington Harbour v Trade Indemnity Co Ltd* [1934] 49 Ll. L. Rep. 430, reversed [1937] A.C. 1.

gaining an unfair advantage over the other, then there would appear to be no reason in principle why the obligation to disclose could not arise, in appropriate cases, at the time of a variation to the guarantee. The case was referred to by Colman J. in *Geest v Fyffes* [1999] 1 All E.R. (Comm) 672 at 682 with apparent approval.[72]

Disclosure to whom?

One matter which does not appear to have been considered in the authorities, but which could have significant practical implications for lenders, is whether any disclosure must be made to the surety personally, or whether disclosure to an agent would suffice. If the surety is represented by a solicitor, the lender would naturally expect any material matters disclosed to the solicitor to be passed on to his client. Indeed it might be seen as a breach of professional etiquette to correspond with the surety directly. However, if the purpose of the disclosure is to ensure that the surety is fully informed about aspects of the transaction which are extraordinary and which may have an impact on his decision to take the risk, it is questionable whether disclosure to any third party would ever suffice to discharge the creditor's duty. Telling an agent could be regarded as an illegitimate attempt to pass the burden onto someone else. It is anticipated that if this issue ever arose in court and the agent had not passed on the information to his principal, there is a real risk that the court would conclude that the creditor had not discharged his duty, which is, after all, a duty to tell the other contracting party, not a duty to take reasonable steps to make the unusual fact known to him. The safest course would be for the creditor to disclose the matter in writing, and try to obtain written confirmation from the surety that he or she has read the relevant document.

5–024

Express provisions requiring disclosure

It is always open to the parties to agree that certain specific matters should be disclosed to the surety, or that the creditor's obligation to make disclosure should be wider, or continuing, though in practice it is unlikely that someone other than a professional commercial surety will have the strength of bargaining power to obtain the agreement of the creditor to such a term. In *Lee v Jones* (1864) 17 C.B. (N.S.) 482 it was held that on the true construction of an extremely elliptical agreement, the creditor was obliged to disclose the prior indebtedness of a del credere agent for whom the guarantee was being given. However, that case could also be regarded as an example of a transaction which was set aside for fraudulent misrepresentation. Perhaps a better example is the agreement in *Formica Ltd v Secretary of State acting by the Export Credit Guarantee Department* [1995] 1 Lloyd's Rep. 692, in which the ECGD guarantee was expressly given on condition that the beneficiary (described as the "insured") "will at

5–025

---

72 For a different view, see O'Donovan & Phillips (English ed.) *op. cit.* at paras 4–15 to 4–16.

all times during the operation of this guarantee promptly disclose all facts in any way affecting the risks guaranteed". It was held by Colman J. that the contractual duty ended when there was no longer any risk of loss which could be affected by any information which could be provided.

Disclosure and the duty of confidentiality

5–026 If the surety expressly requests information from the creditor, and the creditor is in a position where he owes a duty of confidentiality to the principal, which may be broken if he gives the information (*e.g.* if the creditor is a bank and the principal its customer), the creditor may find himself in a difficult situation. How is he to reconcile the duty to answer the surety's questions in a fair and frank manner, with his obligations of confidentiality?

Of course, each situation will depend very much on its own particular facts, and on the nature of the surety's questions. There are two possible solutions to the problem. The first is for the creditor to procure the principal's consent to giving the necessary information to the surety. If the creditor takes this course, it would be prudent either to obtain the consent in writing or to arrange a meeting to be attended by the creditor, principal and surety at which the information may be given by the principal directly. It would usually be a good idea for the creditor to attend such a meeting, because he would then know directly what the surety was told by the principal, and the extent to which he could discuss with the surety any matters which would otherwise be confidential. However, his presence could expose him to a potential liability to correct any misleading statements made in front of him, (including the creation of a misleading impression by partial disclosure of information).

The alternative solution is for the creditor to tell the surety that he is unable to answer his questions because this would breach his duty of confidentiality, and to refer the surety directly to the principal, thus putting the onus on him to make full inquiry from that source. If he does this, however, he takes the risk that an unscrupulous surety might come back and trick him into disclosing further confidential information on the pretext that the principal has said more to him than he actually has, or that the principal has sanctioned the disclosure of further information. This problem could be met by refusing to discuss the matter further without the written consent of the principal, setting up a tripartite meeting as suggested above, or at least contacting him to check the position before saying anything to the surety.

In the absence of an express request for information, the problem may still arise when the limited duty of disclosure obliges the creditor to reveal a matter that is subject to a duty of confidentiality. Since as a matter of principle and public policy there is no duty of confidentiality in respect of fraud or dishonesty, this is unlikely to pose a practical difficulty in a case where the creditor is obliged to disclose a matter of that nature: see, *e.g.* the observations of Brownie J. in *Westpac Banking Corp v Robinson* (1990)

A.S.C. 56–002 at 59–038.[73] However, in the case of other material "unusual facts" there is no clear-cut guidance. It is arguable that by introducing the surety to the creditor, the principal has impliedly waived any duty of confidentiality which may be owed to him in respect of matters which the creditor is legally obliged to reveal to the surety in order to procure a valid security. However, it will often be the case nowadays that the lender tells the principal what he wants by way of security and from whom (*e.g.* personal guarantees from the directors of the borrower) so that there is no such introduction. Moreover that argument would not assist the creditor with regard to dealings involving third parties to whom the creditor owes the duty of confidence. The safest course is probably to obtain express consent, because in this context the option of refusing to reveal the information is not available to the creditor, and if he refers the surety to the principal or to a third party he cannot be certain that the surety will find out everything he needs to know. As a result of the guidance laid down by the House of Lords in *Royal Bank of Scotland v Etridge (No.2)* [2002] 2 A.C. 773 (particularly by Lord Nicholls in para.79(2)) it is likely that financial institutions will include an express provision in the application form that the borrower consents to the dissemination of relevant material to any prospective surety.

Exemption clauses

Apart from taking care to ensure that any information which he does give   **5–027** to the surety is accurate, the creditor may seek to exclude the consequences of misrepresentation by misstatement or non-disclosure, by including an exemption clause in the contract of suretyship: see, *e.g. Trade Indemnity Co Ltd v Workington Harbour and Dock Board* [1937] A.C. 1. Such a clause may, however, be vulnerable under the Unfair Contract Terms Act or under the EU Directive on Unfair Contract Terms now implemented by the Unfair Terms in Consumer Contracts Regulations 1999.[74]

Unconscionable transactions

A contract of suretyship which is entered into under duress or undue   **5–028** influence exerted by the creditor is voidable if the duress or undue influence operated on the mind of the surety at the time when he entered into the agreement.[75] In addition, if the creditor has actual knowledge of any duress or undue influence exerted by the principal over the surety, and fails to take reasonable steps to ensure that the surety enters into the contract of his or her own free will, the transaction is liable to be set aside. The third category of cases in which the transaction may be set aside is where the creditor is fixed with constructive notice of duress or of actual or

---

73 The point was not considered on appeal.
74 See Ch.3, paras 3–035–3–037.
75 See generally *Chitty on Contracts*, 29th ed., (*op. cit.*) Ch.7.

presumed undue influence (or indeed, misrepresentation or some other legal wrong by the principal debtor) which would have entitled the surety to set aside the transaction if he or she had contracted with the principal debtor rather than the creditor.[76] The principles relating to this special category of cases are discussed in detail later, in the context of undue influence.

The burden of proving duress or undue influence by the other contracting party is on the party seeking to set aside the contract, namely the surety.

Duress

5–029 Duress is not confined to threats of physical violence. It may consist of an express or implied threat to prosecute, even if the prosecution would be proper, in the sense that it would be objectively justifiable. For example, in *Mutual Finance Co v Wetton* [1937] 2 K.B. 389, C, a hire-purchase company, obtained a guarantee which purported to be given by S. The guarantee was a forgery by S's brother. On discovering this, C approached S and got him to sign a fresh guarantee on behalf of the family company, in circumstances in which there was an implied threat to procure the prosecution of his brother if he did not. S signed the fresh guarantee because he was concerned about the possibly fatal effect which the shock of such a prosecution might have on his father's health. C knew that this was the reason why S signed. The contract was set aside for what was termed "undue influence", though it is probably more accurately described as a case of duress.[77]

Guarantees and indemnities are quite often entered into in circumstances in which the creditor would otherwise take legal proceedings against the debtor. For example, the directors of a company may give guarantees for the indebtedness of the company to a trade creditor in circumstances in which the creditor says that he will issue a winding-up petition if he does not receive adequate security for the payment of the debts. If the creditor is entitled to take such proceedings against the debtor, or even if he has a bona fide belief that he is so entitled, then it is unlikely that a threat to assert his legal rights would amount to duress, save in wholly exceptional circumstances.[78]

In appropriate circumstances, a guarantee or indemnity may be set aside on the grounds that it was procured by economic duress. However, mere commercial pressure will not suffice; it has to be shown that the economic pressure was illegitimate and that it constituted a sufficient cause inducing

---

76 *Barclays Bank v O'Brien* [1994] 1 A.C. 180; *Royal Bank of Scotland v Etridge (No.2)* [2002] 2 A.C. 773 discussed below at para.5–030 and following.

77 See also *Williams v Bayley* (1866) L.R. 1 H.L. 200; *Davies v London & Provincial Marine Insurance* (1878) 8 Ch. D. 469. However, as the House of Lords acknowledged in *Royal Bank of Scotland v Etridge (No.2)* [2002] 2 A.C. 773 when clarifying the law relating to undue influence, there may be little practical distinction between duress and actual undue influence by coercion (see, *e.g.* Lord Nicholls at para.8).

78 See, *e.g. Powell v Hoyland* (1851) 6 Exch. 67; *Wardley Australia Ltd v McPharlin* (1984) 3 B.P.R. 9500.

the aggrieved party to enter into the relevant contract: *The "Evia Luck"* [1992] 2 A.C. 152 *per* Lord Goff at 165.[79] If he would have entered into the contract with or without the pressure, he cannot rely on the defence of duress.

A good practical example of the difficulties faced by a surety who wishes to establish a defence of duress is to be found in the Australian case of *Wardley Australia v McPharlin* (1984) 3 B.P.R. 9500. The principal fell into arrears, and the creditor informed an existing guarantor that unless the guarantee was extended to cover further advances, he would enforce his securities. The guarantor agreed, under protest, but made a note on the document which he signed stating that it was signed "under duress". It was held by Rogers J. that although it may have been a hard bargain, the creditor was merely threatening to exercise its lawful rights and the defence of economic duress failed. Similarly, in the New Zealand case of *Shivas v Bank of New Zealand* [1990] 2 N.Z.L.R. 327, it was held that although some degree of commercial pressure had been applied by the bank, it was insufficient to amount to duress. Among the matters which played an important part in this conclusion were the fact that the sureties had had plenty of opportunity to obtain advice before signing, and the fact that there was no protest at the time of intolerable pressure and that the allegation of duress was only made two years later. Tipping J., at 351, summarised the position in which the sureties found themselves as one in which they had to weigh up the unpalatable suggestion that they should give a mortgage against the equally unpalatable suggestion that if they declined, the family home might be sold. He commented that "there are many occasions in commerce when people have to make choices between unwelcome alternatives but that does not mean for one moment that having chosen one they can claim to have acted under duress". A different conclusion might be reached, however, if the creditor obtains the consent of the guarantor by threatening to do something which he is not lawfully entitled to do, for example terminating a company's overdraft facility when it is not in breach of its terms, especially if it is known to both parties that the company is completely dependent upon that facility and cannot continue to trade without it.

Undue influence

The principle of undue influence is an equitable doctrine which is wider in scope than duress. A contract of suretyship may be set aside if the surety entered into the contract under the influence of another person in circumstances in which he was prevented from exercising independent judgment. The principle is not confined to cases where the surety has not

5–030

---

79 See also *Pao On v Lau Yiu Long* (1980) A.C. 614, *Universe Tankships of Monrovia v International Transport Workers Federation* [1983] 1 A.C. 366, *Atlas Express v Kafco* [1989] 1 All E.R. 641, and *Huyton SA v Peter Cremer GmbH* [1999] 1 Lloyd's Rep. 620, especially at 635–639.

really wanted to enter into the transaction but has been forced to do so. On the contrary, "the question is not whether [the surety] knew what she was doing, had done, or proposed to do, but how the intention was produced".[80] It is therefore no defence that the victim of the undue influence acted of his or her own free will because equity looks to the conscience of the person procuring the consent, and is concerned with how the consent was procured, rather than whether it was a true and informed consent.

The evidence required to discharge the burden of proof of undue influence will depend on the nature of the alleged undue influence, the personality of the parties, their relationship, the extent to which the transaction cannot be accounted for by the ordinary motives of ordinary persons in that relationship and all the circumstances of the case. Proof that the complainant placed trust and confidence in the other party in relation to the management of the complainant's financial affairs, coupled with a transaction which calls for explanation, will normally be sufficient, failing satisfactory evidence to the contrary, to discharge the burden of proof. Proof of those two factors will shift the evidential burden to the other contracting party to satisfy the court that the inference that the transaction can only have been procured by undue influence should not be drawn.[81]

Traditionally the cases in which a contract may be set aside for undue influence have been divided into two categories: see *Allcard v Skinner* (1887) 36 Ch. D. 145 at 190 and *Barclays Bank v O'Brien* [1994] A.C. 180. As the House of Lords explained in *Royal Bank of Scotland v Etridge (No.2)* [2002] 2 A.C. 773, the categorisation is really an attempt to distinguish different routes by which a complainant can prove that a transaction was tainted by undue influence. The first category is where it is established by direct proof that actual undue influence was used to procure the contract; for example, where coercion has been used, or where one party exercised a "dominating influence" over the mind of the other, so that his or her independence of decision was substantially undermined. The classic example is where a wife is accustomed to obeying her husband without question, and therefore does whatever he tells her to do. This species (labelled "actual" undue influence) is an equitable wrong committed by the dominant party against the other, which makes it unconscionable for the dominant party to enforce his legal rights against the other party. Examples are *Allcard v Skinner* itself, *Bank of Credit and Commerce International v Aboody* [1990] 1 Q.B. 923 and *Barclays Bank v Bennett*, one of the appeals decided in *Royal Bank of Scotland v Etridge* [2002] 2 A.C. 773 at 871–878, though ultimately Mrs Bennett's appeal succeeded on the entirely different ground of non-disclosure. To the extent that coercion is used, the defence overlaps with duress. The pressure complained of may also overlap with other conduct, such as misrepresentation, which gives rise to a defence. In such cases, it is unnecessary to prove that there was a pre-existing

---

80 *Per* Lord Eldon V.-C. in *Hugenin v Baseley* (1807) 14 Ves. 273 at 300.
81 *Royal Bank of Scotland v Etridge (No.2)* [2002] 2 A.C. 773 *per* Lord Nicholls at 796 (paras 13 and 14).

relationship between the parties. Nor is it necessary to establish that the transaction was "manifestly disadvantageous" to the party seeking to upset it, in the sense that it called for an explanation: *CIBC Mortgages v Pitt* [1994] 1 A.C. 200 as explained by Lord Nicholls in *Royal Bank of Scotland v Etridge (No.2)* [2002] 2 A.C. 773.[82] The critical question in this type of case is whether the complainant was allowed to exercise an independent and informed judgment. Thus a wife who proves that undue influence was used, for example by establishing that in practice she signed whatever her husband put in front of her, may be entitled to avoid the transaction without having to show that it was disadvantageous to her in financial terms or in any other way. However, as Lord Nicholls pointed out, in the nature of things, questions of undue influence will not usually arise, and the exercise of undue influence is unlikely to occur, where the transaction is innocuous.

The second category (labelled "presumed undue influence") may occur only where the relationship between the parties is such as to raise a presumption (or an inference) that one party had influence over the party seeking to set aside the transaction, by reason of the trust and confidence reposed by that party in him or her and where, on the facts, the transaction is one which calls for an explanation. Lord Browne-Wilkinson in *Barclays Bank v O'Brien* [1994] A.C. 180 had sub-divided this category into two classes, but in *Royal Bank of Scotland v Etridge (No.2)* [2002] 2 A.C. 773, which has replaced *O'Brien* as the leading authority in this area, those classifications and prior judicial statements about when a presumption of undue influence will arise were strongly criticised, and are now to be deprecated. All that the previous cases have done is to indicate what is needed by way of evidence, in the absence of direct proof of wrongdoing, to raise a rebuttable presumption that the transaction was tainted by undue influence. Certain types of relationship, such as parent and child, or solicitor and client, will give rise to the presumption of influence as a matter of law.[83] However, it has long been established that an automatic presumption of this kind does not arise in the case of husband and wife.[84] In the case of this and other relationships, influence must be established as a matter of fact, by proof that one party placed trust and confidence in the other in relation to the management of his or her financial affairs, either generally or in respect of the impugned transaction. In *Etridge* Lord Scott indicated, in para.159, that in the case of husband and wife this burden will

---

82 In *Royal Bank of Scotland v Etridge* Lord Nicholls in particular at paras 26–29 criticised the label "manifest disadvantage". He said that it was ambiguous and should be discarded in favour of Lord Scarman's formulation in *National Westminster Bank v Morgan* [1985] A.C. 686 at 704 that "the transaction was wrongful in that it constituted an advantage taken of the person subjected to the influence which, failing proof to the contrary, was explicable only on the basis that undue influence had been exercised to procure it". *Cf.* Lord Scott, at para.155, who described Lord Scarman's reasoning as "circular".

83 For a full discussion of the relationships subject to the presumption see *Chitty on Contracts* (*op. cit.*), at paras 7–063–7–066.

84 *Howes v Bishop* [1909] 2 K.B. 390; *Mackenzie v Royal Bank of Canada* [1934] A.C. 468; *King's North Trust v Bell* [1986] 1 W.L.R. 119.

be lightly discharged. He said that he would assume in every case in which a wife and husband are living together that there is a reciprocal trust and confidence between them, and that in the fairly common circumstances that the financial and business decisions of the family are primarily taken by the husband, he would assume that the wife would have trust and confidence in his ability to do so and would support his decisions. Far from expecting evidence to be necessary to establish the existence of that trust and confidence, he would expect it to be necessary to demonstrate its absence. Critically, however, the House of Lords in *Etridge* made it clear that the mere fact that the relationship is one of presumed or actual influence, will not suffice in itself to raise a further presumption or inference in respect of any transaction that it was entered into as a result of the exertion of *undue* influence by the "dominant" party over the vulnerable party. Such a presumption will only arise if the transaction in question is, in the words of Lindley L.J. in *Allcard v Skinner*, "not reasonably to be accounted for on the grounds of friendship, relationship, charity or other ordinary motives on which ordinary men act". As Lord Nicholls pointed out in para.24, and Lord Scott in para.156, it would be absurd for the law to presume that every gift by a child to a parent, or every transaction between a client and his solicitor or between a doctor and his patient has been brought about by undue influence unless the contrary is affirmatively proved. Equally, as Lord Nicholls made clear, in the ordinary course a guarantee given by a wife for her husband's business debts is not to be regarded as a transaction which, failing proof to the contrary, is explicable only on the basis that it has been procured by the exercise of undue influence by the husband. He pointed out that if the husband's business is the source of the family income, the wife has a "lively interest" in doing what she can to support it. However he expressly acknowledged that there will be cases where a wife's signature of a guarantee or charge of her share in the matrimonial home does call for an explanation: see *Etridge* at paras 28–31. Where there *is* something about the transaction which calls for an explanation, then the greater the disadvantage to the vulnerable person, the more cogent must be the explanation before the presumption or inference that the transaction was procured by undue influence will be regarded as rebutted. As Lord Scott put it at para.156, "it is . . . the combination of relationship and the nature of the transaction that gives rise to the presumption and, if the transaction is challenged, shifts the onus to the transferee".

Lord Nicholls went on to sound what he described as a "cautionary note". He pointed out that undue influence has a connotation of impropriety, and thus statements or conduct by a husband which do not pass beyond the bounds of what may be expected of a reasonable husband should not, without more, be castigated as undue influence. A degree of hyperbole is to be expected when the husband is forecasting the future of the business or expressing his hopes or fears, and judges should not be ready to castigate them as misrepresentations. Inaccurate explanations of a proposed transaction are a different matter. So are cases where the husband abuses his influence by preferring his interests to those of his wife and making a choice for them both on that footing. In such event he fails to discharge the obligation of candour and fairness he owes a wife who is looking to him to make the major financial decisions (*ibid.*, paras 32–33).

When the evidential burden has shifted, the court will set aside the transaction unless it is proved by the party seeking to uphold it that the party subject to the presumed undue influence entered into the transaction of his or her own free will and independently of any undue influence. Consequently, in the comparatively rare cases in which the relationship of trust and confidence arose directly between the creditor and the surety, it is unnecessary to prove that the creditor actually exerted undue influence over the surety, once the relationship and the need for an explanation of the transaction have been established. It will be for the creditor to provide a satisfactory innocuous explanation for the transaction or to show that the transaction was entered into by the other party free of such influence, *e.g.* after taking independent legal advice. However, in cases in which the principal is proved to have exercised undue influence over the surety (whether by direct evidence or by raising an irrebutted presumption), the surety will be unable to set aside the transaction as against the creditor on those grounds unless the creditor had actual or constructive notice of the undue influence.[85]

Undue influence by the creditor himself

The relationship between banker and customer is not one which would ordinarily give rise to the presumption of influence as between those parties: *National Westminster Bank v Morgan* [1985] A.C. 686 at 707–709. Nevertheless, on the facts of a particular case undue influence as between the creditor and surety may be established. *Lloyds Bank v Bundy* [1975] Q.B. 326 provides an example:

5–031

> S, the guarantor, was an elderly farmer who had been a customer of the bank for many years. His son formed a company which banked at the same branch. S went to the bank to discuss giving a guarantee to secure the company's overdraft. As a result he charged his only asset, his home, as security for the overdraft. S relied entirely on the bank manager to advise him about the overdraft and said that he always trusted the bank manager and simply sat back and did as he was told.

It was held that the bank owed a duty to ensure that S had formed an independent and informed judgment. Since the bank had not done so, the guarantee and legal charge would be set aside for undue influence.[86]

---

85 *Royal Bank of Scotland v Etridge (No.2)* (above) applying *Barclays Bank v O'Brien, CIBC v Pitt* [1994] 1 A.C. 200 and see paras 5–034–5–037 below.

86 Lord Denning alone decided the case on the wider ground of inequality of bargaining power, but the House of Lords disapproved this attempt at extending existing principles in *National Westminster Bank v Morgan* [1985] A.C. 686, while emphasising that the majority decision in the *Bundy* case was correct. Recent cases have indicated, however, that the more flexible approach to equitable relief adopted by Lord Denning may be receiving more widespread judicial application. See the discussion of unconscionable bargains at para.5–048 below.

Undue influence by the principal or a co-surety

5–032 It is only in the rarest of cases that the creditor is directly responsible for the undue influence. It is more usual for the influence to have been exerted by the principal debtor, or possibly by a co-surety. The question therefore often arises as to the circumstances in which the creditor will be affected by undue influence for which someone else was responsible. That question is answered in the same way as the analogous question in a case involving misrepresentation or some other legal wrong which would entitle the surety to rescind the transaction if it had been made with the wrongdoer: the creditor will only be responsible if the person exerting the undue influence acted as his agent, in the true legal sense of agency, or if he had sufficient notice of the undue influence and did not take reasonable steps to prevent the surety from acting under it.[87]

It is important not to lose sight of the fact that it is an essential aspect of any case of this nature that the surety (on whom the evidential burden initially lies) must prove that the transaction was procured by undue influence or by some other actionable wrongdoing—for example misrepresentation. The decisions of the House of Lords in the conjoined appeals in *Royal Bank of Scotland v Etridge (No.2)* [2002] 2 A.C. 773 make this plain: two of the appeals, *Etridge* itself and *National Westminster Bank Plc v Gill* failed because the surety was unable to cross that threshold. Even if the surety raises the presumption that the transaction was procured by undue influence, the creditor may be able to displace it on the evidence. As a result of the clarification of the law in *Etridge*, cases in which a wife will be able to prove that the transaction was tainted by undue influence will be rare, since in most cases where the wife is standing surety for the husband's business debts or those of the company running the family business, the transaction will be readily explicable: see, *e.g.* the observations of Lord Nicholls at para.30 and Lord Scott at para.159.

Agency

5–033 If the person exerting the undue influence on the surety was the agent of the creditor for the purpose of obtaining the signature of the surety on the contract of suretyship, the contract will be voidable. However, as the Court of Appeal made clear in *Barclays Bank v O'Brien* [1993] Q.B. 109, the fact that the creditor leaves it to the debtor to procure the signature of the surety will not of itself give rise to a relationship of agency such as to make the creditor vicariously responsible for any misrepresentations of the debtor or for his wrongdoing. Scott L.J. said, at 113, that the "agency" approach favoured by the courts in a number of cases decided since 1985 lent an air of unreality to the arguments addressed to the court and masked the true basis on which relief was granted. A bank which tells a husband that it requires a charge over the matrimonial home to be executed by his wife as

---

87 *Barclays Bank v O'Brien* [1994] A.C. 180 as explained and applied in *Royal Bank of Scotland v Etridge (No.2)* [2002] 2 A.C. 773.

security for a loan would be as astonished as the husband to think that this made the husband the agent of the bank. The House of Lords, [1984] 1 A.C. 180, while disagreeing with the Court of Appeal's rationale as to the "true basis" for the relief, agreed that the agency theory was inappropriate save in the cases where, without artificiality, it can properly be held that the principal was acting as the agent of the creditor in procuring the surety to stand as surety, which would be of very rare occurrence.[88]

Even in cases where agency is established, the creditor may not be held responsible for the wrongdoing of the agent so as to relieve the surety from liability, whether in whole or in part. This is illustrated by the decision in Scotland of the Outer House (2nd Division) in *McCabe v Skipton Building Society* (1994) S.L.T. 1272. In that case, somewhat unusually, the bank's solicitor was also the husband allegedly responsible for procuring the wife's agreement to stand surety by fraudulent misrepresentation. A loan was made to the husband and wife jointly to facilitate the purchase of some property, and therefore the case fell within the principles of *CIBC Mortgages v Pitt* [1994] A.C. 200, discussed in para.5–033 below. The husband was a partner in a firm of solicitors and acted for the bank in the preparation and recording of the standard security documentation, as well as for himself and his wife in the execution of the transaction. He subsequently pleaded guilty to a large number of charges of fraud, and was serving a lengthy sentence of imprisonment at the time when the bank sought to enforce its security. His wife asserted that the original standard security for the loan, which she had executed and which was limited to £50,000, was discharged by her husband without her knowledge. He then allegedly induced her to execute in blank a second standard security by fraudulently misrepresenting that the bank required a fresh document to be executed. He completed the new security document by filling in a figure of £70,000 instead of £50,000, and subsequently procured a series of additional advances from the bank, amounting to £260,000, by forging his wife's signature on requests and receipts. She therefore contended that the entire transaction was tainted by his fraud and that she was entitled to be put in the position in which she stood prior to his embarkation upon the fraudulent plan (so that she was only liable for the original £50,000). However, the security documentation made the wife jointly and severally liable with the husband for the advances made by the bank. The court held that although the husband was the common agent of two innocent parties, the bank and the wife, the fraudulent misrepresentation that the bank required a fresh security document to be executed was not made by the husband in his capacity as agent for the bank. The bank gave valuable consideration for the second security, which it relied upon as genuine; in those circumstances, it was in accordance with principle that the loss should fall upon the wife rather than upon the bank.

---

88 *Per* Lord Browne-Wilkinson [1994] A.C. 180 at 194A, 195F–G.

Notice

5–034   If the creditor has actual or constructive notice at the time when the guarantee is executed, that the guarantee or the charge on which it relies has been procured by the exercise of undue influence, misrepresentation, or some other legal wrong which would entitle the surety to set aside the transaction against the wrongdoer, he cannot enforce the transaction.

Actual notice

5–035   Actual notice in this context will include what has sometimes been described as "Nelsonian knowledge", a useful example of which is to be found in the case of *Woodchester Equipment Leasing Co v Capital Belts Ltd* (unreported) CAT No.335 of 1995, April 12, CA. The defendant company leased certain office equipment (photocopiers, and suchlike) from the plaintiff finance company under a hire-purchase type agreement (called a rental plan) which was personally guaranteed by H, a director of the defendant. Payments under the rental plan were to be made by direct debit. The terms of the deal had been negotiated directly between the defendant and the suppliers and the plaintiff had adopted a deliberate policy of non-interference. The suppliers of the equipment fraudulently altered the direct debit form so as to increase the number of payments under the rental plan from 12 to 36. The defendant failed to pay under the plan and the equipment was repossessed and sold with a considerable shortfall. The Court of Appeal held that in order to escape liability, H had to show that the plaintiff acted with wilful or reckless ignorance of the actual terms of the agreement made with the supplier, or closed its eyes to the obvious.[89] On the facts, he succeeded because, among other matters, it must have been obvious to the plaintiff that something was seriously wrong when the supplier's invoice showed the cost was approximately three times as great as what had previously been calculated (and disclosed to them in the correspondence). Despite this they raised no query about it. Nourse L.J. concluded that there was actual knowledge of facts giving rise to the clear inference of fraud or at the least of a major mistake in the offer.

Constructive notice

5–036   Until the seminal case of *Barclays Bank v O'Brien* [1994] A.C. 180, the law was in a state of conflict and confusion. It was difficult to predict whether a wife who could prove that a guarantee or mortgage was executed as a result of her husband's undue influence or other wrongdoing could set it aside as against the lender, let alone to discern any established body of principle which justified the setting aside or refusal to set aside in any given case.[90] In *O'Brien*, a husband had procured his wife's signature of a mortgage as

---

89 Applying *Feuer Leather Corporation v Frank Johnstone & Sons* [1981] Com. L.R. 251, the doctrine of constructive notice had no part to play in this type of commercial transaction.
90 For an exposition of the historical background to *O'Brien* see the previous edition of this work.

security for an overdraft given to his company, by falsely representing to her that it was limited to £60,000 and it would only last for three weeks. The trial judge held that in the absence of evidence that the husband was acting as the bank's agent, the bank was not liable for his misrepresentations and the mortgage was enforceable. The Court of Appeal allowed the wife's appeal and set aside the transaction.[91] The House of Lords [1994] 1 A.C. 180 affirmed the decision of the Court of Appeal, but on different grounds. The leading speech was delivered by Lord Browne-Wilkinson, who acknowledged that policy dictated that sureties known by the creditor to be in a position where, by virtue of their relationship with the debtor, they are particularly susceptible to pressure or misrepresentations by him, should be afforded proper protection. He stated, however, that any such protection should be based on existing legal principles, and should not be so wide as to have the effect of dissuading financial institutions from accepting matrimonial property as valid security altogether. In the light of the confusion caused by earlier cases, a complete restatement of the law was deemed necessary.

In order for the surety to be able to set aside the transaction against the creditor, there must be undue influence, misrepresentation or some other legal wrong by the principal debtor (which would give rise to an equitable right by the surety to set aside the transaction as against him) and either agency (in the true legal sense) or actual or constructive notice by the creditor. Lord Browne-Wilkinson said that a creditor is put on inquiry when a wife offers to stand surety for her husband's debts by the combination of two factors:

(a) the transaction is on its face not to the financial advantage of the wife; and

(b) there is a substantial risk in transactions of that kind that, in procuring the wife to act as surety the husband has committed a legal or equitable wrong that entitles the wife to set aside the transaction.

In such event the creditor will be fixed with constructive notice of any wrongdoing

> "that is ultimately established to have tainted the transaction, unless he takes reasonable steps to satisfy himself that the agreement of the surety has been properly obtained. What is reasonable will depend on the facts and circumstances of the individual case. The principle applies not just to spouses and co-habitees but to any other relationship of trust and confidence known to the creditor."[92]

---

91 [1993] Q.B. 109.
92 1994] 1 A.C. at 196. For the wide variety of relationships which have been held to be relationships of trust and confidence see, *e.g. Massey v Midland Bank Plc* [1995] 1 All E.R. 929; *Shams v United Bank* (unreported, May 24, 1994, Ch. D.); *Banco Exterior Internacional*

This was acknowledged to be an extension of the concept of constructive notice as set out in *BCC v Aboody* [1990] 1 Q.B. 923, and earlier cases, but Lord Browne-Wilkinson stressed that the crucial factor was the self-evident lack of financial advantage to the surety. In *Royal Bank of Scotland v Etridge (No.2)*, discussed below, the House of Lords subsequently acknowledged that this factor is present in any case where the surety is non-commercial.

Unfortunately, instead of having the desired effect of settling the law in this field, over the next eight years *Barclays Bank v O'Brien* spawned numerous further decisions which tested its boundaries and its implications in a variety of different factual scenarios. Ultimately seven of these cases, together with a related solicitor's negligence claim, came before the House of Lords, so that various issues raised by the *O'Brien* decision could be definitively pronounced upon. *Royal Bank of Scotland v Etridge (No.2)* [2002] 2 A.C. 773 is now the leading case. It affirms the authority and soundness of the *O'Brien* principle but eliminates the sources of much of the confusion. The leading speech, delivered by Lord Nicholls, was described by Lord Bingham in para.3 as commanding "the unqualified support of all members of the House". However, Lord Scott and Lord Hobhouse also delivered lengthy concurring speeches and it is important to have regard to them as well.

As discussed above in para.5–030 the House of Lords in *Etridge* restated the matters which need to be proved by a person seeking to set aside a transaction for undue influence, and deprecated the division of cases of undue influence into different categories. The House emphasised that ultimately in any given case the question of whether the transaction was to be set aside for undue influence depended on *proof* that it had been obtained by undue influence, which would depend on the facts and circumstances and the strength of the evidence in each individual case. In the absence of direct proof, the vulnerable party would be able to raise a rebuttable presumption that the transaction was entered into as a result of undue influence by proving that he or she reposed trust and confidence in the person who benefited from the transaction, and that the nature of the transaction was such as to call for an explanation.

On the key issue of when a creditor would be "put on inquiry" or would be fixed with constructive notice, it was held that the passage from Lord Browne-Wilkinson's speech in *O'Brien* quoted above, read in context, meant quite simply that a bank is put on inquiry whenever a wife offers to stand surety for her husband's debts.[93] The points which he made about the

---

v Thomas [1997] 1 W.L.R. 221; *Credit Lyonnais Bank Nederland BV v Burch* [1997] 1 All E.R. 144; *Steeples v Lea* [1998] 1 F.L.R. 138; *Northern Rock Building Society v Hazel Archer* [1999] Lloyd's Rep. Bank 32; *Barclays Bank v Rivett* [1999] 1 F.L.R. 730; *Portman Building Society v Dusangh* [2000] 2 All E.R. (Comm) 221; *Macklin v Dowsett* [2004] EWCA Civ 904, June 14, 2004. *Cf Homes Bridging Plc v Berwin* (unreported) CAT No.0181 of 1984, February 24, 1984, where the Court of Appeal declined to extend the *O'Brien* principle to a business relationship.

93 See Lord Nicholls at paras 44–46; Lord Hobhouse at paras 108–110.

lack of financial advantage and the risk that the husband would commit a legal or equitable wrong were an explanation of why the bank was to be put on inquiry in such cases, and banks were not required to engage in factual inquiries as to the nature of the domestic relationship or the degree of trust and confidence placed by a particular wife in her husband in relation to her financial affairs. Lord Nicholls said in para.41 that the House of Lords in *O'Brien* set a low level for the threshold which must be crossed before a bank is put on inquiry. For practical reasons it is much lower than the level which is required to satisfy a court that, failing contrary evidence, the court may infer that the transaction was procured by undue influence.[94]

The phrase "put on inquiry" is something of a misnomer, as Lord Nicholls acknowledged, because the bank is not required to make any inquiries, but rather to take steps to minimise the risk of wrongdoing (*ibid.*, para.41). As Lord Scott explained in para.147, the bank is put on inquiry as to whether the wife understood the nature and effect of the transaction she was entering into, which is not an inquiry in the traditional constructive notice sense. The bank would not be on notice that undue influence or misrepresentation was to be presumed, unless it had notice of additional facts pointing to such wrongdoing. Instead, it would simply be on notice of the *risk* of such impropriety. If the bank with notice of that risk failed to take the requisite reasonable steps, then if it transpired that the consent of the wife had indeed been procured by the husband's undue influence or misrepresentation, constructive notice that that was so would be imputed to the bank, and the wife would have the same remedies as she would have had if the bank had actual knowledge of the impropriety. Similar rules would apply, in the case of unmarried couples, whether heterosexual or homosexual, where the bank is aware of the relationship. The House of Lords confirmed that the decision in *Massey v Midland Bank Plc* [1995] 1 All E.R. 929 that co-habitation is not essential was correct.[95] As to the type of transactions where a bank is put on inquiry, the case where the wife is standing surety for her husband's debts is straightforward: the bank is always put on inquiry. The same is true where the wife becomes surety for the debts of a company whose shares are held by her and her husband, whether her shareholding is nominal, a minority shareholding or an equal shareholding, and whether or not the wife is also the secretary or director of the company.[96] Lord Nicholls said, at para.49, that the shareholding interests and the identity of the directors are not a reliable guide to the

---

94 Lord Hobhouse, concurring with this description at para.108, said that the advantage of a low threshold is that it assists banks to put in place procedures which do not require an exercise of judgment by their officials.

95 See the cases referred to in n.92 above.

96 This clear statement of principle should eliminate the type of exercise carried out in cases such as *Goode Durrant Administration v Biddulph* (1994) 26 H.L.R. 625, *Barclays Bank v Sumner* [1996] E.G.C.S. 65 and *Bank of Cyprus (London) Ltd v Markou* [1999] 2 F.L.R. 17, of comparing the size of the wife's shareholding in the family company with the financial consequences to her of a default, in order to determine whether the bank was put on inquiry.

identity of the persons who actually have conduct of the company's business. On the other side of the line is the case where money is or has been advanced to the husband and wife jointly. Lord Nicholls, at para.48, confirmed the earlier decision in *CIBC Mortgages Plc v Pitt* [1994] 1 A.C. 200 that in such a case the bank is not put on inquiry unless the bank is aware the loan is being made for the husband's purposes as distinct from their joint purposes.[97] Since the decision in *Etridge* this has been applied in a number of cases: for example, in *Royal Bank of Scotland v Fielding* [2003] EWHC 986, (Ch) May 2, 2003, *The Times*, May 16, 2003, in which Hart J. held that a wife was liable for the debit balance on a joint account with her husband even though she was, for the most part, wholly ignorant of her indebtedness: there was nothing about the facilities to put the bank on notice of some abuse of confidence so as to bring the principle in *O'Brien* (as clarified by *Etridge)* into operation. An appeal to the Court of Appeal on other grounds [2004] EWCA Civ 64, *The Times*, February 26, 2004, was dismissed. In *Chater v Mortgage Agency Services Number Two Ltd* [2003] EWCA Civ 490, [2004] 1 P. & C.R. 4 an elderly lady had borrowed money jointly with her son on the security of her house in order to raise money for the son's business. The house was transferred into their joint names at the same time. The purpose of the loan on the application form did not accord with the true purpose. The net proceeds of the loan went entirely to the son. Mrs Chater was able to raise a presumption of undue influence, which was not rebutted, but the Court of Appeal (presided over by the Master of the Rolls) nevertheless held that there was nothing about the transaction to put the lender on enquiry. The case can be distinguished from *Steeples v Lea* [1998] 1 F.L.R. 138 because the bank in *Chater* was unaware that the proceeds of the loan were going entirely to one of the supposedly joint borrowers.

In *Etridge* Lord Nicholls went on, in paras 82–89, to endorse the extension of the *O'Brien* principle to all relationships where trust and confidence might conceivably exist. He said that the law could not stop at the point where banks were only put on inquiry in cases where the parties have a sexual relationship or the relationship is one where the law presumes the existence of trust and confidence, such as parent and child: this would be an arbitrary boundary and the law had already moved beyond it in *Credit Lyonnais Bank Nederland BV v Burch* [1997] 1 All E.R. 144. There is no rational cut-off point and if a bank was not to be required to

---

97 An example of a case where the bank was put on notice because it was aware that the loan was in fact being used for the purposes of the person who might have procured it by undue influence or other wrongdoing, is *Northern Rock Building Society v Hazel Archer* [1999] Lloyds' Rep. Bank 32, where the true beneficiary was the brother of the mortgagee. Compare the converse situation which arose in *Hedworth v Scotlife Home Loans (No.2) Ltd* [1995] N.P.C. 91. The Court of Appeal held that it was not open to the wife to rely on the stated purpose of the loan ("business expansion") to raise an *O'Brien* defence, when the true purpose, to her knowledge, was to pay off existing mortgages, and thus the transaction fell into the *CIBC v Pitt* category. This case may be explained as an example of the application of the principle that he (or she) who comes to equity must come with clean hands.

evaluate the extent to which its customer has influence over the surety, the only practical way forward is to regard banks as put on inquiry in all cases where the relationship between the debtor and surety is non-commercial. Those engaged in business can be regarded as capable of looking after themselves and understanding the risks involved in giving guarantees. This principle imposes a modest burden on banks and other creditors who should, in future, regulate their affairs accordingly. Lord Hobhouse, at para.109, gave his express endorsement to this approach. He agreed that the burden on financial institutions was reasonable, pointing out that the bank should know who the principal debtor is and what is the purpose of the facility, and it should also know of any factors which are likely to aggravate the risk of undue influence in a given case, because the bank will either have information about the true nature of the transaction and the financial position of the principal debtor to hand, or if it does not, it is in a position to get it and has the expertise to assess it. This is possibly the most important part of the decision in *Etridge*. It is critical for any legal adviser to bear in mind that although the speeches tend, for the most part, to use the example of husband and wife, *the principle of constructive notice is potentially applicable to any lender in a transaction where the relationship between the principal and surety is not of a commercial nature.* It must also be remembered that although undue influence and duress are rarely proved, misrepresentation is less difficult to establish and the *O'Brien* principle covers any wrongdoing which operates on the mind of the surety.

If the surety does establish that the lender is fixed with constructive notice of the principal's wrongdoing, it is unnecessary for him or her to go on and prove that, but for the wrongdoing, he or she would not have signed the charge or the guarantee. In *UCB Corporate Services Ltd v Williams* [2002] EWCA Civ 555, [2002] 3 F.C.R. 448, the Court of Appeal held that the question whether the wife would have executed the charge in any event was relevant only to the question of what loss, if any, the wife had suffered in consequence of the husband's wrongdoing and was not relevant to the question whether the charge should be set aside.

Knowledge by agents
The actual knowledge of the creditor's agent of the true nature of the   **5–037**
transaction or the particular circumstances of the individual surety may be imputed to the creditor so as to bring *O'Brien* principles into play. An illustration of this is the case of *Nightingale Finance Ltd v Scott* (unreported, Ch. D, Carnwath J., November 18, 1997). A wife who mortgaged her home to secure a joint advance to a company in which she had a 19 per cent interest, was allowed to set aside the transaction on *O'Brien* grounds because the knowledge of a fraudulent agent, who was closely connected with the lender, that the transaction was manifestly disadvantageous to her (or, to use the phrase preferred by the House of Lords in *Etridge*, was of a type which called for an explanation), was imputed to the lender. As the law was then understood and applied, the knowledge of the agent probably made all the difference to the outcome of the case: there was nothing on

the face of the transaction itself to indicate to the lender that the loan was substantially for the benefit of the husband and not the wife, and that this was not a simple case of a joint advance to a company in which they were both interested as directors. Now, following the decision in *Etridge*, the lender would have been put on inquiry in any event.

In *Royal Bank of Scotland v Etridge (No.2)* [2002] 2 A.C. 773, the House of Lords settled the vexed issue of whether the knowledge of a solicitor engaged by the bank either to undertake the conveyancing formalities or to explain the nature and effect of the documents to the surety, and confirm to the bank that he has done so, is to be imputed to the bank as their agent. It was confirmed that such knowledge is not to be imputed to the bank, since any solicitor advising the wife is acting for her and for no one else: the bank has no knowledge or control over the advice which he gives and he is not accountable to the bank for the advice which he gives. To impute to the bank knowledge of what passed between the solicitor and the wife would contradict this essential feature of the arrangement.[98] See further para.5–042 below.

What steps should the creditor take?

5–038 The steps which a creditor should take to avoid being fixed with notice of any wrongdoing proved by the surety at trial were the principal area of controversy in the *Etridge* appeals. In *Barclays Bank v O'Brien* [1994] 1 A.C. 180 at 196–197, Lord Browne-Wilkinson said that a bank can reasonably be expected to take steps to bring home to the surety the risk which she or he is running, and advising the surety to take independent legal advice.

He then laid down some guidelines for creditors as to what would be regarded as reasonable steps in the future. In the normal case, he said that it would suffice to insist that the wife has a private meeting (in the absence of the husband) with the creditor at which the creditor will tell her the extent of her liability, warn her of the risks, and urge her to take independent legal advice. This approach was consistent with the voluntary code adopted by banks and building societies in March 1992 (revised in March 1994) but went further by requiring something more than a notice to be contained in the security documentation itself.[99] The personal meeting

---

98 See the speeches of Lord Nicholls at paras 75–78, Lord Hobhouse at para.122, and Lord Scott at paras 176–179. This confirmed the position stated in earlier cases such as *Halifax Mortgage Services Ltd v Stepsky* [1996] Ch. 207, and *Woolwich Plc v Gomm* (unreported) July 27, 1999, CA. Cf. *Steeples v Lea* [1998] 1 FLR 138, and *Midland Bank Plc v Wallace* one of the *Etridge* appeals, [2002] 2 A.C. 773 at 859–863, which were both unusual in that the solicitor concerned was acting throughout for the lender and only the lender. In those cases the knowledge of the solicitor or deficiencies of the solicitor's behaviour were attributed to the bank.

99 *Good Banking—Code of Practice* (1994 ed.) para.14.1 provided that before a private individual gives a guarantee or other third party security, the bank or building society will tell him or her that he or she could become liable as well as or instead of the principal debtor, and advise her to take independent legal advice before signing. He or she will also be advised whether the security is limited or unlimited, and, if it is limited, what the appropriate limit is.

was regarded by Lord Browne-Wilkinson as of critical importance, because previous cases had indicated that written warnings are often not read, and are sometimes intercepted by the husband.[1] He went on to say that if there are further factors pointing to the existence of probable, and not just possible, undue influence, the creditor may have to *insist* that she takes independent legal advice and not simply urge her to do so. These factors may well emerge in the course of the private interview.

The suggestion that the bank should have a personal meeting with the wife was not popular and, as the House of Lords recognised in *Royal Bank of Scotland v Etridge* [2002] 2 A.C. 773, in practice banks eschewed it, considering that they would stand to lose more than they would gain by holding such a meeting. In *Perry v Midland Bank Plc* [1987] Fin. L.R. 237 the bank's solicitor had tried and failed to give a proper explanation to the surety of the effect of the charge over the property which she executed: the trial judge's finding that the bank was liable to her in negligence was not appealed. The Court of Appeal in *Barclay's Bank v O'Brien* [1993] Q.B. 104 had tried to give some comfort to lenders by seeking to draw a distinction between the situation in which the creditor takes the role of advisor upon itself voluntarily, and the situation in which it is doing no more than necessary to protect itself against the risk of having the transaction set aside on *O'Brien* grounds. In the subsequent case of *Midland Bank v Kidwai* [1995] N.P.C. 81 the Court of Appeal confirmed that a bank discharging its responsibilities under *O'Brien* was not assuming the position of an adviser to the surety. Nevertheless, lenders on the whole preferred not to adopt Lord Browne-Wilkinson's suggestion. Instead, the previous practice of requiring the surety to seek legal advice, and of obtaining written confirmation from a solicitor that he had explained the nature and effect of the documents to the wife (or other vulnerable surety), was continued. In general, in the cases since *O'Brien,* those steps had been held by the courts to be sufficient to protect the bank's position, see, *e.g. Midland Bank v Massey* [1995] 1 All E.R. 929.

In the appeals which came before the House of Lords in *Etridge* many of the difficulties which arose were said to have stemmed from deficiencies in the quality of the advice given to the wives. It was submitted that the system was a charade, that in practice the independent legal advice was a fiction, and that it provided little or no protection for the vulnerable surety. Lord Hobhouse, who plainly had some sympathy with that submission, illustrated the many practical difficulties involved for lenders, sureties and solicitors in striking the right balance, in his speech at paras 111–118. It is noteworthy that these misgivings survived attempts by financial institutions to revise their practices so as to remove many of the grounds for criticism—in particular, the move away from requiring unlimited "all moneys" guarantees when they were not really justified.

---

1 See, *e.g. Coldunell v Gallon* [1986] Q.B. 1184 and *Bank of Baroda v Shah* [1988] 3 All E.R. 24.

The House of Lords accepted that it was neither desirable nor practicable to expect the bank to attempt to discover if there had been any actual wrongdoing: the furthest a bank could be expected to go is to take reasonable steps to satisfy itself that the wife has brought home to her, in a meaningful way, the practical implications of the proposed transaction. As Lord Nicholls said in para.54, this does not eliminate the risk of wrongdoing completely, but it "does mean that the wife enters the transaction with her eyes open so far as the basic elements of the transaction are concerned". It would appear from the steps envisaged by Lord Nicholls and concurred in by the rest of the House that the protection must extend beyond a mere explanation of the documents to a full explanation of the *practical implications* that they will have for the surety (see his speech at paras 54 and 79 and the discussion of the role of the independent solicitor in paras 5–042–5–043 below).

For past transactions, the bank will ordinarily be regarded as having discharged its obligations if a solicitor who was acting for the wife in the transaction gave the bank confirmation to the effect that he had brought home to the wife the risks she was running by standing as surety.[2] It would also appear that so far as past transactions are concerned, the bank's failure to disclose to the surety's solicitor such basic and key financial information as information about the existing indebtedness that the security will cover, and the amount of any new money which is to be lent may not, without more, show that the lender had failed to take reasonable steps to avoid being fixed with constructive notice of the principal's wrongdoing (see the observations of Lord Scott in *Etridge* at para.189). Accordingly if the solicitor failed to obtain the basic financial information to be able to advise the surety properly, he would be exposed to a claim for negligence but the transaction would stand. An extreme example of a case in which the bank was protected by a certificate is *Barclays Bank v Coleman*, one of the conjoined appeals heard in *Etridge* [2002] 2 A.C. 773 (see paras 130 and 282–293.) That was a case in which undue influence was proved because on the evidence Mrs Coleman, who like her husband was brought up in the Hassidic form of the Jewish faith, was accustomed to obeying her husband on all matters of finance without question. Nevertheless, since there was no

---

2 Lord Nicholls at para.80, Lord Scott at paras 171, 175 and 191. For a case decided after *Etridge* in which the solicitor's certificate was held to be sufficient, see *Bank of Scotland v Hill and Tudor* (2002) 29 E.G. 152. However there may still be extraordinary cases in which the solicitor's certificate is not good enough. In *National Westminster Bank v Amin* [2002] 1 F.L.R. 735, the House of Lords reversed the decision of the Court of Appeal to strike out an *O'Brien* defence raised by sureties, who were Ugandan Asians who gave a legal charge over their home as security for borrowings by their son. There was considerable doubt as to whether the solicitor whom the bank had requested to "attend to the formalities" by ensuring that the sureties were fully aware of the terms and conditions of the charge, was acting for the sureties, as it seemed more likely on the evidence that he was acting for the bank. Even more significantly, there was no evidence that he spoke Urdu and therefore there was sufficient evidence to go to trial as to whether he had indeed given them an explanation or one which they fully understood. Thus the certificate was insufficient to give the bank summary judgment.

evidence to show that the bank had any knowledge of any greater risk of undue influence than might be present in any case in which a wife was agreeing to become surety for her husband's business debts, the certificate (signed by a legal executive) sufficed to protect them from being fixed with notice of the wife's equity. If the bank has failed to obtain such confirmation, it obviously takes the risk that the solicitor has not given the wife any or any adequate legal advice (as in *Cooke v National Westminster Bank Plc* [1998] 2 F.L.R. 783 and *UCB Corporate Services Ltd v Williams* [2002] EWCA Civ 555, [2002] 3 F.C.R. 448), but if the solicitor has given appropriate advice and has merely omitted to confirm the fact, the bank will not be affected by its failure to obtain that confirmation before completing the transaction. In such a case, the surety would not make out the underlying grounds for equitable relief.

Communication with the surety

For the future, the bank should take steps to check *directly with the wife* the name of the solicitor she wishes to act for her. It should communicate with the wife directly, informing her that for its own protection it will require written confirmation from a solicitor, acting for her, to the effect that the solicitor has fully explained to her the nature of the documents and the practical implications they will have for her. She should be told that the purpose of this requirement is that thereafter she should not be able to dispute she is legally bound by the documents once she has signed them. She should be asked to nominate a solicitor whom she is willing to instruct to advise her, separately from her husband, and act for her in giving the necessary confirmation to the bank. She should be told that if she wishes the solicitor may be the same solicitor as is acting for her husband in the transaction. If a solicitor is already acting for the husband and wife, she should be asked whether she would prefer that a different solicitor should act for her regarding the bank's requirement for confirmation from a solicitor. **5–039**

Lord Nicholls in *Etridge* said that the bank should not proceed with the transaction until it has received an appropriate response directly from the wife. This should avoid the kind of difficulties which arose in past cases where the surety was offered, but refused to take independent legal advice. An example is the case of *Turner v Barclays Bank Plc* [1998] 1 F.L.R. 276, in which the wife had signed a form acknowledging that she had declined to take independent legal advice: Neuberger J. upheld the transaction.[3] It may

---

3 *Cf. Wilkinson v ASB Bank Ltd* [1998] 1 N.Z.L.R. 675 where Blanchard J. said at 691 that if a guarantor declines to get independent advice (and the financier would be wise to have this recorded in writing signed by the guarantor) a prudent financier will endeavour to ensure that someone, preferably a solicitor, explains the documents and their consequences. The financier may be able by that means to obtain reasonable satisfaction that the guarantor has understood the transaction. Unless it can be shown that an explanation was given, it may be hard to argue plausibly that the guarantor did understand . . . The existence of an acknowledgement by the guarantor of an understanding of the transaction may not suffice when unaccompanied by evidence of an explanation from someone competent to give it."

be, of course, that the transaction was not one which called out for an explanation, and that consequently the wife's refusal to take independent legal advice was something on which the lender was reasonably entitled to rely. It remains open to debate whether the same decision would be reached today on those facts. A case at the other extreme is *Credit Lyonnais Bank Nederland BV v Burch* [1997] 1 All E.R. 144. Miss Burch, a junior employee of the borrowing company, in her early twenties, was persuaded by her employer (who was the alter ego of the company) to give a mortgage over her flat (then worth about £100,000 with an equity of £70,000) as security for the increased borrowings of the company on an overdraft facility with the bank. She was not told of the amount of the overdraft (£270,000) nor of the extent of the company's existing indebtedness (£250,000). However, the bank's solicitor wrote to her not once, but twice, pointing out that the charge was unlimited in time and amount and encouraging her to take independent legal advice, which she failed to do. Indeed she wrote a letter to the bank in which she specifically refused such advice.

The Court of Appeal held that the steps taken by the bank were insufficient in the circumstances to displace constructive notice of undue influence, and upheld the decision of Mr Recorder Harrod to set aside the transaction on *O'Brien* grounds. The bank was put on inquiry because it knew that the relationship was one of junior employee and employer working together in a small business, and that Miss Burch had no incentive to enter into the transaction. Although the bank initially took reasonable steps to avoid being fixed with constructive notice of undue influence, by urging Miss Burch to take independent legal advice, the receipt by it of a letter signed by her "obviously at the instance of [the employer] and after consultation with him" declining to take such advice could not reasonably have allayed any suspicion of undue influence; on the contrary it should have confirmed it. This was therefore a case where it was insufficient to urge the surety to take independent advice: it was necessary to procure that she actually did so. Although Miss Burch was repeatedly told that the charge was unlimited, that information was patently insufficient for her to make an informed judgment about entering into the transaction. As Nourse L.J. put it (at 151j)

> "it was not enough for Miss Burch to be told repeatedly that the mortgage was unlimited in time and amount. She could not assess the significance of that without being told of the extent of [the company's] borrowings and the current limit ... Had she known that [the company's] failure could have exposed her, on the figures then current, to the loss of her home and a personal debt of £200,000 on top, her reaction would have been very different."

It is noteworthy that both the Recorder and the Court of Appeal drew attention to the fact that the solicitor acting for the bank did not appear to have been furnished by the bank with the crucial information about the extent of the existing borrowing by the company and the required increase in the overdraft facility, which might have made all the difference to the outcome. As the Recorder put it, "those figures would have been required by any competent adviser advising the defendant about the wisdom of the transaction, and without them it was impossible for her to give an informed consent to the transaction". Under the scheme envisaged in *Etridge*, that situation should not occur in the future.

Providing information to the solicitor

The House of Lords in *Royal Bank of Scotland v Etridge (No.2)* [2002] 2 A.C. 773 indicated its awareness of the difficulty caused by the fact that much of the key information necessary to a proper understanding of the risks involved in the proposed transaction is in the hands of the bank (or the borrower). In the past, there had been no real guidance given by the courts either to financial institutions about what documents they ought to send to the surety's solicitor, or to solicitors about what sort of documents they should be asking for. Lord Nicholls said, in para.79, that if the bank is not willing to undertake the task of explanation itself, it must furnish the wife's solicitor with the financial information he needs for that purpose. What is required will depend on the facts of each case, but ordinarily it will include information on the purpose for which the proposed new facility has been requested, the current amount of the husband's indebtedness, the amount of his current overdraft facility, and the amount and terms of any new facility. If the husband made a written application to the bank for a facility, a copy of that application should be sent to the solicitor. Any necessary consents to the divulging of this confidential information must be procured, otherwise the transaction cannot proceed. In an exceptional case, if the bank believes or suspects that the wife has been misled or is not entering into the transaction of her own free will, the bank must tell the solicitor of the facts giving rise to its belief or suspicion. Although this guidance is specifically directed to the husband/wife situation, it must be remembered that it covers all cases in which the surety is non-commercial. Thus one can expect to see banks and other financial institutions providing such information almost as a matter of course to solicitors representing sureties in standard lending transactions.

5–040

The solicitor's certificate

In every case, the bank should obtain a written confirmation from the solicitor to the effect that the solicitor has fully explained the nature of the documents and their practical implications to the surety.[4]

5–041

It follows that for the future any bank which goes through the steps set out by Lord Nicholls in *Etridge* will be fully protected by the solicitor's certificate. It remains an open question whether it could avoid being fixed

---

4 Lord Nicholls at para.79, see also Lord Hobhouse at paras 120–122 and Lord Scott in paras 191–192.

with constructive notice of any wrongdoing, by other means. Lord Hobhouse, at para.122, said "If the solicitor does not provide the statement and certificate for which the bank has asked, then the bank will not, *in the absence of other evidence*, have reasonable grounds for being satisfied that the wife's agreement has been properly obtained. Its legal rights will be subject to any equity existing in favour of the wife" (emphasis added). He did not venture to express a view on what "other evidence" might assist the lender in such circumstances. A written statement from the wife to the effect that she understood the transaction perfectly and had no wish to take independent legal advice could now be regarded as something of a poisoned chalice.

The independent solicitor

5–042 Prior to the decision in *Royal Bank of Scotland v Etridge (No.2)* [2002] 2 A.C. 773 it had been held in a number of cases that if the surety appears to have proper protection in the form of a legal adviser, the creditor is not obliged to investigate whether that person is in fact acting for the surety or his competence to advise the surety. For example, in *Bank of Baroda v Shah* [1988] 3 All E.R. 24, the sureties were under the undue influence of a third party. The bank entrusted the task of executing the charge to a firm of solicitors in the belief that those solicitors were acting for the sureties; in fact, they were not authorised to act for the sureties, but were acting for the third party. The Court of Appeal held that the charge was enforceable: the bank had no duty to examine the authority of the solicitors whom they believed to be acting for the sureties. So far as the bank was concerned, the sureties had proper independent legal representation.[5] That approach appears to have received the approval of Lord Scott in *Etridge*, (see his speech at para.191(4)) but with the very important proviso that the belief of the creditor that the solicitor is acting for the wife *and has so advised her* (emphasis added) is a reasonable one. However, Lord Scott made it clear that the fact that a solicitor is or appears to be acting for the wife will not suffice in itself to relieve the bank (*ibid.*, para.168) because the bank is not entitled to assume that just because a solicitor is acting for a surety wife, his instructions extend to advising her about the nature and effect of the transaction. Subject to confirmation that he is so instructed, the bank is entitled to assume that he will advise her competently. For transactions entered into since *Etridge* was decided, the situation in which the bank believes a solicitor to be acting for the wife when he is not, or where he is

---

5 A similar approach was adopted in *Banco Exterior Internacional v Mann* [1995] 1 All E.R. 936, *Bank of Baroda v Reyarel* [1995] 2 F.L.R. 376; *Midland Bank v Serter* [1995] 1 F.L.R. 1034; *Halifax Mortgage Services Ltd v Stepsky* [1996] Ch. 207, *Bank of Credit and Commerce International SA v Hussain* (unreported), Ch D, December 15, 1999, Hart J., and *Woolwich Plc v Gomm* (unreported) July 27, 1999, CA. See also *Scottish Equitable Life Plc v Virdee* [1999] 1 F.L.R. 863, where the lender was told by the husband's solicitor that another solicitor had advised the wife. It was held that the lender was entitled to rely on this information without obtaining independent confirmation from the wife's solicitor.

acting for her, but his instructions do not extend to advising her about the nature and implications of the transaction, should not arise. The bank will be expected to obtain direct confirmation from the wife of the identity of the solicitor who is advising her on these matters. It follows that a case like *Mercantile Credit v Fenwick* (unreported, Ch D, July 23, 1997), in which the bank was led to believe that the husband's solicitor was also acting for the wife, could be decided differently today. In that case the bank asked no question of the solicitor as to whether he had advised her to take independent legal advice on her position, and Carnwath J. held that the bank was entitled to assume that he had. Nowadays, a bank which fails to obtain the necessary certificate from the independent solicitor after going through the steps indicated by Lord Nicholls plainly acts at its own peril.

In *Royal Bank of Scotland v Etridge* the House of Lords confirmed that the bank would not normally be liable for any defects in the legal advice which the surety actually obtained, even if the solicitor was asked by the bank itself to give the legal advice to the surety—provided that the solicitor is in fact acting for the surety and not for the bank.[6] This means that it is the surety's misfortune if the legal adviser whom he or she happens to consult is not an expert in the field or (as in *Etridge* itself and other cases) gives false confirmation to the bank that he has advised the surety about the content and legal effect of the security documentation. On the other hand, if the legal adviser is appointed by the creditor, he must choose someone competent: see *Barclays Bank Plc v Thomson* [1997] 4 All E.R. 816, *per* Simon Brown L.J. at 826. In *Midland Bank v Wallace*, one of the appeals heard by the House of Lords in the *Etridge* case, the solicitor concerned was at all material times acting as the bank's solicitor on the bank's instructions. Consequently the bank was not entitled to rely on the (untruthful) certificate which he gave, but was bound by his failure to give any explanation to Mrs Wallace of the nature and effect of the legal charge on ordinary agency principles and by virtue of s.199(1)(ii)(b) of the Law of Property Act 1925: see the speeches in *Etridge* of Lord Scott at paras 179 and 248–266, Lord Nicholls at para.90(1) and Lord Hobhouse at para.125. See also *National Westminster Bank Plc v Amin* [2002] UKHL 9, (2002) 1 F.L.R. 735, *Steeples v Lea* [1998] 1 F.L.R. 138, and *Bertolo v Bank of Montreal* (1986) 33 D.L.R. (4th) 610.

The House of Lords in *Etridge* also addressed the vexed question of whether the bank's position was affected in any way if the solicitor concerned was acting for the bank and/or for the principal debtor as well as for the wife. When the House of Lords in *Barclays Bank v O'Brien* urged

---

6 Confirming, the approach of the Court of Appeal in cases such as *Banco Exterior Internacional SA v Mann* [1995] 1 All E.R. 936 and *Midland Bank Plc v Serter* [1995] 1 F.L.R. 1034. *Cf.* a case such as *Northern Rock Building Society v Hazel Archer* [1999] Lloyd's Rep. Bank 32 where the lender knew that it had not furnished the "independent" solicitor with the critical information that the surety was a surety and not, as appeared on the face of the transaction, one of the principal borrowers. Query whether that case would be decided differently since *Etridge* on the basis that the lender would be entitled to assume that the surety would tell her legal adviser something of that nature herself.

lenders to advise vulnerable sureties to take independent legal advice, and in some cases required them to insist that such advice be taken, there was no consideration of what was meant by "independent" in this context. In *Etridge* the House held that there can be no objection to a solicitor advising the surety if he is also acting for the bank in a purely administrative capacity: see Lord Scott at para.173. This confirmed the previous approach of the courts in cases such as *Halifax Mortgage Services Ltd v Stepsky* [1996] Ch. 207, *Barclays Bank v Thomson* [1997] 4 All E.R. 816 and *National Westminster Bank v Beaton* (1998) 30 H.L.R. 99. The more difficult problem was whether in principle the advising solicitor should always be completely independent of the actual or potential wrongdoer (generally, in this context, the husband). At first sight, there is much to be said for the view that he should, because if one is seeking to ensure that a surety enters into the transaction of his or her own free will, it is surely important to see to it that the person giving the advice is completely unaffected by any desire or motivation to ensure that the transaction is completed. Thus in *Re Coomber* [1911] 1 Ch. 723 at 730, Fletcher Moulton L.J. said:

> "all that is necessary is that some independent person, free from any taint of the relationship, or of the consideration of interest which would affect the act, should put clearly before the person, what are the nature and consequences of the act."

This was echoed in *Zamet v Hyman* [1961] 1 W.L.R. 1442 by Lord Evershed M.R., who said that the purpose of seeking independent advice was to ensure that the vulnerable party entered the transaction after full, free and informed thought.[7]

It was established in *Bank of Baroda v Shah* [1988] 3 All E.R. 24, and reaffirmed in *Banco Exterior v Mann* [1995] 1 All E.R. 936 that the creditor is entitled to assume that the solicitor who undertakes the task of advising the surety is an independent solicitor and need not enquire into his independence or indeed his authority to act on the surety's behalf. In *Bank of Baroda v Raeyarel* [1995] 2 F.L.R. 376 a strong Court of Appeal (Hoffmann, Hirst and Glidewell L.JJ.) decisively rejected the argument that a creditor who knows that the solicitor advising the surety is also acting for the borrower is under a duty to take steps to ensure that the surety is separately advised, if he wishes to avoid being fixed with constructive notice. That approach had been confirmed in numerous subsequent cases, culminating in the combined appeals in *Royal Bank of Scotland v Etridge (No.2)*. When those appeals reached the House of Lords, [2002] 2 A.C. 773, the matter was looked at afresh. Lord Nicholls addressed the point in paras 69–74. He said that a balancing exercise was called for, that there was a need for a simple and clear rule of well-nigh universal application, and he

---

7 See also *Bullock v Lloyd's Bank* [1955] Ch. 317, in which Vaisey J. observed at 326 that an impeachable transaction can only stand "if executed under the advice of a competent adviser capable of surveying the whole field with an absolutely independent outlook".

acknowledged that there were factors which pointed both ways. He agreed that as a matter of general understanding, "independent" advice would suggest that the solicitor should not be acting in the same transaction for the person who, if there is any influence, is the source of that influence. Ultimately, however, the factors weighing in favour of allowing the solicitor to act for both parties should prevail, provided that there was no conflict of interest or duty and the solicitor was satisfied that it was in the wife's best interests. It would add significantly to the cost if the solicitor had to be completely independent, and in any event a solicitor who knows both husband and wife and their family histories is likely to be better placed to advise the wife than a solicitor who is a complete stranger. However, he emphasised that in every case the solicitor concerned must consider carefully whether there is any conflict of interest or, more widely, whether it would be in the best interests of the wife him to accept instructions from her. Lord Scott, at para.174, said that if there was some particular reason known to the bank for suspecting wrongdoing by the husband, then in his view the bank should insist on advice being given to the wife by a solicitor who was independent of the husband, but in other cases there was no reason why the solicitor advising the wife should not also act for the husband. In the ordinary case, the bank is entitled to rely on the professional competence and propriety of the solicitor.

The content of the legal advice
In *Royal Bank of Scotland v Etridge (No.2)* [2002] 2 A.C. 773 at paras   **5–043**
58–68, Lord Nicholls considered the duties of the solicitor and the advice which he could be expected to give to the surety. He rejected the view expressed by the Court of Appeal that the duty of the solicitor is to satisfy himself that his client is free from improper influence and that the first step is to ascertain whether it is one into which she could sensibly be advised to enter if free from such influence. He said that the general rules were those summarised by Fletcher Moulton L.J. in *Re Coomber* [1911] 1 Ch. 723 at 730:

> "All that is necessary is that some independent person, free from any taint of the relationship, or of the consideration of interest which would affect the act, should put clearly before the person what are the nature and consequences of the act. It is for adult persons of competent mind to decide whether they will do an act, and I do not think that independent and competent advice means independent and competent approval. It simply means that the advice shall be removed entirely from the suspected atmosphere, and that from the clear language of an independent mind, they should know precisely what they are doing."[8]

---

8 Lord Scott also expressed the view (in paras 147–148 and 163–165, that a belief by the bank that the surety understands the nature and effect of the transaction is sufficient to exonerate him from inquiry. Lord Hobhouse, at para.111, strongly dissented because "it is [the surety's] weakness which is being protected not [her] inability to comprehend".

Thus it is not for the solicitor advising the surety to veto the transaction by declining to confirm to the bank that he has explained the documents to the wife and the risk she is taking. At the end of the day, the decision whether or not to proceed is the decision of the client alone and she is not to be precluded from entering into a financially unwise transaction if for her own reasons, she wishes to do so. However if there is an exceptional case in which it is glaringly obvious that the wife is being "grievously wronged" then the solicitor should decline to act further. It follows that Lord Nicholls did not agree with the Court of Appeal that if the transaction was "one into which no competent solicitor could advise the wife to enter" the availability of legal advice would not suffice to protect the bank. In other words, if the transaction appeared on its face to be one into which nobody in the surety's position would enter, but a certificate came back from the solicitor, the bank would be entitled to assume that the surety was willing to go ahead regardless, at least if the bank knew it had furnished the solicitor with sufficient information to enable him to give appropriate advice.

The starting point of the solicitor's responsibilities is his contract of retainer. As a first step the solicitor will be required to explain the purpose for which he has become involved at all. He should explain that, should it ever become necessary, the bank will rely on his involvement to counter any suggestion that the wife was overborne by her husband or that she did not properly understand the implications of the transaction. The solicitor will need to obtain confirmation from the wife that she wishes him to act for her in the matter and to advise her on the legal and practical implications of the proposed transaction. After such instructions have been given, the content of the advice will inevitably depend on the circumstances but Lord Nicholls said, as a "core minimum"

(1) He will need to explain the nature of the documents and the practical consequences these will have for the wife if she signs them. She could lose her home if her husband's business does not prosper. Her home may be her only substantial asset, as well as the family home. She could be made bankrupt.

(2) He will need to point out the seriousness of the risks involved. The wife should be told of the purpose of the new facility, the amount and principal terms of that facility, and that the bank might increase the amount of the facility, or change its terms, or grant a new facility, without reference to her. She should be told the amount of her liability under the guarantee. The solicitor should discuss her financial means, including her understanding of the value of the property being charged, and whether she or her husband have any other assets out of which repayment could be made if the business should fail.

(3) The solicitor will need to state clearly that the wife has a choice. The decision is hers and hers alone. Explanation of that choice will call for some discussion of the present financial position, including the amount of the husband's present indebtedness and the amount of his current overdraft facility.

(4) The solicitor should check whether the wife wishes to proceed. She should be asked whether she is content that the solicitor should write to the bank confirming that he has explained to her the nature of the documents and the practical implications, or whether she would prefer him to negotiate the terms of the transaction with the bank. Matters for negotiation could include the sequence in which the various securities will be called upon or a specific or lower limit to her liabilities. The solicitor should not give the bank the confirmation it requires without the wife's authority.

This advice should be couched in suitably non-technical language and should take place at a face to face meeting without the presence of the husband. The solicitor should also obtain from the bank any information he needs, and if the bank fails to provide that information he should not provide the confirmation to the bank. The House of Lords in *Etridge* has confirmed that, at least in the usual case, the solicitor's duty does not extend to advising his client as to the wisdom or otherwise of entering into the transaction: this is consistent with the earlier Privy Council decision in *Clark Boyce v Mouat* [1994] 1 A.C. 428 (though as mentioned above, there may be exceptional cases in which the solicitor should cease to act).

The Court of Appeal in *Etridge* [1998] 4 All E.R. 705 made it clear that where the bank is asking for an "all moneys" charge or guarantee, the solicitor will not discharge his duties by simply explaining that the liability is "unlimited": he must go further and bring it home to his client that she is being asked to undertake liability for the existing indebtedness (even though this was previously unsecured by her) as well as for future indebtedness to an unlimited extent, and not merely for the amount of the contemplated advance or increase in the overdraft. He should warn her that she will have no control over the extent of the liability which she is being asked to undertake, as the bank can advance further credit at any time without reference to her, and inform her of the alternatives which may be open to her including giving a limited guarantee or charge. This is entirely consistent with Lord Nicholls' guidelines.

The practical effect of the combination of *Barclays Bank v O'Brien* and the subsequent authorities culminating in *Royal Bank of Scotland v Etridge (No.2)* is to shift the risk of the wife or other vulnerable person not really understanding the nature of the transaction or the degree of exposure under it away from the creditor onto the person giving her legal advice.[9] It will no doubt have a correspondingly adverse effect on the level of professional indemnity insurance premia. It may also mean that the whole process of lending and taking security becomes more costly and complex, though the decision in *Etridge* that in most cases it will be in order for the solicitor advising the wife to be the family solicitor who is also acting for

---

9 This may be of small consolation to the surety, because her remedies against a solicitor who failed to give her proper advice may well be circumscribed. See the discussion in para.5–047 below.

the husband may remove some of the concerns in that regard. Nevertheless, the small firm or sole practitioner used to dealing with routine domestic matters may consider that the sort of advice which is required in this type of situation is beyond its capabilities or else is too risky to engage upon for fear of a professional negligence action in years to come. As Lord Hobhouse pointed out (at paras 120–122) the advantage of the scheme spelt out by Lord Nicholls is that it should do away with the fiction of free and informed consent where none existed, and the advising solicitor will now appreciate that he cannot give the statement and certificate unless it conforms to the reality. If he is told anything by his client which makes the statement or certificate untruthful, he cannot sign them without being in breach of duty to his client and committing a fraud on the bank. Thus the solicitor must be vigilant to avoid conflicts of interest and the burden which he shoulders in advising the surety is an onerous one. Now that the House of Lords has spelled out the bare minimum steps he must take, he will no longer be able to shelter behind earlier uncertainties in that regard.

Whereas the requirement that the surety should see an independent solicitor may be a useful safeguard against the exertion of undue influence or duress, (which are rarely likely to be proved in practice) it is doubtful whether it is likely to be quite so useful in respect of misrepresentation. A misrepresentation as to the duration or limit of the guarantee is, of course, something that can be dispelled by a proper explanation of the effect of the terms of the security documentation, along the lines indicated by the House of Lords. However, other types of misrepresentation (*e.g.* as to the financial stability of the debtor's company or as to the soundness of any commercial scheme upon which he or that company wishes to embark with the use of the proceeds of the loan) may well be outside the solicitor's remit. In such circumstances, the prudent solicitor is likely to tell the surety that he or she should seek some financial advice about the soundness of the scheme before signing the mortgage or guarantee. The potential overlap between the legal and financial aspects of transactions of this type was a matter which was considered by the New Zealand Court of Appeal in *Wilkinson v ASB Bank Ltd* [1998] 1 N.Z.L.R. 675. At 691, Blanchard J. made the following observations:

> "Generally speaking, it is not part of a solicitor's function to give investment or financial advice unless he or she undertakes to do so. In an Australian case involving unconscionable behaviour by a financier it has been said that the financier cannot shelter behind an assumption that a solicitor's engagement has been extended beyond the usual retainer: *Teacher's Health Investments Pty Ltd v Wynne* (1996) N.S.W. Conv. R. 56,021. But when the financier requires that an explanation and advice about the effect and implications of a guarantee be given by a solicitor, it is obvious that the solicitor cannot adequately fulfil the task without raising questions about the creditworthiness of the principal debtor and pointing out to the guarantor the need to consider the risk which may be involved. The solicitor should ensure

that the guarantor has considered what he or she may be letting himself or herself in for by way of financial exposure and loss of assets. If the guarantor appears not to have the ability to make an adequate assessment in the particular circumstances, either the solicitor should look into that question personally or, if an investigation is beyond his or her competence, should refer the guarantor for advice from someone appropriately qualified. Upon receiving an unqualified certificate the financier may usually assume this has occurred."

It is now clear from *Royal Bank of Scotland v Etridge (No.2)* [2002] 2 A.C. 773 that there is a primary obligation on the advising solicitor to obtain from the bank any information he needs in order to be able to give advice in accordance with the guidelines laid down by the House. Although the bank has no general duty of disclosure, if it does not comply with the solicitor's reasonable requests or the husband refuses to allow it to disclose confidential information the bank is unlikely to get its certificate from the wife's solicitor. However, there are limits to the information which the reasonable solicitor will be expected to obtain. In *Kenyon-Browne v Desmond Banks & Co*, one of the appeals decided in *Etridge (No.2)*, the surety wife complained that the solicitor should have advised her that there was a conflict of interest between her and her husband, that she should take independent legal advice from another solicitor, that the proposed mortgage would confer no benefit on her and that he should have advised her as to the nature and effect of the mortgage. The trial judge held that the solicitor did try to make sure that she understood the nature and effect of the document she was being asked to sign, that there was no obligation to advise her to go to another solicitor, and that the wife was quite clear about what she was doing by entering into the mortgage and wanted to do so despite the solicitor's warning. Nevertheless, the majority of the Court of Appeal [2000] P.N.L.R. 266 (following dicta in the Court of Appeal in *Etridge* [1998] 4 All E.R. 705, at paras 19–26) criticised the solicitor for failing to find out certain information from his client, including the fact that she did not consider the marriage to have any long term future but wished to avoid bringing it to an end until her son was older. When the matter reached the House of Lords, the dicta in question were disapproved. Lord Scott said that there was nothing in the evidence to suggest that the solicitor had reason to suspect that Mrs Kenyon-Browne was the victim of undue influence. If he had been, he would have been under a duty to try and protect her (*Bank of Montreal v Stuart* [1911] A.C. 120 at 138) but if a case of that sort is to be advanced against a solicitor, it must be pleaded. The mere fact that she was standing surety for her husband's business debts did not give rise to such a suspicion. Apart from seeking information on the amount of the then current indebtedness of the husband to the bank, there was no duty on the solicitor to make any of the inquiries referred to by the Court of Appeal, some of which would have been an "unpardonable impertinence".

Real protection for the surety?

5–044 It is still questionable whether the decision in *Royal Bank of Scotland v Etridge* will have the desired effect of giving adequate protection to the disadvantaged surety. Certainly solicitors acting as independent advisers to sureties should be better informed about the scope and nature of their duties. However, if they fall short of what is expected by the House of Lords, the surety may still have little in terms of adequate remedy. Even if it can be proved that there was a breach by the solicitor of his duty of care, it may be difficult to establish a causative link between that advice and any loss. The surety would probably have to prove that he or she would not have proceeded with the transaction, or at least not on those terms, had the solicitor given the advice which he should have done, even though that would not have been an essential ingredient of any claim to set aside the transaction. See, *e.g. Bristol & West Building Society v Mothew (t/a Stapley & Co)* [1998] Ch. 1, and *Etridge v Pritchard Englefield* [1999] P.N.L.R. 839, a postscript to the *Etridge* case. Mrs Etridge sued her solicitor (who admitted that he had given her no independent advice and that he had falsely certified to the bank that he had). The firm successfully defended the action on the grounds that his negligence had caused no loss to Mrs Etridge because she would have signed the charge anyway. In the Court of Appeal, Morritt L.J., which whom May L.J. and Tuckey L.J. agreed, said that:

> "Mrs Etridge might have had cause for complaint if the judge found that it would have made no difference what advice the solicitors gave because the influence of her husband was so strong, but . . . he did not. His conclusion was based on the exigencies of the situation which may well provide a powerful stimulus to enter into the impugned transaction but do not constitute undue influence".

The exigencies to which Morritt L.J. referred were that at the time when Mrs Etridge signed the charge, the matrimonial home had already been sold, and she and her family only had two days left in occupation, and a deposit of over £50,000 had been paid on a new property which would have been lost if the sale transaction had not proceeded on time. Mrs Etridge was therefore not only giving security to finance her husband's business, but also facilitating the purchase of the new property by signing the charge which encumbered her equity. The Court of Appeal agreed with the judge that the transactions had proceeded too far for withdrawal to be a viable option, and there was no evidence that Mr Etridge could complete the purchase with other funds if Mrs Etridge had refused to sign.[10]

A solicitor who acts in transactions of this type, particularly one who acts for the lender and for one or more of the other parties, is not only vulnerable to suit at the instigation of the surety. An example of a case in

---

10 In the event, of course, the House of Lords held in the underlying case against the bank that Mrs Etridge had no equity to set aside the underlying transaction anyway, as there was no proof of undue influence or any other wrongdoing by her husband.

New Zealand in which a transaction was set aside for undue influence and the advising solicitor was held to be liable in negligence to the **lender** is *Racz v Miliszewski* (unreported, April 4, 1996, High Court of Wellington, Greig J.—noted in the N.Z. Case Law Digest 1594 (5th Series) at 0675). The plaintiff loaned $200,000 to the principal debtor (who was a solicitor) to refinance a mortgage; the loan was guaranteed by the borrower's father-in-law and brother-in-law. The defendant solicitor was retained by the plaintiff. She agreed that the borrower should prepare the mortgage documents. The borrower obtained the signatures of the guarantors on the mortgage documentation. It was held that there had been actual undue influence and that the plaintiff, through his solicitor, had constructive notice of it: the guarantee was unenforceable. The defendant solicitor was held liable in negligence to her own client, the lender, not only because she had failed to advise him as to the imprudence of the transaction and the inadequacy of the security taken, but also because a reasonably competent solicitor in the circumstances would have insisted on being satisfied that the guarantors had received or had at least been offered independent legal advice. The lender was able to establish that the transaction would not have gone ahead, but for the solicitor's negligence. Nowadays, however, it is unlikely that a financial institution would be able to blame its own solicitor for failing to advise it to take the steps in *Etridge*, as lenders should all be acquainted with them and implementing them in all cases where the surety is non-commercial.

Limits on the protection of the *O'Brien* principle

A transaction which is entered into as a result of duress or undue influence   **5–045** is voidable and not void. It follows that the right to have the transaction set aside may be lost by express affirmation, or by delay amounting to proof of acquiescence. If the surety fails to take any steps to set aside the transaction within a reasonable time after he is freed from the undue influence or duress, or acquires a proper understanding of the nature of the transaction, he may be held to have acquiesced in the transaction and be barred from setting it aside: *Allcard v Skinner* (1887) 36 Ch. D. 145. In *Moxon v Payne* (1873) L.R. 8 Ch. App. 881 at 885 it was said that there must be "full knowledge of all the facts, full knowledge of the equitable rights arising from those facts, and an absolute release from the undue influence by means of which the frauds were practised".

If, for example, the surety takes independent legal advice on the transaction *after* signing the contract, it is probable that he would have to take steps to set aside the transaction very soon afterwards if he wished to keep that remedy open. Similarly, if the surety leaves it too long to raise an *O'Brien* defence he or she may find it is too late to rely on the right to set aside the transaction. For example, in *Woodel v BM Samuels Finance Group Plc* [1995] P. & C.R. 311, the Court of Appeal refused leave to wives to raise a fresh case on *O'Brien* grounds after the trial had ended, and left them to their remedy, if any, against their legal advisers.

A more recent example of a case in which a surety in an *O'Brien* type case was held to have affirmed the transaction is *Lloyds Bank Plc v Lucken*, which was one of the combined appeals reported with *Royal Bank of Scotland v Etridge (No.2)* [1998] 4 All E.R. 705. This appeal was not taken to the House of Lords. The Court of Appeal reversed the decision of the trial judge that Mrs Lucken was subject to undue influence and that the bank was fixed with constructive notice of it, but then went on to consider, for the sake of completeness, the question whether she had affirmed the relevant transactions, a business loan agreement and a legal charge over the house which she owned. Mrs Lucken was separated from her husband at the time when the contracts were originally executed, in December 1990. In February or March 1991 she consulted a new firm of solicitors with a view to getting back the deeds to her property. The Court of Appeal said that the only reasonable inference which could be drawn is that she would have fully informed the new solicitors of the pressures to which she was subjected before she signed the contracts, and on receipt of such instructions any competent solicitor would immediately think of the decision in *Barclays Bank v O'Brien* and advise his client accordingly. However, far from seeking to set aside the transactions, the evidence showed that Mrs Lucken tried to enforce other parts of the overall arrangements for a period of almost four years, during which time she had separate solicitors advising her. This separate advice was more than sufficient to counteract any initial undue influence exercised by Mr Lucken. Moreover, the consequence of Mrs Lucken not asserting her rights initially was to obtain over a period of three years financial support from the bank which it would not otherwise have given to her. The Court of Appeal held that it would be inequitable to allow Mrs Lucken to set aside the transactions, on the assumption contrary to their primary findings that she had a right to do so, and accordingly dismissed her appeal.

It should also be borne in mind that the *O'Brien* defence is only of practical use in defending claims made on or under the charge which is "tainted" by the constructive notice of the principal's wrongdoing or any substitute charge provided to the same lender (see *Yorkshire Bank Plc v Tinsley* [2004] 3 All E.R. 463, discussed in para.5–046 below). This is illustrated by the case of *Re Zanfarid* (unreported, Ch D, March 6, 1996, Jonathan Parker J.) Mr and Mrs Z jointly charged their matrimonial home in favour of BCCI and executed a personal guarantee to secure all moneys owed by them and a company, S, to BCCI. After BCCI was wound up, the liquidators made a demand for repayment and took proceedings against both husband and wife to enforce the security. Mrs Z defended the claim on what eventually became *O'Brien* grounds (the House of Lords decision having been given in the course of the proceedings). Her husband had no defence to the claim, and a money judgment was entered against him, but a possession order had been refused by the deputy master. As there was sufficient equity in the husband's share to discharge the debt, BCCI dropped the claim for possession and instead took bankruptcy proceedings against him, offering to surrender its charge over his share for the benefit of the general body of creditors (in fact, BCCI was the only creditor of substance). Mrs Z thereupon sought to be joined in the bankruptcy proceedings and both she and her husband argued that those proceedings were an abuse of the process of the court, designed to circumvent the equity raised by the wife. She argued that the trustee in bankruptcy would be in a stronger position than the mortgagee because of s.336 of the Insolvency Act 1996 and that he would therefore be able to obtain an advantage which the bank, as mortgagee, would be unable to obtain under s.30 of the Law of Property Act 1925. The judge had no hesitation in rejecting this clever argument: the principles governing claims to possession under s.30 are the same whether the claim is made by a mortgagee or a trustee in bankruptcy, applying *Re Citro* [1991] Ch. 142 and *Lloyd's Bank v Byrne* [1993] 1 F.L.R. 369, and the approach of the court would be the same in both cases. Accordingly, the perceived detriment to Mrs Z was illusory. If she succeeded in her *O'Brien* defence, the charge would still be good against her husband; as his share was sufficient to satisfy the claim, the bank could seek to enforce its security against him either by seeking an order for possession under s.30 or, as it had done, by commencing bankruptcy proceedings against him. There was no abuse of process: BCCI were merely seeking to avail themselves of their bankruptcy rights. On July 12, 1996, the Court of Appeal refused leave to appeal, on the basis that the bank was perfectly entitled to choose between the alternative remedies which were open to it. Since the decision in *Royal Bank of Scotland v Etridge (No.2)* [2002] 2 A.C. 773, a similar issue was decided by the Court of Appeal in *Bennett v Bank of Scotland* [2004] EWCA Civ 988, July 23, 2004. This was a sequel to *Bank of Scotland v Bennett*, one of the *Etridge* appeals, in which the House of Lords had set aside the charge over the matrimonial home for non-disclosure. This meant that the bank lost its proceedings for possession. The charge had been given to secure a personal guarantee given by Mr Bennett. In order to protect its position in case it ultimately lost the appeal in the possession action, in 2001 the bank commenced a second action against Mr Bennett for a sum due under a default judgment obtained by it in 1995 in respect of the personal guarantee. In due course the bank obtained a default judgment in that action and in 2003 it served a statutory demand on Mr Bennett. It was argued by Mr Bennett that the second action was an abuse of process and that the statutory demand should be set aside, because the bank should have enforced the original default judgment within six years. By starting fresh proceedings when it did, it deprived him of a limitation defence in circumstances where the court had no discretion to extend the limitation period. The Court of Appeal, applying the principles in *ED & F Man (Sugar) Ltd v Haryanto, The Times*, August 9, 1996, decided that the 1995 judgment created a new debt and the bank was entitled to bring proceedings within six years to enforce that debt, which it did. It could not be an abuse of process per se to commence a second action with the object of preserving one's rights to take bankruptcy proceedings.[11]

---

11 In fact the original claim would not have been time-barred, but this made no difference in principle to the outcome.

The effect of an *O'Brien* defence on subsequent transactions with the same lender

5–046   One of the matters which was not considered by the House of Lords in either *Barclays Bank v O'Brien* or *Royal Bank of Scotland v Etridge* was the position if a transaction which was voidable because the lender had actual or constructive notice of the principal's wrongdoing was replaced, possibly some years later, by a transaction which was wholly untainted by such behaviour. That was the situation considered by the Court of Appeal in *Yorkshire Bank Plc v Tinsley* [2004] EWCA Civ 816, [2004] 3 All E.R. 463. The wife in that case had charged her interest in the matrimonial home on two separate occasions, to secure her husband's business debts. When they started divorce proceedings some years later, he persuaded her to deal with all the financial aspects of the divorce by the exchange of the matrimonial home for a smaller property and the payment of a cash sum, which he proposed would be used to discharge the indebtedness secured on the first property, leaving her owning the second property free of any encumbrances. However, the indebtedness secured on the first property exceeded its value. The bank consented to the exchange transaction on condition that the former wife should execute a new "all moneys" charge in its favour over the second property in substitution for the earlier mortgages, which she did. The bank subsequently commenced possession proceedings. The trial judge held that the two earlier mortgages had been procured by the husband's undue influence, of which the bank had constructive notice, but the same was not true of the later charge taken in 1994, at the time of the divorce. The Court of Appeal (Longmore, Rix and Peter Gibson L.JJ.) decided that nevertheless, the later charge was unenforceable. The earlier transaction for which it was substituted was tainted and since the lender was the same lender, there was no reason why the constructive notice of Mr Tinsley's undue influence should be deemed to have disappeared when that mortgage was discharged (applying the principles in *Crowe v Ballard* (1790) 1 Ves. Jun. 215 and *Kempson v Ashbee* (1874) L.R. 10 Ch. App. 15.) Longmore L.J. partly explained the decision on the basis that "the 1994 mortgage was given upon a consideration that in the mind of Mrs Tinsley . . . carried with it a value which it ought not, *viz.* the discharge of the earlier mortgage which was obtained by undue influence" (para.24). Peter Gibson L.J. said that he would be reluctant to reach a decision which would cause significant practical difficulties for lenders in property transactions but he was not persuaded that the Court of Appeal was doing any such thing in that case. It was rightly not suggested that a lender should be put on inquiry about previous transactions to which that lender was not a party. But if the same lender was the mortgagee in the prior voidable mortgage and required the discharge of the prior mortgage and the grant to it of a new mortgage, he could see no sufficient objection to holding the new mortgage taken in substitution for the earlier mortgage also to be voidable. The lender should know from its own records whether or not it protected itself in the earlier transaction.

Peter Gibson L.J. went on to suggest (in paras 35 and 36) that if the lender did not know whether it had protected itself at the earlier stage, it should be able to protect itself by taking the steps envisaged by the House of Lords in *Etridge* at the stage of the proposed substitute transaction, by procuring that the surety had independent legal advice *on the transaction into which she was about to enter.* He said that the independent adviser would be expected to advise the surety at that stage about the discharge of the previous mortgage. The logic of this suggestion is, with respect, somewhat difficult to follow. If the earlier transaction is voidable because the Bank was on constructive notice of wrongdoing at the time when it took place, any steps taken thereafter by the Bank could not affect the validity of that earlier transaction or "undo" the notice of the past wrongdoing. If the wife took legal advice at that stage, when the tainted transaction was discharged, it is possible that she would be deemed to have affirmed the validity of that transaction, but that would depend on the scope of the retainer. It would be stretching *Etridge* beyond its limits to decide that the bank could always reasonably expect the independent solicitor to advise the surety at that stage that the earlier transaction could be set aside (*Lloyds Bank v Lucken*, discussed in para.5–045 above, was a case turning on fairly exceptional facts). Advice given by a solicitor at the time of the substitute transaction would not normally extend to a discussion about the adequacy of the consideration for the substitute transaction (particularly if nobody had raised the possibility with him that the earlier transaction was tainted in some way). Consequently, the letter from the bank to the surety asking her to take such advice would have to be couched in terms which made it clear that the bank was concerned that she had *already* entered into a transaction which she was entitled to set aside against it—a somewhat curious document to expect a lender to send.

Although Rix L.J. agreed with both judgments, he emphasised that the reason why the later transaction was voidable was that there was nothing to render the past abuse by the husband, of which the Bank had constructive notice, to cease to be operative and the fact that there was no new inequity in relation to the later mortgage was not determinative because the inequity of the earlier transactions had not been cured (see paras 38 and 39). Applying that logic, the inequity of the earlier transactions would only be cured if the wife's legal adviser at the time of the later mortgage spotted the problem and advised her to seek to discharge the mortgage, and not to enter into the substitute transaction. It is difficult to see how that would advance the bank's position. On the other hand, if he did not give her that advice, the earlier transaction would remain tainted. The concept that a lender can remove any constructive notice after the event is rather difficult to sustain, though it may be that what Peter Gibson L.J. really had in mind was the possibility of fully informed affirmation by the surety, which is a different matter altogether. In that event, it would probably be unsafe to rely on assumptions about what the legal adviser said, and the lender would be better advised to seek a written confirmation from the surety that, having taken legal advice about the earlier transaction and the proposed substitute transaction, she wishes to go ahead with the latter.

Setting aside on terms

5–047 One question which arose shortly after the decision in *Barclays Bank v O'Brien* was whether, in cases where the principle of constructive notice rendered the transaction susceptible to being set aside at the instigation of the surety, there was jurisdiction in the court to order that it be set aside on terms. For example, suppose the wife was told by her husband that she was signing a guarantee or a mortgage limited to £100,000 when the liability was unlimited. She was content to agree to stand surety to the extent of £100,000. Accordingly, is there any basis upon which the contract of suretyship can be enforced against her to that extent?

There was a divergence of judicial opinion at first instance which appeared to be settled by the Court of Appeal in *TSB Bank Plc v Camfield* [1995] 1 W.L.R. 430. In *Allied Irish Bank v Byrne* (unreported, February 1, 1994) Ferris J. set aside the transaction *in toto*, rejecting the bank's argument that the transaction should be enforced to the extent of £35,000, that being the limit which the husband had misrepresented to the wife. However, eight days later, and in ignorance of that decision, in *Bank Melli Iran v Samadi-Rad* [1995] 1 F.C.R. 465, Robert Walker Q.C., applying the observation of Judge Rich Q.C. in *Midland Bank v Greene* [1994] 2 F.L.R. 827 that terms may be imposed on the grant of equitable relief, set aside the transaction on condition that the wife acknowledged that the bank had a good security on the house to the extent of the misrepresented limit (in that case, £140,000), together with interest and costs from the date of the formal demand upon her.

The Court of Appeal in *TSB Plc v Camfield* endorsed the approach in *Allied Irish Bank v Byrne* and held that once the conditions for *O'Brien* relief had been made out, the remedy was an "all or nothing" right to set aside the transaction which could not be fettered by the imposition of terms, however much this might offend against notions of justice "in the abstract sense". The reasons were twofold. First, terms could not be imposed on the wife's equity to set aside the transaction unless they were appropriate to procure *restitutio in integrum*. That doctrine had no application in these circumstances because there was nothing for the wife to give back and no cause for her to provide compensation. Secondly, in the light of Lord Browne-Wilkinson's speech in *Barclays Bank v O'Brien* [1994] 1 A.C. 180, in particular the passage at 195E–196A, there was no basis in principle for drawing a distinction between a person in the position of the bank and any third party fixed with notice of any other equitable right. In this situation, the right of the surety to rescind the transaction prevailed over any subsequent rights obtained by the creditor who had notice of that right. Roch L.J. gave the further, perhaps more debatable, reason that the court was not granting equitable relief to the wife, to which terms might be attached, but was simply deciding whether or not she had lawfully rescinded the transaction.

Counsel for the bank pointed out that under s.2(2) of the Misrepresentation Act 1967, if the transaction had been between the husband and the wife, the court would have had a discretion to award damages in lieu of rescission and argued that the innocent bank would be in a worse position than the husband if the court had no analogous power. The Court of Appeal recognised that in some cases this anomaly might arise, but said that it was a direct result of the failure of the 1967 Act to deal with the effect of misrepresentations on third parties. Roch L.J. pointed out that the very fact that Parliament had given the court the power to award damages in lieu of misrepresentation in certain transactions indicated that the power did not exist outside that statute.[12]

TSB Plc v Camfield was followed by the Court of Appeal in *Castle Phillips Finance Co v Piddington* [1994] N.P.C. 155. That was a case in which the matrimonial home was owned outright by the wife. A first mortgage had been granted in favour of Lloyds Bank, who had sent her to see a solicitor. Subsequently, a second mortgage over the house was executed in favour of Barclays Bank in respect of a loan to cover the indebtedness to Lloyds as well as some roof repairs. The wife thought that the loan was only going to cover the roof repairs. Barclays did not take steps to ensure that the wife took separate legal advice and the trial judge held that an *O'Brien* defence was made out. The Lloyds' indebtedness was paid off out of the Barclays loan. The husband later approached the plaintiffs for a loan to both himself and his wife on the security of the property and with the aid of a female accomplice, forged a document transferring the property into the joint names of himself and his wife and a legal charge over the property in favour of the plaintiffs. The plaintiffs then made the loan, as they thought, to the husband and wife. The loan was used to pay off the debts to Barclays. The wife, who was completely ignorant of this, only found out after the husband defaulted on the loan. The trial judge set aside the Barclays mortgage, but only on terms that a new charge was created to the extent of the borrowing for the roof repairs. The Court of Appeal allowed the wife's appeal, on the grounds that terms could not be imposed on the grant of relief on the *O'Brien* principle.

The case is important because it illustrates how the operation of the *O'Brien* principle affects rights of subrogation. The plaintiff had paid off the debt which it believed was secured by the Barclays mortgage. It therefore claimed to be subrogated to Barclays' rights under the Barclays mortgage; the Court of Appeal held that because the charge was unenforceable by Barclays against the wife, the plaintiff could not be subrogated to that

---

12 *Cf.* the approach adopted in Australia in the case of *Vadasz v Pioneer Concrete (SA) Pty Ltd* (1994) 62 S.A.S.R. 150, where conditions were imposed on the rescission of a personal guarantee for misrepresentation and under the principles in *Commercial Bank of Australia v Amadio*. That was a case where the wrongdoer was the creditor himself. In *Far Eastern Shipping v Scales Trading Ltd* [2001] 1 All E.R. (Comm.) 319 discussed in para.5–016 above, the Privy Council deliberately left open the question whether the reasoning in *TSB v Camfield* was to be preferred to the reasoning in *Vadasz* in the context of non-disclosure, because on the facts the surety was entitled to an "all or nothing" remedy.

charge.[13] However, because Barclays, by paying off the Lloyds debt acquired rights of subrogation in respect of that debt, and because the wife had consented to the original charge, the plaintiff was entitled to be subrogated to the Lloyds charge over the property.[14] There was consequently "subrogation on subrogation", which had the effect of ensuring that the wife did not gain any advantage by the fortuity of the irregularity of the Barclays loan. At the same time, the plaintiff was forced to pursue the wrongdoers and not another innocent party to recover the balance of its losses.

Although the concept of subrogation on subrogation was novel, the rationale behind it appears to be sound. There appears to be no reason in principle why the creditor who paid off the indebtedness to Barclays should not take over Barclays' position in full. Barclays' rights of subrogation to Lloyds were not security for the new loan, but were still rights which arose as a direct result of making that loan and using the money to pay off Lloyds. Accordingly, regardless of the enforceability or otherwise of the securities given for the refinancing arrangements, Barclays could still have recovered some of its losses by enforcing those rights of subrogation. However, in view of the complexity of the arguments involved, it seems likely that the whole question of the circumstances in which a subsequent lender may be subrogated to the rights of the earlier lender when he pays off the loan, and if so, which rights, will be reviewed by the House of Lords before long.

The idea that the law relating to setting aside on terms was finally settled by *TSB v Camfield* was relatively short-lived. In *Dunbar Bank v Nadeem* [1998] 3 All E.R. 876 the Court of Appeal (Millett, Morritt and Potter L.JJ.) were concerned with a fairly complex loan transaction involving the house occupied by N and his wife, which was on a short lease with three years left to run. N owed the bank over £1 million secured on various properties. He had been offered a new lease on the matrimonial home at a very favourable price, some £140,000 below the estimated market value, and the bank was willing to advance him £260,000 on the security of the new lease of which £210,000 would be used to acquire the lease and the balance to "regularise" his other accounts with the bank. The bank intended this to be a short-term arrangement pending the re-mortgage or sale of the property. The new lease was executed in the joint names of Mr and Mrs N, and so the bank required her to execute both the facility letter and the charge. A second charge over the new lease was given to another bank. Mrs N executed what appeared to be an "all moneys" charge which purportedly charged her interest in the lease with all N's liabilities to the

---

13 If there had been no such problem, the plaintiff would have been entitled to rights of subrogation: see *National Guardian Mortgage Corporation v Roberts* [1993] N.P.C. 149. The idea that the new lender should take an assignment of the earlier mortgage in order to make his position completely secure is no doubt a sensible one, but it would not have availed the plaintiff in the *Castle Phillips* case because an assignee is still in no better position against the mortgagor than the original lender.

14 Applying *Butler v Rice* [1910] 2 Ch. 277 and *Western Trust & Savings v Rock* [1993] N.P.C. 89. *Equity & Law v Prestridge* [1992] 1 W.L.R. 137 was distinguished on its facts.

bank. At first instance, the judge held that Mrs N was entitled to set aside the transaction for presumed undue influence, but he imposed terms requiring her to repay the bank her share of the money advanced together with interest. Both Mrs N and the bank appealed.

The bank's cross-appeal succeeded on the grounds that the transaction was not on its face disadvantageous to Mrs N. She acquired a joint interest in the equity of redemption in the property which had a value of £140,000. The "all moneys" form had been used by mistake, and the bank was only seeking repayment of the £260,000 from the proceeds of the sale or re-mortgage of the property. This meant that it was unnecessary to decide the question whether terms should have been imposed on any order setting aside the transaction on *O'Brien* grounds. The Court of Appeal expressed the view, however, that Mrs N would not have had an unqualified right to rescission; the right was an equitable right which was conditional upon making restitution, and in this particular case restitution would have been possible. The judge's condition was wrong, though, because Mrs N did not acquire the benefit of the loan: she acquired an interest in the equity of redemption in the property and incurred a liability jointly with her husband. If the charge was set aside, her beneficial interest in the property would also disappear and she would be unable to claim priority over either of the chargees. There was therefore no need to impose terms, because restitution was automatic.

Unconscionable bargains

There is a long-established jurisdiction in equity to set aside transactions **5–048** which are unconscionable bargains, which goes back at least as far as the jurisdiction to grant relief in respect of transactions procured by undue influence, albeit that it has been more rarely exercised in modern times. In its original form, such relief was generally utilised to protect the old, the ignorant, the needy and the infirm, and similarly vulnerable members of society. In *Fry v Lane* (1889) 40 Ch. D. 312 at 322, Kay J. reviewed the earlier authorities and said:

> "The result of the decisions is that where a purchase is made from a poor and ignorant man, at a considerable undervalue, the vendor having no independent advice, a Court of Equity will set aside the transaction . . . the circumstances of poverty and ignorance of the vendor and the absence of independent advice, throw upon the purchaser, when the transaction is impeached, the onus of proving, in Lord Selborne's words,[15] that the purchase was 'fair just and reasonable'."

More recently, these principles have been applied in a number of cases, including *Cresswell v Potter* [1978] 1 W.L.R. 255, *Backhouse v Backhouse*

---

15 In *Earl of Aylesford v Morris* (1873) L.R. 8 Ch. App. 484 at 491.

[1978] 1 W.L.R. 243, and *Boustany v Piggott* (1995) 69 P. & C.R. 298. In *Cresswell v Potter* at 257, Megarry J. suggested that the modern equivalent of "poor and ignorant" might be "a member of the lower income group . . . less highly educated", which is an indication of how the classes of persons covered by the jurisdiction in its traditional manifestation can be adapted to fit the modern era.

The jurisdiction is not only flexible but wide-ranging, and is not constrained to the traditional classes of case involving the elderly, infirm or ignorant. Developments in this area have largely taken place in the antipodean jurisdictions, particularly Australia.[16] The landmark decision of the Australian High Court in *Commercial Bank of Australia v Amadio* [1983] 151 C.L.R. 447 established that the court has jurisdiction to grant relief in any case in which (a) one party to a transaction is under a special disadvantage in dealing with the other party, with the consequence that there is an absence of any reasonable degree of equality between them and (b) that disadvantage is sufficiently evident to the stronger party to make it prima facie unfair or "unconscientious" that he procure or accept the weaker party's assent to the impugned transaction in the circumstances in which he procured or accepted it.[17] Where such circumstances are shown to exist, the onus is thrown upon the stronger party to show that the transaction is fair, just and reasonable. This is usually satisfied if he can show that the weaker party was given a proper explanation by him of the circumstances which enabled him to form a proper judgment, or independent advice from a lawyer and, if need be, financial advisor.

It is clear from the authorities that in order for the equitable jurisdiction to come into play there has to be some kind of unfair exploitation by the stronger party of the known weakness of the other party in a manner which is regarded as morally culpable, so that, to use the traditional phrase, the transaction "shocks the conscience of the court" making it inequitable for the stronger party to retain the benefit of that transaction. In the Privy Council case of *Hart v O'Connor* [1985] A.C. 1000, at 1024 Lord Brightman summarised the relevant principles thus:

> ". . . historically a court of equity did not restrain a suit at law on the ground of 'unfairness' unless the conscience of the plaintiff was in some way affected. This might be because of actual fraud . . . or constructive fraud, *i.e.* conduct which falls below the standards demanded by equity, traditionally considered under its more common manifestations of undue influence, abuse of confidence, unconscionable bargains and frauds on a power . . . An unconscionable bargain in this context would be a bargain of an improvident character made by a

---

16 Though the flexibility of the jurisdiction has been recognised in England: see, *e.g. Multiservice Bookbinding Ltd v Marden* [1979] Ch. 84 *per* Browne-Wilkinson J. at 110 and *Alec Lobb Ltd v Total Oil* [1983] 1 W.L.R. 87.

17 See also *Blomley v Ryan* [1956] 99 C.L.R. 362, and the discussion in *Chitty, op. cit.*, at paras 7–042–7–047.

poor or ignorant person acting without independent advice which cannot be shown to be a fair and reasonable transaction. 'Fraud' in its equitable context does not mean, or is not confined to deceit: 'it means an unconscientious use of the power arising out of these circumstances and conditions' of the contracting parties: *Earl of Aylsford v Morris* . . . It is victimisation, which can consist either of the active extortion of a benefit or the passive acceptance of a benefit in unconscionable circumstances."

The jurisdiction therefore does not involve interference with a contractual bargain simply on the basis that it appears to be unreasonable or unfair. As Neuberger J. put it in *Eggleton v Ashridge Investments Ltd* (unreported, Ch. D., April 17, 1997):

"First, however disadvantageous a contract might appear to be to one party, that does not of itself entitle the court to set aside the contract. However and secondly, where the terms of the contract are manifestly unfair to one party, that may be enough to raise a presumption of victimisation such that the contract ought to be set aside; in any event it is a factor which, if other factors are present, should be taken into account in deciding whether there was victimisation. Thirdly, in order to set aside a contract in equity, the party seeking to set it aside must establish some unfair advantage (amounting to unconscionability in equity) had been taken of him by the other party. The taking of such unfair advantage must, in some way or other, amount to victimisation. It may well be that cases such as *Fry v Lane*, and cases of undue influence are examples of the application of the more general equitable power to set aside transactions unconscionably obtained."

There have been a number of cases in Australia, in particular, in which this principle has been invoked successfully by sureties against financial institutions, often in the kind of circumstances in which in England a defence would be run on the basis of the principle in *Barclays Bank v O'Brien* [1994] A.C. 180. The leading authority of *Commercial Bank of Australia v Amadio* (1983) 151 C.L.R. 447 was itself such a case. It concerned sureties who were the elderly parents of the managing director of the borrowing company, who had misled them as to the extent and duration of the guarantee. They also had a limited grasp of English. Their son approached them to sign the guarantee in their kitchen "when Mr Amadio was reading the newspaper after lunch and Mrs Amadio was washing dishes". There was also a significant non-disclosure of the true nature and purpose of the transaction which was not a normal business arrangement. In those circumstances the outcome of the case was hardly surprising.

The judgments in *Amadio* (particularly that of Mason J.) indicate that the position of "special disadvantage" essentially involves some kind of condition or circumstances which seriously affect the ability of the innocent party to make a judgment as to his or her own best interests. Of course, this would include the traditional list of personal disabilities such as age, infirmity, illiteracy or lack of education, and poverty,[18] but it has been extended in Australia and New Zealand to cover lack of business knowledge or acumen[19] and the kind of emotional dependency which may give rise to an *O'Brien* defence.[20] In *Akins v National Australia Bank* [1996] 5 Bank. L.R. 21, the Court of Appeal of New South Wales held that the *Amadio* principle should suffice to protect a wife in an *O'Brien* type of case without the need to resort either to the *O'Brien* principle as expressed by the House of Lords or to the concept of a "special equity" protecting wives (and other vulnerable classes of surety) which the House of Lords rejected. The court held that the mere fact that the wife of the debtor is to stand surety would not suffice in itself to put her in a position of "special disadvantage" within the *Amadio* rule, but the fact that the creditor leaves it to the husband to procure the execution of the guarantee and takes no steps to ensure that the wife understands the liability which she is undertaking or that she is independently advised, would possibly suffice, in appropriate circumstances, to put the creditor on notice that she is in a position of special disadvantage.[21] However, if the wife stood to benefit wholly or partially from the secured advance, the *Amadio* principle would not apply (presumably because in such circumstances the bargain could not be characterised as unfair or unconscionable).[22] Further, if the wife receives advice from someone whom the creditor believes on reasonable grounds to be competent, independent and disinterested, then the circumstances would need to be very exceptional before the creditor could be held bound by any equity arising from the husband's conduct and the wife's actual failure to understand the transaction.[23]

Amadio has been applied in numerous other cases involving sureties, including *Platzer v Commonwealth Bank of Australia* [1997] Qd. R. 266; *Gregg v Tasmanian Trustees Ltd* (1997) 73 F.C.R. 91; *Krambousanos v Jedda Investments Pty Ltd* (1995) 142 A.L.R. 604; *Louth v Diprose* (1992) 175 C.L.R. 621, *National Australia Bank Ltd v Nobile* (1988) 100 A.L.R. 227, *Nolan v Westpac Banking Corporation* (1989) A.T.P.R. 40–982.[24] It has not

---

18 See, *e.g. Blomley v Ryan* (1956) 99 C.L.R. 362.

19 See, *e.g. National Australia Bank Ltd v Nobile* (1988) 100 A.L.R. 227; *Household Financial Services Ltd v Price* (unreported, SA Sup Ct, Burley J. November 14, 1994). However, the failure by solicitors to explain the transaction to a guarantor properly does not put him in a position of special disadvantage for these purposes: see the N.Z. case of *Bradley West Solicitors Nominee Co Ltd v Keeman* [1994] 2 N.Z.L.R. 111 at 126.

20 See, *e.g. Louth v Diprose* (1992) 175 C.L.R. 621; *Gregg v Tasmanian Trustees Ltd* (1997) 73 F.C.R. 91.

21 See, *e.g. Racz v Miliszewski* (unreported, April 4, 1996, HC Wellington, Greig J., noted in N.Z. Case Law Digest (5th Series) 0675).

22 See also *Australian Guarantee Corporation Ltd v McClelland* (1993) A.S.C. 56–230, and *National Australia Bank v di Battista* [1996] 5 Bank. L.R. 225 at 230.

23 An example of a case in which the taking of independent advice by the surety was insufficient to protect the creditor is *ANZ Banking Group Ltd v Guthrie* (1989) 92 A.N.Z. Conv. R. 221, where the advisor was unaware of a recent contingent liability incurred by the principal to the bank.

24 For a fuller discussion of the case law in Australia, see O'Donovan & Phillips, *The Modern Contract of Guarantee*, 3rd (Australian) ed. (1996), pp.176–185, though a shorter discussion will be found at paras 4–155–4–158 of the English ed. (*op. cit.*).

yet been applied directly in England, although in *Credit Lyonnais Bank Nederland NV v Burch* [1997] 1 All E.R. 145, Nourse L.J. indicated (at 151) that if a case had been made below that the transaction was an unconscionable bargain, he would have had little difficulty in setting it aside on those grounds also. Interestingly, *Amadio* and the Australian authorities do not appear to have been cited to the Court of Appeal: Nourse L.J.'s observations were based on the traditional English line of authority in this area, including *Fry v Lane*.

There are many similarities between *Amadio*, the more recent case of *Platzer v Commonwealth Bank of Australia* [1997] 1 Qd. R. 266 and *Credit Lyonnais v Burch*; one notable factor present in each case was the absence of any proper information about the level of the indebtedness of the principal debtor or the amount of the contingent liability to which the surety was going to be exposed. The authors of O'Donovan & Phillips, *The Modern Contract of Guarantee*[25] suggest that a survey of the case law indicates that various factors besides purely personal characteristics of the surety may be regarded as indicative of a position of "special disadvantage" in this context, and that these factors include insufficiency of information which would enable the "disadvantaged" surety to form an independent judgment, such as knowledge of the financial position of the principal debtor. However, in England there is no obligation on the creditor to disclose such matters to the potential surety, and it is therefore unlikely that a surety would be held to be in a position of special disadvantage simply because they were not furnished with that information. On the other hand, if they were already in a position of special disadvantage because, for example, of a relationship of trust and confidence with the principal debtor or the controller of the principal debtor (as in *Credit Lyonnais v Burch*), the absence of sufficient information to form an independent judgment about the risks may well be an important factor in determining whether the transaction was unfair and unconscionable, and indeed whether any independent advice received was sufficient to remove the disadvantage. Another way of looking at the matter, propounded by O'Donovan and Phillips, and supported by the judgment of Mason J. in *Commercial Bank of Australia v Amadio* (1983) 151 C.L.R. 447 at 468, is that once the creditor becomes aware that the surety is in a position of special disadvantage, his duty of disclosure evolves beyond the normal duty to disclose only unusual facts into a duty to disclose all facts which would enable the guarantor to form a proper judgment.

The reported cases indicate that the evidence may establish that a person who may, at first sight, appear to be in a position of special disadvantage, is not in fact in such a position: for example, if he is ill-educated, but nevertheless considerably experienced in matters of business. An example of such a case is *National Australia Bank Ltd v Di Battista* [1996] 5 Bank. L.R. 225, where an employee of the bank persuaded various members of

---

25 3rd ed., see fn. 24 above.

his family to guarantee a loan to a family trust company which was engaged in property speculation. The guarantors sought to run an *Amadio* defence on the basis that they had poor facility in English and poor comprehension. One of the reasons why the defence was rejected was that the judge found that although the defendants had an impaired capacity to deal in English, they were numerate: they had been in Australia for 40 years, they had carried on business as market gardeners and moreover they had entered into personal guarantees for their sons on previous occasions. As Nathan J. succinctly put it (at 230), "you cannot survive 40 years in Australia as a market gardener, buying your house and doing everything else, as most people do, and be absolutely ignorant of what the nature of a mortgage and a guarantee are".[26] Likewise, in New Zealand, it was decided in the case of *ASB Bank Ltd v Harlick* [1996] 1 N.Z.L.R. 655 that a mortgage given by parents over their home as security in respect of borrowings by their daughter and son-in-law was not susceptible to being set aside as an unconscionable bargain, because there was no evidence of any greater element of trust or confidence or reliance than was to be expected between parents and adult children. A similar result occurred in *Portman Building Society v Dusangh* [2000] 2 All E.R. (Comm) where the Court of Appeal rejected a claim by a surety that he could set aside the transaction as an unconscionable bargain. The surety was a retired man of 72 who was illiterate in English and spoke the language poorly. He mortgaged his property to obtain money for his son to use in the purchase of a supermarket. It was held that building societies were not required to police transactions of this nature to ensure that parents, even poor and ignorant ones, were wise in seeking to assist their children. The building society had not exploited the situation nor acted in a morally reprehensible manner and the transaction was neither overreaching nor oppressive.

Although the power to grant relief against unconscionable bargains may be exercised in cases in which an *O'Brien* defence may also be available, it is important to note that it may be granted even in cases where an *O'Brien* defence would fail because, for example, there has been no misconduct by the principal. For example, in *Begbie v State Bank of New South Wales Ltd* (1994) A.T.P.R. 41–288, the *Amadio* principle was applied to relieve the wife even though, on the facts, undue influence was disproved.[27]

It is also important to bear in mind the potential distinction between the type of knowledge of the disadvantage or disability which the creditor has to have in order for the *Amadio* principle to apply (at least in its antipodean manifestation) and the actual or constructive notice which triggers an *O'Brien* defence. In *Amadio* it was said that if the creditor "is aware of facts that would raise the possibility in the mind of any reasonable

---

26 The defence also failed because the transaction was not unconscionable or unfair: the borrowings were for their own benefit and not for the benefit of third parties.

27 Though this case may now be regarded in truth as an example of the application of the separate principle in *Yerkey v Jones*: see *Garcia v National Australia Bank Ltd* (1998) 72 A.L.J.R. 1243.

person" that the surety was in a position of special disadvantage, that would suffice. This test was applied in *ANZ Banking Group Ltd v Guthrie* (1989) 92 A.N.Z. Conv. R. 221, in which it was held that the bank ought to have known of the guarantor's alcoholism, and more recently indorsed by the Federal Court of Australia in *Lisciandro v Official Trustee in Bankruptcy* [1996] A.L.R. 689.[28] Another potential area of distinction relates to the independence of the advice which is given. In the leading English case of *Fry v Lane* (1888) L.R. 40 Ch. D. 312, the solicitor was inexperienced, and was acting for both parties to the transaction which was set aside as an unconscionable bargain, and the fact that the disadvantaged parties were represented by him was no bar to equitable relief. However, that was a case of a purchase at an undervalue, where it was clear that the solicitor could not have performed his duty to the vendor. It remains to be seen whether advice given by a solicitor who is also acting for the lender or the principal would be classified as sufficiently "independent" to meet the requirements of *Amadio*, as it clearly has been in the *O'Brien* context. The answer may well depend on the facts of each case, because the ultimate inquiry in an *Amadio* case is whether the disadvantaged person was in fact able to form a proper judgment.

Ultra vires and illegal transactions

It is rarely the case that a guarantee will be *ultra vires* a company which agrees to act as surety. On the occasions where it is, s.108 of the Companies Act 1989 (which enacted a new s.35, s.35A and s.35B of the Companies Act 1985) should usually protect the creditor.[29] However, there are still situations in which the doctrine of *ultra vires* could prove to be a pitfall for the unwary lender, particularly so far as inter-company guarantees are concerned. A guarantee may be *ultra vires* a company on two different grounds. First, it may amount to an unlawful disposition of capital without any corresponding commercial benefit to the company. Secondly, it may be outside the scope of the powers of the company under its constitution to give a guarantee. When the topic of *ultra vires* transactions arises, the second of these rules tends to overshadow the first which consequently may be overlooked, but it is equally important to bear it in mind.

5–049

It is *ultra vires* a corporation, and a fraud upon its shareholders and creditors, if it disposes of its capital without receiving a benefit in return. As Bowen L.J. put it in *Hutton v West Cork Railway* (1883) 23 Ch. D. 654 at 673: "there are to be no cakes and ale except such as are required for the benefit of the company". It is common practice for inter-company guarantees to be given by members of a group in favour of borrowings by other

---

28 A case which went the other way in New Zealand was *Contractors Bonding Ltd v Snee* [1992] 2 N.Z.L.R. 157, where the defence failed because knowledge of the surety's mental impairment or of her son's undue influence could not be imputed to the creditor.

29 See also ss.109 and 111 of the 1989 Act. For the position where the underlying obligation of a company which is a principal debtor is *ultra vires*, see Ch.6 at para.6–021.

members of that group. Where the guarantee is a so-called "downstream" guarantee, *i.e.* a guarantee given by a parent company for the borrowings of a subsidiary, it is relatively easy to find some benefit to the parent deriving from the increased financial strength of the subsidiary and any corresponding increase in the value of its shares, unless, of course, the subsidiary is insolvent. Likewise, where the guarantee is an "upstream" guarantee given by the subsidiary in favour of the parent, the benefit usually takes the form of financial, technical or other support provided by the parent company, again assuming that the parent company is solvent. The problems are more likely to arise, therefore, in cases where associated companies (*e.g.* two subsidiaries of the same holding company) guarantee each other's indebtedness to a third party, but there is no direct trading relationship between them. It may suffice to create a benefit if each subsidiary gives a guarantee in favour of the other, so there are mutual guarantees. It is important to note, however, that the benefit must be to the individual company giving the guarantee: a benefit to the group as a whole will not usually suffice.

The question whether there is a benefit to the company, and if so, whether it is a sufficient benefit (the greater the risk of the guarantee being called, the greater the benefit the company must derive) will be a question of fact in each particular case. Where any company within the group giving or receiving the benefit of a guarantee is insolvent, or where the giving of the guarantee might create a technical insolvency, the creditor and his advisors should be on their guard.

So far as the powers of the company are concerned, if the company includes the giving of guarantees among its objects, there can be no question of any guarantee being *ultra vires*: *Re Horsley & Weight Ltd* [1982] 3 All E.R. 1045. If the power to guarantee is merely among the ancillary objects of the company, however, it can only be exercised by the directors in the commercial interests of the company. It is a matter of construction of the company's memorandum whether the power to guarantee is a substantive object or an ancillary power: *Rolled Steel Products (Holdings) Ltd v British Steel Corporation* [1986] 1 Ch. 246. Any doubt on this issue could be removed by insisting on a special resolution being passed, which would make the creation of the guarantee a substantive object.

So far as the creditor is concerned, the consequences of the guarantee being *ultra vires* are limited, though entry into the transaction would amount to a misfeasance on the part of the directors. The guarantee can only be set aside as against the creditor if he has actual or imputed knowledge of the directors' misfeasance and if the provisions of the Companies Act 1985 do not protect him. By s.35(1) of the 1985 Act, the validity of an act done by a company should not be called into question on the ground of lack of capacity by reason of anything in its constitution. Section 35(3) provides that it remains the duty of the directors to observe any limitations in the memorandum.

Section 35(A) provides that in favour of a person dealing with a company in good faith, the power of the board of directors to bind the company shall be deemed to be free of any limitation under the company's constitution.

There is a presumption of good faith, and the fact that the third party knows that an act is beyond the powers of the directors under the company's constitution is not enough, in itself, to show that he acted in bad faith. By s.35(B) a party to a transaction with a company is not bound to enquire whether that transaction is permitted by the memorandum or as to any limitation on the powers of the board of directors to bind the company. It is to be noted that these provisions only deal with powers of the directors under the company's constitution, and not with the wider question whether any commercial benefit is derived from the guarantee: consequently that is a matter with which a prudent lender will still be concerned.

If the creditor reasonably believes that the guarantee is in the interests of the company, or that the company is deriving a commercial benefit from giving it, he should be protected, even if it is held by the court that in fact it was not in the company's interests and there was no substantial benefit to be derived from giving the guarantee. There has been some judicial guidance as to what constitutes bad faith in this context. In *International Sales and Agencies Ltd v Marcus* [1982] 3 All E.R. 551, Lawson J. said:

> ". . . lack of . . . good faith in somebody entering into obligations with a company will be found either in proof of his actual knowledge that the transaction was ultra vires . . . or where it can be shown that such a person could not in view of all the circumstances, have been unaware that he was a party to a transaction ultra vires".

In *Re Rapierway Ltd* (unreported, Ch. D. May 17, 1989) Peter Gibson J. said that "genuine and honest absence of notice must . . . also comprehend that the purchaser is not a person who shuts his eyes to the truth". Consequently, the lender who is put on inquiry but fails to make reasonable inquiries could be said to have acted in bad faith. It is very difficult to conceive of situations in which a financial institution might be regarded as acting in bad faith in this context, though one possibility would be where its representatives are made aware that the guarantee, or the transaction of which it forms a part, is not for the benefit of the company but for some entirely extraneous purpose. Accordingly lenders involved in transactions where the objective is to benefit the group as a whole, or a different company within that group, should be particularly vigilant. There is a possibility that any financial institution which was paid under a guarantee which it knew to be given by the directors contrary to the interests of the company would be liable to make restitution as constructive trustee.

Although the legislation is likely to protect the creditor in all but rare instances, he may still wish to give himself additional protection, particularly in the context of a complex inter-company transaction. As already mentioned, he might require a special resolution to be passed. Alternatively, he might insist on the production of minutes of a meeting of the Board of Directors containing statements by the directors as to why they consider that the transaction is in the company's interests (and possibly identify the various benefits in terms).

The doctrine of *ultra vires* still has the capacity to invalidate a guarantee when the surety is a body whose powers are governed by statute. It will be a matter of interpretation of the particular statute whether the surety has the capacity to enter into the guarantee, and that interpretation may be particularly difficult when considering the scope of general powers which are ancillary to the surety's main powers under the statute, such as the power to borrow or raise money. For example, in *Credit Suisse v Borough Council of Allerdale* [1995] 1 Lloyd's Rep. 315, Colman J. held that a local authority had exceeded its statutory powers by entering into a guarantee of £6 million to secure a loan by Credit Suisse to a single-purpose company set up by the council to borrow money for use in various capital projects.[30] Alternatively, if the council had statutory powers to form the company and give the guarantee, it had exercised those powers in a manner which was invalid because the purpose of the scheme was an improper one, namely to evade the borrowing and spending controls on local authorities and to trade in time-share units in order to fund the construction of the time-share accommodation and a swimming pool. Thirdly, the decision to enter into the scheme was irrational under the principles laid down in *Associated Provincial Picture Houses Ltd v Wednesbury Corporation* [1948] 1 K.B. 223 and *ultra vires* for that reason. Consequently, on all these grounds, the guarantee was unenforceable and it did not matter that the bank was ignorant of the irrationality of the decision to enter into the scheme or that the local authority was seeking to rely on the invalidity of that decision.[31] The judgment was upheld by the Court of Appeal [1997] Q.B. 306.

Apart from the illegality of any consideration which may be given for the guarantee (discussed in Chapter 2), or the situation in which the underlying principal obligation is illegal (which is discussed in Chapter 6) a contract of suretyship may be unenforceable for illegality on four main grounds, which may overlap:

(1) If the making of the guarantee is expressly or implicitly prohibited by statute.

(2) If the guarantee appears to be lawful but is made to effect an unlawful purpose.

(3) If the guarantee is to do something which contravenes a statute or is contrary to public policy.

(4) If the guarantee is performed or can only be performed in a manner which contravenes a statute.

Guarantees prohibited by statute

5–050   If a contract is expressly or impliedly prohibited by statute, it is unenforceable whether the parties meant to break the law or not: *St John Shipping Corporation v Joseph Rank Ltd* [1957] 1 Q.B. 267 *per* Devlin J. at 283. The

---

30 Compare *Den Norske Creditbank v The Sarawak Economic Development Corporation* [1989] 2 Lloyd's Rep. 35.
31 See also *Credit Suisse v Waltham Forest LBC* [1997] Q.B. 362; *Morgan Grenfell & Co v Sutton LBC* [1997] 6 Bank. L.R. 156; *Alliance & Leicester Building Society v Marland and Quigley* (unreported) CAT No.163 of 1995, February 17.

question whether a guarantee is prohibited by a particular statute is often difficult to answer and will depend on such factors as the object of the statute, the presence or absence of any penalty for infringement, and the reasonableness or unreasonableness of the result if the contract is unenforceable. The Australian case of *Yango Pastoral Co Ltd v First Chicago Australia Ltd* (1978) 139 C.L.R. 41 is a useful illustration of these principles. In that case it was assumed that the bank had carried on banking business without the authority required by the provisions of the Australian Banking Act 1959. The question which arose was whether this prevented the bank from enforcing a guarantee and a mortgage in support of a loan which it had made in the course of its unauthorised business. Mason J. held that it did not. The statute did not prohibit all the banking transactions which were carried out, and such a result would have been absurd because the logical consequence would have been to prevent depositors with the bank from recovering their money. The penalty imposed by the Act was directed towards the general conduct of banking business and not towards the individual transactions or their method of performance. The relevant statute may specifically cater for the problem by stipulating circumstances in which the guarantee may be enforced. For example, s.330(2) of the Companies Act 1985 expressly prohibits a company from entering into a guarantee in connection with a loan made to a director of the company, or its holding company. Section 330(4) prohibits the company from guaranteeing or providing any security in connection with a credit transaction (such as a hire-purchase agreement) made by any other person for such a director or a person connected with a director. Section 341 of the Act provides that a transaction or arrangement prohibited by s.330 is voidable at the instance of the company unless restitution is impossible, or the company has been indemnified by the director concerned for the loss and damage which it has suffered, or "any rights acquired bona fide for value and without actual notice of the contravention by a person other than the person for whom the transaction or arrangement was made would be affected by its avoidance". This would normally suffice to protect the lender.

These provisions can be contrasted with the prohibition contained in s.151 of the Companies Act 1985 on the giving of financial assistance by a company or any of its subsidiaries to a person for the purpose of acquiring shares in the company. By s.152, "financial assistance" is defined to include financial assistance given by way of guarantee, security or indemnity, other than an indemnity in respect of the indemnifier's own neglect or default, or by way of release or waiver. There are a number of exceptions to the general prohibition, set out in s.153. By virtue of s.155 of the Act, the prohibition is also relaxed somewhat in relation to private companies, provided that the provisions of ss.156–158 are complied with. The potential impact of those sections on guarantees and other security documentation is illustrated by two recent cases, *Anglo Petroleum Ltd v TFB (Mortgages) Ltd* [2003] EWHC 3125, QB and *In the Matter of Hill & Tyler Ltd (In Administration)* [2004] EWHC 1261, Ch, *The Times*, June 11, 2004. In the *Anglo Petroleum* case S, the guarantor of a loan of £15 million from T to a company (P) which had been purchased by another company (K) which was under S's control, successfully defended an application for summary judgment on the basis that it was arguable that T knew that £9 million of the loan was to be used to pay the deferred part of the purchase price due from K for P's shares, and thus contravened s.151(2) of the Act. Jack J held that if that analysis was correct, then both the loan agreement and S's guarantee were arguably unenforceable.

In *In the Matter of Hill & Tyler Ltd* an agreement had been reached whereby one of the directors, L, would buy out the shares of his fellow directors in the company, HT, through a company, J, which was specially formed for that purpose. The purchase price of some £1.3 million was financed by two loans to J, one made by L himself, and a much larger inter-company loan by HT. L's loan was in turn secured by a guarantee and a debenture given by HT to L. The inter-company loan by HT to J was financed by a bank loan, which was secured by a fixed charge granted by HT over two printing presses. There had been an attempt by HT, which was now insolvent, to comply with the requirements of ss.155–158 of the Act so as to render any assistance lawful, and the issue before the court was whether that attempt had been successful. The judge (Richard Sheldon Q.C.) held that there had been sufficient compliance with the requirements of the statute, despite certain inaccuracies in the statutory declaration. However, he stated *obiter* that if the declaration had been found to have been invalid, then as a matter of statutory interpretation the guarantee and debenture given by HT to L would both have been invalid, as would the charge given as security to the bank for its loan, although the loan from the bank would have remained enforceable on the basis that it did not constitute the giving of financial assistance within s.151.

Guarantees made to effect an unlawful purpose

5–051   The guarantee given in the *Credit Suisse* case was one which prima facie contravened this principle, but the local authority would not have been able to rely upon the illegality. Contracts which appear on their face to be lawful, but which are made to effect an underlying purpose which is contrary to public policy or infringes a statute, are generally enforceable at the behest of the other contracting party if he was ignorant of the underlying purpose and was not implicated in the illegality: *Mason v Clarke* [1955] A.C. 778. Consequently the fact that the bank had no involvement in the scheme to circumvent the limitations on the council's borrowing powers would have protected it against a defence of illegality, although it did not assist it in meeting the defence of *ultra vires*.

Guarantees which offend against public policy

5–052   Guarantees which fall within this category are generally guarantees of an underlying transaction which is itself contrary to public policy or contravenes a statute (*e.g.* a guarantee of a contract to sell or supply prohibited drugs or hard-core pornographic material) but they may be independently repugnant, *e.g.* a guarantee to pay the costs of an action which is champertous, or a guarantee aimed at stifling the prosecution of the principal debtor.[32] The question whether cases falling within this category are to be treated in the same way as those in the first category, so that even an innocent creditor could not enforce the guarantee, is probably still open to debate. As a matter of principle, it would appear that the underlying policy would require the guarantee to be unenforceable regardless of any intention on the part of the contracting parties. However, in practice this could produce harsh results. For example, it is an interesting question whether a guarantee provided by a claimant as security for the costs of the defendant in proceedings which are subsequently held to be champertous (at the defendant's behest) would fall within this category. Given that the result would be manifestly unfair to the defendant, it is unlikely that it would.

Guarantees which are not or cannot be performed in a lawful manner

This type of illegality covers a situation in which a contract, on its face, **5–053** appears to be perfectly lawful, but either is performed in a manner which contravenes a statute or can only be performed in such a manner: see, *e.g. B and B Viennese Fashions v Losane* [1952] 1 All E.R. 909. Such transactions are generally enforceable by an innocent party. It is difficult to envisage circumstances in which a guarantee or other contract of suretyship would fall into this class, save perhaps where payment by the prescribed means would infringe exchange control legislation. In such a case the court would probably strive to uphold the guarantee, for example by construing it in such a way as to provide for a lawful means of payment, unless the creditor was implicated in the illegal scheme.

A recent example of a case in which the guarantee was unenforceable by reason of illegality is *Lloyds TSB Bank Plc v Rasheed Bank, The Times*, January 19, 2000. A company, S, had contracted to supply medical products to an Iraqi company. The buyers agreed to advance payment on the strength of a performance guarantee issued by an Iraqi bank which was backed by S's bank, Lloyds. S in turn had deposited money with Lloyds as counter-security for its guarantee. As a result of EU legislation passed in the wake of the Iraqi invasion of Kuwait, it became unlawful for anyone to pay claims arising out of bonds or guarantees given to any Iraqi person. S's liquidator successfully claimed the return of the deposit from Lloyds on the grounds that its guarantee could not be performed and that the prohibition against payment had every appearance of being permanent.

---

32 See the discussion of unlawful consideration in Ch.2, above, at paras 2–016–2–020.

Chapter 6

The Liability of the Surety

The nature of the surety's liability

Secondary nature

6–001 A contract of guarantee is an accessory contract, by which the surety undertakes to ensure that the principal performs the principal obligation.[1] It has been described as a contract to indemnify the creditor upon the happening of a contingency, namely the default of the principal to perform the principal obligation.[2] The surety is therefore under a secondary obligation which is dependent upon the default of the principal[3] and which does not arise until that point.[4] In *Ex p. Gardom* (1808) 15 Ves. 286, it was held that no claim could be brought by the creditor for the price of goods sold and delivered until the period for payment of the price for the goods allowed to the principal had expired. The secondary nature of the surety's liability will preclude the creditor from applying *quia timet* to compel the surety to set aside a fund to provide for the possibility of the debt becoming due from the principal and the principal making default.[5]

However, the surety's liability is not contingent for the purposes of the distribution rules in insolvency.[6] Further, the surety is no more justified in placing the whole of his property out of the reach of the creditor than is the principal. In *Goodricke v Taylor* (1864) 2 De G. J. & Sm. 135 the surety effected a mortgage of his house to secure an existing debt of £1,100 for which he was liable as surety. He was at the time also liable on a promissory

---

1 *Jowitt v Callaghan* [1938] 38 N.S.W. 512; *Moschi v Lep Air Services* [1973] A.C. 331; *NRG Vision Ltd v Churchfield Leasing Ltd* [1988] B.C.L.C. 624; and see Ch.1, paras 1–004–1–007 for a detailed discussion of the nature of a contract of guarantee.

2 *Sampson v Burton* (1820) 4 Moo. C.P. 515. See also *Mallet v Bateman* (1865) L.R. 1 C.P. 163, 171; *Fahey v MSD Spiers Ltd* [1973] 2 N.Z.L.R. 655.

3 *Rees v Berrington* (1795) 2 Ves. Jun 540 at 543, *per* Lord Loughborough L.C.; *Lakeman v Mountstephen* (1874) L.R. 7 H.L. 17 at 24 *per* Lord Selborne L.C. See generally Ch.1, para.1–005.

4 *Pattison v Guardians of the Belford Union* (1856) 1 H. & N. 523; *Rickaby v Lewis* (1905) 1 T.L.R. 130; and see Ch.7 at 7–002.

5 *Antrobus v Davidson* (1817) 3 Mer. 569; see also *Wolmershausen v Gullick* [1893] 2 Ch. 514 at 524.

6 *Atkinson v Grey* (1853) 1 Sm. & G. 577; *Boyd v Robins and Langlands* (1859) 5 C.B.N.S. 597. See also *MS Fashions Ltd v Bank of Credit and Commerce International SA* [1993] Ch. 425.

note for £2,000. He became bankrupt, and the mortgage was held to be void as an assignment to defeat or delay creditors.[7]

The extent of the surety's liability is the same at law and in equity.[8]

The co-extensiveness principle

The most important aspect of the nature of a guarantor's liability as a secondary liability is that it is co-extensive with the liability of the principal. This means that as a general rule, the surety's liability is no greater and no less than that of the principal, in terms of amount, time for payment and the conditions under which the principal is liable.[9] Accordingly, in *Hartland v Jukes* (1863) 1 H. & C. 667, where the principal and surety both gave a promissory note to the creditor as security for advances, no action could be maintained on the note against either principal or surety until an advance was made to the principal by the creditor. Co-extensiveness of liability is one of the essential characteristics of a guarantee that distinguishes it from a contract of indemnity.[10] For example, the guarantee by a surety of the "due fulfilment of any obligation" of a party to a charterparty which contained an arbitration clause covered the principal's liability to pay interest and costs ordered by the arbitrators, as well as the principal amount of the award.[11]

6–002

Where, therefore, the liability of a promisor under an agreement exceeds that of the primary debtor, in that, for example, he may be liable when the primary debtor is not, or for an amount for which he is not, then the agreement is not a guarantee, and the promisor undertakes primary liability himself. In such circumstances the contract in question can only be viewed as an indemnity.[12]

However, the principle of co-extensiveness is not an immutable rule. The precise extent of the liability of the surety will always be governed by the provisions of the guarantee on their true construction,[13] and the parties remain free in certain respects to provide for limitations of the surety's

---

7 See also *Re Ridler, Ridler v Ridler* (1882) 22 Ch. D. 74; *Bludoff v Osachoff* [1928] 3 D.L.R. 170. Transactions in fraud of creditors are now dealt with by the Insolvency Act 1986, s.425 (replacing Law of Property Act 1925, s.172).

8 *Samuell v Howarth* (1817) 3 Mer. 272.

9 *Rees v Berrington* (1795) 2 Ves. Jun. 540 at 543 *per* Lord Loughborough; *Moschi v Lep Air Services Ltd* [1973] A.C. 331; *Hampton v Minns* [2002] 1 W.L.R. 1. See generally Else Mitchell, "Is a Surety's Liability Co-Extensive with that of the Principal?" (1947) 63 L.Q.R. 355; Johan Steyn, "Guarantees: the Co-Extensiveness Principle" (1974) 90 L.Q.R. 246, and see Ch.4, para.4–014; Ch.9, paras 9–019–9–020.

10 See generally Ch.1, paras 1–004–1–005; Ch.4, para.4–014.

11 *Compania Sudamericana de Fletes SA v African Continental Bank Ltd* [1973] 1 Lloyd's Rep. 21, *Sabemo Pty Ltd v De Groot* (1991) 8 B.C.L. 132; *cf. Bruns v Colocotronis (The "Vasso")* [1979] 2 Lloyd's Rep. 412.

12 See *Moschi v Lep Air Services* [1973] A.C. 331; *Board of Trade v Employers' Liability Assurance Corpn* [1910] 2 K.B. 649; *Pattison v Guardians of the Belford Union* (1856) 1 H. & N. 523; *Oastler v Pound* (1863) 11 W.R. 518.

13 As to which see generally Ch.4, esp. paras 4–002–4–003.

liability without detracting from the nature of the contract as a guarantee.[14] Furthermore, the court has not always regarded itself as bound to treat the surety as co-extensively liable with the principal, and there are circumstances where the surety will remain liable notwithstanding the fact that the principal is not, or is no longer, liable for the principal obligation.[15]

One question which often arises is whether the surety's liability sounds in debt or in damages. In *Moschi v Lep Air Services* [1973] A.C. 331, the House of Lords appeared to express a general rule that the surety's liability sounded in damages and not in debt, even where he was guaranteeing a debt.[16] Lord Diplock's penetrating historical analysis of the nature of the secondary liability of a surety revaled that the remedy for the failure by the surety to perform his own obligation to see to it that the principal performed his own obligations, even to pay a sum of money, lay not in indebtitatus assumpsit (debt) but special assumpsit (damages).[17] However, it is clear that this is not an immutable rule of law, but depends (as the House of Lords were careful to say) on the construction of the words of the guarantee.[18] If what is guaranteed is the performance by the principal of his obligations, even payment obligations, then the surety's liability lies in damages. If, on the other hand, the surety's promise is that, on the happening of certain events, he will pay a sum of money, then he is liable once those events have happened.

The distinction between a guarantee of the principal's performance and the promise to pay a sum of money if the principal does not is a fine one and will depend on the precise words of the guarantee. In *Hampton v Minns* [2002] 1 W.L.R. 1, Kevin Garnett Q.C. (sitting as a Deputy High Court Judge), after careful analysis of *Moschi v Lep Air Services*, held that the fact that the sureties had promised to "pay or discharge to" the creditor bank all monies due and owing by the principal created a debt obligation on their part, and not an obligation to pay damages.[19]

---

14 See, *e.g. Fahey v MSD Spiers Ltd* [1973] 2 N.Z.L.R. 655; [1975] 1 N.Z.L.R. 240, PC, where the surety only guaranteed payment for future purchases, and not past indebtedness. See further Ch.4, paras 4–016–4–017.

15 *Moschi v Lep Air Services Ltd* [1973] A.C. 331; *Hyundai Shipbuilding & Heavy Industries Co Ltd v Pournaras* [1978] 2 Lloyd's Rep. 502; *Hyundai Heavy Industries Co Ltd v Papadopoulos* [1980] 1 W.L.R. 1129 *Stocznia Gdanska SA v Latvian Shipping Co* [1998] 1 Ll. Rep. 609; *Hampton v Minns* [2002] 1 W.L.R. 1; and see Johan Steyn, "Guarantees: The Co-Extensiveness Principle" (1974) 90 L.Q.R. 246.

16 See Lord Simon of Glaisdale at 352. The general rule seems to have been assumed.

17 See 347–349.

18 The observation of Peter Smith J. in *Securum Finance v Ashton* [2002] All E.R. (D) 380 at para.58 that it is a *"fundamental principle that a surety liability is a secondary liability to pay damages measured by the failure of the principal debtor to pay"* is not correct so far as the reference to damages is concerned. See further para.6–030 below and Ch.7, para.7–018.

19 See para.99 of his judgment. One question may be whether the instrument creates two obligations (an obligation of guarantee plus a separate obligation to pay losses on demand) or one obligation (a guarantee, with a procedural provision for demand). The answer depends on the precise language of the instrument, but is usually likely to be read as creating only one obligation: see *Romain v Scuba TV* [1997] Q.B. 887, *per* Evans L.J. at 895.

Extent of the surety's liability: the provisions of the contract of guarantee

Limitations upon liability

Prospective and retrospective liability

The liability of the surety may be restricted to obligations of the principal **6–003** which have already arisen prior to the contract of guarantee, or which are incurred after the contract of guarantee is made, or he may be liable both prospectively and retrospectively. As has been mentioned earlier in this work,[20] most modern guarantees will clearly indicate that the guarantee applies to obligations already incurred by the principal towards the creditor as well as those which may fall due in the future. The difficulties which may arise in construing a contract as being prospective, retrospective, or both, are considered in detail in Chapter 4.

The question whether a guarantee is retrospective or prospective arises most crucially in the context of payments made by the principal in satisfaction of his indebtedness to the creditor, and whether these are in extinction or reduction of the guaranteed indebtedness. The rule in *Clayton*'s case,[21] which will operate in the absence of any express appropriation of a particular payment by the principal or the creditor to any particular indebtedness, will mean that the earliest payment is appropriated to the earliest indebtedness. The consequence of this is that in the case of a retrospective guarantee, the payments by the principal which reduce or extinguish his indebtedness will *pro tanto* reduce or extinguish the surety's liability. Where, however, the guarantee is prospective in effect, the earliest payment by the principal will reduce his own liability incurred prior to the execution of the guarantee, but not affect the liability of the surety, who will remain liable in full for the post-guarantee indebtedness.[22] The effect of *Clayton*'s case can be avoided by a specific appropriation of a payment by the principal (or by the creditor in his turn).[23]

Continuing or specific liability

A guarantee may relate to one or more specific transactions,[24] or may relate **6–004** to a series of indefinite transactions.[25] The distinction between these two forms of guarantee can be very important, and is often extremely difficult to draw.[26]

---

20 See Ch.4, para.4–016.

21 *Devaynes v Noble, Clayton*'s case (1816) 1 Mer. 572.

22 See the discussion in Ch.4, para.4–016.

23 For a full discussion of rights of appropriation and the rule in *Clayton*'s case, see Ch.9, paras 9–005–9–008.

24 See, *e.g. Kay v Groves* (1829) 6 Bing. 276; *Walker v Hardman* (1837) 4 Cl. & Fin. 258; *Re Medewe's Trust* (1859) 26 Beav 588; *J Wiseman & Sons Ltd (in liq.) v Harris* [1932] N.Z.L.R. 663; *Phillips Petroleum v Quintin* (1998) L.T.L. March 13, 1998, PC.

25 See, *e.g. Wood v Priestner* (1866) L.R. 2 Exch. 66; *Heffield v Meadows* (1869) L.R. 4 C.P. 595; *Parr's Banking Co v Yates* [1898] 2 Q.B. 460 (illustrating the effect of limitation on interest on a guaranteed account).

26 See the discussion in Ch.4 at para.4–017.

The distinction between a specific and a continuing guarantee is most crucially at issue when the principal makes a payment to the creditor. For example, if the principal borrows £1,000 under an overdraft facility, and the guarantee is for a specific sum of £1,000, the operation of the rule in *Clayton*'s case[27] will mean that a payment by the principal of, say, £500 will reduce the surety's liability *pro tanto*, and if the principal then pays another £500 the surety's liability will be extinguished altogether, even though the principal has borrowed further sums from the creditor in the meantime and is liable for £1,000 newly advanced.[28] However, where the guarantee is a continuing one, the surety will remain liable in full for the principal liability as it arises from time to time, and the payments in will not affect his liability.

Most modern standard form guarantees contain an "all moneys" clause, which provides that the guarantee will cover "all moneys which are now or which may from time to time be owing or remain unpaid", and provide that the guarantee be a "continuing security"; thus the rule in *Clayton*'s case only rarely operates in favour of the surety. However, in the Irish Supreme Court decision of *The Governor and Company of the Bank of Ireland v McCabe* (unreported, September 19, 1994), the bank had taken guarantees from directors of the principal, which was a customer of some years' standing. The guarantees were expressed to be "a continuing security on the guarantors". The bank also held certain stock owed by the principal as security for the guaranteed loan. The bank was asked to release part of that stock so that the principal could sell it, to which it duly agreed. The sale went ahead and the loan was repaid. The bank then loaned the principal further moneys on the security of "any security held however". The bank subsequently claimed repayment under the guarantees. Egan J. held that the bank's claim failed, since the guarantees covered only the original indebtedness which had been discharged, and did not extend to the new advance. The case illustrates the fallibility of the "continuing security" provision in standard form guarantees. Banks would be well advised to spell out in their facility letter exactly what security they are seeking and, if they wish to cover future advances, to include an "all moneys" or similar provision in the guarantee itself.[29]

In *Banner Lane Realisations Ltd (in liq.) v Berisford Plc* [1997] 1 B.C.L.C. 380, the Court of Appeal considered the meaning of the phrase "future indebtedness" in a guarantee contained in a debenture. They rejected the argument advanced by the surety that liability to indemnify the creditor was not a debt and therefore not indebtedness within the meaning of the debenture. They held that "future indebtedness" included not only a present obligation to pay a sum certain in the future, but also an

---

27 See para.4–016, and Ch.9, para.9–007.
28 See *Heffield v Meadows* (1869) L.R. 4 C.P. 595.
29 See *Halsbury's Laws* (4th ed., reissue, 2004), Vol. 20, para.198.

(unquantified) sum in the future or on a contingency.[30] That included an obligation arising in the future.

There is increasing judicial support in Australia for a more restrictive approach to "all moneys" guarantees. In *Estoril Investments Pty Ltd v Westpac Banking Corporation* (1993) 6 B.P.R. 13, 146, Young J. laid down guidelines for construction of "all moneys" mortgages, most importantly that only debts of the same type or character as the original debt are secured by the mortgage, and that once the original debt has been fully discharged the mortgage is extinguished and cannot secure further loans.[31]

The modern approach to "all moneys" provisions
The protection of sureties from the harshness and abuse of all moneys **6–005** clauses is gaining ground in England. *Lloyds Bank Plc v Hawkins* [1998] Lloyd's Rep. Bank. 379 illustrates a significant pitfall for banks when claiming moneys due under an "all moneys" charge.

In March 1982 H charged his house by way of legal mortgage to Lloyds Bank. The mortgage was an "all moneys" security with H covenanting to "pay to the Bank on demand all money and liabilities whether certain or contingent which now are or at any time hereafter may be due owing or incurred by the Mortgagor to the Bank".

In January 1987 H entered into a guarantee with the bank of the borrowings of his company, G. The guarantee was expressed to be in addition to any other security held by the bank. In 1997 the bank issued proceedings against H, seeking possession of his house and a money judgment under the mortgage. These proceedings related to money owed on his overdraft account and a separate loan account as well as unpaid insurance premiums. His total indebtedness to the bank in relation to these items only amounted to £107,948.26. Judgment was entered against him for possession of his house and the sums claimed in the bank's particulars of claim.

The bank had failed to claim an additional £260,000 which H owed under the guarantee. When the bank issued fresh proceedings in an attempt to recover this sum (which had in fact grown to £300,000 by the time the case reached the Court of Appeal), its claim was rejected unanimously. In its first action, the bank had pleaded that the sums claimed were the "amount outstanding under the mortgage". The order made against H reflected the bank's pleaded claim. However, as the mortgage was an "all moneys" security, it also secured H's guarantee of G's debts (which was in place at the time of the first proceedings). The Court of Appeal held that the initial judgment obtained by the bank covered the sums due under the guarantee

---

30 For a comprehensive discussion of the surety's liability for sums owing contingently to the creditor, see *National Bank of Australasia v Mason* (1976) 50 A.L.J.R. 362, and the discussion of that case in O'Donovan & Phillips (*op.cit.*) at pp.247–250, and O'Donovan & Phillips (English ed., 2003) paras 5–74 to 5–78.
31 See also *Burke v State Bank of New South Wales Ltd* [1994] 37 N.S.W.L.R. 53, esp. at 72–73.

as well as H's debts. The bank's failure to pursue sums due under the mortgage effectively rendered the guarantee valueless as a result of cause of action estoppel; its plea that this was simply an oversight was not accepted. Robert Walker L.J. (with whom Buxton and Mantell L.JJ. agreed) held:

> "I fully accept that the bank initially had two separate sets of contractual rights, one of which was backed by security over Mr Hawkins' property. Because of the customarily wide terms of any bank's all moneys charge, these two sets of rights, and the remedies to enforce them, overlapped to a considerable extent. There was nothing secured by the promise in the guarantee that was not also automatically secured by the terms to the all moneys charge in the legal charge. No doubt it was open to the bank, subject to rules of court relating to mortgage actions and subject also to general rules as to abuse of process, to decide to enforce only some of its rights and remedies against Mr Hawkins. It might have decided to seek a money judgment without seeking possession of the farmhouse or it might have decided to take the converse course . . . But what it was not open to the bank to do was to go for possession and for a money judgment in respect (and I quote from para 10 of the particulars of claim) of "the total amount outstanding under the . . . [legal charge]", and having obtained a money judgment and not having made any attempt to get either the judgment varied or the pleadings varied, then to start fresh proceedings in the High Court based on the guarantee . . . Although the guarantee was a continuing guarantee, any claim in respect of money advanced after the date of proceedings against Mr Hawkins would, it seems to me, be the subject-matter of a separate cause of action arising from the continuing nature of the guarantee."

Even though the guarantee relates to a specific transaction undertaken by the principal, the surety may nonetheless be liable for additional amounts incurred in the course of that transaction, if the principal would be so liable as a primary obligor. Accordingly, where the surety guarantees all the obligations of the contractor under a building contract, and the guarantee contemplates further loans being made to the contractor to enable him to complete the works, the surety will be liable if the contractor defaults in repayment of the loans.[32] Further, the court will construe the guarantee as continuing if there are general words which indicate that the principal obligations to be guaranteed arise in the context of an ongoing relationship or course of dealing between the principal and creditor.[33]

The Court has shown a reluctance to read "all moneys" or "all obligations" clauses in guarantees as apt to cover those obligations owed by

---

32 See *Trade Indemnity Co Ltd v Workington Harbour and Dock Board* [1937] A.C. 1; *Melvin International SA v Poseidon Schiffahrt ("The Kalma")* [1999] 2 Ll. Rep. 374 (where Cresswell J. examined the scope of the variation clause in a charterparty guarantee).

33 *Meyer v Isaac* (1840) 6 M. & W. 605; *cf. Nicholson v Paget* (1832) 1 C. & M. 48.

the principal to a third party who then assigns them to the creditor who holds the benefit of the guarantee. In *Clark's Refrigerated Transport Pty Ltd* (1982) V.R. 989, Brooking J. picturesquely expressed the view that the surety would not ordinarily contemplate that debts due by the principal to third parties could be covered by the guarantee following assignment to the creditor. In *Kova Establishment v Sasco Investments Ltd* [1998] 2 B.C.L.C. 83, John Martin Q.C. decided that the all obligations clause in the guarantee before him did not catch assigned debts, on the basis that the contractual interest rate in the guarantee was higher than that whichh the creditor was entitled to receive from the principal. See further the discussion in Chapter 4 at para.4–013.

In *Lloyds TSB Plc v Shorney* [2002] 1 F.L.R. 81, the Court of Appeal refused to allow the bank to take advantage of the "all moneys" nature of the mortgage so as to deprive the mortgagor of her right to be subrogated to the mortgage, having paid off the original amount secured by it. Robert Walker L.J., giving the main judgment, said that in circumstances where the mortgage was given to secure a loan of fixed amount and for a particular purpose, it was not permissible to use the "all moneys" nature of the charge to suggest that the mortgagor contemplated further liabilities being entered into by the principal.[34] The case is important because it shows that lenders may not always be able to rely on "all moneys" provisions in respect of liabilities not (on the facts) contemplated by the surety at the outset. It means that the creditor's right to recovery under such instruments, or the right to enforce securities for the principal's obligations, may be fact-dependent, or at least critically dependent on precisely the ambit of the guarantee or personal covenant for payment in the mortgage.[35]

Limitations on the amount of principal debt

Where the guarantee is a continuing guarantee covering future trans-actions, it will usually be construed as being unlimited as to amount, in the absence of any express stipulation for a limit on liability.[36] On the other hand, the stipulation for a limit is not inconsistent with a continuing guarantee, unless it is clear that the limit was stipulated for in order to tie the guarantee to a specific debt or obligation.[37] Where the creditor uses a standard form of guarantee which provides for a limit but the appropriate

6–006

---

34 In *Shorney*, the liabilities were under personal guarantees given to the bank by the mortgagor's husband in respect of additional loans by the bank to his company. The bank lost its claim to possession on the basis that the mortgagor, having paid off the secured amount, was entitled to be subrogated to the bank's security, even though the bank was still owed money by the principal.

35 If there is one: there is no such covenant in a mortgage over unregistered land. See Ch.13, para.13–022 below.

36 See, *e.g. Coles v Pack* (1869) L.R. 5 C.P. 65 but note the warning of Bovill C.J. in that case that the language of one guarantee affords little or no guide to the construction of another which is given under other and different circumstances.

37 See, *e.g. Kirby v Duke of Marlborough* (1813) 2 M. & S. 18, and the discussion in Ch.4 at paras 4–017–4–021.

space in the guarantee instrument has been left blank, the guarantee will be unlimited.[38]

Any stipulation in the guarantee to limit the surety's liability to a fixed amount will not operate so as to make the surety's liability thereunder conditional upon the principal's liability to the creditor being limited to that sum, so that the creditor is at liberty to make advances to the principal in excess of the guarantee limit without affecting his rights under the guarantee to claim up to the limit from the surety.[39] However, this will not be the case where the surety contracts with the creditor that he should advance a particular sum to the principal, which the surety would guarantee; in such a case, where the creditor advances more than the stipulated sum, he will be in breach of a condition of the guarantee and the surety will be discharged altogether.[40] In Australasia and Canada, courts have proved reluctant to deprive creditors so easily of the benefit of their guarantees.[41] Thus in *Queensland National Bank Ltd v Queensland Trustees Ltd* (1899) Q.L.J. 282, a clause in a guarantee stating that "the limit of the overdraft at No.2 account shall be £50,000" was construed as merely specifying the amount which the principal could draw without further consent of the creditor bank.[42]

Guarantee for the whole or part of the debt

6–007　　Where there is a limitation upon the amount of the surety's liability, it is vitally important to ascertain whether his intention was to guarantee the whole of the debt of the principal, subject to the stipulated limit on the amount of the liability of the surety, or whether the surety's intention was to guarantee only part of the debt.[43]

There are several consequences which flow from this distinction. First, where the guarantee is construed as a guarantee of part of the debt rather than the whole indebtedness (subject to a limit), the surety will be entitled upon payment of the entirety of that part to be subrogated to any securities held by the creditor in respect of the principal debt in the same proportion that the part of the debt satisfied by the surety bore to the whole amount of the debt, as long as the whole of the debt to the creditor has been discharged.[44] Where, on the other hand, the guarantee makes it clear that

---

38 *Caltex Oil (Australia) Pty Ltd v Alderton* (1964) 81 W.N. (N.S.W.) (Pt 1) 297. Such a guarantee will not be regarded as uncertain. See also *Bank of Baroda v ANY Enterprises Ltd* (unreported) CAT No.1088 of 1986, December 4, and the more recent related case, *Bank of Baroda v Patel* [1996] 1 Lloyd's Rep. 391 at 395. See also Ch.3 at para.3–023.

39 *Laurie v Scholefield* (1869) L.R. 4 C.P. 622; *Total Oil Products (Australia) Pty Ltd v Robinson* [1970] 1 N.S.W.L.R. 701.

40 *Philips v Astling* (1809) 2 Taunt. 206.

41 See *Commercial Bank v Moylan* (1870) 1 A.J.L.R. 123; *New Zealand Loan and Mercantile Agency Co Ltd v Willis* [1920] N.Z.L.R. 379; *J. R. Watkins Medical Co v Gray* [1920] W.W.R. 588; *Dime Savings Bank v Mills* (1919) 46 O.R. 492. See also *Parker v Wise* (1817) 6 M. & S. 239.

42 See O'Donovan & Phillips *The Modern Contract of Guarantee* (3rd ed., 1996), p.231 and the cases cited there; see also and O'Donovan & Phillips (English ed., 2003) paras 5–30 to 5–34.

43 See Ch.4, para.4–020.

44 *Gedye v Matson* (1858) 25 Beav. 310; *Dixon v Steel* [1901] 2 Ch. 602; and see Ch.11, paras 11–017–11–028 for a detailed discussion of the surety's rights of subrogation.

the whole of the debt is guaranteed (even though the amount of the surety's liability is limited), the surety who pays the full amount of his liability thereunder is not entitled to share in the creditor's securities until the creditor has been paid in full.[45]

Secondly, where the guarantee is only for part of the debt, the surety will on payment of part of that debt be entitled to prove in the principal's insolvency, and to receive such proportion of dividends as his payment bears to the total debt.[46] For this reason the creditor often insists that the surety should not be entitled to prove until the creditor has received the full amount owed by the principal.[47] Where, on the other hand, the surety has guaranteed the whole debt but with a limitation as to his liability, he has no right of proof until the creditor has been paid in full.[48]

Thirdly, where the surety guarantees a part of the debt, and his co-surety a separate part of the same debt where there is no common liability between them, there will be no rights of contribution between them.[49]

Fourthly, where the surety guarantees the whole of the debt, limited to part, and pays that part to the creditor, there is authority to the effect that the creditor will nonetheless be entitled to claim the full amount from the principal, and (if the principal is insolvent) prove for the full amount in his bankruptcy.[50] In such circumstances, the creditor is subject to a duty to account to the surety for any surplus which he may recover over and above the balance outstanding.

Given the serious consequences of the distinction between a guarantee for the whole debt and a guarantee for part, it is crucial to be able to differentiate between them as a matter of construction.[51] The principles of

---

45 *Re Sass Ex p. National Provincial Bank of England* [1896] 2 Q.B. 12; *cf. Re Howe Ex p. Brett* (1871) 6 Ch. App. 838; the surety may have an equitable interest in the secured property by way of a charge: *Gedye v Matson* (1858) 25 Beav. 310, *Barclays Bank Ltd v TOSG Fund Ltd* [1984] 1 All E.R. 628 at 641. See Ch.11, paras 11–018–11–020, *AE Goodwin Ltd (in liq.) v A. G. Healing Ltd (in liq.)* (1979) 7 A.C.L.R. 481; *Bayley v Gibsons Ltd* (1993) 1 Tas. R. 385, where the point was left open by Zeeman J. whether a surety who pays only part of what he is obliged to pay under the guarantee is entitled to the statutory right of subrogation under the Mercantile Law Amendment Act 1856. See O'Donovan & Phillips (*op. cit.*) p.658, where the authors express the view that the statutory right should be available so long as the creditor is paid in full, in the result, from other sources: see Ch.11, paras 11–021–11–022 below.
46 *Gray v Seckham* (1872) 7 Ch. App. 680; *Seabird Corpn Ltd (in liq.) v Sherlock* (1990) 2 A.C.S.R. 111 at 116. *Re Butler's Wharf Ltd* [1995] 2 B.C.L.C. 43; *Liberty Mutual Insurance Co (UK) Ltd v HSBC Bank Plc* [2001] Ll Rep. Bank 224 (Morritt V.-C.), affd CA [2002] EWCA Civ 691.
47 *Midland Banking Co v Chambers* (1868) L.R. 7 Eq. 179; see also *Re Rees Ex p. National Provincial Bank of England* (1881) 17 Ch. D. 98; *Re Houlder* [1929] 1 Ch. 205.
48 *Ellis v Emmanuel* (1876) 1 Ex. D. 157; *Re Sass Ex p. National Provincial Bank of England* [1896] 2 Q.B. 12. Further, the creditor may, without accounting for the value of security be held for the debt. See Ch.13 for a detailed discussion of the surety's rights of proof in the principal's insolvency, esp. paras 13–004–13–009.
49 See generally Ch.12, esp. paras 12–003–12–008.
50 *Ulster Bank v Lambe* [1966] N.I. 161; *Westpac Banking Corpn v Gollin & Co Ltd* [1988] V.R. 399; *Seabird Corpn Ltd (in liq.) v Sherlock* (1990) 2 A.C.S.R. 111 at 115. There is no reason why the surety's right of indemnity against the principal should be affected.
51 See *Challenge Bank Ltd v Mailman* (N.S.W., CA, May 14, 1993).

construction appropriate for determining which form any particular guarantee takes in this respect are discussed in detail in Chapter 4.[52]

Limitations as to time

6–008   Certain types of guarantee are clearly capable of being construed as being limited in time, even if there is no express statement to that effect. For example, fidelity guarantees are normally construed as being limited to the current term of the principal's employment, where such is itself limited in time.[53] Similarly, where the guarantee relates to the obligations of the tenant under a lease for a fixed period, the guarantee will normally expire by effluxion of time together with the lease, unless there is a specific provision extending it to other leases.[54] On the other hand, a continuing guarantee of future advances will generally be construed as unlimited in duration,[55] although sometimes a specific time limit will be stipulated.[56]

Difficulties arise where, in the case of a guarantee so limited, it is unclear whether the surety's liability has arisen prior to or after the date of the expiry of the guarantee. Certainly, where a loss arises during the life of the guarantee but is only capable of quantification after the guarantee has expired, the surety will remain liable.[57] However, where the guarantee relates to defaults by the principal during the currency of a particular period, such as a line of credit or a term loan, where there is no liability on the part of the principal to repay until the end of the period, a dispute may arise as to whether a default in making repayment at the end of the period is a default to which the guarantee relates. Matters may be compounded by the fact that the principal has not demanded payment at that time because, for example, the principal is negotiating a rescheduling of his debt to the creditor. When this fails, and the creditor calls in the debt and sues the surety, the question arises whether the surety can seek to avoid liability by claiming that the principal's default did not occur until after expiry of the principal agreement, and so after expiry of the guarantee.

This problem arose in *Caisse Populaire de Ste Anne du Madawaska Ltee v Tardif* (1985) 61 N.B.R. (2d) 192. In that case the parents of a woman had guaranteed a mortgage on her house, and at the end of its term the daughter entered negotiations with the creditor as to its renewal. The discussions failed after a few months and the creditor demanded repayment of the balance of the sum owing. The sureties defended a claim of the guarantee on the basis that the guarantee had expired with the mortgage.

---

52 See Ch.4, para.4–020.
53 *Hassel v Long* (1814) 2 M. & S. 363. The guarantee may expressly apply to a subsequent reappointment: *Augero v Keen* (1836) 1 M. & W. 390. See generally the discussion in Ch.4 at para.4–019.
54 *Tayleur v Wildin* (1868) L.R. 3 Exch. 303; *Freeman v Evans* [1922] 1 Ch. 36; *A Plesser & Co Ltd v Davis* (1983) 267 E.G. 1039, and see the discussion in Ch.4 at para.4–019.
55 *Coles v Pack* (1869) L.R. 5 C.P. 65.
56 *Hollond v Teed* (1848) 7 Hare 50; *National House-Building Council v Fraser* [1983] 1 All E.R. 1090.
57 *National House-Building Council v Fraser* [1983] 1 All E.R. 1090.

Doyle J. held that in fact the default had occurred at the end of the principal agreement, and so within the term of the guarantee, when the principal failed to repay as she had been obliged to do, and the defence failed. The judge relied strongly on the fact that the guarantee contained a provision permitting the creditor to grant indulgences of time to the principal without affecting its rights under the guarantee. Although it is to some extent unclear whether the result would have been the same had there been no such provision, it is submitted that it would be commercially unrealistic to allow the surety to avoid liability in such a situation, unless perhaps the creditor could be taken to have waived the breach by his conduct in not pressing immediately for payment.[58]

In the absence of a specific provision in the contract which entitles the surety to give notice of cancellation of the guarantee, it is possible for him to give a valid notice of cancellation of a continuing guarantee, where the underlying consideration is divisible. However, he may not do so if the guarantee is not continuing or relates to a specific obligation which has already been performed by the creditor.[59] Cancellation will not, however, affect rights which have accrued to the creditor under the guarantee prior to the date of the cancellation.[60] Accordingly, cancellation is not a means by which the surety may discharge himself from liability which has already accrued: he may only avoid potential further liability which may arise in the future.

Limitations in respect of the type of principal transaction

It is possible for the guarantee to be limited as to the type of principal **6–009** transaction guaranteed.[61] If the principal transaction intended to be the subject of the guarantee is not clearly identified, the guarantee may be void for uncertainty, such as where a guarantee for the performance of the lessee's obligations under a lease could reasonably refer to two leases.[62] Where the guarantee refers to a particular transaction, the surety will not be liable for a different transaction or one outside the scope of that guaranteed, such as where the guarantee relates to a transaction for a given amount but the transaction proceeds for a larger amount,[63] or where the creditor advances moneys to the principal under a different facility to the one identified in the guarantee,[64] or where the guarantee is limited to

---

58 See also the discussion in O'Donovan & Phillips (*op. cit.*) at pp.433–434; pp.449–450.
59 *Lloyds Bank v Harper* (1880) 16 Ch. D. 290. The surety's rights of revocation and cancellation are considered in detail in Ch.8.
60 *Tooke Bros Ltd v Al-Walters Ltd* [1935] 1 D.L.R. 295, BCCA.
61 See Ch.4 at para.4–021.
62 *Mercantile Credits Ltd v Harry* [1969] 2 N.S.W.L.R. 248.
63 *Philips v Astling* (1809) 2 Taunt. 206; *Sumner v Powell* (1816) 2 Mer. 30 (both bill of exchange cases); a limited guarantee for a loan of a specific amount will not be invalidated by a loan of a larger amount, although the surety will not be liable in excess of his limit: *Williams v Rawlinson* (1825) 3 Bing. 71; *Mason v Pritchard* (1810) 12 East. 227; *Parker v Wise* (1817) 6 M. & S. 239.
64 *Dan v Barclays Australia Ltd* (1983) 57 A.L.J.R. 442.

banking transactions and facilities and the creditor is owed money in respect of debt discounting and goods.[65]

This can sometimes operate harshly from the putative creditor's point of view. In *Chan v Cresdon Pty Ltd* (1989) 168 C.L.R. 242, the High Court of Australia was concerned with a guarantee of the lessee's obligations which was embodied in the lease itself, which was for a five-year term executed in registrable form but not in fact then registered as required by statute. The majority took the view (Toohey J. dissenting) that an equitable lease came into existence, but the surety was not liable. The guarantee of obligations "under this lease", they said, meant exactly that, namely a five-year lease at law duly registered, and the surety's liability did not extend to an equitable lease.[66]

Liability for interest on the principal obligation

6–010   It is a question of construction of the guarantee to what extent and for what period the surety is liable for interest on the principal transaction.[67] Although generally the surety's liability for interest must be stipulated for, and a simple guarantee of the principal debt will not carry an interest obligation with it, the court may look at the surrounding circumstances of the transaction to determine whether interest is guaranteed. Thus in *Fahey v MSD Spiers Ltd* [1975] 1 N.Z.L.R. 240, a guarantee "to pay for any materials purchased from" the creditor was held to cover the elements of the overdue accounts which constituted interest, on the basis that the surety knew the terms on which the materials were supplied to the principal. Further, where the surety guarantees all the obligations of the principal, he will be liable for interest as one of the obligations guaranteed, even though this is not expressly provided for.[68]

Where the surety's liability under the guarantee is limited, the limit is usually expressed to be in respect of the principal sum, and the surety will remain liable for interest accruing on that sum, unless the guarantee specifies that the limit is inclusive of interest.[69] However, the surety will not be liable for interest accruing to the debt to the extent that it exceeds his limit, but only for interest on the sums payable by the surety.[70] Further, where the surety guarantees payment of a specific sum on a certain day inclusive of interest at a fixed rate down to that day, there is no rule that a

---

65 *United Dominion Trust Ltd v Beech* [1972] 1 Lloyd's Rep. 546; see also *Bank of India v Transcontinental Commodity Merchants and Patel* [1982] 1 Lloyd's Rep. 506 and Ch.4 at para.4–020.

66 See also *Tasman Properties v Mayhew* (1994) A.N.Z. Conv. R. 440; *Jaskel v Sophie Nursery Products* [1993] E.G.C.S. 42; *West Horndon Industrial Park Ltd v Phoenix Timber Group Plc* [1995] N.P.C. 42; [1995] 20 E.G. 137.

67 See *Fahey v MSD Spiers Ltd* [1975] 1 N.Z.L.R. 240, PC.

68 *Ackerman v Ehrensberger* (1846) 16 M. & W. 99, where Pollock C.B. took the view that a surety for a bill of exchange is liable for interest from the date it falls due; see also *Dawson v Raynes* (1826) 2 Russ. 466; *Re Dixon, Heynes v Dixon* [1900] 2 Ch. 561.

69 As in *Dow Banking Corpn v Mahnakh Spinning and Weaving Corpn and Bank Mellat* [1983] 2 Lloyd's Rep. 561.

70 *Meek v Wallis* (1872) 27 L.T. 650.

further contract for the payment of interest at the same rate on the principal debt thereafter is to be implied.[71]

Sometimes the surety guarantees interest alone, and not the principal debt. Accordingly a covenant by a surety for the due payment of interest during the currency of a mortgage security obliges him to pay interest so long as the principal debt remains unpaid, and therefore after default by the principal on the due date for payment.[72] If it is intended that the surety should be liable for all the interest which has accrued on the principal sum, even though his liability may be limited to part of the outstanding capital indebtedness, the language of the guarantee must be carefully chosen. In the decision of the Outer House in Scotland, *Huewind Ltd v Clydesdale Bank Plc* (1995) S.L.R. 392, the sureties gave a "top-slice" guarantee of the indebtedness of the principal above the sum of £800,000 "and of all interest due or to become due by the principals thereon". The guarantee went on to provide that their liability should not exceed the sum of £1 million "and interest thereon at the rate or rates foresaid". It was held by Lord Kirkwood[73] that the guarantee plainly limited the guarantors' liability for interest, to the interest on the guaranteed sum in excess of the initial £800,000. They would not be liable for any interest on the first £800,000 of the debt and their overall liability for interest was not to exceed the interest due on the maximum guaranteed sum of £1 million.

Where the principal has ceased to be liable for the principal debt, the surety's obligation to pay interest upon it will also cease. Thus judgment obtained by the creditor against the principal will determine both the principal's and the surety's liability for future interest.[74] The bankruptcy of the principal will put an end to the surety's further liability to pay interest where the surety has become bound while there is any principal debt due,[75] but not where the surety is liable for interest "until payment" on the principal debt.[76] However, the creditor will not be able to prove in the surety's insolvency for interest accruing on the principal debt after the commencement of the insolvency.[77]

Where the creditor's claim against the surety for the principal debt has become time-barred, the creditor may still recover interest from the surety

---

71 *Cook v Fowler* (1874) L.R. 7 H.L. 27 at 37, *per* Lord Selborne.

72 *King v Greenhill* (1843) 6 Man. & G. 59.

73 At 396–397.

74 *Faber v Lathom (Earl)* (1897) 77 L.T. 168; the reason is that the cause of action merges in the judgment, so that interest thereafter accrues pursuant to the rules of court rather than pursuant to the contractual obligation: see *Eagle Star Trustees Ltd v Tai Ping Trading Co Pty Ltd* (unreported, N.S.W. Supreme Court, October 30, 1990).

75 *Re Moss Ex p. Hallett* [1905] 2 K.B. 307, where the surety could not prove for future interest in the principal's bankruptcy to be indemnified in respect of future interest liabilities.

76 *Re FitzGeorge Ex p. Robson* [1905] 1 K.B. 462. The distinction between a guarantee of interest on the principal debt "due" and a guarantee of interest on a principal sum "until payment" is illustrated by *Jowitt v Callaghan* (1938) 38 N.S.W. 512, where the bankruptcy of the principal did not relieve the surety of liability to pay interest on the debt while it remained unpaid by the principal debtor.

77 *Re Amalgamated Investment and Property Co Ltd* [1984] 3 All E.R. 272; and see *Re Standard Insurance Co Ltd (in liq.) and Companies Act 1936* [1970] 1 N.S.W.R. 392.

which had accrued on the principal debt during the period prior to the time-bar attaching, where interest is guaranteed on the same basis as advances of principal.[78] Normally, however, interest is accessory to the principal debt and is not recoverable when a claim for the principal is time-barred.[79]

There is authority that suggests that the surety will be relieved from payment of future interest if the creditor delays in enforcing his rights against the principal.[80] However, this runs contrary to the well-established rule that there is no duty of active diligence by the creditor against the principal under English law,[81] and the decision should be treated with caution.

Liability for costs incurred by the creditor

6–011   Whether the surety is liable for the costs incurred by the creditor in enforcing the principal transaction will turn on the true construction of the guarantee, and of the principal contract. In *Hoole UDC v Fidelity and Deposit Co of Maryland* [1916] 1 K.B. 25, the sureties guaranteed the principal's liability under a building contract. The building contract did not contain any provision to the effect that if the creditor sued the principal the latter, if unsuccessful, would pay the former's legal costs. A dispute arose which was referred to arbitration pursuant to the arbitration clause in the principal contract, and the arbitrator made an award in favour of the creditor which included an order for costs. The arbitration clause had not been strictly complied with, since an arbitrator had been appointed different from the one contemplated by the contract, of which no notice was given to the sureties. The principal's liability did not therefore arise under the principal contract, but under the arbitration award itself, and accordingly the sureties were not liable. Generally, however, where the principal contract, or the guarantee, contains an obligation to pay costs, then the surety will be liable for costs: the *Hoole* case would have had a different result had the arbitration procedure provided for been followed, for then the payment of costs would have been a principal obligation and covered by the guarantee.[82]

The surety will not, however, be liable to pay the costs of a fruitless action by the creditor against the principal where the creditor has given the surety no notice of his intention to sue the principal.[83]

---

78 *Parr's Banking Co v Yates* [1898] 2 Q.B. 460; *cf. Re FitzGeorge Ex p. Robson* [1905] 1 K.B. 462.

79 *Elder v Northcott* [1930] 2 Ch. 422.

80 *Dawson v Raynes* (1826) 2 Russ. 466.

81 See Ch.9, para.9–036: *Wright v Simpson* (1802) 6 Ves. 714.

82 See *Compania Sudamericana de Fletes SA v African Continental Bank Ltd* [1973] 1 Lloyd's Rep. 21, where the surety guaranteed due performance of all obligations under a charterparty, including the arbitration award thereunder and an award of costs; see also *Re Lockey* (1845) 1 P.H. 509.

83 *Baker v Garrett* (1825) 3 Bing. 56.

Where the creditor is obliged to take steps to enforce a security upon the principal's default, the surety will be liable for the costs of doing so where he guarantees the principal's obligations to the creditor in general.[84] Where the costs were reasonably incurred by the creditor in enforcing his rights against the principal, the surety will bear them.[85]

The creditor should ensure, if he wishes to make the surety liable for the costs of enforcing the principal transaction, that there is a clear provision in the guarantee to this effect.

Designation of the parties

Limitation to a particular principal

The guarantee may provide that it is only to be limited to transactions **6–012** undertaken by the creditor with a particular named principal, and if this is the case, the surety will not be liable for obligations undertaken to the creditor by someone other than the named principal. Accordingly, a guarantee which covers advances made to a particular principal will not cover advances to an entity in which the principal is merely a partner or shareholder.[86] The question of the identity of the principal arises most importantly in the context of a change in constitution of the principal, when the surety may be discharged altogether.[87]

Difficulties also arise as to the identity of the principal where mutual guarantees are given, for example, where each company in a group guarantees the liabilities of all the others to a particular creditor. In *Ford & Carter Ltd v Midland Bank Ltd* (1979) 129 N.L.J. 543, HL, each of five companies in a group gave mutual guarantees for the debts of the others, contained in a memorandum signed by all the companies. A sixth company joined the group and signed the memorandum, but the other five companies did not add a fresh signature to the memorandum. It was held by the House of Lords that it was a condition of entering the memorandum that the guarantee would be mutual, and that since the five companies did not give their guarantees to the sixth company, there was no mutuality and it would not be bound by the guarantee it had given by signing the memorandum. It made no difference that the companies were all controlled by one individual: their separate corporate personalities had to be respected, and there was no memorandum in writing from each of them to satisfy s.4 of the Statute of Frauds 1677.

---

84 *Maunsell v Egan* (1846) 9 Ir. Eq. R. 283, where the sureties for a receiver were liable for the costs of the appointment of a new receiver on the discharge of the old; see also *Keily v Murphy* (1837) Sau. & Sc. 479.

85 *Hatch, Mansfield & Co v Weingott* (1906) 22 T.L.R. 366, where the costs incurred by the employer in criminal proceedings against a thieving employee in order to recover property were payable by the surety under a fidelity bond.

86 See for example *Reid Murray Holdings Ltd (in liq.) v David Murray Holdings Pty Ltd* (1972) 5 S.A.S.R. 386.

87 See the discussion in Ch.4 at para.4–013 and see also Ch.9, paras 9–037–9–039.

Limitation to a particular creditor

6–013   Sometimes the creditor who has the benefit of a guarantee gives the consideration for it, such as advances to the principal, through the medium of a subsidiary company for tax or exchange control purposes. This may have the effect that the creditor cannot enforce the guarantee. In *Amalgamated Investment and Property Co Ltd v Texas Commerce International Bank* [1982] Q.B. 84, CA, the plaintiffs were sureties in respect of a loan made to the principal (a company called ANPP) by the defendant bank. The money had been advanced through a subsidiary of the bank called Portsoken, in order to avoid exchange control restrictions.

The terms of the guarantee were that the sureties would guarantee "all moneys which . . . shall . . . be due and owing to [the defendant bank] on any account whatsoever by the principal". On the sureties' liquidation the bank realised securities held by the bank for the sureties' indebtedness in relation to transactions not the subject of the guarantee and sought to apply the proceeds towards the sureties' liability under the guarantee. The sureties' liquidator sought to restrain the bank from taking this course on the grounds that they were not liable under the guarantee because the loan was not owing by ANPP to the bank but to Portsoken. Robert Goff J. was not owing by ANPP to the bank but to Portsoken. Robert Goff J. at first instance accepted this argument, holding that on its true construction the guarantee had been given in respect of ANPP's indebtedness to the bank, and there was no reason to depart from the natural and ordinary meaning of the guarantee.[88] However, the Court of Appeal reversed the decision on this point,[89] holding that the terms of the guarantee were wide enough to include the indebtedness of ANPP to Portsoken, which Portsoken was itself obliged to pass on to the bank. The Court of Appeal had regard to the conduct of the parties in correspondence which showed that the sureties regarded themselves as liable to ensure that the bank was repaid,[90] the conduct of the parties at the time of the transaction,[91] and the fact that Portsoken was merely the alter ego of the bank. The sureties had to pay and could not have their injunction. The decision has been considered to be too liberal in approach, and to ignore the rule that extrinsic evidence is only admissible as an aid to construction of a document where it contains an ambiguity, which this did not.[92]

However, Robert Goff J. and the Court of Appeal were in agreement that the sureties were not entitled to the relief sought because they had conducted themselves throughout on the basis that they would be liable for the loan to ANPP, and the bank had relied on that conduct, so that the sureties were estopped by convention from challenging the claim under the

---

88 [1982] Q.B. 84 at 91.
89 [1982] Q.B. 84 at 118–119 *per* Denning M.R.; 124–125 *per* Eveleigh L.J.; 128–129 *per* Brandon L.J.
90 At 123, *per* Eveleigh L.J.
91 At 118–119, *per* Lord Denning M.R.
92 See O'Donovan & Phillips (*op. cit.*), pp.245–246.

guarantee. This illustrates that the surety's liability under a guarantee may be extended by an estoppel notwithstanding the express words of the instrument.[93]

The effect of the terms of the principal contract

In general, the co-extensiveness principle will mean that, except where he has expressly or by implication limited his liability, the surety's liability to the creditor will be identical in scope with that of the principal. However, there are two important areas in which the surety's liability may be affected by the terms of the principal contract.   **6–014**

Discrepancy between the principal contract and the guarantee
There is very little English authority on this point from which clear guidance can be obtained, but it has been carefully considered in New Zealand. In *Perrott v Newton King Ltd* [1933] N.Z.L.R. 1131, the principal (a mortgagor) was liable to pay interest on the principal sum as long as it remained "unpaid"; the surety was liable under the guarantee to pay arrears of interest while any money remained "owing" on the mortgage. When the principal became bankrupt the surety was held to be released from his liability to pay interest, on the basis that upon the principal's bankruptcy the interest could no longer be said to be "owing". Kennedy J. said that the words in the guarantee and not the words in the principal contract must be taken to define the scope of the surety's liability, and that words in the guarantee could not be taken to have the same meaning as different words in the principal contract.[94] The result would have been different had both instruments used the word "unpaid".   **6–015**

As has been pointed out,[95] this was a case where the words of the guarantee prevailed to reduce the scope of the surety's liability; but Kennedy J. considered that the terms of the guarantee would take priority even if they extended the scope of the surety's liability thereunder.[96] However, it is not easy to see how the surety's liability could be greater in scope than that of the principal unless he was himself liable as a principal or had given an indemnity and not a guarantee.

Where the whole debt is to be paid on principal's default
Difficulties arise where the principal contract provides for the whole amount of the principal debt to be paid in the event of the principal's default, but where the surety guarantees each instalment as it falls due.   **6–016**

---

93 See also *Credit Suisse v Borough Council of Allerdale* [1995] 1 Lloyd's Rep. 315, where Colman J. considered the impact of an estoppel by conduct on a defence based on the Statute of Frauds (at 367–372). Estoppel in this context is discussed in detail at para.6–017 and Ch.3, para.3–031 above.
94 At 1157.
95 See O'Donovan & Phillips (*op. cit.*), pp.255–256.; see O'Donovan & Phillips (English ed., 2003) paras 5–90, 5–91.
96 At 1157–1158.

Again guidance comes from the Australasian cases. In *Parker v Bayly* [1927] G.L.R. 265, the surety guaranteed payment of moneys under a mortgage "whenever the same may under or by virtue of the said memoranda of mortgage ... be due and payable", but the mortgage provided that the entire mortgage debt be repayable upon a default by the principal (the mortgagee). It was held that the guarantee extended only to the instalments as and when they fell due, and not to repayment of the whole sum. The reasoning was that the whole sum was not payable "under or by virtue of" the mortgage but by virtue of a default by the principal. This conclusion was not affected by the presence in the guarantee of a provision deeming the surety to be a principal debtor, since such a provision did not extend the scope of the surety's liability. However, a provision which rendered the surety liable for all the principal's obligation under the principal contract would mean that the surety would be liable for the whole debt upon the principal's default.[97]

Extension of the surety's liability by estoppel

6–017   It is possible for the liability of the surety pursuant to the express contractual terms of a guarantee to be extended by the operation of the doctrine of estoppel. This is acutely illustrated by the case of *Amalgamated Investment and Property Co Ltd v Texas Commerce International Bank* [1982] Q.B. 84, CA, the facts of which have been set out earlier in this chapter, together with the wording of the relevant guarantee.[98] Both Robert Goff J. and the Court of Appeal accepted the contentions of the defendant bank that notwithstanding the words of the guarantee,[99] the sureties were estopped by convention from denying that the true creditors were the defendant bank, and that the loan came within the scope of the guarantee. The parties had proceeded on the basis of an assumption as to certain facts, which were that the sureties were guaranteeing to the bank a loan which was to come from the bank's subsidiary, Portsoken. The bank had relied on the common assumption in acting in a particular way.[1] Brandon L.J. accepted the description of estoppel by convention as follows:

> "This form of estoppel is founded, not on a representation of fact made by a representor and believed by a representee, but on an agreed state of facts, the truth of which has been assumed, by the convention of the parties, as the basis of the transaction into which they are about to enter. When the parties have acted in their transaction upon the agreed assumption that a given state of facts is to be accepted between

---

97 See *Gilmer and Gilmer v Ross* [1932] N.Z.L.R. 507.
98 See para.6–012.
99 As to which Goff J. held that on their true construction the creditor thereunder was not the bank but the bank's subsidiary, on which point the Court of Appeal differed: [1982] Q.B. 84 at 94; at 118–119 *per* Lord Denning M.R.; at 124–125 *per* Eveleigh L.J. and 128–129 *per* Brandon L.J.
1 See [1982] Q.B. 84 *per* Lord Denning M.R. at 121; *per* Brandon L.J. at 131.

them as true, then as regards that transaction each will be estopped against each other from questioning the truth of the statement of facts so assumed."[2]

Accordingly, even if the terms of the instrument of guarantee restrict the liability of the surety to a given principal obligation, or to obligations of a specific principal, or to a specific creditor, the doctrine of estoppel by convention may operate so as to extend the liability of the surety to transactions outside the scope of the written guarantee, or in respect of principals or in favour of creditors not the subject of the written instrument. It is clear that it is not necessary to establish any specific representation or promise in order for this category of estoppel to operate, even though in fact in the *Amalgamated Investment* case there was a representation by the sureties.[3] It was also suggested by Robert Goff J. at first instance[4] that the estoppel may operate to make a guarantee effective even though it would otherwise have no legal effect, so that if the guarantee is unenforceable, for example, for want of consideration, the court may yet give effect to it on the basis that an estoppel operates.[5]

There are a number of aspects of the decision which should be treated with caution. First, it is not altogether clear how a guarantee which has been extended by the operation of estoppel to cover a particular transaction or a particular creditor or principal can be valid if not in writing so as to comply with s.4 of the Statute of Frauds 1677.[6] This point does not appear to have been considered either by Robert Goff J. or by the Court of Appeal in that case, and remains open. There have been subsequent expressions of judicial doubt that a situation could ever arise where the facts gave rise to an estoppel by convention without rendering nugatory the provision of s.4 of the Statute of Frauds. However, in *Credit Suisse v Borough Council of Allerdale* [1995] 1 Lloyd's Rep. 315, at 369–372, Colman J. boldly came to the conclusion, *obiter*, that in appropriate circumstances the creditor would be entitled to raise an estoppel (in that case an estoppel by convention) against a surety to prevent the surety from taking a defence based upon the Statute of Frauds. He held that if, contrary to his primary findings, the consent of a surety to a material variation of the guarantee has to satisfy the requirements of s.4 of the Statute of Frauds, then if the creditor could make out a case of estoppel which would otherwise preclude the surety from raising that defence, he would be entitled to rely on it. He said, at p.371:

---

2 See *ibid.*, at 130–131; see also *per* Lord Denning M.R. at 121; Spencer Bower and Turner, *Estoppel By Representation* (4th ed., 2004), para.VIII.2 at pp.180–184. See also *Hiscox v Outhwaite (No.3)* [1991] 2 Lloyd's Rep. 524; for a recent exposition of the law of estoppel by convention, see *Baird Textile Holdings Ltd v Marks & Spencer Plc* [2002] 1 All E.R. (Comm) 737.
3 See [1982] Q.B. 84 *per* Robert Goff J. at 100.
4 *ibid.*, at 105–107.
5 *ibid.*, at 106.
6 As to which, see Ch.3, para.3–031.

"In as much as s.4 does not strike at the essential validity of a contract of guarantee, I should have held that it did not supersede the court's ability to treat as unconscionable, and therefore to disallow, reliance on discharge of an original guarantee where there has been a giving of time or variation of the principal debt not assented to by the guarantor."

In so holding, Colman J. relied on the dictum of Viscount Radcliffe in *Kok Hoong v Leong Cheong Kweng* [1964] A.C. 993, to the effect that a party could set up an estoppel in the face of a statute which does not strike at essential validity but merely regulates procedure. His approach is also entirely consistent with that of the House of Lords in the more recent case of *Republic of India v India Steamship Co Ltd, The "Indian Grace"* [1993] A.C. 410, in which it was held that a defence based on s.34 of the Civil Jurisdiction and Judgments Act 1982 (essentially a defence of *res judicata*) might be defeated by an estoppel, waiver or contrary agreement. There is much to commend the approach favoured by Colman J. Indeed, it is difficult to justify drawing a distinction between, for example, a surety who has promised not to take a defence based on the Statute of Frauds and thereby induced the creditor to act to his detriment in reliance on that promise, and any other contracting party who promises not to take a defence which is open to him or who acts in a manner which is inconsistent with taking that defence. However, Colman J. was solely concerned with an estoppel which would prevent the surety from taking a defence based on the Statute of Frauds. Like Brooke J. in *Bank of Scotland v Wright* [1991] B.C.L.C.244 he left open the question whether an estoppel by convention could ever affect the terms and scope of a guarantee. In that context, there would appear to be more force in the argument that the application of the doctrine of estoppel, at least estoppel by conduct, would defeat the policy considerations which lie behind s.4 of the Statute of Frauds.[7]

Secondly, there remains a doubt as to the extent to which the doctrine of estoppel by convention can operate to the benefit of a creditor so as to enable him to *enforce* a guarantee in respect of a particular obligation or principal. Traditionally, the scope of the operation of a *promissory* estoppel was as a shield and not as a sword, creating only a defence and not a cause of action.[8] Although on its facts the *Amalgamated Investment* case involved the use by the bank of a defence of estoppel when faced with a claim by the sureties to prevent enforcement of the guarantee, the question of whether the estoppel could be used by the bank in enforcing the guarantee was considered by the Court of Appeal. Eveleigh L.J. doubted that it could be

---

7 See further *Actionstrength Ltd v International Glass Engineering Ltd* [2003] 2 A.C. 541; *Bank of Scotland v Wright* [1991] B.C.L.C. 244; *Coghlan v SH Lock* (1985) 4 N.S.W.L.R. 158; reversed on different grounds (1987) 8 N.S.W.L.R. 88, and see generally the discussion in Ch.3 at para.3–031.
8 See *Combe v Combe* [1951] 2 K.B. 215; *The Proodos C* [1980] 2 Lloyd's Rep. 390; *Brikom Investments Ltd v Seaford* [1981] 1 W.L.R. 863; *Chitty on Contracts* (*op. cit.*), Vol. 1, para.3–098.

so used, since that would involve treating the estoppel "as having the effect of an assumpsit[9]; Brandon L.J. took the view that the bank were not so restricted, although they would have to take the point in their pleading in reply to the sureties" defence that they would not liable on the guarantee on its proper construction.[10] Lord Denning M.R. expressed no view, and accordingly the question remains an open one.[11]

Finally, although Robert Goff J. considered that the estoppel by convention could operate to render an otherwise unenforceable guarantee enforceable, this too remains a matter of doubt. While it is correct that the surety may, by acting in a particular way, waive a defect which makes the guarantee voidable, such as a misrepresentation by the creditor, it is difficult to see how it can render a guarantee which is unenforceable for want of due consideration enforceable without creating an entirely new contract, based, it would seem, on a promissory estoppel. The doctrine of estoppel by convention will not operate to save a contract from essential voidness or invalidity on the grounds, say, of illegality or public policy. Nor will the doctrine of estoppel by convention permit the surety's liability to be extended beyond the liability assumed by the principal which is the subject of the guarantee.[12] There is less difficulty in applying the principles of estoppel by convention in order to limit the surety's liability, notwithstanding widely drafted words in the guarantee.[13]

Extent of the surety's liability: defects in the principal obligation[14]

General principles

As has been explained earlier in this chapter, the guiding principle   **6–018**
applicable to contracts of guarantee is that the liability of the surety is co-extensive with that of the principal. This is because a contract of guarantee is an undertaking to the creditor that the principal will perform his principal obligation.[15] Accordingly, as Lord Selborne said in *Lakeman v Mountstephen* (1874) L.R. 7 H.L. 17 (at 24–25):

---

9 [1982] Q.B. 84 at 126.

10 *ibid.* at 131.

11 See the discussion of this point in *Chitty on Contracts* (*op. cit.*), Vol. 1, paras 3–111 to 3-113, *Hiscox v Outhwaite (No.3)* [1991] 2 Lloyd's Rep. 524. The estoppel was invoked as a defence in *The Vistafjord* [1988] 2 Lloyd's Rep. 343, and in *Shearson Lehman Hutton Inc v Maclaine Watson & Co Ltd* [1989] 2 Lloyd's Rep. 570. See G.H. Treitel, *The Law of Contract* (Sweet & Maxwell, 11th ed., 2003), pp.123–124, where the view is expressed that, like promissory estoppel, estoppel by convention cannot create a new cause of action. See further *Johnson v Gore Wood & Co* [2002] 2 A.C. 1.

12 In *Securum Finance v Ashton* [2002] 2 All E.R. (D) 380, Peter Smith J. said that there was nothing in *Amalgamated Texas* which could lead to the *"bizarre result"* whereby the surety was liable but the principal was not (see para.58).

13 See *National Westminster Finance N.Z. Ltd v National Bank of N.Z. Ltd* [1996] 1 N.Z.L.R. 548.

14 See generally Johan Steyn (*op. cit.*), p.246.

15 *Moschi v Lep Air Services Ltd* [1973] A.C. 331.

". . . until there is a principal debtor, there can be no suretyship. Nor can a man guarantee anyone else's debt unless there is a debt of some other person to be guaranteed."[16]

However, the fact that the principal obligation is in some way defective, either because it is illegal, void, voidable or unenforceable, or because it has been repudiated, will not necessarily release the surety from liability under the guarantee. The surety may find himself liable to the creditor where the principal is not, or under a liability to the creditor different from that of the principal.

Principal obligations which are illegal

6–019   Where the making or the performance of a contract is prohibited by law such that it is void and of no legal effect, the normal result is that the creditor cannot enforce a guarantee of such a contract against the surety. In the case of *Heald v O'Connor* [1971] 1 W.L.R. 497, the defendant bought shares in a company from the plaintiffs for a consideration which was provided by means of a loan by the plaintiffs secured by a debenture creating a floating charge over the assets of the company and which was endorsed with a personal guarantee by the defendant. The plaintiffs sued the defendant on his guarantee and sought summary judgment pursuant to Order 14 of the Rules of the Supreme Court 1965, and it was contended that because the principal contract was illegal and unenforceable because it had involved the provision by the company of financial assistance in breach of s.54 of the Companies Act 1948,[17] the guarantee could not be enforced against him. Fisher J. gave leave to defend on the basis that the guarantee was a contract to pay what principal moneys were due under the debenture, and if the debenture was void then no moneys could be due under it, and so nothing would be due under the guarantee.

The same result will arise where the principal obligation is void for reasons of public policy or on the grounds that it is penal.[18] One analysis of the position is that where the principal obligation cannot be enforced on the grounds that it is entirely void there is no consideration to support the guarantee: this is because quite often the consideration is expressed to be the creditor's entering into or performing (or continuing to perform) the principal contract, and therefore where the principal contract is void, the guarantee is unenforceable for total failure of consideration.[19]

The illegality of the principal obligation will not always discharge the surety. First, there is a view that the creditor who is innocent of the

---

16 See also *Yeoman Credit Ltd v Latter* [1961] 1 W.L.R. 828.
17 Now ss.151–158 of the Companies Act 1985. For a modern example of the application of the principle, see *Anglo Petroleum Ltd v TFB (Mortgages) Ltd* [2003] EWHC 3125, Jack J.
18 See also *Swan v Bank of Scotland* (1836) 10 Bli. (N.S.) 627; *Lougher v Molyneux* [1916] 1 K.B. 718; *De La Rosa v Prieto* (1864) 16 C.B. (N.S.) 578.
19 O'Donovan & Phillips (*op. cit.*), 264; and O'Donovan & Phillips (English ed., 2003), para.5–111.

illegality and who has not participated in it may in certain circumstances still be able to enforce the guarantee against the surety.[20] However, in such a case, the creditor would be able to enforce the principal obligation against the principal as well, and the surety's liability would involve no departure from the co-extensiveness principle. Second, where only certain parts of the principal contract are illegal or contrary to public policy, such as contracts in restraint of trade, such that the court would sever them from the rest of the agreement, leaving the remainder of the contract valid and enforceable, the guarantee would remain similarly enforceable to the same extent, and the surety will be relieved from liability only in respect of the obligation which had been severed.[21]

In *Heald v O'Connor*, Fisher J. distinguished[22] between cases where the surety undertook to pay only those sums which the principal could lawfully be called upon to pay, from cases where the surety undertook to pay those sums which the principal promised to pay, whether he could lawfully be called upon to do so or not. A guarantee will always fall into the former category, and the illegality of the principal obligation will generally absolve the surety from liability, whereas an indemnity may render the surety liable even if the principal contract is void.[23]

Accordingly, the illegality of the principal obligation will render the guarantee of that obligation unenforceable by the creditor against the surety. Where the illegal principal contract can be enforced, the surety will be similarly liable. The principle of co-extensiveness appears, therefore, to operate without exception in the case of illegal principal obligations.

Principal obligations which are void

In accordance with the principle of co-extensiveness, the fact that a principal obligation is void will mean that as a general rule the surety is not liable under his guarantee of the principal's obligations thereunder, for example where the principal obligation is void for uncertainty,[24] or as discussed earlier, for illegality. However, there are a number of different situations in which the general rule does not apply, and the surety will be liable notwithstanding the voidness of the principal obligation.

6–020

Ultra vires

Historically, in England, a contract entered into by a company which was beyond its powers as *ultra vires* was void and of no effect against the company.[25] The position where the contract of suretyship itself is *ultra vires*

6–021

---

20 See G. H. Treitel (*op. cit.*), 484–490; *Archbolds (Freightage) Ltd v Spanglett Ltd* [1961] 1 Q.B. 374; *cf. Mahmoud v Ispahani* [1921] 2 K.B. 716.
21 See *Silverton Ltd v Harvey* [1975] 1 N.S.W.L.R. 659 at 664; *Citicorp Australia Ltd v Hendry* [1985] 4 N.S.W.L.R. 1; *William E Thompson & Associates v Carpenter* (1989) 69 O.R. (2d) 545.
22 [1971] 1 W.L.R. 497, at 506.
23 *Yeoman Credit Ltd v Latter* [1961] 1 W.L.R. 828.
24 *Corser v Commonwealth General Assurance Co Ltd* [1963] N.S.W.R. 225.
25 *Ashbury Railway Carriage and Iron Co Ltd v Riche* [1875] L.R. 7 H.L. 563; and see generally *Palmer's Company Law* (Sweet & Maxwell, 25th ed., 1992), para.2.604.

has been discussed in para.5–049 above. So far as the situation in which underlying obligation guaranteed by a director or other third party is *ultra vires* the company which is the principal in the transaction, matters are slightly more complex. It was established in the nineteenth century that a director's guarantee of a contract *ultra vires* the company was enforceable by the creditor.[26] In *Yorkshire Railway Waggon Co v Maclure* (1881) 19 Ch. D. 478, Kay J. held that the directors of a company who had guaranteed a loan to it *ultra vires* were liable to the creditor. He said (at 491) that "probably the reason in this case for requiring the guarantee was the doubt that existed whether the company could be compelled to pay". It is true that this could have been evidence that the parties intended to enter into a contract of indemnity, where indemnifiers undertake to hold the creditor harmless against loss, and the voidness of the principal contract is irrelevant,[27] as opposed to a guarantee, where the surety guarantees the due performance of the obligations of the principal. However, Kay J. treated the contract as one of guarantee.

In *Garrard v James* [1925] Ch. 616, the directors had guaranteed an *ultra vires* loan to a company in good faith and honestly believing that it was *intra vires*. Lawrence J. held that the directors were liable, holding that although the contract appeared to be one of guarantee, it was intended to bind the directors irrespective of the fact that the company was not legally liable to perform its obligations.[28]

Therefore, even though the court in both these cases held the directors to be sureties as opposed to indemnifiers, the decision to hold the directors liable appears to be based on the evidence of their intention to be bound even though the company may not have been liable. If, as has been suggested,[29] the reality was that the contracts with which the court was concerned in each case were in fact contracts of indemnity and not guarantees, they are of doubtful application to cases involving guarantees and do not illustrate any exception to the co-extensiveness principle. This was the explanation put forward for these cases by Jordan C.J. in *Jowitt v Callaghan* (1938) 38 S.R. (N.S.W.) 512, who also suggested (at 518) that in other cases the directors may be estopped from relying on the *ultra vires* nature of the company's transaction by reason of some implied representation that the company did have the power to enter it.[30]

Whatever the explanation, the principle that a guarantee given by a director of an obligation of a company which is *ultra vires* is nonetheless enforceable against him has found wide acceptance,[31] and has been said to

---

26 *Chambers v Manchester & Milford Ry Co* (1864) 5 B. & S. 588, at 610 *per* Blackburn J. *obiter*.

27 *Yeoman Credit Ltd v Latter* [1961] 1 W.L.R. 828.

28 [1925] 1 Ch. 616, at 619, 622.

29 Johan Steyn (*op. cit.*), at p.250.

30 But see *Ashbury Railway Carriage and Iron Co v Riche* (1875) L.R. 7 H.L. 653. The cases discussed above do not mention any reliance by the creditor on the representations of the directors.

31 See for example Rowlatt, *Principal and Surety* (*op. cit.*), p.131 (para.6–01).

be justifiable on policy grounds, and in particular that a director ought to bear more onerous obligations not least because he is more likely to be acquainted with the powers of the company than is an outsider.[32] It is not clear whether the principle extends to guarantees given by sureties who are not directors, but there is Australian authority to the effect that it does.[33] It has been forcefully suggested that the surety who has no knowledge of the lack of capacity of the principal ought to be released on the grounds of mutual mistake (being mutual to the creditor and the surety), since the mistake goes to the very root of the surety's liability under the guarantee.[34] This would limit the effect of the *ultra vires* exception to those sureties who were not, when they entered the guarantee, under a mistake as to the powers of the principal company.

The operation of this apparent exception to the co-extensiveness principle is now of very little practical interest following the enactment of the Companies Act 1989, ss.108, 109 and 111 of which have effectively put an end to the *ultra vires* doctrine to the extent that it operated to invalidate transactions with third parties. However, the sections have retained the director's personal liability to the company for any loss arising out of *ultra vires* acts.

It should also be noted that the doctrine of *ultra vires* is not confined to companies but may also apply to statutory bodies such as local authorities which exceed the powers given to them by the statute. A recent example is to be found in the cases of *Credit Suisse v Borough Council of Allerdale* [1996] 4 All E.R. 129, *Credit Suisse v Waltham Forest LBC* [1996] 4 All E.R. 176, and *L.B. Sutton v Morgan Grenfell & Co Ltd* [1997] 6 Bank. L.R. 156, CA, where the giving of the guarantee itself was in each case *ultra vires* the local authority. It is not inconceivable, however, that a guarantee might be given for the performance by a local authority of obligations under a contract entered into by the local authority in excess of its statutory powers. See further the discussion at para.5–049, above.

Minors' contracts[35]

In *Wauthier v Wilson* (1911) 27 T.L.R. 582, the creditor had lent money to a   **6–022** minor, whose father had given a promissory note to the creditor as a surety. Although the debt was void under the provisions of the Infants Relief Act 1874, Pickford J. held that the principle in *Yorkshire Ry v Maclure (above)*[36] applied universally to all void debts and that the father was not released

---

32 Johan Steyn (*op. cit.*), p.251.
33 See *Australia Joint Stock Bank v Croudace* (1899) 20 L.R. (N.S.W.) 361, where the mayor and aldermen of a principality guaranteed its bank overdraft which was *ultra vires* the principality's powers, and the guarantee was enforceable. But like directors, they would have known of the ambit of the principality's *vires*. *Quaere*, therefore, where the surety is wholly unfamiliar with the principal company's constitution.
34 See McGuiness, *The Law of Guarantee (op. cit.)*, para.3.12, n.42; *Bell v Lever Bros Ltd* [1932] A.C. 161.
35 See generally E. J. Cohn, "Validity of Guarantees for Debts of Minors" (1947) 10 M.L.R. 40.
36 See para.6–021.

from liability under the note. The Court of Appeal[37] appears to have expressed disapproval of any universal application of a principle whereby the void nature of the principal contract does not release the surety but affirmed the decision on the ground that the father's contract was one of indemnity.

In *Coutts & Co v Browne-Lecky* [1947] K.B. 104, where an adult had guaranteed the overdraft of a minor with a bank, Oliver J. followed *Swan v Bank of Scotland*[38] and held that since the overdraft was absolutely void under the provisions of the Infants Relief Act 1874, the guarantee was unenforceable by the bank: *Wauthier v Wilson* (above) was not followed. Oliver J. (at 111) distinguished the *ultra vires* cases from cases where the principal obligation is rendered void by the express provisions of a statute. The decision has been criticised[39] in particular on the ground that the provisions of the Infants Relief Act 1874 afforded a personal privilege to the minor that was open to him and nobody else. While there are strong arguments as a matter of law and policy for holding liable a surety who guaranteed the debts of a minor in the knowledge of his minority, it is submitted that different considerations might apply where the surety was ignorant of the minority of the principal.[40] In those circumstances there is an argument that the surety should be released from the guarantee on the grounds of mistake, since the capacity of the principal goes to the root of the guarantee.[41] *Coutts & Co v Browne-Lecky* has been followed in Australia and New Zealand.[42] Further, in *Stadium Finance Co Ltd v Helm* (1965) 109 S.J. 447, where a finance company had hired a car to a minor under a hire-purchase agreement which had been co-signed by his mother, the Court of Appeal held that she was a surety for the minor, and not an indemnifier, and that because the minor was not liable under the principal contract she could not be liable under the guarantee. It appears from the judgment of Denning M.R. in the transcript[43] that in fact it was conceded by the finance company that a guarantee of a minor's void debt is unenforceable, and so it may be said to be authority for the proposition that the surety is not liable even where he or she knew of the principal's incapacity.

However, the Court of Appeal in England has expressed doubts about the decision in *Coutts & Co v Browne-Lecky*,[44] and the correctness of the principle that the surety is not liable for the void debts of a minor therefore remains open to question. Certainly it has been authoritatively suggested that where the surety knows of the incapacity, he ought to be liable on the guarantee.[45]

---

37 (1912) 28 T.L.R. 239.
38 (1836) 10 Bli. (N.S.) 627.
39 E. J. Cohn (*op. cit.*), 40.
40 See Johan Steyn (*op. cit.*), p.252, n.31.
41 See para.6–021 above and para.6–025 below.
42 See *Alliance Acceptance Co Ltd v Hinton* (1964) 1 D.C.R. (N.S.W.) 5; *Robinson's Motor Vehicles Ltd v Graham* [1956] N.Z.L.R. 545.
43 CAT No.137A of 1965, p.2.
44 *Argo Caribbean Group v Lewis* [1976] 2 Lloyd's Rep. 289.
45 Johan Steyn (*op. cit.*), pp.246, 253.

The above discussion is of limited application following the enactment of the Minors Contracts Act 1987. Section 1 of that Act repealed the Infants Relief Act 1874, with the effect that the previous common law rules relating to infants now apply.[46] Section 2 of the Act provides that where a guarantee is given in respect of an obligation of a party to a contract made after the commencement of the Act[47] and the obligation is unenforceable against him (or he repudiates the contract) because he was a minor when the contract was made, the guarantee shall not for that reason alone be unenforceable against the surety. It is not clear whether the surety who has paid the creditor has a right of indemnity against the minor principal. The Law Commission Report on Minors' Contracts.[48] suggested that there was a right of recovery only where the minor could, under the common law rules, have been sued by the original creditor.

Void under other statutes

It may be that the principal obligation is rendered void by operation of some other statutory provision, such as, for example, s.127 of the Insolvency Act 1986, which makes void any disposition of the company's property made after the commencement of the winding up. In *Coutts & Co v Stock* [2000] 1 W.L.R. 906, Lightman J. considered the position of the surety for a principal obligation that was rendered void by s.127.[49] He held that a provision in the guarantee which stipulated that the guarantor's liability was not to be affected by "legal limitation, bar or restriction, disability, incapacity or want of borrowing powers of the debtor" did not cover a situation where the principal obligation had been validly incurred but subsequently retrospectively invalidated. He said that "the clearest language is required to impose on a guarantor liabilities of the principal debtor in cases where statute has decreed that the liability of the principal debtor shall be void".

6–023

Principal obligations which are voidable

Obligations voidable by reason of the creditor's conduct

Where the principal obligation is voidable at the suit of the principal because of the act of the creditor, such as his misrepresentation or undue influence, the surety will be discharged *ab initio* where the principal elects to rescind the principal contract. So, for example, where the principal has an accrued right to rescind a contract for the sale of land under a statutory provision, which he exercises, the surety will be automatically discharged.[50] More difficult questions arise where the principal elects not to rescind the contract but affirms it or waives his right to rescind. There is no authority in

6–024

---

46 As to which see *Chitty on Contracts* (*op. cit.*), Vol. 1, para.8–005ff.
47 This came into force on June 9, 1987.
48 Law Com. 134.
49 His analysis was *per incuriam*, because he had already decided that s.127 did not avoid the principal obligation.
50 *Insurance Office of Australia Ltd v TM Burke Pty Ltd* (1935) 35 N.S.W. 438.

English law which affords any guidance, but writers have advanced a number of different views. At one end of the scale is the view that where the principal has elected to affirm a voidable contract, the surety should not be entitled to take advantage of the defence that was open to the principal so as to avoid liability.[51] It has also been said that there is a fundamental difference between the situation where the principal contract is voidable because of the creditor's fraud and where it is voidable because of his innocent misrepresentation; in the case of the former, the surety ought to be released from liability because otherwise the creditor would be able to rely on his own fraud, but in the case of the latter he should not be released.[52]

At the other end of the scale, it has been said that the surety should be allowed to rely on the principal's right to rescind the contract, including a right to rescind for misrepresentation, since he should not be subject to the caprice of the (possibly insolvent) principal from whom he may not be able to recover under his right to an indemnity.[53]

It is submitted that the better view is that the surety is not able, once the principal has elected to affirm to contract, or has waived the right to rescind, to escape liability to the creditor on the grounds of the initial voidability of the principal contract. First, the right to elect is a privilege enjoyed by the principal, and he should be free to exercise this right unencumbered by the possibility that his surety may seek to avoid liability. The principal ought not to have to consult with the surety before making the election. Indeed, there may be commercial advantages to the principal in affirming the contract which may well become unavailable in the absence if the surety ceased to be liable under his guarantee, especially where it is a condition of the principal contract that it is guaranteed.

Secondly, the surety suffers no perceived prejudice by the act of the principal in affirming the contract. He loses no rights against the creditor,[54] and there is no reason to suppose that the enforcement by the surety of his right of indemnity against the principal would be any the more difficult or that the indemnity would be any the less valuable. Indeed, the surety may be in a better position to enforce the indemnity if, as a result of the election to affirm the principal contract, the principal obtains a commercial advantage.

Thirdly, it has been held that the surety is unable to rely upon the right of the principal to counterclaim for unliquidated damages in defence to the creditor's claim under the guarantee where the principal is not before the court.[55] To allow the surety to escape liability under a guarantee of a

---

51 S. Williston, *A Treatise on the Law of Contracts* (3rd ed., 1957), s.1218.
52 Johan Steyn (*op. cit.*), pp.246, 257, where the view was expressed that there is a "fundamental policy consideration that it is in the interests of commerce that the effectiveness of guarantees be upheld unless there are compelling reasons for sanctioning a departure from the general rule".
53 Law Reform Commission of British Columbia, *Report on Guarantees of Consumer Debts* (1979), 86–89.
54 As to which, see Ch.11.
55 *Cellulose Products Pty v Truda* (1970) 92 W.N. (N.S.W.) 561 and see Ch.11, para.11–007 and n.90 below.

contract which has been affirmed by the principal would be inconsistent with this view.

Obligations voidable by reason of the principal's lack of capacity

As has been discussed earlier in this chapter, the prevailing view is that   **6–025** where the principal contract is entered by a minor who lacks capacity, it is void under statute and the surety is not liable, although this is questionable where the surety knew of the lack of capacity when he entered the guarantee. However, where the principal contract is entered by the principal under a disability, such as drunkenness or mental disability, difficulties arise. Where this is the case, the contract is voidable by the principal if the creditor knew that the principal was under the disability, and if the principal did not know what he was doing at the time he entered the contract.[56]

It has been suggested that where the surety guarantees a liability of one under a disability, as opposed to the victim of a fraud or misrepresentation, the intention will be present that he should be liable as a principal, whether the principal was liable or not.[57] However, the authorities given for this view are those which either are expressly decided, or are at least explicable, on the basis that the secondary contract in question was an indemnity and not a guarantee.[58]

There is no authority in English law as to the position where the secondary contract is truly a guarantee and the principal was under a disability when he entered the principal contract. It has been suggested[59] that where the surety did not know that the principal was under a disability when he entered the principal contract, the surety ought not to be liable either where the principal contract is avoided on this ground, or where the contract is affirmed by the principal. Where the surety did know, he should remain liable. There is much to be said for this view on policy grounds and as a matter of legal principle, but the point remains open for judicial consideration.

Principal obligations which are unenforceable

Where the principal contract is time-barred

The situation may arise where the creditor's claim against the principal is   **6–026** barred by the provisions of the Limitation Act 1980, but is not so barred against the surety. This will occur where the creditor has omitted to sue the principal during the limitation period, but has not done anything yet to set

---

56 *Molton v Camroux* (1848) 2 Exch. 487; (1849) 4 Exch. 17; *York Glass Co Ltd v Jubb* (1925) 42 T.L.R. 1; *Hart v O'Connor* [1985] A.C. 1000; *Chitty on Contracts* (*op. cit.*), Vol. 1, paras 8–064, 8–074.

57 Rowlatt, *Principal and Surety* (Sweet & Maxwell, 5th ed., 1999).

58 *Wauthier v Wilson* (1911) 27 T.L.R. 582; *Chambers v Manchester and Mildford Ry Co* (1864) 5 B. & S. 588; *Yorkshire Railway Waggon Co v Maclure* (1881) 19 Ch. D. 478; *Garrard v James* [1925] Ch. 616.

59 Johan Steyn (*op. cit.*), p.259.

time running as against the surety, such as making a demand,[60] or where the principal debt is an ordinary debt with a limitation period of six years, but the guarantee is under seal and has a limitation period of twelve years.[61] In a case where the claim against the principal is time-barred but the claim against the surety is not, the surety will remain liable on the guarantee. This is because "the mere omission to sue does not discharge the surety, because the surety can himself set the law in operation against the debtor".[62] The surety has it in his own hands to set the law in operation against the principal, by compelling him to pay off the principal debt,[63] or by himself making payment to the creditor (or into court) and claiming an indemnity against the principal.

Where he pays the principal debt, the surety remains entitled to sue the principal for an indemnity even though the creditor's claim against him is time-barred, and where the creditor did not sue the surety until after the expiry of the limitation period attaching to the principal contract.[64]

Where the principal contract fails to comply with a statutory requirement

6–027   Where the principal contract is unenforceable because it fails to comply with a statutory requirement, such as contracts for the sale of land,[65] the position is not so clear. In *Eldridge and Morris v Taylor* [1931] 2 K.B. 416, the principal contract was unenforceable because it failed to comply with the requirements of the Money Lenders Act 1927. The Court of Appeal held that because the principal contract had gone, the surety was also discharged. Greer L.J.'s analysis was that the failure on the part of the creditor was analogous to the giving of time to the principal, which discharged the surety;[66] Scrutton and Slesser L.JJ. were of the rather more dogmatic view that the fact that the principal was not liable meant that the surety was not liable either.[67]

In *Temperance Loan Fund Ltd v Rose* [1932] 2 K.B. 522, the same Court of Appeal considered a similar problem under the same Act. However, the conclusion was reached that the surety was not liable solely on the ground that in that case the guarantee was embodied in a promissory note, action upon which was specifically prohibited by the Act in the circumstances.[68] Slesser and Greer L.JJ. agreed, the latter adding that he was bound by the decision in *Eldridge and Morris v Taylor* (above), and that if the surety were held liable in the circumstances, then the statute would give a defence to the principal, who has had the money, but not to the surety, who has not.[69]

---

60 See Ch.7, para.7–005.
61 Limitation Act 1980, s.8.
62 *Carter v White* (1884) 25 Ch. D. 666.
63 See Ch.10, paras 10–25–10–28.
64 *Wolmershausen v Gullick* [1893] 2 Ch. 514; *Hampton v Minns* [2002] 1 W.L.R. 1.
65 Under the Law of Property Act 1925, s.40, as replaced by the Law of Property (Miscellaneous Provisions) Act 1989, s.2.
66 [1931] 2 K.B. 416 at 422.
67 *ibid.* at 422, 423.
68 Namely the absence of a memorandum in writing complying with the Act: see [1932] 2 K.B. 522 at 529–530 *per* Scrutton L.J.
69 [1932] 2 K.B. 522, 531.

In these cases, the unenforceability of the guarantees was entirely justifiable, and the policy of the enactment in question appears to have been that the creditor acted at his peril in not ensuring compliance with its terms. However, it would be dangerous to assume that these cases are necessarily authority that the unenforceability of the principal contract renders every guarantee likewise unenforceable. Each contract and the ground of its unenforceability must be examined on a case-by-case basis.

If the surety pays the principal debt where it is unenforceable by the creditor, the principal has no defence to a claim against him for an indemnity by the surety on those grounds, at least where the basis of the claim for indemnity lies in a contract (express or implied) between the surety and the principal: see *Re Chetwynd's Estate* [1938] Ch. 13. This will not be the case where the surety would have had his own defence to a claim by the creditor under the guarantee: see, *e.g. Re Morris, Coneys v Morris* [1922] 1 I.R. 81, where both the principal and the surety had limitation defences against the creditor.[70]

Provisions preserving liability where the principal contract is defective

A modern guarantee may contain a provision that the surety is to remain **6–028** liable notwithstanding defects in the principal contract rendering it void, voidable or unenforceable. Such a provision may take the form of a "principal debtor" clause which deems the surety to be liable as a principal. In *Heald v O'Connor* [1971] 1 W.L.R. 497, Fisher J. held[71] that the effect of such a clause did not preserve the surety's liability where the principal contract was void for illegality; it did not convert the contract of guarantee into a contract of indemnity. The purpose of the provision was merely to allow the creditor to preserve his rights against the surety in the event that he released or gave time to the principal, where such indulgences would, without this provision, discharge the surety.[72]

However, where the guarantee contains a clause purporting to keep the surety liable notwithstanding the fact that the principal contract is defective, the surety may remain liable. This is either because the contract is one of indemnity, or because the surety is estopped from denying his liability by reason of defects in the principal contract.[73] If such a clause is to be used in

---

70 See further O'Donovan & Phillips (*op. cit.*), p.598, and the discussion there.
71 At 503.
72 As to which see Ch.9, paras 9–010 and 9–029–9–034, see also *MS Fashions Ltd v Bank of Credit and Commerce International Ltd* [1993] Ch. 425, where Hoffmann L.J. (delivering judgment at first instance), reached the same view. *Cf. Canadian Imperial Bank of Commerce v Patel* (1990) 66 D.L.R. (4th) 720, where there was no principal debtor. See also Ch.13, paras 13–019–13–021 below and the discussion of principal debtor clauses in the context of insolvency set-off in *BCCI (No.8)* [1998] A.C. 214.
73 See *Alliance Acceptances Co v Hinton* (1964) 1 D.C.R. (N.S.W.) 5, where this analysis was deployed in relation to a guarantee of principal contract entered by a minor, where the guarantee provided that the surety's liability would not be impaired by reason of the principal being under a disability.

the guarantee, it should be wide enough to cover all the circumstances which may render the principal contract void, voidable or unenforceable. However, this provision, no matter how widely drawn, will not preserve the liability of the surety where the consideration for the guarantee is the act of the creditor in entering or performing the principal contract, or where the guarantee itself is rendered voidable by reason of the surety's mistake as to the principal's capacity to enter the contract.[74] In such cases there will be no guarantee to which such terms can apply.

Extent of the surety's liability: breach of the principal contract by the creditor or principal

Breach of the principal contract by the creditor

6–029　　Where the creditor has committed a repudiatory breach of contract, or is in breach of a condition of that contract, entitling the principal to terminate the contract and be discharged from any further liability, the surety will be likewise discharged from further liability under his guarantee in the event that the principal accepts the repudiation.[75] Where the principal elects to affirm the principal contract or waives the breach, it is submitted that, for the reasons already discussed earlier in this chapter in relation to contracts voidable at the suit of the principal, the surety will remain liable.[76]

Where the creditor has committed a non-repudiatory breach of the principal contract sounding in damages only, the surety will not be discharged unless it involves a "not unsubstantial" departure from a term of the principal contract which has itself been incorporated into the guarantee.[77]

Discharge of the surety in these circumstances is explicable on the basis of a variation of the surety's obligations.[78] Generally, the surety's rights are restricted to the possible ability to utilise the principal's counterclaim or set-off arising out of the creditor's breach in defence of the creditor's claim against him under the guarantee.[79]

Breach of the principal contract by the principal

6–030　　The general rule is that where the principal commits a breach of the principal contract, the surety will be liable to the creditor for the amount representing the damages payable by the principal in respect of the breach.

---

74 As to which, see para.6–025.
75 See Ch.9, para.9–017, and see *Ankhar Pty Ltd v National Westminster Finance (Australia) Ltd* (1987) 162 C.L.R. 549. The principal, and so the surety, will remain liable for any obligation accrued due prior to the acceptance of the repudiation: *Hirji Mulji v Cheong Yue Steamship Co* [1926] A.C. 497, 510.
76 See para.6–025.
77 See *National Westminster Bank v Riley* [1986] B.C.L.C. 268 (especially at 275–276). See also *The Mercers Company v New Hampshire Insurance Co* [1992] 2 Lloyd's Rep. 365.
78 As to which see generally Ch.9.
79 But there are limitations to the exercise of this right: see Ch.11, para.11–007, see also Johan Steyn (*op. cit.*), pp.261–264.

In *Moschi v Lep Air Services Ltd* [1973] A.C. 331,[80] where the performance of the principal contract to pay a sum of money by instalments was guaranteed by the surety, the House of Lords held that it was not open to a surety to say that he had only guaranteed performance of the contract, and not guaranteed to pay damages. Where the surety had guaranteed the performance of the principal contract (as opposed to payment of an instalment due under it) and the principal failed to perform the principal contract, he not only broke his own contract but put the surety in breach of his contract of guarantee: the surety was in breach of his undertaking to ensure that the principal performs the principal contract, and he became liable to the creditor to pay damages.[81]

In such a case, the liability of the surety is co-extensive with that of the principal, in that both are liable to pay damages for breach of contract, and the measure of the principal's liability is also the measure of that of the surety.[82] However, this principal appears to have found an exception where the principal obligation guaranteed is to pay a sum of money by instalments, and certain instalments become accrued due prior to the termination of the contract by reason of the principal's breach in not paying.[83] This is what happened in *Hyundai Shipbuilding & Heavy Industries v Pournaras* [1978] 2 Lloyd's Rep. 502.

In that case the principals were buyers of four ships which were to be built and sold by the plaintiffs, a Korean shipyard. The four principal contracts provided for payment of the contract price by five instalments. The sum of US $1.25 million had been prepaid, and would be applied to the first instalments due under each contract. The contracts were guaranteed by the defendants as follows: "In consideration of your entering into the shipbuilding contract . . . the [defendant] hereby irrevocably and unconditionally guarantees the payment in accordance with the terms of the contract of all sums due or to become due by the buyer to you under the contract and in case the buyer is in default of any such payment the [defendant] will forthwith make the payment in default on behalf of the buyer." There was a default in payment by the buyers and the amount of the prepayments was insufficient to cover the whole of the first instalments payable under the four contracts, and the shipyard sued, treating the contracts as at an end.

Roskill L.J., with whose judgment Stephenson L.J. agreed, held, applying the words of Lords Reid and Diplock[84] in *Moschi v Lep Air Services*, that

---

80 See further Ch.4, para.4–014; Ch.9, paras 9–019–9–020.

81 See the speech of Lord Reid at 343. See also *Nangus Pty Ltd v Charles Donovan Pty Ltd (in liq.)* [1989] V.R. 184; *Womboin Pty Ltd v Savannah Island Trading Pty Ltd* (1990) 19 N.S.W. L.R. 364; *Astilleros Espanoles SA v Bank of America National Trust & Savings Assocn* [1995] 2 Ll. Rep. 352, CA.

82 See *per* Lord Diplock at 349 (quoted in Ch.4, para.4–014).

83 See the speech of Lord Reid at 344–345. The distinction between a promise by a surety that the principal will pay an instalment, and a promise that he will perform the principal contract, is discussed in *NRG Vision Ltd v Churchfield Leasing Ltd* [1988] B.C.L.C. 624; see also *Sunbird Plaza Ltd v Maloney* (1988) 166 C.L.R. 245 and in particular the judgment of Mason C.J. at 255–256; *Keene v Devine* [1986] W.A.R. 217.

84 Respectively at 343 and 350.

the termination of the contract because of the buyers' repudiation, although sounding in damages, did not deprive the yard of the benefit of accrued rights to payment from the buyers, and so the fact that the contracts had come to an end did not free the sureties from their liability in respect of accrued instalments.[85] It was implicit in the judgment that the buyers were also liable to pay the accrued instalments, and there is nothing in this part of the judgment which undermines the co-extensiveness principle.

However, Roskill L.J. went on to state, *obiter*, that even though the buyers could arguably recover the US $1.25 million prepaid[86] to the yard notwithstanding their own repudiatory breach on the basis of the decision of Stable J. in *Dies v International Mining & Finance Corpn Ltd* [1939] 1 K.B. 724,[87] in reduction of their liability, this was not a defence or cross-claim which was open to the sureties.[88] The reasoning underlying this conclusion is, with respect, sparse and appears to be that the commercial purpose of the guarantee was to enable the yard to recover from the sureties even if they could not recover from the buyers, and that to give the sureties the benefit of this defence would nullify the commercial utility of this particular form of guarantee.[89] If Roskill L.J. was determining that, as a matter of construction, the contract in question was really to be regarded as an indemnity, this conclusion would be defensible, but the reasoning hardly justifies such a major derogation from the principle of co-extensiveness if the contract was indeed a guarantee.

This aspect of the case is therefore rather more debatable. There is certainly authority to the effect that the surety may not, in his defence of a claim under the guarantee, take advantage of a cross-claim for *unliquidated* damages which the principal has against the creditor.[90] However, the general rule is that the surety may take advantage of whatever defence is

---

85 At 507, Col. 2. Although not spelt out in the judgment, the reason for this is that a repudiation puts an end to the contract in so far as it is executory, but does not discharge the parties *ab initio*: see *McDonald v Denny Lascelles Ltd* (1933) 48 C.L.R. 457, *per* Dixon J. at 476–468 cited with approval in *Rover International Ltd v Cannon Film Sales Ltd (No.3)* [1989] 3 All E.R. 423 *per* Kerr L.J. at 438. See also *Hirji Mulji v Cheong Yue Steamship Co* [1926] A.C. 497 at 510.

86 Prepayments must be distinguished from deposits: the latter are forfeitable on default, whereas the former may or may not be forfeitable, depending on the construction of the contract: see Goff and Jones, *The Law of Restitution* (5th ed., 1998), pp.535–540.

87 Roskill L.J. expressly did not approve this decision, but proceeded on the assumption that it was correctly decided, saying that the "arguments advanced by Mr Morris K.C. and Mr Denning K.C. (as those two distinguished gentlemen then were) were not without considerable merit": see pp.507–508. The decision was applied directly in *Rover International Ltd v Cannon Film Sales Ltd (No.3)* [1989] 3 All E.R. 423 *per* Kerr L.J. at 440.

88 At 508.

89 *ibid.*

90 *Cellulose Products Pty Ltd v Truda* (1970) 92 W.N. (N.S.W.) 561. See also *Covino v Bandag Manufacturing Pty Ltd* [1983] 1 N.S.W.L.R. 237; *Indrisie v General Credits Ltd* [1985] V.R. 251; *National Westminster Bank Plc v Skelton* [1993] 1 W.L.R. 72; *Ashley Guarantee Plc v Zacaria* [1993] 1 W.L.R. 62; *Elkhoury v Farrow Mortgage Services Pty Ltd (in liq.)* (1993) 114 A.L.R. 541; *Beri Distributors v Pulitano* (1994) 10 S.R. (W.A.) 274; *Trafalgar House Construction (Regions) Ltd v General Surety & Guarantee Co Ltd* [1996] A.C. 199 and see generally Ch.11, para.11–007 on this point.

open to the principal against the creditor,[91] and in the case of the buyers in the *Pournaras* case, their cross-claim based on *Dies* was not one for unliquidated damages, but a claim for a liquidated sum in restitution. Further, if the analysis of the right of restitution in *Dies* is that the prepayments are recoverable in the circumstances where the innocent party is discharged because there has been a total failure of consideration in relation thereto,[92] then it could be argued that the guarantee itself was *pro tanto* unenforceable as not supported by consideration. This is because the consideration given by the creditor for the guarantee is the performance by the creditor of his obligations under the principal contract.

The decision in *Pournaras* was followed shortly afterwards by the House of Lords in *Hyundai Shipbuilding and Heavy Industries Co Ltd v Papadopoulos* [1980] 1 W.L.R. 1129, which dealt with a guarantee in virtually identical terms, and a very similar shipbuilding contract providing for payment of five instalments by the buyers. The shipbuilding contract also contained a clause permitting the yard to cancel the contract where the buyers were in default of payment of any instalment. The buyers failed to pay the second instalment and the yard exercised their rights of cancellation and sued the sureties for the second instalment. It was argued that since the contract had been cancelled pursuant to its terms, there was at that point no accrued right to the second instalment which had become due before the date of the cancellation. This argument was based on the decision of Stable J. in *Dies* and was to the effect that since the first instalment was recoverable by the buyers, and the second would have been likewise recoverable had it been paid prior to the cancellation, there was no claim for the second instalment even though unpaid at the date of the cancellation. Viscount Dilhorne and Lords Edmund-Davies and Fraser held (Lords Russell and Keith dissenting) that the exercise of the contractual right to cancel did not destroy the yard's accrued rights to recover the amount of the second instalment, unless the contract specifically provided for it. They distinguished *Dies* on the basis that it related to a contract for sale of goods, whereas the shipbuilding contract resembled a building contract,[93] and it was assumed that "the increasing proportions of the contract price represented by the five instalments bore some relation to the anticipated rate of [the yard's] expenditure", and that the yard had carried out their part of the bargain up until the date of the cancellation.[94] Further, the majority of their Lordships applied the reasoning deployed in *Pournaras* that the right to recover the prepayment would defeat the commercial utility of the guaran-

---

91 See now *BOC Group Plc v Centeon* [1999] 1 All E.R. (Comm) 970, affirming [1999] 1 All E.R. 53; [1999] 63 Com.L.R. 104.
92 Although in *Hyundai Shipbuilding and Heavy Industries v Papadopoulos* [1980] 1 W.L.R. 1129, Viscount Dilhorne said (at 1134) that was not the basis of Stable J.'s decision in *Dies*, it appears to be suggested in *Rover International Ltd v Cannon Film Sales Ltd (No.3)* [1989] 3 All E.R. 423, 439, 440 *per* Kerr L.J., and further, Viscount Dilhorne's conclusion at 1136A–B is based, at least in part, on this analysis.
93 See 1134, *per* Viscount Dilhorne; 1148–1149 *per* Lord Fraser.
94 At 1148 *per* Lord Fraser.

tee.[95] In holding that the yard could recover the accrued instalment from the sureties, reliance was placed on what was said by Megaw L.J. in *Moschi v Lep Air Services Ltd* in the Court of Appeal.[96]

Papadopoulos was revisited by the House of Lords in *Stocznia Gdanska v Latvian Shipping Co* [1998] 1 W.L.R. 574, a case not actually concerned with the liability of sureties for instalments, but with the rights of the yard directly against the buyers. They held (unanimously) that the buyers were liable for an accrued instalment notwithstanding the exercise by the yard of its contractual right to rescind. They followed, in particular, the reasoning of Lord Fraser in *Papadopoulos* (at 1148–1149) that shipbuilding contracts are not simply contracts of sale and decided that the consideration for the instalment was not simply the sale of the ship, but also the undertaking by the yard of her design and construction. The buyers' argument that the instalment was not payable on the grounds that the construction for it had wholly failed was rejected: the true test was not whether the promisee received a specific benefit, but whether the promisor had performed any part of the contractual duties in respect of which payment was due.

Again, the *ratio* of the decision in *Papadopoulos* does not involve any radical departure from the co-extensiveness principle: the sureties were liable for the accrued but unpaid second instalment in the same way as the buyers were liable for it, notwithstanding the termination of the contract.[97] However, Viscount Dilhorne went rather further, and held that even if the cancellation had deprived the yard of their accrued rights to the second instalment, this would not similarly deprive the yard of its right of recourse against the sureties for that instalment.[98] This view does not seem to be supported by any authority, apart from the *obiter dicta* of Roskill L.J. in *Pournaras*, and this is certainly not what *Moschi v Lep Air Services* decided.

In considering this issue, it is important to remember that the principle in *Dies* is of very limited practical application. If a contract provides for the consideration to be paid by instalments in advance, and in breach of contract the payments cease, the ability of the party in default to recover any instalments already paid or resist liability to pay any instalments which have prima facie accrued, will depend on whether there has been any consideration or part-performance.[99] Consequently, in the case of a ship-building contract, there will almost invariably be a complete answer to an argument based on *Dies*, and this was so in both the *Hyundai* cases.

Secondly, even in a case in which the principal does have a right to recover instalments already paid or resist payment of instalments which have prima facie accrued, on the grounds of total failure of consideration, the principal and the surety will remain liable in damages for the breach of

---

95 See *per* Viscount Dilhorne at 1137–1138; Lord Edmund-Davies at 1143; Lord Fraser at 1152.
96 [1971] 1 W.L.R. 934 at 941.
97 See especially 1137F, *per* Viscount Dilhorne.
98 At 1137F–H.
99 See generally *Rover International Ltd v Cannon Film Sales Ltd (No.3)* [1989] 3 All E.R. 423, especially *per* Kerr L.J. at 432–433.

contract. Those damages may be measured in whole or in part by reference to the amount of the accrued instalments. Thus it is possible to envisage a situation in which the right to recover the instalments is of no practical effect because the damages are equivalent or greater (*e.g.* a substantial claim for loss of profits).

The problem therefore only arises squarely in the limited type of case, such as *Rover v Cannon* itself, where the damages are negligible and there has been a total failure of consideration for the advance payments. In such a case, there can be no justification for creating a situation in which the surety remains liable for the instalments in circumstances in which the principal is not, unless the contract on its true construction is to be regarded as one of indemnity rather than one of guarantee. It is submitted, with the greatest respect, that the suggestion that the surety may be liable for accrued instalments in circumstances in which the principal is not, is plainly wrong and should not be followed.

Both *Pournaras* and *Papadopoulos* were distinguished by Rix J. and the Court of Appeal in *BOC Group Plc v Centeon LLC* [1999] 1 All E.R. (Comm) 970, [1999] 1 All E.R. 53. In that case, the guarantee was for the purchase price of the share capital of a company sold to the principal. The principal refused to pay the third of three instalments of the purchase price on the grounds that the vendor had committed various repudiatory breaches of warranty, and the vendor sued the surety under the guarantee. The warranties had been given not only to the purchaser but also to the surety. Rix. J. held that the guarantee was not intended to make the surety liable to an extent beyond the liability to make payment on the due date of the purchase. If the purchaser had a set-off which entitled him to withhold payment on the due date, so did the surety. In any event, the surety had its own separate defence of set-off arising out of its claim for breach of the warranties given to it.

Chapter 7

Enforcement of Contracts of Suretyship

Introduction

7–001 A creditor who wishes to enforce a contract of guarantee or indemnity against the surety will need to take into account a number of legal and practical considerations before he commences proceedings. First, he has to ensure that his cause of action has accrued, which involves ensuring that all relevant conditions precedent to the surety's liability have been fulfilled. A related matter of concern will be whether or not the action is time-barred. Secondly, he must address the question of jurisdiction: this may be something which is predetermined in the contract, but if it is not, he will need to consider which available forum is the most appropriate for his requirements. Thirdly, he must ensure that he has title to sue, and that all the necessary parties to the action are joined. Fourthly, he must prove his case. Finally, there may be a number of miscellaneous matters to take into consideration in choosing what type of proceedings he should take. These considerations may include the solvency of the surety, and the availability of assets against which he can execute any judgment which he may obtain.

These general considerations arise in any case in which a party to a contract wishes to enforce the obligations of another contracting party. In this chapter, the aspects of these matters which have special relevance to contracts of suretyship are discussed, together with some of the problems which may arise, and a few practical solutions are suggested.

When can the creditor sue the surety?

Default of the principal

7–002 If the contract on which the creditor proposes to sue the surety is a contract of guarantee, the liability of the surety accrues at the earliest when the principal defaults in his obligations.[1] Thus in *Ex p. Gardom* (1808) 15 Ves. 286, it was held that the creditor was unable to sue the surety on a guarantee for the payment of the price of goods supplied to the principal

---

1 *Rawstone v Parr* (1827) 3 Russ. 539; *Browne v Lee* (1827) 6 B. & C. 689; *Holl v Hadley* (1835) 2 Ad. & El. 758; *Haliwell v Counsell* (1878) 38 L.T. 176; *Raymond v Cooper* (1858) 8 C.P. 388 (Can).

before the period of credit allowed to the principal had expired. The fact that the obligations of the guarantor arise only when the principal has defaulted in his obligations to the creditor does not necessarily mean that the creditor has to demand payment from the principal before he can sue the surety.[2] A prior demand on the principal will only be obligatory if such a demand is necessary to complete the creditor's cause of action, or if there is an express or implied contractual obligation on the creditor to make such a demand. Thus the creditor may proceed against the guarantor without making any prior demand on the principal even if the obligation of the principal is itself expressed in terms of a liability to pay "on demand". For example, he may do so if the principal obligation is the repayment of a loan made without any fixed repayment date (and therefore, by implication, repayable on demand), because in such a case the demand is not an essential ingredient of his cause of action against the principal. The underlying principle is that "where a man engages to pay upon demand what is to be considered his own debt, he is liable to be sued upon that engagement, without any previous demand."[3]

Of course, the terms of the agreement may have the effect that the liability of the surety is to accrue at a later time than default by the principal, for example, on the creditor demanding payment from the principal or, more commonly, demanding payment from the surety. If a contract of guarantee expressly or implicitly requires a demand to be made on the surety, or such a demand is required by law, the creditor cannot sue the surety until he has made such a demand even if the underlying obligation does not require a demand to be made on the principal.[4] This is subject to the effect of a "principal debtor" clause, discussed below in para.7–006. Similarly if, after the principal first defaults, the creditor gives him time to pay, with the surety's knowledge and acquiescence, time will not begin to run against the surety for limitation purposes, and the creditor cannot sue him, until the extended time for payment has expired.[5]

On the other hand, if the contract is one of indemnity, the obligation of the surety to the creditor is a primary obligation which is independent of that of the principal, and it will depend on the terms of the contract whether it arises simultaneously with the obligation of the principal,

---

2 *Cutler v Southern* (1667) 1 Saund. 116; *Lilley v Hewitt* (1822) 11 Price 494; *Re Lockey* (1845) 1 Ph. 509; *O'Connor v Sorahan* [1933] I.R. 591, *DFC Financial Services Ltd v Coffey* [1991] B.C.C. 218. As to guarantors of obligations arising under bills of exchange see *Hitchcock v Humfrey* (1843) 5 Mar. & G. 559; *Walton v Mascall* (1844) 13 M. & W. 452; *Carter v White* (1883) 25 Ch. D. 666; *Barber v Mackrell* (1892) 68 L.T. 29; *Re Mayor Ex p. Whitworth* (1841) 2 Mont. D. & De G. 158. *Cf. Hartland v Jukes* (1863) 1 H. & C. 667. See also the discussion in O'Donovan & Phillips, *The Modern Contract of Guarantee* (LBC Information Services, 3rd ed., 1996), pp.486–489 and in the English ed. (Sweet & Maxwell, 2003) at paras 10–110–10–115

3 *Rowe v Young* (1820) 2 Bli. 391 at 465 *per* Bayley J.

4 See, *e.g. Re Brown's Estate, Brown v Brown* [1893] 2 Ch. 300; *Sicklemore v Thistleton* (1817) 6 M. & S. 9; *Bradford Old Bank v Sutcliffe* [1918] 2 K.B. 833.; *Hampton v Minns* [2002] 1 W.L.R. 1. For an example of an implied requirement for a demand see *Morten v Marshall* (1863) 2 H. & C. 305.

5 *Holl v Hadley* (1835) 2 Ad. & El. 758.

afterwards, or even before. Thus it may not be open to the surety to say that because there has been no default, or will be no default, by the principal (*e.g.* if the principal dies or becomes insolvent before the time for performance of his obligations arises) the cause of action against him has not accrued or will never accrue.[6]

Defaults for which the surety is not liable

7–003   A creditor cannot rely upon a default by the principal which is attributable to his own misconduct. Thus in *Halliwell v Counsell* (1878) 38 L.T. 176, a surety for the faithful service of an apprentice was allowed to raise by way of defence the allegation that the apprentice had left the service of the employer under the reasonable apprehension that the employer would inflict grievous bodily harm upon him, because of prior assaults and injuries inflicted on him.[7] However, the fact that the default has been caused by the creditor becoming insolvent may not absolve the surety from liability: see *Re Barber & Co Ex p. Agra Bank* (1870) L.R. 9 Eq. 725. A default which occurs as a result of connivance between the creditor and principal will not render the surety liable, because it would be a fraud on the surety.[8] However, a default which occurs as the result of negligence by the creditor will not relieve the surety. Nothing less than connivance or, in the case of a fidelity bond, reckless disregard of fraud or misconduct by the employee or officeholder, will suffice.[9]

In general terms it is no answer to a claim for breach of contract, or a defence to a claim on a guarantee, to say that the breach was due to circumstances beyond the control of the party in default. However, the contract may be interpreted in such a way as to relieve both the obligor and the surety from liability by finding that there was no relevant breach or default. For example, in *Walker v British Guarantee Association* (1852) 18 Q.B. 277, a guarantee was given for the due and faithful discharge of his duties by the treasurer of a building society. The treasurer was robbed of certain moneys by irresistible violence and without any personal fault. It was held that the sureties were not liable in an action by the trustees of the society based on the allegation that he had not paid those moneys into the society account after receiving them.[10]

---

6 See, *e.g. Atkinson v Grey* (1853) 1 Sm. & G. 577, *Antrobus v Davidson* (1817) 3 Mer. 569; *Boyd v Robins and Langlands* (1859) 5 C.B.N.S. 597; *Buck v Hurst & Bailey* (1866) L.R. 1 C.P. 297. For an example of a hybrid case in which the surety's liability began as that of a guarantor but survived as an independent liability after the occurrence of an event which discharged the principal, see *General Produce Co v United Bank* [1979] 2 Lloyd's Rep. 255.
7 See also *Blest v Brown* (1862) 4 De G. F. & J. 367.
8 *Lodder v Slowey* [1904] A.C. 442; *Dawson v Lawes* (1854) Kay 280; *Sanderson v Aston* (1873) L.R. 8 Exch. 73.
9 *M'Taggart v Watson* (1836) 3 Cl. & Fin. 525; see also *Melville v Doidge* (1848) 6 C.B. 450, *Dawson v Lawes* (above) and *Black v Ottoman Bank* (1862) 15 Moo. P.C. 472, *Shepherd v Beecher* (1725) 2 P. Wms. 288 and *Bank of India v Patel* [1982] 1 Lloyd's Rep. 506 at 515 col. 1, *per* Bingham J., approved on appeal [1983] 2 Lloyd's Rep. 298 at 301–302.
10 See also *Jephson v Hawkins* (1841) 2 Man. & G. 366, where a mistake made by a clerk in a balance sheet was held not to amount to a breach of his duties, but *cf. Melville v Doidge* (1848) 6 C.B. 450, where accidental loss of funds by an employee did make the surety liable.

Demands for payment

Demand on the principal

The normal rule is that the creditor is not obliged to make a demand on the   **7–004**
principal before suing the guarantor, unless there is an express contractual
provision in the guarantee or a relevant statutory provision obliging him to
do so. Thus, if the underlying agreement is regulated by the Consumer
Credit Act 1974, service of a default notice on the principal is necessary
before the creditor can terminate the agreement for breach and enforce any
security: see Chapter 17, para.17–009. For an example of a case where the
contract, on its true construction, required both a default by and a demand
on the principal before any action could be brought against the surety, see
*Commercial Bank of Australia v Colonial Finance Mortgage Investment &
Guarantee Corporation* (1906) 4 C.L.R. 57.

However, if a demand on the principal is essential to complete the
creditor's cause of action against him, then the making of such a demand
on the principal will be an implied condition precedent to the right to sue
the surety, provided, of course, that the surety's obligations are collateral.
Cases falling within this category will include the situation where the
principal obligation is itself a liability as surety for someone else, as in *Bank
of Scotland v Wright* [1991] B.C.L.C. 244, and the situation where the
creditor is seeking to accelerate liability for payment of a debt which would
otherwise have been payable by instalments, as in *Esso Petroleum Co Ltd v
Alstonbridge Properties Ltd* [1975] 1 W.L.R. 1474 and in *Dow Banking
Corporation v Mahnakh Spinning and Weaving Corporation* [1983] 2 Lloyd's
Rep. 561. In *Esso Petroleum* it was necessary to make a demand both on the
surety and on the principal. In principle, a demand on the borrower is
necessary to terminate a bank overdraft facility and require repayment of
the balance: *Rouse v Bradford Banking Co* [1894] A.C. 586, *Cripps & Son
Ltd v Wickenden* [1973] 1 W.L.R. 944 *per* Goff J. at 954–955.[11] Although the
borrower has a direct liability to repay the bank, the amount he is liable to
repay is neither ascertained nor ascertainable until the time for repayment
arrives. The bank cannot sue him until his liability has crystallised. Thus, in
the absence of any contractual provisions to the contrary, a valid demand
cannot be made on a guarantor under a continuing guarantee of an
overdraft unless and until the obligation on the part of the principal to
make repayment has crystallised, which would normally require the termination of the account and a demand on the principal for repayment. Of
course, the terms of the facility letter may provide for automatic termination of the facility on the occurrence of one or more specified events of
default, and thus give rise to an automatic liability to repay the balance on
the date of termination without a need for any further notice or demand. In
such a case, the guarantor's liability arises on the date of the default, or, if

---

11 Likewise if a customer wishes his bank to repay money standing to the credit of his account
a demand is necessary in the absence of a contractual dispensation with this requirement:
Joachimson v Swiss Bank Corporation [1921] 3 K.B. 110.

the guarantee is a demand guarantee, on the date of demand on him. Contrast the position of a continuing guarantee of a current account, where, depending on the construction of the contract, the liability of the guarantor may arise automatically on each and every occasion a sum is advanced by the bank to the principal on overdraft (*Parr's Banking Co Ltd v Yates* [1898] 2 Q.B. 460), or alternatively on the date when a balance is constituted by the excess of total debits over total credits (*Wright v New Zealand Farmers Co-operative Association of Canterbury Ltd* [1939] A.C. 439). Both these cases are discussed in para.7–012 below, in the context of limitation.

Demand on the surety

7–005   The parties to the contract may, of course, agree that the surety is only to be liable if a demand is made on him, or notice is given to him of the relevant default. Modern bank guarantee forms contain an express provision for the guarantor to discharge his liability to the bank on service of a written demand on him (thus avoiding the need, in most cases, to investigate when the underlying liability arose). If the surety promises to pay "on demand", the creditor cannot sue him until after a demand has been made on him.[12] The requirement of a demand is a purely procedural requirement for the benefit of the surety, and therefore can be waived by him.[13] The question whether a demand on the surety (or on a co-surety) is necessary is always a matter of construction of the relevant contracts.[14] In *Stimpson v Smith* [1999] Ch. 340, two co-sureties were jointly and severally liable under a guarantee by which they guaranteed the liabilities of their company up to a maximum of £25,000. The terms of the guarantee provided that a demand had to be in writing and signed by the bank. One of the co-sureties settled with the bank and was released from his liability. He then sought contribution from the other co-surety, who claimed that he was under no liability because no written demand had been made by the bank either on the principal debtor or on the sureties. The Court of Appeal held that the service of a written demand was not a precondition of liability under the guarantee, because there was an express provision entitling the bank to set off the liability of the guarantor to it against any credit balance in any account of either of the co-guarantors with the bank as well before as after demand under the guarantee. If a set-off could be operated without a demand, it was difficult to interpret the contract as intending that a demand should be a precondition of liability in other circumstances. However, even

---

12 *Re Brown's Estate* [1893] 2 Ch. 300; *Sicklemore v Thistleton* (1817) 6 M. & S. 9; *Bradford Old Bank v Sutcliffe* [1918] 2 K.B. 833; *Duchess Theatre Co v Lord* [1993] N.P.C. 163, *Romain v Scuba TV Ltd* [1997] Q.B. 887 at 895, *Hampton v Minns* [2002] 1 W.L.R. 1: see also *Esso Petroleum Co v Alstonbridge Properties Ltd* [1975] 1 W.L.R. 1474, *General Financial Corporation of Canada v Le Jeune* [1918] 1 W.W.R. 372.

13 *Thomas v Nottingham Incorporated Football Club Ltd* [1972] Ch. 596 at 604, *per* Goff J; *Stimpson v Smith* [1999] Ch. 340, CA.

14 *Joachimson v Swiss Bank Corporation* [1921] 3 K.B. 110 *per* Atkin L.J. at 129; *MS Fashions Ltd v BCCI* [1993] Ch. 425 *per* Dillon L.J. at 447.

if this construction was wrong, the provision for a demand had been validly waived by the claimant co-surety who had paid the bank.

The effect of a "principal debtor" clause

If the guarantee covers obligations which prima facie require a demand to be made on the principal before the creditor can sue the guarantor, the device most commonly used to try to exclude this obligation is a "principal debtor" clause. In *Esso Petroleum v Alstonbridge Properties Ltd* [1975] 1 W.L.R. 1474 Walton J. expressed the view, *obiter*, that a clause which provided that as between the sureties and the lenders the sureties were to be considered as principal debtors would obviate the need for a demand, but that view was premised on the basis that the clause turned the contract into one of indemnity, which is not necessarily the case. As other commentators have pointed out, the effect of such a clause is not necessarily to make the guarantor liable as if the principal debt were his own debt, but rather serves the more modest function of allowing the creditor to treat the guarantor as a principal debtor in certain events.[15] In the unreported Australian case of *Commonwealth Bank of Australia v Stow* (February 21, 1989, New South Wales Supreme Court), a demand had been served on the principal debtor requiring payment within 14 days. The creditor sued the guarantor before that period expired; Brownie J. held that this was not a premature action because the "principal debtor" clause in the contract made the guarantor liable to pay the creditor upon demand. In *DFC Financial Services Ltd v Coffey* [1991] B.C.C. 218, the Privy Council construed a principal obligation clause in a debenture as entitling the debenture holder to proceed against the sureties as if they were primary obligors, by making a demand on them for payment (instead of making a demand on the principal debtor).

The effect of a principal debtor clause may even be to overrule an express provision in the contract of suretyship to the effect that payment will be made "on demand". *MS Fashions Ltd v Bank of Credit and Commerce International SA (in liquidation)* [1993] Ch. 425 concerned three company directors who had signed "as principal debtor" an agreement with BCCI whereby as guarantee for repayment of loans by BCCI to their respective companies, the bank could withdraw money from their deposit accounts and apply it to satisfaction of the company's debts. At 447, Dillon L.J. said of the principal debtor clause:

> "the effect of this must be to dispense with any need for a demand in the case of [surety 1] since he has made the companies' debts to BCCI his own debts and thus immediately payable out of the deposit without demand. In the case of [surety 2] there must be immediate liability even though the word "demand" was used, because he accepted

7–006

---

15 O'Donovan & Phillips, *The Modern Contract of Guarantee*, English ed. (Sweet & Maxwell, 2003) at para.10–118. See also *General Produce Co v United Bank Ltd* [1979] 2 Lloyd's Rep. 255 at 259, *per* Lloyd J.

liability as a principal debtor and his deposit can be appropriated without further notice."[16]

It follows, therefore, that if the contract of suretyship is properly classified as an indemnity, even an express statement in the contract that the indemnifier is liable to pay "on demand" may not be construed as requiring the creditor to make a demand on the surety before suing him, for exactly the same reason that the words do not require a demand to be made on the principal. However, since this point has apparently not been conclusively determined by the courts, it would always be a wise precaution for the creditor to serve a demand on the surety if express reference to a demand is made in the body of the contract of suretyship.

Compliance with a contractual requirement for a demand

7–007 If the guarantee does require a demand to be made, and the requirement for a demand is not waived by the guarantor, the question whether a particular demand meets the contractual requirements is a matter of construction in each case. In the Australian case of *Re Colonial Finance, Mortgage Investment and Guarantee Corporation Ltd* (1906) 6 S.R.N.S.W. 6 at 9 Walker J. gave this definition of a valid demand:

"... there must be a clear intimation that payment is required to constitute a demand; nothing more is necessary, and the word "demand" need not be used; neither is the validity of a demand lessened by its being clothed in the language of politeness; it must be of premptory character and uncondiitonal, but the nature of the language is immaterial provided it has this effect".

That definition was subsequently approved in England by Nourse J. in *Re A Company* [1985] B.C.L.C. 37 and by the Court of Appeal in the case of *BCCI v Blattner* (unreported, November 20, 1986). A demand should not be couched in terms of a vague request or wish that payment should be made, a threat to take proceedings (or make a demand) in the future, or a general statement of the principal's indebtedness.[17] A mere notice of the principal debtor's default will not constitute a sufficient demand for payment by implication: *Bank of Montreal v Agnew* (1986) 72 N.B.R. (2d) 276. If there is more than one creditor, it should be made clear on the face of the demand that it is served on behalf of all of the creditors, preferably by

---

16 Surety 2 had signed a guarantee containing a covenant stated to be a "separate and independent obligation" that "on demand in writing the companies' liabilities would be recoverable from him as principal debtor"—see the judgment of Hoffmann J. [1993] Ch. 427 at 430. Although the House of Lords cast doubt on the correctness of the decision in *MS Fashions* in *Re BCCI (No.8)* [1998] A.C. 214, they did so on grounds which did not impugn the validity of the decision on this particular point.

17 See, *e.g. Dow Banking Corporation v Mahnakh Spinning and Weaving Corporation* [1983] 2 Lloyd's Rep. 561 *per* Lloyd J. at 566; *Royal Bank of Canada v Ruben* (1978) 48 A.P.R. 707; *Royal Bank of Canada v Oram* [1978] 1 W.W.R. 564.

ensuring that all the creditors sign it.[18] A demand will normally be made in writing, but there is no reason in principle why a demand could not be made orally, so long as there is no contractual requirement or statutory requirement that it be made in a particular form.[19]

In general terms, the court would not construe an obligation to demand payment from the surety as requiring the creditor to specify the precise sum due and owing, unless the contract clearly says so: *Bank of Baroda v Panessar* [1987] Ch. 335, *NRG Vision Ltd v Churchfield Leasing Ltd* [1988] B.C.L.C. 624. The unreported case of *Donnelly v National Australia Bank* (May 19, 1992) in which the Supreme Court of Western Australia granted guarantors unconditional leave to appeal against a summary judgment on the grounds that they had an arguable defence that the bank demand should have specified the correct amount owing or at least sufficient information to enable them to ascertain that amount, may be regarded as something of a maverick decision.[20] Indeed, it may be virtually impossible for the creditor to ascertain the precise amount which is due at the time when he makes the demand for payment.[21] Thus a demand for more than is actually due may nevertheless constitute a valid demand: see, *e.g. Bank Negara Indonesia 1946 v Taylor* [1995] C.L.C. 255.[22] However, if the contract does require the demand to be made in a particular form, the creditor must comply with that requirement. In *Frans Maas (UK) Ltd v Habib Bank AG Zurich* [2001] Lloyd's Rep. Bank 14, a demand under a performance guarantee which did not state precisely what the contract required, was held to be invalid. It is possible that a less stringent approach might be taken with normal guarantees.[23]

The guarantee will often contain provisions stipulating where the notice of demand is to be served. In that case, the demand must be served at the specified address, unless there is an agreement between the parties to vary the terms of the guarantee. It has been held in Australia that service of the demand on the guarantor's actual business address (notified by the guarantor to the creditor) was invalid even though the address for service stated in the guarantee was no longer occupied by the guarantor.[24] The

---

18 See *Manzo v 555/255 Pitt Street Pty Ltd* (1990) 21 N.S.W.L.R. 1 and the commentary in O'Donovan & Phillips, English ed. (*op cit.*) at para.10–132 fn.10.

19 *e.g.* a statutory demand under s.123(1) or 268(1) of the Insolvency Act 1986, or a demand under s. 103(1) or s.196 of the Law of Property Act 1925 (as amended).

20 See the cogent criticism of this case in *O'Donovan & Phillips*, English ed., *op. cit.,* at paras 10–127–10–130.

21 *Bunbury Foods Pty Ltd v National Bank of Australasia* (1984) 58 A.L.J.R. 199; *O'Day v Commercial Bank of Australia Ltd* (1933) 50 C.L.R. 200 *per* Starke J. at 216; see also *NRG Vision Ltd v Churchfield Leasing Ltd* [1988] 4 B.C.C. 56 at 66, *Re A & K Holdings Pty Ltd* [1964] V.R. 257 at 262.

22 And in the analogous context of mortgages, *Bank of Montreal v Winter* (1981) 101 A.P.R. 385, *Westpac Banking Corporation v Evans* [1986] B.C.L. 1129. *Cf. NRG Vision v Churchfield Leasing Ltd* [1988] B.C.L.C. 624.

23 Compare the judicial approach taken in *Dow Banking Corporation v Mahnakh Spinning and Weaving Corporation* [1983] 2 Lloyd's Rep. 561 and *Re A & K Holdings Pty Ltd* [1964] V.R. 257 with the cases referred to in O'Donovan & Phillips, *The Modern Contract of Guarantee* (English ed.) at para.10–125, fn.93.

24 *Bond v Hongkong Bank of Australia Ltd* (1991) 25 N.S.W.L.R. 286, NSW Supreme Court, CA. See also *Tricontinental Corp Ltd v HDH Ltd* (1990) 21 N.S.W.L.R. 689.

guarantee may also contain provisions dealing with proof of service of the demand, for example, a term providing that the demand will be deemed to have been made within a particular period after an envelope containing it addressed to the guarantor at his last known address has been posted. Proof that the envelope was posted will normally suffice to preclude the guarantor from raising the defence that no demand was actually received by him.[25] In Australia it has been held that a clause which provided that the statement by an officer of the creditor was conclusive evidence of "all other matters stated herein" was wide enough to allow such a statement to stand as conclusive evidence that a demand had been made on the guarantor in accordance with the terms of the guarantee: *Papua New Guinea Development Bank v Manton* [1982] V.R. 1000.

Although provisions of this type are designed to assist the creditor, the case of *Bank of Baroda v Patel* [1996] 1 Lloyd's Rep. 391 illustrates that they can sometimes cause him difficulty. The bank guarantee in that case contained a provision enabling a demand to be sent to the guarantor at his last known place of abode, and stipulated that "a notice of demand so given or made shall be deemed to be given or made on the day it was left or the day following that on which it is posted as the case may be". In August 1985, the creditor bank sent a letter to the defendant guarantor's last known address, and shortly afterwards obtained judgment in default against him for the sums then due on account from the principal debtor. The defendant successfully applied to set aside the judgment on the grounds that he had moved house and never received the demand. In April 1992, the bank sent him a fresh letter of demand relating to the updated (and substantially increased) indebtedness of the principal, and six months later, commenced new proceedings. The defendant successfully argued that the claim was time-barred save for the interest and charges which had accrued within six years before the issue of the writ.

Potter J. held that it was not open to the bank to contend that the first demand was invalid because it did not come to the defendant's attention. The notice provision in the guarantee deemed that demand to have been valid and the bank could not go behind it; nor could the bank adopt the defendant's factual denial that he ever received it. He said (at 395 col. 1):

> "Not only does it seem to me that there is no absurdity inherent in a deeming provision of this kind taking effect despite the fact that actual notice was not received at the time; it also seems to me that, by its stance, the bank is seeking to approbate and reprobate in a manner which is not open to it."

The learned Judge went on to hold, for the avoidance of doubt, that the bank was in effect estopped from contending that the first demand was ineffective, by its conduct in suing the defendant on that demand and

---

25 See, *e.g. Canadian Imperial Bank of Commerce v Haley* (1979) 100 D.L.R. (3d) 470.

contending (until the limitation point was pleaded) that it was a valid notice. Since the first demand was a valid one, it triggered the six-year limitation period and the subsequent notice could not extend it.

If a demand is made, the creditor should usually allow the surety a reasonable time to comply with it before suing him: see, *e.g. Bond v Hongkong Bank of Australia* [1991] 25 N.S.W.L.R. 286, where a period of five days was held to be sufficient.[26] However, if the guarantor has been allowed a reasonable time to pay before a formal demand is made upon him, even a demand to pay "forthwith" may be enforceable: see, *e.g. Federal Business Development Bank v Dunn* [1984] 6 W.W.R. 46, and *Good Motel Co Ltd (in liq.) v Rodeway Pacific International Ltd* (1988) 94 F.L.R. 84.

Compliance with other conditions precedent

If any condition precedent is not fulfilled, the surety is not liable, and consequently his liability does not accrue for limitation purposes until the condition is performed.[27] The question whether a condition precedent exists, and if so, whether the creditor has fulfilled it, will depend on the facts of each particular case, and prior decisions afford little in the way of guidance as to how other contracts will be interpreted.[28] The surety may also be discharged if the creditor is unable to fulfil a condition precedent. In *Rickaby v Lewis* (1905) 22 T.L.R. 130, the contract required the creditor to give a written notice to the principal requiring payment. The principal died before such notice could be given to him. The condition precedent was not fulfilled, and the surety was discharged. However, in *Musket v Rodgers* (1839) 5 Bing NC, it was held that the creditor had not failed to comply with a requirement that he should avail himself to the utmost of any security he held of the principal, by reason of his omission to bring proceedings on a bill of exchange drawn by the principal and accepted by someone who was insolvent.

7–008

The contract may stipulate a time limit for performance of a condition precedent, but this is rare. In theory, therefore, the creditor might prolong the limitation period against the surety, for example by delaying in making a demand or serving a notice which is an express condition precedent to the surety's liability. However, the creditor may be precluded from recovering

---

26 But *cf. Bank of Baroda v Panessar* [1987] Ch. 335 where the requirement to give a reasonable time to pay was specifically rejected, at least so far as the principal debtor was concerned, following the dictum of Blackburn J. In *Brighty v Norton* (1862) 3 B. & S. 305 at 312 that a debtor who is required to pay money on demand should have it ready. See also *Sheppard & Cooper v TSB (No.2)* [1996] B.C.C. 965; *Thermo King Corporation v Provincial Bank of Canada* (1981) 130 D.L.R. (3d) 256 and *Lloyds Bank Plc v Lampert* [1999] 1 All E.R. (Comm) 161, where the CA expressly left the point open.
27 *Rickaby v Lewis* (1905) 22 T.L.R. 130; *London Guarantee Co v Fearnley* (1880) 5 App. Cas. 911; *Re Brown's Estate* [1893] 2 Ch. 300; *Sicklemore v Thistleton* (1817) 6 M. & S. 9; *Bradford Old Bank v Sutcliffe* [1918] 2 K.B. 833. See also, on the effect of delay by the creditor in performing a condition precedent, *Lancaster v Harrison* (1830) 6 Bing. 276.
28 For a discussion of conditions precedent see Ch.4, at para.4–023. See generally *Halsbury's Laws* (4th ed., reissue 2004.), Vol. 20, paras 194–195 and the cases there cited.

against the surety by his unreasonable delay in fulfilling a condition precedent: *Holl v Hadley* (1835) 2 Ad. & El. 758.[29] If the contract provides that notice of the default of the principal shall be given to the surety, this will usually be interpreted in such a way that the creditor will not be obliged to give the notice until he knows that liability has been incurred: *Ward v Law Property Assurance Co* (1856) 27 L.T.O.S. 155.[30] This does not necessarily mean that he can wait until a court ascertains liability: see *Colvin v Buckle* (1841) 8 M. & W. 680, discussed in para.7–012 below.

The creditor may pursue the surety first

7–009   Just as there is generally no requirement to make a demand on the principal before proceeding against the surety, there is no obligation on the part of the creditor to commence proceedings against the principal, whether criminal or civil, or to commence arbitration against him, unless there is an express term in the contract requiring him to do so, or his cause of action does not arise until he obtains a judgment or arbitral award, *e.g.* if the guarantee is confined to payment of a sum awarded by the arbitrators.[31] Likewise, there is no rule that the creditor must avail himself of other securities which the debtor may have given himself or sue a co-surety, before looking to the surety for payment, unless the contract states that he must do so, or he is obliged to do so by a relevant statutory provision.[32] In general terms the creditor has a completely unfettered choice as to how, and against whom, he should proceed to recover the debt or damages to which he is entitled. The creditor may simultaneously bring winding-up proceedings against the principal and sue on the guarantee in separate proceedings: *Permanent Custodians Ltd v Digital Enterprises Pty Ltd* (1992) 8 A.C.S.R. 542.

Thus, in the absence of any condition precedent in the contract, all that the creditor needs to establish to complete his cause of action against the guarantor is that the principal has defaulted: for example, that the last day for repayment of a loan has passed by without payment, or that the principal has committed a relevant breach of contract. Whether or not a

---

29 See also *Lancaster v Harrison* (1830) 6 Bing. 726.
30 See also *Bonthrone v Paterson* (1898) 5 S.L.T. 284; *Britannia Steamship Insurance v Duff Association* [1909] S.C. 1261.
31 *Wright v Simpson* (1802) 6 Ves. 714; *Barber v Mackrell* (1892) 68 L.T. 29; *Lawrence v Walmsley* (1862) 12 C.B.N.S. 799; *Lee v Bayes and Robinson* (1856) 18 C.B. 599; *Palmer v Sheridan-Vickers, The Times*, July 20, 1910; *Bank of Nova Scotia v Vancouver Associated Contractors Ltd* [1954] 3 D.L.R. 72. *Themistocles Navegacion SA v Langton ("The Queen Frederica")* [1978] 2 Lloyd's Rep. 164. See further Ch.11, paras 11–002–11–004.
32 See the discussion in Ch.11. See also *Wilks v Heeley* (1832) 1 Cr. & M. 249; *Gwynne v Burnell* (1840) 6 Bing. N.C. 453, reversing (1835) 2 Bing. N.C. 7, *sub nom.*, *Collins v Gwynne*. Unless he can exercise his right in equity to have the securities marshalled (as to which, see Ch.11, para.11–015) the surety has no right to those securities until after he has paid the debt himself: *Re Howe Ex p. Brett* (1871) L.R. 6 Ch. App. 838 at 841. For an example of an express obligation see *Musket v Rogers* (1839) 8 Scott 51.

default has occurred will depend on the nature of the contract and the circumstances of each particular case.[33]

The general rule that the creditor may proceed directly against the surety has been endorsed by the House of Lords. In *Moschi v Lep Air Services Ltd* [1973] A.C. 331 at 356, Lord Simon cited with approval a passage from Rowlatt on *Principal and Surety* (*op. cit.*) which formulated the rule thus:

> "On default of the principal promisor causing damage to the promisee the surety is, apart from special stipulation, immediately liable to the full extent of his obligation, without being entitled to require either notice of the default, or previous recourse against the principal, or simultaneous recourse against co-sureties."

Lord Simon observed that the rule had not been questioned in the course of argument in the case then under consideration. He also approved the reason given by Rowlatt for the rule, which is that it is the obligation of the guarantor, rather than the obligation of the creditor, to see to it that the principal pays or otherwise performs his obligations.[34]

Preservation of rights against third parties

It has been suggested that the creditor may be obliged to enforce rights **7–010** against third parties which only he can pursue, and which would not be available to the surety under his rights of subrogation after payment.[35] This suggestion emanates from *Cottin v Blane* (1795) 2 Anst. 544, a case decided at a time when England was at war with France. The surety had given a guarantee to the owner of an American ship for a merchant who freighted the ship to Bordeaux. The vessel was detained there by an embargo and the contract of affreightment was terminated by the merchant. The French government had declared itself bound to indemnify all neutral shipowners in respect of the effects of the embargo; the surety, being English, could not avail himself of the indemnity. It was held that the American owner had to endeavour to obtain an indemnity in France before he could sue the surety.

It is submitted that the facts of *Cottin v Blane* are sufficiently unusual to make it unsafe to assume that it lays down any precedent. Certainly it is difficult to ascertain from the report what legal principles were applied in order to achieve the result, though it may perhaps be viewed as a fairly extreme example of the application of the principle that the creditor is

---

33 For an example of the difficulties which may arise, see the cases discussed in Rowlatt, *Principal and Surety* (Sweet & Maxwell, 5th ed., 1999), pp.110–111 and in O'Donovan & Phillips, *the Modern Contract of Guarantee* (English ed.) *op. cit.* at paras 10–145–10–150.
34 *Re Lockey* (1845) 1 Ph. 509 and *Wright v Simpson* (1802) 6 Ves. 714 offer indirect support for the rationale, see Lord Simon, *ibid.* at 357. See further the discussion in Rowlatt (*op. cit.*), at 108; *Chitty on Contracts* (29th ed., 2004), Vol. 2, para.44–040 *et seq.*; *Halsbury's Laws*, 4th ed. (2004 reissue), Vol. 20, paras 191–193.
35 Rowlatt (*op. cit.*), at 145, McGuinness, *The Law of Guarantee* (*op. cit.*), para.7.4, n.17: but see the critique in Ch.11 at para.11.002.

obliged to take reasonable steps to mitigate his loss (in this instance, claiming against the fund). However, even on that analysis, the element of compulsion of the creditor is unique: therefore the case should be treated with considerable caution.

Time of suit is not of the essence

7-011   There is no obligation on the creditor to take proceedings against the guarantor promptly or within a reasonable time after the default of the principal in the absence of an express contractual provision to that effect: *Isbell Dean (Bean) Co v Avery* [1923] 1 D.L.R. (N.S.) 708.[36] The surety has to bear the risk that the principal will become insolvent during the period of the delay, making his right of indemnity worthless. The right of the surety to claim *quia timet* relief against the creditor before demand is made on him is therefore a valuable safeguard.[37]

Limitation of actions

7-012   As stated above, in a contract of guarantee the liability of the surety usually accrues when the principal defaults or when the creditor fulfils any necessary condition precedent.[38] However, *Colvin v Buckle* (1841) 8 M. & W. 680, illustrates a situation in which time began to run from the date on which the creditor became aware of all the facts on which the surety's liability depended:

> C & Co had advanced money to D to enable him to pursue a specific business venture. D was going to transport goods to a foreign port on a vessel which he had chartered from her owner, sell the goods there, and send back the proceeds in goods or bills to C. The proceeds would be used by C to repay the loan and charges and the balance held by them for D. D ran into financial difficulties and asked for a further loan against the expected proceeds of the consignment. In consideration of that further advance, S gave C a guarantee that "we will reimburse you the amount of demand with interest, in the event of your finding it necessary to call upon us to do so, either from the state of D's pending account with you, or from any other circumstances". When the vessel returned to England with a cargo, D had become bankrupt. The owner of the ship caused the goods to be sold to pay off his lien for freight, and the balance of the monies thus realised were paid into court on an interpleader summons. Many years of litigation then ensued between the shipowner, the trustees of D, and C.

It was held that time began to run against S when the cargo was sold, and not when the litigation was terminated, because once the cargo had been sold C were aware of all the facts upon which S's legal liability depended.

---

36 See also *Waung v Subbotovsky* [1968] 3 N.S.W.R. 499; *Heinish v MCC Amusement Enterprises Ltd* (1977) 42 N.S.R. (2d) 195.

37 *Thomas v Nottingham Incorporated Football Club* [1972] Ch. 596, and see the discussion of *quia timet* relief in Ch.10, para.10–026 *et seq.*

38 See, generally *Halsbury's Laws* (*op. cit.*), Vol. 20 para.194.

In the case of an indemnity, time will run either from the date on which the creditor suffers loss (in an indemnity which is akin to a guarantee, this is usually the date of default by the principal), or from the date when he incurs a liability in respect of which the indemnity is given, or, in the case of a contract to indemnify the creditor on the occurrence of a particular event, from the date on which that event occurs.[39]

The relevant period of limitation for an action on a contract of suretyship, as on any other contract, is six years from the accrual of the cause of action, namely when the surety first becomes liable to make payment.[40] If there are successive breaches of the principal contract, time will begin to run afresh from each breach. If the principal has defaulted, it does not matter for the purposes of limitation that the loss suffered by the creditor cannot yet be quantified: see, *e.g. National House-Building Council v Fraser* [1983] 1 All E.R. 1090.

Where no time is stipulated

The question of when the limitation period starts to run in a case where no **7–013** time has been stipulated in the underlying contract for performance of the principal's obligations is slightly more difficult to answer. In general, in such a case the time for performance by the principal will be deemed to be a reasonable time, and therefore the surety's liability will accrue when a reasonable time has elapsed: *Henton v Paddison* (1893) 68 L.T. 405.

However, it was held in *Parr's Banking Co Ltd v Yates* [1898] 2 Q.B. 460 that if a series of sums are advanced by the creditor to the principal under a running account without any specific time for repayment being stipulated, time starts to run under a continuing guarantee from the date of each advance. This contradicted the decision in the earlier case of *Hartland v Jukes* (1863) 1 H. & C. 667 (which was not cited in *Parr's Banking Co Ltd v Yates*) that time starts to run from the date when a balance is struck and a claim is made.

In *Wright v New Zealand Farmers Co-Operative Association of Canterbury Ltd* [1939] A.C. 439, the Privy Council held that if the guarantee is of the balance at any time owing on an account, time will run from the time that the balance which is sued for is constituted, and not from the time at which each individual debit is made in the account. However, no opinion was expressed as to the correctness or otherwise of the decision in *Parr's Banking Co Ltd v Yates*.

Matters have been simplified somewhat by s.6 of the Limitation Act 1980. This provides that if a contract of loan does not provide for repayment of the debt on or before a fixed or determinable date, and does

---

39 See, *e.g. Collinge v Heywood* (1839) 9 Ad. & El. 633; *County District Properties Ltd v C Jenner & Son Ltd* (1974) 230 E.G. 1589; *Adams v Dansey* (1830) 6 Bing. 506; *Carr v Roberts* (1833) 5 B. & Ad. 78; *Huntley v Sanderson* (1833) 1 Cr. & M. 467; *Reynolds v Doyle* (1840) 1 Man. & G. 753. See also *Wolmershausen v Gullick* [1893] 2 Ch. 514, and the discussion in Ch.10 at paras 10–002–10–014 and Ch.12 at para.12–018.
40 Limitation Act 1980, s.5. In the case of an obligation arising under a specialty, *i.e.* a contract or other obligation contained in a document under seal, it is 12 years: *ibid.*, s.8.

not effectively make the obligation to repay conditional on a demand for repayment made by or on behalf of the creditor, time will start to run from the date on which a written demand is made by the creditor for repayment of the debt.[41]

If the balance of indebtedness under a guarantee has accrued due and become payable in consequence of a demand, the creditor cannot start the limitation period running again by including that sum as part of a larger sum which is the subject of a fresh demand: *Australia and New Zealand Banking Group v Douglas Morris Investments Pty Ltd* [1992] 1 Qd. R. 478; *Bank of Baroda v Patel* [1996] 1 Lloyd's Rep. 391.

Interest

7–014 Interest which is expressly guaranteed may be recoverable even if the principal debt is statute-barred, if it has accrued due from the principal within six years prior to the commencement of the proceedings against the surety: *Parr's Banking Co v Yates* [1898] 2 Q.B. 460.[42]

Recovering sums secured by property

7–015 The period of limitation for an action to recover a principal sum secured by a mortgage or other charge on property is 12 years from the date on which the right to receive the money accrued.[43] However, if a claim is made against a principal for a personal remedy under a simple contract, such as a loan, which happens to be secured by a mortgage, and the claim does not involve enforcing the charge, the appropriate time limit is six years and not 12.[44] The question therefore arises whether, if the claim is brought against a surety for a mortgage debt, the period of limitation is six years or 12.

If the surety is party to a separate contract, and not a party to the mortgage deed, it appears that s.20 of the 1980 Act would not apply. In *Re Powers* (1885) 30 Ch. D. 291, (a case decided when the relevant period of limitation in mortgage actions was 20 years), it was held that the claim against a surety on a separate bond was not a proceeding to recover money secured on land, but a proceeding to recover damages because another person failed to pay money secured on land. In *Henton v Paddison* (1893) 68 L.T. 405, a claim by a mortgagee against a surety for the mortgagor under an independent guarantee was held to be time-barred after the lapse of six years from the date on which the cause of action against the principal first accrued (on the facts, this happened to be on the expiry of a reasonable time for suing the principal).

---

41 This provision will not apply if the principal enters into a collateral obligation to pay the amount of the debt or any part of it on terms which would exclude the application of the section if they had applied directly to repayment of the debt; *e.g.* by giving the creditor a promissory note. This is presumably because the collateral obligation will indicate the time for performance.

42 As to the time until which a bank may charge compound interest, see *National Bank of Greece SA v Pinios Shipping Co No.1 (The "Maira" (No.2))* [1990] 1 A.C. 637 and the general discussion in *Paget's Law of Banking*, 12th ed. (*op. cit.*) at paras 13.6–13.12.

43 Limitation Act 1980, s.20.

44 See *Halsbury's Laws* (*op. cit.*), Vol. 28, para.797 and *Barnes v Glenton* [1899] 1 Q.B. 885.

The question whether s.20 would apply if the surety is a party to the mortgage deed was left open by Kay J. and the Court of Appeal in *Re Frisby* (1889) 43 Ch. D. 106. However, given that the time limit for actions on a deed is 12 years, this problem is purely academic.

Rent guarantees

A similar problem arises for consideration where the contract of suretyship **7–016** for rent is made under seal, which is often the case if the contract is encompassed within the lease as an independent covenant. The relevant period of limitation is prima facie 12 years from the date on which the cause of action against the surety accrued, by virtue of s.8 of the Limitation Act 1980. However, s.19 of the Act provides as follows:

> "No action shall be brought, or distress made, to recover arrears of rent, or damages in respect of arrears of rent, after the expiration of six years from the date on which the arrears became due."

In *Romain v Scuba TV Ltd* [1997] Q.B. 887, the Court of Appeal held that s.19 applies not only to actions against a tenant to recover arrears of rent, but also to claims against a guarantor in respect of his undertaking to pay the rent reserved by the lease, on the grounds that such a claim was a claim for "damages in respect of arrears of rent". This conclusion was reached despite the fact that the history of s.19 could be traced back to the Real Property Limitation Act 1833 and the Limitation Act 1623 which, as Evans L.J. fairly conceded, were statutes concerned with the situation of the tenant rather than that of third parties, including sureties. Consequently, although nothing appears on the face of the statute to limit the application of s.19 to claims against the tenant, there might be legitimate grounds for interpreting it as being so confined by implication. It would appear that the main reason for the decision not to adopt that approach was that it was considered to be impossible to give any realistic meaning to the phrase "damages in respect of arrears of rent" if s.19 was confined to claims against the tenant, in the light of the House of Lords decision in *President of India v La Pintada Compania Navigacion SA* [1985] A.C. 104, where it was held that the court has no power to award general damages for late payment or non-payment of a debt. That reasoning overlooks the fact that the House of Lords specifically left open the possibility of a claim for *special* damages for non-payment of a debt, an approach which was specifically endorsed in the subsequent case of *President of India v Lips Maritime Corporation* [1988] 1 A.C. 395. Although it may be rare to find a case in which special damages for non-payment of rent would be recoverable against the tenant, it is by no means an impossibility.

As matters presently stand, therefore, even if the guarantee is made in a deed, the shorter limitation period of six years from the date of the arrears of rent will apply. The curious effect of this decision is that it is possible for time to start accruing against the landlord even before the surety is under a liability to him, for example if the guarantee was one by which a demand on the guarantor was a condition precedent to his liability, because the six-year period would start to run from the moment when the rent fell due, before any demand was made on the guarantor. This means that a creditor under a rent guarantee is uniquely disadvantaged in terms of choosing when to sue the guarantor, for no apparent reason. An even more drastic consequence of the Court of Appeal's interpretation of the phrase "a claim for damages in respect of arrears of rent" is that the claim by the surety for an indemnity from the principal would arguably also be time-barred after six years from the date when the rent fell into arrears, with the obvious risk of injustice to the surety if the claim against him was made at the end of the limitation period. It is respectfully doubted whether these results were what Parliament intended when s.19 (or any of its predecessors) was enacted. Although the alternative interpretation would mean that the surety could remain under a liability to the creditor even after the claim by the creditor against the principal had become time-barred, this is by no means an unusual situation (see Chapter 6 at para.6–026). It remains to be seen whether Parliament will remedy the position, or whether the argument on this point will reach the House of Lords in due course.

Effect of acknowledgment and part-payment

7–017 If the principal makes part-payment of a debt, the limitation period will run afresh against the surety from the time of such payment, though no new cause of action is created: see Limitation Act 1980, ss.29–31. Part-payments of interest are treated as payments in respect of the principal debt: s.20(6).[45]

However, by s.31(6) of the Act, an acknowledgment of any debt or other liquidated pecuniary claim shall bind the acknowledgor and his successors but not any other person.[46] Thus, if the person making the acknowledgment is the principal, or a co-surety, the surety is not bound by that acknowledgment and time will not start to run afresh against him on that ground.[47]

Nature of the claim against the surety

7–018 There has been some judicial debate as to whether a claim on a guarantee is properly framed as a claim in damages or a claim in debt. If the guarantee is not of a debt or liquidated sum but a guarantee of the performance of more general obligations, such as a tenant's obligation to maintain or repair the premises, the claim against the principal and against the guarantor will properly sound in damages. The measure of damages will usually be the same as any sum which would have been recoverable from

---

45 Consequently payment of interest by a surety will make time run against the debtor, and vice versa: see *Re Powers* (1885) 30 Ch. D. 291, *Re Frisby* (1889) 43 Ch. D. 106, *Lewin v Wilson* (1881) 11 App. Cas. 639, and the discussion in *Halsbury's Laws* (*op. cit.*), at para.913.

46 "Successor" means his personal representatives, and any other person on whom the rights of the principal devolve, whether on death or bankruptcy or the disposition of property—*ibid*, s.25(8).

47 The history of these provisions is explained in Rowlatt (*op. cit.*), at 204–205.

the principal by way of damages for breach of the guaranteed obligation: *Moschi v Lep Air Services Ltd* [1973] A.C. 331, and see the discussion in Chapter 6 at paras 6–002 and 6–030.

However, if the principal transaction guaranteed is for a debt or other liquidated sum, then traditionally the action on the guarantee is brought for that sum rather than being framed as an action for damages for breach of contract. In *Moschi v Lep Air Services Ltd* the propriety of this was questioned by Lord Diplock, in particular, who suggested that an action against a guarantor should properly be brought as a claim in damages, because the obligation of the surety is not an obligation to pay a sum of money to the creditor but to see to it that the principal performs his obligation. That view, however, was criticised in Australia by Mason C.J. in *Sunbird Plaza Pty v Maloney* (1988) 166 C.L.R. 245, discussed in Chapter 1, para.1–004. The proper formulation of the claim will probably depend on the construction of the contract and the nature of the underlying obligation in each case. For example, a guarantee which expressly obliges the surety to pay a sum of money to the guarantor on default by the principal is likely to be characterised as giving rise to a debt, as it was in *Hampton v Minns* [2002] 1 W.L.R. 1, discussed in more detail in Chapter 12, para.12–018. In that case, the effect of that construction meant was a claim for contribution by one guarantor against his co-surety in respect of his liability to the creditor under the guarantee was unarguably also a claim in debt. Thus the claim fell outside s.1 of the Civil Liability (Contribution) Act 1978, and was not subject to the two-year limitation period for bringing such claims under s.10 of the Limitation Act 1980.

Although the nature of the claim makes no difference to the limitation period which applies as between creditor and surety, it could affect the rights of the parties in other respects. One advantage of bringing a claim in debt is that there is no duty on the creditor to mitigate his loss. However, it is difficult to see what practical effect an obligation to mitigate would have in this context, given that it is well-established that the creditor may choose to proceed against the surety without first making any claim or taking proceedings against the principal, or a co-surety, even if they are solvent, or realising other securities. The obligation to mitigate would therefore probably be confined to taking any relevant steps to mitigate the underlying loss in respect of which the principal was primarily liable and the surety secondarily liable. Another problem with a liquidated claim is that in certain circumstances the provision under which the underlying obligation arises may be struck out as a penalty, or the obligation on the principal to make payment may be predicated on the occurrence of a specified event which never takes place. In such a case, the creditor's alternative claim for damages would only be available to the extent that it was consistent with the terms of the guarantee. A good illustration of the application of these principles is *Sunbird Plaza Pty v Maloney* (above) where the guarantee was a guarantee of all the purchaser's obligations under a contract of sale including his liability to make payment of "all moneys payable by the purchaser under the contract". The contract itself provided that the balance of the purchase price was payable "on settlement". On the day fixed for settlement, the purchaser repudiated the contract, but the vendor refused to accept the repudiation and sued for specific performance. Although the guarantee, on its true construction, was apposite to allow the creditor to bring a claim for damages, his action in affirming the contract of sale and obtaining an order for specific performance precluded him from claiming damages for loss of profit/loss of bargain.

Where should the creditor sue the surety?

Jurisdiction or arbitration clauses

7–019   Most standard form bank guarantees which relate to transactions which take place in England now contain a clause which expressly provides that the contract is to be governed by English law and that disputes between the parties are to be referred to the English courts. Indeed, it is common to find an English jurisdiction clause in bank guarantees even where the transaction has substantial foreign connections. It is rarer to find English arbitration clauses in guarantees, though these are sometimes included in guarantees or letters of indemnity put up by insurers in order to release a vessel from arrest in a disputed cargo claim.

Exclusive jurisdiction clauses

7–020   If the contract of suretyship contains an exclusive jurisdiction clause, and the creditor brings proceedings in the designated court, he will normally be able to resist any attempts by the surety to have the dispute dealt with by another court. If the creditor does not wish to abide by the exclusive jurisdiction clause, he may still be able to sue the surety somewhere else, but he will risk the possibility that the surety will succeed in getting those proceedings stayed, or that the surety will bring an action against him for damages for breach of the exclusive jurisdiction clause. The probabilities are that the surety would have to go to the court in which the proceedings have been brought in order to obtain a stay or declaration by that court that it has no jurisdiction. The recent decision of the European Court of Justice in Case C–159/02 *Turner v Grovit, The Times*, April 29, 2004 precludes the English court from granting an anti-suit injunction in respect of proceedings within a state which is a party to the Brussels Convention (and by extension, to a state which is a party to the Lugano Convention). It may mean that an English court is now less willing to grant anti-suit injunctions in respect of proceedings outside the EC. Generally the damages for breach of the exclusive jurisdiction clause would be minimal, but in rare cases they could be substantial and might even negate the value of the judgment. If the jurisdiction clause is not exclusive, of course, there would be no claim in damages and the prospects of obtaining a stay would be somewhat diminished.

Arbitration clauses

7–021   Likewise, if the contract contains an arbitration clause which covers the particular dispute, and the creditor brings proceedings in England in breach of that clause, then on the application of the surety, the court must stay the proceedings unless satisfied that the arbitration agreement is null and void, inoperative, or incapable of being performed.[48] If he brings the proceedings abroad, it will depend on the law of the chosen forum whether the proceedings are stayed, but s.32 of the Civil Jurisdiction and Judgments Act 1982 might cause him difficulties in enforcing such a judgment in England.[49] Again, the breach of the arbitration agreement might sound in damages.[50]

No choice of forum

If the contract does not contain an arbitration clause or jurisdiction clause, **7–022** it is open to the parties to reach an *ad hoc* agreement, but more often the creditor will try to sue the surety in a jurisdiction in which he knows or suspects that the surety will have assets available for the enforcement of the judgment. Alternatively, if the surety has assets in England but the creditor is unable to found jurisdiction for his claim here, he would try to choose a forum where the judgment is capable of swift reciprocal enforcement in England.

In a case where the surety is domiciled in another EU state or in an EFTA state which is party to the Lugano Convention of September 16, 1988, the creditor may have to sue him in the state of domicile and then rely on the provisions of the Civil Jurisdiction and Judgments Act 1982 or the Civil Jurisdiction and Judgments Act 1991 to enforce the judgment here or anywhere else in Europe where the surety might have assets. In such a case the creditor can avail himself of interlocutory remedies designed to preserve assets which are likely to disappear before judgment is executed, in any EU or EFTA contracting state.[51] However, if the creditor is domiciled in England himself, he may be able to sue the surety here on the grounds that the place for performance of the surety's obligations under the contract of indemnity is England.[52] He may also be able to join him as an additional defendant in proceedings properly commenced by him in England against the principal, if the principal is domiciled in England (under Art.6(1) of Regulation EC 44/2001 ("the Judgments Regulation") or (where still applicable) the Brussels and Lugano Conventions). Article 6(2) of the Judgments Regulation and the relevant Conventions provides that a person domiciled in a Contracting State may also be sued as a third party in an action on a warranty or guarantee or in any other third-party proceedings in the court seised of the original proceedings, unless these were instituted soley with the object of removing him from the jurisdiction of the court which would be competent in his case. "Third-party proceed-

---

48 Abritration Act 1996, s.9(4).
49 See, *ibid.*, 483–485.
50 See, *e.g. Mantovani v Carapelli* [1978] 2 Lloyd's Rep. 63.
51 See, s.25 of the Civil Jurisdiction and Judgments Act 1982; Art.24 of the Lugano Convention.
52 Thus bringing the case within Art.5(1) of the Judgments Regulation and Brussels Convention and Art.5(1) of the Lugano Convention.

ings" in this context may not be confined to proceedings which would be so categorised under national law: in the Jenard Report, at p.28, such proceedings are "those in which a third party is joined as a party to the action. They are intended to safeguard the interests of the third party, or of one of the parties to the action . . ." It remains to be seen whether the phrase would be interpreted so widely as to encompass the situation in which the creditor brings proceedings against the creditor, or another surety, and the guarantor as co-defendants, but it certainly would cover the situation in which a surety sued in England brings CPR Pt 20 proceedings against a co-surety domiciled in another EU state claiming contribution or an indemnity.

Complicating factors

7–023 In many cases where the creditor seeks to recover money from the surety, he will not wish to pursue the principal. For example, the principal might be insolvent or outside the jurisdiction and it may be cheaper and more convenient to pursue the surety and leave him to seek his remedy against the principal if he can. In a straightforward case, *e.g.* where it is plain and obvious that the principal has defaulted in repayment of a loan, there are few drawbacks to taking this course.

However, in other cases there may well be a substantial dispute as to whether the principal was in breach of the relevant contractual obligations so as to give rise to a claim under the guarantee. The creditor may well consider that in terms of tactics it is preferable to pursue the surety alone, and leave the surety either to try and get the principal to help him by providing him with evidence to prove that he was not in default, or to join him as a CPR Pt 20 defendant and bring all the matters in dispute before the court in that fashion.

Sometimes, however, this tactic will be inappropriate. For example, the creditor might be engaged in proceedings with the principal already. Indeed, the principal might have initiated those proceedings. Even if that is not the case, the creditor might wish to have the question of the principal's liability settled not only as between himself and the surety but also as between himself and the principal.

One of the main problems which the creditor may face in such a situation is that a judgment or arbitral award against the principal in favour of the creditor in respect of the relevant debt, default or miscarriage for which the surety is liable is not binding on the surety unless he was a party to those proceedings: *Re Kitchin Ex p. Young* (1881) 17 Ch. D. 668.[53] *Re Kitchin* was followed and applied by Robert Goff J. in *Bruns v Colocotronis, The Vasso* [1979] 2 Lloyd's Rep. 412, in which it was held that the general words in a guarantee which guaranteed the due performance of all the obligations of the principal did not of themselves have the effect that the surety was

---

53 See also *Mercantile Investment and General Trust Co v River Plate Trust, Loan and Agency Co* [1894] 1 Ch. 578 at 595, *per* Romer J.

bound by an arbitration award, even where that award arose out of a clause in the agreement containing the obligations guaranteed.

Consequently, in the absence of an express agreement by the surety that he will be bound by the findings in such proceedings, the surety is entitled to demand that the matter be relitigated as against him. Multiplicity of proceedings concerning the same subject-matter is not desirable as a general rule, and there is a risk of inconsistent decisions: see *Bank of Nova Scotia v Vancouver Associated Contractors Ltd* [1954] 3 D.L.R. 72. It is therefore preferable in such cases for the creditor to do whatever he can to ensure that the claims against principal and surety are heard by the same court or arbitral tribunal.

The simplest way of doing this is to sue the principal and the surety in the same proceedings, or, if there are two sets of proceedings pending in the same court, *e.g.* if the principal has initiated proceedings against the creditor), to seek consolidation or an order that the actions be tried together. If the creditor does commence proceedings against both, whether in one action or in two, the surety has no right in equity to seek to restrain the creditor from proceeding with the action against him simply on the grounds that the creditor may recover the money from the principal, at least in the absence of proof of circumstances which would prevent the surety from recovering over against the principal if he were forced to pay first: *Jackson v Digby* (1854) 2 W.R. 540.

The arbitration trap

If the creditor sues both the principal and the surety before the English **7–024** court, and one of the relevant contracts contains an arbitration clause which gives rise to a mandatory stay at the option of the principal, it appears that the court would have no means of ensuring that all the parties remained involved in the proceedings before it. In such a case, the surety might rescue the position by bringing the principal into the proceedings as a CPR Pt 20 defendant but that is a matter for him to decide, and he cannot be forced to do so. The surety and the principal may be quite content to put the creditor to the cost and expense of parallel proceedings, especially if they perceive that it would be advantageous in terms of putting pressure on him to settle. This often occurs where the surety and the principal are closely connected, for example, where the principal is an offshore company with few assets, and the surety is a director of the company.

Even if the surety does join the principal in Pt 20 proceedings, the creditor would still probably have to persuade the arbitrators to stay the arbitration pending the outcome of the proceedings in court, if he wished to avoid the prospect of inconsistent decisions and interesting debates about issue estoppel.

This problem has already occurred in practice, and there appears to be no easy solution to it. If the contract between the creditor and the principal contains an arbitration clause, the surety cannot join in the arbitration proceedings without the consent of both parties. One possible answer would be for the contract of suretyship and the underlying contract to contain specific provisions whereby the principal, creditor and surety consent to tripartite arbitration. Alternatively, a clause could be inserted in the contract between creditor and principal whereby the arbitration clause is agreed to be ineffective if the dispute involves questions of liability of a surety, and the principal agrees that he can be sued in the same proceedings and before the same court as the surety. Given the potential disruption to the creditor which an exclusive arbitration clause can cause, however, it is unlikely that a surety or principal would be persuaded to agree to such terms unless the creditor was in a strong enough bargaining position to dictate them. A further solution now arises as a result of the Contracts (Rights of Third Parties) Act 1999, ss.1 and 8, by which a stranger to a contract containing an arbitration clause may be given the right to enforce that clause and be treated as a party to the arbitration agreement. It is not clear how this would work in practice in the context of suretyship, because even if the creditor conferred the right on a surety to participate in an arbitration between the creditor and principal, the surety might not wish to avail himself of it.

High Court or county court?

7–025　　If the creditor is able to commence proceedings against the surety in England, the choice between starting his action in the county court or in the High Court will often depend on such factors as the amount he is claiming and the subject-matter of the claim.[54] However, he may have no choice in the matter: for example, by s.141 of the Consumer Credit Act 1974, any action by a creditor to enforce a regulated agreement or any security related to it must be brought in the county court and nowhere else. If the action is brought in the High Court, it will be transferred to the county court.

If proceedings are commenced in the High Court, the case may fall within a class which is assigned to a particular division, and therefore if it is commenced in a different division it may be susceptible to transfer. For example, an action pertaining to a mortgage or charge over land which is commenced in the High Court should be brought in the Chancery Division.[55] If the matter is not assigned to a particular division, the creditor should choose whichever division appears most suited to the case, bearing in mind the nature of the transaction guaranteed: for example, a case concerning the guarantee of a charterer's obligations under a charterparty would probably be most effectively disposed of in the Commercial Court.

Another important factor which may influence his decision, and which is sometimes overlooked, is the state of the lists. Generally the creditor will be anxious to avoid delay, so in a case which might be brought in the Chancery Division or in the Queen's Bench Division, it is always worthwhile making

---

54 See generally Pt 7 of the Civil Procedure Rules 1999 and the practice direction supplementing it, the High Court and County Courts Jurisdiction Order 1991 (SI 1991/724), the Courts and Legal Services Act 1990 and the County Courts Act 1984.
55 Supreme Court Act 1981, Sch.1.

enquiries to ascertain the likely time it will take the action to come to trial or, in simpler cases, the likely time before an application for summary judgment will be heard. The creditor may then choose to proceed in the division which is likely to deal with the matter most expeditiously.

An application for summary judgment may be made under Pt 24 of the Civil Procedure Rules in either the High Court or county court after service of the claim form. Alternatively, the creditor may decide to serve a statutory demand and then petition for the winding-up or bankruptcy of the surety instead of suing him. However, this is only appropriate in the most straightforward, uncontentious cases, and will backfire on the creditor if he uses it merely as a tactic to encourage the surety to pay quickly: see *Re A Company (No.0012209 of 1991)* [1992] 2 All E.R. 797, Hoffmann J.

Parties to the proceedings

Joint obligors

Quite apart from the difficulties which may arise when the creditor has a **7–026** free choice whether or not to sue both the principal and the surety, there may be situations in which he is bound to sue them both, or to sue all the sureties in the same proceedings. As a general rule, if the liability of the surety is several, or joint and several, the creditor may sue the surety independently without joining in other parties to the action, or he may sue some or all of them.[56] If it is joint, on the other hand, all the relevant parties should be joined because judgment against one would operate as a bar against the rest.[57] Moreover, any surety may prevent the action from continuing without their joinder. If one of the joint promisors dies, the liability will devolve on the survivors. By virtue of s.81 of the Law of Property Act 1925, if a contract is made under seal with two or more persons jointly, it is construed as being joint and several.[58]

Any right which the creditor might have to proceed independently against the principal and any sureties is subject to any statutory obligation which he may have. For example, by s.141(5) of the Consumer Credit Act 1974, unless otherwise provided by rules of court, all the parties to a regulated agreement, and any surety, shall be made parties to any proceedings relating to the agreement.

Guarantees given to more than one creditor

Where the guarantee has been given to more than one creditor, the rules **7–027** are very similar to those stated above. If the guarantee is given to the creditors severally, or s.81 of the Law of Property Act 1925 applies, each creditor may sue upon it by himself, and so may his personal representa-

---

56 See generally CPR Pt 19; *Collins v Prosser* (1823) 1 B. & C. 682; *Fell v Goslin* (1852) 7 Exch. 185; *Ellis v Emmanuel* (1876) 1 Ex. D. 157, *Armstrong v Cahill* (1880) 6 L.R. Ir. 440.
57 *Other v Iveson* (1855) 3 Drew. 177.
58 As to the construction of a guarantee or indemnity as being joint or several see Ch.4 at para.4–011.

tives, though they may all join as plaintiffs in the same action if they so wish.[59] If the guarantee is given to them jointly, all the creditors should be parties to the action.[60] If one of them dies, the survivors, or the personal representatives of the last survivor, may sue upon it.[61]

Guarantees given to partnerships

7–028 If a guarantee is given for the benefit of all the partners in a firm, though it was given to one of them, all the partners may sue on it: *Garrett v Handley* (1825) 4 B. & C. 664.[62] However, if the guarantee is given to one member of the firm personally, on his undertaking not to sue certain debtors of the firm, he will be entitled to sue on the guarantee alone without joining the rest of his partners: *Agacio v Forbes* (1861) 14 Moo. P.C.C. 160. By virtue of RSC Ord. 81, r.1, the partners of a partnership carrying on business within the jurisdiction may sue in the name of the firm of which they were partners at the time when the cause of action accrued.

Trustees and other representatives

7–029 A guarantee may be given to a trustee on behalf of third persons to secure the performance of obligations to such persons, and even though the third persons may be a fluctuating and changing body, the guarantee may be enforced by the trustee against the surety. Thus a guarantee given to the trustees of an unincorporated association may be sued on by the trustees for the benefit of the individual members whom they represent: *Metcalf v Bruin* (1810) 2 Camp. 422. This rule may apply even if the person to whom the guarantee is given is not a trustee in the legal sense, but it is clear that the guarantee is given to him for the benefit of a particular body of persons who are exposed to the relevant loss or damage.[63]

Who may sue on the guarantee?

7–030 Provided that the conditions of s.4 of the Statute of Frauds are met, a guarantee which is not addressed to anyone may be sued on by the person to whom, or for whose benefit, it was given.[64] The parties to the contract may be sufficiently identified if the person for whose benefit it was given signs a written document of acceptance.[65]

---

59 See, *e.g. Place v Delegal* (1838) 4 Bing. N.C. 426; *Palmer v Sparshott* (1842) 4 Man. & G. 137.

60 *Pugh v Stringfield* (1857) 3 C.B.N.S. 2; (1878) 4 C.B.N.S. 364, and see CPR r.19.3.

61 *Anderson v Martindale* (1801) 1 East. 497.

62 This is so *a fortiori* if the partner to whom it was given did not carry on a separate business to which the guarantee could relate: *Walter v Dodson* (1827) 3 C. & P. 162. See also *Moller v Lambert* (1810) 2 Camp. 548.

63 See, *e.g. Lloyd's v Harper* (1880) 16 Ch. D. 290; *Lamb v Vice* (1840) 6 M. & W. 467.

64 If extrinsic evidence is allowed to clarify a guarantee so as to identify the person to whom it was given, only that person may bring an action on the guarantee: *Boral Resources (Q) Pty Ltd v Donnelly* [1988] 1 Qd. R. 506.

65 *Williams v Byrnes* (1863) 1 Moo. P.C.C.N.S. 154 at 198; see also *Walton v Dodson* (1827) 3 C. & P. 162, and *Re Agra and Masterman's Bank* (1867) 2 Ch. App. 391.

Sometimes a person who is not a direct party to a guarantee or indemnity or fidelity bond of suretyship may sue on it as being entitled to the benefit of it. However, he must be able to demonstrate an actual beneficial right which places him in the position of a beneficiary under the contract. Thus in *Re Stratton Ex p. Salting* (1883) 25 Ch. D. 148, a person whose securities had been fraudulently pledged to a bank for a debt of a partnership was held by the Court of Appeal to be entitled to the benefit of a guarantee for payment to the bank of the partnership debts, which had been given by the only partner who was innocent of the fraud.

It is often difficult to evaluate what degree of proximity to the contract of suretyship the alleged "beneficiary" has to show in order to fall within the protected class. In the Irish case of *Kenney v Employers Liability Insurance Corporation* [1901] 1 I.R. 301, the mortgagees of an estate appointed a receiver and a bond was given for the faithful discharge of his duties. The receiver was fraudulent. The mortgagees, who had been paid out of the estate, were held to be entitled to recover under the bond for the benefit of the mortgagor who had suffered loss as a result of the fraud. This decision can be contrasted with *Re British Power Traction and Lighting Company Ltd* [1910] 2 Ch. 470:

> A receiver in a debenture-holders' action, W, was empowered to borrow up to £3,000 to be secured as a first class charge on the assets. He joined in the usual type of surety bond with two sureties, for the proper discharge of his duties. W borrowed in excess of the £3,000 and incurred heavy liabilities to trade creditors. The company was put into liquidation. W lodged his cash account which showed a deficiency of £400, which he could not pay. The court held that he had incurred justifiable debts of £900 in excess of the £3,000, against which the £400 deficiency could be set off (leaving £500 for the benefit of persons claiming in the liquidation). The trade creditors who had supplied W tried to claim the £400 deficiency under the surety bond.

The court held that they were not entitled to do so. The bond had been given to secure the estate, not the creditors, and so they could not enforce it in equity. The estate had suffered no loss, and the creditors only had an indirect claim, through the receiver, which was limited to the net amount of his indemnity, £500. They could not recover the balance from the sureties.

The common law position has now been modified by statute. If the third party is named in the contract, or is a member of a class of persons identified or described in it, and the contract provides that he may enforce its terms, or the terms of the contract confer a benefit on him, he may sue to enforce those terms or obtain that benefit as though he were a party: Contracts (Rights of Third Parties) Act 1999. However, these provisions only apply to contracts made after May 11, 2000, unless the contract was made on or after November 11, 1999 and expressly provides for the Act to apply. The Act does not apply to contracts on a bill of exchange, promissory note or other negotiable instrument.

Assignees

7–031   In the absence of express agreement to the contrary, the creditor is entitled
to assign the guaranteed debt and the securities for the debt to someone
else.[66] The principles which apply are the same as for the assignment of any
other contract, and the assignee acquires all the rights of the assignor, and
may sue in his own name on the guarantee.[67] The surety is not discharged
by the assignment, and it makes no difference to his position whether he is
given notice of it or not, though as a matter of prudence the creditor ought
to give him notice.[68] However, a stranger to the contract may not enforce it
in the absence of at least an informal assignment: *Sacher Investment Pty Ltd
v Forma Steros Consultants Pty Ltd* [1976] 1 N.S.W.L.R. 5.[69] This rule is
subject to (a) the effect of the Contracts (Rights of Third Parties) Act 1999,
discussed in Chapter 2, and (b) the special exception in the case of sureties
for obligations under leases, where the benefit of the covenants by the
surety are enforceable by an assignee of the reversion without express
agreement: *Swift (PBA) Investments v Combined English Stores Group Plc*
[1989] A.C. 632.[70] Although *Sacher Investments v Forma Steros* was a case
about a lease, and therefore it would not be decided in the same way on its
facts today, its general reasoning is probably unimpaired and would apply
to other types of contract of suretyship.

In the contract of suretyship is a guarantee, the assignee of the guarantee
or other security must also be the assignee of the underlying debt. In
Hutchens v Deaville Investments Pty Ltd (1986) 68 A.L.R. 367, the Australian High Court held that the debt owed by a guarantor on default of the
principal is the same debt as is owed by the principal. Accordingly, a
creditor cannot assign the benefit of a guarantee or other security for the
principal debt whilst at the same time purporting to retain the benefit of
the guaranteed debt, thus converting one debt into two, one of which is
owed by the guarantor to the assignee and the other by the principal debtor
to the assignor.

A more difficult question which sometimes arises is whether the assignment by the creditor of his rights under the underlying principal contract
also operates as an implied assignment of his rights under the guarantee. In
many cases it would not, and indeed it might terminate the obligations of
the surety, because there would be a material alteration in the nature of the
principal obligation from an obligation owed to the creditor into an

---

66 *Wheatley v Bastow* (1855) 7 De G. & G. 261; *Bradford Old Bank v Sutcliffe* [1918] 2 K.B.
833 at 841, *per* Pickford L.J. *Cf. Sheers v Thimbleby & Son* (1897) 76 L.T. 709, where the
guarantee was intended for the personal benefit of the creditor only and was therefore
incapable of being assigned.
67 *Wheatley v Bastow* (above); *Re Hallett & Co* [1894] 2 Q.B. 256.
68 *Wheatley v Bastow* (1855) 7 De G. M. & G. 261 *per* Turner L.J. at 280; *Bradford Old Bank v
Sutcliffe* [1918] 2 K.B. 833 at 841, 842, 846 and 852.
69 See also *West v Lee Soon* (1915) 9 W.W.R. 644.
70 Following and approving *Kumar v Dunning* [1989] Q.B. 193. The position in Australia is
now the same, see *Lang v Asemo Pty Ltd* [1989] V.R. 773. These cases are discussed in
detail in Ch.18.

obligation owed to someone else. Even if the assignment of the principal debt does not operate to discharge the guarantor, any right of the creditor to sue the guarantor is suspended until his right to recover the underlying debt is restored to him: see *Clark v Devukaj* [1993] 2 Qd. R. 10.

In the absence of a prohibition against assignment, a contract of indemnity may also be enforced by an assignee. However such contracts depend on their true construction, and if the obligation is intended to be personal, an assignee may not be entitled to enforce it.

Evidence of liability

Conclusive evidence clauses

Once the creditor has proved the existence and terms of the contract,[71] he **7–032** must establish that the surety is liable, which in turn usually involves proving that the principal is liable. A very useful way of cutting short the evidential process is to make sure that the contract of suretyship contains a "conclusive evidence clause" which provides that a notice in a certain form, or a demand by the creditor, shall be conclusive evidence as between creditor and surety that the principal is liable: see *Bache & Co (London) Ltd v Banque Vernes et Commerciale de Paris* [1973] 2 Lloyd's Rep. 437. In that case the Court of Appeal held that the guarantor must usually pay the sum certified to be due, and if it subsequently transpires that he has paid too much, he can institute separate proceedings against the creditor to recover the excess.

The judgment of the Court of Appeal in the case was firmly founded on the rationale that "the commercial practice of inserting conclusive evidence clauses is only acceptable because the bankers or brokers who insert them are known to be honest and reliable men of business who are most unlikely to make a mistake".[72] It therefore remains to be seen whether different considerations might be applied to a clause of this kind in a contract where the creditor does not fall within that category, or an analogous category of professionals, and the surety's safeguard in terms of recouping any overpayment might prove illusory.

A term providing that a certificate as to "the amount of principal and of interest" due may be complied with even if the certificate fails to itemise the principal and interest separately and merely states a global figure: *Je Maintiendrai Pty Ltd v Australia and New Zealand Banking Group Ltd* (1985) 38 S.A.S.R. 70.

Similarly, the creditor may include a term in the contract which is designed to avoid prolonged dispute by the surety about whether there has been a breach of contract by the principal or by himself, by making the creditor the sole arbiter of that issue. This may be tantamount to turning the guarantee into a performance guarantee. An example of such a clause is

---

71 See generally Chs 3 and 4.
72 *Per* Denning L.J. at 440.

to be found in *The "Glacier Bay"* [1996] 1 Lloyd's Rep. 370, where the contract provided that one of the parties to it was to be the "sole judge of the validity of any claim made hereunder". The Court of Appeal held that although it was unusual for one party to be the sole arbiter of the validity of any claim made against it, the agreement was of an unusual nature and was in common use internationally in the oil trade. The validity of the clause was upheld, subject to the (conceded) duty on the party concerned to act fairly in making any such determination. It would appear, therefore, that even in cases where a clause of this nature is inserted in the guarantee, for example one purporting to give the creditor the power to determine whether or not there had been a breach of the principal contract, the Court would retain the power to review any determination made by the creditor if it could be shown that he acted in bad faith or the decision was perverse. See also the discussion of the possible impact on such clauses of the Unfair Terms in Consumer Contracts Regulations 1999 at Chapter 3, paras 3–036 and 3–037 above.

Proof without conclusive evidence clauses

7–033   Conclusive evidence clauses are particularly useful where the accounts as between creditor and principal are fairly complex and it would take a very long time to prove each and every entry on the credit and debit side. In the absence of such a clause, the creditor has to prove the relevant "debt, default or miscarriage", or the event which triggers the liability under an indemnity, in the usual way that any other claimant under a contract would go about proving a breach.[73] He also has to prove that the event on which he relies falls within the terms of the contract of suretyship. In *Bacon v Chesney* (1816) 1 Stark 192, Lord Ellenborough said that "the claim as against a surety is *strictissimi juris*, and it is incumbent on plaintiff to show that the terms of the guarantee have been strictly complied with".[74]

In *Re Kitchin Ex p. Young* (1881) 17 Ch. D. 668, it was held that a judgment or award in an arbitration to which the creditor and principal were parties, but the surety was not, is not even evidence that may be used to establish the liability of the surety. The reason for the rule was explained by James L.J. in these terms at 672:

> "The principal debtor might entirely neglect to defend the surety properly in the arbitration; he might make admissions of various things

---

73 In the case of an indemnity against liability to a third party, a judgment against the creditor in an action brought by the third party which has been bona fide defended is conclusive evidence of such liability: see *Gray v Lewis* (1873) 8 Ch. App. 1035. On the other hand an indemnity against "loss sustained" requires proof of actual loss: *Montagu Stanley & Co v JC Solomon Ltd* [1932] 1 K.B. 611.

74 That was a case in which the creditor was allowed to adduce evidence to establish that an invoice delivered by him to the debtor, which on its face suggested that he had been trading with the debtor on different credit terms from those agreed upon with the surety, contained a mistake, and that the terms had not been varied. See also *Pattison v Belford Union Guardians* (1856) 1 H. & N. 523.

which would be binding as against him, but which would not, in the absence of agreement, be binding as against the surety."[75]

Admissions made by the principal in the course of such proceedings, however, might be used in evidence in the proceedings against the surety subject to the provisions of the Civil Evidence Act 1995, by which all hearsay statements are now admissible in civil proceedings.[76] Apart from any documents which are admissible under the Act, accounts and business records kept by the principal are in some cases admissible to the prejudice of the surety.[77] A receipt signed by a surety may be evidence against him, but is not always conclusive evidence. Thus in *Straton v Rastall* (1788) 2 Term Rep. 366, an annuity bond was granted by two persons jointly, one of whom was known to be only a surety for the other. The bond was void because the creditor failed to comply with certain statutory formalities requiring registration. It was held that he could not recover the consideration money from the surety (who had not received any of it) notwithstanding that the surety and the principal had jointly signed a receipt for it.[78]

It would appear that a creditor may choose to enforce the obligations of the guarantor in part. In *Bank Negara Indonesia 1946 v Taylor* [1995] C.L.C. 255, the defendant had signed an unlimited "all moneys" guarantee in favour of a bank which was intended to cover the indebtedness of company A but which, as a matter of construction, extended to the liabilities of company B. Both companies became insolvent. The bank originally demanded the full amount of the indebtedness due from both companies and sought summary judgment; the guarantor claimed, unsuccessfully, that he had a defence on the grounds of misrepresentation. However, somewhat unusually, at the hearing the bank abandoned its claim for the full amount and sought rectification to limit its claim to the sums due from company A only. The judge granted rectification; the Court of Appeal (Hoffmann, Glidewell and Hirst L.JJ.) held that a plaintiff who relies on a written instrument does not have to prove that the document accorded with the intention of the parties, and the guarantee was enforceable unless the defendant could rely upon some legal or equitable defence based upon an absence of such intent. Consequently, whether or not rectification was available, the bank was entitled to sue on the guarantee as it stood, and it could also limit its claim if it felt that it would be unconscionable to claim

---

75 Similar policy reasons were given by Robert Goff L.J. in *Bruns v Colocotronis (The "Vasso")* [1979] 2 Lloyd's Rep. 412, who pointed out that the surety might otherwise be bound by an award made in the absence of the principal. See also *Compania Sudamericana de Fletes v African Continental Bank* [1973] 1 Lloyd's Rep. 21.

76 At common law, admissions are generally only binding on the person who makes them: see *Evans v Beattie* (1803) 5 Esp. 26, and *Re Kitchin* (1881) 17 Ch. 668 especially *per* Lush L.J. at 673. *Cf. Bacon v Chesney* (above) (admission made by debtor as agent for surety). As to admissions generally, see, *e.g. Perchard and Hamerton v Tindall* (1795) 1 Esp. 394.

77 See, *e.g. Lysaght v Walker* (1881) 5 Bli. N.S. 1; *Abbeyleix Union Guardians v Sutcliffe* (1890) 26 L.R. Ir. 332; *Middleton v Melton* (1829) 5 Man. & Ry. K.B. 264; *Perchard & Hamerton v Tindall* (above).

78 See also *Bristow v Eastman* (1749) 1 Esp. 172.

the full amount which was prima facie due on the face of the document signed by the guarantor. If the bank had not limited its claim in that way, it would have been a matter for the guarantor to seek rectification.

Set-off and counterclaim

7–034 The liability of a surety under a contract of guarantee or indemnity may be made the subject of a set-off or counterclaim in an action brought by him against the creditor: see CPR r.16.6 and Pt 20. Likewise, he may raise a set-off or counterclaim against the creditor in any action brought on the contract of suretyship. The right of the surety to raise a set-off or counterclaim may be expressly excluded by contract, see *The "Fedora"* [1986] 2 Lloyd's Rep. 441 and *Coca Cola Financial Corporation v Finsat International Ltd* [1998] Q.B. 43, although such a clause is unlikely to satisfy the requirements of the Unfair Contract Terms Act or the Unfair Terms in Consumer Contracts Regulations 1999, and therefore is almost certain to be unenforceable if the surety is a consumer: see the discussion in Chapter 3, paras 3–036–3–037.

Miscellaneous considerations

Preserving assets for judgment

7–035 The creditor will wish to ensure that it is worth his while suing the surety. If he has evidence that the surety is likely to remove assets from the jurisdiction or otherwise dissipate them so as to render any judgment against him nugatory, he may apply to the court for a freezing injunction or other appropriate interlocutory relief.[79] The court has power to grant a freezing injunction in aid of proceedings in another EC or EFTA contracting states and (since April 1997) in aid of proceedings anywhere else in the world.[80] A parallel jurisdiction exists in respect of arbitration proceedings in England or elsewhere: Arbitration Act 1996, s.44, s.2(3). The injunction may be expressed in terms which cover assets belonging to the defendant outside the jurisdiction.

Counter-securities

7–036 In the absence of express or implied agreement, the creditor is not entitled to the benefit of any security obtained by the surety from the principal: *Re Walker, Sheffield Banking Co v Clayton* [1892] 1 Ch. 621.[81]

---

79 See CPR r.25.1 and Practice Direction to Pt 25, Interim Injunctions, and generally Gee, *Mareva Injunctions and Anton Piller Orders* (FT Law and Tax, 4th ed., 1995).
80 Civil Jurisdiction and Judgments Act 1982, s.25 as extended by Order in Council made under s.25(3): SI 1997/415; Lugano Convention, Art.24 and see, *e.g. Republic of Haiti v Duvalier* [1990] 1 Q.B. 202.
81 See *Ex p. Waring, Inglis, Clarke* (1815) 19 Ves. 345; *Re Yewdall, Ex p. Barnfather* (1877) 46 L.J. Bcy. 87; *Wilding v Richards* (1845) 1 Coll. 655; *Ex p. Rushforth* (1805) 10 Ves. 409, and the discussion in Rowlatt (*op. cit.*), at 154–155.

Claims against an insolvent surety

A creditor may prove against the estate of an insolvent surety on his **7–037** guarantee.[82] However, he has to prove the extent of the surety's liability. As already noted above, the fact that he may have obtained judgment against the principal will not suffice, because that judgment is not evidence of the liability of the surety: *Re Kitchin Ex p. Young* (1881) 17 Ch. D. 668.

The creditor must give credit for any sum which he has already realised before proving, and for dividends which have been declared in the principal debtor's bankruptcy, even if not actually received by him: *Re Blakeley Ex p. Aachener Disconto Gesellschaft* (1892) 9 Morr. 173. However, if there are several sureties jointly and severally liable to the creditor, the creditor can prove against the estate of one of those sureties who has become bankrupt, for the whole of the debt, without giving credit for any sums received from the co-sureties since the date of the receiving order, provided that he does not recover more than 100 pence in the pound altogether: *Re Houlder* [1929] 1 Ch. 205.[83]

Claims against the surety when the principal is insolvent

Usually if the principal is known to be insolvent, the creditor will bring his **7–038** action against the surety instead. He may, however, prove in the bankruptcy or liquidation of the principal. The effects of his proof on the surety's position are discussed in Chapter 13. However, the question may arise as to the creditor's right to claim against the surety if a payment made by the principal to the creditor is set aside as a wrongful preference, and he has to repay the money to the liquidator or trustee in bankruptcy.[84] The position appears to be that if the creditor was not a party to the preference, he probably can recover the money from the surety, on the grounds that there was no valid payment to him and he has not done anything to discharge the surety on equitable grounds: *Pritchard v Hancock* (1843) 6 Man. & G. 151; *Petty v Cooke* (1871) L.R. 6 Q.B. 790.

Claims against the estate of a deceased surety

If the liability of the surety has not accrued by the time that he dies, the **7–039** general rule is that his personal representatives cannot be forced to set aside a sum out of his estate to meet a potential future liability on the guarantee. In *Antrobus v Davidson* (1817) 3 Mer. 569, an application made by the executor of the deceased creditor against the representatives of the deceased surety, for an order that the latter should set aside a sufficient

---

82 See generally *Halsbury's Laws* (4th ed.), Vol. 3 and Fletcher, *The Law of Insolvency* (Sweet & Maxwell, 1990).
83 Similarly if a co-surety deposits money with the creditor to appropriate towards the debt as he thinks fit, and there has been no appropriation before the creditor proves against the surety's estate, it need not be deducted: *Commercial Bank of Australia Ltd v Wilson & Co's Estate Official Assignee* [1893] A.C. 181.
84 See the discussion in Ch.9 at para.9–002.

sum out of the estate to answer future contingent demands, was dismissed. Grant M.R. said:

> "A person who is as yet no creditor, and who may never become one, is claiming to force out of the hands of the executor the utmost extent of what can ever become due. I cannot make such a decree without laying it down as a rule that, whenever a person bound in an obligation of this sort dies, a court of equity will compel his executor to bring into court the whole amount of the penalty of the bond. I can find no trace of the exercise of any such jurisdiction."

However, if the liability of the surety has already accrued, or if the terms of the guarantee are worded in such a way that he appears to be a principal debtor with a liability to make a payment on a fixed future date, albeit that he is really a surety, a sufficient sum must be set aside out of his estate to meet that liability, even if there is a prospect that the principal debtor might pay the debt instead: *Atkinson v Grey* (1853) 1 Sm. & G. 577. See also *Basch v Stekel* [2001] L. & T.R. 1 discussed in Chapter 18.

Claims by the estate of a deceased creditor

7–040 The personal representatives of a deceased creditor may be entitled to pursue his claim against the surety in the normal way. If the creditor has left a legacy to the surety, there is an alternative open to them. The executor of a deceased creditor is entitled to retain the amount of the debt from such a legacy: *Coates v Coates* (1864) 33 Beav. 249; *Re Melton, Milk v Towers* [1918] 1 Ch. 37. This right will exist notwithstanding that the limitation period for bringing a claim against the surety has expired: *Coates v Coates* (above).

Chapter 8

Revocation of Contracts of Suretyship

Introduction

One of the most important matters which the prospective surety will wish to **8–001** ascertain is the potential duration of his liability once he has entered into a binding contract with the creditor.[1] Is he entitled to terminate the contract of guarantee or indemnity voluntarily, on giving notice to the creditor? If there is no express provision for giving notice, can he terminate on giving reasonable notice, or is his liability co-terminous with the duration of the principal's obligations in the underlying principal contract? Further, what effect on his liability would such a notice have: would it cancel his liability altogether, or only protect him in respect of future transactions between the creditor and principal? Finally, what effect, if any, will a supervening event such as the death or insanity of the principal or a co-surety have on the contract of suretyship?[2]

In most commentaries on this subject, and in the cases, the words "revoke" and "cancel" are used to mean voluntary termination by the surety. This terminology can be somewhat misleading, as both words suggest that the liability of the surety is cancelled *ab initio*, whereas it will be seen that this is not usually the case.

Revocation by the surety

Revocation by express notice

A contract of guarantee or indemnity may expressly state that it may be **8–002** terminated by the surety or the creditor, or both, on the giving of notice.[3] Most modern guarantees will contain such a provision, which will usually state that the notice must be given in writing, and stipulate the identity of the addressee and the address to which it must be sent. The contract may

---

1 As to the revocation of the surety's offer prior to acceptance or part-performance, see the discussion in Ch.2 at paras 2–003–2–007.
2 The effect of insolvency of the principal and changes in the constitution of the parties to the guarantee are considered elsewhere in this work, in particular in Ch.9 and Ch.13.
3 See, *e.g. Solvency Mutual Guarantee Co v Froane* (1861) 7 H. & N. 5; *Boyd v Robins and Langlands* (1859) 5 C.B.N.S. 597; *Morrison v Barking Chemicals Co Ltd* [1919] 2 Ch. 325.

provide that the notice may only be given on performance of certain conditions, or on the occurrence of certain eventualities.

Revocation in the absence of contractual provision

Continuing guarantees

8–003   If the surety enters into a continuing guarantee,[4] under which his liability continues to accrue, the question whether he may revoke it depends on whether the consideration for his promise is divisible or entire; this in turn depends on the nature of the principal contract. If the consideration is divisible, the guarantee is treated as if it were a standing offer by the surety which is accepted *pro tanto* by part-performance of the consideration, and therefore, in accordance with the general rule that an offer may be revoked at any time before it is accepted, the surety may revoke all future liability under the guarantee at any time, save insofar as the contract provides otherwise.[5] Thus, unless the right is excluded by the contract, a continuing guarantee to secure the balance of a running account at a bank is revocable at any time in respect of future advances. The reason was stated by Bowen J. in *Coulthart v Clementson* (1879) 5 Q.B.D. 42 at 46: "The guarantee . . . is divisible as to each advance . . . into an irrevocable promise or guarantee only when the advance is made."[6]

The right to revoke a continuing guarantee is not excluded simply by the fact that it is given under seal, or the fact that it is stated to be for a specified period.[7] It has been said that the right of cancellation is an inherent characteristic of a continuing guarantee,[8] but whilst this is true of many continuing guarantees, it is not true of all, since a continuing guarantee may not be revoked if the consideration for it is indivisible, unless the contract expressly confers such a right on the surety. Thus in *Lloyd's v Harper* (1880) 16 Ch. D. 290, the surety guaranteed the liabilities of his son to Lloyd's on the son's admission to Lloyd's as an underwriter for his life. The admission was irrevocable, and therefore the father could not revoke his guarantee. Cotton L.J. said, at 317, that the guarantee was "given in consideration of an act done once and for all by the persons to whom the guarantee was given". The rationale behind the rule appears to be that if the creditor has entered into an irrevocable transaction in reliance upon the guarantee, he should not be deprived of his security by the

---

4 See Ch.4 at para.4–017.

5 *Re Crace, Balfour v Crace* [1902] 1 Ch. 733; *Offord v Davies* (1862) 12 C.B.N.S. 738; *Brocklebank v Moore* (1823) 2 Stark. 590; *Bastow v Bennett* (1812) 3 Camp. 220; *Lloyd's v Harper* (1880) 16 Ch. D. 290; *Wingfield v De St Croix* (1919) 35 T.L.R. 432; *Royal Bank v TVM Catering Ltd* (1980) B.C.L.R. 199 (Can).

6 See the similar statement by Lush J. in *Lloyd's v Harper* (1880) 16 Ch. D. 290 at 319.

7 *Re Crace, Balfour v Crace*, above, at 738. It was formerly considered that a guarantee given under seal was irrevocable, see, *e.g. Hassell v Long* (1814) 2 M. & S. 363 at 370–371, *per* Lord Ellenborough C.J., but this view no longer obtains: see *Halsbury's Laws* (4th ed., 1993 reissue), Vol. 20, para.290 and the cases cited in n.4, and the discussion in Rowlatt, *Principal and Surety*, (*op. cit.*), pp.60–61.

8 See McGuinness, *The Law of Guarantee* (*op. cit.*), para.6.28.

voluntary act of the surety. Otherwise the creditor might be induced to make a substantial loan to the principal on the faith of a guarantee by the surety, only to find that the surety determines the guarantee voluntarily immediately after the advance has been made, leaving the loan unsecured.

When is the underlying consideration divisible?

It is often difficult to determine whether the consideration for a guarantee is entire or divisible. In the case of a guarantee for rent, if the tenancy is for a fixed period of a number of months or years, then prima facie the consideration is indivisible and the guarantee may not be revoked. On the other hand, a guarantor of rent payable from week to week may give notice of revocation. In *Wingfield v De St Croix* (1919) 35 T.L.R. 432, the principal was a gardener working for the surety, who entered into occupation of a cottage belonging to the creditor. The surety guaranteed the rent for three months and from week to week thereafter. Four months after the tenancy began, the gardener left the service of the surety, and the surety gave the creditor a week's notice of termination of the guarantee. It was held that the guarantee was continuous and that the consideration was divisible, and consequently it could be terminated by notice.

The problem most frequently arises in the context of fidelity guarantees. It has been held that a fidelity bond given to secure the due performance of an office by the principal cannot be revoked, on the ground that the appointment of the principal is an indivisible consideration.[9] However, one matter which does not appear to have been considered by the courts, and which is of particular relevance to fidelity guarantees, is whether the surety may revoke the guarantee if the creditor has a right to terminate the underlying principal contract by giving a specified period of notice. In such a case, it is strongly arguable that the consideration is divisible: the creditor is not prejudiced by the surety having a right to revoke the guarantee, because on receipt of notice of revocation from the surety he may decide whether or not to terminate the underlying transaction.[10]

8–004

Specific guarantees

In the absence of an express term allowing the surety to give notice of termination, the general rule is that a specific guarantee is not determinable. This is because a creditor who has entered into an irrevocable transaction on the strength of a guarantee should not be deprived of his security by its subsequent revocation or cancellation.[11]

8–005

---

9 *Re Crace, Balfour v Crace* [1902] 1 Ch. 733, *Gordon v Calvert* (1828) 4 Russ. 581. See also *Burgess v Eve* (1872) L.R. 13 Eq. 450. Similar results have been reached in other jurisdictions, see, *e.g. R v Leeming Applegarth's Executors* (1850) 7 U.C.R. 306 (Can), *Myingan Municipality v Maung Po Nyun* (1930) I.L.R. 8 Ran. 320 (Ind); *cf. North British Mercantile Insurance Co v Kean* (1888) 16 O.R. 117 (Can).

10 This view is shared by the editors of *Chitty on Contracts* (*op. cit.*): see Vol. 2, at para.44–017.

11 See *Lloyd's v Harper* (1880) 16 Ch. D. 290, and the discussion above.

The effect of revocation

8–006   If the surety is entitled to revoke or cancel a guarantee on giving notice to the creditor, the revocation will not affect rights which have accrued prior to the date of termination.[12] Thus, in the case of a guarantee of an overdraft, the guarantor's liability does not remain static at the date of termination. He will remain liable for the principal amount outstanding at that date, together with any interest which has already accrued on it or which may accrue thereafter, and he is only exonerated in respect of any future advances of further principal sums. He may terminate his liability altogether by paying the creditor the sum outstanding at the date of termination, up to the limit of his guarantee.[13] It has been suggested in Canada that withdrawal from or cancellation of the guarantee is *only* effective if the notice is accompanied by payment of the full amount then due and owing.[14] However, this does not accord with the underlying rationale, or with the majority of the authorities on the subject, which place no such limitation on the right of revocation: the surety's right to revoke a standing offer is not conditional upon his satisfaction of earlier bargains. Further, the amounts advanced by the creditor may not be repayable at the time when the guarantee is cancelled, and if the surety volunteers payment prematurely, he may not be entitled to recover the money from the principal.[15]

The surety is only entitled to call upon the principal to release or indemnify him when his liability to the creditor has accrued; this may occur as soon as he has given notice of cancellation. When the notice expires and possibly before, he may seek *quia timet* relief against the principal.[16]

Once a guarantee has been revoked, the liabilities of the surety cannot be revived unless there is a fresh agreement which complies with all the necessary formalities. In *Silverburn Finance Ltd v Salt* [2001] 2 All E.R. (Comm) 438, the claimant, S, was a finance company which factored invoices on a recourse basis for a company, N, under an agreement dated September 19, 1991. In 1992, the defendants, who were the directors of N, executed written guarantees to pay on demand "any monies due to S in respect of any unpaid invoices re discount charges and all costs and

---

12 *Tooke Bros Ltd v Al-Walters Ltd* [1935] D.L.R. 295; *Westminster Bank Ltd v Sassoon* (1926) 5 Legal Decisions Affecting Bankers 19 CA; *Commercial Bank of Australia Ltd v Cavanaugh* (1980) 7 N.T.R. 12; *AG Canada v Bank of Montreal* (1984) 32 Man. R. (2d) 98; *National Westminster Bank Ltd v French* (unreported) October 20, 1977; *National House-Building Council v Fraser* [1983] 1 All E.R. 1090; see also *JR Watkins Co v Robertson* [1928] 1 D.L.R. 979. Cancellation is not the same as discharge: cancellation exonerates the surety from future liability, whereas discharge frees him from existing liabilities, see *Royal Bank v TVM Catering Ltd* (1980) 23 B.C.L.R. 199.
13 See *Beckett v Addyman* (1882) 9 Q.B.D. 783 at 791, *Burgess v Eve* (1872) L.R. 13 Eq. 450.
14 By Wilson J. in *Benge v Hanna* (1979) 100 D.L.R. (3d) 218 at 226, citing in support *Royal Bank v Sterns* [1924] 3 D.L.R. 1050; *Starrs v Cosgrave Brewing & Malting Co* (1886) 12 S.C.R. 571 at 593–594 and *Burgess v Eve* (1872) L.R. 13 Eq. 450.
15 See further the critique in McGuinness, *The Law of Guarantee* (*op. cit.*), at para.6.30, n.124.
16 *Morrison v Barking Chemicals Co Ltd* [1919] 2 Ch. 325, and see Ch.10 at paras 10–025 *et seq.*

expenses incurred in enforcing payment". Three months later, a fresh factoring agreement was made between S and N. On December 10, 1992, N asked S to terminate the factoring agreement, and S agreed. One of the directors then had a telephone conversation with a representative of S to find out what the position was under the guarantees. She told him that the guarantees would cover all invoices which had been issued up to December 10. In early January 1993, however, the directors of N approached S and asked if they would resume factoring N's invoices. S agreed, but nothing was said at the time about any guarantees. In 1995, N went into receivership and S tried to claim the outstanding indebtedness from the directors under the guarantees. The Court of Appeal (Rix and Mummery L.JJ.) upheld the decision of the trial judge that the guarantees were revoked on December 10, 1992 with regard to any future liabilities of N, and had not been replaced or revived. Although a fresh oral agreement to factor N's invoices was made in January 1993, no new guarantees were given. In any event, even if was arguable that there was an implicit agreement to revive the guarantees, the requirements of s.4 of the Statute of Frauds were not complied with. Rix L.J. expressed the view that it was extremely doubtful whether the old guarantees could be a sufficient note or memorandum of new or revived guarantees, in the absence of an express agreement to that effect.

Demand guarantees

These general rules are subject to a caveat in the case of demand **8–007** guarantees. Under such a guarantee, the liability of the surety to pay is contingent upon demand, and the creditor has no cause of action against him until such time as the demand is made. If, at the time when the notice of termination expires, no such demand has been made, then at least prima facie there is no accrued liability capable of surviving the termination of the contract, even if the principal has defaulted. In *Thomas v Nottingham Incorporated Football Club Ltd* [1972] Ch. 596, a case concerning a demand guarantee, Goff J. observed in passing, at 600, that the exercise by the guarantor of his right to determine his guarantee "did not exonerate him from liability upon it in respect of the position as it then stood, but made it cease to be operative for the future". Although this observation is literally correct, it does not address the issue whether the "liability" from which he is not exonerated may be contingent. The decision in that case that a surety can claim *quia timet* relief against the principal notwithstanding that no demand has yet been made against him can be justified on the basis that a contingent liability to pay an accrued fixed sum is sufficient to give rise to a right to equitable relief. However, nobody appears to have addressed the argument that *quia timet* relief was inappropriate on the facts of the case because no legitimate demand could ever have been made on the guarantor, and the learned judge appears to have proceeded upon the assumption that such a demand could have been made in the future. The wording of the guarantee is not reproduced in the report and therefore it is impossible to tell whether or not this assumption was well-founded.

In *National Westminster Bank v Hardman* [1988] F.L.R. 302, the point arose directly for decision by the Court of Appeal. The case concerned two demand guarantees given by a director of a company. The guarantees stated, in Clause 3, that:

> "this guarantee shall be a continuing security and shall remain in force notwithstanding any disability or death of the guarantor until determined by three months' notice in writing from the Guarantor or the Personal Representatives of the Guarantor.
>
> But such determination shall not affect the liability of the Guarantor for the amount due hereunder at the date of expiration of the notice with interest as herein provided until payment in full."

The guarantor gave notice under Clause 3. About 18 months after the notice expired, the bank demanded payment. It was common ground that there was no cause of action until a demand was made and that the guarantor's liability until demand was, in the words of Parker L.J., "merely a contingent liability which may never crystallise". The judgment of the Court of Appeal was delivered by Parker L.J. He held that on the wording of the first sentence of Clause 3 it appeared that the guarantee ceased to be in force when the notice expired, and if at that time there were only a contingent liability which had not crystallised, one would expect that no liability remained. He then went on to consider whether that prima facie construction was changed by the proviso or by any other clauses in the contract.

The argument that the proviso was to be read as preserving any contingent liabilities was roundly dismissed; there could be no "amount due hereunder" without any prior demand. Not only was the creditor's interpretation contrary to the language of the proviso but it produced a result which the Court of Appeal plainly regarded as unfair. First, the guarantor would remain contingently liable for an indefinite and unascertainable future period; the limitation period could not begin to run against the creditor until there was a demand. Furthermore, if the bank's interpretation was right, it would be entitled without any demand, at any time in the future, to apply balances standing to the credit of the guarantor's account in satisfaction of the principal's indebtedness pursuant to Clause 5 of the standard terms.

Finally, the Court of Appeal considered an argument based on Clause 7 of the guarantee. This provided that:

> "in case this guarantee shall be determined . . . the bank may continue its account with the debtor notwithstanding the determination . . . and the guarantor's liability in respect of the amount due from the debtor at the date when the determination . . . takes effect along with interest . . . until payment in full shall remain regardless of any subsequent dealings in the amount."

As Parker L.J. observed, the purpose of this clause was to give the bank the right to continue its accounts with the principal without affecting the position of the guarantor, thus affording it protection because such dealings would otherwise discharge the surety. It was not a provision which was directed towards the consequences of termination. The most that could be said was that references in it to the guarantor's liability on "determination" might be otiose if the guarantor's construction of Clause 3 was correct. However this was not necessarily the case; if the creditor did make a demand during the notice period, there would be an actual liability and Clause 7 would be relevant. If Clause 7 made Clause 3 ambiguous, then the *contra proferentem* rule required the court to adopt the interpretation more favourable to the guarantor, which in any event was the correct one. Parker L.J. was not impressed by the argument that this interpretation was uncommercial. The bank had the period of notice in which to find alternative security or make a demand. It could wait until a few days before the notice expired before making a demand, and it could cease to make any advances to the principal thereafter. As for the idea that banks would be forced to make demands on all retiring directors when they did not want to do so, Parker L.J. pointed out that if a creditor makes a demand, he need not take any further steps to enforce the guarantee immediately, because he will have the benefit of the limitation period. The demand simply preserves liability and the bank can then reach an appropriate accommodation with the surety, or the surety can apply for *quia timet* relief.

The decision in *National Westminster Bank v Hardman* has been criticised[17] but appears to be entirely in accordance with principle. The idea that the guarantee should be interpreted in such a way that the surety will remain contingently liable for an indefinite period is an unappealing one, whether or not as a matter of practice banks act promptly in realising their securities. The *Hardman* case was considered by the Court of Appeal two years later in *Royal Bank of Scotland v Slinn* (unreported) CAT No.259 of 1989, March 10. This was an appeal against summary judgment in a case in which the judge had decided that no valid notice of termination had been served by the guarantor. He therefore had no need to deal with the argument that since no demand had been made before the notice expired, the guarantor was not liable. The Court of Appeal, however, disagreed with the judge on the question of the validity of the notice of termination, regarding the matter as arguable. The guarantee was worded slightly differently from the guarantees in *Hardman*. It provided that the guarantee was a continuing security and that it should "remain in force . . . until the expiry of one month from the date of receipt by the Bank of written notice by the Guarantor . . . to discontinue this guarantee". The proviso stated that notice of discontinuance shall not affect "the liability of the guarantor for the amount of the debtor's obligations at the date of expiry of the notice".

---

17 Marks, "Guarantees—the Rights and Wrongs of Determination" (1994) J.B.L. 121. The current editors of *Paget's Law of Banking*, (12th ed. Butterworths, 2003) at para.33.23 describe the decision as "questionable" because "it produces a result which seems unlikely to reflect the true intention of the parties objectively judged".

The bank sought to argue that this proviso preserved the contingent liability of the guarantor, and the Court of Appeal concentrated on this point. It therefore appears to have been accepted that, as in *Hardman*, the clause without the proviso would have the effect of discharging the guarantor if no demand was made before the notice expired. Slade L.J., with whom Ormrod L.J. agreed, said that the question of construction was a difficult one, and that he accepted that it was arguable that the proviso was apt to include the contingent liability. However, it was at least equally arguable that it was not, for the same reasons that Parker L.J. rejected the similar argument in *Hardman* on the wording of the proviso in that guarantee. It was clearly arguable that there was no liability of the guarantor for the amount of the debtor's obligations, if no demand had been made and there was no cause of action against the guarantor until demand. Although the Court was careful not to express any final view on the point of construction, the tenor of Slade L.J.'s observations incline towards a preference for the construction which would not involve an indefinite contingent liability surviving the termination.

There is an earlier case in which a similar issue arose, which was apparently not cited to the Court of Appeal in either *Hardman* or *Slinn*. This was the unreported decision of Robert Goff J. in *National Westminster Bank Ltd v French* (October 20, 1977). The first part of the guarantee was identical to the first sentence in Clause 3 of the guarantees in the *Hardman* case, but the proviso was different. This stated that "such determination shall not affect the liability of the Guarantor for the amount *recoverable* at the date of expiration of the notice". Robert Goff J. held that "recoverable" in this context plainly meant "capable of being recovered", and that the mere fact that a demand must be made does not make the money any more or less recoverable. Consequently the effect of the clause was to crystallise the amount of the liability of the guarantor as at the date of expiry of the notice. In other words, the proviso was apt to preserve the contingent liability of the guarantor whilst placing a maximum limit upon it.

As Hobhouse L.J. stressed, in the case of *Bank of Credit and Commerce International v Simjee* [1997] C.L.C. 135, if the document is clearly worded, the court will give full effect to it even if the result is adverse to the surety. *BCCI v Simjee* was the first case in which all the relevant prior authorities (and the various published articles and commentaries about them) were considered by the Court of Appeal. The relevant clause in that case read as follows:

> "This guarantee is to be a continuing security to you notwithstanding any settlement of account or other matter or thing whatsoever but may and shall be determined (save as below provided) and the liability hereunder crystallised (except as regards unascertained or contingent liabilities and the interest charges costs and expenses hereinbefore referred to) at the expiration of three months after the receipt by you from the undersigned of notice in writing to determine it but notwithstanding determination as to one or more of the undersigned this Guarantee is to remain a continuing security as to the other or others."

The surety argued that this clause had a similar effect to that in *National Westminster Bank v Hardman* on the basis that although the guarantee stated that the liability under it would be "crystallised" on the expiration of the notice, the words in parenthesis, namely, "except as regards unascertained or contingent liabilities", specifically precluded the liability of the surety, which was a contingent upon demand, from "crystallising". The leading judgment was delivered by Hobhouse L.J., who produced an illuminating analysis of the nature of continuing guarantee and the function of a demand in the context of such a guarantee. He drew a distinction between two different ways in which the open-ended nature of a continuing guarantee can be brought to an end. The first is by including a provision which enables the surety to give notice of termination of the guarantee contract so that the creditor is given a period of time within which he may if he chooses make a demand upon the surety; if he does not do so, the contract then comes to an end. That was the effect of the provision in *National Westminster Bank v Hardman*. Another is by having a provision which enables the surety by the service of a notice to bring to an end the continuing character of the guarantee, so that from the expiry of the notice its subject matter becomes the obligations of the principal to the creditor at that time. If the provisions of the guarantee are of this latter kind, the guarantee remains in force, but only as a guarantee of the performance of identified obligations. It remains a demand guarantee so that no cause of action will arise unless and until a demand is made on the surety. However, that demand can only relate to such of the obligations of the principal at the time of the expiry of the notice as still remain unperformed at the time of the demand on the surety.

As a matter of construction, the guarantee in the *Simjee* case fell into the latter category; therefore what the surety was to be entitled to determine by notice was its continuing nature as against him. The words at the end of the clause in question made this clear, as the guarantee expressly retained its continuing nature against any other sureties. The reference to "crystallising" put the matter beyond doubt, because the word "crystallise" is typically used to contrast a continuing guarantee with one which has ceased to float. The words in parenthesis were held to refer merely to the unascertained and contingent liabilities of the principal, and not of the guarantor: it was a cross-reference to Clause 1 of the guarantee under which the surety undertook a liability to pay "all moneys which were due owing or incurred by the principal to you whether actually or contingently". The *Hardman* case was of a different nature, because it contained language expressly referring to the time during which the guarantee itself was to remain in force.

The decision in *BCCI v Simjee* has undoubtedly clarified the proper approach to construction of termination provisions in continuing guarantees, even though cases will no doubt still turn on the language used in the specific clause in question. Cases falling within the *Hardman* category are likely to be rare, as notice provisions in standard forms generally follow a *Simjee* type of formulation. Nevertheless there are still provisions which, on their face, appear to relate to the termination of liability rather than merely the continuing nature of the liability.

An interesting variant of the *Hardman* type argument is to be found in the unreported case of *Bank of Baroda v Patel* (CAT No.221 of 1997, February 4), where the surety failed in his somewhat ambitious attempt to persuade the Court of Appeal that the bank should have served a demand on him before his notice of termination expired. The guarantee provided that "the Guarantor may at any time give you notice in writing to determine this guarantee and at a date not less than three calendar months after the receipt by [the bank] of such notice this guarantee shall cease in respect of all future transactions after that date but so that ... the Guarantor shall remain liable to the extent of the amount due to [the bank] from the principal at the same date, with interest at the rate aforesaid and for such costs and expenses as aforesaid." The argument raised was that the express reservation of liability for sums due at the date when the notice took effect was ineffective and meaningless because the words "at a date not less than 3 calendar months after receipt of such notice" rendered uncertain the period after which the guarantee would cease. Accordingly, it was submitted, the second part of the clause should be treated as being of no effect, which meant that the guarantor was free to determine his liability at any time. Peter Gibson L.J. had no difficulty in rejecting this argument. The service of a notice of termination was, he said, a matter for the guarantor. The clause meant that if the guarantor specified a termination date in the notice, it had to be a date not less than three calendar months after the notice was received (and there were other provisions in the guarantee which helped to ascertain when notices were deemed to be received by the bank). If such a notice was served, there would be no problem in ascertaining when it was to take effect. If, on the other hand, the guarantor served a notice without specifying a termination date, it had to be presumed by the bank that it would take effect as soon as possible consistent with the requirement of a minimum three-month period after the notice was received: that interpretation accorded with the decision of Goulding J. in *Dyet Investment Ltd v Moore* [1973] E.G. 945. Again, that posed no difficulty in ascertaining with certainty when the guarantee came to an end; the "saving" provision in the clause was therefore effective to preserve the guarantor's liability at that date.

It is clear that the issue of whether or not the failure to make a demand upon the guarantor before the notice expires is fatal will depend very much upon the language of the guarantee. *National Westminster Bank v French* cannot be regarded as laying down any general principle in respect of demand guarantees; it is a case which turns upon the language of the clause in question. On the other hand, *National Westminster Bank v Hardman* can be read as an indication that if the guarantee is a demand guarantee, the draftsman of the notice of termination clause will have to use precise language if it is intended that the contingent liability of the guarantor to pay on demand should survive termination. The suggestion that as a general rule, in the absence of clear language to the contrary, such provisions should be construed as preserving that liability, because it would not be foreseen by the parties that the creditor's failure to make a demand during the notice period would fortuitously release the surety,[18] would appear to be completely inconsistent with the approach of the Court of Appeal in *Hardman* and *Slinn* and in the more recent case of *BCCI v Simjee* [1997] C.L.C. 135 discussed above. There is nothing "fortuitous" about the release of the surety in such circumstances; he will have given what both parties regard as ample notice to the creditor, and the effect of giving that notice will be that when it expires, both parties will know exactly where they stand. If there is a choice between a construction which promotes commercial certainty and a construction which leaves one party indefinitely exposed to a liability in circumstances in which he is seeking to bring his obligations to an end, the first option may be preferred. As Hobhouse L.J. put it in *BCCI v Simjee* [1997] C.L.C. 135 at 136C "If the wording of the document is not clear, the banks only have themselves to blame if their security is not as extensive or valuable as they had hoped— see particularly Professor Goode at 1988 J.B.L. 264."

Form of notice

In the absence of any express provision in the contract, the surety is not **8–008** required to give any particular form of notice, though it is obviously prudent to give notice in writing. He must ensure that the notice is given in sufficiently precise and clear terms, if it is to be operative. A mere expression of a wish or preference will not suffice. Thus in *Dickson v Royal Bank* (1975) 66 D.L.R. (3d) 242, the guarantor wrote to the creditor stating that he had a firm wish that no additional funds should be advanced to the principal and asked that "all efforts be made to retire the obligation". It was held that this was too equivocal to have the effect of a notice of cancellation.[19]

If there is an express provision which entitles the guarantor to cancel the guarantee, any notice which he gives must clearly indicate a wish to cancel, and notice of an event from which it might be inferred that there is a wish to cancel will not usually suffice. Thus in *Re Silvester, Midland Railway Co v Silvester* [1895] 1 Ch. 573, a joint and several continuing guarantee bond provided that the obligors or any of them, or their respective "representatives" might determine their or his liability by giving a month's notice in writing to the obligees. It was held that a notice given by the executor of one of the obligors, which merely referred to the death of the surety, did not suffice.[20] In order to give an effective notice, the surety must comply strictly with the provisions of the contract. In *Commercial Bank of Australia Ltd v Cavanaugh* (1980) 7 N.T.R. 12, a guarantee was given in respect of a

---

18 See Marks (*op. cit.*), p.127.
19 Affirmed 66 D.L.R. (3d) 253, but *cf. Massey-Ferguson Ltd v Waddell* (1984) 29 Man. R. (2d) 241. See also *Royal Bank v TVM Catering Ltd* (above).
20 See also *Toronto-Dominion Bank v Brot* [1958] O.R. 152, (Can). *Cf. Coulthart v Clementson* (1879) 5 Q.B.D. 42 and the cases discussed in para.8–011.

banking facility. The relevant termination clause stated that the guarantee remained in force until it was determined as to future advances by notice in writing given to, and received by, the manager for the time being of the branch where the customer kept the relevant account, and until the guarantors had paid to the bank the full amount for which the guarantors were liable. It was held that these were cumulative conditions and that receipt of a notice by the bank manager was ineffective to terminate the liability of the surety until there had been payment in full of the outstanding liability of the customer at that time. Similarly, in another Australian case, *Je Maintiendrai Pty Ltd v ANZ Banking Group Ltd* (1985) 38 S.A.S.R. 70, it was held that a purported revocation was ineffective because the relevant notice was not delivered to the creditor.

It is fairly commonplace to find that the provisions regarding revocation require actual receipt of the notice of revocation by the creditor, whereas the provisions for the creditor making demand upon the surety will stipulate that a notice of demand will be deemed to have been validly served in certain circumstances, *e.g.* if it is posted by registered post to the last-known address of the surety. Whilst such provisions relating to demands have been enforced in the past without difficulty, creditors should be aware that in the context of guarantees made with consumers, there is a possibility that the distinction between these two types of notice provisions would be held by a court to be unjustifiable under the Unfair Terms in Consumer Contracts Regulations.[21] Although notice provisions, like conclusive evidence clauses, do not appear to fall within the list in Sch.3, the terms in that list are indicative only, and it would appear that there is a respectable argument that the disparity between the position of the surety and that of the creditor in this context is a "significant imbalance to the detriment of the consumer". Creditors would therefore be well advised to take steps to ensure that in consumer guarantees, the same rules for service and receipt of notices apply, regardless of the identity of the party serving the notice.

Liability during notice period

8–009 It is common for standard form bank guarantees to contain a provision which expressly provides for a period of notice to be given by the surety to the creditor if he wishes to cancel the guarantee, and also provides that he will remain liable for any advances made during that period of notice, whether the obligation to repay matures before or after the notice expires. In the absence of the latter type of provision, the question whether the guarantor is liable for advances made during the currency of the notice has not yet been resolved, and may depend upon the construction of each particular contract. It might be argued that a notice to terminate, which is intended to enable the surety to circumscribe his loss, is of little effect or value to him if the creditor and principal are entitled to run the account up

---

21 Discussed in Ch.3, above, at paras 3–036–3–037.

to its limit after the notice has been received, and that therefore he should not be liable for such advances. One possible legal justification for precluding the creditor from recovering those advances is that the further advances constituted a breach of a duty on the part of the creditor to act equitably towards the surety, though the absence of any consistent judicial recognition of the existence of such a duty may prove a formidable hurdle to overcome when seeking to persuade a court to accept this analysis.[22] Furthermore, if the continuing guarantee is treated in all respects as a standing offer, any notice provision would have to be construed as circumscribing the inherent right of the surety to withdraw that offer at any time.[23] If a strict *contra proferentem* approach were to be adopted, therefore, a construction which made the surety liable for debts accruing during the period of notice might be difficult to support.

On the other hand, the bank and the principal might suffer serious prejudice if they are unable to conduct their relationship in the same way during the notice period as they have done previously; the notice period could be said to be for the purpose of giving them the time and opportunity to find a new surety, and therefore they should be entitled to preserve the *status quo* until it expires. Indeed, on general principles of construction it is strongly arguable that it would make little sense to construe a one-month notice period as cancelling the surety's liability from the date of the notice rather than from the date on which it expires. In most other contracts, such as employment, the rights and liabilities of the parties cease on expiry of the notice period, and contracts of suretyship should not be treated any differently.

Revocation by co-surety

Where there is more than one surety, the question may arise whether one of them may exercise his right of revocation independently of the others. As a general rule, he may, unless the contract expressly or by implication provides otherwise; and if the creditor wishes to exclude this right, the drafting must be precise. In *Kalil v Standard Bank of South Africa Ltd* [1967] 4 S.A. 550, several sureties signed a guarantee which provided that "this guarantee shall remain in force as a continuing guarantee . . . until . . . the bank shall have received notice from us terminating the same". It was held that "notice from us" did not mean that the notice had to be given by all the sureties; since the bank had failed to exclude the right of the individual surety to revoke the continuing guarantee, he was entitled to do so.[24] This case may be compared with *Egbert v National Crown Bank* [1918] A.C. 903, in which six sureties jointly and severally agreed with a bank to

8–010

---

22 The proposition was put forward by the editors of the 9th ed. of *Paget's Law of Banking* (Butterworths, 1982), p.510. Although it has not been repeated in subsequent editions, see the commentary in the 12th ed. in fn.10 to para.33.23, citing *Harriss v Fawcett* (1873) 8 Ch. App. 866.
23 See *Chitty on Contracts* (*op. cit.*), Vol. 2 at para.44–017.
24 See also *North British Mercantile Insurance Co v Kean* (1888) 16 O.R. 117 (Can).

guarantee repayment of the liabilities of a customer "until the undersigned, or the executor or administrator of the undersigned shall have given the bank notice in writing to make no further advances on the security of this guarantee". The Privy Council held that the guarantee remained in force against all the guarantors until each and every one of them (or their personal representatives) gave notice of termination in accordance with the contract.

Revocation by death or insanity

Death or insanity of the surety

8–011   The effect of the insanity of the surety is the same as that of his death: *Bradford Old Bank v Sutcliffe* [1918] 2 K.B. 833. The death of the surety will not of itself operate so as to revoke the contract of guarantee: *Bradbury v Morgan* (1862) 1 H. & C. 249.[25] However, a personal representative of a deceased surety may exercise any right which the surety had to revoke the guarantee on giving reasonable or specified notice of cancellation or termination to the creditor. On the other hand, if the guarantee could not have been revoked by the surety, *e.g.* because the consideration was indivisible, then it cannot be revoked by his death or by notice given by his personal representative: *Lloyd's v Harper* (1880) 16 Ch. D. 290 at 317, *Basch v Stekel* [2001] L. & T. R. 1.[26]

There is also authority that, in the absence of express contractual provision, notice of the *death* of the surety (as opposed to express notice of termination) will automatically revoke a continuing guarantee: *Coulthart v Clementson* (1879) 5 Q.B.D. 42. It was implied in that case that even constructive notice of the death of the surety would suffice.[27] The reason given by Bowen J., that the will of the deceased surety may create new interests in the property which are contradictory to the continued existence of liability under the guarantee, is doubtful, and contrary to the reasoning in *Bradbury v Morgan*. As a result the case has been subjected to criticism.[28] However, it was followed in Ireland in *Re Whelan* [1897] 1 I.R. 575. A similar result was achieved in the case of *Harriss v Fawcett* (1873) L.R. 15 Eq. 311[29] where the principal debtor happened to be the executor of the surety, and failed to give notice of revocation; it was held that knowledge by the creditor of the facts sufficed to bring the guarantee to an end. It is submitted that there is justification for holding that the guarantee is prospectively determined when the death of the surety comes to the actual notice of the creditor, namely that he cannot purport to accept a standing offer to contract in future, made by someone he knows to be deceased,

---

25 See also *Harriss v Fawcett* (1873) 8 Ch. App. 866, *per* Mellish L.J. at 869.
26 See also *Re Crace* [1902] 1 Ch. 733; *Calvert v Gordon* (1828) 3 Man. & Ry. K.B. 124.
27 This was followed in Ireland in *Re Whelan, Dodd v Whelan* [1897] 1 I.R. 575, where it was held that it would suffice if the creditor read an obituary in the newspaper.
28 By Romer J. in *Re Silvester* [1895] 1 Ch. 573 and by Joyce J. in *Re Crace* [1902] 1 Ch. 733.
29 Approved by the CA at (1873) 8 Ch. App. 866.

unless that offer is expressly adopted on behalf of the surety's estate by his executors or administrators.[30] If, as is usual in the case of modern guarantees, the contract provides that it may be terminated by notice given by the surety or by his personal representatives, it is likely to be construed in such a way that notice of the death of the surety, whether actual or constructive, will not suffice to bring the contract to an end; a proper termination notice would have to be given. See *Re Silvester, Midland Railway Co v Silvester*.[31] However, most modern guarantees of a continuing nature Pwill contain a term which expressly provides that the guarantee will not be determined by the guarantor's death, so these considerations are unlikely to arise very often in practice.

Death or insanity of a co-surety

The liability of a joint and several guarantor for future advances, in the event of revocation by a co-surety, essentially depends on the nature of the particular agreement between the parties. It may be that as a matter of construction the unilateral termination of the liability of one co-surety would operate in the same way as a release, and discharge the co-sureties altogether,[32] though it is most unlikely that a court would interpret a contract in such a way as to produce this drastic result unless the wording was very explicit. Alternatively, revocation by one surety might revoke the future liability of his co-sureties. A contract which makes it clear that A will not guarantee the liability of the principal unless B also guarantees that liability, might be interpreted in such a way. Thirdly, the right to revoke might be treated as a wholly independent right in the case of each co-surety, so that the exercise by one co-surety of his right of revocation will not affect the future liability of the others. This is probably the most likely interpretation to be adopted.   **8–012**

Thus it has been held that if the contract contains no provision for notice, the death of one co-surety will not discharge the other, even though the estate of the dead co-surety may be discharged in respect of liabilities occurring after death, once notice has been given to the creditor, in accordance with the principles discussed above: *Beckett v Addyman* (1882) 9 Q.B.D. 783. The contract may, of course, provide that notice of termination must be given by all the sureties or their personal representatives, as it did in *Egbert v National Crown Bank* [1918] A.C. 90, considered above. In that case, however, Lord Dunedin said "it is not necessary to examine what is the law in the case of death when nothing is said in the guarantee about its continuation or not".

If the liability of the co-sureties is joint, it appears to be an open question whether the death of one (or notice of that death given to the creditor), revokes the liability of the other for further advances under a continuing guarantee.[33]

---

30 This view is shared by McGuinness (*op. cit.*), at para.6.33.
31 [1895] 1 Ch. 573.
32 As to which, see Ch.9, at para.9–040.
33 See *Re Sherry, London and County Banking Co v Terry* (1884) 25 Ch. D. 692 at 703, 705, and the Civil Liability (Contribution) Act 1978.

There are a number of cases in which it has been held that an obligation of a surety or co-surety will devolve on his estate in the event of his death. For example, in *Primrose v Bromley* (1739) 1 Atk. 89, it was held that where a joint obligor died, his representative would be charged *pari passu* with the surviving obligor on the payment of a bond. Similarly in *Batard v Hawes, Batard v Douglas* (1853) 2 E. & B. 287, the plaintiff was one of a number of co-sureties, two of whom died before the plaintiff paid the entire debt, and it was held that he would have been entitled, if necessary, to sue the personal representatives of the deceased sureties for contribution.[34] None of these cases, however, expressly considers the position in respect of advances made under a continuing guarantee after the creditor has notice of the death of the co-surety. It is well settled that cancellation, by notice of death or insanity or otherwise, will not affect any pre-existing liabilities, and these authorities appear to do no more than confirm this.

In *Ashby v Day* (1886) 54 L.T. 408, two directors and the solicitor of a company gave a joint guarantee to the bank in respect of the company's bank account. One of the guarantors died, and it was held that the guarantee did not terminate. However, the case cannot be treated as clear authority for the proposition that co-sureties under a joint guarantee will not be discharged from future liabilities by the death of one of their number; it appears that the *ratio* was that, on the facts, the survivors had conducted themselves in such a way as to estop them from denying that their liability on the guarantee continued.[35] A similar result was reached in Canada in the case of *Fennell v McGuire* (1870) 21 U.C.C.P. 134, where there was acknowledgment of continuing liability by the co-surety.

In the absence of such conduct, and in the absence of express contractual provision to the contrary, it is submitted that the revocation of a joint guarantee by one co-surety will release the remaining co-sureties from liability for future advances, because if a standing offer is being made on behalf of two people jointly, it is difficult to see how it can continue to be made, or accepted, if one of them dies.

Death or insanity of the creditor or principal

8–013   Subject to any express provision to the contrary, if the guarantee is of a type which is revocable, the death of the creditor will operate as a revocation of the guarantee. Thus in *Barker v Parker* (1786) 1 Term Rep. 287, the surety under a fidelity bond was not liable for defaults by the principal which occurred after the death of the employer, though the employment had been continued by his executors. Similarly in *Strange v Lee* (1803) 3 East. 484, a surety was discharged from liability for advances made by the surviving members of a banking house to the principal after the death of one of their partners.[36]

---

34 See also *Ramskill v Edwards* (1885) 31 Ch. D. 100; *Stirling v Forrester* (1821) 3 Bli. 575.
35 The point was not dealt with in the Court of Appeal, (1886) 34 W.R. 312.
36 See also *Dance v Girdler* (1804) 1 Bos. & P.N.R. 34; *Weston v Barton* (1812) 4 Taunt. 673; *Pemberton v Oakes* (1827) 4 Russ. 154; *Hollond v Teed* (1848) 7 Hare 50; *Chapman v Beckinton* (1842) 3 Q.B. 703; the Partnership Act 1890, s.18 and the discussion in Ch.9 at para.9–038.

Similar rules will apply in the case of the death of the principal or one of a number of joint principals. Thus in *Simson v Cooke* (1824) 1 Bing. 452, the surety was liable under a bond for such sums as should be advanced to meet bills drawn by J and T, who were in partnership, or by either of them; it was held that this obligation did not extend to bills drawn by J after the death of T.[37] If the liability of the principal ceases upon his death, the liability of the guarantor will also cease: *Sparrow v Sowgate* (1621) W. Jo. 29. Ultimately the question is one of construction of the guarantee; normally the principle of co-extensiveness will operate so as to discharge the guarantor from liability in circumstances in which the creditor would not be entitled to claim against the estate of the deceased principal.

Revocation of contracts of indemnity

There appears to be no direct authority concerning the revocation of **8–014** contracts of indemnity. Although the obligation of the surety under such a contract is a primary obligation, there is no reason in principle why a continuing indemnity should not be subject to the same rules as a continuing guarantee. A person may make a standing offer to indemnify a bank in respect of advances made from time to time to a customer, in the same way as he may make a standing offer to act as guarantor for such advances. It is likely, therefore, that the rules considered above in relation to guarantees will apply equally to contracts of indemnity.

---

37 See also *Backhouse v Hall* (1865) 6 B. & S. 507, *Solvency Mutual Guarantee Co v Freeman* (1861) 7 H. & N. 17; but *cf. Richardson v Horton* (1843) 6 Beav. 185.

Chapter 9

Discharge of the Surety

Discharge of surety by discharge of the principal

9-001 Since the purpose of a guarantee is to secure the performance of the principal's obligations towards the creditor, the surety will be discharged from his liability under the guarantee if the principal pays the debt or performs the obligation which the surety has guaranteed, or if the principal's liability is forgiven. This is an aspect of the principle of co-extensiveness of liability, discussed elsewhere in this work.[1] The position is different where the contract is on its true construction one of indemnity, under which the surety assumes an independent liability from that of the principal which may often be greater in scope. Accordingly he may not necessarily be discharged by reason of the performance by the principal of his obligations, or otherwise by his discharge.[2]

Discharge by payment or performance

Payment or performance by the principal

9-002 Payment of the principal debt by the principal will discharge the surety. In *Western Credit v Alberry* [1964] 1 W.L.R. 945, where a surety guaranteed due performance by a hirer (the principal) of his obligations under a hire-purchase contract, the surety was held to be discharged where the hirer had terminated the hire purchase contract in accordance with its terms and had paid the full amount due under the contract, even though the creditor did not receive the full amounts that it was entitled to receive had the hirepurchase contract run to expiry. This case can be contrasted with

---

1 See Ch.6. In *Canadian Permanent Trust Co v King Art Developments Ltd* [1984] 4 W.W.R. 587, CA, Laycraft J.A. stated, at 643–634: "Prima facie a guarantor's obligations are co-extensive with the principal debtor but the starting point must always be to analyse the nature of the guarantor's undertaking. Depending upon the terms of the guarantor's contract with the debtor, his obligation may persist even though the creditor is temporarily or even permanently disabled from pursuing the debtor to collect the debt. It is also important to an analysis of the problem to remember that although the obligations of the surety and the principal debtor are often co-extensive they are, nevertheless, separate and distinct obligations. Though co-extensiveness of the obligations of the debtor and the surety may be varied by the surety's contract with the creditor, I have difficulty in envisioning the contractual term which would hold a surety liable when the debt guaranteed has been paid. The essence of suretyship contracts is to see that the obligations between debtor and creditor are satisfied."

2 *Goulston Discount Co Ltd v Clark* [1967] 2 Q.B. 493; *cf. Bentworth Finance v Lubert* [1968] 1 Q.B. 680. But now see Consumer Credit Act 1974, s.113.

Goulston Discount Co v Clark [1967] 2 Q.B. 493, where the facts were similar to those in the *Western Credit* case, but because the contract was one of indemnity, it was held that the surety had a liability to make up the shortfall to the discount company on its anticipated profit.

The payment must be a valid and effective payment and not voidable, although this depends largely on matters between the creditor and the principal, and to what extent the principal has accepted the payment or giving of security for it.[3] In *Camidge v Allenby* (1827) 6 B. & C. 373,[4] it was a condition of a surety's bond that the treasurer of a union, who was a banker, should "honestly, diligently and faithfully perform and discharge the duties of his office", one such duty being to pay from the guardians' moneys in his control all orders drawn upon him. He paid an order with his own notes, which the creditors accepted. The bank stopped payment on the notes subsequently, but the sureties were held discharged, on the basis of the principle that a banknote, where taken for a debt at the time of the transaction, is taken at the peril of the taker. The fact that an unconditional acceptance of a payment by the debtor proves ultimately to be valueless does not revive the surety's liability.[5] However, the payment must have been accepted in settlement of the principal liability. This is particularly important where payment is made by cheque, and where a creditor accepts a cheque as conditional payment, its subsequent dishonour will serve to maintain the surety's liability. Accordingly, if a creditor to whom a cheque is tendered by the principal wishes to preserve all his options, he should ensure that his acceptance is clearly expressed to be conditional upon the clearance of the cheque.

The payment must be a good and satisfactory payment.[6] Examples of payments that have been held not to be good and satisfactory payments are a simple balance owing by the creditor to the principal,[7] the assignment of a security by the principal to the creditor,[8] or the reorganisation by the creditor of his internal book-keeping arrangements, such as transferring the principal indebtedness from one account to another.[9]

Where the payment constitutes a preference of the creditor and is avoided by the liquidator or trustee in bankruptcy of the principal under ss.239–241 or ss.340–342 of the Insolvency Act 1986 respectively, the surety

---

3 *Pritchard v Hancock* (1843) 6 M. & G. 151.
4 See *Guardians of the Lichfield Union v Greene* (1857) 1 H. & N. 668, where it was held that where a creditor takes a banknote for a pre-existing debt, and so not at his own peril, if he neglects to present he makes it his own and the liability of the surety is extinguished even though it is the debtor who is the maker of the note.
5 *Guardians of the Lichfield Union v Greene* (above).
6 *Pritchard v Hitchcock* (1843) 6 M. & G. 151.
7 *Harrison v Nettleship* (1833) 2 My. & K. 423.
8 *Halford v Byron* (1701) Prec. Ch. 178.
9 *National Bank of New Zealand v Mee & Reid (Executors of Cramond)* [1885] N.Z.L.R. 3. However, the surety may be discharged where he guaranteed only the principal's liability on that one specific account, and not the principal's liability to the creditor generally.

remains liable, since in equity there has been no discharging event.[10] Where it is sought to challenge a payment as a preference, the surety should be joined as a party.[11] It is submitted that the same principles apply to payments designed to defeat the interests of the principal's creditors, which may be avoided under ss.423–425 of the Insolvency Act 1986, and also to payments or transfers of property which are automatically void under the insolvency legislation.[12]

Partial payment or performance by the principal will discharge the surety *pro tanto*.[13] Where a guaranteed debt is compromised by the creditor and the debtor, the surety is entitled to the benefit of that compromise in total or partial reduction of his liability.[14]

Payment by the surety

9–003   Payment or performance by the surety of his obligations under the guarantee will discharge him, subject to the point made above that the payment or performance must be valid and effective. Where the surety is liable to the creditor both personally and on the guarantee, he should, when making payment, expressly appropriate the payment to a specific debt rather than allowing the creditor to decide to which the payment should be appropriated.[15] Similarly, where the surety makes payment to the principal with the intention that he should use the money to discharge or reduce the obligation guaranteed, and so discharge or reduce the surety's liability under the guarantee, the arrangements and supporting documents should make it clear that the money is being paid for the specific purpose of enabling the principal to pay the guaranteed creditors (and not creditors

---

10 *Pritchard v Hitchcock* (1843) 6 M. & G. 151; *Petty v Cooke* (1871) L.R. 6 Q.B. 790; *Re Seymour* [1937] Ch. 668, where it was held that the surety remained liable where the creditor was not a party to the preference. The old cases on fraudulent preference must be reviewed in the light of the changes brought about by ss.239 and 340 of the Insolvency Act 1986: A director of a principal debtor company who has guaranteed its overdraft with the bank will generally bear a heavy burden in showing that he was not influenced by a desire to prefer the bank in procuring payment by the company, especially where payment would incidentally relieve him of his obligations to it as surety: such payments will be struck down as against the company, and his liability as surety will remain. There is a presumption, in the case of connected persons such as directors, that the preference is influenced by a desire to give it: see s.239(6), and see *re DKG Contractors Ltd* [1990] B.C.C. 903; *Re Beacon Leisure Ltd* [1990] B.C.C. 213; *Re Exchange Travel (Holidays) Ltd* [1996] B.C.C. 933; *Re Shapland Inc* [2000] B.C.C. 106
11 *Re Idenden* [1970] 1 W.L.R. 1015.
12 Such as under s.127 of the Insolvency Act 1986: see *Coutts & Co v Stock* [2000] 1 W.L.R. 906, which was approved by the Court of Appeal (reversing Blackburne J. at first instance) in *Hollicourt (Contracts) Ltd v Bank of Ireland* [2001] 2 W.L.R. 290. In *Hollicourt (Contracts) Ltd v Bank of Ireland*, the Court of Appeal reviewed all the English and Commonwealth authorities and has now decided definitively that s.127 does not impose any restitutionary liability on the bank as the paying agent of the company to make good the account where a payment is void under that section.
13 *Perry v National Provincial Bank* [1910] 1 Ch. 464.
14 *M'Clure v Fraser* (1840) 9 L.J.B.Q. 60.
15 *Waugh v Wren* (1862) 11 W.R. 244; *Commercial Bank of Australia v Wilson & Co's Estate (Official Assignee)* [1893] A.C. 181. As to appropriation between principal and creditor, see para.9–005.

generally): see *Mahoney v McManus* (1981) 55 A.L.J.R. 673[16] Where payments are made by a surety to a running current account the rule in *Clayton's* case (1816) 1 Mer. 529 will apply[17] so that there is a presumption that the earliest payments are treated as discharging the earliest debits. However, there exists no right in the surety to compel either the principal or the creditor to appropriate a payment by the principal in reduction of the guaranteed amount.[18] This rule does not apply where the principal has become insolvent.[19]

The surety sometimes makes a part-payment of the guaranteed debt to the creditor in consideration of his being granted an absolute release. Where this occurs, the part-payment constitutes part-payment of the principal obligation and reduces it *pro tanto* as between the principal and the creditor.[20] In *Milverton Group Ltd v Warner World Ltd* [1995] 32 E.G. 70, Hoffmann J. said that unless this were the case, "a creditor could pick off his debtors one by one and recover in total more than the whole debt". This would operate to the disadvantage of the principal and co-sureties.

Payment by co-sureties

A payment by a co-surety charged with the same liability (*i.e.* severally or   **9–004**
jointly and severally liable) will discharge the surety's liability by payment: the crucial question will be whether, on the true construction of the guarantee, the sureties are so liable or jointly liable only, and to what extent each surety binds himself.[21]

Discharge by appropriation

General principle

In the absence of any express agreement, the mere existence of a surety   **9–005**
does not affect the rights of the creditor and the principal to appropriate payments. Whether there is appropriation is a question of fact, to be determined by the circumstances in which the particular payment was made. It may depend on the intentions of the party making the payment,[22] upon the agreement itself, or upon the nature of the payment received.[23]

---

16 See the discussion of this case in O'Donovan & Phillips (*op. cit.*), pp.278–279 (English ed., 2003, at paras 6–04 to 6–07); see also Ch.12 below, at 12–005.

17 See para.9.07.

18 See *Re Sherry* (1884) 25 Ch. D. 692; *Kinnaird v Webster* (1878) 10 Ch. D. 139. There is no obligation on the creditor to appropriate payments to the guaranteed debt, even where the surety did not know of the existence of the second (unguaranteed) debt: *Kirby v Duke of Marlborough* (1813) 2 M. & S. 18; *Williams v Rawlinson* (1825) 3 Bing. 25. And see Ch.11, paras 11–002–11–003. However a payment by the surety to the principal earmarked for payment to the creditor in discharge of the guaranteed debt may discharge the surety: see Ch.12, para.12–005.

19 See para.9–008.

20 *P & A Swift Investments v Combined English Stores Group Plc* [1989] A.C. 632, at 638 *per* Lord Templeman. *Milverton Group Ltd v Warner World Ltd* [1995] 32 E.G. 70.

21 *Collins v Prosser* (1823) 1 B. & C. 682; *Ellis v Emmanuel* (1876) 1 Ex. D. 157; *Fell v Goslin* (1852) 7 Exch. 185; *Armstrong v Cahill* (1880) 6 L.R. Ir. 440. See Ch.4.

22 *Kinnaird v Webster* (1878) 10 Ch. D. 139; *Lysaght v Walker* (1831) 5 Bli. N.S.1.

23 *Marryatts v White* (1817) 2 Stark. 101, where payment of the exact amount was held to be an appropriation to the guaranteed debt. See also *City Discount Co Ltd v McLean* (1874) L.R. 9 C.P. 692; *A-G for Jamaica v Manderson* (1848) 6 Moo. P.C. 239; *Bank of Montreal v MacFatridge* 17 D.L.R. (2d) 557.

The principal may elect to appropriate a payment to any subsisting debt that he chooses, and if he does not do so, then the creditor may do so.[24] Appropriation by the principal need not be express, provided it can be sufficiently shown by the circumstances. Appropriation by the creditor, on the other hand, is not complete until it is communicated to the principal, and is revocable until then, and thereafter is binding.[25] The right of the creditor to appropriate in the absence of appropriation by the principal does not extend to amounts which could not be appropriated (either because of his ignorance or a legal bar) by the principal.[26] In *Deeley v Lloyds Bank Ltd* [1912] A.C. 756 it was held that where there is an unbroken current account, part of which is covered by a guarantee, there is, in the absence of any appropriation, no presumption that payments in are to be allocated to the unsecured rather than the secured portion, or otherwise than in the normal sequence of "first in first out".

Separate bank accounts

9–006   The circumstances in which the creditor may appropriate a payment are to some extent limited. Where there are separate current accounts and the payment is general the creditor may appropriate, but not where the accounts are blended and treated as one entire indivisible account by all parties.[27] In *Hollond v Teed* (1848) 7 Hare 50, it was held that where a guarantee was given to a banker for a loan account, or advances by way of acceptance of bills, the surety had no right to have any credit balance that may exist from time to time on a running account kept by the principal with the same banker applied in reduction of the account guaranteed, and the balance on the current account existing at the moment that the guarantee terminates may then be paid over by the banker to the principal without affecting his rights against the surety.[28] However, in *Kinnaird v Webster*[29] it was held that where the principal had given promissory notes to the bank as consideration for an advance, and where the surety promised to give a mortgage to the bank to secure the amounts if there was not enough money received by the bank to cover the notes, the bank was not permitted to appropriate the amounts that he held, which were sufficient to cover the notes, to other indebtedness of the principal. This decision can be explained also on the basis that the rule in *Clayton*'s case operated to discharge the guaranteed debt.

---

24 For the general rule see *Simpson v Ingham* (1823) 2 B. & C. 65.

25 *Simpson v Ingham* (1823) 2 B. & C. 65; *Cory Bros & Co Ltd v Owners of the Turkish Steamship "Mecca"* [1897] A.C. 286, at 292 *per* Lord Herschell. Contrast the position in Canada: *Hopkinson v Canadian Imperial Bank of Commerce* [1977] 6 W.W.R. 490 at 493–494.

26 *Walker v Lacey* 1 M. & G. 34.

27 *City Discount Co Ltd v McLean* (1874) L.R. 9 C.P. 692.

28 See *York City & County Banking v Bainbridge* (1880) 43 L.T. 732; *Bradford Old Bank v Sutcliffe* [1918] 2 K.B. 833. For a detailed discussion on the banker's right to appropriate, see Paget, *Law of Banking*, (Butterworths, 12th ed., 2003), Ch.12 at pp.187–8.

29 (1878) 10 Ch. D. 139.

The application of the rule in Clayton's case

The rule in *Clayton's* case[30] is not really a rule at all but a presumption of **9–007** law. Its essence is that in the absence of any appropriation by the debtor and of any contrary intention, any payment credited by the creditor to a current account is presumed to discharge the earliest debit in the account then unpaid. The rule, otherwise known as the "first in first out" rule, does not operate until the fact of the credit is communicated to the debtor[31] and only applies to a running current account. Further, it does not operate to appropriate a payment to debits subsisting in separate accounts, nor debits on a current account which is closed and a new account opened in its place. In *Re Sherry* (1884) 25 Ch. D. 692, where the surety had guaranteed a running account that was then closed, and a new one opened not covered by the guarantee, it was held that the bank was entitled to appropriate payments (by the debtor) to the new account because the debtor had not appropriated them to the old current account, leaving the surety exposed to liability.

It must be remembered that the presumption is only as to the conduct of the *creditor*, and may always be rebutted by appropriate evidence of a contrary intention to appropriate on the part of the debtor.[32] The presumption is of no assistance to a surety who has guaranteed an ultimate balance on an account under a continuing guarantee, and will only ever help a surety for a specific debt carried by the creditor into a running account, or where a continuing guarantee has ceased to cover new items in the account because of death, revocation or effluxion of time.

Insolvency of the principal debtor

The insolvency of the principal debtor creates an exception to the general **9–008** rule that the creditor may appropriate the payment by the surety to a debt not guaranteed by him. In *Re Mason Ex p. Sharp* (1844) 3 Mont. D. & De G. 490, where a guarantee had been given to a bank which had knowledge of the principal's act of bankruptcy, and the surety, in ignorance of the act of bankruptcy,[33] paid the bank to the full extent of his liability under the guarantee without any specific appropriation, it was held that the bank had to apply the payment to the portion of the guaranteed debt which was provable, and not to that portion which was not provable. However, the insolvency of the principal also prevents the surety for a debt payable by instalments, from compelling the creditor to apply his dividend received in respect of the whole debt in discharge of one instalment of it.[34] The dividend must be applied rateably to each instalment as it falls due.[35] But a dividend to the creditor for the capital and interest at the date of the

---

30 *Devaynes v Noble* (1816) 1 Mer. 572.
31 *Simpson v Ingham* (1823) 2 B. & C. 65.
32 See, *e.g.*, *City Discount Co Ltd v McLean* (above).
33 This would now equate to the presentation of a petition.
34 *Martin v Brecknell* (1813) 2 M. & S. 39.
35 See *Thompson v Hudson* (1871) L.R. 6 Ch. App. 320, a case concerning a scheme of arrangement.

insolvency may be applied against the surety's liability for interest accrued since the insolvency, even though not the subject of proof against the insolvent principal.[36]

Discharge arising from set-off

9–009 Where the payment by the principal is effected by means of a set-off against the creditor's corresponding liabilities, the prima facie rule is that the surety is entitled to avail himself of that set-off, and will be discharged.[37] This derives from the principle that the surety is entitled to be indemnified by the principal. The precise extent of this right of set-off is discussed in detail in Chapter 11.[38]

Discharge by agreement or by release

The general rule as to release of the principal

9–010 If the creditor releases the principal from his debt or obligations by a valid and binding legal agreement,[39] then the surety will be discharged.[40] There are two reasons for this rule:

(1) As a matter of basic principle, since the contract is one of guarantee (as opposed to indemnity), the surety's obligation being to pay the debt or perform the obligation of another, once that payment or obligation has been released, there is nothing left in respect of which the surety can be liable.

(2) The effect of the release would deprive the surety of his right to pay off the creditor and sue the principal in the creditor's name.[41]

The rationale behind the rule is that unless the surety is discharged by the principal's release, absurdity results: any claim by the surety against the principal (either in the name of the creditor or for an indemnity) is met by the defence that there is no longer any liability on the part of the debtor, and so the creditor would have unilaterally deprived the surety of a right he would have expected to have had.[42] Further, if a right to an indemnity or to make a subrogated claim did survive a release, so providing the surety with recourse against the debtor, it would render the release nugatory so far as

---

36 *Bower v Marris* (1841) Cr. & Ph. 351.
37 See *Murphy v Glass* (1869) L.R. 2 C.P. 408; *Bechervaise v Lewis* (1872) L.R. 7 C.P. 372; *Bowyear v Pawson* (1881) 6 Q.B.D. 540. See also *BOC Group Plc v Centeon LLC* [1999] 1 All E.R. 53; [1999] 63 Com. L.R. 104.
38 See paras 11–006–11–014.
39 There is no reason to suppose that an agreement enforceable in equity, or a promissory estoppel, should not be similarly effective, although the point has not been decided.
40 *Hawkshaw v Parkins* (1818) 2 Swanst. 539; *Moss v Hall* (1850) 5 Exch. 46; *Mahant Singh v U Ba Yi* [1939] A.C. 601. And see *Perry v National Provincial Bank* [1910] 1 Ch. 464 at 471 *per* Lord Cozens Hardy.
41 See *Mahant Singh v U Ba Yi* [1939] A.C. 601 at 606 *per* Lord Porter.
42 See *Polak v Everett* (1876) 1 Q.B.D. 669 at 673–674.

the principal was concerned.[43] This reasoning has been held to have had no application in circumstances where the creditor reserves his rights against the surety at the time he releases the principal,[44] or where the original contract provides for the enduring liability of the surety notwithstanding the principal's release, since in those circumstances the principal has notice of the surety's continuing liability, and his consequent liability to indemnify the surety. In *Greene King v Stanley* [2001] EWCA Civ 1966, [2002] B.P.I.R. 491 the Court of Appeal rejected the proposition that, in the absence of a provision in the guarantee which permitted him to do so, the creditor could not, as a matter of general law, release the principal and reserve his rights against the surety. The reservation may be made at the time of the release, and not necessarily in the guarantee. As Jonathan Parker L.J. explained (at para.80), the surety's obligation to pay the creditor and then to pursue the principal is unaffected by the release because, in accepting the release subject to the reservation, the principal impliedly consents to the surety's rights against him remaining on foot notwithstanding the release.[45]

The release by the creditor may take the form of an express binding agreement,[46] or it may be included as part of a debtor's composition with all of his creditors,[47] or by the giving by the principal of a new security in substitution for the old one.[48]

Release by substitution is illustrated by the case of *Bolton v Buckenham* [1891] 1 Q.B. 278, where the surety had guaranteed a debt of £450 which was also secured by a mortgage on the principal's property. The principal then agreed with the creditor that various mortgages that he had given the creditor should be consolidated and covenanted to pay £3,200 at a later date. The old debts, including the £450, were substituted by the new arrangements, and the surety was thereby released from liability.

It is important to distinguish cases where fresh security or liability is undertaken in substitution for the existing liability or security, from cases where a new security or liability is taken in addition. In the latter case the liability of the original surety will not be discharged.[49] However, the surety

---

43 *Malleth v Thompson* (1804) 5 Esp. 178; *Oriental Financial Corporation v Overend Gurney & Co* (1871) L.R.7 Ch. App. 142, 150.

44 *Cole v Lynn* [1942] 1 K.B. 142. See the discussion of reservation of rights against the surety in the context of agreements by the creditor not to sue the principal at para.9–011.

45 The decision is also noteworthy for its liberal approach to the admissibility of extrinsic evidence to prove the reservation of rights: see the discussion of this issue in O'Donovan & Phillips (English ed., para.6–70).

46 *Hawkshaw v Parkins* (above).

47 *Cragoe v Jones* (1873) L.R. 8 Exch. 81; *Cole v Lynn* (above). But see para.9–014, where the impact of the voluntary arrangement provisions under Pt VIII of the Insolvency Act 1986 are discussed.

48 *Commercial Bank of Tasmania v Jones* [1893] A.C. 313.

49 *Wyke v Rogers* (1852) 21 L.J.C.H.611. This is so unless there is an agreement, or the intention is manifested, that the original security is not to remain in force: *Overend Gurney & Co v Oriental Financial Corpn* (1874) L.R. 7 H.L. 348; *Munster & Leinster Bank v France* (1889) 24 L.R. Ir. 82. Where a principal and surety are indebted on the same bond, a taking by the creditor of a bond for a larger sum from the principal will not release the surety: *Eyre v Everett* (1826) 2 Russ. 381.

may be discharged where the creditor agrees with the principal only to look to the security, releasing the principal from his personal liability.[50]

The surety will also be discharged where a compromise order is reached which is incorporated in an agreed order of the court, since the agreement substitutes the original liability of the debtor.[51] In the first and second editions of this work, the rule was stated that a surety will be released where the liquidator of the principal disclaims onerous property liabilities in respect of which the surety has given the guarantee.[52] However, following the overruling of *Stacey v Hill* [1901] 1 K.B. 660 by the House of Lords in *Hindcastle v Barbara Attenborough Associates* [1997] A.C. 70, this general principle is no longer the law in the context of statutory disclaimer of leases (under s.178 of the Insolvency Act 1986), and of at least very doubtful application in the context of other property.[53]

Promise by the creditor not to sue

9–011   In the older authorities on this subject, and indeed in the last two editions of this work, there were two distinctions to be borne in mind when considering whether an agreement between the creditor and the principal that the creditor would not sue him had the effect of discharging the surety. The first was between joint and joint and several liability. The second was between a release and a covenant not to sue. In *Deanplan v Mahmoud* [1993] Ch. 151, Judge Paul Baker Q.C., having undertaken an exhaustive and penetrating review of the authorities, concluded (at 170) that a release of one joint contractor will release the others, but not a covenant not to sue, because it is not a release at all; the distinction between them is a question of construction. In respect of joint and several obligations, he said that where one joint and several obligor is released by accord and satisfaction, then all are released.[54] The rationale for this was that otherwise the obligor thus released would still be exposed to indemnity or contribution claims from his co-obligors. In *Johnson v Davies* [1999] Ch. 117, Chadwick L.J. said (at 125) that this rationale had particular force in the context of a release (if it be such) which is part of an arrangement between the principal and a number of his creditors (such as an individual or company voluntary arrangement under the Insolvency Act 1986).

However, in *Watts v Aldington, The Times*, December 16, 1993, 1993 CA transcript 1578, the Court of Appeal considered the statement of general principal as expressed in *Deanplan v Mahmoud*, and disapproved the strict

---

50 *Lowes v Maugham and Fearon* (1884) Cab. & El. 340.
51 *Tatum v Evans* (1885) 54 L.T. 336. More accurately, it merges with the judgment and ceases to have an independent existence. See also *Faber v Earl of Lathom* (1897) L.T. 168.
52 *Stacey v Hill* [1901] 1 K.B. 660; *Morris & Sons v Jeffreys* (1932) 148 L.T. 56; *Hastings Corpn v Letton* [1908] 1 K.B. 378; but *cf. Re Wells* [1933] Ch. 29; *Re AE Realisations Ltd* [1988] 1 W.L.R. 200; *Re Yarmarine* [1992] B.C.C. 28; *WH Smith Ltd v Wyndham Investments Ltd* [1994] B.C.C. 699.
53 See Ch.18. For recent cases applying *Hindcastle v Barbara Attenborough Associates* [1997] AC 70, see *Basch v Stekel* [2000] L. & T.R. 1, and *Capital Prime Properties Plc v Worthgate Ltd* [2000] 1 B.C.L.C. 647.
54 Following *Re EWA Ltd* [1901] 2 K.B. 642.

distinction between a covenant not to sue and a release.[55] The real question was, they said, whether the creditor was in fact reserving the right, in his agreement with the obligor, to sue the co-obligor. Simon Brown L.J. described the rule, that release of one obligor released joint and joint several obligors, as a "juridical relic", and said that the issue was determined by ascertaining the intentions of the parties. Although the liability under consideration by the Court of Appeal in *Watts v Aldington* was joint and several, the co-obligor was not released by the arrangements between the creditor and the principal because there was no intention between them that he should be released, as derived from the documents and the surrounding circumstances. Accordingly, the Court of Appeal upheld the common law rule, subject to the exception that the creditor may agree with a joint debtor to release him but may reserve in his agreement the right to sue his joint obligor.[56]

In *Johnson v Davies*, Chadwick L.J. (at 127) analysed *Deanplan v Mahmoud* and *Watts v Aldington*, and framed the relevant question as "not whether the agreement between the creditor, A, and one of the co-debtors, B, releases the debt which B owes to A" but rather, "whether the agreement between A and B precludes A from enforcing the debt against C [the co-debtor]". He said that the same principle applied whether the obligation was joint or joint and several. In the context of a joint debt, where the rationale of the rule that one joint obligor is released by a release of the other joint obligor is based on the unity of the debt, Chadwick L.J. followed the approach of Neill L.J. to joint obligation adopted in *Watts v Aldington*, the question being whether the release is an absolute release or a release with a reservation over against the joint obligor.

Johnson v Davies was itself analysed by Mr John Martin Q.C. (sitting as a Deputy High Court Judge) in *Sun Life Assurance Society Plc v Tantofex Engineers Ltd* [1999] E.G.L.R. 135. In that case, the claimant had let his premises to the defendant for a term of 25 years, and then had granted a licence to assign to A Ltd. A Ltd covenanted to observe and perform the terms of the lease. Three years later, the claimant granted a licence to A Ltd to assign to four individuals trading as Lamda. The licence contained a clause releasing "the Lessee [*i.e.* A Ltd] and the Surety as from the assignment date . . . from their respective covenants . . . of the licence". Lamda fell into arrears of rent, and the claimant sued the original lessee to recover them. The original lessee relied on the release, but joined A Ltd as third party for an indemnity. It was held that the release of A Ltd did not operate to release the original lessee. The judge drew the distinction between the situation (as in *Deanplan v Mahmoud*) where the release was deemed to be performance (and therefore discharge) of the obligation in question, as opposed (as in *Tantofex*) to a release without performance or

---

55 See particularly the judgment of Neill L.J.
56 That was the pithy summary of the effect of *Watts v Aldington* by Pill L.J. in *Mainwaring v Goldtech Investments (No.2)* [1999] 1 W.L.R. 745 at 749.

deemed performance.[57] Furthermore, given the doubts expressed by the Court of Appeal in *Watts v Aldington* about the rule that release of one joint and several debtor releases the other, it was unsafe to go beyond that and apply the rule to a situation where there was only several liability, and no element of joint liability whatsoever. This approach is consistent with the older principal and surety cases. The authorities draw the distinction between cases where no express reservation has been made against the surety, in which case he may be released,[58] and where there is such a reservation, so that the surety is not released.[59] In *Price v Barker* (1855) 4 E. & B. 760 at 779, Lord Campbell C.J. said:

> "It seems to be a result of the authorities that a covenant not to sue qualified by a reserve of the remedies against sureties is to allow the surety to retain all his remedies over against the principal debtor; and that the covenant not to sue is to operate only so far as the rights of the surety are not affected."

Where there is such an express reservation by the creditor of his rights against the surety, the surety in turn retains his rights over against the principal, the express reservation being sufficient notice to him. The reservation will generally be made in the guarantee.

An agreement not to sue the principal may or may not contain such a reservation, and so may or may not discharge the surety. In *Finley v Connell Associates (a firm)* [1999] Lloyd's Rep. P.N. 895, Richards J. held that in a creditor's agreement not to sue the principal, a reservation of rights against the principal's surety could be implied and would have the same effect as an express reservation, namely to prevent the surety being discharged. He said that none of the authorities laid down any rule of law that a reservation of rights against a surety had to be express, and there was no reason why it could not be implied in an appropriate case. This is consistent with *Johnson v Davies*, in that the question of whether the surety is to be released is to be determined objectively from the intentions of the creditor and the principal, as expressed in the agreement between them.[60] An actual release, by contrast, whether by express agreement, substitution or otherwise, leaves no room for the creditor to reserve any of his rights against the surety,[61] and the presence of such a reservation will encourage the court to

---

57 The judge said (at 137), on the basis of *Johnson v Davies*, that whether there is deemed performance of the obligation in question is in each case a question of construction of the deed of release.

58 *Bailey v Edwards* (1864) 4 B. & S. 761. But see now *Finley v Connell Assocs. The Times* June 23, 1999.

59 *Price v Barker* (1855) 4 E. & B. 760; *Hidson v Barclay* (1865) 3 H. & C. 361; *Green v Wynn* (1868) L.R. 7 Eq. 28; *Bateson v Gosling* (1871) L.R. 7 C.P. 9; *Re Whitehouse, Whitehouse v Edwards* (1877) 37 Ch. D. 683.

60 It is also consistent with *Mallett v Thompson* (1804) 5 Esp. 178, where Lord Ellenborough held that a simple release of the principal was not effective to discharge the surety, who then had a right of indemnity against the principal if he paid the creditor. *Mallett* does not appear to have been cited in either *Finley v Connell* or *Johnson v Davies*.

61 *Commercial Bank of Tasmania v Jones* (above). But see discussion at para.9–034 and *Union Bank of Manchester v Beech* (1865) 12 L.T. 499; *Fletcher Organisation Plc Ltd v Crocus Investments Plc Ltd* [1988] 2 Qd. R. 517.

construe words of release as a mere covenant not to sue.[62] Those advising principals should therefore take care when considering a release, for if it fails adequately to reflect the parties' intention that the surety should also stand released, or fails to reflect the fact that the creditor is *not* reserving his right to sue the surety, the principal will be unprotected from an indemnity claim by the surety. Where there is no doubt that the creditor intends to extinguish the debt (as opposed to intending merely not to sue upon it) and not to reserve his rights the sureties are discharged.[63]

Exceptions to the general rule

The disapproval by the Court of Appeal in *Watts v Aldington* of the   **9–012** distinction between a release and a covenant not to sue has no effect on the principal and surety cases where notwithstanding release (properly so called) the surety remained liable in any event. There are four main situations:

(1) Procurement of release by fraud

If the release of the principal was obtained by fraud, the surety will remain   **9–013** liable even though he was not a party to the fraud. In *Scholefield v Templer* (1859) 4 De G. & J. 429, the surety was not discharged where the creditor was persuaded to release the principal on the strength of a mortgage given by the debtor, the mortgage being over a non-existent property. In *Kingston-Upon-Hull v Harding* [1892] 2 Q.B. 494, where a contractor for works obtained his release and payment of his fees by fraud on the creditor, the surety was not released. These cases can be explained[64] on the basis that a surety cannot claim to be discharged on the ground that his position has been altered by the conduct of the creditor where that conduct has been caused by a fraudulent act against which the surety guaranteed him.[65]

(2) Insolvency of the principal

Section 281(7) of the Insolvency Act 1986 expressly provides that discharge   **9–014** of the principal from his bankruptcy does not release any person from liability as surety for the principal or a person in the nature of such a

---

62 *Solley v Forbes* (1820) 2 B. & B. 38; *Keynes v Elkins* (1864) 5 B. & S. 240; *Bateson v Gosling* (1871) L.R. 7 C.P. 9; *Duck v Mayeu* [1892] 2 Q.B. 511. And see the discussion of the cases relating to the giving of time by the creditor at paras 9–029–9–034 and in particular *Commercial Bank of Tasmania v Jones* [1893] A.C. 313 and *Perry v National Provincial Bank* [1910] 1 Ch. 464. See also *Deanplan Ltd v Mahmoud* [1993] Ch. 151; *Watts v Aldington* (*The Times*, December 16, 1993, CA transcript 1578); *Johnson v Davies* [1999] Ch. 117, *per* Chadwick L.J. at 127; *Sun Life Assurance Socy Plc v Tantofex (Engineers) Ltd*, [1999] 2 E.G.L.R. 135.

63 *Nicholson v Revill* (1836) 4 Ad. & El. 675, explicable as releasing the principal (and so the surety) on the basis of accord and satisfaction: see *Deanplan Ltd v Mahmoud* [1993] Ch. 151 at 165–167, but see now *Johnson v Davies* [1999] Ch. 117.

64 As the *Kingston-Upon-Hull* case was by Bowen L.J. at 504.

65 There is no reason why this principle should not be extended to cover cases where the release has been procured by the negligent misrepresentation of the principal.

surety.[66] Difficult questions arise as to the effect on the surety's liability of the entry by the principal into a voluntary arrangement under Pt VIII of the Insolvency Act 1986. By virtue of s.253(1), these are expressed to include both compositions in satisfaction of a debtor's debts and schemes of arrangement, which under s.16(20) of the Bankruptcy Act 1914 were expressed to have the same effect as a discharge if entered in accordance with that Act.[67] Voluntary arrangements under Pt VIII bind "every person who in accordance with the rules had notice of, and was entitled to vote at, the meeting . . . as if he were a party to the arrangement".[68] There is no provision to the effect that a voluntary arrangement discharges the debtor. It has been suggested that voluntary arrangements are therefore like compositions under the Bankruptcy Act 1869 which had the effect of discharging the surety, being voluntary acts.[69] In the first edition of this work, it was suggested that the better analysis is that since a voluntary arrangement is in effect a statutory variation of pre-existing contractual rights and liabilities, the normal common law rules will apply,[70] with the effect that, unless there is an express reservation by the creditors, the surety will be discharged on a voluntary arrangement by the principal coming into effect. In *RA Securities Ltd v Mercantile Credit Co Ltd* [1994] B.C.C. 598, Jacob J. disapproved this argument (at 602), on the ground that a statutory binding cannot be equated with consent.[71] However, it is difficult to see why the fact that the satisfaction of the debt under the voluntary arrangement is statutory rather than consensual on a creditor by creditor basis should make any difference to the result. Indeed, in *Finch v Jukes* [1877] W.N. 211, it was held that a surety for performance of obligations under a building contract was discharged when the obligations of the principal were altered by an Act of Parliament.[72]

In *Johnson v Davies* [1999] Ch. 117, Chadwick L.J. agreed with the criticisms made of *RA Securities v Mercantile Credit Co* in the second

---

66 This section substantially re-enacted s.28(4) of the Bankruptcy Act 1914, which consolidated the previous equitable rules: *Ex p. Jacobs* (1875) L.R. 10 Ch. App. 211; *cf. Re Moss* [1905] 2 K.B. 307, in which it was held that a surety for interest on a debt would not be liable to the creditor in respect of interest which would have accrued if the debtor had not become bankrupt and had been discharged, as the principal sum was no longer due. See *Bank of Montreal v MacFatridge* 14 D.L.R. (2d) 552 *per* Winter J.; *Quainos v NZ Breweries Ltd* [1991] 1 N.Z.L.R. 161.

67 Compare the Bankruptcy Act 1869, ss.125, 126.

68 Insolvency Act 1986, s.260(1)(b) and s.37 of the Insolvency Act 2000.

69 See *Chitty on Contracts* (27th Ed.) Vol. 2, para.44–047. See now *Chitty* 29th ed., Vol 2 at para.44–083, where the suggestion is not repeated. The cases on schemes of arrangement under the Bankruptcy Act 1869 made it clear that the surety remained liable, the discharge of the principal being by operation of law: see *London Chartered Bank of Australia* [1893] 3 Ch. 540; *Dane v Mortgage Insurance Corporation* [1894] 1 Q.B. 54; *Mortgage Insurance Corporation v Pound* (1894) L.J.Q.B. 394; and see *Ex p. Jacobs* (1875) L.R. 10 Ch. App. 211: *Hill v Anderson Meat Industries Ltd* [1971] 1 N.S.W.L.R. 868; *RA Securities Ltd v Mercantile Credit Co Ltd* [1994] B.C.C. 598 at 602.

70 See paras 9–022–9–028.

71 Followed in *Burford Midland Properties Ltd v Marley Extrusions Ltd* [1994] B.C.C. 604, and by Lightman J. in *March Estates plc v Gunmark Ltd* [1999] 2 B.C.L.C. 1.

72 See also *Pybus v Gibb* (1856) 6 E. & B.902. Neither of these cases was cited to Jacob J. in the *RA Securities* case.

edition of this work and said (*per incuriam*) that a voluntary arrangement under Pt VIII of the Insolvency Act 1986 was not a "statutory binding" which purported to impose the arrangement on a dissenting creditor, but a statutory hypothesis that required him to be treated as if he had consented to the arrangement. He drew a critical distinction between the provisions of the Bankruptcy Act 1869 (ss.125–126), which actually provided (together with the rules thereunder) for the discharge of the principal, and the provisions of Pt VIII of the Insolvency Act. Under Pt VIII of the Insolvency Act the discharge of the debtor depends *entirely* on the terms of the arrangement. The question whether the debtor is discharged by the arrangement and the question whether co-debtors and sureties are discharged by the arrangement is to be answered by treating the arrangement as consensual (and by construing it). That, he said, was the intention of Parliament discernible from the drafting of Pt VIII, and particularly s.260(2). In *Greene King v Stanley* [2001] EWCA Civ 1966, [2002] B.P.I.R. 491 the Court of Appeal took a relaxed view of the fact that the IVA itself in that case did not actually contain the reservation of rights, holding that it was sufficient to have been mentioned in the dealings between the parties which led to the IVA, and in the proposal for the IVA. The Court will therefore look at all the surrounding circumstances to see whether there is a reservation of rights, and not simply the IVA document.

(3) Dissolution of the principal under the Companies Act 1985

Where the principal, being a company, is dissolved under s.653 of the Companies Act 1985, the surety remains liable for the obligations of the company he has guaranteed which are outstanding as at the date of dissolution.[73] It has been held that this is not so where the company is a lessee; its dissolution, without it having assigned the lease, is equivalent to a disclaimer, and the effect is that the surety for rent is discharged: *Hastings Corpn v Letton* [1908] 1 K.B. 378. This is odd: it is suggested that the modern view is that the lease is, upon dissolution of the lessee, vested in the Crown as *bona vacantia*: see *Re Wells* [1933] Ch. 29, and s.654 of the Companies Act 1985, in which case the surety may continue to be liable, at least until there is an actual disclaimer by the Crown. Indeed, *Hastings Corpn v Letton* was not followed in *Re Strathblaine* [1948] Ch. 228.[74] Moreover, following the decision of the House of Lords in *Hindcastle Ltd v Barbara Attenborough Associates* [1997] A.C. 70, that a disclaimer of a lease did not operate to discharge the obligations of the sureties (overruling *Stacey v Hill*), it is submitted that *Hastings Corporation v Letton* is no longer good law.

9–015

---

73 *Re Fitzgeorge Ex p. Robson* [1905] 1 K.B. 462: see also *Ali Shipping Corporation v Jugobanka DD Beograd* [1997] EWCA Civ 2705.
74 See also *Murphy v Sawyer-Hoare* [1994] 1 B.C.L.C. 59; *Allied Dunbar Assurance Plc v Fowle* [1994] 2 B.C.L.C. 197, and the detailed discussion at Ch.18, para.18–015.

(4) Where the surety becomes liable as principal

9–016   A surety will remain liable to the creditor notwithstanding the release of the principal if he has ceased in fact to be a surety and become a principal in relation to the obligation guaranteed,[75] or where he has agreed to pay the guaranteed sum,[76] in consideration of the grant of time to pay, or where he has paid part of the guaranteed debt and given security for the balance.[77] Where the guarantee expressly provides for the surety's continuing liability following release of the principal (as all properly drafted modern bank guarantees should), there is no room for the operation of the rule as to release of the surety, and the surety can remain liable for the balance of the guaranteed debt from which the principal, having paid part, has been released.[78]

Discharge of surety by breach of contract by creditor

Breach of the underlying principal contract

9–017   If the creditor commits a repudiatory breach of his contract with the principal so that the principal is entitled to treat the contract as at an end, the surety is also discharged from further liability. In *Watts v Shuttleworth* (1861) 7 H. & N. 353, the surety agreed to guarantee the due performance of a building contract carried out by the principal for the creditor. The creditor promised as a term of the contract that he would insure against fire risk certain fittings, purchased by the principal with money advanced by the creditor, against the risk of fire. He failed to do this, and the fittings worth £2,300 fitted by the principal were destroyed by fire. It was held that the surety was discharged from liability completely, and not merely *pro tanto* to the benefit he would have obtained from the insurance.[79]

The principal will, however, remain liable in respect of rights which have accrued due prior to the termination, and the surety will be correspondingly liable.[80]

The surety will also be discharged if the creditor fails to perform an obligation under the principal contract which is stipulated for in the guarantee, or enters a wholly different contract from the one which is the subject of the guarantee. In *Clarke v Green* (1849) 3 Exch. 619,[81] the surety guaranteed the repayment by instalments by the principal of a loan given by

---

75 *Reade v Lowndes* (1857) 23 Beav. 361.
76 *Defries v Smith* (1862) 10 W.R. 189.
77 *Hall v Hutchings* (1833) 3 My. & K. 426.
78 *Perry v National Provincial Bank* [1910] 1 Ch. 464, especially at 478 *per* Buckley L.J.
79 See, *e.g. Bank of Montreal v Wilder* (1986) 32 D.L.R. (4th) 9; also the hire-purchase cases: *Bentworth Finance Ltd v Lubert* [1968] 1 Q.B. 680; *Unity Finance Ltd v Woodcock* [1963] 1 W.L.R. 455.
80 *Hirji Mulji v Cheong Yue Steamship Co* [1926] A.C. 497, 510; *Elkhoury v Farrow Mortgage Services Pty Ltd* (1993) 114 A.L.R. 541.
81 See also *De Brettes v Goodman* (1855) 9 Moo. P.C.C., where the parties to the principal contract were different from those envisaged by the guarantee; *Archer v Hudson* (1844) 7 Beav. 551, where the specific advance guaranteed was not made, but a fluctuating overdraft instead; *Bonser v Cox* (1841) 4 Beav. 379, where the loan was not made at the time stipulated in the guarantee.

the creditor. The creditor in fact contracted with the principal on the basis that any default in paying one instalment would result in the whole amount becoming immediately repayable. It was held that the surety was discharged because the principal contract was not the contract in respect of which the surety gave the guarantee.

Further, where the performance of an entire contract is guaranteed by the surety, and the principal is not liable because there has been no complete performance of the contract due to a default by the creditor, the surety is discharged.[82]

There appears to be no direct authority as to how the surety's position is affected when the principal affirms the principal contract which has been repudiated by the creditor. It has been suggested that in the event of an affirmation by the principal, the surety ought to remain liable: it is he who takes the risk of an adverse election by the principal, even though it is to some extent unfair that the liability of the surety should depend upon the "possibly capricious decision of the insolvent principal".[83] It is submitted that this is the better view, for reasons expressed earlier in this work.[84]

A non-repudiatory breach of contract by the creditor, that is, a breach sounding in damages only, will not discharge the surety unless it involves a "not unsubstantial" departure from a term of the principal contract which has itself been incorporated into the guarantee.[85] Discharge of the surety in these circumstances is explicable on the basis of a variation of the surety's obligations.

The usual position is that a non-repudiatory breach of the principal contract by the creditor does not discharge the principal but gives him a right to claim damages for breach of contract. That right enures to the benefit of the surety who may be able to utilise it by raising a set-off by way of a defence to a claim on the guarantee by the creditor.[86] However, the right of a surety to set off against the creditor's claims is limited, and may not extend to a counterclaim for unliquidated damages arising out of a breach of the principal contract, or other unliquidated claim for damages

---

82 *Eshelby v Federated European Bank Ltd* [1932] 1 K.B. 423; Slesser and Scrutton L.JJ. decided the appeal on the basis of a failure to complete the works envisaged by the contract and Greer L.J. on the basis of a failure by the creditor to comply with a condition precedent, namely giving a contractual notice to the surety (Slesser L.J. supporting this ground).

83 See Johan Steyn (*op. cit.*) at 260–261.

84 See Ch.6, paras 6–024–6–025, in relation to contracts voidable at the suit of the principal.

85 See *National Westminster Bank v Riley* [1986] B.C.L.C. 268 (especially at 275–276). See also *The Mercers Company v New Hampshire Insurance Co* [1992] 3 All E.R. 57. But see *Ankhar Pty Ltd v National Westminster Finance (Australia) Ltd* (1987) 162 C.L.R. 549, where the High Court of Australia adopted a somewhat stricter approach, on the basis that any departure by the vendor from the terms of the principal contract may be a breach of condition of the guarantee, or a material innominate term discharging the surety: see Deane J. at 253. Also *Corumo Holdings Pty Ltd v C Itoh Ltd* (1991) 5 A.C.S.R. 720.

86 He may do so if the principal is joined as a party to the proceedings: *Bechervaise v Lewis* (1872) L.R.C.P. 372. See Ch.11, paras 11–006–11–007.

that the principal may have against the creditor.[87] To the extent that the principal has a good defence to the creditor's claims, the surety is entitled to adopt it against the creditor, for example where the creditor has elected to exercise a remedy inconsistent with a claim for damages. In *Hewison v Ricketts* (1894) 63 L.J.Q.B. 711[88] the creditor under a hire-purchase contract sought termination of the contract and a repossession of the goods on the grounds of the principal's default, and he was held to have no claim against the surety for the accrued instalments on the grounds that he had chosen his remedy in terminating the contract. Similarly, a surety has been held to be entitled to the benefit of a defence on the basis that the sum claimed by the creditor is a penalty.[89] He may also assert that the creditor has failed reasonably to mitigate his loss.

It is often difficult to ascertain when a breach of contract will be treated as repudiatory and when it will sound in damages only. In *Lloyds Bowmaker (Commercial) Ltd v Smith* [1965] 1 W.L.R. 855, a motor dealer agreed to indemnify a hire-purchase company in respect of losses suffered by it under hire-purchase agreements between the company and his customers. It was a term of the contract that the company would transfer the vehicle, the subject of the hire-purchase agreement, to the dealer upon his payment to the company of sums due under the indemnity. The company, in a particular instance, inadvertently sold the vehicle, and thereby deprived the dealer of the opportunity to receive it. It was held that the dealer was discharged only to the extent of the value of the vehicle, and not wholly discharged from his indemnity.

This case must be contrasted with *Watling Trust Ltd v Briffault Range Co Ltd* [1938] 1 All E.R. 525, where the surety agreed to guarantee the payment by the principal of goods purchased under a hire-purchase contract. The contract provided that in case of default by the principal the hire purchase company should retake possession of the goods and deliver them to the surety. The debtor in fact absconded with the goods, and the hire-purchase company was unable to perform this obligation: it was held that the surety was wholly discharged from liability. It is hard to draw any meaningful distinction between these two cases, and the matter should perhaps be left to each set of factual circumstances and the terms of the

---

87 *Wilson v Mitchell* [1939] 2 K.B. 869; see the analysis by Isaacs J. in *Cellulose Products Pty Ltd v Truda* (1970) 92 W.N.N.S.W. 561; see Ch.11, esp. para.11–007; also *Hyundai Shipbuilding & Heavy Industries Co v Pournaras* [1978] 2 Lloyd's Rep. 502; *Hyundai Heavy Industries v Papadopoulos* [1980] 1 W.L.R. 1129 and the detailed discussion of these cases in Ch.6, para.6–030 and below at 9–020. It may, however, extend to cross-claims that the surety has in his own right against the creditor, for example, for breaches of warranty in a share sale agreement where the surety guaranteed the purchase price, and himself received the benefit of the warranties from the creditor: *BOC Group Plc v Centeon LLC* [1999] 1 All E.R. 53; [1999] Com. L.R. 104. See the consideration of those cases in *Marubeni Hong Kong and South China Ltd v Mongolian Govt*, 2 Lloyd's Rep. 198, at paras 130–138.
88 (1984) 63 L.J.Q.B. 711. But see *Hyundai Heavy Industries Co v Papadopoulos* [1980] 1 W.L.R. 1129.
89 *Cellulose Products Pty Ltd v Truda* (1970) 92 W.N. N.S.W. 561.

individual guarantee in deciding whether a breach is repudiatory or merely one sounding in damages.[90]

Where the contract is one of indemnity, then the surety will not be entitled to the benefit of the principal's defences; he has contracted to pay on the happening of a specified event, and the fact that the principal could escape liability is immaterial.

Breach of the contract of guarantee

The effect on a surety of a breach of a term of the guarantee by the creditor depends on whether the breach strikes at the root of the contract, in which case the surety will be discharged,[91] or whether it sounds in damages only, giving the surety a counterclaim which reduces his liability *pro tanto*. A failure on the part of the creditor to comply with a condition precedent in the guarantee (for example to give notice of a breach or default by the principal) will serve to discharge the surety.[92]

9–018

Discharge of surety by breach of contract by principal

The general rule

Where the principal commits a repudiatory breach of contract which entitles the creditor to treat the contract as at an end, and the creditor accepts the repudiation, the general rule is that the surety remains liable to the creditor on the guarantee notwithstanding that the principal contract no longer subsists. The leading case is *Moschi v Lep Air Services* [1973] A.C. 331. In that case the creditors agreed to give up liens held by them over goods supplied to the principals in consideration of the principals' agreement to pay £40,000 to the creditors by instalments. The principals defaulted on the payments and the creditors treated the contract as repudiated, and sued the sureties for the amount of the unpaid instalments. The House of Lords held that the sureties remained liable to the creditors. The analysis was that the surety's obligation under a contract of guarantee was to ensure that the principal performed his obligations the subject of the guarantee; a breach by the principal necessarily involved a breach by the surety of his own obligations under the guarantee, for which he is liable in damages to the creditor to the same extent as the principal.[93] On the

9–019

---

90 In O'Donovan & Phillips (English ed., 2003), the authors (at para.8–09, fn.9) suggest that there is a difference, because in the latter case (*Watling Trust*) the hire-purchase company was not in a position to deliver the car and give title to it to the surety on payment by him. However, the inability to deliver the goods to the surety (and thus have a claim to the price enforceable under the guarantee) was a feature of both cases.

91 See, *e.g. Ankhar Pty Ltd v National Westminster Finance (Australia) Ltd* (1987) 162 C.L.R. 549.

92 *Burton v Gray* [1873] C.R.8 Ch. App. 932; *United Dominions Trust (Commercial) Ltd v Eagle Aircraft Services Ltd* [1968] 1 W.L.R. 74; but see *Australia & New Zealand Banking Corp v Beneficial Finance Corpn* (1983) 44 A.L.R. 241; *Barclays Bank v Quincecare Ltd* [1988] F.L.R. 166 at 192 *per* Steyn J. now reported at [1992] 4 All E.R. 363. See also Ch.7 at para.7–005.

93 See *per* Lord Diplock at 351. See now *Hampton v Minns* [2002] 1 W.L.R. 1, Kevin Garnett Q.C. and the discussion in Ch.6 at paras 6–002, 6–030 and Ch.7 at 7–018 above.

repudiation of the contract by the principal, the surety's liability remained, although transmuted by operation of law into an obligation to compensate the creditor by way of damages for his loss suffered by reason of the principal's breach.[94] Lord Simon said[95] that if the surety were not to be liable in these circumstances, he "would lose the benefit of the guarantee at the very moment he most needs it—namely, on a repudiation by the principal promisor of his obligations under the contract".

Liability for instalments: the shipbuilding cases

9–020   The fact that the principals in the *Moschi v Lep Air Services* case were obliged to pay in instalments caused no difficulty, because the sureties had guaranteed the complete performance of the contract by the principals. However, where this is not clear, problems arise. Where a contract provides for payment by instalments by the buyer (the principal), such as is the case with shipbuilding contracts, the creditor's right to claim payment of a particular instalment (whether from the principal or from the surety) only arises (prima facie) once the events specified in the contract have occurred and the instalment is accrued due. Where, therefore, a contract has been terminated prematurely (whether by reason of the principal's breach or for any other reason), then the principal is discharged from further performance, including payment of further instalments, and the surety is also discharged from that liability, although he will remain liable to the extent that the principal has to pay damages to the creditor (the builder) for repudiatory breach. However, the surety will continue to remain liable for instalments which have accrued due, and the fact that the principal's liability has been transmuted into a liability to pay damages to the creditor (representing, prima facie, the difference between the contract price and the market value of the vessel at the time of the breach) which arise by reason of the exercise by the creditor of a contractual right to rescind or cancel the contract will not deprive the creditor of his accrued rights against the surety.[96] Provided that the right to the instalment in question has arisen, it is immaterial (subject to any specific contractual provision to the opposite effect) that the creditor has not exercised his right of rescission or cancellation as against the principal before commencing proceedings against the surety.[97]

It would be unusual if the effect of the cancellation were to be to deprive the creditor of a claim against the principal in respect of instalments which

---

94 See *per* Lord Diplock at 347–351. See *Chatterton v McLean* [1951] 1 All E.R. 761, where Parker J. assumed that the acceptance by the creditor of the principal's repudiation did not release the surety in respect of accrued liabilities of the principal or future liabilities for damages: *cf.* the *Hyundai* cases, and see now *Stocznia Gdanska v Latvian Shipping Co* [1998] 1 W.L.R. 574.

95 At 536.

96 *Hyundai Heavy Industries Co v Papadopoulos* [1980] 1 W.L.R. 1129.

97 Contrast *Hyundai Shipbuilding & Heavy Industries v Pournaras* [1978] 2 Lloyd's Rep. 502 (suit commenced before cancellation) with *Hyundai Heavy Industries Co v Papadopoulos* [1980] 1 W.L.R. 1129 and *Stocznia Gdanska v Latvian Shipping Co* [1998] 1 Ll. Rep. 609 (suit commenced after cancellation). For a detailed discussion of these cases see Ch.6, para.6–030.

had accrued and were due, but if this does occur, for example by reason of a total failure of consideration, the co-extensiveness principle would seem to demand that the surety is not liable to the creditor to any greater extent than the principal. However there have been judicial suggestions that this is not always the case, and that it is possible to have a position where the principal is liable to the creditor in a sum of damages which is less than the amount for which the surety is liable.[98] Whilst the surety will apparently retain his right of indemnity against the principal, this apparently peculiar position has been considered to be an exception to the co-extensiveness principle.[99] It is suggested that the better view is that, in circumstances where the surety may be made liable for a greater amount than the principal, the contract by which he is bound should be regarded as an indemnity to that extent, rather than a guarantee; if it is truly a guarantee, the situation in which the surety is liable for the instalments when the principal is not, should never arise.[1]

Discharge by operation of law

This is not really a separate category of discharge at all, but a description of many of the instances discussed above where the surety is discharged from liability. The various instances of discharge by operation of law can be summarised usefully as follows: **9–021**

(1) The surety for a mortgage debt is discharged by foreclosure and subsequent sale by the mortgagee.[2]

(2) The surety for a hire-purchase debt is discharged when the creditor exercises his right to repossession, discharging the hirer under the Consumer Credit Act 1974.[3]

(3) The surety for interest under a debenture bond issued by a company while the principal sum remains due is discharged on the insolvency of the principal.[4]

---

98 *Dies v British International Mining & Finance Corporation* [1939] 1 K.B. 724, where a party in breach of contract was none the less entitled to recover his deposit from the plaintiff; the surety was not entitled to utilise this cross-claim in *Pournaras* or *Papadopoulos*. See also Goff & Jones, *Law of Restitution* (6th ed.), paras 20–36–20–40. Beatson; "Discharge for Breach: the Position of Instalments, Deposits and Other Payments" (1981) 97 L.Q.R. 389; *Rover International Ltd v Cannon Film Sales Ltd (No.3)* [1989] All E.R. 423, and the detailed critique in Ch.6, para.6–030.
99 See *Chitty on Contracts* (29th ed.), Vol. 2, paras 44–085, 44–086.
1 See Ch.6, paras 6–030 *et seq.*
2 *Lloyds & Scottish Trust v Britten* (1982) 44 P. & C.R. 249.
3 *Unity Finance Ltd v Woodcock* [1963] 1 W.L.R. 455; ss.91 and 113(1) of the Consumer Credit Act 1974 (replacing s.34(2) of the Hire Purchase Act 1965) now provide expressly that this should be the result if the guarantee is a "security" within the meaning of s.189(1), which excludes recourse agreements. See generally Ch.17.
4 *Re Moss Ex p. Hallet* [1905] 2 K.B. 307, although he is not discharged where the company goes into liquidation and is dissolved: *Re Fitzgeorge Ex p. Robson* [1905] 1 K.B. 462; *Jowitt v Callaghan* [1938] 38 N.S.W.L.R. 512.

(4) Under legislation prior to the enactment of the Insolvency Act 1986, a surety for the payment of a composition with creditors was discharged where the debtor was adjudged bankrupt and the composition annulled.[5]

Discharge by alteration of the principal contract

Material alteration of documents

9–022 Section 4 of the Statute of Frauds requires that a guarantee must be in writing or evidenced by a written memorandum.[6] The necessity for written documentation gives rise to the possibility that the guarantee documentation may be physically altered by one or other party following execution. Where it is materially altered by the creditor, the surety is discharged. This rule has its origins in *Pigot's Case* (1614) 11 Co. Rep. 26b,[7] and has been analysed in modern times thus:

> "The rule excluding altered documents, in its modern application, appears to rest on the principle or policy that the law will not assist a party to enforce a bargain who has placed the other party in jeopardy by unilateral alteration of the instrument by which their bargain was made."[8]

So the addition of a seal to the agreement opposite the signature of a party not intending to enter it as a deed will invalidate it and discharge the surety.[9] So will striking out the names of co-sureties,[10] or changing the amount for which one of a number of co-sureties is jointly and severally liable.[11]

The effect of an alteration is not merely that the court ignores the alteration, simply treating it as unaltered, nor that the altered clause is rendered unenforceable, but that the entire document is unenforceable. As Sir George Jessel M.R. said in *Suffell v Bank of England* (1882) 9 Q.B.D. 555 at 561:

> "The policy of the law has already been stated, namely that a man shall not take the chance of committing a fraud, and when that fraud is detected recover on the instrument as it was originally made. In such a

---

5 *Walton v Cook* (1888) 40 Ch. D. 325; Bankruptcy Act 1914, s.16(16). The position now discussed at para.9–014 above.
6 See generally Ch.3.
7 This was considered in *Lombard Finance Ltd v Brookplain Trading Ltd* [1991] 1 W.L.R. 271, and recently by the Court of Appeal in *Raiffeisen Zentralbank Ostereich AG v Crossseas Shipping Ltd* [2000] 1 W.L.R. 1135.
8 *Per* Taylor J., *Petro-Can Exploration Inc. v Tormac Transport Ltd* (1983) 23 B.L.R. 1, BCSC.
9 *Aldous v Cornwell* (1868) L.R. 3 Q.B. 573; *Davidson v Cooper* (1844) 13 M. & W. 343.
10 *Bank of Hindustan, China & Japan v Smith* (1867) 36 L.J.C.P. 241; *Suffell v Bank of England* (1882) 9 Q.B.D. 555.
11 *Ellesmere Brewery v Cooper* [1896] 1 Q.B. 75; *Gardner v Walsh* (1855) 5 E. & B. 83.

case the law intervenes, and says that the deed thus altered no longer constitutes the same deed, and that no person can maintain an action on it . . . And this principle is founded on great good sense, because it tends to prevent the party in whose favour it is made from attempting to make any alteration in it."

Even though the rule is designed to prevent fraud by the creditor, it will apply even if the document is altered by a stranger to the guarantee. It is somewhat harsh that the creditor should lose the benefit of the guarantee if it is not he who made the alteration, but the principle seems to be that the creditor, who has the custody of the document, bears the burden of seeing that it remains unaltered.[12]

The surety will only be discharged by an alteration which is material.[13] A change is material if it has an effect on some contract or right within the transaction, either by giving a new right to one of the parties or by changing the substantive nature of the instrument itself. Accordingly, materiality is restricted to changes which are material to the altered document itself: an alteration is not material simply because it may affect some right or contract not created by the document itself.[14] The surety will not be discharged by any alteration made by himself or with his consent.[15]

An alteration need not be detrimental to be material: any alteration that affects the liability appears to be sufficient. In *Gardner v Walsh* (1855) 5 El. & Bl. 83, where the surety co-signed a promissory note with the principal, it was held that the addition of a further surety to be jointly and severally liable on the note would, without the consent of the first surety at the time he gave his commitment, discharge the first surety. In *Lombard Finance Ltd v Brookplain Trading Ltd* [1991] 1 W.L.R. 271 the Court of Appeal held that an alteration of the identity of the principal in the guarantee from "B. Company Ltd" to "B. Ltd" was not material since it did not go to "the whole or to the essence of the instrument".[16] It seems that stamping the instrument after execution will not be a material variation, although affixing a seal (so that it becomes an instrument under seal) will be material.[17]

The rule in *Pigot's Case* has been analysed most recently by the Court of Appeal in *Raiffeisen Zentralbank Osterreich AG v Crossseas Shipping Ltd* [2000] 1 W.L.R. 1135. There, the guarantee, which was on the claimant bank's standard form, had been altered by the bank without the surety's knowledge or authority, by unilaterally inserting into a service of suit clause

---

12 *Davidson v Cooper* (1844) 13 M. & W. 343.

13 *Bishop of Crediton v Bishop of Exeter* [1905] 2 Ch. 455.

14 *Caldwell v Parker* (1869) 3 I.R. Eq. 519, at 526; *cf. Collins v Prosser* (1823) 1 B. & C. 682. In *CIBC v Hardy Bay Inn Ltd* [1985] 1 W.W.R. 405, BCSC, the addition of a signature of a witness and date and place of execution was held not to be material.

15 *Mason v Booth* (1816) 5 M. & S. 223.

16 See also *Birrell v Stafford* [1988] V.R. 281, where it was held that the act of the bank manager deleting the witness's signature on the guarantee and inserting his own after execution of the guarantee did not constitute material variation.

17 See O'Donovan & Phillips, *The Modern Contract of Guarantee*, (3rd ed., 1998), pp.388–389 and the cases referred to there.

the name, address, telex and fax number of the principal as purported service agent for the surety. These details were inserted in printed spaces designed for the purpose. Cresswell J. held that the application of the rule in *Pigot's Case*, and whether or not a surety was discharged, was to be determined by reference to a distinction between "fundamental" and "procedural" obligations, and that since the alteration was procedural only, it was not material for the purposes of allowing the surety to be discharged under the guarantee. The Court of Appeal, undertook a thorough review of the English and Commonwealth[18] authorities, followed *Pigot's Case* and upheld the result, but disagreed with Cresswell J.'s distinction between "fundamental" and "procedural" alterations. Potter L.J. giving the leading judgment (with which Henry and Thorpe L.JJ. agreed), said that the distinction had no support in the authorities. The real test was whether the alteration has "some prejudicial effect upon the legal obligations of the obligor under the instrument" (at 117 col. 1), by which he meant either having an effect on the rights and obligations arising out of the instrument itself (as *per Caldwell v Parker* (1869) I.R. 3 Eq. 519) or where it nonetheless results in the "alteration of the business utility of the instrument when used for an ordinary business purpose" (as *per Suffell v Bank of England* (1882) 9 Q.B.D. 555) (see 114–115). Furthermore, the question of materiality was not to be answered by reference to whether there was an actual prejudice to the surety, but to whether there was the potential for prejudice (see 116). The Court of Appeal firmly rejected the introduction into English law of a flexible rule based on the actual significance and effect of any particular alteration.[19]

Sometimes the physical nature of the alteration is relevant. In *Co-Operative Bank v Tipper* [1996] 4 All E.R. 366, Judge Roger Cooke had to consider the effect of the alteration, by the creditor bank, of the names of the sureties. The guarantee had erroneously described the sureties as "the customer" (*i.e.* the borrower) and as the sureties. The guarantee was altered in pencil by the bank, following execution, to delete the reference to "customer". The borrower went into liquidation and the bank claimed rectification of the guarantee in order to enforce it. The sureties claimed that, rectification or no rectification, they had been discharged by the alteration. The judge held that since the alteration had been made in pencil, the most natural inference was that it was not intended to be a final and operative alteration: it was "deliberative", and not "final and absolute" as would have been the case if it were in pen (ink or biro). Had it been in

---

18 See in particular *Walsh v Westpac Banking Corpn* (1991) 104 A.C.T.R. 30; and *Farrow Mortgage Services Pty Ltd (in liq.) v Slade & Nelson* (1996) 38 N.S.W.L.R. 636.

19 As expressed in Canada in *CIBC v Skender* [1986] 1 W.W.R. 284, *per* Lambert J.A. at 288. The rejection of a flexible result-based test was justified on the grounds that the rule in *Pigot's Case* is designed to avoid fraud, and should be rigorously applied. It is to be contrasted with the approach of the English court to the application of the test of materiality to the avoidance of insurance contracts on the grounds of breach of the duty of utmost good faith, following *Pan Atlantic Insurance Co v Pine Top Insurance Co* [1995] 1 A.C. 501, which introduced a requirement of reliance.

ink, the judge held that the alteration would most certainly have been material.[20]

Material variation of the terms

The rule in Holme v Brunskill

Any material variation of the terms of the principal contract (*i.e.*, between the creditor and the principal) will discharge the surety. This is known as the rule in *Holme v Brunskill* (1878) 3 Q.B.D. 495. The facts of the case were that the creditor let a farm with sheep on it to the principal, the surety guaranteeing the redelivery of the flock in good condition at the end of the term. During the course of the term the agreement was varied between the creditor and the principal whereby the principal surrendered one of the fields up to the creditor in return for a reduction in rent of £10, without the knowledge or assent of the surety. The Court of Appeal held (Brett L.J. dissenting) that even though the variation made no substantial difference to the tenancy agreement, the surety was discharged from liability. Cotton L.J. said (at 505):

9–023

> "The true rule in my opinion is that if there is any agreement between the principals with reference to the contract guaranteed, the surety ought to be consulted, and if he has not consented to the alteration, although in cases where it is without enquiry evident that the alteration is unsubstantial, or that it cannot otherwise be beneficial to the surety, the surety may not be discharged; yet that if it is not self-evident that the alteration is unsubstantial, or one which cannot be prejudicial to the surety, the Court . . . will hold that in such a case the surety himself must be the sole judge whether or not he will consent to remain liable notwithstanding the alteration, and that if he has not so consented he will be discharged."

Therefore in general terms the surety is entitled to require that his position shall not be altered by any agreement between the creditor and the principal from that in which he stood at the time of *his* contract.[21]

Materiality

A variation of the principal contract is material for the purposes of the rule in *Holme v Brunskill* where it is not necessarily beneficial to the surety or otherwise prejudices him, and where any lack of prejudice or benefit is not evident without enquiry.[22] If the benefit or lack of prejudice is not self-

9–024

---

20 His view was *obiter*, and in any event would be unlikely to stand scrutiny after *Raiffeisen Zentralbank Osterreich v Crossseas Shipping Ltd* [2000] 1 W.L.R. 1135.
21 *Polak v Everett* (1876) 1 Q.B.D. 669.
22 *Egbert v National Crown Bank* [1918] A.C. 903, where it was held that the surety remained liable even though the creditor increased the rate of interest charged to the principal to 8 per cent, the increase being illegal and ineffective; *cf. Holland-Can Mortgage Co v Hutchings* [1936] S.C.R. 165. See also *Manulife Bank of Canada v Conlin* 120 D.L.R. (4th) 234 (1994).

evident, then the court will not embark on an enquiry as to whether the variation was indeed beneficial to the surety or otherwise unprejudicial.[23]

The rule has recently been stated by the High Court of Australia in *Ankhar Pty Ltd v National Westminster Finance (Australia) Ltd* (1987) 162 C.L.R. 549 (at 559) thus:

> "According to the English cases, the principle applies so as to discharge the surety when conduct on the part of the creditor has the effect of altering the surety's rights, unless the alteration is unsubstantial and not prejudicial to the surety. The rule does not permit the courts to enquire into the effect of the alteration. The consequence is that, to hold the surety to its bargain, the creditor must show that the nature of the alteration can be beneficial to the surety only or that by its nature it cannot in any circumstances increase the surety's risk."[24]

Thus, the question of whether a variation is material is answered objectively, without reference to what the parties thought. A surety may be discharged, therefore, if the variation is potentially prejudicial when made, even though it ultimately has little effect on the surety's risk.[25] Accordingly, whenever a creditor seeks a variation in the terms of his contract with the principal without the knowledge or consent of the surety, he does so at his own risk, and unless the benefit or lack of prejudice to the surety is obvious, or there is obviously no possibility of prejudice, the surety will be entitled to be discharged. It is a matter for the surety as to whether he wishes to continue to be bound by the guarantee in the circumstances of the variation of the principal contract, and if the creditor wishes to avoid the risk that the surety will seek to avoid liability under the guarantee, he should obtain the surety's prior consent to the variation.[26]

In *Lloyd's Bank TSB v Shorney* [2001] All E.R. (D) 277, a husband had given a guarantee for the liabilities of a company of up to £150,000, and he and his wife had mortgaged their home in respect of that liability. The mortgage was limited to £150,000. Clause 21 of the mortgage contained a

---

23 (1878) 3 Q.B.D. at 505; *Croydon Gas Co v Dickinson* (1876) 2 C.P.D. 46, *Bank of Baroda v Patel* [1996] 1 Ll. Rep. 391 at 396. See also *Re Darwen and Pearce* [1927] 1 Ch. 176.

24 See also *Corumo Holdings Pty Ltd v C Itoh Ltd* (1991) 5 A.C.S.R. 720, at 729 and 753. These principles were restated by Cresswell J in *Marubeni Hong Kong and South China Ltd v Mongolian Govt* [2004] 2 Lloyd's Rep. 198 at paras 206–209.

25 In *Credit Suisse v Borough Council of Allerdale* [1995] 1 Lloyd's Rep. 315 Colman J. (at 365–366) applied the rule in *Holme v Brunskill* where the variation *might* have been, but would not *inevitably* have been, beneficial to the surety, in holding that the variation was material. See *The Kalma* [1999] 2 Ll. Rep. 374 at 378 col. 1. This is entirely consistent with the approach of the Court of Appeal to the materiality of an alteration of the document embodying the guarantee in *Raiffeisen Zentralbank Osterreich AG v Crossseas Shipping* [2000] Ll. Bank. Rep. 108.

26 See *National Bank of Nigeria v Awolsi* [1964] 1 W.L.R. 1311, [1965] 2 Lloyd's Rep. 389, where the bank took a guarantee over an existing overdrawn bank account, and then opened a new account on which the bank then dealt with the principal; it was held that the opening of the new account was a variation which, without the consent of the surety, discharged him. See also *Bank of New Zealand v West* [1977] 1 N.Z.L.R. 31.

provision which prevented the wife from enforcing any claim against her husband or the bank, or to exercise any subrogation rights, until *all moneys* owed to the bank had been paid off. The bank then lent further sums which were covered by the husband's guarantee. He defaulted, and the bank obtained judgment against the husband for £238,000 and sought a charging order on the home for the balance. The wife paid the £150,000 and claimed to be entitled to be subrogated to the bank's charge. The Court of Appeal held that the bank was not entitled to rely on the all moneys nature of clause 21 in shutting the wife out of her subrogation rights, among other reasons because its conduct in increasing the husband's liability under his guarantee had materially prejudiced the wife's position as mortgagor.[27]

A startling illustration of the operation of the rule in *Holme v Brunskill* was provided by the decision of Morland J. in *Howard de Walden Estates Ltd v Pasta Place Ltd* [1995] 22 E.G. 143. There, the use provision in a lease of a delicatessen was progressively released, to permit sale of wine to customers taking meals, and off-licence use. The sureties were not parties to the variations, but when they were sued for rent after the assignee went into receivership, they successfully pleaded discharge by reason of the variations,[28] on the basis that the variations were not obviously insubstantial or beneficial.

In *Unicomp Inc v Eurodis Electron Plc* (unreported, May 7, 2004, Evans-Lombe J.), the landlord, Fortwilliam had let commercial premises on a long lease to a subsidiary of the claimant, who had guaranteed the payment of the rent under the lease and the due performance of the covenants in it. The guarantee contained a clause by which the claimant agreed that any "neglect or forbearance" by Fortwilliam in endeavouring to obtain payment or to enforce the covenants would not release or exonerate the claimant's liability under the guarantee. The tenant went into liquidation and assigned the lease to an asssignee, who took occupation and began to pay rent. Fortwilliam did not attempt to forfeit or to take the initiative to vary the lease, but simply accepted rent from the assignee on the same terms. Evans-Lombe J. held that Fortwilliam's conduct constitited a forbearance within the meaning of the guarantee and that the claimant was not released by operation of the rule in *Holme v Brunskill.*

A variation is material so as to entitle a surety to full discharge, however, only if it is an act by the creditor which affects the *risk of default by the principal,* and consequently the risk of the surety being called upon to

---

27 The Court of Appeal primarily based their reasoning on the fact that the wife had contemplated that her husband would undertake no liability greater than £150,000, and took the view that clause 16 of the mortgage, which permitted the bank to "renew vary increase or determine any advances accommodation or facilities given or to be given to the Customer or to any other person" without the husband or wife's consent did not catch the taking of further guarantees (from the husband) for those advances.

28 See also *West Horndon Industrial Park v Phoenix Timber* [1995] 20 E.G. 137; also [1995] Conv. 289, where it is suggested that in order to avoid the harsh effects of the rule, landlords should obtain the consent of all sureties for the obligations under leases. See the detailed discussion in Ch.18, para.18–002.

honour the guarantee. Such a variation alters the basis on which the surety agreed to become liable under the guarantee, and not to release the surety in those circumstances would be to allow the creditor and the principal to impose a new bargain upon the surety. In those circumstances, the surety cannot necessarily be compensated by a reduction in the creditor's right to recover against him. An example of this is provided by *Bank of Baroda v Patel* [1996] 1 Lloyd's Rep. 391, where the bank made available a facility to the principal, guaranteed by the surety, which related to import and export transactions to be undertaken by the principal with the benefit of ECGD cover, as required by the terms of the facility. The bank operated the facility in relation to a number of foreign bill transactions without there being ECGD cover in place (as the bank knew). Potter J. held that this amounted to a variation of the terms of the facility which seriously prejudiced the surety. Although he did not spell out the reason, it is clear that the failure on the part of the bank to obtain ECGD cover increased the risk of default by the principal. The result is analogous to the result where the creditor deals with securities to the detriment of the surety's interests.[29] This type of variation must be contrasted with a variation which merely affects the *amount* of the surety's ultimate liability, but which leaves the risk of default by the principal unchanged; this variation will not be material.[30]

Scope of the rule

9–025   The rule in *Holme v Brunskill is* not confined to cases in which the surety and principal have entered into a binding agreement to vary the principal contract. The surety may also be discharged by variation of the principal's liability arising out of an exercise of a right by the creditor,[31] or by an arrangement which removes a security on which the surety is entitled to rely as against the principal.[32] In *Mayhew v Boyes* (1910) 103 L.T. 1 the surety on a composition was discharged from liability to a particular creditor where that creditor (without the knowledge or consent of the surety) obtained an agreement from the principal to be paid all the debts owing to that creditor in full. The surety may also be discharged by any variation in the performance of the principal contract,[33] and a surety for the redemption of an annuity or for shares in a company is discharged by any variation in the mode of redemption.[34]

However, variations to collateral arrangements that may exist outside the scope of the guaranteed contract do not affect the liability of the surety, unless those variations in some way impact on the surety's risk. In

---

29 See below at paras 9–041 *et seq.*
30 See the analysis in McGuinness, *The Law of Guarantee* (*op. cit.*) paras 10.14, 10.15.
31 *Re Darwen and Pearce* [1927] 1 Ch. 176.
32 *General Steam Navigation Co v Rolt* (1858) 6 C.B. (N.S.) 575.
33 *Bellingham v Freer* (1837) Moo. P.C.C. 333; *General Steam Navigation Co v Rolt* (above); *Calvert v London Dock Co* (1838) 2 Keen 638; *Warre v Calvert* (1837) 7 Ad. & El. 143.
34 *Eyre v Bartrop* (1818) 3 Madd. 221; *Polak v Everett* (1876) 1 Q.B.D. 669. *Cf. Nicholson v Burt* (1882) 10 R. 121.

Sanderson v Aston (1873) L.R. Ex. 73 the guarantee was for the good conduct of the servant, whose term of employment was varied to provide for three months' instead of one month's notice. It was held that the term as to notice was not part of the servant's contract, and the variation did not materially add to the surety's risk.[35]

Further, variations which are authorised by the surety or expressly contemplated by the principal contract[36] will not discharge the surety, and nor will those authorised within the guarantee.[37] Plainly, where the surety plays a part in the variation transaction, he will not be discharged, for example where he prepares his own documents,[38] or where he allows the creditor to think that he has consented.[39] However, the surety is not bound to enquire as to whether a variation is to take place, nor is he bound to warn the creditor against carrying it out because of some prejudice he may suffer.[40] In *Credit Suisse v Borough Council of Allerdale* [1995] 1 Lloyd's Rep. 315, the distinction was drawn between mere knowledge of the proposed variation on the part of the surety, and his consent to it (at 361–362).

There is a distinction, so far as the application of the rule is concerned, between a guarantee of a specific contract and a future course of dealing, so that it will be open to the creditor, without discharging the surety, to vary the terms applicable to the future course of dealing so long as it remains within the scope of the guarantee.[41]

Where the surety gives his consent to the variation, that is sufficient to continue to bind him to the guarantee even in the absence of fresh consideration.[42] There is authority that "principal debtor" clauses in guarantees are effective to preclude the surety from being discharged in the

---

35 There is some suggestion in the speech of Pollock B. that the surety would not be discharged, even though the variation was potentially prejudicial to him, if he could not show actual damage to his position. Any such rule was disapproved in *Holme v Brunskill* and does not represent the law.

36 See, *e.g. Stewart v McKean* (1855) 10 Exch. 675, where the creditor was given a discretion as the mode of accounting between himself and the principal.

37 *British Motor Trust Co v Hyams* (1934) 50 T.L.R. 230.

38 *Woodcock v Oxford & Worcester Ry* (1853) 1 Drew. 521.

39 *Hollier v Eyre* (1840) 9 C. & F. 52.

40 *Polak v Everett* (1876) 1 Q.B.D. 669 at 673.

41 *City of London v New Hampshire Insurance Co* (January 18, 1991, Phillips J.), summarised at (1991) 3 J.I.B.F.L. 144; reversed on other grounds *sub nom. Wardens etc of Mercers Co v New Hampshire Insurance Co* [1992] 3 All E.R. 57.

42 *Mayhew v Crickett* (1918) 2 Swanst. 185, *per* Lord Eldon L.C.; *Smith v Winter* (1834) 4 M. & W. 454; *Phillips v Foxall* (1872) L.R. 7 Q.B. 666 at 676–677. The basis for this rule is that consideration is not necessary since the consent simply revives an old obligation rather than creates a new one. This is a peculiar application of the doctrine of consideration, but the rule (perhaps to be limited to principal and surety cases) is now enshrined in the law, and can be explained, it is suggested, on the basis that the surety would be estopped from objecting to the variation, the other parties having relied on his consent in going ahead. See *Credit Suisse v Borough Council of Allerdale* [1995] 1 Lloyd's Rep. 315.

event of a variation to the principal contract.[43] However, "principal debtor" clauses have been scrutinised carefully by the courts, and rarely provide the protection the creditor seeks.[44]

Acceptance or ratification by the creditor of conduct that amounts to a repudiatory breach of the principal contract by the principal does not discharge the surety,[45] and nor do any changes in the relationship between the creditor and the surety which alter their relationship in a way which does not impact upon the surety's risk. While novation of the principal contract will discharge the surety,[46] a mere assignment by the creditor of his rights thereunder will not.[47] A failure of the creditor to exercise a legal right which he has against the principal, or a simple omission, does not amount to a variation of the principal contract sufficient to discharge the surety.[48] When the surety is discharged, he is entitled to be released from any security which he has given in respect of the guaranteed obligation.[49]

Exceptions to the rule

9–026 The rule in *Holme v Brunskill* will not apply notwithstanding that the surety is prejudiced by the variation in two circumstances as described below.

(1) Unenforceability of the variation

9–027 Where the variation is unenforceable on the grounds of illegality, the surety will not be discharged. In *Egbert v National Crown Bank* [1918] A.C. 903 the variation of the interest rate from 7 per cent to 8 per cent was illegal, and so the surety remained liable on the guarantee to the bank. Further, where the variation is obtained by fraud of the principal, the surety is not entitled to be discharged.[50]

---

43 *General Produce Co v United Bank Ltd* [1979] 2 Lloyd's Rep. 255; *Byblos Bank SAL v Al-Khudhairy* [1987] B.C.L.C. 232. In *Marubeni Hong Kong and South China Ltd v Mongolian Govt* [2004] 2 Lloyd's Rep. 198, Cresswell J. analysed whether the liability assumed by the defendant surety was as primary obligor or not and concluded that it was not. However, he said (at para.142) that even if the defendant had undertaken a primary liability, it did not follow that the rule in *Holme v Brunskill* had no application. However, he appears to have based himself on the terms of the documents in that case rather than any authority in support of that proposition. The case is going to the Court of Appeal.
44 In both *Manulife Bank of Canada v Conlin* 120 D.L.R. (4th) 234 (1994) and *Credit Suisse v Borough Council of Allerdale* [1995] 1 Lloyd's Rep. 315, principal debtor clauses failed to prevent variations from discharging the sureties.
45 *Moschi v Lep Air Services* [1973] A.C. 331.
46 *Commerical Bank of Tasmania v Jones* [1893] A.C. 313.
47 *Bradford Old Bank v Sutcliffe* [1918] 2 K.B. 833, *per* Pickford L.J. at 841; *Wheatley v Bastow* (1855) 7 De M. & G. 261 at 279. See *First National Corpn v Goodman* [1983] B.C.L.C. 203 at 210.
48 *Kingston-Upon-Hull Corpn v Harding* [1892] 2 Q.B. 494. This is not the case where the omission relates to something which the creditor has contracted with the surety to do.
49 *Bolton v Salmon* [1891] 2 Ch. 48; *Smith v Wood* [1929] 1 Ch. 14.
50 *Bramley Union Guardians v Guarantee Society* (1900) 64 J.P. 308. It is not clear what the position would be where the variation is obtained by the fraud of the creditor. It is submitted that the surety would be entitled to his discharge, since the creditor could not plead his own fraud in making a claim against the surety.

(2) Divisibility of the principal contract

Where the guarantee extends to one of several distinct debts or obligations, **9–028** a variation of one of these debts or obligations will not release the surety from his guarantee with respect to the others.[51] However, in *Midland Motor Showrooms v Newman* [1929] 2 K.B. 256 it was held that a variation giving the principal time to pay instalments in arrears discharged the surety not only in respect of those instalments but also of any further liability under the principal contract. In *Bank of Baroda v Patel* [1996] 1 Ll. Rep. 391 Potter J. said (at 397) that the payment obligations in *Newman* were properly to be regarded as arising out of one contract only, so that the saving of time in respect of one instalment discharged the surety in respect of all.

Agreement by creditor to give time to the principal

The general rule

Where the creditor enters an agreement with the principal whereby the **9–029** principal is given an extension of time, beyond that contemplated in the original contract, in which to perform his obligation, the surety is discharged.[52] The basis of the rule is that an extension of time deprives the surety of his right at any time to pay the debt and sue the principal in the name of the creditor: the creditor is unable to place his remedies at the disposal of the surety without breaching the agreement as to the extension of time, and so since the surety's right or remedy is suspended, he is discharged altogether.[53] Otherwise, if the surety were able to claim against the principal, this would nullify the effect of the extension of time, and if he were unable to claim, but remained liable to the creditor, it would put the principal in a better position than the surety, which would offend the co-extensiveness principle.[54] The rationale of the rule is elegantly summarised by Cockburn C.J. in *Swire v Redman* (1876) 1 Q.B.D. 536 at 541 as follows:

> "The relation of principal and surety gives to the surety certain rights. Amongst others the surety has a right at any time to apply to the creditor and pay him off, and then (on giving a proper indemnity for

---

51 *Bingham v Corbett* (1864) 34 L.J.B.Q. 37; *Skillett v Fletcher* (1867) L.R. 1 C.P. 217; *Harrison v Seymour* (1866) L.R. 1 C.P. 518; *Croydon Gas Co v Dickinson* (1876) 1 C.P.D. 707; *WR Simmons v Meek* [1939] 2 All E.R. 645. The principle was considered by Potter J. in *Bank of Baroda v Patel* [1996] 1 Ll. Rep. 391 at 396–397.
52 *Nisbet v Smith* (1789) 2 Bro. C.C. 579; *Samuell v Howarth* (1817) 3 Mer. 272; *Swire v Redman* (1876) 1 Q.B.D. 669 at 673–674.
53 See *Bailey v Edwards* (1864) 4 B. & S. 761 *per* Blackburn J.; *Wright v Simpson* (1802) 6 Ves. 714; *Samuell v Howarth* (1817) 3 Mer. 272. And see *Rouse v Bradford Banking Co* [1894] A.C. 586; [1894] 2 Ch. 32 at 75 *per* A.L. Smith L.J., set out in full in Ch.11, para.11–002.
54 See the discussion at para.9–010 above in relation to release of the principal. In *Philpot v Bryant* (1828) 4 Bing. 717, Best C.J. said: "A creditor, by giving time to the principal debtor, in equity, destroys the rights of the sureties; and a court of equity will grant an injunction to restrain a creditor, who has given further time to the principal, from bringing an action against the surety. This equitable doctrine courts of law have applied to cases arising on bills of exchange."

costs) to sue the principal in the creditor's name. We are not aware of any instance in which a surety has in practice exercised this right; certainly the cases in which a surety uses it must be very rare. Still the surety has this right. And if the creditor binds himself not to sue the principal debtor, for however short a time, he does interfere with the surety's theoretical right to sue in his name during such period. It has been settled by decisions that there is an equity to say that such interference with the rights of the surety—in the immense majority of cases not damaging him even to the extent of one shilling—must operate to deprive the creditor of his right to recourse against the surety, though it may be for thousands of pounds."

It may be thought that this is scarcely a reasonable basis for depriving the creditor of valuable rights.[55] The rule may, however, be justified more sympathetically on the basis that the extension of time amounts to a variation of the principal contract which increases the risk of default by the principal and so the risk which the surety has assumed under the guarantee.[56] The variation as to time for performance gives rise not only to the loss of an immediate remedy against the principal, but also to a change in the risk of default by the principal, since payment or performance on a certain day is replaced by a period during which his financial situation may deteriorate.[57]

There is a further justification for releasing the surety when time is given by the creditor to the principal. This is that if the surety were to continue to be liable to the creditor under the guarantee, the principal's liability having been postponed, the creditor might claim against the surety who would then be entitled to claim against the principal, with the effect that the principal loses the benefit of the extension of time which he has bought from the creditor. In other words, unless the surety is released, the creditor will derogate from his grant.[58]

To this extent, the rule that the surety is discharged by reason of the creditor giving time to the principal may be regarded as an aspect of the operation of the rule in *Holme v Brunskill*.[59] Accordingly, the question of actual prejudice is irrelevant to the question whether the surety should be

---

55 The rule has been reversed in Saskatchewan and Manitoba: see McGuinness, *The Law of Guarantee* (*op. cit.*), para.10.27. See the criticisms of the rule in O'Donovan & Phillips (*op. cit.*), p.358.
56 See the discussion at para.9–024 above.
57 This explanation is given in *Philpot v Bryant* (1828) 4 Bing. 717 at 719, *per* Best C.J. In *Oakeley v Pasheller* (1836) 4 Cl. & Fin. 207, Lord Lyndhurst said:"Now the principle of law is that, where a creditor gives time to the principal debtor, there being a surety to secure payment of the debt, and does so without the consent of, or communication with, the surety, he discharged the surety from liability, as he thereby places him in a new situation, and exposes him to a risk and contingency to which he would otherwise not be liable."
58 *Re Natal Investment Co, Nevill's Case* (1870) 6 Ch. App. 43, esp. at 47. See the discussion at para.9–034 below of the question of the validity of express terms in the guarantee giving the creditor the right to give time to the principal while preserving his rights against the surety.
59 See paras 9–023–9–028 above.

discharged, although if the extension is obviously beneficial to the surety, he will remain liable on the guarantee.[60] The consent of the surety will be crucial in order for the creditor to protect his rights under the guarantee. If the extension has been given after the surety has performed his obligations under the guarantee, he will not be discharged, since he has a vested right of indemnity and subrogation which cannot be defeated by any subsequent act of the creditor.[61]

Requirements of the rule

It is not material what form the giving of time by the creditor takes, so long   **9–030**
as there is a legally binding and enforceable agreement by the creditor that he will suspend his rights against the principal.[62] However, at the time of this agreement, the surety's right to pay off the creditor and sue the principal must have accrued; in other words, the principal must be under an obligation to the creditor.[63] The agreement need not be in writing,[64] nor of an express nature, but may be implied from the conduct of the creditor and the principal. However, the intention to vary the principal's obligations must be unequivocal.[65] Mere forbearance to sue, or gratuitous indulgence by the creditor, is not sufficient. In *Rouse v Bradford Banking Co* [1894] A.C. 586, an agreement by a bank with its customer to allow him to increase his overdraft was held not to be an agreement to give time so that the customer was released from the obligation to repay immediately.[66]

The agreement must be made by the creditor with the principal, and enforceable at his suit,[67] since an agreement with a third party, even if enforceable by him, will not affect the surety's risk. An agreement made with the surety will not discharge the surety.[68] In order to affect the surety's

---

60 See Rowlatt, *Principal and Surety* (*op. cit.*), p.163.
61 *Reade v Lowndes* (1857) 23 Beav. 361 at 368 *per* Romilly M.R.
62 *Overend Gurney & Co Ltd v Oriental Financial Corpn Ltd* (1874) L.R. 7 H.L. 348; *Rouse v Bradford Banking & Co Ltd* [1984] A.C. 586 at 594. *Marubeni Hong Kong and South China Ltd v Mongolian Govt* [2004] 2 Lloyd's Rep. 198, Cresswell J. at para.216.
63 *Prendergast v Devey* (1821) 6 Madd. 124. In *Steinbach Credit Union Ltd v Oakridge Gravel Ltd* [1983] 5 W.W.R. 450 it was held that in the case of a loan payable on demand, an agreement to extend time for payment would never discharge the surety, on the ground that the debt is not due until the demand is made by the creditor, and so it is up to him when to fix the moment of liability, without discharging the surety. It is doubtful that this is correct, because the agreement not to make a demand for a period in effect converts the demand loan into a term loan: this is a fundamental variation of the loan agreement which will materially affect the surety, because it increases his risk of non-performance by the principal: see *Oakeley v Pasheller* (1836) 4 Cl. & Fin. 207, *per* Lord Lyndhurst. But see *Unigate Ltd v Bentley* (unreported) November 25, 1986 CAT No.1055, where it was held that the rule only applied where the guarantee related to payment on a fixed date and that date is postponed.
64 See *Re a Debtor No.517 of 1991, The Times*, November 25, 1991, where Ferris J. held that an oral variation could be effective to discharge the surety, but this could only be used as a defence.
65 *Petty v Cooke* (1871) 25 L.T. 90; *Bolton v Buckenham* [1891] 1 Q.B. 278.
66 See especially at 594.
67 *Lyon v Holt* (1839) 5 M. & W. 250; *Clarke v Birley* (1889) 4 Ch. D. 422, where the surety was not released, the contract being made with a co-surety.
68 *Ex p. Smith* (1713) 1 P. Wms. 237.

liability, the agreement with the principle must be supported by consideration[69] unless made under seal, although to the extent that the creditor is
estopped from suing the principal because of some representation, promise
or conduct, it is submitted that the surety will similarly be discharged.
There is no judicial support for this proposition.

The effect of the agreement must be genuinely to give time to the
principal, and not merely to give the creditor an option to require payment
or performance as originally contracted for.[70] Nor will an agreement to give
time conditional upon performance by the debtor of certain acts be
effective to discharge the surety.[71] Where judgment is obtained by consent
against the principal and the creditor agrees not to execute it for a period
no longer than that in which judgment would have been obtained in the
usual course, the surety will not be discharged.[72] Where the principal agrees
to satisfy the judgment by instalments in consideration of a stay of
execution, the surety remains liable where the principal defaults and the
whole judgment sum becomes due.

In the absence of an obligation to pursue him timeously,[73] the surety will
not be discharged by mere passivity on the part of the creditor, that is, an
omission to pursue the principal.[74] This is so even though the principal
subsequently becomes insolvent.[75] The settled view is that it is the responsibility of the surety to see that the principal pays, and not that of the
creditor.[76]

Forms of giving time

9–031   The class of cases where the creditor gives time to the principal is never
closed, and depends on the circumstances of each case. The following are
selected examples from the case law.[77] An agreement to accept payment
from the principal by instalments will discharge the surety,[78] as does an

---

69 *McManus v Bark* (1870) L.R. 5 Exch. 65 at 66; *Tucker v Laing* (1856) 2 K. & J. 745;
   Overend Gurney & Co Ltd v Oriental Financial Corpn Ltd (1874) L.R. 7 H.L. 348.
70 *York City & County Banking Co v Bainbridge* (1880) 43 L.T. 732.
71 *Vernon v Turley* (1836) 1 M. & W. 316; *Badnall v Samuel* (1817) 3 Price 521; *Brickwood v
   Anniss* (1814) 5 Taunt. 614, where the creditor promised time to allow the principal to see
   if his other creditors would accept a composition, in which the creditor would join, and the
   surety was not discharged. See also *Lewis v Jones* (1825) 4 B. & C. 506; *cf. Bailey v Edwards*
   (1864) 4 B. & S. 761.
72 *Ladbroke v Hewitt* (1832) 1 Dowl. 488; *Hulme v Coles* (1827) 2 Sim. 12; *Jay v Warren* (1824)
   1 C. & P. 532.
73 *Price v Edwards* (1829) 10 B. & C. 578; *Croft v Johnson* (1814) 5 Taunt. 319; *Jenkins v
   Robertson* (1854) 2 Drew. 351. But once judgment has been obtained against the principal
   and the surety, the granting of time to the principal to satisfy the judgment does not
   discharge the surety, because the basis of his liability is not now the guarantee but the
   judgment: see *In Re a Debtor* [1913] 3 K.B. 11.
74 See *Holl v Hadley* (1835) 2 Ad. & El. 758.
75 *Shepherd v Beecher* (1725) 2 P.W. 288; *Perfect v Musgrave* (1818) 6 Price 111; *Wright v
   Simpson* (1802) 6 Ves. 714; *Price v Kirkham* (1864) 3 H. & C. 437. See the discussion in
   relation to the availability of the defence of laches to the surety, at para.9–036.
76 *Trent Navigation v Harley* (1808) 10 East. 34.
77 *Wright v Simpson* (above), and see the discussion in Rowlatt, *On Principal and Surety* (*op.
   cit.*) para.4.97.
78 See the cases cited in *Halsbury's Laws* (*op. cit.*) Vol. 20 (2004 reissue), para.317.

agreement to extend time between the instalments;[79] but a change in the number of instalments does not discharge the surety where there is no extension of time as a result.[80] The taking of further security for the guaranteed obligation will discharge the surety where it was obtained by the creditor giving the principal further time.[81] Further, the accepting of a new bill instead of payment,[82] or renewing a promissory note will discharge the surety,[83] as will the acceptance of a further security for the guaranteed debt with a covenant for payment at a later date.[84]

The surety will not be discharged by taking security for a debt at a future point in time while retaining the right to sue on the original debt;[85] equally, where the principal gives the creditor an assignment of chattels by way of security which is not enforceable until a notice period has expired but the principal's personal liability is not postponed, the surety remains liable.[86] Similarly, where the creditor takes as security both a mortgage not enforceable until a date certain and, as a collateral security, a promissory note guaranteed by the surety, the surety is not discharged by the fact that the mortgage was executed subsequently to the promissory note.[87] However, where the receipt of interest by the creditor amounts to an agreement by him not to sue for the principal amount until the date for payment of interest has arrived, the surety will be discharged, this being an agreement to give time.[88]

Scope of the rule

The rule will apply to discharge sureties who originally contracted as co-principals, but before time was given, became sureties, provided the surety (once a co-principal) agrees with the principal and the creditor has notice of the fact.[89] However, where a person contracting originally as surety becomes a principal, he is not released by reason of time being given to the original principal.[90] Nor does the rule serve to discharge a person who does   **9–032**

79 *Clarke v Henty* (1838) 3 Y. & C. Ex. 187.
80 *Howell v Jones* (1834) 1 Cr. M. & R. 97.
81 *WH Malkin v Sherman* (1925) 35 B.C.R.445.
82 *Overend Gurney & Co v Oriental Financial Corpn* (1874) L.R. 7 H.L. 348; *Wyke v Rogers* (1852) 21 L.J. Ch. 611, where the acceptance of a post-dated promissory note by the creditor discharged the surety.
83 *Goldfarb v Bartlett* [1920] 1 K.B. 639.
84 *Provincial Bank of Ireland v Fisher* (1919) 2 I.R.R. 249.
85 *Munster & Leinster Bank v France* (1889) 24 L.R. I.R. 82.
86 *Lindsay v Lord Downes* (1840) 2 Ir. Eq. R. 307, where the creditor had both a bond for the debt then outstanding and bills falling due at different dates.
87 *Twopenny v Young* (1824) 3 C. 208; the mere giving of further security is not, without more, the giving of time: see *Swire v Redman* (1876) 1 Q.B.D. 536.
88 *Boaler v Mayor* (1865) 19 C.B. (N.S.) 76.
89 *Blake v White* (1835) 1 Y. C. Eq. 420.
90 *Rouse v Bradford Banking Co* [1894] 2 Ch. 32, where a partner, who retired from a firm and took a covenant that they would pay the partnership debts and indemnify him, became in effect surety to those creditors with notice of the dissolution. A provision in the covenant to the effect that so long as he was indemnified he was not entitled to insist that they pay the debts did not deprive him of the right to be discharged on the giving of time to the continuing partners.

not in fact occupy the position of surety,[91] such as a company director who is deemed by statutory provision to be liable for the company's debt.[92]

Where the surety is liable for several separate and distinct obligations, time given in respect of one such obligation will not discharge the surety as to the remainder. This is so whether the obligations arise under one contract or under separate contracts.[93] For example, in *Croydon Commercial Gas Co v Dickinson* (1876) L.R. 2 C.P.D. 46 the principal had contracted with the creditor to purchase gas by-products, the surety having guaranteed monthly payment of the price. It was held that time given by the creditor in relation to one monthly payment discharged the surety only in respect of that payment; the surety was not discharged from liability for the principal's obligations otherwise.[94] Similarly in *Bingham v Corbet* (1864) 34 L.J.B.Q. 37, the surety had given a continuing guarantee for a contract for the price of goods to be supplied, and time was given in respect of an amount due, the creditor reserving his rights in relation to future supplies. The surety remained liable in respect of future amounts.[95]

Reservation by the creditor

9–033   Where the creditor reserves his rights to proceed against the surety when giving time to the principal, the surety will not be discharged.[96] It has been seen that one of the justifications for the rule that the surety is released by the giving of time to the principal is that otherwise the creditor would derogate from his grant in leaving the principal still potentially liable to the surety.[97] The justification for the protection of the creditor who reserves his rights against the surety appears to be that the principal has notice that he will continue to be liable to the surety notwithstanding the creditor's agreement with the principal to give him time, and so there is no basis for discharging the surety.[98] However, this rather assumes that the principal has sight of or is a party to the guarantee. Further, as will be seen,[99] the effectiveness of provisions in the guarantee whereby the creditor reserves his rights against the surety is not wholly free from doubt.

The effect of a reservation of time is to transmute the promise of the creditor to extend time into a mere covenant not to sue, as opposed to a

---

91 *Reade v Lowndes* (1857) 23 Beav. 361; *Greenwood v Francis* [1899] 1 Q.B. 312. In the latter case it was left open as to whether a surety could discharge his co-surety by agreeing to give time to the principal.

92 *Way & Hearn* (1862) 11 C.B. (N.S.) 774, where the surety had in fact merely given an indemnity in respect of a particular loss.

93 *British Airways v Parish* [1979] 2 Lloyd's Rep. 361.

94 *Harrison v Seymour* (1866) L.R.1 C.P. 518.

95 See the analysis of this case in *Bank of Baroda v Patel* [1996] 1 Ll. Rep. 391.

96 But see *Midland Motor Showrooms v Newman* (1929) 2 K.B. 256; *WR Simmons v Meek* [1939] 2 All E.R. 645.

97 *Tatum v Evans* (1885) 54 L.T. 336; *Boaler v Mayor* (1865) 19 C.B.N.S. 76; 144 E.R. 714; *Nichols v Norris* (1831) 3 B. & Ad. 41; *Bateson v Gosling* (1871) L.R. 7 C.P. 9; *Overend Gurney & Co v Oriental Financial Corpn* (1874) 7 H.L. 348; *Mahant Singh v U Ba Yi* [1939] A.C. 601; *Greene King v Stanley* [2001] EWCA Civ 1966, [2002] B.P.I.R. 491 a case about release in the context of an IVA (see above para.9–014).

98 See para.9–029 above.

99 *Webb v Hewitt* (1857) 3 K.J. 438.

binding release.[1] The essential difference between giving time and other variations of the principal agreement discharging the surety is that, so long as the creditor reserves his rights against the surety, the consent of the surety is not essential to protect the creditor's rights against him: the surety will remain bound.[2] Further, it is not necessary that the reservation of rights be communicated to the surety.[3] There is no reason, it is suggested, why the reservation should not be made orally to the principal.[4] However, where the guarantee requires that notice of the variation or giving of time be given to the surety, this must be complied with, or the surety will be discharged.[5]

Accordingly, the burden lies upon the surety to establish a binding agreement to give time to the principal. Having established such an agreement, he is entitled to be discharged unless the creditor can show, the burden now being upon him, that he took steps to reserve his rights against the surety.[6] It is a matter of fact whether the creditor has genuinely reserved his rights against the surety, and although a modern standard form bank guarantee will contain such a clause, the court will not be shut out from looking at the transaction as a whole: where the nature and effect of the agreement is fundamentally inconsistent with the reservation of rights, then the true intentions of the parties in giving time (insofar as evidence of them is admissible) will override the express words of the guarantee agreement. This (and the discussion below) is relevant both to the giving of time and releases generally.

Agreements to remain bound

A modern standard form guarantee will contain a clause permitting the creditor to release or give time to the principal without affecting the liability of the surety. The agreement must be directed towards release or giving of time to the principal: an agreement that the creditor should be permitted merely to grant "indulgence" to the principal may not be sufficient.[7] Further, it may follow as a matter of necessary implication from the nature of the obligations guaranteed that the surety is bound to remain liable notwithstanding variations in the performance of the principal contract.[8]

9–034

This principle proceeds upon the assumption that the creditor and the surety are free to contract for the rights and obligations that will bind them

---

1 See para.9–034.
2 *Re Armitage Ex p. Good* (1877) 5 Ch. D. 46.
3 *Kearsley v Cole* (1846) 16 M. W. 128; *Bateson v Gosling* (1871) L.R. 7 C.P. 9.
4 *Webb v Hewitt* (1857) 3 K.J. 438; *Boaler v Mayor* (1865) 19 C.B.N.S. 76. Compare the position in the cases under the rule in *Holme v Brunskill* where the surety's consent to the variation is essential for the surety to remain bound.
5 *Re Blakely* (1854) 4 De G. M. & G. 881 at 889; *Norman v Bolt* (1883) Cab. & El. 77.
6 *Midland Counties Motor Finance Co Ltd v Slade* [1951] 1 K.B. 346; *Guinness Mahon & Co Ltd v London Enterprise Investments Ltd* [1995] 4 Bank L.R. 185.
7 *Nicholson v Revill* (1836) 4 Ad. & El. 675; *Deanplan Ltd v Mahmoud* [1993] Ch.151. But see now *Watts v Aldington* (*The Times* December 16, 1993, CA transcript 1578); *Johnson v Davies* [1999] Ch.117; *Sun Life Assurance Socy Plc v Tantofex (Engineers) Ltd* [1999] 2 E.G.L.R. 135.
8 See *Burnes v Trade Credits Ltd* [1981] 1 W.L.R. 805, where the surety was discharged by the creditor making a fresh loan to the principal at a more advantageous rate of interest.

under the guarantee. However, this is not as simple a matter as it first appears. In *Commercial Bank of Tasmania v Jones* [1893] A.C. 313, the guarantee provided that the liability of the surety would not be affected by reason (*inter alia*) of granting of time to or discharge of the principal. The creditor (the bank) had released the principal from the guaranteed mortgage, and had entered into a new agreement with a new party in place of the principal. The Privy Council held that, because of what amounted in effect to a novation of the principal contract, the bank was precluded from suing the surety on the original guaranteed mortgage, notwithstanding the express terms of the guarantee.[9] The effect of this decision appears to be that where the giving of time in reality amounts to a release of the principal, the express provisions in the guarantee protecting the creditor will be overridden, and the surety will stand discharged. This is wholly at odds with two earlier cases decided in the Court of Exchequer, namely *Cowper v Smith* (1838) 4 M. & W. 519 and *Union Bank of Manchester v Beech* (1865) 12 L.T.499, which decided that an express clause in the guarantee protected the creditor from losing his rights against the surety even though the release was absolute.

The decision in *Jones* was examined in *Perry v National Provincial Bank* [1910] 1 Ch. 464 where the Court of Appeal said that *Jones* would not be given a wide application, and was in conflict with the two earlier cases (which were not cited to the Privy Council). The Court of Appeal held that *Jones* did not decide any general principle in conflict with the earlier cases (and to the extent that it did so it was meaningless), but was a normal application of settled principles, explicable on the basis that on its facts the particular clause relied upon by the creditor did not apply.[10]

This explanation does not wholly relieve the disquiet arising from the *Jones* case. While it is undoubtedly desirable that the terms of the guarantee contract must be upheld and enforced, there remains some difficulty in seeing how, as the Court of Appeal suggested, the guarantee could contain an explicit clause permitting release or novation of the principal contract and yet remain in truth a guarantee: rather, it would become a positive primary undertaking to pay, independent of any liability of a third party. On the one hand, the surety and the creditor should be free to contract for their own rights and obligations; on the other hand, the creditor should not put himself in a position so as to derogate from his grant to the principal. If the principal is not privy to the guarantee, he will

---

9 *Stewart v M'Kean* (1855) 10 Exch. 675.

10 Lord Morris said (at 316): "It may be taken as settled law that where there is an absolute release of a principal debtor, the remedy against the surety is gone because the debt is extinguished, and where such actual release is given no right can be reserved because the debt is satisfied, and no right of recourse remains where the debt is gone. Language importing an absolute release may be construed as a covenant not to sue the principal debtor, when that intention appears, leaving such debtor open to any claims of relief at the instance of his sureties. But a covenant not to sue the principal debtor is a partial discharge only, and although expressly stipulated, is ineffectual if the discharge given is in reality absolute."

not be affected by any reservation of rights by the creditor against the surety; but he will be affected by the exercise of such rights in facing a claim by the surety. Equally, the surety will not be bound by the agreement to give time (or release) between the creditor and the principal, and will not be precluded from suing the principal. The most satisfactory explanation is that where such a clause exists in a guarantee, the surety has waived his right to an indemnity from the principal, and is liable to the creditor as if he were principal, and indeed many standard form bank guarantees state this expressly. However, the extent to which a principal is thereby given a right to defend himself against the surety on the basis of a promise given by him to the creditor is not clear.

There remains, at the heart of this topic, an inherent and problematic conflict between two policy considerations, the one being that the creditor should not derogate from his grant and the other being the freedom of contract. Nor is a tripartite contract between creditor, surety and principal the solution to this problem. Any provision rendering a surety liable where the principal is not effectively liable transmutes the guarantee into an indemnity.[11] In practice a court will generally uphold the express clause in the guarantee in favour of the creditor, following *Perry*,[12] but the problem remains unresolved.

In the recent case of *Finley v Connell Associates (a firm)* [1999] Ll Rep. P.N. 895, the issue arose for consideration whether there could ever be an *implied* reservation of rights against the surety. It was argued on behalf of the surety that nothing short of an express reservation of rights would suffice to preserve the creditor's rights against the surety, relying on *Kearsley v Cole* (1846) M. & W. 128, *Cole v Lynn* [1942] 1 K.B. 142 and dicta in *Mahant Singh v U Ba Yi* [1939] A.C. 601. After an extensive and detailed consideration of the authorities, including the unreported case of *Watts v Aldington* (CA, December 16, 1993), which concerned the reservation of rights against a joint tortfeasor, the judge held that there was no reason in principle why there could not be an implied reservation of rights against a surety in an appropriate case, and that the law applicable to sureties was no different from that applicable to joint debtors. However, the question whether there was such a reservation of rights in a given case would depend on the construction of the agreement against the factual matrix, and the application of the usual test of "strict necessity" referred to in *Watts v Aldington*. In other words, it had to be shown that it was so obvious that it went without saying that the creditor was implicitly reserving his right to sue the surety. In *Greene King v Stanley* [2001] EWCA Civ 1966, [2002] B.P.I.R. 491 however, the Court of Appeal were prepared to look at

---

11 See esp. at 476 *per* Fletcher Moulton L.J. See also *Midland Counties Motor Finance Co v Slade* [1951] 1 K.B. 346, CA, where the creditor had failed to give the surety contractual notice of the principal's default, and the surety was discharged, and *Guinness Mahon & Co v London Enterprise Investment Ltd* [1995] 4 Bank. L.R. 185.

12 Although in *Fletcher Organisation Pty Ltd v Crocus Investments Pty Ltd* [1988] 2 Qd. R. 519 the principal debtor clause was, it appears, sufficient to protect the creditor (see *per* Shepardson J. at 526–527; Ryan J. at 543).

the entire course of dealing between the parties to find the reservation, and did not take a strict constructionist approach.

Agreement by creditor to give time to surety

9–035 The creditor is at liberty to compound with, release or take security from the surety without discharging either the principal or the co-sureties.[13] Where a surety accepted a bill of exchange as surety for the principal, and was then given time by the creditor under a binding agreement, the subsequent release of the principal by all his creditors did not discharge the surety.[14]

Where there are two co-sureties, and the creditor grants a further loan to the principal and takes new security, giving further time to the principal and to one of the co-sureties only without reserving his remedies against the other, that other will be discharged.[15]

Laches of creditor

9–036 Laches is an equitable defence based upon the notion that a court of equity would not give its assistance to a party who had been guilty of negligent or unreasonable delay in asserting its rights or pursuing its claims.[16] Mere delay on the part of the creditor will not, without more, discharge the surety. What is essential is that the creditor omits to do something which he is bound to do for the protection of the surety,[17] so that where his omission results in a variation of the terms of the principal contract (affecting the surety's risk), the surety will be discharged. It is in effect the prejudice to the surety's rights which leads to discharge, rather than mere delay on the part of the creditor or passive acquiescence in acts which do not amount to negligence or fraud.[18]

There is no duty of active diligence placed on the creditor: it is the surety's obligation to see that the principal performs the guaranteed obligation.[19] However, a failure by the creditor to take some step that he is bound to take, either because of some provision in the guarantee, or because such a step is a condition precedent to the surety's liability, will discharge the surety. In *London Guarantee Co v Fearnley* (1880) 5 App.

---

13 As the High Court of Australia did in *Bank of Adelaide v London* (1970) 45 A.L.J.R. 49.

14 *Dunn v Slee* (1817) Moore C.P. 2; *Bedford v Deakin* (1818) 2 B. & Ald. 210. These cases decided that the co-surety remained liable to contribute to the surety; it is submitted that they will likewise remain liable to the creditor under the guarantee.

15 *Defries v Smith* (1862) 10 W.R. 189.

16 *Vyner v Hopkins* (1842) 6 Jur. 889; contrast *Fletcher Organisation Pty Ltd v Crocus Investments Ltd* [1988] 2 Qd. R. 519.

17 See generally Snell's *Principles of Equity*, (30th ed., 2000) paras 3–19.

18 *Mansfield Union Guardians v Wright* (1882) 9 Q.B.D. 683; *Wulff v Jay* (1872) L.R. 7 Q.B. 756; *Watts v Shuttleworth* (1861) 7 H. & N. 353; *Kingston-Upon-Hull Corpn v Harding* [1892] 2 Q.B. 494 at 508.

19 *Durham Corporation v Fowler* (1889) 22 Q.B.D. 394; *Eyre v Everett* (1826) 2 Russ. 381; *Creighton v Rankin* (1840) 7 Cl. & Fin. 325; *Black v Ottoman Bank* (1862) 15 Moo. P.C.C. 472 (a case on fidelity guarantees).

Cas. 911, the creditor was bound by the terms of the guarantee to use his best efforts to recover from the principal before being entitled to claim against the surety, and where he failed to do so the surety was discharged.[20] Where a surety guarantees the honesty of an employee, he is not entitled to be discharged because the employer has failed to use all means in his power to guard against the dishonesty,[21] and failure of the principal, with the creditor's connivance, to do something *reducing* the surety's risk, is not laches so as to discharge the surety.[22] In the fidelity bond cases,[23] the surety for the good behaviour of an employee was not discharged by delay on the part of the creditor in enforcing his rights unless it could be shown that he had connived at an omission by the principal or permitted him to do what he had contracted not to do, and that but for such connivance by the creditor the omission or act would not have occurred.

A failure by a creditor to take all reasonable steps to obtain payment on a bill of exchange prior to the insolvency of the drawer or acceptor will discharge the surety for the bill,[24] however, a surety will not be discharged where the creditor omits to complete the bill of exchange by inserting the drawer's name, and no prejudice results to the surety.[25] Nor will a surety be discharged where the creditor has failed to take legal proceedings which may prove futile (in the absence of a condition precedent that he should do so),[26] nor where the creditor has allowed himself to be time-barred as against the principal, where the surety's claim against the principal is not time-barred,[27] nor where the guarantee provides that the principal's property had to be sold before recourse could be had to the surety and the creditor delays for so long that the principal's goods are seized and sold in his bankruptcy,[28] nor where the creditor had allowed securities for the principal debt to fall in value.[29]

The doctrine of laches, even where it does apply to assist a surety, does not give him a complete discharge but only discharges him *pro tanto* to the extent of the loss he has suffered as a consequence.[30]

---

20 *Wright v Simpson* (1802) 6 Ves. 714.
21 See also *Holl v Hadley* (1835) 2 Ad. & El. 758, *Jephson v Maunsell* (1847) 10 I. Eq. R. 132 at 133 *per* Brady L.J.: *Carter v White* (1883) 25 Ch. D. 666 at 670; these are cases where the creditor was obliged to make the liability of the principal complete before suing the surety, and failure to do so discharged the surety.
22 *Black v Ottoman Bank* (1862) 15 Moo. P.C.C. 472. See the cases relating to employee fidelity guarantees in *Halsbury's Laws* (*op. cit.*) Vol. 20, para.341.
23 *Re Barber & Co Ex p. Agra Bank* (1870) L.R. 9 Eq. 725.
24 See, *e.g. M'Taggart v Watson* (1836) 3 Cl. & Fin. 525; *Dawson v Lawes* (1854) Kay 280; *Mansfield Union Guardians v Wright* (1882) 9 Q.B.D. 683.
25 *Philips v Astling* (1809) 2 Taunt. 206.
26 *Carter v White* (1883) 25 Ch. D. 666.
27 *Musket v Rogers* (1839) 5 Bing. N.C. 728.
28 *Mahant Singh v U Ba Yi* [1939] A.C. 601.
29 *Lancaster v Harrison* (1820) 6 Bing. 726.
30 *China & South Seas Bank v Tan* [1990] 1 A.C. 536; *Skipton Bldg Socy v Bratley* [2000] Ll. Bank. Rep. 34 (*sub nom. Skipton Bldg Socy v Stott* [2001] Q.B. 261); *Silven Properties v Royal Bank of Scotland* [2004] 1 B.C.L.C. 359, CA.

Change in position of parties

In general

9–037 Where a continuing guarantee is given, the change in the nature or position of the creditor or of the principal will result in the discharge of the surety's liability under the guarantee for any act or default subsequent to the change, where the effect of that change is to alter the legal identity or the fundamental role of that party. In *Dance v Girdler* (1804) 1 Bos. & P.N.R. 34 the surety who had given a guarantee to named individuals as governors of a society and their successors was discharged when the creditors, as the society, became incorporated. Equally, where the surety guarantees the acts of a principal in a particular position or office, the surety will be discharged by a change in that position or office.[31]

A mere change in the name of the creditor will not discharge the surety,[32] but an amalgamation, merger or reconstruction of the creditor, being a company, may serve to discharge the surety if the creditor has thereby assumed a different legal identity.[33] In *Bradford Old Bank Ltd v Sutcliffe* [1918] 2 K.B. 833[34] Pickford L.J. (at 841) held that while a novation of an existing debt discharged the surety, the transfer of an existing and ascertained debt to another creditor did not unless it effected a material alteration in his position. However, he said (*obiter*) that the position "would be different if it was sought to make the surety liable for a debt arising out of new dealings between the new creditor and the debtor . . .". The effect of a merger between the creditor and a third party was considered in *First National Finance Corpn v Goodman* [1983] B.C.L.C. 203, where the Court of Appeal considered the effect on the surety's liability of further advances to the principal by the creditor following the merger. The Court of Appeal distinguished the *obiter* remarks of Pickford L.J. in the *Bradford Old Bank* case and held that because of an express provision to that effect in the guarantee, the surety continued to be liable, even for further dealings between the new creditor and the debtor.

Where a creditor has the benefit of the guarantee in a titular or trustee capacity, a change in the identity of the occupant of that role which is not accompanied by a change in the identity of the beneficiaries will not serve to discharge the guarantee.[35] A guarantee given to a holder of a public office will continue in favour of his successor to that office.[36]

---

31 *Polak v Everett* (1876) 1 Q.B.D. 669; *Taylor v Bank of New South Wales* (1886) 11 App. Cas. 596, esp. at 603; *Dale v Powell* (1911) 105 L.T. 291 at 294.

32 *Grant v Budd* (1874) 30 L.T. 319.

33 *Wilson v Craven* (1841) 8 M. & W. 584; *Groux's Improved Soap v Cooper* (1860) 8 C.B.N.S. 800; *Gill and Duffus SA v Rionda Futures* [1994] 2 Lloyd's 67. See also *Housing Guarantee Fund Ltd v Yusef* [1991] 2 W.L.R. 17.

34 See *London Brighton & South Coast Ry Co v Goodwin* (1849) 3 Exch. 320; *Eastern Union Ry Co v Cochrane* (1853) 9 Exch. 197, where the sureties did remain liable because of the preservatory words of the enabling legislation.

35 See also *Prescott, Dimsdale, Cave, Tugwell & Co v Bank of England* [1984] 1 Q.B. 351, a case decided under the Bank Charter Act 1844.

36 See *Truro v McCulloch* (1971) 22 D.L.R.(3d) 293 (NSTD) reversed 30 D.L.R. (3d) 242, CA reversed (*sub nom. Truro v Toronto Gen Insce Co*) 38 D.L.R. (3d) 1 (SCC); *Beswick v Beswick* [1966] Ch. 538 at 555.

Any express provisions in the guarantee will override the position at common law, and the terms will govern the consequences of a change of position of the parties.[37]

Partnerships

The position at common law prior to the enactment of the Partnership Act **9–038** 1890 was that in the absence of a contrary intention, a guarantee to or for a particular person or number of persons did not cover debts or obligations owed by that person or persons together with others, or some only of those persons, nor their executors.[38] The rule as to guarantees is now contained in s.18 of the Partnership Act 1890 as follows:

> "A continuing guaranty . . . given either to a firm or to a third person in respect of the transactions of a firm is, in the absence of agreement to the contrary, revoked as to future transactions by any change in the constitution of the firm to which, or of a firm in respect of the transactions of which, the guaranty . . . was given."

The main concern, therefore, of any draftsman of a guarantee in relation to the obligations of a firm is to see that sufficiently express words appear to provide that the liability of the surety shall continue notwithstanding any change in the constitution of the firm.[39] Similar concerns apply where the firm is the creditor. The old cases indicate that determination or dissolution of a firm has the same effect as a change in its constitution, namely that where the guarantee is given in respect of a partnership, the surety is discharged from further liability on the determination of the partnership, and is not liable for its successor firm.[40]

Where a bond is given for the faithful performance of an employee of a partnership, the surety is discharged from on-going liability where the employee is made a partner, even though the surety knew that this was a possibility when he gave the guarantee.[41] The death of the creditor, and of a partner in a creditor firm, will discharge the surety from ongoing liability arising after the date of the death.[42]

---

37 *M'Gahey v Alston* (1836) 1 M. & W. 386. It has been suggested (McGuinness, *The Law of Guarantee* (*op. cit.*) para.10–045) that this applies similarly to a corporation sole.
38 See *Oswald v Berwick-Upon-Tweed Corporation* (1856) 5 H.L. Cas. 856.
39 *Myers v Edge* (1797) 7 T.R. 254; *Strange v Lee* (1803) East. 484; *Spiers v Houston* (1829) 4 Bligh. (NS) 515; *Backhouse v Hall* (1865) 6 B. & S. 50; *Montefiore v Lloyd* (1863) 15 C.B. (N.S.) 203; *Barker v Parker* (1786) 1 T.R. 287; *Weston v Barton*(1812) 4 Taunt. 673.
40 See *Metcalfe v Bruin* (1810) 12 East. 400; *Strange v Lee* (1807) 3 East. 484. See also Ch.4. It should also cater for the continuing liabilities of the partnership following dissolution: see *Hurst v Bryk* [2000] 2 All E.R. 193.
41 *Cambridge University v Baldwin* (1839) 5 M. & W. 580; *Weston v Barton* (1812) 4 Taunt. 673; *cf. Bank of BNA v Cuvillier* (1861) 14 Moo. P.C. 187, where the wording of the guarantee was held not to discharge the surety despite a change in the nature of the principal; see also *Pease v Hirst* (1829) 10 B. & C. 122.
42 *Montefiore v Lloyd* (1863) 15 C.B.N.S. 203; and see *Mills v Alderbury Union* (1849) 3 Exch. 590, where the surety did not know of the fact that the principal had partners, and was held (in effect) discharged; *cf. Leathley v Spyer* (1870) L.R. 5 C.P. 595, where a renewed guarantee given by the surety with knowledge of the fact that the principal had taken a partner who could deal for him was sufficient to bind the surety for the debts of the partnership.

Fidelity bonds

9–039   It is in the area of fidelity bonds that the rule that a change in the position of the parties discharges the surety is most relevant. The question arises usually where the surety gives a fidelity bond in respect of an employee who is then promoted to a new position. There are two different factual scenarios which call for consideration, namely renewals of employment and promotions. Where the employee is employed for a fixed term only, then the guarantee will expire by effluxion of time upon the employment terminating, and any re-employment of the employee necessitates the obtaining of a fresh fidelity bond (or an extension of the old one).[43] Where, however, the office is for no fixed term, the surety is liable throughout in the absence of any express limitation in the guarantee.[44] The guarantee may also provide for continuing liability on the part of the surety notwithstanding that the employee's term of employment may be fixed, thus allowing re-employment.[45]

The promotion of a bonded employee from his original position in respect of which the guarantee was given may result in the discharge of the surety: this is also true of any substantial changes in the fundamental nature of the employee's employment.[46] The crucial question is whether the promotion of the employee has meant that he has relinquished his old position,[47] or has taken an appointment incompatible with the first.[48] The basis for the discharge of the surety in these circumstances is that the promotion fundamentally alters the accountability of the employee, and so it materially varies the risk to which the surety is exposed.[49] This principle applies similarly to the expansion of the responsibilities of an employee,[50] since to hold the surety liable would be to hold him to a different obligation from the one which he agreed originally to assume; and such an expansion will release the surety from liability for the employee even in respect of duties the subject of the original guarantee.[51] Where the nature of the relationship between the employer and employee has changed by reason of the assumption by the latter of his new duties, the surety will be discharged even in respect of those breaches of duties that in fact also fell within the scope of the original guarantee.[52]

---

43 *Barker v Parker* (1786) 1 Term Rep. 287; this was so even where the principal remained employed by the creditor's executors. See also *Chapman v Beckinton* (1842) 3 Q.B. 703; *Simson v Cooke* (1824) 1 Bing. 452; *Pemberton v Oakes* (1827) 4 Russ. 154.

44 *St Saviours Southwark (Wardens) v Bostock* (1806) 2 Bos. & P.N.R. 175.

45 *Curling v Chalklen* (1815) 3 M. & S. 502.

46 *Augero v Keen* (1836) 1 M. & W. 390.

47 *Pybus v Gibb* (1856) 6 El. & Bl. 902, where it was held that since the change in the nature of the employment was so radical, impacting on the sureties' risk, the sureties were discharged even though the breach by the employee was one arising out of his original duties.

48 *Anderson v Thornton* (1842) 3 Q.B. 271.

49 *Malling Union (Guardians) v Graham* (1870) 22 L.T. 789, especially *per* Bovill C.J. at 793–794.

50 *Worth v Newton* (1854) 10 Exch. 247; *Skillett v Fletcher* (1867) L.R. 2 C.P. 469.

51 *Bartlett v A-G* (1709) Park. 277.

52 *Bamford v Iles & Neale* (1849) 3 Exch. 380; *cf. Frank v Edwards* (1852) 8 Exch. 214.

The question of whether the change in the position of the creditor or of the principal is sufficient to discharge the surety is effectively based on the same principles as those which govern variations in the principal contract, namely whether the risk of the surety has been materially affected.[53]

Discharge of surety by loss of rights of recourse

Loss of co-sureties

One of the rights available to a surety is his right of contribution against his co-sureties, if there are any.[54] As has already been seen in relation to the discharge of a surety by release of the principal,[55] the rationale underlying the discharge of the surety where the principal is no longer liable is that the creditor cannot do anything to put the rights of the surety in danger, for if he does, the surety is entitled to be discharged.[56] Accordingly, where the creditor releases a co-surety who is jointly or jointly and severally liable, the surety's rights of contribution and marshalling of securities are prejudiced, and the release will discharge the surety *in toto,* unless remedies have been reserved against him.[57] This is a manifestation of the general rule of law, that a release of one of a number of joint or joint and several covenantors will discharge the others.[58] Accordingly, where a fresh guarantee is taken from a co-surety, his old guarantee being released, the surety is not discharged, since his right of contribution has not been affected.[59]

9–040

The position in relation to co-sureties who are severally liable was considered in *Ward v National Bank of New Zealand Ltd* (1883) 8 App. Cas. 755, where Sir Robert Collier explained the rule thus (at 764–766):

> "it is no part of the contract of surety that other persons shall join in it, in other words, where he contracts only severally, the creditor does not break that contract by releasing another several surety; the surety cannot therefore claim to be released on ground of breach of contract. . . . The claim of a several surety to be released upon the creditor releasing another surety arises not from the creditor having broken his contract, but from his having deprived the surety of his remedy of contribution in equity. The surety therefore, in order to support his claim, must show that he had a right to contribution and that that right has been injuriously affected."

---

53 *Bonar v McDonald* (1850) 3 H.L. Cas. 226.
54 See discussion at paras 9–023–9–026.
55 See Ch.12 generally.
56 See paras 9–010–9–016.
57 *Mayhew v Crickett* (1818) 2 Swanst. 185; and see *Polak v Everett* (1876) 1 Q.B.D. 669 at 673–674.
58 *Mercantile Bank of Sydney v Taylor* [1893] A.C. 317. See Ch.12, paras 12–020–12–022.
59 *Deanplan Ltd v Mahmoud* [1993] Ch. 151; the principle has been confined somewhat by the Court of Appeal in *Watts v Aldington, The Times,* December 16, 1993, CA transcript 1528; *Johnson v Davies* [1999] Ch. 117; *Sun Life Assurance Socy Plc v Tantofex (Engineering) Ltd* [1999] 2 E.G.L.R. 135.

Accordingly where one of a number of jointly liable co-sureties is released, the remaining co-sureties are wholly discharged. The analysis is that since they are jointly liable, release of one is release of all. However, the rule that this applies to jointly and severally liable sureties has been doubted by the Court of Appeal and must be treated with caution.[60] However, where sureties are jointly liable only, the obtaining of judgment against one of them on a cheque given for their common liability is not a bar to suit by the creditor against the other on the guarantee[61] although satisfaction of the judgment would discharge both surety and his co-surety.[62] Where the sureties contract only severally *inter se* (that it is not a part of the surety's contract that his co-sureties should join in it as such), the release of one will discharge the others *pro tanto* to the extent that each of their rights of contribution and marshalling are prejudiced.[63]

The cases relating to release of the principal apply equally to release of the co-surety. However, a surety will not be discharged where there is no actual release of his co-surety, but merely a forbearance,[64] or a giving of time[65] or a covenant not to sue.[66] Where the creditor releases the co-surety with the consent of the surety, or having reserved his rights against the surety, the surety will not be released, the release of the co-surety having the same effect as a covenant not to sue:[67] if the release of the co-surety is genuinely a release, as opposed to a covenant not to sue, then the surety will be released.[68] Accordingly, the guarantee may expressly provide for the continuation of the surety's liability notwithstanding the release of co-sureties,[69] or the creditor may reserve his rights expressly in the release document. Where one co-surety is released, the security given by the other is also released.[70]

---

60 See now *Watts v Aldington, The Times*, December 16, 1993, CA transcript 1528; *Johnson v Davies* [1999] Ch. 117 and *Sun Life Assurance Society Plc v Tantofex (Engineering) Ltd* [1999] 2 E.G.L.R. 135 and the discussion of these cases in para.9–011 above.
61 *Commercial Bank of Australia v Wilson & Co's Estate (Official Assignee)* [1893] A.C. 181.
62 *Wegg-Prosser v Evans* [1895] 1 Q.B. 108.
63 *Re EWA Ltd* [1901] 2 K.B. 642. *Deanplan Ltd v Mahmoud* [1993] Ch. 151. But see Civil Liability (Contribution) Act 1978, s.3.
64 *Ward v National Bank of New Zealand Ltd* (1883) 8 App. Cas. 755; and see *Wolmershausen v Wolmershausen* (1890) 62 L.T. 541, which contains an exhaustive discussion of the relevant authorities.
65 *Kearsley v Cole* (1846) 16 M. & W. 128 at 136 *per* Parke B.; *cf. Scandinavian American National Bank of Minneapolis v Kneeland* (1913) 4 W.W.R. 944.
66 *Dunn v Slee* (1817) 1 Moo. C.P. 2; *cf.* where time is given to the principal, which will discharge all co-sureties: *Overend Gurney and Co Ltd v Oriental Financial Corpn* (1874) L.R. 7 H.L. 348.
67 *Price v Barker* (1855) 4 E. & B. 760.
68 *Willis v De Castro* (1858) 4 C.B.S. 216.
69 *Liverpool Corn Trade Assn Ltd v Hurst* [1936] 2 All E.R. 309.
70 One is then faced with the problem posed by the conflict between the two policy considerations of non-derogation of grant on the one hand and freedom of contract on the other: see para.9–034 above.

Discharge by loss of securities held by creditor

The general rule

One of the most important rights that a surety has by reason of his position **9–041** is the right to call for all securities held by the creditor for the guaranteed debt in the same state and condition as they were when they were originally received by the creditor, whether given at the time of the guarantee or subsequently, and whether he has notice of them or not.[71] The precise extent of a creditor's obligations in respect of securities is discussed below,[72] but can be summarised briefly: the creditor may not act or neglect to act so as to worsen the position of the surety, and if by his act or neglect the benefit of a security is lost or diminished, the surety will be discharged, either wholly or in part.

In *Barclays Mercantile Business Finance Ltd v Marsh* (unreported, June 25, 2002, CA), Dyson L.J. said (at para.14)[73] that

> "The law is clear: a surety is not released by the loss of a security unless that loss is brought about by the wilful act of the creditor or by his neglect to take some step which the surety has stipulated he should take . . . A surety is not discharged, whether absolutely or pro tanto, unless the creditor has acted or neglected to act so as to lose or diminsh the benefit of the security."

It has been suggested that whether the surety is discharged completely or *pro tanto* to the extent of his loss depends upon whether the existence of the security was an essential condition of the contract of guarantee or not.[74] It is submitted that in fact there are two situations in which neglectful or improper dealing by the creditor with security entitles the surety to be discharged from liability in full, namely:

(a) where the effect of the conduct of the creditor in dealing with the security is to vary the risk of default by the principal[75]; and

(b) where the creditor breaches a condition of the contract of guarantee.

This is to be contrasted with dealings by the creditor with the security that only affect the amount for which the surety will be liable in the event of default by the principal; in this latter situation, discharge is only available to

---

71 *Hodgson v Hodgson* (1837) 2 Keen 704; *Bolton v Salmon* [1891] 2 Ch. 48; *Smith v Wood* [1929] Ch. 14.

72 *Pledge v Buss* (1860) John 663 at 667 *per* Wood V.-C.; *Campbell v Rothwell* (1877) 47 L.J.B.Q. 144; *Newton v Chorlton* (1853) 10 Hare 346; *Pearl v Deacon* (1857) 24 Beav. 186; *Merchants Bank of London v Maud* (1870) 18 W.R. 312, reversed on other grounds (1871) 19 W.R. 657; *Forbes v Jackson* (1882) 19 Ch. D. 615 at 621 *per* Hall V.-C. And see Ch.11 paras 11–017–11–028 for a detailed discussion of the surety's rights of subrogation.

73 Citing with approval paras 9–41 to 9.44 of the third edition of this work.

74 See *Chitty on Contracts (op. cit)* Vol. 2, para.44–102.

75 As in *Watts v Shuttleworth* (1860) 5 H. & N. 235; affirmed (1861) 7 H. & N. 353.

the extent that the surety has actually suffered a loss by reason of the creditor's dealing.[76] It is submitted that the true analysis is that the loss of securities in these circumstances sounds in damages only, giving the surety a right of set-off against the creditor's claim for the full amount guaranteed, rather than constituting a repudiation of the guarantee or an alteration of the surety's risk.[77]

In *Skipton Building Society v Stott* [2001] Q.B. 261, the Court of Appeal reviewed the authorities[78] and firmly rejected the suggestion that a sale of securities for the guaranteed debt at an undervalue by the creditor discharged the surety entirely. He is discharged only *pro tanto* to the amount of the undervalue. Evans L.J. did, however, preserve the possibility of complete discharge where there has been a variation in the principal obligation without the surety's consent. He said (at para.21, at 269):

> "The guarantor may be discharged by a variation in the terms of the debtor's contract, made without his consent, but the creditor's failure to obtain the proper value of a security which he sells reduces pro tanto the amount for which the guarantor is liable."

He went on to say that complete discharge was also possible if the creditor's conduct could properly be regarded as repudiatory of the guarantee. He did not explain the juridical basis for the *pro tanto* reduction in liability; it is suggested that it lies in damages for breach of an express or implied term in the guarantee that the creditor will not damage the value of the surety's subrogation rights. The critical distinction therefore, is whether the creditor's dealings with the securities does or does not vary the risk of default by the principal, as opposed to damaging the money value of the surety's subrogation rights: in *Stott* (as in the majority of cases where the security is enforced by the creditor by sale) the principal is *already* in default. However, the distinction is not easy to tease out of the cases.

In *Wulff v Jay* (1872) L.R. 7 Q.B. 756 the creditors lent the principals £300, guaranteed by the surety. By way of additional security the principals mortgaged to the creditors a business which they owned, but the security was never perfected since the deed of assignment creating the security was not registered. The creditors received notice that the principals were insolvent, but failed to seize the mortgaged property. It was held that the surety was discharged by the failure of the creditors to register the deed and

---

76 See the analysis of this topic by Laskin J.A. in *Rose v Aftenberger* [1970] 1 O.R. 547 (Ontario Court of Appeal), and the critique of the decision by McGuinness, *The Law of Guarantee* (*op. cit.*) paras 10.53–10.54. The case is particularly noteworthy for its discussion of the burden of proof: Laskin J.A. places the burden of disproving neglectful or improper dealings with the security, or proving that the dealing results only in a *pro tanto* discharge, upon the creditor.

77 See *Strange v Fooks* (1863) 4 Giff. 408.

78 Principally *Watts v Shuttleworth* (1860) 5 H. & N. 235; 7 H. & N. 353; *Mutual Loan Fund Association v Sudlow* (1858) 5 C.B.N.S. 449; *Wulff v Jay* (1872) L.R. 7 Q.B. 756; *Pearl v Deacon* (1857) 24 Beav. 186; *Taylor v Bank of New South Wales* (1886) 11 H.L. Cas. 596.

to take possession of the mortgaged property, since they had deprived themselves of the power to assign the mortgaged property to the surety. The discharge operated *pro tanto* to the amount that the mortgaged property was worth.[79] In *Rainbow v Juggins* (1880) 5 Q.B.D. 422 a surety guaranteed an advance by the creditor to the principal which was secured by an insurance policy on the principal's life. The policy lapsed by reason of the principal's failure to pay the premiums, and on the principal's bankruptcy, the creditor proved for the full amount of the debt without valuing the policy.[80] It was held that since the policy was not worth anything the failure to value the policy in the bankruptcy did not alter the surety's position because it had no market value, and so the surety was not discharged in any amount.

In neither case was the giving of security an essential condition of the guarantee, nor did the loss of the right of recourse affect the risk of default by the principal. The prejudice suffered by the surety was the loss of the value of the recourse to the security, and to that extent the surety was discharged.

In *Smith v Wood* [1929] 1 Ch. 14 at 12 persons, by a joint and several memorandum of charge, deposited deeds with the surety as security to relieve her of the burden of a guarantee given by her to the bank for the debts of S & Co, charging the property to which the deeds related with the debt due from S & Co. One of the 12 depositors then took away her deeds, with the consent of the surety, and the bank called in the loan, S & Co having gone into liquidation. The remaining depositors brought an action claiming that they were entitled to have the deeds released from the charge for the debt on the ground that the removal of the deeds by their co-depositor had increased their risk. It was held that since the remaining depositors had not consented to the removal of the deeds by the twelfth, the properties were discharged from the deed; their rights of marshalling had been prejudiced. It was noted that the same reasoning applied whether the sureties offered security or personal liability. This case can be explained on the basis that the depositors (who occupied the analogous position of sureties) had their bargain altered, since their marshalling rights were an inherent part of their contract. This case was not referred to by Evans L.J. in *Skipton BS v Stott* [2001] Q.B. 261.

In *Watts v Shuttleworth* (1861) 7 H. & N. 353 the creditor failed to insure the fittings to be installed by the principal under a building contract, and the surety was held discharged in full on the basis that the obligation on the creditor to insure was a condition of the principal contract imported into the guarantee which had been broken by the creditor's default.[81]

---

79 See also *Strange v Fooks* (1863) 4 Giff. 408; *Capel v Butler* (1825) 2 Sim. & St. 457; *Pearl v Deacon* (1857) 25 L.J. Ch. 761; *Skipton BS v Stott* [2001] Q.B. 261.

80 The creditor has a statutory right not to value his security but to come in and prove for the full debt: Insolvency Act 1986, s.322, Insolvency Rules 1986 (SI 1986/1925), r.6.109(2).

81 See also *China & South Seas Bank Ltd v Tan* [1990] A.C. 536, where Lord Templeman reviewed the cases; see now *Skipton BS v Stott* [2001] Q.B. 261, and *Silven Properties Ltd v Royal Bank of Scotland* [2004] 1 B.C.L.C. 359, in which the Court of Appeal reviewed the law on the mortgagee's (and the receiver's) equitable duties in relation to realisation of securities.

What remains unclear from these cases is whether it is necessary to show actual loss in order to be discharged, or merely a potential prejudice. Clearly in *Smith v Wood*, no actual loss was made out, and the sureties were discharged on the ground, in effect, that their risk had been increased. In *Rainbow v Juggins,* on the other hand, it was necessary for there to be an actual loss in order to discharge the surety *pro tanto*. As stated above, the answer lies in the distinction between dealings by the creditor which increase the risk to the surety, or constitute a repudiatory breach of the guarantee, in which case the surety's discharge is total without any investigation of the actual loss to the surety, and simple breaches of a term of the guarantee which merely give the surety a counterclaim sounding in damages, capable of being set off against the creditor.[82]

When a surety is not discharged by the loss of securities

9–042 There are circumstances when notwithstanding the loss of the rights of recourse to securities held by the creditor, the surety will remain liable under the guarantee. The surety's liability will not be affected by a sale by the principal of the property the subject of the security in a way contemplated by the security deed and with the consent of the creditor.[83] Equally the loss of a right of the creditor which is not strictly speaking a security held in respect of the debt, or which is non-assignable (such as a right to distrain for rent), will not discharge the surety,[84] nor will the loss of a security to which the surety was not entitled.[85]

Where the loss of the securities is not attributable to the fault of the creditor, the surety will not be discharged:[86] similarly where the dealing with the security causes no loss to the surety.[87] So the assignment of the guaranteed debt together with any security in respect thereof does not discharge the guarantee, and the creditor is not obliged to notify the surety

---

82 But see *Continental Illinois National Bank v Papanicolaou* [1986] 2 Lloyd's Rep. 441, where the defence of negligent dealing with securities failed even to provide a resistance to the creditor's claim for summary judgment on the guarantee, on the basis that the surety had contracted to pay free of any counterclaim or set-off. Anti-set-off provisions in guarantees must be approached with caution now, since they are susceptible to being struck down as unreasonable: *Stewart Gill Ltd v Horatio Myer & Co* [1992] 1 Q.B. 600, and see the Unfair Terms in Consumer Contract Regulations (SI 1994/3159), in force from July 1, 1995, and especially Sch.3, para.1(b) discussed in Ch.3, paras 3–035–3–036.

83 *Taylor v Bank of New South Wales* (1886) 11 App. Cas. 596.

84 *Re Russell, Russell v Shoolbred* (1885) 29 Ch. D. 254. Compare this case with the cases that decide that abandonment of execution against the principal will discharge the surety: *Mayhew v Crickett* (1818) 2 Swanst. 185; *Williams v Price* (1824) 1 Sim. & St. 581, especially at 587.

85 *Chatterton v McLean* [1951] 1 All. E.R. 761, especially at 766, where a hire-purchase company which had given up a right to repossess a car remained entitled to hold the surety fully liable for the hirer's debt, since the right to possession was a personal right and not one to which the surety could succeed.

86 *Hardwick v Wright* (1865) 35 Beav. 133; and see *Wheatley v Bastow* (1855) 7 De G. M. & G. 261.

87 *Rainbow v Juggins* (1880) 5 Q.B.D. 138. The position may be otherwise if the loss of securities increases the surety's risk or constitutes a repudiatory breach of contract by the creditor.

in order to make the assignment binding and effectual.[88] Where a surety guarantees against the fraud of the principal, a release of security procured by the principal's fraud will not discharge the surety.[89]

The duties owed by a creditor

In order to understand the circumstances in which the creditor will be at fault in dealing with securities, it is important to know what the creditor may and may not do. The creditor is obliged to deal with the security in a reasonable manner so as to ensure that the maximum amount can be derived from it to satisfy the guaranteed obligation.[90] While the creditor deals with the security in a manner contemplated by the guarantee agreement, the surety will not be discharged.[91] Further, if the guarantee expressly or impliedly authorises the creditor to deal with securities such that no improper or negligent dealing will discharge the surety, prima facie the surety will be bound by that provision.[92] Neither is the creditor obliged to deliver all security to the surety, but merely to ensure that the maximum benefit can be derived from it.[93] In *Rainbow v Juggins* (1880) 5 Q.B.D. 138 Bramwell L.J. said (at 423):

9–043

> "Where a man enters into a contract of suretyship, he, it is true, bargains that he shall not be prejudiced by any improper dealing with the securities to the benefit of which he as surety is entitled; but he makes that bargain with reference to the law of the land, and if the law of the land says that under such and such circumstances certain things must take place in order to enable the creditor to do the best he can for his own protection, then the contract of suretyship must be taken to be made subject to the liability of those things taking place."[94]

It is, therefore, not the security to which the surety is entitled, but the maximum benefit that can be derived from it, so that simple realisation of the security does not of itself give the surety any cause for complaint, since it is not realisation *per se* that increases the surety's risk or the amount of his liability. It is now clear that the creditor, as the chargee or mortgagee, owes a duty of care to the principal to take all steps to realise the security at the best price reasonably obtainable.[95] The question is to what extent the creditor owes such a duty to the surety for that principal.

---

88 *Wheatley v Bastow* (1855) 7 De G. M. & G. 261.
89 *Kingston-Upon-Hull Corpn v Harding* [1892] 2 Q.B. 494.
90 *Mutual Loan Fund v Sudlow* (1858) 5 C.B.N.S. 449.
91 *Taylor v Bank of New South Wales* (1886) 11 App. Cas. 596.
92 See *Bank of Montreal v Bauer* (1978) 19 O.R. (2d) 425.
93 *Polak v Everett* (1876) 1 Q.B.D. 669, esp. at 675 *per* Blackburn J.
94 See also Baggallay L.J. at 424–425.
95 *Gosling v Gaskell* [1897] A.C. 575; *Cuckmere Brick Co v Mutual Finance Ltd* [1971] Ch. 949; *American Express International Banking Corpn v Hurley* [1985] 3 All E.R. 564; *Gomba Holdings (UK) Ltd v Homan* [1986] B.C.L.C. 331; *cf. Parker-Tweedale v Dunbar Bank Plc* [1991] Ch. 12; see also *Downsview Nominees Ltd v First City Corpn Ltd* [1993] B.C.C. 46, for the position *vis-à-vis* subsequent encumbrances; *Yorkshire Bank v Hall* [1999] 1 All E.R. 879 at 893, per Robert Walker L.J., and *Medforth v Blake* [1999] 3 All E.R. 97 and see generally Picarda, *The Law Relating to Receivers and Managers*, 3rd ed. (Butterworths, 2000), pp.130 *et seq*; Paget on *Law of Banking* (*op. cit.*), para.14.18.

There is a line of cases which hold that the creditor owes no duty of care to the surety at all in the realisation of securities for the guaranteed obligation.[96] In *Latchford v Beirne* [1981] 3 All E.R. 705,[97] the question was whether the receiver of a company owed the surety a duty of care in ensuring that the assets of the company were properly accounted for, and in obtaining a proper price for those assets on a sale. Milmo J. held that while the creditor (by his receiver) did owe a duty of care to the principal, he owed no such duty to the surety, on the basis that the surety was simply a contingent creditor of the principal company, and to extend a duty of care to such creditors would be to extend the duty to every creditor of the principal, with unacceptable results.

In *Barclays Bank Ltd v Thienel* (1980) 247 E.G. 385 Thesiger J. held, on the trial of a preliminary issue, that the creditor owed no duty of care to the surety to obtain a reasonable price for the security. In *Scottish Midland Guarantee Trust v Woolley* (1964) 114 L.J. 272, it was held that a hire-purchase company owed no duty, in selling repossessed goods, to obtain the best price reasonably obtainable for them. Further, in *Pratt's Trustee v Pratt* [1936] 3 All E.R. 901, a husband and wife guaranteed a company's overdraft with a bank, and the husband charged certain property to the bank as security for the overdraft. The husband was to be primarily liable on the guarantee, the wife in effect being surety for him. The bank recovered monies from the husband arising from a sale of the charged property by his trustee in bankruptcy, and sued the wife on the guarantee for the balance. She argued that she had an equitable charge on the charged property by reason of her position as surety, and the sale at an undervalue prejudiced her in that had the sale been at a full value, her liability to the bank would have been reduced. Farwell J. held that even assuming a sale at an undervalue, the creditor owed no duty to obtain a proper price.

It is submitted that these cases are either explicable or simply wrongly decided. The *Thienel* case can be explained on the basis that in fact the contract of guarantee expressly excluded the liability of the creditor for loss of securities.[98] In the *Scottish Midland Guarantee Trust* case the surety had an equitable right of subrogation to the right of the creditor in respect of the repossessed car: the sale at an undervalue would have directly affected the surety, and on the basis that the creditor must not, according to principle, prejudice the surety's rights of recourse, the decision is, it is submitted, wrong. Similarly, the *Pratt's Trustee* case is wrongly decided,

---

96 Beginning with *Kingston-Upon-Hull Corpn v Harding* [1892] 2 Q.B. 494; the cases do not, however, form a progressive line of authority.

97 Curiously, the issue was raised by the surety as grounds for his claim rather than by way of defence, but nothing in the decision turns on burden of proof. But see *McManus v Royal Bank* (1985) 55 C.B.R. (N.S.) 238, where it was held that the surety had no cause of action for damages for improper realisation, but could raise it by way of defence to a claim by the creditor.

98 This does not appear from the *Estates Gazette* report; see also *Continental Illinois National Bank v Papanicolaou* [1986] 2 Lloyd's Rep. 441.

since the wife, although not having an equitable charge over the charged property (which is how her case was argued), nevertheless had an equitable right to be subrogated to the securities given by her co-surety,[99] and to have these preserved for her benefit.

The reasoning of Milmo J. in *Latchford v Beirne* demonstrates in particular how these cases are wrong in principle and are contrary to authority. The surety's rights in relation to securities held by the creditor are not derived through the principal nor founded upon any contract with the principal (as was assumed by Milmo J.). They are equitable rights arising independently, and based upon the principle that the creditor should not act so as to prejudice the surety's rights of recourse, whether those rights operate by way of contribution, subrogation or marshalling,[1] and whether against (or in respect of security given by) principal or co-surety. Furthermore, the decisions appear to proceed in ignorance of the prior case law, most notably *Mutual Loan Fund v Sudlow* (1858) 5 C.B.N.S. 499, which established that a creditor owed an obligation to the surety to take care in realising security held in respect of the guaranteed debt (or at least was at risk if he did not do so).

In *Standard Chartered Bank v Walker* [1982] 1 W.L.R. 1410,[2] the Court of Appeal considered the point squarely. There the principal, a company, had given a debenture secured by a fixed and floating charge over its assets present and future to the creditor bank to secure its overdraft; the sureties had guaranteed the company's indebtedness up to £75,000, including interest. The bank appointed a receiver under the terms of the debenture, and the stock (part of the charged assets) was valued at £90,000. The stock was subsequently sold for £42,864, which was absorbed by the costs of realisation and preferential claims. The bank then sued the sureties for the full amount of their guarantees; the sureties defended on the basis that the sale had been conducted negligently. The Court of Appeal held that the receiver owed a duty of care not merely to the company as chargee[3] but also to the company's sureties as persons liable to the same extent as the company. Insofar as the receiver had not used reasonable care, the sureties would be entitled to a credit for the amount which the sale would have realised had it been conducted with reasonable care. Lord Denning M.R. expressly disapproved the *Thienel* case on the ground that a clause in a guarantee rendering the surety liable for a larger sum than the mortgagor could not be enforceable;[4] he refused to follow *Latchford v Beirne* on the

---

99 See Ch.12, para.12–014.

1 *Craythorne v Swinburn* (1807) 14 Ves. 160.

2 See also *Canadian Imperial Bank of Commerce v Haley* (1979) 100 D.L.R. (3d) 470; *McManus v Royal Bank* (1985) 55 C.B.R. (N.S.) 283, NBCA; and as to receivers' obligations, *Bank of Montreal v Western Store Supplies Ltd* (1983) 57 N.S.R. (2d) 118.

3 Relying on the dissenting judgment of Rigby L.J. in *Gaskell v Gosling* [1896] 1 Q.B. 669, upheld by the House of Lords [1897] A.C. 575; *Cuckmere Brick Co Ltd v Mutual Finance Ltd* [1971] 2 All E.R. 633; see also *Bank of Cyprus (London) Ltd v Gill* [1979] 2 Lloyd's Rep. 508.

4 See 1416C–E.

grounds that the surety was proximate enough to the receiver for a duty of care to arise.

The case has been followed on a number of occasions.[5] In *American Express v Hurley* [1986] 3 All E.R. 564 at 571D–F, Mann J. found that the creditor was not assisted by an exclusion clause in the mortgage purporting to relieve him of liability for a negligent sale.[6]

The breadth of the obligations of a creditor, and his receiver, to take care in relation to his dealings with securities was scrutinised by the Privy Council in *China & South Seas Bank Ltd v Tan* [1990] A.C. 536. There the creditor held security in the form of shares: the principal defaulted, and although the shares at the date of the default were worth more than the loan, the creditor allowed them to decline in value. The creditor then sued the surety under the guarantee. The Privy Council held that the creditor owed the surety no duty to exercise its power of sale over the mortgaged securities, and so the surety was not discharged. Lord Templeman giving the judgment of the court, applied established authority[7] in holding that the surety would be discharged if the creditor had done an act injurious to the interests of the surety or acted inconsistently with the surety's rights, or breached any obligation. In the present case none of those applied: the creditor was at liberty to choose which of his remedies to pursue, whether against the principal, the security or the surety. Once the creditor does decide to sell, then he must obtain the current market value,[8] but he must be the author of the decision whether to sell, and he is not obliged to exercise that decision. If he were, this would place an unacceptably heavy burden on a lender. Lord Templeman pointed out that the surety is in fact protected from declining security values by his right to pay off the creditor and have the securities immediately transferred to him.

It is to be noted that the appeal was expressly decided on the basis of equitable principles, since, it was held, the doctrine of the duty of care was not so developed as to supplant equitable principles or contradict contractual promises.[9] This implicitly recognised the creditor's argument that there

---

5 See *American Express International Banking Corpn v Hurley* [1986] 3 All E.R. 564; *Gomba Holdings (UK) Ltd v Homan* [1986] B.C.L.C. 331; *Shamji v Johnson Matthey Bankers Ltd* [1986] B.C.L.C. 278, esp. at 283E–G; and see *National Bank of Greece SA v Pinios Shipping Co (The "Maira") (No.3)* [1988] 2 Lloyd's Rep. 126.

6 See the comments of Simon Brown L.J. in *Circuit Systems Ltd v Zuken Redac (UK) Ltd* [1997] 1 W.L.R. 721 at 739.

7 *Wulff v Jay* (1872) L.R.7 Q.B.756; *Watts v Shuttleworth* (1860) 5 H. & N. 235.

8 In *Palk v Mortgage Services Funding Plc* [1993] Ch. 330, the duties of the mortgagee to the mortgagor or *vis-à-vis* the security were reaffirmed in the light of the *Tan* case. Sir Donald Nicholls V.C. (at 337–378) suggested that any conduct on the part of the mortgagee relating to his rights of leasing or sale of the security which substantially increased the burden on the borrower or guarantor under their personal covenants was a breach of duty by the mortgagee. The decision was approved and applied by the Court of Appeal in *Silven Properties Ltd v Royal Bank of Scotland* [2004] 1 B.C.L.C. 359, and in *Den Norske Bank ASA v Acemex Management Co Ltd ("The Tropical Reefer")* [2004] 1 Ll. Rep. 1. See also *Meftah v Lloyd's TSB Bank Plc* [2001] 2 All E.R. (Comm.) 741 on the duty to expose the property properly to the market when the mortgagee does decide to sell. See also *Cohen v Lloyd's TSB Bank Plc* [2002] 2 B.C.L.C. 32 at paras 55–57 (39–40), Etherton J.

9 See *Socomex Ltd v Banque Bruxelles Lambert SA* [1996] 1 Ll. Rep. 156, at 5198 col. 2.

was no overall duty of care in tort where, as here, there was a contractual relationship between the parties, and (following the arguments of Counsel for the bank) that *Standard Chartered Bank v Walker* had to be regarded in the light of the later development of the tort of negligence.[10] There is no room for any implication into the contract of guarantee of a duty to take care.

In *Mahomed v Morris* [2000] 2 B.C.L.C. 536, the Court of Appeal pointed out in trenchant terms that a mortgagee owes no duty to consult the mortagor about the proposed sale. Peter Gibson L.J. said (at para.34 on 557):

> "I have never heard it suggested that a secured creditor who is contemplating realising the charged assets is under some duty to consult the debtor or the surety of the debtor, even if he is aware that the price he obtains on realisation may mean that the debt is not discharged and so there are no surplus proceeds which the surety might claim by subrogation."

He went on to say that such an suggestion was contrary to authority, specifically *China & South Sea Bank v Tan*, and was unsupported by authority, and said (at para.35 on 558) that to impose such an obligation on the secured creditor would be to impose a serious fetter on his freedom to exercise his power of sale as and when he chooses.[11]

In *Burgess v Auger* [1998] 2 B.C.L.C. 478 the plaintiff was a majority shareholder and a director of a company, A. In 1989 the company granted V a fixed and floating charge over its undertaking. A second such charge was granted to a bank in 1990. In addition, the plaintiff guaranteed A's indebtedness to the bank up to a limit of £60,000.

In 1990 V demanded repayment of the sum of £106,457.45 due from A. When the company failed to pay, V appointed receivers, who sold the company's business to an associated company of V at what the plaintiff alleged to be an undervalue, and a misuse by V of its powers as chargee. The plaintiff claimed that as a consequence of the actions of V and the receivers he had been exposed to liability under the guarantee, and had suffered other loss and damage as a shareholder and employee of A; he claimed that V and the receivers owed him a duty of good faith.

Lightman J. held that the duties owed by V and the receivers were owed only to the persons interested in the equity of redemption; as a director, shareholder, employee and guarantor of A, the plaintiff had no interest in the equity of redemption and accordingly his pleaded claim had to be struck out. The plaintiff tried to amend his claim to plead an interest in the equity of redemption as a guarantor of the secured indebtedness of the

---

10 Most importantly *Tai Hing Cotton Mill Ltd v Liu Chong Hing Bank Ltd* [1986] A.C. 80; *National Bank of Greece SA v Pinios Shipping Co* [1988] 2 Lloyd's Rep. 126.
11 See also *Raja v Austin Gray* [2002] EWCA Civ 1965, [2003] 13 E.G. 117, *per* Peter Gibson L.J. at para.55.

company to the bank, but that claim was bound to fail because he had made no payment to the bank, any liability to the bank was statute barred, and there was no evidence to suggest that a sale of the company's business at a proper value would have left a surplus after discharging V's debt.

The principle that wrongful or neglectful dealings by a creditor with security for the guaranteed obligation will discharge a surety will not assist a surety who has agreed in the guarantee to pay without regard to his defences. In *Continental Illinois National Bank v Papanicolaou* [1986] 2 Lloyd's Rep. 441, where the surety had given a guarantee on terms that all sums payable were to be paid "in full free of set-off or counterclaim", the court enforced the guarantee and held that the defence by the surety based on the creditor's negligent realisation of securities was not sufficiently arguable to resist the creditor's claim for summary judgment, or to give him a stay of execution pending his counterclaim.

In *Barclays Bank v Quincecare* [1992] 4 All E.R. 363,[12] Steyn J. held that the creditor owed no duty of care, or any implied contractual duty, to the surety to see that the loan the subject of the guarantee was applied for the purposes for which it was made.

In *Medforth v Blake* [1999] 3 W.L.R. 922, the Court of Appeal reviewed the authorities, including the judgment of Robert Walker L.J. in *Yorkshire Bank Plc v Hall* [1999] 1 All E.R. 879 (893), and decided that the duty owed by a receiver to a mortgagor was not limited to a duty to act in good faith, but extended to a duty to carry out his functions with due diligence, including managing the charged property and carrying on a business. Those duties did not arise in tort or contract but in equity. This is not a guarantee case, but it is submitted that the equitable duty of due diligence applies with equal force in favour of a surety as it does in favour of the principal who has mortgaged or charged his property. One aspect of that duty is to take reasonable precautions to obtain the true market value of the mortgaged property on the date on which he chooses to sell: see *Meftah v Lloyd's TSB Bank plc* [2001] 2 All E.R. (Comm) 741.

The most recent and authoritative statement on the duties of mortgagees and receivers appointed by them is the judgment of Lightman J. (sitting in the Court of Appeal) in *Silven Properties Ltd v Royal Bank of Scotland* [2004] 1 B.C.L.C. 359. In that case, the question was whether the receivers appointed by the mortgagees were entitled, regardless of whether it was reasonable for them to do so, to sell the properties without delay as they stood, or whether they should have delayed to get a better price. Lightman J. exhaustively reviewed the authorities as to the duties of both mortgagees and receivers and set out the principles to be derived from them. He held (at para.13 and following) that a mortgagee has no duty to exercise his power of sale at any particular time and can remain passive. He is not "a

---

12 And see *Bank of India v Trans Continental Commodity Merchants Ltd* [1983] 2 Lloyd's Rep. 298, where the Court of Appeal held that there is no general principle that irregular conduct on the part of the creditor, even if prejudicial to the surety, will discharge the surety.

trustee of the power of sale" for the mortgagor and has an unfettered discretion to sell when he likes to achieve the repayment of the debt, and his decision is not constrained by the fact that the exercise or non-exercise of the power will occasion damage to the mortgagor. Lightman J. held that the dicta of Lord Denning M.R. in *Standard Chartered Bank Ltd v Walker* [1982] 3 All E.R. 938 that it was arguable that in choosing his timing of the sale, the mortgagee owed the mortgagor a duty of care, could not stand with later authority (*e.g. Tan*); and that the mortgagee may sell the property as it is and is under no duty to improve its value. As and when he decides to sell, the mortgagee then comes under a duty in equity (and not in tort) to tke reasonable precautions to obtain the fair or true market value at the date of the sale; and he cannot simply take a knock-down price in the interests of speed simply to pay off the debt. Lightman J. went on to hold that the same duties apply to receivers appointed by the mortgagees, even though they may be appointed as agents for the mortgagor in the mortgage deed.

An interesting illustration of these principles in action is provided by *Den Norske Bank ASA v Acemex Management Co Ltd* [2004] 1 Lloyd's Rep. 1.[13] The case concerned a ship mortgage. The mortgagor committed an event of default under the loan agreement and mortgage, and so the bank arrested the ship in Panama, where she was laden with bananas. The bananas had to be disposed of rapidly, and were cast overboard. This exposed the mortgagor to a cargo claim and to liability for the expense of the disposal. The mortgagor argued that the bank had acted "negligently" by arresting the ship in Panama, and should instead have allowed her to proceed to Hamburg, the discharge port, and there discharge the bananas; there would then have been no problem about the cargo claim or costs of discharge, both of which took priority to the bank's claim. The Court of Appeal had no hesitation in rejecting the argument. The law as stated in *Silven* cannot, said Longmore L.J. (at para.25), be sidestepped by saying that, in the case of a movable chattel such as a ship, the mortgagee has to take care to sell at the place where the best price is available. He expressed a reservation as to whether the position might not be the same if there was no true market for the chattel concerned at the place where the mortgagee proposes to sell. However, in that case, that was not a relevant consideration because ships are frequently sold in Panama under the recognised Admiralty jurisdiction.

Securities held from co-sureties

As has been discussed above, and is dealt with fully in Chapter 12, the **9–044** surety has a right of contribution, founded in equity, in respect of any payment which he is required to make in respect of the guaranteed debt, in excess of his rateable share of that debt.[14] This right is available against his co-sureties for the same debt. Accordingly, the creditor must take care to

---

13 The appeal in which was heard eight days after the judgment in *Silven* was handed down.
14 *Dering v Winchelsea (Earl)* (1787) 2 Bos. & P. 270; *Stirling v Forrester* (1821) 3 Bli. 575; Mercantile Law Amendment Act 1856, s.5.

deal with any securities held from co-sureties, since the surety who has paid is entitled to be subrogated to those securities, or to marshall them, as a means of exercising his rights of contribution.[15] The creditor owes a duty not to waste or to permit waste of the security.[16]

The surety's right to be discharged which arises as a result of a breach of his right to recover contribution out of the security operates *pro tanto*, so that he remains liable to the creditor to the extent of his proportionate share. However, it is submitted that it is arguable that the surety may in certain circumstances be entitled to be discharged in full by reason of the breach by the creditor in his dealings with the security given by co-sureties, namely where the dealings have increased the surety's risk, or where the dealings amount to a repudiatory breach of the contract of guarantee.[17]

The right to be discharged on the grounds of loss of securities, whether held from the principal or a co-surety, is no longer available to the surety where he has become liable for the debt as a principal.[18]

---

15 *Duncan Fox & Co v North & South Wales Bank* (1880) 6 App. Cas. 1; *Re Downer Enterprises* [1974] 2 All E.R. 1074.
16 *Margrett v Gregory* (1862) 6 L.T. 543. Compare this with *China & South Seas Bank Ltd v Tan* [1990] A.C. 536.
17 See the discussion at para.9–041.
18 *Reade v Lowndes* (1857) 23 Beav. 361.

Chapter 10

Rights of the Surety Against the Principal

Introduction

When the surety has paid the creditor, or has otherwise discharged the **10–001** liability which he has undertaken in the contract of guarantee or indemnity, certain rights of recoupment may then become available to him. However, he may have certain rights in equity even before payment, which in practical terms are often more valuable to him. This chapter considers the rights and remedies available to the surety against the principal debtor other than those which he acquires by way of subrogation to the rights of the creditor after payment, which are dealt with in Chapter 11.

Whilst the rights considered in this chapter are similar to those which the surety possesses against the creditor, they are not identical. They may also differ considerably, both in nature and in scope, from the rights which the creditor may have against the principal.[1]

The right to an indemnity

The right of the surety to be indemnified in respect of his liability to the **10–002** creditor may arise under an express or implied agreement with the principal, or he may have a right of restitution in quasi-contract. However, the restitutionary right only becomes important if the person seeking the indemnity did not become a surety at the express or implied request of the principal.[2] Although there appears to be no express authority on the surety's right to an indemnity where he is liable to the creditor under a contract of indemnity as opposed to a contract of guarantee, there seems to be no doubt that such a right will usually exist.[3]

The surety's liability to the creditor under a guarantee is prima facie co-extensive with that of the principal to the creditor under the underlying contract, but this is not necessarily the case when the surety takes on an

---

1 See the observations made by Stirling J. in *Badeley v Consolidated Bank* (1886) 34 Ch. D. 536 at 556.
2 See, below, paras 10–008–10–011.
3 See, *e.g. Moule v Garrett* (1872) L.R. 7 Ex. 101, the *"Zuhal K" and the "Selin"* [1987] 1 F.T.L.R. 76.

independent primary liability to the creditor under a contract of indemnity. If the surety's liability to the creditor under an indemnity is wider than the principal's underlying liability, the question may arise whether the liability of the principal to indemnify the surety is limited by the terms of his underlying obligation to the creditor, or whether he must reimburse him in full.

There is no general rule which would apply in all cases. The answer is likely to depend on whether the right of indemnity is contractual or quasi-contractual, and upon the terms of the relevant agreements. The probabilities are that if the surety has entered into an agreement with the creditor at the instigation of the principal, the latter would be required to indemnify him in full, whatever the discrepancies in their individual liabilities to the creditor might be. However, if he did not enter into the transaction at the express or implied request of the surety, then on the rare occasions when this would give rise to a right of indemnity, it is likely that his restitutionary rights would be limited by the terms of the principal's direct liability to the creditor.[4]

Independent right of the surety

10–003   Whether the right to an indemnity is founded on contract or quasi-contract in a particular case, it is an independent right of the surety, rather than a right arising out of subrogation to the rights of the creditor; and he may therefore bring an action in his own name against the principal.[5] The action is essentially a claim for the payment of a debt, and therefore the surety's claim is subject to any right of set-off which the principal may be entitled to raise against him: *Thornton v Maynard* (1875) L.R. 10 C.P. 695.

It follows from the independent nature of the right of indemnity that nothing which the creditor does or says may prejudice it; so, for example, an agreement by the creditor that he will not sue the principal, or that he will not rank as a creditor on the principal's insolvency, or a compromise with the principal will not preclude the surety from exercising his right to claim an indemnity if he is called upon to pay and is liable to do so. This is particularly relevant if the contract of guarantee or indemnity between the creditor and the surety contains a clause (to be found in most bank guarantees) to the effect that a release of the principal or the granting of time to the principal or other material variation will not discharge or otherwise affect the liability of the surety.

In the Canadian case of *Brown v Coughlin* (1914) 50 S.C.R. 100 at 109, Duff J. gave the following succinct summary of the rights of the surety to an indemnity:

> "Unless precluded by agreement express or implied or by some equity or estoppel arising from the conduct of the parties the surety (by

---

4 This view is shared by the editors of *Chitty on Contracts*, 29th ed. (2004), Vol. 2, para.44–114; see also Goff & Jones, *The Law of Restitution*, 6th ed. (Sweet & Maxwell 2002), paras 15–020 to 15–021.

5 See the observations of Lord Denning M.R. in *Morris v Ford Motor Co* [1973] 2 All E.R. 1084 at 1089.

reason of the relationship created by the contract of suretyship) is entitled to require the principal debtor to discharge his obligation to the creditor in so far as that may be necessary to relieve the surety. The debtor in other words comes under an obligation to save the surety harmless from any prejudice which might arise from the performance of the principal obligation . . . the surety cannot by any act of the creditor alone be deprived of his right to compel the debtor to protect him by discharging the debt, or to indemnify him against the consequences of his failure to do so."

Express agreement

The principal may enter into an express agreement with the surety to indemnify him or hold him harmless in respect of any liability which he may incur to the creditor under the contract of suretyship.[6] In such a case, the extent and nature of the indemnity are dictated by the contract, and there will be no implied right of indemnity.[7] The surety is therefore bound to sue on the express contract of indemnity rather than on any alleged implied agreement or right to restitution in quasi-contract.[8]   **10–004**

An express agreement may be attractive to the potential surety because it may confer wider rights upon him than an implied agreement; however, he should take care to ensure that the promise is enforceable and that his rights to prove in an insolvency are adequately protected.[9] The principal may also find an express agreement affords him most protection; in particular, if he wishes to ensure that he is not liable to indemnify the surety unless, when the surety pays, the creditor has an enforceable claim against the principal, or that the surety has exhausted all available defences, an express provision is the best means of doing so.[10]

Unenforceable agreements

An interesting question which has not been directly considered in the context of suretyship is whether the court would imply any right to an indemnity where the express agreement between the principal and surety is unenforceable or void. It is unlikely that an implied agreement would ever be found in circumstances where the express agreement is unenforceable or void because of the infringement of some statutory rule or regulation; this would prove too easy a means of circumventing the statute.[11] There may   **10–005**

---

6 See, *e.g. Cooper v Jenkins* (1863) 32 Beav. 337; *Re Moss Ex p. Hallet* [1905] 2 K.B. 307.
7 This is merely an application of the general principle that the express agreement excludes any implied agreement inconsistent with its terms: see, *e.g. Re Richmond Gate Property Co* [1965] 1 W.L.R. 335 at 337; *Upton v Fergusson* (1833) 3 Moo. & S. 88.
8 Thus in *Toussaint v Martinnant* (1787) 2 Term Rep. 100, a surety was precluded from suing in *assumpsit* for money paid to the use of the debtor by his acceptance of a bond from the debtor which stipulated the date on which the surety was to be paid.
9 See, *e.g. Re Moss Ex p. Hallet* [1905] 2 K.B. 307; and compare *Re Simons Ex p. Allard* (1881)16 Ch. D. 505 with *Re Robinson Ex p. Burrell* (1876) 1 Ch. D. 537.
10 See the discussion at paras 10–007 and 10–009–10–011 below.
11 The view is expressed in *Chitty on Contracts* (*op. cit.*), Vol. 2, para.44–114, fn.542 that the defendant in *Yeoman Credit Ltd v Latter* [1961] 1 W.L.R. 828 could hardly have obtained an indemnity from the minor hire-purchaser, but that is probably because as the law then stood, the implied contract of indemnity would have been unenforceable.

also be considerable evidential difficulties, quite apart from the obvious conceptual difficulties, in proving that the surety acted in performance of an implied contract, when in truth he was acting in accordance with the terms of an express contract which was unenforceable.[12]

In principle, there would appear to be no good reason to preclude a restitutionary claim in quasi-contract if the express contract is void and if all the necessary conditions which would give rise to such restitutionary relief have been fulfilled and there is no public policy reason (such as illegality) why the indemnity should not be granted. The position would be the same as if there never was a contract, but nevertheless there was a request by the principal to the surety. There is a precedent for a quasi-contractual remedy being granted in analogous circumstances. In *Craven-Ellis v Canons* [1936] 2 K.B. 403, the Court of Appeal allowed a claim by a director of a company for *quantum meruit* for services rendered by him to the company in circumstances in which the express contract providing for his remuneration was void.

It is more questionable whether a right to restitution would ever arise if the agreement is merely unenforceable. In such circumstances the express agreement by which the parties chose to regulate their conduct still exists, and it appears that the existence of that agreement may preclude any restitutionary remedy, as it would if it had been enforceable. In *Britain v Rossiter* (1879) 11 Q.B.D. 123, an employee whose contract was unenforceable by reason of s.4 of the Statute of Frauds was unable to recover remuneration on a *quantum meruit* basis. However, it appears that the case was argued purely on the basis of an implied agreement (*cf. Craven-Ellis v Canons,* above) and also there was the particular problem in that case that an implied agreement would circumvent the statute. Despite the fact that the right to an indemnity as a matter of implied agreement and as a matter of restitution are very closely linked, the matter is still open to debate.

Implied agreement

10–006   It is more common for the right to an indemnity to arise as a matter of implication. If the surety has undertaken his liability as the result of an express or implied request by the principal, then there are two legal bases on which the right to an indemnity may arise. One is an implied contract between the surety and the principal: see *Re A Debtor* [1937] Ch. 156. Alternatively, the surety may have a right to restitution which arises, in quasi-contract, from the fact that he has been compelled to discharge a liability for which the principal is ultimately liable.[13] The right of indemnity was founded on the old form of action of *indebitatus assumpsit* for recovery of money paid to the use of another.[14]

---

12 See *Britain v Rossiter* (1879) 11 Q.B.D. 123.
13 *Moule v Garrett* (1872) L.R. 7 Ex. 101, 104, and see *Niru Battery Manufacturing Co v Milestone Trading Ltd (No.2)* [2004] 2 Lloyd's Rep. 319. See further paras 10–008–10–011 below.
14 *Morrice v Redwyn* (1731) 2 B.K.B. 26; *Ware v Horwood* (1807) 14 Ves. 28: *Alexander v Vane* (1836) 1 M. & W. 511; *Kearsley v Cole* (1846) 16 M. & W. 128.

In the majority of cases, where the surety has entered into the contract of suretyship with the creditor at the express or implied request of the principal, the court will have no difficulty in finding sufficient evidence of an implied agreement by the principal to indemnify the surety. It is a necessary corollary of the principal asking someone to pay his debt, that he promises that he will repay him. As will be seen from the discussion of the restitutionary remedy, an express or implied request is an almost invariable requirement for a surety claiming in quasi-contract, yet when there is such a request, he would rarely, if ever, need to put his claim on that basis.

Unenforceable agreements between creditor and principal
The nature and extent of the implied promise to repay will depend, of **10–007** course, on the intention of the parties, to be ascertained by the court in each particular case. The importance of discovering this intention is particularly illustrated in two contexts.

If the surety is not legally compellable to pay the debt or discharge the liability of the principal to the creditor, whether because the principal is not legally liable, or because he himself is not legally liable, he cannot claim an indemnity by way of restitution. That does not mean, however, that he is without any remedy if he became a surety at the express or implied request of the principal. In such cases, there is a prima facie presumption that the request of the principal to the surety was "pay if I do not", rather than "pay if I do not and if I am legally compellable to pay". Thus in *Argo Caribbean Group Ltd v Lewis* [1976] 2 Lloyd's Rep. 289, the underlying liability of the principal was unenforceable because of an infringement of the Moneylenders Acts, but the Court of Appeal held that the surety was entitled to an indemnity.[15]

Similarly, in *Alexander v Vane* (1836) 1 M. & W. 511, the surety was entitled to an indemnity notwithstanding that he had paid a claim which was unenforceable against him by reason of the absence of a written note or memorandum as required by s.4 of the Statute of Frauds. On the other hand, it has been held in Ireland that a surety who paid a statute-barred debt had no right to an indemnity: *Re Morris, Coneys v Morris* [1922] 1 I.R. 81, affirmed on appeal [1922] 1 I.R. 136. That was a case in which the claim was treated (possibly erroneously) as arising only in quasi-contract, where the unenforceability of the underlying obligation would normally be an answer to any claim for restitution. If the claim to an indemnity is based on an agreement, then the fact that the underlying claim was time-barred at the time when the surety paid should only preclude recovery if, on its true construction, the request of the principal was "pay if I do not and I am legally compellable to pay".

There are two possible ways for the principal to avoid becoming liable to indemnify the surety for the latter's possibly gratuitous discharge of a

---

15 Following *Re Chetwynd's Estate* [1938] Ch. 13. The Moneylenders Acts were repealed from May 19, 1985 by the Consumer Credit Act 1974, but presumably the same result would follow in respect of s.113 of that Act.

liability for which neither he nor the principal were in fact legally liable. The first is to ensure that when the request is made to the surety, it is made very clear (preferably in writing) that the request is to pay only if the principal does not pay *and* he was legally compellable to do so.[16]

An example of a case in which the evidence rebutted the presumption as to the nature of the request is *Sleigh v Sleigh* (1850) 19 L.J. (N.S.) Ex. 345 whereby the plaintiff had drawn a bill of exchange for the accommodation of the defendant who had accepted it. The plaintiff paid the holder of the bill although no notice of dishonour had been given. He therefore paid at a time when he was under no obligation to do so. His claim for an indemnity was rejected. The case was explained by Greene M.R. in *Re Chetwynd's Estate* [1938] Ch. 13 at 19, 20 as "one . . . where [the court] could not imply from the facts any authority or request by the accommodated party to pay otherwise than in accordance with the ordinary routine applicable to bills of exchange".

The second way in which it has been suggested that the principal may escape liability to indemnify the surety in such circumstances is to "countermand his request before [the surety] had committed himself to the transaction, since in such a case it could truly be said that [the surety] had made a voluntary payment".[17] However, it is difficult to see how this would work in practice. Once the surety has entered into a binding legal obligation with the creditor pursuant to the principal's request, the principal cannot countermand or change the request. It has been held that once the initial request has been made, the principal will be liable to indemnify the surety even if he has subsequently paid the debt against the wishes of the principal, since no further request to pay is necessary.[18]

Consequently, a countermanded request is probably only effective when the countermand is given to the surety before he acts upon it to his detriment, by committing himself to a contract with the creditor—and that is long before any danger of an indemnity in respect of an unjustified payment would arise. It is extremely doubtful whether a countermand prior to payment would ever be regarded as effective, if the surety had made a contract in response to a request to "pay if I do not", especially if that contract placed him under an independent primary liability to the creditor.

One situation in which the court will be particularly concerned to determine the intention of the contracting parties is that in which the principal is the wife and the surety is her husband. In *Anson v Anson* [1953] 1 Q.B. 636 and in *Re Salisbury-Jones* [1938] 3 All E.R. 459 it was held that a husband who had paid a bank under a guarantee of his wife's overdraft was not precluded from recovering an indemnity by the application of the presumption of advancement, although if there had been clear evidence of an intention to make the wife a gift of the money, the husband would have been precluded from reclaiming it. The courts will look closely at the facts of each particular case to see what the husband and wife intended.

---

16 See the observations of Orr L.J. in *Argo v Lewis* [1976] 2 Lloyd's Rep. 289 at 295.
17 *Argo v Lewis* [1976] 2 Lloyd's Rep. 289 *per* Orr L.J.at 295–296.
18 See the observations of Lord Kenyon C.J. in *Exall v Partridge* (1799) 8 Term Rep. 308.

Restitutionary right in quasi-contract

Three conditions must be fulfilled for the right in quasi-contract to arise: **10–008**

(1) The person claiming restitution (the surety) must have been compelled, or have been compellable by law, to make the payment.

(2) He must not have officiously exposed himself to make the payment.

(3) The payment must have discharged a liability of the principal.[19]

If there has been a request by the principal to the surety, there should be no difficulty in establishing the first two conditions. Indeed, in such cases the right to an indemnity may be regarded as an ordinary incident of the suretyship. Thus, in *Batard v Hawes* (1853) 2 E. & B. 287 at 296, Lord Campbell said:

> "To support the action for money paid, it is necessary that there should be a request from the defendant to pay, either express or implied by law. Where one party enters into a legal liability for and at the request of another, a request to pay the money is implied by law from the fact of entering into the engagement."[20]

Of course, if a request is established there is probably no need for the claim to be brought in quasi-contract because the surety should be able to prove an implied agreement. As Greene L.J. said in *Re A Debtor* [1937] 1 Ch. 156 at 166:

> "Where, as in the present case, the implied request for payment is referable to a request to give a guarantee, the contractual basis of the action is apparent, and the difference between the old form of action of *indebitatus assumpsit* and an action on a special contract to indemnify disappears for all practical purposes."

Legal compulsion to discharge

In order for a right of restitution to arise, the surety must have been under   **10–009** a legal liability (as opposed to a moral obligation) to make payment to the creditor. Thus, if the contract of suretyship is unenforceable, there is no restitutionary right to an indemnity. This is illustrated by the case of *Re Cleadon Trust* [1939] 1 Ch. 286. One of the two directors of a company discharged certain company debts at the request of the company secretary, on the understanding that the company would repay him. The debts were incurred by the company as guarantor of the obligations of certain subsidiaries. The secretary had no power to borrow on behalf of the

---

19 See the discussion in Goff & Jones (*op. cit.*), Ch.15 esp. at 15–015 *et seq.*
20 See also *Brittain v Lloyd* (1845) 14 M. & W. 762, *per* Pollock C.B. at 773; *Leigh v Dickeson* (1884) 15 Q.B.D. 60.

company, and therefore the request could not be treated as a request by the company. The payments were treated as loans to the company, and a resolution was passed by the board purporting to confirm this, but unfortunately the resolutions did not comply with the articles of association and were *ultra vires* and void. The court held that the payments were therefore to be treated as if they were voluntary payments and were irrecoverable from the company in subsequent liquidation proceedings.

Self-induced compulsion to pay

10–010   As explained above, once it is established that there was an express or implied request by the principal to the surety that he should pay his debt, there is usually no question of the surety having officiously or voluntarily exposed himself to the liability to make the payment. That is so even if the principal does not want him to make the payment at the time when he does so.

A particular area of difficulty arises where it is arguable that the surety has brought his liability to the creditor upon himself, in circumstances where there was no express or implied request by the principal—for example, if the principal has no knowledge that the surety has offered to provide a guarantee to the creditor.[21] In such a case, his right to an indemnity can only arise in quasi-contract, because there is no basis for implying any agreement to indemnify him. In determining whether or not there is a right to an indemnity in such a situation, two conflicting principles have to be reconciled. The first is that a person who has volunteered to undertake another person's obligations is not entitled to regard himself as that person's creditor; anyone who confers an unsought benefit on another has no right in equity to recoup it.[22] The second is that wherever two persons are liable for the same debt, and as between them, one of them is primarily liable, he is liable to indemnify the other if the other meets the liability.[23]

In *Owen v Tate* [1976] Q.B. 402, the defendants obtained a bank loan for £350 secured by a mortgage over the property of L. The plaintiff was not concerned with that transaction in any way. Subsequently, L wanted the title deeds to the property, deposited with the bank, to be released. The plaintiff, a friend of L, offered to help. He deposited £350 with the bank and signed a form of guarantee limited to £350 due owing or incurred to the bank by the defendants. The defendants had no prior knowledge of this

---

21 It should be noted, however, that the mere fact that the creditor makes an express request for security, or insists on a certain type of security, would not preclude the court from finding an implied, if not an express, request on the part of the principal to the surety to provide it.

22 See *Hodgson v Shaw* (1834) 3 My. & K. 183 at 190, *per* Lord Brougham L.C.; *Leigh v Dickeson* (1884) 15 Q.B.D. 60 at 64, *per* Brett M.R.; *Falcke v Scottish Imperial Insurance Co* (1886) 34 Ch. D. 234.

23 *Moule v Garrett* (above); *Duncan Fox & Co v North & South Wales Bank* (1880) 6 App. Cas. 1 at 11; *Selous Street Properties Ltd v Oronel Fabrics Ltd* (1984) 270 E.G. 643; *Becton Dickinson UK Ltd v Zwebner* [1989] 1 Q.B. 208.

and had not requested the plaintiff to put up the security. Indeed they strongly objected to the title deeds being released. Later, when the bank called in the loan, the defendants not only knew about the plaintiff's position but encouraged the bank to have recourse to the plaintiff.

Despite the behaviour of the defendants, the Court of Appeal refused the plaintiff any right of recourse against them; because he had assumed his obligations voluntarily, there had been no antecedent request from the defendants, and he was not acting out of necessity.[24] Scarman L.J. said at 411:

> "If without an antecedent request a person assumes an obligation or makes a payment for the benefit of another, the law will, as a general rule, refuse him a right of indemnity. But if he can show that in the particular circumstances of the case there was some necessity for the obligation to be assumed, then the law will grant him a right of reimbursement if in all the circumstances it is just and equitable to do so."

On the facts of the particular case, there was no necessity, and the court held that it would not be just and equitable to grant relief because the obligation was initially entered into behind the backs of the defendants and contrary to their wishes. It is difficult to envisage a situation in which anyone would become a surety in circumstances of "necessity", and consequently the effect of *Owen v Tate is* probably to preclude a personal claim for an indemnity in quasi-contract being successfully brought by a surety in circumstances in which there has been no request or no valid request by the principal. Ironically, this is probably the only situation in which the remedy in quasi-contract would be needed.[25]

As demonstrated by the facts of *Re Cleadon Trust* [1939] 1 Ch. 286, the surety who acts in accordance with a request which appears to emanate from the principal but which the principal or his agent is not authorised to make, may find himself precluded from relief on the grounds that he was a volunteer. In the case of requests or agreements which are *ultra vires* a company principal, the surety may be protected by ss.108–111 of the Companies Act 1989.[26]

Whilst these provisions might assist many sureties, it is unlikely that they would provide any remedy for the surety in the situation of the company director in *Re Cleadon Trust;* the statute has retained the director's personal liability to the company for any loss arising out of *ultra vires* acts.

---

24 A person may be acting out of necessity if he has been compelled to pay moneys to the creditor in order to release goods which have been seized in execution of the claim against the debtor, as in *Edmunds v Wallingford* (1885) 14 Q.B.D. 811 and *Johnson v Royal Mail Steam Packet Co* (1867) L.R. 3 C.P. 38. However, it is difficult to envisage a situation in which this type of necessity would arise in the context of suretyship.

25 The possibility of subrogation does not appear to have been considered. Subrogation may be granted when the party who pays off the indebtedness has no relationship with the principal. See further Ch.11, para.11–019.

26 See Ch.6, para.6–021.

Owen v Tate has been the subject of strong criticism.[27] Nevertheless, it has not been overruled, and therefore a potential surety would be foolish to undertake any obligations to the creditor without first making sure, so far as he is able, that there is a specific request by the principal that he should undertake the suretyship and that the person making the request has authority to do so.

It is important to note, however, that *Owen v Tate* does not apply to the situation in which the payer discharges a liability which he has incurred jointly or jointly and severally with the principal (whether or not they are subject to a common demand): for example, where the obligation of the surety is expressed on the face of the contract with the creditor as a primary liability, but the true arrangement as between principal and surety is that the principal is primarily liable and the surety only secondarily liable. In such cases the right to an indemnity arises because, by discharging his own liability, the surety has also discharged a liability of the primary obligor and thus created a situation in which the latter will be unjustly enriched if the surety cannot recover that sum from him: see, *e.g. Niru Battery Manufacturing Co v Milestone Trading Co (No.2)* [2004] 2 Lloyd's Rep. 319 and the discussion in Goff & Jones, *The Law of Restitution* (6th ed. 2002) at para.15–015. Since most modern standard form guarantees contain a clause which makes the surety liable as a "primary obligor", it may be that *Owen v Tate* is unlikely to have much impact in practice.

Discharged liability of the principal

10–011 In the majority of cases, this condition is the easiest of the three requirements to establish. However, if the underlying liability of the principal is void or unenforceable, the surety runs the risk that the principal could avoid liability to indemnify him, on the ground that he made a voluntary payment. An example of such a situation is *Garrard v James* [1925] Ch. 616, where the guarantor of the *ultra vires* borrowings of a company was not entitled to an indemnity from the company even though he remained liable to the lender.[28]

In *Re Law Courts Chambers Co Ltd* (1889) 61 L.T. 669, a director of a company, C, had given a personal guarantee in respect of a debt secured by a mortgage on the company's property. The company assigned the equity of redemption in the property to L Co who covenanted with the company that they would indemnify the company in respect of the mortgage debt, which L Co would pay off. C was not a party to that agreement. The company went into liquidation, and C was called on to pay off the mortgage debt under his personal guarantee. He did so. It was held that C was not entitled

---

27 With which the authors concur. See further Birks and Beatson "Unrequested Payment of Another's Debt" (1976) 92 L.Q.R. 188; see also Goff & Jones, *The Law of Restitution* (*op. cit.*), paras 3–015–3–018, and 15–011; in which it is plausibly argued that the concept of officious exposure to liability has perhaps been too generously interpreted to deny a plaintiff restitution.

28 Though the position may well be different for many sureties since the enactment of ss.108–111 of the Companies Act 1989, see above.

to an indemnity from L Co. There was no contract between L Co and C at any material time, and despite the fact that payment of the mortgage debt had conferred a benefit on L Co, C had not discharged any liability on its part to the creditor bank. Despite the fact that as between L Co and the company L Co was to discharge the mortgage debt the company remained solely liable to the creditor.[29]

In such a situation, if the assignee has given an indemnity to the principal, the surety may be able to enforce it in the principal's name (rather than his own) under his rights of subrogation. Another possible solution would be for the principal to assign him the right of indemnity.

It has already been noted above that the principal's request to the surety, if there was one, is presumed in the absence of contrary evidence to have been "pay if I do not" rather than "pay if I am liable to pay and do not", and that consequently the unenforceability of the principal's underlying obligation will not preclude recovery in contract, save possibly where illegality is involved.[30] It is debatable in the light of the authorities whether it would preclude recovery in quasi-contract. Where there is a request, the surety does not need to rely on quasi-contractual remedies, and so the point is unlikely to arise in practice. If there is no request, there is no reason in principle why the normal requirement of discharge of an enforceable liability should not apply; otherwise the surety cannot legitimately claim to have conferred a benefit upon the principal for which he should have an equitable right to reimbursement.

Accrual of the surety's right of indemnity

The surety's right to an indemnity, prima facie, only arises on actual **10–012** payment by him. "The implied undertaking to indemnify is an undertaking to reimburse the guarantor upon the happening of a contingency, *viz.*, the payment by the guarantor to the creditor, and until that contingency occurs, there is no debt": *Re A Debtor* [1937] Ch. 156, *per* Greene L.J. at 163–164.[31]

This is simply an application of a more general rule that the right to an indemnity does not usually arise until the person entitled to the indemnity has been called upon to pay and his liability has been ascertained.[32] However, this general rule is subject to any different bargain which the contracting parties may have made. This may include an agreement to give

---

29 See also *Crafts v Tritton* (1818) 8 Taunt. 365. An assignee of the equity of redemption does not take over liability to the mortgagee in the absence of an agreement with him to that effect: see *Mills v United Counties Bank Ltd* [1912] 1 Ch. 231 *per* Cozens Hardy M.R. at 237.

30 *Alexander v Vane* (1836) 1 M. & W. 511; *Re Chetwynd's Estate* [1938] Ch. 13; *Argo Carribbean Group Ltd v Lewis* [1976] 2 Lloyd's Rep. 288. *Cf. Re Morris, Coneys v Morris* [1922] 1 I.R. 81, and see para.10–007 above.

31 See also *Re Mitchell, Freelove v Mitchell* [1913] 1 Ch. 201 *per* Parker J. at 206; *Brittain v Lloyd* (1845) 14 M. & W. 762 *per* Pollock C.B. at 733; *Re Richardson* [1911] 2 K.B. 705 at 712; *Re Beavan* [1913] 2 Ch. 595; *Re Fenton* [1931] Ch. 85. As to what constitutes "payment", see the discussion in *Halsbury's Laws*, Vol. 20 (4th ed., 2004 reissue) at para.245.

32 *Telfair Shipping v Inersea Carriers SA* [1985] 1 W.L.R. 553.

the surety a right to bring an action against the principal for the money before he pays anything himself. Accordingly, if the surety and the principal agree that the principal will idemnify the surety on a liability "arising", he may be able to claim the indemnity before he makes payment. So, for example, in *Re Allen* [1896] 2 Ch. 345, there was a covenant between the principal and the surety that the principal would pay the debt on a certain day. When this covenant was broken, the surety had an immediate right to recover the whole of the debt as damages for breach of that covenant.[33] Similarly, in *Spark v Heslop* (1859) 1 E. & E. 563, the plaintiff had agreed to pay the holder the amount of a dishonoured bill of exchange and to bring an action against the acceptor in his own name, in return for a guarantee from the indorser of the bill. The guarantee included a covenant that the indorser would "be answerable to you for all costs damages and expenses which you may sustain by reason of trying the action, and relating and incidental thereto". It was held that this covered the plaintiff's own legal fees, for which he was liable, but which he had not yet paid.

The surety may also be able to enforce his right of indemnity against the principal in equity even if he has not paid the creditor. Thus in *Meates v Westpac Building Corp Ltd* [1991] 3 N.Z.L.R. 385, a guarantor was sued by the creditor and joined the principal in third party proceedings, claiming an indemnity. It may be that this case is best viewed as an example of the operation of the surety's equitable right to claim exoneration from the principal as soon as he is exposed to liability—see the discussion of *quia timet* relief in para.10–025 *et seq.* below.

Despite the fact that the debt between the surety and the principal usually arises on payment, any contract from which the right of indemnity emanates is almost certain to have been made at an earlier date, namely whenever the express or implied request to the surety was made or, at the latest, acted upon: *Re A Debtor* [1937] Ch. 156. This was important on the facts of that particular case. The surety had guaranteed the bank account of a married woman. Subsequently the Law Reform (Married Women and Tortfeasors) Act 1935 was enacted, which provided that no action might be brought against a married woman in respect of a contract or obligation entered into before the passing of the Act. The surety was called upon to pay under the guarantee after the Act was passed, but he could not recover the sum from the woman, because the implied agreement to indemnify him had been made before the Act.

In most cases, the time at which the contract or obligation to indemnify arose is unlikely to be of importance, since nowadays legislation which invalidates transactions retrospectively is rarely passed.

Effect of date of accrual

10–013   The general rule that no right of indemnity (or debt) accrues until payment by the surety has several consequences in the following contexts: periods of limitation, administration of estates, and bankruptcy and liquidation. The

---

33 For other examples of express rights arising before payment see *Bosma v Larsen* [1966] 1 Lloyd's Rep. 22; *National House-Building Council v Fraser* [1983] 1 All E.R. 1090.

first two are dealt with in this chapter. The effect of the rule in the context of insolvency is dealt with in Chapter 13.

Limitation period

In the absence of agreement to the contrary, the limitation period will not start to run against the surety in favour of the principal until he has paid the creditor: *Collinge v Heywood* (1839) 9 Ad. & El. 633; *Re Mitchell* [1913] 1 Ch. 201. If the surety has only paid part of the debt, the limitation period will run only in respect of that part: *Davies v Humphreys* (1840) 6 M. & W. 153.

10–014

Administration of estates

In *Re Mitchell, Freelove v Mitchell* [1913] 1 Ch. 201, the question which arose was whether the release of "all debts" to a principal debtor by a surety's will affected the right of his executors to claim against the debtor's beneficial interest under the will for an indemnity against claims under the guarantee made by the creditor after the surety's death. Parker J. held that it did not. The right of the surety to an indemnity did not become a debt until he (or his estate) had paid the creditor; accordingly the reference to "all debts" in the will did not apply to this future contingent liability which might never accrue. It follows that careful drafting of the will is necessary to avoid frustration of the testator's intention in such circumstances.

10–015

There is a conflict of authority as to whether an executor who is surety for the debt of the testator can exercise a right of retainer from the testator's estate. In *Re Orme* (1883) 50 L.T. 51, Kay J. held that no right of retainer arose until after payment of the debt by the surety, but he gave the surety the opportunity to make the payment so as to enable him to exercise the right of retainer. In *Re Harrison* [1886] L.R. 32 Ch. D. 395, the question arose whether the executor could exercise a right of retainer in respect of a debt paid off by him after he had parted with the assets of the testator to a receiver; Pearson J. held that he could not, because at the time when the debt arose there were no assets in his hands against which he could have exercised that right. Again, it was a fundamental part of this decision that the right of retainer could not arise until payment of the debt.

Despite these two cases, in *Re Giles* [1896] 1 Ch. 956, it was held by Kekewich J. that although nothing was due to the executor before he was called on to pay, there was an "equitable debt" which gave rise to a right to retain even before payment. That case was not followed in *Re Beavan* [1913] 2 Ch. 595. Neville J. referred to, and approved of *Re Orme* and *Re Harrison*. He explained that if the executor has a right in equity to an order, such as that in *Re Orme*, allowing him an opportunity to pay the debt and thereafter exercise his right of retainer, the court might provide for immediate payment of the debt so as to give effect to the right of retainer straight away; but that was quite different from holding that he had a right of retainer before he paid the debt. There was no such thing as an "equitable right to retain". *Re Giles* was in direct conflict with the earlier authorities and was not in accordance with the underlying principle that a right of retainer only arises on payment of the debt. Accordingly, he declined to follow it. It is likely that in a similar situation today, the court would follow the reasoning in *Re Beavan*.

Payment by surety before the due date

10–016   The situation frequently arises in which the surety becomes concerned that the liability of the principal to the creditor is increasing and that he has no immediate means of controlling his potential liability. This is a particular concern when, for example, the director of a company, who has given an unlimited guarantee to a bank for the company's overdraft, resigns from the company. The guarantee may enable him to terminate it on giving notice to the creditor, which will at least protect him in respect of future liabilities accruing after the notice takes effect, but that does not provide a complete solution to the problem if he does not wish to remain exposed to liability for the indebtedness which has already accrued.

It will be seen below and in the following chapter that there are a number of equitable remedies available to the surety even before he makes payment to the creditor. However, apart from those remedies, once there is default by the principal, or the guaranteed liability crystallises for any other reason, the surety can make payment and look to the principal for reimbursement, without waiting for a claim to be made against him. Payment at that stage will not prejudice his right to an indemnity on the basis that the payment was "voluntary" or premature. If the guarantee is to "pay on demand", the surety's right to pay the creditor and seek an immediate indemnity will not be prejudiced if he fails to wait for the demand, even though in such a case the demand is a condition precedent to his liability.[34] In *Stimpson v Smith* [1999] Ch. 340 the Court of Appeal held that the requirement that there be a written demand was a condition inserted for the benefit of the guarantor, and thus he is entitled to waive it without prejudicing his right to claim contribution from a co-surety.[35] The Court of Appeal based their decision on the authorities relating to *quia timet* relief (discussed in para.10–025 and following below), from which they drew the principle that the right to claim exoneration from the principal arises as soon as the principal is liable, regardless of whether or not there has been a demand on the surety. They then extended that principle by

---

34 Though the demand will not be a condition precedent if the liability of the surety to the creditor is primary, for example if the contract is one of indemnity. For example in *Pitt v Purssord* (1841) 8 M. & W. 538, the person claiming a right of contribution was a direct signatory to a promissory note, and therefore a demand was not a condition precedent to his liability on it. See generally the discussion in Ch.7 above at 7–002–7–006.

35 See also *Moulton v Roberts* [1977] Qd. Rep. 135; *Thomas v Nottingham Incorporated Football Club Ltd* [1972] Ch. 596 at 604, *per* Goff J. The authors of O'Donovan & Phillips *The Modern Contract of Guarantee* (English ed., Thompson Sweet & Maxwell, 2003) suggest at para.12–12 that a guarantor who pays off the principal debt before receiving a demand from the creditor does not have the immediate right to an indemnity which a guarantor enjoys upon discharging the principal debt after default by the debtor and demand by the creditor, but that proposition appears to be directly contrary to the decision of the Court of Appeal in *Stimpson v Smith*: see, *e.g.* the observations of Judge L.J. at 352F.

analogy to claims for contribution. That decision was plainly correct, since there is no justification for drawing a distinction between the time at which the surety can claim an indemnity from the principal and the time at which he can claim contribution from his co-sureties.

Once the principal's liability has accrued, the surety is at risk under his guarantee and his payment to the creditor cannot be characterised as voluntary, nor would it be right to regard it as premature. If there would be no defence to the claim on the guarantee, once any demand was made, there appears to be no better reason why the surety should have to wait for a demand to be made against him, than that he should have to wait to be sued before making payment. In the Australian case of *Green v Parr* (1870) 4 S.A.L.R. 126, the surety guaranteed to a bank the repayment by the principal of a certain sum "when called upon". The bank never specifically called upon the surety to pay, but it was held that he was entitled to pay and sue for the amount guaranteed whenever he thought proper, without waiting to be called upon.[36] The fact that the surety may have ulterior motives or derive some collateral benefit from making the payment without waiting to be sued or waiting for a demand will not affect his right to claim an indemnity: for example he may consider that moment to be his best chance of achieving a satisfactory compromise with the creditor, as the claimant did in *Stimpson v Smith*.

However, in the absence of express agreement, the surety would not be entitled to accelerate his right to an indemnity by discharging the principal obligation before it is due to be fulfilled, for example by paying the creditor before the liability which he has guaranteed has accrued.[37] Although there is no direct English authority for this proposition,[38] it is stated in De Colyar's *Law of Guarantee and Principal and Surety* (3rd ed. 1900), pp.305–306, and the statement was approved by the Saskatchewan Court of Appeal in *Drager v Allison* (1958) 13 D.L.R. (2d) 204 at 216.[39]

In that case, the guarantor had paid the balance owing under an agreement for the sale of land, before there was any default in payment by the purchasers. It was held by the Canadian Supreme Court [1959] S.C.R. 661 that this payment did not operate as a gift to the principal or the creditor, or turn the guarantor into a mere volunteer, but that generally the surety could not make a claim against the principal for an indemnity until such time as the payment fell due and he could have been sued by the

---

36 See also *Read v McLean* [1925] 3 D.L.R. 716.

37 If the principal liability cannot be discharged before a specific period has elapsed, the guarantor will not be entitled to an indemnity if he pays before that period expires. See *e.g. Bellingham v Freer* (1837) 1 Moo. P.C. 333.

38 Support is to be derived from the analogous case of *Coppin v Gray* (1842) 1 Y. & C. Ch. Cas. 205 in which Knight-Bruce V.-C. stated at 210 (of the acceptor of a bill of exchange): "the mere fact that he paid the bill before the time when according to its tenor it became due would not, I apprehend, give him a right of suit before that time against the drawer by way of loan to whom he accepted it". This view also appears to be shared by the editors of *Halsbury's Laws* (Vol. 20, 1994 reissue) at para.246.

39 Reversed on other grounds by the Canadian Supreme Court: *Drager v Allison* [1959] S.C.R. 661.

creditor. However, the surety might start an action against the principal once it became clear that the principal had definitely repudiated his obligations to the creditor and had asserted an intention to act in disregard of the surety's rights, even though the guaranteed debt was not then due.

This decision is in keeping with the prima facie rule that the principal's request to the surety is to be construed as "pay if I do not" rather than "pay if I do not and I am liable to pay". It remains to be seen whether the same result could be achieved if the request is plainly "pay if I am liable to pay" and payment is made before any such liability accrues and there is no question of any actual or anticipatory repudiation by the principal of his obligations to the creditor at that time. It is one thing for the surety to have the right in equity to pay off the debt when it matures, without waiting to be sued; it is quite another for him to try to pay it before it even falls due.

It is thought that the observations by Cockburn C.J. in *Swire v Redman* (1876) L.R.1 Q.B. 536 at 541 that "the surety has a right at any time to apply to the creditor and pay him off, and then (on giving proper indemnity for costs) to sue the principal in the creditor's name" do not affect this proposition. That is a description of the exercise of rights of subrogation (discussed in Chapter 11). Such rights can normally be exercised by someone who has paid off another person's liability, if the latter would otherwise be unjustly enriched by the payment. In such event, the party who is subrogated may enforce the personal and proprietary rights of the original creditor, and there is no necessity for there to be any relationship, contractual or otherwise, between the payer and the person whose debts or liabilities have been discharged by the payment (though, generally speaking, a debt cannot be discharged unless the debtor consents or ratifies the payment). For the purposes of subrogation, there should be no distinction in principle between the position of a refinancing lender who pays off the original loan, and a surety who does so. The right to an indemnity, by contrast, is a personal right and can only arise when the underlying liability has matured.

Amount of indemnity

10-017   The surety is entitled to be fully indemnified to the extent of the loss which he has suffered and no more. The right of each surety is separate and distinct, which means that if there is more than one surety, each may sue the principal for the amount which he has paid, irrespective of whether the guarantee is joint, several or joint and several. A surety may decide to pay off only part of the debt and sue the principal for that part, or he may compromise the claim against him and seek an indemnity in that amount, see, *e.g. Lord Newborough v Schroder* (1849) 7 C.B. 342 at 399. In *Davies v Humphreys* (1840) 6 M. & W. 153, Parke B. stated at 167:

"It is clear that each sum the plaintiff, the surety, paid, was paid in ease of the principal and ought to have been paid in the first instance by him, and that the plaintiff had a right of action against him the instant he paid it for so much money paid to his use. However convenient it might be to limit the number of actions in respect of one suretyship, there is no rule of law which requires the surety to pay the whole debt before he can call for reimbursement."

The claim for an indemnity is usually a claim in debt, and consequently there is no obligation on the surety to mitigate his loss (for example, by defending the creditor's claim or seeking a compromise). Moreover, in the absence of express contractual provision, it is not usually open to the principal to argue that instead of paying the creditor, the surety should have availed himself of defences which may have been available to him on the guarantee alone, or even that he should have raised defences which may or would have been available to the principal—unless of course the claim to an indemnity is purely based on principles of restitution and the guarantor must prove that he was liable or otherwise made the payment under compulsion.[40] If the claim against the guarantor is compromised, an argument by the principal that he could have obtained more favourable terms is unlikely to avail him, for much the same reasons. Since it appears that the guarantor may not be entitled to an indemnity from the principal in respect of the costs of defending a claim on the guarantee when the defence would only benefit the guarantor (see para.10–020 below), then there would appear to be no justification for a rule which obliges the guarantor to incur those costs prior to claiming his indemnity. Accordingly, in the normal case, and absent any contractual term to the contrary, the guarantor who does have arguable defences under the guarantee alone would appear to have a free choice as to whether he should pay in full, compromise the claim, or raise those defences.

Principal and interest

As a general principle, "on a contract to indemnify the person to be indemnified should be put in the same position as if the man who had contracted to indemnify him had in fact done what he had contracted to do, that is, had paid the money at the proper time".[41] Thus the surety is entitled to recover the sum which he paid to discharge the liability of the principal to the creditor, together with interest on that sum running from the date on which it was paid.[42] However if he pays only part of the debt and the creditor releases him from liability for the rest, he will not be treated as if he had paid the whole, and will only be entitled to recover what he has paid: *Soutten v Soutten* (1822) 5 B. & Ald. 852.

    It appears that the surety's entitlement to interest on what he has paid to the creditor, from the date of payment is unaffected by the fact that the

10–018

---

40 See, *e.g.* Alexander v Vane (1836) 1 M. & W. 511; *McColl's Wholesale Pty Ltd v State Bank (NSW)* [1984] 3 N.S.W.L.R. 365; *Re Chetwynd's Estate* [1938] Ch. 13; *Argo Caribbean Group Ltd v Lewis* [1976] 2 Lloyd's Rep. 289, and the discussion in paras 10–009–10–010 above.

41 *Re Fox, Walker & Co Ex p. Bishop* (1880) 15 Ch. D. 400, *per* Cotton L.J. at 421–422.

42 *Re Fox, Walker & Co Ex p. Bishop* (1880) 15 Ch. D. 400, *Hitchman v Stewart* (1850) 3 Drew 271; *Re Watson* [1896] 1 Ch. 925 at 937.

underlying debt was paid free of interest.[43] This is plainly right, as his claim against the surety is no different from any other claim for repayment of a debt, and prima facie he should be entitled to interest to compensate him for being kept out of his money until he recovers it from the principal. Despite this, in *Rigby v Macnamara* (1795) 2 Cox. 50, it was held that the indemnity does not entitle the surety to claim interest from the date of payment, on interest paid by him which accrued on the underlying debt.

This decision was disapproved, *obiter*, by Malins V.-C. in *Re Maria Anna & Steinbank Coal & Coke Company, McKewan's Case* (1877) 6 Ch. D. 447 at 455 and appears to be contrary to the principle of full indemnity. The sum which the surety is obliged to pay the creditor, for the principal's benefit, will usually consist of a principal debt together with interest which has accrued on it, and he ought to be entitled to recover all of this from the principal once he has paid it. Given that both the principal and the interest elements of the underlying obligation form part of the overall indebtedness of the principal to the surety, there is no reason why interest should only run on part of it from the date of payment.

It is likely that in exercising its statutory discretion to award interest under s.35A of the Supreme Court Act 1981, the court would not follow *Rigby v Macnamara*. The rate of interest to be awarded from the date of payment by the surety would also be a matter of discretion, though in general the surety should be entitled to claim the same rate as he was obliged to pay to the creditor. The position might be different if the surety, through his own fault, increased the amount of the interest which had to be paid. Thus in *Hawkins v Maltby* (1868) L.R. 6 Eq. 505, a case analogous to suretyship, the plaintiff was entitled to an indemnity from the defendant in respect of calls made on some shares which the latter had purchased. The plaintiff delayed for four months before paying the calls with interest which had accrued at 11 per cent per annum, and claimed reimbursement together with interest at that rate from the date of payment. The court held that he was only entitled to interest at 4 per cent per annum, because he should have paid the calls at once.

Consequential damages and expenditure

10–019 If, by reason of the debtor's failure to pay, the surety has suffered any loss or incurred expenditure beyond the principal and interest which he was obliged to pay to the creditor, he is entitled to recover it under the indemnity: *Badeley v Consolidated Bank* (1886) 34 Ch. D. 536 *per* Stirling J. at 556. However there are limits to the extent of such recovery. For example, in *Re Empire Paper Ltd (in liq.)* [1999] B.C.C. 406 the surety's claims against the insolvent principal were compromised on terms which expressly allowed him to prove in respect of any further subrogated claims which he might have by virtue of payment of his admitted claims as guarantor. It was held that the agreement did not cover either interest or

---

43 *Re Swan's Estate* (1869) 4 I.R. Eq. 209.

costs incurred by the principal's liquidator to the creditor, as these were not part of any subrogated claim arising out of the principal debtor's default.

Costs of defending creditor's action

The question of whether, in a particular case, the surety is entitled to **10–020** recover from the principal costs which he has incurred in resisting a claim against him by the creditor is not easy to answer. The case law in this area is somewhat confused. However, the basic principle appears to be that such costs are recoverable if they are reasonably incurred in the interests of the principal.[44] Thus, for example, in *Re Empire Paper Ltd (in liq.)* [1999] B.C.C. 406 at 412 it was said that the surety was entitled to recover the costs reasonably incurred by him in investigating the validity and quantum of the creditor's claim against the principal. In *Smith v Howell* (1851) 6 Exch. 730, Pollock C.B. described the principle thus at 731: "It is now considered that by a contract of indemnity it is meant that the party indemnified may recover all such charges as necessarily and reasonably arise out of the circumstances under which the party charged became responsible."[45]

Therefore, costs incurred with the principal's authority are recoverable: *Garrard v Cottrell* (1847) 10 Q.B. 679.[46] So are costs incurred in running a reasonable defence, even if it fails: see, *e.g. Wolmerhausen v Gullick* [1893] 2 Ch. 514 *per* Wright J. at 529–530 and *McColl's Wholesale Pty Ltd v State Bank (NSW)* [1984] N.S.W.L.R. 365 in which the costs were said to be recoverable as damages for breach of an implied contract to indemnify the surety. If the costs are unavoidable, they may also be recoverable. For example, in *Pierce v Williams* (1854) 23 L.J. Ex. 322, the first notification that the surety had of any default by the principal was the service upon him of a writ; in those circumstances he was entitled to recover the costs of the writ. However, he was not entitled to recover the costs of the subsequent proceedings (presumably on the basis that there was no defence) or the costs of execution, since these were incurred solely as a result of the surety failing to satisfy the judgment.

A surety is not entitled to recover from the principal costs which he incurs in unreasonably defending a claim against him by the creditor. This rule does not simply cover unmeritorious defences, but may extend to a situation where the costs of the running defence would outweigh the benefits to be gained. See, *e.g. Gilleff v Rippon* (1829) Mood. & M. 406 in

---

44 In Goff & Jones, *The Law of Restitution* (*op. cit.*), para.15–020, fn.25, reference is made to the contrary argument that since the benefits accruing to the principal from the defence of an action brought against the surety are merely incidental, there should be no right to recover the costs and expenses incurred in defending the action, at least if the claim is quasi-contractual. Though the observations of Warrington J. in *Shepheard v Bray* [1906] 2 Ch. 235 at 254 tend to support this view, it does not appear to have found any general favour.

45 See also *Hornby v Cardwell* (1881) 8 Q.B.D. 329; especially *per* Brett L.J. at 337 and Cotton L.J. at 339; *Baxendale v London, Chatham & Dover Railway Co* (1874) L.R. 10 Exch. 35 *per* Quain J. at 44; *Broom v Hall* (1859) 7 C.B.N.S. 503.

46 See also *Crampton v Walker* (1860) 3 E. & E. 321.

which the guarantor spent £60 in defending a claim for £6. Lord Tenterden C.J. said: "A man has no right merely because he has an indemnity to defend an action to put the person guaranteeing to useless expense." It follows that if there is no defence to the claim, the surety should make the best compromise he can with the creditor. This might involve his paying in full before the creditor resorts to legal action. Such a payment would not be regarded as a voluntary payment and the surety's right to an indemnity would be unimpaired: *Lord Newborough v Schroder* (1849) 7 C.B. 342 at 399.[47]

Even if the creditor's claim is not clear-cut, the surety may reach a reasonable compromise with him. So long as the settlement is reasonable, the surety is entitled to recover what he has paid, even if that is more than the surety might have been obliged to pay if the matter had been taken to trial. He may also recover the reasonable costs of effecting such a compromise: *Lord Newborough v Schroder*, above. Although there is no obligation on the part of the surety, in the absence of express agreement, to notify the principal before he enters into a settlement with the creditor, it is generally prudent for the surety to do so.[48] If such a notice is given, it may severely limit the scope of the principal's ability to challenge the reasonableness of the settlement agreement.[49]

It has been said that if costs are incurred in running a defence which is purely beneficial to the surety, the costs will not be recoverable.[50] Whilst it is understandable that the cost of unreasonably resisting a claim should not be added to the principal's burden, the rationale behind refusing the guarantor an indemnity in respect of the costs of raising a good arguable defence on the guarantee which he nonetheless ultimately loses, simply because the defence is discrete and will not directly benefit the principal, is perhaps more difficult to justify. On the other hand, if the guarantor undertakes the defence with the authority of the principal debtor, he should normally be entitled to recover the costs of doing so [51] and it will probably not be open to the principal to argue in those circumstances that the defence was not reasonably undertaken or that it only benefited the surety.

When costs are recoverable from the principal, it is likely that the surety would be entitled to an order that they be assessed on the indemnity basis, this being the basis which now comes closest to a full indemnity. Prior to the introduction of the new bases of assessment, there was authority that the surety was entitled to his costs on the common fund basis: *Howard v Lovegrove* (1870) L.R. 6 Exch. 43.

---

47 See also *Pitt v Purssord* (1841) 8 M. & W. 538.
48 *Smith v Compton* (1832) 3 B. & Ad. 407. See also the discussion in O'Donovan & Phillips (*op. cit.*) at para.12–50 and the cases there cited.
49 See, *e.g.* the observations of Buller J. in *Duffield v Scott* (1789) 3 Term Rep. 374 at 377.
50 See *Re International Contract Co, Hughes' Claim* (1872) L.R. 13 Eq. 623 at 624, 625, *per* Wickens V.C.; *Pierce v Williams* (above) *Baxendale v London, Chatham & Dover Railway Co* (1874) L.R. 10 Exch. 35.
51 See, *e.g. Crampton v Walker* (1860) 3 E. & E. 321; *Garrard v Cottrell* (1847) 10 Q.B. 679;

Surety's loss other than cash

In the majority of cases the surety would discharge his liability to the **10–021**
creditor by making a payment, but there is generally no reason why he
should be precluded from doing so by transferring property to him, such as
a share in real estate, a valuable chattel, or some stocks and shares.
Further, in some cases the surety's liability may only be satisfied by
execution of a judgment against his assets.

As a general rule, the right of the surety to an indemnity in those
circumstances is no different from the position if he had paid in cash. In
Fahey v Frawley (1890) 26 L.R. I.R. 78 at 90 Holmes J. said: "Where a
person is expressly or by implication requested by another to pay his debt
and where he arranges with the creditor to pay it in whole or in part, by the
transfer of property . . . it is as far as the debtor is concerned the same as
money paid." Thus the surety was entitled to recover the value of a
mortgage security which he had transferred to the creditor in discharge of
the principal debt.

Similarly in *Rodgers v Maw* (1846) 15 M. & W. 444, execution was levied
against the surety and money was paid over to the judgment creditor by the
sheriff. It was held that he was entitled to maintain an action for money
paid against the defaulting principal, and on the facts of the case he was
entitled to set off the amount realised in a claim brought by the principal
against him. Pollock C.B. said at 448: "We cannot see upon what principle
a man may not set off money paid by the produce of his goods, as well as
money paid indirectly without the sale of his goods."

If the surety has procured the discharge of the principal debt by giving
the creditor a promissory note or bond payable on a due date, the
authorities conflict as to whether the surety can claim against the principal
immediately he hands over the note or bond, or only when it falls due. In
Barclay v Gooch (1797) 2 Esp. 571, it was held that the surety could claim
at once; this is supported by dicta in *Rodgers v Maw* at 449 and three Irish
cases: *M'Kenna v Harnett* (1849) 13 I.L.R. 206, *Gore v Gore* [1901] 2 I.R.
269 and *Fahey v Frawley* (1890) 26 L.R. I.R. 78. However in *Maxwell v
Jameson* (1818) 2 B. & Ald. 51 and *Taylor v Higgins* (1802) 3 East. 169 it
was held that the surety could not sue until the bond matured. The
rationale for this was explained by Bayley J. in *Maxwell v Jameson* on the
basis that "no money has yet come out of the plaintiff's pocket, and non
constat that it ever will"—there still being a possibility that the principal
might pay the creditor before the bond matured.

The view has been expressed that *Maxwell v Jameson* is correct, on the
basis that in most cases the payment can only be considered to be a
conditional discharge of the debt between the surety and the creditor, and
thus only *quia timet* relief would be available until the creditor actually
receives payment.[52] However, the presumption that a bill of exchange or
cheque operates as a conditional payment may be displaced by express or

---

52 See McGuinness, *The Law of Guarantee* (*op. cit.*), para.8–009 (219–230).

implied agreement: see *Allen v Royal Bank of Canada* (1926) 95 W.P.C. 17; *Re Romer & Halsam* [1893] 2 Q.B. 286; *Bolt & Nut Co (Tipton) Ltd v Rowlands, Nicholls & Co Ltd* [1964] 2 Q.B. 10. It may be that the question of whether a right of action has accrued will depend on the nature of the particular instrument given to the creditor by the surety and the terms of the relevant agreement between them.

If a bond given by the surety to the creditor is merely replaced by another bond in discharge of the original debt, the surety cannot prove against the principal for money paid: *Re Parkinson Ex p. Seargeant* (1822) 1 Gl. & J. 183, affirmed (1825) 2 Gl. & J. 23.

Loss by surety of right of indemnity

10–022 It is open to a surety to make an express agreement with the principal that he will not pursue his right of indemnity or that he is to have no such right, but such agreements are rare. The right to an indemnity is so integral a part of the bargain between the surety and the principal that a court would hesitate long before concluding that it had been given up. Thus the onus of proving that such an agreement exists may be difficult to discharge.

For example, in *Close v Close* (1853) 4 De G.M. & G. 176 the principals entered into a composition deed with their creditors which contained express reservation of the rights of the creditors against any surety. The effect of this was to continue the right of the surety to an indemnity from the principals.[53] One of the creditors who was party to the deed also happened to be a residuary legatee of a surety for the compounding principals, and one of the compounding principals was that surety's executor. It was argued that any right of the surety's estate to an indemnity had been abandoned. The court held that the legatee creditor's accession to the deed merely related to the debt arising directly between himself and the executor/principal. He was not thereby precluded from insisting that the surety's estate was to be indemnified by the principals.

Even when it is intended to abandon a right of indemnity, the language which has to be used must be precise and clear; in *Re Mitchell, Freelove v Mitchell* [1913] 1 Ch. 201, the testator clearly intended that his estate should not pursue the executor under the indemnity in respect of the debt which arose after his death, but because the will only released existing debts to the executor, his intentions were frustrated.

If the surety and the principal make arrangements for the repayment of the indebtedness which are plainly inconsistent with the right to an indemnity, the court may hold that the original agreement to indemnify has been varied or superseded, or that the surety is estopped from claiming an indemnity. However, a mere representation by the surety of his intention to abandon his right may not suffice to raise an estoppel: *Chadwick v Manning* [1896] A.C. 231, applying *Jorden v Money* (1854) 5 H.L.C. 185.[54]

---

53 See further *Cole v Lynn* [1942] 1 K.B. 142.

54 Though the law on equitable estoppel has moved on considerably since that time: see generally the discussion of promissory estoppel and estoppel by convention in *Chitty on Contracts* (*op. cit.*), Vol. 1, Ch.3, esp. at paras 3–085 *et seq.* and 3–107.

Unenforceable indemnities

The surety will be unable to claim an indemnity from the debtor if the **10–023** express or implied agreement to indemnify him is illegal and it is likely that he will be unable to claim an indemnity if a statute or other rule of law provides that such an agreement is unenforceable.[55] Similarly, he would not be entitled to recover a debt paid under a contract which is illegal (*e.g.* a wrongful preference) or void for immorality, whether he claims his indemnity under an express or implied contract or in quasi-contract.[56] If the surety has to rely on a restitutionary remedy, the court will not grant any such equitable relief to him if it would be contrary to public policy to do so or if he does not "come to equity with clean hands".

In the event that the agreement by the principal to indemnify the surety is accompanied by some additional security for the promise, the surety should take care to ensure that his acceptance of this security does not fetter his rights against the principal.[57] He should also check that any such security is valid; a bill of sale given by way of indemnity to a surety will be void because the statutory form cannot apply to such a security: *Hughes v Little* (1886) 18 Q.B.D. 32.[58]

Surety's rights before payment

Despite the fact that in most cases no right of indemnity accrues against the **10–024** principal until after the surety has paid the debt or otherwise discharged the underlying liability, certain rights are available to the surety before this.

Quia timet relief

Nature of relief

As soon as the creditor has acquired the right to enforce the surety's **10–025** obligations under the contract of suretyship, the surety has the right in equity to compel the principal to relieve him from his obligations, even though he has not yet discharged them.[59] The surety can enforce this right by suing in a *quia timet* action for a declaration that he is entitled to be exonerated and an order that the principal should pay whatever is due to

---

55 See above and generally *Halsbury's Laws*, Vol. 20 (4th ed., reissue 2004) at paras 248 and 357 and the cases cited thereunder. For an example of a case in which a statute precluded recovery, see *Re A Debtor* [1937] 1 Ch. 156.

56 *Chambers v Manchester & Milford Railway Co* (1864) 5 B. & S. 588, especially *per* Blackburn J. at 612; *Byrant v Christie* (1816) 1 Stark. 329. *Cf.,* however, *Alexander v Vane* (1836) 1 M. & W. 511, *Re Chetwynd's Estate* [1938] Ch. 13 and *Argo Caribbean Group v Lewis* [1976] 2 Lloyd's Rep. 288. The two lines of authority may be reconciled by construing the principal's request as "pay if I do not" but not as "pay if it would be illegal or fraudulent to pay".

57 For example, if he accepts a promissory note payable on a certain future date, he may be precluded from suing the principal at all before that date.

58 See also *Brown Shipley & Co Ltd v Amalgamated Investment (Europe) BV* [1979] 1 Lloyd's Rep. 488; Ch.11 at para.11–026.

59 *Earl Ranelaugh v Hayes* (1683) 1 Vern. 189; *Nisbet v Smith* (1789) 2 Bro. C.C. 579, *per* Lord Thurlow at 582.

the creditor.[60] For example, in *Salcedo v Mawarie Mining Co Pty Ltd* (1991) 6 A.C.S.R. 197, the judge ordered that funds realised by the sale of the principal's assets by a receiver appointed by the court in earlier proceedings be paid directly to the creditor. Alternatively he may be entitled to an order that the principal set aside a particular fund to pay the creditor, or that he should pay the money into court, though this is perhaps more questionable, since the threat to the surety would not be discharged by any action by the principal short of actual payment.[61]

The right to *quia timet* relief—relief to prevent an anticipated "injury" before it is suffered—is based upon the equitable principle that "though the surety is not troubled or molested for the debt, yet at any time after the money becomes payable on the original bond, this court will decree the principal to discharge the debt; it being unreasonable that a man should always have such a cloud hang over him."[62]

The remedy is available both to a guarantor and to a person who has assumed a primary liability to the creditor although as between himself and the principal, he is a surety. Thus in *Watt v Mortlock* [1964] Ch. 84 the plaintiff and the defendant had jointly covenanted with a bank to repay the balance on the latter's bank account, and the plaintiff had charged her property with repayment of the sum. As between the plaintiff and the defendant, the plaintiff was a surety, but both were under a primary liability to the bank. The defendant failed to comply with demands for repayment and the bank gave notice that it would enforce the security. The plaintiff successfully applied for *quia timet* relief against the defendant.[63]

However, it is unlikely that *quia timet* relief against the principal would be available to someone who did not become a surety at the express or implied request of the principal. He may not be entitled to an indemnity even as a restitutionary remedy; and even if he is, it is arguable that he has no rights prior to payment because his rights of restitution would only arise on payment (whereas the obligation to indemnify flowing from an express or implied contract arises when the request is made by the principal, and that obligation is capable of specific performance by making the principal pay the creditor when the surety is under imminent threat of having to pay). The same difficulties would apply to a "volunteer" surety whose only potential remedy derives from his rights of subrogation, which again only arise on payment of the creditor.[64]

---

60 *Wooldridge v Norris* (1868) L.R. 6 Eq. 410 at 413 *per* Giffard V.-C.; *Ascherson v Tredegar Dry Dock & Wharf Co Ltd* [1909] 2 Ch. 401. The surety cannot, of course, obtain an order that the principal should pay him, because that would not discharge either his own or the principal's liability to the creditor.

61 see *Re Richardson* [1911] 2 K.B. 705, *per* Cozens-Hardy M.R. at 709; *Flight v Cook* (1755) 2 Ves. Sen. 619; *Rankin v Palmer* (1912) 16 C.L.R. 285 at 290–291. See also *Papamichael v National Westminster Bank* [2002] 1 Lloyd's Rep. 332 where the nature of the *quia timet* relief granted was akin to a freezing order to prevent dissipation of assets by the principal debtor.

62 *Earl Ranelaugh v Hayes* (above) *per* Lord Keeper North at 190.

63 See also *Tate v Crewdson* [1938] Ch. 869.

64 This view appears to be shared by the editors of *Chitty on Contracts* (*op. cit.*), Vol. 2 at para.44–115.

Quia timet relief is not confined to relief against the principal himself. It may consist of the enforcement of the obligations of a third party who has given the surety an indemnity or security for the implied or express indemnity of the principal. Thus *Wooldridge v Norris* (1868) L.R. 6 Eq. 410 was a claim for *quia timet* relief against the estate of the father of the principal debtor who had given the surety a bond. In such a case, the proper order is probably not that the stranger pay the creditor (because he is not the person ultimately liable to discharge the underlying debt), but rather that he should pay the surety in accordance with the obligations *inter se*, because what is sought is in effect equitable specific performance of the contract to indemnify.[65]

Conditions precedent to relief

The right of a surety to be exonerated arises at the moment when the **10–026**
obligation which the surety has guaranteed has accrued due—*i.e.* as soon as the principal becomes liable. It has been stated that the surety must show that his liability to the creditor has accrued, in the sense that the creditor could proceed against him forthwith—which necessarily involves proof that the principal is liable unless the contract of suretyship is not a guarantee but an indemnity, in which case the surety must prove that the creditor can make a claim against him.[66] Thus relief was refused in *Morrison v Barking Chemicals Company Ltd* [1919] 2 Ch. 325, a case in which the guarantee of a bank account could be terminated either by the bank closing the account, ascertaining the amount due, and demanding payment, or by the guarantor giving three months' notice to terminate the guarantee. Neither of these steps had been taken.[67] As a result, the principal was not yet liable to repay the money to the bank and the guarantor's liability had not yet crystallised. However in the case of a guarantee payable "on demand" this requirement does not extend to proving that a demand has already been made, or even that a demand is going to be made imminently. It appears to be enough to show that all other conditions necessary for a demand to be made have been fulfilled, and that the creditor could "proceed" against the surety forthwith in the sense of proceeding to make a demand.[68]

Subject to this, as a general rule, the liability of the surety must have accrued at the time when he makes his application; so, for example, the guarantor of an overdraft would normally have to wait until the account was closed by the bank, or the expiry of a notice to terminate the guarantee, before he could bring the proceedings.[69] The fact that a debt may be shown after the taking of accounts will not be sufficient: *Antrobus v Davidson*

---

65 See the way in which this argument was put in *Re Law Guarantee, Liverpool Mortgage Insurance Company's Case* [1914] 2 Ch. 617 at 627.
66 *Tate v Crewdson* [1938] Ch. 869, *Morrison v Barking Chemicals Co Ltd* [1919] 2 Ch. 325.
67 See also *Re Ledgard, Attenborough v Ledgard* [1922] W.N. 105, 66 Sol. Jo. 404; *cf.* the analogous case of *Hughes-Hallett v Indian Mammoth Gold Mines Co* (1883) 22 Ch. D. 561.
68 *Thomas v Nottingham Incorporated Football Club* [1972] Ch. 596, discussed below.
69 See, *e.g. Morrison v Barking Chemicals Co Ltd* (above); compare the facts of *Thomas v Nottingham Incorporated Football Club* [1972] Ch. 596.

(1817) 3 Mer. 569. However, in *Re Anderson-Berry* [1928] Ch. 290, it was suggested by Lord Hanworth M.R. that it may be sufficient to establish a definite liability, albeit for an unascertained but quantifiable amount.[70] In that case, the application for *quia timet* relief was made by sureties to an administration bond, who had been told by the administrator that he was going to distribute the estate even though he knew that there were liabilities still outstanding and not yet determined.

Lord Hanworth said at 304:

> "It is not contested . . . that there is a right on the part of the surety to exoneration by his principal, and that as soon as any definite sum of money has become payable to the creditor, the surety has a right to have it paid by the principal and his own liability in respect of it brought to an end. But it is said that that right only arises as and when a definite sum of money has become payable. I think that this is too narrow a view. I think that from the cases that have been cited there is a right of the surety to ask that he should be protected from a cloud that hangs over him, and if there is a liability, even though the amount of that liability will be ascertained in subsequent proceedings, I think the surety has a right to ask for protection. There is the liability, quantified though it may be by subsequent proceedings and at a subsequent date; but once the liability has appeared then I think the right of the surety has accrued."

The following example illustrates how this might assist a surety in practice:

> S has given a guarantee to C for the due performance by D of his obligations under a contract for the supply of a quantity of goods to C. The goods are supplied, but there is clear evidence that a large proportion are below the contractual standard. C has a claim in damages against D, the full extent of which may not be ascertained for some time; he also has an immediate right to claim against S.

In those circumstances, S ought not to be precluded from seeking some form of *quia timet* relief from D simply by reason of the fact that the sum which he has to pay to C is unascertained. In *Papamichael v National*

---

70 In *Rowland v Gulfpac* [1999] 1 Lloyd's Rep. 86 and *Papamichael v National Westminster Bank Plc* [2002] 1 Lloyd's Rep. 332 it was even suggested that the cause of action need not have accrued, provided that there was "reasonably good, perhaps clear evidence, that a liability will fall on the party entitled to be indemnified and that the person obliged to indemnify clearly proposes to ignore his obligations". However the equitable relief under consideration in those cases, as in *Re Anderson-Berry,* was designed to preclude the dissipation of assets by the person who would ultimately be responsible for indemnifying the party seeking the relief. They must therefore be treated with a degree of caution if reliance is sought to be placed on them in circumstances where, for example, the principal is merely impecunious. Cf. *Hughes-Hallett v Indian Mammoth Gold Mines Co* (1882) 22 Ch. D. 561 at 564, where Fry J. said that *quia timet* relief will not be granted where the surety's liability is not yet established.

Westminster Bank [2002] 1 Lloyd's Rep. 332 at 339 H.H. Judge Chambers Q.C., sitting as a Judge of the Commercial Court, considered *Re Anderson-Berry* and the more recent decision of Rix J. in *Rowland v Gulfpac* [1999] 1 Lloyd's Rep. Bank 86, and appeared to contemplate that the jurisdiction to grant such relief was flexible enough to embrace a claim for indemnity where the underlying claim is a claim in damages, though the claim in that case did relate to a specific sum. This approach is to be welcomed, since it may be a matter of pure chance whether the surety's obligation sounds in debt or in damages and the cloud hanging over the surety's head (see below) is likely to be just as threatening in the latter case as it is in the former. However, the form of order which the surety may obtain is unlikely to be an order for the payment of a specific sum of money by D to C, unless the quantum of the damages has been ascertained before the hearing of S's application. In this type of case, it would probably be more appropriate for D to be ordered to set aside a particular fund for the payment of the creditor or to provide some other form of security for the debt. If this is not done, S may be confined to obtaining declaratory relief, which is less likely to be of practical use to him.

It has already been noted above that the fact that no demand has been made on either the principal or the surety is no bar to *quia timet* relief. In *Thomas v Nottingham Incorporated Football Club Ltd* [1972] Ch. 596, Goff J. resolved the previous uncertainty as to whether a surety can seek *quia timet* relief when the guarantee is payable on demand and no demand has been made by the creditor. In the earlier case of *Bradford v Gammon* [1925] Ch. 132, the overdraft of a partnership was repayable only on demand. The executor of one of the partners was refused *quia timet* relief against the surviving partners, based on an express indemnity in the articles of partnership, because no demand had been made for repayment. In *Thomas v Nottingham FC* Goff J. distinguished the case as turning on the particular terms of the contract. After reviewing all the authorities, he held that relief was available to the surety even though no demand had been made:

> "The principle is that the surety is entitled to remove the cloud which is hanging over him. It would be strange indeed, as it seems to me, if he can do that where no demand is required, notwithstanding there is no present likelihood of any attempt to recover against him, and yet when his liability arises as between himself and the creditor only on demand, he cannot seek to remove the cloud until it has started to rain, especially as the provision in the contract of suretyship that the creditor must make a demand upon the surety is clearly a provision for the benefit of the surety."[71]

If this reasoning is correct, however, it is difficult to ascertain why any distinction should be drawn between the absence of a demand and the non-

---

71 *ibid.*, at 606.

fulfilment of any other condition precedent to liability of the surety. The rationale behind the judgment appears to be that the surety is entitled to relief in equity at any time after the principal debt becomes repayable to the creditor,[72] If that is so, it is difficult to see what value may be placed on a contract of suretyship in many cases—for example where the guarantee is of a loan repayable on demand. Nevertheless, the case has stood unchallenged for over 30 years, and was applied by the Court of Appeal in *Stimpson v Smith* [1999] Ch. 340. In *Papamichael v National Westminster Bank* [2002] 1 Lloyd's Rep. 332 (not a case of suretyship) the Court went further, and held that a Bank was entitled to *quia timet* relief on the basis that the claimant had a good arguable case against it in respect of a claim, which, if proved, would entitle the bank to a full indemnity against the Pt 20 defendant. That case was a rather special one, however, where there was evidence that the Pt 20 defendant had been dishonest and was likely to dissipate his assets so as to avoid liability to the bank. The *quia timet* jurisdiction was used to get round the technical argument that the cause of action against him had not yet arisen and that a freezing injunction could not be granted in such circumstances. It remains to be seen whether a similar approach would be adopted in the context of a claim by a guarantor against a principal debtor who does not display similar characteristics.

It is unnecessary for the surety to establish that the creditor has threatened to sue him, or that the creditor has refused to sue the principal: *Ascherson v Tredegar Dry Dock & Wharf Co Ltd* [1909] 2 Ch. 401 at 408, disapproving *dicta* to the contrary in *Padwick v Stanley* [1852] 9 Hare 627.[73] However it may be that the Court will not grant him an order for exoneration unless it considers that he is insufficiently protected by his right to call on the principal to indemnify him after payment—for example because there is evidence that the principal will ignore those obligations or that he is unlikely to be able to meet them because of his worsening financial state. In *Rowland v Gulfpac Ltd* [1999] 1 Lloyd's Rep. Bank. 86 Rix J. said at 98:

> "Equity . . . will give relief in circumstances where the common law will not, and even give relief in a situation of quia timet before a loss has actually occurred, but only when there is reasonably good, perhaps clear evidence, that a liability will fall on the party entitled to be indemnified and that the person obliged to indemnify clearly proposes to ignore his obligations. What is needed is a sufficiently clear right to an indemnity even if the cause of action at law is not yet complete, together with a clear indication that the indemnifier is going to ignore his obligations".

In *Papamichael v National Westminster Bank* [2002] 1 Lloyd's Rep. 332 Judge Chambers Q.C. cited that passage with approval. He said (in para.61)

---

72 See the passage from the judgment of Swinfen Eady J. in *Ascherson v Tredegar Dry Dock and Wharf Co Ltd* [1909] 2 Ch. 401 at 406 relied upon by Goff J. at 601.
73 See also *Mathews v Saurin* (1893) 31 L.R. I.R. 181.

that *Re Anderson-Berry* showed that the threat [to the surety] did not necessarily have to be a great one before the discretion to grant such relief could be exercised: a cloud had to be clearly visible, but it did not have to be especially ominous. He also said that the nature of *quia timet* relief was not yet fixed, and that what needs to be clearly shown if the jurisdiction is to be exercised is that in the event of the occurrence of a contingency, there will be a right over against the person against whom the relief is sought.

It has been suggested that the guarantor should admit his own liability in respect of the guaranteed obligation, but this is not something which the leading commentators in this field have ever regarded as an essential prerequisite of *quia timet* relief.[74] It has already been seen that a guarantor who has discrete defences under his guarantee may not be able to recover from the principal the costs of unsuccessfully defending an action brought by the creditor against him, if those defences would only assist the guarantor. It is one thing for the principal to object to an order for exoneration on the basis that he, the principal, is not liable to the creditor and that the guarantor should first resist payment on that basis (because it would be unfair to make him pay in those circumstances). It is quite another for the principal to object on the basis that the guarantor should first raise any independent defences which are or may be available to him (at his own expense) and seek exoneration only if he loses. If the principal is facing a claim for an indemnity he is unlikely to be able to challenge it on the grounds that the guarantor should not have paid. It is submitted that the better view is that it is not incumbent on the guarantor to admit his own liability before he seeks *quia timet* relief, and that all he needs to do is prove that the *principal's* liability has accrued, and that the creditor may make a claim against him on the guarantee. He does not have to go further and prove that the claim on the guarantee is bound to succeed or that he has exhausted all available defences. Indeed the *Papamichael* case suggests that all he needs to show that there is a cloud hanging over him is a good arguable case that he is liable to the creditor. If the principal is liable to the creditor, then it is difficult to see why he has any basis for objecting to an order requiring him to discharge that liability and thereby release the guarantor from any liability which he may (arguably) have to the creditor. However, since the relief is equitable, it is arguable that the availability of discrete defences under the guarantee is a factor which the court may be entitled to take into account when determining whether it is appropriate to grant an immediate order.

It also appears to be irrelevant that the principal may not be in a position to comply with the order. In *Watt v Mortlock* [1964] 1 Ch. 84 at 87–88,

---

74 *Mathews v Saurin* (fn.73 above), *Hughes-Hallett v Indian Mammoth Gold Mines Co* (1882) 22 Ch. D. 561 at 564; and see the way in which the matter was put in argument in *Watt v Mortlock* [1964] 1 Ch. at 86: "A surety has a right in equity to compel his principal debtor to relieve him from his admitted liability under a guarantee." See the discussion in O'Donovan & Phillips (English ed., Sweet & Maxwell, 2003) at paras 11–130 to 11–156; *Halsbury's Laws* (Vol. 20, 4th ed. reissue 2004) at para.239; *Chitty on Contracts* (*op. cit.*) Vol. 2, para.44–115.

Wilberforce J. considered certain of the earlier cases and remarked that either it was apparent that the principal had sufficient assets to pay the debt, or there was no evidence either way. In *Watt v Mortlock* itself, the defendant had not defended the proceedings and the judge was clearly troubled about the prospects of enforcing any order which he made. He held that the appropriate course would be to provide in the order that the plaintiff should have liberty to apply in the event of the defendant failing to pay. On such an application the court would then consider, in the light of the facts and in particular, the defendant's circumstances, what, if any, further relief should be granted.[75] This is now included in the usual form of order. In the Australian case of *Salcedo v Mawarie Mining Co Pty Ltd* (1991) 6 A.C.S.R. 197, the judge recognised that the payment which he ordered the receivers to make directly to the guaranteed creditor might be challenged as a preference if the principal was wound up, but saw no alternative because there was a substantial risk that if the proceeds of sale of the company's plant and equipment were paid to the directors, they might be dissipated and thus render nugatory the surety's claim to an indemnity.

Procedure

10–027   Like any order for the payment of money, an order granting *quia timet* relief is unlikely to be granted "without notice": see the observations of Megarry J. in *Felton v Callis* [1969] 1 Q.B. 200 at 218–219.[76] The same reasoning would generally preclude the grant of interim *quia timet* relief, save in a very exceptional case. If there is some very good reason why the surety's application should be dealt with expeditiously, he would be best advised to seek a speedy trial of his application. The action would normally be commenced in the Chancery Division of the High Court, though the facts of a particular case may make some other division more suitable.

In *Wolmershausen v Gullick* [1893] 2 Ch. 514 it was suggested that the creditor should be made a party to an action in which it is sought to obtain an order that the principal should pay the creditor. This is the normal practice, and obviously makes sense, because it ensures that the creditor is bound by the decision of the Court, and the court will be in a position to ensure that he cannot undermine the value of the relief by seeking to recover from the guarantor first. Although it has been said that it is only in "exceptional circumstances"[77] that the court will restrain the creditor from enforcing the guarantee against the surety, the court would surely wish to

---

75 This could prove problematic. The Debtors Acts 1869 and 1878 would probably preclude any order for committal or sequestration in the normal case: see RSC Ord. 45, r.1 especially the commentary at 45/1/24 and 45/1/32–6, Administration of Justice Act 1970, s.11, and *Felton v Callis* [1969] 1 Q.B. 200. In an appropriate case, the court might appoint a receiver.

76 The case was concerned with an application for a writ *ne exeat regno*, but the proceedings were *quia timet* proceedings.

77 *Per* Lawrence L.J. in *Re Anderson-Berry* [1928] 1 Ch. 290 at 309 and see *Mahoney v Mcmanus* (1981) 55 A.L.J.R. 673 at 675.

ensure that any form of relief granted to the surety was not rendered nugatory and it is only by having all three parties before it that it can be certain of this. If there is any evidence of collusion between the principal and the creditor, or dealings between them which might prejudice his position, then the guarantor will be in a strong position to seek an order restraining the creditor from enforcing the guarantee. For example, the guarantee might contain a clause entitling the creditor to release the principal or reach a compromise with him or release securities without releasing the guarantor, but an arrangement under which the creditor did release other securities to the principal might be sufficient to persuade the court that it would be inequitable to allow him to enforce the guarantee until a certain time had elapsed, to enable an order for *quia timet* relief to be complied with. Obviously if any form of order is sought against the creditor as well as the principal, he should be joined as a defendant. Likewise, if there is any dispute between the principal and the creditor about whether the former is liable, it is essential that it be resolved in proceedings to which they are both made parties. Indeed it may be impossible for the surety to find out the relevant facts without disclosure by both creditor and principal of the dealings between them: a classic example is where the creditor has made a demand on the guarantor under a guarantee of an overdraft, but the guarantor does not know whether the underlying account is still operative, or whether a demand has been made on the principal to repay, or whether some other event of default has triggered a liability to repay the overdraft in the absence of a demand. In such a case, if the creditor is uncooperative, the guarantor may not have sufficient time to seek pre-action disclosure from him, and joining him as party to the *quia timet* proceedings may be the most prudent course to adopt. If the creditor is not made a party, the Court will be unable to order the principal or his representative to put the surety in funds to meet the demand, instead of paying the creditor directly, because this would not discharge the principal's liability to the creditor and the principal would be at risk of having to pay twice. Nevertheless, there are a number of reported decisions of *quia timet* relief being granted without the creditor being joined, and joinder of the creditor, though desirable, is not an essential requirement.[78]

Practical considerations

The right to *quia timet* relief is potentially a very powerful weapon in the hands of the surety, though in practical terms it is unlikely to create any real advantage if the principal is already insolvent or becomes insolvent before paying the creditor. Despite that drawback, it is one of the most

10–028

---

78 The objection was taken, but not pressed, in *Ascherson v Tredegar Dry Dock and Wharf Co Ltd* [1909] 1 Ch. 401, and Swinfen Eady J. granted the relief sought. For other examples of cases in which the creditor was not joined see *Tate v Crewdson* [1938] Ch. 869; *Watt v Mortlock* (above); *Thomas v Nottingham Incorporated Football Club Ltd* [1972] Ch. 596.

effective ways for a surety to safeguard himself against the risks which he undoubtedly runs if he has to pay first.

The surety may be entitled to obtain an order that the principal should pay the creditor at a time when neither the principal nor the creditor wishes this to happen. A prime example is where the directors of a company fall out, and one of their number terminates his guarantee of the company's overdraft at a time when the remaining directors need the overdraft to run the company and most of the assets which could be used to meet the company's obligations are not easily or readily liquifiable. It may be that the bank is perfectly happy with the situation, and has no immediate intention of claiming against either the company or the ex-director. It is also possible that the ex-director is motivated by ill-will, but unless it can be shown that his behaviour is such as to debar him from seeking equitable relief (on the basis that he is not coming to equity with clean hands), the likelihood is that he could obtain an order which could seriously damage the company.

From the surety's point of view this may well put him in a superior bargaining position. The only practical solution from the principal's point of view may be to persuade the creditor to accept some new form of security in place of the guarantee, and to release the surety from his contract.

Accordingly, it may be that the only certain way to avoid this type of difficulty would be for the agreement between the principal and the surety to expressly exclude the latter's right to *quia timet* relief. The enforceability of such an agreement does not appear to have been considered judicially, probably because it is still quite rare for a written agreement to be made between the principal and surety. On the other hand, some standard form bank guarantees do contain terms which either purport to exclude the right to *quia timet* relief altogether, or seek to postpone it until at least after a demand has been made on the surety. It remains to be seen whether such a provision would be upheld by a court, even in cases where the surety is not a consumer. If the surety has mortgaged property, the term might be susceptible to attack on the grounds that it is a clog on the equity of redemption. It might also be regarded as contrary to public policy to purport to exclude the right to seek equitable relief (though the courts appear to be willing to recognise an agreement not to rely on an estoppel). In any event, it is difficult to see what such a term would actually achieve, because it is unlikely that the creditor could prove that he had suffered any loss by reason of a breach. Accordingly, the practical efficacy of such a term in the guarantee is questionable unless the principal is also a party, and the addressee of the promise not to seek such relief (subject to the Contracts (Rights of Third Parties) Act 1999, discussed in Chapter 2, at para.2–007).

Right to petition for winding-up

10–029   The Companies Act 1948, s.224, first enabled a contingent creditor of a company to present a petition for its winding-up. The relevant statutory provision is now s.124(1) of the Insolvency Act 1986. Since a guarantor of the company's debts is a contingent creditor, this right is available to him.[79] The former requirement that such a creditor must give such security for costs as the court thinks reasonable and show a prima facie case for winding-up (*e.g.* that the company is unable to pay its debts as they fall due), before the court could hear the petition, was repealed by Sch.12 to the Insolvency Act.

In practice, this right could prove useful, as the following example illustrates:

> S, a director and surety of D Co, has guaranteed its trading account with the bank. D has suffered major trading losses and S is concerned that it has no realistic prospect of trading itself out of its present financial difficulties. Meanwhile the account at the bank is seriously overdrawn and S's contingent liability to the bank as guarantor is increasing. S's co-directors disagree with him about the state of the company. Whether or not he decides to resign as director, or terminates the guarantee on notice to the bank and seeks *quia timet* relief, S may present a petition to wind up the company in his capacity as guarantor of its debts.

One major drawback to this course of action is that the surety will be unable to prove in the winding-up unless he has paid the company's debt: *Re Fenton Ex p. Fenton Textile Association Ltd* [1931] 1 Ch. 85.[80] He could therefore find that by precipitating the winding-up of the company he has damaged, rather than improved, his position: if the company is insolvent, there is every reason for the creditor to pursue him and he may have prevented any possibility of recoupment.

Right to recover damages

Where the principal has expressly covenanted with the surety to pay him a certain sum by way of indemnity or payment for the surety undertaking the obligations of suretyship, and makes default, the surety may sue him in accordance with the terms of the covenant regardless of whether he has paid any sum to the creditor.[81]   **10–030**

Similarly, if the principal, creditor and surety enter into a tripartite contract under which the principal agrees to pay the creditor on a certain day, and he fails to do so, the surety may sue him for damages and recover the full sum due to the creditor. However, in either case the surety is then obliged to pay the amount recovered to the creditor: *Loosemore v Radford* (1842) 9 M. & W. 657.[82] If the principal pays the creditor directly, after he

---

79 Reversing the position under *Re Vron Colliery Co* (1882) 20 Ch. D. 442.
80 For the rights of a surety who has not paid the creditor in full, on the insolvency of the principal, see Ch.13, at para.13–005.
81 *Martin v Court* (1788) 2 Term Rep. 640; *Toussaint v Martinnant* (1787) 2 Term Rep. 100.
82 See also *Re Richardson* [1911] 2 K.B. 705. *Cf.* the position if a third party indemnifies the surety: see *Re Law Guarantee Trust and Accident Society Ltd, Liverpool Mortgage Insurance Co's case* [1914] 2 Ch. 617, *per* Buckley L.J. at 622–623.

should have paid the surety, the surety would probably only be entitled to nominal damages.[83]

---

83 *ibid.*

Chapter 11

Rights of the Surety Against the Creditor

Nature and origin of rights

The surety is entitled, by virtue of having assumed liability under the **11–001** guarantee, to a number of equitable rights which the creditor must respect. If the creditor fails to respect those rights, the surety may be discharged.[1] The common origin of these rights is the equitable principle that the person primarily liable for a debt or obligation should bear its whole burden in relief of those who may be secondarily liable for the debt or obligation.[2] If there is deficient performance on the part of the principal, the burden should then be borne equally by those who are subject to a similar secondary liability.[3] In *Anson v Anson* [1953] 1 Q.B. 636 at 641–642, Pearson J. analysed this principle as based on the contractual intention of the parties. He said:

> "The intention as between the two . . . normally is that the principal debtor shall remain the principal debtor; it is his debt and his obligation and he is expected to pay it. If the surety is called upon to pay and does pay, that for the time being defeats the intention of the parties that the debt shall be and remain that of the principal debtor. In order to put that position right, and to restore it to the position intended by the two of them by their original contractual intention, it is necessary that the right of reimbursement should be read into the contract or inferred to be one of the terms of the contract. The essence of the matter is that the principal debt is the primary obligation of the principal debtor, while the liability of the surety is only a secondary liability, and it is the intention as between the surety and the principal debtor that the position should be preserved. That is the explanation on contractual lines of the implied term which confers the right of reimbursement."

By contrast, in *Brooks Wharf & Bull Wharf Ltd v Goodman Bros* [1937] 1 K.B. 523 at 544 and 545, Lord Wright M.R. explained the right of

---

1 See Ch.9 *passim*, and especially paras 9–041 *et seq.*
2 *Duncan, Fox & Co v North & South Wales Bank* (1880) 6 App. Cas. 1, esp. 19–20 *per* Lord Selbourne L.C.; *Anson v Anson* [1953] 1 Q.B. 636.
3 *Dering v Winchelsea (Earl)* (1787) 2 Bos. & P. 270.

recoupment by a secondary debtor against a principal debtor as arising out of the enrichment of the principal debtor by the discharge of his liability, and upon what the court perceives to be the justice of the case.[4]

It is on the same basis that equity confers upon the surety certain rights against the creditor, namely that the surety should not be liable other than co-extensively with the principal, and that once the surety is liable, the creditor should not be permitted to bring down the whole weight of the obligation on the surety alone.[5] The surety's rights fall into two categories, namely rights which protect the surety from prejudicial dealing by the creditor, and rights of subrogation, which allow the surety to stand in the shoes of the creditor. These rights do not necessarily arise upon discharge of the obligation of the principal, but at the time the surety assumes his obligations under the guarantee, and upon the creditor having notice that he is acting as surety.[6] From the time of that notice, the creditor must do nothing to prejudice the rights of the surety.[7] Where the nature of the role of the surety is not apparent, the burden lies on the surety to prove that the creditor was aware that he was acting as such.[8] The creditor's agreement is unnecessary insofar as the assumption of the role of surety affects the principal,[9] and if the creditor knows that a person who contracts with him as principal is in fact undertaking the liability as a surety, then the creditor will be bound by that person's rights as surety even though the contract was under seal.[10] The creditor is bound to respect the surety's rights as such by the equitable doctrine of notice, and not by contract, and notice received after the contract is entered into is sufficient to bind the creditor.[11]

The rights of the surety arise not from the contract of guarantee but from the relationship arising between the surety and the creditor.[12] Although they can be varied by the contractual provisions of the guarantee, these rights form part of every guarantee relationship.

---

4 There is a view that the approach of Lord Wright M.R. is to be preferred to that of Pearson J.: see McGuinness, *The Law of Guarantee* (*op. cit.*), p.193. However, see Goff and Jones, *The Law of Restitution* (6th ed., 2002) paras 15–020, 15–021, where the view is expressed that the surety holds a contractual right of indemnity against the principal which can be exercised regardless of any benefit conferred on him by the discharge of the liability by the surety. The authorities show, however, that the rights of a surety against the creditor do not arise out of the contract but the treatment of the relationship of surety and creditor in equity: see, *e.g. Greenough v McLelland* (1860) 2 E. & E. 429; *Pooley v Harradine* (1857) 7 E. & B. 431.

5 *Dering v Winchelsea (Earl)* (1787) 2 Bos. & P. 270; *Craythorne v Swinburne* (1807) 14 Ves. 160; but see the discussion at para.11–002 below.

6 *Strong v Foster* (1855) 17 C.B.201; *Pooley v Harradine* (1857) 7 E. & B. 431; *Dixon v Steel* [1901] 2 Ch. 602; but see *Ewart v Latta* (1865) 4 Macq. 983. Extrinsic evidence is admissible to prove that the creditor had notice: but see *Hollier v Eyre* (1840) 9 Cl. & Fin. 1.

7 See *Rouse v Bradford Banking Co* [1894] A.C. 586.

8 *Harris v Ferguson* (1922) 63 D.L.R. 672.

9 *Rouse v Bradford Banking Co* [1894] A.C. 586.

10 *Wythes v Labouchere* (1859) 3 De G. & J. 593; *White v Corbett* (1859) 1 E. & E. 692.

11 *Greenough v McLelland* (1860) 2 E. & E. 429.

12 See n.4 above.

Rights of the surety before payment or performance

Rights of the surety before demand

Is there a right to compel the creditor to pursue the principal?

Before the surety has been called upon to perform the guaranteed **11–002** obligation, but after that obligation has accrued, it has been said that the surety has the right to compel the creditor himself to press the principal for performance.[13] This right is said to arise from the equitable principle that a creditor could "be controlled and prevented from enforcing its legal right inequitably against one alone of the sureties".[14] It has also been said that the right arises in order to ensure that the principal bears the whole burden of the guaranteed debt in relief of his sureties.[15] The most commonly cited authority for the existence of this right is the *obiter* statement of A. L. Smith L.J. in *Rouse v Bradford Banking Co* [1894] 2 Ch. 32 at 75, where he said, in the course of explaining the reason why a surety is discharged by the giving of time to the principal:[16]

> "I apprehend that the main reason is that a *surety is entitled at any time to require the creditor to call upon the principal debtor to pay off the debt,* or himself to pay off the debt, and that when he has paid it off he is at once entitled in the creditor's name to sue the principal debtor, and if the creditor has bound himself to give time to the principal debtor, the surety cannot do either one or the other of these things until the time so given has elapsed, and it is said that by reason of this the surety's position is altered to his detriment without his consent."[17] (*Emphasis added*)

Certainly, the right did exist under Roman law, where sureties could compel the creditor to exhaust his remedies against the principal before having recourse to the sureties unless the creditor could show that this would be futile because the principal was absent or insolvent or had expressly waived their right.[18] Many jurisdictions whose domestic law is based on Roman civil law have adopted it.[19] It is this, together with the

---

13 See *Halsbury's Laws* (reissue 2004) Vol. 20, para.219; Rowlatt, *Principal and Surety* (4th ed.), pp.132–133 (1982); the views of the editors of Rowlatt have changed somewhat in the 5th ed. (1999): see below.

14 *Wolmershausen v Gullick* [1893] 2 Ch. 514 at 522 *per* Wright J.; *Dering v Winchelsea (Earl)* (1787) 2 Bos. & P. 270; *Craythorne v Swinburne* (1807) 14 Ves. 160.

15 *Anson v Anson* [1953] 1 Q.B. 636.

16 As to which see Ch.9, paras 9–029–9–034.

17 See Ch.9. See also *Newton v Chorlton* (1853) 10 Hare 346, *per* Turner V.-C. at 652; *Craythorne v Swinburne* (1807) 14 Ves. 160; *Wolmershausen v Gullick* [1893] 2 Ch. 514.

18 De Colyar, *Law of Guarantee*, (3rd ed., 1897), p.148.

19 As have certain common law jurisdictions: a significant minority of states in the USA have adopted the doctrine of *Pain v Packard* 13 Johns (NY) 174 (1816) either judicially or by legislation. This case decided that where the defendant is merely a surety and he requests the creditor to go against a solvent principal when the debt is due, the creditor is bound to

authorities cited above, which appears to have prompted the editors of Rowlatt, *Principal and Surety*, (4th ed., 1982) to depart from the views of their eminent predecessor in the 3rd edition in suggesting that the surety has an equitable right to compel the creditor to pursue the principal. It is submitted that this view is untenable, is contrary to authority, and has no basis in English law or equity. In the 5th edition of Rowlatt, the editors have implicitly retreated from this view, although they have said that the contrary is "still arguable".[20] The point therefore continues to merit attention.

The editors of Rowlatt rely strongly on the dicta of Wright J. in *Wolmershausen v Gullick* [1893] 2 Ch. 514, and the authorities cited there, including the views of Lord Eldon in *Craythorne v Swinburne* (1807) 14 Ves. 160 who decided (at 163) that *Dering v Winchelsea (Earl)* (1787) 2 Bos. & P. 270 was authority for the proposition that "the creditor, who can call upon all, shall not be at liberty to fix one with the payment of the whole debt".

However, Wright J.'s remarks were directed at the surety's rights to recover contribution from his co-sureties. In that context it is true that the creditor may be prevented from imposing the entire burden of the debt on one surety alone, in the sense that equity will adjust the surety's position, if he has paid more than his pro rata burden of the debt, by giving him rights of contribution against his co-sureties. Furthermore, the surety is entitled, as against the creditor, to have his rights against his co-sureties preserved. This cannot, however, be equated with an equitable right to prevent the creditor bringing down the burden upon the surety *as opposed to the principal.* What Lord Eldon meant in *Craythorne v Swinburne* was that the creditor should not unduly burden one surety of several, rather than the surety instead of the principal. Indeed it is settled law that the creditor is at liberty to fix one surety with payment of the principal debt. Where the principal fails to perform his obligation when called upon to do so by the creditor, the surety, in the absence of express stipulation,[21] may not compel the creditor to sue the principal before claiming or commencing action against the surety,[22] even though he is solvent.[23] Nor is the surety entitled,

---

use due diligence against the principal to exonerate the surety. In New South Wales, Victoria and Western Australia, the Credit Act 1984 in some circumstances requires prior proceedings against the principal, or requires the surety and principal to be sued jointly. See also O'Donovan & Phillips, *The Modern Contract of Guarantee* 3rd ed., 1996), pp.463–465; and see O'Donovan & Phillips, English ed. (2003), paras 11–11 *ff.*

20 See Rowlatt (5th ed., 1999), p.144; see also the discussion in O'Donovan & Phillips (3rd ed., 1996), pp.537–541; and see O'Donovan & Phillips, English ed. (2003), paras 11–13 to 11–28.

21 When rights of marshalling may arise, see para.11–015 below.

22 This principle seems to have been implicitly applied in *China & South Seas Bank v Tan* [1990] 1 A.C. 536, PC and in *TSB Bank Plc v Dickson* (unreported, July 24, 1998, CA), but see *Cottin v Blane* (1795) 2 Anst. 544 and the discussion below. See also *Re Marley* [1976] 1 W.L.R. 952; *cf. Re Mitchell Houghton Ltd* [1970] 14 C.B.R.301, Ont Supreme Ct.

23 In *Holl v Hadley* (1828) 5 Bing. 54, the guarantee provided that it was a condition precedent to the surety's liability that the creditor should use "utmost efforts and legal proceedings against the principal". In *Musket v Rodgers* (1839) 5 Bing. N.C. 728, the creditor undertook first to go against available securities.

at least before the creditor has made a demand of him,[24] to insist that the creditor have recourse first to securities for the obligation before suing him.[25] Nor is he entitled to insist that the creditor sues his co-sureties.[26] The surety's liability usually arises on default by the principal, even though in certain cases a demand may be necessary.[27] Even where the surety deposits the amount of the guaranteed debt, he is still bound to indemnify the creditor against risk, delay and expense before he can compel the creditor to sue the principal.[28] Any unequal or unfair distribution of the burden of the debt between the sureties *inter se is* regulated by the surety's rights of contribution.[29]

The correct view of the law is, therefore, that the surety who has not paid the principal for which he is liable cannot require the creditor to proceed against the principal, or co-surety, or against any security for the debt guaranteed, before having recourse to the surety. This has the highest authority. In *Ewart v Latta* (1865) 4 Macq. 983, HL, Lord Westbury said (at 987):

> "until [the surety] has discharged himself of his liability, until he has fulfilled his own contract, he has no right to dictate terms, to prescribe any duty or to make any demand upon his creditor."

And at 989:

> "It is quite a misapprehension of the principle of equity which entitles the surety to call upon the creditor to discuss the principal debtor. Unquestionably the surety had no such right except he undertook to pay the whole debt."

Further, in *Jackson v Digby* (1854) 2 W.R. 540, the Court of Appeal held that a surety, in the absence of circumstances to prevent him from recovering over against the principal, had no equity to restrain the creditor from proceeding against him on the grounds that he could recover against the principal. In *McLean v Discount and Finance Ltd* (1939) 64 C.L.R. 312, Latham C.J. said (at 328):

> "A creditor to whom guarantees have been given may compel any surety to pay according to his contract. He is not bound to take any steps to distribute the burden among the sureties. Thus a surety who has guaranteed the whole of the debt may be compelled to pay the whole debt even though there are other sureties."

---

24 *Belfast Banking v Stanley* (1867) 15 W.R. 989; *Rede v Farr* (1817) 6 M. & S. 121; *Lilley v Hewitt* (1822) 11 Price 494; *Re Brown, Brown v Brown* [1893] 2 Ch. 300.
25 *Wright v Simpson* (1802) 6 Ves. 714, where it was observed that there was no obligation on the part of the creditor of active diligence against the principal.
26 See *e.g. McLean v Discount and Finance Ltd* (1939) 64 C.L.R. 312, at 328 *per* Latham C.J.
27 See the discussion of when a surety's liability arises in Ch.7, paras 7–002–7–011.
28 *Wright v Simpson* (1802) 6 Ves.714.
29 As to which see Ch.12.

The rationale of this principle is that it is the duty of the surety, and not that of the creditor, to ensure that the principal performs his obligations to the creditor,[30] and the creditor should be entirely at liberty to pursue whichever remedies his contract affords him, without having to adopt a course of action at the compulsion of a person who remains his debtor.[31]

In support of the "arguable" right to compel the creditor, the editors of Rowlatt have put forward illustrations of cases where the surety has been able to compel his creditor to exercise a particular right of recourse. *Cottin v Blane* (1795) 2 Anstr. 544 is cited as authority for the proposition that the creditor is compellable by the surety where the creditor has the opportunity to recover the debt from the principal which is not open to the surety. In that case the surety had guaranteed due performance of a charterparty. The vessel was detained by the French government, which was prepared to pay compensation to the (neutral) American owners but not to the surety (who was not neutral). It was held that the creditor should be compelled to seek compensation from the fund before pursuing the surety. However, this decision can be justified on the basis:

(a) that the creditor was not compelled to go against the principal, but an independent fund provided by a third party not as security for the performance of the charterparty but as compensation for its non-performance;

(b) that the fund was personal to the creditor, and the surety could never have had recourse to it even by rights of subrogation; and

(c) that relief was granted only upon the surety paying the debt into court.[32]

It has also fair to regard that case as having been decided on its own facts and as an exercise in pragmatism rather than as containing any statement of principle.[33]

In *Re Westzinthus* (1833) 5 Ad. & B. 817, the creditor held goods from the principal and from the surety to secure the guaranteed debt, and he was compelled to apply the proceeds from the principal's goods in satisfaction of the debt before the proceeds of those of the surety. However, this is an illustration of marshalling[34] rather than of any right to compel the creditor to sue the principal, the goods having been sold and the proceeds received by the creditor; it is explicable on the basis that the receipt of the proceeds constituted payment by the principal.[35] In *Ex p. Goodman* (1818) 3 Madd.

---

30 *Moschi v Lep Air Services Ltd* [1973] A.C. 331.
31 This reflects the modern approach: see *China & South Seas Bank v Tan* [1990] 1 A.C. 536, PC.
32 See the discussion of *Cottin v Blane* in Rowlatt (5th ed., 1999), p.145.
33 That was the view of Humphrey Lloyd Q.C. in *Laing Management Ltd v Aegon Insurance Co (UK) Ltd* (1997) 86 B.L.R. 70 at 116.
34 See below, para.11–015.
35 See also *Duncan, Fox and Co v North and South Wales Bank* (1880) 6 App. Cas. 1, where (at 14) Lord Selbourne L.C. said that where a creditor had received the proceeds from the securities, it is difficult to distinguish the receipt of such a sum from payment on account by the principal.

373 it was held that the sureties had an equity that the creditor should first prove his debt against the insolvent principal's estate before proceeding against the sureties' security. There is no other authority to support this proposition, and it is thought to be incorrect.[36]

In *Law v East India Co* (1799) 4 Ves. 824, the creditor had extracted a payment from the surety by means of duress. It was ordered to refund the amount to the surety pending the determination of the rights of the parties. This is not, as the editors of Rowlatt in the 4th edition said that it was, an example of the exercise of an equity by the surety against the creditor: first, the court did not compel action by the creditor against the principal, and second, the sum paid by the surety would in any event have been recoverable as having been paid under duress. In the 5th edition, the editors rightly recognise that *Law v East India Co* was a special case, turning on its own facts.

Accordingly, the suggestion that the surety has a right to compel the creditor to sue the principal is wholly at odds with the freedom of the creditor to claim against the surety. Since the weight of authority supports the principle that the creditor, in the absence of any agreement to the contrary, should not be obliged to pursue the principal before claiming from the surety, it would seem that any right to compel the creditor to pursue the principal may, in most ordinary cases, very simply be defeated by the creditor making a demand of the principal, notwithstanding that the creditor has not made a demand of the surety. Further, it is difficult to see why this right should exist universally. In many cases the guarantee will provide that the surety's liability is not to arise until the principal has defaulted or there has been a demand on the surety.[37] It would seem that in such cases, on the basis of the authorities that suggest the existence of a right in the surety to compel the creditor to pursue the principal, such a right would exist without any corresponding liability on the part of the surety having yet arisen, and where such might never arise. In such a situation there is no justification for equity to come to the assistance of the surety.

Further still, in many cases the surety may revoke the guarantee as to future liabilities,[38] and so it is hard to see to what practical use the right

---

36 See O'Donovan & Phillips, English ed. (2003), para.11–24. The case of *Re Westzinthus* (1833) 5 Ad. & B. 817 relates to the position after sale of the securities, when the surety may marshal them in his favour.

37 Certainly any such right that the surety might have to compel the creditor to pursue the principal would have to be circumscribed by the contractual relationship between the creditor and the principal. For example, where the creditor has made a term loan to the principal, he may not be entitled, absent a breach of the loan contract by the principal or a clcear provision in the loan agreement, to make a demand on him for the full amount until the term has expired: Paget's *Law of Banking* (*op. cit.*), pp.189–90. See *Lloyds Bank Plc v Lampert* [1999] Ll. Rep. Bank. 138, and *Bank of Ireland v AMCD (Property Holdings) Ltd* [2001] 2 All E.R. (Comm) 894, in which the loan agreements did contain clear terms. It would seem that if the creditor was not entitled to make a demand, the surety certainly could have no right to compel him to do so.

38 See Ch.8.

may be put. It is submitted, therefore, that the alleged right to compel the creditor to pursue the principal before proceeding against the surety is an invention. Lord Westbury L.C.'s notion as expressed in *Ewart v Latta* that the surety should not be entitled to dictate to the creditor has found sympathy in modern times;[39] and is consistent with guarantees being a low-cost and relatively burden-free form of personal security for the creditor.

The right to pay off and sue

11–003 At any time after the principal obligation has fallen due, the surety is entitled to pay off the creditor (or perform the obligation) and to sue the principal. The authority for this proposition is *Swire v Redman* (1876) 1 Q.B.D., *per* Cockburn C.J. (at 53).[40] Prior to the Mercantile Law Amendment Act 1856 the surety who sought to exercise this right was obliged to sue in the creditor's name, joining the creditor as a party to the action against the principal and giving the creditor an indemnity for his costs.[41] Section 4 of that enactment abolished the requirement that the surety had to sue in the creditor's name, and presumably also the requirement that an indemnity be provided. In *Swire v Redman*, Blackburn J. observed that he knew of no reported case where the right has ever been exercised.[42] It is difficult to envisage a situation in which the surety would wish to avail himself of this right. However, in *China & South Seas Bank Ltd v Tan* [1990] 1 A.C. 536, PC, it was suggested that the way for the surety to avoid the consequences of a continuing failure by the creditor to deal with securities for the debt which were declining in value was for him to pay off the debt and obtain a transfer of the securities to him from the creditor so that he could sell them. It does seem, therefore, that the right does have some practical use.

Where the surety has received securities from the principal for the guaranteed obligation, the creditor is not, generally, entitled to them,[43] unless he can establish that they have been given to the surety on trust to apply the proceeds in satisfaction of the debt.[44] The surety may make an assignment to the creditor of securities held from the principal in satisfaction of his

---

39 See *China & South Seas Bank v Tan* [1990] 1 A.C. 536, PC, a case which concerned the creditor's obligations in respect of securities held for the debt; see also *TSB Bank Plc v Dickson* (unreported, July 24, 1998, CA); *Re BCCI (No.8)* [1997] 3 W.L.R. 909; and *Mahomed v Morris* [2000] 2 B.C.L.C. 536.

40 See also *Rouse v Bradford Banking Co* [1894] 2 Ch. 32 at 75, namely the passage quoted at the beginning of para.11–002.

41 *Wright v Simpson* (1802) 6 Ves. 714.

42 It did happen in *Drager v Allison* [1959] 19 S.C.R. 661.

43 *Ex p. Waring* (1815) 19 Ves. 345. See also the cases cited in Rowlatt, *Principal and Surety*, (5th ed., 1999), pp.154–155, although those that relate to sureties for compositions are of little value following the enactment of the Insolvency Act 1986: see *Re A Debtor (No.2 of 1987)* [1989] 1 W.L.R. 271 *per* Nicholls L.J. at 276, and *Smith (SJ), Re Ex p. Braintree District Council* [1990] 2 A.C. 215 *per* Lord Jauncey at 237–238. It is doubtful whether they apply in the context of voluntary arrangements under the IA 1986, Pt VIII.

44 *Ex p. Waring* (1815) 19 Ves. 345; *Ex p. Rushforth* (1805) 10 Ves. 409. Compare this case with *Wilding v Richards* (1845) 1 Coll. 655, where the creditor had no notice of the conveyance to the surety and could not take advantage of it. See also Ch.13, para.13–017.

obligation.[45] However, it has been suggested that the right to make an assignment of security in satisfaction of the guaranteed debt is a right of the surety against the principal, and requires the consent of the creditor.[46] Where the creditor refuses to accept the payment, it is always open for the surety to pay the money into court and then proceed against the creditor.[47]

Fidelity bonds
Where the surety has guaranteed the good behaviour of an officeholder or employee, particular rights arise in his favour. If the surety discovers that the employee has been guilty of misconduct rendering him liable to dismissal, then the surety can insist upon the employer dismissing the employee.[48] Where the surety demands the employee's dismissal, but the employer fails to comply with the demand, the surety is discharged from future liability under the bond.[49] Where the employer discovers the employee's misconduct but the surety is ignorant of it, and the employer fails to disclose it to the surety but keeps the employee on, the surety will be discharged from liability for any further misconduct of the employee from the time of the discovery by the employer of the original misconduct.[50] Where he discovers that the employee is guilty of misconduct, the surety should demand that the bond be cancelled and delivered up to him, otherwise he runs the risk of being taken to consent to remaining liable in spite of the misconduct.[51]

11–004

However, the surety will not be discharged where the power of dismissal is not vested in the employer (*i.e.* the obligee under the bond) but in some third party who is not party to the bond, and where that party refuses to exercise the power.[52] However, where the employer does not request that the employee be dismissed, the surety may be discharged, on the grounds that the employer has acted to increase the surety's risk under the bond.

Rights of the surety upon demand

The right to raise the principal's defences
The general rule is that once payment has been demanded of him, the surety is entitled to raise against the creditor all legal and equitable defences to which the principal is entitled at the moment of demand.[53] In

11–005

---

45 *Paton v Wilkes* (1860) 8 Gr. 252 (Can).
46 See McGuinness, *The Law of Guarantee*, (*op. cit.*) para.7.05.
47 *Carter v White* (1884) 25 Ch. D. 666.
48 *Sanderson v Aston* (1873) L.R. 8 Exch. 73 at 77; *Burgess v Eve* (1872) L.R. 13 Eq. 450.
49 *Phillips v Foxall* (1872) L.R. 7 Q.B. 666.
50 *Sanderson v Aston* (1873) L.R. 8 Exch. 73; *Philips v Foxall* (1872) L.R. 7 Q.B. 666; *Enright v Falvey* (1879) 4 L.R.I.R. 397. Where circumstances show that the surety must have known of the misconduct, the onus is on him to prove his ignorance: *Caxton and Arrington Union v Dew* (1899) 68 L.J.Q.B. 380 at 383.
51 *Shepherd v Beecher* (1725) 2 P. Wms. 288.
52 *Caxton and Arrington Union v Dew* (1899) 68 L.J.Q.B. 380.
53 *Bechervaise v Lewis* (1872)L.R. 7 C.P. 372; *Oastler v Pound* (1863) 7 L.T. 852; *Murphy v Glass* (1869) L.R. 2 P.C. 408; *Alcoy and Gandia Ry and Harbour Co v Greenhill* (1897) 76 L.T. 542, (1898) 79 L.T. 257. See also generally Derham, *Set-Off* (3rd ed. 2003), Ch.18. Wood, *English and International Set-Off* (Sweet & Maxwell, 1989), paras 10.93 *et seq.*

Bechervaise v Lewis (1872) L.R. 7 C.P. 372, Willes J. (at 377) explained the basis of this right thus:

> "we have a creditor who is equally liable to the principal as the principal to him and against whom the principal has a good defence in law and equity and a surety who is entitled in equity to call upon the principal to exonerate him. In this state of things we are bound to conclude that the surety has a good defence in equity to the creditor."

Accordingly, not only must the defence or right of set-off be one which is available to the principal,[54] but it must be one which law and equity will recognise. For example, where the directors of a company guarantee borrowings by the company that are *ultra vires* the company, the directors cannot resist a claim by the creditor on the grounds that the principal obligation is unenforceable against the company on the grounds that it would be inequitable to allow the directors to take advantage of an *ultra vires* act of their own procuring.[55]

While a principal obligation which is unenforceable as being *ultra vires* the principal does not afford a defence to the surety, the surety will have a defence where the principal obligation is illegal.[56] Further, it is not generally necessary to join the principal to any action where the surety is raising a defence against the creditor that was open to the principal, but this may be desirable so that the surety may be bound by the result.[57]

Cross-claims and rights of set-off[58]

11–006 The general rule is that where the principal has a right of set-off or cross-claim against the creditor giving the principal a defence to the debt the subject of the guarantee, the surety is entitled to raise it as a defence to the

---

54 *Bowyear v Pawson* (1881) 6 Q.B.D. 540.

55 *Chambers v Manchester and Milford Ry Co* (1864) 5 B. & S. 588; *Yorkshire Railway Wagon Co v Maclure* (1881) 19 Ch. D. 478; *Garrard v James* [1925] Ch. 616. See the discussion on these cases in Ch.6, para.6–020. In any event these cases must be reviewed in the light of the Companies Act 1989, ss.108, 109 and 111, which have put an end to the *ultra vires* doctine insofar as it operated to invalidate transactions with third parties, although retaining directors' personal liability to the company for any loss arising out of *ultra vires* acts.

56 *Heald v O'Connor* [1971] 1 W.L.R. 497, where the sureties were entitled to defend the claim against them on the guarantee on the basis that the debenture which they had guaranteed was executed in contravention of s.54 of the Companies Act 1948 (now ss.151–8 of the Companies Act 1985). The contrast between the effects of illegality and *ultra vires* of the principal on the guarantee can be explained on the basis that in the former case the guarantee is tainted with the illegality of the principal contract making it itself unenforceable on that ground, whereas *ultra vires* has no such tainting effect. Fisher J. in that case (at 506) distinguished cases where the surety guaranteed only those sums which the creditor could lawfully demand from cases where the surety guaranteed sums which the principal had promised to pay but had not paid, whether the demand was lawful or not. The curious result is that sureties guaranteeing a company's liabilities are in a better position if the principal contract is illegal than if it is simply *ultra vires*: see further Ch.6, paras 6–018–6–020.

57 *Murphy v Glass* (1869) L.R. 2 P.C. 408. See further below paras 11–006–11–012.

58 See generally, Derham, *Set-Off* (3rd ed. 2003), Ch.18; Wood, *English and International Set-Off* (*op. cit.*) para.10.193; and the illuminating article by Professor John Phillips, "When should the guarantor be permitted to rely on the principal's set-off?" in [2001] L.M.C.L.Q. 321, 383.

creditor's claim.[59] For example, in *Bechervaise v Lewis* (1872) L.R. 7 C.P. 372, the surety who had joined in a promissory note given by the principal as the consideration for the assignment to him of certain debts was permitted to set off against a demand on the note certain of the debts which had been collected by the creditor but not yet paid over to the principal.

The surety is not seeking here to set up the principal's defence against the creditor as a set-off against his own liability under the contract of guarantee, since there is no assignment of the benefit of the principal's cross-claim: the surety is not in a position of assignee *vis-à-vis* the principal. What in fact the surety has is an equitable right to be exonerated from liability under the guarantee to the extent that the principal has a defence to the creditor's claim arising out of cross-demands between them.[60] This right is paramount to the principal's right to raise it by separate action against the creditor.[61]

Liquidated and unliquidated cross-claims

The right of the surety to take all his principal's cross-claims against the creditor by way of defence has its limitations. In *Cellulose Products Pty Ltd v Truda* (1970) 92 W.N. (NSW) 561, Isaacs J. reviewed all the authorities and held that a surety cannot claim unliquidated damages, either by way of set-off or counterclaim, in law or equity, which arose from a breach of contract between the creditor and the principal, or arising from any other claim for unliquidated damages that the principal may have against the creditor.[62] Nor can a surety take advantage of any claim that the principal debtor may have had to rescind the contract.[63] There are a number of justifications for this restriction.[64] These are that:

11–007

(a) the cross-claim is not a mere failure of consideration but is an independent claim, and not being due to the surety cannot be invoked by him;

(b) the principal has a right to decide whether to bring his claim in his own action or by counterclaim in an action by the creditor;

---

59 *Murphy v Glass* (1869) L.R. 2 P.C. 408; *Bechervaise v Lewis* (1872) L.R. 7 C.P. 372; *Cape of Good Hope Bank (liquidators) v Forde & Co* (1890) S.C. 30, S.Af.; *Business Computers Ltd v Anglo African Leasing Ltd* [1977] 2 All E.R. 741. For a detailed discussion as to what rights of set-off will and will not be available to the surety, see paras 11–008–11–013.

60 *Bechervaise v Lewis* (1872) L.R. 7 C.P. 372; *Alcoy and Gandia Railway and Harbour Co Ltd v Greenhill* (1897) 76 L.T. 452.

61 See *Cellulose Products Pty Ltd v Truda* (1970) 92 W.N. (NSW) 561 at 572, 575; *Indrisie v General Credit Ltd* [1985] V.R. 251, 254, and see Derham, *Set-Off* (3rd ed. 2003), Ch.18, esp paras 18–12 and 18–21.

62 See *Wilson v Mitchell* [1939] 2 K.B.869, *per* Finlay L.J.; *Hyundai Shipbuilding & Heavy Industries v Pournaras* [1978] 2 Lloyd's Rep. 502, *per* Roskill L.J. at 508; *Westco Motors (Distributors) Pty Ltd v Palmer* (1979) 2 N.S.W.L.R. 93; Steyn, *The Co-Extensiveness Principle* (1974) 90 L.Q.R. 246, and see Chs 6 and 9.

63 *First National Bank of Chicago v Moorgate Properties Ltd*, *The Times*, October 20, 1975, CA.

64 Williston on *Contracts* (*op. cit.*), s.151, p.799; see *Cellulose Products Pty Ltd v Truda* (1970) 92 W.N. (NSW) 561.

(c) if the surety is allowed to set up the counterclaim it must bar a future action by the principal, and that since the amount of the cross-claim might be greater than the creditor's demand under the guarantee, the mere setting it up as a defence would deprive the principal of his right to recover the whole amount;

(d) the surety should not be allowed to assert the cross-claim to the exclusion of his co-sureties, among whom there should be parity of treatment; and

(e) a claim by the surety for unliquidated damages may deprive the creditor of the right to full recovery, since the principal will be able to set up the unliquidated damages claim himself against the creditor subsequently, not being bound by any judgment between the creditor and the surety.

The surety can, however, utilise the principal's cross-claim for unliquidated damages against the creditor in his defence if he joins the principal as a third party to the action brought by the creditor against him, claiming his indemnity. The principal can then join the creditor as fourth party and pursue his claim for damages. This will give the surety his remedy of whole or partial indemnity without the creditor having to face two claims, and without the principal being deprived of the opportunity to reduce his overall liability when faced with an indemnity claim from the surety:[65] this way each party receives his just entitlement.[66] However, this procedure does not in fact give the surety a *defence* to the creditor's claim: all it does is ensure that the surety pays the creditor, the principal indemnifies the surety and the creditor satisfies the principal's cross-claim. It does not directly give effect to the surety's equity of exoneration from the principal debt, and exposes the parties to risks of insolvency of the other. Accordingly, it has been suggested that the better way would be to join the principal as co-defendant.[67]

In *National Westminster Bank Plc v Skelton* [1993] 1 W.L.R. 72, two mortgagees of property who had given the mortgage as sureties for the debts of the principal to the creditor sought to resist an order for possession of the property claimed by the creditor, where defaults had occurred under the terms of the mortgage, on the grounds that the principal had unliquidated claims for damages for breach of the banker—customer contract between them. Slade L.J. held that neither the fact that the unliquidated cross-claims might give rise to a defence of equitable set-off nor the fact that the mortgage had been given not by the principal but by sureties for the principal prevented the operation of the established

---

65 Against whom the principal could not raise the cross-claim.
66 *Cellulose Products Pty Ltd v Truda* (1970) 92 W.N. (NSW) 561 at 588 *per* Isaacs J.; *Elkhoury v Farrow Mortgage Services Pty Ltd (in liq.)* (1993) 114, A.L.R. 541; *cf. Beri Distributions Pty Ltd v Pulitano* (1994) 10 S.R. (WA) 274.
67 See Derham, *Set-Off* (3rd ed. 2003), Ch.18 at paras 18–23, 18–24.

rule[68] that a legal mortgagee's right to possession cannot be defeated by a cross-claim on the part of the mortgagor, even if liquidated and admitted.[69] However, Slade L.J. expressly declined to decide whether there was any general principle that a surety cannot avail himself of the remedies open to the principal as against the creditor. He pointed out that in *Hyundai Shipbuilding and Heavy Industries Co Ltd v Pournaras* [1978] 2 Lloyd's Rep. 502, the Court of Appeal accepted as correct the statement of principle contained in *Halsbury's Laws of England*[70] that a surety may, on being sued by the creditor, avail himself of any right to set off or counterclaim which the principal may have against the creditor. It appears, therefore, that there is some divergence between English and Australian law on this point,[71] and it is suggested that the Australian authorities to the effect that the surety has no defence to the creditor's claim based on the principal's rights of set-off should be approached with a degree of caution.[72]

Where the cross-claim is for a debt or liquidated damages, it does not, however, appear to be necessary to have the principal before the court for the surety to take advantage of his defence.[73] However, most of the Australian cases have required that the principal must be joined unless he is insolvent.[74] The aim is to ensure that the principal does not bring his cross-claim independently against the creditor, and can be bound by the judgment.[75] It is difficult, however, to see why the insolvency of the principal should make any difference to this requirement: his estate is still

---

68 See *Mobil Oil Co Ltd v Rawlinson* (1982) 43 P. & C.R. 221; *Samuel Keller (Holdings) v Martins Bank Ltd* [1971] 1 W.L.R. 43; *Citibank Trust v Ayivor* [1987] 1 W.L.R. 1157.

69 See also *Ashley Guarantee Plc v Zacaria* [1993] 1 W.L.R. 62, where the Court of Appeal (esp. at 69, *per* Nourse L.J.) expressly held that there was no distinction between a case where the mortgagor is the principal and one where he is a surety.

70 The statement is now contained in Vol. 20, para.223 (reissue 2004), in slightly revised form.

71 In *Elkhoury v Farrow Mortgage Services Pty Ltd (in liq.)* (1993) 114 A.L.R. 541, the Federal Court of Australia identified this divergence in clear terms (at 549). See the discussion in O'Donovan & Phillips (3rd ed., 1996), pp.545–546.

72 It should be noted, however, that *National Westminster Bank Plc v Skelton* was an appeal from a striking-out application, and not unnaturally Slade L.J. felt some diffidence in deciding the point (see 79F–G). See the criticisms of this decision by Professor Phillips [2001] 1 L.M.C.L.Q. 383 at 388.

73 Certainly the principal was not before the court in *Murphy v Glass* (1869) L.R. 2 P.C. 408 nor in *Alcoy and Gandia Railway and Harbour Co v Greenhill* (1897) 76 L.T. 542 nor in *Board of Trade v Employers' Liability Assurance Corpn Ltd* [1910] 2 K.B. 649. Since the surety is not an assignee of the principal's cross-claim or defence, the strict rules requiring assignees to join their assignors in proceedings have no application. But see *Cellulose Products Pty Ltd v Truda* (1970) 92 W.N. (NSW) 561, 585; *Elkhoury v Farrow Mortgage Services Pty Ltd (in liq.)* (1993) 114 A.L.R. 541.

74 *ibid.*, and see *Langford Concrete Pty Ltd v Finlay* [1978] 1 N.S.W.L.R. 14, *Indrisie v General Credit Ltd* [1985] V.R. 251, *Covino v Bandag Manufacturing Pty Ltd* [1983] 1 N.S.W.L.R. 237, 241; *cf. Beri Distributions Pty Ltd v Pulitano* (1994) 10 S.R. (WA) 274. See further Derham, *Set-Off* (*op. cit.*), Ch.18, paras 18–23 to 18–25; and compare *Electricity Meter Manufacturing Company Ltd v D'Ombrain* (1927) 44 W.N. (NSW) 131, where James J. allowed a defence of set-off to be brought without joining the (solvent) principal as a party to the action.

75 Thus avoiding one of the principal objections voiced by Isaacs J. in *Cellulose Products Pty Ltd v Truda* (1970) 92 W.N. (NSW) 561, 588.

capable of pursuing the cross-claim independently against the creditor and is still amenable to suit.[76]

Where the creditor sues the surety alone without giving the principal an opportunity to establish his set-off, the latter is entitled to have himself joined to the action to seek a declaration that the cross-claim set-off exists in his favour, his interest in doing so being to protect himself from any claim over by the surety.[77]

It is open to question whether a surety who fails to take advantage of a set-off or defence open to his principal, and who simply pays the creditor in full, remains entitled to claim a full indemnity from the principal, or whether the principal may rely on his set-off against the surety in reduction of his liability to indemnify the surety. It is submitted that the surety is not obliged to raise any set-off that the principal may have, and his failure to do so does not preclude him from making a claim for a full indemnity from the principal. The principal suffers no loss by the surety's failure to raise the set-off, since he may always assert his claim against the creditor at a later stage.[78] Conversely, it would be unfair to deprive a surety who had paid the creditor in ignorance of the principal's right of set-off of his right to a full indemnity. Further, there would be no mutuality between the principal's claim against the creditor and the surety's claim against the principal for an indemnity, even if the surety is standing in the creditor's shoes by being subrogated to his rights.[79]

It is entirely open for the parties to provide in the guarantee that the surety should not be entitled to set up the principal's cross-claims, liquidated or unliquidated, by way of defence to the creditor's claims.[80]

Where there is no insolvency set-off

11–008 There are various types of set-off available where the parties are solvent.[81] The most important are: those which arise out of a common transaction, those arising out of a common account, those arising independently, and those which belong to co-sureties. Not all such set-offs which may exist against the creditor are available to the surety in defence of a claim under the guarantee.

(1) Set-off arising out of a common transaction

11–009 The surety is entitled to be exonerated by the principal and to set off his cross-claims against the creditor which arise out of the same transaction as the creditor's claim for the principal debt. For example, in *Murphy v Glass*

---

76 Although leave would be required to join him (by his trustee) in the proceedings under the Insolvency Act 1986, s.285, and for companies in compulsory liquidation, under s.130(2). Since the purpose of seeking to join the principal would be to have a defence of exoneration determined, rather than a point in the insolvency, leave ought ordinarily to be granted: see by analogy *Re Hutton* [1969] 2 Ch. 201 and *Langford Concrete Pty Ltd v Finlay* [1978] 1 N.S.W.L.R. 14, 16.

77 *Ex p. Hanson* (1806) 12 Ves. 346; *Ex p. Hippins* (1826) 2 Gl. & J. 93.

78 Even if the creditor is insolvent so that the principal has to prove, the surety's involvement has only come about because of the principal's initial default in paying the principal debt.

79 See *Re Jeffery's Policy* (1872) 20 W.R. 857. It would seem that this would also be the case under the statutory insolvency set-off provisions.

80 *Langford Concrete Pty Ltd v Finlay* [1978] 1 N.S.W.L.R. 14.

81 See Wood, *English and International Set-Off* (*op. cit.*), paras 10.194–205; 10.216–25.

(1869) L.R. 2 P.C. 408, the surety guaranteed the price of lands bought by the principal, any dispute in relation to which was to be referred to arbitration. The principal was awarded an abatement in the price because of deficiencies in the acreage, and the surety was permitted to set off the amount of this award against the creditor's claim under the guarantee. Further, in *Langford Concrete Pty Ltd v Finlay* [1978] 1 N.S.W.L.R. 14, the surety guaranteed that the principal, a builder, would pay to the contractor "all monies which are now payable or may in the future become payable by [the principal] to the contractor". The principal went into liquidation, and the contractor sued the surety for the price of goods and services. The surety pleaded that the contractor's work was defective and that he was *pro tanto* exonerated. This defence was upheld on the basis that the surety had only guaranteed to pay what the principal was liable to pay, which was the price reduced by the defective work.[82]

However, in *Indrisie v General Credit Ltd* [1985] V.R. 251, the surety guaranteed the rental payments for amusement machines leased to the principal under a sale and lease-back agreement, the guarantee being secured by a mortgage on property of the surety. The principal defaulted in the rental payments and the creditor, the lessor, claimed to enforce the mortgage. The surety claimed that the creditor had failed to make available in full a loan to the principal, and that damage had been caused as a result which should go to reduce the guarantee liability. It was held that this cross-claim did not afford the surety a right of set-off, since it was not sufficiently connected to the claim for the rentals, and further that it was an unliquidated claim and the principal was not a party to the action.[83]

These cases are not to be confused with cases where the principal is not liable to pay because some condition precedent has not been fulfilled by the creditor, or where the creditor is in breach of a condition of the principal contract.[84] These are not cases of set-off but of discharge by the disappearance of the principal liability. Generally, in such a case, the surety will be likewise discharged, since there will no longer be any principal obligation to which his guarantee can attach. However, it has been held that even where a principal who has repudiated the principal contract may have a cross-claim for restitution of an amount prepaid under the contract,[85] the surety cannot utilise this cross-claim in reduction of his liability under the

---

82 See also *Bechervaise v Lewis* (1872) L.R. 7 C.P. 372; *Electricity Meter Manufacturing Co Ltd v D'Ombrain* (1927) 44 W.N. 131; *The Aliakmon Progress* [1978] 2 Lloyd's Rep. 499.
83 See para.11–007 above.
84 See Ch.9, paras 9–017–9–018, and esp. *Eshelby v Federated European Bank* [1931] 1 K.B. 423; *Watts v Shuttleworth* (1861) 5 H. & N. 235. Similarly, if a condition precedent to the surety's liability is not fulfilled, the surety need not pay: *Burton v Gray* [1873] L.R. 8 Ch.App. 932 and Ch.9, para.9–017.
85 On the basis of the decision of Stable J. in *Dies v British and International Mining and Finance Ltd* [1939] 1 K.B. 724; also *Rover International Ltd v Cannon Film Sales Ltd (No.3)* [1989] 3 All E.R. 423.

guarantee.[86] To the extent that the principal's claim to restitution is based upon a total failure of consideration by the creditor,[87] it is difficult to see why the surety is not entitled to rely on this as a defence, at least *pro tanto*. The consideration given for the guarantee is the performance by the creditor of his obligations under the principal contract, and where this consideration has wholly failed (because, for example, the contract has been repudiated by the principal before the creditor could begin to perform) the guarantee is itself not supported by consideration, and is unenforceable, at least to the extent that consideration for it has failed.

(2) Set-off arising out of a current account

11–010   Where the surety guarantees one of two current accounts held by the principal with the creditor, there is no mutuality sufficient to permit the surety to compel the creditor to appropriate to the guaranteed account any payments to the creditor, or to set off receipts against the guaranteed liability. In the absence of agreement to the contrary, the principal may appropriate any payment to any particular account; if he does not do so, then the creditor may appropriate, and if neither appropriates, then the presumption in *Clayton's Case* (1816) 1 Mer. 572 applies, namely first in first out.[88] This is not something that the surety can control.

Accordingly, the creditor is entitled to apply a payment in satisfaction of the unsecured debt while maintaining the debt as the subject of the guarantee,[89] whether the surety knew of the pre-existing debt or not.[90] Such circumstances will not give rise to any set-off, since the requirement of mutuality is absent. Where, however, the surety guarantees the ultimate balance of a bank account, the creditor cannot appropriate against the surety by dividing the account artificially and charge him for the debits while depriving him of credits.[91]

(3) Set-off arising independently

11–011   Where there is a balance to the amount of the debt owed by the creditor to the principal on another transaction, this balance cannot enure to the benefit of the surety so as to give him a defence to the creditor's claim.[92] In

---

86 *Hyundai Shipbuilding and Heavy Industries Co Ltd v Pournaras* [1978] 2 Lloyd's Rep. 503, where Roskill L.J. (at 508) said that to allow the surety to use the defence would nullify the commercial utility of the guarantee in question; see also *Hyundai Heavy Industries Co Ltd v Papadopoulos* [1981] 1 W.L.R. 1129 and *BOC Group Plc v Centreon* [1999] 1 All E.R. 53; [1999] 63 Com. L.R. 104. See Ch.6, para.6–030 for a detailed discussion of these cases.

87 In *Papadopoulos*, the analysis of *Dies* was disavowed by Viscount Dilhorne at 1134, although it formed part of the decision (1137B) and seems to underpin the decision in *Rover International Ltd v Cannon Film Sales Ltd (No.3)* [1989] 3 All E.R. 423, *per* Kerr L.J. at 439–440. See the discussion in Ch.6 at para.6–030.

88 *Simpson v Ingham* (1823) 2 B. & C. 65, and see the detailed discussion in Ch.9, para.9–007.

89 *Re Sherry* (1884) 25 Ch. D. 692; *Hollond v Teed* (1848) 7 Hare 50; and see Ch.9, paras 9–005–9–008.

90 *Kirby v Duke of Marlborough* (1813) 2 M. & S. 18; *Williams v Rawlinson* (1825) 3 Bing. 71.

91 *Re Sherry* (1884) 25 Ch. D. 693, at 706; *Mutton v Peak* [1900] 2 Ch. 79; *National Bank of Nigeria v Awolesi* [1964] 1 W.L.R. 1311; see Ch.9, para.9–006.

92 See *Bowyear v Pawson* (1881) 6 Q.B.D. 540.

Harrison v Nettleship (1833) 2 My. & K. 423, the principal purchased land leaving half the purchase price on credit, and this debt was guaranteed by the surety who provided promissory notes. Further transactions ensued between the principal and the creditor by which the creditor owed more to the principal than he was owed by the principal, who then became insolvent. The creditor claimed the sum due under the promissory notes from the surety, who pleaded the creditor's liability to the principal. It was held that he failed, on the basis that the mere fact that the principal had a set-off against the creditor did not oblige him to use it so as to reduce the surety's liability, or oblige the creditor to bring his liabilities into account. The decision is a somewhat obscure one, and it is not clear why the insolvency set-off did not apply, since there was mutuality of capacity and the cross-debts were accrued and due.

In *National Bank of Australasia v Swan* (1872) 3 V.R. (L) 168, the Supreme Court of Victoria refused to allow the administrator of the estate of a deceased surety to set off debts due from a bank to the administrator in that capacity against a liability which had not yet accrued against the estate under the guarantee: there was no express promise by the administrator to pay the guaranteed debt, and the necessary mutuality was absent because the administrator was not and could never be liable in his personal capacity for the debt unless he promised to pay it.[93]

In neither case was there sufficient connection between the cross-debts at law for there to be any set-off of which the surety could take advantage.

However, in cases where the creditor's action is for a money sum, the surety can claim a legal set-off if it arises out of the arrangements under which his guarantee was given, and it seems that he can set off against his liability under the guarantee a debt due from the creditor which arose before the guarantee was given.[94]

(4) Set-off available to co-surety

Where the surety is sued by the creditor, he cannot reduce or extinguish **11–012** his liability by relying on a right of set-off which his co-surety has against the creditor. The surety has no right to be exonerated by his co-surety, and must pursue his claim for contribution separately.[95] For example, in *Bowyear v Pawson* (1881) 6 Q.B.D. 540, the creditor sued the surety in respect of the principal's debt. The creditor owed the co-surety a debt, which the co-surety had assigned to himself and the surety jointly and severally equally as tenants in common. The surety claimed to be entitled to set off one half of the claim against the portion of the debt owed by the

---

93 See esp. Stawall C.J. at 171. Compare this case with *Crawford v Stirling* (1802) 4 Esp. 207; *Morley v Inglis* (1837) 4 Bing. (NC) 58, where the creditor could not set off a debt owed to him by the principal against a claim brought by the surety.
94 Even where the debt arose as between the surety and a partnership comprising the creditor and the principal: *Cheetham v Crook* (1825) M'Cle. & Yo. 307, approved in *Emerson v Wreckair Pty Ltd* (1991) 103 A.L.R. 404 at 412. This was in fact a case of insolvency set-off, and so the essential requirement of mutuality was satisfied.
95 As to which see Ch.12.

creditor, and as to the other half, he claimed that since he was entitled to be exonerated by his co-surety and call upon him to contribute, he could set off the remaining portion of the debt against the co-surety's right against the creditor. This defence failed on the grounds that the surety had no right to call upon the co-surety to appropriate the debt due from the creditor to the exoneration of the surety, and had no contract with the creditor to accept a set-off of the co-surety's debt as a payment in discharge of the surety.

Where there is insolvency set-off

11–013   Set-off in insolvency is rather broader in ambit that at common law or in equity and is governed by the Insolvency Act 1986, s.323 in the case of individuals and by the Insolvency Rules 1986 (SI 1986/1925) r.4.90 in the case of companies.[96] The requirement is that there be mutual debts, mutual credits or other mutual dealings,[97] and where there are, then there is a mandatory set-off in the insolvency. The balance is taken in the course of the administration of the insolvent estate, whenever it is necessary to do so. It relates back to the position between the parties as at the date of the bankruptcy or winding-up order (with the benefit of hindsight, taking into account all relevant contingent liabilities which have accrued due since that date), and only the balance is "due".[98]

In *Stein v Blake* [1996] 1 A.C. 243, the House of Lords has now made it clear that the word "due" in the relevant parts of the insolvency legislation denotes a single net balance of account which must be paid either by or to the insolvent estate. The mutual credits, debits or dealings which are to be set off against each other do not survive the commencement of the insolvency as separate cross-claims save for the purposes of calculating the net balance of account. Lord Hoffmann said (at 969):

> "I think that 'due' merely means treated as having been owing at the bankruptcy date with the benefit of hindsight and, if necessary, estimation provided by the bankruptcy law."

In reaching his conclusion, Lord Hoffmann (at 969) rejected the argument, propounded in *Derham on Set-Off* (Oxford University Press, 1988), p.74

---

96 See generally Sealy & Milman, *Annotated Guide to the Insolvency Legislation* (6th ed., 2002), pp.836–838; and Williams and Muir Hunter, *Law and Practice in Bankruptcy*, (19th ed., Sweet & Maxwell, 1979), pp.188–204 for the cases on s.31 of the Bankruptcy Act 1914, the predecessor to the modern provisions. See also Philip Wood, *English and International Set-Off* (*op. cit.*) esp. paras 206–214; Derham, *Set-Off* (*op. cit.*), Ch.18, para.18–30.

97 See Williams and Muir Hunter *Law and Practice in Bankruptcy* (*op. cit.*), pp.188–204 as to the meaning of mutuality in this context.

98 *MS Fashions Ltd v Bank of Credit and Commerce International SA* [1993] Ch. 425, especially *per* Hoffmann L.J. at 432–423; *Stein v Blake* [1996] 1 A.C. 243, HL, applying *Gye v McIntyre* (1991) 171 C.L.R. 609, where the High Court of Australia held (at 622) that "the section is self-executing in the sense that its operation is automatic and not dependent upon 'the option of either party'": See also, *per* Lord Selborne L.C. in *Re Deveze Ex p. Barnett* (1874) L.R. 9 Ch. App. 293 at 295. See now *BCCI (No.8)* [1998] A.C. 214, and the detailed discussion of that case in Ch.13. As to the eligibility of debts that were contingent as at the insolvency date, see the recent decision of the House of Lords in *Re West End Networks Ltd* [2004] 2 All E.R. 1042, discussed in Ch.13 below.

(and derived from a dictum of Mason J. in *Day & Dent Constructions (Pty) Ltd v North Australian Properties (Pty) Ltd* (1982) 150 C.L.R. 85) that the separate cross-claims did not cease to exist until the account under the section or rule had been taken, and he approved the conclusions of Neill J. in *Farley v Housing and Commercial Developments Ltd* [1984] B.C.L.C. 442, which the Court of Appeal in *Stein v Blake* [1993] 4 All E.R. 225 had overruled. The House of Lords accordingly reversed the Court of Appeal on this point.

In the recent case of *BCCI v Prince Al-Saud* [1997] 6 Bank. L.R. 121, the Court of Appeal considered *Stein v Blake* and the extent of the mutuality requirement in the context of deposit accounts containing mixed funds. The bank claimed against the Prince under his guarantee, and he sought to set-off moneys standing to the credit of accounts held by a third party who, the Prince contended, held the sums as his nominee beneficially for him, relying on r.4.90 of the Insolvency Rules 1986. He contended that the rule was wide enough to permit set-off in his favour even though the Court would have to enquire about his beneficial ownership as at the date of the winding-up. The bank contended that, for there to be mutuality under the rule, the Prince's beneficial ownership at the date of the winding-up had to be clear and free from doubt. The Court of Appeal found for the bank, applying the principles enunciated by Brett L.J. in *Re Willis, Percival & Co Ex p. Morier* (1879) 12 Ch. D. 491, to the effect that there is no mutual debit, credit or dealing within the statute if there must be enquiry about the beneficial entitlement of the party claiming the set-off.[99] *Stein v Blake* did not, the Court of Appeal held, change the law or impliedly overrule *Ex p. Morier*. However, it is to be observed that in *Stein v Blake*, Lord Hoffmann described (at 252E) the techniques employed under r.4.90 to ascertain the amount "due" in hindsight as at the winding-up date, and made it clear that it involved the taking of an account on both sides. The Court of Appeal in *BCCI v Prince Al-Saud* did not critically analyse why that account-taking could not include the account-taking or enquiry by the Prince as to the amounts beneficially owned by him at the date of the winding-up, and there is no good practical reason why it should not do so. Neill L.J. relied on the suggestion by the bank that it would be "expensive" for the liquidator, but it is submitted that there is no reason why that expense should not be borne by the party seeking the benefit of the set-off rather than the insolvent estate. Futhermore, the same objection about expense applies to any set-off in respect of cross-demands which are contingent at the date of the winding-up but which subsequently mature. Neill L.J. further relied (at 126) on the fact that Lord Hoffmann did not appear to be considering that he was changing the law. However, it should be noted that *Ex p. Morier* was not cited to the House of Lords in *Stein v Blake*.

Where the principal or creditor is insolvent, it is generally accepted that the surety is not limited to the right of set-off that a solvent principal could

---

99 Then s.69 of the Bankruptcy Act 1869, which as Neill L.J. pointed out at 126, was in materially the same terms as r.4.90 of the Insolvency Rules 1986.

have raised as a defence to an action at law brought by a solvent creditor,[1] and he can rely on the principal's statutory set-off in reduction or extinction of the claim by the creditor under the guarantee. The creditor cannot avoid the effect of the insolvency set-off by claiming under the guarantee before proving in the insolvency.[2] The analysis of the surety's right in these circumstances is that right of insolvency set-off is analogous to a form of security which would have entitled the creditor not to have to prove in the principal's insolvency. The creditor is generally obliged to preserve securities for the guaranteed obligation for the benefit of the surety so that he can, upon payment, exercise his rights of subrogation against them.[3] Although the creditor is not obliged, in the absence of any stipulation to the contrary, to look to a particular security before suing the surety, nonetheless the creditor is compelled to realise a right of set-off for the surety's benefit. This is because a right of set-off is not a right to which the surety can be subrogated, and unless the surety could compel the creditor to set off under the statutory insolvency set-off provisions, he would be forced to pay the debt and prove in the principal's insolvency for his indemnity. This would be inconsistent with his right to be exonerated by the principal.[4]

The usual rule is that the surety should not be able to dictate to the creditor which remedies he should exercise, and attempts have been made to explain the surety's right to compel the creditor to exercise a set-off as an exception to that rule.[5] In fact, it is not an exception. The true analysis of the right is that the surety is entitled, upon demand being made of him, to marshal the creditor's securities in his favour,[6] and this would include rights of set-off which operate as a security in the creditor's hands where the principal is insolvent.[7]

Accordingly, where the principal and the surety are jointly liable, the principal being primarily liable, then the principal should be entitled to set-off an amount owed by the creditor against his claim, and the surety

---

1 But see *Westco Motors (Distributors) Pty Ltd v Palmer* [1979] 2 N.S.W.L.R. 93, where even though the principal was insolvent, the surety's claim for set-off was rejected on the grounds that there was no sufficient connection between the cross-demands.

2 *Ex p. Hanson* (1806) 12 Ves. 346; *Bechervaise v Lewis* (1872) L.R. 7 C.P.372; *Alcoy and Gandia Railway and Harbour Co Ltd v Greenhill*(1897) 76 L.T. 452.

3 See Ch.9 paras 9–041–9–043; and see paras 11–017 *et seq.*

4 *Alcoy and Gandia Railway and Harbour Co Ltd v Greenhill* (1897) 76 L.T. 542.

5 See Wood, *English and International Set-Off* (*op. cit.*), para.10–208, where the view is expressed that this is an example of the operation of the equitable principle that the creditor should not have the whole burden of the debt brought down upon him, citing Rowlatt at p.132. However, this is, as between the principal and the surety, not the law: the creditor has an unencumbered choice of remedies. See para.11.02 above for detailed discussion.

6 See para.11–015.

7 Objection has been made to the availability to the surety of the principal's insolvency set-off on the grounds of absence of mutuality between the creditor and the surety: see O'Donovan & Phillips, *The Modern Contract of Guarantee* (3rd ed., 1996), pp.554–555. However, all that is required is mutuality between creditor and *principal* in order that the surety is advantaged. *Cf.* O'Donovan & Phillips, English ed., at paras 12–52–12–53.

entitled to plead this in diminution or extinction of his own liability.[8] In *Ex p. Hanson* (1806) 12 Ves. 346, the principal and surety were partners, and the principal borrowed a sum from the creditor bank for his partnership capital. The surety was jointly liable for the loan although he was only the surety in respect of it. The creditor bank became insolvent, owing a separate debt to the principal. It was held that the surety could set off the mutual debts in reduction of his liability under the guarantee.[9]

The surety himself has the right to exercise his own insolvency set-off against the creditor.[10] Where the surety is severally liable with the principal, and he has deposited moneys with the creditor, he may compel the insolvent creditor, before the trustee or liquidator has sued the principal, to apply such moneys in satisfaction of the debt.[11] A surety who is jointly liable with the principal can at any time compel the creditor to apply securities in the creditor's hand (or their proceeds) pledged for the joint debt, even though owned severally by the surety.[12] However, it is now clear that it is unnecessary to take an active step to assert any right of set-off (if one exists) prior to the insolvency. The "mandatory principle" underlying modern insolvency set-off means that it is immaterial that the surety does not know of his right of set-off until after the commencement of the insolvency.[13] Where the creditor has a right of set-off against the surety, he is not obliged to realise that set-off before proving in the principal's insolvency.[14]

It appears that the insolvent principal's set-off can be exercised rateably between guaranteed and unguaranteed debts. For example, where the

---

8 *Ex p. Hanson* (1806) 12 Ves. 346; *Ex p. Hippins* (1826) 2 Gl. & J. 93; *Owen v Wilkinson* (1858) 5 C.B. (N.S.) 526; and see *Re Marley* [1976] 1 W.L.R. 952 for an example of the surety who has mortgaged property jointly with the principal being entitled to throw the burden of the debt onto the principal's share and have his own share exonerated.

9 See also *Ex p. Hippins* (1826) 2 Gl. & J. 93.

10 *Cheetham v Crook* (1825) M'Cl. & Yo. 307; *Emerson v Wreckair Pty Ltd* (1991) 103 A.L.R. 404.

11 *Ex p. Stephens* (1805) 11 Ves. 24; *Middleton v Pollock* (1875) L.R. 20 Eq. 515; Wood, *English and International Set-Off* (*op. cit.*), para.14.68. But this is not a right of set-off which belongs to the principal, since the principal would not have been entitled to compel the creditor to look to the security rather than his own personal liability. What the surety and the creditor do as to any security provided by the surety is no concern of the principal debtor, and does not give rise to a right of which the principal can take advantage. The surety's right is in any event not strictly a set-off but a right to claim an account of the proceeds of the security which have not been utilised (or ought not to be utilised) in satisfaction of the secured debt: see *Vulliamy v Noble* (1817) 3 Mer. 621, as explained in *Middleton v Pollock* (above). However, where the surety covenants with the creditor as principal debtor, then he may be entitled to compel the creditor to set off deposits provided by the surety as security against the liability of the principal: *MS Fashions Ltd v Bank of Credit and Commerce International SA* [1993] Ch. 425, and see *Stein v Blake* [1996] 1 A.C. 243; *Re West End Networks Ltd* [2004] 2 All E.R. 1042.

12 *Middleton v Pollock* (1875) L.R. 20 Eq. 515, at 519 *per* Sir George Jessel M.R., explaining *Vulliamy v Noble* (1817) 3 Mer. 621.

13 *MS Fashions v Bank of Credit and Commerce International SA* [1993] Ch. 425, esp. 437–438, where Hoffmann L.J. (at first instance) expressed disquiet at why Sir George Jessel M.R. had found it necessary for the surety to be relieved (and entitled to a set-off) on the grounds of fraud by the creditor, where the set-off was clear and undisputed.

14 See *Crosse v Smith* (1813) 1 M. & S. 545; *Re Kensington Ex p. Burton* (1812) 1 Rose. 320 (bill of exchange cases).

principal owes the creditor £100 which is guaranteed and £50 which is not, and the creditor owes the principal £10, the £10 set-off should be applied rateably between the guaranteed and unguaranteed debts, *i.e.* £5 against £100 and £5 against £50.[15] Further, where the guaranteed debt is payable by instalments and the creditor has been paid in part by operation of a set-off in the principal's bankruptcy, the dividends should be applied rateably between instalments, and not against one instalment so as to extinguish it altogether.[16] Usually, however, all instalments would be accelerated upon the principal's insolvency.

Where a surety under a performance bond performs the bonded contract and becomes entitled to be paid in place of the principal, the creditor may not retain in set-off against the surety amounts which he is owed by the principal on some unrelated transaction.[17]

Where a guarantee secures an English debt, but is to be construed in accordance with a foreign law which would afford a set-off to the principal, the surety is entitled to raise in his defence the fact that the foreign law would have permitted a set-off to the principal against the creditor in extinction of the debt.[18]

Other defences open to the surety

11–014   The surety will be able to take advantage of any pure defences open to the principal which reduce or extinguish the principal debt. Thus where the principal sum claimed is in the nature of a penalty and unenforceable either wholly or *pro tanto,* the surety can take advantage of the fact in his own defence.[19] Where a hire-purchase company retakes possession of goods in exercise of its remedies so that it is not entitled to sue the principal for the price, it cannot sue the surety either.[20]

Where the principal contract has been rendered voidable at the suit of the principal by reason of the vitiating act of the creditor, such as undue influence or misrepresentation, the surety will be discharged *ab initio*, at least if the principal elects to rescind.[21] However, where the principal elects to affirm the contract or waives his right to rescind the principal contract, it is submitted that the surety will also remain liable, and will not be able to utilise the fact that the principal contract was voidable in defending himself against a claim by the creditor under the guarantee.[22]

---

15 See *Raikes v Todd* (1838) 8 Ad. & El. 846, where dividends in the principal's composition were received by the creditor rateably between guaranteed and unguaranteed portions of the debt.
16 *Martin v Brecknell* (1813) 2 M. & S. 39.
17 *Employers Liability Assurance Corporation v R* [1969] 2 Ex. C.R. 246, at 255 *per* Gibson J.
18 *Allen v Kemble* (1848) 6 Moo. P.C.C. 314; explained in *Rouquette v Overmann* (1875) L.R. 10 Q.B. 525.
19 See, *e.g. Sterling Industrial Facilities v Lydiate Textiles* (1962) 106 S.T. 669.
20 *Hewison v Ricketts* (1894) 63 LJQB711; *Brooks v Beirnstein* [1909] 1 K.B. 98. See Ch.9, para.9–017.
21 See Ch.6, para.6–024.
22 See Ch.6, *ibid*.

Right to marshal securities in the hands of the creditor

Marshalling is an equitable doctrine which is designed to achieve equity **11–015** between two creditors, each of whom is owed debts by the same debtor, but where one creditor has recourse to a choice of securities or funds from the debtor over which to enforce his debt, but the other creditor has recourse to only one security or fund. In such circumstances, the latter creditor can require the former creditor to satisfy himself so far as possible out of the securities or funds over which the latter creditor has no rights.[23] The doctrine applies to guaranteed debts. Once a demand is made of him by the creditor, the surety has the right to compel the creditor first to have recourse to a security held by that creditor before suing him. Generally, for this right to operate, the creditor should hold the security in respect of the guaranteed debt.[24] A surety may not marshal in his favour securities held in respect of different debts or of a different part of the same debt.[25] In *Wilkinson v London & County Banking Co* (1884) 1 T.L.R. 63, the surety guaranteed the general balance of the account of the principal's account. On the principal's bankruptcy he owed £1,000 on his general account. The principal had given the creditor securities for each and every specific advance, which he had received back again when he paid the advance off. It was held that the advances were each a separate transaction to be regarded apart from and independently of the guarantee and the guaranteed account, and on the repayment of each such advance, the principal was entitled to have the securities back regardless of the continuing liability of the surety.

However, where the creditor holds security for a debt different from that guaranteed by the surety, and holds security for the guaranteed debt, the surety is entitled to have the security for the other debt marshalled in his favour provided that the securities can be consolidated.[26] In *Praed v Gardiner* (1788) 2 Cox. Eq. Cas. 86, the principal had borrowed an amount from the creditor and deposited various securities for that advance. He then borrowed a further amount, which the surety guaranteed. The securities in the hands of the creditor were more than enough to pay off the first debt. The surety was entitled to have the benefit of the surplus from the securities in reduction of his own liability to the creditor. In *Heyman v Dubois* (1871) L.R. 13 Eq. 158, the surety had guaranteed to the creditor a

---

23 For a recent summary of the doctrine of marshalling, see *Re BCCI (No.8)* [1997] 3 W.L.R. 909, *per* Lord Hoffmann at 921–922. See also generally *Aldrich v Cooper* (1803) 8 Ves. 382; *Trimmer v Bayne (No.2)* (1803) 9 Ves. 209; *Webb v Smith* (1885) 30 Ch. D. 192; *Re Cohen, National Provincial Bank v Katz* [1960] 1 Ch. 179 at 190; *Re Marley* [1976] 1 W.L.R. 952, at 955 *per* Foster J.; Snell's *Principles of Equity*; (30th ed., Sweet & Maxwell 2000, pp.503–504); Meagher Heydon and Leeming, *Equity Doctrines and Remedies*, (4th ed., 2002), Ch.11 at para.11–045.
24 *Ex p. Kendall* (1811) 17 Ves. 514.
25 *Wade v Coope* (1827) 2 Sim. 155; *Re Butlers Wharf Ltd* [1995] 2 B.C.L.C. 43; *Liberty Mutual Insurance Co (UK) Ltd v HSBC Bank Plc* [2002] EWCA Civ 691.
26 The right to consolidated mortgages only exists if stipulated for: Law of Property Act 1925, s.93.

loan secured by policies on the life of the principal; the creditor held another policy from the principal as security for another loan to him. The principal became bankrupt. The surety paid part of the debt, and when the policies fell in, he was entitled to have them marshalled in his favour so as to be paid in full, including his costs of the action.[27]

Where the creditor holds a security for two debts, one of which is guaranteed and the other not, the surety seems to be entitled to marshal in his favour a share of that security pro rata to his liability.[28] The same would appear to apply where the surety has guaranteed part of a debt wholly secured.

The surety's right to marshal the creditor's securities has priority to encumbrances which pre-date the accrual of the right to marshal but which rank behind the creditor's interest in the security. In *Drew v Lockett* (1863) 32 Beav. 499 the principal mortgaged his estate to the creditor for a debt, and the surety guaranteed the debt. The principal then created a mortgage over the estate in favour of a third party who took with notice of the first mortgage. The first mortgage was paid off, partly by the surety, and the legal estate was conveyed to the second mortgagee. It was held that the surety was entitled to have the legal estate marshalled in his favour in priority to the second mortgagee to the extent that the surety had paid off the principal debt. The rationale is that the surety stands in the shoes of the creditor he pays off, and is entitled to his securities *in pari materia*. The subsequent encumbrancer is not prejudiced by the surety's prior right, since it is not additional to that of the original creditor, and it is immaterial that the subsequent encumbrancer did not have notice of the guarantee.[29]

Where the guaranteed debt is secured by the mortgage of two funds, one of which is subject to a second mortage, and the guaranteed debt is paid from the fund which is twice mortgaged, the surety is obliged, if he pays the debt, to marshal the securities in favour of the second mortgagee. The second mortgagee will be entitled to the balance of the other fund, after the mortgage on it is satisfied, to the extent of the fund mortgaged to him.[30] Where the principal and the surety jointly mortgage a property for one debt to the creditor, the surety has an equitable interest by way of a charge on the estate of the principal for the enforcement of his indemnity, and a right to have the burden of the debt thrown upon the principal's estate in priority to his own.[31]

The right to marshal securities operates in reduction of the surety's liability to the creditor, once a demand for payment has been made of him,

---

27 The case shows that the liquidator or trustee is bound by the equity of marshalling. See also *Duncan, Fox & Co v North & South Wales Bank* (1880) 6 App. Cas. 1, especially at 15; *Re Holland Ex p. Alston* (1868) 4 Ch. App. 168; *Re Stratton Ex p. Salting* (1883) 25 Ch. D. 148.
28 *Coates v Coates* (1864) 3 Beav. 249. It seems that this right may only be exercised where the creditor has not himself appropriated the security to a particular debt: *Perrie v Roberts* (1861) 1 Vern. 34.
29 *Drew v Lockett* (1863) 32 Beav. 499 at 505–506.
30 *South v Bloxham* (1865) 2 Hem. & M. 457. See the discussion of the surety's right to tack at para.11–025.
31 *Gee v Liddell* [1913] 2 Ch. 62; *Re Marley* [1976] 1 W.L.R. 952.

and is available before or after payment.[32] It is not to be confused with the right of subrogation which, as will be seen, arises upon payment or performance by the surety. Although several of the cases cited above illustrate what securities the surety may be entitled to call for, they are examples of the operation of the doctrine of marshalling once the right of the surety to be subrogated has arisen.[33]

Rights of the surety after payment or performance

The right of recovery

Money wrongly paid by the surety to the creditor in ignorance of a relevant fact can normally be recovered from him. In *Mills v Alderbury Union* (1849) 3 Exch. 590 the plaintiff was co-surety in a bond given by the principal to the guardians of a union for the due accounting to them of moneys received by him as treasurer. At the time the bond was entered into, the principal was a member of a banking firm into which monies of the union were afterwards paid, and then drawn out by the guardians in their own name. The firm became bankrupt and the guardians demanded the balance from the plaintiff, who paid. It was held that he was entitled to recover the moneys paid over to the guardians because he had done so in ignorance of the fact that the surety was not liable on the bond.[34]

11–016

However, where a payment is made by the surety to the creditor in ignorance of the law, it used to be generally accepted that he cannot recover it.[35] However, this was never an absolute rule,[36] and there were some notable exceptions, such as where payment had been made by personal representatives and trustees,[37] by an officer of the court,[38] by the court itself,[39] or where the mistake is one of foreign law, which is treated as a mistake of fact.[40] However, this entire line of authority is probably now otiose in the light of the decision of the House of Lords in *Kleinwort Benson Ltd v Lincoln City Council* [1999] 2 A.C. 349.

The right of subrogation

Origin and nature

A surety who has performed the obligations of the principal which are the subject of his guarantee is entitled to stand in the shoes of the creditor and to enjoy all the rights that the creditor had against the principal.[41] This is an

11–017

---

32 *Heyman v Dubois* (1871) L.R. 13 Eq. 158.
33 Subrogation is discussed in detail later in this chapter at paras 11–017 *et seq.*
34 See *Geary v Gore Bank* (1856) 5 Gr. 536 (Can); *United States Fidelity & Guarantee Co v Union Bank* (1917) 36 D.L.R. 724.
35 *Re Carnac Ex p. Simmonds* (1885) 16 Q.B.D. 308; generally, *Bilbie v Lumley* (1802) 2 East. 469.
36 See generally Goff and Jones, *The Law of Restitution* (6th ed., 2002), Ch.5.
37 *Dibbs v Goren* (1849) 11 Beav. 483; *cf. Re Horne* [1905] 1 Ch. 76; *Ministry of Health v Simpson* [1951] A.C. 251.
38 *Ex p. James* (1874) L.R. 9 Ch. App. 609; *Re Carnac Ex p. Simmonds* (1885) 16 Q.B.D. 308, esp. at 312; *Re Byfield* [1982] Ch. 267.
39 *Re Birkbeck Permanent Benefit Building Society* [1915] 1 Ch. 91.
40 *Lazard Bros & Co v Midland Bank Ltd* [1933] A.C. 289.
41 *Morgan v Seymour* (1638) 1 Rep. Ch. 120; *Ex p. Crisp* (1744) 1 Atk. 133; *Aldrich v Cooper* (1803) 8 Ves. 382; *Newton v Chorlton* (1853) 10 Hare 346.

equitable right analogous to the right to contribution from his co-sureties,[42] and was described thus by Sir Samuel Romilly in *Craythorne v Swinburne* (1807) 14 Ves. 160:

> "a surety will be entitled to every remedy, which the creditor has against the principal debtor; to enforce every security and all means of payment; to stand in the place of the creditor; not only through the medium of contract, but even by means of securities, entered into without the knowledge of the surety; having a right to have those securities transferred to him; though there was no stipulation for that, and to avail himself of all those securities against the debtor. This right of a surety also stands, not upon contract but upon a principle of natural justice: the same principle, upon which one surety is entitled to contribution from another."

Subrogation is not a right deriving from the contract of guarantee, and the surety does not (and cannot be expected to) "stipulate for the benefit of the security which the principal debtor has given".[43] It is a right that arises out of the relationship of surety and creditor itself. Equity intervenes to assist the surety because, he having paid off the principal debt (or at least that part for which he is liable as surety), it would be unconscionable for the principal then to recover the securities from the creditor while remaining under an obligation to indemnify the surety for the payment,[44] and for the creditor to throw the whole liability onto the surety by electing not to avail himself of the security for the guaranteed debt.[45] The right of subrogation therefore rests on the same principles as those governing the right of marshalling. It is also possible to bring the doctrine of subrogation in the context of the relationship between surety, principal and creditor, within the (broader) doctrine of unjust enrichment, providing a restitutionary remedy against property: see *Banque Financière de la Cité v Parc (Battersea) Ltd* [1999] 1 A.C. 221.[46] On that analysis, the doctrine operates to treat the security, which is strictly speaking actually discharged by the payment to the creditor, as if it were still available to the surety to assist him in recovering the amount he has paid in reduction or extinction of the principal debt.[47]

Subrogation is in effect a class right, and a claim of set-off based upon it cannot succeed. In *AE Goodwin Ltd v AG Healing Ltd* (1979) 7 A.C.L.R.

---

42 See Ch.12.

43 *Yonge v Reynell* (1852) 9 Hare 809 *per* Turner V.-C.; *Duncan Fox & Co v North & South Wales Bank* (1880) 6 App. Cas. 1, *per* Lord Selborne at 13.

44 *ibid.*; and see *Aldrich v Cooper* (1803) 8 Ves. 382, at 389 *per* Lord Eldon L.C.; *Nicholas v Ridley* [1904] 1 Ch. 192.

45 *Aldrich v Cooper* (1803) 8 Ves. 382, at 389 *per* Lord Eldon L.C.; *Lord Harburton v Bennett* (1829) Beat. 386.

46 See para.11–015; *Heyman v Dubois* (1871) L.R.13 Eq. 158; *Duncan, Fox & Co v North and South Wales Bank* (1880) 6 App Cas 1. See also *Boscawen v Bajwa* [1996] 1 W.L.R. 328, *per* Millett L.J. at 777; *Liberty Mutual Insurance Co (UK) Ltd v HSBC Bank Plc* [2002] EWCA Civ 691 at paras 43 to 46, *per* Rix L.J.

47 See *Banque Financière de la Cité v Parc (Battersea) Ltd* [1999] 1 A.C. 221 at 742.

481, all the sureties who contributed towards the payment of the principal debt were subrogated to the creditor's rights against the principal, and the principal was not entitled to set up against such rights the fact that some of the sureties owed him more than the amount of their individual contributions to the principal debt.[48]

How and when the right of subrogation arises

The surety's right to be subrogated to all the creditor's rights in respect of **11–018** the guaranteed debt is traditionally said to arise at the moment he has paid in full all that he must pay to the creditor under the guarantee,[49] unless he has waived the right.[50] In fact, the strict position is that the rights of the surety to the benefit of a security given by the principal arise when the guarantee is entered into, rather than upon payment or performance of the guaranteed obligation.[51] Thus the creditor owes an obligation to the surety to deal with securities in a reasonable and prudent manner,[52] and may discharge the surety if he does not.[53] Pending payment or performance, the surety can (following a demand by the creditor) have the securities marshalled in his favour.[54] However, the surety's right to *enforce* the right of subrogation by calling upon the creditor to transfer or assign to him the security to which he has become entitled does not arise until the surety has paid or performed the obligation guaranteed.[55]

The surety's right does not depend upon his knowledge of the existence of the security at the time he gave the guarantee.[56] This is so even if the creditor is a preferential creditor of the principal and the securities came into existence after the giving of the guarantee.[57] If he strikes a bargain with

---

48 This case made it clear that the surety is, in equity, *not himself* required to satisfy the creditor in full before becoming entitled to exercise rights of subrogation, but is only required to have performed all of his own obligations, even if the balance of the guaranteed debt is discharged by others, such as co-sureties. It has been followed on numerous occasions in Australasia: see *McColl's Wholesale Pty Ltd v State Bank of New South Wales* [1984] 3 N.S.W.L.R. 365; *Russel Pty Ltd (in liq.) v Bach* (unreported, Supreme Court of New South Wales, June 23, 1988); *Raffle v AGC (Advances) Ltd* [1989] A.S.C. 58, 528; *Bayley v Gibsons Ltd* [1993] 1 Tas. R. 385.

49 *Re Howe Ex p. Brett* (1871) 6 Ch. App. 838, at 841 *per* Mellish L.J.; and see *Smith v Bloxham* (1865) 2 Hem. & M. 457 *per* Wood V.-C. See *Lloyd's TSB Bank Plc v Shorney* [2001] EWCA Civ 1161, where Mrs Shorney, as the co-mortgagor, was entitled to be subrogated to the bank's mortgage interest held from the husband because she had paid all that she was liable to pay under her personal covenant for repayment. Despite the fact that the mortgage was an "all moneys" mortgage, it did not secure the husband's liability under later additional guarantees given by him.

50 See para.11–028.

51 *Dixon v Steel* [1901] 2 Ch. 602.

52 See Ch.9, para.9–043.

53 See, *e.g. Watts v Shuttleworth* (1861) 7 H. & N. 353; *Lloyd's TSB Bank Plc v Shorney* [2001] EWCA Civ 1161.

54 As to marshalling see para.11–015, above.

55 Certainly the rights of the surety under the Mercantile Law Amendment Act 1856, s.5 do not arise until this point.

56 *Aldrich v Cooper* (1803) 8 Ves. 382; *Mayhew v Crickett* (1818) 2 Swanst. 185, at 191 *per* Lord Eldon; *Lake v Brutton* (1854) 18 Beav. 34; *Pearl v Deacon* (1857) 24 Beav. 186, 191 *per* Romilly M.R.; *Newton v Chorlton* (1953) 10 Hare 646, *per* Page-Wood V.-C.; *Duncan, Fox & Co v North and South Wales Bank* (1880) 6 App. Cas. 1.

57 *Lake v Brutton* (1854) 18 Beav. 34; *Campbell v Rothwell* (1877) 38 L.T. 33; *Forbes v Jackson* (1882) 19 Ch. D. 615.

the creditor and discharges the debt at a discount, the surety may be subrogated to the creditor's rights, but only to the value of what he actually paid, and no more.[58]

Does the surety have a right of subrogation where he has paid all he is liable to pay under the guarantee, but has not satisfied the entirety of the liability owed by the principal to the creditor? In *Re Howe Ex p. Brett* (1871) 6 Ch. App. 838, Mellish L.J. said (at 841):

> "a surety is not entitled to the securities which the principal creditor may hold until he pays the debt: he has no bargain that the securities shall be given up to him, and it is merely after he has paid in full that the rule of equity comes in and says that he is entitled to the securities; but until payment, the securities are in no sense securities on property of his."

Further, there is some support for this view in *Ewart v Latta* (1865) 4 Marq. 983.[59] However, there is a great weight of modern Australian authority to the effect that although the creditor must be paid in full in order for rights of subrogation to arise, it is not necessary that the surety must *himself* have paid the creditor in full. In *AE Goodwin Ltd v AG Healing Ltd* (1979) 7 A.C.L.R. 481, Powell J. held (at 487) that if the surety was required himself to discharge the debt in full in order to be entitled to exercise rights of subrogation,

> "it would, in my view, permit the whole concept of subrogation, which is intended to prevent a creditor from acting in a capricious way to the detriment of the surety, itself to operate capriciously."

Powell J. simply refused to follow Mellish L.J. in *Re Howe Ex p. Brett*.[60] The decision in *AE Goodwin* has been followed unhesitatingly on numerous occasions in Australasia.[61]

It is submitted that the views of the Australasian courts and writers would be followed in England, and the law as expressed in *Ewart v Latta* and *Re Howe Ex p. Brett* would either not be followed or would be distinguished, for the following reasons:

(1) There is ancient English authority which supports the modern Australasian view, namely *Gedye v Matson* (1858) 25 Beav. 310, in which Sir John Romilly M.R. stated that "to the extent to which the surety

---

58 *Reed v Norris* (1837) 2 Myl. & Cr. 361, at 375 *per* Lord Cottenham.
59 In the passage quoted in para.11–002 above.
60 He also refused to follow dicta of Mellish L.J. and James L.J. in *Re Fothergill Ex p. Turquand* (1876) 3 Ch. D. 445 at 450–451.
61 *McColl's Wholesale Pty Ltd v State Bank (NSW) Ltd* [1984] N.S.W.L.R. 365; *Russet Pty Ltd (in liq.) v Bach* (unreported, Supreme Court of New South Wales, June 23, 1988); *Raffle v AGC (Advances) Ltd* [1989] A.S.C. 58, 528; *Bayley v Gibsons Ltd* (1993) 1 Tas. R. 385. See also O'Donovan & Phillips, *The Modern Contract of Guarantee* (*op. cit.*), pp.657–658.

has paid off the debt, he has a right to the benefit of the remedies of the mortgagee" (at 312). This case does not appear to have been cited in *Ewart v Latta* or *Re Howe Ex p. Brett*.

(2)   If it were necessary that the surety should pay the whole debt in order to obtain a right of subrogation, it would be contrary to the concept of subrogation, which is intended to prevent the creditor acting to the detriment of the surety, so that the surety has some protection when enforcing his rights of indemnity against the principal debtor: Powell J.'s sentiments expressed in the *Healing* case at 487 are entirely consistent with the body of English authority on the nature of subrogation.

(3)   The cases of *Ewart v Latta* and *Re Howe* were concerned with creditors who had not been paid in full at all, and so to the extent that these cases laid down any general rule, they were *obiter* in that regard.[62]

It has been suggested that where the surety seeks to invoke the rights conferred by s.5 of the Mercantile Law Amendment Act 1856, then the creditor must have been satisfied in full *vis-à-vis* the principal indebtedness, and not simply that part for which the surety was liable.[63] However, in *Bayley v Gibsons Ltd* [1993] 1 Tas. R. 385, Zeeman J. considered (*obiter*, at 400–401) that this view did not represent the law, and that the phrase "debt ... of another" in s.5 of the Mercantile Law Amendment Act 1856[64] referred to not only the entire debt but also any part of it.[65]

When the right may not arise: the officious surety

Generally, the surety who makes a payment under a mistake of fact or law   **11–019**
is entitled to rights of subrogation since he has made the payment in performance of a legal duty.[66] There is some doubt whether the surety will be able to claim any rights of subrogation against the creditor whom he pays where he has officiously undertaken the role of surety without the agreement of the principal that he should do so. In *Owen v Tate* [1976] 1 Q.B. 402, the officious surety had made a payment to the creditor and sought an indemnity from the principal.[67] It was never argued that there should be subrogation to the creditor's rights, but it has been suggested by leading commentators.[68] that although there was no right of indemnity

---

62 See the remarks of Zeeman J. in *Bayley v Gibsons Ltd* [1993] 1 Tas. R. 385 at 394.
63 See O'Donovan & Phillips, *The Modern Contract of Guarantee* (*op. cit.*), p.658; O'Donovan & Phillips, English ed. (2003), paras 12–272 to 12–274.
64 In fact, Zeeman J. was considering the Australian equivalent, namely the Mercantile Law Act 1935, s.13(1), where the relevant wording is (on this point) identical.
65 See para.11–021 below.
66 See Goff and Jones, *The Law of Restitution* (6th ed., 2002), paras 3–012 to 3–19 and *Banque Financière de la Cité v Parc (Battersea) Ltd* [1999] 1 A.C. 221.
67 See the discussion of this case in the context of the surety's rights to an indemnity at Ch.10, para.10–010.
68 Goff and Jones, *The Law of Restitution* (6th ed., 2002), paras 3–016 to 3–018. See also P. Birks and J. Beatson, "Unrequested Payment of Another's Debt" (1976) 92 L.Q.R. 188.

available, the surety would be entitled to be subrogated to the creditor's rights. This would certainly be the case where the payment by the surety had discharged the debt, but the payment of a debt by another can only discharge that debt where it is consented to or subsequently ratified. In *Owen v Tate* there was no such consent or ratification[69] (and had there been, the surety would have been entitled to his indemnity, and certainly to subrogation). But the creditor had accepted the surety's giving of the guarantee and had released another surety in consideration of it, and thus the payment by the surety was not officious *vis-à-vis* the creditor. The creditor did not accept the payment mistakenly thinking it was a gift in effect to the principal such that the creditor would have been entitled to refuse to assign the debt to the surety. Accordingly, even though the principal could not be liable to indemnify his officious surety, the surety should nonetheless be entitled to be subrogated to the rights of the creditor to prevent his unjust enrichment, since without subrogation, the creditor would remain entitled to sue the principal.

Although this argument is highly persuasive (and indeed is probably correct) it would be a peculiar result if equity came to the aid of the surety in giving him rights of subrogation to the creditor's rights while refusing him a right of indemnity against the principal.[70] They are both equitable rights based upon identical equitable considerations: indeed in *Yonge v Reynell* (1852) 9 Hare 809 it was pointed out (at 818) that the right of subrogation is derived from the obligation of the principal to indemnify his surety. The effect of the right of subrogation is ultimately the same as that of the right of indemnity in this situation, namely that the principal must pay the surety what he owed the creditor, and it makes no difference in the end whether the payment was officious *vis-à-vis* the creditor or the debtor. It would therefore seem impossible to justify the denial of a right of indemnity to the surety while at the same time permitting him to retain a right of subrogation to the creditor's rights against the principal. Those rights either stand or fall together: see further the analysis by the Court of Appeal of the relationship between subrogation and the rights of recoupment and contribution in *Niru Battery Manufacturing Co v Milestone Trading (No.2)* [2004] 2 Lloyd's Rep. 319. Accordingly, it is submitted, if *Owen v Tate* is rightly decided, the officious surety should not be entitled in equity to be subrogated to the creditor's rights. If, on the other hand, the officious surety would have a right to subrogation based on unjust enrichment, there would appear to be no reason in principle to deny him a personal right of indemnity.

However, the argument based on unjust enrichment is unnecessary given the existence of the surety's rights under s.5 of the Mercantile Law Amendment Act 1856, which gives the surety rights of subrogation where he is "surety for the debt or duty of another", without it being necessary to

---

69 [1976] 1 Q.B. 402, at 410.
70 See Putnam, *Suretyship* (Oyez, 1981), p.85.

have become so at the request or with the consent of the principal. It seems that the plaintiff in *Owen v Tate* would have been entitled to exercise his statutory rights of subrogation notwithstanding that he was officiously a surety *vis-à-vis* the principal, on the basis that he was liable as surety to the creditor. Of course, had he not been liable at all, because for example he had not even assumed a role of surety *vis-à-vis* the creditor, he would not have had any such statutory rights. The view has been expressed that the Mercantile Law Amendment Act 1856 was intended to confirm the principle that the discharge of a creditor's security at law is not a bar to subrogation in equity and indeed is a precondition of the remedy of subrogation.[71]

The extent of the right of subrogation

(1) In respect of what amount

A surety for part of the principal debt is subrogated to the same rights that   **11–020**
the creditor has in respect of that part, and is entitled, on payment of that part, to share *pro rata* in any security which the creditor holds for the entirety of the debt.[72] This is so even if the security is given without the knowledge of the surety and to secure a further debt in addition to that in respect of which he gave the guarantee.[73] However, the surety is not entitled to be subrogated to a security held by the creditor in respect of a part of the debt to which the guarantee does not extend.[74] Further, in *Re Sass Ex p. National Provincial Bank of England* [1896] 2 Q.B. 12, the Court of Appeal held that where surety gave a guarantee for the whole amount limited to a specified sum, which he paid to the creditor, the creditor was nonetheless entitled to prove in the bankruptcy of the principal without deducting the amount of his debt received from the surety. Vaughan Williams L.J. said that even though the surety had guaranteed the whole of the debt, he had only paid a limited amount, and the creditor was entitled to hold all the securities given for the principal's liability until the whole amount of the debt was discharged.[75] Accordingly, it is of vital importance to distinguish between the surety's liability for a part of the debt, payment

---

71 See O'Donovan & Phillips (*op. cit.*), p.658 and see *Boscawen v Bajwa* [1996] 1 W.L.R. 328.
72 *Goodwin v Gray* (1874) 22 W.R. 312; *Ward v National Bank of New Zealand Ltd* (1889) 8 N.Z.L.R. (S.C.) 10. In *Re Butlers Wharf Ltd* [1995] 2 B.C.L.C. 43 Richard Sykes Q.C. held that *Goodwin v Gray* was good law and that the doubtful decision in *Farebrother v Woodhouse* (1853) 23 Beav. 18 cast no doubt on the principle set out in the text above: see further below at para.11–028. *Re Butler's Wharf Ltd* [1995] 2 B.C.L.C. 43 was approved by the Court of Appeal in *Liberty Mutual Insurance (UK) Ltd v HSBC Bank Plc* [2002] EWCA Civ 691, *per* Rix L.J. at paras 47 and 48.
73 *Scott v Knox* (1838) 2 Jon. Ex. 778; see the facts of *Praed v Gardner* (1788) 2 Cox. Eq. Cas. 86.
74 See the cases cited at para.11–015 above in relation to marshalling, especially *Wade v Coope* (1827) 2 Sim. 155; *Wilkinson v London and County Banking Co* (1884) 1 T.L.R. 63.
75 See *Liberty Mutual Insurance Co (UK) Ltd v HSBC Bank Plc* [2001] Ll. Rep. Bank 224, *per* Morritt V.-C. at para.11; affirmed [2002] EWCA Civ 691, CA. See also Ch.13, para.13–008. The surety may have an equitable interest in the secured property by way of a charge: *Gedye v Matson* (1858) 25 Beav. 310.

of which will entitle him to an immediately exercisable right of subrogation, and the surety's liability for the whole debt, limited in amount, payment of which amount does not give the surety an exercisable right of subrogation until the creditor has been paid in full.[76]

(2) Satisfied securities: The Mercantile Law Amendment Act 1856, s.5

11–021 Prior to the enactment of the Mercantile Law Amendment Act 1856, the common law position was that a surety was only entitled to be subrogated to the securities held by the creditor which had not been satisfied or extinguished by the payment.[77] Thus payment by the surety who was jointly liable with the principal discharged the debt, and the surety had only his right of indemnity against the principal. That rule was abrogated by s.5 of that enactment, which provided that the surety who has paid the debt or performs the duty in full is entitled to have assigned to him all judgments, specialties or securities held in respect of the debt or obligation, whether or not such were deemed at law to have been satisfied or not by the payment or performance. He is further entitled, upon giving the creditor a proper indemnity, to use the creditor's name in pursuing the principal to enforce such subrogated rights.

Where the surety is jointly liable with others, and pays the entire debt,[78] he is entitled by virtue of s.5 to an assignment to him of a judgment obtained by the creditor against the principal, and it is no answer to a claim by the surety for an assignment that the judgment had been satisfied by the surety's payment under it.[79] This useful principle cannot be extended beyond contractual joint liability.[80]

Where a person who is liable jointly with the principal becomes a surety for him, he may, upon giving notice of the fact to the creditor of this change, be entitled on payment to a right of subrogation against the creditor's rights in respect of the principal debt.[81] It is sufficient to notify the creditor subsequent to the transaction whereby the co-principal becomes surety.[82] Conversely, where one of two sureties assumes the primary liability under the guarantee, the co-surety retains his rights of subrogation on payment of the principal debt.[83]

The right to take an assignment under s.5 can be enforced by action, and an action for damages will lie against the creditor for failure to assign the

---

76 See Ch.6, para.6–006.
77 *Gammon v Stone* (1749) 1 Ves. Sen. 339; *Woffington v Sparks* (1754) 2 Ves. Sen. 569; *Copis v Middleton* (1823) Turn. & R. 224.
78 But see *Bayley v Gibsons Ltd* [1993] 1 Tas. R. 385, and n.142 above.
79 *Batchellor v Lawrence* (1861) 9 C.B.N.S. 543.
80 In *The Englishman and the Australian* [1895] P. 212, one of two joint tortfeasors paid the damages due under a judgment against them, but was not entitled to an assignment of the judgment even though he had a statutory right of contribution under what is now the Civil Liability (Contribution) Act 1978.
81 *Duncan, Fox & Co v North and South Wales Bank* (1880) 6 App. Cas. 1 at 12; and see *Re Marley* [1976] 1 W.L.R. 952.
82 *Rouse v Bradford Banking Co* [1894] A.C. 586.
83 *Parsons v Briddock* (1708) 2 Vern. 608.

judgment, right or security, provided a loss can be shown.[84] Generally the measure of damages will be the value of the specific assets which would have been available for execution under the judgment (or the value of the right or security) if assigned, without having to show that there were any other assets available against which the surety could enforce his right of indemnity against the principal.[85] However, there is no reason why the creditor should not be able to reduce his liability in damages if he can show that the surety has not reasonably mitigated his loss. The actual right of the surety to stand in the place of the judgment creditor under s.5 is not affected by the fact that no actual assignment has been effected; accordingly a surety who has a right to the assignment of a judgment can non the less prove for that debt in the principal's bankruptcy, even though the creditor has not yet assigned it.[86] The right to an assignment of a security, specialty or judgment under the section is not a personal right but a proprietary right in the subject of the assignment.

The surety seeking to enforce a judgment to which he is entitled under s.5 must obtain the leave of the court under RSC Ord. 46, r.2 which has been preserved in the Civil Procedure Rules 1999, Sch.1.[87] In exercising its discretion as to whether permission ought to be given, the court is entitled to consider the state of account between the parties to the judgment (*i.e.* the creditor and the principal), and their legal and equitable rights and liabilities.[88] The surety's right to receive an assignment from the creditor is subject to whatever equities may exist between the creditor and the principal, and the surety cannot be in any better position in respect of the rights sought to be assigned than the creditor.[89]

The other major effect of s.5 is that the surety succeeds to the priority enjoyed by the creditor in respect of those rights against the principal to which he has become entitled.[90] This has been regarded as somewhat unfair to the principal's other creditors,[91] but its justification lies in the fact that the surety who is subrogated to the creditor's rights stands in his shoes, and the subsequent encumbrancers are not prejudiced because they took notice of the prior encumbrance, it making no difference whether the security is enforced by the creditor, his assignee or the surety.[92] That is not to say that

---

84 *Phillips v Dickson* (1860) 8 C.B.N.S. 391; *Dale v Powell* (1911) 105 L.T. 291; *Kayley v Hothersall* [1925] 1 K.B. 607; *Brown v Cork* [1985] B.C.L.C. 363 (co-sureties).

85 *Oddy v Hallett* (1885) Cab. & El. 532.

86 *Re McMyn, Lightbown v McMyn* (1886) 33 Ch. D. 575.

87 An application for permission under that rule is not the commencement of proceedings for the purposes of the Limitation Act 1980, s.38(2): *National Westminster Bank Plc v Powney* [1991] Ch. 339.

88 *Kayley v Hothersall* [1925] 1 K.B. 607.

89 *Dale v Powle* (1911) 105 L.T. 291.

90 *Re McMyn, Lightbown v McMyn* (1886) 33 Ch. D. 575; *Re Lord Churchill* (1888) 39 Ch. D. 174; *Re Lamplugh Iron Ore Co* [1927] 1 Ch. 308 and see *Badeley v Consolidated Bank* (1888) 38 Ch. D. 238, CA; *Re Davison's Estate* (1893) 31 L.R.I.R. 249.

91 See Goff and Jones, *The Law of Restitution* (6th ed., 2002), paras 3–026–3–027.

92 *Re Davison's Estate* (1893) 31 L.R. I.R. 249, *per* Monroe J. at 255, where he distinguishes the position of the surety enforcing the security from that of the principal paying it off himself. See also *Drew v Lockett* (1863) 32 Beav. 499; and para.11–015.

notice need not be given to anyone. In *Re Jason Construction Ltd* (1975) 25 D.L.R. (3d) 340, the bank which took from a building company a general assignment of the book debts by way of floating charge as security for continuing advances was not postponed to a surety who completed the work after the company's default and who was subrogated to the claims against the building owners for amounts outstanding. Since both the bank's assignment and the surety's rights to which he was subrogated were equitable claims, priority was given to the person who first perfected his interest by giving notice to the building owner who was liable to the company.[93]

The surety may be subrogated to the rights of the Crown.[94] The rights to which a surety may become entitled under s.5 will not be available to someone who was not under any liability to make the payment to the creditor.[95]

(3) To what rights and securities the surety can be subrogated

11–022   As has been stated above, the surety is entitled to the benefit of all securities held in respect of the guaranteed debt or obligation, including both those which were in existence at the date the guarantee was given,[96] and those which came into existence after the assumption of liability by the surety.[97] It is immaterial that the securities were given to the creditor by the principal,[98] by the co-surety,[99] or by the principal's partner,[1] so long as it is held for the principal obligation.[2] In *Pledge v Buss* (1860) John. 663, Wood V.-C. said:

> "the law is now well established that a person having a mortgage for a guaranteed debt is bound to hold it for the benefit of the surety, so as to enable him, on paying the debt which he has guaranteed, to take the security in its original condition unimpaired."

The rationale for this rule was explained by Hall V.-C. in *Forbes v Jackson* (1882) 19 Ch. D. 615:

> "The principle is that the surety bargains that the securities that the creditor takes shall be for him, if and when he shall be called upon to make any payment, and it is the duty of the creditor to keep the

---

93 This is the rule in *Dearle v Hall* (1828) 3 Russ. 1.
94 *R. v Robinson* (1855) 1 H. & N. 275; *R. v Salter* (1856) 1 H. & N. 274; and see Crown Proceedings Act 1947, Sch.1.
95 See para.11–019.
96 *Forbes v Jackson* (1882) 19 Ch. D. 615; *Campbell v Rothwell* (1877) 38 L.T. 33.
97 *Mayhew v Crickett* (1818) 2 Swanst. 185, at 919 *per* Lord Eldon L.C.; *Pledge v Buss* (1860) John. 663; *Lake v Brutton* (1854) 18 Beav. 34.
98 *Mayhew v Crickett* (1818) 2 Swanst. 185; *Goddard v Whyte* (1860) 2 Giff. 449.
99 *Dering v Winchelsea (Earl)* (1787) 2 Bos. & P. 270.
 1 *Goddard v Whyte* (1860) 2 Giff. 449.
 2 *Duncan, Fox & Co v North and South Wales Bank* (1880) 6 App. Cas. 1; *cf. Chatterton v McLean* [1951] 1 All E.R. 761.

securities; not to give them up nor to burthen them with further advances."

The surety is entitled to the securities held for the principal debt at the time he pays it off, and to the benefit of any securities taken in substitution of those securities, to the extent that he has not been discharged thereby.[3] Further, it has been suggested that if the creditor abandons securities without the consent of the surety, then the surety is entitled to a pro rata reduction in the amount of his liability, but this is difficult to reconcile with authority.[4] This is rather different from the situation where the creditor fails to obtain the full market value for securities that he sells: *Skipton Building Society v Stott* [2001] 1 Q.B. 261.[5]

The term "security" has been given a wide meaning by the courts. In *Re Stratton Ex p. Salting* (1883) 25 Ch. D. 148, it was held that a guarantee of one partner in a firm under which the creditor had a right of proof against the separate estate of that partner as well as a right against the partnership property was a security to which the surety could resort. A sum of money standing to the credit of the principal, but appropriated to a particular purpose under a contract, is a security to which the surety may become subrogated.[6] A policy of insurance over life or property is a security the benefit of which the surety is entitled to enjoy.[7] An unpaid seller's lien over goods and his rights of stoppage in transit,[8] documents of title, promissory notes, a lien on shares,[9] and seller's rights under a reservation of title clause,[10] are all examples of rights to which the surety may be subrogated. The surety may also be subrogated to moneys appropriated to the principal transaction.[11]

---

3 See *Ward v National Bank of New Zealand* (1889) 8 N.Z.L.R. (S.C.) 10.

4 See O'Donovan & Phillips, *The Modern Contract of Guarantee* (*op. cit.*), p.668, relying on *Pearl v Deacon* (1857) 24 Beav. 186. Their view is repeated in O'Donovan & Phillips, English ed. (2003), para.12–304. However, this is not what that case actually says, and is in any event not the modern view: see *China & South Seas Bank v Tan* [1990] 1 A.C. 536, PC. In *Mahomed v Morris* [2000] 2 B.C.L.C. 536, Peter Gibson L.J. said (at para.27, p.555) that a surety seeking to exercise subrogation rights is not a creditor In the liquidation of the principal, but is seeking to enforce rights outside liquidation. Schiemann L.J. said (at para.42, 560) that "a creditor who holds disputed security from a debtor is not under a duty to give notice to the debtor's surety before the creditor enters into a compromise agreement with the debtor whereunder sone of the alleged security is surrendered to the debtor".

5 See the discussion of this case in Ch.9, para.9–041.

6 *Re Sherry* (1884) 25 Ch. D. 692, esp at 702.

7 See, *e.g. Watts v Shuttleworth* (1861) 7 H. & N. 353.

8 *Imperial Bank v London and St Katharine Dock Co* (1877) 5 Ch. D. 195, and see *Re Westzinthus* (1833) 5 B. and Ad. 817, where the lien arose as a result of a custom. A surety cannot stop the goods against the principal in his own name, but must use the name of the vendor (*i.e.* the creditor): *Siffken v Wray* (1805) 6 East. 371.

9 *Brandon v Brandon* (1859) 3 De G. & J. 524.

10 *Aluminium Industrie Vaassen BV v Romalpa Aluminium Ltd* [1976] 1 W.L.R. 676. This will be so whether or not the reservation of title clause actually gives rise to a security interest in the strict sense, or a mere contractual right: the surety is subrogated to the creditor's rights against the principal in relation to the goods, whether proprietary or personal.

11 *Employers' Liability Assurance v R.* [1969] 2 Ex. C.R. 246.

The discussion earlier in this chapter in relation to over what securities the surety will be entitled to exercise his rights of marshalling applies equally to subrogation.[12] Where, therefore, the principal owes the creditor two debts, and has given security for one of them only, the other being the subject of the guarantee given by the surety, the surety is entitled to have the benefit of the surplus from the securities in reduction of his own liability to the creditor.[13] However, where the principal has given the creditor security for particular advances which are expressly returnable on repayment of each advance, then the surety who has guaranteed the general balance will not be entitled to be subrogated to these securities.[14] As has been explained above,[15] the general rule is that the surety cannot be subrogated to security given for a different debt or a different part of the same debt: in order for the surety to be subrogated to the creditor's rights in respect of security not actually given for the guaranteed obligation, the creditor must have security for a debt that can be consolidated with the guaranteed debt.

The surety may be subrogated not only to securities held by the creditor from the principal, but also to those given by co-sureties, as a means of enforcing his right of contribution against them,[16] where he has paid more than his common liability. Further, where the surety's liability under the guarantee has been itself guaranteed, the surety under that latter guarantee is entitled to be subrogated to the creditor's security against the co-sureties in prior degree.[17] Similarly, the surety's right of subrogation (certainly under s.5) includes judgments obtained against his co-sureties, but not where he has been sued by the creditor as sole defendant, and satisfied the judgment, because there will be nothing to assign.[18]

It seems that in certain circumstances the surety may also be subrogated to the creditor's rights against third parties. In *Re Miller, Gibb and Co Ltd* [1957] 1 W.L.R. 703 the English Board of Trade, which had guaranteed an exporter's losses due to foreign exchange control, was held to be subrogated to the exporter's right to a certain fund as soon as it came to hand, having been permitted by the foreign exchange authority.[19]

It is not altogether clear whether floating charges are securities which are subject to the doctrine of subrogation. In Australia, floating charges have been held to be security rights to which the surety cannot become

---

12 See para.11–015.
13 *Praed v Gardner* (1788) 2 Cox. Cas. Eq. Cas. 86; *Heyman v Dubois* (1871) L.R. 13 Eq. 158.
14 *Wilkinson v London and County Banking Co* (1884) 1 T.L.R. 63.
15 See para.11–020.
16 See Mercantile Law Amendment Act 1856, s.5; *Greenside v Benson* (1745) 3 Atk. 248; *Duncan, Fox & Co v North and South Wales Bank* (1880) 6 App. Cas. 1; *Re Parker, Morgan v Hill* [1894] 3 Ch. 400; *Smith v Wood* [1929] 1 Ch. 14.
17 See *Parsons v Briddock* (1708) Vern. 608; *Wright v Morley* (1805) 11 Ves. 12; *Standard Brands Ltd v Fox* (1974) 44 D.L.R. (3d) 69; *Fox v Royal Bank of Canada* (1975) 59 D.L.R. (3d) 258, and the discussion in Rowlatt, *Principal and Surety* (*op. cit.*), p.158, n.38.
18 *Hardy v Johnson* (1880) 6 V.L.R. (L.) 190.
19 See also *City of Prince Albert v Underwood McLellan and Associates* (1968) 3 D.L.R. (3d) 385.

subrogated.[20] This is because the nature of a floating charge is as an inchoate equitable assignment which allows the chargor company to utilise the assets which upon crystallisation would become subject to the charge in the ordinary course of its business:[21] this is wholly at odds with the exercise of a right of subrogation, which entitles the surety to call for the assets the subject of the security immediately upon payment. In *O'Day v Commercial Bank of Australia* (1933) 50 C.L.R. 200, Dixon J. said:

> "A floating charge operates to secure monies over an undertaking without giving to the creditor any legal or equitable interest in any specific piece of property comprised in the undertaking until the event occurs upon which it becomes a fixed security. The creditor obtains neither the possession nor property in any part of the assets. He has nothing to retransfer or to redeliver to the debtor upon payment of the debt. The debtor retains control of the assets and the power to dispose of them in the ordinary course of business. The rule of equity invoked is that "if a creditor holding security sues for his debt, he is under an obligation on payment of the debt to hand over the security; and if having improperly made away with the security, he is unable to return it to his debtor, he cannot have judgment for the debt" (*per* Viscount Cave L.C., *Ellis and Co's Trustee v. Dixon-Johnson* [1925] A.C. 000, at 491). This doctrine is entirely inapplicable to a charge which remains floating where nothing is vested in or handed over to the creditor."

This view has not been followed by later Commonwealth and Dominion authority,[22] and there are strong arguments in favour of floating charges being subject to the doctrine of subrogation. Although the surety is entitled in the usual course of events to call for the securities, neither the doctrine of subrogation nor the effect of s.5 of the Mercantile Law Amendment Act 1856 puts the surety in a better position with regard to such securities than the creditor himself. Since the creditor is not entitled to a transfer to him of the assets subject to the floating charge until a crystallising event occurs (as is provided for in the debenture), the surety is similarly not entitled to call for a transfer of the assets the subject of the charge. This does not mean

---

20 *O'Day v Commercial Bank of Australia Ltd* (1933) 50 C.L.R. 200 at 220–221.
21 See *Re Yorkshire Woolcombers Association Ltd* [1903] 2 Ch. 284; *Siebe Gorman & Co Ltd v Barclays Bank Ltd* [1972] 2 Lloyd's Rep. 142; *Re Brightlife* [1987] 2 W.L.R. 197; *Re a Company (No.005009) Ex p. Copp* [1989] B.C.L.C. 13; *Re New Bullas Trading Ltd* [1994] B.C.C. 36; *Royal Trust Bank v National Westminster Bank Plc* [1996] 2 B.C.L.C. 682; *Re Westmaze* [1999] B.C.C. 441; *Re Hamlet International Plc* [1999] 2 B.C.L.C. 506. As to the position concerning fixed or floating charges over book debts, see *Re New Bullas Trading Ltd* [1994] B.C.C. 36; *National Westminster Bank Plc v Spectrum Plus Ltd* [2004] EWCA Civ 670. In *Agnew v CIR* [2002] 1 A.C. 710, the Privy Council disapproved *Re New Bullas Trading Ltd*, but the decision of the Privy Council in *Agnew* was itself not followed by the Court of Appeal in *Natwest v Spectrum*.
22 See *National Bank of New Zealand v Chapman* [1975] N.Z.L.R. 480; *Roynat Ltd v Denis* (1982) 139 D.L.R. (3d) 265; see also O'Donovan & Phillips, *The Modern Contract of Guarantee* (*op. cit.*), p.674; O'Donovan & Phillips, English ed. (2003), para.12–320. The *O'Day* case was examined and distinguished in *Re Selvas Pty Ltd* (1990) 52 S.A.S.R. 449.

that the surety is therefore not entitled to the creditor's security interest in those assets; on the contrary, there is no reason why the surety should not be entitled to call for an assignment of the floating charge and have himself registered as the holder, or even simply to await a crystallising event and enforce the security in the creditor's name.

Most cases relating to subrogation will involve the surety claiming to be entitled to enforce securities held by the creditor for the debt which he has discharged. Prior to the decision in *Banque Financiere v Parc (Battersea) Ltd* [1999] 1 A.C. 221 there was some authority to the effect that subrogation is not available in respect of rights which are personal to the creditor. For example, in *Chatterton v McLean* [1951] 1 All E.R. 761, the surety was held not to be subrogated to the hire purchase company's right to seize the goods because, it was held, this was a personal right.[23] It has also been held that a right to distrain for rent is not a right to which the surety can be subrogated.[24] However, more recent authorities have deprecated any such limitation on the equitable remedy, at least in cases where in the absence of such a remedy, there would be unjust enrichment. See, *e.g. Cheltenham and Gloucester Plc v Appleyard* [2004] EWCA Civ 291, *The Times*, March 29, 2004, in which Neuberger L.J. said (at para.36):

"Fifthly, although the classic case of subrogation involves a lender who expected to receive security (in the proprietary sense—e.g. a mortgage) claiming subrogation to another security, it can apply to personal rights. In *Re Wrexham, Mold and Connah's Quay Railway Co* [1899] 1 Ch. 440 at 458, Vaughan Williams LJ referred to the claim for subrogation being to "the rights of the creditor who has been paid off" and does not appear to have linked those rights to proprietary rights".

That passage was cited with approval by the Court of Appeal in *Filby v Mortgage Express (No.2) Ltd* [2004] EWCA Civ 759; [2004] N.P.C. 98. That case did not concern the rights of a surety to be subrogated to the creditor's rights against the principal debtor but rather, the rights of a lender under an invalid security to be subrogated to the rights of an earlier unsecured lender. A mortgage deed was apparently executed between Mr and Mrs F as mortgagors and the lenders as mortgagees. The lenders' solicitors believed that they were also instructed by Mr and Mrs F, on instructions received from Mr F. The lenders obtained a possession order and, on discovering that Mrs F had abandoned the property, took possession and sold the house. It then transpired that Mrs F's apparent signature on the mortgage application form and mortgage deed was a forgery. Mrs F claimed a full half share in the proceeds of sale, on the grounds that the mortgage was a nullity and she was not bound by it. It was conceded by her (on the principle of *Boscawen v Bajwa* [1996] 1 W.L.R. 328) that the

---

23 *Dalby v India and London Life Assurance Co* (1854) 15 C.B. 365.
24 *Re Albert Life Assurance Co Ex p. Western Life Assurance Society* (1870) L.R. 11 Eq. 164.

lenders were entitled to be subrogated to the rights of an earlier mortgagee whose mortgage had been discharged by the loan. That left an argument as to whether the lenders were also entitled to be subrogated to the rights of Midland Bank, an unsecured lender, on the grounds that the money advanced by the respondents had also been used to reduce the indebtedness of Mr and Mrs F on joint account to Midland. The lenders succeeded, the Court of Appeal holding that although the classic case of subrogation involves the lender claiming subrogation to another security, it can apply to personal rights, and there was no reason in principle not to apply the principles of unjust enrichment as laid down in *Banque Financiere* to this situation. Mrs F was enriched to the extent that the loan reduced her joint indebtedness to Midland. It would be inequitable to leave the lender without a remedy against her. In those circumstances the lender was entitled to a right equivalent to the unsecured personal rights of Midland arising under the joint loan account, including the right to accumulated interest.

Applying the reasoning in those cases, there would appear to be no reason in principle why a surety should not also be entitled to be subrogated to unsecured personal claims by the creditor against third parties, or even against the principal debtor himself.

Rights and securities to which the surety cannot be subrogated

The surety cannot be subrogated in the case of a number of rights and securities: **11–023**

(1)   Private insurance policies. The doctrine of subrogation does not extend to a policy on the life of the debtor taken out and maintained by the creditor at his own expense; the creditor may retain the policy even if the principal debt is paid.[25] Nor will the surety be entitled to be subrogated to an insurance policy taken out by a co-surety at his own expense to protect himself against the liability he might incur under the guarantee.[26] However, a policy of insurance deposited as security for the principal obligation will be subject to subrogation.[27]

(2)   Rights wrongfully or preferentially obtained by the creditor. The doctrine of subrogation will not extend to security interests which the creditor has obtained as a result of a voidable transaction. Indeed, it seems that a third party whose property has been charged to the creditor will be permitted to use the guarantee to secure the release of the property, since he will be entitled to have the property relieved of any encumbrance by any property of the principal pledged for the same debt at the expense of the surety for the debt.[28]

---

25 See *Rainbow v Juggins* (1880) 5 Q.B.D. 422.
26 This case was cited without disapproval in *Moschi v Lep Air Services Ltd* [1973] A.C. 331 although it is difficult to see why the right of seizure was a personal right.
27 *Re Russell, Russell v Shoolbred* (1885) 29 Ch. D. 254 and see Ch.18.
28 *Ex p. Altson* (1868) 4 Ch. App. 168.

(1) Transfer of mortgages and other securities

11–024   Where the guaranteed debt is secured by a mortgage executed by the principal, the surety is entitled to call for a transfer of the mortgage to himself upon satisfaction of the principal obligation.[29] Prior to the transfer, the surety has an equitable charge on the mortgaged property to the extent of the payment made by the surety.[30] It seems that these rights, although they arise in equity, remain inchoate until the time of the transfer and are not registrable as interests in land.[31] Where the mortgage debt was paid out of the proceeds of securities provided by the surety, he was entitled to call for a transfer of the mortgage notwithstanding a proviso in the mortgage deed to the effect that on satisfaction of the mortgage debt, whether by the principal or his surety, the mortgage was to be reconveyed to the principal.[32]

Where the surety redeems a mortgage by the principal, he is deemed to do so for his own benefit and is not presumed, like the mortgagor, to have done so for the benefit of the subsequent encumbrancers, and he receives the property in priority to them, even though their securities were created before the contract of guarantee.[33] A contract of guarantee need not necessarily involve personal liability, and a surety who mortgages his property for another's debt is no less a surety than the surety who undertakes personal liability, with the same rights against the creditor,[34] although, following *BCCI (No.8)* [1998] A.C. 214, there is a substantive, albeit artificial, difference in the position of a surety who personally covenants for repayment of the principal debt and a surety who does not, in that the latter may not be entitled to take advantage of insolvency set-off as against the creditor.[35] But it must still be good law that a surety who has mortgaged his property for the principal's debt, the principal having also provided security for that debt, has an interest in that property and should be made party to an action to redeem or foreclose on that property,[36] and he has the right, in the exercise of his right of subrogation, to redeem that property.[37] A surety will also have a right of redemption where he joins in the mortgage of the principal so as to be surety for the principal liability secured.[38]

---

29 *South v Bloxham* (1865) 2 Hem. & M. 457, where Page-Wood V.-C. appeared to doubt whether the right arose until payment; but see *Dixon v Steel* [1901] 2 Ch. 602, where it was clarified that the surety's rights to security arise when he enters the guarantee; see also *Lake v Brutton* (1856) 18 Beav. 34; *Pledge v Buss* (1860) John. 663.
30 *Gedye v Matson* (1858) 25 Beav. 310; *Allen v de Lisle* (1856) 3 Jur. N.S. 928; *Re Davison's Estate* (1893) 31 L.R. I.R. 249.
31 *Kennedy v Campbell* [1899] 1 I.R. 59, at 63 *per* Kenny J.
32 *M'Neale v Reed* (1857) 7 I. Ch. R. 251.
33 *Re Davison's Estate* (1893) 31 L.R. I.R. 249; *Sawyer v Goodwin* (1875) 1 Ch. D. 351.
34 *Bolton v Salmon* [1891] 2 Ch. 48.
35 See Ch.13, paras 13–019 *et seq.*
36 *Stokes v Clendon* (1790) 3 Swan. 150; see also *Re Marley* [1976] 1 W.L.R. 952 for a case involving joint mortgagors.
37 *Dixon v Steel* [1901] 2 Ch. 602.
38 *Green v Wynn* (1869) 4 Ch. App. 204.

(2) Tacking and consolidation

It is now tolerably clear that the surety's right on payment of the principal **11–025**
debt to be subrogated to the creditor's securities cannot be postponed
merely by the creditor giving further advances to the principal on those
securities.[39] In *Williams v Owen* (1843) 13 S.M. 597, it was held that the
creditor could tack against the surety who had joined in a covenant in a
mortgage deed on the basis that he must have known and impliedly
consented to the right.[40] However, that authority was not followed in
Dawson v Bank of Whitehaven (1877) 4 Ch. D. 639 nor in *Forbes v Jackson*
(1882) 19 Ch. D. 615, where the surety either was not postponed and was
wholly ignorant of the subsequent advances or where such advances were
not contemplated at the time of the loan. Hall V.-C. laid down the principle
that the security which is taken by the creditor is for the surety, and is not
to be given up nor burdened with further advances.[41]

There is nothing preventing the creditor from expressly providing for a
right to make subsequent advances on securities provided by the principal,
and sometimes the principal is given the right to call for them, in which
case the surety may be taken to have agreed that the creditor could tack
further advances against him.[42] Further, where the person claiming rights as
surety in fact contracted as principal, he will not be entitled to rights as if
he were a surety, and the creditor will be entitled to tack against him.[43]

The principle of consolidation permits a creditor who holds two mortgages, each made by the same mortgagor, to refuse to allow the mortgagor
to redeem one mortgage without redeeming the other. The right to
consolidate mortgages is restricted by s.93 of the Law of Property Act 1925,
which provides that it is only to exist if stipulated for. The creditor is not
entitled to exercise this right against a surety, and this restriction binds the
mortgage securities into whomsoever's hands they come.[44] Like tacking, the
right of consolidation can be exercised against one who contracts not in fact

---

39 Tacking has been abolished except as to further advances made either by arrangement with
a subsequent mortgagee or without notice of a subsequent mortgage at the time of the
further advance and under an obligation imposed by the mortgage: Law of Property Act
1925, s.94. In *Liberty Mutual Insurance Co (UK) Ltd v HSBC Bank Plc* [2001] Ll. Rep. Bank
224, Morritt V.-C. said that a clause in the guarantee which provided that it was separate
from the creditor's other securities and a continuing agreement were not clear words
effective to exclude or postpone the right of subrogation on payment, and the bank's "short
answer", that otherwise the creditor and the debtor could, by the creation of further
liabilities, postpone forever the right of subrogation, was correct (see paras 16, 17). The
decision was affirmed on appeal (see [2002] EWCA Civ 691).
40 This decision was followed in *Farebrother v Woodhouse* (1853) 23 Beav. 18; see also *Bowker
v Bull* (1850) 1 Sim. N.S. where it was neither cited nor followed. In *Re Butlers Wharf Ltd*
[1995] 2 B.C.L.C. 43, *Farebrother v Woodhouse*'s subsequent treatment in later cases was
described as "not one of universal acclaim": see *Re Kirkwood's Estate* (1878) 1 L.R. I.R.
108; *Nicholas v Ridley* [1904] 1 Ch. 192.
41 See the passage quoted above at para.11–022.
42 *West v Williams* [1899] 1 Ch. 132.
43 *Nicholas v Ridley* [1904] 1 Ch. 192, applying *Newton v Chorlton* (1853) 10 Hare 346;
Duncan, Fox & Co v North and South Wales Bank (1880) 6 App. Cas. 1.
44 *Bowker v Bull* (1850) 1 Sim. N.S. 29. In *Farebrother v Wodehouse* (1856) 23 Beav. 18, the
surety knew that there were two securities, although he had only given one.

as surety but as principal, where it could be exercised against the principal.[45] The right only arises where the mortgages were created by the same mortgagor, and not where the equities of redemption have been acquired by assignment.[46] The right of consolidation will apply against a surety where the mortgage is subject to consolidation upon its creation, for example where the creditor takes a charge for another debt simultaneously with the giving of the guarantee.

Loss of the right of subrogation

11–026   Where the creditor himself realises the securities held for the principal debt and applies them in reduction or extinction of that debt, the surety will lose his rights of subrogation, although this is immaterial since by applying the securities to the debt, the surety will usually be taken to have been *pro tanto* discharged.[47] Further, where the creditor prejudices the surety's right of subrogation, the surety may, if the obtaining and preserving of securities was a condition of the guarantee, be absolutely discharged, and where it is not such a condition, be *pro tanto* discharged.[48]

Payment under a counter-guarantee can operate to deprive the original sureties of their rights of subrogation. In *Brown Shipley and Co Ltd v Amalgamated Investment (Europe) BV* [1979] 1 Lloyd's Rep. 488, the plaintiffs guaranteed a loan by a bank to the defendant. As security they took a counter-guarantee from the defendant's parent company. When the plaintiffs were called on under their guarantee they called in turn on the parent company under its counter-guarantee, which satisfied its liability under the counter-guarantee with the aid of a loan from the plaintiffs. The plaintiffs then sued the defendant on the basis that it was subrogated to the bank's rights and remedies as creditor. Donaldson J. held that these rights of subrogation were no longer available to the plaintiffs, having been transferred by operation of law to the parent company when it discharged its liability under the counter-guarantee. Since the plaintiffs had in effect surrendered their rights under the counter-guarantee, they also lost their rights of subrogation against the defendant. This result could have been avoided by the plaintiffs themselves discharging the indebtedness to the bank instead of providing the parent company with a loan which it used to discharge its counter-guarantee.

Effect of death and insolvency

11–027   Far from destroying the right of subrogation, the death of the surety may in fact enhance its enforcement. Where the principal is a legatee under the surety's will, the executors of the will are entitled to retain the amount of

---

45 *Nicholas v Ridley* [1904] 1 Ch. 192.
46 *Sharp v Rickards* [1909] 1 Ch. 109.
47 See Ch.9, para.9–002.
48 It is necessary to find a duty on the part of the creditor to take care in relation to securities he holds for the guaranteed obligation, and where none exists the surety may not be discharged at all: see *China & South Seas Bank v Tan* [1990] 1 A.C. 536, PC; *Burgess v Auger* [1998] 2 B.C.L.C. 478; *Skipton Building Society v Stott* [2001] 1 Q.B. 261; *Silven Properties Ltd v Royal Bank of Scotland* [2004] 1 B.C.L.C. 359; and see Ch.9, para.9–043.

the surety's claim to an indemnity plus a reasonable sum for interest out of the legacy due to the principal.[49] This rule operates notwithstanding the insolvency of the principal after the death of the surety, and even if the surety's claim would be time-barred. Further, even where the principal had entered an assignment for the benefit of his creditors, to which the creditor had assented, the surety's executors were entitled to retain the amount of the principal debt out of the legacy payable to the principal instead of proving in the creditor's place.[50]

Generally, the insolvency of the principal or co-surety will not affect the surety's rights of subrogation. There is, however, a special rule which applies where there is a concurrent insolvency of two parties liable on a bill of exchange. This is known as the rule in *Ex p. Waring* (1815) 19 Ves. 345,[51] which states that where, as between the drawer and acceptor of a bill of exchange a security has, by virtue of the contract between them, been specifically appropriated to meet the bill at maturity, and has been lodged by the drawer with the acceptor for that purpose, the holder of the bill is entitled, upon the insolvency of both the drawer and acceptor, to have the specifically appropriated security applied towards payment of the bill.

Waiver of the right of subrogation

The right of subrogation can be expressly excluded by clear words in the   **11–028**
contract of guarantee.[52] However, a clause in a guarantee to the effect that the creditor is at liberty to treat the surety as if he were a principal, and that he is not to be discharged by a giving of time or accommodation to the principal, will not exclude the surety's rights of subrogation to which he is entitled upon payment.[53] Further, in *Re Butlers Wharf Ltd* [1995] 2 B.C.L.C. 43, Richard Sykes Q.C. held that a provision which expressed the guarantee to be additional to any other security held by the creditor was not sufficient to oust or postpone the surety's rights of subrogation.[54] In doing so, he declined to apply, or to give any weight to, an obiter contrary indication in the judgment of Peter Oliver in *Barclays Bank Ltd v TOSG Trust Fund Ltd* [1984] 1 A.C. 626, at 643–634.

Richard Sykes Q.C.'s approach in *Re Butler's Wharf Ltd* was followed by Sir Andrew Morritt V.-C. in *Liberty Mutual Insurance (UK) Ltd v HSBC*

---

49 *Re Watson* [1896] 1 Ch. 925.
50 *Re Whitehouse* (1887) 37 Ch. D. 683. It is doubtful whether the rule still applies in relation to voluntary arrangements under Pt VIII of the Insolvency Act 1986.
51 See Ch.13, para.13–017.
52 *Re Fernandes Ex p. Hope* (1844) 3 Mont. D. & De G. 270; *Earle v Oliver* (1848) 2 Exch. 71; *Re Porter Ex p. Miles* (1848) De G. 623; *Midland Banking Co v Chambers* (1869) 4 Ch. App. 398; *Re Sellers Ex p. Midland Banking Co* (1878) 38 L.T. 395; *Re Rees Ex p. National Provincial Bank of England* (1881) 17 Ch. D. 98; *Barclays Bank Ltd v TOSG Fund Ltd* [1984] 1 All E.R. 628; *Re Butler's Wharf Ltd* [1995] 2 B.C.L.C. 43 (Richard Sykes Q.C.); *Liberty Mutual Insurance Co (UK) Ltd v HSBC Bank Plc* [2001] Lloyds Rep. (Bank) 224, (affd, Court of Appeal [2002] EWCA Civ 691, esp. *per* Rix L.J. at para.59).
53 *Re Kirkwood's Estate* (1878) 1 L.R. Ir. 108; and see *Equity Trustees Agency v New Zealand Loan and Mercantile Agency Co Ltd* [1940] V.L.R. 201.
54 See the critique of this case in [2000] 116 L.Q.R. 121, Ward and McCormack.

Bank Plc [2001] Lloyd's Rep. (Bank) 224. In that case, OMMIA, a P&I Club, had had an arrangement with HSBC Bank whereby the latter would provide guarantees of OMMIA's members liabilities which it would issue to procure the release of those members' vessels from arrest. The bank took a fixed charge over OMMIA's book debts for all of OMMIA's liabilities to the bank, both to indemnify the bank under the bank's guarantees issued in respect of its members and in respect of OMMIA's other liabilities to it. The bank also had the benefit of a guarantee from Liberty Mutual in respect only of OMMIA's liability to indemnify the bank under the bank's guarantees issued in respect of OMMIA's members. The Liberty Mutual guarantee contained a clause providing that "This Agreement is separate from any other security or right of indemnity taken in respect of the Guarantee from any person . . . This Agreement shall be a continuing Agreement and binding on the Surety, its successors and assigns." Liberty Mutual had paid the entirety of the amounts owed by OMMIA to the bank which were covered by the Liberty Mutual guarantee, and sought to be subrogated to the bank's rights in respect of the book debts, *pari passu* with the bank. The bank argued that the words quoted above meant that Liberty Mutual's rights of subrogation were postponed until the bank had satisfied itself as far as it could out of the book debts. It argument was founded on Oliver L.J.'s dictum in *Barclays Bank Ltd v TOSG Trust Fund Ltd* [1984] 1 A.C. 626, at 643–644, in which Oliver L.J. appeared to rely on the judgment of Vaughan Williams L.J. in *Re Sass* [1896] 2 QB 12. Sir Andrew Morritt V.-C. rejected the argument. He analysed *Re Sass*, and particularly the language and structure of the guarantee in that case, and held that Vaughan-Williams L.J. was not, in deciding that the surety's rights of subrogation were postponed, relying on the clause akin to the words quoted above, but on other parts of the guarantee which made it clear that they were. Consequently, Oliver L.J.'s observation in TOSG was effectively wrong. Such words of postponement present in the *Re Sass* guarantee were absent from the OMMIA guarantee (as they were from the guarantee in *Re Butler's Wharf*).[55]

Sir Andrew Morritt V.-C. went on to say that clear words are required to exclude, reduce or postpone the right of subrogation, which was not effected by the rather oblique words, of uncertain purpose, quoted above (see para.15 of the judgment). He also said that postponement made no commercial sense, because if on payment in full of the liability under the guarantee, the surety's rights were thus postponed until all of OMMIA's other liabilities were discharged as well, the practical effect would be to extend liability under the guarantee. That, he said, led to the untenable position that, if the security given by the debtor was "all monies", the creditor and the debtor could postpone for ever the rights of subrogation of

---

55 There is also a major point of distinction, in that the guarantee in *Re Sass* was for the entirety of the principal's liabilities to the creditor, the surety's liability thereunder being limited in amount, whereas in *Liberty Mutual v HSBC Bank*, the guarantee was not limited, but Liberty Mutual had paid all the amounts due from the principal covered thereby.

the surety by the creation of further principal liabilities (see para.16 of the judgment).

In the Court of Appeal,[56] Rix L.J. gave the leading judgment and reached the same conclusions. In particular, he focussed on the purpose of the "separate from other securities" clause, and said that its purpose was to emphasise that the rights under the guarantee could be exercised separately from the other securities held by the bank, and that it was the guarantee that was separate, not any other security or indemnity. He also pointed out that the clause did not refer to postponement or even subrogation, and that separation of the security is not necessarily the same thing as postponement.

The right of subrogation may also be excluded by an implied term in the guarantee, but it cannot be excluded or waived by a course of dealing.[57] It seems that the statutory right of subrogation may also be excluded by sufficient words or conduct. The surety may be taken to have waived his right of subrogation where he accepts an indemnity from the principal in lieu of the right he would otherwise have had,[58] or by expressly or impliedly permitting the creditor to use the security as covering any further advances to the principal he might make.[59] The surety cannot be deprived of his rights of subrogation by an agreement between the creditor and the principal to that effect.[60]

---

56 [2002] EWCA Civ 691.

57 *Re Bulmer, Ex p. Johnson* (1853) 3 De G.M. & G. 218.

58 *Cooper v Jenkins* (1863) 32 Beav. 337; but the surety would not waive his rights of subrogation where he accepted the indemnity or security from the principal in ignorance of the fact that the principal had given security to the creditor: *Lake v Brutton* (1856) 18 Beav. 34.

59 *Waugh v Wren* (1862) 11 W.R. 244.

60 *Steel v Dixon* (1881) 17 Ch. D. 825, by analogy.

Chapter 12

Rights of the Surety Against Co-Sureties

Nature and origin of rights

12–001   Where two or more persons guarantee the same debt, whether jointly, severally or jointly and severally, they are co-sureties. In general, the law of restitution permits co-obligees such as co-contractors, co-insurers and co-trustees to recover contributions from each other should one of them be required by the creditor to pay more than their due share of a common obligation for which they are all liable.[1]

It is doubtful whether there was any common law action for contribution prior to the beginning of the nineteenth century, on the basis that to admit such a claim would be a "great cause of suits".[2] The courts of equity, however, had developed the principle in the early seventeenth century that, "who can pay must not only contribute their own shares but they must also make good the shares of those who are unable to furnish their own contribution".[3] At common law, therefore, the insolvency of one of the co-sureties did not proportionately increase the liability of the solvent sureties to contribute,[4] whereas in equity the solvent sureties had to make good the contributions of their insolvent co-sureties.[5] Since the Judicature Act 1873 the equitable rules have prevailed.

The surety's right of contribution is based upon the equitable principle that the creditor should not be permitted to bring down the burden of the whole debt upon one surety only,[6] and recognises that the co-sureties have a common interest and a common burden.[7] It is a right that arises

---

[1] See Goff and Jones, *The Law of Restitution* (6th ed., 2002), 381, 385 *et seq.*

[2] *Wormleighton v Hunter* (1614) Godb. 243.

[3] *Lowe & Sons v Dixon & Sons* (1885) 16 Q.B.D. 455 at 458 *per* Lopes J.; *Peter v Rich* (1629/1630) 1 Chan. Rep. 34; *Morgan v Seymour* (1637/1638) 1 Chan. Rep. 120.

[4] *Batard v Hawes* (1853) 2 El. & Bl. 287; *Browne v Lee* (1827) 6 B. & C. 689.

[5] *Hole v Harrison* (1673) 1 Chan. Cas. 246; *Dallas v Wells* (1879) 29 L.T. 599; *Lowe v Dixon* (1885) 16 Q.B.D. 455 *per* Lopes J.

[6] *Dering v Winchelsea (Earl)* (1787) 1 Cox. Eq. Cas. 318; *Craythorne v Swinburne* (1807) 16 Ves. 160; *Wolmershausen v Gullick* [1893] 2 Ch. 514; and see the discussion of these cases in Ch.11, para.11.002.

[7] *Dering v Winchelsea (Earl)* (1787) 2 Bos. & P. 270; *Ellesmere Brewery v Cooper* [1896] 1 Q.B. 75 at 79 *per* Lord Russell C.J.; *Albion Insurance Co Ltd v Government Insurance Office of New South Wales* (1969) 121 C.L.R. 342; *Eagle Star Ltd v Provincial Insurance Plc* [1993] 3 W.L.R. 257.

independently of contract, from the essence of the relationship of co-surety itself, and the notion that the burdens and the benefits of that position should be shared.[8] Where a surety pays more than his rateable proportion of the debt, he is entitled to exercise this right against his co-surety, because he has discharged their obligations to the creditor.[9] It exists only where the two sureties guarantee the same debt. In *Dering v Winchelsea (Earl)* (1787) 1 Cox. Eq. Cas. 318, Eyre C.B. said:

> "In the particular case of sureties, it is admitted that one surety may compel another to contribute to the debt for which they are jointly bound. On what principle? Can it be because they are jointly bound? What if they are jointly and severally bound? What if severally bound by the same or different instruments? In every one of those cases sureties have a common interest and a common burden. They are bound as effectually *quoad* contribution, as if bound in one instrument, with this difference only that the sums in each instrument ascertain the proportions, whereas if they were joined in the same engagement they must all contribute equally."[10]

It follows, therefore, that it is immaterial that the sureties are jointly, severally or jointly and severally liable, that they are bound by different instruments.[11] or at different times,[12] or that they know nothing of each others' existence as such,[13] or that the first surety agreed to be bound before the co-surety was approached.[14] In *Capital Cashflow Finance v Southall* [2004] EWCA Civ 817, the Court of Appeal decided that there is no relief in equity wider than that provided by the common law, and that the question whether a surety's liability is conditional upon the signature of an intended co-surety on a joint and several guarantee is a simply a question of construction. There is no wider discretion in equity based on

12–002

---

[8] *Dering v Winchelsea (Earl)* (1787) 1 Cox. Eq. Cas. 318; *Stirling v Forrester* (1821) 3 Bli. 575; *Ramskill v Edwards* (1885) 31 Ch. D. 100; *American Surety Co of New York v Wrightson* (1910) 103 L.T. 663 at 667; *Shepheard v Bray* [1906] 2 Ch. 235; *Eagle Star Ltd v Provincial Insurance Plc* [1993] 3 W.L.R. 257.

[9] *ibid.*

[10] See also *Ex p. Gifford* (1802) 6 Ves. 805, *per* Lord Eldon L.C. at 808; *Molson Bank v Kovinsky* [1924] 4 D.L.R. 330, *per* Orde J.A. at 336: "But sureties have other rights not based upon contract at all but resulting from the equitable right to contribution in all cases where they are sureties for the same debt, even though bound by different instruments, for different amounts and in different terms. In all such cases the extent of the surety's rights must depend not only upon the terms of the instrument by which the other sureties are bound, and the extent of his relief may be measured by the extent to which the conduct of the creditor has affected the surety's right to contribution."

[11] *Ellesmere Brewery v Cooper* [1896] 1 Q.B. 75; *Mayhew v Crickett* (1818) 2 Swanst. 185; *Pendlebury v Walker* (1841) 4 Y. & C. Ex. 424.

[12] *Whiting v Burke* (1871) 6 Ch. App. 342.

[13] Although a surety may agree to be bound on the condition that there are co-sureties with him, and of course if this condition is not met that surety may be discharged: *Leaf v Gibbs* (1830) 4 C. & P. 466; *Evans v Bembridge* (1855) 2 K. & J. 174. See *James Graham & Co (Timber) Ltd v Southgate Sands* [1986] Q.B. 80, where a signature of a co-surety was forged.

[14] See *Scholefield Goodman & Sons Ltd v Zyngier* [1985] 3 W.L.R. 953.

expectation, not amounting to a term or condition. The Court of Appeal went on to say that there is a relevant distinction between the situation where a single document is intended to be signed by different persons undertaking liability as surety, and the situation where different documents are prepared (as in the case before them), and it is not enough to relieve surety A from liability under his guarantee where the signature of surety B on a separate guarantee was intended as part of a larger transaction but is never obtained.[15] Mance L.J. said, at para.17:

> "Where a single document is prepared for signature by several persons, the document on its face points to a conclusion that the signatures of all are essential to its validity. Where separate documents are prepared, each for separate signature by a separate individual, the contrary applies. Of course there are cases where an individual document is, according to its express terms or impliedly when construed in the light of its express terms and all the surrounding circumstances, conditional upon the signature of another document: see eg *Greer v Kettle*.[16] But it is not by itself sufficient that the documents are all part of a larger transaction . . . Further, even if the signature of all such documents by their intended signatories is regarded as important by the parties seeking the same, it cannot be assumed without more that each intended signatory also regards the other's signature as critical, let alone that he regards it as critical that the other is signing an identical document."

So long as:

(a)   the surety and his co-surety have guaranteed a common liability;[17]

(b)   the surety has paid more, or is about to pay more, than his rateable proportion of the total guaranteed debt,[18] *qua* surety;[19]

(c)   the right to contribution has not been contractually excluded or lost;

the right of contribution will apply as a feature of co-suretyship.

---

[15] See also *Byblos Bank Sal v Al Khudhairy* [1987] B.C.L.C. 232; *TCB v Gray* [1988] 1 All E.R. 108.

[16] [1938] A.C. 156.

[17] *Coope v Twynam* (1823) Turn. & R. 426 at 429 *per* Lord Eldon L.C.

[18] In *Re Snowdon Ex p. Snowdon* (1881) 17 Ch. D. 44, Cotton L.J. said:"What we have to decide is whether a surety who has only paid his proportion for the debt for which he is liable can present a bankruptcy petition against his co-surety for contribution. In my opinion he cannot. To entitle him to contribution it is [not] necessary that he should pay more than his proportion of the sum secured by the bond by which he became surety." The word "not" is an obvious error and should be omitted: *Stirling v Burdett* [1911] 2 Ch. 418, *per* Warrington J.

[19] *Trotter v Franklin* [1991] 2 N.Z.L.R. 92 at 102.

The operation of the right of contribution

When the right to contribution arises

Before payment by the surety: quia timet relief

Just as the surety is entitled to seek *quia timet* relief against the principal,[20] so he is entitled to seek *quia timet* relief against his co-sureties even before he has made payment or incurred a loss under the guarantee.[21] The precise extent of the relief available to the surety prior to his payment of the principal debt is not clear, but the statement of Wright J. in *Wolmershausen v Gullick* [1893] 2 Ch. 514 is established authority that a surety can, even before payment, compel his co-sureties to contribute towards the discharge of the common liability.[22] In that case, the executrix of a deceased surety brought *quia timet* action against co-sureties where the creditor had merely lodged a claim against the deceased's estate for the whole amount of the principal debt. Had the claim been admitted in full, it would have been equivalent to judgment against the estate for the full amount. Wright J. granted *quia timet* relief against the co-sureties, holding that contribution could be effected either by an order that the co-surety pay his proportionate share to the creditor if he is a party to the proceedings, or, where the creditor is not a party, by a prospective order that, upon payment by the surety of his own share, the co-surety indemnify him from further liablity.

In *Wolmershausen v Gullick,* Wright J. allowed contribution on the basis that the admission of the claim was equivalent to judgment, and a surety against whom judgment had been obtained by the creditor for the full amount (or in any event for more than his rateable share) had a right to contribution from co-sureties. Quite how imminently the surety must be liable to pay the creditor before his right to contribution arises is not wholly clear. Wright J.'s decision is very wide in ambit, and he was prepared (at 529) to make an order that the plaintiff was entitled to enforce contribution "whenever she has paid any sum beyond her share". It seems therefore that the principle upon which a co-surety may be liable to make contribution prior to payment by the surety is flexible enough to entitle the surety to seek a contribution order even though judgment has not yet been obtained by the creditor for the full amount. It has been suggested that it may be enough for the creditor, having a present right to recover the whole debt from the surety, to threaten to do so.[23] Certainly this view was adopted by Orde J.A. in *Tucker v Bennett* [1927] 2 D.L.R.

12–003

---

[20] See Ch.10 at paras 10–026–10–029.

[21] *Craythorne v Swinburne* (1807) 14 Ves. 160 at 164; *Wolmershausen v Gullick* [1893] 2 Ch. 514 at 520.

[22] See also the remarks of James L.J. in *Re Snowdon Ex p. Snowdon* (1881) 17 Ch. D. 44 at 47.

[23] See Goff and Jones, *The Law of Restitution* (*op. cit.*), 390; *cf.* Rowlatt, *Principal and Surety* (*op. cit.*), 172. See O'Donovan & Phillips, *The Modern Contract of Guarantee* (*op. cit.*), 624–626, where the argument in favour of the necessity for the surety to have paid prior to being entitled to claim contribution is put forward. See O'Donovan & Phillips, English ed. (2003), paras 12–158 to 12–160.

42. In *Woolmington v Bronze Lamp Restaurant Pty Ltd* [1984] 2 N.S.W.R. 242, it was held to be sufficient for the surety merely to satisfy the court that he was willing, able and prepared to pay the full amount of the debt.

It is submitted that, strictly speaking, there is no restriction upon the time at which a surety can apply for relief against his co-sureties, provided that the account between the principal and creditor is closed and there is an immediate liability due and payable under the guarantee such that the amount of the contribution can be precisely ascertained. It is immaterial that the creditor has not yet demanded payment, or even that the creditor is obliged under the terms of the guarantee to make a demand before the surety is liable. It is enough that the creditor could enforce the guarantee, either forthwith or after making a demand, for more than the surety's rateable share. This is certainly the case with *quia timet* relief against the principal for an indemnity,[24] and there is no reason why the same should not apply against the co-surety for contribution.[25] This is entirely consistent with Wright J.'s approach in *Wolmershausen v Gullick,* since in that case, although the claim in the administration was tantamount to a judgment, there was no immediate and pressing threat of execution which had driven the plaintiff to apply to court: she simply wished to obtain the relief in advance so that she could pay out the creditor when the time came.

The views expressed in the last paragraph above in the second edition of this work have now been approved by the Court of Appeal in *Stimpson v Smith* [1999] 2 W.L.R. 1292.[26] In that case, the plaintiff had, jointly and severally with the defendant as co-surety, guaranteed the liabilities of the principal to the bank. The principal's business failed and the bank threatened to put in the receivers. Unknown to the co-surety, the surety negotiated his release from the guarantee in return from a payment by him in reduction of the principal's indebtedness to the bank. He then sued the co-surety for contribution, who objected that the bank had made no demand on the surety and that therefore he was not liable to contribute as co-surety. The Court of Appeal held that the surety was entitled to contribution from the co-surety even though there had been no written demand served by the bank as required by the terms of the guarantee, and even though the co-surety had no knowledge of the payment made by the surety. The amount of the liability the subject-matter of the guarantee was ascertained, or at least easily ascertainable,

---

[24] See, *e.g.* the discussion of the cases in *Rowland v Gulfpac Ltd* [1999] Ll. Rep. Bank. 86 at 96–99, *per* Rix J; now see *Papamichael v National Westminster Bank* [2002] 1 Ll. Rep. 332.

[25] This is the approach adopted in Australia: see *Moulton v Roberts* [1977] Qd. R. 135, where Williams J. applied a surety's right to *quia timet* relief against the principal as stated in *Thomas v Nottingham Football Club Ltd* [1972] 1 Ch. 596 to a claim by the surety for contribution; *Woolmington v Bronze Lamp Restaurant Pty Ltd* [1984] 2 N.S.W.L.R. 242; O'Donovan & Phillips, *The Modern Contract of Guarantee (op. cit.),* 625–626, English ed. (2003) paras 12–159 to 160 . This approach also has support in Canada:see *Agnes & Jennie Mining Co v Zen* [1984] 1 W.W.R. 90; McGuinness, *The Law of Guarantee (op. cit.),* para.9.11.

[26] See *per* Gibson L.J. at 1300D–H.

and a demand under the guarantee could be reasonably anticipated in the absence of a negotiated settlement, and the settlement was not to the co-surety's disadvantage. The requirement of a demand in the guarantee was evidentiary or procedural only, and not a pre-condition of liability under the guarantee, and the surety could waive it without jeopardising his right to claim contribution. Critically, the payment by the surety was not voluntary or officious, viewed commercially in the circumstances which he faced.

Notwithstanding the flexibility of the circumstances in which pre-payment *quia timet* relief will be granted, it is vital to bear in mind that no such relief will be available unless the right to contribution is present.[27] This depends on a number of matters, not least of which is whether the surety can show that the right has not been excluded or waived, or more importantly, whether he can show that recourse against the principal will be futile.[28] Further, although *quia timet* relief will be available against co-sureties prior to the surety's having paid the creditor more than his share, he will not be able to *enforce* an order for contribution against the co-sureties until he has paid.[29]

Where a surety holds an indemnity for his liability under an indemnity bond, he may enforce that indemnity bond after he has been called upon to pay, but before he has actually paid.[30]

After payment by the surety

The general rule: payment in excess of rateable share
As soon as the surety has paid more than his rateable share of the common liability for the principal debt as between himself and his co-sureties, he is entitled to demand contribution from them in proportion to their respective liabilities.[31] The common liability for the principal debt must be owed by the same debtor.[32] Accordingly, where the burden of a guaranteed debt is assigned with the consent of the creditor, or the creditor assigns the debt, and a new guarantee is taken for it, the new surety cannot seek contribution from the previous surety, because they are not liable on a common demand.[33]

The manner in which co-sureties are bound together for the principal debt will not affect the right of contribution, whether they are bound jointly, severally or jointly and severally,[34] nor will the fact that they knew

12–004

---

[27] As to which see below.
[28] Or that this can be inferred: *Hay v Carter* [1935] Ch. 397, and see para.12.007 below.
[29] See the order proposed by Wright J. in *Wolmershausen v Gullick* [1893] 2 Ch. 514 at 529.
[30] *Wooldridge v Norris* (1868) L.R.6 Eq. 410.
[31] *Ex p. Gifford* (1802) 6 Ves. 805; *Davies v Humphreys* (1840) 6 M. & W. 153; *Re Snowdon Ex p. Snowdon* (1881) 17 Ch. D. 44; *Stirling v Burdett* [1911] 2 Ch. 418.
[32] *Ellesmere Brewery Co v Cooper* [1896] 1 Q.B. 75 at 79.
[33] *ibid.*
[34] *Dering v Winchelsea (Earl)* (1787) 2 Bos. & P. 270; *Stirling v Forrester* (1821) 3 Bli. 575, *per* Lord Redesdale at 590; *Mahoney v McManus* (1981) A.L.J.R. 673 at 675 *per* Gibbs C.J.; *cf. Underhill v Horwood* (1804) 10 Ves. 209 *per* Lord Eldon. However, the nature of the respective liabilities of the co-sureties *inter se* may be important in considering the effect of the death or release of one of them: see paras 12–020–12–022 and 12–025.

nothing of each other's existence at the time they entered the guarantee.[35] It is unnecessary even to show that the different instruments binding the sureties are expressly connected with each other.[36]

The surety is entitled to contribution once his payment exceeds his rateable share even if it is less than the total limit of his liability, but he may not sue his co-sureties for contribution as soon as he has paid simply any part of the principal debt.[37] In *Re Snowdon Ex p. Snowdon* (1881) 17 Ch. D. 44, three sureties had joined in a bond for the principal for £2,000, the liability of each limited to £1,000. The creditor called on one of the sureties under the bond (the principal debt being at that time £1,082) and the surety paid £541, and sought contribution from his co-sureties. The Court of Appeal held that the surety was not entitled to recover. James L.J. said (at 46–47):

> "It is impossible to say, when one party has paid part of a debt, until the whole debt is paid in respect of which all the co-sureties are jointly liable, what the right of contribution is . . . there must be an actual legally ascertainable debt. The co-surety cannot know what is the debt due to him by his co-surety until he knows what has been done in respect of the residue of the debt for which he is equally liable . . . But, until the whole debt has been paid by one surety, or so much of it as to make it clear that, as between himself and his co-sureties, he has paid all that he can ever be called upon to pay, there can be no equitable debt from them to him in respect of it."

Where the guaranteed debt is payable by instalments, the surety does not acquire a right to contribution by simply paying more than his share of each instalment unless they constitute separate debts or unless each such instalment creates a discrete liability.[38] In *Stirling v Burdett* [1911] 2 Ch. 418, the surety and co-sureties had executed a deed guaranteeing repayment of a mortgage advance, not to be repayable within ten years, plus premiums and interest. The sureties paid more than their rateable share of premiums and interest, but not of the entire debt, and sought contribution from the co-sureties. Warrington J. held that the principal sum, premiums and interest constituted one entire and indivisible debt, and that the sureties were not entitled to contribution, since although they had paid more than their share of premiums and interest, they had not paid more than their share of the whole debt.

Although the essential requirement of the right to contribution is that the surety should pay the creditor an amount in excess of his rateable

---

[35] *Dering v Winchelsea (Earl)* (1787) 1 Cox. Eq. Cas. 318; *Craythorne v Swinburne* (1807) 14 Ves. 160 at 165.

[36] See *Molson's Bank v Kovinsky* [1924] 4 D.L.R. 330 at 335.

[37] *Davies v Humphreys* (1840) 6 M. & W. 153; *Re Snowdon Ex p. Snowdon* (1881) 17 Ch. 44.

[38] *Re McDonald Ex p. Grant* (1888) W.N. 130; *Stirling v Burdett* [1911] 2 Ch. 418, and see 20 *Halsbury's Laws* (4th ed., 2004 reissue), para.257, n.3.

share, he may also be entitled to contribution where he pays an amount which is not in excess of his rateable share but which is accepted by the creditor in full satisfaction of the whole of the guaranteed liability.[39] It is advisable to give co-sureties an opportunity to consider such a settlement, for this will deprive them later of any defence to a claim for contribution on the grounds that it was an improvident bargain.[40] The rationale is that where the creditor forgives some of the debt in this way equity will redistribute the burden of the debt equally among the co-sureties. Further, a surety who has paid his full share has a right of contribution once he pays anything further.[41] Similarly, where the sureties share a common liability for part of the principal debt, a right of contribution will exist between them in relation to that part. For example, if A guarantees the debt up to a limit of £10,000, and B guarantees the debt without limit, they may claim contribution from each other to the extent of the common liability.[42]

It is always open for the surety to pay the guaranteed debt once it becomes due and then seek contribution, without waiting for any action by the creditor.[43] It appears that there is no requirement in order to found a claim for contribution that the creditor should resort to the guarantee at all before the surety pays under it,[44] provided he is under a present and enforceable liability to the creditor. The payment must be made at least in part out of the surety's own funds or assets, or at least funds or assets treated as such. In *Geopel v Swinden* (1844) 1 Dow. & L. 888, it was held that a surety who was forgiven a debt owing by himself to the principal (as a means of securing the former's rights of indemnity) was not entitled to contribution, having not paid more than the amount forgiven by the principal. This case can be contrasted with *Fahey v Frawley* (1890) 26 L.R. I.R. 78, where the transfer of mortgage security held by the surety was payment giving rise to a right to contribution from co-sureties.

Payment with assistance of third party

Where payment is made with the assistance of a third party, to whom **12–005** securities for the guaranteed debt are then assigned by the creditor, the court will treat the surety and the third party as one person, and in making his claim for contribution the surety must account for any amounts received in respect of such securities, net of realisation expenses.[45] This is best illustrated by *Re Arcedeckne, Atkins v Arcedeckne* (1883) 24 Ch. D. 709, in which four heirs to landed estates joined as co-sureties for the principal in promissory notes to secure the sum of £13,000

---

[39] *Lawson v Wright* (1786) 1 Eq. Cas. 275; *Re Snowdon Ex p. Snowdon* (1881) 17 Ch. D. 44 *per* James L.J. at 47.
[40] *Smith v Compton* (1832) 3 B. & Ad. 407. See para.12–019.
[41] *Davies v Humphreys* (1840) 6 M. & W. 153.
[42] As to the amount of the contribution, see paras 12–012–12–014.
[43] *Pitt v Purssord* (1841) 8 M. & W. 583.
[44] *Moulton v Roberts* [1977] Qd. R. 135.
[45] *Re Arcedeckne, Atkins v Arcedeckne* (1883) 24 Ch. D. 709.

loan and interest. The debt was further secured by policies on the life of the principal for £10,000. One of the four co-sureties, H, then paid off the debt with the assistance of his father by means of a mortgage on the family estates, which were settled on the father as life tenant and on H as remainderman, and obtained an assignment of the policies from the creditor. The father then insured the principal's life for £1,000. The principal then died, and the policy moneys were received by the father. Another co-surety then died, and H sought to be admitted to proof in the administration of his estate for a rateable share of the £13,000 plus interest. It was held that H and his father must be treated as one person for the purposes of claiming contribution, and had to give credit for the £10,000 (net of premiums and expenses) received in respect of the earlier life policies, but not the £1,000 received in respect of the policy taken out by the father.

Payment must be in partial or total discharge of guarantee

12–006 In order to found a right of contribution, the payment by the surety must be made in partial or total discharge of the guaranteed liability.[46] This usually requires that the principal is entitled to receive it.[47] However, it has been suggested that the surety should be entitled to contribution where he has paid the principal in reduction of his liability under the guarantee. In *Mahoney v McManus* (1981) 55 A.J.L.R. 673, this was held to be sufficient to give rise to the right to contribution, even where the amount paid was different from the principal debt and the principal's internal documents showed the payment by the surety as a loan, and not in reduction of the principal debt.

Although the decision has attracted criticism for its application of law to the facts of the case,[48] it is in keeping with the English approach to payments made for specific purposes,[49] and provided the payment to the principal is clearly earmarked as payment for the purposes of discharging the guaranteed liability, the surety will be entitled either to compel the principal to apply it to the principal debt or to restore it to him, depending upon his intentions. In particular, where the surety's object in making the payment to the principal was to save the principal from bankruptcy, and where the surety has an interest of his own, separate from any interest of the principal, in seeing that the money is applied towards its stated purpose, the principal will come under a duty to the surety to apply it for such purpose. Upon communication of the arrangement to the creditor, the surety's equitable interest is vested in the creditor, who can enforce the trust and compel payment to himself.[50]

---

[46] As to what constitutes discharge of the principal debt, see Ch.9, paras 9–002–9–010.

[47] *Mann v Stennett* (1845) 8 Beav. 189.

[48] See O'Donovan & Phillips, *The Modern Contract of Guarantee (op. cit.)*, 628–9; English ed. (2003), paras 12–167 to 12–171.

[49] *Barclays Bank Ltd v Quistclose Investments Ltd* [1970] A.C. 567; and see P. J. Millett Q.C., "The Quistclose Trust:Who Can Enforce It?" (1985) 101 L.Q.R. 269; see now *Twinsectra Ltd v Yardley* [2002] 2 A.C. 164, HL.

[50] The surety's mandate will remain revocable until communication to the creditor, when it will become irrevocable: see Millett Q.C., "The Quistclose Trust: Who Can Enforce It?" (*op. cit.*) at 290–291.

Payment must be made under a legal obligation

In order to be entitled to contribution, the surety must be under a legal **12–007**
obligation to pay the guaranteed debt, and where the payment is
premature or officious, no right to contribution will arise.[51] This is equally
true where payment is effected by the realisation of a security given by the
surety to the creditor for the guaranteed obligation: accelerated realisation and recoupment by the creditor cannot accelerate the rights of
contribution, and the co-sureties are only liable to pay once their own
liability under the guarantee has arisen.[52] Further, where the surety makes
the payment under a mistake of law as to his obligation to pay, or where
there is a valid procedural or substantive defence, at common law he
would not be able to recover contribution from his co-sureties.[53] However,
the surety may have statutory rights to contribution under the Civil
Liability (Contribution) Act 1978 where he can bring himself within its
requirements.[54]

Principal must be insolvent or otherwise not worth pursuing

There is one crucially important condition which must be satisfied before **12–008**
the surety can claim contribution from his co-sureties. This is that the
surety must demonstrate at least by inference that a claim against the
principal would be futile because he is insolvent or otherwise not worth
pursuing.[55] This was laid down in *Hay v Carter* [1935] Ch. 397, where the
Court of Appeal held that in an action for contribution between co-
sureties, the principal should be made a party unless it can be proved or
inferred that the principal is insolvent or that there is good reason why he
should not be joined.

This is obviously sensible, since it would be inequitable to permit the
surety to claim from the co-sureties where the surety retains a right

---

[51] *Barry v Moroney* (1837) 8 I.R.C.L. 554; *Pawle v Gunn* (1838) 4 Bing. N.C. 445.
[52] *McLean v Discount and Finance Ltd* (1939) 64 C.L.R. 312.
[53] *Smith v Compton* (1832) 3 B. & Ad. 407; *Pettman v Keble* (1850) 9 C.B. 701.
[54] In order to invoke the assistance of that Act, the surety must show that his liability arose out
of a claim in damages as opposed to debt. Although it is arguable that such an opportunity
would be rare, on the basis that a claim on a guarantee by the creditor is a claim in debt and
not in damages, this reasoning would appear to be contrary to *Moschi v Lep Air Services*
[1973] A.C. 351 and is unlikely to succeed. In *Barclays Bank Plc v Miller* [1990] 1 All E.R.
1040, the Court of Appeal described the question of whether the Act applied to
contribution claims between co-sureties as a difficult one, and left it open. In *Friends
Provident Life Office v Hillier Parker May and Rowden* [1995] 4 All E.R. 260, Auld L.J.
accorded a very wide meaning to the word "damage" in the 1978 Act and supported the
view that the 1978 Act may govern contribution claims between co-sureties, particularly
where the guarantee is of the principal's performance of his obligations: see Goff & Jones,
The Law of Restitution (*op. cit.*), 382–383 and now *Royal Brompton Hospital National Health
Service Trust v Hammond* [2002] 2 All ER 801, HL. In *Hampton v Minns* [2002] 1 W.L.R. 1,
Kevin Garnett Q.C. decided that s.1 of the 1978 Act applies to damages and not debt, and
that if, on a true construction of the guarantee, the surety had promised to pay a sum of
money if certain events occurred, the liability was in debt and not in damages and s.1 had no
application.
[55] See Goff & Jones, *The Law of Restitution* (*op. cit.*), 388; *Lawson v Wright* (1786) 1 Cox 275,
per Lord Kenyon; *Hay v Carter* [1935] Ch. 397, CA.

against the principal for an indemnity in respect of the whole of the debt guaranteed. Further, if the principal could fruitfully be joined but is not joined, there would be a risk of proliferation of suits by co-sureties against him, each for an indemnity for their rateable share.[56]

The rule may be seen as a corollary of the rule that the surety must bring into hotchpot for the benefit of his co-sureties any security received from the principal for the guaranteed obligation, as to which see para. 12–016.

When the right to contribution does not arise

12–009 Generally, the right to contribution will not arise where the factors mentioned above are not satisfied. For example, there is no right of contribution where the co-sureties are not subject to a common demand,[57] nor where the sureties are bound by different instruments for different and distinct portions of the same debt due from the principal, where each suretyship is a separate and distinct transaction,[58] nor where the surety has not paid more than his rateable share.[59] This also applies where the surety's contract of guarantee has stipulated that each is only to be individually liable for a particular portion of the principal debt,[60] and where the sureties limit their liabilities under the guarantee, they cannot be compelled to pay more than that limit.[61] The court will look at the substance of the transaction, and what exactly the parties had guaranteed and not merely the fact that the instruments were separate.[62]

There is no right of contribution where the sureties guarantee different debts or obligations of the principal.[63] Where A, therefore, guarantees repayment of the principal's overdraft, and B guarantees repayment of a separate overdraft of the principal, no right of contribution will lie between A and B. Equally, where sureties have guaranteed separate and distinct portions of the same principal debt, there is no right of contribution between them.[64]

There is no right of contribution where the surety induced the co-surety to assume liability by means of a fraud. However, there is no general duty of disclosure between co-sureties, and so the surety is not obliged to inform his co-sureties of any dealings he has with the principal, for example the existence of a debt owed to him by the principal.[65] Further,

---

[56] *Craythorne v Swinburne* (1807) 14 Ves. 160.
[57] *Hunter v Hunt* (1845) 1 C.B. 300; *Johnson v Wild* (1890) 44 Ch. D. 146 (an indemnity case); *American Surety Co of New York v Wrightson* (1910) 103 L.T. 663, at 665 *per* Hamilton J.
[58] *Coope v Twynam* (1823) Turn. & R. 426.
[59] *Re Snowdon Ex p. Snowdon* (1881) 17 Ch. D. 44.
[60] *Pendlebury v Walker* (1841) 4 Y. & C. Ex. 424.
[61] *Dering v Winchelsea (Earl)* (1787) 2 Bos. & P. 270.
[62] *Davies v Humphreys* (1840) 6 M. & W. 153.
[63] *Coope v Twynam* (1823) 1 Turn. & R. 426; *Dering v Winchelsea (Earl)* (1787) 1 Cox. Eq. Cas. 318.
[64] *Pendlebury v Walker* (1841) 4 Y. & C. Ex. 424: *Coope v Twynam* (1823) 1 Turn. & R. 426.
[65] *Mackreth v Walmesley* (1884) 51 L.T. 19.

the right to contribution will not (or is said not to) arise in two particular instances.

Against persons not co-sureties

The right to contribution will *not* arise where there is no relationship of co-surety *inter se*. A surety who has his own obligations under the guarantee guaranteed in turn by a sub-surety is not entitled to seek contribution from that sub-surety upon payment to the creditor.[66] The position is that the sub-surety does not occupy the position of co-surety in a common liability with the surety, but as guarantor for the obligations of the surety, who is the principal for that purpose. Although the sub-surety cannot be made liable for contribution to the surety, he can claim an indemnity from his surety in prior degree, and be subrogated to the creditor's securities and rights against that surety.[67]

12–010

Where, on the true construction of his contract, a person is not a co-surety but jointly liable as co-debtor, there will be no right of contribution,[68] although the surety may have a right to contribution under the Civil Liability (Contribution) Act 1978, if he can bring himself within its terms.[69]

Where a bill of exchange is given as security for a debt, both the drawer and the acceptor are sureties *vis-à-vis* the principal, but as between themselves, the drawer is surety only for the acceptor. In the absence of agreement the acceptor bears the primary obligation with no right of contribution against the drawer.[70]

Co-suretyship at the request of the surety: Turner v Davies

There is also authority for the proposition that there is no right to contribution where the co-surety assumes the position as such at the request of the surety. In *Turner v Davies* (1796) 2 Esp. 478, Lord Kenyon said: "there is no pretence for saying that he shall be liable to be called upon by the person at whose request he entered into the surety".[71] However, this purported rule has been doubted by more recent writers,[72] and is difficult to square with the classic statements of principle in relation to contribution from co-sureties: that if the surety and the co-surety are liable for the same debt in a common demand, there is no reason why the obligation to pay contribution should not apply where one surety becomes bound at the request of another.[73] *Turner v Davies* may be explicable on

12–011

---

[66] *Craythorne v Swinburne* (1807) 14 Ves. 160; *Re Denton's Estate* [1904] 2 Ch. 178; *Ward v National Bank of New Zealand* (1883) 8 App. Cas. 755.

[67] See Ch.11, para.11–022 and *Fox v Royal Bank of Canada* (1975) 59 D.L.R. (3d) 258.

[68] *Re Denton's Estate* [1904] 2 Ch. 178.

[69] See n.52 above.

[70] *Ex p. Hunter* (1825) 2 Gl. & J. 7.

[71] At 479.

[72] See Goff & Jones, *The Law of Restitution (op. cit.)*, p.387; McGuinness, *The Law of Guarantee (op. cit.)*, para.9.06; O'Donovan & Phillips, *The Modern Contract of Guarantee (op. cit.)*, 622–3; English ed. (2003), paras 12–150 to 12–155.

[73] Note that there is no principle that the surety should not be entitled to an indemnity where he assumes the role as such at the request of the principal, which would be the case, by analogy, if Lord Kenyon's statement in *Turner v Davies* (above) were correct.

the basis that in that case the surety had received security from the principal in respect of his liability under the guarantee, and if this had been given with a view to discharging the surety then no right of contribution would have arisen.[74]

Of course, the court will be astute to ascertain whether the co-surety did actually become a co-surety, and if there are circumstances, such as the taking of a security by the surety from the purported co-surety, which suggest that in fact the latter is a sub-surety, contribution will not be available to the surety. This may afford another explanation of *Turner v Davies*.

Modification or exclusion

12–012   It is clear that a surety can modify or exclude his right to contribution by express agreement with his co-sureties.[75] Such an agreement will not affect the rights of the creditor.[76] An agreement to modify or exclude the surety's rights of contribution can be vitiated on the grounds of fraud or fraudulent concealment,[77] or a failure to satisfy a condition precedent.[78] An agreement between the surety and the co-surety that the surety would indemnify the co-surety against any liability to which he might be exposed as a result of giving the guarantee operates to exclude the surety's right of contribution.[79] It has been held in Australia that a provision in the guarantee itself that the surety will not "make a claim or enforce" the right of contribution will be effective to vary the surety's equitable rights, but not to oust the court's jurisdiction: *Hongkong Bank of Australia Ltd v Larobi Pty Ltd* (1991) 23 N.S.W.L.R. 593.[80]

The right of the surety to recover contribution from his co-surety may be excluded or restricted by the nature of the obligation assumed by that co-surety. Where the co-sureties have each contracted, in distinct instruments, to be liable for the guaranteed obligation in a particular sum, there is no right of contribution.[81] Similarly, where the co-sureties all agree that one of their number shall pay the first tranche of the principal debt, or where liability is not distributed equally between them, the right to contribution will be excluded.[82] However, an express clause in one guarantee limiting or excluding the right to contribution will not affect the

---

[74] *Done v Walley* (1848) 2 Exch. 198; and see the cases discussed in relation to the hotchpot rule at para.12–016.

[75] *Craythorne v Swinburne* (1807) 14 Ves. 160; *Dering v Winchelsea (Earl)* (1787) 2 Bos. & P. 270; *Pendlebury v Walker* (1841) 4 Y. & C. Ex. 424; *Arcedeckne v Howard (Lord)* (1872) 27 L.T. 194, affirmed (1875) 45 L.J. Ch. 622, HL.

[76] See *Bater v Kare* [1964] S.C.R. 206; *Hampton v Minns* [2002] 1 W.L.R. 1.

[77] *Mackreth v Walmesley* (1884) 51 L.T. 19 at 30, *per* Kay J. The surety's obligations of disclosure to the co-sureties are no greater than those of the creditor to them.

[78] *Re Arcedeckne, Arcedeckne v Lord Howard* (1875) 45 L.J. Ch. 622.

[79] *Rae v Rae* (1857) 6 I. Ch. R. 490.

[80] See also *Bond v Larobi Pty Ltd* (1992) 6 W.A.R. 489.

[81] *Coope v Twynam* (1823) Turn. & R. 426; *Pendlebury v Walker* (1841) 4 Y. & C. Ex. 424; *Re Denton's Estate* [1904] 2 Ch. 178.

[82] *Molson's Bank v Kovinsky* [1924] 4 D.L.R. 330.

rights of contribution of the co-sureties where they are sureties for the same principal and principal debt under a different instrument which does not exclude or limit such rights.

Since its origin lies in equity, and not the contractual relationship of the parties, the court will be slow to imply a term to the effect that the surety has abandoned his rights of contribution. However, it is possible to infer from the conduct of the surety an intention on his part to abandon such rights. For example, where the surety fails to perform his duties towards his co-sureties, for example by refusing to bring security into hotchpot or by joining the co-surety in suing the principal for an indemnity, he may be taken to have waived or abandoned his rights of contribution.[83]

The amount of contribution

The principal amount
The rule at common law was that each surety was liable for his own share **12–013** and his right to contribution depending on the number of co-sureties, irrespective of the insolvency of any co-surety.[84] In equity, the rule was that the amount of contribution depended upon the number of solvent sureties at the time when the contribution was sought, and this is now the prevailing rule.[85]

The general rule is that all the sureties are liable to contribute equally towards the common debt, and if they are not liable in equal proportions, then they must contribute a pro rata amount.[86] Accordingly, where co-sureties guarantee the whole of the principal debt but their liabilities are limited to certain amounts, they share the burden of the principal debt on the basis of the proportion of their maximum liability. In *Ellesmere Brewery v Cooper* [1896] 1 Q.B. 75, the liabilities of the four sureties were limited to £50 each as to two sureties and £25 each as to the other two. Had they been liable for contribution, where one surety paid out £48, the £50 sureties would have borne £16 each as their rateable share and the £25 sureties would have borne £8 each.

Matters are more complex where, on the other hand, the sureties guarantee different parts of the common debt. Assume that A, B and C each guarantee a debt of £1,000 in the proportions £200, £300 and £500, and that they are truly co-sureties for the same debt. Where, for example, the creditor accepts £500 from C in satisfaction of the entire debt, it would appear that A and B would have to contribute £100 and £150,

---

[83] *Steel v Dixon* (1881) 17 Ch. D. 825. As to hotchpot, see para.12–016.
[84] *Cowell v Edwards* (1800) 2 Bos. & P. 268; *Browne v Lee* (1827) 6 B. & C. 689. It seems that the number of sureties was taken as at the time when the guarantee was given, and not when the payment was made: *Batard v Hawes* (1853) 2 E. & B. 287.
[85] *Hitchman v Stewart* (1855) 3 Drew. 271; *Lowe v Dixon* (1885) 16 Q.B.D. 455.
[86] *Dering v Winchelsea (Earl)* (1787) 1 Cox. Eq. Cas. 318; *Pendlebury v Walker* (1841) 4 Y. & C. Ex. 424 at 441 *per* Alderson B.; *Ellesmere Brewery v Cooper* [1896] 1 Q.B. 75; *Coope v Twynam* (1823) Turn. & R. 426; *Re MacDonaghs* (1876) 10 Ir. Eq. 269.

being the proportion of the payment made by the surety which their maximum liability bore to the entire guaranteed debt.[87]

The insolvency of a co-surety will affect the rights of contribution of the remaining co-sureties. Thus where A, B and C are sureties for a debt of £600, and both the principal and A become insolvent, B and C are liable to contribute in equal proportions, and if C pays the whole debt, he can recover £300 from B (rather than £150 from each of A and B, which is what he would be entitled to if A were solvent). Where A, B and C agree to bear the debt in proportions of respectively £150, £300 and £150, then C may recover £400 from B, £300 being his own share plus £100 (two-thirds of A's share of £150). The two-thirds represents the 2:1 ratio which B's share bears to C's share.[88]

It has often been said that the effect of the equitable rule is that only solvent co-sureties are obliged to contribute.[89] What this actually means is that it is the solvent co-sureties who bear the initial burden of contribution, and the estate of the insolvent co-surety remains liable to contribute, the obligation being a provable debt, although the rule against double proof will prevent the surety who has not paid the whole of the guaranteed debt from proving for the amount for which the creditor is entitled to prove.[90] Where the surety proves in the co-surety's bankruptcy, he will be obliged to share any dividends he receives with his co-sureties, or give credit for them, in rateable proportions equivalent to their share, or equally if they remain equally liable.[91]

Interest

12–014 The surety can recover interest from his co-surety on the sum due for contribution: interest will run from the date on which the surety paid the creditor more than his due share.[92] It is immaterial that the principal debt did not carry interest.[93] Further, it seems that a surety who has paid his share is able to compel his co-sureties to exonerate him from further interest accruing to the creditor on his co-sureties' unpaid shares.[94]

---

[87] *See Ellesmere Brewery v Cooper* [1896] 1 Q.B. 75; and see *Ellis v Emmanuel* (1876) 1 Ex. D. 157, where at 162 Blackburn J. indicated that the limits put upon each surety's share of the guaranteed debt would affect the amount which each was liable to contribute, without saying exactly how. See further *Re MacDonaghs* (1876) 10 Ir. Eq. 269 and *Commercial Union Assurance Co Ltd v Hayden* [1977] Q.B. 804 at 815.

[88] See *Pendlebury v Walker* (1841) 4 Y. & C. Ex. 424; *Ellesmere Brewery v Cooper* [1896] 1 Q.B. 75 at 81 *per* Lord Russell C.J.; *Re Price* (1978) 85 D.L.R. (3d) 554.

[89] *Ellesmere Brewery Co v Cooper* [1896] 1 Q.B. 75 at 81; *Mahoney v McManus* (1981) 55 A.J.L.R. 673.

[90] See para.12–024.

[91] *Re Hendry Ex p. Murphy* [1905] S.A.L.R. 116.

[92] *Lawson v Wright* (1786) 1 Cox. Eq. Cas. 275; *Hitchman v Stewart* (1855) 3 Drew. 271; *Re Swan's Estate* (1869) I.R.Eq. 209; *Re Fox, Walker Ex p. Bishop* (1880) 15 Ch. D. 400; and see *Petrie v Duncombe* (1851) 2 L.M. & P. 107 as to interest payable in respect of the principal debt.

[93] *Re Swan's Estate* (1869) 4 Ir. Eq. 209.

[94] Rowlatt, *Principal and Surety (op. cit.)*, p.173.

Costs

The surety cannot as a rule recover as part of his claim for contribution   **12–015**
his costs of defending an action against him by the creditor,[95] unless either
he was specifically authorised by the co-sureties to defend the action or he
was prudent and reasonable in doing so.[96] Where by defending the claim
the common liability of the co-sureties is materially reduced, the surety
may recover these costs in contribution from his co-sureties.[97] However, if
a surety raises a defence that is personal to himself, he will not be entitled
to his costs by way of contribution, because his defence has not and could
not have led to any relief of his co-sureties.[98]

The right of the surety to securities

Subrogation to creditor's securities
A surety who has paid more than his rateable share of the common   **12–016**
liability is entitled to have assigned to him all the creditor's rights and
securities, whether satisfied or not, for the purpose of obtaining contribution,[99] and this includes securities received by the creditor from co-
sureties for the guaranteed obligation.[1] This is because once the creditor
has been paid by the surety, he is bound in equity to make available to the
surety all the rights and remedies against other debtors liable for the same
debt.[2] He is entitled to have recourse to any securities given by the co-
sureties, and may rely on s.5 of the Mercantile Law Amendment Act 1856
in getting them in.[3] The creditor must, in dealing with these securities, act
with similar care for the surety's interests as when the security is given by
the principal.[4] The surety may prove or claim against a co-surety's
insolvent estate standing in the shoes of the creditor, whether or not there
has been an assignment of the security or right by the creditor to him.[5]

Similarly, the surety is entitled to the rateable benefit of any counter-
security received by the co-surety in respect of the guaranteed obligation,
or any judgment obtained by the creditor against the principal and the co-
sureties.[6]

---

[95] *Knight v Hughes* (1828) 3 C. & P. 467; *Roach v Thompson* (1843) 5 Man. & G. 405.
[96] *Tindall v Bell* (1843) 11 M. & W. 228; *Kemp v Finden* (1844) 12 M. & W. 421; *Broom v Hall* (1859) 7 C.B.N.S. 503; *Williams v Buchanan, Anderson Third Party* (1891) 7 T.L.R. 226 at 27 *per* Lord Esher; *The Millwall* [1905] P. 155. See the doubts expressed in Goff & Jones, *The Law of Restitution* (*op. cit.*), 391, n.74.
[97] *Wolmershausen v Gullick* [1893] 2 Ch. 514 at 529–530.
[98] *Re International Contract Co, Hughes' Claim* (1872) L.R. 13 Eq. 623 at 625 *per* Wickens V.-C.; *South v Bloxham* (1865) 2 Hem. & M.457.
[99] As to the surety's right of subrogation, see Ch.11, paras 11–017 *et seq*.
[1] *Ex p. Crisp* (1744) 1 Atk. 133 at 135; *Greenside v Benson* (1745) 3 Atk. 248; *Stirling v Forrester* (1821) 3 Bli. 575 at 590, *per* Lord Redesdale; *Duncan, Fox & Co v North and South Wales Bank* (1880) 6 Ch. App. 1 at 19 *per* Lord Blackburn; *Brown v Cork* [1985] B.C.L.C. 363.
[2] *Stirling v Forrester* (1821) 3 Bli. 575 at 590, *per* Lord Redesdale.
[3] *Re Parker, Morgan v Hill* [1894] 3 Ch. 400; *Aldrich v Cooper* (1803) 8 Ves. 382. The property subject to the security is not subject to set-offs between co-sureties: *Brown v Cork* (above); *A E Goodwin Ltd (In liq.) v AG Healing Ltd (In liq.)* (1979) 7 A.C.L.R. 481.
[4] See Ch.9, paras 9–043–9–044.
[5] *Re M'Myn, Lightbown v M'Myn* (1886) 33 Ch. D. 575.
[6] *Done v Walley* (1848) 2 Exch. 198.

Counter-security given by the principal: hotchpot

12–017 A surety who obtains a counter-security from the principal to which he may look for indemnification should he be called upon to pay under the guarantee is obliged to hold such counter-security for the benefit of his co-sureties. This is known as the principle of hotchpot. The surety must bring into hotchpot for distribution among all his co-sureties for the debt for which the counter-security is given any amount which he receives from the realisation of that counter-security, even though he only became a surety on condition that he was secured as to his liability, and even though the co-sureties were ignorant of the existence of the counter-security.[7] The rationale of the rule is that co-sureties are to be accorded equal treatment in equity, and that counter-security held by one surety stands for security for the full amount of the indemnity which all the co-sureties may claim.[8] This principle will operate even though the surety accepted the counter-security on terms that it would not extend to co-sureties.[9] It applies even where the surety who holds the counter-security is insolvent.[10] Where the surety has paid the principal debt and recouped himself out of the counter-security given to him by the principal and has shared this amount with his co-sureties, he is again entitled to recover out of the counter-security what he handed over, whereupon the co-sureties' rights to participate again arise, and so on until the whole of the amount paid by the co-sureties on account of the principal debt has been refunded or the counter-security exhausted.[11]

It has been suggested that the surety will lose his right of contribution where he gives up the security.[12] This suggestion is analogous with the principle that a creditor who gives up a security for the principal debt may discharge the surety,[13] and it is submitted that it ought to operate in the same way in relation to co-sureties, namely that the surety will lose his rights of contribution *in toto* where he has increased the co-sureties' risk or has breached a condition of the co-suretyship in giving up the security, and otherwise *pro tanto* to the extent of the benefit lost.

A paying surety who takes over the securities from the creditor by exercise of his rights of subrogation must bring such securities into hotchpot for the benefit of his co-sureties, by giving credit or allowing set-off in relation thereto.[14] The surety need not, however, bring into hotchpot the proceeds of a policy of life insurance taken out by the surety at his own expense on the life of the principal.[15] The principle of hotchpot

---

[7] *Steel v Dixon* (1881) 17 Ch. D. 825; *Re Arcedeckne, Atkins v Arcedeckne* (1883) 24 Ch. D. 709.
[8] *Berridge v Berridge* (1890) 44 Ch. D.168.
[9] *Steel v Dixon* (1881) 17 Ch. D. 825.
[10] *Duncan, Fox & Co v North and South Wales Bank* (1880) 6 App. Cas. 1 at 19.
[11] *Berridge v Berridge* (1890) 44 Ch. D.168.
[12] See Rowlatt, *Principal and Surety (op. cit.)*, p.172, relying on the US authority of *Ramsey v Lewis* (1859) 30 Barb. (NY) 403.
[13] See Ch.9, para.9–041, and see *Moorhouse v Kidd* (1898) 25 O.A.R. 221.
[14] *Re Albert Life Assurance Co Ltd* (1870) L.R.11 Eq. 164 at 172 *per* Bacon V.-C.; *Re Arcedeckne, Atkins v Arcedeckne* (1883) 24 Ch. D. 709.
[15] *ibid.*

does not extend to securities or benefits given to the surety by a stranger, as opposed to the principal. These securities or benefits need not be brought into hotchpot, since they never formed part of the principal's estate and so were never available to the co-sureties in enforcement of their rights of indemnity.[16]

Enforcement of the right of contribution

Action for contribution

Parties and procedure

Before the Judicature Acts, the surety who had paid more than his rateable proportion of the guaranteed debt could maintain an action for contribution or money he had received to the use and benefit of his co-sureties;[17] to succeed in the action it was necessary to prove that the payment had been made at the express or implied request of the co-sureties.[18] Following the Judicature Act 1873 the action for contribution became the usual method of enforcing a surety's rights against his co-sureties. There, an action for contribution will not be available unless the amount of the contribution can be ascertained:[19] this need not be delayed until the creditor commences an action, but can be brought on a *quia timet* basis against the co-sureties before suit is brought by the creditor.[20] A claim for an account is not a sufficient way of presenting the claim for contribution, and a specific sum must be claimed.[21]

12–018

The common practice is to join the principal and all solvent sureties to the action, so that the rights of all the parties can be determined in one inquiry,[22] and if the principal or his personal representatives are not joined as a party, the claimant surety must be prepared to prove or at least show that it can be inferred that the principal is insolvent or otherwise not worth suing.[23] Further, where one of the co-sureties is insolvent, his trustee or personal representatives should be joined.[24] Where a co-surety has died, his personal representatives should be joined as parties to the contribution proceedings, since he is liable to the extent of the assets in the estate.[25]

The creditor ought to be made a party to an action for contribution, so that the court can order payment to the creditor by the co-sureties

---

[16] *Goodman v Keel* [1923] 4 D.L.R. 468.

[17] See *McLean v Discount and Finance Ltd* (1939) 64 C.L.R. 312 at 341.

[18] *Batard v Hawes* (1853) 2 El. & Bl. 287.

[19] *Sharpe v Cummings* (1844) 2 Dow. & L. 504; *Bates v Townley* (1848) 2 Exch. 152.

[20] *Wolmershausen v Gullick* [1893] 2 Ch. 514, and see para.12–002.

[21] *Blackie v Osmaston* (1884) 28 Ch. D. 119; particulars of a demand must also be given.

[22] *Craythorne v Swinburne* (1807) 14 Ves. 160 at 164 *per* Lord Eldon L.C.

[23] *Lawson v Wright* (1786) 1 Cox. Eq. Cas. 275; *Cowell v Edwards* (1800) 2 Bos. & P. 268; *Hay v Carter* [1935] 1 Ch. 397; and see para.12–007.

[24] *Hole v Harrison* (1673) Cas. Temp. Finch. 15.

[25] *Primrose v Bromley* (1739) 1 Atk. 89; *Batard v Hawes* (1853) 2 El. & Bl. 287; as to the effect of death, see para.12–025.

directly, thereby discharging the principal debt. In the absence of the creditor before the court, the surety can obtain a prospective order that the co-sureties should pay their contribution to him whenever he pays the creditor.[26]

Where the creditor sues the surety, the appropriate course for the surety is to join the co-sureties by means of Pt 20 proceedings in the creditor's action, pursuant to Pt 20 of the Civil Procedure Rules, whether or not the co-sureties have already been joined as defendants by the creditor. Again, this avoids a multiplicity of proceedings.[27] Permission of the Court is required under CPR Pt 20.7 before a Pt 20 claim can be made, unless the Pt 20 claim is issued before or at the same time as the defence is filed. Where the co-surety, joined as a third party, defends the action separately from the surety, he may have to bear the costs of doing so even though the creditor fails against the surety.[28]

Limitation of claims for contribution

12–019   A surety's claim for contribution is not a claim for a specialty debt, but a simple debt, and has a limitation period of six years.[29] No claim for contribution accrues so as to start the limitation period running until a surety has paid more than his rateable share of what is unpaid by the principal,[30] even if his liability could have been ascertained at an earlier time.[31] Similarly, the limitation periods in relation to contribution claims arising out of successive payments to the creditor in excess of the surety's rateable share run from the date of each payment.[32] Where the surety pays an amount less than his rateable share, and the principal later discharges the entire principal debt, time runs from the latter date if by that date the surety has not paid more than his rateable share: his right to contribution will only arise at that time.[33]

The fact that the creditor's claim against the surety has become time-barred at the time the surety's claim for contribution is made will not affect the contribution claim.[34]

It is difficult to square the notion of the surety's liability beginning to run at the time of payment with the availability to the surety of *quia timet* relief. It could be said that it is open to a co-surety faced with a claim for

---

[26] *Wolmershausen v Gullick* [1893] 2 Ch. 514.

[27] *Baxter v France* [1895] 1 Q.B. 455 at 493, *per* Lord Esher M.R.; *Barclays Bank v Tom* [1923] 1 K.B. 221 at 223, 225; *Standard Securities v Hubbard* [1967] Ch. 1056.

[28] *Williams v Buchanan* (1891) 7 T.L.R. 226.

[29] See the Limitation Act 1980, ss.5 and 8. Where a claim for a contribution is based on s.1 of the Civil Liability (Contribution) Act 1978, the time limit for the bringing of claims is two years from when the right to contribution accrues: Limitation Act 1980, s.10. However, it is doubtful whether this Act applies to claims for contribution between co-sureties:see n.52 above. This passage and footnote were referred to with approval in *Hampton v Minns* [2002] 1 W.L.R. 1 at 21 (para.77ff).

[30] *Ex p. Gifford* (1802) 6 Ves. 805; *Re Snowdon Ex p. Snowdon* (1881) 17 Ch. D. 44.

[31] *Wolmershausen v Gullick* [1893] 2 Ch. 514.

[32] *Davies v Humphreys* (1840) 6 M. & W. 153.

[33] *Davies v Humphreys* (1840) 6 M. & W. 153.

[34] *ibid.*

contribution to defend on the basis that the surety could have applied more than six years ago for *quia timet* relief against him, his right to contribution having accrued when his liability to the creditor was ascertained and immediate. Some support for this argument can be found in *Wolmershausen v Gullick* itself,[35] where Wright J. said that time did not begin to run as against the surety until his liability was ascertained. However, it is submitted that the surety's cause of action for a contribution does not in fact need to have arisen in order to enable him to apply for *quia timet* relief; such an application would be the enforcement of an equitable right to relief[36] which may arise before the limitation period has begun to run.[37] This analysis is supported by the reasoning of Rix J. in *Rowland v Gulfpac Ltd* [1999] Ll. Rep. Bank 86 at 98, where he granted a freezing order on a *quia timet* basis in equity to support an indemnity claim even though the cause of action for an indemnity was not complete at common law.[38]

Defences to claims for contribution

The co-surety may, of course, take in his defence any point to the effect that he is not liable to contribute, including the fact that no such liability has arisen,[39] or that such liability has been expressly excluded or waived by the surety,[40] or that he is not really a co-surety,[41] or that the claim is time-barred.[42] **12–020**

Where the surety has settled with the creditor for less than the full amount of the guaranteed debt, or indeed pays in full, it may be open to the co-sureties to defend a contribution claim on the grounds that the creditor's claim could have been resisted or settled on better terms,[43] unless the co-sureties have sanctioned the arrangement or declined an opportunity to participate.[44] Where the co-surety can show that the payment or compromise was improvident or that he "might have obtained better terms if the opportunity had been given him",[45] he will be discharged.

This is not the case where the Civil Liability (Contribution) Act 1978 applies. Section 1(4) entitles a person who has entered a bona fide settlement or compromise of a claim in respect of any damage to recover regardless of whether he was ever in fact liable, provided that the factual basis of the claim against him could be established.[46]

---

[35] [1895] 2 Ch. 514.
[36] Rather like applying for an injunction to restrain a nuisance before it actually occurs.
[37] See Ch.10, para.10–014.
[38] Thus avoiding the vicissitudes of the *Veracruz I* [1992] 1 Ll. Rep. 353 and *Zucker v Tyndall Holdings Plc* [1992] 1 W.L.R. 1127; see also *Papamichael v National Westminster Bank Plc* [2002] 1 Ll. Rep. 332.
[39] See para.12–008.
[40] See para.12–011.
[41] See para.12–009.
[42] See para.12–018.
[43] *Smith v Compton* (1835) 3 B. & Ad. 407.
[44] *Stewart v Braun* [1925] 2 D.L.R. 423.
[45] *Compton v Smith* (1832) 3 B. & Ad. 407 at 408.
[46] But see n.52 above.

Where the co-surety has a counterclaim or right of set-off against the creditor, he may not invoke this in his defence to a claim by the surety against him for contribution, and any such defence could only be taken with the principal before the court.[47] Further, it has been doubted that the co-surety can rely, in defence of a claim against him for contribution, upon a defence which would normally be open to the surety against the creditor.[48]

Defences based on the conduct of the creditor

12–021 It is well established that a release or indulgence given by the creditor to the principal will, in the absence of any agreement to the contrary or a reservation of rights, discharge the surety and his co-sureties,[49] although if he has paid an amount of the principal debt before the creditor releases the principal, he is entitled to claim an indemnity from the principal, and to the extent that the payment exceeds his rateable share, to claim contribution from his co-sureties.[50] However, where the creditor releases the surety, the co-sureties will not thereby be discharged unless their liability is joint or joint and several,[51] or it is an express condition of the guarantee that they be released in that event. It seems that such discharge will be entire and automatic, on the principle that release of one joint debtor is the release of all.[52] Where the surety is severally liable, however, his claim:

> " . . . to be released upon the creditor releasing another surety, arises not from the creditor having broken his contract, but from his having deprived the surety of his remedy for contribution in equity. The surety, therefore, in order to support his claim, must show that he had a right to contribution, and that that right has been taken away or injuriously affected."[53]

In other words, release of a surety who is jointly or jointly and severally liable will discharge the co-sureties; release of a surety severally liable will discharge co-sureties *pro tanto* to the extent that they have lost the value of a right of contribution.

---

[47] *Wilson v Mitchell* [1939] 2 Q.B. 869.
[48] *Greenwood v Francis* [1899] 1 Q.B. 312; *cf. Griffith v Wade* (1966) 60 D.L.R. (2d) 62; and see para.12–021.
[49] See Ch.9, para.9–010.
[50] See *Reade v Lowndes* (1857) 23 Beav. 361 at 368, and Goff & Jones, *The Law of Restitution* (*op. cit.*), 393.
[51] See Ch.9, paras 9–011 and 9–035; *Mercantile Bank of Sydney v Taylor* [1893] A.C. 317; see also *Cheetham v Ward* (1797) 1 Bos. & P. 630; *Nicholson v Revill* (1836) 4 Ad. & El. 675; *Re EWA* [1901] 2 K.B. 642; *Watts v Baron Aldington* (unreported) December 16, 1992, CA. *Johnson v Davies* [1999] Ch. 117. But see the Civil Liability (Contribution) Act 1978, s.3, which provides that judgment for a debt or damages against a person jointly liable shall not bar an action against any other person jointly liable, abrogating the effect of the common law rule that the cause of action mergers in the judgment. See Ch.9, para.9–040.
[52] *Bonser v Cox* (1841) 4 Beav. 379; *Nicholson v Revill* (1836) 4 Ad. & El. 675.
[53] *Ward v National Bank of New Zealand* (1883) 8 App. Cas. 755, *per* Sir Robert Collier at 766. See also Ch.9, para.9–040; *Wolmershausen v Wolmershausen* (1890) 62 L.T. 541.

However, the mere act of forbearance[54] or giving of time to the surety does not release the co-sureties.[55] This is because such an indulgence enures to the benefit of the co-sureties and cannot adversely affect the obligation to make contribution. In contrast, where the creditor gives time to the principal, the surety and all the co-sureties are released.[56]

Defences based on the conduct of the surety

Surety releasing or giving time to the principal

Once the surety has paid the principal debt and has become entitled to the creditor's rights, it is he and not the creditor who is in a position to release the principal from his obligations, which have themselves become transmuted into an obligation to indemnify the surety. Where the surety does release the principal, the co-sureties are thereby released from their obligation to contribute to the surety for the payment he has made.[57] However, the matter is not wholly free from doubt. In *Greenwood v Francis* [1899] 1 Q.B. 312, the Court of Appeal doubted that a co-surety would be so released, since he could not rely on defences which would normally be open to the surety when sued by the creditor.[58] However, that view was expressly rejected by the Appellate Division of the Alberta Supreme Court in *Griffith v Wade* (1966) 60 D.L.R. (2d) 62, where the principal had been released by the surety who then sought contribution from the co-surety. It was held that, by the release of the principal, the co-surety had been discharged from his obligation to contribute to the surety, since he had been deprived of his right of indemnity from the principal. Johnson J.A. said:

12–022

> "If . . . a surety is discharged by an act of the creditor which affects his right of contribution,[59] it should follow that the co-surety should also be released from contribution by any act which deprives him of his right of reimbursement from the principal debtor. The test would therefore be whether prejudice had been suffered by the surety's act in dealing with the principal debtor."[60]

It is submitted that this is the correct view. The doubts expressed by the Court of Appeal in *Greenwood v Francis* were *obiter* by way of query, and

---

[54] *Kearsley v Cole* (1846) 16 M. & W. 128, *per* Parke B.

[55] *Dunn v Slee* (1817) 1 Moo. C.P. 2.

[56] *Overend Gurney & Co v Oriental Financial Corporation* (1871) 7 Ch. App. 142 at 152 *per* Lord Hatherley L.C.

[57] *Way v Hearn* (1862) 11 C.B.N.S. 774, *per* Earle J. at 782; *Griffith v Wade* (1966) 60 D.L.R. (2d) 62.

[58] See especially A. L. Smith L.J. at 320.

[59] As to which see para.12–020.

[60] (1966) 60 D.L.R. (2d) 62 at 69–70. See also *Ward v National Bank of New Zealand* (1883) L.R. 8 App. Cas. 755, where the test propounded was that the right of contribution should be taken away or injuriously affected; see Goff & Jones, *The Law of Restitution* (*op. cit.*), p.393, where the view is taken that in such a case the co-surety's release should be limited to the extent of the contribution he could have claimed from the released surety.

on the facts it was held that because of the particular terms of the bond in which all the sureties had joined, the giving of time by the sureties did not release the co-sureties. Further, the *Griffith v Wade* approach is consistent with the principle that in order to found a claim for contribution, the principal must either be before the court or be shown or inferred to be insolvent or otherwise not worth pursuing,[61] since the surety's primary line of recourse should always be against the principal for an indemnity. However, where it is provided in the guarantee (or several guarantees) that the co-sureties shall not be so discharged, or that as between themselves and the creditor they shall be liable as principals, this defence will not be open to a co-surety.

Even though *Greenwood v Francis* was a case where time was given by the surety to the principal, and *Griffiths v Wade* involved an outright release, it is submitted that there is no difference in principle, and that, just as the surety is discharged where the creditor releases, gives time to or varies the obligations of the principal,[62] so any such indulgence by the surety will similarly discharge the co-surety. The surety now stands in the creditor's shoes for the purposes of enforcing his right of indemnity. The only difference between the effect of a release of the principal by the creditor and a release by the surety is that the surety who is discharged by indulgence granted by the creditor to the principal need not show that he has actually been prejudiced by the indulgence,[63] whereas the co-surety who claims to be discharged by the release of the principal by the surety must show actual prejudice.[64] This can be explained by the distinction between the surety's right of contribution, which is secondary to his right of indemnity against the principal and necessitates either joinder of the principal or showing him to be insolvent or otherwise not worth pursuing,[65] and the creditor's rights conferred by the guarantee, which give him a primary right of recourse without the necessity of joining the principal or showing him not to be worth suing.

Surety releasing or giving time to a co-surety

12–023   There is no direct authority on the effect of a release or grant of time by one surety to a co-surety on the remaining co-sureties. It has been suggested[66] that the release of a co-surety by a surety does not discharge the remaining co-sureties from their obligations to contribute, because the fact that there are fewer co-sureties does not increase the burden of those who have not been released nor deny them a right of recovery. However, it is submitted that the surety who has paid the principal debt stands in the creditor's shoes, and any release by him of a co-surety

---

[61] *Hay v Carter* [1935] Ch. 397.
[62] See Ch.9, paras 9–010–9–011, 9–023–9–028 and 9–029–9–033.
[63] See Ch.9, especially at para.9–029.
[64] *Ward v National Bank of New Zealand* (1883) L.R. 8 App. Cas. 755.
[65] *Hay v Carter* [1935] Ch. 397.
[66] McGuinness, *The Law of Guarantee* (*op. cit.*), para.9.19.

discharges the other co-sureties, on the basis of the identical principles that govern the release given to a principal by a creditor discussed at para.12–020 above,[67] namely, whether the co-sureties were jointly or jointly and severally liable, or severally liable, and if severally whether they have suffered any prejudice by the release.

This view is supported by American authority,[68] and by English and Commonwealth academic writers.[69] It can be justified on the basis that the discharge of one co-surety does indeed increase the risk that those co-sureties remaining may have to pay more in contribution. This is because there are fewer co-sureties, and so there is an increased risk that, on the insolvency of one of them, the proportion of contribution which each solvent co-surety will have to bear will become larger. This is an aspect of the principle that the burden of contribution is shared pro rata between the solvent co-sureties.[70]

It is, however, established that where a surety holds the benefit of an indemnity from a third party in respect of his liability under the guarantee, and he releases his co-surety from his obligation to contribute, he releases the third party from the indemnity *pro tanto*.[71]

Surety dealing with counter-securities

It is no defence to a claim for contribution that the surety took counter-security from the principal for the guaranteed liability.[72] However, under the hotchpot principle,[73] the surety must give credit for any such counter-security when making his claim for contribution, and he owes his co-sureties a corresponding obligation to preserve counter-securities for their benefit.[74] Where the surety has lost or impaired the benefit of such security, the co-sureties may set this up as a defence to a claim for contribution. The extent of the duties of the surety in relation to such counter-securities is not entirely clear, nor is the question of whether the surety owes the co-sureties any duty of care to deal with the counter-securities in a reasonable manner. It is probable that the surety owes similar duties to the co-sureties in relation to counter-securities held by him as the creditor owes to the surety in relation to securities held by him from the principal.[75] Accordingly, any unreasonable dealing with the counter-securities by the surety may discharge the co-sureties *pro tanto*.

12–024

---

[67] And at Ch.9, paras 9–010–9–016.

[68] *Fletcher v Grover* (1840) 11 N.H. 368.

[69] See O'Donovan & Phillips, *The Modern Contract of Guarantee* (*op. cit.*), pp.640–641; English Edition (2003) paras 12–210 to 214.; Goff & Jones, *The Law of Restitution* (*op. cit.*), pp.394–395.

[70] See para.12–013.

[71] *Hodgson v Hodgson* (1837) 2 Keen 704.

[72] *Knight v Hughes* (1823) 3 C. & P. 467.

[73] See para.12–016.

[74] *Steel v Dixon* (1881) 17 Ch. D. 825.

[75] As to which see Ch.9, para.9–043, and especially *China and South Seas Bank v Tan* [1990] 1 A.C. 536, where it was held that the creditor was under no obligation to the surety to sell securities he held even though they were declining in value; see the recent analysis of this area of the law by Lightman J. in the Court of Appeal) in *Silven Properties Ltd v Royal Bank of Scotland Plc* [2004] 1 B.C.L.C. 359.

Death and bankruptcy

The effect of bankruptcy

12–025   A surety's claim for contribution is in the nature of a simple debt, which can found a bankruptcy petition against the co-surety.[76] Further, the surety's claim is provable in the co-surety's bankruptcy,[77] and in principle this right extends to future claims.[78] Where the creditor has lodged a proof in the co-surety's bankruptcy, the surety who pays the creditor in full will be entitled to take over the creditor's proof for the principal debt,[79] and to recover dividends in the bankruptcy on the whole of that sum.[80] Where the creditor is paid in full by the surety but has not yet lodged a proof in the co-surety's bankruptcy, the surety can still prove in the name of the creditor for the whole amount of the principal debt, and recover dividends on that amount in the bankruptcy up to the amount of the contribution.[81] This is so whether or not the creditor has actually assigned the benefit of the debt or the proof to the surety.[82] The surety will be obliged to share any dividends he receives in excess of his rateable share with his co-sureties, or give credit for them.[83] Alternatively, the surety who has paid the whole of the guaranteed debt can prove in his own name, but his proof is limited to the bankrupt co-surety's share of the principal debt. Accordingly, the better course for a surety who has paid the whole debt is either to take over the creditor's proof or, if no such proof has been made, to lodge a proof in the name of the creditor.

Where the surety has paid more than his rateable share of the guaranteed debt but less than the whole amount, he is precluded from proving in the co-surety's bankruptcy because his proof would compete with that of the creditor and would accordingly offend the rule against double proof.[84] It is only where the creditor has waived or in some way agreed to give up his right to prove in the co-surety's bankruptcy that the surety may then prove, since the rule will not be offended.

In addition, an express term in the guarantee may prohibit the surety from proving in his co-surety's bankruptcy until the creditor has been paid in full. It is even possible for a guarantee to provide that the surety should not prove in the co-surety's bankruptcy in competition with a proof by the creditor for any debt, even one distinct from the guaranteed debt.

Whether the discharge of a co-surety from bankruptcy relieves him of his liability to contribute depends on the nature of how the liability to

---

[76] *Re Snowdon Ex p. Snowdon* (1881) 17 Ch. D. 44.
[77] *Re Parker, Morgan v Hill* [1894] 3 Ch. 400.
[78] *Wolmershausen v Gullick* [1893] 2 Ch. 514.
[79] Under the Mercantile Law Amendment Act 1856, s.5.
[80] *Re Parker, Morgan v Hill* [1894] 3 Ch. 400.
[81] *ibid.*, and see *Ex p. Stokes* (1848) De G. 618. This right is confirmed by s.5 of the Mercantile Law Amendment Act 1856.
[82] *Re McMyn, Lightbown v McMyn* (1886) 33 Ch. D. 575.
[83] *Re Hendry Ex p. Murphy* [1905] S.A.L.R. 116.
[84] *ibid.*, and see *Ex p. Stokes* (1848) De G. 618.

contribute was incurred. If it was incurred by means of a breach of trust, for example where a director of a company helps to procure an unauthorised advance by the company, he will not be released by discharge from bankruptcy from his obligation to contribute to his co-director similarly liable.[85]

The effect of death

Whether the death of a surety releases his estate from its duty to contribute to the common liability depends on the nature of the relationship between the co-sureties. Even though the death of a surety may, in the absence of any agreement to the contrary, discharge his liability to the creditor once the creditor has notice of the death,[86] his co-sureties will of course remain liable. The surety's estate remains liable to contribute to the common liability on the basis of ordinary equitable principles provided he was bound with his co-sureties jointly and severally or simply severally. However, where the co-sureties were jointly liable to the creditor it is doubtful whether the estate of one such co-surety will be obliged to contribute.[87] This is an aspect of the common law notion that death discharges the joint contractor from his obligations, and equity follows the law on this.

12–026

It appears, therefore, to be necessary to establish something over and above the mere fact of co-suretyship before the estate of a co-surety jointly liable can be compelled to contribute. His estate might be required to contribute where it can be inferred that he intended his estate to pay his original share of the principal debt.[88] Such an inference may be drawn from the fact that the guarantee is to provide a continuing benefit to his estate, for example by ensuring the continuity of a loan to a company in which it had shares.[89] In *Ashby v Ashby* (1827) 7 B. & C. 444, Bayley J. said (at 451):

"To put a plain case, suppose two persons are jointly bound as sureties, one dies, the survivor is sued and is obliged to pay the whole debt. If the deceased had been living, the survivor might have sued him for contribution in an action for money paid, and I think he is entitled to sue the executor of the deceased for money paid to his use

---

[85] *Ramskill v Edwards* (1885) 31 Ch. D. 100. This is not a guarantee case, but illustrates the exception to statutory discharge in cases of breach of trust under what is now s.281 of the Insolvency Act 1986.

[86] *Other v Iveson* (1855) 3 Drew 177; *Re Denton's Estate* [1904] 2 Ch. 178.

[87] See *Ashby v Ashby* (1827) 7 B. & C. 444, 451; *Batard v Hawes* (1853) 2 El. & Bl. 287, 298; *Prior v Hembrow* (1841) 8 M. & W. 873, 889; Rowlatt, *Principal and Surety (op. cit.)*, p.170.

[88] *Prior v Hembrow* (1841) 8 M. & W. 873, where the circumstances were said to be those which "stand on the same footing as that of several persons jointly contracting for a chattel to be made or procured for the common benefit of all—the building of a ship, for instance, or the furnishing of a house—and as to which the executors of any party dying before the work is completed are by agreement to stand in the place of the party dying".

[89] *ibid.*, and Rowlatt, *Principal and Surety (op. cit.)*, p.170.

as executor . . . and when money is paid to his use as executor, justice requires that the person who made that payment should have the liberty of looking to the fund which the executor has in that character."

However, it is not easy to see why Bayley J. thought that the estate would benefit from the payment in that case.

On the whole, the authorities in this area are inconclusive, and should be approached with caution. Those which have allowed a contribution claim to proceed have done so on the basis of some implied contract between the parties or some benefit accruing by means of the payment by the surety to the creditor.

Chapter 13

Insolvency

The insolvency of the principal

When the principal becomes insolvent, a number of matters may arise for consideration, such as whether payments to the creditor made by the principal which would normally discharge the surety are impugnable by the liquidator or trustee-in-bankruptcy as preferences,[1] or as transfers at an undervalue, or whether security given by the principal during the period prior to insolvency can be avoided. These questions raise issues of general insolvency law applicable not only to guarantee cases but to all commercial relationships, and are therefore outside the scope of this work.[2] The main area of concern in the context of contracts of suretyship is the question of whether and in what circumstances the surety has a right of proof in the insolvency of the principal for his indemnity.

The rule against double proof

The general rule
The respective rights of the creditor and the surety to prove in the insolvency of the principal are governed by the rule against double proof. The essence of this rule is that the insolvent estate should not be compelled to entertain more than one proof in respect of the same debt, for to do so would unfairly distort the *pari passu* principle of distribution in insolvency. It prevents two creditors from proving in the insolvency of the principal in respect of what is in effect the same debt, so that there is no doubling-up of dividends.[3]

The claim by the surety to be indemnified is a mirror image of the creditor's claim against the principal for the principal debt, and is a contingent claim until the surety has paid the creditor in full under the guarantee so that his right to indemnity from the principal arises.[4] Although

13–001

13–002

---

[1] See Ch.9, para.9–002 and n.10.
[2] For a useful review of the problems that arise in guarantee cases where the principal is insolvent, see R. M. Goode, *Legal Problems of Credit and Security*, (3rd ed., 2003), paras 8.16 to 8.35.
[3] See *Re Oriental Commercial Bank* (1871) L.R. 7 Ch. 99; *Re Moss Ex p. Hallett* [1905] 2 K.B. 307; *Re Fenton* [1931] 1 Ch. 85; *Barclays Bank v TOSG Fund Ltd* [1984] 1 All E.R. 628, CA; *Stotter v Equiticorp Australia Ltd* [2002] 2 N.Z.L.R. 686 at para.48.
[4] *Ex p. Turquand; Re Fothergill* (1876) 3 Ch. D. 445. This may be seen as somewhat hard on the surety, who is entitled, where the principal is solvent, to recover a *pro tanto* indemnity from him to the extent of the amount of the principal debt discharged by the surety: see *Re Sass* [1896] 2 Q.B. 12 and Ch.10, para.10–017 above, and paras 13–008–13–009 below. See also *Stotter v Equitcorp Australia Ltd* [2002] 2 N.Z.L.R. 686.

contingent claims are provable by statute,[5] the rule against double proof will protect the insolvent estate from having to entertain a proof from the surety where the creditor retains a claim and the surety has not discharged the whole of the guaranteed indebtedness.[6] The debt to the creditor and the contingent claim by the surety are both extinguished by the one payment out of the insolvent estate to the creditor, and so the creditor is the senior creditor of the insolvent estate. As will be seen below (at para.13–012), where the creditor renounces his right of proof or releases the principal while reserving his rights against the surety,[7] the surety becomes the senior creditor (even though still contingent), and there is no longer a possibility of double proof.

In *Re Polly Peck Plc* [1996] 2 All E.R. 433, Robert Walker J. had to decide the question of whether two notices of claim in Polly Peck Plc's scheme of arrangement relating to its bond issues, one from creditor banks and one from a lending company within the Polly Peck group, constituted a single claim, attracting the rule against double proof, or whether they were two separate claims. After setting out some of the basic principles (at 442), he said that the basis of the rule was that "the surety's contingent claim is not regarded as an independent free-standing debt, but only as a reflection of the real debt—that in respect of money which the principal creditor had loaned to the principal debtor." The question of whether the debts are separate or in fact only a "reflection of the real debt" is, he said, one of legal substance, and not economic substance.[8] Accordingly, the fact that the surety is a member of the same group of companies as the principal debtor or otherwise closely economically linked will not of itself render the debt substantially the same so as to attract the rule against double proof. There was, he said, no justification for ignoring the separate legal status of the companies within the same group simply in order to apply the rule against double proof.

The time at which the rule operates

13–003 The question of the time at which the rule against double proof comes into operation is not settled, and there appear to be two schools of thought. The generally accepted view is that the rule operates at the moment when the creditor lodges his proof in the principal's insolvency, so that in order to have a right to prove in the principal's insolvency, the surety must have paid in full before the creditor lodges his proof.[9] In other words, there cannot be

---

[5] See the Insolvency Act 1986 (hereinafter IA 1986), s.382(3) in the case of individuals and the Insolvency Rules 1986, r.30.12 in the case of companies.

[6] *Re Fenton* [1931] 1 Ch. 85, *per* Romer L.J. at 118–120; *Barclays Bank Ltd v TOSG Fund Ltd* [1984] 1 All E.R. 628 at 641F–G; *Re Fitness Centre Ltd* [1986] B.C.L.C. 518, *per* Hoffmann J. at 521. See further paras 13–004–13–009.

[7] *Re Fenton* [1931] 1 Ch. 85 at 118 *per* Romer L.J.

[8] He relied on the test as stated by Oliver L.J. in *Barclays Bank v TOSG Fund Ltd* [1984] A.C. 626 at 636 that it is "whether two claims are, in substance, claims for the payment of the same debt twice over".

[9] *ibid.* at 118. Philip Wood, *English and International Set-Off (op. cit.)*, para.10.97; Williams and Muir Hunter, *Law and Practice in Bankruptcy (op. cit.)*, p.187.

two proofs in respect of the one debt, and the proof by the creditor precludes proof by the surety.

However, there is powerful judicial support for the proposition that the time at which the rule comes into operation is the date on which the creditor's dividend is paid.[10] This is, it is said, because the rule against double proof is in effect a rule against "double-dividend" designed to prevent payment of two dividends on one and the same debt.[11] In guarantee cases, the question whether the rule arises or not can usually only be determined with any certainty at the time when a dividend payment has been made to the creditor.

It has been suggested that there are good reasons for preferring the date of lodgment over the date of payment of dividend.[12] In particular, it is said, if the rule does not operate until the creditor is paid, the surety will be able, prior to payment to the creditor, to exercise any right of insolvency set-off he may have against the principal.[13] Since the exercise of an available insolvency set-off is tantamount to payment to the surety of the balance of the account due, the mischief of the rule against double proof will be offended since the creditor remains entitled to prove in respect of the amount the subject of the surety's set-off.[14] Further, this would be consistent with the position where the surety is insolvent. Where the creditor proves in the surety's insolvency, he must give credit for any amounts received in reduction of the principal indebtedness prior to the date of lodgment of his proof in the surety's insolvency.[15]

---

[10] *Barclays Bank Ltd v TOSG Fund Ltd* [1984] 1 All E.R. 628 at 636 at 637E–F , *per* Oliver L.J. See O'Donovan & Phillips, English ed. (2003) para.12-67, where this view is adopted. The view of the authors in footnote 1 to that paragraph, that *Barclays Bank Ltd v TOSG Fund Ltd* contains no explicit support for this proposition, is incorrect: see *per* Oliver L.J. at 637E–F, where he said: "I can see no logical justification for seeking to fix the position at the commencement of the insolvency. One has, as it seems to me, to look at the position at the point at which the dividend is about to be paid and to ask the question then whether two payments are being sought for a liability which, if the company were solvent, could be discharged as regards both claimants by one payment."

[11] See also *Re Oriental Commercial Bank* (1871) L.R. 7 Ch. 99, *per* Mellish L.J. at 103, where he said: "The true principle is that there is only to be one dividend in respect of what in substance is the same debt, although there may be two separate contracts." See also *Gray v Seckham* (1872) 7 Ch. Ap. 680, especially *per* Mellish L.J. at 684.

[12] See Philip Wood, *English and International Set-Off (op. cit.)*, para.10.98.

[13] Under the IA 1986, s.323 (individuals) and the Insolvency Rules 1986, r.4.90 (companies).

[14] Under the statutory insolvency set-off provisions, the set-off is exercised by means of an account taken in the insolvency, with only the balance being payable. The statutory provisions operate automatically as at the date of the bankruptcy or liquidation, and the account "must be taken whenever it is necessary for *any* purpose to ascertain the effect which the section had": *Stein v Blake per* Lord Hoffmann at [1996] 1 A.C. 243, at 253. See also *Gye v McIntyre* (1991) 171 C.L.R. 609. See now *Re West End Networks Ltd (In liq.)* [2004] 2 All E.R. 1042, in which Lord Hoffmann (at paras 22–25) gave an extended meaning to the word "dealings" in the statute, applying *Gye v McIntyre* and disapproving Millett J.'s more restrictive approach in *Re Charge Card Services Ltd* [1987] Ch. 150 at 189. Lord Hoffmann was able to do so because the House was overruling *Re a Debtor (No.66 of 1955)* [1956] 2 All E.R. 94.

[15] *Re Blakeley* (1892) 9 Morr. 173; *Re Houlder* [1929] 1 Ch. 205; *Re Amalgamated Investment & Property Co Ltd* [1985] 1 Ch. 349, and see now *Stotter v Equiticorp Australia Ltd* [2002] 2 N.Z.L.R. 686 at paras 42–46 and 62–66. See further below, para.13–013. This is also consistent with the position in relation to the right of a surety to prove in the insolvency of his co-surety for contribution, as to which see Ch.12, para.12–023.

Despite these arguments, it is submitted that the views of Oliver L.J. in *Barclays Bank Ltd v TOSG Fund Ltd* are the more attractive, and that the crucial cut-off date for payment by the surety which would qualify him to prove in the principal's insolvency is the date of the payment of a dividend to the creditor. Lodgment of proof by the creditor is merely a procedural step in the insolvency, and has no substantive significance. The proof can be withdrawn, rejected or expunged, and the liquidator or trustee is not bound to admit the proof or pay the dividend proved for.[16] Indeed, even once a dividend in the insolvency is declared in favour of the creditor, it is not a debt recoverable by action against the liquidator or trustee.[17] The admission of proof and the calculation of dividend are procedural matters for the liquidator or trustee, and it is unsatisfactory that the right of the surety to prove should be dependent upon something so arbitrary as the date on which the creditor lodges his proof. The mischief of the rule against the double proof is to prevent a doubling-up of dividends, and the fact that there are two proofs for the same debt is something that can be dealt with by the liquidator or trustee when he calculates and pays the dividend, making unnecessary the application of any rule of law at any earlier stage.

In the first edition of this work, it was suggested, in the course of supporting the views of Oliver L.J. in *Barclays Bank Ltd v TOSG Fund Ltd*, that insolvency set-off was not a self-help remedy in the hands of the surety, in that he could not in fact exercise his rights of insolvency set-off against the principal until the principal's liquidator or trustee took the account of what was due. However, in *MS Fashions Ltd v Bank of Credit and Commerce International SA* [1993] Ch. 425 Hoffmann L.J. (as he then was)[18] and in *Stein v Blake* [1996] 1 A.C. 243 Lord Hoffmann has now decided that the insolvency set-off account is mandatory, self-executing, and operates as at the date of the liquidator or bankruptcy, but with the benefit of hindsight, so that contingencies which have matured after that date by the time the account comes to be taken are to be included in that account. In *Stein v Blake*, he cast doubt on a dictum of Mason J. in *Day & Dent Constructions Ltd v North Australian Properties Pty Ltd* (1982) 150 C.L.R. 85 to the effect that "due" in the Australian equivalent of s.323(2) of the IA 1986 meant due at the date when the account came to be taken, and said[19] that "due" merely means treated as having been owing at the bankruptcy date with the benefit of hindsight and, if necessary, estimation prescribed by the bankruptcy law.[20]

---

[16] For the procedure on admission or rejection of proofs, and the creditor's right of challenge, see the IR 1986, rr.6.104, 6.105 (individuals), and rr.4.82, 4.83 (companies).

[17] *Prout v Gregory* (1889) 24 Q.B.D. 281; *Spence v Coleman* [1901] 2 K.B. 199; where the creditor has not received a declared dividend, the creditor must apply to the court for an order that the liquidator or trustee perform his statutory duties.

[18] Delivering judgment at first instance.

[19] [1996] 1 A.C. 243 at 256.

[20] The House of Lords reversed the decision of the Court of Appeal [1994] Ch. 17, who had overruled *Farley v Housing and Commercial Developments Ltd* [1984] B.C.L.C. 442. Lord Hoffmann approved the decision of Neill J. in that case, to the effect that under the statutory insolvency provisions, cross-claims cease to have a separate existence as choses in action and are replaced by a balance of account.

However, the decision of the House of Lords in *Stein v Blake* provides no particular support for the view that the date of the operation of the rule against double proof is the date of lodgment of proof by the creditor. The surety who has paid a part of the guaranteed debt to the creditor will still be able to insist on the set-off account being taken as between himself and the insolvent principal at any time during the insolvency, even *before* lodgment of proof by the creditor for the unpaid balance of the debt. In this way, he will always be able to use insolvency set-off to avoid the vicissitudes of the rule against double proof. Perhaps this is a compensation for the harshness of the rule in depriving him of his right to prove for any amount in the principal's insolvency until the creditor is paid in full once the rule does apply.

Accordingly, it is submitted that the better view is that where the surety has paid the creditor in full *prior to the payment to the creditor of a dividend in the principal's insolvency*, the surety is entitled himself to prove in full. Once the surety has discharged the guaranteed indebtedness, he is free to exercise any right of insolvency set-off against the principal which he may have in order to obtain payment of his indemnity; he would not be free to do this if the creditor had been paid a dividend prior to the payment by the surety.[21]

Furthermore, the decision of the House of Lords in *Stein v Blake* does not have the effect of interpolating the statutory insolvency set-off rules in such a way as to abrogate the rule against double proof. In *Re Glen Express Ltd* [2000] B.P.I.R. 456, the defendant was a director of a company (the principal) which had gone into liquidation. He owed it £100,000 on a directors' loan account at the date of winding up. However, he had also provided a guarantee to the company's bankers which was secured over three properties, and at the date of winding up the company it owed the bank £170,000 which was caught by the director's guarantee. The liquidator of the company sued the director for recovery of the loan, and the director claimed that this contingent right to an indemnity from the company (arising by reason of his liability to the bank as surety under his guarantee) should be set off under the statutory insolvency rules against his liability to repay the loan to the company. Neuberger J. held that the liquidator was entitled to rely on the rule against double proof: there was nothing in the operation of the statutory insolvency set-off rules as analysed by Lord Hoffmann in *Stein v Blake* which affected the rule against double proof. The fact that the director, as surety, had not paid anything to the creditor bank meant that, although he had a contingent claim against the company, it was not a provable debt by reason of the very operation of the rule

---

[21] This is because the statutory right of set-off only applies to provable claims: see *Re Daintry* [1900] 1 Q.B. 546 at 555 *per* Wright J. Equally, where the the surety has paid part only of the debt (having guaranteed the whole), there can be no insolvency set-off between the surety's claim for an indemnity and any claim by the principal against the surety, since the indemnity claim remains subject to the rule against double proof and is not provable: *Re Fenton* [1931] 1 Ch. 85; Philip Wood, *English and International Set-Off (op. cit.)*, paras 10.116, 10.117. See now *Re West End Networks (In liq.)* [2004] 2 All E.R. 1042.

against double proof, and it would not become so until he had paid the creditor either wholly or *pro tanto*. Since the claim to an indemnity was not a provable debt, it did not fall to be set off under the statutory insolvency set-off rules. This rule is enshrined in *Re Fenton* [1931] 1 Ch. 85, and has now received the approval of the House of Lords in *Re West End Networks (In liq.)* [2004] 2 All E.R. 1042, at para.13 in the speech of Lord Hoffmann.

The rule against double proof is therefore unaffected by the fact that the surety's claim for an indemnity was contingent at the date of the commencement of the insolvency, and has since become due and payable: contingent claims are (otherwise) provable.[22] In *Re Moseley Green Coal & Coke Co Ltd, Barrett's Case (No.2)* (1864) De G. J. & S. 754, the surety guaranteed a mortgage debt to the creditor. The mortgage liability was then taken over by a company who issued a promissory note to the creditor as further security. The surety was a contributory in the company and liable to contribute on its liquidation. Following the liquidation the mortgage fell due and the surety paid it, taking a transfer of the note from the creditor. The note fell due and the company failed to pay it. It was held that the surety was entitled to set off against a call by the liquidator for contribution the amount owing by the company to him under the note, since he had paid off the debt which the note secured in his capacity as surety and had acquired it by subrogation. Lord Westbury said that even though the claim under the note by the surety became accrued due after the commencement of the insolvency, it was the result of a liability incurred or a contract entered prior to the commencement of the insolvency.[23]

In *Day & Dent Constructions Ltd v Northern Australian Pty Ltd* (1982) 56 A.J.L.R. 347, the surety had guaranteed the principal's debt, and owed the principal a sum arising out of a loan transaction. The surety paid off the creditor and sought an indemnity, and was met with a defence of insolvency set-off. It was held that the principal's claim to set-off succeeded under the Australian statutory insolvency set-off provision.[24] The court held that the date at which the availability of the set-off is determined is the date of the commencement of the insolvency. It was sufficient, however, that the obligation sought to be set off was contingent as at that date, provided that it had become an actual liability when the set-off account came to be taken (*i.e.* after lodgment of proofs but before payment of dividends): it was not

---

[22] See the IA 1986, s.382(2) and the IR 1986, r.30.12. See further *Re Daintry* [1900] 1 Q.B. 546; *Re Charge Card Services Ltd* [1987] Ch. 150.

[23] Wood, *English and International Set-Off (op. cit.)*, p.760. See *Re West End Networks (In liq.)* [2004] 2 All E.R. 1042 at para.12.

[24] Section 86(1) of the Australian Bankruptcy Act 1966, similar to the Bankruptcy Act 1914, s.31, and now the IA 1986, s.323 and the IR 1986, r.4.90. See *Stein v Blake* [1995] 2 All E.R. 961, where Lord Hoffmann (at 969A) disapproved a dictum of Mason J. that was "due" meant due at the point the set-off account was taken. Lord Hoffmann expressly said that the point was not necessary for the decision in *Day & Dent Construction Ltd v Northern Australian Pty Ltd*, and that case is therefore still good law in its result.

necessary for the debt to have accrued due at the date of the commencement of the liquidation.[25]

In *Re West End Networks (In liq.)* [2004] 2 All E.R. 1042, the House of Lords has now followed the approach of the High Court of Australia in *Day & Dent Constructions* in its disapproval of the decision of the Court of Appeal in *Re a Debtor (No.66 of 1955)* [1956] 2 All E.R. 94. In the latter case, Lord Evershed M.R. and Hodson L.J. appear to have decided that, as a broad rule, a surety under a pre-insolvency guarantee is not entitled to set-off unless he had actually paid the debt before the insolvency date. In *Re West End Networks (In liq.)*, Lord Hoffmann considered that in *Re A Debtor* the narrower reason for denying the set-off, namely the absence of mutuality, was "convincing" (this was the reason relied by the Divisional Court in bankruptcy), but he thought that the broader ground enunciated by the Court of Appeal in that case was "wrong". *Re a Debtor* has therefore now been overruled to the extent that it is authority for a broad rule against permitting a surety to set off where he has not paid the debt before the insolvency date

Where the surety pays the creditor the whole of the guaranteed indebtedness after the date on which the latter is paid a dividend, the surety cannot himself prove. However, the creditor must hold the dividend on trust for the surety, since the surety has a right of subrogation against the creditor in respect of such dividends.[26] Where the surety guarantees part of the debt,[27] and pays that part in full after the creditor has received dividend, then similarly the surety has a right to share pro rata in the dividends received by the creditor, and the portion of such dividends is impressed with a trust in favour of the surety.[28]

Payment in full by the surety

As has been seen, the surety who guarantees the whole debt may only prove in the insolvency of the principal once the creditor has been paid in full.[29] However, it remains open to debate whether the creditor must have been paid in full by the surety, or whether in certain circumstances the surety can

13–004

---

[25] See also *Hiley v Peoples Prudential Assurance Co Ltd* (1938) 16 C.L.R. 468; *Sovereign Life Assurance Co v Dodd* [1892] 1 Q.B. 405; 2 Q.B. 573, CA: *Re Charge Card Services Ltd* [1987] Ch. 150. The court in *Day & Dent* refused to follow dicta to the contrary in *Re a Debtor (No.66 of 1955)* [1956] 2 All E.R. 94, which suggests that contingencies must have accrued due before the insolvency date to qualify for set-off *See MS Fashions Ltd v Bank of Credit and Commerce International SA* [1993] Ch. 425 for a review of these authorities, and now see *Re West End Networks (In liq.)* [2004] 2 All E.R. 1042, HL in which *Re a Debtor (No.66 of 1955)* has been overruled.

[26] *Re Sass* [1896] 2 Q.B. 12 at 15. In *Re Butlers Wharf Ltd* [1995] 2 B.C.L.C. 43, Richard Sykes Q.C. rejected the existence of any distinction between dividends in the principal's insolvency and the proceeds of realisation of security: both are eligible to be shared rateably between the surety and the creditor: see *Goodwin v Gray* (1874) 22 W.R. 312. The decision of Richard Sykes Q.C. in *Re Butlers' Wharf* has now been approved by the Court of Appeal in *Liberty Mutual Insurance Co (UK) Ltd v HSBC Bank Plc* [2002] EWCA Civ 691.

[27] As to which generally see paras 13–008–13–009.

[28] *Gray v Seckham* (1872) L.R. 7 Ch. App. 680.

[29] *Ex p. Turquand; Re Fothergill* (1876) 3 Ch. D. 445.

prove in respect of a part-payment when the creditor has received the balance of the indebtedness from another source (see the discussion below at paras 13–005–13–008). Obviously, the surety must have discharged a liability of the principal to the creditor before he is entitled to prove in the former's insolvency. Unless he has done so, he has no right to prove at all, and so the rule against double proof does not arise.

Payment of the creditor in full by the surety may occur in a number of different practical ways, such as by actual payment, set-off, realisation of a security given by the surety for the guaranteed obligation, execution by the creditor or the payment of a dividend in the surety's own insolvency. Once the creditor has recovered in full from the surety, he will lose his right to prove against the principal since he cannot claim more than 100 pence in the pound, and there is no longer any possibility of a double proof.

However, the question of whether a payment by a surety constitutes payment in full so as to entitle him to prove in the principal's insolvency depends upon the nature of the surety's liability under the guarantee. There are distinctions between cases where a surety pays part of the amount guaranteed, cases where he pays in full the guaranteed part of the whole debt, and cases where he pays his maximum limit, but not the whole amount. It is of particular importance to distinguish, as a matter of construction, between guarantees of part of the principal debt and guarantees for the whole of the principal debt limited to a maximum amount.[30]

Payment by the surety of part of his liability under the guarantee

13–005   Where the surety is liable for £100 under the guarantee and pays the creditor £75 only in part discharge of his indebtedness, the question arises to what extent the surety is entitled to prove for an indemnity in relation to the part paid, and whether the creditor is obliged to give credit, in proving against the principal, for the £75 received from the surety, thus removing any double proof in relation to that part. The answer depends upon whether the surety's obligations arise under an ordinary guarantee or under a negotiable instrument.

(1) Part payment under an ordinary guarantee

13–006   Where the principal is insolvent and the surety makes a part payment to the creditor before the creditor has been paid a dividend, the rule is that the surety has no right to prove, and the creditor does not have to give credit by reducing his proof by the amount received from the surety, so long as the creditor does not receive more than 100 pence in the pound.[31] The creditor

---

[30] See *Ellis v Emmanuel* (1876) 1 Ex. D. 157; *Re Sass* [1896] 2 Q.B. 12; *Barclays Bank Ltd v TOSG Fund Ltd* [1984] 1 All E.R. 628, at 641H, *per* Oliver L.J; *Re Butlers Wharf Ltd* [1995] 2 B.C.L.C. 43, Richard Sykes Q.C; *Liberty Mutual Insurance Co (UK) Ltd v HSBC Bank Plc* [2002] EWCA Civ 691. See generally Ch.4, para.4–019 and Ch.6, para.6–006.

[31] *Ellis v Emmanuel* (1876) 1 Ex. D. 157; *Re Sass* [1896] 2 Q.B. 12; *Ulster Bank Ltd v Lambe* [1966] N.I. 161. The opposite was suggested in Rowlatt, *Principal and Surety* (4th ed., 1982), 199, but the authorities cited there were of dubious support for this proposition and have been removed from the 5th ed. (1999): see, *e.g. Ex p. Gilbey* (1878) 8 Ch. D. 248, a case involving a composition between the principal and the creditors.

can prove for the full amount and the surety is barred from proving at all. It makes no difference that the payment was before or after the commencement of the insolvency.[32] The basis for the rule is that the surety has undertaken to be responsible for the full sum guaranteed, including whatever may remain due to the creditor after receipt of dividends in the principal's insolvency, and cannot prove (or more correctly, receive a dividend) in competition with the creditor for a right of indemnity.[33] Since the creditor is himself entitled to prove for the whole amount without giving credit for sums received from the surety, the rule against double proof will, upon the creditor proving for the whole amount of the debt, preclude the surety from proving (or claiming a set-off against the principal's estate) in relation to the part paid.[34]

The effect of the operation of this principle is that where the surety pays only a part of his total indebtedness under the guarantee, he will never be able to claim for an indemnity in relation to that part (unless the creditor is satisfied in full by a payment of the balance from another source, as to which see below): the principal becomes discharged on the completion of the insolvency, and the surety's claim does not survive it.[35]

Where the surety pays part only, and the balance is paid by the principal so that the creditor is paid in full, it appears that the surety is still precluded from proving for the part he has paid where he relies on a right of subrogation in support of his claim for an indemnity. In *Re Fenton* [1931] 1 Ch. 85, Lawrence L.J. said (at 115):

> "Even where the principal creditor has been paid in full partly by a dividend from the estate of the insolvent surety and partly by a dividend from the estate of the insolvent principal debtor, the trustee of the insolvent surety will not be allowed to prove against the estate of the principal debtor for the amount which the estate of the surety had contributed towards payment of the debt, as it is only when the surety has paid the full amount of the debt that he will be subrogated to the rights of the principal creditor: see *In Re Oriental Commercial Bank* (1871) L.R. 7 Ch. 99, 102".

Where the surety must rely on a right of subrogation to the creditor's rights in order to enforce his claim for an indemnity against the principal, then

---

[32] *Re Sass* [1896] 2 Q.B. 12. But see the analysis of the comparison between payments made by the surety pre-insolvency with those made post-insolvency by Fisher J. in *Stotter v Equiticorp Australia Ltd* [2002] 2 N.Z.L.R. 686 at paras 66 and 67. Fisher J. concluded that there was a difference, in that amounts received by the creditor from the surety before the liquidation are to be deducted from the creditor's proof, and that a "whole of money" (all moneys) clause is ineffective to avoid that result; he also concluded that this is not inconsistent with *Re Sass*, a case in which the surety had paid the creditor after the commencement of the insolvency.

[33] See R. M. Goode, *Legal Problems of Credit and Security (op. cit.)*, para.8.18.

[34] See *Re Fenton (No.2)* [1932] 1 Ch. 178.

[35] *Re Fenton* [1931] 1 Ch. 85, at 120 *per* Romer L.J.

this passage is clear authority that he has no right of proof unless he has acquired that right of subrogation, *i.e.* where he has paid in full.[36]

However, the surety's right to an indemnity from the principal often arises independently of, and prior to, the acquisition by him of the right of subrogation (which only arises on full payment). In many cases the right to an indemnity *pro tanto* will arise expressly or by implication on payment of any part of the debt to the creditor.[37] Accordingly, it is submitted that where the surety does not need to rely on a right of subrogation in order to enforce his claim for an indemnity because he has an express or implied right to an indemnity, and he has made a part-payment, and the creditor has been paid the balance of the indebtedness by the principal or by a co-surety, then the surety may prove in the principal's insolvency for the amount which he has paid to the creditor. The same consequence should follow if the creditor has been paid in full by a co-surety and the surety has made a payment to the co-surety in contribution. In either case there is no possibility of a double proof, because the creditor has been satisfied in full and would recover in excess of 100 pence in the pound. If the surety could not prove in these circumstances, the creditor would be proving in the insolvency of the principal solely for the benefit of the surety, and would be obliged to hold any dividend which he recovered on trust for him.

(2) Part payment under a negotiable instrument

13–007   A drawer and an indorser of a negotiable instrument are liable to the holder as if they were sureties of the acceptor who does not pay it on presentation.[38] Where the holder has been paid part of the debt the subject of the negotiable instrument by the drawer or indorser before he has received a dividend in the acceptor's insolvency, he is only entitled to prove for the balance which he has not received,[39] and the drawer and indorser are entitled to prove for the amount they have paid. It is also possible that the creditor should give credit for any dividend received (or declared) in the drawer's or indorser's insolvency.[40]

Where the holder of a negotiable instrument receives a part-payment from the indorser or drawer after he has lodged a proof in the acceptor's

---

[36] It is not easy to reconcile this dictum with the line of (mainly Australian) cases to the effect that a surety *will* acquire (*pro tanto*) rights of subrogation where the creditor is satisfied in full, partly by the surety and partly from other sources (*e.g.* co-sureties); *Gedye v Matson* (1858) 25 Beav. 310; *AE Goodwin Ltd (In liq.) v AG Healing Ltd (In liq.)* (1979) 7 A.C.L.R. 481; *McColl's Wholesale Pty Ltd v State Bank (NSW)* [1984] 3 N.S.W.L.R. 365; *Raffle v AG Advances Ltd* [1989] A.S.C. 58, 528; *Bayley v Gibsons Ltd* (1993) 1 Tas. R. 385; see further Ch.11, para.11–018.

[37] *Davies v Humphreys* (1840) 6 M. & W. 153, at 157 *per* Parke B.; see Ch.10, para.10–017.

[38] Bills of Exchange Act 1882, ss.55, 56 and 82, and see *Duncan Fox & Co v North and South Wales Bank* (1880) 6 App. Cas. 1; *Re Conley* [1938] 2 All E.R. 127, *per* Lord Greene M.R. at 133.

[39] *Cooper v Pepys* (1781) 1 Atk. 107; *Re Houghton, Ex p. Taylor* (1857) 26 L.J. Bank. 58; this rule is confined to negotiable instruments: *Re Blackburne* (1892) 9 Mor. 249; *Re Houlder* [1929] 1 Ch. 205.

[40] Certainly, where the holder receives a part-payment by the acceptor, he must give credit for it in proving against the drawer or acceptor: see *Re Stein* (1815) 19 Ves. 310; see Wood, *English and International Set-Off* (*op. cit.*), para.10.120.

insolvency,[41] he is entitled to maintain his proof for the entire debt under the instrument and need not give credit for the sums received. In such circumstances the drawer or indorser is not entitled to prove for the amount paid.[42]

Payment of the whole of the guaranteed part of the debt

Where the surety has guaranteed part of a debt, and pays the creditor the amount guaranteed by him in full prior to the creditor receiving a dividend in the principal's insolvency, he is entitled himself to prove in the principal's insolvency for the amount paid by him. In *Re Sass* [1896] 2 Q.B. 12, Vaughan Williams J. said (*obiter*, at 15): **13–008**

> ". . . it is quite true that where the surety is a surety for a part of the debt as between the principal creditor and the debtor, the right of the surety arises merely by payment of a part because that part, as between him and the principal creditor, is the whole".[43]

The rationale for permitting the surety to prove is that the part of the debt guaranteed by the surety is treated, for the purposes of proof, as a separate debt from the part not guaranteed. When the surety pays that part in full, he has fully performed his obligations to the creditor, and becomes subrogated to the creditors' right to prove for that part.[44] Where the surety pays this amount after the creditor receives the dividend, then it would seem that the creditor stands in the position of a trustee for the surety in respect of the dividend received in the insolvency which would be payable to the surety where he able to prove.[45]

Payment by the surety of the limited maximum under the guarantee

Where the surety guarantees the whole of the principal debt (as opposed to part) but his liability is limited to a maximum amount, and he pays that maximum amount, then the creditor is entitled to prove for the full amount of the debt in the principal's insolvency without giving a credit for the amount received from the surety, and the surety may not prove in the insolvency for the amount he has paid. It is immaterial that the amount is received before or after the creditor has lodged his proof or received a **13–009**

---

[41] The authorities cited below do suggest that this is the crucial date, but the argument advanced at para.13–003 above applies equally to negotiable instrument cases.

[42] *Re London, Bombay & Mediterranean Bank Ex p. Cama* (1874) L.R. 9 Ch. 686; *Re Fothergill Ex p. Turquand* (1876) 3 Ch. D. 445.

[43] See also *Ex p. Rushforth* (1805) 10 Ves. 409; *Paley v Field* (1806) 12 Ves. 435; *Bardwell v Lydall* (1831) 7 Bing. 489; *Hobson v Bass* (1871) 6 Ch. App. 792; *Gray v Seckham* (1872) L.R. 7 Ch. App. 680; *Barclays Bank Ltd v TOSG Fund Ltd* [1984] 1 All E.R. 628, *per* Oliver L.J. at 641 G–J; *Re Butlers Wharf Ltd* [1995] 2 B.C.L.C. 43, Richard Sykes Q.C.; *Liberty Mutual Insurance Co (UK) Ltd v HSBC Bank Plc* [2002] EWCA Civ 691; contrast *Ellis v Emmanuel* (1876) 1 Ex. D. 157. Contrast also *Stotter v Equiticorp Australia Ltd* [2002] 2 N.Z.L.R. 686 in respect of payments made pre-insolvency.

[44] *Westpac Banking Co v Gollin & Co Ltd* [1988] V.R. 397 at 405.

[45] See para.13–014.

dividend, since the payment is not payment of the whole indebtedness under the guarantee.[46]

In *Re Sass* [1896] 2 Q.B. 12, the surety had guaranteed to the creditor bank the payment of all sums which were then or which might thereafter from time to time become due or owing to the bank from the customer, the principal. The total amount of the surety's liability was not to exceed £300. The guarantee was expressed to be a continuing security for the whole amount due and owing to the creditor bank, in addition to and without prejudice to any other securities which the bank might hold to the account of the principal, and it further provided that any dividends received in the principal's insolvency where not to prejudice the bank's right to recover in full the balance from the surety. The principal became insolvent and the surety, prior to the lodgment of a proof by the bank, paid the £300. The bank nonetheless proved for the full amount of the principal's indebtedness without giving any credit for the sums received: this was challenged by the principal's trustee. Vaughan-Williams J. held that the bank were entitled to prove for the whole amount without deduction.[47]

In *Barclays Bank Ltd v TOSG Fund Ltd* [1984] 1 All E.R. 628, Oliver L.J. suggested (at 644) that a provision that a guarantee is to be in addition to and without prejudice to any other securities held from or on account of the principal and that it is to be a continuing security notwithstanding settlement, is probably sufficient to exclude the surety's right (where it arises) to prove in priority to the creditor in the principal's insolvency. In doing so, Oliver L.J. expressly relied on *Re Sass*. However, in *Re Butlers Wharf Ltd* [1995] 2 B.C.L.C. 43, Richard Sykes Q.C. considered *Re Sass* and the terms of the guarantee in question in that case. He held that Vaughan Williams J., in concluding that the guarantee was in respect of the whole debt, had not relied upon the words of the guarantee which expressed it to be additional to and without prejudice to any other securities held by the creditor from the principal, rather than the general words expressing the guarantee to be for the whole debt, and the provision that receipt of dividends in the principal's insolvency was not to prejudice the creditor's rights to recover in full from the surety. In *Re Butlers Wharf Ltd*, Richard Sykes Q.C. held that the existence of a provision that the guarantee was

---

[46] *Re Sass* [1896] 2 Q.B. 12; *Re Rees* (1881) 17 Ch. D. 98; *Re Fernandes Ex p. Hope* (1843) 3 Mont. D. & D. 720; *Earle v Oliver* (1848) 2 Ex. Ch. 71; *Midland Banking Co v Chambers* (1869) 4 Ch. App. 398; *Seabird Corpn Ltd (In liq.) v Sherlock* (1990) 2 A.C.S.R. 111 at 115–116.

[47] This case appears not to have been cited to the Court of Appeal in *M S Fashions Ltd v Bank of Credit and Commerce International SA* [1993] Ch. 425. This may explain Dillon L.J.'s remark (at 448D) that "A creditor cannot sue the principal debtor for an amount of the debt which the creditor has already received from a guarantor". This remark, it is respectfully submitted, should be treated with some caution. See also *Ulster Bank v Lambe* [1966] N.I. 161; *Re Hawkins* (unreported) February 2, 1978, Walton J. However, Fisher J.'s reasoning in *Stotter v Equiticorp Australia Ltd* [2002] 2 N.Z.L.R. 686 relies on Dillon L.J.'s remark in support of his conclusion that, so far as pre-insolvency receipts from the surety are concerned, the creditor must deduct them from his proof. That *Re Sass* was not cited to the Court of Appeal in *MS Fashions* is a good reason to treat *Stott* with some degree of caution, while retaining admiration for the closeness and thoroughness of the analysis.

additional to other security held from the principal, was ineffective to preclude the sureties from being entitled to exercise rights of subrogation and participate in the security rateably with the creditors.[48] In reaching his conclusion, he said that it was not necessary to attribute the weight he would otherwise have done to the dictum of Oliver L.J. in *Barclays Bank Ltd v TOSG Fund*.[49]

If the surety pays the limited amount before the principal becomes insolvent, and is then released from further liability by the creditor, there is a view that the creditor will then be restricted to proving only for the balance outstanding from the principal, and the surety will be free to prove for the amount he has paid.[50] This is, it appears, because the effect of the release is that the surety is no longer liable for the full amount of the debt, and he is treated as having paid the whole of a part of the debt. However, this view has been disapproved in Australia[51] In the earlier editions of this work, it was submitted that the better view is that the creditor will not be restricted in the amount of his proof where the guarantee is for the whole debt, even if the surety has paid the amount of his limit before the principal's insolvency. That view must be revisited in the light of the penetrating analysis of the cases by Fisher J. in the High Court of New Zealand in *Stotter v Equiticorp Australia Ltd* [2002] 2 N.Z.L.R. 686. In that case, Fisher J. concluded that a creditor was bound to give credit, in proving in the principal's insolvency, for amounts received from the surety prior to the insolvency date. That view is not inconsistent with *Re Sass*, a case about post-insolvency receipts, is consistent with earlier authority[52], and has the merit of apparent fairness. There are, however, competing policy considerations which offer reasons to be cautious about accepting Fisher J.'s view too warmly[53]. Furthermore, it is hard to see why there should be such a fundamental distinction between payments made by the surety prior to the insolvency and those made after insolvency has supervened. There is also a powerful case for saying that if the guarantee is for the whole of the debt, then the creditor is entitled to treat the surety as

---

[48] By parity of reasoning, the surety would also not be precluded by such a provision from sharing rateably in the dividends in the principal's insolvency: Richard Sykes Q.C. expressly rejected any distinction between sharing in securities and sharing in distribution of the principal's insolvent estate.

[49] See the valuable critique of this case at (2000) 116 L.Q.R. 121, Ward and McCormack.

[50] *Mackinnon's Trustee v Bank of Scotland* [1915] S.C. 411.

[51] In *Westpac Banking Corpn v Gollin & Co Ltd* [1988] V.R. 397, where Tadgell J. (at 406-407) followed Lowry J. in *Ulster Bank v Lambe* [1966] N.I. 161, in which Lowry J. disapproved *McKinnon's Trustee v Bank of Scotland* [1915] S.C. 411. In *Stotter v Equiticorp Australia Ltd* [2002] 2 N.Z.L.R. 686, Fisher J. either distinguished or refused to follow *Westpac* and *Ulster Bank*. There is now therefore, on the current state of the law, a tension between the Australian and the New Zealand authorities on this subject.

[52] *Re Blakeley* (1892) 9 Morr 173; *Re Amalgamated Investment & Property Co* [1985] 1 Ch. 349.

[53] As expressed by Prof R. M. Goode in *Legal Problems of Credit and Security* (3rd ed., 2003) at para.8.18 (although without any commentary by him on the *Stotter* case, which was reported the previous year). Fisher J. did avert to these policy considerations at paras 55 to 57 of his judgment, and proceeded to recognise these "at a theoretical level" but said that they were not of any consequence in practice.

having not performed his obligation until he has seen to it that the entire debt has been paid.[54]

Suspense accounts and non-competition clauses

Suspense account clauses

13–010 Some guarantees may contain a suspense account clause[55] which entitles the creditor to keep separate any payment made by the surety until the creditor has received all that is due to him from the principal. The effect of these clauses is that the creditor is not obliged to give credit, in proving in the principal's insolvency, for any amounts received from the surety unless the creditor appropriated these payments to the principal debt: equally, the creditor who holds security from the surety for the full amount does not have to give credit for it when proving against the principal's insolvent estate.[56] Since the payment by the surety is not (as yet) in discharge of the guaranteed indebtedness, and there is no obligation to use such sums for that purpose, the surety has no right of indemnity in any event, and so no question of double proof even arises, the surety not having a provable claim.

Non-competition clauses

13–011 The other main clause in a guarantee precluding the rule from arising is one in which the creditor provides that the surety should not prove in competition with him. Again, the rule against double proof will not arise because the surety is contractually prevented from proving for the same debt which is the subject of the creditor's proof. However, many standard form guarantees go further than this and preclude the surety from proving for a debt which is independent of the surety's claim for an indemnity (to which the rule against double proof does not apply in any event). This has been forcefully criticised as folly,[57] since it benefits not only the creditor himself but all the other unsecured creditors: and it is said that what the creditor should do is provide that the surety must prove for the independent liability in the principal's insolvency, and hold any dividend he receives on trust for the creditor (with a power of attorney to the creditor to lodge a proof in the surety's name), up to the amount necessary to discharge the amount due under the guarantee.[58] This carries with it a protection for the

---

[54] See O'Donovan & Phillips (English ed., 2003), paras 10-40 to 10-42, citing *Barclays Bank Ltd v TOSG Fund Ltd* [1984] 1 All E.R. 628, at 641, per Oliver L.J. Again, the editors offered no comment on *Stotter*.

[55] For a precedent of which see Precedent 1, clause 8.3.

[56] *Commercial Bank of Australia Ltd v Wilson* [1893] A.C. 181.

[57] See R. M. Goode, *Legal Problems of Credit and Security* (*op. cit.*), para.8.24, a view which Prof. Goode described as having come to him one night in the bath.

[58] This suggestion has been reflected in the precedent for a standard form bank guarantee, Precedent 1, clause 6.4. The precedent is slightly different from that suggested by Prof. Goode in that it gives the creditor a *power* to compel the surety to prove for non-competing claims rather than *obliging* the surety to do so, thus enabling the creditor to retain a discretion as to what are and what are not non-competing claims.

creditor in the event of the surety's own insolvency, since the creditor would hold a security interest in the dividend receivable by the surety's estate. Further, it seems that such a trust would not be registrable as a charge on book debts.

Release of the principal by the creditor

Where the creditor releases the principal while reserving his rights against the surety, or renounces his rights of proof against the principal's insolvent estate, the rule against double proof will not arise, since the creditor is no longer proving. The effect of the reservation of rights against the surety, or a clause in the guarantee preserving such rights notwithstanding the release of the principal, is that the surety retains his rights of indemnity over against the principal, and may prove in respect of an indemnity claim.[59] In *Re Fenton* [1931] 1 Ch. 85, Romer L.J. said (at 118):

13–012

> "But I cannot agree that a surety who had not paid off the principal creditor can prove in the bankruptcy of the principal debtor so as to share in the distribution of his assets unless the principal creditor has renounced in some way his right to lodge a proof himself while preserving, of course, his rights against the surety."

The insolvency of the surety

The creditor's right of proof

The creditor has a right of proof in the insolvency of the surety, even though the surety's liability remains contingent and there is no debt accrued due.[60] The creditor can maintain this proof at the same time as a proof for the full amount from the principal and any co-sureties, provided that they are each liable for the whole debt and the creditor does not receive more than 100 pence in the pound.[61] However, he is required to give credit in his proof against the insolvent surety's estate for any amounts received from the principal, by way of payment, realisation of securities or of dividend, prior to the date on which the creditor *lodges his proof* in the surety's insolvency.[62]

13–013

Where the surety has guaranteed only part of the debt, the question of whether a payment by the principal is to be attributed to the guaranteed part of the debt or the unguaranteed balanced is a matter of appropriation by the creditor: the surety's office-holder has no right to compel the

---

[59] See *Perry v National Provincial Bank* [1910] 1 Ch. 464, and Ch.9, paras 9–010–9–016 and 9–033–9–034.
[60] See IA 1986, s.322. See also *Re Fitzgeorge* [1905] 1 K.B. 462; in practice it may be difficult to value the contingent debt.
[61] *Ex p. Rushforth* (1805) 10 Ves. 409; *Re Houlder* [1929] 1 Ch. 205.
[62] *Re Blakeley* (1892) 2 Morr. 173; *Re Houlder* [1929] 1 Ch. 205; *Re Amalgamated Investment & Property Co Ltd* [1985] 1 Ch. 349; *cf. Westpac Banking Corpn v Gollin & Co Ltd* [1988] V.R. 397.

creditor to appropriate the creditor to apply the payment in reduction of the indebtedness the subject of the guarantee.[63]

However, where the creditor receives a payment or security from sources not primarily liable for the guaranteed debt, such as co-sureties, he is not bound to apply the payment, or to realise the security and apply the proceeds, in reduction of his proof in the surety's insolvency. In *Re Houlder* [1929] 1 Ch. 205, the principals took a loan from the creditor of which £8,000 was outstanding, and it was guaranteed by three sureties. One of the sureties became insolvent. The creditor, prior to its lodging a proof in that surety's insolvency, received £5,372 from the co-sureties. It then proved for the full amount without giving credit for the £5,000 received from the co-sureties. Astbury J. held that the creditor was entitled to prove for the full amount without deduction.[64] Similarly, the creditor may still prove even though he has given up his rights against a co-surety, provided that he does not receive more than the surety's net share, allowing for the contribution he would have received from the co-surety.[65]

Negotiable instruments

13–014 In *Re Houlder*, Astbury J. distinguished the position where negotiable instruments were concerned.[66] There, the holder who proves against an insolvent indorser (or drawer), who occupies the position of a surety,[67] must deduct amounts received from other indorsers (in the position of co-sureties) prior to the lodging of a proof by the holder. Accordingly, the holder must apply such receipts in reduction of the indebtedness the subject of the negotiable instrument, and cannot keep it in suspense so as to maximise his claim on the insolvent indorser's estate.

Where, however, the holder receives payment from the *acceptor* prior to his lodging a proof in the indorser's or drawer's insolvency, then the rule is the same as with ordinary guarantees: the holder must give credit for such receipts.[68]

The insolvency of both principal and surety

The general rule

13–015 Where both the principal and the surety are insolvent, the creditor is entitled to prove in both insolvencies for the full amount of the debt, and he is not obliged to reduce his proof in one insolvency for dividends

---

[63] *Re Sherry* (1884) 25 Ch. D. 692; this will be so unless the presumption in *Clayton's* case (1816) 1 Mer. 572 applies in favour of the surety.

[64] See also *Commercial Bank of Australia Ltd v Wilson* [1893] A.C. 181, a case involving a suspense clause; further, the discussion of these cases in O'Donovan & Phillips, *The Modern Contract of Guarantee (op. cit.)*, 472–5; English ed. (2003), paras 10-40 to 10-60.

[65] *Ex p. Gifford* (1802) 6 Ves. 805.

[66] At 210, referring to *Re Blackburne* (1892) 9 Morr. 249.

[67] See *Duncan Fox & Co v North and South Wales Bank* (1880) 6 App. Cas. 1; *Re Conley* [1938] 2 All E.R. 127.

[68] *Ex p. Leers* (1802) 6 Ves. 644; *Re Stein* (1815) 19 Ves. 310.

declared or received in the other, provided that he does not receive more than 100 pence in the pound overall.[69]

Negotiable instruments

Where the insolvent principal and the insolvent surety are liable as such **13–016** because they are, respectively, the acceptor and the indorser or drawer of a negotiable instrument held by the holder as creditor, the holder must, when proving in the insolvency of the principal, give credit for any dividends declared or paid in the insolvency of the surety prior to the time at which he lodged his proof in the principal's insolvency. The same applies vice versa to dividends received in the insolvency of the principal.[70] The holder need not give credit when proving in one insolvency nor give credit for any sums received (or dividends declared) in the other insolvency after the date at which he lodged his proof in the former.[71]

The rule in *Ex p. Waring*[72]

This rule states that where a drawer of a negotiable instrument deposits **13–017** money with the acceptor to meet his liability to the holder thereunder, the holder is entitled, upon the insolvency of both the acceptor and the drawer, to have the amount of the deposit paid to him in full, it not being available for distribution among the general body of the acceptor's creditors. This is because the deposit was made for a specific purpose, namely payment to the holder, and is accordingly impressed with a trust for that purpose: the court applies the property in such a way as will carry out the equities between the two insolvent estates.[73]

The creditor is entitled to prove in the surety's insolvency for the balance of the guaranteed debt not satisfied by the receipt by him of the deposited amount, and in lodging his proof, the creditor must give credit for the amount received, and must refund any dividends received over and above the amount of the reduced proof.[74]

Although the rule in *Ex p. Waring* derives from negotiable instrument cases, the principle of an enforceable purpose trust is one of the general application,[75] and there is no reason why it should not apply to ordinary guarantees.

The insolvency of the creditor: set-off

The insolvency of the creditor does not commonly give rise to any **13–018** particular questions peculiar to the law of guarantees, and most problems which arise can usually be resolved by reference to the general law of

---

[69] *Ex p. Rushforth* (1805) 10 Ves. 409, at 417; *Cooper v Pepys* (1741) 1 Atk. 107; *Ex p. Wildman* (1750) 1 Atk. 109; *Ex p. Turquand* (1876) 3 Ch. D. 445, 450, *Re Blakeley* (1892) 9 Morr. 173.
[70] *Cooper v Pepys* (1741) 1 Atk. 107; *Re Stein* (1815) 19 Ves. 310.
[71] *Re Fothergill* (1876) 3 Ch. D. 445; *Re London, Bombay & Mediterranean Bank* (1874) L.R. 9 Ch. App. 686.
[72] (1815) 19 Ves. 345.
[73] See *Ex p. Dever (No.2)* (1885) 14 Q.B.D. 611, the analysis of the basis of the rule, especially at 623 *per* Brett M.R.
[74] *Re Barned's Banking Co* (1875) L.R. 10 Ch. App. 198.
[75] See Ch.12, para.12–005.

insolvency and equitable principles. However, there are important questions that arise in relation to rights of set-off in the creditor's insolvency with respect to the insolvent creditor's claim under the guarantee.

Plainly, where the creditor's claim against the surety has accrued due as at the date of the commencement of the insolvency, there is no difficulty in applying the statutory insolvency set-off provisions so that a surety may be entitled to require his claim against the insolvent creditor's estate to be set off against the estate's claim against him under the guarantee, with only the balance payable.[76] However, the creditor's claim against the surety may be contingent as at the date the creditor becomes insolvent, for example because no demand may have been made against him at that time. In such circumstances the question arises whether the benefit of the statutory insolvency set-off provisions are available in relation to this contingent claim. The answer is that where the insolvent is a *creditor* in respect of a contingent claim as opposed to a *debtor*, and owes a cross-debt eligible for statutory insolvency set-off, there is no method for valuing the contingency as there is with contingent debts owed by the insolvent.[77] Accordingly, there should be no set-off, since otherwise, if the set-off were allowed and the account were duly taken, the guarantee would then in effect be paid before the surety was obliged to pay, even though the risk of default by the principal was small. The value of the set-off would then bear no relation to the value of the surety's real liability.

However, where the contingency accrues due after the date of the commencement of the insolvency, but prior to some point during the insolvency, it is capable of set-off provided the transaction which created it existed at the former date.[78] In *Re Daintrey* [1900] 1 Q.B. 546, the leading case on this point, it seems to be suggested that it is sufficient that the claim should have accrued due by the time the account comes to be taken,[79] and it is submitted that this makes perfect sense.[80] Accordingly, provided the obligations giving rise to the surety's contingent liability are present at the commencement of the insolvency of the creditor, they will be available for set-off in the creditor's insolvency at the moment they accrue due, provided they do so in the course of the insolvency. It is up to the liquidator or trustee as to when he takes the set-off account, and if no claim has yet

---

[76] Under IA 1986, s.323 (individuals) and IR 1986 r.4.90 (companies).

[77] See *Stein v Blake* [1996] A.C. 243, at 253.

[78] *Re Daintrey* [1900] 1 Q.B. 546; *Re Charge Card Services Ltd* [1986] 3 All E.R. 289.

[79] See at 555 *per* Wright J. although what Romer L.J. says at 574, namely that "it is sufficient if the account can be taken when the set-off arises", is somewhat obscure. The dicta in *Re a Debtor (No.66) of 1955* [1956] 2 All E.R. 94 to the effect that the contingency must have accrued due at the commencement of the insolvency to be available for set-off are incorrect and have been expressly disapproved by the House of Lords in *Re West End Networks (In liq.)* [2004] 2 All E.R. 1042, following *Day & Dent Construction Ltd v Northern Australian Pty Ltd* (1982) 56 A.J.L.R. 347.

[80] The anomaly created by the decision in *MS Fashions* was graphically illustrated by the Privy Council in *Tam Wing Chuen v Bank of Credit and Commerce Hong Kong Ltd* [1996] B.C.C. 388, where the surety struggled in vain to show that he was personally liable to the bank in order to take the benefit of the statutory insolvency set-off.

accrued to the insolvent estate, he will not (and cannot) take it. Of course, the set-off will immediately become available if the liquidator or trustee claims under the guarantee, since he will be estopped from denying that the surety's liability remains contingent, even though on its terms the surety may not yet be liable.

Personal covenant for repayment

The question whether or not a surety is entitled to compel his insolvent **13–019** creditor to set off his liability against the claim which the insolvent estate may have against the principal (or against security provided by the principal) is difficult. The answer depends on whether the surety has given the creditor a personal covenant to repay the debt or perform the obligation guaranteed. In *MS Fashions v Bank of Credit and Commerce International SA* [1993] Ch. 425, the Court of Appeal permitted set off in those circumstances. The core of the reasoning was that since, on the particular provisions of the security documentation, the sureties' liability was expressed to be that of principal, the guarantees were construed, in order to give effect to those provisions, as creating a personal liability on the part of the sureties in favour of the creditor as principal obligors for the guaranteed liability. That personal liability was held to be subject to the right in the surety to set off the creditor's obligation to repay a deposit provided by the surety as security for the principal obligation, with the result that the surety could avail himself of rule 4.90 of the Insolvency Rules 1986 in compelling the creditor to set off its claim against the principal against the principal's claim to recover or redeem the deposit, thus discharging the principal from liability.

This decision was analysed and distinguished as "anomalous" in what is now the leading case on insolvency set-off, the decision of the House of Lords in *BCCI (No.8)* [1998] A.C. 214.[81] Delivering the leading opinion, Lord Hoffmann said that the distinction between situations where the surety had given a personal covenant for repayment, and those where he had not, but had merely charged his property to the creditor as security for the principal's obligations, was an artificial one, since the creditor would in no case wish to rely on the personal liability of the chargor (whether *qua* principal or *qua* surety). He described the decision in *MS Fashions* as a trap for the unwary in the context of a bank *"thinking of becoming insolvent"*. He noted the difficulty of reconciling the nature of statutory insolvency set-off as automatic and self-executing with the principle that joint and several debtors are liable for the same debt, so that payment or deemed payment (in the case of set-off) by the one discharges the other. Lord Hoffmann identified two arguments in favour of why there should be no set-off in the case of a charged deposit. The first (rejected in *MS Fashions* at first instance "somewhat cursorily" by him) is that the existence of the charge in

---

[81] For a full critique of the debate, see the casenote on *BCCI (No.8)*, *sub nom. Morris v Agrichemicals Ltd* [1996] Ch. 245, "Pleasing Paradoxes" [1997] L.Q.R.

favour of the creditor destroys the mutuality of dealings required for the operation of the statutory set-off, since the creditor's claim is in its own right, but the depositor's claim is subject to the equitable security interest of the creditor. The second argument, suggested by the Court of Appeal in *BCCI (No.8)* itself, is that set-off works in the order in which things naturally occur, so that the recovery of the debt from the principal takes place immediately before the operation of the statutory set-off, and by discharging the debt, prevents set-off from taking place at all. He recorded the debate without comment, saying simply that it would only arise for resolution in the unlikely event of documentation like that in the *MS Fashions* case appearing in another liquidation. It was not germane in *BCCI (No.8)* because the letter of charge over the deposits provided by the surety could not be construed as creating a personal joint and several obligation on the part of the surety and principal.[82] However, Lord Hoffmann was plainly attracted by the first of these two arguments: he decided that there was no mutuality for the purposes of insolvency set-off between the principals and the creditor because the statutory rule required that there be at least the existence in the creditor of a right to make a money demand, and that the creditor's merely having a right under a charge to appropriate property under its control to a particular debt was not a right to make a money demand on the other party to the (purportedly) mutual dealings (*i.e.* the principals).

The most important impact of *BCCI (No.8)* is that, in deciding that there was no personal obligation on the part of the surety to make payment to the creditor, the House of Lords had to consider whether it was conceptually possible for a bank to take a charge over a deposit made with it by a borrower or a surety as security for his or another's obligations. This was necessary because the principals contended that if such a charge was indeed conceptually impossible, then the only effect that could be given to the charge given by the surety was as a personal covenant for repayment. As Lord Hoffmann noted, this had been a matter of some controversy in banking circles since 1986, when the doctrine of conceptual impossibility had been propounded by Millett J. in *Re Chargecard Services Ltd* and affirmed by the Court of Appeal in *BCCI (No.8)* [1996] Ch. 245.[83] Lord Hoffmann said that he could not see why if the charge was a true charge, which created a genuine proprietary interest in the bank not requiring any formal assignment or vesting of title in the bank, with the chargor retaining an equity of redemption, there was no problem with the bank having a proprietary interest by way of charge over the debt it owes the chargor.

It is a trap for the unwary to think that the only source of a personal covenant for repayment is the security documentation. On the contrary, where the security is registered land, then s.28 of the Land Registration Act

---

[82] See Philip Wood, *English and International Set-Off (op. cit.)*, para.10.59. See also *Kent v Monroe* (1904) 4 O.W.R. 468, Ont SC; *Re The West Australian Lighterage, Stevedore & Transport Co Ltd* (1903) 5 W.A.L.R. 132.

[83] In which Millett L.J. gave the judgment of the court.

1925 implies a personal covenant for repayment unless negatived by "suitable words" in the instrument. What constitutes "suitable words" will be construed in favour of the mortgagor, particularly where he has received nothing from the mortgagee.[84]

The insolvency of co-sureties

The right of the surety to prove in the insolvency of his co-surety for contribution has been dealt with in full in Chapter 12 of this work.[85] It should be noted that the rule against double proof applies to the surety's right to prove, and that this arises at the date upon which the creditor lodges his proof in the co-surety's insolvency. **13–020**

---

[84] See *Fairmile Portfolio Management v Davies Arnold Cooper (a firm)* (1998) E.G.C.S. 149; *The Times*, November 17, 1998.

[85] See paras 12–024–12–025.

Chapter 14

Bank Guarantees and Related Transactions

Introduction

14–001   Of all the many businesses which involve the giving and taking of guarantees, banking is probably the one in which guarantees play the most important everyday role, ranging from the personal guarantees ancillary to mortgage transactions and personal loans, to the often complex bank guarantees which form an important part of major commercial transactions. In general terms, a bank is no different from any other creditor or surety, and there are no special rules which apply to its rights or liabilities. However, there are a number of matters which may be of particular significance to a bank, which therefore merit independent discussion in this chapter.

Duty of care

Duty in relation to securities held by the bank

14–002   A bank, like any other creditor, is obliged to deal with the security which it holds in a reasonable manner so as to ensure that the maximum benefit can be derived from it to satisfy the guaranteed obligation. However, the duty of care of a mortgagee (and any receiver appointed by him) in respect of the sale of the mortgaged property only extends to persons with an interest in the equity of redemption: *Burgess v Auger* [1998] 2 B.C.L.C. 478. Lightman J. held that although this might include a guarantor of the secured indebtedness, it would only do so if he has already acquired such an interest at the time of the events complained of, by making payment under his guarantee.[1] The reported cases on this topic are generally concerned with the situation in which the security has been realised, and the surety contends that the creditor or his agent obtained less than the best available market price.[2] These are considered elsewhere in this work.[3] However,

---

1 See the discussion in Ch.9 para.9–043.
2 See, *e.g. Standard Chartered Bank Ltd v Walker* [1982] 1 W.L.R. 1410; *Medforth v Blake* [2000] Ch. 86; *Skipton Building Society v Stott* [2001] Q.B. 26; *Mahomed v Morris* [2000] 2 B.C.L.C. 536, *Silven Properties Ltd v Royal Bank of Scotland* [2004] 1 B.C.L.C. 359, *Den Norske Bank ASA v Acemex Management Co Ltd* [2004] 1 Lloyds' Rep 1.
3 See Ch.9 paras 9–041–9–044.

another problem which may arise at an earlier stage, and which has particular relevance to a creditor bank, is whether there is any duty on the bank to exercise reasonable care to ensure that the value of the security is preserved for the benefit of the surety before it is sold. This was considered by the Court of Appeal in *National Bank of Greece v Pinios Shipping Company (No.1) (The "Maira") (No.3)* [1990] 1 A.C. 637.[4]

In that case, the plaintiff bank had guaranteed the due payment by a one-ship company of a series of promissory notes in respect of the purchase price of a vessel from her Japanese builders. The notes were payable, in yen, to a Japanese bank, which had a first mortgage over the vessel. The plaintiff bank was secured by a second mortgage over the vessel and a personal guarantee given by T. Both the mortgages required the vessel to be insured in US dollars for not less than 130 per cent of the total balances, including interest, currently due under both mortgages.

There was a substantial decline in the shipping market and the company failed to honour the first promissory note. Rather than lose the use of the vessel altogether, at the insistence of the bank, the company entered into a tripartite agreement with the bank and G, a management company, under which G took over the management of the vessel as the company's agent, and agreed to apply its trading profits to reduce the indebtedness. The company effectively gave up all responsibility for the vessel and had no means of controlling G, but G was obliged to act in accordance with the instructions of the bank. At a time when the value of the US dollar had declined sharply against the yen, G renewed the vessel's insurance at a dollar figure which was insufficient to cover the company's liability to the Japanese bank and to the bank, and shortly afterwards the vessel became a total loss. Although it was held that G owed a duty of care to the company[5] this proved to be of no use to the company or to T, because G was insolvent. Consequently, when the bank sued the company and T for the balance due on the loan account together with a substantial amount of interest, it was sought to allege by way of defence that the bank was itself in breach of a duty to take reasonable care to preserve the value of the securities.

Despite a finding by the trial judge, Leggatt J., that the bank "knew and approved" of the level of insurance, the Court of Appeal held that the bank owed no duty of care either to its customer or to the surety. A distinction was drawn between the situation in which there is positive interference by the bank with the security (*e.g.* where the bank *tells* the manager to insure for a particular sum, which it knows or ought to know will be insufficient) and the case in which there is passive acquiescence in what might be a breach of duty by some other person.[6] Subsequently, in *China and South Seas Bank Ltd v Tan* [1990] 1 A.C. 536, this approach was effectively

---

4 Leave to appeal to the House of Lords was refused on this point.
5 *Glafki Shipping Company SA v Pinios Shipping Co (No.1) (The "Maira") (No.2)* [1986] 2 Lloyd's Rep. 12, HL.
6 See the judgment of Lloyd L.J. at 646–651 and Nicholls L.J. at 660–661.

endorsed by the Privy Council which held that the creditor was not liable for allowing the security, in that case shares, to decline in value.[7]

Consequently, if a surety wishes to protect his position, he would be well advised to ensure that there is an express term in the contract of suretyship which obliges the bank (or other creditor) to take reasonable care to preserve the value of other securities to which it may have recourse, and to achieve the best possible price for them if it decides to sell them. Likewise, if a third party is introduced by the bank to manage assets, any fresh contractual arrangement should include terms which make the bank vicariously liable for defaults of that manager either generally, or when the action taken by the manager is subject to the prior approval of the bank.

Explaining the nature and effect of security documents

14–003 Another topic which may be of particular interest to a bank is whether, and if so in what circumstances, a creditor bank owes a duty to a prospective surety to advise him about the meaning and effect of the bank guarantee before he signs it, or to tell him to seek independent legal advice.

Best practice—the Banking Code

14–004 In 1987 the Government established a committee, headed by Professor Jack, to review the law and practice of banking services. In its report (1989 Cmnd 622) the Jack Committee recommended the introduction of a Code of Banking Practice covering the relations between banks and building societies and their personal customers. The first edition of the Code was published in 1991 and subsequent versions were published in 1994, 1997 and 1998. The most recent version of the Code came into force on January 1, 2001 but it was updated in March 2002. The Code is not intended to be read as a rigorous legal document but financial institutions are expected to abide by the spirt as well as the letter of the Code. The Code provides guidance as to best practice: it does not necessarily follow that a financial institution which does not adhere to that guidance will undertake any legal liability.

One of the Jack Committee's key recommendations was that prospective guarantors should be adequately warned of the legal effects and possible consequences of their guarantee and of the importance of receiving independent advice. As a result, the first Code of Banking Practice contained the following provision:

> "Banks and buildings societies will advise private individuals proposing to give them a guarantee or other security for another person's liabilities that: (i) by giving the guarantee or third party security he or she might become liable instead of or as well as that other person; (ii) he or she should seek independent legal advice before entering into

---

7 See further the discussion in Ch.9, at para.9–043, and the speech of Lord Hoffmann in *Re Bank of Credit and Commerce International (No.8)* [1998] A.C. 214 at 222D–E and 231B.

the guarantee or third party security. Guarantees and other third party security forms will contain a clear and prominent notice to the above effect."

As a result, prominent warning notices were printed on the first as well as on the last page of the standard form documentation used by banks. By the time that the Code was revised in 1994, banks had also adopted the practice of sending standard letters to all types of guarantor in the following, or similar terms:

"You should appreciate in giving the guarantee that, if our customer does not repay the bank, you may have to pay instead. The bank strongly recommends that you seek independent legal advice before signing the guarantee. Please let me know the name and address of the solicitor you have chosen. I will then arrange to send the guarantee to your solicitor for signature, and you will no doubt arrange to call and see him."

The 2001 edition of the Code provides as follows in Clause 11.2:

"If you want us to accept a guarantee or other security from someone for your liabilities, we may ask you for your permission to give confidential information about your finances to the person giving the guarantee or other security, or to their legal adviser. We will also

• Encourage them to take independent legal advice to make sure that they understand their commitment and the possible consequences of their decision (where appropriate, the documents we ask them to sign will contain this recommendation as a clear and obvious notice)
• Tell them that by giving the guarantee or other security they may become liable instead of or as well as you; and
• Tell them what their liability will be. We will not take an unlimited guarantee."

The Code goes on to explain that it is important that guarantors or grantors of security receive independent legal advice to help them understand the full nature of their commitment and the potential implications of their decision. It says that subscribers to the code may wish to go further and actually get the potential surety who refuses to take legal advice to sign a declaration to that effect.

Transactions involving non-commercial sureties

The recent decision of the House of Lords in *Royal Bank of Scotland v Etridge (No.2)* [2002] 2 A.C. 773 has now established that in any case where the surety is "non-commercial",[8] it is incumbent on a bank or other lender

14–005

---

8 The House of Lords does not define this term. It seems clear from Lord Nicholls' speech that it covers company directors, even if they have a significant shareholding in the company. Probably the safest approach for lending institutions to take is that which the Code already advocates, namely to treat all individual sureties alike: corporate sureties or professional bond issuers plainly fall into a different category.

to take certain steps (set out in para.79 of Lord Nicholls' speech) which are designed to procure that the surety takes independent legal advice before entering into the transaction. Those steps (discussed in more detail in Chapter 5) go beyond what is set out in the Code, but not to the extent that the burden on banks will be unduly onerous. One area which remains open to debate is what the financial institution should do if the surety refuses to take independent legal advice. Prior to *Etridge*, obtaining written confirmation (as the Code suggests) may well have been sufficient to protect the bank, but Lord Nicholls appears to contemplate that unless the surety responds in a satisfactory manner to the bank's initial letter, the transaction should not proceed, and therefore if a bank goes ahead in the face of even a written refusal, it does so at its own peril. Presumably, though, a bank will be able to decide for itself whether the surety falls into a category where the commercial risk is worth taking, as in many situations, the prospect of the surety having any equity to set aside the transaction is slender.

It should be emphasised that the steps laid down in *Etridge* are for the lender's own protection, in that if they are taken the lender will be freed from constructive notice of any wrongdoing which might otherwise be proved to have tainted the transaction, for example misrepresentation or undue influence exerted by the principal debtor on the surety. However, the bank or other lender is not under a legal *duty* to anyone to take these steps, and its failure to do so will not give rise to a claim in damages. The basic rule that a creditor owes no duty of care to a prospective surety has survived intact. As Lord Hobhouse put it in *Etridge* in para.114: "Seeing that the solicitor is adequately informed is not the performance of a *duty* owed by the bank to the wife. It is simply a necessary step to be taken by the bank so that it may be satisfied that the wife entered into the obligation freely and in knowledge of the true facts."

The decision in *Royal Bank of Scotland v Etridge* has moved away from the idea originally proposed by Lord Browne-Wilkinson in *Barclay's Bank v O'Brien* [1994] 1 A.C. 180 that banks should have a face to face meeting with wives or other potentially vulnerable sureties and undertake to explain the security documents themselves. Financial institutions were understandably chary of undertaking such explanations, among other reasons because of the risk that they might be held liable in negligence if the explanation was inaccurate. In the *O'Brien* case in the Court of Appeal [1993] Q.B. 109, Scott L.J. (at 140–141) had stated that a duty of care would not arise simply by reason of the fact that a creditor tried to explain the documents or the transaction to the surety in circumstances in which the creditor might otherwise be susceptible to an equitable defence arising out of the undue influence or other wrongdoing of the principal *vis-à-vis* the surety. He said that if the explanation was inadequate, the security might not be enforceable, but it would not follow that any liability in damages would attach. The reason was that equity should not place creditors in the dilemma of having to choose between, on the one hand, risking the security being unenforceable and on the other hand, undertaking a duty of care. In *Midland Bank v Kidwai* [1995] N.P.C. 81 the Court of Appeal confirmed that a bank which was taking the steps envisaged by Lord Browne-Wilkinson to free itself of constructive notice did not thereby assume the role of adviser to the surety. Whilst this may have provided some reassurance, it clearly did not sufficiently assuage the fears of lending institutions. Now the *Etridge* guidelines mean that banks should not find themselves undertaking explanations of this kind at all in the future.

Transactions involving commercial sureties

This means that the only circumstances in which the issue whether the bank **14–006** had a duty to explain security documentation to the prospective surety will be raised in future are those in which the prospective surety falls within the class of sureties envisaged by the House of Lords to be in no need of any special protection—which rather points towards the issue being resolved in favour of the absence of such a duty. This is entirely in accordance with the preponderance of modern authority prior to the decision in *Royal Bank of Scotland v Etridge* [2002] 2 A.C. 773, most notably the decision of Thomas Morison Q.C. (as he then was) in *Barclays Bank v Khaira* [1992] 1 W.L.R. 623 and Clarke J. in *Union Bank of Finland v Lelakis* [1995] C.L.C. 20.[9] In that case, the defendant guarantor was a Greek shipowner who had fair experience of both London arbitration and litigation. He had entered into personal guarantees in respect of substantial loans made to his shipowning company by the plaintiff bank. One of the grounds on which he sought to set aside a judgment in default which the bank had entered against him was that he had an arguable defence on the merits because the bank owed him a duty of care to give him a fair and proper explanation of the guarantees and his obligations thereunder, or at least to advise him of the importance of taking independent legal advice. It was alleged that the duty arose out of a voluntary assumption of responsibility by the bank to give such an explanation, or alternatively by reason of the fact that the bank knew or ought to have known by making appropriate enquiry from the defendant that he had not taken independent legal advice and that he was relying on the bank to give him a fair and unbiased explanation of the guarantees.

Clarke J. had little difficulty in rejecting this defence. He considered the relevant English authorities, and in particular *Barclays Bank Plc v Khaira* and *Barclays Bank v O'Brien*, and stated his agreement with what Thomas

---

9 See also *Chetwynd-Talbot v Midland Bank Ltd* (unreported), June 21, 1982, McCullough J.; *O'Hara v Allied Irish Banks Ltd* [1985] B.C.L.C. 52; *Westpac Banking Corporation v McCreanor* [1990] 1 N.Z.L.R. 580; *Shivas v Bank of New Zealand* [1990] 2 N.Z.L.R. 327; *Barclays Bank v Schwartz, The Times*, August 2, 1995; *Citibank NA v Ercole Ltd* (unreported) May 24, 2001, Bell J. The "tentative" view expressed by Kerr L.J. in *Cornish v Midland Bank Plc* [1985] 3 All E.R. 513 that banks may owe a duty of care to their customers to explain security documents was strongly criticised both academically (*e.g.* in the 10th ed. of *Paget's Law of Banking* and by Stuart Walker, (1990) N.Z.L.J. 120) and judicially (*e.g.* in *Barclays Bank v Khaira*) and is almost impossible to reconcile with the long-established line of cases to the effect that there is no fiduciary relationship between a creditor and prospective surety or between a banker and his customer, see, *e.g. Hamilton v Watson* (1845) 12 Cl. & Fin. 109; *Westpac v Dickie* [1991] 1 N.Z.L.R. 657 and the observations of Lord Woolf C.J. in *Bank of Scotland v A* [2001] 1 W.L.R. 751.

Morison Q.C. had said in the former case. He said (at 45) that there may be circumstances in which a bank assumes responsibility to give advice or explanations to a prospective guarantor and that if it does so, a duty of care will no doubt exist, as envisaged in *Hedley Byrne v Heller* [1964] A.C. 465. There may also be other circumstances in which a duty of care may be held to exist, and in deciding whether or not such a duty arises it may be necessary to have regard to any relevant banking practice. Nevertheless he was not persuaded that a bank owed a general duty of care to every prospective guarantor of the kind alleged, even though the Code of Banking Practice, revised in 1994, had given rise to standard letters being sent by banks to all types of guarantor and not just to wives or others falling within the *O'Brien* category.The reasons for this conclusion were summarised thus by Clarke J. at 47–48:

"(1) None of the cases supports the proposition that a bank always owes a duty of care to a prospective guarantor whatever the circumstances.

(2) I do not think that in *Cornish v Midland Bank Plc* Kerr L.J. intended to say that it does, or indeed that he had a case like this in mind. If he did, the views of McCullough J. in *Chetwynd-Talbot v Midland Bank Ltd* and of Morison J. in *Barclays Bank v Khaira* are to be preferred.

(3) Whether a duty of care is owed depends on all the circumstances of the case.

(4) One of the circumstances of the case includes relevant evidence of banking practice. In the instant case there is no relevant evidence of banking practice which relates to a bank like the plaintiffs' which proposes to take a personal guarantee from a shipowner like the defendant. I do not think that Lord Browne-Wilkinson had such a person in mind during any part of his speech in [*Barclays Bank v O'Brien*].

(5) None of the cases supports the existence of a duty of care in a case such as the present. That includes both the cases relied upon by [Counsel for the defendant] and *Caparo Industries Plc v Dickman* [1990] 2 A.C. 605.

(6) The relevant facts of the case are these . . . [The learned judge then summarised the facts including the fact that the defendant was an experienced shipowner, that he had no difficulty in instructing experienced solicitors in London if he wanted to, and that he had had every opportunity to do so before signing the personal guarantees, and concluded:] The defendant could not, in my judgment, reasonably have expected at the time to receive advice of the kind suggested by [his counsel]. [Counsel for the bank]'s submission was that it was entirely a matter for the defendant whether or not he simply signed the document or took legal advice. There was no reason whatever for the bank to give him advice what to do. I accept that submission. It is, in my

judgment, a startling suggestion that experienced shipowners like Mr Lelakis should be given advice or warnings of the kind suggested by an international bank, especially if that bank is being asked to lend moneys to a borrower wholly owned by the guarantor. That is so whatever the position may be in the kind of case contemplated by the codes referred to above or by the Barclays Bank letter, as to which I express no opinion."

A similar approach was adopted by Judge Geddes in *Lloyds TSB Bank v Shelton* (unreported, QBD, June 20, 2000). The original guarantee had been extended by a deed which effectively doubled the amount for which the directors of the borrowing company, including Mr S, were liable. S contended that there was a breach of fiduciary duty by the bank in failing to advise him of the impact of the deed on his interests. The judge held that the transactions were part of the normal banker-customer relationship and that no duty to advise arose.

Voluntary assumption of a duty of care

As Clarke J. acknowledged in *Union Bank of Finland v Lelakis* [1995] C.L.C. 20 there may be circumstances in which a bank embarks upon an explanation of the security documents, in which case it may well be held to owe a duty of care to explain them fully and properly. *Cornish v Midland Bank Plc* [1985] 3 All E.R. 513 was a case in which it was conceded that a duty of care had arisen, and that was the basis on which the appeal was decided.[10] Another example is *Perry v Midland Bank* [1987] Fin. L.R. 237, in which the bank was held liable for the negligent explanation given by its solicitor to the prospective surety. However, in the light of *Royal Bank of Scotland v Etridge* [2002] 2 A.C. 773 it is envisaged that the circumstances in which a bank would embark upon an explanation of the security documents, if it would ever do so in future, will be extremely rare.

14–007

Bank guarantees and legal proceedings

There are a number of situations in which a party to an action proceeding before the court or in arbitration, or sometimes a third party, is required to give security, either to another party to the litigation, or to the court. Among the most common examples are security for costs, security provided to release an injunction, security for the release of a ship or aircraft from arrest, and security given for the due performance by a receiver of his office. In certain commercial contracts, there may even be an express contractual requirement that in the event of a dispute, one of the parties should procure a bank guarantee to secure payment of any judgment or arbitration award.[11]

14–008

---

10 See the judgments of Croom-Johnson L.J. at 516–518, Glidewell L.J. at 520, and Kerr L.J. at 521.
11 See, *e.g.* the condition in the contract in *Chiswell Shipping Ltd v State Bank of India Ltd (The "World Symphony")* [1987] 1 Lloyd's Rep. 165.

Bank guarantees as security

14–009 In all such cases, a guarantee given by a bank may be an acceptable form of security, and in the first two examples given above, such guarantees have probably overtaken payments into court as the normal form of security. This reflects the commercial reality that such guarantees are rarely dishonoured, because banks generally honour their contractual obligations, and are unlikely to become insolvent. However, this does not mean that such a guarantee is invariably accepted. It is fairly common practice for agreements to give security, or court orders for the provision of security, to refer to a guarantee being given by "a first class bank" or "a first class London bank". This is not a term of art, and will not be found in any of the rules of court. However, it is an expression which is indicative of the general practical approach to such matters, which is that whereas a guarantee offered by one of the major clearing banks will generally be regarded by the court as an acceptable alternative to a payment into court, a guarantee offered by a licensed deposit taker or a bank which has no assets which are readily susceptible to enforcement within the jurisdiction will not be so regarded.

Guarantees of this type are usually provided for a limited period, often for a year, with liberty to renew, or a provision for automatic renewal subject to the fulfilment of certain conditions (*e.g.* the continued prosecution of the action). Whether the guarantee is expressed in indefinite or renewable form, care should be taken to provide for a means of termination. There is a danger that once a party to an action achieves a measure of security, he will lose the incentive to prosecute the case with the requisite degree of diligence; although the changes to the Civil Procedure Rules have gone some way towards safeguarding against undue delay, a provision in any relevant contract or court order which entitles the party providing the security to apply to the court to have the security discharged if the action does not proceed for a stated period, or if it does not come to trial by a certain date, would provide additional protection and act as an incentive to the claimant to get on with the case.

It is also important from the bank's perspective that any counter-security which it obtains from its customer in respect of the guarantees which it, itself, puts up, is commensurate with the obligations which it has undertaken, so that it does not leave itself exposed. The case of *Liberty Mutual Insurance Co (UK) Ltd v HSBC Bank Plc* [2002] EWCA Civ 691, May 16, 2002, provides a cautionary tale. The Court of Appeal heard three conjoined appeals from two decisions of Sir Andrew Morritt V.-C. and a decision of Patten J. on various preliminary issues concerning the construction of certain surety bonds issued in standard form by two insurance companies, to secure liabilities which the bank had entered into at the request of its customer, OMMIA, a P&I Club which was now in liquidation. As part of its business activities, OMMIA was regularly called upon to provide security for its members in order to obtain the release of their vessels when they were arrested in various ports around the world. OMMIA entered into an arrangement with the bank that enabled it to procure guarantees (or admiralty bonds) directly from HSBC or, more commonly, guarantees from local correspondent banks in the jurisdiction where the vessel had been arrested. In the latter situation, HSBC would provide the correspondent bank with a counter-indemnity. The guarantees put up as security for the release of the vessels from arrest were conditional, in that they were only payable on production of a judgment or arbitral award in favour of the arresting party. The counter-indemnities were in the form of undertakings to pay on the correspondent bank's first demand, provided that the correspondent bank stated that it was liable to pay in accordance with the terms of its guarantee. The insurers issued surety bonds to support and secure the bank's engagements, most of which arose under the counter-indemnities.

One of the issues was whether the insurers were liable in circumstances where OMMIA had requested the bank to procure an admiralty bond/guarantee for one year, but in fact the bank had procured guarantees which were automatically renewable every 12 months, and a claim had been made under the counter-indemnity by a correspondent bank in respect of a demand made against it after the first twelve months. Patten J. held that in such circumstances the insurers were not liable, and the Court of Appeal upheld that decision for the same reasons. Rix L.J. in the Court of Appeal was concerned that the preliminary issue which the court had to determine was too narrowly focused, but ultimately agreed that as a matter of construction of the surety bond, the liability which it secured was that of that bank arising from it having procured the execution of a guarantee of the kind requested by OMMIA, and not some different kind of guarantee. Consequently if OMMIA requested a one-year guarantee but the guarantee was renewable, any liability incurred after the first year would not be covered by the bond.

A guarantee which is intended to secure payment under an arbitration award or judgment may contain provisions for the amount to be reduced *pro tanto* by any payments which have been made in partial satisfaction of the award or judgment. If this is done, careful wording should be employed in order to avoid the possibility of payments being appropriated by the payee to other debts outstanding between the parties. See generally *Chiswell Shipping Ltd v State Bank of India (The "World Symphony") (No.1)* [1987] 1 Lloyd's Rep. 165.

Expense of such guarantees

Banks will make a charge for providing such a guarantee, and will usually require counter-security (which may involve further expense). Unfortunately from the point of view of the person who has to provide the security, there appears to be no means by which he can recover these costs on taxation or otherwise, even if he succeeds, since they are probably not part of his legal costs or disbursements. He would be well advised, therefore, to make express provision for the recovery of these costs, in any relevant contract or court order pertaining to the provision of the security.

One possible exception is the defendant who provides a bank guarantee in place of a freezing injunction under reservation of his right to challenge

14–010

the imposition of the injunction, and succeeds in persuading the court that the injunction should not have been granted (*e.g.* if it was obtained by material and culpable non-disclosure). It is an open question whether the court has jurisdiction to order the guarantee to be discharged in such circumstances,[12] but if it does, it is possible that the defendant would be entitled to recover the costs of putting up the security under the cross-undertaking in damages.

Cheque guarantee cards

14–011   Although it is well established that a cheque, like any other bill of exchange, should generally be treated as the equivalent of cash, with the consequence that there are few defences available to an action brought on a cheque, in practice retailers are increasingly unlikely to accept a cheque in payment for goods or services without the added protection afforded by the production of a cheque guarantee card. Cheque guarantee cards are a relatively recent phenomenon, and as a result there is very little case law about them. The effect of using such a card was explained by Millett J. in *Re Charge Card Services* [1987] Ch. 150 at 166 (at first instance) as being that the bank, through the agency of its customer, and subject to the conditions of issue, undertakes to the payee not to dishonour the cheque on presentation *for want of funds in the account* (emphasis added), with the result that the bank is obliged, if necessary, to advance sufficient funds to the customer's account to enable the cheque to be met.

The object of the card is to relieve the retailer from concerning himself with the relationship between drawer and drawee; all he is concerned with is that the bank's conditions governing use of the card are satisfied: *R. v Kassim* [1992] 1 A.C. 9 at 19. Those conditions are likely to be prescribed by the rules of the UK Domestic Cheque Guarantee Card Scheme: see Paget's Law of Banking (12th ed., Butterworths, 2002), para.16.4.

The relationship between bank and payee

14–012   Despite the fact that the cards are referred to as cheque guarantee cards, the relationship between the bank and the payee is not one of creditor and guarantor: the bank's liability to put its customer in funds sufficient to meet the cheque is an entirely independent primary obligation, and is probably not co-extensive with that of the customer.[13] Accordingly, it would probably not be open to the bank to justify refusing payment even on the grounds of a total failure of consideration for the cheque. Indeed, the customer normally undertakes to the bank that he will not countermand payment of a "guaranteed" cheque, and if he does, the bank may have a claim against him for damages equal to any sum which the bank may have been obliged to pay to the supplier. Thus the risk of a fraud by the supplier is probably

---

12 See the discussion in Ch.15, at para.15–022.
13 See the observations of Evans L.J. in *First Sport Ltd v Barclays Bank Plc* [1993] 1 W.L.R. 1229 at 1235–1236.

ultimately borne by the customer rather than by the bank, though this proposition has yet to be tested in court; it may be that an analogy would be drawn between the obligation under a cheque guarantee card and the obligation under a performance guarantee or letter of credit, so that in a sufficiently clear case the customer might be able to obtain an injunction to restrain payment by the bank.

Unauthorised use

The rights and liabilities of the parties in the situation in which the cheque **14–013** and card have been presented to the supplier by an unauthorised person, such as a thief, have only been considered by the court in one reported case *First Sport Ltd v Barclays Bank Plc* [1993] 1 W.L.R. 1229, though the rights and liabilities of a banker who, acting in good faith, pays on a cheque which bears a forged signature or indorsement, are catered for extensively by statute.[14] The customer may have reported the theft prior to the transaction in question, and the account may have been frozen by the bank so that all payments will be countermanded. As between the bank and the customer, it is strongly arguable that the latter's undertaking not to countermand payment should not operate in circumstances in which a theft (or loss) of the chequebook and cheque card has been discovered. The contract between the bank and the customer usually provides for a maximum liability of the customer to the bank for losses suffered by the bank in consequence of such loss or theft, provided that the customer has reported the loss or theft to the police and to the bank within a stipulated time limit after discovering it, and has complied with certain other conditions (which usually include keeping the cheque card in a separate place from the chequebook). Thus if the bank has to pay the supplier, it may have no right of recourse against the customer, or its rights may be limited to recovering a relatively small sum.

Despite this, it is now established that the bank could be obliged to pay the supplier in such circumstances, even though the cheque card would have been used by someone who had no actual authority to create a contract between the bank and the supplier.[15] It is possible therefore, that at least, if the theft was undiscovered at the time of presentation, the bank might be able to recover a payment made to the innocent supplier out of its own funds, though this again would turn on the precise terms of the contract between the bank and its customer.

If the undertaking by the bank is as Millett J. described it, in effect an undertaking to put the customer in funds to meet the cheque, rather than a

---

14 See, *e.g.* s.1 of the Cheques Act 1957, s.60 of the Bills of Exchange Act 1882 and *Chitty on Contracts* (*op. cit.*), Vol. 2, Ch.34.
15 See *First Sport Ltd v Barclays Bank Plc* [1993] 1 W.L.R. 1229 in which a majority of the Court of Appeal (Sir Thomas Bingham M.R. and Evans L.J.) held that the thief has ostensible authority to convey an offer to the supplier on behalf of the bank. The case turned on the terms of the statement on the cheque guarantee card addressed to suppliers; and it seems clear that if these had contained a clear and unequivocal statement that the bank would not, under any circumstances, accept liability on a cheque which was not signed by the authorised signatory of the card, the outcome would have been different.

general undertaking to the payee to honour the cheque, then contrary to popular assumption, it probably affords little or no additional protection to the supplier in a case where the cheque has been stolen or the card is used by someone without authority.[16] Although the person who presents it represents to the payee that he has authority from the bank to make a contract with the payee that the bank will honour the cheque on presentation,[17] a claim against a thief or receiver of stolen cheques and a cheque card for breach of warranty of authority is likely to afford the payee little consolation.

The undertaking of the bank is normally subject to the express conditions under which the cheque card is made available to the customer (see *Paget's Law of Banking, op. cit.*). These typically include a requirement that the payee (not the cardholder) shall write the number of the card on the reverse of the cheque after it has been signed, though with the advent of the "chip and PIN" system this may change. The card will be subject to a maximum guaranteed limit. Initially the usual limit was £50, but some clearing banks have now introduced a regular limit of £100, and certain customers who are considered to be a good credit risk may be issued with cards with a limit of £250. The undertaking or guarantee of payment relates to transactions within that limit (and to avoid abuse, the use of more than one cheque for the same transaction, *e.g.* two £50 cheques drawn on the same account, each backed by a £50 cheque card, for one transaction of £100, is normally expressly prohibited). The cheque must be dated before the expiry date of the cheque card, and must normally be signed in the presence of the payee.

A cheque operates as conditional payment only, unless the parties otherwise agree expressly or by implication.[18] In *Re Charge Card Services*, Millett J. stated, *obiter*, that the presumption of conditional payment would not be displaced merely by the fact that the cheque was accompanied by a bank card.[19] He said that the only risk was that of the default or insolvency of the bank, and this risk, though unlikely to be in the contemplation of the parties, is equally present whether or not the cheque is accompanied by a bank card. On appeal, the point was expressly left open by the Court of Appeal: [1989] Ch. 497 at 517. If this is correct, the acceptance of the "guaranteed" cheque does not restrict the payee to pursuing the bank in the event of dishonour, though in the normal course of events the payee would look to the bank for payment, leaving the risk of the customer's insolvency to fall upon the bank.

---

16 Though the increase in frauds using stolen cheques and cheque cards has been used in the past by the clearing banks as justification for maintaining the £50 limit.

17 *Metropolitan Police Commissioner v Charles* [1977] A.C. 177, *per* Lord Diplock at 182.

18 *Re Romer & Halsam* [1893] 2 Q.B. 286, *Bolt & Nut Co (Tipton) Ltd v Rowlands Nicholls & Co Ltd* [1964] 2 Q.B. 10.

19 [1987] 1 Ch. at 166.

Letters of comfort

The situation sometimes arises in which a third party is unable or unwilling **14–014** to provide a guarantee for a loan made to a borrower,[20] but is prepared to give a written assurance to the lender of its continued support for, interest in, or dealings with, the borrower. These written assurances are known as letters of comfort, because they are intended to afford "comfort" to the lender by indicating to him that the borrower is likely to be able to repay the loan. Although the use of letters of comfort is not confined to banking transactions, they are perhaps most prevalent in this area, and are often given by parent companies in respect of prospective loans to their less affluent subsidiaries. They may also be given by an existing lender in order to encourage the injection of further capital into a borrowing company, or additional financial support, and indeed may be relied on by a prospective surety. See for example *Morgan Grenfell Development Capital Syndications Ltd v Arrows Autosport Ltd* [2003] EWHC (Ch) 333, February 28, 2003, in which Pumfrey J. held that a letter sent by a lender (MG) to a borrower (Arrows) following discussions between them about the latter's liquidity crisis and the need to attract an injection of further capital was "best described as a letter of comfort for anyone contemplating an investment in Arrows. It indicates how that new investor can expect MG to react, and the general structure of a deal which they can be expected to accept" (para.73 of the judgment).

The contents of a letter of comfort may range from a statement that the parent company intends to continue to hold a controlling interest in the subsidiary, and to use that controlling interest so as to procure that the subsidiary conducts its affairs in a particular way, to an assurance that it will ensure that the subsidiary keeps sufficient reserves to enable it to meet its obligations to repay the loan. A bank which is offered a letter of comfort in place of a guarantee would be well advised to study the proposed wording very carefully before accepting it. Sometimes there will be a clear indication that the promise is not intended to be binding. For example in *Re Atlantic Computer Plc (in Administration), National Australia Bank Ltd v Soden* [1995] B.C.C. 696, two letters from the parent company of a borrower to the bank stated that if the subsidiary could not meet its commitments, the parent would take steps to ensure that its subsidiary's present and future obligations to the bank were met. However the letters expressly provided that this was an "expression of present intention by way of comfort only". On that basis, Chadwick J. held that the parent company was entitled to enter into a subsequent arrangement which rejected the bank's claims as a creditor, the statements of its existing intentions were not to be construed as a promise as to its future conduct. It should be borne in mind that, in the

---

20 *e.g.*: if it would be *ultra vires* for a company to give a guarantee for its subsidiary; or if it would be undesirable to give a guarantee because its contingent liability would have to appear in its balance sheet.

absence of such a clear statement, the question whether the letter of comfort gives rise to a binding legal obligation is often difficult to resolve.[21]

Statements of promises and present intention

14–015 There is a clear distinction between a statement which involves a promise to ensure that a particular state of affairs exists or continues to exist, and a statement of present intention. The former may give rise to a binding contractual obligation (in an appropriate case, it may even amount to a guarantee or indemnity) whereas, provided the latter is an honest statement of the writer's intention at the time when it is made, there is nothing legally to prevent the giver of the letter of comfort from changing his mind at any time in the future. The distinction is illustrated by the case of *Kleinwort Benson Ltd v Malaysian Mining Corporation Bhd* [1989] 1 W.L.R. 379, in which the Court of Appeal had to construe the following statement in a letter written by a parent company to a bank: "It is our policy to ensure that the business of [the subsidiary] is at all times in a position to meet its liabilities to you under the above arrangements". The subsidiary became insolvent and the loan was not repaid.

Although the bank had relied on the letter when advancing money to the subsidiary, and there was evidence that both the bank and the parent company had treated it as a matter of commercial importance, it was held, reversing the decision of Hirst J.,[22] that the letter of comfort merely stated the parent company's present intention. Since the statement was honestly made, the only obligation on the parent company to maintain that policy was a moral one, and therefore a subsequent change in its intention did not entitle the bank to claim damages.[23] The statement had to be construed in the context of the rest of the letter, and against the factual matrix, which included a refusal by the parent company throughout the negotiations to assume any legal liability for repayment of the loan. In the light of all these factors, there was no binding promise.[24] Similarly in *Autocar Equipment Ltd v Motemtronic Ltd and Searle* (unreported) CAT No.656 of 1996, June 20, the Court of Appeal, by a majority, held that an oral statement by the chairman and majority shareholder of a company, M, that he would "make sure" that the money was there to repay a substantial sum of money to the plaintiff if the agreement was cancelled was a mere "comfort", even though

---

21 In business matters there is usually a presumption that an agreement is intended to create legal relations unless the opposite intention is clearly shown: see *Rose & Frank Co v JR Crompton & Bros Ltd* [1923] 2 K.B. 261 esp. *per* Bankes L.J. at 282. However, contrast *Morgan Grenfell Development Capital Syndications Ltd v Arrows Autosport Ltd* [2003] EWHC (Ch) 333, discussed above.

22 [1988] 1 W.L.R. 799.

23 Of course, if the person making the statement "changed his mind" very shortly after the loan was advanced, a court might be persuaded that the statement was not made honestly in the first place. The person who gives the letter of comfort must therefore be prepared to justify any change in his position.

24 This approach is to be contrasted with that of Hirst J., who had pointed out that even if a formal guarantee has been rejected, that does not mean that the parties are not willing to enter into some other contractual obligation.

the statement was made at a late stage in the negotiations after a company search on M had revealed that it did not have the means to effect repayment itself.

These cases can be contrasted with *Chemco Leasing SpA v Rediffusion Plc* [1987] 1 F.T.L.R. 201, in which the parent company had given a letter of comfort in these terms:

> "We assure you that we are not contemplating the disposal of our interests in [the subsidiary] and undertake to give Chemco prior notification should we dispose of our interest during the life of the leases. If we dispose of our interest we undertake to take over the remaining liabilities to Chemco of [the subsidiary] should the new shareholders be unacceptable to Chemco."

The Court of Appeal held that the parent company was not liable, because Chemco had failed to give it reasonable notice that the new shareholders were unacceptable to it (and thus an implied condition precedent to the undertaking in the second sentence had not been fulfilled). However, it appears that the decision of Staughton J. that the parent company was liable as guarantor would have been upheld but for this.

In *Banque Brussels Lambert SA v Australian National Industries Ltd* [1989] 21 N.S.W.L.R. 502 the New South Wales Supreme Court held that a letter of comfort gave rise to a legally binding obligation. In that case the letter stated "we . . . take this opportunity to confirm that it is our practice to ensure our affiliate . . . will at all times be in a position to meet its financial obligations as they fall due". It may be that apart from the slight variations in wording, the crucial point of distinction between this case and the *Kleinwort Benson* case was the absence of a similar factual matrix pointing towards a refusal to accept liability. More recently, the Court of Appeal rejected an attempt by ABTA to avoid responsibility for promises made in its widely promulgated Notice to Travellers on the grounds that they were merely intended to reassure consumers and were not intended to give rise to legally binding obligations: *Bowerman v Association of British Travel Agents* (1995) 145 N.L.J. Rep. 1815. Of course, it is rarely the subjective intention of the person giving the letter of comfort to make a binding legal commitment to the person receiving it. For the avoidance of any doubt, therefore, the company which gives the letter may insist that it includes an express statement that the contents are not intended to give rise to any enforceable legal obligation on the part of the writer, as in *Re Atlantic Computer* (para.14–014 above). In order to strengthen its position still further, it may also insist that the bank signs and returns a copy of the letter accepting that it does not give rise to any binding contract. Such disclaimers are now common. A bank may be prepared to accept such a letter of comfort from a business whose financial standing is well known to it, on the basis that failure to adhere to its promise would cause it such commercial damage that the risk of default would be minimal. On the other hand, if the bank has had no prior dealings with the companies involved, it is more likely to insist that there should be some form of binding legal obligation even if it falls short of a guarantee, such as a letter in the terms of the first sentence of the relevant paragraph in the *Chemco* case.

Even if the letter of comfort does give rise to a binding contract, it will not afford the bank the same degree of protection as a guarantee or indemnity. The subsidiary may become insolvent and fail to repay the loan, but that will not necessarily involve any breach of its obligations by the parent company. Furthermore, even if a parent does renege on its promise by withdrawing support from the subsidiary or selling its shareholding, the bank will have to establish a sufficient causal connection between that default and any loss which it suffers. This may be a difficult task, because the failure by the parent company to do what it promised may not have precipitated the insolvency of the subsidiary.

The absence of a binding contract may not deprive the addressee of the letter of comfort of all legal remedy. It is possible that the terms of the letter will contain representations as to existing fact which, if false, could give rise to a claim for damages for deceit or negligent misstatement on the basis of the principles enunciated in *Hedley Byrne v Heller* [1964] A.C. 465 . The difficulty of proving deceit is illustrated by the recent case of *Daniel v Gregory* [2002] EWCA Civ 566, April 12, 2002. That case concerned the sale of shares in a company. A firm of accountants had given the prospective purchaser a letter of comfort in the following terms:

> "To the best of our knowledge and belief when accounts for the year ending 30 September 1992 have been prepared we consider that it is unlikely that the results shown in the unaudited consolidated accounts will show a position which differs from that at 30 September 1991 by plus or minus 5%"

The Court of Appeal reversed the trial judge's findings that this statement was false and that it had been made recklessly. They held that it was not a statement in relation to the net worth of the company or a guarantee of the accuracy of the company's accounts. It had been relied on by the purchaser purely as a reassurance about the cashflow and profitability of the company. In fact the results shown in the 1992 accounts differed from the 1991 accounts by no more than about 1 per cent, well within the 5 per cent figure referred to in the letter. Accordingly the accountants were not liable to the purchaser in deceit.

Of course, statements as to the parent company's existing intention may be difficult to attack as misrepresentations, but if the subsidiary is allowed to go into liquidation shortly after the parent has stated an intention to support it, the court may subject the explanation for the change of policy to considerable scrutiny before concluding that the expressed intention was genuine at the time when the statement was made.

Chapter 15
International Commerce

Introduction

Guarantees, indemnities and insurance play a vital part in everyday **15–001** business transactions concerning the international sale and supply of goods and services, and the international carriage of goods. This chapter focuses upon certain special types of guarantee or related instruments which have particular applications in this context.

Export credit guarantees

There are a number of ways in which a person supplying goods or services **15–002** abroad may seek to protect himself against non-payment by the overseas purchaser. In a straightforward sale transaction, this may be done by stipulating that the price, or a large part of it, shall be paid by an irrevocable letter of credit, issued or confirmed by a bank in the seller's own country. Alternatively, the seller may require a performance bond or bank guarantee, which could cover the performance of other contractual obligations besides the payment of the purchase price. He may also choose to insure himself against commercial risks of non-payment, such as the insolvency of the buyer.

The seller or supplier may also face non-payment through the operation of political risks such as the imposition of foreign exchange control regulations, a foreign embargo on certain imports, or the outbreak of a civil war. It is rare for private insurers to offer insurance against political risks as opposed to commercial risks, and even when such cover is available, it is often expensive and severely circumscribed by exceptions. If this type of risk is perceived to be a real obstacle to making a bid for a tender for what might otherwise be regarded as a lucrative project, an export credit guarantee, provided by the Export Credits Guarantee Department ("ECGD") or by private sector insurers who generally provide similar instruments in respect of short-term insurance,[1] may be the solution.

The types of "guarantee" granted by ECGD[2] fall into three broad categories, namely:

---

1 See para.15–007 below.
2 Though, as regards ECGD's customer, they are almost certainly contracts of insurance rather than contracts of guarantee. ECGD now uses the acronym "EXIG" (an abbreviation for Export Insurance/Guarantee) when it refers to its products.

(a) credit insurance, granted to suppliers to protect them against non-payment by the overseas purchaser;

(b) guarantees granted to approved banks who, on the strength of ECGD support, make advances to the supplier to finance contracts of sale or supply to overseas purchasers ("supplier credit financing facilities"); and

(c) guarantees granted to approved banks for the finance of overseas purchasers who wish to purchase goods manufactured in the UK ("buyer credit financing facilities").[3]

An export credit guarantee has the additional attraction of assisting the supplier to raise finance for the transaction, which is often a matter of considerable importance if the obligation to pay the bulk of the price does not accrue until several months, or even years, have expired, as is often the case with overseas construction projects. An optional facility is insurance against the unwarranted call on a performance bond which the supplier may be required to give as a condition of the tender for the contract. ECGD support will usually result in the bank offering the supplier far more favourable terms (including interest rates) than it would be prepared to offer without such backing, and may give him a competitive edge when making his tender for an overseas project.

The powers of the ECGD

15–003 The ECGD, which has existed since 1919, is a separate government department, which exercises the powers conferred upon the Secretary of State[4] by statute (currently the Exports and Investment Guarantees Act 1991).[5] Part I of the Act defines the powers of the ECGD. Section 1 empowers the Secretary of State to make arrangements for providing financial facilities or assistance in any form, including guarantees[6] and insurance, for the purpose of facilitating the supply abroad of goods and services by UK businesses and of rendering economic assistance to countries outside the UK.[7] Section 2 empowers the Secretary of State to provide insurance against risks of certain specified losses,[8] arising in connection with any investment of resources by the insured in enterprises

---

3 These are broadly similar to supplier credit facilities, save that the financing bank lends money to the buyer rather than to the seller.

4 This means one of the principal Secretaries of State (Interpretation Act 1978, s.5 and Sch.1). The relevant person is the Secretary of State for Trade.

5 The Act came into force on October 23, 1991, and repeals the Export Guarantees and Overseas Investment Act 1978, re-enacting and supplementing most of its provisions. It was also intended to facilitate the privatisation of the insurance services business of ECGD, as to which see para.15–007 below.

6 Defined by s.4(3) as including an indemnity.

7 The UK is defined by s.4(4) as including the Isle of Man and the Channel Islands.

8 That is, losses resulting directly or indirectly from war, expropriation, restrictions on remittance and other similar events.

carried on outside the UK, or in connection with guarantees given by the insured in respect of any investment of resources by others in such enterprises, being enterprises in which the insured has an interest. Section 3 empowers the Secretary of State to make arrangements which he believes to be in the interests of the proper management of the ECGD portfolio, including the power to lend and to provide and take out insurance and guarantees. Section 4 provides, *inter alia,* that the powers of the Secretary of State under ss.1 to 3 are exercisable only with the consent of the Treasury. Section 5 enables the Secretary of State to provide and charge for information and services related to credit insurance.

Limits on ECGD commitments

Section 6 of the 1991 Act sets out the monetary limits for the aggregate amount of the ECGD's commitments under arrangements relating to export and insurance.[9] The current limit for contracts under which the commitments are expressed in sterling is £35,000 million, and for contracts where the commitments are expressed in foreign currencies, is £30,000 million special drawing rights.[10] The Secretary of State was empowered by s.4(4) and (7) to increase or further increase the limits to a measured extent by order, with the consent of the Treasury: however that limit has now been reached. **15–004**

International aspects

Export credit guarantee schemes exist in many other countries besides the UK. The Berne Union, an organisation of credit insurers,[11] was established in 1934 with the specific objective of maintaining restrictions on competition in the field of credit insurance by the exchange of information between members about terms of cover which are under consideration and about claims experiences and defaulting purchasers. Since 1974 it has also become a centre for consultation on overseas investment insurance. **15–005**

Within the EU, steps for the harmonisation of the terms of export credit guarantees have been under consideration for some years. There have been a number of draft directives, and the Commission published a "Background Report on Export and Credit Insurance" on July 22, 1977. However, a proposal in 1992 for a Council Decision on co-ordination and information procedures in export credit guarantees has not yet been passed and to date there has not been a final harmonisation of standard policies and guarantees provided within the European Union. Nevertheless, the steps which have been taken have resulted in a degree of uniformity as regards limits on ECGD cover, *i.e.* what percentage of the loss is recoverable. If an exporter

---

9 Defined as meaning arrangements under ss.1 and 2 of the 1991 Act and arrangements made under the old law (the 1978 Act) other than arrangements for giving grants.

10 Export and Investment Guarantees (Limit on Foreign Currency Commitments) Order 2000, SI 2000/2087. The SDR is the unit of account maintained by the International Monetary Fund since 1972.

11 Not governments themselves, though some statutory bodies are members.

in the UK is involved in a joint export project with an exporter from another country, he may be able to take advantage of one of the "One Stop Shop" agreements entered into by the ECGD with its equivalent Export Credit Agency (ECA) in the other country. Currently the ECGD has negotiated agreements of this kind with 24 other countries. Under such an arrangement, the ECA in the country whose exporter has the largest share of the deal will provide export credit support on its own terms for the whole deal and the other ECA will generally provide reinsurance.

Facilities available from ECGD

15-006 The types of facility which the ECGD offers have changed in their nature and scope over the years, and the standard forms have been adapted accordingly. In particular, there has been a growing trend towards introducing or reinforcing obligations on the part of the applicant and the bank financing him to disclose material facts to ECGD. In the light of the fairly constant changes and updates, it is unlikely to be helpful or desirable to try to describe in detail in this chapter all the various facilities currently available to suppliers or to overseas buyers, which are set out on the ECGD website. The ECGD also publishes a number of booklets which are available from its office and which describe the facilities available in considerable detail. A useful overall guide is to be found in "ECGD—A Short Guide to ECGD Facilities". However, it is possible to illustrate the main types of facility which are available, by reference to the medium-term facilities introduced before privatisation of the short-term facilities agency in 1991. In general terms the ECGD facilities complement the private sector, and do not compete with it. Unlike the private sector, however, ECGD does not aim to make a profit from its activities though it does seek to break even. Following a major review of the "Mission and Status" of the ECGD in 2000 it was concluded that it was not desirable to privatise ECGD's portfolio of medium-term and longer-term facilities because private sector insurers were not willing to take on these risks. Thus if the ECGD stopped offering those facilities, UK exporters would be put at a disadvantage as regards trade competitors from other countries who had the benefit of such support from their own ECAs. Prior to discussing these facilities, we consider the effects of the privatisation and the types of policy which are available from NCM and other short-term risk insurers.[12]

Privatisation of part of the ECGD functions

15-007 The EU Commission expressed a clear view that any direct or indirect government involvement in short-term[13] export credit insurance was potentially anti-competitive and in breach of the Treaty of Rome. The 1991 Act

---

12 A more detailed description is to be found in Benjamin's *Sale of Goods*, (Sweet & Maxwell, 6th ed., 2002), Ch.24, and in Jones, "Some Legal Aspects of Political Risk Insurance" *Project Finance Yearbook 1994/95* (Euromoney Publications), pp.73–75, but potential applicants should contact ECGD or look at its website which is www.ecgd.gov.uk or the websites of one of the relevant private sector insurers: www.ncmgroup.com, www.eulergroup.com or www.coface.uk.com in order to obtain up-to-date information about the facilities on offer.

13 Less than two years.

therefore made provision for the privatisation of the limb of ECGD, based in Cardiff, which had been dealing with such insurances. In December 1991, Britain became the first member of the European Union to privatise its short-term export credit agency. It sold the business to a privately owned Dutch credit insurer named Nederlandse Credietverzekering Maatschappij NV, which set up a subsidiary, NCM Credit Insurance Ltd (NCM) to administer the run-off on existing short-term guarantees issued by ECGD and to issue new policies in its own name on similar terms to those which ECGD previously offered.

NCM took over most of the existing Cardiff personnel and therefore acquired the benefit of the existing ECGD expertise. Initially it adopted the style and wording of the existing ECGD documents, but it is gradually replacing them with newer-style "plain English" policies.[14] The privatisation appears to have been a success. NCM offers a Comprehensive Short Term (International) Guarantee under which the applicant is generally required to insure all eligible business with NCM. This prevents the applicant from choosing to insure only the contracts which he perceives to be the most risky, and thus helps to keep the cost of premiums down. There are other private sector insurers offering cover similar to that on offer from NCM group: for example, in the UK, EULER Trade Indemnity and Coface UK.

As with medium-term and long-term facilities, the insurance will only cover a proportion of the loss (generally between 90 and 95 per cent) and the customer will have to bear the risk of the uninsured percentage. There may also be a specific credit limit placed on transactions with a particular buyer. The eligible contracts are contracts for the sale of goods or services made with buyers in countries for which the insurer offers cover,[15] which do not give more than 180 days' credit.[16] If pre-shipment cover is required, (that is, insurance against the possibility of the manufacturer becoming insolvent before the goods are shipped), the shipment date must usually be no more than 12 months from the date of the contract.[17] Premiums are assessed and fixed in the same way as any other insurer would do so, with

---

14 Since acquiring ECGD's short-term business, NCM has developed other policies which are tailored to the needs of different businesses. In 1992 NCM launched a domestic policy which covers UK buyer insolvency risks, which has proved to be remarkably successful. The number of insurances under that policy may well exceed those under the export policy in future years. In 1996 NCM introduced a global policy which enables the assured to cover all his transactions in just one facility. This is particularly useful for multinational groups who have different branches in countries all over the world. Among other policies offered by NCM are a "commercial risks" policy which covers buyer risks but excludes political risks, a "compact policy" for smaller UK businesses, and an "international policy" for UK companies with turnovers in excess of £5 million, who wish to insure both UK and export trade debts.

15 The world's major markets are all included, and the total number of countries in NCM's list exceeds 200. The currency of payment will probably also have to fall within a stipulated list.

16 This may be extended by agreement to up to two years, upon payment of an additional premium.

17 This period may be extended to 24 months by agreement upon payment of an additional premium.

higher premiums (called Market Rate Additions or MRAs) being charged for contracts involving those markets which are perceived as a higher risk. A small annual administration charge is also made. The commercial and political risks covered by the short-term policy and the exclusions are more or less the same as those covered by the medium-term SIP discussed below.

Facilities offered by ECGD

Export Insurance Policies

15–008 ECGD will issue an Export Insurance Policy ("EXIP") to an exporter from the UK on a case by case basis. Such policies insure against the risk of non-payment. Since they are negotiated individually the risks covered may be commercial, political or both, and the premium will depend on the assessment of the risk in the individual case. ECGD also offers supplementary policies, such as the Bond Insurance Policy referred to in para.15–010 below and other facilities which are described in detail on the ECGD website. Apart from the one-off facilities, ECGD also offers the Supplier Credit Facility ("SCF") discussed in para.15–009. This is the only comprehensive facility which is still available from ECGD. The EXIP, as its name implies, is an insurance policy[18] under which ECGD agrees to indemnify the supplier against a specified percentage of loss.[19] emanating from up to 11 defined causes, of which three relate to losses resulting from events within the UK, and the remainder relate to losses emanating from events outside the UK. ECGD will not insure the supplier against losses covered by other insurances.[20]

The insured categories.[21] are as follows:

(1) The insolvency of the overseas purchaser or any surety.

(2) The failure of the overseas purchaser or any surety to pay to the supplier any amount owing in respect of the element of the goods and services supplied under the contract which is covered by the policy (defined as the "insured element").[22]

---

18 A predecessor, a "Comprehensive Guarantee (Shipments)", which covered the supplier's exports to Brazil, was held to be a contract of insurance rather than a guarantee by Wynn-Parry J. in *Re Miller, Gibb & Co Ltd* [1957] 1 Lloyd's Rep. 258. Subsequent versions of this type of facility, including the "suppliers' credit policy" which was the subject of *L Lucas Ltd v ECGD* [1974] 1 W.L.R. 909, included a clause which specifically entitled ECGD to be subrogated to the supplier's rights against the purchaser. Clause 18 of the present standard SIP entitles ECGD to seek to recover the loss directly from the defaulting purchaser, and even if ECGD allows the supplier to pursue the purchaser, clause 20 obliges the supplier to hold any recoveries in trust for ECGD in a separate bank account until they are allocated in accordance with clause 18.8.

19 Generally 90%. There will also be an overall maximum policy limit.

20 See clause 7.1.12 of the standard policy terms.

21 These are enumerated in clause 5 of the standard policy wording. The applicable heads of loss covered by the individual contract will be specified in para.8.3 of the schedule to the policy. The first four causes of loss are not insurable under this type of policy if the overseas purchaser is an associated company of the supplier.

22 ECGD may decline cover or SCF support for part of the goods or services to be supplied. If it does so, the supplier must make entirely independent financing arrangements in respect of the excluded element.

(3) The failure of the overseas purchaser or any surety to pay to the supplier a sum due in respect of any final judgment or award[23] in connection with a claim in respect of the insured element within six months following the date of the judgment or award.

(4) If the overseas purchaser is defined as an "overseas public purchaser",[24] failure or refusal by him to pay the supplier any amount owing in respect of the insured element within six months following the due date of payment or to fulfil any of the terms of the contract.

(5) A law, decree or regulation in the overseas purchaser's country which has the effect of discharging him from liability for any debt in respect of the insured element when he makes payment in a currency other than the currency of the contract.[25]

(6) Prevention of, or delay in transfer of funds in respect of the insured element resulting from the occurrence outside the UK of political events, economic difficulties, legislative or administrative measures, or a general moratorium.

(7) Any measure or decision by a foreign government (including the non-renewal or cancellation of an export licence) which prevents performance of the insured element either in whole or in part.

(8) The occurrence outside the UK of hostilities, civil disturbance or natural disaster which prevents performance of the insured element in whole or in part.

(9) The cancellation or non-renewal of a UK export licence.

(10) Any UK restrictions introduced after the date of the contract which prevent performance of the insured element.[26]

(11) If the EXIP is ancillary to an SCF, the withdrawal of the ECGD-supported finance arrangements under the SCF facility by means of a written notice sent by ECGD to the supplier.[27]

Like any other insurance contract, an EXIP contract is one of the utmost good faith, and the prospective assured has a duty to disclose to ECGD all material facts of which he is or ought to be aware, prior to the entry into the contract. This duty is also specified in the express terms of the contract,

---

23 Which is not subject to appeal.
24 Such a foreign government or State-owned entity. The purchaser has to be defined as an overseas public purchaser by ECGD in clause 8.2 of the Schedule to the EXIP.
25 Provided that the discharge is not a valid discharge under the proper law of the contract, and that there is an actual loss produced by paying in a different currency.
26 Other than the refusal to grant any relevant licence or authorisation which was required at the date of the contract.
27 This particular head of loss is severely circumscribed. The policy does not protect the supplier if ECGD withdraws its support on account of a misrepresentation by the supplier. In any event losses are restricted to those suffered before the date of the written notice, or in certain specified cases, to losses occurring within 90 days thereafter.

particularly clause 9 of the standard policy, but is expanded by clause 13, which obliges the insured supplier to provide certain information and reports to ECGD during the currency of the policy.

Other express terms of which the prospective applicant should take careful note include clause 7 (which stipulates the conditions precedent to liability and places the burden of proving compliance with them on the assured); clause 8 (exclusions); and clause 11, which obliges the supplier to notify ECGD in writing within 30 days of the occurrence of any variation in or departure from the terms of the underlying contract.[28]

Whereas, in the past, the supplier could use an ECGD policy as a means of raising finance by assigning his rights under it in whole or in part to his bank,[29] the standard policy terms make it a condition precedent to ECGD's liability that the supplier has not, at the time of making any claim in respect of an insured loss, assigned or charged his right to recover in respect of the loss, or any interest which he has under the contract, and has given a written declaration to that effect to ECGD.

Supplier Credit Finance Facilities

15–009 On July 1, 1991, ECGD introduced the Supplier Credit Finance Facility (SCF) for contracts of supply involving medium-term credit (two years or more).[30] Under the SCF scheme, in return for the payment to ECGD of what is described as a premium,[31] the successful applicant obtains support from ECGD for finance to be granted to him by a bank approved by ECGD, in respect of a specified contract for the supply of goods or services to an overseas purchaser (which may be an associated company), under which the purchaser is granted credit terms in an acceptable form.[32] The bank must be one of the banks participating in the SCF scheme and will become a party to a standard form Master Guarantee Agreement ("MGA") with ECGD. Participating banks all have an established place of business in the UK, though they are not all domestic in origin. The MGA is an "umbrella document" which sets out the principal terms and conditions in which ECGD guarantees payment to the bank which makes finance available to the applicant.

If ECGD issues a certificate of approval, the bank will grant finance to the supplier by purchasing from the supplier at face value, usually without

---

28 The exception to this obligation is a variation agreed in writing which does not cause the total amount payable by the overseas purchaser in respect of the insured element to increase by more than 10%, does not extend any relevant period for performances of the contract by more than 12 months, does not change the nature of the goods or sevices under the contract, and does not alter the proportion of the value of goods and services under the contract which are of UK origin.

29 See, *e.g. Paul and Frank Ltd v Discount Bank (Overseas) Ltd* [1967] Ch. 348.

30 Replacing the "Comprehensive Extended Terms" and Associated Bank Guarantee Facilities.

31 A separate premium is payable is respect of the SCF facility and any ancillary EXIP.

32 Defined as "approved credit terms". Basically the purchaser must secure payment of the element of the price for which credit is given, by means of bills of exchange or promissory notes.

recourse,[33] bills of exchange or promissory notes drawn on the overseas purchaser or his bank as payment of part of the contract price.[34] Each bill or note presented to the bank must be indorsed in blank by the supplier, and accompanied by a warranty signed on behalf of the supplier by an authorised person, which is in standard form and basically confirms that the bill or note is given in payment for goods or services supplied under the relevant contract, that the relevant goods have been exported or the work done, that the overseas purchaser has no right of rejection, and that the supplier is not receiving finance from any other source. The contract may require other documents to be produced by the supplier to evidence the due performance by him of the contract. The bills or notes may also be required to be secured by an aval or independent guarantee or standby letter of credit given by another bank, generally the purchaser's own bank. The security must be of a kind which is freely transferable by assignment or otherwise to the UK financing bank.[35]

Both the supplier and the financing bank are required to accept ECGD's offer of support for finance, and must do so separately.[36] ECGD's offer will stipulate the maximum amount of finance to be granted by the bank (generally the total amount of the contract approved for finance, plus a 10 per cent tolerance). If the bills or promissory notes are dishonoured, the bank will have a right of recourse against ECGD under the MGA.[37] ECGD's offer will stipulate the maximum overall liability of ECGD in respect of any loss sustained by the bank.[38]

---

33 ECGD may require that the contract between the bank and the supplier will allow recourse to be taken to the supplier in limited circumstances: for example, if the underlying contract of supply has been terminated by the overseas purchaser because of the supplier's own default. See *ECGD v Universal Oil Products Co* [1983] 2 Lloyd's Rep. 152 for an illustration of how a recourse agreement operates in similar circumstances (though that was a case of a recourse agreement made directly between ECGD and the supplier). Any recourse obligation will be set out in the terms of the contract.

34 Typically the payment terms will provide for a deposit or down payment of between 5% and 10%, and a second tranche secured by irrevocable letter of credit, with the balance (generally up to 85%) payable by means of bills of exchange or promissory notes.

35 The financing bank is required to satisfy itself of the validity and enforceability of such security before it buys any negotiable instrument to which it relates. Failure to do so may absolve ECGD from liability to the bank if the additional security proves worthless.

36 The bank must sign a financing declaration and acceptance, in standard terms, addressed to ECGD, which states, *inter alia*, that the bank is not aware of any circumstances that might adversely affect the support to be given by ECGD.

37 Despite an increasing tendency to try to import obligations of utmost good faith, and in particular obligations of disclosure, into the contract between ECGD and the bank, that contract is still a contract of guarantee or indemnity rather than a contract of insurance: see *Credit Lyonnais Bank Nederland v ECGD* [1996] 1 Lloyd's Rep 200. The same comment applies to the independent SCF contract made directly between ECGD and the supplier, under which ECGD essentially promises to assume liability for the due performance of obligations owed by the purchaser to the bank in respect of the relevant negotiable instruments. This view is shared by the editors of Benjamin (*op. cit.*), see para.24–037.

38 The bank must independently agree that this it to be ECGD's maximum liability for losses sustained by the bank, unless ECGD otherwise agrees in writing: this is a term of the standard Bank's Financing Declaration and Acceptance.

As the bank is purchasing bills or notes, the risk of default is minimised, because in general terms the existence of a dispute by the purchaser about the performance of the supplier's contractual obligations (whether genuine or otherwise) will not prevent the bank, as a holder for value, from obtaining payment. The risk of the supplier's fraud or insolvency is still ultimately borne by ECGD, but the new scheme is far less vulnerable to these contingencies than one in which the bills or notes are drawn on the supplier, and timed to mature when the tranches are due to be paid by the overseas purchaser, or a scheme in which the bank merely makes an overdraft facility available to the supplier up to a given limit. As an optional extra, the supplier may also take out an ancillary EXIP to cover any additional losses which he may incur in connection with the contract financed under the SCF facility.

Performance bond risk insurance

15–010 The ECGD does not itself issue performance bonds, but it can assist an exporter to obtain such an instrument from a bank or other financial institution by providing counter-security to the issuer of the bond. ECGD will normally provide for a right of recourse against the exporter for any sums paid by it under its counter-guarantee, unless it is established that the call on the underlying bond was unjustified (because the exporter was not in default) or that any default was due to causes beyond his control. In addtion, any person who holds one of ECGD's main facilities, such as an SCF, has the option of asking ECGD to insure him under a Bond Insurance Policy against a percentage of the loss which he may incur as a result of claims being made on a performance bond which the supplier or his bank is required to give to the overseas purchaser in connection with the contract covered by the ECGD facility. He may be required to pay an additional premium for this cover. Under a Bond Insurance Policy, when certain of the political risks insured against under the SIP have occurred, or when ECGD gives notice to terminate the SCF facility resulting in the withdrawal of finance by the bank, the supplier is protected not only against the loss which he may suffer as a result of the buyer's failure to pay him, but also against the loss sustained by paying a call made on the performance bond.[39] In addition, the supplier may be insured against the risk of unwarranted calls against the bond by the purchaser:

(a) when there is no default or risk of default by the supplier; or

(b) when any failure by the supplier to perform the contract is solely attributable to a failure or refusal by the purchaser to perform the contract, or to repay any amount already called under the bond which

---

39 Essentially the same events which constitute numbers 6 to 11 of the main contract heads of loss, including such matters preventing due performance of the insured element of the contract as hostilities in the country of export, the operation of exchange control in that country, or the non-renewal or cancellation of an export licence.

a court or arbitral tribunal has ordered him to repay to the supplier within 60 days of the award or judgment.

ECGD may exclude certain types of bonds from this cover, and may impose special conditions on the grant of such insurance, depending on the nature of the risk and the underlying contract. Clause 34.1 of the standard policy provides that any claim under the bond risk cover must be made within one year of the date on which the insured supplier sustained the bond risk loss. An important additional condition precedent to ECGD's liability under this extended cover is that if the supplier is insolvent when the bond loss occurs, he must satisfy ECGD that there are adequate undertakings or security available to secure payment of all amounts which may be or become payable by him to ECGD.[40]

Other ECGD facilities

ECGD currently operates two schemes under which it gives support in the form of guarantees to financial institutions who make finance available to overseas buyers under high value export or construction contracts. The "buyer credit guarantee"[41] is available for contracts worth £5 million or more made between an identified UK exporter or supplier and an overseas customer. The buyer can negotiate the loan with the lender directly, and then seek either a "simple guarantee" in respect of the repayment of instalments alone, or more complex cover from ECGD, for which he will pay a premium based on the risks covered and the value of the contract. Normally ECGD will require the purchaser to pay at least 15 per cent of the contract price as a downpayment, so that its maximum exposure is 85 per cent. The scheme operates in a manner which is almost identical to the SCF scheme. ECGD will also issue lines of credit for smaller projects or contracts with foreign governments, government agencies, private industrial companies or financial institutions.[42] Since 1972 ECGD has made Overseas Investment Policies available to certain UK individuals and companies who wish to invest in developing countries or HIPCs ("heavily indebted poor countries"). More recently, it has introduced several new types of facility covering project finance and exchange control risk.[43] A detailed consideration of such facilities is outside the scope of this work.

15–011

Obtaining cover from ECGD

It is possible for a supplier (or a broker acting for him)[44] to approach ECGD for an informal indication of the likely premium and interest rates and terms of cover which might be made available in respect of a particular

15–012

---

40 Clause 28.1.2. In such circumstances care must be taken by both parties to ensure that any arrangements made to secure ECGD are not liable to be set aside in the liquidation or bankruptcy proceedings.
41 Described in more detail in Benjamin, *op. cit.* at paras 24–034–24–042.
42 See Benjamin, para.24–043.
43 See Benjamin, paras 24–044–24–050.
44 Only ECGD-approved brokers working in respect of EXIPs will be eligible for payment of brokerage by ECGD. Brokerage is not paid by ECGD in respect of SCF cover.

project. The inquiry may also be made by the prospective financing bank. The person making the inquiry may do so by completing a request for a costing indication form, which informs ECGD of the basic details of the contract, the identity of the overseas purchaser, the country of performance, the contract period, the terms of payment, and the nature of any security to be provided. Alternatively, he may use the form as a checklist and compose a fax or telex to ECGD which makes the request for an indication. Any indication will be given without commitment on the part of ECGD, except that the premium and interest rates will be committed for a particular period, generally up to six months. This may assist the supplier in his financial projections prior to making a tender for the contract or entering into a firm contractual commitment. The indication will generally also inform the applicant of any further information which ECGD would require if a formal proposal for cover is to be considered in the future.

It is generally a good idea for the prospective applicant to discuss the matter with the prospective financing bank prior to approaching ECGD, or even prior to making a tender or entering into detailed negotiations with the overseas purchaser. This is particularly important if there are elements of the contract which will have to be financed independently if they are not approved for ECGD support. The supplier need not approach a bank before making a firm application to ECGD. However, if he has not already discussed the matter with the bank, he is faced with the potentially difficult task of approaching a bank and persuading it to provide such finance strictly in conformity with the terms of ECGD's offer to him, after that offer has been made. He cannot accept that offer until he is able to identify to ECGD an acceptable bank which will provide the finance. Banks may be more amenable if they have been involved in a project from the very outset, than if they are faced with an inflexible *fait accompli*.

If the supplier wishes to make a formal application for an ECGD facility, he must complete a proposal form, and a short proposal form for any EXIP and bond risk cover required. Detailed guidance notes are available from ECGD to assist the supplier in filling in the forms.[45] If the application is considered favourably, ECGD will send a formal offer of support (and, if relevant, an offer of any ancillary EXIP) which the supplier and the bank must each accept by completing separate forms of declaration and acceptance, and these are returned to ECGD together with the appropriate premiums. On receipt of these documents, ECGD will send the bank a Certificate of Approval for support, which the bank must acknowledge. Any relevant EXIP will be sent to the supplier together with a copy of the Certificate of Approval. The bank and the supplier may then commence the operation of the facility.

---

45 Applications for cover should be sent initially to the SCF Central Unit of ECGD, Marketing and Business Development Division, 2 Exchange Tower, Harbour Exchange Square, London E14 9GS. In certain circumstances the applicant may be entitled to contact the ECGD underwriters directly to find out whether cover is available on a particular market. Contact numbers are available from the SCF Central Unit.

Carnets

ATA carnets are international customs documents issued by chambers of commerce in many major countries throughout the world[46] for the purpose of facilitating the temporary importation of goods into another country without the necessity of paying customs duties or taxes, or raising bonds or depositing amounts for duty, and without completing customs documentation, which may be complex and time-consuming. They may be used for a simple entry and exit into one country, or for numerous entries into and exits from different destinations during the period of validity of the carnet.[47] Carnets are therefore particularly useful for salesmen travelling with samples into various countries to exhibit at trade fairs, or for professionals, such as engineers, travelling to a site abroad and taking equipment with them. However, the possession of a carnet does not absolve the holder from observing the customs regulations of the countries operating the scheme, and therefore he may still require an export licence or import licence.

15–013

The ATA system is quite independent of, and should not be confused with, the TIR system under the Convention on the International Transport of Goods under cover of TIR Carnets, which was entered into in Geneva on November 14, 1975, and to which all EU Member States are party. That system regulates goods travelling between EU Member States and other countries in secure vehicles or containers under customs seal, where part of the transit is by road, and provides that duties and taxes at risk during the journey are covered by an internationally valid guarantee.[48]

Types of goods

The types of goods covered by the system fall into three broad categories:

15–014

(a) commercial samples and advertising film;

(b) goods for international exhibition; and

(c) professional equipment (which must be used solely by or under the personal supervision of the carnet holder or his nominated representative).

---

46 Basically the countries which are parties to the ATA Convention of December 6, 1961. These include the United Kingdom and other Member States of the European Union, Japan, Australia, New Zealand, the United States and Canada. At present an ATA carnet covers goods temporarily exported to 59 countries, but not goods moving within the Member States of the EU. Agreement has now been reached between the EU, Taiwan, and the International Chamber of Commerce to establish a system of carnets similar to that for ATA carnets which covers goods temporarily imported or exported between Taiwan and the EU. The free movement of goods within the EU States is now regulated by the EC Treaty, and the regulations and directives made thereunder, and is outside the scope of this work.

47 Which may not exceed one year.

48 See further Council Regulation EEC No.719/91 on the use in the Community of TIR Carnets and ATA Carnets as transit documents, and Commission Regulation EEC No.1593/91 [1991] OJ L148/11 which provided for the implementation of the Council Regulation.

The goods which are temporarily imported under the carnet system must not be sold to another person within the territory of temporary import. If they are, the holder of the carnet becomes liable to pay customs charges to the relevant customs authorities, unless those authorities sanctioned the arrangement by, for example, allowing the purchaser to re-export the goods without paying any duty. Carnets cannot be used for certain types of goods, including goods which are to be sold or hired out abroad for financial gain, perishable or consumable items (because they would not normally be re-exported), goods which are temporarily exported for processing or repair, goods used as a means of transport, goods which are unaccompanied or sent by post, and certain types of construction equipment. They cannot be used for foreign goods temporarily imported into the EU under a Customs Temporary Importation Concession, or for goods on which a Common Agricultural Policy refund will be claimed. Alternative arrangements can be found on the DTI website at www.tradepartners.gov.uk.

How the ATA carnet system operates

15–015 By the ATA Convention, each Convention State undertakes to accept, instead of its national customs documents, a carnet covering the temporary importation of the goods into its territory. The carnet is issued by the issuing chamber of commerce of another Convention State,[49] but is guaranteed by one of the national chambers of commerce of the State into which the goods are imported, designated with the agreement of the customs administration of that State as the national guaranteeing organisation. The national guaranteeing organisation is a chamber of commerce or group of chambers of commerce—there being one organisation of chambers of commerce per country adhering to the ATA Convention—which has been recognised by the customs authorities of its country to guarantee therein the import duties and taxes due to them on goods covered by foreign ATA carnets and has organised, together with the relevant chambers of commerce, a national guarantee system under the following conditions:

(1) The carnets are delivered under the IBCC[50] monogram, and under the seal of the national guaranteeing organisation.

(2) The carnets are numbered according to the procedure set up by the guaranteeing organisation or by the issuing chamber of commerce in order to make it possible to find the issuing chamber of commerce, the file for the operation and, if necessary, the year of issue by means of the number given.

---

49 Namely, a chamber of commerce which has been recognised as such by the customs authorities of its country by virtue of Art.1(e) of the ATA Convention or which, if not itself the national guaranteeing organisation, issues ATA carnets under the guarantee and authority of that organisation.
50 International Bureau of Chambers of Commerce.

(3) Guarantees are granted on the responsibility of the issuing chamber of commerce, under the terms of the agreements signed with or by the national guaranteeing organisation.

(4) The issuing chamber of commerce has undertaken:

(a) to refund immediately to the national guaranteeing organisation any sums the latter may have to pay either to the customs authorities of its country or to foreign guaranteeing organisations for carnets issued under their responsibility; and

(b) to claim repayment of the sums thus advanced from the holders of the carnets.

The English national guaranteeing organisation under the ATA Convention is the London Chamber of Commerce and Industry ("LCCI") (for further information see its website at www.londonchamber.co.uk.)

If the goods are not exported from the country of import within the time stipulated in the carnet, the guaranteeing organisation becomes liable to pay to the customs authorities of the country of import the customs duties and any other sums (*e.g.* penalties) payable in that event. This liability is joint and several with the liability of the persons from whom the duties and charges are primarily due.[51] The customs authorities of the country of import cannot claim payment from the guaranteeing association if they have unconditionally discharged a carnet, or if a year or more has elapsed since the expiry of the carnet.[52]

The issuing chamber of commerce must refund immediately to the national guaranteeing organisation any sums which the latter may have to pay, and it is that chamber of commerce which then becomes responsible for claiming repayment from the carnet user. The carnet user is liable to refund to the issuing chamber of commerce and/or the guaranteeing association all the sums paid by the latter, and all the costs it has incurred as a result of the failure to re-export the goods covered by the carnet. If the carnet user disputes the validity or extent of the customs charges, it is his responsibility to take this up with the customs authorities and is not a matter for the issuing or guaranteeing chambers of commerce.

By virtue of Art.8(3) of the Convention, the guaranteeing association may refuse to pay, on the grounds that the customs authorities of the country of import have waived re-exportation of the goods, but it may do so only if the relevant customs authorities have certified that position by endorsing the carnet. Accordingly, it is not open to the guaranteeing association to refuse to pay the customs charges demanded on the grounds that they have been wrongly levied or wrongly computed; equally, it is not open to the issuing chamber of commerce to refuse to reimburse the guaranteeing association on those grounds. It follows that it is not open to

---

51 Art.6 of the Convention.
52 Art.6(3) and (4). Arts 7 and 8 set out the time-limits for proving that the goods have been re-exported, and the form which such proof shall take.

the beneficiary of the carnet to refuse to reimburse the issuing or guaranteeing associations on those grounds either. The carnet user is ultimately at risk, whatever the reason for the failure to re-export the goods. Thus it is no excuse that the equipment, or even the carnet itself, has been lost or stolen.

The carnet system therefore operates in a manner very similar to a performance bond. The system would not operate properly if this were not the case; the *quid pro quo* for allowing temporary importers of goods to avoid the necessity of going through customs formalities is the certainty that if the goods are not re-exported, the relevant duties are going to be borne by the chamber of commerce which issued the carnet, which takes upon itself the risk of the user's insolvency. Thus it is the practice of the issuing chamber of commerce to require the applicant for the carnet to provide security or to obtain insurance cover for the chamber of commerce at his own expense, or both. The LCCI requires the holder of carnets which it issues to provide security for an amount equal to the highest rate of duty and taxes applicable to any country of destination. This may be done by means of a bank or insurance company guarantee, which must be given on the issuing chamber's official form.

Alternatively the LCCI has set up an "in house" Carnet Indemnity Scheme with Lloyds of London which simplifies the means by which security is provided by the carnet holder, for a premium which may be as little as £75. A proposal form can be downloaded from the LCCI website. If the amount of duty is not capable of ready assessment, the LCCI may fix the amount of the security.

Obtaining a carnet

15–016   A carnet may be issued in the UK in the name of an individual or a company which is permanently resident in the UK. However, it may be used by someone other than the carnet holder (*e.g.* an agent) provided that he has a letter of authority from the carnet holder in the appropriate form, which is set out on the LCCI website. The procedure for obtaining a carnet in the UK is relatively straightforward. The applicant must complete an official application form which identifies the persons who will use the carnet, the category of goods for which the carnet is required, the country of destination, any relevant countries of transit, and the number of visits being made. The forms must be typed; they can now be downloaded from the LCCI website.

Lodging an application form

15–017   The official application form also includes an undertaking by the applicant to re-export the goods within such period as may be stipulated by any customs authority (and in any event within the period of the carnet). If the goods are not re-exported within such period, the applicant undertakes to accept responsibility for any negotiations or proceedings with any customs authority and to pay all duties, taxes or charges which may result from his failure to re-export or his failure to observe customs regulations and requirements in the UK or abroad. He also agrees to pay the issuing chamber of commerce immediately on receipt of its demand in writing "all or any such sum or sums of money which it may have paid or be called upon to pay in respect of any professional or other fees, costs, liabilities, and expenses of any nature whatsoever incurred by the Chamber as a result of, or in connection with, the issue of the carnet".

When the applicant lodges the application form, he must also pay the relevant fee and lodge the appropriate security required by the LCCI. The security has to be valid for a minimum period of 31 months from the date of issue of the carnet.[53] Frequent users of the system may use an approved form of continuing guarantee with the consent of the relevant issuing chamber of commerce. Despite the requirement that the security should be valid for 31 months, the LCCI has a discretion to grant a "conditional discharge" and to return the security in appropriate cases. Thus, if the carnet is only used for a few weeks, and is returned to the LCCI and appears to be in order, a cash deposit might be returned to the carnet holder.

Listing the goods and completing the form

On receipt of the application form and security, the LCCI will issue a blank carnet form to the applicant, together with standard information sheets showing him how to fill it in. The applicant must type onto the form a general list which precisely itemises all the goods or equipment covered by the carnet (giving details such as serial numbers where appropriate), stating their weight or volume, their country of origin, and their individual values, as well as a total value. Goods of foreign origin may be included, but then the applicant must state in the list that UK customs duty has been paid on them or that they are in free circulation within the EU. The general list cannot be amended by anyone once the carnet has been issued. Any other alterations can only be made before the carnet is used. If there is a change in the goods or equipment, the holder of the carnet has to notify the Customs and Excise who will note this in a special certificate box inside the front cover of the carnet and certify this by placing an official stamp over the box.

15–018

When the list is completed, the form is returned to the LCCI, which will then allocate a number to the carnet. The number is stamped on the cover of the carnet and on each page. A back cover is attached and the carnet is given a validity date and signed on behalf of the LCCI. If these formalities are not completed, the carnet will be invalid. The LCCI retains a photocopy of the carnet and sends the completed carnet to the applicant. He must sign it on receipt. Before the goods are exported, the carnet holder must have them examined by the UK customs authorities either at the point of

---

53 This being the period for which the issuing chamber of commerce is at risk: 12 months for the validity of the carnet, 12 months for the period during which claims may be made by the guaranteeing organisation under the Convention, and an additional seven months for finalising such claims.

departure or at his own premises, and they will note the fact of the examination on the carnet cover. The carnet holder then presents the carnet to the relevant foreign customs authorities as and when required, and the various counterfoils will be stamped on exit and entry as necessary. The carnet must be returned to the LCCI intact after its use, and at the latest on its expiry date.

P&I club guarantees and bail bonds

Security for the release of maritime vessels

15–019 One of the most effective means of obtaining security for certain types of maritime claim, such as a claim for damage to cargo, is to arrest the ship on which it was carried, or a sister ship.[54] It is not uncommon for a vessel to be arrested in one jurisdiction even if substantive proceedings in respect of the claim have been commenced in another, or are required by contract or by legislation to be brought in another jurisdiction or arbitrated.[55] When a vessel is arrested in English territorial waters, the party making the application for arrest must state in the declaration filed with the Admiralty Court the amount of security sought, if known: CPR r.61.5(3)(b) and form ADM 5.

Bail bonds

15–020 The traditional means of securing the release of the vessel was the provision of a bail bond, under which one or more sureties covenant to pay the claimant such sum as may be awarded to him by the court or an arbitral tribunal, or agreed by way of settlement, if the defendant defaults.[56] Bail by bond is now a rarity.

The undertaking by the surety is given to the court, and consequently if a surety defaults, the court may enforce his obligations by making an order for execution against his property.[57] The claimant must ensure that the bail is sufficient for his purposes, because he is not entitled to re-arrest the vessel after judgment in order to make good any difference between the existing bail and the amount which he has been awarded.[58] The claimant is

---

54 See generally the International Convention relating to the Arrest of Seagoing Vessels (Brussels, 1952).

55 The shipowner may therefore have a right to claim damages for breach of contract or to seek a stay of the proceedings commenced by the arrest, but even if a stay is granted, the court retains a discretion to retain security or to require security to be given for the release of the vessel: see The Civil Jurisdiction and Judgments Act 1982, s.26, after which it became permissible to arrest a vessel as security for arbitration proceedings. *Cf.* the position if the court decides it would be appropriate to release the vessel from arrest altogether, when the security may also be released: see, *e.g. The "Vasso" (formerly "Andria")* [1984] Q.B. 477 (though the particular abuse of process in that case would no longer be an abuse since the 1982 Act came into force).

56 See generally CPR Pt 61, Admiralty Claims, at Section 2D of the *White Book* Vol. 2.

57 See the observations of Brandon J. in *The "Wladislaw Lokotiek"* [1978] 2 Lloyd's Rep. 520 at 533.

58 See *The "Point Breeze"* [1928] P. 135, *The "Alletta"* [1974] 1 Lloyd's Rep. 40. As to arrest or rearrest before judgment, see *The "Hero"* (1865) Br. & Lush. 447; *The "Flora"* (1866) 1 A. & E. 45.

generally entitled to security in the amount of the damages, interest and reasonable costs which he may be awarded on his best arguable case, though this must not exceed the value of the arrested ship or any undisputed limitation figure which the shipowner may claim under a relevant international maritime convention.[59] In the event of a dispute as to the appropriate amount of security, an application may be made to the court to determine what is a sufficient sum. In reaching its decision, the court will be guided by the principle that the power to exact security must not be used oppressively: see *The "Moscanthy"* [1971] 1 Lloyd's Rep. 37, especially at 44–47. The Court has the power to reduce the amount of any security given, under CPR 61.6 (*White Book*, Vol. 2, para.2D-40). It may stay the claim until that order is complied with. A surety under a bail bond does not assume all the rights and liabilities of a guarantor of the shipowner. The rights of the claimant against him are limited by the terms of the bail bond, so that if the bail is insufficient to meet the damages which he ultimately obtains, he cannot look to the surety for the difference: *"The Majfrid" (Owners)* (1944) 77 Ll. L. Rep. 127.

Other means of "sufficient security"

As an alternative to a bail bond, the shipowner may furnish sufficient security[60] for the release of the vessel by paying an appropriate sum of money into court, by providing a bank guarantee or bond guarantee,[61] or by procuring his Protection and Indemnity Insurers to furnish a club guarantee.[62] This is a letter of undertaking by the P&I club, as surety, to pay the amount of any judgment, arbitral award or settlement agreement in the event of default by the defendant.[63] The rules used to make specific provision in the Admiralty Practice Direction for a person who has filed an acknowledgment of service to make an application to the Admiralty Court **15–021**

---

59 *The "Charlotte"* [1920] P.78, now enshrined in the rules at CPR r.61.6(3).

60 See generally the notes to CPR Pt 61.8 at paras 2D-47 to 2D-48 of Vol. 2 of the *White Book*.

61 Otherwise known as "admiralty bonds". These are provided by insurance companies: for an illustration see *The "Zuhal K" and "Selin"* [1987] 1 Lloyd's Rep. 151. See also *Liberty Mutual Insurance Co (UK) Ltd v HSBC Bank Plc* [2002] EWCA Civ 691, May 16, 2002, discussed in Ch.14, above, at para.14–009, a case which illustrates how important it is to ensure that any security and any counter-security provided by the P&I Club, the owner, or a bank at their behest to the issuer of an admiralty bond, is identical in scope. In that case the Court of Appeal heard three conjoined appeals on separate issues of construction which arose when the P&I Club went into liquidation and disputes arose between the insurers who had issued bonds in favour of the bank which had provided security (or counter-security) for the release of the vessels from arrest. The result left the bank theoretically exposed to the possibility that it had incurred liabilities for which it was not insured.

62 A club may also provide a guarantee to prevent a vessel from being arrested, but it will only do so if a claim has arisen against the ship or shipowner. See the discussion at para.15–023 below.

63 If the ship is chartered, it is almost invariably the shipowner's club rather than the charterer's club which puts up the guarantee, see the discussion in para.15–023 below. Sometimes this may be required as a matter of law in the jurisdiction where the vessel is arrested. See, *e.g. The "Spirit of Independence"* [1999] 1 Lloyd's Rep. 43 (France).

for an order specifying the amount and form of security to be provided. Now the only guide to the procedure is to be found in the footnotes to CPR r.61.8 at para.2D 47, which suggest that the application should be made to the Admiralty Registrar by application notice in the claim asking for the release of the property on provision of security for a specific amount. The club guarantee is probably the most popular and common means of obtaining the release of an arrested vessel, and will generally be accepted by an English court as sufficient security, unless there is good reason to challenge the financial standing of the club or the wording of the guarantee is insufficient to afford reasonable protection to the arresting party. Unlike a bail bond, the undertaking in the club guarantee is given personally to the beneficiary, and is not an undertaking to the court. Thus the obligations of the club cannot usually be enforced by execution against its property unless and until a judgment or award has been obtained against it on the letter of guarantee.

Despite the fact that the guarantee is a private contract between the club, the defendant and the claimant, and in theory the doctrine of privity of contract would prevent any interference with its terms, in practice the court has held that it is empowered to order its cancellation, release or surrender in circumstances in which it would release a bail bond or order the payment out of money paid into court by way of security: see *The "Wladislaw Lokotiek"* [1978] 2 Lloyd's Rep. 520 and *The "Vasso" (formerly "Andria")* [1984] Q.B. 477. Thus if the court holds that the arrest was an abuse of the process of the court, it may release the P&I club from its undertaking.[64]

Cases analogous to arrest

15–022   A vessel can be made the subject of a freezing injunction, if the claimant can establish the necessary prerequisites for the exercise of this jurisdiction,[65] though this procedure is generally only advisable when the claim against the owner falls outside the specific heads of claim which would entitle the claimant to arrest the ship, or where an arrest would otherwise be impractical or an abuse of the process. In such event, the owner may procure a P&I club guarantee as an alternative to a bank guarantee or payment into court, as a means of securing the release of the injunction. Such a guarantee puts the claimant into a stronger position than the

---

64 As Sheen J. rightly pointed out in *The "Jalamatsya"* [1987] 2 Lloyd's Rep. 164, Robert Goff L.J.'s observations in *The "Vasso"* must be qualified by the subsequent enactment of s.26 of the Civil Jurisdiction and Judgments Act 1982, but that does not affect the general proposition that if the court declines jurisdiction on grounds of an abuse of the process it is likely to release any security. Compare the position in other jurisdictions, see, *e.g. Sea Melody Enterprises SA v Bulktrans (The "Merak S")* [2000] 1 Lloyd's Rep. 619, where a court in South Africa held that it was not empowered to reduce or vary the terms of a guarantee provided to release a vessel which had been arrested in its territorial waters, because the terms of the guarantee were a private contract between the arresting party and the owners.

65 See, *e.g. The "Rena K"* [1978] 1 Lloyd's Rep. 545. In cases where an arrest is possible, the claimant is far less vulnerable to claims by innocent third parties affected by the detention of the ship, such as the owners of cargo on board, if he chooses to arrest.

freezing injunction, since the latter affords him no protection in the event of the insolvency of the owner.

It remains to be seen whether a court which subsequently comes to the conclusion that the injunction should not have been granted (*e.g.* because of a material non-disclosure by the claimant) would be empowered to order the release of the club guarantee or any other security which replaced the injunction. It is possible that an equitable jurisdiction analogous to the one which apparently empowers the court to release club guarantees provided to secure the release of a vessel from arrest, might be invoked.[66] However, it would appear to require an extremely generous interpretation of the standard third party cross-undertakings (which refer to persons who suffer loss or damage or incur expense by reason of the freezing order or compliance with it, or who are otherwise affected by it), for the club to be able to claim directly under those cross-undertakings: similarly it is difficult to ascertain a basis on which the club would have *locus standi* to apply to the court to be released from its guarantee. Since the cross-undertaking in damages would almost certainly cover any liability of the defendant to reimburse the club, this problem may be more academic than practical, unless the defendant is insolvent or has not been required to give counter-security to the club.

A further situation analogous to an arrest, in which the shipowner's club may issue a guarantee to secure the release of the vessel, is where a public authority or similar governmental or quasi-governmental body (such as a port-authority or Customs and Excise) has detained the vessel for non-payment of duties or fines. Once again, however, the availability of such security will initially depend on whether liability for such fines is insured under the relevant club cover for that vessel.

Form of club guarantees

P&I clubs generally use a standard form of wording for their letters of **15–023** guarantee. The consideration will usually consist of a promise by the claimant to release the relevant vessel from arrest or to refrain from arresting that vessel or any other vessel in the same ownership, associated ownership, or management, as security for the relevant claim, and to refrain from commencing any fresh proceedings elsewhere in respect of his claim. The club will undertake to pay (usually on demand, rather than on proof of default by its member) the amount of any judgment or award in favour of the claimant, including interest and costs, up to a specified maximum sum. The recipient of the guarantee should ensure that the undertaking is

---

66 See *The "Wladislaw Lokotiek"* [1978] 2 Lloyd's Rep. 520 at 533. It should be noted, however, that this case, like *The "Putbus"* [1969] P. 136, was concerned with the statutory power under s.5 of the Merchant Shipping (Liability of Shipowners and Others) Act 1958 (see now the Merchant Shipping Act 1979, ss.17 *et seq.*, and Sch.4) to release a ship from arrest when satisfactory security has previously been given in the UK or elsewhere. Brandon J. equated release of the ship in this context with the release of any club guarantee provided in order to release it from arrest.

couched in sufficiently wide terms to oblige the club to pay the amount of any judgment or award of any competent court or tribunal, unless there is a clear and unambiguous submission by the defendant to the jurisdiction of the court of arrest. If the wording is restricted to a judgment of a specific court, the claimant could be exposed if that court subsequently declines jurisdiction or stays the proceedings.[67]

The situation often occurs in which the vessel arrested or threatened with arrest is chartered. In such a case, the cargo claimant may have claims against both owner and charterer, or the owner may have a claim against the charterer for an indemnity or contribution in respect of the cargo claim. If the owner and charterer are entered in the same P&I Club, problems are unlikely to arise. However when they are entered in different clubs it is important for the owners, or their club, to ensure that any corresponding security which is obtained from the charterers' club is couched in appropriate terms and, in particular, that there is an adequate mechanism for dispute resolution.

The case of *Newcastle Protection and Indemnity Association Ltd v Assurance Foreningen Gard Gjensidig* [1998] 2 Lloyd's Rep. 387 provides an illustration of the kind of problems which might arise in this situation. A cargo claim was made in respect of some fishmeal which had overheated and caught fire while it was being discharged. Damage was caused by the fire and the seawater which was used to extinguish it. The cargo receivers threatened to arrest the vessel and demanded security in excess of US$1 million from the owners and charterers. The owners' club, Newcastle, put up a guarantee on behalf of the owners. After further discussion it agreed with the charterers' club, Gard, that the guarantee would be extended to cover charterers' liability on condition that Gard provided counter-security. Gard provided a letter of guarantee agreeing to indemnify Newcastle in respect of all sums payable under the terms of its guarantee which were agreed or found "in accordance with the arbitration clause contained in the charter party" to be the direct and sole liability of the charterers. The letter required Newcastle to inform Gard immediately of any proposed terms of settlement of the cargo claim.

In due course the cargo claim was compromised, but Gard were not notified in advance, nor was there any apportionment of liability between owners and charterers in the settlement agreement. The letter of guarantee expressly provided that the lack of notice would not operate as a bar or defence to the claim on the letter of guarantee, but could be taken into account in assessing the reasonableness of any compromise. The charterers went into liquidation. Newcastle sought an indemnity from Gard under the guarantee alleging that the cause of the fire was a matter for which charterers were entirely to blame. Gard argued that as the charterers were in liquidation, arbitration proceedings could not be commenced by the owners against them to determine their liability under the charterparty.

---

67 This would not necessarily result in the release of the security—see above, n.64.

This meant that a necessary condition precedent to Gard's liability under the letter of guarantee had not been and could not be fulfilled. Colman J. held that as a matter of construction there was no such condition precedent. As the parties had agreed on a means of resolving questions which might arise and which had to be resolved in order to ascertain liability, but the means agreed on was incapable of being used despite the wishes of the parties to use it, in the absence of agreement as to the matters in issue they must be resolved by the Court. Consequently the court had to determine whether the charterers were liable and apportion liability under the letter of guarantee in respect of the settlement of the claims, which was found to be reasonable.

Under English procedural rules, the acknowledgment of service of particulars of claim does not in itself consititute a submission to the jurisdiction, and the defendant may apply within the period prescribed by CPR r.15.4 for filing a defence, under CPR r.11 to have the action stayed or struck out. Indeed if he intends to challenge the jurisdiction of the court he *must* file an acknowledgment of service under CPR r.10.1(3)(b). A club guarantee will frequently include an undertaking by the club that it will instruct solicitors to accept service of the writ on behalf of the shipowner, and file an acknowledgment of service.[68] It may also be drafted in such a way as to expressly preserve any right of the defendant shipowner to challenge the jurisdiction of the court of arrest, for example by stipulating that nothing in the guarantee shall constitute an agreement by or on behalf of the defendant that the English High Court shall have jurisdiction in respect of the claim or an agreement to refer the claim to arbitration in England, or a waiver of any procedural or other irregularity.[69]

If a guarantee is proffered in this form, the claimant should take care to ensure that his promise not to arrest or re-arrest the vessel or a sister ship, or to commence proceedings in another jurisdiction, is also made expressly contingent on the English High Court (or an English arbitral tribunal, as the case may be) having jurisdiction over his claim, or on a submission by the defendant to the jurisdiction of that court or tribunal. If he does not do so, he is in danger of finding that even if he has no choice but to litigate in a different jurisdiction, he would be in breach of the terms of the guarantee if he did so. Consequently, he could be deprived of his security altogether if a challenge to the jurisdiction proved successful (even if the court does not set aside the letter of guarantee). If this reservation is not acceptable to the P&I club, the claimant would probably have a reasonable prospect of

---

68 In *The "Berny"* [1977] 2 Lloyd's Rep. 533 it was held that this type of undertaking is given by the club as agent for the shipowner.

69 This is intended to get round the difficulties which became apparent in cases such as *The "Lloydiana"* [1983] 2 Lloyd's Rep. 313 and *The "Pia Vesta"* [1984] 1 Lloyd's Rep. 169, where the effect of the wording of the club guarantees was to prevent the defendant from challenging the jurisdiction (in the latter case it was even held to have varied an exclusive jurisdiction clause in the underlying contract of carriage). Compare these cases with *The "Berny"* (above), in which the undertaking to "enter an appearance", under the old procedure, was held to encompass entering a conditional appearance.

persuading the court that the terms of the guarantee were insufficient to constitute satisfactory security for the release of the vessel from arrest under CPR 61.8.

If the guarantee does not contain an express preservation of the right to challenge the validity of the proceedings it may be taken to have been waived. An example is the case of *Galaxy Energy International Ltd v Assuranceforeningen Skuld* ("*the Oakwell*") [1999] 1 Lloyd's Rep. 249. The vessel was chartered for a voyage from Odessa to Beirut with two parcels of fuel oil which were rejected by cargo receivers on grounds of contamination. An extension of the limitation period for cargo claims under the Hague Rules was negotiated and the owners' P&I Club issued a letter of undertaking which stated:

> "we undertake that we will, within 14 days of the receipt from you of a request to do so, instruct solicitors to accept on behalf of the shipowners service at your option of *in personam* or *in rem* proceedings brought by the cargo owners in the English High Court of Justice and file acknowledgment of service thereof."

Before any proceedings were commenced, the vessel was sold for scrap. Writs *in rem* and *in personam* were issued on behalf of the cargo interests but service was refused by the club on the grounds that the writ *in rem* was invalid (having been issued after the sale of the vessel). The judge held that the purpose of the undertakings was to ensure that cargo interests were not prejudiced by awaiting the outcome of settlement negotiations before issuing proceedings. The undertaking to accept service and acknowledge service was unqualified and if the owners and their club had tried to introduce a qualification to the effect that proceedings *in rem* could only be commenced if the vessel remained in the same ownership, no doubt cargo interests would have rejected it. He remarked that "sensible and experienced solicitors do not, as a matter of course, go out and issue writs in rem when they are already protected by a club undertaking". In the circumstances the cargo interests were entitled to take full advantage of the extension of time for service which they had negotiated.

The provision of a club guarantee is invariably a matter of discretion for the managers of the club, rather than a right to which the insured member is entitled.[70] However, the shipowner who seeks the issue of such a guarantee by his club must comply with any necessary prerequisites laid down in the relevant club rules. Thus he must usually ensure that his calls are fully paid up at the time when he seeks the provision of the security. The claim against the owner or the vessel must fall within the terms of the club cover and the owner's particular entry, although the decision to

---

70 Thus clubs do not run the risk of liability to their members for any loss or damage occasioned by a refusal to provide a guarantee, and it is unlikely that a liability would arise in respect of delay in providing such a guarantee, unless the club entered into a binding agreement to provide one within a specific time.

provide a guarantee will not amount to an admission by the club of its liability to indemnify the owner in respect of the substantive claim.[71] Likewise, the vessel which is arrested, or (if a sister ship is arrested) the vessel which is said to be responsible for the damage, must have been entered in the club at the time of the incident giving rise to the claim, because otherwise the security would be in respect of a claim for which the club had no liability to indemnify the member.

The club may require the owner to put up counter-security. Sometimes this is stipulated in the club rules, but it may be left to the discretion of the managers on a case by case basis. If other insurers are liable for a percentage of the risk (*e.g.* hull and machinery underwriters, in the case of collision claims) the club may require an undertaking from the other insurers that they will bear their respective percentages, before providing security for the entire claim. The club may also require the owner's undertaking to be backed by a bank guarantee.[72]

The cost of security or counter-security

If the litigation or the arbitration continues for any substantial period of time, as is often the case, the cost of providing and maintaining the security can accumulate into a substantial amount of money, which the owner of the vessel may well find it difficult to afford. The question of who should bear the cost of the security, whether initially or ultimately, is therefore one which it is important to address at the very outset, and something which those advising shipowners should be diligent to consider.

It may be argued with some force that since the security is in place for the benefit of the claimant, who has yet to prove his case, it is wrong to penalise the shipowner financially by making him pay for being allowed to use his own vessel. On the other hand, the claimant might contend that he is entitled by international convention to arrest a ship as security, no matter what adverse effect that arrest might have on other persons, and therefore if the owner wants to release his vessel, he should be the one who pays for the privilege.

It would appear from the general tenor of the approach of the court in *The "Moscanthy"* [1971] 1 Lloyd's Rep. 37 that the court would be empowered to determine any dispute between the parties as to which of them should bear the expense of providing the security; this could be an inherent part of the process of deciding what type of security is appropriate and sufficient. However, there appears to be no reported case in which this point has been considered. No doubt each dispute would turn on its own

15–024

---

71 If there is doubt whether the claim is included or excluded (*e.g.* if there is an allegation of fraud) the club may still issue the guarantee provided that the owner gives it an undertaking, backed by adequate counter-security, to reimburse the club if it transpires that the claim falls outside the terms of the cover. The club rules may also require him to pay the club's expenses or a fee for providing the security in such event.

72 This is often provided by a bank to which the vessel has been mortgaged, which may have the largest interest in the vessel in any event.

particular facts, because whereas it might be oppressive to require the shipowner to bear even the initial costs in certain circumstances, in others it might be entirely inappropriate to make the arresting party pay. For example, if the arrest is wrongful, the costs of maintaining the security might be recovered as part of the damages, as was envisaged in *Winter Maritime Ltd v Maritime Oil Trading Ltd* [2000] 2 Lloyd's Rep. 298.

It may be that a fair compromise in the majority of cases would be for the costs to be borne initially by the shipowner, but for the claimant to agree to reimburse him in full in the event that the claim is unsuccessful. In order to achieve this, however, there would have to be an agreement or an order to that effect at the time when the alternative security is put in place. In the absence of an agreement or order, there appears to be no way in which the shipowner could recover the costs from the claimant, if the arrest was lawful.

Indemnities for port agents

15–025   In certain jurisdictions, a ship's agent at the port of discharge may be held legally liable to the cargo receiver for claims against the vessel or her owners, if the vessel has sailed when the claim is brought. He may also be personally responsible for the payment of certain types of port dues and taxes. Consequently, if an agent is approached to act for a particular vessel, he may ask the shipowner to provide what is known as an "anticipatory guarantee" before the ship arrives; essentially a guarantee that all claims against the ship will be met. However, P&I clubs do not provide this type of guarantee. This is a matter of policy, because it is feared that the presence of security would encourage the arrest of vessels in cases where there is no genuine claim. Nevertheless, the port agent may be satisfied with a letter of indemnity from the shipowner which holds him harmless in the event of his being held liable to the cargo owners, which he may require to be supported by a bank guarantee. A club may be prepared to give this more limited form of indemnity on behalf of its member.

Indemnities given to or by cargo receivers

15–026   If the cargo is damaged before the vessel reaches its destination, the receiver may refuse to take delivery. This may cause considerable practical difficulties for the shipowner, particularly if the cargo is of a perishable nature. It may be impractical to wait for a court to determine whether the receiver is entitled to refuse delivery, and whether the carrier has the right to dispose of the cargo. If the cargo claim falls within the carrier's club cover, his P&I club may be prepared to give a letter of indemnity or guarantee to the receiver (or to the bill of lading holder) which essentially provides security for the cargo claim while at the same time preserving all the rights and defences open to the carrier under the contract of carriage. In practice, a receiver will usually be prepared to take delivery of the cargo on provision of such an indemnity or alternative acceptable security such as a bank guarantee.

It should be noted, however, that a shipowner who issues a clean bill of lading when the cargo has been damaged prior to shipment is likely to be guilty of fraud; his club cover will often exclude any liability arising as a result of such behaviour and his club may refuse to provide security to release his vessel from arrest or to persuade the receiver to take delivery. If the shipowner obtains a letter of indemnity from the person who persuaded him to load the unsound cargo without clausing the bills of lading, and that indemnity is subject to English law, he runs the risk that it will be unenforceable as a matter of public policy: see, *e.g. Brown Jenkinson & Co v Percy Dalton* [1957] 2 Q.B. 621.

Another difficult situation which may arise is where the shipowner is requested by the receiver, or the charterer, to deliver the cargo without production of the bills of lading. If he delivers the cargo to someone who has no right to it, he may be liable to the true owner of the goods, or to the bill of lading holder, in damages for conversion and breach of contract. The problem is most frequently encountered when the bills of lading have been indorsed to a bank which has advanced the purchase price to the seller of the goods and has not yet received reimbursement from the buyer. The buyer may be unable to repay the bank until he delivers the goods to his own sub-purchaser and receives payment; however, the documents of title will remain with the bank until he repays the advance.

The delivery of goods without production of the bills of lading is discouraged by P&I clubs in their literature, and the liability of the owner consequential on such delivery is often excluded from club cover. Indeed, it may justify a decision to refuse to provide a bail bond or club guarantee.[73] Nevertheless, in practice delivery of goods without production of the bills of lading does occur, and charterers giving orders to the master to do so have been held liable to indemnify the owners in respect of any consequential loss, damage or expense which they might incur.

Thus for example in *The "Sagona"* [1984] 1 Lloyd's Rep. 194, the vessel was arrested by the true owners of the cargo and a second mortgage had to be raised in order to procure its release. This took nearly two months. The charterers were held liable for the vessel's loss of earnings and for expenditure incurred by the owners on the grounds that the arrest was a direct result of compliance with their orders, albeit that the orders were unlawful and the master was not bound to obey them.[74] However, it is important to note that there was an express finding that there was nothing to excite the suspicions of the master, and that there were express orders given by the charterers to deliver the cargo to the particular receivers. Given the possible scope for argument about an implied indemnity, the owner is better protected if the receiver or charterer furnishes him with a suitable letter of indemnity (preferably backed by a bank guarantee or

---

73 See *The "Sagona"* [1984] 1 Lloyd's Rep. 194 *per* Staughton J. at 196.
74 Applying *Strathlorne Steamship Co Ltd v Andrew Weir & Co* (1934) 49 Ll. L. Rep. 306, upheld on appeal (1934) 50 Ll. L. Rep. 185.

other security).[75] Perhaps in recognition of this commercial reality, many P&I clubs are able to provide advice on the appropriate form of wording (and may even have standard forms of indemnity available for the use of their members).

---

75 Indeed in Scotland it has been held that refusal to deliver against an appropriate indemnity was so unreasonable that the owner could not claim demurrage for delay resulting from that refusal: *Carlberg v Weymss Co* [1915] S.C. 616. It is doubtful whether this would be followed in England, in the light of the finding in *The "Sagona"* that an order to deliver without production of the bill of lading is unlawful.

Chapter 16

Performance Bonds

The nature of performance bonds

Performance bonds (or performance guarantees or demand guarantees as **16–001** they are sometimes known) are essentially unconditional undertakings to pay a specified amount to a named beneficiary, usually on demand, and sometimes on the presentation of certain specified documents.[1] They range in type from an undertaking to pay the beneficiary on simple demand, or on demand coupled with a statement by the beneficiary that the person at whose request the bond was issued ("the account party") is in default (a "demand guarantee"), to an undertaking to pay only upon proof of default by the account party, such as the production of an arbitration award or judgment in favour of the beneficiary, or a signed admission of default by the account party. See, *e.g.* the provision for expert determination of damages in the bond used in *Odebrecht Oil & Gas Services v North Sea Production Co Ltd* (unreported) May 10, 1999, Dyson J. An intermediate position is achieved by a bond which requires production of a demand together with a certificate of default from a third party, such as an architect, engineer or surveyor.[2] A performance bond will usually be given by a bank, although it may be provided by some other financial institution such as an insurance company.[3]

The essential character of a performance bond is more akin to a promissory note than to a true guarantee.[4] It is an undertaking to pay a

---

1 The term "performance guarantee" or "performance bond" is sometimes used to denote a genuine contract of guarantee or indemnity. To make matters even more confusing, such guarantees or indemnities may be given in circumstances in which one might expect to find true performance bonds As the Singapore Court of Appeal noted in *American Home Assurance Co v Hong Lam Marine Pte Ltd* [1999] 3 S.L.R. 683, "the nature of the particular contract, whether it happens to be a guarantee or an indemnity, or a performance bond, and whether the normal incidents of a contract of that class have been modified, is ultimately a question of construction in each case, and is often very difficult to resolve".

2 For example, in *GUR Corporation v Trust Bank of Africa Ltd* (unreported) October 28, 1986, Leggatt J., the guarantee was payable on receipt of a claim accompanied by a certificate from the beneficiary approved and signed by a registered quantity surveyor, that such amount was payable by the account party. Examples of different types of performance bonds, divided into lower-risk texts and higher-risk texts, are to be found in Pierce, *Demand Guarantees in International Trade* (Sweet & Maxwell, 1993).

3 If the contract specifies that the beneficiary has the right to approve the person giving the bond, a term may be implied that such approval may not be unreasonably withheld; *Arbiter Investments v Wiltshier* (1987) 14 Con. L.R. 16 (note).

4 See *Edward Owen Engineering Ltd v Barclays Bank International Ltd* [1978] Q.B. 159 *per* Lord Denning M.R. at 170 and Geoffrey Lane L.J. at 175.

specified sum to the beneficiary in the event of a breach of contract, rather than a promise to see to it that the contract will be performed. Similarly, the obligations of the bank or other financial institution which issues the performance bond are much more analogous to obligations arising under a letter of credit than to those arising under a guarantee.[5] In practice these instruments are treated as substitutes for cash. Thus, the various equitable defences which are available to a surety are not available to the issuer of a performance bond, and as a general rule he will not be concerned with the rights or wrongs of any underlying dispute between the beneficiary and the account party, or with the factual accuracy or otherwise of any statement made to him by the beneficiary or the genuineness of any document presented to him in order to obtain payment. His obligation to pay in accordance with the terms of the agreement is entirely independent of the underlying contract between the account party and the beneficiary.[6]

It is well established that if the beneficiary seeks payment in accordance with the terms of the bond, the bank must pay, regardless of how unfair that might be to the account party. This is exemplified by the leading case of *Edward Owen Engineering Ltd v Barclays Bank International Ltd* [1978] Q.B. 159, in which the performance bond was payable "on first of our demand without any conditions or proof". The bond was called on by a buyer who had failed to provide a letter of credit, after the suppliers had accepted this as a repudiation of the contract. The Court of Appeal held that the bank had to honour the bond in accordance with its terms. Similarly, if the performance bond is expressed in terms that the bank will pay if the account party fails to do something, such as deliver goods to the beneficiary, the bank is obliged to pay regardless of any justification which might exist for the non-delivery.[7] As with letters of credit, once a demand has been made (or documents produced) in accordance with the requirements of the bond, the sole basis on which a bank may justify a refusal to pay (and, at least in theory, the account party may obtain an order restraining the bank from payment), is where the bank has notice of fraud at the time when the beneficiary calls on the bond, or where payment by the bank would in itself be fraudulent.[8]

It is important to note that a performance bond is a guarantee of due performance, and is not to be treated as a pre-estimate of the amount of damages to which the beneficiary may be entitled in respect of the alleged

---

5 See, *e.g. United City Merchants (Investments) Ltd v Royal Bank of Canada* [1983] 1 A.C. 168 *per* Lord Diplock at 184; *Edward Owen Engineering Ltd v Barclays Bank International Ltd* [1978] Q.B. 159 *per* Lord Denning M.R. at 169; *Howe-Richardson Scale Co Ltd v Polimex-Cekop* [1978] 1 Lloyd's Rep. 161 *per* Roskill L.J. at 165.

6 *Howe-Richardson Scale Co Ltd v Polimex-Cekop* [1978] 1 Lloyd's Rep. 161; *Edward Owen Engineering Ltd v Barclays Bank International Ltd* [1978] 1 Q.B. 159; *Attaleia Marine Co Ltd v Bimeh Iran ("The Zeus")* [1993] 2 Lloyd's Rep. 497; *Esal (Commodities) Ltd v Oriental Credit Ltd* [1985] 2 Lloyd's Rep. 546; *United Trading Corporation v Allied Arab Bank Ltd* [1985] 2 Lloyd's Rep. 554n; *Siporex Trade SA v Banque Indosuez* [1986] 2 Lloyd's Rep. 146. See also *Wood Hall Ltd v Pipeline Authority* (1979) 53 A.J.L.R. 487.

7 See, *e.g. Howe-Richardson Scale Co Ltd v Polimex Cekop* [1978] 1 Lloyd's Rep. 161.

8 See the discussion at paras 16–021 and following *et seq.* below.

breach of contract which gave rise to the right to call on the bank to make payment under it. The issuer will not be concerned with the rights and wrongs of disputes arising between the beneficiary and the account party under the underlying contract. It will pay what it is called upon to pay under the bond. However, if at some future stage the rights and obligations of those parties in respect of that contract are resolved, and it transpires either that there was no breach of contract at all, or that the relevant breach of contract occasioned loss and damage which was either greater or less than the amount paid under the bond, then in the absence of clear language in the bond to the contrary, it is implicit that there will be an accounting between the parties to the underlying contract. If the beneficiary has suffered no loss, or if he has been paid more than the loss which he sustained, he will be liable to repay the account party; if, on the other hand, his loss and damage is greater than the amount of the bond he will be entitled to recover the excess from the account party: see *Comdel Commodities Ltd v Siporex Trade SA* [1997] 1 Lloyd's Rep. 424 *per* Potter L.J. at 431, and *Cargill International SA v Bangladesh Sugar and Food Industries Corporation* [1998] 1 W.L.R. 461, and the discussion in paras 16–033– 16–035 below. On the other hand, the right to an adjustment may be displaced by clear wording in the contract: see the observations of Langley J. in *Seepong Engineering Construction Co Ltd v Formula One Administration Ltd* (unreported) February 25, 1999.

Performance bond or true guarantee?

The question whether a particular contract is a performance bond or a true **16–002** contract of suretyship conditioned on proof of actual breach or non-performance, is a matter of construction to be determined on a case by case basis.[9] There are certain factors which may be indicative of the nature of the instrument, but these are not necessarily decisive. For example, the fact that the document is issued by a bank or other financial institution, or by an insurer or professional bond issuer, and that it appears from its language to be conditioned on a demand will point towards it being a performance guarantee, particularly if the underlying contract is made between parties in different jurisdictions. Another indication that the contract is a performance bond is a stipulation that payment will be made on presentation of documents, such as a letter from the beneficiary stating that a default has occurred and giving particulars of the nature of the default. However, an instrument which appears on a literal interpretation to be conditioned on

---

9 This can be a particularly difficult exercise the context of bonds given to secure performance under construction projects, discussed in para.16–004 below. See, *e.g. Trade Indemnity Co v Workington Harbour and Dock Board* [1937] A.C. 1; *General Surety & Guarantee Co v Parker Ltd* (1977) 6 B.L.R. 16; *Wardens of the Commonalty and Mystery of Mercers of the City of London v New Hampshire Insurance Co* [1992] 2 Lloyd's Rep. 365; *Trafalgar House Construction (Regions) Ltd v General Surety and Guarantee Co Ltd* [1996] 1 A.C. 199, and *cf. Northwood Development Co v Aegon Insurance Co (UK) Ltd* [1994] 10 Const. L.J. 157.

actual default, rather than an assertion of default, may still be held to be a performance bond, as in *Esal (Commodities) Ltd v Oriental Credit Ltd* [1985] 2 Lloyd's Rep. 546. On the other hand, a document which contains an "unconditional pledge to pay to you upon your simple demand all amounts payable under the Agreement if not paid when the same becomes due" may be held to be a guarantee, as in *Marubeni Hong Kong and South China Ltd v The Mongolian Government* [2004] 2 Lloyd's Rep. 198. As other commentators have rightly pointed out,[10] and the Court of Appeal has accepted,[11] a demand guarantee can hardly avoid making some reference to the underlying contract for which it is security or the circumstances in which a legitimate demand can be made, namely a default by one of the contracting parties. Thus a reference of that kind will not in itself be decisive of the nature of the instrument.

Another factor which may point towards a document being a performance bond is the absence of a clause which excludes or limits the defences available to a surety, since such a clause would usually serve no commercial purpose in this context. However, the presence of such a clause in the contract will not preclude the court from coming to the conclusion that it is a performance bond. In *Gold Coast Ltd v Caja de Ahorras del Mediterraneo* [2002] 1 Lloyd's Rep. 617, the buyer under a shipbuilding contract was obliged to make stage payments to the builder, with a final payment on delivery of the vessel. The buyer's obligation to make each stage payment was conditional upon the simultaneous delivery of a "refund guarantee" from issuers acceptable to the buyer's bank, Lloyds, who had taken an assignment of the refund guarantees by way of security for their financing of the transaction. The defendant banks issued the refund guarantees, each of which provided that: *"in consideration of your payment of the instalment under the shipbuilding contract we do hereby irrevocably and unconditionally undertake . . . that we will pay you within five days of your written demand . . . amounts due to you under this guarantee"*. The guarantees also provided that the issuers would pay upon receipt of a certificate issued by Lloyds Bank stating the amount of the instalment paid to the builder, the date of such payment, that the buyer had become entitled to a refund pursuant to the Agreements and that the builder had not made such refund. However they also included a provision, in Clause 5, that *"any variation, amendment to or waiver given in respect of the Agreements will not limit, reduce or exonerate our liability under this Guarantee, always provided such variation, amendment or waiver will not increase our maximum liability assumed under this Guarantee"*. The buyer declared the builder in default and rescinded the contract on the ground of delayed delivery, by which time seven instalments had been paid. The builder disputed the buyer's right to declare default, and the dispute was referred to arbitration. Meanwhile, a demand was

---

10 *Paget's Law of Banking* (12th ed., Butterworths, 2002), para.34.4; Jack, Malek and Quest, *Documentary Credits* (3rd ed., Butterworths 2001), para.12.57.
11 *Gold Coast Ltd v Caja de Ahorros del Mediterraneo* [2002] 1 Lloyd's Rep. 617 at 621 col.1 (para.18).

made under the refund guarantees accompanied by a certificate from Lloyds Bank in a form which satisfied the requirements of the guarantees. There was evidence that Lloyds had taken legal advice prior to issuing that certificate. The Court of Appeal upheld the decision of Thomas J. that the refund guarantees were performance bonds, as they bore all the hallmarks of such an instrument, and that the inclusion of Clause 5 did not detract from that conclusion. They accepted the argument that there were possible reasons for including such a clause in an instrument which was intended to be autonomous, including the avoidance of any argument that variation of the shipbuilding contract by postponing a stage payment or remitting part of it in settlement of a cross-claim would imperil recovery under the refund guarantees. Tuckey L.J. said that it could have been inserted simply to ensure that the rule applicable to true guarantees did not apply to these instruments.[12]

The commercial role of performance bonds

Performance bonds (or similar instruments) have assumed an extremely important status in modern commerce.[13] They perform the role of an effective safeguard against non-performance, inadequate performance or delayed performance. The underlying commercial purpose of a performance bond is to provide a security which is to be readily, promptly and assuredly realisable when the prescribed event occurs.[14] It has been described by one commentator as a "risk redistributing device" which transfers the risk of default from the beneficiary to the account party.[15]   **16–003**

In theory, in the event that a claim is wrongly made, the account party should have a remedy against the beneficiary; and if that remedy is potentially difficult or impossible to pursue, or there is a real risk of a dishonest demand, then he should be able to reflect these factors by charging more for his goods or services. This theoretical ability to readjust the balance of the risk may not be easy to put into practice. However, despite the many drawbacks which are involved, the use of performance bonds is becoming increasingly prevalent in commerce. They are particularly common in the construction industry (where they have evolved as a replacement for the traditional forms of bonds which were in the nature of normal guarantees or indemnities and required proof of loss) and in the field of international sales contracts, especially those involving supplies to and from state-owned corporations or government departments.

---

12 At para.25, 622 col.2.
13 In the United States of America, standby letters of credit are used to fulfil the same function: see below, paras 16–031–16–032. They are less common in Europe. For a comparative survey see Ellinger, "Uses of Letters of Credit and Bank Guarantees in the Insurance Industry" (1978) 6 *International Business Lawyer* 604.
14 *Per* Hirst J. in *Siporex v Banque Indosuez* [1986] 2 Lloyd's Rep. 146 at 158.
15 Coleman (1990) L.M.C.L.Q. 223.

Construction projects

16–004　In the construction industry, both in England and abroad, cash-flow problems are common, particularly in a time of recession. The employer therefore runs the risk of a project worth millions of pounds being abandoned at a critical stage because the contractor or a subcontractor has suddenly become insolvent. The insolvency of a subcontractor may also leave the principal contractor in an extremely vulnerable position. He may face the prospect of having to find the money to complete the job himself, or to engage a new subcontractor, or of having to pay substantial damages to the employer, without having any effective means of recourse against the subcontractor, which may precipitate his own insolvency.

Many building contracts are commissioned by government (or local government) departments or bodies, after seeking bids for the tender from various contractors. Anyone awarding large contracts out of public funds will usually be particularly concerned to ensure that the successful bidder for the contract has sufficient technical and financial resources to undertake the project in accordance with its terms. Such employers are often equally concerned to ensure that moneys advanced on account will be used for the purposes of the project, and not as part of the contractor's general working capital.

Traditionally in the construction industry, these problems were met by the practice of requiring the contractor to provide a guarantee from a bank or, more often, an insurance company, to secure the performance of his obligations. These guarantees would normally take the form of a conditional bond or "surety bond", an extension of the concept of a fidelity bond. They are normally given under seal, in order to eliminate any problems in ascertaining what the consideration is for the promise by the person giving the bond.

Although there is no particular form which must be adopted, all such bonds will contain an undertaking that the contractor will perform a particular obligation, such as repay a deposit, or supply goods and materials to another contractor working on the same project, or simply do the work which he has contracted to carry out. It is also common for the bond to provide that the obligation of the issuer will cease either upon the performance by the contractor of his obligations, or the payment of damages for any breach, or alternatively that the promise of the issuer to pay is to become null and void in such an event. In the absence of a specific provision, the bond will not necessarily terminate when the works are completed, because it may extend to cover any loss occasioned by latent defects. Sometimes the bond states that the issuer has the option of paying a sum of money or completing the works himself.[16]

However, these types of traditional bond, which are often drafted in archaic language, do not always afford the employer the kind of protection he requires. In the absence of a specific provision to the contrary effect, he

---

16 See generally Keating, *Building Contracts* (Sweet & Maxwell, 7th ed., 2001), 10–40–10–47.

would normally have to prove the contractor's default and how much it has cost him, before he can recover under the bond.[17] Furthermore, depending on the nature of the contract the issuer may have all the rights and defences of a surety. This was held by the House of Lords to be the effect of the bond in *Trafalgar House Constructions (Regions) Ltd v General Surety and Guarantee Company Ltd* [1996] 1 A.C. 199. The plaintiffs were the main contractors on a project for the construction of a leisure complex for Maidstone Borough Council. They subcontracted certain groundworks to subcontractors named Chambers. The plaintiffs took a bond from Chambers and the defendants for an amount equal to 10 per cent of the subcontract value. The bond provided that Chambers and the defendants (who were described as "the Surety"):

> "are held and firmly bound unto [the contractor] in the sum of £101,285 for the payment of which sum the subcontractor and the surety bind themselves, their successors and assigns jointly and severally by these presents. . .
>
> if the subcontractor shall duly perform and observe all the terms provisions conditions and stipulations of the said subcontract . . . or if on default by the said subcontractor the surety shall satisfy and discharge the damages sustained by the main contractor thereby up to the amount of the above-written Bond then this obligation shall be null and void but otherwise shall be and remain in full force and effect but no alteration in terms of the said subcontract made by agreement between the main contractor and the subcontractor or in the extent or nature of the subcontract works to be constructed and completed thereunder and no allowance of time by the main contractor under the said subcontract nor any forbearance or forgiveness in or in respect of any matter or thing concerning the said subcontract on the part of the main contractor shall in any way release the surety from any liability under the above-written Bond."

Chambers went into receivership before the groundworks were completed, and the plaintiffs completed those works. A claim was made by the plaintiffs for summary judgment against the defendants for the full amount of the bond. The main question to be determined was whether the bond was a contract of guarantee, entitling the defendant to raise claims of set-off which could have been relied on by Chambers in defence to an action for damages for breach of contract, or whether it was a performance bond. The Court of Appeal (Sir Thomas Bingham M.R., Saville L.J. and Beldam L.J.) upheld the decision of Mr Recorder Knight Q.C. granting the plaintiffs summary judgment, on the grounds that the bond was not a

---

17 See, *e.g. Nene Housing Society v National Westminster Bank*(1980) 16 B.L.R. 22; *Guyana and Trinidad Mutual Fire Insurance Co Ltd v Plummer and Associates Ltd* (1992) 8 Const. L.J. 171; *Perar v General Surety and Guarantee Co Ltd* (1994) 66 B.L.R. 72 (discussed below).

contract of suretyship, but gave rise to an entirely independent obligation to pay on demand the damages sustained by the plaintiffs by reason of the failure of the subcontractors to carry out the subcontract. Although the bond was silent as to a demand, the Court held that a demand had to be implied in order to give effect to the correct interpretation of the contract, and any such demand had to be made in good faith. Saville L.J. said that the obligation under the bond was to pay, up to the amount of the bond, that which the main contractors asserted in good faith to be the amount of the damages. The decision was largely influenced by what the Court of Appeal perceived to be the underlying commercial nature of the bond, namely, to provide a security which was capable of prompt realisation in the event that extra costs were incurred by the main contractor as a result of the subcontractor's breach. Saville L.J. said that:

> "it is obvious that any significant default by the subcontractors is likely to put the main contractor in or at risk of breach of the main contract, or at least risk interruption of the cashflow under that contract, if remedial action is not taken immediately. It goes without saying that remedial action is likely to cost money. What the main contractor wants, therefore, is some assurance of immediate funds in this event."

The language of the bond was consistent with an immediate undertaking to pay, which would only be released on the occurrence of the specific events referred to in the second part of the clause, namely performance by the subcontractor of his obligations or payment by him of the damages.

The construction of the bond by the Court of Appeal as giving rise to an on-demand autonomous obligation proved to be extremely unpopular both with surety companies and building contractors who had to pay the "premiums" for such bonds to be issued. This was particularly because until then, courts had always treated bonds of this type as guarantees and, as a result, this is how they were regarded in the trade: see, *e.g. Calvert v London Dock Co* (1838) 2 Keen. 638; *Clydebank and District Water Trustees v Fidelity Deposit of Maryland* [1915] S.C. 362 at 372; *Trade Indemnity Co Ltd v Workington Harbour and Dock Board* [1937] A.C. 1 at 17; *City of Glasgow District Council v Excess Insurance Co Ltd* [1986] S.L.T. 585; *Tins Industrial Coal v Kono Insurance* (1987) 42 B.L.R. 110. More recently, but before the *Trafalgar House* case, a differently constituted Court of Appeal (Parker, Scott and Nolan L.JJ.) in the case of *The Wardens and Commonalty of the Mystery of Mercers of the City of London v New Hampshire Insurance Co* [1992] 2 Lloyd's Rep. 365, had been faced with the task of construing an "Advance Payment Bond" which was in equally archaic language, and which also included a joint and several liability. They held that it was not a performance bond but a guarantee.

The bond in question related to an advance payment of a sum in excess of £4 million made by Mercers to the contractors, RTL, under a building contract. The building contract provided for Mercers to give possession of the site to RTL in mid-May 1989, but allowed that period to be deferred until about the end of June 1989. In fact possession was not given until July 24. RTL went into receivership before completing the contract, which automatically terminated the contract. About 75 per cent of the advance payment remained unapplied and it was no longer capable of being applied for the purposes of the contract. As in the *Trafalgar House* case, the bond was entered into by RTL and the defendant insurers as joint obligors. It stated that it was "given to save the obligee (Mercers) harmless against any and all losses which may result from the failure of the Principal (RTL) to faithfully employ for the purpose of the said contract and liquidate in accordance with the terms and conditions of the said contract all or any portion of the advance payments so made". As in the *Trafalgar House* case, it contained a condition that the obligation under the bond would be void on the occurrence of a specific contingency: in this case "if the aforementioned advance ... is liquidated in accordance with the terms and conditions of the said contract and is faithfully employed for the purpose of the said contract".

The Court of Appeal deprecated the language (Parker L.J. described the bond as "a most unsatisfactory document" and Scott L.J. said that it "resists tidy categorization") but had no difficulty in construing it as a genuine contract of suretyship. They held that the plain purpose of the bond was to ensure that, in the event and to the extent that RTL did not earn under the contract the full amount of the advance payment, RTL and the defendants would be jointly and severally primarily liable to Mercers for the balance. This was not a guarantee of performance, but a guarantee of payment. Much the same reasoning could have been applied to the bond in the *Trafalgar House* case, but despite the obvious similarities between the two bonds, there was no discussion of the *Mercers* case by the Court of Appeal in *Trafalgar House*.

When the *Trafalgar House* case reached the House of Lords, Lord Jauncey, who gave the leading speech, was clearly strongly influenced by the fact that bonds of a similar form had existed for more than 150 years and had been treated by the parties thereto and by the courts as guarantees. There were indications in the bond itself that it was to be regarded as a guarantee (*e.g.* the definition of the giver of the bond as "the Surety" and the provision that the granting of time or variation of the underlying contract would not discharge him). He said that the second part of the bond, which provided the circumstances in which the bond was to be null and void, in no way detracted from the nature of the first part, which was a plain and simple guarantee of payment. It was not, as the Court of Appeal had construed it, a binding and immediate obligation to pay with provision for release on the happening of one or other of two specified events.

The practice of obtaining bonds containing the archaic wording which the Court of Appeal so deprecated in the *Mercers* case, in conjunction with modern standard form construction contracts, can give rise to enormous difficulties for the party trying to place reliance on them, regardless of whether they are construed as a guarantee, properly so-called. For example, in *Perar v General Surety and Guarantee Co Ltd* (1994) 66 B.L.R. 72, a bond, in the same archaic form as was used in *Trafalgar House*, was given to the employer as security for the obligations of the main contractor under the JCT standard form of building contract with contractor's design (1981 ed.). Clause 27.2 of that contract had the effect of automatically terminating the employment of the main contractor if he went into administrative receivership. When this occurred, and the works were still incomplete, the guarantor successfully persuaded the judge and the Court of Appeal that there had been no "default" (*i.e.* no breach of the main contractor's obligations) by reason of the receivership because the contractor was discharged from his obligations to complete the works. Consequently, the guarantor was not liable to make payment. Commercially this had the effect of depriving the employer of the financial protection he would have expected in those circumstances.

Perar was followed in the case of *Paddington Churches Housing Association v Technical and General Guarantee Co Ltd* [1999] B.L.R. 244, Judge Bowsher Q.C. In that case, the bond was in a slightly modified form which provided that either on default or on valid determination (*i.e.* termination) of the contractor's employment under Clause 27 of the contract, the guarantor would discharge the "net established and ascertained damages" sustained by the employee. The contractor became insolvent, and the employer terminated the contract and engaged someone else to complete the works.[18] His claim under Clause 27 was dismissed as being premature, because there had been no "default", and although there had been a valid termination under Clause 27, the damages had not yet been "ascertained and established" by the taking of a proper account.

Another potential area of concern for the unwary claimant relates to the time and content of any notice which must be given under the bond. In *Oval (717) Ltd v Aegon Insurance Company (UK) Ltd* (1997) 85 B.L.R. 97, the employer was defeated by his breach of a term requiring the issuer of the bond to be "notified by the employer in writing of any non-performance or non-observance on the part of the contractors . . . within one month after such non-performance or non-observance shall have come to the knowledge of the employer or his authorised representative(s) having supervision of the said contract".

In *Odebrecht Oil & Gas Services Ltd v North Sea Production Co Ltd* (unreported) May 10, 1999, Dyson J., the bond had a much more sophisticated system for notification and determination of the payee's liability. The bond guaranteed payment of any damages sustained by the employer as a result of the contractor's breach of contract. Clause 2(a) provided for notice to be given by the employer to the contractor and guarantor specifying the nature of the breach and his estimate of damages

---

18 In *Laing Management Ltd v Aegon Insurance Co (UK) Ltd* (1998) 88 B.L.R. 70, it was held that the employer who terminated the contract under the contractual mechanism for appointing administrative receivers over the assets and undertaking of the subcontractor was entitled to recover under the bond the additional cost of completing the works, in exactly the same way as if there had been acceptance of a repudiatory breach.

arising from it. If the breach or the amount of damages was not agreed, the matter would then be referred to an expert, who would have power to make a binding determination of quantum, subject to an express power to revise that figure at a later stage. Any payment made under the guarantee pursuant to the expert's determination would be provisional and subject to later adjustment. The works were not completed on time, and the employer gave notice under Clause 2(a) claiming certain heads of damages. The expert determined that the contractor had a cross-claim for payment for additional works, which exceeded the quantum of the damages claimed in respect of delay. He certified that the amount payable to the employer was nil. Nothing daunted, the employer sent a further letter purporting to make fresh claims under Clause 2(a), some of which overlapped with the heads of damage previously claimed. On a trial of preliminary issues, it was held that the second notice was sufficiently specific in its terms to satisfy the requirements of Clause 2(a), but that the employer could not give a fresh notice in respect of breaches which had already been ruled on by the expert.

The tendency of the courts to construe such bonds as guarantees has meant that it is becoming increasingly common for the employer to use performance bonds, properly so called, as a means of ensuring that either the contractor does the work which he has undertaken or, if he does not, there will be adequate compensation in the form of readily available cash from a reputable source. The contractor, who has to provide such bonds, will take similar bonds from his subcontractor. The money paid under the bonds can be used to enable the project to be completed, without the employer or principal contractor having to find money from his own resources. In many construction contracts, performance bonds are also used as a means of ensuring that the timetable for completing the project is adhered to, or that advance payments made to the contractor are repaid if he defaults in his obligations. Thus, for example, part of the price, known as retention money, which is to be retained under the contract until the work is certified as completed and all the maintenance obligations of the contractor are fulfilled, may be released in whole or in part to the contractor against a bond which secures its repayment to the employer should the contractor then fail to complete the work.

International sales

Similar considerations apply in international contracts for the sale of goods. **16–005** The buyer, who often buys the goods unseen, and yet is usually obliged to pay by means of a letter of credit, will use the bond as a safeguard against late delivery, non-delivery or delivery of goods which are not in accordance with the contractual specification, as well as protection against fraud. His right of recourse to a performance bond may be particularly important if he has sold the goods on back-to-back terms, or needs them to fulfil a particular project or contract which is subject to time limits. If the buyer is a government, or a state-owned entity, the supplier will almost invariably have had to bid for a tender, and, as with construction contracts, the government will be concerned to ensure that the supplier performs the contract in conformity with the tender. Consequently, performance bonds are almost invariably required in such contracts.

In its briefing note on the Uniform Rules for Demand Guarantees (ICC publication No.458, discussed in para.16–019 below) the ICC has identified the main uses of performance bonds in international commerce as follows:

1. **Tender or bid guarantee**—this is to safeguard the party inviting the tenders against the withdrawal of a tender after the tender closing date from or the non-signing of the resulting contract by the successful tenderer. It is also provided to safeguard against the successful tenderer signing the contract, but not providing the agreed performance guarantee.

2. **Performance guarantee**—A performance guarantee is to safeguard the importer against the consequences of non-performance of the contract by the exporter.

3. **Advance payment guarantee**—An advance payment guarantee is to safeguard the importer against giving an advance payment and the exporter subsequently failing to perform the contract.

4. **Retention guarantee**—A retention guarantee safeguards the importer against the early release of retention moneys (required as a form of warranty security), as opposed to stage payments, and the exporter failing to perform what remains of the guarantee.

5. **Warranty guarantee**—A warranty guarantee safeguards the importer against the non-performance of the warranty by the exporter.

The advantages of performance bonds

Comparative cost

16–006   Although it may be possible to insure against the contingencies which would trigger payment under the performance bond, insurance is often a more expensive option. The charges made by the bank issuing the performance bond may be comparatively small, reflecting the fact that the bank should not have to become involved in an investigation of the factual basis for any demand made against it, or in any litigation between the account holder and the beneficiary if the demand was allegedly unjustified. These lower charges may be favourably reflected in the price of the goods or services to be supplied under the underlying contract, although the account party may need to adjust the price in order to reflect the degree of risk of an unjustified or dishonest claim being made against the bond.[19] Of

---

19 See, *e.g.* the observations of Geoffrey Lane L.J. in *Edward Owen v Barclays Bank* [1978] 1 Lloyd's Rep. 166 at 174 and of Ackner L.J. in *United Trading v Allied Arab Bank* [1985] 2 Lloyd's Rep. 554 at 566.

course, his practical ability to reflect that risk in the price may be curtailed by other commercial considerations, especially if he is bidding for a tender against numerous competitors.

Obtaining immediate payment

An insurer may also take much longer to pay even a fairly straightforward **16–007** claim under the insurance contract than a bank will take to pay under a performance bond. In the case of the archaic forms used by the construction industry, insurers issuing bonds tend to be more enthusiastic about resisting payment than banks. This is possibly due to the fact that a bank will invariably require the account party to furnish back to back security for the full amount, whereas the premium demanded by the insurer could be substantially lower than the potential outlay to which he is exposed. The insurer under an insurance contract or who issues that type of bond also has more potential scope for resisting payment, as does a genuine surety, whereas, as the case law demonstrates, it is generally extremely difficult to resist or to prevent payment under normal performance bonds. This gives the beneficiary the advantage that he will obtain payment before any underlying disputes are determined, which naturally strengthens his bargaining position.

In *Bolivinter Oil SA v Chase Manhattan Bank NA* [1984] 1 W.L.R. 392 at 393, Sir John Donaldson M.R. observed of irrevocable letters of credit and performance bonds or guarantees:

> "The unique value of such a letter, bond or guarantee is that the beneficiary can be completely satisfied that whatever disputes may thereafter arise between him and the bank's customer in relation to the performance or indeed existence of the underlying contract, the bank is personally undertaking to pay him provided that the specified conditions are met. In requesting his bank to issue such a letter, bond or guarantee, the customer is seeking to take advantage of this unique characteristic."

Securing the performance of unenforceable obligations

Performance bonds may also be used to secure the performance of **16–008** obligations which may not otherwise be enforceable; for example, if there is an intention to enter into a binding contract but the contract has not been finalised. The most common examples of the use of performance bonds in this context are bid bonds, and bonds securing the performance of counter-trade obligations.

Bid or tender bonds

A building contractor or supplier of goods bidding for a tender may be **16–009** required to provide a bid bond. The bid bond will normally provide for payment of a particular sum if a contract is not entered into on the terms of the tender or such other terms as may be mutually agreed between the beneficiary and the successful bidder.[20] Such bonds are taken at the pre-tender stage to ensure that only genuine and serious bids are made and to ensure that a successful bidder for the tender does not subsequently change his mind and refuse to sign a contract on the terms of the tender.

It is also common for the tender to stipulate a condition precedent that performance guarantees for the underlying contract must be procured by the contractor; the bid bond will therefore usually provide for payment of a particular sum in the event that the contractor fails to perform that condition precedent.

Securing counter-trade obligations

16–010   A contract for the supply of a specific commodity (usually to a foreign government or state agency) may contain a "counter-trade" obligation, whereby the supplier agrees that in the future he will purchase a quantity of a different commodity from the other contracting party. The counter-trade obligation may not be enforceable: it may be a mere agreement to agree, or it may simply be too vague in its terms. One way in which the moral commitment of the original supplier to contract in the future may be enforced is by providing in the original contract that a performance bond in respect of the counter-trade shall be given by the original supplier's bank. If the bond is worded in sufficiently clear terms, the obligation to pay need not depend on the existence of an underlying binding contract—like a bid bond, it may operate if the original supplier subsequently refuses to, or fails to enter into a binding contract.[21]

Freeing of other assets

16–011   A potential advantage for the account party in procuring a performance bond is that it may be an attractive alternative to depositing, as security for his obligations, money which he may need as working capital. It was common practice, prior to the evolution of the bid bond, for the bidder to be required to deposit a substantial sum (often up to 10 per cent of the contract price) with his bid. This could cause considerable inconvenience, since that money could be tied up for a significant amount of time while all the bids were considered, and then there would be no certainty that his bid would be accepted. Whilst the bank which issues the performance bond will invariably require a counter-indemnity, and this may have to be secured in turn, the bank might be more flexible in its arrangements than the beneficiary, and in most cases the account party would not be required to tie up his working capital in order to obtain the performance bond.

---

20 However a "bid bond" on its true construction, may be a normal guarantee or less stringent indemnity than a demand guarantee, for example, if the sum which the issuer promises to pay is the difference between the amount of the tender and the price at which the beneficiary is able to arrange a contract with some other person. See further the discussion in McGuinness, *The Law of Guarantee* (*op. cit.*) at 12.04–12.08.
21 For an example of such an arrangement, see *State Trading Corporation of India v Golodetz* [1989] 2 Lloyd's Rep. 277.

Nevertheless the ICC has identified cash flow problems, particularly for smaller companies, as one of the main drawbacks to providing a performance bond.

The provision of performance bonds

The performance bond may be given directly by a bank to the beneficiary, **16–012** but more frequently it will be given by a bank in the beneficiary's own country against a counter-bond or guarantee or indemnity given to that bank by the supplier's or contractor's own bank. Indeed, there may be a chain of banks in different countries involved in a particular transaction. For example, where the account party's bank does not have a correspondent in the beneficiary's country, a third bank may act as an intermediary, and will give the bank issuing the performance bond an indemnity in return for an indemnity or counter-guarantee from the account party's bank: see, *e.g.* the arrangements in *Turkiye is Bankasi As v Bank of China* [1998] 1 Lloyd's Rep. 250. The terms of the contracts between the last bank and the beneficiary, between the first bank and the account party, and between the various banks in the chain, may differ considerably, and may be governed by different laws, and therefore it is always important to consider the rights and obligations of the parties to each contract in the chain separately. The indemnities which the banks in the chain give to each other are usually drafted in such a way as to ensure that there is reimbursement without argument about whether the bank claiming the reimbursement should have paid. However a requirement that a demand should be accompanied by a statement by the bank that it was obliged to pay will be enforced.[22]

One common distinction between performance bonds given by banks and those issued by surety companies is that the former will usually consist of an undertaking to pay money either in the event of breach of the relevant contract, or simply on demand (with or without the production of documents), whereas the latter will more often consist of an undertaking to pay on evidence of a loss caused by the contractor's failure.

As a condition of giving a performance bond, the bank or surety company will invariably require a counter-indemnity from the person whose performance it secures. The indemnity is likely to be couched in wider terms than the bond itself, requiring the account party to pay the bank whatever amount it actually pays under the bond, rather than requiring him to indemnify the bank in respect of such sums as it may be *obliged* to pay, because the latter form would enable the account party to question the basis of payment.[23] The bank may require the counter-indemnity to be secured, for example by the deposit of funds sufficient to cover the moneys advanced, by a personal guarantee, or by the execution of a fixed or floating charge. Thus if the bank does pay, the account party and any surety will

---

22 See, *e.g.* the approach adopted in *IE Contractors Ltd v Lloyds Bank Plc and Rafidain Bank* [1990] 2 Lloyd's Rep. 496.
23 See, *e.g.* the indemnity in the *Edward Owen* case [1978] Q.B. 159 at 167.

usually have to reimburse it. Depending on the wording of the counter-indemnity, he may even be obliged to pay the bank before there is any default. An extreme example of this is the case of *Technical & General Guarantee Co Ltd v Patterson* (unreported) September 11, 2003.

The claimant, T&G, had entered into a performance bond to guarantee the correct performance by a contractor, S, of its obligations under a construction contract, up to a maximum of 10 per cent of the contract price. In consideration of the bond the defendant, a director of S, had given a personal guarantee to T&G. S entered into an agreement with T&G under which it agreed to indemnify T&G in respect of the performance guarantee and also agreed to place T&G on demand in cleared funds sufficient to cover S's actual and contingent liabilities. S became insolvent and failed to complete the works. T&G served a demand on S for 10 per cent of the contract price and when S failed to pay under the counter indemnity, T&G started bankruptcy proceedings against the defendant under his personal guarantee. It was held that because the counter-indemnity obliged S to put T&G in funds at any time, whether or not a demand had been made under the performance bond, the demand by T&G on S gave rise to an immediate liquidated obligation to make that payment and consequently the guarantor had no defence to the bankruptcy proceedings.

The account party will therefore be concerned to ensure that the bank is only obliged to pay in fair cases. This is something which it may be difficult to achieve. His liability (or that of his bank) to reimburse the paying bank may arise even in circumstances in which the underlying performance bond is invalid, illegal or unenforceable: a recent example is to be found in the case of *Gulf Bank KSC v Mitsubishi Heavy Industries Ltd (No.2)* [1994] 2 Lloyd's Rep. 145, where the obligation of the bank under the relevant guarantee (an advance payment guarantee) was characterised by the court as an obligation to pay on demand with no questions asked. The customer's cross-indemnity was expressed to be "against any and all claims, demands, liabilities, costs losses damages and expenses which may be made of the Bank or which the Bank may incur or sustain under or in connection with the issue of the Guarantee". The case went to trial on the basis of an assumption that by the proper law of the guarantee, which was Kuwaiti law, in the events which had occurred it was to be taken as never having had any legal effect. It was held by Tuckey J. and the Court of Appeal that there was no legitimate distinction to be drawn in this context between a guarantee which had become legally invalid, and a guarantee which never had any legal validity in the first place, and that the customer was obliged to indemnify the bank.[24]

---

24 *Cf. Wahda Bank v Arab Bank Plc* [1993] 2 Bank. L.R. 233, where Phillips J. held on a trial of a preliminary issue that any payments under a performance bond relating to a contract of supply, the performance of which would have contravened UK regulations imposing sanctions on trade with Libya (SI 1992/975), would also contravene the UK regulations. The consequence of this was that the plaintiff bank's claim for reimbursement under counter-guarantees given by the defendant bank in respect of the relevant performance bonds was defeated by illegality.

An example of a case in which the issuer of the performance guarantee was obliged to pay even if the underlying transaction was non-existent, or a fraudulent device to extract money from unsuspecting banks, is *Standard Bank London Ltd v Canara Bank* (unreported) May 22, 2002. In that case, a claim was brought by Standard as trustee for a syndicate of lending banks to recover the sum of US$10 million under a performance guarantee issued by Canara in support of a contract for the sale of tin made between Canara's customer Drayva Chemicals Ltd ("Drayva") as seller and Solo Industries Ltd ("Solo") as buyer. As part of the complex financing arrangements, and as a condition precedent to the contract of sale, Solo had agreed to make substantial "pre-export advances" to Drayva, which would be repaid by setting off monthly tranches agains the price due in respect of the goods supplied under the contract. Those advances were financed by a syndicated loan. Canara issued a performance guarantee in the sum of US$10 million to Solo, ostensibly as security for the performance of Drayva's obligations under the contract, which Solo then assigned to Standard as security for its obligations in respect of the pre-export advances.

Canara alleged that the underlying contract between Drayva and Solo was a sham, that Canara had been induced by fraud to give the performance guarantee, and that it had justifiably rescinded it. Moore-Bick J. held that on the evidence, Canara had failed to prove that the underlying contract was a sham, but that even if it had proved that it was, it was still liable to pay Standard under the performance guarantee. The guarantee had contained a provision which said that the liability of Canara was not reduced, discharged or adversely affected by any actual or purported illegality of the purchase contract and thus it was impossible to imply a term into the performance guarantee that the purchase contract should be genuine. The guarantee was only one element in a complex transaction and the context in which it was given was important. The commercial purpose of taking the guarantee was not so much to secure the performance of obligations by Drayva, as to secure the pre-export advance which had been made by Solo and financed by Standard, without which the purchase contract would never have been made. It was plainly contemplated by all the parties that Standard, the lender to whom the guarantee was assigned, needed special protection. Moreover, on the true construction of the assignment, which provided that Canara agreed to pay "all amounts payable by us pursuant to or otherwise in relation to the assigned property", the rights under the demand guarantee had been assigned free of all cross-claims and equities (including any claim to avoid it on grounds of fraud). This was therefore an example of the kind of commercial arrangement contemplated by Waller L.J. in *Banco Santander v Bayfern* [2000] Lloyd's Rep. Bank 165, where by virtue of the relevant agreements, an assignee was given better protection against fraud than the original beneficiary. Canara was not entitled to rely on any matters arising out of the relationship between Canara, Solo and Drayva to avoid its liability.

The construction of performance bonds

16–013 The question of whether or not the bank is obliged to pay under the performance bond depends on whether, as a matter of construction, the beneficiary has made any necessary demand and produced any necessary documents in conformity with the requirements of the bond. If he does not produce the necessary documents within any time limit specified by the bond, he will be precluded from claiming under it.[25] Since each contract will depend on its own wording, previous case law is of little assistance in determining how this question should be answered in any given case.[26] However, the cases are indicative of the general approach which the courts will adopt.

The question whether or not there has been compliance is a matter for the bank (or issuer of the bond) alone to determine at the time when a demand is made. It is not open to the account party to seek an injunction to restrain the bank from paying on grounds of non-compliance. This was established in the case of *Ermis Skai Radio & Television v Banque Indosuez SA* (unreported, Commercial Court, Thomas J., February 26, 1997). The account party had obtained an *ex parte* injunction to restrain payment under a performance guarantee in response to a demand which had been made, and to restrain the making of any further demands before the guarantee expired. A positive case of fraud was not alleged, but rather an "absence of honest belief" by the beneficiary of entitlement to the sum demanded. It was also asserted that certain terms of the performance guarantee, which on one view could be characterised as conditions precedent to payment, had not been fulfilled. When the matter came back *inter partes* after the guarantee had expired, Thomas J. held that there was no basis for the implication of a term into the contract between the bank and the beneficiary that the latter should not make a demand for sums which it did not honestly believe were due.[27] He also held that a stranger to the contract, such as the account party, had no *locus standi* to restrain the bank from paying on the grounds of non-fulfilment of a term of the guarantee.

Ironically, having discharged the injunction, the judge then went on to hold that the bank had been justified in refusing to make payment in response to the demand, because the form of the demand did not in fact conform to the requirements of the guarantee. The preamble to the guarantee had recited that a representative of the beneficiary had told the bank that a contract, having certain characteristics, "would shortly be signed" between the beneficiary and the account party. There had been a slight delay in the issue of the performance bond, but no modification of

---

25 See, *e.g. Clydebank & District Water Trustees v Fidelity & Deposit Co of Maryland* [1916] S.C. (HL) 69.

26 For an analysis of the particular wordings used in several of the leading cases, see Jack, Malek and Quest, *op. cit.*, 12.52–12.56.

27 Compare *State Trading Corporation of India Ltd v ED & F Man (Sugar) Ltd* [1981] Com. L.R. 235.

the text, with the result that the underlying contract, to which reference had been made, had already been executed on the day before the performance guarantee was issued by the bank. It was held that although the contract which had been executed was undoubtedly the contract which was referred to in the bond, the demand was non-compliant because it made specific reference to the date of the contract, which pre-dated the guarantee. The effect of this was probably to render the bond commercially useless from its inception, since any demand would necessarily refer to the contract which pre-dated it. However, even if a demand could have been reformulated to get around this problem, the injunction had precluded any fresh demand from being made before the guarantee expired. It is questionable whether, in the circumstances, the learned judge's construction would have been upheld by the Court of Appeal had the matter gone further.

This case can be compared with recent developments in the law relating to letters of credit. In *Deutsche Ruckversicherung AG v Walbrook* [1995] 1 W.L.R. 1017, Phillips J. at first instance stated, consistently with Thomas J., that the Court would not imply a term into the contract between the applicant and beneficiary of a letter of credit a term that the latter would not draw down on the letter of credit unless payment under the underlying contract was in fact due. On the other hand if an express agreement had been made to that effect, there was no reason for the court not to give effect to it. In *Sirius International Insurance Ltd v FAI General Insurance Ltd* [2003] 1 W.L.R. 2214 the Court of Appeal held that the principle of autonomy did not preclude an injunction from being granted to restrain the beneficiary from drawing down under a letter of credit in circumstances in which he had expressly agreed not to do so unless certain conditions were fulfilled, and those conditions had not in fact been fulfilled. This potentially leaves it open to the person on whose instructions a performance guarantee was issued to seek injunctive relief against a beneficiary who threatens to make a demand on the guarantee when express conditions precedent to the demand have not been fulfilled. See further the discussion in para.16–025 below.

It is still open to debate whether the party making the demand will be required to comply strictly with the requirements set out in the contract, as is undoubtedly the case under a letter of credit. Different judges have expressed different views, and the answer may well depend on the language of the particular performance bond. In *Siporex Trade SA v Banque Indosuez* [1986] 2 Lloyd's Rep. 146 at 159, Hirst J. observed that there was a substantial difference between letters of credit and performance bonds, since in the former case exact compliance with documentary requirements is imperative but in the latter, precise wording may not be essential. In that particular case, however, the guarantee required a "declaration to the effect" that a certain event had occurred, and therefore it did not contemplate precision. Nevertheless this distinction was endorsed by Staughton L.J. in *IE Contractors Ltd v Lloyds Bank and Rafidain Bank* [1990] 2 Lloyd's Rep. 496 at 500, subject to the caveat that the degree of compliance required by each particular bond always depends on its true construction.[28] On the other hand, in the same case at first instance Leggatt J. said that "the demand must conform strictly to the terms of the bond in the same way that documents tendered under a letter of credit must conform strictly to the terms of the credit. In particular, it is important to determine whether the bond is on simple first demand, or on first demand in a specified, form, or on first demand supported by a specified document. Where courts seem to have deviated from these simple principles they may have only been responding to the wording of the particular bonds under consideration".[29]

There is much to commend the strict construction approach.[30] As Eveleigh L.J. pointed out in *Potton Homes Ltd v Coleman Contractors Ltd* (1984) 28 B.L.R. 19 at 29, "when a bank pays under a letter of credit on receipt of documents, the documents provide some security, namely title to the goods themselves. There is no such security in the case of the performance bond."[31] This additional disadvantage should justify the courts in taking an approach to performance bonds which is at least as protective of the rights of the issuer or the account party as the strict approach which undoubtedly applies to letters of credit. However, there are few signs that this argument has commended itself to the courts. The traditional view that commercial men are well able to look after themselves and that if a performance bond is requested, they can refuse, or take out insurance, or increase their price to take account of the risks inherent in giving such a bond, has tended to prevail. Thus if the language of the performance bond is unclear or ambiguous, the account party runs a risk that the bank may pay against an imprecise demand.

Proper law

16–014 In the absence of an express choice of law clause, (something which is still comparatively rarely found in such instruments) the proper law of a performance guarantee, as with a letter of credit, will usually be the law of the country where the bank is obliged to make payment to the beneficiary rather than, for example, the law of the country of the beneficiary or account party's own domicile or the law which governs the underlying contract. The place of payment will normally be the place where demand is made, see *Britten Norman Ltd v State Ownership Fund of Romania* [2000] Lloyd's Rep. Bank 315.[32] In *Bank of Baroda v Vysya Bank* [1994] 2 Lloyd's Rep. 87, a case concerning a letter of credit, Mance J. had to consider the

---

28 The approach of the Court of Appeal was approved and followed by the Supreme Court of Kuala Lumpur in *Esso Petroleum Malaysia Inc v Kago Petroleum Sdn Bhd* [1995] 1 M.L.J. 149 at 157.
29 [1989] 2 Lloyd's Rep. 205 at 207.
30 This view is supported by the editors of Jack, Malek and Quest, (*op. cit.*) at 12–66.
31 This note of caution was echoed by Parker L.J. in the subsequent case of *GKN Contractors v Lloyds Bank* (1985) 30 B.L.R. 48.
32 Part of the reasoning of the judge is cogently criticised by the authors of Brindle and Cox, *The Law of Bank Payments* (3rd ed., Sweet & Maxwell, 2004), 8–110, 8–111, but the basic principle he applied is correct.

effect of the Rome Convention on the Law Applicable to Contractual Obligations, which was incorporated into English law by the Contracts (Applicable Law) Act 1990, with effect from April 1, 1991. Article 4(2) raises a presumption that the contract is most closely connected with the country where the party who is to effect the performance which is characteristic of the contract (*i.e.* the bank or issuer of the guarantee) has his habitual residence or central administration, or, if the contract is entered into in the course of that party's trade or profession, the country in which the principal's place of business is situated. However that presumption is likely to be displaced where payment is to be made by the bank in another jurisdiction, and that is the view taken by Mance J. in the *Bank of Baroda* case. Since performance bonds are very similar to letters of credit, it is therefore likely that the law of the place of performance of the obligation to pay on demand will displace the place of residence or business of the issuing bank as the proper law of such transactions, on the basis that this is the system of law with which the transaction has its most close and real connection. However, where a counter-guarantee is given, it may be inferred that the parties intended it to be governed by the same law as governed the guarantee: *Wahda Bank v Arab Bank Plc* [1996] 1 Lloyd's Rep. 470.[33] This has the salutary effect of ensuring that the same system of law governs all the relevant contracts in the chain.

Article 27 of the ICC Uniform Rules for Demand Guarantees provides that "unless otherwise provided in the Guarantee or Counter-Guarantee, its governing law shall be that of the place of business of the Guarantor or Instructing Party (as the case may be) or, if the guarantor or Instructing Party has more than one place of business, that of the branch that issued the Guarantee or Counter-Guarantee". In *Wahda Bank v Arab Bank Plc* Staughton L.J. pointed out that such a solution would not be very attractive to bankers. It may be one reason why the Uniform Rules are not more widely adopted. The choice of the proper law proved important when that case came to trial before Timothy Walker J. [1998] C.L.C. 689. The proper law of the performance bonds was Libyan law, and the courts in Libya gave judgment for the claimant on two out of the four instruments (it accepted that the claims on the others were fraudulent). The defendant bank (which had given counter-guarantees) unsuccessfully argued that it was incumbent on the paying bank to raise certain arguments which it had raised as grounds for non-payment. The court held that there was no such obligation under Libyan law, and the defendant was liable to reimburse the claimant bank in the absence of proof of fraud.

Liability without proof of breach

In *IE Contractors v Lloyds Bank Plc and Rafidain Bank* [1990] 2 Lloyd's Rep. 496, Staughton L.J. (with whom Purchas L.J. agreed) said that there is a presumption in favour of the construction which holds a performance

16–015

---

[33] Distinguishing *Attock Cement Company v Romanian Bank for Foreign Trade* [1989] 1 W.L.R. 1147. See also *Turkiye Is Bankas AS v Bank of China* [1998] 1 Lloyd's Rep. 250.

bond to be conditioned upon documents rather than facts.[34] In other words, in cases of ambiguity, a construction which would require the bank to investigate whether a state of affairs asserted by the beneficiary genuinely exists will not be favoured. However, that presumption would not be irrebuttable if the meaning was plain. Accordingly, it is possible to draft a performance bond which requires proof by the beneficiary of a breach by the account party, though such a bond would be unlikely to be as attractive or acceptable to a beneficiary as a demand bond.[35]

Demand

16–016   In the same case, Staughton L.J. stated that he would hesitate long before construing a performance bond as being payable on oral demand by the beneficiary.[36] It may be that the commercial context in which such instruments are given would require a general presumption that the word "demand" be construed as "written demand" unless oral demands are specifically catered for.

The question whether a demand has been made in accordance with the provisions of the bond will depend on its construction. In *Frans Maas (UK) Ltd v Habib Bank AG Zurich* [2001] Lloyd's Rep. Bank 14, a demand was held to be invalid because it failed to assert, as the guarantee required, that there had been a failure to **pay**, but stated instead that there had been "a failure to meet contractual obligations". This mattered, because some of the money claimed was in respect of sums which were as yet unascertained, and thus any claim that there had been a failure to pay that amount would have been untruthful. It was held that under a demand guarantee, a bank was not obliged to accept without investigation a demand which was ambiguous or potentially misleading, as this one was.

Unless the performance bond otherwise provides, or its period of validity has expired, there is nothing to prevent a party from making a fresh demand if the first demand is rejected as non-conforming.

In *Gold Coast Ltd v Caja de Ahorras del Mediterraneo* [2002] 1 Lloyd's Rep. 617, several demands were made before the one which was accom-

---

34 Staughton L.J. relied upon *Esal (Commodities) Ltd v Oriental Credit Ltd* [1985] 2 Lloyd's Rep. 546.

35 For example, the bond might be made payable on production of an arbitral award or judgment of a court in which it is held that the account party was in breach, or on production of a written admission by the account party that he was in breach. Article 9 of the original ICC Uniform Rules for Contract Guarantees, (1978) ICC Publication No.325, introduced a requirement that an award or judgment or written approval by the account party of the claim and the amount to be paid should be provided if the guarantee either does not specify the documentation to be produced or specifies only a statement of claim by the beneficiary. However these rules only apply if expressly incorporated by the contracting parties, and to date have not been widely adopted because of the view that they are too protective of the account party. The ICC subsequently introduced the Uniform Rules for Demand Guarantees (1992) ICC Publication No.458, discussed at para.16–019 below, which substitutes a written statement by the beneficiary of the breach for any actual proof.

36 *ibid.*, at 499.

panied by the certificate from Lloyds bank which was eventually held to be enforceable.

Stating the basis of the claim

The question whether as a general rule of construction, a "demand"   **16–017**
performance bond requires the demand to be accompanied by a statement by the beneficiary of the basis on which the demand is made, (for example, asserting a breach of contract), has also been the subject of judicial observation. In *Esal (Commodities) Ltd v Oriental Credit Ltd* [1985] 2 Lloyd's Rep. 546, Ackner L.J. (with whom Glidewell L.J. agreed) expressed the opinion that a guarantee which provided that "we undertake to pay the said amount on your written demand in the event that the supplier fails to execute the contract in perfect performance" was not a guarantee payable on simple demand, and that the beneficiary should also allege a breach by the supplier. He described this result as "salutary", in that such a requirement may prevent some of the abuses of the performance bond procedure that undoubtedly occur.[37] However, Neill L.J. expressed reservations about this approach, and preferred to leave the matter open, saying that he would be reluctant to introduce into this field any rule which provided scope for an argument that the qualifying event had not been sufficiently identified.[38]

The matter was considered again by Leggatt J. and the Court of Appeal in *IE Contractors v Lloyds Bank Plc and Rafidain Bank*[39] Although a different result was reached on the construction of two of the three bonds involved in that particular case, the approach of all the judges in that case to this particular issue was very similar. Leggatt J. said that there was no reason why a beneficiary should accept a term on the basis that its observance by him would be "salutary", and that the question of whether the demand had to specify a breach depended on the construction of the contract. The court should adopt a twofold approach; first, it must construe the bond to see what the beneficiary has to do for the purpose of making a valid demand under it, and secondly, it must construe the call and any associated document in order to see whether the beneficiary has complied with those obligations.

The Court of Appeal agreed with this approach. However, while agreeing with Leggatt J. that a particular construction cannot be adopted simply because the result is salutary, Staughton L.J. echoed the observations of Ackner L.J. in the *Esal (Commodities)* case by saying that a construction requiring the demand to assert the breach of contract was "a construction which one would wish to adopt, since it requires the beneficiary to state in plain terms that which he must, if honest, be prepared to assert—and may

---

37 *ibid.*, at 550.
38 *ibid.*, at 554.
39 [1989] 2 Lloyd's Rep. 205: [1990] 2 Lloyd's Rep. 496. See also *Belleli SpA v AIG Europe (UK) Ltd* (unreported) Commercial Court, July 4, 1996, Rix J.

place him in peril of a charge of obtaining money by deception if it is untrue to his knowledge".

It would appear, therefore, that whilst there is no general rule of construction to the effect that the beneficiary must assert a breach, the court may be inclined to construe a demand guarantee in that way even if there is no express requirement. However, the "salutary nature" of that result is open to question; it is difficult to see what additional protection it really affords the account party against dishonesty. The demand itself would generally carry with it the implicit representation that there had been a breach of the underlying contract, and the psychological burden on a false claimant is unlikely to be significantly increased by making him tell a lie expressly.

However, the idea that the additional psychological pressure caused by requiring an express statement of the breach to accompany the demand may help to protect against some of the more blatant abuses of the banking system in this context has obviously commended itself to the ICC. Article 20(a) of the Uniform Rules for Demand Guarantees, ICC Publication No.458[40] contains a provision requiring the demand to be accompanied by a written statement

> "i that the Principal is in breach of his obligation(s) under the underlying contract(s) or, in the case of a tender guarantee, the tender conditions, and
>
> ii. the respect in which the Principal is in breach."

However, this provision may be expressly excluded by the terms of the guarantee or counter-guarantee, and therefore the key provision in the rules is effectively optional.

It is quite common for performance guarantees to contain provisions of this nature, whether or not the ICC Uniform Rules for Demand guarantees are expressly incorporated. One interesting issue which has yet to be resolved is whether a demand can be made under such a guarantee if the breach in question has been cured, or if there has been a settlement between the parties to the underlying contract. This issue arose in the recent case of *Manx Electricity Authority v JP Morgan Chase Bank* [2003] EWCA Civ 1324, October 3, 2003, in which the Court of Appeal reversed the decision of Tomlinson J. to strike out part of the claim made against the defendant bank under a performance guarantee in respect of a second (precautionary) demand.

The performance guarantee in that case was issued in support of a contract between the claimant, MEA, and Nepco Europe Ltd ("Nepco"), part of the Enron group, under which Nepco was to design and construct a generating station in the Isle of Man. It provided that the bank would pay the amount specified upon written demand by MEA stating (a) that Nepco,

---

40 Discussed in para.16–019 below.

as the contractor and named principal, is in breach of its obligation or obligations under the contract and (b) the respect in which the principal is in breach. The demand also had to be accompanied by a certified copy of a written notice given by MEA to Nepco under the contract specifying the breach and notifying it of MEA's intention to make demand on the bank under the bond. When Enron collapsed in late 2001, Nepco repudiated the contract with MEA and vacated the construction site on December 1, 2001. On December 14, 2001, MEA made its first demand under the guarantee. A few days later, MEA and Nepco's administrators entered into a settlement agreement. That agreement released and discharged Nepco from any claims but expressly provided that this was without prejudice to MEA's rights under the bond, and "shall in no circumstances be deemed to constitute a waiver of Nepco's breaches as referred to in the notifications sent by MEA to Nepco". The bank challenged the validity of the first demand on a number of technical grounds relating to its form. In October 2002, MEA made a second demand which stated, in conformity with the language of the guarantee, that Nepco "*is in breach* of its obligations under the contract." The demand relied upon the breaches specified in the first demand. The bank took the objection that as at October 2002, when that demand was served, Nepco was no longer in breach of any obligations under the contract.

Tomlinson J. acceded to the bank's application for summary judgment on the basis that Nepco's breach in December 2001 had been an anticipatory breach, and that when the settlement agreement was made, that breach could no longer be said to exist, since no further performance was required. In the Court of Appeal it appears to have been realistically accepted by the bank that this part of his reasoning could not be sustained, and the Court of Appeal agreed. Instead, the bank argued that even if the breaches by Nepco had been actual rather than anticipatory, the guarantee required the breach which formed the basis of the demand to be actionable at the time of the demand. It was submitted that a performance guarantee cannot bite unless the principal can continue to perform, at any rate in the sense that he can continue to perform his secondary obligation to pay damages. The settlement agreement released and discharged Nepco from all further liability and thus the breaches complained of were no longer actionable at the time of the second demand. Rix L.J. accepted in para.40 that the competing arguments on the issue whether the guarantee does or does not apply to accrued, existing but non-actionable breaches were capable of being well balanced. However, he was less impressed by the bank's argument that the guarantee contemplated the continuing performance by the principal of his primary obligations under the contract, or his secondary obligation to pay damages for breach. He said "I would have thought that the parties to a performance guarantee contemplate that it will continue to provide security to its beneficiary in exactly those situations where the principal is in substance able to perform neither his primary nor his secondary obligations." However he preferred not to express a final view on the subject because the competing arguments would have to be dealt with at trial.

Implied terms

16–018 The nature of performance guarantees is such that it is very difficult to persuade a court to imply terms into them. In *Cauxell Ltd v Lloyds Bank Plc, The Times*, December 26, 1995, Bank Melli provided a demand guarantee required by the Iranian Meat Corporation as a condition for signing a contract with the claimant for the supply of meat. A counter-guarantee was provided by Lloyds Bank which stipulated that Lloyds' liability would commence on receipt by Bank Melli of a confirmation from Lloyds that the underlying contract had been signed and the associated letter of credit was satisfactory to its principals. That confirmation was never forthcoming and consequently the counter-guarantee never became operative. Bank Melli argued that there was an implied term that Lloyds should take reasonable steps to procure the confirmation. Cresswell J. rejected this argument. He said that the court would rarely imply terms into first demand guarantees, emphasising that the need for certainty in such instruments is particularly important.

The ICC Uniform Rules for Demand Guarantees (ICC Publication No.458)

16–019 These rules, (known as the "URDG"), which were published in April 1992,[41] aim to strike an even balance between the interests of the beneficiary and the party for whose account the performance bond is opened, and to curb abuse in the unfair calling of performance bonds. They also seek to achieve certainty and clarity, not entirely successfully. The URDG were introduced in an attempt to reflect international practice in the use of demand guarantees more closely than their predecessors, the 1978 Uniform Rules for Contract Guarantees.[42] The earlier rules were unpopular because, insofar as they required proof of breach by production of an award or judgment, they were widely regarded as being too favourable to the account party. However the current rules are still a long way from commanding the same kind of international acceptance as the Uniform Customs and Practice for Documentary Credits.[43] Despite strong encouragement from the ICC, and the adoption of the URDG by the International Federation of Construction Engineers in February 1999, SITPRO's report on the Use of Demand Guarantees in the UK (July 2003) found that very few demand guarantees are in fact issued subject to URDG. It may be that the fact that parties can opt out of Art.20 has something to do with this, as the requirement of a written statement that

---

41 The full text of the Rules appears in an appendix to Jack, Malek and Quest (*op. cit.*). The ICC has also published a Guide to the Rules by Professor Roy Goode, ICC Publication No.510.

42 1978, ICC Publication No.325.

43 (1993 Revision), ICC Publication No.500 ("the UCP 500"). See also the supplement to UCP known as eUCP, which provides an additional set of rules where the documents which are the subject of the credit are to be presented electronically.

there has been a breach and particulars of the breach was supposed to be the main protection afforded by the URDG to those who are required to procure such guarantees. The World Bank has now given further impetus to the international acceptance of the URDG by incorporating reference to them in their standard forms of guarantee.

The URDG will only apply when they are expressly incorporated into the Performance Bond. Article 2(b) reflects the legal principle that the person who issues the guarantee (called "the Guarantor") is in no way concerned with or bound by the underlying contract, and that his duty is to pay the sum or sums specified in the guarantee on presentation of a written demand for payment and any other documents specified in the guarantee which appear on their face to be in accordance with its terms. By Art.2(d) the expression "written" encompasses an authenticated teletransmission or tested electronic data interchange message equivalent thereto.

Article 2(c) is more controversial. It defines "counter guarantee" as any guarantee, bond or other payment undertaking of the "Instructing Party" (that is a bank or other body or person acting on the instructions of the principal) given in writing for the payment of money to the Guarantor on presentation in conformity with the terms of the undertaking of a written demand for payment and other documents specified in the Counter-Guarantee conforming with its terms. It goes on to state that "Counter-Guarantees are by their nature separate transactions from the Guarantees to which they relate . . . and Instructing Parties are in no way concerned with or bound by such Guarantees." In *Wahda Bank v Arab Bank* [1996] 1 Lloyds' Rep. 470, Staughton L.J. (with whom Henry and Pill L.JJ. agreed) said at 474 col.1: "I would not agree with that at all, I must say. The party who gives the performance bond is vitally concerned, I would say, in the counter guarantee".

Article 3 requires instructions for the issue of guarantees (or amendments to them) to be clear and precise and to avoid excessive detail. The guarantee should identify the principal, the beneficiary, the guarantor and the underlying transaction requiring the issue of the guarantee. It should stipulate the maximum amount payable and the currency of payment, the terms for demanding payment and any provision for reduction of the guarantee amount (catered for by Art.8). It should also state either an expiry date or "expiry event" or both. Expiry is dealt with in Arts 22 to 26. The "expiry event" is defined by Art.22 as "the presentation of the documents specified for the purpose of expiry". Quite what documents the parties are likely to have in mind in this context is a matter for speculation —it cannot be the documents which trigger payment. Possibly this would cover a judgment or award in favour of the principal which makes it clear that the beneficiary would not be entitled to claim under the guarantee. If both an expiry date and an expiry event are stipulated, Art.22 provides that the guarantee will expire when the first of these occurs. Article 23 provides that the beneficiary's written release from liability will cancel the guarantee irrespective of whether the guarantee or any amendments to it are also returned. Article 26 deals with the situation which commonly arises in which the beneficiary requests an extension of the validity of the guarantee as an alternative to a demand for payment. In such event the Guarantor must inform the principal without delay and suspend payment "for such time as is reasonable" to permit the principal and the beneficiary to reach agreement on the granting of an extension. Unless an extension is granted within that time the guarantor must pay against any conforming demand, and he will not be liable to the beneficiary for any loss arising out of a delay in payment as a result of following this procedure. It will be seen that this provision potentially leaves a great deal of scope for argument about whether a demand which is expressed in the alternative is valid, how much time is to be regarded as reasonable to allow the principal and a guarantor to reach agreement, how the bank is going to assess what is a reasonable time for this purpose, and whether any delay in payment is actionable at the behest of the beneficiary or not.

Article 4 prohibits the Beneficiary from assigning the right to make a demand under the guarantee unless express provision is made in the guarantee or any amendment to it; on the other hand he may assign the *proceeds* to which he may become entitled without such express provision. Article 5 provides that all guarantees and counter-guarantees are irrevocable unless otherwise indicated. Article 6 provides that a guarantee takes effect from the date of its issue in the absence of express provision to the contrary, and Art.7 deals with the situation where the guarantor is unable to comply with instructions to issue a guarantee because of a legal prohibition in the country of issue.

Many of the rules in the URDG reflect the rules which apply to letters of credit under the UCP 500. For example, Arts 9 and 10 oblige the bank or other guarantor to examine the documents presented with care to see whether or not they conform with the terms of the guarantee, and give him a reasonable time to carry out this examination and decide whether or not to pay. Article 11 reflects the normal rule that the guarantor is not responsible for or liable for the truth or falsity of any documents presented to him or any statements made in such documents. However it goes further and states that there is no liability for the sufficiency or accuracy of such documents. On the face of it, therefore, the bank would appear to be protected from liability even if it paid out against wholly inadequate documentation or a demand which was plainly non-conforming. Yet Art.15 states that Guarantors are not excluded from liability under the terms of Art.11 for their failure to act in good faith and with reasonable care. A bank which fails to act in good faith would not be protected in any event, but the problems which may arise in reconciling Art.11 with Art.15 if there is an allegation of negligence on the part of the bank may be one reason for the reluctance of international traders to adopt the URDG. Another may be Arts 12 to 14 which give a wide degree of protection from suit to the guarantor in the event of delays or errors in transmitting messages, force majeure events and failures by others whose services they have used to give effect to the principal's instructions, and Art.16 which caps any liability of the Guarantor to the Beneficiary at an amount "not exceeding that stated in the Guarantee and any amendments thereto". It may be that these provisions put the account party at no real disadvantage compared with the terms of any counter-indemnity which he may be required to give to his bank, but it is understandable why they would be regarded as a disincentive to adopt the URDG.

Safeguards against wrongful demands or fraud

The nature of performance bonds clearly leaves them open to abuse by an   **16–020** unscrupulous beneficiary. Despite this, in practice there may be substantial commercial limitations on the extent to which the account party may safeguard himself against the possibility of fraud or a wrongful calling-in of the bond. If he is in a sufficiently strong bargaining position, but not strong enough to persuade the beneficiary to dispense with the requirement for a performance bond altogether, his best means of protection is probably to ensure that the guarantee requires a document to be produced to the bank which gives independent confirmation of the breach, for example, a certificate given by a reputable third party, such as an engineer, surveyor or architect. Care should be taken to ensure that the wording only allows the certificate to be given by someone who would have direct knowledge of the breach, *e.g.* the architect or engineer appointed under the underlying construction contract.[44] Failing this, a minimum degree of protection may be achieved by at least insisting that the performance bond is subject to the URDG discussed above, and by ensuring that Art.20 is not excluded, or, if there are aspects of the URDG which are unpalatable, by negotiating a term which is similar to Art.20.

Another possible safeguard is a clause which provides for the obligations of the bank under the performance bond to cease upon production to the bank by the account party of evidence that the contract has been fully and properly performed by him. In order to avoid abuse by the account party, the beneficiary may only agree to such a clause if independent evidence of performance is produced to the bank.

In order to safeguard against the beneficiary claiming on the performance guarantee when he is himself in breach of his obligation to open a letter of credit, or a similar fundamental obligation, it may be possible to make the validity of the performance bond expressly contingent on the opening of the letter of credit (or performance of the relevant obligation) within a particular time.[45]

Similarly, the account party may afford himself some limited protection by ensuring that the performance bond is given for a limited period, or that a time limit for claiming under it is specified, as with a letter of credit, and

---

44 In *GUR v Trust Bank of Africa Ltd* (unreported) October 28, 1986, Leggatt J. held that a requirement to present a certificate signed by a "registered quantity surveyor" was not to be interpreted as confined to the surveyor appointed under the underlying construction contract.
45 See, *e.g.* Kvaerner *Singapore Pte Ltd v UDL Shipbuilding (Singapore) Pte Ltd* [1993] 3 S.L.R. 350.

stipulating that it should be delivered up to him immediately upon expiry.[46] However, he should bear in mind that the unscrupulous beneficiary may be in a position to force extensions of the time limit by threatening to make a claim under the performance bond if it is not extended. The extent to which the beneficiary would be able to exert such pressure would depend on how far it was open to him to produce any necessary documents to the bank, but it may be easier to abuse a performance bond in this way than a letter of credit, particularly if the performance bond is couched in terms of a simple written demand by the beneficiary. Finally, if the account party is unsatisfied with such safeguards as he has been able to include in the contract (which can never fully protect him), he may consider it prudent to insure against the contingency of a wrongful demand.[47]

Injunctive relief

Against the issuing or paying bank

16–021　In an earlier edition of this work we expressed the view that it was highly unlikely that the account party would ever succeed in persuading an English court to grant him an injunction restraining the bank which issued the performance bond (or, if there is a chain, the bank which is liable to pay under it) from making payment, once a demand has been made against it in accordance with its terms.

As recently as 1995, Phillips J. was able to say that he knew of no reported case in which the grant of an injunction based on the fraud exception was upheld *inter partes*; *Deutsche Rückversicherung AG v Walbrook Insurance Co Ltd* [1995] 1 W.L.R. 1017 at 1030E. Since then, Cresswell J. has upheld an injunction granted under the fraud exception: *Kvaerner John Brown v Midland Bank Plc* [1998] C.L.C. 446, but as Rix J., pointed out in *Czarnikow-Rionda v Standard Bank* [1999] 2 Lloyd's Rep. 187 at 190, in that case there was no consideration of the balance of convenience. It remains the case that the grant of injunctions to restrain payment is likely to be very rare indeed: see the judgment of Rix J. in *Czarnikow-Rionda* (esp. at 204), discussed below.

It has been repeatedly stated that performance bonds and irrevocable letters of credit are "the lifeblood of international commerce" and that consequently the court will not intervene and disturb the mercantile practice of treating the rights of the beneficiary as the equivalent of cash in hand.[48] The sole exception to the bank's liability to pay under a perfor-

---

46 Article 5 of the earlier ICC Uniform Rules for Contract Guarantees, (1978) ICC Publication No.325, assumes that the bond will have an expiry date. Article 6 provides for the return of a guarantee which has expired or ceased to be valid. The URDG , also contain provisions relating to expiry and cancellation (Arts 22–26), see para.16–019 above.

47 Such insurance may be available through the Export Credit Guarantee Department or in the private sector: see Ch.15.

48 The expression was first used by Kerr J. in *Harbottle (Mercantile) Ltd v National Westminster Bank Ltd* [1978] Q.B. 146 at 155.

mance bond is where there is a clear case of fraud of which the bank has notice.[49] In *Bolivinter Oil SA v Chase Manhattan Bank* [1984] 1 W.L.R. 392, Sir John Donaldson M.R. set out the requirements of the fraud exception thus:

> "The wholly exceptional case where an injunction may be granted is where it is proved that the bank knows that any demand for payment already made or which may thereafter be made will clearly be fraudulent. But the evidence must be clear, both as to the fact of fraud and as to the bank's knowledge."

The time at which the Bank has to have knowledge of the fraud was considered in the context of letters of credit in *Group Josi v Walbrook Insurance* [1996] 1 Lloyd's Rep. 345 by Staughton L.J., who, after discussing the facts of the *United City Merchants* case said at 360:

> "As the decision in that case shows, it is nothing to the point that at the time of trial the beneficiary knows, and the bank knows, that the documents presented under the letter of credit were not truthful in a material respect. It is the time of presentation that is critical."

The same rule obviously applies to performance bonds, where it is the time of demand which matters. Where there is more than one bank involved in the transaction, there may be a hiatus between the time of demand and the time at which the obligation to pay arises. The position where discovery of the fraud occurs in the intervening period was considered in *Czarnikow-Rionda v Standard Bank* [1999] 2 Lloyd's Rep. 187, a case involving letters of credit (in respect of which this problem is more likely to arise in practice). The letters of credit provided for deferred payment, and the confirming banks had discounted the proceeds of the letters of credit before they matured, and long before any question of fraud was raised. The fraud, if there was one, had therefore succeeded. After a very careful analysis of all the preceding cases, Rix J. came to the conclusion (at 202) that the interest in the integrity of banking contracts under which banks make themselves liable on their letters of credit or their guarantees is so great that not even fraud can be allowed to intervene unless the fraud comes to the notice of the bank (a) in time, *i.e.* in any event before the beneficiary is paid, and (b) in such a way that it can be said that the bank had knowledge

---

49 *Sztejn v J Henry Schroder Banking Corporation* (1941) 31 N.Y.S. 2d 631 as approved in *United City Merchants (Investments) Ltd v Royal Bank of Canada* [1983] 1 A.C. 168 *per* Lord Diplock at 183–184 and *Edward Owen Engineering Ltd v Barclays Bank International Ltd* [1978] Q.B. 159 *per* Lord Denning at 171; see also *Harbottle (Mercantile) Ltd v National Westminster Bank Ltd* [1978] Q.B. 146; *Howe-Richardson Scale Co Ltd v Polimex-Cekop* [1978] 1 Lloyd's Rep. 161; *State Trading Corporation of India v ED & F Man (Sugar) Ltd* [1981] Com. L.R. 235; *Bolivinter Oil SA v Chase Manhattan Bank* [1984] 1 W.L.R. 392, fully reported at [1984] 1 Lloyd's Rep. 251; *United Trading Corporation v Allied Arab Bank Ltd* [1985] 2 Lloyd's Rep. 554; *GKN Contractors v Lloyds Bank Plc* (1985) 30 B.L.R. 48.

of the fraud. A month after that judgment, however, a gloss was introduced by Langley J. in *Banco Santander SA v Bayfern Ltd* [2000] 1 All E.R. (Comm.) 776. This was a trial of preliminary issues on the basis of an assumption that both the issuing and confirming banks had knowledge of the beneficiary's fraud before the maturity date of the letter of credit, but after the confirming bank had made a discounted payment. The question of injunctive relief therefore did not arise. It was held that the risk of the fraud in those circumstances fell on the confirming bank, and that the issuing bank was not obliged to reimburse it under Art.10 of the UCP 500. An appeal against that judgment was dismissed by the Court of Appeal [2000] Lloyd's Rep. Bank 165.

These two judgments are difficult to reconcile, though the latter case depends on the particular nature of the obligation undertaken by the confirming bank and on the type of credit itself. It is also explicable on the basis that it was open to the banks in the transaction to have given themselves adequate protection by contract. It is theoretically possible that, although the account party could not rely on the fraud exception to restrain the issuing bank from paying the confirming bank, the issuing bank would be under no liability to make such payment as a matter of contract, and would be in breach of his duties to the account party if he did so. However in practice this problem is unlikely to arise, particularly in the light of the way in which the case law has since developed. The time at which fraud has to be established was next examined by the Court of Appeal in *Balfour Beatty Civil Engineering v Technical & General Guarantee Co* [2000] C.L.C. 252. Waller L.J. considered the position where fraud was not established at the time of the demand but sufficient evidence of fraud came to light by the time the matter reached court. He said it would be absurd if the court in that situation felt bound to give summary judgment in such circumstances. If the evidence was clear enough to establish fraud, the bank would have a claim against the beneficiary for fraudulent misrepresentation which would cancel out any claim by the beneficiary for payment. If the evidence was not that clear-cut, but was still powerful, the court might be justified in granting summary judgment but staying execution, or alternatively deferring consideration of the beneficiary's claim until after the counterclaim had been tried.

In *Safa Ltd v Banque du Caire* [2000] 2 Lloyd's Rep. 600, the Court of Appeal upheld the decision of Timothy Walker J. to refuse summary judgment to the assignee of the beneficiary of the letter of credit. That case, however, turned on very special circumstances where the bank not only had an arguable case that a fraudulent demand had been made (which had a real prospect of success at trial) but also had an arguable case that it had been deceived into believing that what it was agreeing to pay under the letter of credit was premium to a reinsurance company when in fact it was agreeing to pay it to someone else. As Waller L.J. pointed out, it was unusual for the bank to be involved in the underlying transaction to the extent that this bank was.

The most recent examination of the underlying principles by the Court of Appeal was in *Solo Industries UK Ltd v Canara Bank* [2001] 1 W.L.R. 1800, a case involving a performance bond which the bank claimed to have avoided on the grounds that it was induced to issue it by fraud. The Court of Appeal upheld the decision of the judge (H.H. Judge Hallgarten) to refuse summary judgment. The leading judgment was given by Mance L.J., who examined all the authorities. He accepted the submission that banks and their customers accept the risks inherent in the terms of the instruments that they issue, including the risk that a benficiary may make a demand that is unjustified or fraudulent, but has to be met because it cannot be clearly established to be so. The cash principle means that short of established fraud, any claim that a bank may acquire against a beneficiary who makes a fraudulent demand must be pursued separately. However he said that these principles assume the integrity of the instrument that the bank has issued: it does not follow that banks accept the risk that the instrument itself has been induced by fraud. He could see no principled basis for the argument that once an instrument has been issued, the bank is bound to pay under it. After considering Waller L.J.'s judgment in *Balfour Beatty,* Mance L.J. indicated that the justification for refusing summary judgment in a case where the fraud came to light between the making of the demand and the application to court could equally be founded on the principle that "fraud unravels all". If the court allowed judgment to be given in favour of the beneficiary, whatever the merits of the bank's earlier behaviour, it would be tantamount to allowing the court's process to be used to effect a fraud.

The Court of Appeal did not agree with Waller L.J.'s view stated in *Balfour Beatty* and *Safa* that if the evidence of fraud was "powerful" but insufficient to establish fraud, "an arguable case that a fraudulent demand had been made with a real prospect of success would entitle the bank to resist an application for summary judgment". In para.31 Mance L.J. said "short of established fraud, a bank will not normally be allowed to raise any defence or set off based on alleged impropriety affecting the demand". He distinguished the situation in which the bank was seeking to attack the letter of credit or performance bond itself as having been induced by fraud. It would appear, therefore, that in all other cases the rule in *Bolivinter* has not been watered down.[50]

Common law fraud

The majority of cases in which an injunction has been sought to restrain **16–022** payment by a bank under a performance bond or letter of credit because of fraud have involved allegations of what Parker L.J. described in *GKN Contractors v Lloyds Bank Plc* as "common law fraud, that is to say, a case where the named beneficiary presents a claim which he knows at the time to be an invalid claim, representing to the bank that he believes it to be a valid claim".[51] This would include the situation where he knows he has

---

50 See also the critique in *Brindle and Cox, The Law of Bank Payments (op. cit.)* at 8–089–8–091, with which we respectfully agree.
51 (1985) 30 B.L.R. 48 at 63.

failed to perform a condition precedent to making a demand. Thus, if the beneficiary honestly believes that there has been a default by the seller at the time when he makes the claim, there would be no fraud by him.[52] If the claim is dishonest, then the bank must either be aware of the beneficiary's fraud at the time of payment, or else reckless, in that the only realistic inference to be drawn in the circumstances is that the demand was fraudulently made.[53] A seriously arguable case that there is good reason to suspect that the demand is dishonest is not good enough. At the interim stage the test is "have the plaintiffs established that it is seriously arguable that, on the material available, the only realistic inference is that [the beneficiary] could not honestly have believed in the validity of its demands on the performance bond?"[54]

This requirement places a very heavy burden of proof on a bank seeking to resist payment, or (in a far more common situation) on an account party seeking to restrain the bank from making such payment. A mere assertion of fraud will not suffice, and the court would normally require strong corroborative evidence (usually in the form of contemporaneous documents) and would also normally expect the person accused of the fraud to have been given an opportunity to answer the allegation and to have failed to provide any or any adequate answer in circumstances in which one could properly be expected.[55] It may often prove to be impossible, as a matter of practicality, for the account party to comply with these requirements in time to seek an injunction; further, the fact that the beneficiary chooses to remain silent may not count against him, as there may be perfectly valid reasons for his refusal to get involved in English litigation.[56]

Unjustified demand

16–023　In the *GKN Contractors* case, Parker L.J. suggested that the scope of the fraud exception might embrace a different situation, namely that in which the beneficiary genuinely believed that there was a breach of contract, and made a demand, but the bank knew that there was not, and that the

---

52 See *United City Merchants (Investments) Ltd v Royal Bank of Canada* [1983] 1 A.C. 168 at 184, and the observations of Lord Denning in *State Trading Corporation of India v ED & F Man (Sugar) Ltd* CAT No.307 of 1981, (July 17), reported in part at [1981] Com. L.R. 235.
53 In the *GKN Contractors* case Parker L.J. paraphrased this as "the only reasonable inference". It is unlikely that this was intended to be a broader test or to set a lower standard of proof.
54 *United Trading Corporation v Allied Arab Bank* [1985] 2 Lloyd's Rep. 554, and see *Solo Industries v Canara Bank* [2000] 1 W.L.R. 1800 and the cases cited in para.16–021 above. See further, *Society of Lloyd's v Canadian Imperial Bank of Commerce* [1993] 2 Lloyd's Rep. 579; *Group Josi Re v Walbrook Insurance* [1996] 1 Lloyd's Rep. 345 at 358; *Turkiye Is Bankasi AS v Bank of China* [1998] 1 Lloyd's Rep. 250, *Czarnikow-Rionda v Standard Bank* [1999] 2 Lloyd's Rep. 187 at 200. The "clear case of fraud" requirement of the English courts has been disapproved in other jurisdictions, on the grounds that it may be too high a burden for an interlocutory application: see, *e.g. CDN Research & Development v Bank of Nova Scotia* (1981) 136 D.L.R. (3d) 656, *per* Smith J. at 662.
55 *United Trading v Allied Arab Bank* [1985] 2 Lloyd's Rep. 554 *per* Ackner L.J. at 561.
56 See, *e.g.* the observations by Kerr J. in *Harbottle (Mercantile) Ltd v National Westminster Bank* [1978] Q.B. 146 at 157–158.

demand was therefore unjustified. In such circumstances it might be established that the bank itself would be guilty of a fraud on its customer if it made the payment. Although it would seem that such a case might be a justified extension to the fraud exception, the courts are likely to be very reluctant to move towards a position in which it may be suggested that the bank should have investigated the underlying facts or the documents presented to it. In the Singaporean case of *Rajaram v Ganesh* [1995] 1 S.L.R. 159 at 164, Kan Ting Chiu J. said "It is doubtful that fraud on the part of a receiving bank can vitiate a bank guarantee if the beneficiary is innocent of it. There is no basis for denying payment to that beneficiary because of the fraud of the bank. The position is different if the beneficiary is guilty of the same fraud, in which case payment would be denied even without the bank's complicity, so long as the bank knows of the beneficiary's fraud". Although the judge was addressing the situation in which the beneficiary's own bank receiving the payment fraudulently represented to the paying bank that the beneficiary was entitled to payment when it knew that he was not, his remarks would appear to apply equally to a situation in which the paying bank knows that the beneficiary is not entitled to receive payment. In any event, the chances of proving dishonesty on the part of a bank are probably even more remote than those of establishing that the only realistic inference to be drawn from the evidence is that the beneficiary has made a fraudulent demand.

Other problems

Even if the account party manages to surmount these considerable diffi- **16–024** culties and prove fraud, he may still be left without the remedy of an injunction against the bank. The first problem lies in establishing a cause of action against the bank which issued the performance bond. If the bank which has issued the bond is the account holder's own bank, then there is no difficulty. There would be a direct contractual relationship, and if necessary, a term would readily be implied prohibiting the bank from paying any claims which the bank knew to be fraudulent (which of course it would, once the court had been satisfied on the evidence that there was a clear case of fraud by the beneficiary and this had been communicated to the bank).

However, if, as is more likely, the account holder's own bank is merely indemnifying the bank which issued the performance bond, it would almost invariably have to be established that the issuing bank owed the account holder a duty of care, and that it would be liable in deceit or negligence if it paid a claim knowing the claim to be fraudulent or having reasonable grounds for believing it to be fraudulent.

This argument was raised in the *United Trading Corporation* and *GKN Contractors* cases. In both cases it was accepted that there was a good arguable case sufficient to satisfy the requirements for an interim injunction and that the bank owed a duty of care to the account holder. However, in the latter case Parker L.J. remarked that the cause of action was one which he had some difficulty in appreciating. Although there might be good commercial reasons for imposing a duty of care in these circumstances,[57] the relationship may not be regarded as sufficiently proximate in the light of the trend in recent cases on the law of negligence of restricting the circumstances giving rise to a duty of care.

Secondly, if the bank which is to pay is outside the jurisdiction, the beneficiary must find a basis for establishing that the English court has jurisdiction over it, under one or more of the heads of CPR rr.6.19 or 6.20. For example, if the loss or damage occasioned to the account party by the arguable tort of the overseas bank is not suffered in England, he may not be able to take proceedings here to restrain payment.

Assuming that a cause of action can be made out and that jurisdiction is established, the next, and potentially insurmountable, obstacle is that if there is a sufficiently clear and strong case of fraud to be made out, and there would be a cause of action against the bank or bond issuer if it paid, damages would normally be an adequate remedy, because the bank or bond issuer is usually likely to be of sufficient financial standing to be able to afford to compensate the account party if it pays out wrongly. On the other hand, the damage to the reputation of a bank, if it transpires that the injunction was wrongly granted, is likely to outweigh any compensation which could be afforded it under the cross-undertaking in damages. The balance of convenience is therefore likely to be weighed heavily against the account party. This was described by Kerr J. in *Harbottle (Mercantile) Ltd v National Westminster Bank* [1978] Q.B. 146 at 155 as an "insuperable difficulty" and subsequent cases have echoed and approved his observations.[58] For example, in *Czarnikow-Rionda v Standard Bank* [1999] 2 Lloyd's Rep. 187, Rix J. refused an injunction on the balance of convenience, being particularly swayed by the availability of alternative relief in the form of what used to be called a Mareva injunction to freeze the proceeds of the letter of credit or guarantee in the hands of the beneficiary. He stated, at 204:

> "I do not know that it can be affirmatively stated that a court would never, as a matter of balance of convenience, injunct a bank from making payment under its letter of credit or performance guarantee obligations in circumstances where a good claim within the fraud exception was accepted by the Court at a pre-trial stage. I do not regard Mr Justice Kerr and the other Courts which have approved or applied the logic of his 'insuperable difficulty' as necessarily saying that

---

57 As Ackner L.J. stated in the *United Trading Corporation* case, [1985] 2 Lloyd's Rep. at 561: "it cannot be in the interests of international commerce or the banking community as a whole that this important machinery that is provided for traders should be misused for the purposes of fraud".

58 *GKN Contractors v Lloyd's Bank Plc* (1985) 30 Build. L.R. 48 at 64–65; *United Trading Corporation SAT v Allied Arab Bank Ltd* [1985] 2 Lloyd's Rep. 554n at 565; *Tukan Timber Ltd v Barclays Bank Plc* [1987] 1 Lloyd's Rep. 171 at 177. See also *Esso Petroleum Malaysia Inc v Kago Petroleum Sdn Bhd* [1995] 1 M.L.J. 149 at 159, but *cf.* the approach of the High Court of Singapore in *Rajaram v Ganesh* [1995] 1 S.L.R. 159 at 165–166.

it could *never* be done. It is perhaps wise to expect the unexpected, even the presently unforeseeable. All that can be said is that the circumstances in which it should be done have not so far presented themselves, and that it would of necessity take extraordinary facts to surmount this difficulty."

The case contains pithy and cogent criticisms of the two reported English cases in which injunctive relief has been upheld *inter partes*, *Kvaerner John Brown v Midland Bank Plc* [1998] C.L.C. 446 and *Themehelp Ltd v West* [1996] Q.B. 84 discussed at para.16–025 below. Indeed if there is clear evidence of fraud the bank may decide that it will not pay, so that an injunction becomes unnecessary.[59]

A dispute may arise between the account party and the bank, or between two banks in the chain, as to whether the demand which has been made is in accordance with the terms of the contract. In such circumstances, as in the *IE Contractors* case, it may be possible to obtain declaratory relief. However, it is now established that a court will not grant an injunction to restrain the bank from paying in such circumstances since this would subvert the policy underlying the fraud exception: see *Ermis Skai v Programma Europa* (unreported) Commercial Court, February 26, 1997, Thomas J. Further, as in a case where there is reason to believe that the demand, though proper in form, was made fraudulently, if the bank pays when it should not, the account party should have an adequate remedy in damages.

Injunction against the beneficiary

In the second edition of this work we questioned whether the attitude of the court to granting injunctive relief to stop the beneficiary from making a claim under the performance bond would, or should, be different to its attitude in respect of injunctive relief against the bank. In most of the reported cases, a demand has been made by the beneficiary before the injunctive relief is sought, and therefore the beneficiary was not joined as a party to the proceedings. The policy reason for refusing to restrain the bank from making payment in those circumstances is clear, and has been considered above.

16–025

We referred in this context to decisions of the High Court of Singapore in which the Court granted an injunction against the beneficiary of the performance bond restraining him either from receiving payment after a demand has been made, or from demanding payment under it.[60] The first type of injunction would have the same effect in practical terms as granting an injunction against the bank, provided that the bank was put on notice of

---

59 This is what happened in *Tukan Timber Ltd v Barclays Bank Plc* [1987] 1 Lloyds Rep. 171.
60 *Kvaerner Singapore Pte Ltd v UDL Shipbuilding (Singapore) Pte Ltd* [1993] 3 S.L.R. 350, and *Rajaram v Ganesh t/a Golden Harvest Trading Corporation* [1995] 1 S.L.R. 159. *Cf. Esso Petroleum Malaysia Inc v Kago Petroleum Sdn Bhd* [1995] 1 M.L.J. 149, a decision of the Supreme Court of Kuala Lumpur.

the injunction before it complied with any demand. We pointed out, however, that the same policy considerations did not necessarily apply where the beneficiary had not yet made a demand upon the bank. In that situation, the bank has not yet been placed in any embarrassing position. In a case in which a buyer of goods has given the seller a post-dated cheque for the price, and then discovers that the seller has shipped empty containers stuffed with newspaper, instead of the goods, he may be entitled to obtain an injunction restraining the seller from presenting the cheque to the bank for payment, notwithstanding that as a bill of exchange the cheque is notionally treated as cash in hand. The injunction would be directed against the seller rather than against the bank. It is difficult to see why a buyer who has opened a letter of credit, or a contracting party who has procured a performance bond, should be placed in a worse position when a fraud is committed against him.

As to the balance of convenience, although it is true that a bank which pays when there is clear evidence of fraud may be able to satisfy a claim for damages, it is arguably unfair to the bank to make it bear the economic burden of the fraud if an alternative remedy could be made available against the fraudster before any harm is done to the account holder, and before the bank is called upon to honour any contractual obligation to pay. It may be that once a claim has been made against it, bearing that economic burden is part of the price which the bank, and its customer, has to pay for achieving commercial certainty; but if no claim has yet been made, the bank's reputation surely does not stand in jeopardy if the *beneficiary,* rather than the bank, is restrained from making a claim on the bond.

In such circumstances we pointed out that a refusal to grant the injunction might well be open to criticism on the ground that the courts really would be allowing the performance bond to be used as an instrument of fraud. If it were minded to grant such an injunction against the beneficiary, the court would of course take into account the possible damage which he would suffer if the fraud was not proved at the trial (which would almost certainly take place after the time for claiming under the performance bond had expired) and it is unlikely that such an injunction would be granted without any substantial fortification of the cross-undertaking in damages or the extension of the time for claiming under the performance bond until after trial.

These matters were considered by the Court of Appeal in the first reported case in which an English court has exercised its jurisdiction to grant an injunction against the beneficiary to restrain him from presenting the documents, *Themehelp Ltd v West* [1996] Q.B. 84. The case concerned a performance guarantee in respect of the third, and largest, instalment of the purchase price of a business. After paying the first instalment, the buyers allegedly discovered that a fraudulent misrepresentation had been made to them prior to the contract of sale. They started proceedings against the sellers claiming rescission of the contract and damages for fraudulent misrepresentation, but on the facts it appeared unlikely that rescission would be an available remedy. The buyers then applied for, and obtained, an interlocutory injunction restraining the sellers from demanding payment of the third instalment under the performance guarantee. The Court of Appeal, by a majority (Waite and Balcombe L.JJ.), upheld the injunction.

Waite L.J. essentially adopted the arguments canvassed above, and held that the exercise of the jurisdiction of the court in such circumstances did not threaten the autonomy of the guarantee. He said[61] that if no demand had yet been made, there was no risk to the integrity of the performance guarantee, and therefore no occasion for involving the guarantor in any question as to whether or not fraud was established. The injunction amounted to no more than an instance of equity intervening to restrain the beneficiary—until the day when his conscience stood trial at the main hearing—from enforcement of his legal rights against a third party. Although the law recognised the prima facie right of the guarantor to be sole arbiter on the question whether or not payment should be refused by it on grounds of fraud,[62] this did not affect the rights and remedies which were available to the account party against the beneficiary. An injunction could be granted to restrain a demand by the beneficiary, on the basis of a serious argument that on the available material before the court the only reasonable inference to be drawn was that a fraud had been committed. The burden had been satisfied in the present case. Balcombe L.J. delivered a concurring judgment.

Although the recognition of the jurisdiction to grant an injunction against the beneficiary in appropriate circumstances may be regarded as a welcome development it would appear that the acceptance by the Court of Appeal that a distinction could be drawn between injunctions against the bank and injunctions against the beneficiary was *per incuriam*. In the subsequent case of *Group Josi Re v Walbrook Insurance Co Ltd* [1996] 1 Lloyd's Rep. 345 it was pointed out by Staughton L.J. that the argument had been raised (and dismissed) in numerous earlier decisions of the Court of Appeal, most notably the unreported case of *Dong Jin Metal Co Ltd v Raymet Ltd*, July 13, 1993. He said "in my opinion the effect on the life blood of commerce will be precisely the same whether the bank is restrained from paying or the beneficiary is restrained from asking for payment. That was the view of Sir John Donaldson M.R. in *Bolivinter Oil SA v Chase Manhattan Bank NA* [1984] 1 Lloyd's Rep. 251 at 256, of Lord Justice Donaldson in *Intraco Ltd v Notis Shipping Corporation* [1981] 2 Lloyd's Rep. 256, of Lord Justice Lloyd in the *Dong Jin Metal* case and of both Mr Justice Clarke and Mr Justice Phillips in the present case. The contrary view has the support of Lords Justices Balcombe and Waite in *Themehelp Ltd v West* . . . and to a very limited extent the support of Lord Justice Evans as well. But none of these remarks were essential to the

---

61 At 98–99.
62 Relying on *dicta* of Lord Diplock in *United City Merchants (Investments) Ltd v Royal Bank of Canada* [1983] 1 A.C. 168 at 186.

decision. While I share the view of Lord Justice Balcombe, if such it was, that the law on this topic is not wholly satisfactory, it is in my opinion too well established for change to take place in this Court."

As Staughton L.J. recognised, the *Themehelp* case was one in which reliance was being placed on the fraud exception. A further problem, however, was that the alleged fraud was not of the usual character, *i.e.* a fraudulent misrepresentation to the bank that the beneficiary was entitled to be paid. Instead, it was an allegedly fraudulent misrepresentation which induced the innocent party to enter into the underlying contract. It was not argued that this fraudulent misrepresentation also induced the procuring of the performance guarantee, and of course that could not have affected the position as between the bank and the beneficiary. If the fraud had no effect upon the validity of the demand, the court would be interfering with the operation of the performance bond on grounds well outside the established parameters. The case can therefore be compared and contrasted with *Safa Ltd v Banque du Caire* [2000] 2 Lloyd's Rep 600 and *Solo Industries v Canara Bank* [2000] 1 W.L.R. 1800.

In his powerful dissenting judgment in *Themehelp*, Evans L.J. (formerly a judge of the Commercial Court) pointed out[63] that there was no evidence, on the facts, that the fraud exception to the general rule would have been available to the paying bank and that there were considerable dangers involved in allowing the plaintiff to have a "pre-emptive strike" of this kind. However, he did not dispute the jurisdiction to grant direct injunctive relief against the beneficiary in an appropriate case, for example where there was a good arguable case that the contract was voidable or otherwise invalid.[64] His main concern was that if the contract could not be rescinded, the demand on the bank was not affected in any way by the alleged fraud. The bank's obligation to pay under the performance bond remained intact, and the injunction was therefore an unwarranted interference with the contract. The buyer had undertaken that the seller would have the benefit of the performance guarantee; the court was taking steps to enable him to resile from that undertaking. He regarded this development as potentially harmful to the banking system, pointing out the commercial advantages to the bank and its customer of taking a course which enabled the customer to obtain temporary relief from the bank's obligation to pay in circumstances in which the bank itself could not or might not have been able to refuse to pay on grounds of the recognised fraud exception. He said that the integrity of the bank's separate undertaking in such a case would be undermined.[65]

There was a further perceived problem, which was that there was a time limit imposed by the contract on making a demand. If the seller was prohibited by the court from making a demand within the time scale, the

---

63 At 103.
64 At 103–104.
65 Although he did not specifically consider the position where a clear case of fraud was established against the beneficiary but the bank felt that it had insufficient knowledge to refuse payment under the performance bond.

bank would be forced to extend time, and this would mean that the court was effectively imposing on a contracting party a variation of the contract together, possibly, with the obligation to incur ancillary charges. In his opinion, the appropriate remedy was a Mareva injunction (now known as a freezing injunction) over the proceeds of the performance guarantee, if necessary coupled with an ancillary order to pay the proceeds into court (following *United Norwest Co-operatives Ltd v Johnstone, The Times*, February 24, 1994). Evans L.J. dismissed the majority view that it was a pertinent consideration that the defendants might become insolvent, and that it was unfair that the plaintiffs should be out of pocket pending the trial, pointing out quite rightly that in exercising the Mareva jurisdiction it was no part of the function of the court to protect the plaintiff against the potential insolvency of the defendant. The Mareva solution did not commend itself to Balcombe L.J., who said that if the bank paid under the guarantee it would have the right to reimbursement from the plaintiff, and that it would be wrong in principle to make the plaintiff pay in such circumstances. However it gained considerable support from Rix J. in *Czarnikow-Rionda v Standard Bank* [1999] 2 Lloyd's Rep. 187. See the discussion in para.16–027 below.

On the facts of the case, there would appear to be considerable force in Evans L.J.'s analysis that the court was indulging in an unwarranted extension of the Mareva jurisdiction in the guise of exercising its jurisdiction to grant injunctive relief against the beneficiary in a case of fraud. There is nothing in his judgment, however, which suggests that in an appropriate case, *e.g.* where the demand for payment would clearly be fraudulent, direct relief against the beneficiary should not be granted; indeed his judgment goes further and appears to accept that even in a case where there is no allegation of fraud, such relief might be granted if the underlying contract is voidable or otherwise invalid.[66]

Indeed the recent indication by the Court of Appeal that an injunction might be granted against a beneficiary who calls on a letter of credit or performance bond in breach of an express term appears to support the grant of relief in such circumstances.[67]

No court has yet gone so far as to say that the majority decision in *Themehelp* was wrong. However it has been substantially undermined by the discussion in *Group Josi Re v Walbrook* [1996] 1 Lloyd's Rep. 345 and *Czarnikow-Rionda v Standard Bank* [1999] 2 Lloyd's Rep. 187. It is fair to assume that in future, the decision is likely to be treated as turning on its own particular facts and that Evans L.J.'s dissenting judgment is more likely to be preferred.

---

66 At 103–104. See the discussion of *Elian and Rabbath v Matsas and Matsas* [1966] 2 Lloyd's Rep. 495 and *Potton Homes Ltd v Coleman Contractors Ltd* (1984) 28 B.L.R. 19.
67 See, *e.g. Sirius International Insurance Cpn v FAI General Insurance Co Ltd* [2003] 1 W.L.R. 2214 discussed in para.16–013 above.

Cases not involving fraud

16–026 Despite the general tenor of the cases it is not yet completely settled whether, in cases simply involving the parties to the underlying contract (which do not concern any claim against the bank to restrain it from paying, because the time for making payment has not yet arisen), an injunction would only be granted against the beneficiary in clear cases of fraud, or whether such an injunction could be granted in other circumstances—for example if it were shown that it would be unlawful to pay (under the proper law of the bond or letter of credit). In *Howe-Richardson v Polimex Cekop* [1978] 1 Lloyd's Rep. 161, and in *Intraco v Notis Shipping Corporation, The "Bhoja Trader"* [1981] 2 Lloyd's Rep. 256, the Court of Appeal stated that such an injunction should not be granted against the beneficiary unless fraud was involved, and this has been echoed more recently by Staughton L.J. in the *Group Josi* case. However, *Howe-Richardson* was a case in which the demand had already been made under the guarantee, and although the injunction which was sought and refused was one restraining the beneficiary from claiming under the guarantee, in effect it was sought too late: the bank was already in a position where it was legally obliged to pay.

Intraco v. Notis Shipping may have concerned a different situation. It is not clear from the report of that case whether, at the time when the injunction was sought, any demand had been made. If it had, it is understandable why the court refused to countenance an injunction restraining the bank from making payment. However, it is difficult to see why the observations of Donaldson L.J. in that case (at 257) about the proceeds of letters of credit and bank guarantees being treated as cash in hand would justify refusing to restrain the beneficiary from making a demand under the letter of credit or guarantee. The dishonour of a bill of exchange might be justified on the grounds of a total failure of consideration; prima facie, there is no reason why this should not also be a reason for preventing the beneficiary of the performance bond from making a demand under it, or the beneficiary of the letter of credit from tendering documents under it in order to obtain payment. The bank would not be put in a position whereby it had to decide which of the two disputing parties was right or wrong, nor would it be placed in a position where it was contractually obliged to pay.

This view is supported by the observations made by Eveleigh L.J. in *Potton Homes Ltd v Coleman Contractors Ltd* (1984) 28 B.L.R. 19 at 28:

> "If the seller has lawfully avoided the contract, prima facie, it seems to me that he should be entitled to restrain the buyer from making use of the performance bond. Moreover, in principle I do not think it possible to say that in no circumstances whatsoever apart from fraud will the court restrain the buyer. The facts of each case must be considered. If the contract is avoided or if there is a failure of consideration between the seller and the buyer for which the seller undertook to procure the issue of the performance bond, I do not see why as between the seller and the buyer the seller should be unable to prevent a call upon the

bond by the mere assertion that the bond is to be treated as cash in hand. . ."

It is noteworthy that the only reported case in which an injunction was granted, *Elian and Rabbath v Matsas and Matsas* [1966] 2 Lloyd's Rep. 495, was one in which it was sought by one of the parties to the underlying contract against the other contracting party. The charterers of a vessel had procured a bank guarantee in order to secure the release of their cargo, which was subject to a lien by the owners of the vessel. As soon as the guarantee was put up, the owners purported to exercise a fresh lien on the cargo and refused to release it until further security was put up. An injunction was granted restraining the owners from claiming under the guarantee, and the Court of Appeal upheld the order, on the grounds that the owners' behaviour was at the very least a breach of a contractual obligation to release the goods. It is difficult to categorise that behaviour as fraudulent, though on the facts there may well have been a total failure of consideration so as to bring the case within the extended category subsequently envisaged by Eveleigh L.J. in *Potton Homes.* Although *Elian and Rabbath v Matsas* has been described as a "very special case"[68] the approach of the Court of Appeal is arguably justifiable. The point was expressly left open for argument on a future occasion by the Court of Appeal in *Themehelp Ltd v West*. In Singapore, an injunction has been granted against a beneficiary on grounds of non-performance of a condition precedent, see *Kvaerner Singapore Plc Ltd v UDL Shipbuilding (Singapore) Plc Ltd* [1993] 3 S.L.R. 350, expressly applying the *dicta* of Eveleigh L.J. in *Potton Homes* (at 353). The jurisdiction to grant such relief was also expressly recognised by the Supreme Court of Kuala Lumpur in *Esso Petroleum Malaysia Inc v Kago Petroleum Sdn Bhd* [1995] 1 M.L.J. 149 at 158. In the unreported case of *Ermis Skai Radio & Television v Banque Indosuez SA* (February 26, 1997) Thomas J. held that the account party had no *locus standi* to seek such relief on grounds of non-performance of a condition of the guarantee or of a condition precedent to payment However in *Sirius International Insurance Corporation v FAI General Insurance Co Ltd* [2003] 1 W.L.R. 2214 the Court of Appeal recognised that injunctive relief could be granted against a beneficiary who sought to draw down a letter of credit in breach of the express terms of the underlying contract when a condition precedent had not been fulfilled. It has been clearly established, however, that the court will not imply a term in the underlying contract between account party and beneficiary, or construe it as giving rise to an obligation on the part of the beneficiary not to make demand under the guarantee unless there is actual default. In *State Trading Corporation of India Ltd v ED & F Man (Sugar) Ltd*[69] Shaw L.J. said, "It seems to me that the implication of such a term, so far from giving

---

68 By Lord Roskill in *Howe-Richardson v Polimex-Cekop* [1978] 1 Lloyd's Rep. 161 at 165.
69 CAT No.307 of 1981, July 17; incompletely reported at [1981] Com. L.R. 235, and in *The Times*, July 22, 1981.

business efficacy to the arrangement relating to the provision of a performance bond, goes far to erode its legitimate commercial object."[70]

This observation was expressly approved by the Court of Appeal in the subsequent unreported case of *Costain International v Davy McKee (London) Ltd*.[71] That case concerned a construction contract under which a bank guarantee was given on behalf of a subcontractor to a contractor in lieu of a retention of 10 per cent of the price, with the amount reducing to 5 per cent on completion. By the guarantee the bank stated, "We unconditionally and irrevocably guarantee to pay [the contractor] on its first demand in writing without reference to any other authorisation or justification . . ." the guaranteed sum. The subcontractor sought an injunction against the contractor restraining it from claiming under the guarantee (an attempt to restrain the bank was abandoned). The sole question before the court was whether there was any inhibition upon the subcontractor calling on the bank to pay, in circumstances where there was a genuine dispute between the parties, but no fraud was alleged.

The Court of Appeal did not state in terms that an injunction could only be granted against the beneficiary in a case of fraud, but held that on the true construction of the particular contract, there was no breach by the beneficiary in calling upon the guarantee in these circumstances, and that there was no basis for implying a term that the beneficiary could only demand payment if it had a reasonably arguable claim against the account party. It held that an injunction would strike at the whole object of the guarantee, which was to provide a safeguard and security to the contractor, counterbalanced by the advantage to the subcontractor in obtaining 100 per cent of the value of the work as it progressed.[72] Consequently, even if the basis on which injunctive relief may be sought against the beneficiary (rather than the bank) is wider than the fraud exception, it seems unlikely that the grounds would be extended by an English court any further than, at the very most, a clear case of total failure of consideration, illegality or failure to comply with a condition precedent. Any wider exception would be too likely to subvert the value of the performance bond as a commercial instrument, to find favour with the court.

Freezing injunctions

16–027 Even if it proves impossible for the account party to prevent the bank from making payment under the performance guarantee, in an appropriate case he may be able to obtain relief in the form of a freezing injunction (previously known as a Mareva injunction) restraining the beneficiary from dealing with the proceeds of the guarantee.[73] Of course, he must be able to

---

70 In the same case, Lord Denning said that honest belief by the beneficiary that there had been default would suffice to enable him to claim under an "on demand" bond; lack of such honest belief might bring the case within the fraud exception.

71 CAT No.1009 of 1990, November 26.

72 See also *Deutsche Ruckversicherung AG v Walbrook* [1995]1 W.L.R. 1017.

73 *Intraco v Notis Shipping Corporation* [1981] 2 Lloyd's Rep. 256.

establish a good arguable case in respect of a cause of action against the beneficiary which is actionable either in England or in another EU or EFTA contracting state,[74] and the real risk of dissipation of assets or other steps being taken by the defendant to render a judgment against him nugatory. In a case involving clear evidence of fraud, it may be relatively easy for the account party to establish this risk to the satisfaction of the court, and in view of the difficulties involved in obtaining an injunction restraining the bank from making payment, it may be a preferable course for him to seek a freezing injunction. It was the view of Rix J. in *Czarnikow-Rionda v Standard Bank* [1999] 1 Lloyd's Rep. 187 at 203 that although such an injunction is not a complete solution to all the problems of a claimant in such circumstances, the availability of such relief must be a highly important consideration which goes very far to undermine the account party's complaint about the difficulties of his position if payment is made under the letter of credit or performance guarantee.

Of course, this type of relief is not confined to cases involving fraud, and may be obtained in circumstances involving a simple claim for breach of contract, or tort, provided that a real risk of dissipation of assets can be established. As a condition of obtaining such relief, the claimant must be prepared to give cross-undertakings in damages covering the defendant and any third party (including a bank) who may be adversely affected by the imposition of the injunction. He must also undertake to pay the reasonable costs and expenses incurred by such a third party in consequence of the imposition of the injunction. In appropriate cases (for example, if the claimant is outside the jurisdiction and has no substantial assets within the jurisdiction), the court may order the cross-undertakings to be fortified by a bank guarantee or payment of a sum of money into court.[75]

Extra-territorial freezing injunctions

It has been established in recent years that the jurisdiction of the court to **16–028** grant freezing injunctions extends in exceptional cases to assets of the defendant in countries other than England.[76] Therefore it is possible that in an appropriate case (which would probably include one in which a likely fraud is established), the court would grant a freezing injunction relating to the proceeds of a performance bond payable outside the jurisdiction. However, in practical terms such an order is unlikely to be of substantial value to the claimant unless either he can rapidly obtain a similar order, or an order enforcing the injunction, in the jurisdiction in which the payment is made, or the defendant is within the jurisdiction of the English court so that the sanction of contempt proceedings against him is a potentially

---

74 Civil Jurisdiction and Judgments Act 1982, s.25.
75 For a full discussion of this topic, see Steven Gee, Commercial Injunctions (5th ed.) (Sweet and Maxwell, 2004).
76 See, *e.g. Maclaine Watson v International Tin Council (No.2)* [1989] Ch. 286; *Republic of Haiti v Duvalier* [1990] 1 Q.B. 202; *Babanaft v Bassatne* [1990] Ch. 13; *Derby v Weldon (No.1)* [1990] Ch. 48; *Derby v Weldon (Nos 3 and 4)* [1990] Ch. 65.

effective deterrent from disobedience. Thus a freezing injunction is more likely to be of value to the account party if the performance bond is payable within the jurisdiction than if there is a banking chain, with the monies being payable in the beneficiary's own country or some other jurisdiction. In theory, an alternative to trying to extend the injunction to accounts situated abroad could be an ancillary order requiring the money to be paid into court; this was suggested by Evans L.J. in *Themehelp Ltd v West* [1996] Q.B. 84 at 103e–f. However, the court would probably not do this if the performance bond, on its true construction, required the payment to be made abroad: see *Britten-Norman Ltd v State Ownership Fund of Romania* [2000] Lloyd's Rep. Bank. 315.

Third party rights

16–029   It should also be borne in mind that a freezing injunction is of little or no use to the claimant if some third party has a prior right to the assets, for example if the proceeds of the performance bond have already been assigned by the beneficiary. It is standard practice for a freezing injunction to include a proviso which enables any bank which has an existing right of set-off against monies in the defendant's account to exercise that right without further application to the court. In a sale transaction which involves both payment by letter of credit and a performance bond being given on behalf of the seller, it is quite common for both instruments to be issued by the buyer's bank (with an indemnity or covering bond from the seller's bank). However, it may be prudent for the seller to try to ensure that the letter of credit and performance bond are not both issued by the same bank. If they are, and a freezing injunction is granted restraining disposal of the proceeds of the performance bond, the bank may be in a position to use the funds to reimburse itself in respect of any payment made by it under the letter of credit.

Anticipatory freezing orders

16–030   The account party who wishes to seek a freezing injunction may face a further problem relating to the timing of his application. It was held by the House of Lords in *Siskina v Distos, The Siskina* [1979] A.C. 210, that the Mareva relief must be ancillary to an existing cause of action over which the English court has jurisdiction.[77] This was subsequently interpreted as meaning that the cause of action has to exist at the time when the application for the injunction is made, though the House of Lords did not consider the timing of any application in the *Siskina* itself.[78] In effect this

---

77 The rule was upheld, after the enactment of s.37(1) of the Supreme Court Act 1981, by the House of Lords in *South Carolina Insurance v Assurantie Maatschappij "de Zeven Provincien"* [1987] A.C. 24 and *Pickering v Liverpool Post Plc* [1991] 2 W.L.R. 513 (rejecting the wider views expressed by Lord Denning in *Chief Constable of Kent v V* [1983] Q.B. 34). Subsequently s.25 of the Civil Jurisdiction and Judgments Act 1982 created a statutory exception to the rule in the *Siskina*; see *Channel Tunnel Group Ltd v Balfour Beatty Construction Ltd* [1993] A.C. 334.

78 See *Siporex Trade SA v Comdel Commodities Ltd* [1986] 2 Lloyd's Rep. 428 at 436; *Steamship Mutual Underwriting Association (Bermuda) Ltd v Thakur Shipping Co Ltd* [1986] 2 Lloyd's Rep. 439 at 440.

interpretation ignored the long-standing power of the court to grant *quia timet* relief in the form of an injunction to restrain an anticipated wrong, a matter which was not canvassed or adverted to in the *Siskina*. The *Siskina* concerned a claim which could never be actionable in the English courts unless the defendants submitted to the jurisdiction, and therefore the point never arose.

In recognition of the injustice which the practical difficulties of waiting for a cause of action to accrue and then rushing to court to make an *ex parte* application might cause in certain cases, the practice grew up in the Commercial Court of granting relief in the form of a conditional injunction which would only take effect when the cause of action accrued. This followed the pioneering decision of Saville J. in *A v B* [1989] 2 Lloyd's Rep. 423. It is strongly arguable that this practice did not contravene the rule in the *Siskina,* properly understood, since the injunction would always be ancillary to an existing cause of action when it took effect, and that the suggestion that there must be an existing cause of action *at the time of the application,* rather than at the time when the injunction takes effect, is based on a misconception of the *ratio* in the *Siskina.*

However, that salutary practice was halted by the Court of Appeal. In *Veracruz Transportation Inc v VC Shipping Co Inc (The "Veracruz 1")* [1992] 1 Lloyd's Rep. 353, the Court of Appeal decided, while expressing some regret, that it was bound by the *Siskina* and subsequent authorities to hold that the cause of action must already exist at the time when the injunction is sought, and that a fear or apprehension of a future breach of contract or other wrong, however well founded, is not good enough to found a claim for a freezing order.

As matters presently stand, therefore, an injunction cannot be granted on terms that it will only take effect when the cause of action is complete, even if such an order would be just and equitable, as well as commercially expedient and sensible. In *The Veracruz 1* Sir John Megaw said (at 361):

> "I see no valid reason, in logic or practical convenience in the interest of justice, why jurisdiction should not exist in respect of Mareva injunctions, with the qualification which Mr Justice Saville applied; namely that such a Mareva injunction should not operate unless and until the anticipated cause of action has arisen. But we are precluded by authority from so deciding on this question of technical jurisdiction."

In the previous edition we expressed the hope that if this situation was not remedied by the House of Lords in the near future, the power to grant such relief would be established by legislation. However, despite the wholesale revision of Civil Procedure in recent times, none has yet been enacted.

The decision in the *Veracruz 1 is* likely to have an unfortunate impact which is not confined to cases involving ship sales, which have their own peculiar difficulties. In most cases involving performance bonds, the account party and the beneficiary will be in a contractual relationship. It is possible, therefore, that a breach of contract by the beneficiary, giving rise to a right in damages, may have occurred before demand is made under the performance bond—for example, failure to open a letter of credit, or failure to pay the purchase price. Such cases are relatively straightforward.

However, there are likely to be cases in which the only arguable breach would be the unjustified demand by the beneficiary for payment under the bond, or (more commonly) cases in which the only relevant claim against him lies in tort, which is not complete until the account party suffers damage, and the earliest that may be is when the demand is made on the bank. In some cases, where there is no breach of contract involved in making a demand without justification, no prior breach of contract, and no fraud, it might be said that the account party has no cause of action against the beneficiary save, possibly, a future claim for an account for any moneys had and received by him over and above any damages to which he would be entitled in respect of the account party's alleged breach of contract which triggered the demand. Such a claim would arise at the earliest upon payment of the bond, and would depend on a number of factors, including whether there was an arguable legal basis for any such duty to account.[79]

All these scenarios could pose considerable practical difficulties for the account party, in that he may be unable to apply to court in time to obtain an order before payment has been made, and an order made afterwards may be too late. He may also find himself entirely dependent on the goodwill of the paying bank in notifying him timeously of any demand. In the last mentioned situation referred to above, even if the application is made after the bank has paid the money to the beneficiary, the task of establishing a sufficient cause of action against him for its repayment may be extremely onerous. Consequently, the potential availability of a freezing injunction is not necessarily as effective a safeguard against abuse of the performance bond by an unscrupulous beneficiary as it may seem at first. However, recent developments in the case law on *quia timet* relief has indicated that the problem is not insurmountable and that relief may be granted even if a freezing order is not available because the cause of action is not yet complete: see, *e.g.* the decisions of Rix J. in *Rowland v Gulfpac Ltd* [1999] 1 Lloyd's Rep. Bank 86 and of H.H. Judge Chambers in *Papamichael v National Westminster Bank* [2002] 1 Lloyd's Rep. 332, discussed in Chapter 10 at para.10–026.

Standby letters of credit

16–031   A standby letter of credit is a special form of letter of credit which essentially fulfils the same function as a performance guarantee. It is an alternative means by which the beneficiary may obtain payment in the event of a default by the account party in performance of his obligations. Although the purpose for which a standby letter of credit is used is completely different from the purpose for which an ordinary documentary

---

79 See below, paras 16–033–16–035.

letter of credit is used, in that it is a safeguard against non-performance by the seller rather than non-payment by the buyer, the same general legal principles apply to it. A discussion of those principles is outside the scope of this work.[80]

Advantages and disadvantages

Like any other letter of credit, a standby letter of credit is an irrevocable **16–032** undertaking by the bank to pay certain drafts drawn on it, or to pay on demand by the beneficiary, in either case on presentation to it of certain specified documents, and that undertaking is entirely independent of any underlying transaction between the account party and beneficiary. The Uniform Customs and Practice for Documentary Credits may apply to standby credits if they are expressly incorporated in them but the ICC has developed an entirely separate series of more pertinent rules, the ISP 98.[81]

Some countries, particularly in the Middle East, will not accept performance bonds with an expiry date, as this may not be enforceable under the local law. Therefore the local bank guarantor may not be prepared to cancel the liability, even after expiry, without the beneficiary's agreement. This can cause problems, especially an open-ended balance sheet liability. In certain countries it has been possible to overcome resistance to expiry dates in performance bonds by using instead a standby letter of credit, which will include an expiry date if it is made subject to UCP500 (Art.42) or ISP98 (Arts 47–49). Of course this will not eliminate the risk of the beneficiary threatening to call for payment unless the instrument is extended.

As with a performance bond, the documents which have to be presented to the bank may range from a simple written demand to an arbitration award or certificate of default given by some third party, or some other documentary evidence of non-performance. The protection afforded to the account party will depend on the nature and extent of the documents which must be provided by the beneficiary. The bank has an obligation to scrutinise the documents presented to it and to satisfy itself that they are in conformity with the requirements of the credit. One possible advantage to the account party of using a standby letter of credit rather than a performance guarantee is that the principle of strict compliance will definitely apply to the former, whereas doubt has been raised about whether it applies to the latter.[82] In practical terms, however, this potential distinction is unlikely to make a major difference to the choice of instrument in a particular case.

---

80 For a fuller discussion of standby letters of credit and of the American and Canadian case law relating to them, see Jack, Malek and Quest, *Documentary Credits* (*op. cit.*), Ch.12; McGuinness, *The Law of Guarantee* (*op. cit.*), Ch.12; Ellinger (1978) 8 *International Business Lawyer* 604.

81 The 1993 Revision to the Uniform Customs (ICC Publication No.500) refers expressly to standby letters of credit in Art.2. For a commentary on the effct of applying these rules to such a credit see Jack, Malek and Quest *Documentary Credits* (*op. cit.*), Ch.12.

82 See the comments of Hirst J. in *Siporex Trade SA v Banque Indosuez* [1986] 2 Lloyd's Rep. 146 at 159, and para.16–013 above.

A possibly more significant distinction, which is disadvantageous to the account party, is that it is perhaps more likely that third parties may acquire rights in respect of a letter of credit. Such rights are most commonly acquired as holders of drafts drawn on the bank, but if the letter of credit is not restricted in its terms to paying only one named beneficiary, it is always possible for someone else to present the requisite documents for payment under its terms. Indeed, the beneficiary may use the letter of credit to raise finance: standby letters of credit may be purchased at a discount in certain futures markets.

The account party may therefore find that someone other than the party with whom he has contracted, such as a creditor of the beneficiary, or a purchaser of the letter of credit or the drafts drawn under it, claims payment from the bank on the basis of documents purporting to evidence nonperformance; and even if that allegation is made wrongfully by the beneficiary in order to enable an innocent third party to obtain payment, the court will be more reluctant than ever to interfere with the operation of the letter of credit. By way of contrast, although it may be possible to assign a performance guarantee, the scope for anyone other than the person to whom it is addressed claiming under it is likely to be more circumscribed by the terms of the bank's undertaking, than it is with a letter of credit.

Standby letters of credit originated in the United States of America, as a means of getting round the legal prohibition on the issue of guarantees by federally chartered banking associations. Their origin has meant that they are commonly used in the United States and other countries, such as Japan, where similar prohibitions apply. They are much less common in England, where banks and similar financial institutions would normally issue performance guarantees, and tend to be found only in international transactions where one of the banks in the chain of payment happens to be in the United States, Japan or a country where performance guarantees are prohibited. Consequently there are few reported cases in England concerning the interpretation, operation and effect of standby letters of credit.[83] Those which do exist tend to confirm that such instruments are to be treated in the same way as any other letter of credit.

In practical terms, it may make little difference to the account party whether the instrument issued by the bank is in the form of a standby letter of credit or a performance bond. They share most, if not all, of the same advantages and disadvantages from his perspective; on the other hand, they have many advantages for the beneficiary. In many cases, where tenders are concerned, the account party may have no choice but to take the risk of providing a bond or standby letter of credit if he wishes to tender for the project. However, if he does have a choice, he would be advised to consider the matter carefully before agreeing to provide such an instrument. Among the factors which should be taken into consideration should be the financial

---

83 *Hongkong and Shanghai Banking Corporation v Kloeckner* [1989] 2 Lloyd's Rep. 323 and *Offshore International SA v Banco Central SA* [1977] 1 W.L.R. 399 appear to be the main cases featuring standby letters of credit.

soundness of the beneficiary, the nature of the underlying contract, the amount of the bond or standby letter of credit and its relationship to any sums which might be claimed by way of damages for non-performance, the practical ability of the account party to pursue the beneficiary in the event of a wrongful demand, his ability to reflect the risk in the price which he charges and the availability of insurance.

Despite the risks involved, performance bonds and standby letters of credit continue to play a very important role in modern commerce. It remains to be seen whether the case law in England will develop in such a way as to afford the account party better protection against an unscrupulous beneficiary, as it has in the United States.

Duty to account for the proceeds of the bond

One important matter which (until quite recently) received very little **16–033** attention from either commentators or the courts is the extent to which the beneficiary of a performance bond is liable to account to the account party for any sum received under it, if and when the extent (if any) of his damages for breach of the underlying contract has been determined. If his damages turn out to be greater than the sum which he receives, it is highly unlikely that the court would allow him any double recovery, and the payment via the bond would almost certainly be treated as a payment on account of the damages. However, more difficult problems could arise if the account party requires repayment in whole or in part.

Repayment when there has been no breach

It has been seen that it may not be a breach of contract for the beneficiary **16–034** to make a demand on the performance bond when there has not, in fact, been a breach by the account party. However, if there has been no breach, the beneficiary will usually have been unjustly enriched. If, in the context of the overall transaction, this was a situation which objectively both parties agreed to risk and to tolerate, the beneficiary may be entitled to keep his windfall. However, as discussed in para.16–001 above, the Court of Appeal has held that the performance bond must expressly provide for this. See also the observations of Langley J. in *Seepong Engineering Construction Co Ltd v Formula One Administration Ltd* (unreported) February 25, 1999. In the absence of such a provision, the beneficiary must pay the money back: *Comdel Commodities Ltd v Siporex Trade SA* [1997] 1 Lloyd's Rep. 424 *per* Potter L.J. at 431, and *Cargill International SA v Bangladesh Sugar and Food Industries Corporation* [1998] 1 W.L.R. 461. The precise legal route by which the obligation to account arises probably does not matter, but it may be an implied term of the underlying contract, an implied collateral contract to make repayment or simply an operation of the basic equitable principles of restitution (founded on the unjust enrichment of the beneficiary).

The liability of the beneficiary to account therefore depends very much upon the terms of the particular contract. Problems may arise, for example, if the underlying contract contains an express clause stating that the written terms constitute the whole agreement between the parties, or if the moneys were not paid to the beneficiary himself but to a third party.

The duty to account would also arise in a situation in which the account party was indeed in breach of contract, but the sum which the beneficiary received as a result of the demand bears no relationship to the actual loss and damage which he suffers as a result. In an early edition of this work we suggested that it might be more difficult in such a case to imply a term that the moneys received shall be accounted for, but the Court of Appeal in *Comdel v Siporex* [1997] 1 Lloyd's Rep. 424 appears to have regarded it as an obvious implication in the absence of clear wording to the contrary. The suggestion was made by the distinguished editor of *Keating on Building Contracts*[84] that if a building contractor has procured an unconditional "on demand" bond there may be greater scope for implying a term that the employer is under a duty to account for any overpayment, than there may be in the case of international sales contracts. Although the distinction could be drawn, because the amount of a performance bond given in the context of a construction project may bear a closer relationship to a likely pre-estimate of the employer's loss than the amount of a performance bond given in other contexts, and because the relationship may be one in which a running account is quite normal, an argument by counsel for the beneficiary in the *Comdel v Siporex* case that the principle should be confined to performance bonds in building cases received no judicial sympathy from Potter L.J.

Interest

16–035 If a repayment of the proceeds of the performance bond (or standby letter of credit) is ordered, or taken into account in producing a final figure on balance of accounts between the parties, a further problem arises in respect of interest. Should the beneficiary of the performance bond be required to pay interest from the date on which he received payment under the bond, or from some other date? If the demand was made in compliance with the terms of the contract and was otherwise lawful, then the beneficiary was arguably entitled to the use of that money from that date.

On that basis, although the account party will have paid, or been debited with, a similar sum on or about the date of payment by the bank, it is strongly arguable that interest should not run until it has at least been established that there is a duty to account for a specific surplus. The beneficiary should not be liable to compensate the account party for keeping him out of his money unless and until his obligation to repay that money has accrued. On the other hand, it might be said that if the overpayment occurred when the demand under the bond was met, interest should run from the date of the overpayment, and that this would not be unfair if it transpired that the beneficiary had no right to the money or part of it. It remains to be seen which of these views finds favour with the court.

---

84 (6th ed., 1995), 276, n.77.

Chapter 17

Consumer Credit Transactions

Introduction

It has already been seen that, as a general rule, the surety is expected to **17–001**
look after himself, and that the remedies available at common law and in
equity if he makes a harsh bargain are limited. This is a concomitant of the
basic principle of freedom of contract. However, in practice the inequality
of bargaining power between the principal (and his surety) on the one
hand, and the creditor, on the other, is often such that there is no real
freedom of contract and the creditor is free to impose whatever terms he
likes upon the agreements. The Consumer Credit Act 1974 was enacted in
order to attempt to redress the balance in areas in which it was felt to be
necessary, by establishing a new common system for the control of credit,
hire and hire-purchase transactions relating to certain types of debtor or
hirer ("consumers"), leaving business credit uncontrolled.[1]

In essence, the Act regulates the supply of credit not exceeding £25,000
to individuals (including partnerships and sole traders) under consumer
credit agreements and consumer hire agreements.[2] It imposes a system of
licensing on persons carrying on a business which involves the making of
consumer credit and consumer hire agreements. It also specifies the form
and content which such agreements must take, and requires certain
information to be disclosed to the debtor, hirer or surety in respect of such
an agreement or a "linked transaction".[3] It also regulates the withdrawal
from, and cancellation and termination of such agreements, and the steps
which must be taken by the creditor before enforcing any security.

The protection of consumer agreements

The Act is the first attempt by the legislature to provide a coherent pattern **17–002**
of rules governing the taking and enforcement of security in respect of
consumer credit and consumer hire agreements. The protection which it

---

1 For the background to the Act, see the report of the Committee on Consumer Credit (the
  Crowther Report), Cmnd 4596 (1984).
2 Defined respectively in ss.8(2) and 15.
3 As defined by s.19(1). For example, if a finance company has pre-existing arrangements
  with a car dealer, and the dealer puts the debtor in touch with the finance company, which
  then makes him a loan to enable him to buy the car, the contract of sale is a linked
  transaction.

provides does not derogate from any other rights and remedies which may be available to the surety at common law or in equity. The principal areas of control provided for by the Act and regulations made under it can be summarised as follows:

(1) Certain documents and information are required to be supplied by the creditor[4] to prospective and actual sureties, in a specified and readily comprehensible form; the objective is to ensure so far as is possible that the surety knows precisely what obligations he is guaranteeing, and what his rights and obligations are.

(2) The form and content of security instruments (*i.e.* documents containing a guarantee or indemnity provided in relation to a regulated agreement)[5] are specified: again the objective is to set out all the rights and obligations of the parties in clear and readily comprehensible terms.

(3) The Act provides a system of control over the realisation and enforcement of securities, and provides that in certain circumstances the securities will be treated as invalid and ineffective.

(4) It applies the principle of co-extensiveness to all contracts of suretyship in respect of regulated agreements, and prevents evasion of the system of regulation and control by the device of taking security for the principal's obligations either from the principal or from a third party.

In addition to these main areas of control, the Act also contains special provisions which relate to pledges, and restricts the taking and negotiation of negotiable instruments in connection with a regulated agreement. These matters are outside the scope of this work.

Protected sureties

17–003   The Act adopts an extremely wide definition of a "surety" in s.189(1):

> "Surety means the person by whom any security is provided, or the person to whom his rights and duties in relation to the security have passed by assignment or operation of law."

By the same section, "security", in relation to an actual or prospective consumer credit agreement or consumer hire agreement, or any linked transaction, means "a mortgage, charge, pledge, bond, debenture, indemnity, guarantee, bill, note or other right provided by the debtor or hirer, or

---

4 The Act uses the expression "creditor or owner" in order to cover persons who own and hire out goods under consumer hire and hire-purchase agreements. For ease of reference, the expression "creditor" is used in this chapter to refer to all such persons.
5 S.105(2), and see below, para.17–004.

at his request (express or implied) to secure the carrying out of the obligations of the debtor or hirer under the agreement".[6]

Accordingly, for the purposes of the Act no distinction is drawn between a surety under a contract of indemnity and a guarantor; indeed, the definitions are so wide that the debtor or hirer himself may be regarded as a "surety" for the purposes of the Act, if he provides security (*e.g.* a mortgage) for the performance of his obligations under the regulated agreement. An important exception is a person who provides security at the request of the *creditor* only. When this happens, the security is outside the protection of the Act regardless of whether it has been provided in respect of a regulated agreement.

No distinction is drawn in the definition section between personal securities (*e.g.* a contract of guarantee) and real securities (*e.g.* a mortgage or charge over property). However, this does not mean that it can be assumed that wherever the word "security" or the expression "security instrument" appears in the Act or in regulations made under it, it necessarily refers to all types of security or to securities provided by anyone falling within the wide definition of a "surety". Although several provisions of the Act relate to all types of security, certain of the controls presently relate only to certain types of security: for example, it will be seen below that the provisions governing formalities of security instruments currently only apply to guarantees and indemnities.

Furthermore, some of the regulations in the Act which relate to securities are currently restricted to securities provided by the debtor or hirer himself, and not to securities provided by third parties. Thus, if a creditor ordinarily requires the provision of security by the debtor or hirer in respect of any credit or hire facilities which he advertises in certain types of advertisement, the advertisement must contain a statement indicating the requirement in question.[7] However, there is presently no obligation on the creditor to reveal in such an advertisement that he would normally require security to be provided by a third party, even if the debtor would be responsible for procuring such security.

The rights and obligations of the creditor in respect of sureties and securities are mostly contained in Pt VIII of the Act (ss.105–126) and the regulations made under those provisions.

Formalities

If the surety is someone other than the debtor or hirer, any security **17–004** provided in relation to a regulated agreement must be expressed in writing.[8] That requirement applies to all types of "security" as defined by the Act. If regulations prescribe the form and contents of the documents which express

---

6 See Guest and Lloyd, *Encyclopedia of Consumer Credit*, paras 2–106–2–127.
7 Consumer Credit (Advertisement) Regulations 1989 (SI 1989/1125). There is a similar obligation in respect of credit or hire quotations: see Sch.2 to the Consumer Credit (Quotations) Regulations 1989 (SI 1989/1126).
8 S.105(1) and (6).

the security, those documents are defined in the Act as "security instruments" and must conform to the requirements of the relevant regulations.[9] A security instrument must also contain all the express terms of the contract, be signed by or on behalf of the surety, and be in a readily legible form when it is presented to or sent to the surety for his signature.[10]

So far, the only regulations made under this section are the Consumer Credit (Guarantees and Indemnities) Regulations 1983 (SI 1983/1556). Thus there is no requirement in this Act as to the particular form which a mortgage of land must take, other than that it must be in writing, and the Bills of Sale Acts 1878 and 1882 continue to apply to mortgages of chattels. The only "security instruments" defined by and regulated by the Act at present are contracts of guarantee and indemnity, and the requirements of s.105(4), (5) and (7)(b) only apply to those types of contract.

The formal requirements for such contracts are slightly less complex than the requirements for the underlying regulated agreements.[11] The surety need not sign the guarantee or indemnity personally (someone may sign it on his behalf)[12] and the creditor need not sign it at all. The instrument must contain a prominent heading on the first page in one of the forms of words specified in Pt I of the Schedule to the Regulations denoting the type of contract it is: *i.e.* "Guarantee subject to the Consumer Credit Act 1974", "Indemnity subject to the Consumer Credit Act 1974", or "Guarantee and Indemnity subject to the Consumer Credit Act 1974". If the agreement contains both primary and secondary obligations, or is susceptible of being so read, the last of these headings should be used.[13]

The document must contain the names and postal addresses of the creditor, debtor and surety, and a description of the subject-matter of the security.[14] It must also set out a statement of the rights of the surety in the form specified in Pt III of the Schedule.[15] There must be a signature box in the appropriate one of four forms specified in Pt IV of the Schedule, and the signature of the surety must be in the space on the document in the signature box indicated for that purpose.[16] Words shown in capitals in the forms prescribed in Pts III and IV of the Schedule must be afforded more prominence than any other lettering except that in the prescribed statement of the surety's rights, and no less prominence than that given to any other information in the security instrument apart from the heading, trade names, names of parties or lettering inserted in handwriting.[17] The lettering of the

---

9 S.105(2). These requirements go beyond the requirements of the Banking Code, and apply to any guarantee or indemnity given in respect of an overdraft which falls within the ambit of the Act as a regulated agreement.

10 Section 105(4). Thus the requirements of s.4 of the Statute of Frauds are extended in this field to contracts of indemnity, and are generally amplified.

11 See generally the Consumer Credit (Agreements) Regulations 1983 (SI 1983/1553) as amended by SI 1984/1600, SI 1985/666 and SI 1988/2047.

12 S.105(4)(c).

13 Reg.3(1)(a).

14 Reg.3(1)(b).

15 Reg.3(1)(c).

16 Reg.4(2). A witness may, however, sign outside the box: reg. 4(3).

17 Reg.3(5).

terms of security included in the instrument must be easily legible, and of a colour readily distinguishable from the colour of the paper used.[18]

The surety must be presented with or sent a copy of the guarantee or indemnity at the same time as he is presented with or sent the original for his signature.[19] If the guarantee is provided before the regulated agreement (*e.g.* a loan to a consumer debtor) is made, the surety must be given a copy of the executed agreement and a copy of any other document referred to in it within seven days after that agreement is made. If the security is provided at the same time as the regulated agreement, or afterwards, the surety must be given a copy of the executed agreement and a copy of any other document referred to in it, at the time when the security is provided.[20]

Sanctions for non-compliance with formal requirements

Failure to comply with any of these requirements will mean that the **17–005** guarantee or indemnity is not properly executed. This means that the creditor cannot enforce the security without first obtaining an order for enforcement from the court under s.127 of the Act.[21] The same sanction applies if any other type of security is not expressed in writing, in contravention of s.105(1).[22] The Act does not prescribe all the considerations which should be taken into account by the court in exercising its discretion under s.127, though specific reference is made to the degree of prejudice caused to any person by the contravention in question, and the degree of culpability for it.[23]

If an application for an order for enforcement is dismissed in these circumstances, other than on technical grounds, (which the court must certify under s.189(5)) the security will be treated as if it never had effect, by virtue of the application of s.106.[24] As a result, any property lodged with the creditor solely for the purposes of the security must be returned by him forthwith, any amount paid to the creditor on realisation of the security must be repaid by him, and he must take any necessary steps to ensure that any entries on any register relating to security so provided are removed or cancelled.[25]

---

18 Reg.4(1).
19 S.105(4)(d). Any copy of the security instrument supplied must conform with the requirements of the Consumer Credit (Cancellation Notices and Copies of Documents) Regulations 1983 (SI 1983/1557).
20 S.107(5). It is probable that the time at which the security is "provided" in this context means the time when the surety enters into the contract and not any later time when the security takes effect.
21 S.105(7)(b).
22 S.105(7)(a).
23 S.127(1)(i).
24 S.105(8).
25 Subject to s.177 which preserves certain rights of proprietors of registered charges and bona fide purchasers where a mortgagee has exercised a power of sale. If the surety suffers loss and damage by reason of the operation of s.177 he may claim a full indemnity from the creditor under s.177(4).

The right of the surety to change his mind

17–006 By s.113(6) of the Act, any security provided in relation to a prospective regulated agreement is only enforceable after the regulated agreement has been made; at any time until then, the surety has the opportunity to change his mind and require that the security be treated as ineffective under s.106. The rights of the surety in this regard are similar to the rights of the prospective debtor or hirer to cancel the underlying agreement.

Information to be supplied

17–007 Quite apart from the obligation to give the surety any information or documents under s.105 of the Act, the creditor is obliged to supply him with certain documents and information under ss.107–109 within the prescribed period[26] after receipt of a written request and payment of the statutory fee.[27] Unlike the requirements of s.105(4) and (5) these obligations are not restricted to situations in which the security is a guarantee or indemnity.

These sections require the creditor to supply the surety with a copy of the security instrument (if any) and a copy of the underlying regulated agreement and any documents referred to in it.[28] They also enable the surety to find out, *inter alia,* the state of accounts as between the creditor and debtor or hirer. However, these provisions do not apply to non-commercial agreements (*i.e.* those not made by a creditor or owner in the course of a business carried on by him).[29] Agreements under which no sum is or will or may become payable by the debtor or hirer are also excluded. In order to avoid a creditor being overwhelmed by continuous "nuisance" requests for information, it is expressly provided that he has no duty to answer a request made less than one month after a previous request relating to the same agreement has been complied with.

Similarly, s.110 obliges the creditor to supply the debtor or hirer within the prescribed period with a copy of any security instrument (*i.e.* guarantee or indemnity) executed in relation to the agreement after the making of the agreement, upon written request and payment of the statutory fee.[30] The exclusions are identical to those under ss.107–109.

---

26 Currently 12 working days, see Consumer Credit (Prescribed Periods for Giving Information) Regulations 1983 (SI 1983/1569).

27 Currently 50p.

28 Although these requirements overlap to a certain extent with s.105, they are additional to s.105 which may mean that the creditor has to supply copies of the same documents to the surety at different times.

29 As defined by s.189(1).

30 It is unclear why this obligation is confined to instruments executed after the underlying regulated agreement has been made. While it is likely that the debtor would be entitled to a copy of a security instrument executed prior to the regulated agreement under other provisions of the Act—*e.g.* if it is referred to in the main agreement—the reason for drawing a distinction between prior and subsequent securities is not apparent. Nor, indeed, is the reason for confining the right to copies of guarantees or indemnities. A debtor might be just as concerned to see a third-party mortgage: but see s.58.

Sanctions for non-compliance with information requirements

If the creditor fails to comply with the requirements of any of these sections **17–008** he cannot enforce the security while he remains in default. If the default lasts for more than one month, he commits an offence.[31] The Act is silent as to what sanctions are available to the surety if the creditor goes ahead and enforces the security regardless of the default. In particular, there is no provision which applies s.106 to the security in this context. The difficulties to which this may give rise are considered below.[32]

Termination and enforcement

Sections 87–89 of the Act oblige the creditor to serve a default notice on a **17–009** debtor or hirer under a regulated agreement before he is entitled to terminate the agreement for breach of contract by the debtor or hirer, and before he can take certain other steps such as recovering possession of any goods or land or enforcing any security. These obligations override the provisions of s.7(1) of the Bills of Sale Act 1878 and the Bills of Sale Amendment Act 1882, which permit the mortgagee to exercise a right of immediate possession of the secured chattel for default in payment.[33] If the default is remedied within the period specified in the notice, the creditor cannot take the matter any further.

Similar provisions for the service of a notice by a creditor who wishes to terminate the regulated agreement or take certain other types of action without termination, such as demanding early payment or recovering possession of goods or land, in circumstances other than breach by the debtor or hirer, are contained in ss.76 and 98.

For reasons which are not apparent, s.76(1), unlike s.87(1)(e), does not specifically refer to the enforcement of any security.[34] Thus, if the security consisted of a chose in action, and the contract was drafted in an appropriate manner, the anomalous situation might arise in which, prima facie, the creditor would be entitled to enforce that security against both the debtor and the surety without prior notice in a case not involving a breach of contract or termination, but would have to give them notice in a case of breach.[35]

By s.111(1) of the Act, a copy of the default notice or notice under ss.76 or 98 must be served on any relevant third party surety. There is no time limit specified for service, nor is there any requirement that the copy be served at the same time as the notice is served on the debtor. As a result these requirements afford very little protection to the surety. In theory

---

31 Ss.107(4), 108(4), 109(4) and 110(4).
32 See para.17–013.
33 See s.7A of the 1882 Act.
34 Though s.76(1)(b) makes reference to the recovery of possession of any goods or land.
35 It is likely that a credit agreement which enabled the creditor to enforce the security without a breach would be vulnerable to being reopened under s.137 as an extortionate credit bargain. That section will not, however, afford protection to the surety if the contract of suretyship entitles him to do this, though s.113(1) might.

there is probably no reason why the creditor should not wait until after the time for compliance with the default notice has expired before he serves the copy on the surety. Furthermore, the creditor is only obliged to serve a copy of the particular default notice on which he relies; so that if an earlier default notice has been complied with, and a fresh breach is alleged and a new notice is served in respect of that breach, he only has to serve the surety with a copy of the latter notice. Thus the surety is not necessarily fully appraised of any likely pattern of default, and may not find out the true state of affairs between the creditor and debtor in time to do something about it.

Failure to comply with s.111(1) means that the security is enforceable against the surety in respect of the breach or other matter to which the notice relates, on an order of the court only. Once again, however, there is no provision in the Act which applies s.106 to the security if an order for enforcement is refused or if the creditor purports to enforce without a court order.

Realisation and enforcement of securities

17–010 Section 113(1) of the Act provides that where a security is provided in relation to a regulated agreement, it shall not be enforced so as to benefit the creditor to an extent greater than would be the case if the security were not provided, and the obligations of the debtor under the agreement were carried out to the extent to which they would be enforced under the Act. This section does not make the security wholly ineffective, but it prevents the creditor from recovering more from the surety than he can recover under the Act from the debtor.[36] The object of s.113 therefore goes beyond applying the principle of co-extensiveness to security given for regulated agreements regardless of whether the contract is one of indemnity or guarantee, so that if the underlying transaction is cancelled, the security arrangements fall with it. It is primarily intended to ensure that the effect of the regulatory provisions of the Act is not evaded by the simple device of taking security. Thus the creditor who fails to execute a regulated agreement in compliance with the requirements of the Act cannot avoid the necessity of an application to court for an enforcement order by taking a mortgage or pledge from the debtor or from a third party surety and enforcing that instead.

The operation of s.113 can be illustrated by the following example.

At the request of D, S agrees to mortgage his property in favour of C to secure advances made by C to D under a prospective regulated loan agreement, and also to give a personal guarantee. The mortgage and guarantee are both ineffective until the loan agreement is made, and at any time before then, D can cancel the loan agreement, or S can

---

36 See *Wilson v First County Trust Ltd* [2001] Q.B. 407; *Wilson v Secretary of State for Trade and Industry* [2003] UKHL 40, [2003] 3 W.L.R. 568.

require s.106 to apply to the security. In either event, S is entitled to the return of the land certificate and title deeds. If the loan agreement is entered into, and the mortgage is executed, any provision in the mortgage or the guarantee which purportedly allows C to go into possession at any time or to call for payment under the mortgage on demand is ineffective to the extent that it gives C a better right against S than he has against D. If either the loan agreement or the guarantee is improperly executed, in that it is in the wrong form or S is not provided with copies of the guarantee and the loan documentation at the appropriate time, C cannot enforce the guarantee without an order of the court. (He cannot enforce the mortgage without a court order in any event.) If an order for enforcement is refused on any ground which is not purely technical, (for example, on the basis that the underlying loan agreement is an extortionate credit bargain within the meaning of s.138) s.106 will entitle S to the return of his title deeds and land certificate and to the cancellation of the guarantee. If the mortgage has to be enforced because of s.177, S is entitled to a full indemnity from C in respect of any loss which he suffers as a result.

If a regulated agreement is enforceable on an order of the court or of the OFT only, any security provided in relation to the agreement is enforceable only where such an order has been made in relation to the agreement, and not otherwise: s.113(2). The same rule applies where security is provided in relation to an actual or prospective linked transaction: s.113(8). Thus the creditor cannot evade the protections of the Act by dint of taking a security which is drafted so widely as to apparently give him a full indemnity regardless of the enforceability of the underlying agreement. Likewise, if the Court makes a time order in favour of the principal debtor under s.129, the creditor cannot accelerate payment by demanding the money immediately from a surety because of the provisions of s.113.[37] Given that the power to make time orders extends to almost all applications and actions connected with the enforcement of a regulated agreement or security provided in relation to such an agreement, it is unlikely in practice that the court would not have taken the position of the surety into account when it made such an order.

By virtue of s.126 of the Act, a land mortgage securing a regulated agreement is enforceable (so far as is provided in relation to that agreement) on an order of the court only. However, s.127 appears to give the court no discretion to refuse such an order, though the court may make a time order under s.129 or impose conditions or suspend the operation of the order under s.135.

Section 112 provides that, subject to s.121 (which relates to pawned items), regulations may provide for any matters relating to the sale or other

---

37 On the exercise of the power of the Court to make time orders, see *Southern & District Finance Plc v Barnes* [1995] C.C.L.R. 62, CA. See also *First National Bank v Syed* [1991] 2 All E.R. 250.

realisation by the creditor of property over which any right has been
provided by way of security in relation to an actual or prospective regulated
agreement, other than a non-commercial agreement. As at August 1, 2004 ,
no such regulations have been enacted.

Cancelled or unenforceable agreements

17–011   If any of the events prescribed by s.113(3) to (6) occurs, s.106 applies to the
security in whole or in part. The situations covered by s.113 are as follows:

(a)   where the underlying regulated agreement is cancelled under s.69(1)
or becomes subject to s.69(2);

(b)   where the regulated agreement is terminated under s.91;

(c)   where the creditor or broker introducing the business was unlicensed
under the Act, and the Office of Fair Trading ("OFT") dismisses an
application under ss.40(2) or 149(2) (except on technical grounds);[38]

(d)   where the regulated agreement has been improperly executed, and the
court has dismissed an application for an enforcement order under
s.65(1) other than on technical grounds;[39]

(e)   where there has been a breach of the restrictions on taking and
negotiating instruments under s.123 and the court has dismissed an
application for an enforcement order under s.124(1) or (2) other than
on technical grounds;

(f)   where a declaration is made by the court under s.142(1) refusing an
enforcement order, except on technical grounds; and

(g)   where a notice has been given by the surety requiring s.106 to apply to
the security at a time prior to the making of the regulated agreement.

If s.106 applies, the security will be treated as if it never had effect.[40]

Contracts with minors or the incapacitated

17–012   Section 113(7), as amended by s.4(1) of the Minors' Contracts Act 1987,
provides as follows:

> "Where an indemnity or guarantee is given in a case where the debtor
> or hirer is a minor, or an indemnity is given in a case where he is not
> otherwise of full capacity, the reference in subs (1) to the extent to
> which his obligations would be enforced shall be read in relation to the

---

38 For the power of the OFT or court to certify that a dismissal is on technical grounds see
s.189(5).
39 This is the mirror of s.105(8), which applies s.106 if the security instrument is improperly
executed.
40 See para.17–005 above.

indemnity or guarantee as a reference to the extent to which those obligations would be enforced were he of full capacity."

Sanctions for wrongful or premature enforcement

One of the major problems in the Act, which still remains to be resolved, is **17–013** what happens if the regulated agreement or the security is unenforceable, but s.106 does not expressly apply. For example, s.77(1) provides that the creditor is under an obligation to give certain information to a debtor under a regulated fixed-sum credit agreement, and s.77(4)(a) provides that the creditor is not entitled to enforce the agreement while he is in default.[41] Examples of similar provisions which provide that in the event of default, the creditor is not entitled to enforce the security, are to be found in ss.107–111, discussed above.

Although it is clear from s.113(1) that the creditor cannot evade the consequences of s.77(4)(a) by trying to enforce his security instead of proceeding against the debtor, there is no express application of s.106 to the security in those circumstances. Similarly, in s.107(4)(a) it is expressly provided that failure to comply with s.107(1) means that the creditor is not entitled to enforce the security while the default continues, but s.106 is not applied to the security. In all these types of case, the Act is completely silent as to the sanction if the creditor purports to enforce the security at a time when he is not entitled to do so.

The first question which arises is whether there is an implied operation of s.106, so that if the creditor remains in default under s.77 or a like provision he is obliged to return any property lodged by way of security or any money which he obtains by reason of the wrongful enforcement.

Whilst there is no authority directly in point under the 1974 Act, it has been held in respect of enactments as to unenforceable securities in the Moneylenders Act 1927[42] that if the security is unenforceable, it is implicit that the creditor must return the property: see, *e.g. Barclay v Prospect Mortgages Ltd* [1974] 1 W.L.R. 837.[43]

Despite the persuasiveness of the reasoning in the cases on the prior legislation, it seems likely that defaults under ss.77–79 and similar provisions of the 1974 Act are distinguishable, on the grounds that the default under those sections is potentially remediable and therefore the unenforceability may be temporary rather than permanent. It is noteworthy that all the situations in ss.113 and 105(8) which expressly apply s.106 are ones in which the agreement, the security, or both, are permanently unenforceable. It is therefore strongly arguable, as a matter of plain construction, that the legislation deliberately excludes unenforceability under any other sections from the draconian effects of s.106.

---

41 See also, *e.g.* s.78(6), which applies similar rules to running-account credit agreements, and s.79(3), which applies to consumer hire agreements.

42 Repealed by s.192(2) of the 1974 Act.

43 Applying the reasoning of the Privy Council in *Kasumu v Baba Egbe* [1956] A.C. 539, a decision on the Nigerian Moneylenders Ordinance.

If s.106 does not apply, the absence of any express sanction for enforcing an agreement when the creditor is not entitled to do so raises a considerable problem. This problem is compounded by s.170(1), which expressly states that a breach of any requirement made by or under the Act (other than one made by the court) shall incur no civil or criminal sanction except as provided by the Act.

This provision appears to rule out the possibility of suing the creditor for damages for breach of statutory duty. By s.170(3) the right to seek an injunction is preserved, but the right to prevent enforcement is of little consolation to the injured party if the damage has already been done. It is possible that a surety whose property has been wrongfully sold or seized at a time when the security was unenforceable might obtain a mandatory injunction requiring the creditor to return his property, but again that is of no real value if the property has been sold or otherwise disposed of. In those circumstances, it is arguable that s.170(1) is an obstacle to any tracing remedy, claim for an account, or claim for damages under the Torts (Interference with Goods) Act 1977. The ultimate sanction available is for the credit licence of the creditor to be suspended or revoked, but the use of such a weapon as a means of deterring the creditor from enforcing a temporarily unenforceable agreement or security may be regarded as disproportionately draconian.

One possible solution would be for the debtor, or indeed the surety, to apply to court under s.142(1)(b) for a declaration of unenforceability. If the application is successful, s.106 would then apply to the security by virtue of s.113(3)(d). Although it may be regarded as rather artificial for the surety or the debtor to seek a declaration of unenforceability after the agreement or the surety has been wrongfully enforced, in the hope of making s.106 apply, this may still be the most effective solution to the problem. In taking this step, the surety or the debtor will run the risk that the creditor would succeed in getting an enforcement order by means of a cross-application, but in that situation the court may well impose conditions on the grant of an enforcement order, which could include compensating the surety or the debtor for the premature and illegal enforcement.[44]

Extortionate credit bargains

17–014 One of the most important aspects of the Act is the power conferred upon the court to reopen the credit agreement so as to do justice between the parties if it finds a credit bargain extortionate.[45] The definition of "credit agreement" in this context extends to any agreement between an individual ("the debtor") and any other person ("the creditor") by which the creditor provides the debtor with credit of any amount. Consequently it will apply to virtually any personal loan transaction. The main exemption is an agree-

---

44 See s.135(1)(a). The court also has the power to vary any agreement or security in consequence of a term of any order which it may make: see s.136.
45 Ss.137–140.

ment falling under s.16(6C) of the Act, namely a transaction secured by a land mortgage where the lender is carrying on a regulated activity for the purposes of the Financial Services and Markets Act 2000. The power of the court is to examine and if necessary re-open the *bargain*, which is not therefore confined to the terms of the underlying credit agreement but will extend to the terms of any ancillary transaction including any agreement to provide security.

It is no doubt for this reason that a surety, as well as the debtor, has the power to make an application to the court for the credit agreement to be reopened, and he can do so even if the creditor has not started any proceedings against him or the debtor. He also has the standing to ask the court to reopen the agreement in any proceedings to which he and the debtor are parties, being proceedings to enforce the credit agreement, any security relating to it or any linked transaction, or in any other proceedings where the amount paid or payable under the credit agreement is relevant.[46] The relief which the court may grant on such an application, under s.139(2) includes an order directing the return to the surety of any property provided for the purposes of the security, and the court may also alter the terms of the credit agreement or any security instrument.

If a surety alleges that the credit bargain is extortionate, it is for the creditor to prove the contrary (s.171(7)). Nevertheless the statutory test of "extortionate" is high: the general principle, set out in s.138(1), is that a credit bargain is extortionate if it requires the debtor or a relative of his to make payments (unconditionally or on certain contingencies) which are "grossly extortionate" or it otherwise "grossly contravenes ordinary principles of fair dealing". In practice this threshold is rarely crossed. For example, in *Nash v Paragon Finance Plc* [2002] 1 W.L.R. 685, the borrowers who had secured their matrimonial homes by mortgage in favour of the lenders on terms which contained variable interest clauses, sought to reopen the mortgages on the basis that the agreements became extortionate when the lenders, Paragon, failed from time to time to reduce their interest rates in line with the Bank of England's prevailing market rates. The Court of Appeal held that although a commercial mortgage lender was under an implied obligation not to set rates of interest dishonestly, capriciously or arbitrarily, there were sound commercial reasons for the lender's behaviour in this particular case. It also held that it was not permissible to take subsequent changes in interest rates into account when determining whether the loan agreements were extortionate credit bargains, because the transaction had to be judged on the basis of the "total charge for credit" as determined at the outset of the agreement, which expressly excluded variations in interest rates.

In determining whether the bargain was extortionate, one of the most material factors is the degree of risk accepted by the creditor, having regard to the value of any security provided. For example, good security may

---

46 See s.139.

render the interest rate charged open to challenge even if if would not be regarded as excessive for an unsecured loan. The nature of the security is also important: personal security is likely to be regarded as more precarious than security over land, shares or goods.[47]

---

47 See further the discussion of extortionate credit bargains in *Chitty on Contracts* (29th ed. Sweet & Maxwell, 2004) Vol. 2 at 38–192 *et seq.*

Chapter 18

Landlord and Tenant

Introduction

The surety for the obligations of a lessee, his assignee or a sub-lessee is in general terms no different from any other surety. However, time may start to run against the landlord under s.19 of the Limitation Act 1980 much earlier than the landlord anticipates: see *Romain v Scuba TV Ltd* [1997] Q.B. 887, discussed in Chapter 7, above. The obligations of this type of surety will often be strictly construed. In *Jaskel v Sophie Nursery Products* [1993] E.G.C.S. 42 the sureties guaranteed the payment of rent under a lease of commercial premises. The landlord and tenant subsequently entered into an agreement for payment of a rent deposit, which was signed by the sureties, although they were not made parties to it. The sureties successfully defended a claim by the landlord that the guarantee extended to the rent deposit; it was held that the second agreement did not vary the lease and it was impossible to construe the documents together as constituting a single agreement.[1] Such a surety cannot rely on his own non-performance of a condition precedent to avoid liability. Thus in *Cerium Investments Ltd v Evans*, *The Times*, February 14, 1991 the Court of Appeal held that sureties who had convenanted to guarantee payment of rent and performance of covenants by an assignee of the lease could not escape liability because the licence had not been registered within one month, even though it contained a provision that in such event it would be "null and void". The licence became effective upon signature and the obligation to pay rent accrued during the month of grace, and in any event the sureties could not rely on their own wrongdoing as an excuse.

Variations of the lease
If the surety is a guarantor, the normal rule that a variation in the terms of the underlying agreement, in this case the lease, without the consent of the surety releases him from liability under the guarantee, will apply.[2] A good

18–001

18–002

---

1 Compare the approach to construction of a limited guarantee in *Menwald Properties v Hargrave House Ltd* (unreported) January 24, 2002, Ch D.
2 At least if it is a material variation which actually or potentially prejudices the surety: *Holme v Brunskill* (1878) 3 Q.B.D. 495, and see generally the discussion of this rule in Ch.9. However this will not prevent an assignee of the leasehold reversion from enforcing the obligation of the surety to pay rent: *Swift (PBA) Investments v Combined English Stores Group Plc* [1989] 1 A.C. 632, *Kumar v Dunning* [1989] Q.B. 193, discussed at later in this chapter at para.18–005.

modern illustration of the operation of the rule in *Holme v Brunskill* in this particular context is *West Horndon Industrial Park v Phoenix Timber* [1995] 20 E.G. 137, where the lease guaranteed by the defendant was assigned pursuant to a licence to assign which imposed additional burdens on the original tenant in respect of the rent payable on review, the potential insurance liability and the repair obligations. The operation of the rule may be excluded by agreement, and in this case the landlord argued that a provision in the covenant of guarantee which stated that the guarantor would be liable for the default of the tenant "notwithstanding . . . any other act or thing whereby but for this provision the guarantor would have been released" meant that the guarantor continued to be liable for the tenant's obligations. This argument was rejected by the judge, Mr Roger Kaye Q.C., who held that the words relied on were apt to cover the situation where, for example, the landlord released some other security for the rent, but they were not wide enough to cover the situation where the underlying obligations of the tenant became greater than those under the lease which it was clear the guarantor had agreed to guarantee.

A similar result was achieved in *Howard de Walden Estates v Pasta Place Ltd* [1995] 22 E.G. 143, where the express protection afforded to the landlord was limited to neglect or forbearance in enforcing covenants against the tenant, and therefore did not extend to variations of the lease by consent. The lease originally contained a provision restricting the use of the premises to a delicatessen, but the landlord granted a licence to the tenant to install tables for use by its customers, and progressively widened its scope to permit the sale of wine to customers taking meals, and to permit use as an off-licence. The lease was subsequently assigned and the licence was renewed. When the assignee and its guarantor both became insolvent, the landlord sought to recover arrears of rent from the original tenant and its guarantors: the latter successfully argued that the licence was a variation to which they had not consented and that they were discharged.

These cases may be contrasted with *Metropolitan Properties Co (Regis) Ltd Bartholomew* (1996) 72 P. & C.R. 380. The defendants were guarantors of the obligations of M, the assignee of the original tenant under a licence to assign dated December 15, 1988. Those obligations were "to pay the rents reserved by the lease and to perform and observe all the original tenant's covenants therein contained". In 1990 there was a further assignment of the underlease by M. This contained a provision entitling the new assignee, C, to allow other companies within the same group as C to occupy the demised premises as licensee. Mitchell J. held that this was a variation of the alienation covenant in the underlease and that the variation was relevant to the obligations of the tenant and to the liability of the surety. However, he rejected the argument by the sureties that the variation released them from their liability, on the grounds that the 1990 deed did not actually vary the contractual terms of the 1988 licence which gave rise to the obligations of M which the surety had guaranteed. He drew a distinction between a variation of the earlier contractual terms (which would release the surety) and a variation of an obligation created under the terms of that contract, which variation itself encompassed those same terms (which would not). His judgment was upheld by the Court of Appeal. Millett L.J.'s analysis was straightforward:

> "By the 1990 Licence the plaintiff at M's request and with its consent granted M licence to assign the Underlease to C and granted C a concession while it was a tenant. M could not object to the grant of the concession to C which it had requested and to which it had consented, but it did not agree to any modification or variation in the terms of the obligation which it had undertaken in the 1988 Licence. Since the terms of the 1988 Licence remain unaltered, the defendants are not discharged."

He stressed the importance of distinguishing between a material variation in the nature or extent of M's obligations in the 1988 licence, which may have discharged the sureties, and conduct which merely affected the cost of complying with those obligations, which would not.

The guarantee may, of course, contain an express provision protecting the landlord from the effect of the rule in *Holme v Brunskill* or any other act or omission which might otherwise release a guarantor. In *Eurodis Electron Plc v Unicomp Inc* [2004] EWHC 979 (May 7, 2004) a 20-year lease had been granted over the premises on terms which included a covenant that the tenant, CEM, would not assign or transfer the lease without the prior written consent of the landlord. CEM's parent company, C, guaranteed due payment of the rent and performance of the covenants under the lease. The guarantee contained a clause by which C agreed that any "neglect or forbearance" by the landlord in endeavouring to obtain payment or to enforce the covenants would not release or exonerate C's liability under the guarantee. Subsequently C sold its shares in CEM, under a share sale agreement which included an obligation on the purchaser, H, to use its best endeavours to procure that C was released from its guarantee, and to indemnify C from all liabilities in connection with the lease pending release. Another party to the share sale agreement, D, also agreed to indemnify C. CEM got into financial difficulty and went into voluntary liquidation. H then gave notice to the landlord that a related company of CEM was in occupation of the premises and paying the rent. Since the landlord had not consented, this was a breach of the covenant against assignment, but the landlord continued to accept rent from the other company and took no steps to forfeit the lease. However, negotiations with the landlord to obtain its consent to the assignment ultimately failed. The landlord began proceedings against C as guarantor, which were compromised. C then took steps to recover the money from H and D under their indemnities. One of the defences raised by D was that, by tolerating the breach of covenant by CEM and taking no steps to forfeit the lease, the landlord had materially altered the risk borne by C as surety and discharged it from liability. However, Evans-Lombe J. held that even if there had been any material prejudice, it arose from the forbearance of the landlord to enforce a covenant in the lease, which fell squarely within the proviso to the guarantee, and consequently C was not released.

Instead of relying upon the traditional type of contractual provision to the effect that a variation does not release the guarantor, the landlord may prefer to include a provision in the guarantee which requires him to give notice of the proposed variation to the guarantor and provides that unless the guarantor objects in writing within a given period, he will be deemed to have consented to the variation: see, *e.g. BM Samuels Finance Group Plc v Beechmanor* (1994) 67 P. & C.R. 282.

Subject to any statutory provisions[3] the consent of a surety to a variation in the lease will be binding on him: *Apus Properties v Douglas Farrow & Co* [1989] 2 E.G.L.R. 265. In *BM Samuels Finance Group Plc v Beechmanor* (above) the situation which would arise if some of the sureties consented (or were deemed to consent) to the variation, and others objected, was left unclear. This could pose a particular difficulty if the original liability was expressed to be joint, rather than joint and several. The difficulty might be resolved by treating any express consent as giving rise to a fresh and independent contract of suretyship between the landlord and the consenting sureties, or by the operation of the doctrine of estoppel, but both these solutions could prove awkward to apply in the context of a clause deeming the surety to have consented because he did not object within a given time.

Although it is common for the surety's consent to be recorded in writing as part of the deed of variation of the lease, the question whether or not a surety has consented to a variation may be answered by reference to extraneous evidence. In *Goodaston Ltd v FH Burgess Plc* [1999] L. & T. R. 46, FHB had guaranteed a lease of which G were the landlords. In 1982 FHB, G and the tenant had all entered into a deed of variation to extend the term of the lease. FHB argued that they were not liable under the varied lease, as the 1982 deed failed to spell out that they were to be guarantors. Jacob J. unsurprisingly gave this argument short shrift; the terms of the 1982 deed satisfied s.4 of the Statute of Frauds 1677 and it was clear from all the surrounding circumstances that FHB were intending to continue as guarantors of the lease.

A variation of a lease by court order under s.38 of the Landlord and Tenant Act 1987 will be binding on a surety who has guaranteed performance of any obligation varied by the court order, even if he has not been made party to the proceedings or served with notice of the application under s.35(5) of the Act and the relevant procedural rules:[4] *ibid.* s.39(2). The surety will be taken to have guaranteed the performance of that obligation as so varied.

Effect of termination of the lease

18–003   The question whether or not the surety's obligations are co-extensive with those of the principal will depend on the true construction of the contract of suretyship, and the terms of that contract will also provide the answer to

---

3 See the provisions of s.18(3) of the Landlord and Tenant (Covenants) Act 1995, discussed in para.18–008 below.
4 See CPR r.97.17.

the question whether the liability of the surety survives for the future after the forfeiture of the lease, or its termination for other reasons, *e.g.* the expiry of a fixed term or release of the principal debtor. If quarterly rent is payable in advance, the guarantor's liability will extend to the whole quarterly payment even if the lease is forfeited during the quarter in question: *Capital and City Holdings Ltd v Dean Warburg Ltd* [1989] 25 E.G. 97. In *Collin Estates Ltd v Buckley* [1992] 40 E.G. 151, proceedings by the landlord against the tenant were settled on terms that the tenant paid a particular sum by way of compromise without admitting liability. The landlord sued the guarantor and the guarantor argued that there had been a compromise and a novation and he was released from liability. Nolan L.J. acknowledged the force of the argument, but held that the terms of the guarantee were wide enough, on their true construction, to cover the liability accepted in the consent order.[5]

In the absence of express wording, the obligations of the guarantor will not cover the obligations of the tenant under a statutory continuation of the tenancy after the lease expires.[6] Nor will he be obliged to pay interim rent in excess of the contractual rate under s.24A of the Landlord and Tenant Act 1954 unless there is express provision: *City of London Corporation v Fell* [1993] Q.B. 589. An example of such an express provision is to be found in *Collin Estates Ltd v Buckley* (above). Of course, the termination of the lease will not affect any liability of the surety which has already accrued: see, *e.g. Apus Properties Ltd v Douglas Farrow & Co Ltd* [1989] 2 E.G.L.R. 265; *Pierce & Thames (Manufacturing) Co v Perrotts* (1984) P. & C.R. 1. The acceptance by the landlord of the repudiation of a lease by the tenant has no different effect on the liability of the surety than the acceptance by the creditor of the repudiation of any other contract; the rule in *Lep Air v Moschi* [1973] A.C. 331 still applies.[7]

In the important case of *Ivory Gate Ltd v Spetale* (1999) 77 P. & C.R. 141 the Court of Appeal held that sureties for the obligations of a tenant under a lease remain under a continuing liability to pay rent for the period between the service of proceedings seeking possession of the demised property and the termination of those proceedings. In June 1993, the landlord served a notice under s.146 of the Law of Property Act 1925 on the grounds that the tenant had appointed receivers. He subsequently issued and served proceedings claiming forfeiture, but the proceedings were compromised in February 1994 and the lease was transferred to the

---

5 The guarantee covered "all losses costs damages and expenses occasioned to [the landlord] by non-payment of said rents or any part thereof or breach non-observance or non-performance of any of said covenants stipulations and conditions".

6 *Junction Estates v Cope* (1974) 2 P. & C.R. 482; *Plesser v Davis* (1983) 267 E.G. 1039; *Associated Dairies v Pierce* (1982) 265 E.G. 127. See also, on the question whether the creditor can enforce an obligation in the contract to extend the guarantee to a renewed lease, the Australian case of *Verdi La Fontana Pty Ltd v Mabrook Pty Ltd* [1992] N.S.W. Conv. R. 59, 606, also reported in (1992) 5 B.P.R. 11, 557, a decision of the New South Wales Supreme Court (Court of Appeal).

7 See, *e.g. Nough Pty Ltd v Charles Donovan Pty Ltd (in liq.)* [1989] V.R. 184.

landlord. The settlement agreement expressly provided that it was not intended to release the sureties from their liability under the lease.

The Court of Appeal restated the principle, approved on many prior occasions, that the service of a writ claiming forfeiture and possession does not by itself bring a lease to an end, but operates as an unequivocal election by the landlord to rely on the breach of covenant to found the forfeiture. The apparently contrary observation by Lord Templeman in *Billson v Residential Apartments Ltd* [1992] 1 All E.R. 142 that "the effect of issuing and serving a writ is precisely the same as the effect of re-entry; in each case the lease is determined" should not be taken out of context: it was made in response to a submission by a landlord that a tenant could not apply for relief from forfeiture where a landlord had physically re-entered the premises without order. In fact, the lease continues, subject to a final determination of its status. If the court holds that there was no breach of covenant, so that the notice under s.146 was ineffective, the lease subsists. It would only be if the defence to the action for possession and any counterclaim for relief from forfeiture both failed, that the lease would be treated as determined retrospectively from the date of service of the writ. Thus the liability of the surety to pay rent, if the tenant fails to do so, continues unless and until the tenant's application for relief is dismissed. If possession is ordered, mesne profits will be payable from the date of the possession order until the delivery up of possession; alternatively mesne profits could be backdated to the date of service of the writ, with the payments which would have been characterised as rent (if the tenant's application for relief had succeeded) being re-cast as mesne profits.

Effect of assignment of the lease

18–004　In a normal case, the mere act of assigning the lease will not release the surety because, in the absence of express release, the assignor will remain liable to pay the rent and observe the covenants of the lease despite the assignment; see *Cheverell Estates Ltd v Harris* [1998] 1 E.G.L.R. 27. The same rule applies to an assignee under a licence to assign who covenants directly with the landlord that he will pay the rents reserved by the lease and observe the covenants in the lease, and then assigns the lease to someone else.[8] When the assignment takes effect, then, unless as a matter of construction the covenant to pay rent contained in the first licence to assign clearly only applies to the period when the lease is vested in the assignee, and does not extend to the full duration of the lease, the first assignee will remain liable to pay the rent and so will any surety for his obligations under the licence to assign: *Estates Gazette Ltd v Benjamin Restaurants Ltd* [1994] 1 W.L.R. 1528.[9] However, a guarantee which is

---

8 Likewise, if the assignee covenants with the original tenant to pay the rent and observe the covenants in the lease, he is assuming a primary obligation and is not a surety for the obligations of the tenant: see *Baynton v Morgan* (1888) 22 Q.B.D. 74.

9 Similarly, the release of a guarantor of an assignee will not release the original tenant from his liability: *Allied London Investments Ltd v Hambro Life Assurance Ltd* (1985) 274 E.G. 81. One may query, however, whether it might release the surety for the original tenant by causing material prejudice to his rights on subrogation.

expressed to be for "so long as the term hereby granted is vested in the tenant" will not survive an assignment so as to make the surety liable on default by the assignee: *Johnsey Estates v Webb* [1990] 19 E.G. 84.

Effect of transfer of the freehold reversion

For some time it was doubtful whether the transfer by the landlord of the freehold reversion of the property automatically transferred the benefits of any guarantees given to the landlord in respect of the obligations under the lease, so that the new landlord could enforce the covenants in the lease directly against the sureties. In the Australian case of *Sacher Investments v Forma Stero Consultants Pty Ltd* [1976] 1 N.S.W.L.R. 5, although the expression "lessor" was defined in the lease as "the lessor, its successors and assigns", it was held by Yeldman J. that the covenants by the guarantors in the lease were not enforceable by the transferee of the reversion without an express assignment. The case was followed in England in *Pinemain Ltd v Welbeck International Ltd* [1984] 272 E.G. 1168 and *Re Distributors and Warehousing Ltd* [1986] B.C.L.C. 129.

18–005

However, in *Kumar v Dunning* [1989] 1 Q.B. 193, Sir Nicholas Browne-Wilkinson V.-C. cast doubt upon those cases, and held that the covenant by the surety "touched and concerned" the land, in consequence of which the benefit of the covenant passed automatically to the assignee of the reversion without the need for a separate assignment to be executed. This decision was approved by the House of Lords in *Swift (PBA) Investments v Combined English Stores Group Plc* [1989] A.C. 632. The House of Lords held that the benefit of the covenant by the surety could be enforced by an assignee of the reversion without express agreement if the covenant was one which "touched and concerned" the land, and that the covenant in respect of the obligation to pay rent fell into that category. It was held that if the underlying obligation of the tenant touches and concerns the land, then the obligation of the guarantor also touches and concerns the land, even if it is an obligation to pay money. Lord Oliver, at 642, formulated the following working test for whether, in any given case, a covenant touches and concerns the land:

(1) the covenant benefits only the reversioner for the time being, and if separated from the reversion ceases to be of benefit to the covenantee;

(2) the covenant affects the nature, quality, mode of user or value of the land to the reversioner;

(3) the covenant is not expressed to be personal (*i.e.* it is not given only to a specific reversioner nor in respect of the obligations only of a specific tenant).

If these three conditions are fulfilled, the fact that a covenant is to pay a sum of money will not prevent it from touching and concerning the land, if the covenant is connected with something to be done on, to or in relation to the land. Thus the assignment of the reversionary interest in the underlease carried with it the benefit of the guarantee. The position of the guarantor was explained by Lord Templeman at 638 in the following simple sporting metaphor:

> "a surety for a tenant is a quasi-tenant who volunteers to be a substitute or 12th man for the tenant's team and is subject to the same rules and regulations as the player he replaces. A covenant which runs with the reversion against the tenant runs with the reversion against the surety."[10]

By s.3 of the Landlord and Tenant (Covenants) Act 1995, the benefit of a covenant by a surety guaranteeing the tenant's convenants will pass on assignment to the landlord's assignee whether or not it "touches and concerns the land". The rule, which is subject to the qualifications in s.3 (3), applies to all new tenancies, *i.e.* those granted after January 1, 1996, when the Act came into force, except those granted pursuant to a court order or agreement made before that date. The Act is discussed in more detail in para.18–008 below.

Rent reviews

18–006 The surety will normally covenant not just to pay the rents reserved by the lease but all rents (including increased rents after a rent review). Forfeiture of the lease will not release the surety from liability for accrued obligations, including an obligation to pay rent which has not yet been quantified under a rent review clause at the date of forfeiture: *Torminster Properties v Green* [1983] 1 W.L.R. 676. Unless the contract makes express provision, the surety will have no right to participate in a rent review. It is fairly common to find a provision in a modern lease by which the tenant creates the guarantor his attorney for the purpose of participation in the rent review. Such a clause could pose difficulties if the lease is subsequently assigned, because it is hard to envisage how the original tenant can bind a future assignee to make the guarantor the attorney of the *assignee* for the purposes of any rent review. It may be preferable for the guarantor to insist that he be given the contractual right to participate in his own name and on his own behalf.

Relief against forfeiture

18–007 A surety has no right to seek relief against forfeiture unless he happens to be in the position of equitable mortgagee, *e.g.* if the tenant agrees that if the surety calls upon him to do so, he will execute a mortgage of the lease

---

10 The same reasoning has been adopted in Australia: *Lang v Asemo Pty Ltd* [1989] V.R. 773, Supreme Court of Victoria.

in favour of the surety: *Re Good's Lease* [1954] 1 W.L.R. 309.[11] Nowadays it is fairly common to find provisions requiring the tenant to assign the lease to the surety in the event of his default, coupled with a covenant by the landlord to consent to such an assignment (such consent not to be unreasonably withheld). In order to try to prevent a claim arising under the guarantee without his having been given sufficient warning to be able to take steps to protect himself, the surety may insist on including terms requiring the landlord to serve on the surety copies of all notices served by him on the tenant, and requiring the landlord to tell the surety within a particular period if the tenant or any assignee falls into arrears in paying the rent on a specified number of occasions, or is otherwise in breach of covenant. However, a degree of statutory protection has been introduced in the Landlord and Tenant (Convenants) Act 1995, discussed in para.18–008 below.[12]

If a surety offers to pay arrears of rent, there is some authority for the proposition that the landlord may refuse to accept the payment if this would prejudice him by depriving him of the right to forfeit: *Richards v De Freitas* [1974] 29 P. & C.R. 1. In that case, the offer to make payment was made not by a surety, but by the receiver of a company which was in possession of the premises under licence. The reasoning of May J. in that case and in the earlier authorities referred to in it, was expressly approved by the Court of Appeal in *Milverton Group v Warner World* [1995] 2 E.G.L.R. 28.

If the payment is accepted, the surety will be entitled to claim from the tenant, by way of indemnity, any rent which he had paid, in accordance with usual principles. He will also be entitled to be subrogated to the landlord's claim for the rent against any other party who is liable to pay, such as a defaulting assignee (see the discussion in para.18–017 below).

Once the surety has paid the outstanding arrears, then as between the landlord and any other person against whom a claim for the rent could have been made, payment by the surety will extinguish the debt and he is not entitled to double recovery: *Milverton Group v Warner World* (above) explaining the earlier decision of the Court of Appeal in *London and County (A & D) Ltd v Wilfred Sportsman Ltd* [1971] Ch. 764. Hoffmann L.J. said that the analysis of Russell L.J. in that case, to the effect that a payment under the guarantee was not a payment of "rent", could not survive the decision of the House of Lords in *P & A Swift Investments v Combined English Stores* [1989] A.C. 632 (see para.18–005 above). The correct analysis was that of Megarry J. in *Re Hawkins, deceased* [1972] Ch. 714 at 723–729, namely that a single set of obligations is owed by the tenant

---

11 The surety was a person "having an agreement for an underlease" within the meaning of s.146(5)(d) of the Law of Property Act 1925, and therefore entitled to apply for relief from forfeiture under s.146(4) of that Act. On the right of a mortgagee to intervene in forfeiture proceedings see *Egerton v Jones* [1939] 2 K.B. 702.
12 Further protection against a secret accumulating liability may be afforded to the surety by including a term requiring the landlord to enforce the covenants in the lease against the tenant or any assignee before claiming on the surety.

and the guarantor to pay rent and perform the covenants in the lease. Accordingly if a surety pays the rent in full, or the landlord accepts a smaller sum from him in satisfaction of the outstanding rent, he cannot look to the tenant to pay the money again or to pay the balance and the landlord would therefore have no entitlement to forfeit the lease. Likewise, any payments made by a surety towards future rent will be taken into account in determining the amount which the tenant is obliged to pay. If the payment by the surety covers an element relating to both past and future rent, then it is up to the landlord to make an appropriation.

The Landlord and Tenant (Covenants) Act 1995

18–008 This Act, which came into force on January 1, 1996, contains provisions which have considerable impact on the liabilities of guarantors for the obligations of lessees.[13] The most important sections in this regard are ss.16–18.

Section 5 of the Act has the effect of releasing a former tenant from his covenants under the lease immediately upon assignment of the tenancy. His obligations (and his corresponding rights under the covenants by the landlord) devolve upon the assignee, who stands in his shoes and is treated to all intents and purposes as if he were the original tenant. Section 16, which applies only to new tenancies, allows the tenant who has assigned the lease to enter into an "authorised guarantee agreement" with the landlord with respect to the performance of the covenants by the assignee. Such an agreement will only be authorised if it is entered into in fulfilment of a condition, lawfully imposed by the landlord, on the giving of his consent to the assignment, where the assignment cannot be effected without such consent, and it otherwise satisfies the requirements of s.16. The contract of suretyship may be an "authorised guarantee agreement" even if it is more properly described as a contract of indemnity, but it cannot impose on the tenant any liability in relation to any period after the assignee is released from his liability in respect of the covenant, or which is more onerous than the assignee's liability, or which requires him to guarantee the liability of anyone else besides the assignee—s.16(4). Section 16(8) provides that the rules of law relating to guarantees, and in particular those relating to the release of sureties, apply to such a guarantee agreement in the same way as to any other guarantee.

Section 16 partly implemented a recommendation by the Law Commission[14] that a landlord whose consent has to be obtained should be able to impose a condition that the assignor guarantees the assignee's performance

---

13 For a full discussion of the Act see Woodfall, *Landlord & Tenant* (Sweet & Maxwell), Vol. 1, Ch.16.
14 Law Commission Report "Landlord and Tenant Law: Privity of Contract and Estate" (Law Com. No.174). A useful commentary on the Act, by T. M. Aldridge, Q.C., was published by Pearson Professional Ltd in 1995. It contains a precedent of an authorised guarantee agreement.

of the lease covenants, to last until but only until the date of the next assignment. It was felt appropriate that a landlord should be able to insist on a guarantee of the performance of a substitute tenant whom the assignor has nominated, but not of any further assignees in whose selection he may have played no part. It will be noted that the wording of s.16(1) is permissive; this was deliberate. It was designed to avoid the guarantee being used by the landlord as a device for retaining the tenant's privity of contract liability after he had assigned the lease, thereby circumventing s.5. The landlord cannot force the tenant to give such a guarantee, but he can probably legitimately withhold his consent to the assignment if he refuses. In *Wallis Fashion Group Ltd v CGU Life Assurance Ltd* [2000] L. & T.R. 520, it was decided that a landlord cannot demand, as of right, that a requirement of an authorised guarantee agreement be included in the assignment provisions in a new tenancy granted under Pt II of the 1954 Act. Neuberger J. held that an authorised guarantee agreement may be "lawfully imposed" under s.16(3)(b) of the 1995 Act only where it is reasonable to do so. He also held that the terms of the authorised guarantee agreement also had to be reasonable. Section 16(6) applies to a situation where the tenant has made an unlawful assignment or the lease has been assigned to a new tenant by operation of law. When the first tenant is released from his covenants on assignment by the first assignee, if the first assignee has entered into an authorised guarantee agreement, the landlord may require the first tenant to enter into such a guarantee as well, so that he and his assignee are both sureties of the second assignee.

Section 16(7) makes it clear that where a tenant who entered into an authorised guarantee agreement either takes back the assigned lease on a disclaimer following his assignee's insolvency (see para.18–014 below) or enters into a new lease under the authorised guarantee agreement, the provisions of s.16(1) to (5) will still apply in the event that he subsequently assigns the new lease or re-acquired lease to someone else.

If an agreement relating to a tenancy excludes, modifies or would otherwise frustrate the operation of any provision of the Act it will be void by virtue of s.25. This will include any guarantee agreement which falls within s.16(4).

Sections 17 and 18 apply new restrictions on the liability of a former tenant or his surety for rent or service charges under the tenancy agreement,[15] and when the tenancy agreement is subsequently varied. Both sections apply to new and existing tenancies. Section 17 introduces a statutory condition precedent requiring the landlord, within six months beginning with the date when any fixed charge (including rent) falls due for payment under a covenant, to serve a notice in prescribed form on the former tenant and on the guarantor. The notice will fix the maximum amount of the tenant or guarantor's liability unless it (a) informs him of the

---

15 It does not apply to any obligations under an agreement to surrender the lease, see *BSE Trading v Hands* [1996] E.G.C.S. 99.

possibility that his liability may be subsequently determined to be for a greater amount (*e.g.* by virtue of a forthcoming rent review), (b) his liability is determined to be greater, and (c) within three months from such determination the landlord serves on him a further notice informing him that the landlord intends to recover that greater amount from him, plus interest where payable. When the surety or the former tenant has paid the full amount required under a s.17 notice, together with any interest, he will become entitled to call on the landlord to grant him an overriding lease of the premises under s.19. This has the virtue of enabling him to pursue remedies directly against the defaulting tenant, if he is still in occupation and still solvent, or to take possession of the property in the manner which the Court of Appeal held was open to the surety in *London and County (A & D) Ltd v Wilfred Sportsman Ltd* [1971] Ch. 764, discussed in para.18–007 above.

A notice under s.17 will be properly served if it is sent to the recipient at his last residential address, even if it is not received by him: *Commercial Union Life Assurance v Moustafa* [1999] 24 E.G. 155. If the notice provisions are not adhered to, the landlord will be precluded from recovering the fixed charge from the former tenant or the guarantor as the case may be. In *Cheverell Estates v Harris* [1998] 1 E.G.L.R. 27, the guarantor, on whom a notice had been duly served under s.17(3), took the objection that a notice under s.17(2) had not been served on the former tenant and argued that as the principal was not liable to pay the rent, the relevant six months having expired, his own liability had been extinguished. It was held that there was no necessity for the landlord to serve a notice on the former tenant, if he chose not to sue him as well as the guarantor. This accords with normal principles of the law of suretyship; see Chapter 7, para.7–002 above. The fact that no notice had been served on the tenant by the landlord would not have prejudiced the surety's rights to claim an indemnity from him in the usual way.

When the surety has paid the rent or another "fixed charge", and seeks to recover contribution or an indemnity from the tenant or a third party, the provisions of s.17 have no application as between the surety and the other party. This was confirmed by Judge Brandt in the Ipswich county court in *Fresh (Retail) Ltd v Emsden* (unreported), January 18, 1999, where the person claiming contribution or an indemnity was the original tenant, T. T assigned the lease to A, who assigned to B, who assigned to C. In 1992, A went bankrupt and in 1993, C defaulted. The landlord sued T, who took an assignment from A's trustee in bankruptcy of all the rights and benefits of the statutory covenants. T claimed indemnity or a contribution from B and B's guarantor, G. They argued that conditions precedent to their liability had not been fulfilled because notices in the prescribed form had not been served on them by T under s.17 of the Act: it was held that T's action was not vicarious enforcement of the landlord's claim to payment of a fixed charge, but a claim for an indemnity or contribution in quasi-contract and therefore the Act did not apply.

Section 18 of the Act deals with variations of tenancy covenants after an assignment. It applies to all tenancies, but only to new variations of tenant covenants. Section 18(3) provides that where a "relevant" variation of a lease [16] does not wholly discharge the guarantor of a former tenant from liability, he will not be liable to pay any amount in respect of the tenant's covenants to the extent that the amount is referable to any such variation. Thus for example, if the lease contains a clause which enables the landlord to vary its terms without releasing the guarantor, and he agrees with the assignee to permit the premises to be used for additional purposes on payment of an increased sum, when the assignee defaults, the guarantor will only be liable for the original amount of rent. It would appear that this provision cannot be contracted out of, and consequently even if the guarantor expressly covenants to pay all moneys covenanted to be paid under the terms of lease as varied from time to time, the landlord will be unable to claim the increase from him. It is arguable, on the basis of s.25(1), that a guarantee which contained such a provision would be void, and not simply unenforceable as regards the offending clause, but this can hardly have been the result which Parliament intended. The contrary argument is supported by the language of s.18(3), which implicitly recognises that the guarantor retains some liability. It is important to note that s.18 is confined to variations which the landlord has (or would have had) an absolute right to *refuse*. It therefore does not apply to variations which the landlord has the right to make, such as an increase in the rent or service charges (if the terms of the original lease are not worded in such a way as to make these a facet of the tenant's original obligations rather than variations).

Substitution clauses

In view of the fact that a guarantor of the obligations in a lease will be unable to revoke the guarantee if the lease is for a fixed term,[17] and that he is prima facie liable throughout the term of the lease not only in respect of the obligations of the original tenant, but in respect of subsequent assignees, it is generally prudent for the guarantor to seek to include a term enabling him to retire upon finding a reasonable substitute guarantor who is acceptable to the landlord.[18] There will usually be a provision for notice to be given to the landlord and for him to give his consent (not to be unreasonably withheld) within a specified time. A refusal of consent will be unreasonable if the landlord has no objection to the substitute but seeks to link his consent to variations in the terms of the lease, see, *e.g. Roux Restaurants Ltd v Jaison Property Development Co Ltd* [1997] 74 P. & C.R. 357, (a case concerning consent to an assignment). The question whether or not the landlord is behaving reasonably in withholding his consent or

18–009

---

16 Defined in s.18(4) as a variation which the landlord had an absolute right to refuse to allow or would have had if he had not been deprived of that right between the time of the assignment and the time of the variation.

17 See the discussion in Ch.8 above.

18 See, *e.g. Grovewood (LE) v Lundy Properties* (1995) 69 P. & C.R. 507.

imposing certain conditions upon it will of course depend on the facts and circumstances of each particular case.[19] However, it will not necessarily be unreasonable for the landlord to require evidence that the proposed sureties are able to meet *all* their financial liabilities and not just their liabilities as sureties. This is illustrated by the case of *Mount Eden Land Ltd v Towerstone Ltd* (2002) 31 E.G. 97 (again, a case concerning consent to an assignment). This was an action by a landlord to action to forfeit the lease of business premises which were occupied by a company, D. The tenant of the premises was another company owned and run by a husband and wife, who had since separated. They had agreed that the business would be taken over by D, which was controlled solely by the husband, H. In consequence of that agreement, D took over possession of the premises. Some years later, the original tenant sought the landlord's permission to assign the residue of the term of the lease to D. The lease provided that in the event that an assignment to a limited company was proposed, the landlord might require two or more directors to stand as sureties. The landlord invoked that provision, and asked for references for three of D's directors. In the event, references were provided for only two directors including H, whose references revealed that he had other contingent liabilities, most notably to D's bankers. The landlord refused to give consent to the proposed assignment unless there were three sureties, and the references for H satisfied the landlord that H could meet all his contingent liabilities, and not just the guarantee liability which he was proposing to take on. D argued that this was an unreasonable refusal to grant consent. The judge, however, refused to grant relief from forfeiture. He held that requiring three sureties was not unreasonable, since it was not a requirement for such a large number of sureties as to make the assignment provisions unworkable. In any event, it would not have been unreasonable for the landlord to seek references which spoke of H's ability to meet all his contingent liabilities and not just the liability which would arise under the prospective guarantee.

Similar provisions may protect the tenant from the exercise by the landlord of a right of re-entry on the death, insolvency or receivership of the surety: see, *e.g. Grovewood (LE) Ltd v Lundy Properties Ltd* [1995] 69 P. & C.R. 507, where Jonathan Parker J. held that as a matter of construction a provision entitling the tenant to serve notice indicating that one or more surety was to be released, and requiring the landlord to enter into a deed of release "provided always that . . . the tenant shall procure for the landlord such person as shall be required to act as substitute guarantor . . . and such substitute shall simultaneously enter into a direct covenant with the landlord" meant that the release of the surety did not come into effect until a substitute had been provided or the landlord agreed to waive his rights under that clause.

---

19 For discussion of what has and has not been held to be reasonable, see *Woodfall*, (*op. cit.*) Vol. 1 at 11.121 and 11.138.

Effect of disclaimer of the lease

In the second edition of this work a considerable part of this chapter was **18–010** devoted to the difficulties which used to arise when one of the parties in the leasing chain (whether a lessee or an assignee) became insolvent and the lease was disclaimed. In the light of the decision of the House of Lords in *Hindcastle Ltd v Barbara Attenborough Associates Ltd* [1997] A.C. 70 most of those difficulties have disappeared and the legal position on disclaimer can be much more simply stated. If the party concerned is an individual, his trustee in bankruptcy may disclaim the lease under s.315 of the Insolvency Act 1986.[20] A similar right is given to the liquidator of an insolvent company by virtue of s.178 of that Act.[21] Likewise, if a company is dissolved after being struck off the register under s.652 of the Companies Act 1985, its property (including any lease) initially vests in the Crown as *bona vacantia* under s.654. By virtue of s.656, the Crown then has the right to disclaim that lease. This has a twofold effect; first, the execution of the notice of disclaimer means that the disclaimed lease is deemed not to have vested in the Crown under s.654 (s.657(1)), and secondly, the Crown's disclaimer is to be treated as if it were a disclaimer by a liquidator immediately prior to the dissolution of the company (s.657(2)). This has the effect of bringing into operation ss.178(4) and 179–182 of the Insolvency Act 1986.[22]

Neither a receiver nor an administrator may disclaim a lease. A tenant company which is in administration or receivership therefore continues to be liable under the lease unless and until it expires, is forfeited by the landlord or otherwise terminates.

Effect of disclaimer

Section 178(4) of the Insolvency Act 1986 provides that a disclaimer: **18–011**

"(a) operates to determine, as from the date of the disclaimer, the rights interest and liabilities of [the insolvent company] in or in respect of the property disclaimed; but

(b) does not, except so far as is necessary for the purpose of releasing [the company] from any liability, affect the rights or liabilities of any other person."[23]

---

20 A detailed discussion of these provisions in this context is to be found in *Woodfall, Landlord & Tenant (op. cit.)* Vol 1 at paras 16–208 *et seq.*

21 The wording of the present legislation dates back to s.55 of the Bankruptcy Act 1883, introduced at a time when only a trustee-in-bankruptcy had a right to disclaim. The right of the liquidator to disclaim with the leave of the court was introduced by s.267 of the Companies Act 1929: see *Re Katherine et Cie* [1932] 1 Ch. 70 at 73–74. The legal consequences of disclaimer are the same for the person whose interests are being disclaimed and for any surety, whether the disclaimer is by a trustee in bankruptcy or a liquidator. A very good concise history of the legislation is to be found in the judgment of Vinelott J. in *Re AE Realisations Ltd* [1987] 3 All E.R. 83.

22 *Per* Millett J. in *Re Yarmarine (IW) Ltd* [1992] B.C.C. 28 at 30.

23 Identical language is used in s.315(3) which applies to bankruptcy.

A person who sustains loss or damage in consequence of the operation of a disclaimer is entitled to prove in the bankruptcy or liquidation. The disclaimer therefore determines the interests of the person whose interests have been disclaimed in the lease, and releases him and his estate from all future liability thereunder, including the liability to pay rent for any period after the disclaimer, and substitutes a statutory liability on the part of his estate to compensate any person injured by the disclaimer, including the landlord.

Disclaimer on insolvency of the original tenant

18–012   If the insolvent person is the original tenant, the prevailing view in the authorities appears to be that the disclaimer terminates the lease itself and not just the obligations of the tenant: see, *e.g. Hindcastle Ltd v Barbara Attenborough Associates* [1997] A.C. 70 *per* Lord Nicholls at 87E–G, applied by the Court of Appeal in *Christopher Moran Holdings Ltd v Bairstow* [1999] 1 E.G.L.R. 1.[24] The termination of the head lease by the disclaimer also simultaneously terminates any sub-lease, although a sub-tenant may apply to the court for an order that the lease be vested in him: *Re AE Realisations (1985) Ltd* [1988] 1 W.L.R. 200.[25] Although the sub-lease is terminated by the disclaimer, the position as between the landlord and the sub-tenant is that the head lease is to be treated as though it still existed, and consequently the sub-tenant may still remain in occupation of the term of the sub-lease. The landlord cannot directly enforce any covenants in the lease against him unless (as is usually the case) the sub-tenant has entered into a direct contract with the landlord under which he has covenanted to pay the rent. However, if the sub-tenant does not perform the covenants in the original lease, he will be liable to forfeiture or to be distrained upon for rent by the landlord.[26] The disclaimer will not destroy the right of a tenant, sub-tenant or mortgagee, who is in the same position, to make an application to the court for relief from forfeiture: *Barclays Bank Plc v Prudential Assurance Co* [1998] 10 E.G. 159. In order to protect his position, the sub-tenant may apply to the court for an order vesting the

---

24 See also *Re Morrish Ex p. Hart Dyke* (1882) 21 Ch. D. 410 *per* Jessel M.R. at 425–426; *Stacey v Hill* [1901] 1 K.B. 660 *per* A.L. Smith M.R. at 664; *Re Finley* (1888) 21 Q.B.D. 475; *Richmond v Savill* [1926] 2 K.B. 530.

25 Applying *Re Finley Ex p. Clothworkers' Co* (1888) 21 Q.B.D. 475. See also *Stacey v Hill* [1901] 1 K.B. 660 *per* A. L. Smith L.J. at 664 and *per* Romer L.J. at 667; *Warnford Investments Ltd v Duckworth* [1979] 1 Ch. 127 at 135. The sub-tenancy will also terminate if the landlord exercises his right to forfeit the head lease: *Great Western Railway v Smith* (1876) 2 Ch. D. 235, subject to the right to seek relief against forfeiture and the special rules which apply to business tenancies under Part II of the Landlord and Tenant Act of 1954. The sub-tenancy will also terminate at common law if either the landlord or the tenant serves a notice to quit or exercises a "break" clause: *Pennell v Payne* [1995] 6 E.G. 152. It does not terminate on surrender or merger; ss.139 and 150 of the Law of Property Act 1925, and see *Fairweather v St Marylebone Property Co Ltd* [1963] A.C. 510.

26 *Re AE Realisations Ltd* [1988] 1 W.L.R. 200, applying the cases of *Smalley v Hardinge* (1881) 7 Q.B.D. 524 and *Ex p. Walton, In re Levy* (1881) 17 Ch. D. 746, decided on the wording of the 1869 Act, and the Court of Appeal decision in *Re Finley, ex p. Clothworkers' Co* (1888) 21 Q.B.D. 475, which was decided after the 1883 Act.

property in him. If he does not do so, the landlord may put him to his election: see *Re AE Realisations* (above).

If the surety is a guarantor of the obligations of the original tenant and the disclaimer is by the liquidator or trustee in bankruptcy of that tenant, he will not be released by the disclaimer, even though the lease ceases to exist: *Hindcastle Ltd v Barbara Attenborough Associates Ltd* (above), applying *Hill v East and West India Dock Co* (1884) 9 App. Cas. 448 and overruling *Stacey v Hill* [1901] 1 K.B. 660. The decision in *Stacey v Hill* was founded on the principle of co-extensiveness—if the lease terminates, no further rent can fall due under it and therefore there was no primary liability for the surety to guarantee. The problem with this analysis was that the statutory provision which was then in force (s.55(3) of the Bankruptcy Act 1883) provided that the disclaimer should not "except so far as is necessary for the purpose of releasing the bankrupt and his property and the trustee from liability, affect the rights or liabilities of any other person". The House of Lords in *Hindcastle* held that the modern re-enactment of that provision, with slight modification, in s.178(4) of the Insolvency Act 1986 was a statutory exception to the common law principle. Two members, of the Court of Appeal in *Stacey v Hill*, A. L. Smith M.R. and Romer L.J., had sought to apply the proviso to a surety by reasoning that in order to release the insolvent party from his liabilities in respect of the lease, it was necessary that the guarantor should also be released. In *Hindcastle* the House of Lords said that this was not so; all that was necessary was to release the insolvent party from his liability to indemnify the surety. In the Court of Appeal, the potential injustice which this interpretation would produce obviously weighed heavily with Millett L.J., who said:[27]

"It would . . . require very clear statutory language to deprive a surety of his right to indemnity while leaving his liability unimpaired. No such language is to be found in subsection 4(b) . . ."

However, in the House of Lords Lord Nicholls demonstrated the fallacy of this approach by showing that the effect of the statute is that the surety is no worse off by the loss of his right of indemnity. He would be just like any other unsecured creditor of the insolvent party. He pointed out that the fundamental purpose of an ordinary guarantee is that the risk of the debtor's insolvency shall fall on the guarantor and not the creditor, and referred to the fact that the discharge of a bankrupt principal from his bankruptcy does not release a guarantor.[28] Although the guarantor loses his right to an indemnity, he is entitled to prove as a creditor in the insolvent party's estate, which is exactly what he would be entitled to do if he had an indemnity. The statute, far from taking away the guarantor's rights, leaves him in the same position. Moreover, he could be better off, because it

---

27 [1995] Q.B. 95 at 195.
28 S.281(1) and (7) of the Insolvency Act 1986.

would be open to him to take steps to obtain some return from the property by seeking a vesting order under ss.181(2)(b) and 182(3) of the Insolvency Act 1986.[29] Lord Nicholls also suggested that he might even be entitled to an overriding lease under s.19 of the Landlord and Tenant (Covenants) Act 1995, though this is debatable in the light of s.19(7) which provides that the landlord is not obliged to grant an overriding lease under that section at any time when the relevant tenancy has been determined.

Covenants by the surety to take on a new lease from the date of the disclaimer

18–013   There is commonly an express provision in the lease requiring the guarantor to take a new lease for the remainder of the term in the event of a disclaimer by the liquidator or trustee in bankruptcy of the original tenant. It has been held that such an obligation is not personal to the surety and thus will bind his executors: *Basch v Stekel* [2001] L. & T.R. 1, Buxton and Chadwick L.JJ. Interesting questions arise in this context, when the guarantor has been party to the lease prior to January 1, 1996 and is required to take up the fresh lease thereafter, as to whether the Landlord and Tenant (Covenants) Act applies to the new lease. In such a case it is arguable that, by virtue of the transitional provisions in the 1995 Act, s.1(3) and (6), the old regime continues to apply. Matters are more open to debate, perhaps, where the guarantor becomes party to a pre-1996 lease after January 1, 1996.[30]

It would appear that such covenants may be enforced by a person who acquires the landlord's interest in the premises even after the disclaimer, regardless of whether or not there is an express assignment by the original landlord. In *Scottish Widows Plc v Jane Tripipatkul* [2003] EWHC 1874, [2004] B.C.C. 200, a lease was granted by the landlord, G, to a company, T Ltd, on November 28, 1996. T was surety for the obligations of T Ltd under the lease. The lease contained a clause which provided that if T Ltd went into liquidation, and the lease was disclaimed, then within three months after the disclaimer G could demand that T, as surety, should take a new lease for a term equal to the residue of the lease. However, if G did not require the surety to take a new lease, "the surety shall neverthless upon demand pay to the Landlord a sum equal to the rents and other payments that would have been payable under this Lease but for the disclaimer or forfeiture until the expiration of six months therefrom or until the demised premises shall have been re-let by the Landlord whichever shall first occur". In March 2000, T Ltd went into liquidation and the liquidator subsequently disclaimed the lease. G then sold the premises to S. The issue was whether T was liable as surety for the rent which fell due in the six month period

---

29 See *Re AE Realisations (1985) Ltd* [1988] 1 W.L.R. 200. The decision of Hoffmann J. in *Re No.1 London Ltd* [1991] B.C.L.C. 28 to the contrary effect must now be treated as incorrect in the light of *Hindcastle*.
30 For a commentary on this see Slessinger (2000) 144 S.J. 724.

immediately following the disclaimer of the lease by the liquidator of T Ltd, and if so, whether either S or G was entitled to enforce the covenant of suretyship. T argued that even if, as a result of *Hindcastle v Barbara Attenborough Associates* [1997] A.C. 70 she was still liable to pay rent to G, that obligation was not enforceable by S. She contended that Lord Nicholls' speech in *Hindcastle* made it clear that as between landlord and tenant the reversion was extinguished. Therefore, as there was no reversionary interest at the date of the transfer to S, there was nothing with which the surety's covenant could run.

The master had held that the reversion to a disclaimed lease "may be regarded as continuing in a notional sense despite the termination of the lease, like the Cheshire Cat's grin in Lewis Carroll's Alice". Pumfrey J. agreed, subject to the caveat that it must be remembered that "the grin remains only as between the surety and the landlord." Although it might be thought that the idea of a "notional reversion" was to pile artificiality upon artificiality, the judge said it was a necessary and logical application of the principles that Lord Nicholls had articulated. As a result of s.178(4), the lease remained on foot to the extent to which its provisions were relevant to the liabilities and rights of the landlord and the surety *inter se*, and if the dead lease was deemed to subsist as between them, there was no reason why the "notional reversion" could not be assigned to a purchaser with the benefit of the covenant annexed to it as if the lease had not been disclaimed. The judge also held that, in any event, the benefit of the relevant clause of the lease had been expressly assigned by G to S. He preferred to leave open for another occasion the contention that the benefit of the clause containing the surety's covenants was annexed to the freehold reversion expectant on the head lease of the premises.

If the landlord terminates the original lease by taking possession or accepting its surrender before any disclaimer, then, (subject to relief from forfeiture) he not only loses the right to claim rent from the surety for the future, but also loses the right to require the surety to take on a new lease for the remainder of the term. In *Scottish Widows v Tripipatkul* (above) the surety unsuccessfully contended that there had been re-entry on the basis that it was to be inferred from the fact that the premises had been sold with the benefit of vacant possession. In *Active Estates Ltd v Parness* [2002] EWHC 893 (Ch), [2002] 36 E.G. 147, the main issue was whether, as a matter of principle, if a landlord recovers possession of the land *after* there has been a disclaimer, he is likewise precluded from enforcing a covenant by the surety to take up a new lease for the residue of the original term. Although Neuberger J. acknowledged the force of the argument that there is, on the face of it, no inconsistency between a landlord taking possession and thereafter seeking to enforce a contractual option in his favour to require a third party to take on a new lease, he decided that the landlord cannot do so. He gave five main reasons for his decision:

(1) In *Hindcastle* the House of Lords confirmed that in principle, a covenant by the guarantor to pay rent ends on repossession by the landlord after a disclaimer. Lord Nicholls said at 89B:

"When a landlord acts in this way, he is no longer merely the involuntary recipient of a disclaimed lease. By his own act of taking possession he has demonstrated that he regards the lease as ended for all purposes. His conduct is inconsistent with there being a continuing liability on others to perform the tenant covenants in the lease. He cannot have possession of the property and, at the same time, claim rent for the property from others".

Although Lord Nicholls was specifically directing his remarks to the obligation to pay rent, the obligation of the surety to take on a new lease is integrally linked to the obligation to pay rent. The taking on of the new lease has been described as a means of giving effect to the surety's obligation to procure compliance with the terms of the old lease: see *Coronation Street Industrial Properties v Ingall Industries Plc* [1989] 1 All E.R. 979 at 981, *per* Lord Templeman. If that is so, then the retaking of possession by the landlord is just as incompatible with the enforcement of an option to require the surety to execute a new lease, as it is with requiring him to pay rent under the old one.

(2) The retaking of possession after a disclaimer is also inconsistent with requiring a new lease to be taken as from the date of the disclaimer, as it would be peculiar if the landlord could be entitled to charge rent for a period during part of which he had possession of the property.

(3) Section 178(4)(b) of the Insolvency Act 1986 suggests that there should be no difference in principle between the effect of repossession before and after a disclaimer on the relationship between landlord and surety.

(4) The conclusion would not do violence to the language of the usual form of covenant, because the "guarantor" must still be a "guarantor" when the option is sought to be enforced against him;

(5) The Court of Appeal in *Basch v Stekel* [2001] L. & T.R. 1 proceeded on the assumption that the landlord could not enforce the option if he took possession after a disclaimer.

A further argument deployed by the sureties in *Active Estates Ltd v Parness* was that the clause requiring them to take up a new lease was unenforceable because the provisions of s.2 of the Law of Property (Miscellaneous Provisions) Act were not complied with. Although the contract creating the option in favour of the landlord was in writing and signed by the surety, it was argued that the contract arising as the result of the exercise of that option was not recorded in writing, and that therefore the provisions of the Act were not satisfied. However, Neuberger J. held that the statute was sufficiently complied with if the grant of the option was evidenced in writing and signed by the surety.

In practice, it may be difficult for the surety to prove that the landlord has accepted the surrender of the old lease or taken possession. For example in *Bhogal v Cheema* [1998] 2 E.G.L.R. 50 the landlord accepted rent from an associated company of the tenant company, which then went into liquidation. When the landlord made a demand on the surety for payment of the arrears of rent, it was held that there was no implied surrender of the old lease by the insolvent tenant, and no implied acceptance of surrender by the landlord in allowing the associated company into possession and accepting rent from it, since the landlord had made it clear that it regarded any payments by the associated company as being payments for the account of the tenant. Sir John Vinelott also held that there was no obligation on the landlord to mitigate his loss by taking possession of the property—it was up to the surety to seek a vesting order if he wished to mitigate his own position. Likewise, in *Active Estates Ltd v Parness* (above) the sureties were unable to establish on the evidence that the landlord had taken possession of the property after the disclaimer, although again the landlord had allowed an associated company of the insolvent tenant to occupy the premises. The landlord had agreed, prior to the disclaimer, to grant the associated company a right of occupation upon disclaimer. However, that right of occupation was in the nature of a licence, and all rent demands continued to be addressed to the insolvent company.

Disclaimer on insolvency of a sub-tenant or assignee of the lease

The decision in *Hindcastle* finally put paid to the apparent anomaly **18–014** between the position of the original tenant and the guarantor, when the disclaimer was by the trustee or liquidator of an assignee of the lease. It had been established long before *Stacey v Hill* that disclaimer by an assignee's trustee in bankruptcy did not release the original tenant from his obligation to pay the rent: *Hill v East and West India Dock Co* (1884) 9 App. Cas. 448, applying *Ex p. Walton, In re Levy* (1881) 17 Ch. D. 746. The obligations of the original tenant are primary, and not secondary, so the requirement that the insolvent party's obligations should survive did not apply to the tenant. However, if the lease was terminated by the disclaimer, it would be difficult to see how any future rent could be claimed from anyone. Moreover, the much-criticised second ground for the decision in *Stacey v Hill*, namely that it was "necessary" to release the surety from liability in order to release the insolvent estate from its liability to indemnify him, applied equally to tenants, who would also have a right of indemnity. The Court of Appeal in *Stacey v Hill* had sought to distinguish the earlier authorities on the basis of the wording of the Bankruptcy statute which was in force at the time when they were decided, but it was apparent that the decisions could not easily be reconciled.

It was another 77 years before the position of the original tenant (and any surety for his obligations) fell to be considered by an English court in the light of *Stacey v Hill* and the changes in wording of the Bankruptcy legislation since *Hill v East and West India Dock Co* was decided. It was considered in the interim in New Zealand by McGregor J. in *Re Ice Rinks (Timaru) Ltd* [1955] N.Z.L.R. 641 and Australia by Gowans J. in *Re Teller Home Furnishers Pty Ltd (in liq.)* [1967] V.R. 313, which concerned statutory provisions which were identical to the corresponding terms in the

English statute. In both cases it was decided that the obligations of the original tenant survived the disclaimer; in the latter case Gowans J. also, somewhat reluctantly, followed *Stacey v Hill* and held that the sureties for the obligations of the assignee to the landlord were discharged. The question finally came before Sir Robert Megarry V.-C. in *Warnford Investments v Duckworth* [1979] 1 Ch. 127. Somewhat surprisingly, neither of these Commonwealth authorities was cited to the court. Nevertheless, Megarry V.-C. reached the same conclusion as McGregor J. and Gowans J. that the obligations of the original tenant survived the disclaimer despite the second ground of the decision in *Stacey v Hill*. He held that the law in this regard was the same as it was before the enactment of the 1883 Act, which merely spelled out something which the courts had previously construed into the language of the previous statute so as to avoid the perpetration of an injustice to the landlord. The 1883 Act had the effect of making explicit what the courts had held to be implicit for the purposes of avoiding injustice and absurdity and made it clear that the legislature "resoundingly approved of the law which was shortly to find its final expression by the House of Lords in *Hill v East and West India Dock Co*". However, the reasoning by which he reached the conclusion that the tenant remained liable was largely founded upon the proposition that the lease remained in existence despite the disclaimer, which he said merely released the insolvent assignee and his estate from liability under it.[31] That proposition was plainly impossible to reconcile with *Stacey v Hill*.

The reasoning of Megarry V.-C. must be treated as incorrect, in the light of the confirmation by the House of Lords in *Hindcastle* that the lease *does* end on disclaimer, and not merely become "cataleptic". However, the decision in *Hindcastle* affirms the correctness of his conclusions. If the lease is disclaimed, both the original tenant and any surety will remain liable. Lord Nicholls expressly acknowledged the artificiality of the concept that there would be no subsisting lease (unless a vesting order was made) and yet claims for rent could still be made, but he said that this awkwardness was inherent in the statutory operation: see [1997] A.C. at 89D–E.

Effect of disclaimer by the Crown

18–015   In *Re No.1 London Ltd* [1991] B.C.L.C. 501, and *Re Yarmarine (IW) Ltd* [1992] B.C.C. 28 the disclaimer by the Crown on dissolution of the company was equated with a disclaimer by a liquidator. Both those cases followed *Stacey v Hill* and held that the disclaimer terminated the liability of the guarantor in respect of any future rent or breaches of the covenants in the lease; in the light of *Hindcastle Ltd v Barbara Attenborough Ltd* they must be treated as wrongly decided on this aspect, but there is no reason to doubt the correctness of treating the disclaimer by the Crown as equivalent to disclaimer by a liquidator or trustee in bankruptcy.

---

31 A disclaimer by the trustee-in-bankruptcy of an insolvent assignee does not merely disclaim his interest under the licence to assign, but disclaims the interest of the bankrupt in the lease itself: *MEPC Plc v Scottish Amicable* [1993] N.P.C. 44.

A company which is dissolved after being struck off the register for failing to file statutory accounts, unlike a company which is placed in liquidation, may be revived and restored to the register.[32] In *Allied Dunbar Assurance Plc v Fowle* [1994] 2 B.C.L.C. 197, Garland J. held that the effect of restoration of a dissolved company to the register was to revive the liability of all sureties for the company's obligations.[33] In that case, the company was the assignee of the lease and the sub-tenant; the sureties were its directors. The lease vested in the Crown as *bona vacantia* under s.654 of the Insolvency Act 1986 and the Crown then disclaimed the lease at the instigation of the sureties. Subsequently the company was restored to the register. The landlord tried to distinguish *Stacey v Hill* and argued that the liability of the sureties survived the disclaimer, but Garland J. reluctantly felt constrained by earlier authority to hold that there was no valid distinction to be drawn between a disclaimer on liquidation and disclaimer by the Crown. The sureties argued that the disclaimer took effect from the moment that the leasehold interest vested in the Crown and that they were discharged from liability at that time; the disclaimer was a "disposition" under s.655 of the Companies Act 1985, and the landlord's remedy was to seek compensation. The landlord and the original tenant argued, successfully, that the effect of the restoration of the company to the register was that it was deemed to have continued as if it had not been struck off. Consequently, the lease was deemed never to have vested in the Crown and the company, and original sureties, remained liable.

This decision was easy to justify, given that the argument advanced by the sureties would have meant that, in theory, unscrupulous sureties who happened to be directors of the tenant or sub-tenant company could terminate their liability simply by dint of ensuring that it did not file its annual returns and was struck off; the landlord or an intermediate assignee would then have to rely on the Crown not to disclaim the lease, because restoration to the register would leave him with a remedy only against the company. In the light of the decision in *Hindcastle*, the obligations of the guarantor would probably survive the disclaimer regardless of whether the company was restored to the register, and so restoration may not matter so much to the landlord, though it could be of importance to the surety. A guarantor of a company's obligations under a lease is put in a difficult position when the company is dissolved, because the extent of his liability remains unresolved even if the Crown disclaims the lease. Although the revival of the company will revive its primary liability, this may not provide much of a safeguard: companies which have been struck off for failing to file their annual returns are often in financial difficulties and if the company went into liquidation shortly after its restoration the surety would have no remedy save for his right to prove in the liquidation. This is quite likely to

---

32 See ss.652–653 of the Companies Act 1985.
33 This is *not* the case if a bankruptcy is annulled after the trustee-in-bankruptcy has disclaimed the interest in the lease: see *Re Hyams* (1923) 93 L.J. Ch. 184. However, this may not matter because of the decision in *Hindcastle*.

happen if the person who petitions the court for restoration is a creditor—possibly the landlord himself. The surety's best course may well be to sue the company for *quia timet* relief as soon as it is restored to the register; he cannot sue for such relief before then, as once it has been dissolved the company no longer exists and cannot be sued. Consequently if he has the *locus standi* to procure that the company is restored to the register, by making an application to the court under ss.653 or 651 of the 1985 Act, it may be in his best interests to do so as soon as possible.[34]

Voluntary arrangements

18–016 The surrender of a lease in the course of a voluntary arrangement under Pt 1 of the Insolvency Act 1986 will not absolve the original tenant or his sureties from liability, for exactly the same policy reasons as were employed in *Hill v East and West India Dock Co. RA Securities Ltd v Mercantile Credit Co Ltd* [1994] B.C.C. 599 concerned a claim by landlords for rent against the original tenants and assignors of the lease. The lease had been assigned by the tenants to a bank, and by the bank to a company which had entered into the voluntary arrangement. The agreement made under the voluntary arrangement provided that "each lessor accepts a surrender of the respective lease". By s.5(2) of the Insolvency Act 1986, such a voluntary arrangement binds "every person who in accordance with the rules had notice of and was entitled to vote at" the creditors' meeting. The landlords had been given such notice but did not attend the meeting. The original tenants were not parties to the meeting. Jacob J. held that although the voluntary arrangement was binding on the landlords, there was no accord and satisfaction as regards the original tenants; the purpose of a voluntary arrangement is to enable a company to come to a composition with its creditors in order to stay in business, and is not for the benefit of a solvent party who also happens to owe debts owed by that company. The voluntary arrangement may not release the surety for the person entering into that arrangement.[35] However, this will probably depend upon the precise wording of the contract of suretyship; if the guarantee is for payment of "rent which remains due and owing", a discharge of the principal debtor under the terms of the voluntary arrangement may also discharge the guarantor.[36]

---

34 But query whether he would qualify as a "creditor" under s.653(2).
35 A scheme of arrangement sanctioned by the court will not usually release the guarantor: *Ex p. Jacobs* (1875) L.R. 10 Ch. App. 211; *Dane v Mortgage Insurance Corporation* [1894] 1 Q.B. 54 at 63–64, *per* Kay L.J. See also the Australian cases of *Hill v Anderson Meat Industries Ltd* [1971] 1 N.S.W.L.R. 868 at 874–876 *per* Street J. (*affirmed* on appeal [1972] 2 N.S.W.L.R. 704) and *Caratti v Hillman* [1974] W.A.R. 92 at 95, in which the same reasoning was applied to a scheme of arrangement pursuant to statutory provisions outside the context of winding-up or bankruptcy proceedings.
36 See *Johnson v Davies* [1999] Ch. 117; *Greene King v Stanley* [2001] EWCA Civ 1966 and the discussion in Ch.9 at para.9–014 above.

Rights of the surety after payment

The surety who discharges the obligations of the tenant or of an assignee **18–017** has the same rights of indemnity and subrogation as any other surety who has paid. He will usually have an express contractual right of indemnity against the person whose obligations he has discharged. He may also take over the remedies and securities of the landlord to enforce his rights to contribution or an indemnity.[37] Thus in *Re Downer Enterprises Ltd* [1974] 1 W.L.R. 1460, an assignee paid the arrears of rent to the landlord, after the company to which the assignee had in turn assigned the lease went into liquidation. The liquidator decided not to disclaim the lease and it was eventually sold. Pennycuick J. held that he was entitled to be paid in full out of the assets of the company, as an expense in the liquidation, the sum realised on the sale of the lease, because he was subrogated to the landlord's right to claim that money in respect of rent which had accrued due after the commencement of the liquidation.[38] This would no doubt apply equally to any surety who paid the rent.

In *Re Russell, Russell v Shoolbred* (1885) 29 Ch. D. 254, the question arose whether the surety who paid the landlord would be entitled to distrain for the rent, though it did not arise directly in the context of any claim by the surety to distrain, but rather in the context of a claim by a tenant against an assignee under a contract of indemnity. The tenant, H, had bought the leasehold interest in four properties from the landlord's liquidators after they had sued him for the rent, which H had paid. He had a claim under a contract of indemnity against the estate of his former business partner, R, to whom he had previously assigned all his interest in the property. R had covenanted to pay the rents and observe the covenants under the lease, and to keep H indemnified against them. H made a claim against R's estate for the rent which he had paid. The estate defended the claim on a number of grounds, one of which was that H, on payment of the rent, had become entitled to a right of distress, which he had destroyed by taking an assignment of the leases from the landlord. It was contended that if R had paid that rent to H, he would have been entitled to an assignment of that right of distress as a "security" under s.5 of the Mercantile Law Amendment Act 1865[39] and that H had therefore discharged R as surety by releasing a remedy to the benefit of which R was entitled. There is little doubt that the argument was unmeritorious because as between H and R it was plainly intended that R should bear the ultimate obligation to pay the rent, so the arrangement was not a classic case of suretyship. The Court of Appeal rejected the argument on the basis that the right to distrain for rent

---

37 See s.5 of the Mercantile Law Amendment Act 1865, discussed in Ch.11, above. It is common to find a provision in the lease requiring the landlord to co-operate with the surety in enforcing the landlord's subrogated rights.
38 Applying *Re ABC Coupler & Engineering Co Ltd (No.3)* [1970] 1 W.L.R. 702.
39 See the discussion in Ch.11 particularly at para.11–021.

in arrear is not a "security", which is no doubt correct. However they went on to decide (slightly more hesitantly) that it was not a "remedy" which the person paying the debt is entitled to use within the meaning of s.5, because the remedies there referred to are confined to proceedings in which but, for the statute, payment might have been pleadable. Even if this narrow reading of the reference to "remedies" in s.5 of the 1865 Act is correct, (which is doubtful), the Act should not be regarded as exhaustive of a surety's rights of subrogation.[40]

In *BSE Trading Ltd v Hands* [1998] 75 P. & C.R. 138, three sureties, two of whom were B and H, guaranteed the obligations of the tenant, T, under a lease. B paid the outstanding rent under a settlement with the landlord, and claimed contribution from H. H argued that pursuant to the rule in *Lord Harberton v Bennett* (1829) Beatty 386, B could recoup payments out of the land and that it should exhaust its remedies against the principal debtor, T, before seeking contribution from him. The Court of Appeal rejected this argument. It held that the rule did not apply where the lessor was the creditor and the tenant the principal debtor. A surety could not use the remedy of distress and re-entry, as this would terminate the lease, and the title of the creditor had to be preserved. However, it allowed H to defend the claim for contribution on other grounds. That decision does not depend on any general principle that the remedy of distress is unavailable to a surety, but on the rather special facts of the case. In the context of suretyship there is no general obligation on a surety to exhaust his remedies against the principal before claiming contribution or an indemnity from his co-surety.

In the light of more recent case law, which has shed further light on the nature of the doctrine of subrogation, and which has confirmed the right of the subrogated party to succeed to personal as well as proprietary claims,[41] it is debatable whether the decision in *Re Russell* that a surety who has paid the rent cannot distrain can be regarded as good law today.

If the surety succeeds to the freehold reversion, he may also acquire the landlord's right to forfeit the lease for non-payment of the rent by the tenant. In those circumstances it is debatable whether it is open to the tenant or any other party to say that the rent has been paid, and the right to forfeiture lost, because the surety himself has paid it to the landlord. On normal principles of subrogation the fact that a debt has been paid will not preclude it being treated as still subsisting in equity for the purpose of preventing unjust enrichment. On the other hand, a distinction may be drawn between the right on the part of the subrogated party to claim payment of the debt, and the specific powers available to a landlord to

---

40 *cf. Selous Street Properties v Oronel Fabrics Ltd* [1984] 270 E.G. 643.
41 See, *e.g. Banque Financiere v Parc (Battersea) Ltd* [1999] A.C. 221; *Niru Battery Manufacturing Co v Milestone Trading (No.2)* [2004] 2 Lloyd's Rep. 319; [2004] *Cheltenham and Gloucester Plc v Appleyard* [2004] EWCA Civ 291, *The Times*, March 29, 2004; *Filby v Mortgage Express (No.2) Ltd* [2004] EWCA Civ 759, [2004] N.P.C. 98, and the discussion in Ch.11 at para.11–023.

enforce that payment. In principle, if the right to distrain can be acquired by subrogation then there would appear to be no good reason to distinguish the right of forfeiture.

Precedent 1

Standard Form Bank Guarantee[1]

THIS IS AN IMPORTANT DOCUMENT. SIGN ONLY IF YOU WANT TO BE   **P1–001**
LEGALLY BOUND. YOU ARE RECOMMENDED TO TAKE INDEPEN-
DENT LEGAL ADVICE BEFORE SIGNING.[2]

[*space for the Guarantor to initial*]
Dated the 7th day of December 1992

TO: THE ROYAL BANK OF ELSINORE LIMITED (herein called
              'the Bank')

FROM: HAMLET PRINCE of The Castle, Castle Hill, Elsinore,
              Denmark (herein called 'the Guarantor')

In consideration of the Bank making or continuing advances or otherwise giving
credit or affording banking facilities or other financial accommodation or granting
time to such extent and for so long as the Bank may think fit to ELSINORE
ENTERPRISES LTD (herein called 'the Debtor'):

IT IS HEREBY AGREED AS FOLLOWS:

1 Definitions

'the Bank'	the Royal Bank of Elsinore Limited, its successors **P1–002** and assigns, including any bank into which it may be absorbed or with which it may amalgamate
'the Debtor'	shall include the personal representatives of the Debtor, and where the Debtor is a partnership, the persons from time to time being members of the partnership, and where the Debtor is a company, any company into which it may be absorbed or with which it may amalgamate or any new company constituted by a merger with or by reconstruction of the Debtor company
'Debtor's Obligations'	all the Debtor's liabilities to the Bank of any kind whatsoever (whether present or future, whether actual or contingent, whether incurred as principal or as a surety or in any other capacity whatsoever, and whether incurred alone or jointly or severally with any other person),[3] including liabilities in respect of Interest, Expenses, banking charges and commission and any liabilities arising during the [*three months'*] period of notice referred to in clause 3.2[4]

'Expenses'	all costs and other expenses of whatsoever nature (on a full indemnity basis) incurred by the Bank or its agents in connection with the enforcement of the Debtor's Obligations in whole or in part, or the enforcement of this Guarantee in whole or in part, or the exercise of any power under this Guarantee or under any agreement between the Bank and the Debtor, including (without prejudice to the generality of the foregoing) any legal costs and disbursements, together with Interest or Guarantee Interest from the date on which the Expenses are incurred
'Guarantee Interest'	Interest at the rate of [2%] above the Bank's published base rate from time to time with [*three monthly*] rests [*or at the rate of 10% per annum compounded quarterly whichever is the greater*]
'Interest'	Interest (whether simple or compound) as well after as before judgment, at the rate or rates charged by the Bank to the Debtor from time to time, or as may be awarded by a court or arbitral tribunal or stipulated by statute
'Security'	shall include a Guarantee, Indemnity, Charge, Mortgage or Deposit, Letter of Credit or any other form of security real or personal and whether or not negotiable.

2 Guarantee and indemnity[5]

P1–003 **2.1** the Guarantor hereby unconditionally guarantees to discharge the Debtor's Obligations to the Bank on demand in writing by the Bank to the Guarantor [*without deduction, set-off, or counterclaim*[6],] together with Guarantee Interest thereon from the date of such demand.

2.2 The Guarantor further agrees that if any of the Debtor's Obligations are at any time void or unenforceable against the Debtor for any reason whatsoever (whether known to the Bank or not), the Guarantor will be liable to the Bank as a principal debtor by way of indemnity for the same amount as that for which the Guarantor would have been liable had the Debtor's Obligations not been void or unenforceable, and further agrees to discharge the amount of that liability on demand in writing by the Bank to the Guarantor without deduction set-off or counterclaim, together with Guarantee Interest thereon from the date of such demand.

2.3 The Guarantor further agrees to pay Expenses to the Bank on demand in writing, together with Guarantee Interest thereon from the date of such demand.

PROVIDED THAT the amount recoverable from the Guarantor under this Guarantee (whether as surety or by way of indemnity) shall not exceed the total of [*£1,000,000 (one million pounds sterling)*)] together with Interest on that sum since the date on which Interest was last compounded in the books of the Bank, and Guarantee Interest on that total from the date of demand, and Expenses (including any Interest or Guarantee Interest accruing thereon).[7]

3 Continuing security

P1–004 **3.1**This Guarantee is and shall remain a continuing security for the Debtor's Obligations to the Bank at any time and shall not be satisfied or otherwise affected by any repayment or recovery from time to time of the whole or any part of any amount which may then be due and owing from the Debtor to the Bank.

3.2 This Guarantee shall remain in force notwithstanding the death or disability of the Guarantor, or notice of his death or disability, and shall be binding on his personal representatives or persons legally entitled to represent him,[8] but may be discontinued and the liability hereunder crystallised (except as regards unascertained or contingent liabilities and any liability for Interest, Guarantee Interest and Expenses) by [*three months'*] notice in writing to the Bank from the Guarantor or his personal or legal representatives.[9]

3.3 If notice of discontinuance under Clause 3.2 is given, the Guarantor will be liable for the amount of the Debtor's Obligations at the date of the expiry of such notice whether or not any demand has been made on the Guarantor or on the Debtor before that date. Such notice shall not affect the liability to the Bank of any Guarantor or surety other than the Guarantor giving notice.[10]

3.4 This Guarantee shall continue and shall be enforceable notwithstanding any change in the name of the Bank or any change in the constitution of the Bank, its successors or assigns or by its absorption of or by its amalgamation with any other bank or banks.[11]

3.5 Where the Debtor is a partnership, the Debtor's Obligations shall include those (in relation to the partnership business) of the persons from time to time being members of the partnership and the Guarantor's liability hereunder shall continue despite any change in the constitution of the partnership and shall not be prejudiced by any such change. However, the Debtor's Obligations shall only include obligations undertaken by a partner or partners on behalf of the partnership firm.[12]

3.6 Where the Debtor is a company,[13] the Debtor's Obligations shall include those undertaken by the Debtor under a different name or style to that stated in this Guarantee and the Guarantor's liability hereunder shall continue without any prejudice and this Guarantee shall be available to the Bank despite any change in the name or business of the Debtor or change in the constitution of the Debtor (whether by amalgamation consolidation reconstruction or otherwise). In the event of such a change, the expressions 'Debtor' and 'Debtor's Obligations' shall be deemed to apply to the new or amalgamated or reconstituted company and its obligations to the Bank as if it had been the company whose obligations were originally guaranteed, as well as to the original company and its obligations to the Bank incurred prior to the change, and this Guarantee shall be interpreted accordingly.[14]

4 Arrangements with the debtor and others

The Bank may in its absolute discretion as it thinks fit and without the consent of the Guarantor and without releasing or reducing or otherwise affecting whatsoever the liability of the Guarantor under this Guarantee or the validity of the security hereby created do any of the following:[15] **P1–005**

4.1 enter into, renew, vary or determine any agreement or other arrangement with the Debtor or any other person; and without prejudice to the generality of the foregoing, grant to the Debtor any new or increased facility and increase any rate of interest or charge;

4.2 renew, vary, hold over, exchange, modify, assign, release or refrain from enforcing or perfecting any present or future security from the Debtor or any other person which is now or may be held by the Bank hereafter in respect of the Debtor's Obligations;

4.3 grant time or indulgence to or compound with the Debtor or any other person;

4.4 refuse at any time without notice to the Guarantor or to the Debtor to grant any further loans or advances or credit or banking or credit facilities or other accommodation to the Debtor notwithstanding that the limit of this Guarantee shall not have been reached;

4.5 resort to any other means of payment of the Debtor's Obligations or any of them at any time and in any order which the Bank thinks fit;

4.6 make a demand under or enforce this Guarantee either with or without first resorting to other means of payment or to other securities and with or without making a demand from, or taking proceedings against, the Debtor or any co-surety;

and the security hereby created shall not be discharged nor shall the liability of the Guarantor under Clause 2 be affected by anything which would not have discharged, released, reduced or otherwise affected the liability of the Guarantor if the Guarantor had been a principal Debtor of the Bank instead of a guarantor.

5 Additional security

P1–006   **5.1** This Guarantee shall be additional to any other security which the Bank may hold now or at any time hereafter from the Guarantor or the Debtor or from any other person in respect of the Debtor's Obligations, and shall not merge with or prejudice or otherwise affect such other security or any contractual or legal rights of the Bank.[16]

5.2 This Guarantee and the liability of the Guarantor hereunder shall not be affected by the invalidity or unenforceability of or any defect, irregularity or informality of any other security held by the Bank in respect of the Debtor's Obligations.

6 Preservation of bank's claims against the debtor

P1–007   Until all claims of the Bank in respect of the Debtor's Obligations have been discharged in full:

6.1 The Guarantor shall not be entitled to share in any security held by the Bank or money received by the Bank in respect of the Debtor's Obligations or to stand in the place of the Bank in respect of any security or money.

6.2 The Guarantor [*has not taken and*] will not take any security from the Debtor or from any co-surety in respect of this Guarantee without the written consent of the Bank. Any security taken by the Guarantor or by any person on behalf of the Guarantor from the Debtor or any co-surety (whether taken prior to or subsequent to the date of this Guarantee) shall be held in trust for the Bank as security for the Guarantor's liability to the Bank under this Guarantee.[17]

6.3 If the Debtor becomes bankrupt or, being a company, is wound up, or reconstructed in insolvency proceedings, or the Debtor makes any composition or arrangement with his creditors, then notwithstanding any payment which may have been made under this Guarantee, the Bank may rank as creditors and prove for the full amount of the Debtor's Obligations. Any dividends or payments which the Bank may receive from the Debtor or his estate or any other person shall be taken and applied as payments in gross and shall not prejudice the right of the Bank to recover from the Guarantor to the full extent of the security hereby created the ultimate balance of the Debtor's Obligations which, after the receipt of such dividends or payments, remains outstanding. The Guarantor's obligations under this Guarantee shall remain in force and the full amount hereby guaranteed shall be payable by the Guarantor until the Bank has received from all sources one hundred pence in the pound in respect of the Debtor's Obligations.[18]

6.4 The Guarantor shall not in competition with or in priority to the Bank seek to enforce repayment or to exercise any other rights or legal remedies of whatsoever kind which may accrue to him in respect of any amount which may have been paid by the Guarantor to the Bank hereunder, and in particular (without prejudice to the generality of the foregoing) shall not make any claim against the Debtor or any co-surety or their respective estates nor make any claim in the bankruptcy or liquidation of the Debtor or any co-surety nor enforce any security from or against the Debtor or any co-surety.

PROVIDED THAT on making a claim under this Guarantee the Bank may in its sole discretion instruct the Guarantor to take any of the steps referred to in Clause 6.4. The Guarantor shall comply with any such instructions at his own expense and any monies or other benefit thereby obtained by the Guarantor shall be held in trust by the Guarantor for the Bank.[19]

7 Preservation of the bank's rights against the guarantor

7.1 Any settlement, discharge or release between the Guarantor and the Bank shall   **P1–008**
be conditional upon no security or payment to the Bank by the debtor or any other person being avoided or reduced by virtue of any provisions or enactments relating to bankruptcy or liquidation from time to time in force. Subject to any limit in the total amount recoverable under the security hereby created, the Bank shall be entitled:

7.1.1 in the event of such avoidance or reduction, to recover the value or amount of any such security or payment from the Guarantor subsequently as if such settlement or discharge had not occurred;

7.1.2 to retain any security held by it for the Guarantor's liability until it is satisfied that it will not have to make any repayment under such law.[20]

7.2 This Guarantee will remain the property of the Bank after any release or settlement of the Guarantor's liability to the Bank.

8 Appropriation

8.1 Subject to Clause 8.2 the Bank may appropriate all payments received in respect   **P1–009**
of the Debtor's Obligations in reduction of any part of the Debtor's obligations as the Bank decides.

8.2 After this Guarantee has been discontinued in accordance with Clause 3.2 or otherwise terminated or the Bank has demanded payment from the Guarantor, the Bank may continue any account or accounts with the Debtor notwithstanding such discontinuance, termination or demand, or may open a new account or accounts for the Debtor. In any event, no payment received by the Bank for the account of the Debtor after such discontinuance, termination or demand, if followed by a payment out of or debit to or any other dealings with the Debtor's account or accounts, shall be appropriated towards or deemed to be appropriated towards or have the effect of discharging any part of the Debtor's Obligations outstanding at the time of such discontinuance termination or demand.[21]

8.3 The Bank may place to the credit of a suspense account for so long as it considers desirable any money received under this Guarantee without any obligation to apply it towards discharge of the Debtor's Obligations.[22]

9 Lien and set-off[23]

9.1 In respect of the liability of the Guarantor under this Guarantee, the Bank shall   **P1–010**
have a lien on all securities or other property of the Guarantor held by the Bank whether for safe custody or otherwise.

9.2 The Bank shall be entitled (both before and after demand hereunder) to set off the liability of the Guarantor to the Bank under this Guarantee against any credit balance on any account of the Guarantor with the Bank (whether current or otherwise or subject to notice or not).

9.3 Notwithstanding any term to the contrary in relation to any deposit or credit balance on any account of the Guarantor with the Bank, no such deposit or credit balance shall be repayable by the Bank to the Guarantor until all liability of the Guarantor to the Bank under this Guarantee has been discharged.

10 Certificate of debtor's obligations

P1–011 A certificate signed by an official of the Bank as to the amount of the Debtor's Obligations or the amount due from the Guarantor under this Guarantee shall be conclusive evidence of that amount save in the case of manifest error.[24]

11 Notices and demands

P1–012 **11.1** Any demand made under this Guarantee shall be in writing signed by an authorised official of the Bank.

11.2 Any such demand may be served personally on the Guarantor or left for him at his address or place of business last known to the Bank or sent by post or by facsimile or telex to that address.

11.3 If such demand is sent by post, it shall be sent by first-class or registered mail and addressed to the Guarantor at his address or place of business last known to the Bank.

11.4 Any demand which has not been served personally on the Guarantor shall be considered as having been duly made and shall be deemed to have reached the addressee within [*48*] hours of posting, transmission, or delivery by hand at the said address, whether or not the same be later returned undelivered and notwithstanding the death of the Guarantor.

11.5 Any notice of discontinuance or other notice given by the Guarantor or his personal representatives on the Bank hereunder shall be served by sending the same by first class or registered mail addressed to the Bank at [*Castle Street branch, Elsinore*] marked for the attention of [*the Branch Manager*] and, in the absence of evidence to the contrary, shall be deemed to have been received by the Bank within [*48*] hours after posting.

12 Governing law and jurisdiction

P1–013 **12.1** This Guarantee shall be governed by and construed in accordance with the laws of England.

12.2 The Bank shall be at liberty to enforce this Guarantee by taking action or proceedings against the Guarantor in the High Court of Justice of England and Wales or elsewhere in its absolute discretion. If such proceedings are commenced in the High Court of Justice aforesaid the Guarantor agrees to submit to the jurisdiction of the said court in respect of all matters concerned with his obligations and liabilities under or arising out of or otherwise connected with this Guarantee.

12.3 Subject to Clause 12.2 above, any dispute or difference arising under or otherwise in connection with this Guarantee shall be referred to the exclusive jurisdiction of the High Court of Justice of England and Wales.[25]

13 Entire agreement[26]

P1–014 This Guarantee embodies all the agreements and all the terms agreed between the parties hereto relating to the Guarantor's liabilities to the Bank in respect of the Debtor's Obligations, and the Guarantor hereby acknowledges that there have been no representations warranties or promises made to him by or on behalf of the Bank and agrees that none of the parties hereto shall be bound by any representation or promise or agreement which is not embodied herein, or any variation to the terms of this Guarantee which is not agreed by the Bank in writing.

14 Interpretation

In this Guarantee, unless the context clearly admits a contrary interpretation: P1–015

14.1 Words importing the singular number include the plural number and vice versa.

14.2 Words importing the masculine gender include the feminine and neuter genders.

14.3 Reference to a person or persons shall include companies or other legal entities.

14.4 If two or more persons are included in the expression 'Debtor', then that expression shall be deemed to refer to such persons both together and separately and any reference to the Debtor's Obligations shall be a reference to their joint and several obligations.

14.5 Where this Guarantee is made by or on behalf of more than one person as Guarantor (other than as agents for a named principal) the agreements, obligations and liabilities on the part of the Guarantor contained herein shall take effect as joint and several agreements, liabilities and obligations and all references herein to 'the Guarantor' shall mean such persons or any of them, and none of them shall be released from liability hereunder by reason of this Guarantee not binding or ceasing for any reason to bind any other or others of them, whether or not by agreement with the Bank.[27]

14.6 Interest will be calculated both before and after judgment on a daily basis and compounded quarterly on such days as the Bank may select.

14.7 Each of the provisions of this Guarantee shall be severable and distinct from one another and if one or more of such provisions is invalid or unenforceable the remaining provisions shall not be affected in any way.

IN WITNESS WHEREOF THIS DEED HAS BEEN DULY EXECUTED SIGNED SEALED AND DELIVERED by[28]

(signature)
The above-named Guarantor
In the presence of:

(Witness's name in full): HORATIO FRIEND
(Signature)
(Address) 17 Castle Street, Elsinore
(Occupation) Mature Student

Notes

[1] This precedent is drafted in a form which is suitable for use when there are two   P1–016
or more sureties, or where the surety is a company, although the example given is
one in which the surety is an individual.

[2] See generally Chapters 5 and 14. The warning may appear at the end of the Guarantee, but it should be prominent. The Guarantee may also include an acknowledgment by the Guarantor that he has read the warning and that he has either decided not to take legal advice or that he has taken independent legal advice before signing; this usually appears at the end of the Guarantee. A space can be left for the countersignature of the independent legal adviser, if desired. If there is no acknowledgment clause, it is standard practice for the Guarantor to initial the warning to indicate that he has read it.

[3] This is drafted as widely as possible; it will be noted that under this form of wording, the Guarantor will be liable for any sums which the principal debtor may be liable to pay if it takes on liability as a surety for some other party. This is explicitly included, to avoid any argument about what constitutes a 'contingent' liability.

[4] This is to make it clear that liabilities incurred during the notice period are covered by the Guarantee, and enables the Bank to continue an overdraft facility pending the substitution of alternative security.

[5] Most standard form Bank Guarantees are drafted so as to attempt to avoid the consequences of the unenforceability of the principal contract by, in effect, making the guarantee an indemnity. However, such clauses are not always effective to protect the Bank—see eg *Associated Japanese Bank v Credit du Nord* [1989] 1 WLR 255 at 269–70. The form of draft used in Clause 2.2 is not intended to meet the problem encountered in that case by the creditor. However, it is couched in the widest possible terms so as to cover any reason for the invalidity or unenforceability of the principal contract, while at the same time limiting the liability of the Guarantor under the indemnity to the liability which he would have had under the Guarantee. An alternative, and wider form of indemnity would be an agreement by the Guarantor to indemnify the Bank against all and any loss damage and expense which it may sustain by reason of the avoidance, nullity or unenforceability of the principal contract.

[6] These words should be omitted if the Guarantor is a consumer. Other provisions in the standard form may also be susceptible to being struck out as unreasonable in the context of a consumer guarantee, see generally Chapter 3. However we have not sought to amend the terms of this precedent or to indicate those which may be vulnerable if included in a consumer guarantee because it is virtually impossible to do so at this time.

[7] This is a Guarantee for the whole sum, but limited in amount. However, this particular form of words favours the Bank, because the limit will not apply to the interest charged to the principal, nor to expenses. If interest on the principal debt is to be included in the limit, it is important to draw an express distinction between that interest and the interest which is charged to the Guarantor if he fails to pay on demand.

[8] This is intended to exclude the possibility that notice of death or disability operates as a revocation of the Guarantee—see generally Chapter 8.

[9] The appropriate notice period will depend on the circumstances of the Guarantee but should be long enough to enable alternative security to be obtained; usually it is no less than one month. The Guarantee may also contain a provision entitling the Guarantor, upon giving notice of discontinuance, to receive a statement from the Bank of the amount needed to discharge his liability under the Guarantee. This is useful evidence for the purposes of *quia timet* proceedings against the principal.

[10] It is important to include this clause to avoid any doubt about the effect of the notice of discontinuance. See *National Westminster Bank plc v Hardman* [1988] FLR 302, and the discussion in Chapter 8, para 8.07.

[11] This sub-clause, and the following two, are intended to exclude the rule that a change in the parties to the Guarantee will release the Guarantor.

[12] This is to prevent the Guarantor from being released by reason of a change in the partners of the principal firm. However the prospective Guarantor should insist

that there is a proviso which limits the Guarantee to matters which can properly be categorised as obligations of the partnership. Otherwise he might find himself inadvertently guaranteeing a personal loan made by the Bank to one of the partners.

[13] Many standard form guarantees include a term which covers changes to a debtor which is an unincorporated association, but this has not been included in the precedent because the situation is not one which commonly arises, and if it does, it is preferable to draft a special clause which suits the circumstances of the particular case.

[14] This provision should protect the Bank against a Guarantor who controls the principal debtor company using his influence to assign the assets and liabilities of that company to a fresh company and winding up the first company, then claiming that he is discharged from the Guarantee because of the change in the principal debtor. However if the Guarantor is independent, he may wish to ensure that he is only liable for the debts of a specific company, in which case he will seek to exclude this provision.

[15] These provisions are designed to avoid rules which would otherwise release the Guarantor, as well as expressly stipulating the freedom of the Bank to pursue, or not to pursue, the Debtor, the Guarantor, and any other sureties or securities as and when it thinks fit.

[16] This prevents the argument that it can be inferred that the Bank has intended to release the Guarantor by taking another security.

[17] This is designed to prevent the Guarantor from adversely affecting the Bank's rights against the principal by taking security from the principal in priority to the Bank. Some standard Guarantees merely prohibit the Guarantor from taking security from the principal or any co-surety, but this will not protect the Bank if the Guarantor has been clever enough to take the security before he enters into the Guarantee.

[18] This is designed to exclude the possibility that the Guarantor may be released from liability by virtue of the fact that the debt is deemed to be satisfied by payments made in liquidation, bankruptcy or composition: see Chapter 13.

[19] An alternative would be to include a clause which obliges the Surety to prove for noncompeting claims, but this might cause considerable argument as to what is a competing claim. The version in the precedent is designed to enable the Bank to decide for itself when a claim is or is not a competing claim. See Chapter 13.

[20] These provisions are designed to protect the Bank against the exposure which might occur if a payment made by the principal in satisfaction of the indebtedness is avoided in insolvency proceedings, and the Bank has released the Guarantor.

[21] This is intended to remove the application of the presumption in *Clayton's* case, see Chapter 9.

[22] See Chapter 13. This provision is one which could be very hard on the prospective Guarantor, and may be of a kind which could be vulnerable under the new Unfair Terms in Consumer Contracts Regulations. The danger is that the Bank could abuse its power to put the money in a suspense account while allowing the debtor to accumulate large arrears of interest. It is therefore a provision which the prospective Guarantor should try to exclude.

[23] It is common for this type of provision to be included in the standard form Bank Guarantee; it is also one of the provisions which the prospective Guarantor is least likely to understand. If he is a customer of the Bank, he may incur the risk that monies which he has paid towards the discharge of his mortgage are in jeopardy: it is therefore important to give careful consideration to the ramifications of these provisions and to modify the draft accordingly.

[24] This avoids the delays and difficulties which the Bank may encounter in proving the amount of the indebtedness. Some Guarantees will also include a term which provides that any admission of liability or acknowledgment in writing of the amount of the indebtedness by the principal, or judgment against the principal by the Bank is to be binding on the Guarantor and conclusive evidence of liability and quantum.

[25] The jurisdiction clauses are designed to give the Bank an option to start proceedings anywhere against the Guarantor which will assume jurisdiction over him, but to fetter the Guarantor's choice. The Bank may require this flexibility in order to pursue the Guarantor, if possible, in the place where his most valuable assets are to be found, and to prevent him from taking his assets somewhere where an English judgment will not be recognised or enforced. Without these clauses, in the example given, the Bank might find itself constrained to sue the Guarantor in Denmark (being a Danish domiciliary).

[26] This is intended to make it as difficult as possible for the Guarantor to establish misrepresentation or non-disclosure, or to rely on an alleged collateral contract or estoppel.

[27] This excludes the rule that the release of a co-surety will release the Guarantor.

[28] Deeds executed by individuals no longer need a seal: Law of Property (Miscellaneous Provisions) Act 1989, s1(1)(*b*), which came into force on 31 July 1990. However, the deed must be witnessed.

Precedent 2

Notice of Revocation[1]

TO: THE ROYAL BANK OF ELSINORE LIMITED
        Elsinore High Street Branch
        Elsinore, Denmark

For the attention of Polonius Chamberlain, Branch Manager.

1 January 1993

Dear Sir,

By a contract of guarantee made in writing and dated 7 December 1992 ('the Guarantee') I, Hamlet Prince of The Castle, Castle Hill, Elsinore, Denmark, guaranteed the obligations to you of Elsinore Enterprises Limited on the terms and conditions therein contained. Since I have tendered my resignation to the Board of Directors as Managing Director of Elsinore Enterprises with effect from 1 April 1993, by this letter I give you three months' notice pursuant to Clause 3.2 of the Guarantee that I revoke and determine the Guarantee with effect from 1 April 1993 and declare that my liability under the Guarantee shall wholly cease and be determined from and after that date.

Yours faithfully,

(*Signature*)

Notes

P2–002   ¹ There is generally no prescribed form for a Notice of Revocation, so long as it
clearly expresses the intention of the Guarantor to discontinue acting as surety
with effect from the expiry date of the notice (or forthwith, if the agreement
between the parties allows him to revoke with immediate effect).

   If the Guarantee specifies the length of the notice, the place to which it should
be sent, the person to whom it should be addressed, and any particular contents,
these should be followed.

Precedent 3

Deed of Release of Surety from Bank Guarantee

THIS RELEASE is given this 1st day of April 1993
BY: THE ROYAL BANK OF ELSINORE LIMITED
     (herein called 'the Bank')

P3–001

WHEREAS by a Guarantee made in writing and dated the 7th day of December 1992 HAMLET PRINCE (herein called 'the Guarantor') undertook to pay to the Bank on demand the liabilities to the Bank of ELSINORE ENTERPRISES LTD (herein called 'the Debtor') defined in the said Guarantee as 'the Debtor's Obligations';

AND WHEREAS in accordance with Clause 3.2 of the said Guarantee the Guarantor served notice of discontinuance upon the Bank on 1 January 1993 and has tendered to the Bank the sum of £500,000 ('the settlement amount') representing the amount of the Debtor's Obligations to the Bank as at 1 April 1993, being the date of expiry of the said notice of discontinuance, and demanded the cancellation and surrender to him of the Guarantee.

In consideration of the payment by the Guarantor to the Bank of the settlement amount (receipt of which is hereby acknowledged) IT IS AGREED AS FOLLOWS:

(1) The Bank hereby releases and discharges the Surety from all past present and future liability to the Bank under the Guarantee and also from all actions, suits accounts claims and demands whatsoever for, upon account of or in respect of the Guarantee.

(2) The Bank hereby cancels the Guarantee and surrenders it and delivers it up to the Guarantor.[2]

IN WITNESS WHEREOF the Bank has caused this Deed of Release to be signed, sealed and delivered by its authorized officers this First day of April One Thousand Nine Hundred and Ninety Three

(Signatures and seals)

Notes

P3–002   [1] The form of release may be modified to take account of any conditions placed on the release of the surety. For example. if the release is consequential on payment of a sum to the Bank by the principal debtor or a co-surety, the Deed of Release may include an express reservation of the right of the Bank to pursue the guarantor in the event that the payment is avoided or reduced in subsequent insolvency proceedings—reflecting Clause 7 of Precedent 1.

[2] The Deed of Release will not necessarily accompany the surrender of the Guarantee, though this draft contemplates that the release and surrender are to be simultaneous. The Bank may have reserved the right to keep the Guarantee; or the Bank may state in the Deed of Release that it will deliver up the Guarantee on demand by the released Guarantor; or it may state that it will deliver up the Guarantee subject to being satisfied that none of the payments received by the Bank are likely to be avoided or reduced in insolvency proceedings.

Letter of Comfort

The Royal Bank of Elsinore
Castle Street Branch
15 Castle Street
Elsinore
Denmark

For the attention of Polonius
Chamberlain Esq, Manager

7 December 1992

Dear Sirs,

We understand from the Directors of our subsidiary Elsinore Enterprises Limited ('the Company') that an application has been made to you for a short-term loan facility and for the issue by you of a Performance Bond in connection with a contract for the supply of widgets by the Company to Fortinbras Import and Export A/S of Norway.

In consideration of your affording these and any additional banking facilities to the Company, we, Danish King Holdings Ltd, hereby give you our faithful assurance that we are not contemplating the disposal of our majority interests in the Company and we undertake to give you at least 48 hours' written notice of any disposal of those interests should such disposal occur during the next two years.

Yours faithfully,

(*Signature*)
Claudius King
Managing Director
For and on behalf of Danish King Holdings Limited

Precedent 5

On Demand Unconditional Performance Bond

P5–001   TO: FORTINBRAS IMPORT AND EXPORT A/S, NORWAY[1]

Our Performance Guarantee No 1992 ex 78910 dated 7th Day of December 1992

We understand from our customer ELSINORE ENTERPRISES LTD ('the Supplier') that it has tendered for[2] a contract for the supply and delivery of a quantity of [*600,000 metric tonnes of widgets*] to you in [*three*] shipments as follows:

100,000 mt to be shipped no later than 1 January 1993
200,000 mt to be shipped no later than 1 February 1993
300,000 mt to be shipped no later than 1 July 1993[3]

At the request of the Supplier and in consideration of your entering into a contract with the Supplier for the supply and delivery of the said goods on the terms and conditions aforesaid,[4] in the event that the Supplier fails to fulfil any of its obligations under the said contract in accordance with its terms (or such variations thereof as may have been agreed with you [*in writing*] with the Supplier) we THE ROYAL BANK OF ELSINORE LTD of 15 Castle Street Elsinore Denmark, hereby irrevocably undertake to pay you[5] promptly on demand and without proof or conditions,[6] such amount as may be demanded by you in writing up to a maximum of [*£100,000*] [*being 10 per cent of the contract price*][7]

Our undertaking herein shall not become effective unless and until we have been notified by the Supplier in writing that all conditions precedent otherwise required to bring the contract into effect have been fulfilled by you.[8]

Our liability hereunder shall cease on whichever of the following events first occur, upon which event this Bond shall be returned to us for cancellation:

(1) On [*date*][9] unless before that date we have received your written demand at this branch, namely 15 Castle Street, Elsinore.

(2) When we have paid to you the maximum amount for which we are liable under this Bond.

(3) On receipt of written notice from you that this Bond is to be discharged.[10]

Yours faithfully,

(*Signature*)
Polonius Chamberlain
Manager
For and on behalf of the Royal Bank of Elsinore

Notes

[1] Name of Buyer or Buyer's Bank.
[2] This precedent assumes that the performance bond is a prerequisite of the tender. If it is put up *after* the contract is entered into, it is normal practice to avoid all mention of the consideration in the text of the bond. Even if the only consideration is past consideration, in practice these bonds, like letters of credit, will be enforced.
[3] Here set out the salient details of the contract. These may include the price.
[4] or, 'on the terms and conditions of the said tender'.
[5] Alternatively it may be a promise to pay the Buyer's bank or to indemnify the Buyer's bank in respect of any payment which it has made to the Buyer under a back-to-back bond.
[6] This is one of the strictest forms of wording to be found in a performance bond and affords little protection to the supplier against fraudulent claims.
[7] The maximum figure in the Bond may be related to a percentage of the price in the contract of supply (usually no more than 10 per cent) or it may be wholly unrelated.
[8] This is designed to protect the supplier from the abuse of the bond by a buyer who fails to comply with a condition precedent, such as putting up a letter of credit for the price, while at the same time preventing the non-fulfilment of a condition precedent by the supplier from rendering the bond useless.
[9] This date is often linked to the latest time for fulfilment of the contract by the supplier.
[10] Some bonds will provide for discharge if the contract is terminated for any reason other than breach by the Supplier, but this is unlikely to be satisfactory to the Buyer, who may wish the bond to protect him in the event of non-fulfilment of the contract by reason of matters other than breach, eg *force majeure* events.

Precedent 6

Conditional
Performance Bond[1]

P6–001   TO: FORTINBRAS IMPORT AND EXPORT A/S, Norway ('the Buyer')
   BY: THE ROYAL BANK OF ELSINORE LTD, 15 Castle Street, Elsinore,
   Denmark ('the Bank')

Performance Bond No XYZ 1234 given this 7th Day of December 1992

WHEREAS:

(1) ELSINORE ENTERPRISES LTD ('the Supplier') has entered into a contract
('the Supply Contract') for the supply and delivery to the Buyer cif Southampton of a quantity of 600,000 metric tonnes of widgets ('the goods') in three
shipments as follows:
   (a) 100,000 mt to be shipped no later than 1 January 1993 ('the First
   Quantity');
   (b) 200,000 mt to be shipped no later than 1 February 1993 ('the Second
   Quantity');
   (c) 300,000 mt to be shipped no later than 1 July 1993 (the 'Third Quantity');
   (together referred to as 'the Contract Quantities').

(2) It is a condition of the Supply Contract that performance guarantees be issued
by the Bank against non-shipment in respect of each such shipment.

(3) At the request of the Supplier [*and the Buyer*] the Bank has agreed to issue this
Performance Bond in favour of the Buyer.

IT IS AGREED AS FOLLOWS:

1 Definitions

P6–002   In this Bond the words and phrases set out below shall have the following meaning
and shall be interpreted accordingly:

'Due Demand'   A demand by notice in writing (including telex) to the
Bank at 15 Castle Street aforesaid within seven days
after the expiration of the Shipment Date in respect of
the Contract Quantity to which it relates, which must be
accompanied by a Certificate of Non-Shipment signed
by Independent Lloyd's Agents at the port of shipment
giving details of the non-shipment and certifying the
basis of calculation of the amounts claimed in the said
demand.[2]

'Shipment'   The loading of the relevant contractual quantity of the
goods in accordance with the Supply Contract on board
a vessel at Southampton England or such other port as
may be agreed [*in writing*] between the Supplier and the
Buyer and notified in writing to the Bank [*by the Buyer*]

'First Shipment Date'	The date (being no later than 1 January 1993) by which shipment of the First Quantity is required to be made by the Supply Contract, or such later date for shipment of the First Quantity as may be agreed [*in writing*] between the Supplier and the Buyer and notified in writing to the Bank [*by the Buyer*]
'Second Shipment Date'	The date (being no later than 1 February 1993) by which shipment of the Second Quantity is required to be made by the Supply Contract, or such later date for shipment of the Second Quantity as may be agreed [*in writing*] between the Supplier and the Buyer and notified in writing to the Bank [*by the Buyer*]
'Third Shipment Date'	The date (being no later than 1 July 1993) by which shipment of the Third Quantity is required to be made by the Supply Contract, or such later date for shipment of the Third Quantity as may be agreed [*in writing*] between the Supplier and the Buyer and notified in writing to the Bank [*by the Buyer*]
'Non-Shipment'	Failure to make shipment of the relevant quantity of goods on or before the relevant shipment date in accordance with the terms of the Supply Contract or any written variation thereof

2 Matters to be disregarded in ascertaining whether there has been non-shipment

For the purposes of determining whether there has been non-shipment, account shall be taken only of whether shipment of the relevant Quantity of the goods has been made by the relevant Shipment Date and there shall be also disregarded:

P6–003

(a) any other breach or non-performance by the Supplier of its obligations under the Supply Contract; and
(b) any non-shipment arising or resulting from act of God, fire (unless caused by the actual fault or privity of the Supplier), war, insurrection, act of public enemies, strikes or lock-outs at the port of shipment or at any factory producing the goods, riots, civil commotion, arrest or restraint of princes, insufficiency of packing, insufficiency or inadequacy of marks, wastage in bulk or weight or any other matter arising from inherent defect quality or vice of the goods, latent defects of containers not discoverable by due diligence, or any other cause arising without negligence on the part of the carrier, his servants agents or subcontractors.[3]

3 The Bank's Undertaking

The Bank hereby undertakes:

P6–004

(a) in the event that there shall be a Non-Shipment of the First Quantity by the First Shipment date, or
(b) in the event that there shall be a Non-Shipment of the Second Quantity by the Second Shipment Date, or
(c) in the event that there shall be a Non-Shipment of the Third Quantity by the Third Shipment Date,

on receipt of Due Demand promptly to pay to the Buyer a sum equal to one per cent of the contract value of the relevant Shipment for every complete period of ten days or fraction thereof during the period in respect of which there shall have been Non-Shipment PROVIDED THAT in no event shall the Bank be liable to pay more than one per cent only aforesaid in respect of every complete period of ten days in respect of which there shall have been Non-Shipment, and that in no event shall this undertaking oblige the Bank to pay the Buyer more than £100,000 in respect of the Non-Shipment of any one Quantity of goods.[4]

4 Condition Precedent

P6–005 This Performance Bond is conditional upon the provision by the Buyer of an irrevocable Letter of Credit pursuant to the terms of the Contract of Supply by no later than 15 December 1992 and in the event that such Letter of Credit is not provided by that date this Bond shall become absolutely null and void and shall be returned to us for cancellation.[5]

5 Termination

P6–006 This Performance Bond shall become absolutely null and void and cease to be of any effect whatsoever, on the occurrence of either of the following events, in which event this Bond shall be returned to us for cancellation:

(a) when shipment has been made of all the Contract Quantities of the goods on the relevant Shipment Dates as stated in the Supply Contract or as varied [*in writing*] by the Supplier and the Buyer and notified in writing to the Bank;

(b) if the Supplier ceases for any reason to have any obligation to supply the goods or any Quantity of them to the Buyer pursuant to the Supply Contract.[6]

This performance bond shall be governed by English law and any dispute which may arise between the Buyer, the Bank [*and the Supplier*] in connection with this Bond shall be referred to the jurisdiction of the English courts.

Yours sincerely,

(*Signature*)
Polonius Chamberlain
Manager
For and on Behalf of the Royal Bank of Elsinore Ltd

Notes

P6–007   [1] This is still a 'demand' Performance Bond, but unlike Precedent 5 there rare a number of features included for the protection of the Supplier.

[2] This is defined to avoid unfair calling of the bond without proof or condition, and to provide for a means of independent confirmation of the non-shipment.

[3] A 'force majeure' clause should be included in the Performance Bond if the underlying supply contract would excuse non-shipment in such circumstances, and then it should accurately reflect the terms of the underlying contract. In many cases such a clause would not be considered acceptable to the Buyer because it would allow the possibility of argument about the legitimacy of payment by the Bank.

[4] Alternatively an overall maximum limit could be specified, decreasing in tranches on due shipment of each quantity of goods.

[5] This is intended to prevent the Buyer from calling in the Performance Bond when the non-shipment has been due to his failure to perform any necessary conditions precedent to the underlying contract of supply.

[6] This is an additional safeguard against the non-fulfilment by the Buyer of conditions precedent to the underlying contract, and also ensures that the bond becomes inoperative if the Buyer accepts a repudiation of the underlying contract by the Supplier, so that the Supplier has no further obligation to ship the goods.

Precedent 7

Counter-Indemnity to a Bank Issuing a Performance Bond

TO: THE ROYAL BANK OF ELSINORE LIMITED ('the Bank')   **P7–001**

In consideration of the Bank issuing a Performance Bond ('the Bond') in favour of Fortinbras Import and Export Ltd ('the Buyer') in the terms of the draft appended hereto, and in consideration of our payment to the Bank of such bank charges for the issue and maintenance of the Bond as you may notify to us from time to time, we, Elsinore Enterprises Ltd, [*and the undersigned Directors of Elsinore Enterprises Ltd*] hereby [*jointly and severally*] agree to indemnify the Bank and keep the Bank fully indemnified in respect of any sums up to the limit of the Bank's liability under the Bond which may be paid by the Bank to the Buyer on any demand on the Bond made or purporting to be made by or on behalf of the Buyer.

We further hereby acknowledge and accept that any payments under the Bond may be made by the Bank in response to such demand without further inquiry or confirmation or verification and without reference to us. We agree that as between ourselves and the Bank, any such demand shall be conclusive evidence that the sum demanded therein is properly due and payable. The Bank is hereby authorised to debit any of [*our/Elsinore Enterprises Ltd's*] accounts kept with the Bank with the whole or any part of any payment which the Bank may make under the Bond.

Yours faithfully,

(*Signature*)   (*Signature*)
HAMLET PRINCE,   ULF ROZENCRANTZ
Managing Director   Director

for and on behalf of [*ourselves and*] Elsinore Enterprises Ltd.

Precedent 8

P&I Club Letter of Undertaking

From the Hampstead & Highgate Mutual P&I Club
[*Address*]
19 April 1993

P8–001   To the owners of the cargo lately laden on board the mv 'Player King' ('the Vessel')[1]

Dear Sirs,

In consideration of your refraining from taking action resulting in the arrest of the Vessel or any other vessel in the same ownership, associated ownership or management[2] in respect of your claim for alleged damage to a cargo said to consist of 200,000 mt of widgets shipped on the said vessel on a voyage from Southampton to Trondheim under Bills of Lading Nos 1 and 2 dated 1 February 1993:[3]

(1) We hereby undertake to pay to you or to your solicitors on your behalf on first written demand[4] without set-off, counterclaim or any other deduction whatsoever, such sum as Mousetrap Shipping Corporation of Panama SA, (hereinafter referred to as 'the Owners')[5] may be adjudged liable to pay you in respect of your said claim in proceedings commenced or to be commenced by you in the High Court of Justice, Queen's Bench Division, Admiralty Court, or on appeal therefrom,[6] together with interest and costs (including any costs that may be awarded on taxation if not agreed), or such sums in respect of principal interest and costs as may be agreed by us in writing to be recoverable by you from the Owners in respect of the said claim, interest and costs.[7]

PROVIDED ALWAYS that our liability hereunder shall on no account exceed the sum of [£600,000] [*or the equivalent in the currency of your claim, at the rate of exchange in force on the date of final judgment in the action or agreement prior to such judgment*].[8]

(2) We further undertake that we will, within [*14*] days after receipt from you or your solicitors of a request [*in writing*] to do so, instruct solicitors to accept on behalf of the Owners service of proceedings brought by you in the High Court of Justice aforesaid and to acknowledge service of the said proceedings on behalf of the Owners.[9]

(3) The undertakings given in Paragraphs 1 and 2 herein are without prejudice to any application which may be made to the Court for the stay or dismissal of the said proceedings and further or alternatively for an order that the security comprised herein be released or varied.[10]

(4) Without prejudice to any other matters which may terminate our liability hereunder, the undertakings in Paragraph (1) of this letter shall terminate and we shall thereupon cease to be under any liability to you whatsoever, whether in respect of any matters occurring prior to the said termination or subsequently

thereto, on the 7th December 1993[11] unless by that date you have received written confirmation from us of the renewal of our undertakings for a further period which we shall then specify, and on the occurrence of any one of the following events:

(a) when the Owners and/or any other person have paid to you or your solicitors in full either:
  (i) the amount of any judgment[12] (not being an interim judgment) in the proceedings referred to in paragraph (1); or
  (ii) the amount agreed by us [*in writing*] to be recoverable by you from the Owners as contemplated in paragraph (1); or
  (iii) an amount agreed by you [*in writing*] to be in full and final settlement of your claims in respect of the alleged cargo damage;

(b) when the Owners and/or any other person have provided you with security of equivalent amount to this letter of undertaking, or upon the establishment of a limitation fund in respect of the Vessel in England or any other jurisdiction;[13]

(c) on the expiry of twelve months after the date of the judgment aforesaid[14] or the date of our or your agreement [*in writing*] aforesaid.[15]

(5) This letter of undertaking is governed by English law. All disputes arising out of or otherwise connected with this letter of undertaking shall be referred to the exclusive jurisdiction of the High Court of Justice in London, to which jurisdiction you hereby agree to submit.

(*Signed*)
For and on behalf of the Hampstead & Highgate Mutual P&I Club

We confirm that we have read the terms of the above letter of undertaking and that they are acceptable to us.

(*Countersigned*)[16]
Oscar Fortinbras
Managing Director
For and on behalf of Fortinbras Import and Export A/S of Norway

Notes

[1] Alternatively insert here the name of the addressee or addressees. The letter may be addressed to the solicitors for the Plaintiffs, but if the vessel has not yet been arrested it is more likely to be addressed to the Plaintiffs themselves. **P8–002**

[2] or, as the case may be: 'in consideration of your consenting to the release of the 'Player King' from arrest and in consideration of your refraining from taking action resulting in the rearrest of the said vessel or the arrest of any other vessel in the same ownership associated ownership or management . . .'.

[3] If the Club letter reserves the right to challenge the jurisdiction of the court, whether expressly or implicitly, the potential Plaintiff should endeavour to protect his position by including a provision either in the letter of undertaking itself, or in a side letter, which preserves his right to seek to arrest the vessel or a sister ship in the event that the English High Court declines jurisdiction over the claim or makes an order which releases the security. See the discussion in Chapter 15 at para 15.21.

[4] Alternatively, the letter of undertaking could require production of a copy of the judgment or court order or arbitral award, or even a letter from the Plaintiff's solicitors confirming that the judgment or award had not been paid by the Defendant.

[5] Insert here the name of the Club member on whose behalf the undertaking is given.

[6] Alternatively, 'such sum as may be awarded to you by Final Award in arbitration proceedings commenced or to be commenced by you in London'.

[7] Alternatively the undertaking may refer to any sum which is agreed by the Club member in writing to be payable, but this is less advisable if the Club wishes to guard against having to pay a sum which it considers to be unacceptably high. In practice, the Club would expect to be fully involved in any settlement negotiations.

[8] The limit will be the equivalent of the vessel's limitation fund or a figure estimated by reference to the likely recovery, rounded up, whichever is the lower. P&I Clubs often express the limit in US dollars. It is preferable to use the currency of claim in the action as the currency of the guarantee, to avoid confusion and any argument about rates of exchange. If for any reason this cannot be done, it is preferable to avoid future argument by specifying a date on which the rate of exchange will be taken. The precedent refers to the date of the judgment or the date of the settlement agreement, if earlier, but some other date, such as the date of demand, could be chosen.

[9] This paragraph might contain an express submission to the jurisdiction; if it does not, the agreement to acknowledge service will not amount to a submission to the jurisdiction. If the substantive dispute is to be referred to arbitration, the Club will undertake to accept notice of the appointment of an arbitrator, or whatever other step is required in order to commence the arbitral process. This will almost inevitably result in a submission to the jurisdiction of the arbitrators and thus the reservation of rights as in Clause 3 would usually be omitted, or varied by simply preserving the right to challenge for wrongful arrest or set aside or vary the amount of the security.

[10] This will be omitted, or its scope will be narrowed, if Clause 2 contains a submission to the jurisdiction.

[11] Or alternatively, 'on the first anniversary of the date of this letter', or 'on the expiry of 12 months from the date of this letter', or on some other date. This limitation may be omitted altogether, but is worth including as it acts as an incentive to the Plaintiff to ensure that the litigation progresses with due speed.

[12] Or Final Award, as the case may be.

[13] See the Merchant Shipping Act 1979, s 17 and following, and Sched 4.

[14] Or the date of the publication of the Final Award aforesaid, whichever is appropriate.

[15] The purpose of this provision is to ensure that the liability under the letter of undertaking is not kept open indefinitely once an award or judgment has been obtained or a settlement reached. Alternatively, the letter could simply provide for a specific termination date. Thus if the undertaking is renewable annually, there may be no need for a further time limit referable to the date of the relevant judgment, award, or agreement. Care should be taken to ensure that the time limit allows for the taxation of costs or the exhaustion of any appeal process: provisions designed to deal with these contingencies appear in Precedent 12.

[16] It is somewhat unusual to see a space for a countersignature on a Club letter, but it is sensible to have a record that the terms of the letter have been accepted by the other contracting party and this is one means of providing that record.

Precedent 9

Guarantee of Dividends on Shares

P9–001

TO: LARS GUILDENSTERN

In consideration of your having at my request applied for and having been allotted one hundred ordinary shares (each being of the nominal value of £1) in ELSINORE ENTERPRISES LIMITED ('the Company') and in consideration of your paying the full nominal amount for the said shares in cash forthwith,[1]

I, ULF ROSENCRANTZ undertake that in the event of the Company paying in any one year no dividend on the said shares or a dividend at a rate less than [*10%*] per annum, then within 30 days after the Annual General Meeting of the Company I will pay you a sum equivalent to such dividend or so much of it as the Company shall not pay.

This Guarantee is to continue in force for five years and no longer.

In the event of the Company being wound up or going into liquidation within [*1 year*] from the date of this Guarantee, I further undertake to pay to you during the remainder of the period of this Guarantee a sum equal to 10 per cent per annum upon the nominal amount of the shares less any sums which you may have received in the winding-up or liquidation in respect of dividends on the shares,[2] such payments to be made by me on the 1st day of December each year.

Yours faithfully

(*Signature*)
Ulf Rosencrantz

Notes

P9–002

[1] Care should be taken to ensure that the consideration is not past consideration or expressed in terms which are ambiguous. If in doubt, a deed should be executed.
[2] The surety has subrogated rights, but will not rank as a creditor: *Re Walters' Deed of Guarantee* [1933] Ch 321.

Precedent 10

Guarantee of Ascertained Debt

1 January 1993

P10–001   TO: SHYLOCK ENTERPRISES (VENICE) SpA
of Numero Uno, Via Ventura, Venice, Italy

In consideration of your having at my request agreed to discontinue for a period of [*four weeks*][1] the action commenced by you in the High Court of Justice, Queen's Bench Division, 1992 B No 1234 against BASSANIO TRADING LTD (hereinafter called 'the Debtor') and in further consideration of your agreeing to forbear from taking any legal or other proceedings against the Debtor within that period, whether in England or in any other jurisdiction[2] in respect of the principal sum of £100,000 and interest which has already accrued thereon in the sum of £10,000 (together referred to as 'the guaranteed amount') now due and owing to you by the Debtor,

I, the undersigned ANTONIO MERCHANT hereby guarantee the payment by the Debtor on [*date*][3] of the guaranteed amount[4] together with all interest which may have accrued thereon from the date of this Guarantee at a rate of [*18*] per cent per annum, [calculated *daily and compounded monthly*][5] and the reasonable legal and other costs charges and expenses [up *to but not exceeding £5,000*] which you have incurred prior to the date of this Guarantee in endeavouring to recover the guaranteed amount from the Debtor, provided that it shall be a condition precedent to my liability to you hereunder that all payments received by you on or after the date of this Guarantee from me or from the Debtor shall be applied by you in reduction of the guaranteed amount.

Yours sincerely,
(*Signature*)

Antonio Merchant

Notes

P10–002   [1] It is preferable to have a specified period of discontinuance or forbearance, to prevent the creditor from reviving the proceedings in too short a space of time.

[2] This prevents the creditor from discontinuing one action only to commence a fresh and different action against the principal within the period of discontinuance. However a promise to forbear which does not have a specified time limit will usually be construed as a promise to forbear at least until any period for payment referred to in the text expires: see eg *Board v Hoey* (1948) TLR 43.

[3] The specified date will coincide with the expiry of the stipulated period of discontinuance and forbearance.

[4] An alternative formula is 'I guarantee the payment to you of the guaranteed amount or such part of it as the Debtor shall not have repaid to you within [6] months from the date of this Guarantee'.

[5] These figures should correspond with the obligations of the principal debtor under his agreement with the creditor.

Agreement for the Release of a Surety[1]

P11–001   This agreement is made the 15th day of January 1993 BETWEEN:

(1)   SHYLOCK ENTERPRISES (VENICE) SPA ('the Creditor')
(2)   BASSANIO TRADING LTD ('the Debtor')
(3)   ANTONIO MERCHANT ('the Retiring Surety')
(4)   PORTIA BELMONT ('the New Surety')

WHEREAS:

(1)   The Debtor is indebted to the Creditor in the sum of £100,000 ('the principal indebtedness') and interest thereon under a Loan Agreement made on [*date*].

(2)   By an agreement made in writing and dated 1 January 1993 ('the Guarantee') the Retiring Surety guaranteed the payment by the Debtor on [*date*] of the principal indebtedness together with interest and the reasonable legal and other costs charges and expenses (up to but not exceeding £5,000) incurred by the Creditor prior to the date of the Guarantee in endeavouring to recover the principal indebtedness and interest thereon from the Debtor, (hereinafter referred to as 'the Expenses') on the terms and conditions therein contained.

(3)   The Retiring Surety desires to be released and discharged from his liability under the Guarantee.

(4)   At the request of the Debtor, the Retiring Surety and the New Surety, the Creditor has agreed to release and discharge the Retiring Surety upon the New Surety guaranteeing the payment to the Creditor of the principal indebtedness together with interest thereon and the Expenses:

IT IS AGREED AS FOLLOWS:

(1)   In consideration of the release by the Creditor of the Retiring Surety, the New Surety hereby guarantees the payment of the principal indebtedness, interest and Expenses to the Creditor upon the same terms and conditions as are contained in the Guarantee as if the New Surety were a party to the Guarantee, and her name were inserted in it in place of the name of the Retiring Surety.

(2)   The Creditor accepts the liability and guarantee of the New Surety in substitution for the liability and guarantee of the Retiring Surety, and hereby releases and discharges the Retiring Surety from all past present and future liability whatsoever under the Guarantee and from all actions suits, accounts, claims and demands whatsoever for, upon account of or in respect of the Guarantee.

Note

P11–002   [1] This type of agreement is unlikely to be suitable if the original Guarantee agreement was complex in nature; in general terms it is preferable in all but the simplest cases for the new surety to enter into a fresh guarantee agreement and for the Creditor to execute a separate deed of release which will recite the fact of the substitution.

Precedent 12

Bank Guarantee in Respect of Security for Costs

P12–001 To: Bassanio Trading Ltd

Whereas proceedings have been commenced by Shylock Enterprises (Venice) SpA ('Shylock Enterprises') against you in the High Court of Justice, Queen's Bench Division, action 1992 B No 1234 ('the action') and you have issued a summons in that action for an order that Shylock Enterprises do provide security for your costs of the said action in the sum of £_____ and that pending the provision of such security all proceedings in the action be stayed;[1]

We hereby agree as follows:

(1) As security for your costs of the action [*up to and including discovery*][2], and in consideration of your refraining from pursuing the said application or any further application for security for your costs[3] [*up to and including discovery*] we hereby undertake to pay you or your solicitors on your behalf,[4] on first written demand[5] [*and upon production of documents evidencing our liability to pay in accordance with paragraph 2 or paragraph 3 below*][6] without set-off, counterclaim or any other deduction whatsoever:[7]

    (a) such sum in respect of your costs of the action [*up to and including discovery*] as Shylock Enterprises may be ordered by the court to pay to you (including any costs that may be awarded on taxation if not agreed by the parties);
    or
    (b) such sum in respect of your costs of the action [*up to and including discovery*] as Shylock Enterprises may agree in writing to pay to you; and
    (c) interest on the said costs at the rate of [*15%*] per annum from [*2*] days after your written demand.[8]

PROVIDED ALWAYS THAT:
(A) our total liability hereunder shall on no account exceed the sum of £_____,[9]

and

(B) the costs which we are liable to pay you under this guarantee exclude the costs of any appeal by you to the Court of Appeal, whether interlocutory or final.[10]

(2) In the event that the demand made hereunder relates to costs which are the subject of a court order or orders, proof of our liability to make payment hereunder shall consist of:

(a) a copy of the relevant court order or orders, together with a copy of any subsequent written agreement between the parties quantifying the costs payable to you, or a copy of any relevant certificate of taxation (as the case may be); and

(b) written confirmation from [*you or*] your solicitors that the award of costs in your favour has not been satisfied by Shylock Enterprises in full within [7] days of the issue of the relevant certificate of taxation,[11] or the date of agreement as to the quantification of costs, whichever is applicable and, if the costs have been paid in part, confirmation that your demand relates only to the unpaid balance.[12]

(3) In the event that the demand made hereunder relates to costs which are the subject of an agreement between yourselves and Shylock Enterprises other than an agreement as to quantum made in consequence of a court order for the payment of those costs, proof of our liability to make payment hereunder shall consist of:

(a) a copy of the relevant agreement; and

(b) written confirmation from [*you or*] your solicitors that the agreed costs have not been paid by Shylock Enterprises in full within [77] days of the date of that agreement, and, if the said costs have been paid in part, confirmation that your demand relates only to the unpaid balance.

(4) Without prejudice to any other matters which may terminate our liability hereunder, the undertaking in Paragraph (1) of this letter shall terminate and we shall thereupon cease to be under any liability to you whatsoever, whether in respect of any matters occurring prior to the said termination or subsequently thereto, on [*date*][13] unless by that date you have received written confirmation from us of the renewal of our undertaking for a further period of [*one year*], and on the occurrence of any one of the following events:

(a) when we and/or Shylock Enterprises and/or any other person have paid to you or your solicitors in full either the sum of £ _____ being the maximum amount of our liability hereunder, or, if less than that sum, the full amount of your costs of the action due and payable to you by Shylock Enterprises being the amount specified in—

   (i) all relevant court orders (whether interim or final)[14] which provide for costs to be paid to you by Shylock Enterprises;

   (ii) all relevant agreements between yourself and Shylock Enterprises by which a sum is payable by Shylock Enterprises to you in respect of your costs of the action;

   (iii) all relevant Certificates of Taxation.

(b) On the expiry of [*six*] months after the date of a Final Judgment or Summary Judgment [*under RSC Order 14*] in the action in favour of Shylock Enterprises unless within that time we receive written notice from you or your solicitors on your behalf that steps have been taken by you to appeal against the said judgment within the time limits prescribed by Rules of Court;[15]

(c) in any event, on the expiry of [*twelve months*] after the date of the latest agreement or Certificate of Taxation by which the costs are quantified;[16]

(d) when we have received [*written*] notification from you or your solicitors that you have received in full your costs in the action from Shylock Enterprises, such notification to be given by you or your solicitors within [7 *days*] after receipt by you of the said costs in full [*in cleared funds*];

(e) when we have received written notification from you or your solicitors, or joint notification by Shylock Enterprises (or their solicitors) and yourselves (or your solicitors), that this Guarantee should be discharged.

(5) Subject to our maximum liability under this Guarantee of £ _____ aforesaid, this Guarantee shall be continuing relating to all costs incurred in the

Action [*up to and including discovery*] both before and after its date and will be additional to any other guarantee or other security given at any time by us or any other person on behalf of Shylock Enterprises.

(6) Our liability hereunder shall not be affected in any way by any of the following matters:

   (a) the bankruptcy, liquidation, receivership or insolvency of Shylock Enterprises;

   (b) our amalgamation or reconstruction or any transfer which we may make of any assets;

   (c) your taking any other or further securities in respect of your costs of the action;

   (d) your varying, releasing, discharging or omitting or neglecting to enforce any such further securities;

   (e) your giving time for payment or granting any other indulgences whatsoever to Shylock Enterprises or making any other arrangement with ourselves or with Shylock Enterprises.

(7) This Guarantee is governed by English law. All disputes arising out of or otherwise connected with this letter of undertaking shall be referred to the exclusive jurisdiction of the High Court of Justice in London, to which jurisdiction you hereby agree to submit.

(8) Any demand hereunder may [*or shall*] be made by [*here set out the means of service of the demand, eg notice in writing sent by first class or registered post addressed to the Bank at its registered office*].

Dated the 7th day of December 1992

[*Signatures and seal, if given under seal*]

Notes

P12–002   [1] Or otherwise reflect the terms of the summons; in the Commercial Court the applicant will generally seek an order for the provision of security by a certain time with liberty to apply to the court in case of default.

   [2] It is possible, but unusual, to find a limitation in the guarantee which refers to the stage of the action up to which the costs are provided. The more common practice is to limit the right of the Defendant to apply for further security in respect of his costs up to and including the particular stage of the proceedings for which the guarantee is provided. However, such a limitation is more commonly, and appropriately, to be found in the agreement between the Plaintiff and Defendant and not in the text of the Bank Guarantee itself. The restriction on the right to apply for further security will depend on the circumstances of the particular application; if the security is expressed to be up to and including the trial of the action, the right to seek further security is likely to be circumscribed altogether.

   [3] If no summons has been issued, the letter should begin 'in consideration of your refraining from making an application to the court in Action No .... for security for your costs up to and including [*the relevant stage of the action*]'. If an order for security has already been made, the consideration clause is more difficult to draft. It may be worded thus: 'as security for your costs of the action and pursuant to an Order of the Honourable Mr Justice Shallow dated 24th September 1992 and in consideration of your refraining from applying to the court for the stay or dismissal of the action in respect of any alleged non-compliance by [*the Plaintiffs*]

with the said order'. However, this is highly artificial, and possibly insufficient, if the order is in the normal form which allows the Plaintiff to put up security in terms agreed by the parties, because there is then no breach of the order entitling any further application to be made to the court. A safer alternative is to provide for the payment of a nominal sum to be made to the Bank. Since the consideration should move from the beneficiary of the guarantee, it should be paid by the Defendant. However, the Plaintiff ordinarily bears at least the initial expense of providing the security, and where this is the case, the wording of the consideration clause should state that the payment is made by the Plaintiff on the Defendant's behalf.

4 The guarantee may be addressed to the Defendant's solicitor rather than the Defendant, but this should be avoided, since, unless great care is taken in the drafting, it leaves open the possibility that the undertaking cannot be enforced by the Defendants if they change their legal advisers in the course of the action without getting a fresh guarantee.

5 Or, 'within £ ____ days after our receipt of your written demand'. It has been known for some guarantees for security for costs to provide for payment on demand and within a specified number of days after the relevant court order, the issue of a certificate of taxation or the date of an agreement to pay the costs. However, that formulation is open to the possible construction that if the demand is made more than the specified number of days after the order, certificate or agreement, there is no liability, and is therefore best avoided.

6 The 'proof of liability' provisions are a safeguard against unfair claims, and if they are inserted are ultimately for the benefit of the Plaintiff. However, it is still common for this type of guarantee to be drafted as a plain demand guarantee.

7 This form can be adapted to cover other forms of security, eg security fortifying the Plaintiff's cross-undertakings in damages given in respect of a freezing injunction or similar order. In that case the words 'without set-off counterclaim or other deduction whatsoever' are possibly more pertinent than in a straightforward undertaking in respect of costs, where they are often omitted.

8 Note that this formula is intended to provide for interest to be paid by the Bank if it does not pay immediately on demand; it does not cover interest which may have accumulated on the costs themselves prior to that demand.

9 This is an example of a limit which applies both to the costs and to any interest. If interest is to be excluded from the total, this should be stated expressly. If the costs are likely to include costs or disbursements incurred in another currency, the limit could be expressed as '£ ____ or the equivalent in the currency or currencies of the costs at the rate of exchange in force on the date of the relevant certificate of taxation or agreement to pay costs'.

10 This provision is often excluded, but is worth including to avoid later argument as to whether the guarantee of the costs of the action includes the costs of an appeal. Interlocutory appeals from the master or district judge to the judge would normally be included. In arbitral proceedings the proviso would exclude any appeals to the High Court under the Arbitration Act 1996.

11 The precedent effectively requires the beneficiary to wait for a period before making a claim on the Bank. It does not, however, provide for any interest lost during that period to be recoverable under the Guarantee. If such interest is to be covered, Clause 1c should be amended to cover interest during the periods referred to in Clauses 2b and 3b.

12 This provision, like paragraph 3, is inserted for the protection of the Bank against unjustified demands and is optional.

13 Or alternatively, 'on the first anniversary of the date of this letter', or 'on the expiry of 12 months from the date of this letter', or on some other date. This limitation may be omitted, but many banks dislike giving guarantees which are unlimited in time, and thus guarantees which are renewable every year are fairly common. The agreement between the Plaintiff and the Defendant should provide that if the Bank refuses to renew its guarantee, the Defendant will have the right to apply to court for alternative security.

[14] Or Arbitral awards, as the case may be. Care must be taken to adopt a formula which does not release the Bank from liability on payment of costs awarded in an interim award or interlocutory judgment. This is why many guarantees of this type refer only to final awards and judgments. However, that formula may lead to doubt as to whether interlocutory costs are recoverable under the guarantee, particularly if the action never reaches the stage of a final award or judgment.

[15] If the substantive matters are to be dealt with by arbitration, references to awards will be substituted. In order to prevent the discharge of the guarantee if there is an interlocutory ruling on a minor matter in favour of the Plaintiff, the phrase 'judgment on the merits' could be used, though this could give rise to argument as to its meaning. Reference only to a final judgment or award, however, arguably prevents the guarantee from terminating if the Plaintiff obtains summary judgment under CPR Part 24. Specific reference to that procedure, where appropriate, may be preferred to the more general formulation in the precedent.

[16] This ensures that liability under the guarantee is not maintained indefinitely after an award or judgment has been obtained. If the guarantee is renewable annually, there may be no need for a further time limit referable to the date of the relevant judgment or award. There may be some need to cater for the effect of any possible appeal, but the permutations are too many for this to be dealt with in the precedent. It may be important to make the time limit run from the date of any certificate of taxation rather than final judgment, in view of the delay which taxation can cause.

Precedent 13

Indemnity for the Fidelity of an Employee

THIS AGREEMENT is made this 1st day of December 1992 BETWEEN: **P13–001**

The COUNTESS OLIVIA of GRIEF of Willow Mansion, Love Lane, Illyria (herein referred to as 'the Employer')

and

SIR TOBIAS BELCH also of Willow Mansion, Love Lane, Illyria and SIR ANDREW AGUECHEEK lately of Castle Adamant, Arden and temporarily of The Plough Inn, Illyria (herein referred to as 'the Sureties')

In consideration of the Employer having at our request agreed to employ one MALVOLIO PROUD ('the Employee') in the office of Steward with effect from 7 December 1992, we the Sureties hereby jointly and severally agree as follows:

(1) The Sureties hereby undertake that they will be answerable to the Employer for the honest, due and faithful fulfilment by the Employee of such duties as the Employer may reasonably call upon and require him to perform in connection with the said office, and for his faithful and honest conduct during his service in that office, for so long as he shall be in her service and employed by her in that office, and in particular (without prejudice to the generality of the foregoing) that he will:

    (a) timeously and satisfactorily account for and pay over and deliver to the Employer all monies and securities for money, goods and other property whatsoever which the Employee shall receive for the use of the Employer or which shall at any time or times be entrusted to the care of the Employee by the Employer or by any other persons to whom the Employer is or may be liable or accountable therefor; and

    (b) not steal, embezzle, or otherwise convert to his own use any monies or other property of whatsoever nature of the Employer or of any other persons to whom the Employer is or may be liable or accountable for the safe custody or keeping of the said property.

(2) Without prejudice to Clause 1 above, the Sureties each agree to indemnify the Employer against all loss damage costs and expenses of whatsoever nature which she may incur or sustain by reason of any misconduct (whether criminal or otherwise) or dishonesty or negligence on the part of the Employee during the course of his employment in that office or by reason of any failure by the Employee duly to fulfil and perform the duties required of him in connection with that office.

(3) The maximum liability of each of the Sureties individually and the total amount recoverable from both of the Sureties together under Clauses 1 and 2 above in respect of all defaults of the Employee shall not exceed £1,000 and shall not exceed £250 in respect of any one act or omission.[1] Subject to these limits, the

Sureties shall be liable to indemnify the Employer in respect of all sums which she may lose and all loss and damage which she may sustain by reason of any act, omission or default of the Employee in the course of his employment in the office aforesaid, and not merely those amounts for which the Employee might be liable to the Employer.

(4) The agreements liabilities and obligations on behalf of the Sureties contained herein shall take effect as joint and several agreements, liabilities and obligations and neither of the Sureties shall be released from liability hereunder by reason of this Indemnity not binding or ceasing for any reason to bind the other of them (whether by agreement with the Employer or otherwise).

(5) This Indemnity shall be a continuing contract and shall remain in operation until the dismissal of the Employee from the office or until his contract of employment has otherwise terminated or until the Sureties have received notice in writing of his death in service, provided that:

(a) each of the Sureties shall be at liberty to give to the Employer one month's written notice of revocation of this Indemnity with respect to his future liabilities hereunder;

(b) the obligations of the Sureties under Clauses 1 and 2 herein and this Indemnity shall continue in effect after termination of the contract of employment or the death of the Employee or the time at which any notice of revocation of this Indemnity takes effect, and the Sureties shall remain liable in respect of all acts omissions defaults or liabilities which have occurred or arisen prior to such termination, death or revocation.

(6) The Sureties hereby acknowledge and accept that their liabilities and obligations hereunder are undertaken as principal obligors and shall not be diminished, prejudiced, impaired or discharged by reason of any dealings between the Employer and Employee of whatsoever nature or treated as co-extensive with any liabilities of the Employee to the Employer.

Signed
Sir Tobias Belch, Knight

Sir Andrew Aguecheek, Knight

In the presence of

Maria Scullion
(Occupation) Lady's Maid
At Willow Mansion, Love Lane, Illyria

Note

P13–002 [1] This is intended to stop one of the sureties from arguing that if the limit is £100, he is only liable for £50, and to stop the employer from arguing that he is entitled to recover £100 from each surety.

Precedent 14

Rent Guarantee[1]

This Agreement is made on the 6th day of January 1993 BETWEEN: **P14–001**

ORSINO DUKE of 17 Palace Gardens, Illyria (hereinafter referred to as 'the Landlord')

and

ALAN CEDRIC CAPTAIN of Smuggler's Cottage, The Waterfront, Illyria ('hereinafter referred to as the Surety')

Whereas the Landlord has agreed at the request of the Surety to accept Cesario Incognito ('the Tenant') as the tenant of the Landlord's freehold premises known as 12, Christmas Crescent, Illyria ('the premises') upon the terms and conditions of an agreement of even date herewith, ('the Tenancy Agreement') at a rent of £12,000 per annum payable by equal monthly instalments in arrear on the first day of each calendar month.

The Surety hereby guarantees the payment by the Tenant to the Landlord of the rent and the performance and observance by him of the terms of the Tenancy Agreement upon the following conditions:

(1) If the Tenant defaults in the payment of the rent for the period of [*one week*] after the same falls due, the Surety will pay the month's rent which is in arrear to the Landlord forthwith on receipt of the Landlord's written demand.

(2) If the Tenant defaults in the performance or observance of any of the covenants [*or other obligations*] on his part contained in the Tenancy Agreement, the Surety will pay to the Landlord forthwith on receipt of the Landlord's written demand all losses damages expenses and costs which the Landlord shall be entitled to recover by reason of the Tenant's default [*to the extent to which the Landlord is unable to recover them from the Tenant*].

(3) This Guarantee shall continue only for the period of [*2 years*] from the date hereof, and shall apply to the acts omissions and defaults of the Tenant in respect of the Tenant's obligations and liabilities under the Tenancy Agreement during that period only. During that period the Guarantee shall not be revocable by the Surety, nor shall it be discharged by his death or notice thereof, or by the death or insolvency of the Tenant.

(4) During the period of the Guarantee referred to in Clause 3 the Surety shall not be discharged by the Landlord giving time to the Tenant in which to meet his rent or other obligations under the Tenancy Agreement or affording the Tenant any other indulgence in respect of his obligations under that Agreement.

(5) If the Tenancy Agreement is assigned with or without the consent of the Landlord, or is terminated by agreement or by re-entry or otherwise, or if the Tenant acquires rights of occupation of the premises under a statutory tenancy, the liability of the Surety hereunder shall cease with effect from the date of the said assignment, termination, or commencement of the statutory tenancy.

(*Signature*)
AC Captain

Note

P14–002   [1] This is a very simple form of Guarantee and only includes the basic minimum of the types of clause which are commonly to be found in such agreements. Many of the standard form clauses set out in Precedent 1 could be included with appropriate modifications.

Appendix

Legislation

Statute of Frauds 1677

4 No action against executors, etc, upon a special promise, or upon any agreement,   A–001
or contract for sale of lands, etc, unless agreement, etc, be in writing, and signed

. . . noe action shall be brought . . . whereby to charge the defendant upon any speciall promise to answere for the debt default or miscarriages of another person . . . unlesse the agreement upon which such action shall be brought or some memorandum or note thereof shall be in writing and signed by the partie to be charged therewith or some other person thereunto by him lawfully authorised.

*   *   *   *   *

Statute of Frauds Amendment Act 1828

6 Action not maintainable on representations of character, etc, unless they be in   A–002
writing signed by the party chargeable

No action shall be brought whereby to charge any person upon or by reason of any representation or assurance made or given concerning or relating to the character, conduct, credit, ability, trade, or dealings of any other person, to the intent or purpose that such other person may obtain credit, money, or goods upon, unless such representation or assurance be made in writing, signed by the party to be charged therewith.

*   *   *   *   *

Mercantile Law Amendment Act 1856

A–003
1,2 (*Repealed.*)

3 Written guarantee not to be invalid by reason that the consideration does not   A–004
appear in writing

No special promise to be made by any person . . . to answer for the debt, default, or miscarriage of another person, being in writing, and signed by the party to be charged therewith, or some other person by him thereunto lawfully authorised, shall be deemed invalid to support an action, suit, or other proceeding to charge the person by whom such promise shall have been made, by reason only that the consideration for such promise does not appear in writing, or by necessary inference from a written document.

4 (*Repealed.*)   A–005

5 Surety who discharges the liability to be entitled to assignment of all securities   A–006
held by the creditor, and to stand in the place of the creditor

Every person who, being surety for the debt or duty of another, or being liable with another for any debt or duty, shall pay such debt or perform such duty, shall be entitled to have assigned to him, or to a trustee for him, every judgment, specialty, or other security which shall be held by the creditor in respect of such debt or duty, whether such judgment, specialty, or other security shall or shall not be deemed at law to have been satisfied by the payment of the debt or performance of the duty, and such person shall be entitled to stand in the place of the creditor, and to use all the remedies, and, if need be, and upon a proper indemnity, to use the name of the creditor, in any action or other proceeding, at law or in equity, in order to obtain from the principal debtor, or any co-surety, co-contractor, or co-debtor, as the case may be, indemnification for the advances made and loss sustained by the person who shall have so paid such debt or performed such duty, and such payment or performance so made by such surety shall not be pleadable in bar of any such action or other proceeding by him: Provided always, that no co-surety, co-contractor, or co-debtor shall be entitled to recover from any other co-surety, co-contractor, or co-debtor, by the means aforesaid, more than the just proportion to which, as between those parties themselves, such last-mentioned person shall be justly liable.

*　*　*　*　*

Bills of Exchange Act 1882

A–007　**55 Liability of drawer or indorser**

(1) The drawer of a bill by drawing it—

    (a) Engages that on due presentment it shall be accepted and paid according to its tenor, and that if it be dishonoured he will compensate the holder or any indorser who is compelled to pay it, provided that the requisite proceedings on dishonour be duly taken;

    (b) Is precluded from denying to a holder in due course the existence of the payee and his then capacity to indorse.

(2) The indorser of a bill by indorsing it—

    (a) Engages that on due presentment it shall be accepted and paid according to its tenor, and that if it be dishonoured he will compensate the holder or a subsequent indorser who is compelled to pay it, provided that the requisite proceedings on dishonour be duly taken;

    (b) Is precluded from denying to a holder in due course the genuineness and regularity in all respects of the drawer's signature and all previous indorsements;

    (c) Is precluded from denying to his immediate or a subsequent indorsee that the bill was at the time of his indorsement a valid and subsisting bill, and that he had then a good title thereto.

A–008　**56 Stranger signing bill liable as indorser**
Where a person signs a bill otherwise than as drawer or acceptor, he thereby incurs the liabilities of an indorser to a holder in due course.

*　*　*　*　*

Partnership Act 1890

A–009　**18 Revocation of continuing guaranty by change in firm**
A continuing guaranty or cautionary obligation given either to a firm or to a third person in respect of the transactions of a firm is, in the absence of agreement to the contrary, revoked as to future transactions by any change in the constitution of the firm to which, or of the firm in respect of the transactions of which, the guaranty or obligation was given.

* * * * *

Consumer Credit Act 1974

PART VIII
SECURITY

General

105 Form and content of securities A–010

(1) Any security provided in relation to a regulated agreement shall be expressed in writing.

(2) Regulations may prescribe the form and content of documents ('security instruments') to be made in compliance with subsection (1).

(3) Regulations under subsection (2) may in particular—

    (a) require specified information to be included in the prescribed manner in documents, and other specified material to be excluded;

    (b) contain requirements to ensure that specified information is clearly brought to the attention of the surety, and that one part of a document is not given insufficient or excessive prominence compared with another.

(4) A security instrument is not properly executed unless—

    (a) a document in the prescribed form, itself containing all the prescribed terms and conforming to regulations under subsection (2), is signed in the prescribed manner by or on behalf of the surety, and

    (b) the document embodies all the terms of the security, other than implied terms, and

    (c) the document, when presented or sent for the purpose of being signed by or on behalf of the surety, is in such state that its terms are readily legible, and

    (d) when the document is presented or sent for the purpose of being signed by or on behalf of the surety there is also presented or sent a copy of the document.

(5) A security instrument is not properly executed unless—

    (a) where the security is provided after, or at the time when, the regulated agreement is made, a copy of the executed agreement, together with a copy of any other document referred to in it, is given to the surety at the time the security is provided, or

    (b) where the security is provided before the regulated agreement is made, a copy of the executed agreement, together with a copy of any other document referred to in it, is given to the surety within seven days after the regulated agreement is made.

(6) Subsection (1) does not apply to a security provided by the debtor or hirer.

(7) If—

    (a) in contravention of subsection (1) a security is not expressed in writing, or

    (b) a security instrument is improperly executed,

the security, so far as provided in relation to a regulated agreement, is enforceable against the surety on an order of the court only.

(8) If an application for an order under subsection (7) is dismissed (except on technical grounds only) section 106 (ineffective securities) shall apply to the security.

(9) Regulations under section 60(1) shall include provision requiring documents embodying regulated agreements also to embody any security provided in relation to a regulated agreement by the debtor or hirer.

A–011 106 Ineffective securities

Where, under any provision of this Act, this section is applied to any security provided in relation to a regulated agreement, then, subject to section 177 (saving for registered charges),—

(a) the security, so far as it is so provided, shall be treated as never having effect;

(b) any property lodged with the creditor or owner solely for the purposes of the security as so provided shall be returned by him forthwith;

(c) the creditor or owner shall take any necessary action to remove or cancel an entry in any register, so far as the entry relates to the security as so provided; and

(d) any amount received by the creditor or owner on realisation of the security shall, so far as it is referable to the agreement, be repaid to the surety.

A–012 107 Duty to give information to surety under fixed-sum credit agreement

(1) The creditor under a regulated agreement for fixed-sum credit in relation to which security is provided, within the prescribed period after receiving a request in writing to that effect from the surety and payment of a fee of [£1],[1] shall give to the surety (if a different person from the debtor)—

(a) a copy of the executed agreement (if any) and of any other document referred to in it;

(b) a copy of the security instrument (if any); and

(c) a statement signed by or on behalf of the creditor showing, according to the information to which it is practicable for him to refer,—

(i) the total sum paid under the agreement by the debtor,

(ii) the total sum which has become payable under the agreement by the debtor but remains unpaid, and the various amounts comprised in that total sum, with the date when each became due, and

(iii) the total sum which is to become payable under the agreement by the debtor, and the various amounts comprised in that total sum, with the date, or mode of determining the date, when each becomes due.

(2) If the creditor possesses insufficient information to enable him to ascertain the amounts and dates mentioned in subsection (1)(c)(iii), he shall be taken to comply with that sub-paragraph if his statement under subsection (1)(c) gives the basis on which, under the regulated agreement, they would fall to be ascertained.

(3) Subsection (1) does not apply to—

(a) an agreement under which no sum is, or will or may become, payable by the debtor, or

(b) a request made less than one month after a previous request under that subsection relating to the same agreement was complied with.

(4) If the creditor under an agreement fails to comply with subsection (1)—

(a) he is not entitled, while the default continues, to enforce the security, so far as provided in relation to the agreement; and

(b) if the default continues for one month he commits an offence.

(5) This section does not apply to a non-commercial agreement.

[1] Substituted by Consumer Credit (Further Increase of Monetary Amounts) Order (SI 1998/997) Sch.1, para.1.

A–013 108 Duty to give information to surety under running-account credit agreement

(1) The creditor under a regulated agreement for running-account credit in relation to which security is provided, within the prescribed period after receiving a

request in writing to that effect from the surety and payment of a fee of [£1],[1] shall give to the surety (if a different person from the debtor)—

(a) a copy of the executed agreement (if any) and of any other document referred to in it;

(b) a copy of the security instrument (if any); and

(c) a statement signed by or on behalf of the creditor showing, according to the information to which it is practicable for him to refer,—

(i) the state of the account, and

(ii) the amount, if any, currently payable under the agreement by the debtor to the creditor, and

(iii) the amounts and due dates of any payments which, if the debtor does not draw further on the account, will later become payable under the agreement by the debtor to the creditor.

(2) If the creditor possesses insufficient information to enable him to ascertain the amounts and dates mentioned in subsection (1)(c)(iii), he shall be taken to comply with that sub-paragraph if his statement under subsection (1)(c) gives the basis on which, under the regulated agreement, they would fall to be ascertained.

(3) Subsection (1) does not apply to—

(a) an agreement under which no sum is, or will or may become, payable by the debtor, or

(b) a request made less than one month after a previous request under that subsection relating to the same agreement was complied with.

(4) If the creditor under an agreement fails to comply with subsection (1)—

(a) he is not entitled, while the default continues, to enforce the security, so far as provided in relation to the agreement; and

(b) if the default continues for one month he commits an offence.

(5) This section does not apply to a non-commercial agreement.

[1] Substituted by Consumer Credit (Further Increase of Monetary Amounts) Order (SI 1998/997) Sch.1, para.1.

109 Duty to give information to surety under consumer hire agreement   A–014

(1) The owner under a regulated consumer hire agreement in relation to which security is provided, within the prescribed period after receiving a request in writing to that effect from the surety and payment of a fee of [£1],[1] shall give to the surety (if a different person from the hirer)—

(a) a copy of the executed agreement and of any other document referred to in it;

(b) a copy of the security instrument (if any); and

(c) a statement signed by or on behalf of the owner showing, according to the information to which it is practicable for him to refer, the total sum which has become payable under the agreement by the hirer but remains unpaid and the various amounts comprised in that total sum, with the date when each became due.

(2) Subsection (1) does not apply to—

(a) an agreement under which no sum is, or will or may become, payable by the hirer, or

(b) a request made less than one month after a previous request under that subsection relating to the same agreement was complied with.

(3) If the owner under an agreement fails to comply with subsection (1)—

(a) he is not entitled, while the default continues, to enforce the security, so far as provided in relation to the agreement; and

(b) if the default continues for one month he commits an offence.

(4) This section does not apply to a non-commercial agreement.

[1] Substituted by Consumer Credit (Further Increase of Monetary Amounts) Order (SI 1998/997) Sch.1, para.1.

A–015   110 Duty to give information to debtor or hirer

(1) The creditor or owner under a regulated agreement, within the prescribed period after receiving a request in writing to that effect from the debtor or hirer and payment of a fee of [£1][1] shall give the debtor or hirer a copy of any security instrument executed in relation to the agreement after the making of the agreement.

(2) Subsection (1) does not apply to—

(a) a non-commercial agreement, or
(b) an agreement under which no sum is, or will or may become, payable by the debtor or hirer, or
(c) a request made less than one month after a previous request under subsection (1) relating to the same agreement was complied with.

(3) If the creditor or owner under an agreement fails to comply with subsection (1)—

(a) he is not entitled, while the default continues, to enforce the security (so far as provided in relation to the agreement); and
(b) if the default continues for one month he commits an offence.

[1] Substituted by Consumer Credit (Further Increase of Monetary Amounts) Order (SI 1998/997) Sch.1, para.1.

A–016   111 Duty to give surety copy of default etc notice

(1) When a default notice or a notice under section 76(1) or 98(1) is served on a debtor or hirer, a copy of the notice shall be served by the creditor or owner on any surety (if a different person from the debtor or hirer).

(2) If the creditor or owner fails to comply with subsection (1) in the case of any surety, the security is enforceable against the surety (in respect of the breach or other matter to which the notice relates) on an order of the court only.

A–017   112 Realisation of securities

Subject to section 121, regulations may provide for any matters relating to the sale or other realisation, by the creditor or owner, of property over which any right has been provided by way of security in relation to an actual or prospective regulated agreement, other than a non-commercial agreement.

A–018   113 Act not to be evaded by use of security

(1) Where a security is provided in relation to an actual or prospective regulated agreement, the security shall not be enforced so as to benefit the creditor or owner, directly or indirectly, to an extent greater (whether as respects the amount of any payment or the time or manner of its being made) than would be the case if the security were not provided and any obligations of the debtor or hirer, or his relative, under or in relation to the agreement were carried out to the extent (if any) to which they would be enforced under this Act.

(2) In accordance with subsection (1), where a regulated agreement is enforceable on an order of the court or the [OFT][1] only, any security provided in relation to the agreement is enforceable (so far as provided in relation to the agreement) where such an order has been made in relation to the agreement, but not otherwise.

(3) Where—

(a) a regulated agreement is cancelled under section 69(1) or becomes subject to section 69(2), or

(b) a regulated agreement is terminated under section 91, or

(c) in relation to any agreement an application for an order under section 40(2), 65(1), 124(1) or 149(2) is dismissed (except on technical grounds only), or

(d) a declaration is made by the court under section 142(1) (refusal of enforcement order) as respects any regulated agreement,

section 106 shall apply to any security provided in relation to the agreement.

(4) Where subsection (3)(d) applies and the declaration relates to a part only of the regulated agreement, section 106 shall apply to the security only so far as it concerns that part.

(5) In the case of a cancelled agreement, the duty imposed on the debtor or hirer by section 71 or 72 shall not be enforceable before the creditor or owner has discharged any duty imposed on him by section 106 (as applied by subsection (3)(a)).

(6) If the security is provided in relation to a prospective agreement or transaction, the security shall be enforceable in relation to the agreement or transaction only after the time (if any) when the agreement is made; and until that time the person providing the security shall be entitled, by notice to the creditor or owner, to require that section 106 shall thereupon apply to the security.

(7) Where an indemnity or guarantee is given in a case where the debtor or hirer is a minor, or an indemnity is given in a case where he is otherwise not of full capacity, the reference in subsection (1) to the extent to which his obligations would be enforced shall be read in relation to the indemnity or guarantee as a reference to the extent to which those obligations would be enforced if he were of full capacity.

(8) Subsections (1) to (3) also apply where a security is provided in relation to an actual or prospective linked transaction, and in that case—

(a) references to the agreement shall be read as references to the linked transaction, and

(b) references to the creditor or owner shall be read as references to any person (other than the debtor or hirer, or his relative) who is a party, or prospective party, to the linked transaction.

[1] Substituted by Enterprise Act 2002, Sch.25, para.6.

Pledges

114 Pawn-receipts
A–019

(1) At the time he receives the article, a person who takes any article in pawn under a regulated agreement shall give to the person from whom he receives it a receipt in the prescribed form (a 'pawn-receipt').

(2) A person who takes any article in pawn from an individual whom he knows to be, or who appears to be and is, a minor commits an offence.

(3) This section and sections 115 to 122 do not apply to—

(a) a pledge of documents of title or of bearer bonds, or

(b) a non-commercial agreement.

115 Penalty for failure to supply copies of pledge agreement, etc
A–020

If the creditor under a regulated agreement to take any article in pawn fails to observe the requirements of sections 62 to 64 or 114(1) in relation to the agreement he commits an offence.

A–021   **116 Redemption period**

(1) A pawn is redeemable at any time within six months after it was taken.

(2) Subject to subsection (1), the period within which a pawn is redeemable shall be the same as the period fixed by the parties for the duration of the credit secured by the pledge, or such longer period as they may agree.

(3) If the pawn is not redeemed by the end of the period laid down by subsections (1) and (2) (the 'redemption period'), it nevertheless remains redeemable until it is realised by the pawnee under section 121, except where under section 120(1)(a) the property in it passes to the pawnee.

(4) No special charge shall be made for redemption of a pawn after the end of the redemption period, and charges in respect of the safe keeping of the pawn shall not be at a higher rate after the end of the redemption period than before.

A–022   **117 Redemption procedure**

(1) On surrender of the pawn-receipt, and payment of the amount owing, at any time when the pawn is redeemable, the pawnee shall deliver the pawn to the bearer of the pawn-receipt.

(2) Subsection (1) does not apply if the pawnee knows or has reasonable cause to suspect that the bearer of the pawn-receipt is neither the owner of the pawn nor authorised by the owner to redeem it.

(3) The pawnee is not liable to any person in tort or delict for delivering the pawn where subsection (1) applies, or refusing to deliver it where the person demanding delivery does not comply with subsection (1) or, by reason of subsection (2), subsection (1) does not apply.

A–023   **118 Loss etc of pawn-receipt**

(1) A person (the 'claimant') who is not in possession of the pawn-receipt but claims to be the owner of the pawn, or to be otherwise entitled or authorised to redeem it, may do so at any time when it is redeemable by tendering to the pawnee in place of the pawn-receipt—

> (a) a statutory declaration made by the claimant in the prescribed form, and with the prescribed contents, or
>
> (b) where the pawn is security for fixed-sum credit not exceeding [£75][1] or running-account credit on which the credit limit does not exceed £75[2], and the pawnee agrees, a statement in writing in the prescribed form, and with the prescribed contents, signed by the claimant.

(2) On compliance by the claimant with subsection (1), section 117 shall apply as if the declaration or statement were the pawn-receipt, and the pawn-receipt itself shall become inoperative for the purposes of section 117.

[1] Substituted by Consumer Credit (Further Increase of Monetary Amounts) Order (SI 1998/997) Sch.1, para.1.
[2] Substituted by Consumer Credit (Further Increase of Monetary Amounts) Order (SI 1998/997) Sch.1, para.1.

A–024   **119 Unreasonable refusal to deliver pawn**

(1) If a person who has taken a pawn under a regulated agreement refuses without reasonable cause to allow the pawn to be redeemed, he commits an offence.

(2) On the conviction in England or Wales of a pawnee under subsection (1) where the offence does not amount to theft, [section 148 of the Powers of Criminal Courts (Sentencing) Act 2000 (restitution orders)[1] shall apply as if the pawnee had been convicted of stealing the pawn.

(3) On the conviction in Northern Ireland of a pawnee under subsection (1) where the offence does not amount to theft, section 27 (orders for restitution) of the Theft Act (Northern Ireland) 1969, and any provision of the Theft Act (Northern Ireland) 1969 relating to that section, shall apply as if the pawnee had been convicted of stealing the pawn.

[1] Substituted by Powers of Criminal Courts (Sentencing) Act 2000, Sch.9, para.45.

120 Consequence of failure to redeem

A–025

(1) If at the end of the redemption period the pawn has not been redeemed—

(a) notwithstanding anything in section 113, the property in the pawn passes to the pawnee where the redemption period is six months and the pawn is security for fixed-sum credit not exceeding [£75][1] or running-account credit on which the credit limit does not exceed [£75][2]; or

(b) in any other case the pawn becomes realisable by the pawnee.

(2) Where the debtor or hirer is entitled to apply to the court for a time order under section 129, subsection (1) shall apply with the substitution, for 'at the end of the redemption period' of 'after the expiry of five days following the end of the redemption period'.

[1] Substituted by Consumer Credit (Further Increase of Monetary Amounts) Order (SI 1998/997) Sch.1, para.1.
[2] Substituted by Consumer Credit (Further Increase of Monetary Amounts) Order (SI 1998/997) Sch.1, para.1.

121 Realisation of pawn

A–026

(1) When a pawn has become realisable by him, the pawnee may sell it, after giving to the pawnor (except in such cases as may be prescribed) not less than the prescribed period of notice of the intention to sell, indicating in the notice the asking price and such other particulars as may be prescribed.

(2) Within the prescribed period after the sale takes place, the pawnee shall give the pawnor the prescribed information in writing as to the sale, its proceeds and expenses.

(3) Where the net proceeds of sale are not less than the sum which, if the pawn had been redeemed on the date of the sale, would have been payable for its redemption, the debt secured by the pawn is discharged and any surplus shall be paid by the pawnee to the pawnor.

(4) Where subsection (3) does not apply, the debt shall be treated as from the date of sale as equal to the amount by which the net proceeds of sale fall short of the sum which would have been payable for the redemption of the pawn on that date.

(5) In this section the 'net proceeds of sale' is the amount realised (the 'gross amount') less the expenses (if any) of the sale.

(6) If the pawnor alleges that the gross amount is less than the true market value of the pawn on the date of sale, it is for the pawnee to prove that he and any agents employed by him in the sale used reasonable care to ensure that the true market value was obtained, and if he fails to do so subsections (3) and (4) shall have effect as if the reference in subsection (5) to the gross amount were a reference to the true market value.

(7) If the pawnor alleges that the expenses of the sale were unreasonably high, it is for the pawnee to prove that they were reasonable, and if he fails to do so subsections (3) and (4) shall have effect as if the reference in subsection (5) to expenses were a reference to reasonable expenses.

122 Order in Scotland to deliver pawn

A–027 **(1) As respects Scotland where—**

(a) a pawn is either—
(i) an article which has been stolen, or
(ii) an article which has been obtained by fraud, and a person is convicted of any offence in relation to the theft or, as the case may be, the fraud; or
(b) a person is convicted of an offence under section 119(1),

the court by which that person is so convicted may order delivery of the pawn to the owner or the person otherwise entitled thereto.

(2) A court making an order under subsection (1)(a) for delivery of a pawn may make the order subject to such conditions as to payment of the debt secured by the pawn as it thinks fit.

Negotiable instruments

A–028 **123 Restrictions on taking and negotiating instruments**

(1) A creditor or owner shall not take a negotiable instrument, other than a bank note or cheque, in discharge of any sum payable—

(a) by the debtor or hirer under a regulated agreement, or
(b) by any person as surety in relation to the agreement.

(2) The creditor or owner shall not negotiate a cheque taken by him in discharge of a sum payable as mentioned in subsection (1), except to a banker (within the meaning of the Bills of Exchange Act 1882).

(3) The creditor or owner shall not take a negotiable instrument as security for the discharge of any sum payable as mentioned in subsection (1).

(4) A person takes a negotiable instrument as security for the discharge of a sum if the sum is intended to be paid in some other way, and the negotiable instrument is to be presented for payment only if the sum is not paid in that way.

(5) This section does not apply where the regulated agreement is a non-commercial agreement.

(6) The Secretary of State may by order provide that this section shall not apply where the regulated agreement has a connection with a country outside the United Kingdom.

A–029 **124 Consequences of breach of s 123**

(1) After any contravention of section 123 has occurred in relation to a sum payable as mentioned in section 123(1)(a), the agreement under which the sum is payable is enforceable against the debtor or hirer on an order of the court only.

(2) After any contravention of section 123 has occurred in relation to a sum payable by any surety, the security is enforceable on an order of the court only.

(3) Where an application for an order under subsection (2) is dismissed (except on technical grounds only) section 106 shall apply to the security.

A–030 **125 Holders in due course**

(1) A person who takes a negotiable instrument in contravention of section 123(1) or (3) is not a holder in due course, and is not entitled to enforce the instrument.

(2) Where a person negotiates a cheque in contravention of section 123(2), his doing so constitutes a defect in his title within the meaning of the Bills of Exchange Act 1882.

(3) If a person mentioned in section 123(1)(*a*) or (*b*) ('the protected person') becomes liable to a holder in due course of an instrument taken from the protected person in contravention of section 123(1) or (3), or taken from the protected person and negotiated in contravention of section 123(2), the creditor or owner shall indemnify the protected person in respect of that liability.

(4) Nothing in this Act affects the rights of the holder in due course of any negotiable instrument.

Land mortgages

126 Enforcement of land mortgages

A–031

A land mortgage securing a regulated agreement is enforceable (so far as provided in relation to the agreement) on an order of the court only.

---

189 Definitions

A–032

(1) In this Act, unless the context otherwise requires—
  'advertisement' includes every form of advertising, whether in a publication, by television or radio, by display of notices, signs, labels, showcards or goods, by distribution of samples, circulars, catalogues, price lists or other material, by exhibition of pictures, models or films, or in any other way, and references to the publishing of advertisements shall be construed accordingly;
  'advertiser' in relation to an advertisement, means any person indicated by the advertisement as willing to enter into transactions to which the advertisement relates;
  'ancillary credit business' has the meaning given by section 145(1);
  'antecedent negotiations' has the meaning given by section 56;
  'appeal period' means the period beginning on the first day on which an appeal to the Secretary of State may be brought and ending on the last day on which it may be brought or, if it is brought, ending on its final determination, or abandonment;

* * * * *

  'associate' shall be construed in accordance with section 184;
  [. . .]¹
  'bill of sale' has the meaning given by section 4 of the Bills of Sale Act 1878 or, for Northern Ireland, by section 4 of the Bills of Sale (Ireland) Act 1879;
  'building society' means a building society within the meaning of the Building Societies Act 1986;
  'business' includes profession or trade, and references to a business apply subject to subsection (2);
  'cancellable agreement' means a regulated agreement which, by virtue of section 67, may be cancelled by the debtor or hirer;
  'canvass' shall be construed in accordance with sections 48 and 153;
  'cash' includes money in any form;
  'charity' means as respects England and Wales a charity registered under [the Charities Act 1993]² or an exempt charity (within the meaning of that Act), and as respects Scotland and Northern Ireland an institution or other organisation established for charitable purposes only ('organisation' including any persons administering a trust and 'charitable' being construed in the same way as if it were contained in the Income Tax Acts);

'conditional sale agreement' means an agreement for the sale of goods or land under which the purchase price or part of it is payable by instalments, and the property in the goods or land is to remain in the seller (notwithstanding that the buyer is to be in possession of the goods or land) until such conditions as to the payment of instalments or otherwise as may be specified in the agreement are fulfilled;

'consumer credit agreement' has the meaning given by section 8, and includes a consumer credit agreement which is cancelled under section 69(1), or becomes subject to section 69(2), so far as the agreement remains in force;

'consumer credit business' means any business so far as it comprises or relates to the provision of credit under regulated consumer credit agreements;

'consumer hire agreement' has the meaning given by section 15;

'consumer hire business' means any business so far as it comprises or relates to the bailment or (in Scotland) the hiring of goods under regulated consumer hire agreements;

'controller', in relation to a body corporate, means a person—

(a) in accordance with whose directions or instructions the directors of the body corporate or of another body corporate which is its controller (or any of them) are accustomed to act, or

(b) who, either alone or with any associate or associates, is entitled to exercise, or control the exercise of, one third or more of the voting power at any general meeting of the body corporate or of another body corporate which is its controller;

'copy' shall be construed in accordance with section 180;

*   *   *   *   *

'court' means in relation to England and Wales the county court, in relation to Scotland the sheriff court and in relation to Northern Ireland the High Court or the county court;'credit' shall be construed in accordance with section 9;

'credit-broker' means a person carrying on a business of credit brokerage;

'credit brokerage' has the meaning given by section 145(2);

'credit limit' has the meaning given by section 10(2);

'creditor' means the person providing credit under a consumer credit agreement or the person to whom his rights and duties under the agreement have passed by assignment or operation of law, and in relation to a prospective consumer credit agreement, includes the prospective creditor;

'credit reference agency' has the meaning given by section 145(8);

'credit-sale agreement' means an agreement for the sale of goods, under which the purchase price or part of it is payable by instalments, but which is not a conditional sale agreement;

'credit-token' has the meaning given by section 14(1);

'credit-token agreement' means a regulated agreement for the provision of credit in connection with the use of a credit-token;

'debt-adjusting' has the meaning given by section 145(5);

'debt-collecting' has the meaning given by section 145(7);

'debt-counselling' has the meaning given by section 145(6);

'debtor' means the individual receiving credit under a consumer credit agreement or the person to whom his rights and duties under the agreement have passed by assignment or operation of law, and in relation to a prospective consumer credit agreement includes the prospective debtor;

'debtor-creditor agreement' has the meaning given by section 13;

'debtor-creditor-supplier agreement' has the meaning given by section 12;

'default notice' has the meaning given by section 87(1);

'deposit' means [(except in section 16(10) and 25(1B))][3] any sum payable by a debtor or hirer by way of deposit or down-payment, or credited or to be credited to him on account of any deposit or down-payment, whether the sum is to be or has been paid to the creditor or owner or any other person, or is to be or has been discharged by a payment of money or a transfer or delivery of goods or by any other means;

[. . .]⁴

'electric line' has the meaning given by [the Electricity Act 1989] or, for Northern Ireland, the Electricity (Northern Ireland) Order 1992;

'embodies' and related words shall be construed in accordance with subsection (4);

'enforcement authority' has the meaning given by section 161(1);

'enforcement order' means an order under section 65(1), 105(7)(*a*) or (*b*), 111(2) or 124(1) or (2);

'executed agreement' means a document, signed by or on behalf of the parties, embodying the terms of a regulated agreement, or such of them as have been reduced to writing;

'exempt agreement' means an agreement specified in or under section 16;

'finance' means to finance wholly or partly and 'financed' and 'refinanced' shall be construed accordingly;

'file' and 'copy of the file' have the meanings given by section 158(5);

'fixed-sum credit' has the meaning given by section 10(1)(*b*);

'friendly society' means a society [or treated as registered [or treated as registered under the Friendly Societies Act 1974 or the Friendly Societies Act 1992]⁵;

[. . .]⁶

'future arrangements' shall be construed in accordance with section 187;

'general notice' means a notice published by the [OFT]⁷ at a time and in a manner appearing to [it]⁸ suitable for securing that the notice is seen within a reasonable time by persons likely to be affected by it;

'give', means deliver or send by post to;

'goods' has the meaning given by section 61(1) of the Sale of Goods Act 1979;

'group licence' has the meaning given by section 22(1)(*b*);

'High Court' means Her Majesty's High Court of Justice, or the Court of Session in Scotland or the High Court of Justice in Northern Ireland;

'hire-purchase agreement' means an agreement, other than a conditional sale agreement, under which—

(*a*) goods are bailed or (in Scotland) hired in return for periodical payments by the person to whom they are bailed or hired, and

(*b*) the property in the goods will pass to that person if the terms of the agreement are complied with and one or more of the following occurs—

    (i) the exercise of an option to purchase by that person,

    (ii) the doing of any other specified act by any party to the agreement,

    (iii) the happening of any other specified event;

'hirer' means the individual to whom goods are bailed or (in Scotland) hired under a consumer hire agreement, or the person to whom his rights and duties under the agreement have passed by assignment or operation of law, and in relation to a prospective consumer hire agreement includes the prospective hirer;

'individual' includes a partnership or other unincorporated body of persons not consisting entirely of bodies corporate;

'installation' means—

(*a*) the installing of any electric line or any gas or water pipe,

(*b*) the fixing of goods to the premises where they are to be used, and the alteration of premises to enable goods to be used on them,

(*c*) where it is reasonably necessary that goods should be constructed or erected on the premises where they are to be used, any work carried out for the purpose of constructing or erecting them on those premises;

[. . .]⁹

'land', includes an interest in land, and in relation to Scotland includes heritable subjects of whatever description;

'land improvement company' means an improvement company as defined by section 7 of the Improvement of Land Act 1899;

'land mortgage' includes any security charged on land;

'licence' means a licence under Part III (including that Part as applied to ancillary credit businesses by section 147);

'licensed', in relation to any act, means authorised by a licence to do the act or cause or permit another person to do it;

'licensee', in the case of a group licence, includes any person covered by the licence;

'linked transaction' has the meaning given by section 19(1);

'local authority', in relation to England [. . .]¹⁰, means . . . a county council, a London borough council, a district council, the Common Council of the City of London, or the Council of Isles of Scilly, [in relation to Wales means a county council or a county borough council]¹¹ and in relation to Scotland, [council constituted under section 2 of the Local Government etc. (Scotland) Act 1994]¹², and, in relation to Northern Ireland, means a district council;

* * * * *

'modifying agreement' has the meaning given by section 82(2);

* * * * *

'multiple agreement' has the meaning given by section 18(1);

'negotiator' has the meaning given by section 56(1);

'non-commercial agreement' means a consumer credit agreement or a consumer hire agreement not made by the creditor or owner in the course of a business carried on by him;

'notice' means notice in writing;

'notice of cancellation' has the meaning given by section 69(1);

["OFT" means the Office of Fair Trading;']¹³

'owner' means a person who bails or (in Scotland) hires out goods under a consumer hire agreement or the person to whom his rights and duties under the agreement have passed by assignment or operation of law, and in relation to a prospective consumer hire agreement, includes the prospective bailor or persons from whom the goods are to be hired;

'pawn' means any article subject to a pledge;

'pawn-receipt' has the meaning given by section 114;

'pawnee' and 'pawnor' include any person to whom the rights and duties of the original pawnee or the original pawnor, as the case may be, have passed by assignment or operation of law;

'payment' includes tender;

'personal credit agreement' has the meaning given by section 8(1);

'pledge' means the pawnee's rights over an article taken in pawn;

'prescribed' means prescribed by regulations made by the Secretary of State;

'pre-existing arrangements' shall be construed in accordance with section 187;

'principal agreement' has the meaning given by section 19(1);

'protected goods' has the meaning given by section 90(7);

'quotation' has the meaning given by section 52(1)*(a)*;

'redemption period' has the meaning given by section 116(3);

'register' means the register kept by the [OFT]¹⁴ under section 35;

'regulated agreement' means a consumer credit agreement, or consumer hire agreement, other than an exempt agreement, and 'regulated' and 'unregulated' shall be construed accordingly;

'regulations' means regulations made by the Secretary of State;

'relative', except in section 184, means a person who is an associate by virtue of section 184(1);

'representation' includes any condition or warranty, and any other statement or undertaking, whether oral or in writing;

'restricted-use credit agreement' and 'restricted-use credit' have the meanings given by section 11(1);

'rules of court', in relation to Northern Ireland means, in relation to the High Court, rules made under section 7 of the Northern Ireland Act 1962, and, in relation to any other court, rules made by the authority having for the time being power to make rules regulating the practice and procedure in that court;

'running-account credit' shall be construed in accordance with section 10;

'security', in relation to an actual or prospective consumer credit agreement or consumer hire agreement, or any linked transaction, means a mortgage, charge, pledge, bond, debenture, indemnity, guarantee, bill, note or other right provided by the debtor or hirer, or at his request (express or implied), to secure the carrying out of the obligations of the debtor or hirer under the agreement;

'security instrument' has the meaning given by section 105(2);

'serve on' means deliver or send by post to;

'signed' shall be construed in accordance with subsection (3);

'small agreement' has the meaning given by section 17(1), and 'small' in relation to an agreement within any category shall be construed accordingly;

'specified fee' shall be construed in accordance with section 2(4) and (5); all

'standard licence' has the meaning given by section 22(1)*(a)*;

'supplier' has the meaning given by section 11(1)*(b)* or 12*(c)* or 13*(c)* or, in relation to an agreement falling within section 11(1)*(a)*, means the creditor, and includes a person to whom the rights and duties of a supplier (as so defined) have passed by assignment or operation of law, or (in relation to a prospective agreement) the prospective supplier;

'surety' means the person by whom any security is provided, or the person to whom his rights and duties in relation to the security have passed by assignment or operation of law;

'technical grounds' shall be construed in accordance with subsection (5);

'time order' has the meaning given by section 129(1);

'total charge for credit' means a sum calculated in accordance with regulations under section 20(1);

'total price' means the total sum payable by the debtor under a hire-purchase agreement or a conditional sale agreement, including any sum payable on the exercise of an option to purchase, but excluding any sum payable as a penalty or as compensation or damages for a breach of the agreement;

'unexecuted agreement' means a document embodying the terms of a prospective regulated agreement, or such of them as it is intended to reduce to writing;

'unlicensed' means without a licence, but applies only in relation to acts for which a licence is required;

'unrestricted-use credit agreement' and 'unrestricted-use credit' have the meanings given by section 11(2);

'working day' means any day other than—

(a) Saturday or Sunday,

(b) Christmas Day or Good Friday,

(c) a bank holiday within the meaning given by section 1 of the Banking and Financial Dealings Act 1971.

(2) A person is not to be treated as carrying on a particular type of business merely because occasionally he enters into transactions belonging to a business of that type.

(3) Any provision of this Act requiring a document to be signed is complied with by a body corporate if the document is sealed by that body.
This subsection does not apply to Scotland.

(4) A document embodies a provision if the provision is set out either in the document itself or in another document referred to in it.

(5) An application dismissed by the court or the [OFT][15] shall, if the court or the [OFT][16] (as the case may be) so certifies, be taken to be dismissed on technical grounds only.

(6) Except in so far as the context otherwise requires, any reference in this Act to an enactment shall be construed as a reference to that enactment as amended by or under any other enactment, including this Act.

(7) In this Act, except where otherwise indicated—

  (a) a reference to a numbered Part, section or Schedule is a reference to the Part or section of, or the Schedule to, this Act so numbered, and
  (b) a reference in a section to a numbered subsection is a reference to the subsection of that section so numbered, and
  (c) a reference in a section, subsection or Schedule to a numbered paragraph is a reference to the paragraph of that section, subsection or Schedule so numbered.

[1] Repealed by Financial Services and Markets Act 2000 (Consequential Amendments and Repeals) Order (SI 2001/3649) art.176.
[2] Substituted by Charities Act 1993, Sch.6, para.30.
[3] Inserted by Financial Services and Markets Act 2000 (Consequential Amendments and Repeals) Order (SI 2001/3649) art.176.
[4] Repealed by Enterprise Act 2002, Sch.25, para.6, Sch.26.
[5] Substituted by by Financial Services and Markets Act 2000 (Consequential Amendments and Repeals) Order (SI 2001/3649) art.176.
[6] Repealed by Friendly Societies Act 1992, Sch.22, para.1.
[7] Substituted by Enterprise Act 2002, Sch.25, para.6.
[8] Substituted by Enterprise Act 2002, Sch.25, para.6.
[9] Repealed by by Financial Services and Markets Act 2000 (Consequential Amendments and Repeals) Order (SI 2001/3649) art.176.
[10] Repealed by Local Government (Wales) Act 1994, Sch.18, para.1.
[11] Inserted by Local Government (Wales) Act 1994, Sch.16, para.45.
[12] Substituted by Local Government etc. (Scotland) Act 1994, Sch.13, para. 94.
[13] Inserted by Enterprise Act 2002, Sch.25, para.6.
[14] Substituted by Enterprise Act 2002, Sch.25, para.6.
[15] Substituted by Enterprise Act 2002, Sch.25, para.6.
[16] Substituted by Enterprise Act 2002, Sch.25, para.6.

* * * * *

Unfair Contract Terms Act 1977

Avoidance of liability for negligence, breach of contract, etc

A–033 **2 Negligence liability**

(1) A person cannot by reference to any contract term or to a notice given to persons generally or to particular persons exclude or restrict his liability for death or personal injury resulting from negligence.

(2) In the case of other loss or damage, a person cannot so exclude or restrict his liability for negligence except in so far as the term or notice satisfies the requirement of reasonableness.

(3) Where a contract term or notice purports to exclude or restrict liability for negligence a person's agreement to or awareness of it is not of itself to be taken as indicating his voluntary acceptance of any risk.

Explanatory provisions

11 The 'reasonableness' test A–034

(1) In relation to a contract term, the requirement of reasonableness for the purposes of this Part of this Act, section 3 of the Misrepresentation Act 1967 and section 3 of the Misrepresentation Act (Northern Ireland) 1967 is that the term shall have been a fair and reasonable one to be included having regard to the circumstances which were, or ought reasonably to have been, known to or in the contemplation of the parties when the contract was made.

(2) In determining for the purposes of section 6 or 7 above whether a contract term satisfies the requirement of reasonableness, regard shall be had in particular to the matters specified in Schedule 2 to this Act; but this subsection does not prevent the court or arbitrator from holding, in accordance with any rule of law, that a term which purports to exclude or restrict any relevant liability is not a term of the contract.

(3) In relation to a notice (not being a notice having contractual effect), the requirement of reasonableness under this Act is that it should be fair and reasonable to allow reliance on it, having regard to all the circumstances obtaining when the liability arose or (but for the notice) would have arisen.

(4) Where by reference to a contract term or notice a person seeks to restrict liability to a specified sum of money, and the question arises (under this or any other Act) whether the term or notice satisfies the requirement of reasonableness, regard shall be had in particular (but without prejudice to subsection (2) above in the case of contract terms) to—

   (a) the resources which he could expect to be available to him for the purpose of meeting the liability should it arise; and
   (b) how far it was open to him to cover himself by insurance.

(5) It is for those claiming that a contract term or notice satisfies the requirement of reasonableness to show that it does.

A–035

SCHEDULE 2

'GUIDELINES' FOR APPLICATION OF REASONABLENESS TEST

The matters to which regard is to be had in particular for the purposes of sections 6(3), 7(3) and (4), 20 and 21 are any of the following which appear to be relevant—

   (a) the strength of the bargaining positions of the parties relative to each other, taking into account (among other things) alternative means by which the customer's requirements could have been met;
   (b) whether the customer received an inducement to agree to the term, or in accepting it had an opportunity of entering into a similar contract with other persons, but without having to accept a similar term;
   (c) whether the customer knew or ought reasonably to have known of the existence and extent of the term (having regard, among other things, to any custom of the trade and any previous course of dealing between the parties);

(d) where the term excludes or restricts any relevant liability if some condition is not complied with, whether it was reasonable at the time of the contract to expect that compliance with that condition would be practicable;

(e) whether the goods were manufactured, processed or adapted to the special order of the customer.

* * * * *

Unfair Terms in Consumer Contracts Regulations 1999 (SI 1999/2083)

A–036 **1 Citation and commencement**
These Regulations may be cited as the Unfair Terms in Consumer Contracts Regulations 1999 and shall come into force on 1st October 1999.

A–037 **2 Revocation**

The Unfair Terms in Consumer Contracts Regulations 1994 are hereby revoked.

A–038 **3 Interpretation**

(1) In these Regulations—
'the Community' means the European Community;
'consumer' means any natural person who, in contracts covered by these Regulations, is acting for purposes which are outside his trade, business or profession;
'court' in relation to England and Wales and Northern Ireland means a county court or the High Court, and in relation to Scotland, the Sheriff or the Court of Session;
'Director' means the Director General of Fair Trading;
'EEA Agreement' means the Agreement on the European Economic Area signed at Oporto on 2 May 1992 as adjusted by the protocol signed at Brussels on 17th March 1993;
'Member State' means a State which is a contracting party to the EEA Agreement;
'notified' means notified in writing;
'qualifying body' means a person specified in Schedule 1;
'seller or supplier' means any natural or legal person who, in contracts covered by these Regulations, is acting for purposes relating to his trade, business or profession, whether publicly owned or privately owned;
'unfair terms' means the contractual terms referred to in regulation 5.

(2) In the application of these Regulations to Scotland for references to an 'injunction' or an 'interim injunction' there shall be substituted references to an 'interdict' or 'interim interdict' respectively.

A–039 **4 Terms to which these Regulations apply**

(1) These Regulations apply in relation to unfair terms in contracts concluded between a seller or a supplier and a consumer.

(2) These Regulations do not apply to contractual terms which reflect—

(a) mandatory statutory or regulatory provisions (including such provisions under the law of any Member State or in Community legislation having effect in the United Kingdom without further enactment);

(b) the provisions or principles of international conventions to which the Member States or the Community are party.

A–040 **5 Unfair terms**

(1) A contractual term which has not been individually negotiated shall be regarded as unfair if, contrary to the requirement of good faith, it causes a significant imbalance in the parties' rights and obligations arising under the contract, to the detriment of the consumer.

(2) A term shall always be regarded as not having been individually negotiated where it has been drafted in advance and the consumer has therefore not been able to influence the substance of the term.

(3) Notwithstanding that a specific term or certain aspects of it in a contract has been individually negotiated, these Regulations shall apply to the rest of a contract if an overall assessment of it indicates that it is a pre-formulated standard contract.

(4) It shall be for any sellor or supplier who claims that a term was individually negotiated to show that it was.

(5) Schedule 2 to these Regulations contains an indicative and non-exhaustive list of the terms which may be regarded as unfair.

6 Assessment of unfair terms   A–041

(1) Without prejudice to regulation 12, the unfairness of a contractual term shall be assessed, taking into account the nature of the goods or services for which the contract was concluded and by referring, at the time of conclusion of the contract, to all the circumstances attending the conclusion of the contract and to all the other terms of the contract or of another contract on which it is dependent.

(2) In so far as it is in plain intelligible language, the assessment of fairness of a term shall not relate—

- (*a*) to the definition of the main subject matter of the contract, or
- (*b*) to the adequacy of the price or remuneration, as against the goods or services supplied in exchange.

7 Written contracts   A–042

(1) A seller or supplier shall ensure that any written term of a contract is expressed in plain, intelligible language.

(2) If there is doubt about the meaning of a written term, the interpretation which is most favourable to the consumer shall prevail but this rule shall not apply in proceedings brought under regulation 12.

8 Effect of unfair term   A–043

(1) An unfair term in a contract concluded with a consumer by a seller or supplier shall not be binding on the consumer.

(2) The contract shall continue to bind the parties if it is capable of continuing in existence without the unfair term.

9 Choice of law clauses   A–044

These Regulations shall apply notwithstanding any contract term which applies or purports to apply the law of a non-Member State, if the contract has a close connection with the territory of the Member States.

10 Complaints—consideration by Director   A–045

(1) It shall be the duty of the Director to consider any complaint made to him that any contract term drawn up for general use is unfair, unless—

- (*a*) the complaint appears to the Director to be frivolous or vexatious; or
- (*b*) a qualifying body has notified the Director that it agrees to consider the complaint.

(2) The Director shall give reasons for his decision to apply or not to apply, as the case may be, for an injunction under regulation 12 in relation to any complaint which these Regulations require him to consider.

(3) In deciding whether or not to apply for an injunction in respect of a term which the Director considers to be unfair, he may, if he considers it appropriate to do so, have regard to any undertakings given to him by or on behalf of any person as to the continued use of such a term in contracts concluded with consumers.

A–046 **11 Complaints—consideration by qualifying bodies**

(1) If a qualifying body specified in Part One of Schedule 1 notifies the Director that it agrees to consider a complaint that any contract term drawn up for general use is unfair, it shall be under a duty to consider that complaint.

(2) Regulation 10(2) and (3) shall apply to a qualifying body which is under a duty to consider a complaint as they apply to the Director.

A–047 **12 Injunctions to prevent continued use of unfair terms**

(1) The Director or, subject to paragraph (2), any qualifying body may apply for an injunction (including an interim injunction) against any person appearing to the Director or that body to be using, or recommending use of, an unfair term drawn up for general use in contracts concluded with consumers.

(2) A qualifying body may apply for an injunction only where—

    (a) it has notified the Director of its intention to apply at least fourteen days before the date on which the application is made, beginning with the date on which the notification was given; or

    (b) the Director consents to the application being made within a shorter period.

(3) The court on an application under this regulation may grant an injunction on such terms as it thinks fit.

(4) An injunction may relate not only to use of a particular contract term drawn up for general use but to any similar term, or a term having like effect, used or recommended for use by any person.

A–048 **13 Powers of the Director and qualifying bodies to obtain documents and information**

(1) The Director may exercise the power conferred by this regulation for the purpose of—

    (a) facilitating his consideration of a complaint that a contract term drawn up for general use is unfair; or

    (b) ascertaining whether a person has complied with an undertaking or court order as to the continued use, or recommendation for use, of a term in contracts concluded with consumers.

(2) A qualifying body specified in Part One of Schedule 1 may exercise the power conferred by this regulation for the purpose of—

    (a) facilitating its consideration of a complaint that a contract term drawn up for general use is unfair; or

    (b) ascertaining whether a person has complied with—

        (i) an undertaking given to it or to the court following an application by that body, or

        (ii) a court order made on an application by that body,

        as to the continued use, or recommendation for use, of a term in contracts concluded with consumers.

(3) The Director may require any person to supply to him, and a qualifying body specified in Part One of Schedule 1 may require any person to supply to it—

    (a) a copy of any document which that person has used or recommended for use, at the time the notice referred to in paragraph (4) below is given, as a pre-formulated standard contract in dealings with consumers;

    (b) information about the use, or recommendation for use, by that person of that document or any other such document in dealings with consumers.

(4) The power conferred by this regulation is to be exercised by a notice in writing which may—

    (a) specify the way in which and the time within which it is to be complied with; and

    (b) be varied or revoked by a subsequent notice.

(5) Nothing in this regulation compels a person to supply any document or information which he would be entitled to refuse to produce or given in civil proceedings before the court.

(6) If a person makes default in complying with a notice under this regulation, the court may, on the application of the Director or of the qualifying body, make such order as the court thinks fit for requiring the default to be made good, and any such order may provide that all the costs or expenses of and incidental to the application shall be borne by the person in default or by any officers of a company or other association who are responsible for its default.

14 Notification of undertakings and orders to Director A–049

A qualifying body shall notify the Director—

    (a) of any undertaking given to it by or on behalf of any person as to the continued use of a term which that body considers to be unfair in contracts concluded with consumers;

    (b) of the outcome of any application made by it under regulation 12, and of the terms of any undertaking given to, or order made by, the court;

    (c) of the outcome of any application made by it to enforce a previous order of the court.

15 Publication, information and advice A–050

(1) The Director shall arrange for the publication in such form and manner as he considers appropriate, of—

    (a) details of any undertaking or order notified to him under regulation 14;

    (b) details of any undertaking given to him by or on behalf of any person as to the continued use of a term which the Director considers to be unfair in contracts concluded with consumers;

    (c) details of any application made by him under regulation 12, and of the terms of any undertaking given to, or order made by, the court;

    (d) details of any application made by the Director to enforce a previous order of the court.

(2) The Director shall inform any person on request whether a particular term to which these Regulations apply has been—

    (a) the subject of an undertaking given to the Director or notified to him by a qualifying body; or

    (b) the subject of an order of the court made upon application by him or notified to him by a qualifying body;

and shall give that person details of the undertaking or a copy of the order, as the case may be, together with a copy of any amendments which the person giving the undertaking has agreed to make to the term in question.

(3) The Director may arrange for the dissemination in such form and manner as he considers appropriate of such information and advice concerning the operation of these Regulations as may appear to him to be expedient to give to the public and to all persons likely to be affected by these Regulations.

A–051   **16 The functions of the Financial Services Authority**

[The functions of the Financial Services Authority under these Regulations shall be treated as functions of the Financial Services Authority under the [Financial Services and Markets Act 2000][1]][2].

[1] Substituted by Financial Services and Markets 2000 (Consequential Amendments and Repeals) Order (SI 2001/3649) art.583.
[2] Reg.16 added by Unfair Terms in Consumer Contracts (Amendment) Regulations (SI 2001/1186) reg.2.

A–052   SCHEDULE 1   Regulation 3

                                   QUALIFYING BODIES

                                        PART ONE

[**1**. The Information Commissioner.][1]
[**2**. The Gas and Electricity Markets Authority.][2]
[**3**. The Director General of Electricity Supply for Northern Ireland.][3]
[**4**. The Director General of Gas for Northern Ireland.][4]
[**5**. The Office of Communications.][5]
[**6**. The Director General of Water Services.][6]
[**7**. The Rail Regulator.][7]
[**8**. Every weights and measures authority in Great Britain.][8]
[**9**. The Department of Enterprise, Trade and Investment in Northern Ireland.][9]
[**10**. The Financial Services Authority.][10]

[1] Substituted by Unfair Terms in Consumer Contracts (Amendment) Regulations (SI 2001/1186) reg.2.
[2] Substituted by Unfair Terms in Consumer Contracts (Amendment) Regulations (SI 2001/1186) reg.2.
[3] Substituted by Unfair Terms in Consumer Contracts (Amendment) Regulations (SI 2001/1186) reg.2.
[4] Substituted by Unfair Terms in Consumer Contracts (Amendment) Regulations (SI 2001/1186) reg.2.
[5] Substituted by Communications 2003 (Consequential Amendments No.2) Order (SI 2003/3182) art.2.
[6] Substituted by Unfair Terms in Consumer Contracts (Amendment) Regulations (SI 2001/1186) reg.2.
[7] Substituted by Unfair Terms in Consumer Contracts (Amendment) Regulations (SI 2001/1186) reg.2.
[8] Substituted by Unfair Terms in Consumer Contracts (Amendment) Regulations (SI 2001/1186) reg.2.
[9] Substituted by Unfair Terms in Consumer Contracts (Amendment) Regulations (SI 2001/1186) reg.2.
[10] Substituted by Unfair Terms in Consumer Contracts (Amendment) Regulations (SI 2001/1186) reg.2.

PART TWO

11. Consumers' Association.

SCHEDULE 2

Regulation 5(5)   **A–053**

INDICATIVE AND NON-EXHAUSTIVE LIST OF TERMS WHICH MAY BE REGARDED AS UNFAIR

1. Terms which have the object or effect of—

(a) excluding or limiting the legal liability of a seller or supplier in the event of the death of a consumer or personal injury to the latter resulting from an act or omission of that seller or supplier;

(b) inappropriately excluding or limiting the legal rights of the consumer vis-à-vis the seller or supplier or another party in the event of total or partial non-performance or inadequate performance by the seller or supplier of any of the contractual obligations, including the option of offsetting a debt owed to the seller or supplier against any claim which the consumer may have against him;

(c) making an agreement binding on the consumer whereas provision of services by the seller or supplier is subject to a condition whose realisation depends on his own will alone;

(d) permitting the seller or supplier to retain sums paid by the consumer where the latter decides not to conclude or perform the contract, without providing for the consumer to receive compensation of an equivalent amount from the seller or supplier where the latter is the party cancelling the contract;

(e) requiring any consumer who fails to fulfil his obligation to pay a disproportionately high sum in compensation;

(f) authorising the seller or supplier to dissolve the contract on a discretionary basis where the same facility is not granted to the consumer, or permitting the seller or supplier to retain the sums paid for services not yet supplied by him where it is the seller or supplier himself who dissolves the contract;

(g) enabling the seller or supplier to terminate a contract of indeterminate duration without reasonable notice except where there are serious grounds for doing so;

(h) automatically extending a contract of fixed duration where the consumer does not indicate otherwise, when the deadline fixed for the consumer to express his desire not to extend the contract is unreasonably early;

(i) irrevocably binding the consumer to terms with which he had no real opportunity of becoming acquainted before the conclusion of the contract;

(j) enabling the seller or supplier to alter the terms of the contract unilaterally without a valid reason which is specified in the contract;

(k) enabling the seller or supplier to alter unilaterally without a valid reason any characteristics of the product or service to be provided;

(l) providing for the price of goods to be determined at the time of delivery or allowing a seller of goods or supplier of services to increase their price without in both cases giving the consumer the corresponding right to cancel the contract if the final price is too high in relation to the price agreed when the contract was concluded;

(m) giving the seller or supplier the right to determine whether the goods or services supplied are in conformity with the contract, or giving him the exclusive right to interpret any term of the contract;

(n) limiting the seller's or supplier's obligation to respect commitments undertaken by his agents or making his commitments subject to compliance with a particular formality;

(*o*) obliging the consumer to fulfil all his obligations where the seller or supplier does not perform his;

(*p*) giving the seller or supplier the possibility of transferring his rights and obligations under the contract, where this may serve to reduce the guarantees for the consumer, without the latter's agreement;

(*q*) excluding or hindering the consumer's right to take legal action or exercise any other legal remedy, particularly by requiring the consumer to take disputes exclusively to arbitration not covered by legal provisions, unduly restricting the evidence available to him or imposing on him a burden of proof which, according to the applicable law, should lie with another party to the contract.

2. Scopes of paragraphs 1(g), (j) and (l)

(*a*) Paragraph 1(g) is without hindrance to terms by which a supplier of financial services reserves the right to terminate unilaterally a contract of indeterminate duration without notice where there is a valid reason, provided that the supplier is required to inform the other contracting party or parties thereof immediately.

(*b*) Paragraph 1(j) is without hindrance to terms under which a supplier of financial services reserves the right to alter the rate of interest payable by the consumer or due to the latter, or the amount of other charges for financial services without notice where there is a valid reason, provided that the supplier is required to inform the other contracting party or parties thereof at the earliest opportunity and that the latter are free to dissolve the contract immediately.

Paragraph 1(j) is also without hindrance to terms under which a seller or supplier reserves the right to alter unilaterally the conditions of a contract of indeterminate duration, provided that he is required to inform the consumer with reasonable notice and that the consumer is free to dissolve the contract.

(*c*) Paragraphs 1(g), (j) and (l) do not apply to:
—transactions in transferable securities, financial instruments and other products or services where the price is linked to fluctuations in a stock exchange quotation or index or a financial market rate that the seller or supplier does not control;
—contracts for the purchase or sale of foreign currency, traveller's cheques or international money orders denominated in foreign currency;

(*d*) Paragraph 1(l) is without hindrance to price indexation clauses, where lawful, provided that the method by which prices vary is explicitly described.

* * * * *

Civil Liability Contribution Act 1978

Proceedings for contribution

A–054   **1 Entitlement to contribution**

(1) Subject to the following provisions of this section, any person liable in respect of any damage suffered by another person may recover contribution from any other person liable in respect of the same damage (whether jointly with him or otherwise).

(2) A person shall be entitled to recover contribution by virtue of subsection (1) above notwithstanding that he has ceased to be liable in respect of the damage in question since the time when the damage occurred, provided that he was so liable immediately before he made or was ordered or agreed to make the payment in respect of which the contribution is sought.

(3) A person shall be liable to make contribution by virtue of subsection (1) above notwithstanding that he has ceased to be liable in respect of the damage in question since the time when the damage occurred, unless he ceased to be liable by virtue of the expiry of a period of limitation or prescription which extinguished the right on which the claim against him in respect of the damage was based.

(4) A person who has made or agreed to make any payment in bona fide settlement or compromise of any claim made against him in respect of any damage (including a payment into court which has been accepted) shall be entitled to recover contribution in accordance with this section without regard to whether or not he himself is or ever was liable in respect of the damage, provided, however, that he would have been liable assuming that the factual basis of the claim against him could be established.

(5) A judgment given in any action brought in any part of the United Kingdom by or on behalf of the person who suffered the damage in question against any person from whom contribution is sought under this section shall be conclusive in the proceedings for contribution as to any issue determined by that judgment in favour of the person from whom the contribution is sought.

(6) References in this section to a person's liability in respect of any damage are references to any such liability which has been or could be established in an action brought against him in England and Wales by or on behalf of the person who suffered the damage; but it is immaterial whether any issue arising in any such action was or would be determined (in accordance with the rules of private international law) by reference to the law of a country outside England and Wales.

2 Assessment of contribution   A–055

(1) Subject to subsection (3) below, in any proceedings for contribution under section 1 above the amount of the contribution recoverable from any person shall be such as may be found by the court to be just and equitable having regard to the extent of that person's responsibility for the damage in question.

(2) Subject to subsection (3) below, the court shall have power in any such proceedings to exempt any person from liability to make contribution, or to direct that the contribution to be recovered from any person shall amount to a complete indemnity.

(3) Where the amount of the damages which have or might have been awarded in respect of the damage in question in any action brought in England and Wales by or on behalf of the person who suffered it against the person from whom the contribution is sought was or would have been subject to—

(a) any limit imposed by or under any enactment or by any agreement made before the damage occurred;
(b) any reduction by virtue of section 1 of the Law Reform (Contributory Negligence) Act 1945 or section 5 of the Fatal Accidents Act 1976; or
(c) any corresponding limit or reduction under the law of a country outside England and Wales;

the person from whom the contribution is sought shall not by virtue of any contribution awarded under section 1 above be required to pay in respect of the damage a greater amount than the amount of those damages as so limited or reduced.

Proceedings for the same debt or damage

3 Proceedings against persons jointly liable for the same debt or damage   A–056

Judgment recovered against any person liable in respect of any debt or damage shall not be a bar to an action, or to the continuance of an action, against any other person who is (apart from any such bar) jointly liable with him in respect of the same debt or damage.

A–057 **4 Successive actions against persons liable (jointly or otherwise) for the same damage**

If more than one action is brought in respect of any damage by or on behalf of the person by whom it was suffered against persons liable in respect of the damage (whether jointly or otherwise) the plaintiff shall not be entitled to costs in any of those actions, other than that in which judgment is first given, unless the court is of the opinion that there was reasonable ground for bringing the action.

*   *   *   *   *

Insolvency Act 1986

A–058 **239 Preferences (England and Wales)**

(1) This section applies as does section 238.

(2) Where the company has at a relevant time (defined in the next section) given a preference to any person, the office-holder may apply to the court for an order under this section.

(3) Subject as follows, the court shall, on such an application, make such order as it thinks fit for restoring the position to what it would have been if the company had not given that preference.

(4) For the purposes of this section and section 241, a company gives a preference to a person if—

(a) that person is one of the company's creditors or a surety or guarantor for any of the company's debts or other liabilities, and

(b) the company does anything or suffers anything to be done which (in either case) has the effect of putting that person into a position which, in the event of the company going into insolvent liquidation, will be better than the position he would have been in if that thing had not been done.

(5) The court shall not make an order under this section in respect of a preference given to any person unless the company which gave the preference was influenced in deciding to give it by a desire to produce in relation to that person the effect mentioned in subsection (4)(b).

(6) A company which has given a preference to a person connected with the company (otherwise than by reason only of being its employee) at the time the preference was given is presumed, unless the contrary is shown, to have been influenced in deciding to give it by such a desire as is mentioned in subsection (5).

(7) The fact that something has been done in pursuance of the order of a court does not, without more, prevent the doing or suffering of that thing from constituting the giving of a preference.

*   *   *   *   *

A–059 **281 Effect of discharge**

(7) Discharge does not release any person other than the bankrupt from any liability (whether as partner or co-trustee of the bankrupt or otherwise) from which the bankrupt is released by the discharge, or from any liability as surety for the bankrupt or as a person in the nature of such a surety.

323 Mutual credit and set-off
A–060

(1) This section applies where before the commencement of the bankruptcy there have been mutual credits, mutual debts or other mutual dealings between the bankrupt and any creditor of the bankrupt proving or claiming to prove for a bankruptcy debt.

(2) An account shall be taken of what is due from each party to the other in respect of the mutual dealings and the sums due from one party shall be set off against the sums due from the other.

(3) Sums due from the bankrupt to another party shall not be included in the account taken under subsection (2) if that other party had notice at the time they became due that a bankruptcy petition relating to the bankrupt was pending.

(4) Only the balance (if any) of the account taken under subsection (2) is provable as a bankruptcy debt or, as the case may be, to be paid to the trustee as part of the bankrupt's estate.

* * * * *

Insolvency Rules 1986 (SI 1986/1925)

4.90 Mutual credit and set-off
A–061

(1) This Rule applies where, before the company goes into liquidation there have been mutual credits, mutual debts or other mutual dealings between the company and any creditor of the company proving or claiming to prove for a debt in the liquidation.

(2) An account shall be taken of what is due from each party to the other in respect of the mutual dealings, and the sums due from one party shall be set off against the sums due from the other.

[(3) Sums due from the company to another party shall not be taken into account under paragraph (2) if—

    (a) that other party had notice at the time they became due that a meeting of creditors had been summoned under section 98 or (as the case may be) a petition for the winding up of the company was pending;

    (b) the liquidation was immediately preceded by an administration and the sums became due during the administration; or

    (c) the liquidation was immediately preceded by an administration and the other party had notice at the time that the sums became due that—
        (i) an application for an administration order was pending; or
        (ii) any person had given notice of intention to appoint an administrator.][1]

(4) Only the balance (if any) of the account is provable in the liquidation. Alternatively (as the case may be) the amount shall be paid to the liquidator as part of the assets.

[1] Substituted by Insolvency (Amendment) Rules (SI 2003/1730) Sch.1, para.19.

* * * * *

Minors' Contracts Act 1987

1 Disapplication of Infants Relief Act 1874 etc
A–062

The following enactments shall not apply to any contract made by a minor after the commencement of this Act—

(a) the Infants Relief Act 1874 (which invalidates certain contracts made by minors and prohibits actions to enforce contracts ratified after majority); and

(b) section 5 of the Betting and Loans (Infants) Act 1892 (which invalidates contracts to repay loans advanced during minority).

A–063 **2 Guarantees**

Where—

(a) a guarantee is given in respect of an obligation of a party to a contract made after the commencement of this Act, and

(b) the obligation is unenforceable against him (or he repudiates the contract) because he was a minor when the contract was made, the guarantee shall not for that reason alone be unenforceable against the guarantor.

Index